HARPER COLLINS

ITALIAN-ENGLISH

◆

ENGLISH-ITALIAN

ITALIAN DICTIONARY

HarperPaperbacks

A Division of HarperCollinsPublishers

HarperPaperbacks *A Division of* HarperCollins*Publishers*
10 East 53rd Street, New York, N.Y. 10022

This book was published in Great Britain in 1990 by William Collins Sons & Co. Ltd.

First HarperPaperbacks printing: August 1991

Printed in the United States of America

HarperPaperbacks and colophon are trademarks of HarperCollins*Publishers*

10 9 8 7 6 5 4 3 2 1

INTRODUCTION

This dictionary of Italian and English is designed to provide the user with wide-ranging and up-to-date coverage of the two languages, and is ideal for both school and reference use.

A special feature of HarperCollins dictionaries is the comprehensive "signposting" of meanings on both sides of the dictionary, guiding the user to the most appropriate translation for a given context. We hope you will find this dictionary easy and pleasant to consult for all your study and reference needs.

ABBREVIAZIONI

ABBREVIATIONS

aggettivo	a	adjective
abbreviazione	abbr	abbreviation
avverbio	ad	adverb
amministrazione	ADMIN	administration
aeronautica, viaggi aerei	AER	flying, air travel
aggettivo	ag	adjective
agricoltura	AGR	agriculture
amministrazione	AMM	administration
anatomia	ANAT	anatomy
architettura	ARCHIT	architecture
astronomia, astrologia	ASTR	astronomy, astrology
l'automobile	AUT	the motor car and motoring
avverbio	av	adverb
aeronautica, viaggi aerei	AVIAT	flying, air travel
biologia	BIOL	biology
botanica	BOT	botany
inglese della Gran Bretagna	Brit	British English
consonante	C	consonant
chimica	CHIM, CHEM	chemistry
congiunzione	cj	conjunction
familiare (! da evitare)	col(!)	colloquial usage (! particularly offensive)
commercio, finanza, banca	COMM	commerce, finance, banking
informatica	COMPUT	computers
congiunzione	cong	conjunction
edilizia	CONSTR	building
sostantivo usato come aggettivo, non può essere usato né come attributo, né dopo il sostantivo qualificato	cpd	compound element: noun used as adjective and which cannot follow the noun it qualifies
cucina	CUC, CULIN	cookery
davanti a	dav	before
determinativo: articolo, aggettivo dimostrativo o indefinito etc	det	determiner: article, demonstrative etc
diritto	DIR	law
economia	ECON	economics
edilizia	EDIL	building
elettricità, elettronica	ELETTR, ELEC	electricity, electronics
esclamazione	escl, excl	exclamation
femminile	f	feminine
familiare (! da evitare)	fam(!)	colloquial usage (! particularly offensive)
ferrovia	FERR	railways
figurato	fig	figurative use
fisiologia	FISIOL	physiology
fotografia	FOT	photography
(verbo inglese) la cui particella è inseparabile dal verbo	fus	(phrasal verb) where the particle cannot be separated from main verb

ABBREVIAZIONI

ABBREVIATIONS

nella maggior parte dei sensi; generalmente	**gen**	in most or all senses; generally
geografia, geologia	**GEO**	geography, geology
geometria	**GEOM**	geometry
impersonale	**impers**	impersonal
informatica	**INFORM**	computers
insegnamento, sistema scolastico e universitario	**INS**	schooling, schools and universities
invariabile	**inv**	invariable
irregolare	**irg**	irregular
grammatica, linguistica	**LING**	grammar, linguistics
maschile	**m**	masculine
matematica	**MAT(H)**	mathematics
termine medico, medicina	**MED**	medical term, medicine
il tempo, meteorologia	**METEOR**	the weather, meteorology
maschile o femminile, secondo il sesso	**m/f**	either masculine or feminine depending on sex
esercito, lingua militare	**MIL**	military matters
musica	**MUS**	music
sostantivo	**n**	noun
nautica	**NAUT**	sailing, navigation
numerale (aggettivo, sostantivo)	**num**	numeral adjective or noun
	o.s.	oneself
peggiorativo	**peg, pej**	derogatory, pejorative
fotografia	**PHOT**	photography
fisiologia	**PHYSIOL**	physiology
plurale	**pl**	plural
politica	**POL**	politics
participio passato	**pp**	past participle
preposizione	**prep**	preposition
psicologia, psichiatria	**PSIC, PSYCH**	psychology, psychiatry
tempo passato	**pt**	past tense
sostantivo che non si usa al plurale	**q**	uncountable noun: not used in the plural
qualcosa	**qc**	
qualcuno	**qn**	
religione, liturgia	**REL**	religions, church service
sostantivo	**s**	noun
	sb	somebody
insegnamento, sistema scolastico e universitario	**SCOL**	schooling, schools and universities
singolare	**sg**	singular
soggetto (grammaticale)	**sog**	(grammatical) subject
	sth	something
congiuntivo	**sub**	subjunctive
soggetto (grammaticale)	**subj**	(grammatical) subject
termine tecnico, tecnologia	**TECN, TECH**	technical term, technology
telecomunicazioni	**TEL**	telecommunications
tipografia	**TIP**	typography, printing

ABBREVIAZIONI

ABBREVIATIONS

televisione	**TV**	television
tipografia	**TYP**	typography, printing
inglese degli Stati Uniti	**US**	American English
vocale	**V**	vowel
verbo	**vb**	verb
verbo o gruppo verbale con funzione intransitiva	**vi**	verb or phrasal verb used intransitively
verbo riflessivo	**vr**	reflexive verb
verbo o gruppo verbale con funzione transitiva	**vt**	verb or phrasal verb used transitively
zoologia	**ZOOL**	zoology
marchio registrato	®	registered trademark
introduce un'equivalenza culturale	≈	introduces a cultural equivalent

TRASCRIZIONE FONETICA

PHONETIC TRANSCRIPTION

CONSONANTS CONSONANTI

NB The pairing of some vowel sounds only indicates approximate equivalence/La messa in equivalenza di certi suoni indica solo una rassomiglianza approssimativa.

puppy	p	*padre*
baby	b	*bambino*
tent	t	*tutto*
daddy	d	*dado*
cork kiss chord	k	*cane che*
gag guess	g	*gola ghiro*
so rice kiss	s	*sano*
cousin buzz	z	*svago esame*
sheep sugar	ʃ	*scena*
pleasure beige	ʒ	
church	tʃ	*pece lanciare*
judge general	dʒ	*giro gioco*
farm raffle	f	*afa faro*
very rev	v	*vero bravo*
thin maths	θ	
that other	ð	
little ball	l	*letto ala*
	ʎ	*gli*
rat brat	r	*rete arco*
mummy comb	m	*ramo madre*
no ran	n	*no fumante*
	ɲ	*gnomo*
singing bank	ŋ	
hat reheat	h	
yet	j	*buio piacere*
wall bewail	w	*uomo guaio*
loch	x	

VOWELS VOCALI

NB **p, b, t, d, k, g** are not aspirated in Italian/sono seguiti da un'aspirazione in inglese.

heel bead	i: i	*vino idea*
hit pity	ɪ	
	e	*stella edera*
set tent	ɛ	*epoca eccetto*
apple bat	æ a	*mamma amore*
after car calm	ɑ:	
fun cousin	ʌ	
over above	ə	
urn fern work	ə:	
wash pot	ɔ	*rosa occhio*
born cork	ɔ:	
	o	*ponte ognuno*
full soot	u	*utile zucca*
boon lewd	u:	

DIPHTHONGS DITTONGHI

ɪə	*beer tier*
ɛə	*tear fair there*
eɪ	*date plaice day*
aɪ	*life buy cry*
au	*owl foul now*
əu	*low no*
ɔɪ	*boil boy oily*
uə	*poor tour*

MISCELLANEOUS

VARIE

* per l'inglese: la "r" finale viene pronunciata se seguita da una vocale.

' precedes the stressed syllable/precede la sillaba accentata.

ITALIAN PRONUNCIATION

VOWELS

Where the vowel **e** or the vowel **o** appears in a stressed syllable it can be either open [ɛ], [ɔ] or closed [e], [o]. As the open or closed pronunciation of these vowels is subject to regional variation, the distinction is of little importance to the user of this dictionary. Phonetic transcription for headwords containing these vowels will therefore only appear where other pronunciation difficulties are present.

CONSONANTS

c before "e" or "i" is pronounced *tch*.

ch is pronounced like the "k" in "kit".

g before "e" or "i" is pronounced like the "j" in "jet".

gh is pronounced like the "g" in "get".

gl before "e" or "i" is normally pronounced like the "lli" in "million", and in a few cases only like the "gl" in "glove".

gn is pronounced like the "ny" in "canyon".

sc before "e" or "i" is pronounced *sh*.

z is pronounced like the "ts" in "stetson", or like the "d's" in "bird's-eye".

Headwords containing the above consonants and consonantal groups have been given full phonetic transcription in this dictionary.

NB All double written consonants in Italian are fully sounded: eg. the *tt* in "tutto" is pronounced as in "ha*t t*rick".

ITALIANO - INGLESE
ITALIAN - ENGLISH

A

a *prep* (*a* + *il* = **al**, *a* + *lo* = **allo**, *a* + *l'* = **all'**, *a* + *la* = **alla**, *a* + *i* = **ai**, *a* + *gli* = **agli**, *a* + *le* = **alle**) **1** (*stato in luogo*) at; (: *in*) in; essere alla stazione to be at the station; essere ~ casa/~ scuola/~ Roma to be at home/at school/in Rome; è ~ 10 km da qui it's 10 km from here, it's 10 km away

2 (*moto a luogo*) to; andare ~ casa/~ scuola to go home/to school

3 (*tempo*) (*epoca, stagione*) in; alle cinque at five (o'clock); ~ mezzanotte/ Natale at midnight/Christmas; al mattino in the morning; ~ maggio/ primavera in May/spring; ~ cinquant'anni at fifty (years of age); ~ domani! see you tomorrow!

4 (*complemento di termine*) to; dare qc ~ qn to give sth to sb

5 (*mezzo, modo*) with, by; ~ piedi/ cavallo on foot/horseback; fatto ~ mano made by hand, handmade; una barca ~ motore a motorboat; ~ uno ~ uno one by one; all'italiana the Italian way, in the Italian fashion

6 (*rapporto*) a, per; (: *con prezzi*) at; prendo 500.000 lire al mese I get 500,000 lire a o per month; pagato ~ ore paid by the hour; vendere qc ~ 500 lire il chilo to sell sth at 500 lire a o per kilo.

a'bate *sm* abbot.

abbacchi'ato, a [abbak'kjato] *ag* downhearted, in low spirits.

abbagli'ante [abbaʎ'ʎante] *ag* dazzling; ~**i** *smpl* (AUT): accendere gli ~**i** to put one's headlights on full (*Brit*) o high (*US*) beam.

abbagli'are [abbaʎ'ʎare] *vt* to dazzle; (*illudere*) to delude; **ab'baglio** *sm* blunder; prendere un abbaglio to blunder, make a blunder.

abbai'are *vi* to bark.

abba'ino *sm* dormer window; (*soffitta*) attic room.

abbando'nare *vt* to leave, abandon, desert; (*trascurare*) to neglect; (*rinunciare a*) to abandon, give up; ~**rsi** *vr* to let o.s. go; ~**rsi a** (*ricordi, vizio*) to give s. up to; **abban'dono** *sm* abandoning; neglecting; (*stato*) abandonment; neglect; (*SPORT*) withdrawal; (*fig*) abandon; in abbandono (*edificio, giardino*) neglected.

abbas'sare *vt* to lower; (*radio*) to turn down; ~**rsi** *vr* (*chinarsi*) to stoop; (*livello, sole*) to go down; (*fig*:

umiliarsi) to demean o.s.; ~ **i fari** (AUT) to dip o dim (US) one's lights.

ab'basso *escl*: ~ **il re!** down with the king!

abbas'tanza [abbas'tantsa] *av* (*a sufficienza*) enough; (*alquanto*) quite, rather, fairly; **non è** ~ **furbo** he's not shrewd enough; **un vino** ~ **dolce** quite a sweet wine, a fairly sweet wine; **averne** ~ **di qn/qc** to have had enough of sb/sth.

ab'battere *vt* (*muro, casa*) to pull down; (*ostacolo*) to knock down; (*albero*) to fell; (: *sog: vento*) to bring down; (*bestie da macello*) to slaughter; (*cane, cavallo*) to destroy, put down; (*selvaggina, aereo*) to shoot down; (*fig: sog: malattia, disgrazia*) to lay low; ~**rsi** *vr* (*avvilirsi*) to lose heart; **abbat'tuto, a** *ag* (*fig*) despondent, depressed.

abba'zia [abbat'tsia] *sf* abbey.

abbece'dario [abbetʃe'darjo] *sm* primer.

abbel'lire *vt* to make beautiful; (*ornare*) to embellish.

abbeve'rare *vt* to water; ~**rsi** *vr* to drink.

'abbi, 'abbia, abbi'amo, 'abbiano, abbi'ate *forme del vb* avere.

abbicci [abbit'tʃi] *sm inv* alphabet; (*sillabario*) primer; (*fig*) rudiments *pl*.

abbi'ente *ag* well-to-do, well-off.

abbi'etto, a *ag* = abietto.

abbiglia'mento [abbiʎʎa'mento] *sm* dress *q*; (*indumenti*) clothes *pl*; (*industria*) clothing industry.

abbigli'are [abbiʎ'ʎare] *vt* to dress up.

abbi'nare *vt*: ~ (**a**) to combine (with).

abbindo'lare *vt* (*fig*) to cheat, trick.

abbocca'mento *sm* talks *pl*, meeting.

abboc'care *vt* (*tubi, canali*) to connect, join up // *vi* (*pesce*) to bite; (*tubi*) to join; ~ (**all'amo**) (*fig*) to swallow the bait.

abboc'cato, a *ag* (*vino*) sweetish.

abbona'mento *sm* subscription; (*alle ferrovie etc*) season ticket; **fare l'**~ to take out a subscription (o season ticket).

abbo'narsi *vr*: ~ **a un giornale** to take out a subscription to a newspaper; ~ **al teatro/alle ferrovie** to take out a season ticket for the theatre/the train; **abbo'nato, a** *sm/f* subscriber; season-ticket holder.

abbon'dante *ag* abundant, plentiful; (*giacca*) roomy.

abbon'danza [abbon'dantsa] *sf* abundance; plenty.

abbon'dare *vi* to abound, be plentiful; ~ in *o* di to be full of, abound in.

abbor'dabile *ag* (*persona*) approachable; (*prezzo*) reasonable.

abbor'dare *vt* (*nave*) to board; (*persona*) to approach; (*argomento*) to tackle; ~ una curva to take a bend.

abbotto'nare *vt* to button up, do up.

abboz'zare [abbot'tsare] *vt* to sketch, outline; (*SCULTURA*) to rough-hew; ~ un sorriso to give a hint of a smile; **ab'bozzo** *sm* sketch, outline; (*DIR*) draft.

abbracci'are [abbrat'tʃare] *vt* to embrace; (*persona*) to hug, embrace; (*professione*) to take up; (*contenere*) to include; ~rsi *vr* to hug *o* embrace (one another); **ab'braccio** *sm* hug, embrace.

abbreviazi'one [abbrevjat'tsjone] *sf* abbreviation.

abbron'zante [abbron'dzante] *ag* tanning, sun *cpd*.

abbron'zare [abbron'dzare] *vt* (*pelle*) to tan; (*metalli*) to bronze; ~rsi *vr* to tan, get a tan; **abbronza'tura** *sf* tan, suntan.

abbrusto'lire *vt* (*pane*) to toast; (*caffè*) to roast.

abbru'tire *vt* to exhaust; to degrade.

abbu'ono *sm* (*COMM*) allowance, discount; (*SPORT*) handicap.

abdi'care *vi* to abdicate; ~ a to give up, renounce.

aberrazi'one [aberrat'tsjone] *sf* aberration.

a'bete *sm* fir (tree); ~ rosso spruce.

abi'etto, a *ag* despicable, abject.

'abile *ag* (*idoneo*): ~ (a qc/a fare qc) fit (for sth/to do sth); (*capace*) able; (*astuto*) clever; (*accorto*) skilful; ~ al servizio militare fit for military service; **abilità** *sf inv* ability; cleverness; skill.

abili'tato, a *ag* qualified; (*TEL*) which has an outside line; **abilitazi'one** *sf* qualification.

a'bisso *sm* abyss, gulf.

abi'tacolo *sm* (*AER*) cockpit; (*AUT*) inside; (: di camion) cab.

abi'tante *smf* inhabitant.

abi'tare *vt* to live in, dwell in // *vi*: ~ in campagna/a Roma to live in the country/in Rome; **abi'tato, a** *ag* inhabited; lived in // *sm* (*anche*: centro abitato) built-up area; **abitazi'one** *sf* residence; house.

'abito *sm* dress *q*; (*da uomo*) suit; (*da donna*) dress; (*abitudine, disposizione, REL*) habit; ~i *smpl* clothes; in ~ da sera in evening dress.

abitu'ale *ag* usual, habitual; (*cliente*) regular.

abitu'are *vt*: ~ qn a to get sb used *o* accustomed to; ~rsi a to get used to, accustom o.s. to.

abitudi'nario, a *ag* of fixed habits //

sm/f regular customer.

abi'tudine *sf* habit; aver l'~ di fare qc to be in the habit of doing sth; d'~ usually; per ~ from *o* out of habit.

abo'lire *vt* to abolish; (*DIR*) to repeal.

abomi'nevole *ag* abominable.

abo'rigeno [abo'ridʒeno] *sm* aborigine.

abor'rire *vt* to abhor, detest.

abor'tire *vi* (*MED: accidentalmente*) to miscarry, have a miscarriage; (: deliberatamente) to have an abortion; (*fig*) to miscarry, fail; **a'borto** *sm* miscarriage; abortion; (*fig*) freak.

abrasi'one *sf* abrasion; **abra'sivo, a** *ag*, *sm* abrasive.

abro'gare *vt* to repeal, abrogate.

A'bruzzo *sm*: l'~, gli ~i the Abruzzi.

'abside *sf* apse.

a'bulico, a, ci, che *ag* lacking in will power.

abu'sare *vi*: ~ di to abuse, misuse; (*alcool*) to take to excess; (*approfittare, violare*) to take advantage of; **a'buso** *sm* abuse, misuse; excessive use.

a.C. *ad abbr* (= avanti Cristo) B.C.

'acca *sf* letter H; non capire un'~ not to understand a thing.

acca'demia *sf* (*società*) learned society; (*scuola: d'arte, militare*) academy; **acca'demico, a, ci, che** *ag* academic // *sm* academician.

acca'dere *vb impers* to happen, occur; **acca'duto** *sm*: raccontare l'accaduto to describe what has happened.

accalappi'are *vt* to catch; (*fig*) to trick, dupe.

accal'care *vt* to crowd, throng.

accal'darsi *vr* to grow hot.

accalo'rarsi *vr* (*fig*) to get excited.

accampa'mento *sm* camp.

accam'pare *vt* to encamp; (*fig*) to put forward, advance; ~rsi *vr* to camp.

accani'mento *sm* fury; (*tenacia*) tenacity, perseverance.

acca'nirsi *vr* (*infierire*) to rage; (*ostinarsi*) to persist; **acca'nito, a** *ag* (*odio, gelosia*) fierce, bitter; (*lavoratore*) assiduous, dogged; (*fumatore*) inveterate.

ac'canto *av* near, nearby; ~ a *prep* near, beside, close to.

accanto'nare *vt* (*problema*) to shelve; (*somma*) to set aside.

accapar'rare *vt* (*COMM*) to corner, buy up; (*versare una caparra*) to pay a deposit on; ~rsi qc (*fig: simpatia, voti*) to secure sth (for o.s.).

accapigli'arsi [akkapiʎ'ʎarsi] *vr* to come to blows; (*fig*) to quarrel.

accappa'toio *sm* bathrobe.

accappo'nare *vi*: far ~ la pelle a qn (*fig*) to bring sb out in goosepimples.

accarez'zare [akkaret'tsare] *vt* to caress, stroke, fondle; (*fig*) to toy with.

acca'sarsi *vr* to set up house; to get

married.

accasci'arsi [akkaʃˈʃarsi] vr to collapse; (fig) to lose heart.

accat'tone, a sm/f beggar.

accaval'lare vt (gambe) to cross; ~rsi vr (sovrapporsi) to overlap; (addensarsi) to gather.

acce'care [attʃeˈkare] vt to blind // vi to go blind.

ac'cedere [atˈtʃedere] vi: ~ a to enter; (richiesta) to grant, accede to.

accele'rare [attʃeleˈrare] vt to speed up // vi (AUT) to accelerate; ~ il passo to quicken one's pace; **accele'rato** sm (FERR) slow train; **accelera'tore** sm (AUT) accelerator; **accelerazi'one** sf acceleration.

ac'cendere [atˈtʃendere] vt (fuoco, sigaretta) to light; (luce, televisione) to put o switch o turn on; (AUT: motore) to switch on; (COMM: conto) to open; (fig: suscitare) to inflame, stir up; ~rsi vr (luce) to come o go on; (legna) to catch fire, ignite; **accen'dino** sm, **accendi'sigaro** sm (cigarette) lighter.

accen'nare [attʃenˈnare] vt to indicate, point out; (MUS) to pick out the notes of; to hum // vi: ~ a (fig: alludere a) to hint at; (: far atto di) to make as if; ~ un saluto (con la mano) to make as if to wave; (col capo) to half nod; accenna a piovere it looks as if it's going to rain.

ac'cenno [atˈtʃenno] sm (cenno) sign; nod; (allusione) hint.

accensi'one [attʃenˈsjone] sf (vedi accendere) lighting; switching on; opening; (AUT) ignition.

accen'tare [attʃenˈtare] vt (parlando) to stress; (scrivendo) to accent.

ac'cento [atˈtʃento] sm accent; (FONETICA, fig) stress; (inflessione) tone (of voice).

accen'trare [attʃenˈtrare] vt to centralize.

accentu'are [attʃentuˈare] vt to stress, emphasize; ~rsi vr to become more noticeable.

accerchi'are [attʃerˈkjare] vt to surround, encircle.

accerta'mento [attʃertaˈmento] sm check; assessment.

accer'tare [attʃerˈtare] vt to ascertain; (verificare) to check; (reddito) to assess; ~rsi vr: ~rsi (di) to make sure (of).

ac'ceso, a [atˈtʃeso] pp di **accendere** // ag lit; on; open; (colore) bright.

acces'sibile [attʃesˈsibile] ag (luogo) accessible; (persona) approachable; (prezzo) reasonable; (idea): ~ a qn within the reach of sb.

ac'cesso [atˈtʃesso] sm (anche INFORM) access; (MED) attack, fit; (impulso violento) fit, outburst.

acces'sorio, a [attʃesˈsɔrjo] ag secondary, of secondary importance; ~i smpl accessories.

ac'cetta [atˈtʃetta] sf hatchet.

accet'tabile [attʃetˈtabile] ag acceptable.

accet'tare [attʃetˈtare] vt to accept; ~ di fare qc to agree to do sth; **accettazi'one** sf acceptance; (locale di servizio pubblico) reception; accettazione bagagli (AER) check-in (desk).

ac'cetto, a [atˈtʃetto] ag: (ben) ~ welcome; (persona) well-liked.

accezi'one [attʃetˈtsjone] sf meaning.

acchiap'pare [akkjapˈpare] vt to catch.

acci'acco, chi [atˈtʃakko] sm ailment.

acciai'eria [attʃajeˈria] sf steelworks sg.

acci'aio [atˈtʃajo] sm steel.

acciden'tale [attʃidenˈtale] ag accidental.

acciden'tato, a [attʃidenˈtato] ag (terreno etc) uneven.

acci'dente [attʃiˈdente] sm (caso imprevisto) accident; (disgrazia) mishap; **non si capisce un ~** it's as clear as mud; **~i!** (fam: per rabbia) damn (it)!; (: per meraviglia) good heavens!

accigli'ato, a [attʃiʎˈʎato] ag frowning.

ac'cingersi [atˈtʃindʒersi] vr: ~ a fare to be about to do.

acciuf'fare [attʃufˈfare] vt to seize, catch.

acci'uga, ghe [atˈtʃuga] sf anchovy.

accla'mare vt (applaudire) to applaud; (eleggere) to acclaim; **acclamazi'one** sf applause; acclamation.

acclima'tare vt to acclimatize; ~rsi vr to become acclimatized.

ac'cludere vt to enclose; **ac'cluso, a** pp di **accludere** // ag enclosed.

accocco'larsi vr to crouch.

accogli'ente [akkoʎˈʎente] ag welcoming, friendly; **accogli'enza** sf reception; welcome.

ac'cogliere [akˈkɔʎʎere] vt (ricevere) to receive; (dare il benvenuto) to welcome; (approvare) to agree to, accept; (contenere) to hold, accommodate.

accol'lato, a ag (vestito) high-necked.

accol'tellare vt to knife, stab.

ac'colto, a pp di **accogliere**.

accoman'dita sf (DIR) limited partnership.

accomia'tare vt to dismiss; ~rsi vr: ~rsi (da) to take one's leave (of).

accomoda'mento sm agreement, settlement.

accomo'dante ag accommodating.

accomo'dare vt (aggiustare) to repair, mend; (riordinare) to tidy; (conciliare) to settle; ~rsi vr (sedersi) to sit down; **s'accomodi!** (venga avanti) come in!; (si sieda) take a seat!

accompagna'mento [akkompaɲɲaˈmento] sm (MUS) accompaniment.

accompa'gnare [akkompaɲˈɲare] vt to accompany, come o go with; (MUS) to accompany; (unire) to couple; ~ la porta to close the door gently.

accomu'nare *vt* to pool, share; (*avvicinare*) to unite.

acconcia'tura [akkontʃa'tura] *sf* hairstyle.

accondi'scendere [akkondiʃ'ʃendere] *vi*: ~ a to agree *o* consent to; **accondi'sceso, a** *pp di* **accondiscendere.**

acconsen'tire *vi*: ~ (a) to agree *o* consent (to).

acconten'tare *vt* to satisfy; ~rsi di to be satisfied with, content o.s. with.

ac'conto *sm* part payment; pagare una somma in ~ to pay a sum of money as a deposit.

accoppia'mento *sm* coupling, pairing off; mating; (*TECN*) coupling.

accoppi'are *vt* to couple, pair off; (*BIOL*) to mate; ~rsi *vr* to pair off; to mate.

accorci'are [akkor'tʃare] *vt* to shorten; ~rsi *vr* to become shorter.

accor'dare *vt* to reconcile; (*colori*) to match; (*MUS*) to tune; (*LING*): ~ qc con qc to make sth agree with sth; (*DIR*) to grant; ~rsi *vr* to agree, come to an agreement; (*colori*) to match.

ac'cordo *sm* agreement; (*armonia*) harmony; (*MUS*) chord; essere d'~ to agree; andare d'~ to get on well together; d'~! all right!, agreed!

ac'corgersi [ak'kordʒersi] *vr*: ~ di to notice; (*fig*) to realize; **accorgi'mento** *sm* shrewdness *q*; (*espediente*) trick, device.

ac'correre *vi* to run up.

ac'corto, a *pp di* **accorgersi** // *ag* shrewd; stare ~ to be on one's guard.

accos'tare *vt* (*avvicinare*): ~ qc a to bring sth near to, put sth near to; (*avvicinarsi a*) to approach; (*socchiudere: imposte*) to half-close; (: *porta*) to leave ajar // *vi* (*NAUT*) to come alongside; ~rsi a to draw near, approach; (*fig*) to support.

accovacci'arsi [akkovat'tʃarsi] *vr* to crouch.

accoz'zaglia [akkot'tsaʎʎa] *sf* (*peg: di idee, oggetti*) jumble, hotchpotch; (: *di persone*) odd assortment.

accredi'tare *vt* (*notizia*) to confirm the truth of; (*COMM*) to credit; (*diplomatico*) to accredit; ~rsi *vr* (*fig*) to gain credit.

ac'crescere [ak'kreʃʃere] *vt* to increase; ~rsi *vr* to increase, grow; **accresci'tivo, a** *ag, sm* (*LING*) augmentative; **accresci'uto, a** *pp di* **accrescere.**

accucci'arsi [akkut'tʃarsi] *vr* (*cane*) to lie down.

accu'dire *vt* (*anche*: *vi*: ~ a) to attend to.

accumu'lare *vt* to accumulate.

accura'tezza [akkura'tettsa] *sf* care; accuracy.

accu'rato, a *ag* (*diligente*) careful; (*preciso*) accurate.

ac'cusa *sf* accusation; (*DIR*) charge; la pubblica ~ the prosecution.

accu'sare *vt*: ~ qn di qc to accuse sb of sth; (*DIR*) to charge sb with sth; ~ ricevuta di (*COMM*) to acknowledge receipt of.

accu'sato, a *sm/f* accused; defendant.

accusa'tore, 'trice *sm/f* accuser // *sm* (*DIR*) prosecutor.

a'cerbo, a [a'tʃerbo] *ag* bitter; (*frutta*) sour, unripe; (*persona*) immature.

'acero ['atʃero] *sm* maple.

a'cerrimo, a [a'tʃerrimo] *ag* very fierce.

a'ceto [a'tʃeto] *sm* vinegar.

ace'tone [atʃe'tone] *sm* nail varnish remover.

A.C.I. ['atʃi] *sigla m* (= *Automobile Club d'Italia*) ≈ A.A.

'acido, a ['atʃido] *ag* (*sapore*) acid, sour; (*CHIM*) acid // *sm* (*CHIM*) acid.

'acino ['atʃino] *sm* berry; ~ d'uva grape.

'acne *sf* acne.

'acqua *sf* water; (*pioggia*) rain; ~e *sfpl* waters; fare ~ (*NAUT*) to leak, take in water; ~ in bocca! mum's the word!; ~ corrente running water; ~ dolce fresh water; ~ minerale mineral water; ~ potabile drinking water; ~ salata salt water; ~ tonica tonic water.

acqua'forte, pl acque'forti *sf* etching.

a'cquaio *sm* sink.

acqua'ragia [akkwa'radʒa] *sf* turpentine.

a'cquario *sm* aquarium; (*dello zodiaco*): A~ Aquarius.

acqua'santa *sf* holy water.

ac'quatico, a, ci, che *ag* aquatic; (*sport, sci*) water *cpd*.

acqua'vite *sf* brandy.

acquaz'zone [akkwat'tsone] *sm* cloudburst, heavy shower.

acque'dotto *sm* aqueduct; waterworks *pl*, water system.

'acqueo, a *ag*: vapore ~ water vapour.

acque'rello *sm* watercolour.

acquie'tare *vt* to appease; (*dolore*) to ease; ~rsi *vr* to calm down.

acqui'rente *sm/f* purchaser, buyer.

acqui'sire *vt* to acquire.

acquis'tare *vt* to purchase, buy; (*fig*) to gain; **a'cquisto** *sm* purchase; fare acquisti to go shopping.

acqui'trino *sm* bog, marsh.

acquo'lina *sf*: far venire l'~ in bocca a qn to make sb's mouth water.

a'cquoso, a *ag* watery.

'acre *ag* acrid, pungent; (*fig*) harsh, biting.

a'crobata, i, e *sm/f* acrobat.

acu'ire *vt* to sharpen.

a'culeo *sm* (*ZOOL*) sting; (*BOT*) prickle.

a'cume *sm* acumen, perspicacity.

a'custica *sf* (*scienza*) acoustics *sg*; (*di una sala*) acoustics *pl*.

a'cuto, a *ag* (*appuntito*) sharp, pointed; (*suono, voce*) shrill, piercing; (*MAT, LING, MED*) acute; (*MUS*) high-pitched; (*fig: dolore, desiderio*) intense; (*: perspicace*) acute, keen.

ad *prep* (*dav V*) = **a.**

adagi'are [ada'dʒare] *vt* to lay *o* set down carefully; **~rsi** *vr* to lie down, stretch out.

a'dagio [a'dadʒo] *av* slowly // *sm* (*MUS*) adagio; (*proverbio*) adage, saying.

adatta'mento *sm* adaptation.

adat'tare *vt* to adapt; (*sistemare*) to fit; **~rsi** (a) (*ambiente, tempi*) to adapt (to); (*essere adatto*) to be suitable (for).

a'datto, a *ag*: **~** (a) suitable (for), right (for).

addebi'tare *vt*: **~** qc a qn to debit sb with sth; (*fig: incolpare*) to blame sb for sth.

ad'debito *sm* (*COMM*) debit.

adden'sare *vt* to thicken; **~rsi** *vr* to thicken; (*nuvole*) to gather.

adden'tare *vt* to bite into.

adden'trarsi *vr*: **~** in to penetrate, go into.

ad'dentro *av* (*fig*): essere molto **~** in qc to be well-versed in sth.

addestra'mento *sm* training.

addes'trare *vt*, **~rsi** *vr* to train; **~rsi in** qc to practise (*Brit*) *o* practice (*US*) sth.

ad'detto, a *ag*: **~** a (*persona*) assigned to; (*oggetto*) intended for // *sm* employee; (*funzionario*) attaché; **commerciale/stampa** commercial/press attaché; **gli ~i ai lavori** authorized personnel; (*fig*) those in the know.

addì *av* (*AMM*): **~ 3 luglio 1978** on the 3rd of July 1978 (*Brit*), on July 3rd 1978 (*US*).

addi'accio [ad'djattʃo] *sm* (*MIL*) bivouac; **dormire all'~** to sleep in the open.

addi'etro *av* (*indietro*) behind; (*nel passato, prima*) before, ago.

ad'dio *sm, escl* goodbye, farewell.

addirit'tura *av* (*veramente*) really, absolutely; (*perfino*) even; (*direttamente*) directly, right away.

ad'dirsi *vr*: **~** a to suit, be suitable for.

addi'tare *vt* to point out; (*fig*) to expose.

addi'tivo *sm* additive.

addizio'nare [addittsjo'nare] *vt* (*MAT*) to add (up); **addizi'one** *sf* addition.

addob'bare *vt* to decorate; **ad'dobbo** *sm* decoration.

addol'cire [addol'tʃire] *vt* (*caffè etc*) to sweeten; (*acqua, fig: carattere*) to soften; **~rsi** *vr* (*fig*) to mellow, soften.

addolo'rare *vt* to pain, grieve; **~rsi (per)** to be distressed (by).

ad'dome *sm* abdomen.

addomesti'care *vt* to tame.

addormen'tare *vt* to put to sleep; **~rsi** *vr* to fall asleep, go to sleep.

addos'sare *vt* (*appoggiare*): **~** qc a qc to lean sth against sth; (*fig*): **~ la colpa a qn** to lay the blame on sb; **~rsi** qc (*responsabilità etc*) to shoulder sth.

ad'dosso *av* (*sulla persona*) on; **mettersi ~ il cappotto** to put one's coat on; **non ho soldi ~** I don't have any money on me; **~ a** *prep* (*sopra*) on; (*molto vicino*) right next to; **stare ~ a qn** (*fig*) to breathe down sb's neck; **dare ~ a qn** (*fig*) to attack sb.

ad'durre *vt* (*DIR*) to produce; (*citare*) to cite.

adegu'are *vt*: **~** qc a to adjust *o* relate sth to; **~rsi** *vr* to adapt; **adegu'ato, a** *ag* adequate; (*conveniente*) suitable; (*equo*) fair.

a'dempiere, adem'pire *vt* to fulfil, carry out.

ade'rente *ag* adhesive; (*vestito*) close-fitting // *sm/f* follower; **ade'renza** *sf* adhesion; **aderenze** *sfpl* (*fig*) connections, contacts.

ade'rire *vi* (*stare attaccato*) to adhere, stick; **~ a** to adhere to, stick to; (*fig: società, partito*) to join; (*: opinione*) to support; (*richiesta*) to agree to.

ades'care *vt* to lure, entice.

adesi'one *sf* adhesion; (*fig*) agreement, acceptance; **ade'sivo, a** *ag, sm* adhesive.

a'desso *av* (*ora*) now; (*or ora, poco fa*) just now; (*tra poco*) any moment now.

adia'cente [adja'tʃente] *ag* adjacent.

adi'bire *vt* (*usare*): **~** qc a to turn sth into.

adi'rarsi *vr*: **~** (con *o* contro qn per qc) to get angry (with sb over sth).

a'dire *vt* (*DIR*): **~ le vie legali** to take legal proceedings.

'adito *sm*: **dare ~ a** to give rise to.

adocchi'are [adok'kjare] *vt* (*scorgere*) to catch sight of; (*occhieggiare*) to eye.

adole'scente [adoleʃ'ʃente] *ag, sm/f* adolescent; **adole'scenza** *sf* adolescence.

adope'rare *vt* to use; **~rsi** *vr* to strive; **~rsi per qn/qc** to do one's best for sb/sth.

ado'rare *vt* to adore; (*REL*) to adore, worship.

adot'tare *vt* to adopt; (*decisione, provvedimenti*) to pass; **adot'tivo, a** *ag* (*genitori*) adoptive; (*figlio, patria*) adopted; **adozi'one** *sf* adoption.

adri'atico, a, ci, che *ag* Adriatic // *sm*: **l'A~, il mare A~** the Adriatic, the Adriatic Sea.

adu'lare *vt* to adulate, flatter.

adulte'rare *vt* to adulterate.

adul'terio *sm* adultery.

a'dulto, a *ag* adult; (*fig*) mature // *sm* adult, grown-up.

adu'nanza [adu'nantsa] *sf* assembly, meeting.

adu'nare *vt*, **~rsi** *vr* to assemble,

gather; **adu'nata** *sf* (*MIL*) parade, muster.

a'dunco, a, chi, che *ag* hooked.

a'ereo, a *ag* air *cpd*; (*radice*) aerial // *sm* aerial; (*aeroplano*) plane; ~ **a reazione** jet (plane); **ae'robica** *sf* aerobics *sg*; **aerodi'namico, a, ci, che** *ag* aerodynamic; (*affusolato*) streamlined // *sf* aerodynamics *sg*; **aero'nautica** *sf* (*scienza*) aeronautics *sg*; **aeronautica militare** air force; **aero'plano** *sm* (aero)plane (*Brit*), (air)plane (*US*); **æero'porto** *sm* airport; **aero'sol** *sm inv* aerosol.

'afa *sf* sultriness.

af'fabile *ag* affable.

affaccen'darsi [affattʃen'darsi] *vr*: ~ **intorno a qc** to busy o.s. with sth.

affacci'arsi [affat'tʃarsi] *vr*: ~ **(a)** to appear (at).

affa'mato, a *ag* starving; (*fig*): ~ **(di)** eager (for).

affan'nare *vt* to leave breathless; (*fig*) to worry; ~**rsi** *vr*: ~**rsi per qn/qc** to worry about sb/sth; **af'fanno** *sm* breathlessness; (*fig*) anxiety, worry; **affan'noso, a** *ag* (*respiro*) difficult; (*fig*) troubled, anxious.

af'fare *sm* (*faccenda*) matter, affair; (*COMM*) piece of business, (business) deal; (*occasione*) bargain; (*DIR*) case; (*fam: cosa*) thing; ~**i** *smpl* (*COMM*) business *sg*; **ministro degli A~i esteri** Foreign Secretary (*Brit*), Secretary of State (*US*); **affa'rista, i** *sm* profiteer, unscrupulous businessman.

affasci'nante [affaʃʃi'nante] *ag* fascinating.

affasci'nare [affaʃʃi'nare] *vt* to bewitch; (*fig*) to charm, fascinate.

affati'care *vt* to tire; ~**rsi** *vr* (*durar fatica*) to tire o.s. out.

af'fatto *av* completely; **non ... ~** not ... at all; **niente ~** not at all.

affer'mare *vt* (*dichiarare*) to maintain, affirm; ~**rsi** *vr* to assert o.s., make one's name known; **affermazi'one** *sf* affirmation, assertion; (*successo*) achievement.

affer'rare *vt* to seize, grasp; (*fig: idea*) to grasp; ~**rsi** *vr*: ~**rsi a** to cling to.

affet'tare *vt* (*tagliare a fette*) to slice; (*ostentare*) to affect; **affet'tato, a** *ag* sliced; affected // *sm* sliced cold meat.

affet'tivo, a *ag* emotional, affective.

af'fetto *sm* affection; **affettu'oso, a** *ag* affectionate.

affezio'narsi [affettsjo'narsi] *vr*: ~ **a** to grow fond of.

affezi'one [affet'tsjone] *sf* (*affetto*) affection; (*MED*) ailment, disorder.

affian'care *vt* to place side by side; (*MIL*) to flank; (*fig*) to support; ~ **qc a qc** to place sth next to *o* beside sth; ~**rsi a qn** to stand beside sb.

affia'tarsi *vr* to get on well together.

affibbi'are *vt* (*fig: dare*) to give.

affida'mento *sm* (*DIR: di bambino*) custody; (*fiducia*): **fare ~ su qn** to rely on sb; **non dà nessun ~** he's not to be trusted.

affi'dare *vt*: ~ **qc o qn a qn** to entrust sth *o* sb to sb; ~**rsi** *vr*: ~**rsi a** to place one's trust in.

affievo'lirsi *vr* to grow weak.

af'figgere [af'fiddʒere] *vt* to stick up, post up.

affi'lare *vt* to sharpen.

affili'are *vt* to affiliate; ~**rsi** *vr*: ~**rsi a** to become affiliated to.

affi'nare *vt* to sharpen.

affinché [affin'ke] *cong* in order that, so that.

af'fine *ag* similar; **affinità** *sf inv* affinity.

affio'rare *vi* to emerge.

affissi'one *sf* billposting.

af'fisso, a *pp di* **affiggere** // *sm* bill, poster; (*LING*) affix.

affit'tare *vt* (*dare in affitto*) to let, rent (out); (*prendere in affitto*) to rent; **af'fitto** *sm* rent; (*contratto*) lease.

af'fliggere [af'fliddʒere] *vt* to torment; ~**rsi** *vr* to grieve; **af'flitto, a** *pp di* **affliggere**; **afflizi'one** *sf* distress, torment.

afflosci'arsi [affloʃ'ʃarsi] *vr* to go limp; (*frutta*) to go soft.

afflu'ente *sm* tributary; **afflu'enza** *sf* flow; (*di persone*) crowd.

afflu'ire *vi* to flow; (*fig: merci, persone*) to pour in; **af'flusso** *sm* influx.

affo'gare *vt, vi* to drown; ~**rsi** *vr* to drown; (*deliberatamente*) to drown o.s.

affol'lare *vt*, ~**rsi** *vr* to crowd; **affol'lato, a** *ag* crowded.

affon'dare *vt* to sink.

affran'care *vt* to free, liberate; (*AMM*) to redeem; (*lettera*) to stamp; (: *meccanicamente*) to frank (*Brit*), meter (*US*); ~**rsi** *vr* to free o.s.; **affranca'tura** *sf* (*di francobollo*) stamping; franking (*Brit*), metering (*US*); (*tassa di spedizione*) postage.

af'franto, a *ag* (*esausto*) worn out; (*abbattuto*) overcome.

af'fresco, schi *sm* fresco.

affret'tare *vt* to quicken, speed up; ~**rsi** *vr* to hurry; ~**rsi a fare qc** to hurry *o* hasten to do sth.

affron'tare *vt* (*pericolo etc*) to face; (*assalire: nemico*) to confront; ~**rsi** *vr* (*reciproco*) to come to blows.

af'fronto *sm* affront, insult.

affumi'care *vt* to fill with smoke; to blacken with smoke; (*alimenti*) to smoke.

affuso'lato, a *ag* tapering.

a'foso, a *ag* sultry, close.

'Africa *sf*: l'~ Africa; **afri'cano, a** *ag*, *sm/f* African.

afrodi'siaco, a, ci, che *ag, sm* aphrodisiac.

a'genda [a'dʒɛnda] *sf* diary.

a'gente [a'dʒɛnte] *sm* agent; ~ **di cambio** stockbroker; ~ **di polizia** police officer; **agen'zia** *sf* agency; (*succursale*) branch; **agenzia di collocamento** employment agency; **agenzia immobiliare** estate agent's (office) (*Brit*), real estate office (*US*); **agenzia pubblicitaria/viaggi** advertising/travel agency.

agevo'lare [adʒevo'lare] *vt* to facilitate, make easy.

a'gevole [a'dʒevole] *ag* easy; (*strada*) smooth.

agganci'are [aggan'tʃare] *vt* to hook up; (*FERR*) to couple.

ag'geggio [ad'dʒeddʒo] *sm* gadget, contraption.

agget'tivo [addʒet'tivo] *sm* adjective.

agghiacci'ante [aggjat'tʃante] *ag* (*fig*) chilling.

agghin'darsi [aggin'darsi] *vr* to deck o.s. out.

aggior'nare [addʒor'nare] *vt* (*opera, manuale*) to bring up-to-date; (*seduta etc*) to postpone; ~**rsi** *vr* to bring (*o* keep) o.s. up-to-date; **aggior'nato, a** *ag* up-to-date.

aggi'rare [addʒi'rare] *vt* to go round; (*fig: ingannare*) to trick; ~**rsi** *vr* to wander about; **il prezzo s'aggira sul milione** the price is around the million mark.

aggiudi'care [addʒudi'kare] *vt* to award; (*all'asta*) to knock down; ~**rsi qc** to win sth.

ag'giungere [ad'dʒundʒere] *vt* to add; **aggi'unto, a** *pp di* **aggiungere** // *ag* assistant *cpd* // ~ *sm* assistant // *sf* addition; **sindaco aggiunto** deputy mayor.

aggius'tare [addʒus'tare] *vt* (*accomodare*) to mend, repair; (*riassettare*) to adjust; (*fig: lite*) to settle; ~**rsi** *vr* (*arrangiarsi*) to make do; (*con senso reciproco*) to come to an agreement.

agglome'rato *sm* (*di rocce*) conglomerate; (*di legno*) chipboard; ~ **urbano** built-up area.

aggrap'parsi *vr*: ~ **a** to cling to.

aggra'vare *vt* (*aumentare*) to increase; (*appesantire: anche fig*) to weigh down, make heavy; (*fig: pena*) to make worse; ~**rsi** *vr* (*fig*) to worsen, become worse.

aggrazi'ato, a [aggrat'tsjato] *ag* graceful.

aggre'dire *vt* to attack, assault.

aggre'gare *vt*: ~ **qn a qc** to admit sb to sth; ~**rsi vr** to join; ~**rsi a** to join, become a member of; **aggre'gato, a** *ag* associated // *sm* aggregate; **aggregato urbano** built-up area.

aggressi'one *sf* aggression; (*atto*) attack, assault.

aggres'sivo, a *ag* aggressive.

aggrot'tare *vt*: ~ **le sopracciglia** to frown.

aggrovigli'are [aggroviʎ'ʎare] *vt* to tangle; ~**rsi** *vr* (*fig*) to become complicated.

agguan'tare *vt* to catch, seize.

aggu'ato *sm* trap; (*imboscata*) ambush; **tendere un** ~ **a qn** to set a trap for sb.

agguer'rito, a *ag* fierce.

agi'ato, a [a'dʒato] *ag* (*vita*) easy; (*persona*) well-off, well-to-do.

'agile ['adʒile] *ag* agile, nimble; **agilità** *sf* agility, nimbleness.

'agio ['adʒo] *sm* ease, comfort; ~**i** *smpl* comforts; **mettersi a proprio** ~ to make o.s. at home *o* comfortable.

a'gire [a'dʒire] *vi* to act; (*esercitare un'azione*) to take effect; (*TECN*) to work, function; ~ **contro qn** (*DIR*) to take action against sb.

agi'tare [adʒi'tare] *vt* (*bottiglia*) to shake; (*mano, fazzoletto*) to wave; (*fig: turbare*) to disturb; (*: incitare*) to stir (up); (*: dibattere*) to discuss; ~**rsi** *vr* (*mare*) to be rough; (*malato, dormitore*) to toss and turn; (*bambino*) to fidget; (*emozionarsi*) to get upset; (*POL*) to agitate; **agi'tato, a** *ag* rough; restless, fidgety; upset, perturbed; **agitazi'one** *sf* agitation; (*POL*) unrest, agitation; **mettere in agitazione qn** to upset *o* distress sb.

'agli ['aʎʎi] *prep + det vedi* **a**.

'aglio ['aʎʎo] *sm* garlic.

a'gnello [aɲ'ɲɛllo] *sm* lamb.

'ago, pl aghi *sm* needle.

ago'nia *sf* agony.

ago'nistico, a, ci, che *ag* athletic; (*fig*) competitive.

agoniz'zare [agonid'dzare] *vi* to be dying.

agopun'tura *sf* acupuncture.

a'gosto *sm* August.

a'grario, a *ag* agrarian, agricultural; (*riforma*) land *cpd* // *sf* agriculture.

a'gricolo, a *ag* agricultural, farm *cpd*; **agricol'tore** *sm* farmer; **agricol'tura** *sf* agriculture, farming.

agri'foglio [agri'foʎʎo] *sm* holly.

agrimen'sore *sm* land surveyor.

agritu'rismo *sm* farm holidays *pl*.

'agro, a *ag* sour, sharp; ~**dolce** *ag* bittersweet; (*salsa*) sweet and sour.

a'grume *sm* (*spesso al pl: pianta*) citrus; (*: frutto*) citrus fruit.

aguz'zare [agut'tsare] *vt* to sharpen; ~ **gli orecchi** to prick up one's ears.

a'guzzo, a [a'guttso] *ag* sharp.

'ai *prep + det vedi* **a**.

'Aia *sf*: **l'**~ the Hague.

'aia *sf* threshing-floor.

ai'rone *sm* heron.

aiu'ola *sf* flower bed.

aiu'tante *sm/f* assistant // *sm* (*MIL*) adjutant; (*NAUT*) master-at-arms; ~ di campo aide-de-camp.

aiu'tare *vt* to help; ~ qn (a fare) to help sb (to do).

ai'uto *sm* help, assistance, aid; (*aiutante*) assistant; venire in ~ di qn to come to sb's aid; ~ chirurgo assistant surgeon.

aiz'zare [ait'tsare] *vt* to incite; ~ i cani contro qn to set the dogs on sb.

al *prep* + *det vedi* **a.**

'ala, *pl* **'ali** *sf* wing; fare ~ to fall back, make way; ~ destra/sinistra (*SPORT*) right/left wing.

'alacre *ag* quick, brisk.

a'lano *sm* Great Dane.

a'lare *ag* wing *cpd*.

'alba *sf* dawn.

Alba'nia *sf*: l'~ Albania.

'albatro *sm* albatross.

albeggi'are [albed'dʒare] *vi*, *vb impers* to dawn.

albera'tura *sf* (*NAUT*) masts *pl*.

alberghi'ero, a [alber'gjero] *ag* hotel *cpd*.

al'bergo, ghi *sm* hotel; ~ della gioventù youth hostel.

'albero *sm* tree; (*NAUT*) mast; (*TECN*) shaft; ~ genealogico family tree; ~ a gomiti crankshaft; ~ di Natale Christmas tree; ~ maestro mainmast; ~ di trasmissione transmission shaft.

albi'cocca, che *sf* apricot; **albi'cocco, chi** *sm* apricot tree.

'albo *sm* (*registro*) register, roll; (*AMM*) notice board.

'album *sm* album; ~ da disegno sketch book.

al'bume *sm* albumen.

'alce [ˈaltʃe] *sm* elk.

al'colico, a, ci, che *ag* alcoholic // *sm* alcoholic drink.

alcoliz'zato, a [alcolid'dzato] *sm/f* alcoholic.

'alcool *sm* alcohol; **alco'olico** *etc vedi* **alcolico** *etc*.

al'cuno, a *det* (*dav sm*: **alcun** +*C, V*, **alcuno** + *s impura, gn, pn, ps, x, z*; *dav sf*: **alcuna** +*C*, **alcun'** +*V*) (*nessuno*): non ... ~ no, not any; ~i(e) *det pl*, *pronome pl* some, a few; non c'è ~a fretta there's no hurry, there isn't any hurry; senza alcun riguardo without any consideration.

aldilà *sm*: l'~ the after-life.

a'letta *sf* (*TECN*) fin; tab.

alfa'beto [ˈaldʒebra] *sf* alphabet.

alfi'ere *sm* standard-bearer; (*MIL*) ensign; (*SCACCHI*) bishop.

al'fine *av* finally, in the end.

'alga, ghe *sf* seaweed *q*, alga.

'algebra [ˈaldʒebra] *sf* algebra.

Alge'ria [aldʒe'ria] *sf*: l'~ Algeria.

ali'ante *sm* (*AER*) glider.

'alibi *sm inv* alibi.

a'lice [aˈlitʃe] *sf* anchovy.

alie'nare *vt* (*DIR*) to alienate, transfer; (*rendere ostile*) to alienate; ~rsi qn to alienate sb; **alie'nato, a** *ag* alienated; transferred; (*fuor di senno*) insane // *sm* lunatic, insane person; **alienazi'one** *sf* alienation; transfer; insanity.

ali'eno, a *ag* (*avverso*): ~ (da) opposed (to), averse (to) // *sm/f* alien.

alimen'tare *vt* to feed; (*TECN*) to feed; to supply; (*fig*) to sustain // *ag* food *cpd*; ~i *smpl* foodstuffs; (*anche*: negozio di ~i) grocer's shop; **alimentazi'one** *sf* feeding; supplying; sustaining; (*gli alimenti*) diet.

ali'mento *sm* food; ~i *smpl* food *sg*; (*DIR*) alimony.

a'liquota *sf* share; (*d'imposta*) rate.

alis'cafo *sm* hydrofoil.

'alito *sm* breath.

all. *abbr* (= allegato) encl.

'alla *prep* + *det vedi* **a.**

allacci'are [allat'tʃare] *vt* (*scarpe*) to tie, lace (up); (*cintura*) to do up, fasten; (*due località*) to link; (*luce, gas*) to connect; (*amicizia*) to form.

alla'gare *vt*, ~rsi *vr* to flood.

allar'gare *vt* to widen; (*vestito*) to let out; (*aprire*) to open; (*fig: dilatare*) to extend.

allar'mare *vt* to alarm.

al'larme *sm* alarm; ~ aereo air-raid warning.

allar'mismo *sm* scaremongering.

allat'tare *vt* to feed.

'alle *prep* + *det vedi* **a.**

alle'anza [alleˈantsa] *sf* alliance.

alle'arsi *vr* to form an alliance; **alle'ato, a** *ag* allied // *sm/f* ally.

alle'gare *vt* (*accludere*) to enclose; (*DIR: citare*) to cite, adduce; (*denti*) to set on edge; **alle'gato, a** *ag* enclosed // *sm* enclosure; in allegato enclosed.

allegge'rire [alleddʒeˈrire] *vt* to lighten, make lighter; (*fig: sofferenza*) to alleviate, lessen; (: *lavoro, tasse*) to reduce.

alle'gria *sf* gaiety, cheerfulness.

al'legro, a *ag* cheerful, merry; (*un po' brillo*) merry, tipsy; (*vivace: colore*) bright // *sm* (*MUS*) allegro.

allena'mento *sm* training.

alle'nare *vt*, ~rsi *vr* to train; **alle'natore** *sm* (*SPORT*) trainer, coach.

allen'tare *vt* to slacken; (*disciplina*) to relax; ~rsi *vr* to become slack; (*ingranaggio*) to work loose.

aller'gia, 'gie [allerˈdʒia] *sf* allergy; **al'lergico, a, ci, che** *ag* allergic.

alles'tire *vt* (*cena*) to prepare; (*esercito, nave*) to equip, fit out; (*spettacolo*) to stage.

allet'tare *vt* to lure, entice.

alleva'mento *sm* breeding, rearing;

(*luogo*) stock farm.

alle'vare *vt* (*animale*) to breed, rear; (*bambino*) to bring up.

allevi'are *vt* to alleviate.

alli'bire *vi* to be astounded.

allibra'tore *sm* bookmaker.

allie'tare *vt* to cheer up, gladden.

alli'evo *sm* pupil; (*apprendista*) apprentice; (MIL) cadet.

alliga'tore *sm* alligator.

alline'are *vt* (*persone, cose*) to line up; (TIP) to align; (*fig: economia, salari*) to adjust, align; ~**rsi** *vr* to line up; (*fig: a idee*): ~**rsi a** to come into line with.

'allo *prep* + *det vedi* **a**.

al'locco, a, chi, che *sm* tawny owl // *sm/f* oaf.

allocuzi'one [allokut'tsjone] *sf* address, solemn speech.

al'lodola *sf* (sky)lark.

alloggi'are [allod'dʒaɾe] *vt* to accommodate // *vi* to live; **al'loggio** *sm* lodging, accommodation (*Brit*), accommodations (*US*); (*appartamento*) flat (*Brit*), apartment (*US*).

allontana'mento *sm* removal; dismissal.

allonta'nare *vt* to send away, send off; (*impiegato*) to dismiss; (*pericolo*) to avert, remove; (*estraniare*) to alienate; ~**rsi** *vr*: ~**rsi (da)** to go away (from); (*estraniarsi*) to become estranged (from).

al'lora *av* (*in quel momento*) then // *cong* (*in questo caso*) well then; (*dunque*) well then, so; **la gente d'~** people then *o* in those days; **da ~ in poi** from then on.

allor'ché [allor'ke] *cong* (*formale*) when, as soon as.

al'loro *sm* laurel.

'alluce ['allutʃe] *sm* big toe.

alluci'nante [allutʃi'nante] *ag* awful; (*fam*) amazing.

allucinazi'one [allutʃinat'tsjone] *sf* hallucination.

al'ludere *vi*: ~ **a** to allude to, hint at.

allu'minio *sm* aluminium (*Brit*), aluminum (*US*).

allun'gare *vt* to lengthen; (*distendere*) to prolong, extend; (*diluire*) to water down; ~**rsi** *vr* to lengthen; (*ragazzo*) to stretch, grow taller; (*sdraiarsi*) to lie down, stretch out.

allusi'one *sf* hint, allusion.

alluvi'one *sf* flood.

al'meno *av* at least // *cong*: (**se**) ~ if only; (**se**) ~ **piovesse!** if only it would rain!

a'lone *sm* halo.

'Alpi *sfpl*: **le** ~ the Alps.

alpi'nismo *sm* mountaineering, climbing; **alpi'nista, i, e** *sm/f* mountaineer, climber.

al'pino, a *ag* Alpine; mountain *cpd*.

al'quanto *av* rather, a little; ~, **a** *det a*

certain amount of, some // *pronome* a certain amount, some; ~**i(e)** *det pl*, *pronome pl* several, quite a few.

alt *escl* halt!, stop! // *sm*: **dare l'~** to call a halt.

alta'lena *sf* (*a funi*) swing; (*in bilico, anche fig*) seesaw.

al'tare *sm* altar.

alte'rare *vt* to alter, change; (*cibo*) to adulterate; (*registro*) to falsify; (*persona*) to irritate; ~**rsi** *vr* to alter; (*cibo*) to go bad; (*persona*) to lose one's temper.

al'terco, chi *sm* altercation, wrangle.

alter'nare *vt*, ~**rsi** *vr* to alternate; **alterna'tivo, a** *ag* alternative // *sf* alternative; **alter'nato, a** *ag* alternate; (ELETTR) alternating; **alterna'tore** *sm* alternator.

al'terno, a *ag* alternate; **a giorni** ~**i** on alternate days, every other day.

al'tezza [al'tettsa] *sf* height; width, breadth; depth; pitch; (GEO) latitude; (*titolo*) highness; (*fig: nobiltà*) greatness; **essere all'~ di** to be on a level with; (*fig*) to be up to *o* equal to; **altez'zoso, a** *ag* haughty.

al'ticcio, a, ci, ce [al'tittʃo] *ag* tipsy.

altipi'ano *sm* = **altopiano**.

alti'tudine *sf* altitude.

'alto, a *ag* high; (*persona*) tall; (*tessuto*) wide, broad; (*suono, acque*) deep; (*suono*) high(-pitched); (GEO) upper; (*settentrionale*) northern // *sm* top (part) // *av* high; (*parlare*) aloud, loudly; **il palazzo è** ~ **20 metri** the building is 20 metres high; **il tessuto è** ~ **70 cm** the material is 70 cm wide; **ad** ~**a voce** aloud; **a notte** ~**a** in the dead of night; **in** ~ up, upwards; at the top; **dall'~ in** *o* **al basso** up and down, **degli** ~**i e bassi** (*fig*) ups and downs; ~**a fedeltà** high fidelity, hi-fi; ~**a moda** haute couture.

alto'forno *sm* blast furnace.

altolo'cato, a *ag* of high rank, highly placed.

altopar'lante *sm* loudspeaker.

altopi'ano *sm*, *pl* **altipiani** plateau, upland plain.

altret'tanto, a *ag*, *pronome* as much; (*pl*) as many // *av* equally; **tanti auguri!** — **grazie,** ~ all the best! — thank you, the same to you.

'altri *pronome inv* (*qualcuno*) somebody; (*: in espressioni negative*) anybody; (*un'altra persona*) another (person).

altri'menti *av* otherwise.

'altro, a ◆ *det* **1** (*diverso*) other, different; **questa è un'~a cosa** that's another *o* a different thing

2 (*supplementare*) other; **prendi un** ~ **cioccolatino** have another chocolate; **hai avuto** ~**e notizie?** have you had any more *o* any other news?

3 (*nel tempo*): **l'~ giorno** the other day;

l'altr'anno last year; l'~ ieri the day before yesterday; domani l'~ the day after tomorrow; quest'~ mese next month

4: d'~a parte on the other hand

◆ *pronome* **1** (*persona, cosa diversa o supplementare*): un ~, un'~a another (one); lo farà un ~ someone else will do it; ~i(e) others; gli ~i (*la gente*) others, other people; l'uno e l'~ both (of them); aiutarsi l'un l'~ to help one another; da un giorno all'~ from day to day; (*nel giro di 24 ore*) from one day to the next; (*da un momento all'altro*) any day now **2** (*sostantivato: solo maschile*) something else; (: in espressioni interrogative) anything else; non ho ~ da dire I have nothing else *o* I don't have anything else to say; più che ~ above all; se non ~ at least; tra l'~ among other things; ci mancherebbe ~! that's all we need!; non faccio ~ che lavorare I do nothing but work; contento? — ~ che! are you pleased? — and how!; *vedi* **senza, noialtri, voialtri, tutto.**

al'tronde *av*: d'~ on the other hand.

al'trove *av* elsewhere, somewhere else.

al'trui *ag inv* other people's // *sm*: l'~ other people's belongings *pl*.

altru'ista, i, e *ag* altruistic.

al'tura *sf* (*rialto*) height, high ground; (*alto mare*) open sea; **pesca d'~** deep-sea fishing.

a'lunno, a *sm/f* pupil.

alve'are *sm* hive.

'alveo *sm* riverbed.

al'zare [al'tsare] *vt* to raise, lift; (*issare*) to hoist; (*costruire*) to build, erect; ~**rsi** *vr* to rise; (*dal letto*) to get up; (*crescere*) to grow tall (*o* taller); ~ **le spalle** to shrug one's shoulders; ~**rsi in piedi** to stand up, get to one's feet; **al'zata** *sf* lifting, raising; **un'alzata di spalle** a shrug.

a'mabile *ag* lovable; (*vino*) sweet.

a'maca, che *sf* hammock.

amalga'mare *vt*, ~**rsi** *vr* to amalgamate.

a'mante *ag*: ~ **di** (*musica etc*) fond of // *sm/f* lover/mistress.

a'mare *vt* to love; (*amico, musica, sport*) to like.

amareggi'ato, a [amared'dʒato] *ag* upset, saddened.

ama'rena *sf* sour black cherry.

ama'rezza [ama'rettsa] *sf* bitterness.

a'maro, a *ag* bitter // *sm* bitterness; (*liquore*) bitters *pl*.

ambasci'ata [ambaʃ'ʃata] *sf* embassy; (*messaggio*) message; **ambascia'tore, 'trice** *sm/f* ambassador/ambassadress.

ambe'due *ag inv*: ~ **i** ragazzi both boys // *pronome inv* both.

ambien'tare *vt* to acclimatize; (*romanzo, film*) to set; ~**rsi** *vr* to get

used to one's surroundings.

ambi'ente *sm* environment; (*fig: insieme di persone*) milieu; (*stanza*) room.

am'biguo, a *ag* ambiguous; (*persona*) shady.

am'bire *vt* (*anche: vi:* ~ **a**) to aspire to.

'ambito *sm* sphere, field.

ambizi'one [ambit'tsjone] *sf* ambition; **ambizi'oso, a** *ag* ambitious.

'ambo *ag inv* both.

'ambra *sf* amber; ~ **grigia** ambergris.

ambu'lante *ag* travelling, itinerant.

ambu'lanza [ambu'lantsa] *sf* ambulance.

ambula'torio *sm* (*studio medico*) surgery.

amenità *sf inv* pleasantness *q*.

a'meno, a *ag* pleasant; (*strano*) funny, strange; (*spiritoso*) amusing.

A'merica *sf*: l'~ America; l'~ **latina** Latin America; **ameri'cano, a** *ag, sm/f* American.

ami'anto *sm* asbestos.

a'mica *sf vedi* **amico.**

ami'chevole [ami'kevole] *ag* friendly.

ami'cizia [ami'tʃittsja] *sf* friendship; ~**e** *sfpl* (*amici*) friends.

a'mico, a, ci, che *sm/f* friend; (*amante*) boyfriend/girlfriend; ~ **del cuore** *o* intimo bosom friend.

'amido *sm* starch.

ammac'care *vt* (*pentola*) to dent; (*persona*) to bruise; ~**rsi** *vr* to bruise.

ammaes'trare *vt* (*animale*) to train; (*persona*) to teach.

ammai'nare *vt* to lower, haul down.

amma'larsi *vr* to fall ill; **amma'lato, a** *ag* ill, sick // *sm/f* sick person; (*paziente*) patient.

ammali'are *vt* (*fig*) to enchant, charm.

am'manco, chi *sm* (*ECON*) deficit.

ammanet'tare *vt* to handcuff.

ammas'sare *vt* (*ammucchiare*) to amass; (*raccogliere*) to gather together; ~**rsi** *vr* to pile up; to gather; **am'masso** *sm* mass; (*mucchio*) pile, heap; (*ECON*) stockpile.

ammat'tire *vi* to go mad.

ammaz'zare [ammat'tsare] *vt* to kill; ~**rsi** *vr* (*uccidersi*) to kill o.s.; (*rimanere ucciso*) to be killed; ~**rsi di lavoro** to work o.s. to death.

am'menda *sf* amends *pl*; (*DIR, SPORT*) fine; **fare** ~ **di qc** to make amends for sth.

am'messo, a *pp di* **ammettere** // *cong*: ~ **che** supposing that.

am'mettere *vt* to admit; (*riconoscere: fatto*) to acknowledge, admit; (*permettere*) to allow, accept; (*supporre*) to suppose.

ammez'zato [ammed'dzato] *sm* (*anche: piano* ~) mezzanine, entresol.

ammic'care *vi*: ~ (**a**) to wink (at).

amminis'trare *vt* to run, manage;

(*REL, DIR*) to administer; **ammini-stra'tivo, a** *ag* administrative; **amministra'tore** *sm* administrator; (*di condominio*) flats manager; **amministratore delegato** managing director; **amministrazi'one** *sf* management; administration.

ammiragli'ato [ammiraʎ'ʎato] *sm* admiralty.

ammi'raglio [ammi'raʎʎo] *sm* admiral.

ammi'rare *vt* to admire; **ammira'tore, 'trice** *sm/f* admirer; **ammirazi'one** *sf* admiration.

ammis'sibile *ag* admissible, acceptable.

ammissi'one *sf* admission; (*approvazione*) acknowledgment.

ammobili'are *vt* to furnish.

am'modo, a 'modo *av* properly // *ag inv* respectable, nice.

am'mollo *sm*: lasciare in ~ to leave to soak.

ammo'niaca *sf* ammonia.

ammoni'mento *sm* warning; admonishment.

ammo'nire *vt* (*avvertire*) to warn; (*rimproverare*) to admonish; (*DIR*) to caution.

ammon'tare *vi*: ~ a to amount to // *sm* (*total*) amount.

ammorbi'dente *sm* fabric conditioner.

ammorbi'dire *vt* to soften.

ammortiz'zare [ammortid'dzare] *vt* (*ECON*) to pay off, amortize; (*: spese d'impianto*) to write off; (*AUT, TECN*) to absorb, deaden; **ammortizza'tore** *sm* (*AUT, TECN*) shock-absorber.

ammucchi'are [ammuk'kjare] *vt*, ~**rsi** *vr* to pile up, accumulate.

ammuf'fire *vi* to go mouldy (*Brit*) o moldy (*US*).

ammutina'mento *sm* mutiny.

ammuti'narsi *vr* to mutiny.

ammuto'lire *vi* to be struck dumb.

amnis'tia *sf* amnesty.

'amo *sm* (*PESCA*) hook; (*fig*) bait.

a'more *sm* love; ~**i** *smpl* love affairs; il tuo bambino è un ~ your baby's a darling; fare l'~ o all'~ to make love; per ~ o per forza by hook or by crook; amor proprio self-esteem, pride; **amo'revole** *ag* loving, affectionate.

a'morfo, a *ag* amorphous; (*fig: persona*) lifeless.

amo'roso, a *ag* (*affettuoso*) loving, affectionate; (*d'amore: sguardo*) amorous; (*: poesia, relazione*) love cpd.

ampi'ezza [am'pjettsa] *sf* width, breadth; spaciousness; (*fig: importanza*) scale, size.

'ampio, a *ag* wide, broad; (*spazioso*) spacious; (*abbondante: vestito*) loose; (*: gonna*) full; (*: spiegazione*) ample, full.

am'plesso *sm* (*eufemismo*) embrace.

ampli'are *vt* (*ingrandire*) to enlarge; (*allargare*) to widen.

amplifi'care *vt* to amplify; (*magnificare*) to extol; **amplifica'tore** *sm* (*TECN, MUS*) amplifier.

am'polla *sf* (*vasetto*) cruet.

ampu'tare *vt* (*MED*) to amputate.

anabbagli'ante [anabbaʎ'ʎante] *ag* (*AUT*) dipped (*Brit*), dimmed (*US*); ~**i** *smpl* dipped (*Brit*) o dimmed (*US*) headlights.

a'nagrafe *sf* (*registro*) register of births, marriages and deaths; (*ufficio*) registration office.

analfa'beta, i, e *ag, sm/f* illiterate.

anal'gesico, a, ci, che [anal'dʒeziko] *ag, sm* analgesic.

a'nalisi *sf inv* analysis; (*MED: esame*) test; ~ **grammaticale** parsing; **ana'lista, i, e** *sm/f* analyst; (*PSIC*) (psycho)analyst.

analiz'zare [analid'dzare] *vt* to analyse; (*MED*) to test.

analo'gia, 'gie [analo'dʒia] *sf* analogy.

a'nalogo, a, ghi, ghe *ag* analogous.

'ananas *sm inv* pineapple.

anar'chia [anar'kia] *sf* anarchy; **a'narchico, a, ci, che** *ag* anarchic(al) // *sm/f* anarchist.

'ANAS *sigla f* (= *Azienda Nazionale Autonoma delle Strade*) national roads department.

anato'mia *sf* anatomy; **ana'tomico, a, ci, che** *ag* anatomical; (*sedile*) contoured.

'anatra *sf* duck.

'anca, che *sf* (*ANAT*) hip; (*ZOOL*) haunch.

'anche ['anke] *cong* (*inoltre, pure*) also, too; (*perfino*) even; vengo anch'io I'm coming too; ~ se even if.

an'cora *av* still; (*di nuovo*) again; (*di più*) some more; (*persino*): ~ più forte even stronger; non ~ not yet; ~ una volta once more, once again; ~ un po' a little more; (*di tempo*) a little longer.

'ancora *sf* anchor; gettare/levare l'~ to cast/weigh anchor; **anco'raggio** *sm* anchorage; **anco'rare** *vt*, ancorarsi *vr* to anchor.

anda'mento *sm* progress, movement; course; state.

an'dante *ag* (*corrente*) current; (*di poco pregio*) cheap, second-rate // *sm* (*MUS*) andante.

an'dare *sm*: a lungo ~ in the long run // *vi* to go; (*essere adatto*): ~ a to suit; (*piacere*): il suo comportamento non mi va I don't like the way he behaves; ti va di andare al cinema? do you feel like going to the cinema? **andarsene** to go away; questa camicia va lavata this shirt needs a wash o should be washed; ~ a cavallo to ride; ~ in macchina/aereo to go by car/plane; ~ a fare qc to go and do sth; ~ a pescare/sciare to go fishing/skiing; ~ a male to go bad; come va?

(*lavoro, progetto*) how are things?; come va? — **bene, grazie!** how are you? — fine, thanks!; va fatto entro oggi it's got to be done today; ne va della nostra vita our lives are at stake; **an'data** *sf* going; (*viaggio*) outward journey; **biglietto di sola andata** single (*Brit*) *o* one-way ticket; **biglietto di andata e ritorno** return (*Brit*) *o* round-trip (*US*) ticket; **anda'tura** *sf* (*modo di andare*) walk, gait; (*SPORT*) pace; (*NAUT*) tack.

an'dazzo [an'dattso] *sm* (*peg*): **prendere un brutto ~** to take a turn for the worse.

andirivi'eni *sm inv* coming and going.

'andito *sm* corridor, passage.

an'drone *sm* entrance hall.

a'neddoto *sm* anecdote.

ane'lare *vi*: **~ a** (*fig*) to long for, yearn for.

a'nelito *sm* (*fig*): **~ di** longing *o* yearning for.

a'nello *sm* ring; (*di catena*) link.

a'nemico, a, ci, che *ag* anaemic.

a'nemone *sm* anemone.

aneste'sia *sf* anaesthesia; **anes'tetico, a, ci, che** *ag*, *sm* anaesthetic.

anfite'atro *sm* amphitheatre.

an'fratto *sm* ravine.

an'gelico, a, ci, che [an'dʒɛliko] *ag* angelic(al).

'angelo ['andʒelo] *sm* angel; **~ custode** guardian angel.

anghe'ria [ange'ria] *sf* vexation.

an'gina [an'dʒina] *sf* tonsillitis; **~ pectoris** angina.

angli'cano, a *ag* Anglican.

angli'cismo [angli'tʃizmo] *sm* anglicism.

anglo'sassone *ag* Anglo-Saxon.

ango'lare *ag* angular.

angolazi'one [angolat'tsjone] *sf* (*FOT etc*, *fig*) angle.

'angolo *sm* corner; (*MAT*) angle.

an'goscia, sce [an'gɔʃʃa] *sf* deep anxiety, anguish *q*; **angosci'oso, a** *ag* (*d'angoscia*) anguished; (*che dà angoscia*) distressing, painful.

angu'illa *sf* eel.

an'guria *sf* watermelon.

an'gustia *sf* (*ansia*) anguish, distress; (*povertà*) poverty, want.

angusti'are *vt* to distress; **~rsi** *vr*: **~rsi (per)** to worry (about).

an'gusto, a *ag* (*stretto*) narrow; (*fig*) mean, petty.

'anice ['anitʃe] *sm* (*CUC*) aniseed; (*BOT*) anise.

a'nidride *sf* (*CHIM*): **~ carbonica/solforosa** carbon/sulphur dioxide.

'anima *sf* soul; (*abitante*) inhabitant; **non c'era ~ viva** there wasn't a living soul.

ani'male *sm*, *ag* animal.

ani'mare *vt* to give life to, liven up; (*incoraggiare*) to encourage; **~rsi** *vr* to become animated, come to life;

ani'mato, a *ag* animate; (*vivace*) lively, animated; (*: strada*) busy; **anima'tore, 'trice** *sm/f* guiding spirit; (*CINEMA*) animator; (*di festa*) life and soul; **animazi'one** *sf* liveliness; (*di strada*) bustle; (*CINEMA*) animation; **animazione teatrale** amateur dramatics.

'animo *sm* (*mente*) mind; (*cuore*) heart; (*coraggio*) courage; (*disposizione*) character, disposition; **avere in ~ di fare qc** to intend *o* have a mind to do sth; **perdersi d'~** to lose heart.

'anitra *sf* = anatra.

anna'cquare *vt* to water down, dilute.

annaffi'are *vt* to water; **annaffia'toio** *sm* watering can.

an'nali *smpl* annals.

annas'pare *vi* to flounder.

an'nata *sf* year; (*importo annuo*) annual amount; **vino d'~** vintage wine.

annebbi'are *vt* (*fig*) to cloud; **~rsi** *vr* to become foggy; (*vista*) to become dim.

annega'mento *sm* drowning.

anne'gare *vt*, *vi* to drown; **~rsi** *vr* (*accidentalmente*) to drown; (*deliberatamente*) to drown o.s.

anne'rire *vt* to blacken // *vi* to become black.

an'nesso, a *pp di* **annettere** // *ag* attached; (*POL*) annexed; **... e tutti gli ~i e connessi** ... and so on and so forth.

an'nettere *vt* (*POL*) to annex; (*accludere*) to attach.

annichi'lare, annichi'lire [anniki'lare, anniki'lire] *vt* to annihilate.

anni'darsi *vr* to nest.

annienta'mento *sm* annihilation, destruction.

annien'tare *vt* to annihilate, destroy.

anniver'sario *sm* anniversary.

'anno *sm* year.

anno'dare *vt* to knot, tie; (*fig: rapporto*) to form.

annoi'are *vt* to bore; (*seccare*) to annoy; **~rsi** *vr* to be bored; to be annoyed.

anno'tare *vt* (*registrare*) to note, note down; (*commentare*) to annotate; **annotazi'one** *sf* note; annotation.

annove'rare *vt* to number.

annu'ale *ag* annual.

annu'ario *sm* yearbook.

annu'ire *vi* to nod; (*acconsentire*) to agree.

annul'lare *vt* to annihilate, destroy; (*contratto, francobollo*) to cancel; (*matrimonio*) to annul; (*sentenza*) to quash; (*risultati*) to declare void.

annunci'are *vt* to announce; (*dar segni rivelatori*) to herald; **annuncia'tore, 'trice** *sm/f* (*RADIO, TV*) announcer; **l'Annunciazi'one** *sf* the Annunciation.

an'nuncio [an'nuntʃo] *sm* announcement; (*fig*) sign; **~ pubblicitario**

advertisement; ~i **economici** classified advertisements, small ads.

'annuo, a *ag* annual, yearly.

annu'sare *vt* to sniff, smell; ~ **tabacco** to take snuff.

'ano *sm* anus.

anoma'lia *sf* anomaly.

a'nomalo, a *ag* anomalous.

a'nonimo, a *ag* anonymous // *sm* (*autore*) anonymous writer (*o painter etc*); **società ~a** (*COMM*) joint stock company.

anor'male *ag* abnormal // *sm/f* subnormal person; (*eufemismo*) homosexual.

ANSA *sigla f* (= *Agenzia Nazionale Stampa Associata*) press agency.

'ansa *sf* (*manico*) handle; (*di fiume*) bend, loop.

'ansia, ansietà *sf* anxiety.

ansi'mare *vi* to pant.

ansi'oso, a *ag* anxious.

'anta *sf* (*di finestra*) shutter; (*di armadio*) door.

antago'nismo *sm* antagonism.

an'tartico, a, ci, che *ag* Antarctic // *sm*: **l'A~** the Antarctic.

antece'dente [antetʃe'dɛnte] *ag* preceding, previous.

ante'fatto *sm* previous events *pl*; previous history.

antegu'erra *sm* pre-war period.

ante'nato *sm* ancestor, forefather.

an'tenna *sf* (*RADIO, TV*) aerial; (*ZOOL*) antenna, feeler; (*NAUT*) yard.

ante'prima *sf* preview.

anteri'ore *ag* (*ruota, zampa*) front; (*fatti*) previous, preceding.

antia'ereo, a *ag* anti-aircraft.

antia'tomico, a, ci, che *ag* antinuclear; **rifugio ~** fallout shelter.

antibi'otico, a, ci, che *ag, sm* antibiotic.

anti'camera *sf* anteroom; **fare ~** to wait (for an audience).

antichità [antiki'ta] *sf inv* antiquity; (*oggetto*) antique.

antici'pare [antitʃi'pare] *vt* (*consegna, visita*) to bring forward, anticipate; (*somma di denaro*) to pay in advance; (*notizia*) to disclose // *vi* to be ahead of time; **anticipazi'one** *sf* anticipation; (*di notizia*) advance information; (*somma di denaro*) advance; **an'ticipo** *sm* anticipation; (*di denaro*) advance; **in anticipo** early, in advance.

an'tico, a, chi, che *ag* (*quadro, mobili*) antique; (*dell'antichità*) ancient; **all'~a** old-fashioned.

anticoncezio'nale [antikontʃettsjo'nale] *sm* contraceptive.

anticonfor'mista, i, e *ag, sm/f* nonconformist.

anti'corpo *sm* antibody.

anti'furto *sm* (*anche: sistema ~*) antitheft device.

An'tille *sfpl*: **le ~** the West Indies.

antin'cendio [antin'tʃɛndjo] *ag inv* fire *cpd*.

antio'rario [antio'rarjo] *ag*: **in senso ~** anticlockwise.

anti'pasto *sm* hors d'œuvre.

antipa'tia *sf* antipathy, dislike; **anti'patico, a, ci, che** *ag* unpleasant, disagreeable.

antiquari'ato *sm* antique trade; **un oggetto d'~** an antique.

anti'quario *sm* antique dealer.

anti'quato, a *ag* antiquated, oldfashioned.

antise'mita, i, e *ag* anti-Semitic.

anti'settico, a, ci, che *ag, sm* antiseptic.

antista'minico, a, ci, che *ag, sm* antihistamine.

antolo'gia, 'gie [antolo'dʒia] *sf* anthology.

anu'lare *ag* ring *cpd* // *sm* third finger.

'anzi ['antsi] *av* (*invece*) on the contrary; (*o meglio*) or rather, or better still.

anzianità [antsjani'ta] *sf* old age; (*AMM*) seniority.

anzi'ano, a [an'tsjano] *ag* old; (*AMM*) senior // *sm/f* old person; senior member.

anziché [antsi'ke] *cong* rather than.

anzi'tutto [antsi'tutto] *av* first of all.

apa'tia *sf* apathy, indifference.

'ape *sf* bee.

aperi'tivo *sm* aperitif.

a'perto, a *pp di* **aprire** // *ag* open; **all'~** in the open (air).

aper'tura *sf* opening; (*ampiezza*) width, spread; (*POL*) approach; (*FOT*) aperture; ~ **alare** wing span.

'apice ['apitʃe] *sm* apex; (*fig*) height.

apicol'tore *sm* beekeeper.

ap'nea *sf*: **immergersi in ~** to dive without breathing apparatus.

a'polide *ag* stateless.

apoples'sia *sf* (*MED*) apoplexy.

a'postolo *sm* apostle.

a'postrofo *sm* apostrophe.

appa'gare *vt* to satisfy; ~**rsi** *vr*: ~**rsi di** to be satisfied with.

ap'palto *sm* (*COMM*) contract; **dare/prendere in ~ un lavoro** to let out/undertake a job on contract.

appan'nare *vt* (*vetro*) to mist; (*metallo*) to tarnish; (*vista*) to dim; ~**rsi** *vr* to mist over; to tarnish; to dim; to grow dim.

appa'rato *sm* equipment, machinery; (*ANAT*) apparatus; ~ **scenico** (*TEATRO*) props *pl*.

apparecchi'are [apparek'kjare] *vt* to prepare; (*tavola*) to set // *vi* to set the table; **apparecchia'tura** *sf* equipment; (*macchina*) machine, device.

appa'recchio [appa'rekkjo] *sm* piece of apparatus, device; (*aeroplano*) aircraft *inv*; ~ televisivo/telefonico television set/telephone.

appa'rente *ag* apparent; **appa'renza** *sf* appearance; in *o* **all'apparenza** apparently, to all appearances.

appa'rire *vi* to appear; (*sembrare*) to seem, appear; **appari'scente** *ag* (*colore*) garish, gaudy; (*bellezza*) striking.

apparta'mento *sm* flat (*Brit*), apartment (*US*).

appar'tarsi *vr* to withdraw; **appar'tato, a** *ag* (*luogo*) secluded.

apparte'nere *vi*: ~ a to belong to.

appassio'nare *vt* to thrill; (*commuovere*) to move; ~rsi a qc to take a great interest in sth; to be deeply moved by sth; **appassio'nato, a** *ag* passionate; (*entusiasta*): **appassionato (di)** keen (on).

appas'sire *vi* to wither.

appel'larsi *vr* (*ricorrere*): ~ a to appeal to; (*DIR*): ~ **contro** to appeal against; **ap'pello** *sm* roll-call; (*implorazione, DIR*) appeal; **fare appello a** to appeal to.

ap'pena *av* (*a stento*) hardly, scarcely; (*solamente, da poco*) just // *cong* as soon as; (*non*) ~ **furono arrivati ...** as soon as they had arrived ...; ~ **... che** *o* **quando** no sooner ... than.

ap'pendere *vt* to hang (up).

appen'dice [appen'ditʃe] *sf* appendix; **romanzo d'~** popular serial.

appendi'cite [appendi'tʃite] *sf* appendicitis.

Appen'nini *smpl*: **gli ~** the Apennines.

appesan'tire *vt* to make heavy; ~rsi *vr* to grow stout.

ap'peso, a *pp di* **appendere**.

appe'tito *sm* appetite; **appeti'toso, a** *ag* appetising; (*fig*) attractive, desirable.

appia'nare *vt* to level; (*fig*) to smooth away, iron out.

appiat'tire *vt* to flatten; ~rsi *vr* to become flatter; (*farsi piatto*) to flatten o.s.; ~rsi al suolo to lie flat on the ground.

appic'care *vt*: ~ **il fuoco a** to set fire to, set on fire.

appicci'care [appittʃi'kare] *vt* to stick; (*fig*): ~ qc a qn to palm sth off on sb; ~rsi *vr* to stick; (*fig: persona*) to cling.

appi'eno *av* fully.

appigli'arsi [appiʎ'ʎarsi] *vr*: ~ a (*afferrarsi*) to take hold of; (*fig*) to cling to; **ap'piglio** *sm* hold; (*fig*) pretext.

appiso'larsi *vr* to doze off.

applau'dire *vt, vi* to applaud; **ap'plauso** *sm* applause.

appli'care *vt* to apply; (*regolamento*) to enforce; ~rsi *vr* to apply o.s.; **applicazi'one** *sf* application; enforcement.

appoggi'are [appod'dʒare] *vt* (*mettere contro*): ~ qc a qc to lean *o* rest sth against sth; (*fig: sostenere*) to support;

~rsi *vr*: ~rsi a to lean against; (*fig*) to rely upon; **ap'poggio** *sm* support.

appollai'arsi *vr* (*anche fig*) to perch.

ap'porre *vt* to affix.

appor'tare *vt* to bring.

apposita'mente *av* specially; (*apposta*) on purpose.

ap'posito, a *ag* appropriate.

ap'posta *av* on purpose, deliberately.

appos'tare *vt* to lie in wait for; ~rsi *vr* to lie in wait.

ap'prendere *vt* (*imparare*) to learn; (*comprendere*) to grasp.

appren'dista, i, e *sm/f* apprentice.

appren'sione *sf* apprehension; **appren'sivo, a** *ag* apprehensive.

ap'presso *av* (*accanto, vicino*) close by, near; (*dietro*) behind; (*dopo, più tardi*) after, later // *ag inv* (*dopo*): **il giorno ~** the next day; ~ **a** *prep* (*vicino a*) near, close to.

appres'tare *vt* to prepare, get ready; ~rsi *vr*: ~rsi a fare qc to prepare *o* get ready to do sth.

ap'pretto *sm* starch.

apprez'zabile [appret'tsabile] *ag* noteworthy, significant.

apprezza'mento [apprettsa'mento] *sm* appreciation; (*giudizio*) opinion.

apprez'zare [appret'tsare] *vt* to appreciate.

ap'proccio [ap'prɔttʃo] *sm* approach.

appro'dare *vi* (*NAUT*) to land; (*fig*): **non ~ a nulla** to come to nothing; **ap'prodo** *sm* landing; (*luogo*) landing-place.

approfit'tare *vi*: ~ di to make the most of, profit by.

approfon'dire *vt* to deepen; (*fig*) to study in depth.

appropri'ato, a *ag* appropriate.

approssi'marsi *vr*: ~ a to approach.

approssima'tivo, a *ag* approximate, rough; (*impreciso*) inexact, imprecise.

appro'vare *vt* (*condotta, azione*) to approve of; (*candidato*) to pass; (*progetto di legge*) to approve; **approvazi'one** *sf* approval.

approvvigio'nare [approvvidʒo'nare] *vt* to supply; ~rsi *vr* to lay in provisions, stock up; ~ qn di qc to supply sb with sth.

appunta'mento *sm* appointment; (*amoroso*) date; **darsi ~** to arrange to meet (one another).

appun'tato *sm* (*CARABINIERI*) corporal.

ap'punto *sm* note; (*rimprovero*) reproach // *av* (*proprio*) exactly, just; **per l'~!, ~!** exactly!

appu'rare *vt* to check, verify.

apribot'tiglie [apribot'tiʎʎe] *sm inv* bottleopener.

a'prile *sm* April.

a'prire *vt* to open; (*via, cadavere*) to open up; (*gas, luce, acqua*) to turn on // *vi* to open; ~rsi *vr* to open; ~rsi a qn to

confide in sb, open one's heart to sb.
apris'catole *sm inv* tin (*Brit*) o can opener.

a'quario *sm* = **acquario**.

'aquila *sf* (*ZOOL*) eagle; (*fig*) genius.

aqui'lone *sm* (*giocattolo*) kite; (*vento*) North wind.

A'rabia 'Saudita *sf*: l'~ Saudi Arabia.

'arabo, a *ag*, *sm/f* Arab // *sm* (*LING*) Arabic.

a'rachide [a'rakide] *sf* peanut.

ara'gosta *sf* crayfish; lobster.

a'raldica *sf* heraldry.

a'rancia, ce [a'rantʃa] *sf* orange; **aranci'ata** *sf* orangeade; **a'rancio** *sm* (*BOT*) orange tree; (*colore*) orange // *ag inv* (*colore*) orange; **aranci'one** *ag inv*: (*color*) arancione bright orange.

a'rare *vt* to plough (*Brit*), plow (*US*).

a'ratro *sm* plough (*Brit*), plow (*US*).

a'razzo [a'rattso] *sm* tapestry.

arbi'trare *vt* (*SPORT*) to referee; to umpire; (*DIR*) to arbitrate.

arbi'trarlo, a *ag* arbitrary.

ar'bitrio *sm* will; (*abuso, sopruso*) arbitrary act.

'arbitro *sm* arbiter, judge; (*DIR*) arbitrator; (*SPORT*) referee; (*: TENNIS, CRICKET*) umpire.

ar'busto *sm* shrub.

'arca, che *sf* (*sarcofago*) sarcophagus; l'~ di Noè Noah's ark.

ar'cangelo [ar'kandʒelo] *sm* archangel.

ar'cano, a *ag* arcane, mysterious.

ar'cata *sf* (*ARCHIT, ANAT*) arch; (*ordine di archi*) arcade.

archeolo'gia [arkeolo'dʒia] *sf* arch(a)eology; **arche'ologo, a, gi, ghe** *sm/f* arch(a)eologist.

ar'chetto [ar'ketto] *sm* (*MUS*) bow.

archi'tetto [arki'tetto] *sm* architect; **architet'tura** *sf* architecture.

ar'chivio [ar'kivjo] *sm* archives *pl*; (*INFORM*) file.

arci'ere [ar'tʃere] *sm* archer.

ar'cigno, a [ar'tʃiɲɲo] *ag* grim, severe.

arci'vescovo [artʃi'veskovo] *sm* archbishop.

'arco *sm* (*arma, MUS*) bow; (*ARCHIT*) arch; (*MAT*) arc.

arcoba'leno *sm* rainbow.

arcu'ato, a *ag* curved, bent; **dalle gambe ~e** bow-legged.

ar'dente *ag* burning; (*fig*) burning, ardent.

'ardere *vt*, *vi* to burn.

ar'desia *sf* slate.

ar'dire *vi* to dare // *sm* daring; **ar'dito, a** *ag* brave, daring, bold; (*sfacciato*) bold.

ar'dore *sm* blazing heat; (*fig*) ardour, fervour.

'arduo, a *ag* arduous, difficult.

'area *sf* area; (*EDIL*) land, ground.

a'rena *sf* arena; (*per corride*) bullring;

(*sabbia*) sand.

are'narsi *vr* to run aground.

areo'plano *sm* = **aeroplano**.

'argano *sm* winch.

argente'ria [ardʒente'ria] *sf* silverware, silver.

argenti'ere [ardʒen'tjere] *sm* silversmith.

Argen'tina [ardʒen'tina] *sf*: l'~ Argentina; **argen'tino, a** *ag*, *sm/f* Argentinian.

ar'gento [ar'dʒento] *sm* silver; ~ **vivo** quicksilver.

ar'gilla [ar'dʒilla] *sf* clay.

'argine ['ardʒine] *sm* embankment, bank; (*diga*) dyke, dike.

argomen'tare *vi* to argue.

argo'mento *sm* argument; (*motivo*) motive; (*materia, tema*) subject.

argu'ire *vt* to deduce.

ar'guto, a *ag* sharp, quick-witted; **ar'guzia** *sf* wit; (*battuta*) witty remark.

'aria *sf* air; (*espressione, aspetto*) air, look; (*MUS: melodia*) tune; (*: di opera*) aria; **mandare all'~ qc** to ruin o upset sth; **all'~ aperta** in the open (air).

'arido, a *ag* arid.

arieggi'are [arjed'dʒare] *vt* (*cambiare aria*) to air; (*imitare*) to imitate.

ari'ete *sm* ram; (*MIL*) battering ram; (*dello zodiaco*): **A~** Aries.

a'ringa, ghe *sf* herring *inv*.

'arista *sf* (*CUC*) chine of pork.

aristo'cratico, a, ci, che *ag* aristocratic.

arit'metica *sf* arithmetic.

arlec'chino [arlek'kino] *sm* harlequin.

'arma, i *sf* weapon, arm; (*parte dell'esercito*) arm; **chiamare alle ~i** to call up (*Brit*), draft (*US*); **sotto le ~i** in the army (o forces); **alle ~i!** to arms!; ~ **da fuoco** firearm.

ar'madio *sm* cupboard; (*per abiti*) wardrobe.

armamen'tario *sm* equipment, instruments *pl*.

arma'mento *sm* (*MIL*) armament; (*: materiale*) arms *pl*, weapons *pl*; (*NAUT*) fitting out; manning.

ar'mare *vt* to arm; (*arma da fuoco*) to cock; (*NAUT: nave*) to rig, fit out; to man; (*EDIL: volta, galleria*) to prop up, shore up; **~rsi** *vr* to arm o.s.; (*MIL*) to take up arms; **ar'mata** *sf* (*MIL*) army; (*NAUT*) fleet; **arma'tore** *sm* shipowner; **arma'tura** *sf* (*struttura di sostegno*) framework; (*impalcatura*) scaffolding; (*STORIA*) armour q, suit of armour.

armeggi'are [armed'dʒare] *vi*: ~ (**intorno a qc**) to mess about (with sth).

armis'tizio [armis'tittsjo] *sm* armistice.

armo'nia *sf* harmony; **ar'monico, a, ci, che** *ag* harmonic; (*fig*) harmonious // *sf* (*MUS*) harmonica; **armoni'oso, a** *ag* harmonious.

armoniz'zare [armonid'dzare] *vt* to

harmonize; (*colori, abiti*) to match // *vi* to be in harmony; to match.

ar'nese *sm* tool, implement; (*oggetto indeterminato*) thing, contraption; **male in** ~ (*malvestito*) badly dressed; (*di salute malferma*) in poor health; (*di condizioni economiche*) down-at heel.

'arnia *sf* hive.

a'roma, i *sm* aroma; fragrance; ~**i** *smpl* herbs and spices; **aro'matico, a, ci, che** *ag* aromatic; (*cibo*) spicy.

'arpa *sf* (*MUS*) harp.

ar'peggio [ar'peddʒo] *sm* (*MUS*) arpeggio.

ar'pia *sf* (*anche fig*) harpy.

arpi'one *sm* (*gancio*) hook; (*cardine*) hinge; (*PESCA*) harpoon.

arrabat'tarsi *vr* to do all one can, strive.

arrabbi'are *vi* (*cane*) to be affected with rabies; ~**rsi** *vr* (*essere preso dall'ira*) to get angry, fly into a rage; **arrabbi'ato, a** *ag* rabid, with rabies; furious, angry.

arraf'fare *vt* to snatch, seize; (*sottrarre*) to pinch.

arrampi'carsi *vr* to climb (up).

arran'care *vi* to limp, hobble.

arran'giare [arran'dʒare] *vt* to arrange; ~**rsi** *vr* to manage, do the best one can.

arre'care *vt* to bring; (*causare*) to cause.

arreda'mento *sm* (*studio*) interior design; (*mobili etc*) furnishings *pl*.

arre'dare *vt* to furnish; **arreda'tore, 'trice** *sm/f* interior designer; **ar'redo** *sm* fittings *pl*, furnishings *pl*.

ar'rendersi *vr* to surrender.

arres'tare *vt* (*fermare*) to stop, halt; (*catturare*) to arrest; ~**rsi** *vr* (*fermarsi*) to stop; **ar'resto** *sm* (*cessazione*) stopping; (*fermata*) stop; (*cattura, MED*) arrest; **subire un arresto** to come to a stop *o* standstill; **mettere agli arresti** to place under arrest; **arresti domiciliari** house arrest *sg*.

arre'trare *vt, vi* to withdraw; **arre'trato, a** *ag* (*lavoro*) behind schedule; (*paese, bambino*) backward; (*numero di giornale*) back *cpd*; **arretrati** *smpl* arrears.

arric'chire [arrik'kire] *vt* to enrich; ~**rsi** *vr* to become rich.

arricci'are [arrit'tʃare] *vt* to curl; ~ **il naso** to turn up one's nose.

ar'ringa, ghe *sf* harangue; (*DIR*) address by counsel.

arrischi'are [arris'kjare] *vt* to risk; ~**rsi** *vr* to venture, dare; **arrischi'ato, a** *ag* risky; (*temerario*) reckless, rash.

arri'vare *vi* to arrive; (*accadere*) to happen, occur; ~ **a** (*livello, grado etc*) to reach; **lui arriva a Roma alle 7** he gets to *o* arrives at Rome at 7; **non ci arrivo** I can't reach it; (*fig: non capisco*) I can't understand it.

arrive'derci [arrive'dertʃi] *escl* goodbye!

arrive'derla *escl* (*forma di cortesia*) goodbye!

arri'vista, i, e *sm/f* go-getter.

ar'rivo *sm* arrival; (*SPORT*) finish, finishing line.

arro'gante *ag* arrogant.

arro'lare *vb* = **arruolare**.

arros'sire *vi* (*per vergogna, timidezza*) to blush, flush; (*per gioia, rabbia*) to flush.

arros'tire *vt* to roast; (*pane*) to toast; (*ai ferri*) to grill.

ar'rosto *sm, ag inv* roast.

arro'tare *vt* to sharpen; (*investire con un veicolo*) to run over.

arroto'lare *vt* to roll up.

arroton'dare *vt* (*forma, oggetto*) to round; (*stipendio*) to add to; (*somma*) to round off.

arrovel'larsi *vr*: ~ (**il cervello**) to rack one's brains.

arruf'fare *vt* to ruffle; (*fili*) to tangle; (*fig: questione*) to confuse.

arruggi'nire [arruddʒi'nire] *vt* to rust; ~**rsi** *vr* to rust; (*fig*) to become rusty.

arruo'lare (*MIL*) *vt* to enlist; ~**rsi** *vr* to enlist, join up.

arse'nale *sm* (*MIL*) arsenal; (*cantiere navale*) dockyard.

'arso, a *pp di ardere* // *ag* (*bruciato*) burnt; (*arido*) dry; **ar'sura** *sf* (*calore opprimente*) burning heat; (*siccità*) drought.

'arte *sf* art; (*abilità*) skill.

arte'fatto, a *ag* (*cibo*) adulterated; (*fig: modi*) artificial.

ar'tefice [ar'tefitʃe] *sm/f* craftsman/woman; (*autore*) author.

ar'teria *sf* artery.

'artico, a, ci, che *ag* Arctic.

artico'lare *ag* (*ANAT*) of the joints, articular // *vt* to articulate; (*suddividere*) to divide, split up; **articolazi'one** *sf* articulation; (*ANAT, TECN*) joint.

ar'ticolo *sm* article; ~ **di fondo** (*STAMPA*) leader, leading article.

'Artide *sm*: **l'**~ the Arctic.

artifici'ale [artifi'tʃale] *ag* artificial.

arti'ficio [arti'fitʃo] *sm* (*espediente*) trick, artifice; (*ricerca di effetto*) artificiality.

artigia'nato [artidʒa'nato] *sm* craftsmanship; craftsmen *pl*.

artigi'ano, a [arti'dʒano] *sm/f* craftsman/woman.

artiglie'ria [artiʎʎe'ria] *sf* artillery.

ar'tiglio [ar'tiʎʎo] *sm* claw; (*di rapaci*) talon.

ar'tista, i, e *sm/f* artist; **ar'tistico, a, ci, che** *ag* artistic.

'arto *sm* (*ANAT*) limb.

ar'trite *sf* (*MED*) arthritis.

ar'trosi *sf* osteoarthritis.

ar'zillo, a [ar'dzillo] *ag* lively, sprightly.

a'scella [aʃ'ʃɛlla] *sf* (*ANAT*) armpit.

ascen'dente [aʃʃen'dɛnte] *sm* ancestor; (*fig*) ascendancy; (*ASTR*) ascendant.

ascensi'one [aʃʃen'sjone] *sf* (*ALPINISMO*) ascent; (*REL*): l'A~ the Ascension.

ascen'sore [aʃʃen'sore] *sm* lift.

a'scesa [aʃ'ʃesa] *sf* ascent; (*al trono*) accession.

a'scesso [aʃ'ʃɛsso] *sm* (*MED*) abscess.

'ascia, *pl* **'asce** ['aʃʃa] *sf* axe.

asciugaca'pelli [aʃʃugaka'pelli] *sm* hairdrier.

asciuga'mano [aʃʃuga'mano] *sm* towel.

asciu'gare [aʃʃu'gare] *vt* to dry; ~**rsi** *vr* to dry o.s.; (*diventare asciutto*) to dry.

asci'utto, a [aʃ'ʃutto] *ag* dry; (*fig: magro*) lean; (: *burbero*) curt; **restare a bocca ~a** (*fig*) to be disappointed.

ascol'tare *vt* to listen to; **ascolta'tore, 'trice** *sm/f* listener; **as'colto** *sm*: **essere o stare in ascolto** to be listening; **dare o prestare ascolto (a)** to pay attention (to).

as'falto *sm* asphalt.

asfissi'are *vt* to suffocate, asphyxiate; (*fig*) to bore to tears.

'Asia *sf*: l'~ Asia; **asi'atico, a, ci, che** *ag*, *sm/f* Asiatic, Asian.

a'silo *sm* refuge, sanctuary; ~ **(d'infanzia)** nursery(-school); ~ **nido** crèche; ~ **politico** political asylum.

'asino *sm* donkey, ass.

'asma *sf* asthma.

'asola *sf* buttonhole.

as'parago, gi *sm* asparagus *q*.

aspet'tare *vt* to wait for; (*anche COMM*) to await; (*aspettarsi*) to expect // *vi* to wait; ~**rsi** *vr* to expect; ~ **un bambino** to be expecting (a baby); **questo non me l'aspettavo** I wasn't expecting this; **aspetta'tiva** *sf* wait; expectation; **inferiore all'aspettativa** worse than expected; **essere in aspettativa** (*AMM*) to be on leave of absence.

as'petto *sm* (*apparenza*) aspect, appearance, look; (*punto di vista*) point of view; **di bell'~** good-looking.

aspi'rante *ag* (*attore etc*) aspiring // *sm/f* candidate, applicant.

aspira'polvere *sm inv* vacuum cleaner.

aspi'rare *vt* (*respirare*) to breathe in, inhale; (*sog: apparecchi*) to suck (up) // *vi*: ~ **a** to aspire to; **aspira'tore** *sm* extractor fan.

aspi'rina *sf* aspirin.

aspor'tare *vt* (*anche MED*) to remove, take away.

'aspro, a *ag* (*sapore*) sour, tart; (*odore*) acrid, pungent; (*voce, clima, fig*) harsh; (*superficie*) rough; (*paesaggio*) rugged.

assaggi'are *vt* to taste.

as'sai *av* (*molto*) a lot, much; (: *con ag*) very; (*a sufficienza*) enough // *ag inv* (*quantità*) a lot of, much; (*numero*) a lot of, many; ~ **contento** very pleased.

assa'lire *vt* to attack, assail.

as'salto *sm* attack, assault.

assassi'nare *vt* to murder; to assassinate; (*fig*) to ruin; **assas'sinio** *sm* murder; assassination; **assas'sino, a** *ag* murderous // *sm/f* murderer; assassin.

'asse *sm* (*TECN*) axle; (*MAT*) axis // *sf* board; ~ **f da stiro** ironing board.

assedi'are *vt* to besiege; **as'sedio** *sm* siege.

asse'gnare [asseɲ'ɲare] *vt* to assign, allot; (*premio*) to award.

as'segno [as'seɲɲo] *sm* allowance; (*anche*: ~ **bancario**) cheque (*Brit*), check (*US*); **contro ~** cash on delivery; ~ **circolare** bank draft; ~ **sbarrato** crossed cheque; ~ **di viaggio** traveller's cheque; ~ **a vuoto** dud cheque; ~**i familiari** ≈ child benefit *q*.

assem'blea *sf* assembly.

assen'nato, a *ag* sensible.

as'senso *sm* assent, consent.

as'sente *ag* absent; (*fig*) faraway, vacant; **as'senza** *sf* absence.

asses'sore *sm* (*POL*) councillor.

assesta'mento *sm* (*sistemazione*) arrangement; (*EDIL, GEOL*) settlement.

asses'tare *vt* (*mettere in ordine*) to put in order, arrange; ~**rsi** *vr* to settle in; ~ **un colpo a qn** to deal sb a blow.

asse'tato, a *ag* thirsty, parched.

as'setto *sm* order, arrangement; (*NAUT, AER*) trim; **in ~ di guerra** on a war footing.

assicu'rare *vt* (*accertare*) to ensure; (*infondere certezza*) to assure; (*fermare, legare*) to make fast, secure; (*fare un contratto di assicurazione*) to insure; ~**rsi** *vr* (*accertarsi*): ~**rsi (di)** to make sure (of); (*contro il furto etc*): ~**rsi (contro)** to insure o.s. (against); **assicu'rato, a** *ag* insured // *sf* (*anche*: **lettera assicurata**) registered letter; **assicurazi'one** *sf* assurance; insurance.

assidera'mento *sm* exposure.

assi'eme *av* (*insieme*) together; ~ **a** *prep* (together) with.

assil'lare *vt* to pester, torment.

as'sillo *sm* (*fig*) worrying thought.

as'sise *sfpl* (*DIR*) assizes; **Corte f d'A~** Court of Assizes, ≈ Crown Court (*Brit*).

assis'tente *sm/f* assistant; ~ **sociale** social worker; ~ **di volo** (*AER*) steward/stewardess.

assis'tenza [assis'tɛntsa] *sf* assistance; ~ **ospedaliera** free hospital treatment; ~ **sanitaria** health service; ~ **sociale** welfare services *pl*.

as'sistere *vt* (*aiutare*) to assist, help; (*curare*) to treat // *vi*: ~ **(a qc)** (*essere presente*) to be present (at sth), to attend (sth).

'asso *sm* ace; **piantare qn in** ~ to leave sb in the lurch.

associ'are [asso't∫are] vt to associate; (rendere partecipe): ~ qn a (affari) to take sb into partnership in; (partito) to make sb a member of; ~rsi vr to enter into partnership; ~rsi a to become a member of, join; (dolori, gioie) to share in; ~ qn alle carceri to take sb to prison.

associazi'one [assot∫at'tsjone] sf association; (COMM) association, society; ~ a o per delinquere (DIR) criminal association.

asso'dato, a ag well-founded.

assogget'tare [assoddʒet'tare] vt to subject, subjugate.

asso'lato, a ag sunny.

assol'dare vt to recruit.

as'solto, a pp di **assolvere**.

assoluta'mente av absolutely.

asso'luto, a ag absolute.

assoluzi'one [assolut'tsjone] sf (DIR) acquittal; (REL) absolution.

as'solvere vt (DIR) to acquit; (REL) to absolve; (adempiere) to carry out, perform.

assomigli'are [assomiλ'λare] vi: ~ a to resemble, look like.

asson'nato, a ag sleepy.

asso'pirsi vr to doze off.

assor'bente ag absorbent // sm: ~ igienico sanitary towel; ~ interno tampon.

assor'bire vt to absorb; (fig: far proprio) to assimilate.

assor'dare vt to deafen.

assorti'mento sm assortment.

assor'tito, a ag assorted; matched, matching.

as'sorto, a ag absorbed, engrossed.

assottigli'are [assottiλ'λare] vt to make thin, to thin; (aguzzare) to sharpen; (ridurre) to reduce; ~rsi vr to grow thin; (fig: ridursi) to be reduced.

assue'fare vt to accustom; ~rsi a to get used to, accustom o.s. to.

as'sumere vt (impiegato) to take on, engage; (responsabilità) to assume, take upon o.s.; (contegno, espressione) to assume, put on; (droga) to consume; **as'sunto, a** pp di **assumere** // sm (tesi) proposition.

assurdità sf inv absurdity; dire delle ~ to talk nonsense.

as'surdo, a ag absurd.

'asta sf pole; (modo di vendita) auction.

astan'te'ria sf casualty department.

aste'nersi vr: ~ (da) to abstain (from), refrain (from); (POL) to abstain (from).

aste'risco, schi sm asterisk.

astice ['astit∫e] sm lobster.

asti'nenza [asti'nentsa] sf abstinence; essere in crisi di ~ to suffer from withdrawal symptoms.

'astio sm rancour, resentment.

as'tratto, a ag abstract.

'astro sm star.

'astro... prefisso: **astrolo'gia** [astrolo'dʒia] sf astrology; **as'trologo, a, ghi, ghe** sm/f astrologer; **astro'nauta, i, e** sm/f astronaut; **astro'nave** sf space ship; **astrono'mia** sf astronomy; **astro'nomico, a, ci, che** ag astronomic(al).

as'tuccio [as'tutt∫o] sm case, box, holder.

as'tuto, a ag astute, cunning, shrewd; **as'tuzia** sf astuteness, shrewdness; (azione) trick.

A'tene sf Athens.

ate'neo sm university.

'ateo, a ag, sm/f atheist.

at'lante sm atlas.

at'lantico, a, ci, che ag Atlantic // sm: l'A~, l'Oceano A~ the Atlantic, the Atlantic Ocean.

at'leta, i, e sm/f athlete; **at'letica** sf athletics sg; atletica leggera track and field events pl; atletica pesante weightlifting and wrestling.

atmos'fera sf atmosphere.

a'tomico, a, ci, che ag atomic; (nucleare) atomic, atom cpd, nuclear.

'atomo sm atom.

'atrio sm entrance hall, lobby.

a'troce [a'trot∫e] ag (che provoca orrore) dreadful; (terribile) atrocious.

attacca'mento sm (fig) attachment, affection.

attacca'panni sm hook, peg; (mobile) hall stand.

attac'care vt (unire) to attach; (cucendo) to sew on; (far aderire) to stick (on); (appendere) to hang (up); (assalire: anche fig) to attack; (iniziare) to begin, start; (fig: contagiare) to pass on // vi to stick, adhere; ~rsi vr to stick, adhere; (trasmettersi per contagio) to be contagious; (afferrarsi): ~rsi (a) to cling (to); (fig: affezionarsi): ~rsi (a) to become attached (to); ~ discorso to start a conversation; **at'tacco, chi** sm (azione offensiva: anche fig) attack; (MED) attack, fit; (SCI) binding; (ELETTR) socket.

atteggia'mento [atteddʒa'mento] sm attitude.

atteggi'arsi [atted'dʒarsi] vr: ~ a to pose as.

attem'pato, a ag elderly.

at'tendere vt to wait for, await // vi: ~ a to attend to.

atten'dibile ag (storia) credible; (testimone) reliable.

atte'nersi vr: ~ a to keep o stick to.

atten'tare vi: ~ a to make an attempt on; **atten'tato** sm attack; attentato alla vita di qn attempt on sb's life.

at'tento, a ag attentive; (accurato) careful, thorough; stare ~ a qc to pay attention to sth // escl be careful!

attenu'ante sf (DIR) extenuating

circumstance.

attenu'are vt to attenuate; (dolore, rumore) to lessen, deaden; (pena, tasse) to alleviate; ~rsi vr to ease, abate.

attenzi'one [atten'tsjone] sf attention // escl watch out!, be careful!

atter'raggio [atter'radd3o] sm landing.

atter'rare vt to bring down // vi to land.

atter'rire vt to terrify.

at'teso, a pp di **attendere** // sf waiting; (tempo trascorso aspettando) wait; essere in attesa di qc to be waiting for sth.

attes'tato sm certificate.

'attico, ci sm attic.

at'tiguo, a ag adjacent, adjoining.

attil'lato, a ag (vestito) close-fitting, tight; (persona) dressed up.

'attimo sm moment; in un ~ in a moment.

atti'nente ag: ~ a relating to, concerning.

atti'rare vt to attract.

atti'tudine sf (disposizione) aptitude; (atteggiamento) attitude.

atti'vare vt to activate; (far funzionare) to set going, start.

attività sf inv activity; (COMM) assets pl.

at'tivo, a ag active; (COMM) profit-making, credit cpd // sm (COMM) assets pl; in ~ in credit.

attiz'zare [attit'tsare] vt (fuoco) to poke.

'atto sm act; (azione, gesto) action, act, deed; (DIR: documento) deed, document; ~i smpl (di congressi etc) proceedings; mettere in ~ to put into action; fare ~ di fare qc to make as if to do sth.

at'tonito, a ag dumbfounded, astonished.

attorcigli'are [attortʃiʎ'ʎare] vt, ~rsi vr to twist.

at'tore, 'trice sm/f actor/actress.

at'torno av, ~ a prep round, around, about.

at'tracco, chi sm (NAUT) docking q; berth.

attra'ente ag attractive.

at'trarre vt to attract; **attrat'tiva** sf (fig: fascino) attraction, charm; **at'tratto, a** pp di **attrarre**.

attraversa'mento sm: ~ pedonale pedestrian crossing.

attraver'sare vt to cross; (città, bosco, fig: periodo) to go through; (sog: fiume) to run through.

attra'verso prep through; (da una parte all'altra) across.

attrazi'one [attrat'tsjone] sf attraction.

attrez'zare [attret'tsare] vt to equip; (NAUT) to rig; **attrezza'tura** sf equipment q; rigging; **at'trezzo** sm tool, instrument; (SPORT) piece of equipment.

attribu'ire vt: ~ qc a qn (assegnare) to give o award sth to sb; (quadro etc) to attribute sth to sb; **attri'buto** sm attribute.

at'trice [at'tritʃe] sf vedi **attore**.

at'trito sm (anche fig) friction.

attu'ale ag (presente) present; (di attualità) topical; (che è in atto) actual; **attualità** sf inv topicality; (avvenimento) current event; **attual'mente** av at the moment, at present.

attu'are vt to carry out; ~rsi vr to be realized.

attu'tire vt to deaden, reduce.

au'dace [au'datʃe] ag audacious, daring, bold; (provocante) provocative; (sfacciato) impudent, bold; **au'dacia** sf audacity, daring; boldness; provocativeness; impudence.

audiovi'sivo, a ag audiovisual.

audizi'one [audit'tsjone] sf hearing; (MUS) audition.

'auge ['aud3e] sf: in ~ popular.

augu'rare vt to wish; ~rsi qc to hope for sth.

au'gurio sm (presagio) omen; (voto di benessere etc) (good) wish; essere di buon/cattivo ~ to be of good omen/be ominous; fare gli ~i a qn to give sb one's best wishes; tanti ~i! all the best!

'aula sf (scolastica) classroom; (universitaria) lecture theatre; (di edificio pubblico) hall.

aumen'tare vt, vi to increase; **au'mento** sm increase.

au'reola sf halo.

au'rora sf dawn.

ausili'are ag, sm, sm/f auxiliary.

aus'picio [aus'pitʃo] sm omen; (protezione) patronage; sotto gli ~i di under the auspices of.

aus'tero, a ag austere.

Aus'tralia sf: l'~ Australia; **au'strali'ano, a** ag, sm/f Australian.

'Austria sf: l'~ Austria; **aus'triaco, a, ci, che** ag, sm/f Austrian.

au'tentico, a, ci, che ag (quadro, firma) authentic, genuine; (fatto) true, genuine.

au'tista, i sm driver.

'auto sf inv car.

autoade'sivo, a ag self-adhesive // sm sticker.

autobiogra'fia sf autobiography.

auto'botte sf tanker.

'autobus sm inv bus.

auto'carro sm lorry (Brit), truck.

autocorri'era sf coach, bus.

au'tografo, a ag, sm autograph.

auto'linea sf bus company.

au'toma, i sm automaton.

auto'matico, a, ci, che ag automatic // sm (bottone) snap fastener; (fucile) automatic.

automazi'one [automat'tsjone] sf automation.

auto'mezzo [auto'mɛddzo] *sm* motor vehicle.

auto'mobile *sf* (motor) car.

autono'mia *sf* autonomy; (*di volo*) range.

au'tonomo, a *ag* autonomous, independent.

autop'sia *sf* post-mortem (examination), autopsy.

auto'radio *sf inv* (*apparecchio*) car radio; (*autoveicolo*) radio car.

au'tore, 'trice *sm/f* author; l'~ **del furto** the person who committed the robbery.

auto'revole *ag* authoritative; (*persona*) influential.

autori'messa *sf* garage.

autorità *sf inv* authority.

autoriz'zare [autorid'dzare] *vt* (*permettere*) to authorize; (*giustificare*) to allow, sanction; **autorizzazi'one** *sf* authorization.

autoscu'ola *sf* driving school.

autos'top *sm* hitchhiking; **autostop'pista, i, e** *sm/f* hitchhiker.

autos'trada *sf* motorway (*Brit*), highway (*US*).

auto'treno *sm* articulated lorry (*Brit*), semi (trailer) (*US*).

autove'icolo *sm* motor vehicle.

autovet'tura *sf* (motor) car.

au'tunno *sm* autumn.

avam'braccio, *pl(f)* **cia** [avam'brattʃo] *sm* forearm.

avangu'ardia *sf* vanguard.

a'vanti *av* (*stato in luogo*) in front; (*moto: andare, venire*) forward; (*tempo: prima*) before // *prep* (*luogo*): ~ **a** before, in front of; (*tempo*): ~ **Cristo** before Christ // *escl* (*entrate*) come (*o* go) in!; (*MIL*) forward!; (*coraggio*) come on! // *sm inv* (*SPORT*) forward; ~ **e indietro** backwards and forwards; **andare** ~ to go forward; (*continuare*) to go on; (*precedere*) to go (on) ahead; (*orologio*) to be fast; **essere** ~ **negli studi** to be well advanced with one's studies.

avanza'mento [avantsa'mento] *sm* progress; promotion.

avan'zare [avan'tsare] *vt* (*spostare in avanti*) to move forward, advance; (*domanda*) to put forward; (*promuovere*) to promote; (*essere creditore*): ~ **qc da qn** to be owed sth by sb // *vi* (*andare avanti*) to move forward, advance; (*fig: progredire*) to make progress; (*essere d'avanzo*) to be left, remain; **avan'zata** *sf* (*MIL*) advance; **a'vanzo** *sm* (*residuo*) remains *pl*, leftovers *pl*; (*MAT*) remainder; (*COMM*) surplus; **averne d'avanzo di qc** to have more than enough of sth; **avanzo di galera** (*fig*) jailbird.

ava'ria *sf* (*guasto*) damage; (: *meccanico*) breakdown.

a'varo, a *ag* avaricious, miserly // *sm* miser.

a'vena *sf* oats *pl*.

a'vere ◆ *sm* (*COMM*) credit; **gli ~i** (*ricchezze*) wealth *sg*

◆ *vt* **1** (*possedere*) to have; **ha due bambini/una bella casa** she has (got) two children/a lovely house; **ha i capelli lunghi** he has (got) long hair; **non ho da mangiare/bere** I've (got) nothing to eat/drink, I don't have anything to eat/drink

2 (*indossare*) to wear, have on; **aveva una maglietta rossa** he was wearing *o* he had on a red tee-shirt; **ha gli occhiali** he wears *o* has glasses

3 (*ricevere*) to get; **hai avuto l'assegno?** did you get *o* have you had the cheque?

4 (*età, dimensione*) to be; **ha 9 anni** he is 9 (years old); **la stanza ha 3 metri di lunghezza** the room is 3 metres in length; *vedi* **fame, paura** etc

5 (*tempo*): **quanti ne abbiamo oggi?** what's the date today?; **ne hai per molto?** will you be long?

6 (*fraseologia*): **avercela con qn** to be angry with sb; **cos'hai?** what's wrong *o* what's the matter (with you)?; **non ha niente a che vedere** *o* **fare con me** it's got nothing to do with me

◆ *vb ausiliare* **1** to have; **aver bevuto/mangiato** to have drunk/eaten

2 (+ *da* + *infinito*): ~ **da fare qc** to have to do sth; **non hai che da chiederlo** you only have to ask him.

'avi *smpl* ancestors, forefathers.

avia'tore, 'trice *sm/f* aviator, pilot.

aviazi'one [avjat'tsjone] *sf* aviation; (*MIL*) air force.

avidità *sf* eagerness; greed.

'avido, a *ag* eager; (*peg*) greedy.

avo'cado *sm* avocado.

a'vorio *sm* ivory.

Avv. *abbr* = **avvocato**.

avvalla'mento *sm* sinking *q*; (*effetto*) depression.

avvalo'rare *vt* to confirm.

avvam'pare *vi* (*incendio*) to flare up.

avvantaggi'are [avvantad'dʒare] *vt* to favour; ~**rsi** *vr*: ~**rsi negli affari/sui concorrenti** to get ahead in business/of one's competitors.

avvele'nare *vt* to poison.

avve'nente *ag* attractive, charming.

avveni'mento *sm* event.

avve'nire *vi, vb impers* to happen, occur // *sm* future.

avven'tarsi *vr*: ~ **su** *o* **contro qn/qc** to hurl o.s. *o* rush at sb/sth.

avven'tato, a *ag* rash, reckless.

avven'tizio, a [avven'tittsjo] *ag* (*impiegato*) temporary; (*guadagno*) casual.

av'vento *sm* advent, coming; (*REL*): **l'A~** Advent.

avven'tore *sm* (regular) customer.

avven'tura sf adventure; (amorosa) affair.

avventu'rarsi vr to venture.

avventu'roso, a ag adventurous.

avve'rarsi vr to come true.

av'verbio sm adverb.

avver'sario, a ag opposing // sm opponent, adversary.

av'verso, a ag (contrario) contrary; (sfavorevole) unfavourable.

avver'tenza [avver'tɛntsa] sf (ammonimento) warning; (cautela) care; (premessa) foreword; ~e sfpl (istruzioni per l'uso) Instructions.

avverti'mento sm warning.

avver'tire vt (avvisare) to warn; (rendere consapevole) to inform, notify; (percepire) to feel.

av'vezzo, a [av'vettso] ag: ~ a used to.

avvia'mento sm (atto) starting; (effetto) start; (AUT) starting; (: dispositivo) starter; (COMM) goodwill.

avvi'are vt (mettere sul cammino) to direct; (impresa, trattative) to begin, start; (motore) to start; ~rsi vr to set off, set out.

avvicen'darsi [avvitʃen'darsi] vr to alternate.

avvici'nare [avvitʃi'nare] vt to bring near; (trattare con: persona) to approach; ~rsi (a qu/qc) to approach (sb/sth), draw near (to sb/sth).

avvi'lire vt (umiliare) to humiliate; (degradare) to disgrace; (scoraggiare) to dishearten, discourage; ~rsi vr (abbattersi) to lose heart.

avvilup'pare vt (avvolgere) to wrap up; (ingarbugliare) to entangle.

avvinaz'zato, a [avvinat'tsato] ag drunk.

av'vincere [av'vintʃere] vt to charm, enthral.

avvinghi'are [avvin'gjare] vt to clasp; ~rsi vr: ~rsi a to cling to.

avvi'sare vt (far sapere) to inform; (mettere in guardia) to warn; **av'viso** sm warning; (annuncio) announcement; (: affisso) notice; (inserzione pubblicitaria) advertisement; a mio avviso in my opinion.

avvis'tare vt to sight.

avvi'tare vt to screw down (o in).

avviz'zire [avvit'tsire] vi to wither.

avvo'cato, 'essa sm/f (DIR) barrister (Brit), lawyer; (fig) defender, advocate.

av'volgere [av'voldʒere] vt to roll up; (avviluppare) to wrap up; ~rsi vr (avvilupparsi) to wrap o.s. up; **avvol'gibile** sm roller blind (Brit), blind.

avvol'toio sm vulture.

azi'enda [ad'dzjɛnda] sf business, firm, concern; ~ agricola farm.

azio'nare [attsjo'nare] vt to activate.

azi'one [at'tsjone] sf action; (COMM) share; **azio'nista, i, e** sm/f (COMM) shareholder.

a'zoto [ad'dzɔto] sm nitrogen.

azzan'nare [attsan'nare] vt to sink one's teeth into.

azzar'darsi [addzar'darsi] vr: ~ a fare to dare (to) do; **azzar'dato, a** ag (impresa) risky; (risposta) rash.

az'zardo [ad'dzardo] sm risk.

azzec'care [attsek'kare] vt (risposta etc) to get right.

azzuf'farsi [attsuf'farsi] vr to come to blows.

az'zurro, a [ad'dzurro] ag blue // sm (colore) blue; **gli ~i** (SPORT) the Italian national team.

B

bab'boo sm simpleton.

'babbo sm (fam) dad, daddy; B~ natale Father Christmas.

bab'buccia, ce [bab'buttʃa] sf slipper; (per neonati) bootee.

ba'bordo sm (NAUT) port side.

ba'cato, a ag worm-eaten, rotten.

'bacca, che sf berry.

baccalà sm dried salted cod; (fig peg) dummy.

bac'cano sm din, clamour.

bac'cello [bat'tʃɛllo] sm pod.

bac'chetta [bak'ketta] sf (verga) stick, rod; (di direttore d'orchestra) baton; (di tamburo) drumstick; ~ magica magic wand.

baci'are [ba'tʃare] vt to kiss; ~rsi vr to kiss (one another).

baci'nella [batʃi'nɛlla] sf basin.

ba'cino [ba'tʃino] sm basin; (MINERALOGIA) field, bed; (ANAT) pelvis; (NAUT) dock.

'bacio ['batʃo] sm kiss.

'baco, chi sm worm; ~ da seta silkworm.

ba'dare vi (fare attenzione) to take care, be careful; (occuparsi di): ~ a to look after, take care of; (dar ascolto): ~ a to pay attention to; bada ai fatti tuoi! mind your own business!

ba'dia sf abbey.

ba'dile sm shovel.

'baffi smpl moustache sg; (di animale) whiskers; ridere sotto i ~ to laugh up one's sleeve; leccarsi i ~ to lick one's lips.

bagagli'aio [bagaʎ'ʎajo] sm luggage van (Brit) o car (US); (AUT) boot (Brit), trunk (US).

ba'gagli [ba'gaʎʎi] smpl luggage sg.

bagli'ore [baʎ'ʎore] sm flash, dazzling light; un ~ di speranza a ray of hope.

ba'gnante [baɲ'ɲante] sm/f bather.

ba'gnare [baɲ'ɲare] vt to wet; (inzuppare) to soak; (innaffiare) to water; (sog: fiume) to flow through; (: mare) to wash, bathe; ~rsi *vr* (*al mare*) to go swimming *o* bathing; (*in vasca*) to have a bath.

ba'gnato, a [baɲˈɲato] *ag* wet.

ba'gnino [baɲˈɲino] *sm* lifeguard.

'bagno ['baɲɲo] *sm* bath; (*locale*) bathroom; ~i *smpl* (*stabilimento*) baths; fare il ~ to have a bath; (*nel mare*) to go swimming *o* bathing; fare il ~ a qn to give sb a bath; mettere a ~ to soak; ~ schiuma bubble bath.

bagnoma'ria [baɲɲomaˈria] *sm*: cuocere a ~ to cook in a double saucepan.

'baia *sf* bay.

baio'netta *sf* bayonet.

balaus'trata *sf* balustrade.

balbet'tare *vi* to stutter, stammer; (*bimbo*) to babble // *vt* to stammer out.

balbuzi'ente [balbutˈtsjɛnte] *ag* stuttering, stammering.

bal'cone *sm* balcony.

baldac'chino [baldakˈkino] *sm* canopy.

bal'danza [balˈdantsa] *sf* self-confidence, boldness.

'baldo, a *ag* bold, daring.

bal'doria *sf*: fare ~ to have a riotous time.

ba'lena *sf* whale.

bale'nare *vb impers*: balena there's lightning // *vi* to flash; mi balenò un'idea an idea flashed through my mind; ba'leno *sm* flash of lightning; in un baleno in a flash.

ba'lestra *sf* crossbow.

ba'lia *sf*: in ~ di at the mercy of.

'balla *sf* (*di merci*) bale; (*fandonia*) (tall) story.

bal'lare *vt, vi* to dance; bal'lata *sf* ballad.

balle'rina *sf* dancer; ballet dancer; (*scarpa*) ballet shoe.

balle'rino *sm* dancer; ballet dancer.

bal'letto *sm* ballet.

'ballo *sm* dance; (*azione*) dancing *q*; essere in ~ (*fig: persona*) to be involved; (: *cosa*) to be at stake.

ballot'taggio [ballotˈtaddʒo] *sm* (POL) second ballot.

balne'are *ag* seaside *cpd*; (*stagione*) bathing.

ba'locco, chi *sm* toy.

ba'lordo, a *ag* stupid, senseless.

'balsamo *sm* (*aroma*) balsam; (*lenimento, fig*) balm.

'Baltico *sm*: il (mar) ~ the Baltic (Sea).

balu'ardo *sm* bulwark.

'balza ['baltsa] *sf* (*dirupo*) crag; (*di stoffa*) frill.

bal'zare [balˈtsare] *vi* to bounce; (*lanciarsi*) to jump, leap; 'balzo *sm* bounce; jump, leap; (*del terreno*) crag.

bam'bagia [bamˈbadʒa] *sf* (*ovatta*) cotton wool (*Brit*), absorbent cotton (*US*); (*cascame*) cotton waste.

bam'bina *ag, sf vedi* bambino.

bambi'naia *sf* nanny, nurse(maid).

bam'bino, a *sm/f* child.

bam'boccio [bamˈbɔttʃo] *sm* plump child; (*pupazzo*) rag doll.

'bambola *sf* doll.

bambù *sm* bamboo.

ba'nale *ag* banal, commonplace.

ba'nana *sf* banana; ba'nano *sm* banana tree.

'banca, che *sf* bank; ~ dei dati data bank.

banca'rella *sf* stall.

ban'cario, a *ag* banking, bank *cpd* // *sm* bank clerk.

banca'rotta *sf* bankruptcy; fare ~ to go bankrupt.

ban'chetto [banˈketto] *sm* banquet.

banchi'ere [banˈkjere] *sm* banker.

ban'china [banˈkina] *sf* (*di porto*) quay; (*per pedoni, ciclisti*) path; (*di stazione*) platform; ~ cedevole (AUT) soft verge (*Brit*) *o* shoulder (*US*).

'banco, chi *sm* bench; (*di negozio*) counter; (*di mercato*) stall; (*di officina*) (work-)bench; (GEO, *banca*) bank; ~ di corallo coral reef; ~ degli imputati dock; ~ di prova (*fig*) testing ground; ~ dei testimoni witness box.

'Bancomat *sm inv* ® automated banking; (*tessera*) cash card.

banco'nota *sf* banknote.

'banda *sf* band; (*di stoffa*) band, stripe; (*lato, parte*) side; ~ perforata punch tape.

banderu'ola *sf* (METEOR) weathercock, weathervane.

bandi'era *sf* flag, banner.

ban'dire *vt* to proclaim; (*esiliare*) to exile; (*fig*) to dispense with.

ban'dito *sm* outlaw, bandit.

bandi'tore *sm* (*di aste*) auctioneer.

'bando *sm* proclamation; (*esilio*) exile, banishment; ~ alle chiacchiere! that's enough talk!

'bandolo *sm*: il ~ della matassa (*fig*) the key to the problem.

bar *sm inv* bar.

'bara *sf* coffin.

ba'racca, che *sf* shed, hut; (*peg*) hovel; mandare avanti la ~ to keep things going.

bara'onda *sf* hubbub, bustle.

ba'rare *vi* to cheat.

'baratro *sm* abyss.

barat'tare *vt*: ~ qc con to barter sth for, swap sth for; ba'ratto *sm* barter.

ba'rattolo *sm* (*di latta*) tin; (*di vetro*) jar; (*di coccio*) pot.

'barba *sf* beard; farsi la ~ to shave; farla in ~ a qn (*fig*) to do sth to sb's face; che ~! what a bore!

barbabi'etola *sf* beetroot (*Brit*), beet (*US*); ~ da zucchero sugar beet.

bar'barico, a, ci, che *ag* barbarian; barbaric.

'barbaro, a *ag* barbarous; **~i** *smpl* barbarians.

barbi'ere *sm* barber.

bar'bone *sm* (*cane*) poodle; (*vagabondo*) tramp.

bar'buto, a *ag* bearded.

'barca, che *sf* boat; **~ a remi** rowing boat; **barcai'olo** *sm* boatman.

barcol'lare *vi* to stagger.

bar'cone *sm* (*per ponti di barche*) pontoon.

ba'rella *sf* (*lettiga*) stretcher.

ba'rile *sm* barrel, cask.

ba'rista, i, e *sm/f* barman/maid; bar owner.

ba'ritono *sm* baritone.

bar'lume *sm* glimmer, gleam.

ba'rocco, a, chi, che *ag, sm* baroque.

ba'rometro *sm* barometer.

ba'rone *sm* baron; **baro'nessa** *sf* baroness.

'barra *sf* bar; (*NAUT*) helm; (*linea grafica*) line, stroke.

barri'care *vt* to barricade; **barri'cata** *sf* barricade.

barri'era *sf* barrier; (*GEO*) reef.

ba'ruffa *sf* scuffle.

barzel'letta [bardzel'letta] *sf* joke, funny story.

ba'sare *vt* to base, found; **~rsi** *vr*: **~rsi su** (*sog: fatti, prove*) to be based *o* founded on; (*: persona*) to base one's arguments on.

'basco, a, schi, sche *ag* Basque // *sm* (*copricapo*) beret.

'base *sf* base; (*fig: fondamento*) basis; (*POL*) rank and file; **di ~** basic; **in ~ a** on the basis of, according to; **a ~ di caffè** coffee-based.

ba'setta *sf* sideburn.

ba'silica, che *sf* basilica.

ba'silico *sm* basil.

bassi'fondi *smpl* (*fig*) dregs.

'basso, a *ag* low; (*di statura*) short; (*meridionale*) southern // *sm* bottom, lower part; (*MUS*) bass; **la ~a Italia** southern Italy.

bassorili'evo *sm* bas-relief.

'basta *escl* (that's) enough!, that will do!

bas'tardo, a *ag* (*animale, pianta*) hybrid, crossbreed; (*persona*) illegitimate, bastard (*peg*) // *sm/f* illegitimate child, bastard (*peg*).

bas'tare *vi, vb impers* to be enough, be sufficient; **~ a qn** to be enough for sb; **basta chiedere** *o* **che chieda a un vigile** you only *o* need only ask a policeman.

basti'mento *sm* ship, vessel.

basto'nare *vt* to beat, thrash.

baston'cino [baston'tʃino] *sm* (*SCI*) ski pole.

bas'tone *sm* stick; **~ da passeggio** walking stick.

bat'taglia [bat'taʎʎa] *sf* battle; fight.

bat'taglio [bat'taʎʎo] *sm* (*di campana*) clapper; (*di porta*) knocker.

battagli'one [battaʎ'ʎone] *sm* battalion.

bat'tello *sm* boat.

bat'tente *sm* (*imposta: di porta*) wing, flap; (*: di finestra*) shutter; (*batacchio: di porta*) knocker; (*: di orologio*) hammer; **chiudere i ~i** (*fig*) to shut up shop.

'battere *vt* to beat; (*grano*) to thresh; (*percorrere*) to scour // *vi* (*bussare*) to knock; (*urtare*): **~ contro** to hit *o* strike against; (*pioggia, sole*) to beat down; (*cuore*) to beat; (*TENNIS*) to serve; **~rsi** *vr* to fight; **~ le mani** to clap; **~ i piedi** to stamp one's feet; **~ le ore** to strike the hours; **~ su un argomento** to hammer home an argument; **~ a macchina** to type; **~ bandiera italiana** to fly the Italian flag; **~ in testa** (*AUT*) to knock; **in un batter d'occhio** in the twinkling of an eye.

bat'teri *smpl* bacteria.

batte'ria *sf* battery; (*MUS*) drums *pl*.

bat'tesimo *sm* baptism; christening.

battez'zare [batted'dzare] *vt* to baptize; to christen.

batticu'ore *sm* palpitations *pl*; **avere il ~** to be frightened to death.

batti'mano *sm* applause.

batti'panni *sm inv* carpet-beater.

battis'tero *sm* baptistry.

battis'trada *sm inv* (*di pneumatico*) tread; (*di gara*) pacemaker.

battitap'peto *sm* upright vacuum cleaner.

'battito *sm* beat, throb; **~ cardiaco** heartbeat; **~ della pioggia/dell'orologio** beating of the rain/ticking of the clock.

bat'tuta *sf* blow; (*di macchina da scrivere*) stroke; (*MUS*) bar; beat; (*TEATRO*) cue; (*frase spiritosa*) witty remark; (*di caccia*) beating; (*POLIZIA*) combing, scouring; (*TENNIS*) service.

ba'ule *sm* trunk; (*AUT*) boot (*Brit*), trunk (*US*).

'bava *sf* (*di animale*) slaver, slobber; (*di lumaca*) slime; (*di vento*) breath.

bava'glino [bavaʎ'ʎino] *sm* bib.

ba'vaglio [ba'vaʎʎo] *sm* gag.

'bavero *sm* collar.

ba'zar [bad'dzar] *sm inv* bazaar.

baz'zecola [bad'dzekola] *sf* trifle.

bazzi'care [battsi'kare] *vt* to frequent // *vi*: **~ in/con** to frequent.

be'ato, a *ag* blessed; (*fig*) happy; **~ te!** lucky you!

bec'caccia, ce [bek'kattʃa] *sf* woodcock.

bec'care *vt* to peck; (*fig: raffreddore*) to pick up, catch; **~rsi** *vr* (*fig*) to squabble.

beccheggi'are [bekked'dʒare] *vi* to pitch.

bec'chino [bek'kino] *sm* gravedigger.

'becco, chi *sm* beak, bill; (*di caffettiera etc*) spout; lip.

Be'fana *sf* old woman who, according to legend, brings children their presents at the Epiphany; *(Epifania)* Epiphany; *(donna brutta)*: b~ hag, witch.

'beffa *sf* practical joke; **farsi ~e di qn** to make a fool of sb; **bef'fardo, a** *ag* scornful, mocking; **bef'fare** *vt* (*anche:* **beffarsi di**) to make a fool of, mock.

'bega, ghe *sf* quarrel.

'begli ['bɛʎʎi], **'bei, bel** *ag vedi* **bello.**

be'lare *vi* to bleat.

'belga, gi, ghe *ag, sm/f* Belgian.

'Belgio ['bɛldʒo] *sm*: il ~ Belgium.

bel'lezza [bel'lettsa] *sf* beauty.

'bello, a *ag* (*dav sm* **bel** +*C*, **bell'** +*V*, **bello** + *s impura, gn, pn, ps, x, z, pl* **bei** +*C*, **begli** + *s impura etc o V*) beautiful, fine, lovely; *(uomo)* handsome // *sm* *(bellezza)* beauty; *(tempo)* fine weather // *sf* *(SPORT)* decider // *av*: **fa ~** the weather is fine, it's fine; **una ~a cifra** a considerable sum of money; **un bel niente** absolutely nothing; **è una truffa ~a e buona!** it's a real fraud!; **è bell'e finito** it's already finished; **adesso viene il ~** now comes the best bit; **sul più ~** at the crucial point; **cosa fai di ~?** are you doing anything interesting?; **belle arti** fine arts.

'belva *sf* wild animal.

belve'dere *sm inv* panoramic viewpoint.

benché [ben'ke] *cong* although.

'benda *sf* bandage; *(per gli occhi)* blindfold; **ben'dare** *vt* to bandage; to blindfold.

'bene *av* well; *(completamente, affatto)*: **è ben difficile** it's very difficult // *ag inv*: **gente ~** well-to-do people // *sm* good; **~i** *smpl (averi)* property *sg*, estate *sg*; **io sto ~/poco ~** I'm well/not very well; **va ~** all right; **volere un ~ dell'anima a qn** to love sb very much; **un uomo per ~** a respectable man; **fare ~** to do the right thing; **fare ~ a** *(salute)* to be good for; **fare del ~ a qn** to do sb a good turn; **~i di consumo** consumer goods.

bene'detto, a *pp di* **benedire** // *ag* blessed, holy.

bene'dire *vt* to bless; to consecrate; **benedizi'one** *sf* blessing.

benedu'cato, a *ag* well-mannered.

benefi'cenza [benefi'tʃɛntsa] *sf* charity.

bene'ficio [bene'fitʃo] *sm* benefit; **con ~ d'inventario** *(fig)* with reservations.

be'nefico, a, ci, che *ag* beneficial; charitable.

beneme'renza [beneme'rɛntsa] *sf* merit.

bene'merito, a *ag* meritorious.

be'nessere *sm* well-being.

benes'tante *ag* well-to-do.

benes'tare *sm* consent, approval.

be'nevolo, a *ag* benevolent.

be'nigno, a [be'niŋno] *ag* kind, kindly; *(critica etc)* favourable; *(MED)* benign.

benin'teso *av* of course.

bensì *cong* but (rather).

benve'nuto, a *ag, sm* welcome; **dare il ~ a qn** to welcome sb.

ben'zina [ben'dzina] *sf* petrol *(Brit)*, gas *(US)*; **fare ~** to get petrol *(Brit)* o gas *(US)*; **benzi'naio** *sm* petrol *(Brit)* o gas *(US)* pump attendant.

'bere *vt* to drink; **darla a ~ a qn** *(fig)* to fool sb.

ber'lina *sf* *(AUT)* saloon (car) *(Brit)*, sedan *(US)*.

Ber'lino *sf* Berlin.

ber'noccolo *sm* bump; *(inclinazione)* flair.

ber'retto *sm* cap.

bersagli'are [bersaʎ'ʎare] *vt* to shoot at; *(colpire ripetutamente, fig)* to bombard; **bersagliato dalla sfortuna** dogged by ill fortune.

ber'saglio [ber'saʎʎo] *sm* target.

bes'temmia *sf* curse; *(REL)* blasphemy.

bestemmi'are *vi* to curse, swear; to blaspheme // *vt* to curse, swear at; to blaspheme.

'bestia *sf* animal; **andare in ~** *(fig)* to fly into a rage; **besti'ale** *ag* beastly; animal *cpd*; *(fam)*: **fa un freddo bestiale** it's bitterly cold; **besti'ame** *sm* livestock; *(bovino)* cattle *pl.*

'bettola *sf (peg)* dive.

be'tulla *sf* birch.

be'vanda *sf* drink, beverage.

bevi'tore, 'trice *sm/f* drinker.

be'vuto, a *pp di* **bere** // *sf* drink.

bi'ada *sf* fodder.

bianche'ria [bjanke'ria] *sf* linen; **~ intima** underwear, lingerie; **~ da donna** ladies' underwear, lingerie.

bi'anco, a, chi, che *ag* white; *(non scritto)* blank // *sm* white; *(intonaco)* whitewash // *sf* white, white man/woman; **in ~** *(foglio, assegno)* blank; *(notte)* sleepless; **in ~ e nero** *(TV, FOT)* black and white; **mangiare in ~** to follow a bland diet; **pesce in ~** boiled fish; **andare in ~** *(non riuscire)* to fail; **~ dell'uovo** egg-white.

biasi'mare *vt* to disapprove of, censure; **bi'asimo** *sm* disapproval, censure.

'bibbia *sf* bible.

bibe'ron *sm inv* feeding bottle.

'bibita *sf (soft)* drink.

biblio'teca, che *sf* library; *(mobile)* bookcase; **bibliote'cario, a** *sm/f* librarian.

bicarbo'nato *sm*: **~ (di sodio)** bicarbonate (of soda).

bicchi'ere [bik'kjɛre] *sm* glass.

bici'cletta [bitʃi'kletta] *sf* bicycle; **andare in ~** to cycle.

bidé *sm inv* bidet.

bi'dello, a *sm/f (INS)* janitor.

bi'done *sm* drum, can; *(anche:* **~ dell'immondizia)** *(dust)*bin; *(fam: truffa)* swindle; **fare un ~ a qn** *(fam)* to

let sb down; to cheat sb.
bien'nale *ag* biennial.
bi'ennio *sm* period of two years.
bi'etola *sf* beet.
bifor'carsi *vr* to fork; **biforcazi'one** *sf* fork.
bighello'nare [bigello'nare] *vi* to loaf (about).
bigiotte'ria [bidʒotte'ria] *sf* costume jewellery; (*negozio*) jeweller's (*selling only costume jewellery*).
bigli'ardo [biʎʎardo] *sm* = **biliardo**.
bigliette'ria [biʎʎette'ria] *sf* (*di stazione*) ticket office; booking office; (*di teatro*) box office.
bigli'etto [biʎ'ʎetto] *sm* (*per viaggi, spettacoli etc*) ticket; (*cartoncino*) card; (*anche*: ~ **di banca**) (bank)note; ~ **d'auguri/da visita** greetings/visiting card; ~ **d'andata e ritorno** return (ticket), round-trip ticket (*US*).
bignè [bin'ɲe] *sm inv* cream puff.
bigo'dino *sm* roller, curler.
bi'gotto, a *ag* over-pious // *sm/f* church fiend.
bi'lancia, ce [bi'lantʃa] *sf* (*pesa*) scales *pl*; (*: di precisione*) balance; (*dello zodiaco*): B~ Libra; ~ **commerciale/dei pagamenti** balance of trade/payments; **bilanci'are** *vt* (*pesare*) to weigh; (*: fig*) to weigh up; (*pareggiare*) to balance.
bi'lancio [bi'lantʃo] *sm* (*COMM*) balance(-sheet); (*statale*) budget; **fare il ~ di** (*fig*) to assess; ~ **consuntivo** (final) balance; ~ **preventivo** budget.
'bile *sf* bile; (*fig*) rage, anger.
bili'ardo *sm* billiards *sg*; billiard table.
'bilico, chi *sm*: **essere in ~ to be** balanced; (*fig*) to be undecided; **tenere qn in ~ to keep sb in suspense.
bi'lingue *ag* bilingual.
bili'one *sm* (*mille milioni*) thousand million; (*milione di milioni*) billion (*Brit*), trillion (*US*).
'bimbo, a *sm/f* little boy/girl.
bimen'sile *ag* fortnightly.
bimes'trale *ag* two-monthly, bimonthly.
bi'nario, a *ag* (*sistema*) binary // *sm* (railway) track *o* line; (*piattaforma*) platform; ~ **morto** dead-end track.
bi'nocolo *sm* binoculars *pl*.
bio... *prefisso*: **bio'chimica** [bio'kimika] *sf* biochemistry; **biodegra'dabile** *ag* biodegradable; **biogra'fia** *sf* biography; **biolo'gia** *sf* biology; **bio'logico, a, ci, che** *ag* biological.
bi'ondo, a *ag* blond, fair.
bir'bante *sm* rogue, rascal.
biri'chino, a [biri'kino] *ag* mischievous // *sm/f* scamp, little rascal.
bi'rillo *sm* skittle (*Brit*), pin (*US*); ~i *smpl* (*gioco*) skittles *sg* (*Brit*), bowling (*US*).
'biro *sf inv* ® biro ®.
'birra *sf* beer; **a tutta ~** (*fig*) at top

speed; **birre'ria** *sf* ≈ bierkeller.
bis *escl, sm inv* encore.
bis'betico, a, ci, che *ag* ill-tempered, crabby.
bisbigli'are [bisbiʎ'ʎare] *vt, vi* to whisper.
'bisca, sche *sf* gambling-house.
'biscia, sce ['biʃʃa] *sf* snake; ~ **d'acqua** grass snake.
bis'cotto *sm* biscuit.
bises'tile *ag*: **anno** ~ leap year.
bis'lungo, a, ghi, ghe *ag* oblong.
bis'nonno, a *sm/f* great grandfather/grandmother.
biso'gnare [bizoɲ'ɲare] *vb impers*: **bisogna che tu parta/lo faccia** you'll have to go/do it; **bisogna parlargli** we'll (*o* I'll) have to talk to him.
bi'sogno [bi'zoɲɲo] *sm* need; ~i *smpl*: **fare i propri** ~i to relieve o.s.; **avere ~ di qc/di fare qc** to need sth/to do sth; **al ~, in caso di ~** if need be; **biso'gnoso, a** *ag* needy, poor; **bisognoso di** in need of, needing.
bis'tecca, che *sf* steak, beefsteak.
bisticci'are [bistit'tʃare] *vi*, ~rsi *vr* to quarrel, bicker; **bis'ticcio** *sm* quarrel, squabble; (*gioco di parole*) pun.
'bisturi *sm* scalpel.
bi'sunto, a *ag* very greasy.
'bitter *sm inv* bitters *pl*.
bi'vacco, chi *sm* bivouac.
'bivio *sm* fork; (*fig*) dilemma.
'bizza ['biddza] *sf* tantrum; **fare le** ~e (*bambino*) to be naughty.
biz'zarro, a [bid'dzarro] *ag* bizarre, strange.
biz'zeffe [bid'dzeffe]: **a** ~ *av* in plenty, galore.
blan'dire *vt* to soothe; to flatter.
'blando, a *ag* mild, gentle.
bla'sone *sm* coat of arms.
blate'rare *vi* to chatter, blether.
blin'dato, a *ag* armoured.
bloc'care *vt* to block; (*isolare*) to isolate, cut off; (*porto*) to blockade; (*prezzi, beni*) to freeze; (*meccanismo*) to jam; ~rsi *vr* (*motore*) to stall; (*freni, porta*) to jam, stick; (*ascensore*) to stop, get stuck.
'blocco, chi *sm* block; (*MIL*) blockade; (*dei fitti*) restriction; (*quadernetto*) pad; (*fig: unione*) coalition; (*il bloccare*) blocking; isolating; cutting-off; blockading; freezing; jamming; **in ~** (*nell'insieme*) as a whole; (*COMM*) in bulk; ~ **cardiaco** cardiac arrest.
blu *ag inv, sm* dark blue.
'blusa *sf* (*camiciotto*) smock; (*camicetta*) blouse.
'boa *sm inv* (*ZOOL*) boa constrictor; (*sciarpa*) feather boa // *sf* buoy.
bo'ato *sm* rumble, roar.
bo'bina *sf* reel, spool; (*di pellicola*) spool; (*di film*) reel; (*ELETTR*) coil.

'bocca, che *sf* mouth; **in ~ al lupo!** good luck!

boc'caccia, ce [bok'kattʃa] *sf* (*malalingua*) gossip; **fare le ~ce** to pull faces.

boc'cale *sm* jug; **~ da birra** tankard.

boc'cetta [bot'tʃetta] *sf* small bottle.

bocchegg'iare [bokkeg'dʒare] *vi* to gasp.

boc'chino [bok'kino] *sm* (*di sigaretta, sigaro: cannella*) cigarette-holder; cigar-holder; (*di pipa, strumenti musicali*) mouthpiece.

'boccia, ce ['bottʃa] *sf* bottle; (*da vino*) decanter, carafe; (*palla*) bowl; **gioco delle ~ce** bowls *sg*.

bocci'are [bot'tʃare] *vt* (*proposta, progetto*) to reject; (*INS*) to fail; (*BOCCE*) to hit; **boccia'tura** *sf* failure.

bocci'olo [bot'tʃɔlo] *sm* bud.

boc'cone *sm* mouthful, morsel.

boc'coni *av* face downwards.

'boia *sm inv* executioner; hangman.

boi'ata *sf* botch.

boicot'tare *vt* to boycott.

'bolide *sm* meteor; **come un ~** like a flash, at top speed.

'bolla *sf* bubble; (*MED*) blister; **~ papale** papal bull; **~ di consegna** (*COMM*) delivery note.

bol'lare *vt* to stamp; (*fig*) to brand.

bol'lente *ag* boiling; boiling hot.

bol'letta *sf* bill; (*ricevuta*) receipt; **essere in ~** to be hard up.

bollet'tino *sm* bulletin; (*COMM*) note; **~ di spedizione** consignment note.

bol'lire *vt, vi* to boil; **bol'lito** *sm* (*CUC*) boiled meat.

bolli'tore *sm* (*CUC*) kettle; (*per riscaldamento*) boiler.

'bollo *sm* stamp.

'bomba *sf* bomb; **tornare a ~** (*fig*) to get back to the point; **~ atomica** atom bomb.

bombarda'mento *sm* bombardment; bombing.

bombar'dare *vt* to bombard; (*da aereo*) to bomb.

bombardi'ere *sm* bomber.

bom'betta *sf* bowler (hat).

'bombola *sf* cylinder.

bo'naccia, ce [bo'nattʃa] *sf* dead calm.

bo'nario, a *ag* good-natured, kind.

bo'nifica, che *sf* reclamation; reclaimed land.

bo'nifico, ci *sm* (*riduzione, abbuono*) discount; (*versamento a terzi*) credit transfer.

bontà *sf* goodness; (*cortesia*) kindness; **aver la ~ di fare qc** to be good *o* kind enough to do sth.

borbot'tare *vi* to mumble; (*stomaco*) to rumble.

'borchia ['borkja] *sf* stud.

borda'tura *sf* (*SARTORIA*) border, trim.

'bordo *sm* (*NAUT*) ship's side; (*orlo*) edge; (*striscia di guarnizione*) border, trim; **a ~ di** (*nave, aereo*) aboard, on board; (*macchina*) in.

bor'gata *sf* hamlet.

bor'ghese [bor'geze] *ag* (*spesso peg*) middle-class; bourgeois; **abito ~** civilian dress; **borghe'sia** *sf* middle classes *pl*; bourgeoisie.

'borgo, ghi *sm* (*paesino*) village; (*quartiere*) district; (*sobborgo*) suburb.

'boria *sf* self-conceit, arrogance.

boro'talco *sm* talcum powder.

bor'raccia, ce [bor'rattʃa] *sf* canteen, water-bottle.

'borsa *sf* bag; (*anche: ~ da signora*) handbag; (*ECON*): **la B~ (valori) the Stock Exchange**; **~ nera** black market; **~ della spesa** shopping bag; **~ di studio** grant; **borsai'olo** *sm* pickpocket; **borsel'lino** *sm* purse; **bor'setta** *sf* handbag; **bor'sista, i, e** *sm/f* (*ECON*) speculator; (*INS*) grant-holder.

bos'caglia [bos'kaʎʎa] *sf* woodlands *pl*.

boscai'olo *sm* woodcutter; forester.

'bosco, schi *sm* wood; **bos'coso, a** *ag* wooded.

'bossolo *sm* cartridge-case.

bo'tanico, a, ci, che *ag* botanical // *sm* botanist // *sf* botany.

'botola *sf* trap door.

'botta *sf* blow; (*rumore*) bang.

'botte *sf* barrel, cask.

bot'tega, ghe *sf* shop; (*officina*) workshop; **botte'gaio, a** *sm/f* shopkeeper; **botte'ghino** *sm* ticket office; (*del lotto*) public lottery office.

bot'tiglia [bot'tiʎʎa] *sf* bottle; **bottiglie'ria** *sf* wine shop.

bot'tino *sm* (*di guerra*) booty; (*di rapina, furto*) loot.

'botto *sm* bang; crash; **di ~** suddenly.

bot'tone *sm* button; **attaccare ~ a qn** (*fig*) to buttonhole sb.

bo'vino, a *ag* bovine; **~i** *smpl* cattle.

boxe [bɔks] *sf* boxing.

'bozza ['bɔttsa] *sf* draft; sketch; (*TIP*) proof; **boz'zetto** *sm* sketch.

'bozzolo ['bɔttsolo] *sm* cocoon.

BR *sigla fpl* = **Brigate Rosse**.

brac'care *vt* to hunt.

brac'cetto [brat'tʃetto] *sm*: **a ~** arm in arm.

bracci'ale [brat'tʃale] *sm* bracelet; (*distintivo*) armband; **braccia'letto** *sm* bracelet, bangle.

bracci'ante [brat'tʃante] *sm* (*AGR*) day labourer.

bracci'ata [brat'tʃata] *sf* (*nel nuoto*) stroke.

'braccio ['brattʃo] *sm* (*pl(f)* **braccia**: *ANAT*) arm; (*pl(m)* **bracci**: *di gru, fiume*) arm; (: *di edificio*) wing; **~ di mare** sound; **bracci'olo** *sm* (*appoggio*) arm.

'**bracco, chi** sm hound.
bracconi'ere sm poacher.
'**brace** ['bratʃe] sf embers pl; **braci'ere** sm brazier.
braci'ola [bra'tʃɔla] sf (CUC) chop.
bra'mare vt: ~ qc/di fare to long for sth/to do.
'**branca, che** sf branch.
'**branchia** ['brankja] sf (ZOOL) gill.
'**branco, chi** sm (di cani, lupi) pack; (di uccelli, pecore) flock; (peg: di persone) gang, pack.
branco'lare vi to grope, feel one's way.
'**branda** sf camp bed.
bran'dello sm scrap, shred; a ~i in tatters, in rags.
bran'dire vt to brandish.
'**brano** sm piece; (di libro) passage.
bra'sato sm braised beef.
Bra'sile sm: il ~ Brazil; **brasili'ano, a** ag, sm/f Brazilian.
'**bravo, a** ag (abile) clever, capable, skilful; (buono) good, honest; (: bambino) good; (coraggioso) brave; ~! well done!; (al teatro) bravo!
bra'vura sf cleverness, skill.
'**breccia, ce** ['brettʃa] sf breach.
bre'tella sf (AUT) link; ~e sfpl braces.
'**breve** ag brief, short; in ~ in short.
brevet'tare vt to patent.
bre'vetto sm patent; ~ di pilotaggio pilot's licence (Brit) o license (US).
'**brezza** ['breddza] sf breeze.
'**bricco, chi** sm jug; ~ del caffè coffeepot.
bric'cone, a sm/f rogue, rascal.
bric'iola ['britʃola] sf crumb.
bric'iolo ['britʃolo] sm (specie fig) bit.
'**briga, ghe** sf (fastidio) trouble, bother; pigliarsi la ~ di fare qc to take the trouble to do sth.
brigadi'ere sm (dei carabinieri etc) ~ sergeant.
bri'gante sm bandit.
bri'gata sf (MIL) brigade; (gruppo) group, party.
'**briglia** ['briλλa] sf rein; a ~ sciolta at full gallop; (fig) at full speed.
bril'lante ag bright; (anche fig) brilliant; (che luccica) shining // sm diamond.
bril'lare vi to shine; (mina) to blow up // vt (mina) to set off.
'**brillo, a** ag merry, tipsy.
'**brina** sf hoarfrost.
brin'dare vi: ~ a qn/qc to drink to o toast sb/sth.
'**brindisi** sm inv toast.
'**brio** sm liveliness, go; **bri'oso, a** ag lively.
bri'tannico, a, ci, che ag British.
'**brivido** sm shiver; (di ribrezzo) shudder; (fig) thrill.
brizzo'lato, a [brittso'lato] ag (persona) going grey; (barba, capelli) greying.

'**brocca, che** sf jug.
broc'cato sm brocade.
'**broccolo** sm broccoli sg.
'**brodo** sm broth; (per cucinare) stock; ~ ristretto consommé.
brogli'accio [broλ'λattʃo] sm scribbling pad.
'**broglio** ['brɔλλo] sm: ~ elettorale gerrymandering.
bron'chite [bron'kite] sf (MED) bronchitis.
'**broncio** ['brontʃo] sm sulky expression; tenere il ~ to sulk.
'**bronco, chi** sm bronchial tube.
bronto'lare vi to grumble; (tuono, stomaco) to rumble.
'**bronzo** ['brondzo] sm bronze.
bru'care vt to browse on, nibble at.
brucia'pelo [brutʃa'pelo] a ~ av pointblank.
bruci'are [bru'tʃare] vt to burn; (scottare) to scald // vi to burn; **brucia'tore** sm burner; **brucia'tura** sf (atto) burning q; (segno) burn; (scottatura) scald; **bruci'ore** sm burning o smarting sensation.
'**bruco, chi** sm caterpillar; grub.
brughi'era [bru'gjera] sf heath, moor.
bruli'care vi to swarm.
'**brullo, a** ag bare, bleak.
'**bruma** sf mist.
'**bruno, a** ag brown, dark; (persona) dark(-haired).
'**brusco, a, schi, sche** ag (sapore) sharp; (modi, persona) brusque, abrupt; (movimento) abrupt, sudden.
bru'sio sm buzz, buzzing.
bru'tale ag brutal.
'**bruto, a** ag (forza) brute cpd // sm brute.
brut'tezza [brut'tettsa] sf ugliness.
'**brutto, a** ag ugly; (cattivo) bad; (malattia, strada, affare) nasty, bad; ~ tempo bad weather; **brut'tura** sf (cosa brutta) ugly thing; (sudiciume) filth; (azione meschina) mean action.
Bru'xelles [bry'sɛl] sf Brussels.
'**buca, che** sf hole; (avvallamento) hollow; ~ delle lettere letterbox.
buca'neve sm inv snowdrop.
bu'care vt (forare) to make a hole (o holes) in; (pungere) to pierce; (biglietto) to punch; ~rsi vr (con eroina) to mainline; ~ una gomma to have a puncture.
bu'cato sm (operazione) washing; (panni) wash, washing.
'**buccia, ce** ['buttʃa] sf skin, peel; (corteccia) bark.
bucherel'lare [bukerel'lare] vt to riddle with holes.
'**buco, chi** sm hole.
bu'dello sm intestine; (fig: tubo) tube; (vicolo) alley; ~a sfpl bowels, guts.
bu'dino sm pudding.

'**bue** *sm* ox; (*anche:* carne di ~) beef.
'**bufalo** *sm* buffalo.
bu'fera *sf* storm.
'**buffo, a** *ag* funny; (*TEATRO*) comic.
bu'gia, 'gie [bu'dʒia] *sf* lie; (*candeliere*) candleholder; **bugi'ardo, a** *ag* lying, deceitful // *sm/f* liar.
bugi'gattolo [budʒi'gattolo] *sm* poky little room.
'**buio, a** *ag* dark // *sm* dark, darkness; **fa ~ pesto** it's pitch-dark.
'**bulbo** *sm* (*BOT*) bulb; ~ **oculare** eyeball.
Bulga'ria *sf:* **la ~** Bulgaria.
bul'lone *sm* bolt.
buona'notte *escl* good night! // *sf:* **dare la ~ a** to say good night to.
buona'sera *escl* good evening!
buon gi'orno [bwon'dʒorno] *escl* good morning (*o* afternoon)!
buongus'taio, a *sm/f* gourmet.
buon'gusto *sm* good taste.
bu'ono, a *ag* (*dav sm* **buon** + *C o V,* **buono** + *s* impura, *gn, pn, ps, x, z;* dav *sf* **buon'** +*V*) good; (*benevolo*) ~ (con) good (to), kind (to); (*adatto*): ~ **a/da** fit for/to // *sm* good; (*COMM*) voucher, coupon; **alla buona** simple // *av* in a simple way, without any fuss; **buona fortuna** good luck; **buon compleanno** happy birthday; **buon divertimento** have a nice time; **a buon mercato** cheap; **di buon'ora** early; ~ **di cassa** cash voucher; ~ **di consegna** delivery note; ~ **fruttifero** bond bearing interest; ~ **a nulla** good-for-nothing; ~ **del tesoro** Treasury bill; **buon riposo** sleep well; **buon senso** common sense; **buon viaggio** bon voyage, have a good trip.
buontem'pone, a *sm/f* jovial person.
burat'tino *sm* puppet.
'**burbero, a** *ag* surly, gruff.
'**burla** *sf* prank, trick; **bur'lare** *vt:* **burlare qc/qn**, **burlarsi di qc/qn** to make fun of sth/sb.
burocra'zia [burokrat'tsia] *sf* bureaucracy.
bur'rasca, sche *sf* storm; **burras'coso, a** *ag* stormy.
'**burro** *sm* butter.
bur'rone *sm* ravine.
bus'care *vt* (*anche:* ~rsi: raffreddore) to get, catch; **buscarle** (*fam*) to get a hiding.
bus'sare *vi* to knock.
'**bussola** *sf* compass; **perdere la ~** (*fig*) to lose one's bearings.
'**busta** *sf* (*da lettera*) envelope; (*astuccio*) case; **in ~ aperta/chiusa** in an unsealed/sealed envelope; ~ **paga** pay packet.
busta'rella *sf* bribe, backhander.
'**busto** *sm* bust; (*indumento*) corset, girdle; **a mezzo ~** (*foto*) half-length.
but'tare *vt* to throw; (*anche:* ~ via) to throw away; ~ **giù** (*scritto*) to scribble down, dash off; (*cibo*) to gulp down; (*edificio*) to pull down, demolish; (*pasta, verdura*) to put into boiling water; ~rsi **dalla finestra** to jump *o* throw o.s. out of the window.

C

ca'bina *sf* (*di nave*) cabin; (*da spiaggia*) beach hut; (*di autocarro, treno*) cab; (*di aereo*) cockpit; (*di ascensore*) cage; ~ **telefonica** call *o* (tele)phone box.
ca'cao *sm* cocoa.
'**caccia** ['kattʃa] *sf* hunting; (*con fucile*) shooting; (*inseguimento*) chase; (*cacciagione*) game // *sm inv* (*aereo*) fighter; (*nave*) destroyer; ~ **grossa** big-game hunting; ~ **all'uomo** manhunt.
cacciabombardi'ere [kattʃabombar'djere] *sm* fighter-bomber.
cacciagi'one [kattʃa'dʒone] *sf* game.
cacci'are [kat'tʃare] *vt* to hunt; (*mandar via*) to chase away; (*ficcare*) to shove, stick // *vi* to hunt; ~rsi *vr* (*fam:* mettersi): ~rsi **tra la folla** to plunge into the crowd; **dove s'è cacciata la mia borsa?** where has my bag got to?; ~rsi **nei guai** to get into trouble; ~ **fuori** qc to whip *o* pull sth out; ~ **un urlo** to let out a yell; **caccia'tore** *sm* hunter; **cacciatore di frodo** poacher.
caccia'vite [kattʃa'vite] *sm inv* screwdriver.
'**cactus** *sm inv* cactus.
ca'davere *sm* (dead) body, corpse.
ca'dente *ag* falling; (*casa*) tumbledown.
ca'denza [ka'dentsa] *sf* cadence; (*andamento ritmico*) rhythm; (*MUS*) cadenza.
ca'dere *vi* to fall; (*denti, capelli*) to fall out; (*tetto*) to fall in; **questa gonna cade bene** this skirt hangs well; **lasciar ~** (*anche fig*) to drop; ~ **dal sonno** to be falling asleep on one's feet; ~ **dalle nuvole** (*fig*) to be taken aback.
ca'detto, a *ag* younger; (*squadra*) junior *cpd* // *sm* cadet.
ca'duta *sf* fall; **la ~ dei capelli** hair loss.
caffè *sm inv* coffee; (*locale*) café; ~ **macchiato** coffee with a dash of milk; ~ **macinato** ground coffee.
caffel'latte *sm inv* white coffee.
caffetti'era *sf* coffeepot.
cagio'nare [kadʒo'nare] *vt* to cause, be the cause of.
cagio'nevole [kadʒo'nevole] *ag* delicate, weak.
cagli'are [kaʎ'ʎare] *vi* to curdle.
'**cagna** ['kaɲɲa] *sf* (*ZOOL, peg*) bitch.
ca'gnesco, a, schi, sche [kaɲ'ɲesko] *ag* (*fig*): **guardare qn in ~** to scowl at sb.
cala'brone *sm* hornet.

cala'maio *sm* inkpot; inkwell.

cala'maro *sm* squid.

cala'mita *sf* magnet.

calamità *sf inv* calamity, disaster.

ca'lare *vt* (*far discendere*) to lower; (*MAGLIA*) to decrease // *vi* (*discendere*) to go (o come) down; (*tramontare*) to set, go down; ~ **di peso** to lose weight.

'calca *sf* throng, press.

cal'cagno [kal'kaɲɲo] *sm* heel.

cal'care *sm* limestone // *vt* (*premere coi piedi*) to tread, press down; (*premere con forza*) to press down; (*mettere in rilievo*) to stress; ~ **la mano** to overdo it, exaggerate.

'calce ['kaltʃe] *sm*: **in** ~ at the foot of the page // *sf* lime; ~ **viva** quicklime.

calces'truzzo [kaltʃes'truttso] *sm* concrete.

calci'are [kal'tʃare] *vt, vi* to kick; **calcia'tore** *sm* footballer.

cal'cina [kal'tʃina] *sf* (lime) mortar.

'calcio ['kaltʃo] *sm* (*pedata*) kick; (*sport*) football, soccer; (*di pistola, fucile*) butt; (*CHIM*) calcium; ~ **d'angolo** (*SPORT*) corner (kick); ~ **di punizione** (*SPORT*) free kick.

'calco, chi *sm* (*ARTE*) casting, moulding; cast, mould.

calco'lare *vt* to calculate, work out, reckon; (*ponderare*) to weigh (up); **calcola'tore, 'trice** *ag* calculating // *sm* calculator; (*fig*) calculating person // *sf* (*anche*) **macchina calcolatrice** calculator; **calcolatore elettronico** computer.

'calcolo *sm* (*anche MAT*) calculation; (*infinitesimale etc*) calculus; (*MED*) stone; **fare i propri** ~**i** (*fig*) to weigh the pros and cons; **per** ~ out of self-interest.

cal'daia *sf* boiler.

caldeggi'are [kalded'dʒare] *vt* to support.

'caldo, a *ag* warm; (*molto* ~) hot; (*fig: appassionato*) keen; hearty // *sm* heat; **ho** ~ I'm warm; I'm hot; **fa** ~ it's warm; it's hot.

calen'dario *sm* calendar.

'calibro *sm* (*di arma*) calibre, bore; (*TECN*) callipers *pl*; (*fig*) calibre; **di grosso** ~ (*fig*) prominent.

'calice ['kalitʃe] *sm* goblet; (*REL*) chalice.

ca'ligine [ka'lidʒine] *sf* fog; (*mista con fumo*) smog.

'callo *sm* callus; (*ai piedi*) corn.

'calma *sf* calm.

cal'mante *sm* sedative, tranquillizer.

cal'mare *vt* to calm; (*lenire*) to soothe; ~**rsi** *vr* to grow calm, calm down; (*vento*) to abate; (*dolori*) to ease.

calmi'ere *sm* controlled price.

'calmo, a *ag* calm, quiet.

'calo *sm* (*COMM: di prezzi*) fall; (: *di volume*) shrinkage; (: *di peso*) loss.

ca'lore *sm* warmth; heat; **in** ~ (*ZOOL*) on heat.

calo'ria *sf* calorie.

calo'roso, a *ag* warm.

calpes'tare *vt* to tread on, trample on; "**è vietato** ~ **l'erba**" "keep off the grass".

ca'lunnia *sf* slander; (*scritta*) libel.

cal'vario *sm* (*fig*) affliction, cross.

cal'vizie [kal'vittsje] *sf* baldness.

'calvo, a *ag* bald.

'calza ['kaltsa] *sf* (*da donna*) stocking; (*da uomo*) sock; **fare la** ~ to knit; ~**e di nailon** nylons, (nylon) stockings.

cal'zare [kal'tsare] *vt* (*scarpe, guanti: mettersi*) to put on; (: *portare*) to wear // *vi* to fit; **calza'tura** *sf* footwear.

calzet'tone [kaltset'tone] *sm* heavy knee-length sock.

cal'zino [kal'tsino] *sm* sock.

calzo'laio [kaltso'lajo] *sm* shoemaker; (*che ripara scarpe*) cobbler; **calzole'ria** *sf* (*negozio*) shoe shop.

calzon'cini [kaltson'tʃini] *smpl* shorts.

cal'zone [kal'tsone] *sm* trouser leg; (*CUC*) savoury turnover made with pizza dough; ~**i** *smpl* trousers (*Brit*), pants (*US*).

cambi'ale *sf* bill (of exchange); (*pagherò cambiario*) promissory note.

cambia'mento *sm* change.

cambi'are *vt* to change; (*modificare*) to alter, change; (*barattare*): ~ (**qc con qn/qc**) to exchange (sth with sb/for sth) // *vi* to change, alter; ~**rsi** *vr* (*variare abito*) to change; ~ **casa** to move (house); ~ **idea** to change one's mind; ~ **treno** to change trains.

'cambio *sm* change; (*modifica*) alteration, change; (*scambio, COMM*) exchange; (*corso dei cambi*) rate (of exchange); (*TECN, AUT*) gears *pl*; **in** ~ **di** in exchange for; **dare il** ~ **a qn** to take over from sb.

'camera *sf* room; (*anche*: ~ **da letto**) bedroom; (*POL*) chamber, house; ~ **ardente** mortuary chapel; ~ **d'aria** inner tube; (*di pallone*) bladder; **C**~ **di Commercio** Chamber of Commerce; **C**~ **dei Deputati** Chamber of Deputies, ≈ House of Commons (*Brit*), ≈ House of Representatives (*US*); ~ **a gas** gas chamber; ~ **a un letto/a due letti/ matrimoniale** single/twin-bedded/double room; ~ **oscura** (*FOT*) dark room.

came'rata, i, e *sm/f* companion, mate // *sf* dormitory.

cameri'era *sf* (*domestica*) maid; (*che serve a tavola*) waitress; (*che fa le camere*) chambermaid.

cameri'ere *sm* (man)servant; (*di ristorante*) waiter.

came'rino *sm* (*TEATRO*) dressing room.

'camice ['kamitʃe] *sm* (*REL*) alb; (*per medici etc*) white coat.

cami'cetta [kami'tʃetta] *sf* blouse.

ca'micia, cie [ka'mitʃa] *sf (da uomo)* shirt; *(da donna)* blouse; ~ **di forza** straitjacket; **camici'otto** *sm* casual shirt; *(per operai)* smock.

cami'netto *sm* hearth, fireplace.

ca'mino *sm* chimney; *(focolare)* fireplace, hearth.

'camion *sm inv* lorry *(Brit)*, truck *(US)*; **camion'cino** *sm* van.

cam'mello *sm* (ZOOL) camel; *(tessuto)* camel hair.

cammi'nare *vi* to walk; *(funzionare)* to work, go.

cam'mino *sm* walk; *(sentiero)* path; *(itinerario, direzione, tragitto)* way; **mettersi in ~** to set *o* start off.

camo'milla *sf* camomile; *(infuso)* camomile tea.

ca'morra *sf* camorra; racket.

ca'moscio [ka'moʃʃo] *sm* chamois.

cam'pagna [kam'paɲɲa] *sf* country, countryside; (POL, COMM, MIL) campaign; **in ~** in the country; **andare in ~** to go to the country; **fare una ~** to campaign; **campa'gnolo, a** *ag* country *cpd // sf* (AUT) cross-country vehicle.

cam'pale *ag* field *cpd*; *(fig)*: **una giornata ~** a hard day.

cam'pana *sf* bell; *(anche: ~ di vetro)* bell jar; **campa'nella** *sf* small bell; *(di tenda)* curtain ring; **campa'nello** *sm (all'uscio, da tavola)* bell.

campa'nile *sm* bell tower, belfry; **campani'lismo** *sm* parochialism.

cam'pare *vi* to live; *(tirare avanti)* to get by, manage.

cam'pato, a *ag*: ~ **in aria** unsound, unfounded.

campeggi'are [kamped'dʒare] *vi* to camp; *(risaltare)* to stand out; **campeggia'tore, 'trice** *sm/f* camper; **cam'peggio** *sm* camping; *(terreno)* camp site; **fare (del) campeggio** to go camping.

cam'pestre *ag* country *cpd*, rural.

campio'nario, a *ag*: **fiera ~a** a trade fair *// sm* collection of samples.

campio'nato *sm* championship.

campi'one, 'essa *sm/f* (SPORT) champion *// sm* (COMM) sample.

'campo *sm* field; (MIL) field; *(: accampamento)* camp; *(spazio delimitato: sportivo etc)* ground; field; *(di quadro)* background; **i ~i** *(campagna)* the countryside; ~ **da aviazione** airfield; ~ **di concentramento** concentration camp; ~ **di golf** golf course; ~ **da tennis** tennis court; ~ **visivo** field of vision.

campo'santo, *pl* **campisanti** *sm* cemetery.

camuf'fare *vt* to disguise.

'Canada *sm*: **il ~** Canada; **cana'dese** *ag, sm/f* Canadian *// sf (anche:* **tenda** *canadese)* ridge tent.

ca'naglia [ka'naʎʎa] *sf* rabble, mob; *(persona)* scoundrel, rogue.

ca'nale *sm (anche fig)* channel; *(artificiale)* canal.

'canapa *sf* hemp.

cana'rino *sm* canary.

cancel'lare [kantʃel'lare] *vt (con la gomma)* to rub out, erase; *(con la penna)* to strike out; *(annullare)* to annul, cancel; *(disdire)* to cancel.

cancelle'ria [kantʃelle'ria] *sf* chancery; *(quanto necessario per scrivere)* stationery.

cancelli'ere [kantʃel'ljɛre] *sm* chancellor; *(di tribunale)* clerk of the court.

can'cello [kan'tʃɛllo] *sm* gate.

can'crena *sf* gangrene.

'cancro *sm* (MED) cancer; *(dello zodiaco):* C~ Cancer.

can'dela *sf* candle; ~ **(di accensione)** (AUT) spark(ing) plug.

cande'labro *sm* candelabra.

candeli'ere *sm* candlestick.

candi'dato, a *sm/f* candidate; *(aspirante a una carica)* applicant.

'candido, a *ag* white as snow; *(puro)* pure; *(sincero)* sincere, candid.

can'dito, a *ag* candied.

can'dore *sm* brilliant white; purity; sincerity, candour.

'cane *sm* dog; *(di pistola, fucile)* cock; **fa un freddo ~** it's bitterly cold; **non c'era un ~** there wasn't a soul; ~ **da caccia/guardia** hunting/guard dog; ~ **lupo** alsatian.

ca'nestro *sm* basket.

cangi'ante [kan'dʒante] *ag* iridescent.

can'guro *sm* kangaroo.

ca'nile *sm* kennel; *(di allevamento)* kennels *pl*; ~ **municipale** dog pound.

ca'nino, a *ag, sm* canine.

'canna *sf (pianta)* reed; *(: indica, da zucchero)* cane; *(bastone)* stick, cane; *(di fucile)* barrel; *(di organo)* pipe; ~ **fumaria** chimney flue; ~ **da pesca** (fishing) rod; ~ **da zucchero** sugar cane.

can'nella *sf* (CUC) cinnamon.

cannel'loni *smpl* pasta tubes stuffed with sauce and baked.

cannocchi'ale [kannok'kjale] *sm* telescope.

can'none *sm* (MIL) gun; *(: STORIA)* cannon; *(tubo)* pipe, tube; *(piega)* box pleat; *(fig)* ace.

can'nuccia, ce [kan'nuttʃa] *sf* (drinking) straw.

ca'noa *sf* canoe.

'canone *sm* canon, criterion; *(mensile, annuo)* rent; fee.

ca'nonico, ci *sm* (REL) canon.

ca'noro, a *ag (uccello)* singing, song *cpd*.

canot'taggio [kanot'taddʒo] *sm* rowing.

canotti'era *sf* vest.

ca'notto *sm* small boat, dinghy; canoe.

cano'vaccio [kano'vattʃo] *sm* (*tela*) canvas; (*strofinaccio*) duster; (*trama*) plot.

can'tante *sm/f* singer.

can'tare *vt*, *vi* to sing; **cantau'tore, 'trice** *sm/f* singer-composer.

canti'ere *sm* (EDIL) (building) site; (*anche:* ~ **navale**) shipyard.

canti'lena *sf* (*filastrocca*) lullaby; (*fig*) sing-song voice.

can'tina *sf* (*locale*) cellar; (*bottega*) wine shop.

'canto *sm* song; (*arte*) singing; (REL) chant; chanting; (*poesia*) poem, lyric; (*parte di una poesia*) canto; (*parte, lato*): **da un ~ on the one hand; d'altro ~ on the other hand.

canto'nata *sf* corner; **prendere una ~** (*fig*) to blunder.

can'tone *sm* (*in Svizzera*) canton.

can'tuccio [kan'tuttʃo] *sm* corner, nook.

canzo'nare [kantso'nare] *vt* to tease.

can'zone [kan'tsone] *sf* song; (POESIA) canzone; **canzoni'ere** *sm* (MUS) songbook; (LETTERATURA) collection of poems.

'caos *sm inv* chaos; **ca'otico, a, ci, che** *ag* chaotic.

C.A.P. *sigla m* = **codice di avviamento postale.**

ca'pace [ka'patʃe] *ag* able, capable; (*ampio, vasto*) large, capacious; **sei ~ di farlo?** can you o are you able to do it?; **capacità** *sf inv* ability; (DIR, *di recipiente*) capacity; **capaci'tarsi** *vr*: **capacitarsi di** to make out, understand.

ca'panna *sf* hut.

capan'none *sm* (AGR) barn; (*fabbricato industriale*) (factory) shed.

ca'parbio, a *ag* stubborn.

ca'parra *sf* deposit, down payment.

ca'pello *sm* hair; **~i** *smpl* (*capigliatura*) hair *sg*.

capez'zale [kapet'tsale] *sm* bolster; (*fig*) bedside.

ca'pezzolo [ka'pettsolo] *sm* nipple.

capi'enza [ka'pjentsa] *sf* capacity.

capiglia'tura [kapiʎʎa'tura] *sf* hair.

ca'pire *vt* to understand.

capi'tale *ag* (*mortale*) capital; (*fondamentale*) main, chief // *sf* (*città*) capital // *sm* (ECON) capital; **capita'lismo** *sm* capitalism; **capita'lista, i, e** *ag, sm/f* capitalist.

capi'tano *sm* captain.

capi'tare *vi* (*giungere casualmente*) to happen to go, find o.s.; (*accadere*) to happen; (*presentarsi: cosa*) to turn up, present itself // *vb impers* to happen; **mi è capitato un guaio** I've had a spot of trouble.

capi'tello *sm* (ARCHIT) capital.

ca'pitolo *sm* chapter.

capi'tombolo *sm* headlong fall, tumble.

'capo *sm* head; (*persona*) head, leader; (: *in ufficio*) head, boss; (: *in tribù*) chief; (*di oggetti*) head; top; end; (GEO) cape; **andare a ~ to start a new paragraph; da ~ over again; ~ di bestiame** head *inv* of cattle; **~ di vestiario** item of clothing.

'capo... *prefisso*: **capocu'oco, chi** *sm* head cook; **Capo'danno** *sm* New Year; **capo'fitto: a capofitto** *av* headfirst, headlong; **capo'giro** *sm* dizziness *q*; **capola'voro, i** *sm* masterpiece; **capo'linea, pl capi'linea** *sm* terminus; **capo'lino** *sm*: **fare capolino** to peep out (o in *etc*); **capolu'ogo, pl ghi** o **capilu'oghi** *sm* chief town, administrative centre.

capo'rale *sm* (MIL) lance corporal (*Brit*), private first class (US).

'capo... *prefisso*: **capostazi'one, pl capistazi'one** *sm* station master; **capo'treno, pl capi'treno** o **capo'treni** *sm* guard.

capo'volgere [kapo'voldʒere] *vt* to overturn; (*fig*) to reverse; **~rsi** *vr* to overturn; (*barca*) to capsize; (*fig*) to be reversed; **capo'volto, a** *pp di* **capovolgere.**

'cappa *sf* (*mantello*) cape, cloak; (*del camino*) hood.

cap'pella *sf* (REL) chapel; **cappel'lano** *sm* chaplain.

cap'pello *sm* hat.

'cappero *sm* caper.

cap'pone *sm* capon.

cap'potto *sm* (over)coat.

cappuc'cino [kapput'tʃino] *sm* (*frate*) Capuchin monk; (*bevanda*) frothy white coffee.

cap'puccio [kap'puttʃo] *sm* (*copricapo*) hood; (*della biro*) cap.

'capra *sf* (*she-*)goat; **ca'pretto** *sm* kid.

ca'priccio [ka'pritttʃo] *sm* caprice, whim; (*bizza*) tantrum; **fare i ~i** to be very naughty; **capricci'oso, a** *ag* capricious, whimsical; naughty.

Capri'corno *sm* Capricorn.

capri'ola *sf* somersault.

capri'olo *sm* roe deer.

'capro *sm* billy-goat; **~ espiatorio** (*fig*) scapegoat.

'capsula *sf* capsule; (*di arma, per bottiglie*) cap.

cap'tare *vt* (RADIO, TV) to pick up; (*cattivarsi*) to gain, win.

cara'bina *sf* rifle.

carabini'ere *sm* member of Italian military police force.

ca'raffa *sf* carafe.

cara'mella *sf* sweet.

ca'rattere *sm* character; (*caratteristica*) characteristic, trait; **avere un buon ~** to be good-natured; **caratte'ristico, a, ci, che** *ag* characteristic // *sf* characteristic, trait, peculiarity; **caratteriz'zare** *vt* to characterize, distinguish.

car'bone *sm* coal.

carbu'rante *sm* (motor) fuel.

carbura'tore *sm* carburettor.

car'cassa *sf* carcass; *(fig: peg: macchina etc)* (old) wreck.

carce'rato, a [kartʃe'rato] *sm/f* prisoner.

'carcere ['kartʃere] *sm* prison; *(pena)* imprisonment.

carci'ofo [kar'tʃɔfo] *sm* artichoke.

car'diaco, a, ci, che *ag* cardiac, heart *cpd*.

cardi'nale *ag, sm* cardinal.

'cardine *sm* hinge.

'cardo *sm* thistle.

ca'renza [ka'rɛntsa] *sf* lack, scarcity; *(vitaminica)* deficiency.

cares'tia *sf* famine; *(penuria)* scarcity, dearth.

ca'rezza [ka'rettsa] *sf* caress; **carez'zare** *vt* to caress, stroke, fondle.

'carica *sf vedi* **carico**.

cari'care *vt* to load; *(aggravare: anche fig)* to weigh down; *(orologio)* to wind up; *(batteria, MIL)* to charge.

'carico, a, chi, che *ag (che porta un peso)*: ~ **di** loaded *o* laden with; *(fucile)* loaded; *(orologio)* wound up; *(batteria)* charged; *(colore)* deep; *(caffè, tè)* strong // *sm (il caricare)* loading; *(ciò che si carica)* load; *(fig: peso)* burden, weight // *sf (mansione ufficiale)* office, position; *(MIL, TECN, ELETTR)* charge; **persona a** ~ dependent; **essere a** ~ **di qn** *(spese etc)* to be charged to sb; **ha una forte** ~**a di simpatia** he's very likeable.

'carie *sf (dentaria)* decay.

ca'rino, a *ag* lovely, pretty, nice; *(simpatico)* nice.

carità *sf* charity; **per** ~! *(escl di rifiuto)* good heavens, no!

carnagi'one [karna'dʒone] *sf* complexion.

car'nale *ag (amore)* carnal; *(fratello)* blood *cpd*.

'carne *sf* flesh; *(bovina, ovina etc)* meat; ~ **di manzo/maiale/pecora** beef/pork/mutton; ~ **tritata** mince *(Brit)*, hamburger meat *(US)*, minced *(Brit)* o ground *(US)* meat.

car'nefice [kar'nefitʃe] *sm* executioner; hangman.

carne'vale *sm* carnival.

car'noso, a *ag* fleshy.

'caro, a *ag (amato)* dear; *(costoso)* dear, expensive.

ca'rogna [ka'roɲɲa] *sf* carrion; *(fig: fam)* swine.

caro'sello *sm* merry-go-round.

ca'rota *sf* carrot.

caro'vana *sf* caravan.

caro'vita *sm* high cost of living.

carpenti'ere *sm* carpenter.

car'pire *vt*: ~ **qc a qn** *(segreto etc)* to

get sth out of sb.

car'poni *av* on all fours.

car'rabile *ag* suitable for vehicles; "**passo** ~" "keep clear".

car'raio, a *ag*: **passo** ~ vehicle entrance.

carreggi'ata [karred'dʒata] *sf* carriageway *(Brit)*, (road)way.

car'rello *sm* trolley; *(AER)* undercarriage; *(CINEMA)* dolly; *(di macchina da scrivere)* carriage.

carri'era *sf* career; **fare** ~ to get on; **a gran** ~ at full speed.

carri'ola *sf* wheelbarrow.

'carro *sm* cart, wagon; ~ **armato** tank.

car'rozza [kar'rottsa] *sf* carriage, coach.

carrozze'ria [karrottse'ria] *sf* body, coachwork *(Brit)*; *(officina)* coachbuilder's workshop *(Brit)*, body shop.

carroz'zina [karrot'tsina] *sf* pram *(Brit)*, baby carriage *(US)*.

'carta *sf* paper; *(al ristorante)* menu; *(GEO)* map; plan; *(documento, da gioco)* card; *(costituzione)* charter; ~**e** *sfpl (documenti)* papers, documents; **alla** ~ *(al ristorante)* à la carte; ~ **assegni** bank card; ~ **assorbente** blotting paper; ~ **bollata** *o* **da bollo** official stamped paper; ~ **di credito** credit card; ~ **(geografica)** map; ~ **d'identità** identity card; ~ **igienica** toilet paper; ~ **d'imbarco** *(AER, NAUT)* boarding card; ~ **da lettere** writing paper; ~ **libera** *(AMM)* unstamped paper; ~ **da parati** wallpaper; ~ **verde** *(AUT)* green card; ~ **vetrata** sandpaper; ~ **da visita** visiting card.

cartacar'bone, *pl* **cartecar'bone** *sf* carbon paper.

car'taccia, ce [kar'tattʃa] *sf* waste paper.

cartamo'neta *sf* paper money.

carta'pecora *sf* parchment.

carta'pesta *sf* papier-mâché.

car'teggio [kar'teddʒo] *sm* correspondence.

car'tella *sf (scheda)* card; *(custodia: di cartone)* folder; *(: di uomo d'affari etc)* briefcase; *(: di scolaro)* schoolbag, satchel; ~ **clinica** *(MED)* case sheet.

car'tello *sm* sign; *(pubblicitario)* poster; *(stradale)* sign, signpost; *(ECON)* cartel; *(in dimostrazioni)* placard; **cartel'lone** *sm (pubblicitario)* advertising poster; *(della tombola)* scoring frame; *(TEATRO)* playbill; **tenere il cartellone** *(spettacolo)* to have a long run.

carti'era *sf* paper mill.

car'tina *sf (AUT, GEO)* map.

car'toccio [kar'tɔttʃo] *sm* paper bag.

cartole'ria *sf* stationer's (shop).

carto'lina *sf* postcard.

car'tone *sm* cardboard; *(ARTE)* cartoon; ~**i animati** *smpl (CINEMA)* cartoons.

car'tuccia, ce [kar'tuttʃa] *sf* cartridge.

'casa *sf* house; *(specialmente la propria casa)* home; *(COMM)* firm, house; **essere**

a ~ to be at home; **vado a ~ mia/tua** I'm going home/to your house; **~ di cura** nursing home; **~ dello studente** student hostel; **~e popolari** ≈ council houses (o flats) (*Brit*), ≈ public housing units (*US*).

ca'sacca, che *sf* military coat; (*di fantino*) blouse.

casalingo, a, ghi, ghe *ag* household, domestic; (*fatto a casa*) home-made; (*semplice*) homely; (*amante della casa*) home-loving // *sf* housewife; **~ghi** *smpl* household articles; **cucina ~a** plain home cooking.

cas'care *vi* to fall; **cas'cata** *sf* fall; (*d'acqua*) cascade, waterfall.

'casco, schi *sm* helmet; (*del parrucchiere*) hair-drier; (*di banane*) bunch.

casei'ficio [kazei'fitʃo] *sm* creamery.

ca'sella *sf* pigeon-hole; **~ postale** (C.P.) post office box (P.O. box).

casel'lario *sm* filing cabinet; **~ giudiziale** court records *pl*.

ca'sello *sm* (*di autostrada*) toll-house.

ca'serma *sf* barracks *pl*.

ca'sino *sm* (*confusione*) row, racket; (*casa di prostituzione*) brothel.

casinò *sm inv* casino.

'caso *sm* chance; (*fatto, vicenda*) event, incident; (*possibilità*) possibility; (*MED, LING*) case; **a ~** at random; **per ~** by chance, by accident; **in ogni ~, in tutti i ~i** in any case, at any rate; **al ~** should the opportunity arise; **nel ~ che** in case; **~ mai** if by chance; **~ limite** borderline case.

'cassa *sf* case, crate, box; (*bara*) coffin; (*mobile*) chest; (*involucro: di orologio etc*) case; (*macchina*) cash register; (*luogo di pagamento*) checkout (counter); (*fondo*) fund; (*istituto bancario*) bank; **~ automatica prelievi** automatic telling machine, cash dispenser; **~ continua** night safe; **~ integrazione** mettere in **~ integrazione** ≈ to lay off; **~ mutua** o **malattia** health insurance scheme; **~ di risparmio** savings bank; **~ toracica** (*ANAT*) chest.

cassa'forte, *pl* **casseforti** *sf* safe.

cassa'panca, *pl* **cassapanche** o **cassepanche** *sf* settle.

casseru'ola, casse'rola *sf* saucepan.

cas'setta *sf* box; (*per registratore*) cassette; (*CINEMA, TEATRO*) box-office takings *pl*; **film di ~** box-office draw; **~ di sicurezza** strongbox; **~ delle lettere** letterbox.

cas'setto *sm* drawer; **casset'tone** *sm* chest of drawers.

cassi'ere, a *sm/f* cashier; (*di banca*) teller.

'casta *sf* caste.

cas'tagna [kas'taɲɲa] *sf* chestnut.

cas'tagno [kas'taɲɲo] *sm* chestnut (tree).

cas'tano, a *ag* chestnut (brown).

cas'tello *sm* castle; (*TECN*) scaffolding.

casti'gare *vt* to punish; **cas'tigo, ghi** *sm* punishment.

castità *sf* chastity.

cas'toro *sm* beaver.

cas'trare *vt* to castrate; to geld; to doctor (*Brit*), fix (*US*).

casu'ale *ag* chance cpd.

cata'comba *sf* catacomb.

ca'talogo, ghi *sm* catalogue.

catarifran'gente [catarifran'dʒɛnte] *sm* (*AUT*) reflector.

ca'tarro *sm* catarrh.

ca'tasta *sf* stack, pile.

ca'tasto *sm* land register; land registry office.

ca'tastrofe *sf* catastrophe, disaster.

catego'ria *sf* category.

ca'tena *sf* chain; **~ di montaggio** assembly line; **~e da neve** (*AUT*) snow chains; **cate'naccio** *sm* bolt.

cate'ratta *sf* cataract; (*chiusa*) sluice-gate.

cati'nella *sf*: **piovere a ~e** to pour, rain cats and dogs.

ca'tino *sm* basin.

ca'trame *sm* tar.

'cattedra *sf* teacher's desk; (*di università*) chair.

catte'drale *sf* cathedral.

catti'veria *sf* malice, spite; naughtiness; (*atto*) spiteful act; (*parole*) malicious o spiteful remark.

cattività *sf* captivity.

cat'tivo, a *ag* bad; (*malvagio*) bad, wicked; (*turbolento: bambino*) bad, naughty; (*: mare*) rough; (*odore, sapore*) nasty, bad.

cat'tolico, a, ci, che *ag, sm/f* (Roman) Catholic.

cat'tura *sf* capture.

cattu'rare *vt* to capture.

cauc'ciù [kaut'tʃu] *sm* rubber.

'causa *sf* cause; (*DIR*) lawsuit, case, action; **a ~ di, per ~ di** because of; **fare** o **muovere ~ a qn** to take legal action against sb.

cau'sare *vt* to cause.

cau'tela *sf* caution, prudence.

caute'lare *vt* to protect; **~rsi** *vr*: **~rsi (da)** to take precautions (against).

'cauto, a *ag* cautious, prudent.

cauzi'one [kaut'tsjone] *sf* security; (*DIR*) bail.

cav. *abbr* = **cavaliere.**

'cava *sf* quarry.

caval'care *vt* (*cavallo*) to ride; (*muro*) to sit astride; (*sog: ponte*) to span; **caval'cata** *sf* ride; (*gruppo di persone*) riding party.

cavalca'via *sm inv* flyover.

cavalcioni [kaval'tʃoni]: **a ~ di** *prep* astride.

cavali'ere *sm* rider; (*feudale, titolo*) knight; (*soldato*) cavalryman; (*al ballo*) partner; **cavalle'resco, a, schi, sche** *ag* chivalrous; **cavalle'ria** *sf* chivalry; (*milizia a cavallo*) cavalry.

cavalle'rizzo, a [kavalle'rittso] *sm/f* riding instructor; circus rider.

caval'letta *sf* grasshopper.

caval'letto *sm* (*FOT*) tripod; (*da pittore*) easel.

ca'vallo *sm* horse; (*SCACCHI*) knight; (*AUT: anche:* ~ **vapore**) horsepower; (*dei pantaloni*) crotch; **a** ~ **on** horseback; **a** ~ **di** astride, straddling; ~ **di** battaglia (*fig*) hobby-horse; ~ **da corsa** racehorse.

ca'vare *vt* (*togliere*) to draw out, extract, take out; (*: giacca, scarpe*) to take off; (*: fame, sete, voglia*) to satisfy; **cavarsela** to get away with it; to manage, get on all right.

cava'tappi *sm inv* corkscrew.

ca'verna *sf* cave.

'cavia *sf* guinea pig.

cavi'ale *sm* caviar.

ca'viglia [ka'viʎʎa] *sf* ankle.

ca'villo *sm* quibble.

'cavo, a *ag* hollow // *sm* (*ANAT*) cavity; (*grossa corda*) rope, cable; (*ELETTR, TEL*) cable.

cavolfi'ore *sm* cauliflower.

'cavolo *sm* cabbage; (*fam*): **non m'importa un** ~ I don't give a damn; ~ **di Bruxelles** Brussels sprout.

cazzu'ola [kat'tswola] *sf* trowel.

c/c *abbr* = **conto corrente.**

ce [tʃe] *pronome, av vedi* **ci.**

cece ['tʃetʃe] *sm* chickpea.

cecità [tʃetʃi'ta] *sf* blindness.

Cecoslo'vacchia [tʃekozlo'vakkja] *sf*: **la** ~ Czechoslovakia; **cecoslo'vacco, a, chi, che** *ag, sm/f* Czechoslovakian.

'cedere ['tʃedere] *vt* (*concedere: posto*) to give up; (*DIR*) to transfer, make over // *vi* (*cadere*) to give way, subside; ~ **(a)** to surrender (to), yield (to), give in (to); **ce'devole** *ag* (*terreno*) soft; (*fig*) yielding.

'cedola ['tʃedola] *sf* (*COMM*) coupon; voucher.

'cedro ['tʃedro] *sm* cedar; (*albero da frutto, frutto*) citron.

C.E.E. ['tʃe] *sigla f* = **Comunità Economica Europea.**

'ceffo ['tʃeffo] *sm* (*peg*) ugly mug.

cef'fone [tʃef'fone] *sm* slap, smack.

ce'larsi [tʃe'larsi] *vr* to hide.

cele'brare [tʃele'brare] *vt* to celebrate; **celebrazi'one** *sf* celebration.

'celebre ['tʃelebre] *ag* famous, celebrated; **celebrità** *sf inv* fame; (*persona*) celebrity.

'celere ['tʃelere] *ag* fast, swift; (*corso*) crash *cpd*.

ce'leste [tʃe'leste] *ag* celestial; heavenly; (*colore*) sky-blue.

'celibe ['tʃelibe] *ag* single, unmarried // *sm* bachelor.

'cella ['tʃella] *sf* cell.

'cellula ['tʃellula] *sf* (*BIOL, ELETTR, POL*) cell.

cemen'tare [tʃemen'tare] *vt* (*anche fig*) to cement.

ce'mento [tʃe'mento] *sm* cement; ~ **armato** reinforced concrete.

'cena ['tʃena] *sf* dinner; (*leggera*) supper.

ce'nare [tʃe'nare] *vi* to dine, have dinner.

'cencio ['tʃentʃo] *sm* piece of cloth, rag; (*per spolverare*) duster.

'cenere ['tʃenere] *sf* ash.

'cenno ['tʃenno] *sm* (*segno*) sign, signal; (*gesto*) gesture; (*col capo*) nod; (*con la mano*) wave; (*allusione*) hint, mention; (*breve esposizione*) short account; **far** ~ **di si/no** to nod (one's head)/shake one's head.

censi'mento [tʃensi'mento] *sm* census.

cen'sore [tʃen'sore] *sm* censor.

cen'sura [tʃen'sura] *sf* censorship; censor's office; (*fig*) censure.

cente'nario, a [tʃente'narjo] *ag* (*che ha cento anni*) hundred-year-old; (*che ricorre ogni cento anni*) centennial, centenary *cpd* // *sm/f* centenarian // *sm* centenary.

cen'tesimo, a [tʃen'tezimo] *ag, sm* hundredth.

cen'tigrado, a [tʃen'tigrado] *ag* centigrade; **20 gradi** ~**i** 20 degrees centigrade.

cen'timetro [tʃen'timetro] *sm* centimetre.

centi'naio, *pl(f)* **aia** [tʃenti'najo] *sm*: **un** ~ **(di)** a hundred; about a hundred.

'cento ['tʃento] *num* a hundred, one hundred.

cen'trale [tʃen'trale] *ag* central // *sf*: ~ **telefonica** (telephone) exchange; ~ **elettrica** electric power station; **centrali'nista** *sm/f* operator; **centra'lino** *sm* (telephone) exchange; (*di albergo etc*) switchboard.

cen'trare [tʃen'trare] *vt* to hit the centre of; (*TECN*) to centre.

cen'trifuga [tʃen'trifuga] *sf* spin-drier.

'centro ['tʃentro] *sm* centre; ~ **commerciale** shopping centre; (*città*) commercial centre.

'ceppo ['tʃeppo] *sm* (*di albero*) stump; (*pezzo di legno*) log.

'cera ['tʃera] *sf* wax; (*aspetto*) appearance, look.

ce'ramica, che [tʃe'ramika] *sf* ceramic; (*ARTE*) ceramics *sg*.

cerbi'atto [tʃer'bjatto] *sm* (*ZOOL*) fawn.

'cerca ['tʃerka] *sf*: **in** *o* **alla** ~ **di** in search of.

cer'care [tʃer'kare] *vt* to look for, search for // *vi*: ~ **di fare qc** to try to do sth.

'**cerchia** ['tʃerkja] *sf* circle.

'**cerchio** ['tʃerkjo] *sm* circle; (*giocattolo, di botte*) hoop.

cere'ale [tʃere'ale] *sm* cereal.

ceri'monia [tʃeri'mɔnja] *sf* ceremony; **cerimoni'oso, a** *ag* formal, ceremonious.

ce'rino [tʃe'rino] *sm* wax match.

'**cernia** ['tʃernja] *sf* (ZOOL) stone bass.

cerni'era [tʃer'njera] *sf* hinge; ~ **lampo** zip (fastener) (*Brit*), zipper (*US*).

'**cernita** ['tʃernita] *sf* selection.

'**cero** ['tʃero] *sm* (church) candle.

ce'rotto [tʃe'rɔtto] *sm* sticking plaster.

certa'mente [tʃerta'mente] *av* certainly, surely.

cer'tezza [tʃer'tettsa] *sf* certainty.

certifi'cato *sm* certificate; ~ **medico/di nascita** medical/birth certificate.

'**certo, a** ['tʃerto] ◆ *ag* (*sicuro*): ~ (**di/che**) certain *o* sure (of/that)
◆ *det* **1** (*tale*) certain; **un ~ signor Smith** a (certain) Mr Smith
2 (*qualche; con valore intensivo*) some; **dopo un ~ tempo** after some time; **un fatto di una ~a importanza** a matter of some importance; **di una ~a età** past one's prime, not so young
◆ *pronome*: ~**i(e)** *pl* some
◆ *av* (*certamente*) certainly; (*senz'altro*) of course; **di ~** certainly; **no (di) ~!, ~ che no!** certainly not!; **sì ~** yes indeed, certainly.

cer'tuni [tʃer'tuni] *pronome pl* some (people).

cer'vello, *pl* **i** (*anche: pl(f)* **a** *o* **e**) [tʃer'vɛllo] *sm* brain.

'**cervo, a** ['tʃervo] *smf* stag/doe // *sm* deer; ~ **volante** stag beetle.

ce'sello [tʃe'zɛllo] *sm* chisel.

ce'soie [tʃe'zɔje] *sfpl* shears.

ces'puglio [tʃes'puʎʎo] *sm* bush.

ces'sare [tʃes'sare] *vi, vt* to stop, cease; ~ **di fare qc** to stop doing sth; **cessate il fuoco** *sm* ceasefire.

'**cesso** ['tʃesso] *sm* (*fam: gabinetto*) bog.

'**cesta** ['tʃesta] *sf* (large) basket.

ces'tino [tʃes'tino] *sm* basket; (*per la carta straccia*) wastepaper basket; ~ **da viaggio** (FERR) packed lunch (*o* dinner).

'**cesto** ['tʃesto] *sm* basket.

'**ceto** ['tʃeto] *sm* (social) class.

cetrio'lino [tʃetrio'lino] *sm* gherkin.

cetri'olo [tʃetri'ɔlo] *sm* cucumber.

cfr. *abbr* (= *confronta*) cf.

CGIL *sigla f* (= *Confederazione Generale Italiana del Lavoro*) trades union organization.

che [ke] ◆ *pronome* **1** (*relativo: persona: soggetto*) who; (*: oggetto*) whom, that; (*: cosa, animale*) which, that; **il ragazzo ~ è venuto** the boy who came; **l'uomo ~ io vedo** the man (whom) I see; **il libro ~ è sul tavolo** the book which *o* that is on the table; **il libro ~ vedi** the book (which

o that) you see; **la sera ~ ti ho visto** the evening I saw you
2 (*interrogativo, esclamativo*) what; ~ (**cosa**) **fai?** what are you doing?; **a ~ (cosa) pensi?** what are you thinking about?; **non sa ~ (cosa) fare** he doesn't know what to do; **ma ~ dici!** what are you saying!
3 (*indefinito*): **quell'uomo ha un ~ di losco** there's something suspicious about that man; **un certo non so ~** an indefinable something
◆ *det* **1** (*interrogativo: tra tanti*) what; (*: tra pochi*) which; ~ **tipo di film preferisci?** what sort of film do you prefer?; ~ **vestito ti vuoi mettere?** what (*o* which) dress do you want to put on?
2 (*esclamativo: seguito da aggettivo*) how; (*: seguito da sostantivo*) what; ~ **buono!** how delicious!; ~ **bel vestito!** what a lovely dress!
◆ *cong* **1** (*con proposizioni subordinate*) that; **credo ~ verrà** I think he'll come; **voglio ~ tu studi** I want you to study; **so ~ tu c'eri** I know (that) you were there; **non ~: non ~ sia sbagliato, ma ...** not that it's wrong, but ...
2 (*finale*) so that; **vieni qua, ~ ti veda** come here, so (that) I can see you
3 (*temporale*): **arrivai ~ eri già partito** you had already left when I arrived; **sono anni ~ non lo vedo** I haven't seen him for years, it's years since I saw him
4 (*in frasi imperative, concessive*): ~ **venga pure!** let him come by all means!; ~ **tu sia benedetto!** may God bless you!
5 (*comparativo: con più, meno*) than; *vedi anche* **più, meno, così** *etc.*

cheti'chella [keti'kɛlla]: **alla ~** *av* stealthily, unobtrusively.

'**cheto, a** ['keto] *ag* quiet, silent.

chi [ki] *pronome* **1** (*interrogativo: soggetto*) who; (*: oggetto*) who, whom; ~ **è?** who is it?; **di ~ è questo libro?** whose book is this?, whose is this book?; **con ~ parli?** who are you talking to?; **a ~ pensi?** who are you thinking about?; ~ **di voi?** which of you?; **non so a ~ rivolgermi** I don't know who to ask
2 (*relativo*) whoever, anyone who; **dillo a ~ vuoi** tell whoever you like
3 (*indefinito*): ~ **... ~ ...** some ... others ...; ~ **dice una cosa, ~ dice un'altra** some say one thing, others say another.

chiacchie'rare [kjakkje'rare] *vi* to chat; (*discorrere futilmente*) to chatter; (*far pettegolezzi*) to gossip; **chiacchie'rata** *sf* chat; **chi'acchiere** *sfpl*: **fare due** *o* **quattro chiacchiere** to have a chat; **chiacchie'rone, a** *ag* talkative, chatty; gossipy // *smf* chatterbox; gossip.

chia'mare [kja'mare] *vt* to call; (*rivolgersi a qn*) to call (in), send for; ~**rsi** *vr* (*aver nome*) to be called; **mi**

chiamo Paolo my name is Paolo, I'm called Paolo; ~ alle armi to call up; ~ in giudizio to summon; **chia'mata** *sf* (*TEL*) call; (*MIL*) call-up.

chia'rezza [kja'rettsa] *sf* clearness; clarity.

chia'rire [kja'rire] *vt* to make clear; (*fig: spiegare*) to clear up, explain; ~**rsi** *vr* to become clear.

chi'aro, a ['kjaro] *ag* clear; (*luminoso*) clear, bright; (*colore*) pale, light.

chiaroveg'gente [kjaroved'dʒɛnte] *sm/f* clairvoyant.

chi'asso ['kjasso] *sm* uproar, row; **chias'soso, a** *ag* noisy, rowdy; (*vistoso*) showy, gaudy.

chi'ave ['kjave] *sf* key // *ag inv* key *cpd*; ~ **d'accensione** (*AUT*) ignition key; ~ **inglese** monkey wrench; ~ **di volta** (*anche fig*) keystone; **chiavis'tello** *sm* bolt.

chi'azza [kjattsa] *sf* stain; splash.

'chicco, chi ['kikko] *sm* (*di cereale, riso*) grain; (*di caffè*) bean; ~ **d'uva** grape.

chi'edere ['kjedere] *vt* (*per sapere*) to ask; (*per avere*) to ask for // *vi*: ~ **di** qn to ask after sb; (*al telefono*) to ask for o want sb; ~ **qc a** qn to ask sb sth; to ask sb for sth.

chi'erico, ci ['kjɛriko] *sm* cleric; altar boy.

chi'esa ['kjɛza] *sf* church.

chi'esto, a *pp di* **chiedere.**

'chiglia [kiʎʎa] *sf* keel.

'chilo ['kilo] *sm* kilo; **chilo'grammo** *sm* kilogram(me); **chi'lometro** *sm* kilometre.

'chimico, a, ci, che ['kimiko] *ag* chemical // *sm/f* chemist // *sf* chemistry.

'china ['kina] *sf* (*pendio*) slope, descent; (*BOT*) cinchona; (**inchiostro di**) ~ Indian ink.

chi'nare [ki'nare] *vt* to lower, bend; ~**rsi** *vr* to stoop, bend.

chi'nino [ki'nino] *sm* quinine.

chi'occia, ce ['kjɔttʃa] *sf* brooding hen.

chi'occiola ['kjɔttʃola] *sf* snail; **scala a** ~ spiral staircase.

chi'odo ['kjɔdo] *sm* nail; (*fig*) obsession.

chi'oma ['kjɔma] *sf* (*capelli*) head of hair; (*di albero*) foliage.

chi'osco, schi ['kjɔsko] *sm* kiosk, stall.

chi'ostro ['kjɔstro] *sm* cloister.

chiro'mante [kiro'mante] *sm/f* palmist.

chirur'gia [kirur'dʒia] *sf* surgery; **chi'rurgo, ghi** o **gi** *sm* surgeon.

chissà [kis'sa] *av* who knows, I wonder.

chi'tarra [ki'tarra] *sf* guitar.

chi'udere ['kjudere] *vt* to close, shut; (*luce, acqua*) to put off, turn off; (*definitivamente: fabbrica*) to close down, shut down; (*strada*) to close; (*recingere*) to enclose; (*porre termine*) to end // *vi* to close, shut; to close down, shut down; to end; ~**rsi** *vr* to shut,

close; (*ritirarsi: anche fig*) to shut o.s. away; (*ferita*) to close up.

chi'unque [ki'unkwe] *pronome* (*relativo*) whoever; (*indefinito*) anyone, anybody; ~ **sia** whoever it is.

chi'uso, a ['kjuso] *pp di* **chiudere** // *sf* (*di corso d'acqua*) sluice, lock; (*recinto*) enclosure; (*di discorso etc*) conclusion, ending; **chiu'sura** *sf* closing; shutting; closing o shutting down; enclosing; putting o turning off; ending; (*dispositivo*) catch; fastening; fastener.

ci [tʃi] (*dav lo, la, li, le, ne diventa* **ce**) ◆ *pronome* **1** (*personale: complemento oggetto*) us; (: *a noi: complemento di termine*) (to) us; (: *riflessivo*) ourselves; (: *reciproco*) each other, one another; (*impersonale*): ~ **si veste** we get dressed; ~ **ha visti** he's seen us; **non** ~ **ha dato niente** he gave us nothing; ~ **vestiamo** we get dressed; ~ **amiamo** we love one another o each other

2 (*dimostrativo: di ciò, su ciò, in ciò etc*) about (o on o of) it; **non so cosa far**~ I don't know what to do about it; ~ **puoi contare** you can depend on it; **che c'entro io?** what have I got to do with it? ◆ *av* (*qui*) here; (*lì*) there; (*moto attraverso luogo*): ~ **passa sopra un ponte** a bridge passes over it; **non** ~ **passa più nessuno** nobody comes this way any more; **esser**~ *vedi* **essere.**

C.ia *abbr* (= *compagnia*) Co.

cia'batta [tʃa'batta] *sf* mule, slipper.

ci'alda ['tʃalda] *sf* (*CUC*) wafer.

ciam'bella [tʃam'bella] *sf* (*CUC*) ring-shaped cake; (*salvagente*) rubber ring.

ci'ao ['tʃao] *escl* (*all'arrivo*) hello!; (*alla partenza*) cheerio! (*Brit*), bye!

ciarla'tano [tʃarla'tano] *sm* charlatan.

cias'cuno, a [tʃas'kuno] (*dav sm*: **ciascun** +*C, V*, **ciascuno** +*s impura, gn, pn, ps, x, z*; *dav sf*: **ciascuna** +*C*, **ciascun'** +*V*) *det, pronome* each.

'cibo ['tʃibo] *sm* food.

ci'cala [tʃi'kala] *sf* cicada.

cica'trice [tʃika'tritʃe] *sf* scar.

'cicca ['tʃikka] *sf* cigarette end.

'ciccia ['tʃittʃa] *sf* (*fam: carne*) meat; (: *grasso umano*) fat, flesh.

cice'rone [tʃitʃe'rone] *sm* guide.

ci'clismo [tʃi'klizmo] *sm* cycling; **ci'clista, i, e** *sm/f* cyclist.

'ciclo ['tʃiklo] *sm* cycle; (*di malattia*) course.

ciclomo'tore [tʃiklomo'tore] *sm* moped.

ci'clone [tʃi'klone] *sm* cyclone.

ci'cogna [tʃi'koɲɲa] *sf* stork.

ci'coria [tʃi'kɔria] *sf* chicory.

ci'eco, a, chi, che ['tʃɛko] *ag* blind // *sm/f* blind man/woman.

ci'elo ['tʃɛlo] *sm* sky; (*REL*) heaven.

'cifra ['tʃifra] *sf* (*numero*) figure; numeral; (*somma di denaro*) sum, figure; (*monogramma*) monogram, initials *pl*;

(*codice*) code, cipher.

'ciglio ['tʃiʎʎo] *sm* (*margine*) edge, verge; (*pl(f)* **ciglia**: *delle palpebre*) (eye)lash; (eye)lid; (*sopracciglio*) eyebrow.

'cigno ['tʃippo] *sm* swan.

cigo'lare [tʃigo'lare] *vi* to squeak, creak.

'Cile ['tʃile] *sm*: il ~ Chile.

ci'lecca [tʃi'lekka] *sf*: far ~ to fail.

cili'egia, gie *o* **ge** [tʃi'ljedʒa] *sf* cherry; **cili'egio** *sm* cherry tree.

cilin'drata [tʃilin'drata] *sf* (*AUT*) (cubic) capacity; **una macchina di grossa** ~ a big-engined car.

ci'lindro [tʃi'lindro] *sm* cylinder; (*cappello*) top hat.

'cima ['tʃima] *sf* (*sommità*) top; (*di monte*) top, summit; (*estremità*) end; **in ~ a** at the top of; **da ~ a fondo** from top to bottom; (*fig*) from beginning to end.

'cimice ['tʃimitʃe] *sf* (*ZOOL*) bug; (*puntina*) drawing pin (*Brit*), thumbtack (*US*).

cimini'era [tʃimi'njera] *sf* chimney; (*di nave*) funnel.

cimi'tero [tʃimi'tɛro] *sm* cemetery.

ci'murro [tʃi'murro] *sm* (*di cani*) distemper.

'Cina ['tʃina] *sf*: la ~ China.

cin'cin, cin cin [tʃin'tʃin] *escl* cheers!

'cinema ['tʃinema] *sm inv* cinema; **cine'presa** *sf* cine-camera.

ci'nese [tʃi'nese] *ag, sm/f, sm* Chinese *inv*.

ci'netico, a, ci, che [tʃi'nɛtiko] *ag* kinetic.

'cingere ['tʃindʒere] *vt* (*attorniare*) to surround, encircle; ~ **la vita con una cintura** to put a belt round one's waist.

'cinghia ['tʃingja] *sf* strap; (*cintura, TECN*) belt.

cinghi'ale [tʃin'gjale] *sm* wild boar.

cinguet'tare [tʃingwet'tare] *vi* to twitter.

'cinico, a, ci, che ['tʃiniko] *ag* cynical // *sm/f* cynic; **ci'nismo** *sm* cynicism.

cin'quanta [tʃin'kwanta] *num* fifty; **cinquan'tesimo, a** *num* fiftieth.

cinquan'tina [tʃinkwan'tina] *sf* (*serie*): **una ~ (di)** about fifty; (*età*): **essere sulla ~** to be about fifty.

'cinque ['tʃinkwe] *num* five; **avere ~ anni** to be five (years old); **il ~ dicembre 1988** the fifth of December 1988; **~** (*ora*) at five (o'clock).

cinque'cento [tʃinkwe'tʃɛnto] *num* five hundred // *sm*: **il C~** the sixteenth century.

'cinto, a ['tʃinto] *pp di* **cingere**.

cin'tura [tʃin'tura] *sf* belt; ~ **di salvataggio** lifebelt (*Brit*), life preserver (*US*); ~ **di sicurezza** (*AUT, AER*) safety *o* seat belt.

ciò [tʃɔ] *pronome* this; that; ~ **che** what; ~ **nonostante** *o* **nondimeno** nevertheless, in spite of that.

ci'occa, che ['tʃɔkka] *sf* (*di capelli*) lock.

ciocco'lata [tʃokko'lata] *sf* chocolate; (*bevanda*) (hot) chocolate; **ciocco'latino** *sm* chocolate; **ciocco'lato** *sm* chocolate.

cioè [tʃo'ɛ] *av* that is (to say).

ciondo'lare [tʃondo'lare] *vi* to dangle; (*fig*) to loaf (about); **ci'ondolo** *sm* pendant.

ci'otola ['tʃɔtola] *sf* bowl.

ci'ottolo ['tʃɔttolo] *sm* pebble; (*di strada*) cobble(stone).

ci'polla [tʃi'polla] *sf* onion; (*di tulipano etc*) bulb.

ci'presso [tʃi'presso] *sm* cypress (tree).

'cipria ['tʃiprja] *sf* (face) powder.

'Cipro ['tʃipro] *sm* Cyprus.

'circa ['tʃirka] *av* about, roughly // *prep* about, concerning; **a mezzogiorno ~** about midday.

'circo, chi ['tʃirko] *sm* circus.

circo'lare [tʃirko'lare] *vi* to circulate; (*AUT*) to drive (along), move (along) // *ag* circular // *sf* (*AMM*) circular; (*di autobus*) circle (line); **circolazi'one** *sf* circulation; (*AUT*): **la circolazione** (the) traffic.

'circolo ['tʃirkolo] *sm* circle.

circon'dare [tʃirkon'dare] *vt* to surround.

circonfe'renza [tʃirkonfe'rentsa] *sf* circumference.

circonvallazi'one [tʃirkonvallat'tsjone] *sf* ring road (*Brit*), beltway (*US*); (*per evitare una città*) by-pass.

circos'critto, a [tʃirkos'kritto] *pp di* **circoscrivere**.

circos'crivere [tʃirkos'krivere] *vt* to circumscribe; (*fig*) to limit, restrict; **circoscrizi'one** *sf* (*AMM*) district, area; **circoscrizione elettorale** constituency.

circos'petto, a [tʃirkos'petto] *ag* circumspect, cautious.

circos'tante [tʃirkos'tante] *ag* surrounding, neighbouring.

circos'tanza [tʃirkos'tantsa] *sf* circumstance; (*occasione*) occasion.

cir'cuito [tʃir'kuito] *sm* circuit.

CISL *sigla f* (= *Confederazione Italiana Sindacati Lavoratori*) trades union organization.

'ciste ['tʃiste] *sf* = **cisti**.

cis'terna [tʃis'terna] *sf* tank, cistern.

'cisti ['tʃisti] *sf* cyst.

C.I.T. [tʃit] *sigla f* = *Compagnia Italiana Turismo*.

ci'tare [tʃi'tare] *vt* (*DIR*) to summon; (*autore*) to quote; (*a esempio, modello*) to cite; **citazi'one** *sf* summons *sg*; quotation; (*di persona*) mention.

ci'tofono [tʃi'tɔfono] *sm* entry phone; (*in uffici*) intercom.

città [tʃit'ta] *sf inv* town; (*importante*) city; ~ **universitaria** university campus.

cittadi'nanza [tʃittadi'nantsa] *sf* citizens

pl, inhabitants *pl* of a town (*o* city); (*DIR*) citizenship.

citta'dino, a [tʃitta'dino] *ag* town *cpd*; city *cpd // sm/f (di uno Stato)* citizen; (*abitante di città*) townsman, city dweller.

ci'uco, a, chi, che ['tʃuko] *sm/f* ass, donkey.

ci'uffo ['tʃuffo] *sm* tuft.

ci'vetta [tʃi'vetta] *sf* (*ZOOL*) owl; (*fig: donna*) coquette, flirt *// ag inv:* **auto/nave ~** decoy car/ship.

'civico, a, ci, che ['tʃiviko] *ag* civic; (*museo*) municipal, town *cpd*; municipal, city *cpd.*

ci'vile [tʃi'vile] *ag* civil; (*non militare*) civilian; (*nazione*) civilized *// sm* civilian.

civilizzazi'one [tʃiviliddzat'tsjone] *sf* civilization.

civiltà [tʃivil'ta] *sf* civilization; (*cortesia*) civility.

'clacson *sm inv* (*AUT*) horn.

cla'more *sm* (*frastuono*) din, uproar, clamour; (*fig*) outcry; **clamo'roso, a** *ag* noisy; (*fig*) sensational.

clandes'tino, a *ag* clandestine; (*POL*) underground, clandestine *// sm/f* stowaway.

clari'netto *sm* clarinet.

'classe *sf* class; **di ~** (*fig*) with class; of excellent quality.

'classico, a, ci, che *ag* classical; (*tradizionale: moda*) classic(al) *// sm* classic; classical author.

clas'sifica *sf* classification; (*SPORT*) placings *pl.*

classifi'care *vt* to classify; (*candidato, compito*) to grade; **~rsi** *vr* to be placed.

'clausola *sf* (*DIR*) clause.

'clava *sf* club.

clavi'cembalo [klavi'tʃembalo] *sm* harpsichord.

cla'vicola *sf* (*ANAT*) collar bone.

cle'mente *ag* merciful; (*clima*) mild; **cle'menza** *sf* mercy, clemency; mildness.

'clero *sm* clergy.

cli'ente *sm/f* customer, client; **clien'tela** *sf* customers *pl*, clientèle.

'clima, i *sm* climate; **cli'matico, a, ci, che** *ag* climatic; **stazione climatica** health resort; **climatizzazi'one** *sf* (*TECN*) air conditioning.

'clinico, a, ci, che *ag* clinical *// sm* (*medico*) clinician *// sf* (*scienza*) clinical medicine; (*casa di cura*) clinic, nursing home; (*settore d'ospedale*) clinic.

clo'aca, che *sf* sewer.

'cloro *sm* chlorine.

cloro'formio *sm* chloroform.

club *sm inv* club.

c.m. *abbr* = **corrente mese.**

coabi'tare *vi* to live together, live under the same roof.

coagu'lare *vt* to coagulate *// vi, ~rsi vr* to coagulate; (*latte*) to curdle.

coalizi'one [koalit'tsjone] *sf* coalition.

co'atto, a *ag* (*DIR*) compulsory, forced.

'COBAS *sigla mpl* (= *Comitati di base*) independent trades unions.

coca'ina *sf* cocaine.

cocci'nella [kottʃi'nɛlla] *sf* ladybird (*Brit*), ladybug (*US*).

'coccio ['kɔttʃo] *sm* earthenware; (*vaso*) earthenware pot; **~i** *smpl* fragments (of pottery).

cocci'uto, a [kot'tʃuto] *ag* stubborn, pigheaded.

'cocco, chi *sm* (*pianta*) coconut palm; (*frutto*): **noce di ~** coconut *// sm/f (fam)* darling.

cocco'drillo *sm* crocodile.

cocco'lare *vt* to cuddle, fondle.

co'cente [ko'tʃente] *ag* (*anche fig*) burning.

co'comero *sm* watermelon.

co'cuzzolo [ko'kuttsolo] *sm* top; (*di capo, cappello*) crown.

'coda *sf* tail; (*fila di persone, auto*) queue (*Brit*), line (*US*); (*di abiti*) train; **con la ~ dell'occhio** out of the corner of one's eye; **mettersi in ~** to queue (up) (*Brit*), line up (*US*); to join the queue (*Brit*) *o* line (*US*); **~ di cavallo** (*acconciatura*) ponytail.

co'dardo, a *ag* cowardly *// sm/f* coward.

'codice ['koditʃe] *sm* code; **~ di avviamento postale (C.A.P.)** postcode (*Brit*), zip code (*US*); **~ fiscale** tax code; **~ della strada** highway code.

coe'rente *ag* coherent; **coe'renza** *sf* coherence.

coe'taneo, a *ag, sm/f* contemporary.

'cofano *sm* (*AUT*) bonnet (*Brit*), hood (*US*); (*forziere*) chest.

'cogli ['koʎʎi] *prep + det vedi* **con.**

'cogliere ['kɔʎʎere] *vt* (*fiore, frutto*) to pick, gather; (*sorprendere*) to catch, surprise; (*bersaglio*) to hit; (*fig: momento opportuno etc*) to grasp, seize, take; (*: capire*) to grasp; **~ qn in flagrante** *o* **in fallo** to catch sb red-handed.

co'gnato, a [koɲ'ɲato] *sm/f* brother-/sister-in-law.

cognizi'one [koɲɲit'tsjone] *sf* knowledge.

co'gnome [koɲ'ɲome] *sm* surname.

'coi *prep + det vedi* **con.**

coinci'denza [kointʃi'dɛntsa] *sf* coincidence; (*FERR, AER, di autobus*) connection.

coin'cidere [koin'tʃidere] *vi* to coincide; **coin'ciso, a** *pp di* **coincidere.**

coin'volgere [koin'vɔldʒere] *vt:* **~ in** to involve in; **coin'volto, a** *pp di* **coinvolgere.**

col *prep + det vedi* **con.**

cola'brodo *sm inv* strainer.

cola'pasta *sm inv* colander.

co'lare vt (liquido) to strain; (pasta) to drain; (oro fuso) to pour // vi (sudore) to drip; (botte) to leak; (cera) to melt; ~ a picco vt, vi (nave) to sink.

co'lata sf (di lava) flow; (FONDERIA) casting.

colazi'one [kolat'tsjone] sf (anche: prima ~) breakfast; (anche: seconda ~) lunch; fare ~ to have breakfast (o lunch).

co'lei pronome vedi **colui**.

co'lera sm (MED) cholera.

'colica sf (MED) colic.

'colla prep + det vedi **con** // sf glue; (di farina) paste.

collabo'rare vi to collaborate; ~ a to collaborate on; (giornale) to contribute to; **collabora'tore, 'trice** sm/f collaborator; contributor.

col'lana sf necklace; (collezione) collection, series.

col'lant [kɔ'lɑ̃] sm inv tights pl.

col'lare sm collar.

col'lasso sm (MED) collapse.

collau'dare vt to test, try out; **col'laudo** sm testing q; test.

'colle sm hill.

col'lega, ghi, ghe sm/f colleague.

collega'mento sm connection; (MIL) liaison.

colle'gare vt to connect, join, link; ~rsi vr (RADIO, TV) to link up; ~rsi con (TEL) to get through to.

col'legio [kol'lɛdʒo] sm college; (convitto) boarding school; ~ elettorale (POL) constituency.

'collera sf anger.

col'lerico, a, ci, che ag quick-tempered, irascible.

col'letta sf collection.

collettività sf community.

collet'tivo, a ag collective; (interesse) general, everybody's; (biglietto, visita etc) group cpd // sm (POL) (political) group.

col'letto sm collar.

collezio'nare [kollettsjo'nare] vt to collect.

collezi'one [kollet'tsjone] sf collection.

colli'mare vi to correspond, coincide.

col'lina sf hill.

col'lirio sm eyewash.

collisi'one sf collision.

'collo sm neck; (di abito) neck, collar; (pacco) parcel; ~ del piede instep.

colloca'mento sm (impiego) employment; (disposizione) placing, arrangement.

collo'care vt (libri, mobili) to place; (persona: trovare un lavoro per) to find a job for, place; (COMM: merce) to find a market for.

col'loquio sm conversation, talk; (ufficiale, per un lavoro) interview; (INS) preliminary oral exam.

col'mare vt: ~ di (anche fig) to fill with; (dare in abbondanza) to load o overwhelm with; **'colmo, a** ag: colmo (di) full (of) // sm summit, top; (fig) height; al colmo della disperazione in the depths of despair; è il colmo! it's the last straw!

co'lombo, a sm/f dove; pigeon.

co'lonia sf colony; (per bambini) holiday camp; (acqua di) ~ (eau de) cologne; **coloni'ale** ag colonial // sm/f colonist, settler.

co'lonna sf column; ~ vertebrale spine, spinal column.

colon'nello sm colonel.

co'lono sm (coltivatore) tenant farmer.

colo'rante sm colouring.

colo'rare vt to colour; (disegno) to colour in.

co'lore sm colour; a ~i in colour, colour cpd; **farne di tutti i ~i** to get up to all sorts of mischief.

colo'rito, a ag coloured; (viso) rosy, pink; (linguaggio) colourful // sm (tinta) colour; (carnagione) complexion.

co'loro pronome pl vedi **colui**.

co'losso sm colossus.

'colpa sf fault; (biasimo) blame; (colpevolezza) guilt; (azione colpevole) offence; (peccato) sin; di chi è la ~? whose fault is it?; è ~ sua it's his fault; per ~ di through, owing to; **col'pevole** ag guilty.

col'pire vt to hit, strike; (fig) to strike; **rimanere colpito da qc** to be amazed o struck by sth.

'colpo sm (urto) knock; (: affettivo) blow, shock; (: aggressivo) blow; (di pistola) shot; (MED) stroke; (rapina) raid; di ~ suddenly; fare ~ to make a strong impression; ~ di grazia coup de grâce; ~ di sole sunstroke; ~ di Stato coup d'état; ~ di telefono phone call; ~ di testa (sudden) impulse o whim; ~ di vento gust of wind).

coltel'lata sf stab.

col'tello sm knife; ~ a serramanico clasp knife.

colti'vare vt to cultivate; (verdura) to grow, cultivate; **coltiva'tore** sm farmer; **coltivazi'one** sf cultivation; growing.

'colto, a pp di **cogliere** // ag (istruito) cultured, educated.

'coltre sf blanket.

col'tura sf cultivation.

co'lui, co'lei, pl **co'loro** pronome the one; ~ che parla the one o the man o the person who is speaking; **colei che amo** the one o the woman o the person (whom) I love.

'coma sm inv coma.

comanda'mento sm (REL) commandment.

coman'dante sm (MIL) commander,

commandant; (*di reggimento*) commanding officer; (NAUT, AER) captain.

coman'dare *vi* to be in command // *vt* to command; (*imporre*) to order, command; ~ a qn di fare to order sb to do; **co'mando** *sm* (*ingiunzione*) order, command; (*autorità*) command; (TECN) control.

co'mare *sf* (*madrina*) godmother.

combaci'are [komba'tʃare] *vi* to meet; (*fig: coincidere*) to coincide, correspond.

com'battere *vt* to fight; (*fig*) to combat, fight against // *vi* to fight; **combat-ti'mento** *sm* fight; fighting *q*; (*di pugilato*) match.

combi'nare *vt* to combine; (*organizzare*) to arrange; (*fam: fare*) to make, cause; **combinazi'one** *sf* combination; (*caso fortuito*) coincidence; per combinazione by chance.

combus'tibile *ag* combustible // *sm* fuel.

com'butta *sf* (*peg*): in ~ in league.

'come ♦ *av* 1 (*alla maniera di*) like; ti comporti ~ lui you behave like him *o* like he does; bianco ~ la neve (as) white as snow; ~ se as if, as though
2 (*in qualità di*) as a; lavora ~ autista he works as a driver
3 (*interrogativo*) how; ~ ti chiami? what's your name?; ~ sta? how are you?; com'è il tuo amico? what is your friend like?; ~? (*prego?*) pardon?, sorry?; ~ mai? how come?; ~ mai non ci hai avvertiti? why on earth didn't you warn us?
4 (*esclamativo*): ~ sei bravo! how clever you are!; ~ mi dispiace! I'm terribly sorry!
♦ *cong* 1 (*in che modo*) how; mi ha spiegato ~ l'ha conosciuto he told me how he met him
2 (*correlativo*) as; (*con comparativi di maggioranza*) than; non è bravo ~ pensavo he isn't as clever as I thought; è meglio di ~ pensassi it's better than I thought
3 (*appena che, quando*) as soon as; ~ arrivò, iniziò a lavorare as soon as he arrived, he set to work; *vedi* così, tanto.

'comico, a, ci, che *ag* (TEATRO) comic; (*buffo*) comical // *sm* (*attore*) comedian, comic actor; (*comicità*) comic spirit, comedy.

co'mignolo [ko'miɲɲolo] *sm* chimney top.

cominci'are [komin'tʃare] *vt, vi* to begin, start; ~ a fare/col fare to begin to do/by doing.

comi'tato *sm* committee.

comi'tiva *sf* party, group.

co'mizio [ko'mittsjo] *sm* (POL) meeting, assembly.

com'mando *sm inv* commando (squad).

commandant; (*di reggimento*)

com'media *sf* comedy; (*opera teatrale*) play; (*: che fa ridere*) comedy; (*fig*) playacting *q*; **commedi'ante** *sm/f* (*peg*) third-rate actor/actress; (*: fig*) sham.

commemo'rare *vt* to commemorate.

commenda'tore *sm* official title awarded for services to one's country.

commen'tare *vt* to comment on; (*testo*) to annotate; (RADIO, TV) to give a commentary on; **commenta'tore, 'trice** *sm/f* commentator; **com'mento** *sm* comment; (*a un testo*, RADIO, TV) commentary.

commerci'ale [kommer'tʃale] *ag* commercial, trading; (*peg*) commercial.

commerci'ante [kommer'tʃante] *sm/f* trader, dealer; (*negoziante*) shopkeeper.

commerci'are [kommer'tʃare] *vt, vi*: ~ in to deal *o* trade in.

com'mercio [kom'mertʃo] *sm* trade, commerce; essere in ~ (*prodotto*) to be on the market *o* on sale; essere nel ~ (*persona*) to be in business; ~ all'ingrosso/al minuto wholesale/retail trade.

com'messo, a *pp di* **commettere** // *sm/f* shop assistant (*Brit*), sales clerk (*US*) // *sm* (*impiegato*) clerk // *sf* (COMM) order; ~ viaggiatore commercial traveller.

commes'tibile *ag* edible; ~i *smpl* foodstuffs.

com'mettere *vt* to commit.

com'miato *sm* leave-taking.

commi'nare *vt* (DIR) to threaten; to inflict.

commissari'ato *sm* (AMM) commissionership; (*: sede*) commissioner's office; (*: di polizia*) police station.

commis'sario *sm* commissioner; (*di pubblica sicurezza*) ≈ (police) superintendent (*Brit*), (police) captain (*US*); (SPORT) steward; (*membro di commissione*) member of a committee *o* board.

commissio'nario *sm* (COMM) agent, broker.

commissi'one *sf* (*incarico*) errand; (*comitato, percentuale*) commission; (COMM: *ordinazione*) order; ~i *sfpl* (*acquisti*) shopping *sg*.

commit'tente *sm/f* (COMM) purchaser, customer.

com'mosso, a *pp di* **commuovere**.

commo'vente *ag* moving.

commozi'one [kommot'tsjone] *sf* emotion, deep feeling; ~ cerebrale (MED) concussion.

commu'overe *vt* to move, affect; ~rsi *vr* to be moved.

commu'tare *vt* (*pena*) to commute; (ELETTR) to change *o* switch over.

comò *sm inv* chest of drawers.

como'dino *sm* bedside table.

comodità *sf inv* comfort; convenience.

'comodo, a *ag* comfortable; *(facile)* easy; *(conveniente)* convenient; *(utile)* useful, handy // *sm* comfort; convenience; **con ~** at one's convenience *o* leisure; **fare il proprio ~** to do as one pleases; **far ~** to be useful *o* handy.

compae'sano, a *sm/f* fellow countryman; person from the same town.

com'pagine [kom'padʒine] *sf* *(squadra)* team.

compa'gnia [kompaɲ'nia] *sf* company; *(gruppo)* gathering.

com'pagno, a [kom'paɲɲo] *sm/f* *(di classe, gioco)* companion; *(POL)* comrade; **~ di lavoro** workmate.

compa'rare *vt* to compare.

compara'tivo, a *ag, sm* comparative.

compa'rire *vi* to appear; **com'parso, a** *pp di* **comparire** // *sf* appearance; *(TEATRO)* walk-on; *(CINEMA)* extra.

compartecipazi'one [kompartetʃipat'tsjone] *sf* sharing; *(quota)* share; **~ agli utili** profit-sharing.

comparti'mento *sm* compartment; *(AMM)* district.

compas'sato, a *ag* *(persona)* composed.

compassi'one *sf* compassion, pity; **avere ~ di qn** to feel sorry for sb, to pity sb.

com'passo *sm* (pair of) compasses *pl*; callipers *pl*.

compa'tibile *ag* *(scusabile)* excusable; *(conciliabile, INFORM)* compatible.

compa'tire *vt* *(aver compassione di)* to sympathize with, feel sorry for; *(scusare)* to make allowances for.

com'patto, a *ag* compact; *(roccia)* solid; *(folla)* dense; *(fig: gruppo, partito)* united, close-knit.

com'pendio *sm* summary; *(libro)* compendium.

compen'sare *vt* *(equilibrare)* to compensate for, make up for; **~ qn di** *(rimunerare)* to pay *o* remunerate sb for; *(risarcire)* to pay compensation to sb for; *(fig: fatiche, dolori)* to reward sb for; **com'penso** *sm* compensation; payment, remuneration; reward; **in compenso** *(d'altra parte)* on the other hand.

'compera *sf* *(acquisto)* purchase; **fare le ~e** to do the shopping.

compe'rare *vt* = **comprare**.

compe'tente *ag* competent; *(mancia)* apt, suitable; **compe'tenza** *sf* competence; **competenze** *sfpl* *(onorari)* fees.

com'petere *vi* to compete, vie; *(DIR: spettare)*: **~ a** to lie within the competence of; **competizi'one** *sf* competition.

compia'cente [kompja'tʃɛnte] *ag* courteous, obliging; **compia'cenza** *sf* courtesy.

compia'cere [kompja'tʃere] *vi*: **~ a** to gratify, please // *vt* to please; **~rsi** *vr* *(provare soddisfazione)*: **~rsi di** *o* **per qc** to be delighted at sth; *(rallegrarsi)*: **~rsi con qn** to congratulate sb; *(degnarsi)*: **~rsi di fare** to be so good as to do; **compiaci'uto, a** *pp di* **compiacere.**

compl'angere [kom'pjandʒere] *vt* to sympathize with, feel sorry for; **compi'anto, a** *pp di* **compiangere.**

'compiere *vt* *(concludere)* to finish, complete; *(adempiere)* to carry out, fulfil; **~rsi** *vr* *(avverarsi)* to be fulfilled, come true; **~ gli anni** to have one's birthday.

com'pire *vt* = **compiere.**

compi'tare *vt* to spell out.

'compito *sm* *(incarico)* task, duty; *(dovere)* duty; *(INS)* exercise; *(: a casa)* piece of homework; **fare i ~i** to do one's homework.

com'pito, a *ag* well-mannered, polite.

comple'anno *sm* birthday.

complemen'tare *ag* complementary; *(INS: materia)* subsidiary.

comple'mento *sm* complement; *(MIL)* reserve (troops); **~ oggetto** *(LING)* direct object.

complessità *sf* complexity.

comples'sivo, a *ag* *(globale)* comprehensive, overall; *(totale: cifra)* total.

com'plesso, a *ag* complex // *sm* *(PSIC, EDIL)* complex; *(MUS: corale)* ensemble; *(: orchestrina)* band; *(: di musica pop)* group; **in o nel ~** on the whole.

comple'tare *vt* to complete.

com'pleto, a *ag* complete; *(teatro, autobus)* full // *sm* suit; **al ~** full; *(tutti presenti)* all present.

compli'care *vt* to complicate; **~rsi** *vr* to become complicated; **complicazi'one** *sf* complication.

'complice ['kɔmplitʃe] *sm/f* accomplice.

complimen'tarsi *vr*: **~ con** to congratulate.

compli'mento *sm* compliment; **~i** *smpl* *(cortesia eccessiva)* ceremony *sg*; *(ossequi)* regards, compliments; **~i!** congratulations!; **senza ~i!** don't stand on ceremony!; **make yourself at home!**; **help yourself!**

com'plotto *sm* plot, conspiracy.

compo'nente *sm/f* member // *sm* component.

componi'mento *sm* *(DIR)* settlement; *(INS)* composition; *(poetico, teatrale)* work.

com'porre *vt* *(musica, testo)* to compose; *(mettere in ordine)* to arrange; *(DIR: lite)* to settle; *(TIP)* to set; *(TEL)* to dial.

comporta'mento *sm* behaviour.

compor'tare *vt* (*implicare*) to involve; (*consentire*) to permit, allow (of); **~rsi** *vr* (*condursi*) to behave.

composi'tore, 'trice *sm/f* composer; (*TIP*) compositor, typesetter.

composizi'one [kompozit'tsjone] *sf* composition; (*DIR*) settlement.

com'posta *sf vedi* composto.

compos'tezza [kompos'tettsa] *sf* composure; decorum.

com'posto, a *pp di* comporre // *ag* (*persona*) composed, self-possessed; (: *decoroso*) dignified; (*formato da più elementi*) compound *cpd* // *sm* compound // *sf* (*CUC*) stewed fruit *q*; (*AGR*) compost.

'compra *sf* = compera.

com'prare *vt* to buy; **compra'tore, 'trice** *sm/f* buyer, purchaser.

com'prendere *vt* (*contenere*) to comprise, consist of; (*capire*) to understand.

comprensi'one *sf* understanding.

compren'sivo, a *ag* (*prezzo*): **~ di** inclusive of; (*indulgente*) understanding.

com'preso, a *pp di* comprendere // *ag* (*incluso*) included.

com'pressa *sf vedi* compresso.

compressi'one *sf* compression.

com'presso, a *pp di* comprimere // *ag* (*vedi comprimere*) pressed; compressed; repressed // *sf* (*MED: garza*) compress; (: *pastiglia*) tablet.

com'primere *vt* (*premere*) to press; (*FISICA*) to compress; (*fig*) to repress.

compro'messo, a *pp di* compromettere // *sm* compromise.

compro'mettere *vt* to compromise.

compro'vare *vt* to confirm.

com'punto, a *ag* contrite.

compu'tare *vt* to calculate; (*addebitare*): **~ qc a qn** to debit sb with sth.

com'puter *sm inv* computer.

computiste'ria *sf* accounting, book-keeping.

'computo *sm* calculation.

comu'nale *ag* municipal, town *cpd*, ≈ borough *cpd*.

co'mune *ag* common; (*consueto*) common, everyday; (*di livello medio*) average; (*ordinario*) ordinary // *sm* (*AMM*) town council; (: *sede*) town hall // *sf* (*di persone*) commune; **fuori del** ~ out of the ordinary; **avere in** ~ to have in common, share; **mettere in** ~ to share.

comuni'care *vt* (*notizia*) to pass on, convey; (*malattia*) to pass on; (*ansia etc*) to communicate; (*trasmettere: calore etc*) to transmit, communicate; (*REL*) to administer communion to // *vi* to communicate; **~rsi** *vr* (*propagarsi*): **~rsi a** to spread to; (*REL*) to receive

communion.

comuni'cato *sm* communiqué; **~ stampa** press release.

comunicazi'one [komunikat'tsjone] *sf* communication; (*annuncio*) announcement; (*TEL*): **~ (telefonica)** (telephone) call; **dare la ~ a qn** to put sb through; **ottenere la ~** to get through.

comuni'one *sf* communion; **~ di beni** (*DIR*) joint ownership of property.

comu'nismo *sm* communism; **comu'nista, i, e** *ag, sm/f* communist.

comunità *sf inv* community; **C~ Economica Europea (C.E.E.)** European Economic Community (EEC).

co'munque *cong* however, no matter how // *av* (*in ogni modo*) in any case; (*tuttavia*) however, nevertheless.

con *prep* (*nei seguenti casi con può fondersi con l'articolo definito: con + il* = **col**, *con + gli* = **cogli**, *con + i* = **coi**) with; **partire col treno** to leave by train; **~ mio grande stupore** to my great astonishment; **~ tutto ciò** for all that.

co'nato *sm*: **~ di vomito** retching.

'conca *sf* (*GEO*) valley.

con'cedere [kon't∫edere] *vt* (*accordare*) to grant; (*ammettere*) to admit, concede; **~rsi qc** to treat o.s. to sth, to allow o.s. sth.

concentra'mento [kont∫entra'mento] *sm* concentration.

concen'trare [kont∫en'trare] *vt*, **~rsi** *vr* to concentrate; **concentrazi'one** *sf* concentration.

conce'pire [kont∫e'pire] *vt* (*bambino*) to conceive; (*progetto, idea*) to conceive (of); (*metodo, piano*) to devise.

con'cernere [kon't∫ernere] *vt* to concern.

concer'tare [kont∫er'tare] *vt* (*MUS*) to harmonize; (*ordire*) to devise, plan; **~rsi** *vr* to agree.

con'certo [kon't∫erto] *sm* (*MUS*) concert; (: *componimento*) concerto.

concessio'nario [kont∫essjo'narjo] *sm* (*COMM*) agent, dealer.

con'cesso, a [kon't∫ɛsso] *pp di* concedere.

con'cetto [kon't∫etto] *sm* (*pensiero, idea*) concept; (*opinione*) opinion.

concezi'one [kont∫et'tsjone] *sf* conception.

con'chiglia [kon'kiʎʎa] *sf* shell.

'concia ['kɔnt∫a] *sf* (*di pelle*) tanning; (*di tabacco*) curing; (*sostanza*) tannin.

conci'are [kon't∫are] *vt* (*pelli*) to tan; (*tabacco*) to cure; (*fig: ridurre in cattivo stato*) to beat up; **~rsi** *vr* (*sporcarsi*) to get in a mess; (*vestirsi male*) to dress badly.

concili'are [kont∫i'ljare] *vt* to reconcile; (*contravvenzione*) to pay on the spot; (*favorire: sonno*) to be conducive to, induce; (*procurare: simpatia*) to gain; **~rsi qc** to gain *o* win sth (for o.s.); **~rsi**

qn to win sb over; ~**rsi con** to be reconciled with; **conciliazi'one** *sf* reconciliation; (*DIR*) settlement.

con'cilio [kon'tʃiljo] *sm* (*REL*) council.

con'cime [kon'tʃime] *sm* manure; (*chimico*) fertilizer.

con'ciso, a [kon'tʃizo] *ag* concise, succinct.

conci'tato, a [kontʃi'tato] *ag* excited, emotional.

concitta'dino, a [kontʃitta'dino] *sm/f* fellow citizen.

con'cludere *vt* to conclude; (*portare a compimento*) to conclude, finish, bring to an end; (*operare positivamente*) to achieve // vi (*essere convincente*) to be conclusive; ~**rsi** *vr* to come to an end, close; **conclusi'one** *sf* conclusion; (*risultato*) result; **conclu'sivo, a** *ag* conclusive; (*finale*) final; **con'cluso, a** *pp di* **concludere**.

concor'danza [konkor'dantsa] *sf* (*anche LING*) agreement.

concor'dare *vt* (*tregua, prezzo*) to agree on; (*LING*) to make agree // vt to agree; **concor'dato** *sm* agreement; (*REL*) concordat.

con'corde *ag* (*d'accordo*) in agreement; (*simultaneo*) simultaneous.

concor'rente *sm/f* competitor; (*INS*) candidate; **concor'renza** *sf* competition.

con'correre *vi*: ~ **(in)** (*MAT*) to converge *o* meet (in); ~ **(a)** (*competere*) to compete (for); (: *INS*: *a una cattedra*) to apply (for); (*partecipare: a un'impresa*) to take part (in), contribute (to); **con'corso, a** *pp di* **concorrere** // *sm* competition; (*INS*) competitive examination; **concorso di colpa** (*DIR*) contributory negligence.

con'creto, a *ag* concrete.

concussi'one *sf* (*DIR*) extortion.

con'danna *sf* sentence; conviction; condemnation.

condan'nare *vt* (*DIR*): ~ **a** to sentence to; ~ **per** to convict of; (*disapprovare*) to condemn; **condan'nato, a** *sm/f* convict.

conden'sare *vt*, ~**rsi** *vr* to condense; **condensazi'one** *sf* condensation.

condi'mento *sm* seasoning; dressing.

con'dire *vt* to season; (*insalata*) to dress.

condi'videre *vt* to share; **condi'viso, a** *pp di* **condividere**.

condizio'nale [kondittsjo'nale] *ag* conditional // *sm* (*LING*) conditional // *sf* (*DIR*) suspended sentence.

condizio'nare [kondittsjo'nare] *vt* to condition; **ad aria condizionata** airconditioned.

condizi'one [kondit'tsjone] *sf* condition; ~**i** *sfpl* (*di pagamento etc*) terms, conditions; **a ~ che** on condition that, provided that.

condogli'anze [kondoʎ'ʎantse] *sfpl* condolences.

condo'minio *sm* joint ownership; (*edificio*) jointly-owned building.

condo'nare *vt* (*DIR*) to remit; **con'dono** *sm* remission; **condono fiscale** *conditional amnesty for people evading tax.*

con'dotta *sf vedi* **condotto**.

con'dotto, a *pp di* **condurre** // *ag*: **medico ~** local authority doctor (*in country district*) // *sm* (*canale, tubo*) pipe, conduit; (*ANAT*) duct // *sf* (*modo di comportarsi*) conduct, behaviour; (*di un affare etc*) handling; (*di acqua*) piping; (*incarico sanitario*) country medical practice controlled by a local authority.

condu'cente [kondu'tʃente] *sm* driver.

con'durre *vt* to conduct; (*azienda*) to manage; (*accompagnare: bambino*) to take; (*automobile*) to drive; (*trasportare: acqua, gas*) to convey, conduct; (*fig*) to lead // vi to lead; **condursi** *vr* to behave, conduct o.s.

condut'tore *ag*: **filo ~** (*fig*) thread // *sm* (*di mezzi pubblici*) driver; (*FISICA*) conductor.

con'farsi *vr*: ~ **a** to suit, agree with.

confederazi'one [konfederat'tsjone] *sf* confederation.

confe'renza [konfe'rɛntsa] *sf* (*discorso*) lecture; (*riunione*) conference; ~ **stampa** press conference; **conferenzi'ere, a** *sm/f* lecturer.

confe'rire *vt*: ~ **qc a qn** to give sth to sb, bestow sth on sb // vi to confer.

confer'mare *sf* confirmation.

confer'mare *vt* to confirm.

confes'sare *vt*, ~**rsi** *vr* to confess; **andare a ~rsi** (*REL*) to go to confession; **confessio'nale** *ag*, *sm* confessional; **confessi'one** *sf* confession; (*setta religiosa*) denomination; **confes'sore** *sm* confessor.

con'fetto *sm* sugared almond; (*MED*) pill.

confezio'nare [konfettsjo'nare] *vt* (*vestito*) to make (up); (*merci, pacchi*) to package.

confezi'one [konfet'tsjone] *sf* (*di abiti: da uomo*) tailoring; (: *da donna*) dressmaking; (*imballaggio*) packaging; ~**i** *sfpl* garments, clothes; ~ **regalo** gift pack.

confic'care *vt*: ~ **qc in** to hammer *o* drive sth into; ~**rsi** *vr* to stick.

confi'dare *vi*: ~ **in** to confide in, rely on // vt to confide; ~**rsi con qn** to confide in sb; **confi'dente** *sm/f* (*persona amica*) confidant/confidante; (*informatore*) informer; **confi'denza** *sf* (*familiarità*) intimacy, familiarity; (*fiducia*) trust, confidence; (*rivelazione*) confidence; **confidenzi'ale** *ag* familiar, friendly; (*segreto*) confidential.

configu'rarsi *vr*: ~ a to assume the shape *o* form of.

confi'nare *vi*: ~ con to border on // *vt* (*POL*) to intern; (*fig*) to confine; ~rsi *vr* (*isolarsi*): ~rsi in to shut o.s. up in.

Confin'dustria *sigla f* (= *Confederazione Generale dell'Industria Italiana*) *employers' association*, ≈ CBI (*Brit*).

con'fine *sm* boundary; (*di paese*) border, frontier.

con'fino *sm* internment.

confis'care *vt* to confiscate.

con'flitto *sm* conflict.

conflu'enza [konflu'ɛntsa] *sf* (*di fiumi*) confluence; (*di strade*) junction.

conflu'ire *vi* (*fiumi*) to flow into each other, meet; (*strade*) to meet.

con'fondere *vt* to mix up, confuse; (*imbarazzare*) to embarrass; ~rsi *vr* (*mescolarsi*) to mingle; (*turbarsi*) to be confused; (*sbagliare*) to get mixed up; ~ le idee a qn to mix sb up, confuse sb.

confor'mare *vt* (*adeguare*): ~ a to adapt *o* conform to; ~rsi *vr*: ~rsi (a) to conform (to).

conforme'mente *av* accordingly; ~ a in accordance with.

confor'tare *vt* to comfort, console; **confor'tevole** *ag* (*consolante*) comforting; (*comodo*) comfortable; **con'forto** *sm* comfort, consolation; comfort.

confron'tare *vt* to compare.

con'fronto *sm* comparison; in *o* a ~ di in comparison with, compared to; nei miei (*o tuoi etc*) ~i towards me (*o you etc*).

confusi'one *sf* confusion; (*chiasso*) racket, noise; (*imbarazzo*) embarrassment.

con'fuso, a *pp di* **confondere** // *ag* (*vedi confondere*) confused; embarrassed.

confu'tare *vt* to refute.

conge'dare [kondʒe'dare] *vt* to dismiss; (*MIL*) to demobilize; ~rsi *vr* to take one's leave; **con'gedo** *sm* (*anche MIL*) leave; prendere congedo da qn to take one's leave of sb; congedo assoluto (*MIL*) discharge.

conge'gnare [kondʒeɲ'ɲare] *vt* to construct, put together; **con'gegno** *sm* device, mechanism.

conge'lare [kondʒe'lare] *vt*, ~rsi *vr* to freeze; **congela'tore** *sm* freezer.

congestio'nare [kondʒestjo'nare] *vt* to congest.

congesti'one [kondʒes'tjone] *sf* congestion.

conget'tura [kondʒet'tura] *sf* conjecture, supposition.

con'giungere [kon'dʒundʒere] *vt*, ~rsi *vr* to join (together).

congiunti'vite [kondʒunti'vite] *sf* conjunctivitis.

congiun'tivo [kondʒun'tivo] *sm* (*LING*)

subjunctive.

congi'unto, a [kon'dʒunto] *pp di* **congiungere** // *ag* (*unito*) joined // *sm/f* relative.

congiun'tura [kondʒun'tura] *sf* (*giuntura*) junction, join; (*ANAT*) joint; (*circostanza*) juncture; (*ECON*) economic situation.

congiunzi'one [kondʒun'tsjone] *sf* (*LING*) conjunction.

congi'ura [kon'dʒura] *sf* conspiracy; **congiu'rare** *vi* to conspire.

conglome'rato *sm* (*GEO*) conglomerate; (*fig*) conglomeration; (*EDIL*) concrete.

congratu'larsi *vr*: ~ con qn per qc to congratulate sb on sth.

congratulazi'oni [kongratulat'tsjoni] *sfpl* congratulations.

congrega, ghe *sf* band, bunch.

con'gresso *sm* congress.

congu'aglio [kon'gwaʎʎo] *sm* balancing, adjusting; (*somma di denaro*) balance.

coni'are *vt* to mint, coin; (*fig*) to coin.

co'niglio [ko'niʎʎo] *sm* rabbit.

coniu'gare *vt* (*LING*) to conjugate; ~rsi *vr* to get married; **coniu'gato, a** *ag* (*sposato*) married; **coniugazi'one** *sf* (*LING*) conjugation.

'coniuge ['kɔnjudʒe] *sm/f* spouse.

connazio'nale [konnattsjo'nale] *sm/f* fellow-countryman/woman.

connessi'one *sf* connection.

con'nesso, a *pp di* **connettere**.

con'nettere *vt* to connect, join // *vi* (*fig*) to think straight.

conni'vente *ag* conniving.

conno'tati *smpl* distinguishing marks.

'cono *sm* cone; ~ gelato ice-cream cone.

cono'scente [konoʃ'ʃente] *sm/f* acquaintance.

cono'scenza [konoʃ'ʃentsa] *sf* (*il sapere*) knowledge *q*; (*persona*) acquaintance; (*facoltà sensoriale*) consciousness *q*; perdere ~ to lose consciousness.

co'noscere [ko'noʃʃere] *vt* to know; ci siamo conosciuti a Firenze we (first) met in Florence; **conosci'tore, 'trice** *sm/f* connoisseur; **conosci'uto, a** *pp di* **conoscere** // *ag* well-known.

con'quista *sf* conquest.

conquis'tare *vt* to conquer; (*fig*) to gain, win.

consa'crare *vt* (*REL*) to consecrate; (*: sacerdote*) to ordain; (*dedicare*) to dedicate; (*fig: uso etc*) to sanction; ~rsi a to dedicate o.s. to.

consangu'ineo, a *sm/f* blood relation.

consa'pevole *ag*: ~ di aware *o* conscious of; **consapevo'lezza** *sf* awareness, consciousness.

'conscio, a, sci, sce ['kɔnʃo] *ag*: ~ di aware *o* conscious of.

consecu'tivo, a *ag* consecutive;

(*successivo: giorno*) following, next.
con'segna [kon'seɲɲa] *sf* delivery; (*merce consegnata*) consignment; (*custodia*) care, custody; (*MIL: ordine*) orders *pl*; (*: punizione*) confinement to barracks; **pagamento alla ~** cash on delivery; **dare qc in ~ a qn** to entrust sth to sb.

conse'gnare [konse'ɲɲare] *vt* to deliver; (*affidare*) to entrust, hand over; (*MIL*) to confine to barracks.

consegu'enza [konse'gwɛntsa] *sf* consequence; **per o di ~** consequently.

consegu'ire *vt* to achieve // *vi* to follow, result.

con'senso *sm* approval, consent.

consen'tire *vi*: **~ a** to consent o agree to // *vt* to allow, permit.

con'serva *sf* (*CUC*) preserve; **~ di frutta** jam; **~ di pomodoro** tomato purée.

conser'vare *vt* (*CUC*) to preserve; (*custodire*) to keep; (*: dalla distruzione etc*) to preserve, conserve; **~rsi** *vr* to keep.

conserva'tore, 'trice *sm/f* (*POL*) conservative.

conservazi'one [konservat'tsjone] *sf* preservation; conservation.

conside'rare *vt* to consider; (*reputare*) to consider, regard; **~ molto qn** to think highly of sb; **considerazi'one** *sf* consideration; (*stima*) regard, esteem; **prendere in considerazione** to take into consideration; **conside'revole** *ag* considerable.

consigli'are [konsiʎ'ʎare] *vt* (*persona*) to advise; (*metodo, azione*) to recommend, advise, suggest; **~rsi** *vr*: **~rsi con qn** to ask sb for advice; **consigli'ere, a** *sm/f* adviser // *sm*: **consigliere d'amministrazione** board member; **consigliere comunale** town councillor; **con'siglio** *sm* (*suggerimento*) advice *q*, piece of advice; (*assemblea*) council; **consiglio d'amministrazione** board; **il Consiglio dei Ministri** (*POL*) ≈ the Cabinet.

consis'tente *ag* thick; solid; (*fig*) sound, valid; **consis'tenza** *sf* consistency, thickness; solidity; validity.

con'sistere *vi*: **~ in** to consist of; **consis'tito, a** *pp di* **consistere**.

conso'lare *ag* consular // *vt* (*confortare*) to console, comfort; (*rallegrare*) to cheer up; **~rsi** *vr* to be comforted; to cheer up.

conso'lato *sm* consulate.

consolazi'one [konsolat'tsjone] *sf* consolation, comfort.

'console *sm* consul // [kon'sɔl] *sf* (*quadro di comando*) console.

conso'nante *sf* consonant.

'consono, a *ag*: **~ a** consistent with, consonant with.

con'sorte *sm/f* consort.

con'sorzio [kon'sɔrtsjo] *sm* consortium.

con'stare *vi*: **~ di** to consist of // *vb impers*: **mi consta che** it has come to my knowledge that, it appears that.

consta'tare *vt* to establish, verify; **constatazi'one** *sf* observation; **constatazione amichevole** *jointly-agreed statement for insurance purposes*.

consu'eto, a *ag* habitual, usual; **consue'tudine** *sf* habit, custom; (*usanza*) custom.

consu'lente *sm/f* consultant; **consu'lenza** *sf* consultancy.

consul'tare *vt* to consult; **~rsi** *vr*: **~rsi con qn** to seek the advice of sb; **consultazi'one** *sf* consultation; **consultazioni** *sfpl* (*POL*) talks, consultations.

consu'mare *vt* (*logorare: abiti, scarpe*) to wear out; (*usare*) to consume, use up; (*mangiare, bere*) to consume; (*DIR*) to consummate; **~rsi** *vr* to wear out; to be used up; (*anche fig*) to be consumed; (*combustibile*) to burn out; **consuma'tore** *sm* consumer; **consumazi'one** *sf* (*bibita*) drink; (*spuntino*) snack; (*DIR*) consummation; wear; use; **con'sumo** *sm* consumption.

consun'tivo *sm* (*ECON*) final balance.

con'tabile *ag* accounts *cpd*, accounting // *sm/f* accountant; **contabilità** *sf* (*attività, tecnica*) accounting, accountancy; (*insieme dei libri etc*) books *pl*, accounts *pl*; (*ufficio*) accounts department.

conta'dino, a *sm/f* countryman/woman; farm worker; (*peg*) peasant.

contagi'are [konta'dʒare] *vt* to infect.

con'tagio [kon'tadʒo] *sm* infection; (*per contatto diretto*) contagion; (*epidemia*) epidemic; **contagi'oso, a** *ag* infectious; contagious.

conta'gocce [konta'gottʃe] *sm inv* (*MED*) dropper.

contami'nare *vt* to contaminate.

con'tante *sm* cash; **pagare in ~i** to pay cash.

con'tare *vt* to count; (*considerare*) to consider // *vi* to count, be of importance; **~ su qn** to count o rely on sb; **~ di fare qc** to intend to do sth; **conta'tore** *sm* meter.

contat'tare *vt* to contact.

con'tatto *sm* contact.

'conte *sm* count.

conteggi'are [konted'dʒare] *vt* to charge, put on the bill; **con'teggio** *sm* calculation.

con'tegno [kon'teɲɲo] *sm* (*comportamento*) behaviour; (*atteggiamento*) attitude; **darsi un ~** to act nonchalant; to pull o.s. together.

contem'plare *vt* to contemplate, gaze at; (*DIR*) to make provision for.

contemporanea'mente *av* simultaneously; at the same time.

contempo'raneo, a *ag, sm/f* contemporary.

conten'dente *sm/f* opponent, adversary.

con'tendere *vi* (*competere*) to compete; (*litigare*) to quarrel // *vt:* ~ qc a qn to contend with o be in competition with sb for sth.

conte'nere *vt* to contain; **conteni'tore** *sm* container.

conten'tare *vt* to please, satisfy; ~rsi di to be satisfied with, content o.s. with.

conten'tezza [konten'tettsa] *sf* contentment.

con'tento, a *ag* pleased, glad; ~ di pleased with.

conte'nuto *sm* contents *pl*; (*argomento*) content.

con'teso, a *pp di* **contendere** // *sf* dispute, argument.

con'tessa *sf* countess.

contes'tare *vt* (DIR) to notify; (*fig*) to dispute; **contestazi'one** *sf* (DIR) notification; dispute; (*protesta*) protest.

con'testo *sm* context.

con'tiguo, a *ag:* ~ (a) adjacent (to).

continen'tale *ag, sm/f* continental.

conti'nente *ag* continent // *sm* (GEO) continent; (: *terra ferma*) mainland; **conti'nenza** *sf* continence.

contin'gente [kontin'dʒɛnte] *ag* contingent // *sm* (COMM) quota; (MIL) contingent; **contin'genza** *sf* circumstance; (ECON): (**indennità di**) **contingenza** cost-of-living allowance.

continu'are *vt* to continue (with), go on with // *vi* to continue, go on; ~ a fare qc to go on o continue doing sth; **continuazi'one** *sf* continuation.

con'tinuo, a *ag* (*numerazione*) continuous; (*pioggia*) continual, constant; (ELETTR): **corrente** ~a direct current; **di** ~ continually.

'conto *sm* (*calcolo*) calculation; (COMM, ECON) account; (*di ristorante, albergo*) bill; (*fig: stima*) consideration, esteem; **fare i** ~i con qn to settle one's account with sb; **fare** ~ **su** qn/qc to count o rely on sb; **rendere** ~ a qn di qc to be accountable to sb for sth; **tener** ~ di qn/qc to take sb/sth into account; **per** ~ di on behalf of; **per** ~ **mio** as far as I'm concerned; **a** ~i **fatti, in fin dei** ~i all things considered; ~ **corrente** current account; ~ **alla rovescia** countdown.

con'torcere [kon'tortʃere] *vt* to twist; (*panni*) to wring (out); ~rsi *vr* to twist, writhe.

contor'nare *vt* to surround.

con'torno *sm* (*linea*) outline, contour; (*ornamento*) border; (CUC) vegetables *pl*.

con'torto, a *pp di* **contorcere**.

contrabbandi'ere, a *sm/f* smuggler.

contrab'bando *sm* smuggling, contraband; **merce di** ~ contraband, smuggled

goods *pl*.

contrab'basso *sm* (MUS) (double) bass.

contraccambi'are *vt* (*favore etc*) to return.

contraccet'tivo, a [kontratt∫et'tivo] *ag, sm* contraceptive.

contrac'colpo *sm* rebound; (*di arma da fuoco*) recoil; (*fig*) repercussion.

con'trada *sf* street; district.

contrad'detto, a *pp di* **contraddire**.

contrad'dire *vt* to contradict; **contraddit'torio, a** *ag* contradictory; (*sentimenti*) conflicting // *sm* (DIR) cross-examination; **contraddizi'one** *sf* contradiction.

contraf'fare *vt* (*persona*) to mimic; (*alterare: voce*) to disguise; (*firma*) to forge, counterfeit; **contraf'fatto, a** *pp di* **contraffare** // *ag* counterfeit; **contraffazi'one** *sf* mimicking q; disguising q; forging q; (*cosa contraffatta*) forgery.

contrap'peso *sm* counterbalance, counterweight.

contrap'porre *vt:* ~ qc a qc to counter sth with sth; (*paragonare*) to compare sth with sth; **contrap'posto, a** *pp di* **contrapporre**.

contraria'mente *av:* ~ a contrary to.

contrari'are *vt* (*contrastare*) to thwart, oppose; (*irritare*) to annoy, bother; ~rsi *vr* to get annoyed.

contrarietà *sf* adversity; (*fig*) aversion.

con'trario, a *ag* opposite; (*sfavorevole*) unfavourable // *sm* opposite; **essere** ~ a qc (*persona*) to be against sth; **in caso** ~ otherwise; **avere** qc **in** ~ to have some objection; **al** ~ on the contrary.

con'trarre *vt*, **contrarsi** *vr* to contract.

contrasse'gnare [kontrasseɲ'ɲare] *vt* to mark; **contras'segno** *sm* (*distintivo*) distinguishing mark; **spedire in contrassegno** to send C.O.D.

contras'tare *vt* (*avversare*) to oppose; (*impedire*) to bar; (*negare: diritto*) to contest, dispute // *vi:* ~ (**con**) (*essere in disaccordo*) to contrast (with); (*lottare*) to struggle (with); **con'trasto** *sm* contrast; (*conflitto*) conflict; (*litigio*) dispute.

contrat'tacco *sm* counterattack.

contrat'tare *vt*, *vi* to negotiate.

contrat'tempo *sm* hitch.

con'tratto, a *pp di* **contrarre** // *sm* contract; **contrattu'ale** *ag* contractual.

contravvenzi'one [kontravven'tsjone] *sf* contravention; (*ammenda*) fine.

contrazi'one [kontrat'tsjone] *sf* contraction; (*di prezzi etc*) reduction.

contribu'ente *sm/f* taxpayer; ratepayer (Brit), property tax payer (US).

contribu'ire *vi* to contribute; **con-tri'buto** *sm* contribution; (*tassa*) tax.

'contro *prep* against; ~ **di me/lui** against me/him; **pastiglie** ~ **la tosse** throat lozenges; ~ **pagamento** (COMM) on payment // prefisso: **contro'battere** vt (fig: a parole) to answer back; (: confutare) to refute; **controfi'gura** sf (CINEMA) double; **controfir'mare** vt to counter-sign.

control'lare vt (accertare) to check; (sorvegliare) to watch, control; (tenere nel proprio potere, fig: dominare) to control; **con'trollo** sm check; watch; control; **controllo delle nascite** birth control; **control'lore** sm (FERR, AUTOBUS) (ticket) inspector.

controprodu'cente [kontroprodu'tʃɛnte] ag counterproductive.

contro'senso sm (contraddizione) contradiction in terms; (assurdità) nonsense.

controspio'naggio [kontrospio'naddʒo] sm counterespionage.

contro'versia sf controversy; (DIR) dispute.

contro'verso, a ag controversial.

contro'voglia [kontro'vɔʎʎa] av unwillingly.

contu'macia [kontu'matʃa] sf (DIR) default.

contur'bare vt to disturb, upset.

contusi'one sf (MED) bruise.

convale'scente [konvaleʃ'ʃɛnte] ag, sm/f convalescent; **convale'scenza** sf convalescence.

convali'dare vt (AMM) to validate; (fig: sospetto, dubbio) to confirm.

con'vegno [kon'veɲɲo] sm (incontro) meeting; (congresso) convention, congress; (luogo) meeting place.

conve'nevoli smpl civilities.

conveni'ente ag suitable; (vantaggioso) profitable; (: prezzo) cheap; **conveni'enza** sf suitability; advantage; cheapness; **le convenienze** sfpl social conventions.

conve'nire vi (riunirsi) to gather, assemble; (concordare) to agree; (tornare utile) to be worthwhile // vb impers: conviene fare questo it is advisable to do this; conviene andarsene we should go; ne convengo I agree.

con'vento sm (di frati) monastery; (di suore) convent.

convenzio'nale [konventsjo'nale] ag conventional.

convenzi'one [konven'tsjone] sf (DIR) agreement; (nella società) convention; **le ~i** sfpl social conventions.

conver'sare vi to have a conversation, converse.

conversazi'one [konversat'tsjone] sf conversation; **fare ~** to chat, have a chat.

conversi'one sf conversion; **~ ad U** (AUT) U-turn.

conver'tire vt (trasformare) to change; (POL, REL) to convert; **~rsi** vr: **~rsi (a)** to be converted (to); **conver'tito, a** sm/f convert.

con'vesso, a ag convex.

con'vincere [kon'vintʃere] vt to convince; **~ qn di qc** to convince sb of sth; **~ qn a fare qc** to persuade sb to do sth; **con'vinto, a** pp di **convincere; convinzi'one** sf conviction, firm belief.

convis'suto, a pp di **convivere.**

con'vitto sm (INS) boarding school.

con'vivere vi to live together.

convo'care vt to call, convene; (DIR) to summon; **convocazi'one** sf meeting; summons sg.

convogli'are [konvoʎ'ʎare] vt to convey; (dirigere) to direct, send; **con'voglio** sm (di veicoli) convoy; (FERR) train.

con'vulso, a ag (pianto) violent, convulsive; (attività) feverish.

coope'rare vi: **~ (a)** to cooperate (in); **coopera'tiva** sf cooperative; **coopera-zi'one** sf cooperation.

coordi'nare vt to coordinate; **coor-di'nate** sfpl (MAT, GEO) coordinates; **coordi'nati** smpl (MODA) coordinates.

co'perchio [ko'perkjo] sm cover; (di pentola) lid.

co'perta sf cover; (di lana) blanket; (da viaggio) rug; (NAUT) deck.

coper'tina sf (STAMPA) cover, jacket.

co'perto, a pp di **coprire** // ag covered; (cielo) overcast // sm place setting; (posto a tavola) place; (al ristorante) cover charge; **~ di** covered in o with.

coper'tone sm (telo impermeabile) tarpaulin; (AUT) rubber tyre.

coper'tura sf (anche ECON, MIL) cover; (di edificio) roofing

'copia sf copy; **brutta/bella ~** rough/final copy.

copi'are vt to copy; **copia'trice** sf copier, copying machine.

copi'one sm (CINEMA, TEATRO) script.

'coppa sf (bicchiere) goblet; (per frutta, gelato) dish; (trofeo) cup, trophy; **~ dell'olio** oil sump (Brit) o pan (US).

'coppia sf (di persone) couple; (di animali, SPORT) pair.

coprifu'oco, chi sm curfew.

copri'letto sm bedspread.

co'prire vt to cover; (occupare: carica, posto) to hold; **~rsi** vr (cielo) to cloud over; (vestirsi) to wrap up, cover up; (ECON) to cover o.s.; **~rsi di** (macchie, muffa) to become covered in.

co'raggio [ko'raddʒo] sm courage, bravery; **~!** (forza!) come on!; (animo!) cheer up!; **coraggi'oso, a** ag courageous, brave.

co'rallo sm coral.

co'rano sm (REL) Koran.

co'razza [ko'rattsa] sf armour; (di animali) carapace, shell; (MIL) armour(-plating); **coraz'zata** sf battleship.

corbelle'ria sf stupid remark; **~e** sfpl

nonsense *q*.

'**corda** *sf* cord; (*fune*) rope; (*spago*, *MUS*) string; **dare ~ a qn** to let sb have his (*o* her) way; **tenere sulla ~ qn** to keep sb on tenterhooks; **tagliare la ~** to slip away, sneak off; **~e vocali** vocal cords.

cordi'ale *ag* cordial, warm // *sm* (*bevanda*) cordial.

cor'doglio [kor'dɔʎʎo] *sm* grief; (*lutto*) mourning.

cor'done *sm* cord, string; (*linea: di polizia*) cordon; **~ ombelicale** umbilical cord.

Co'rea *sf*: **la ~** Korea.

coreogra'fia *sf* choreography.

cori'andolo *sm* (*BOT*) coriander; **~i** *smpl* confetti *sg*.

cori'care *vt* to put to bed; **~rsi** *vr* to go to bed.

'**corna** *sfpl vedi* **corno**.

cor'nacchia [kor'nakkja] *sf* crow.

corna'musa *sf* bagpipes *pl*.

cor'netta *sf* (*MUS*) cornet; (*TEL*) receiver.

cor'netto *sm* (*CUC*) croissant; **~ acustico** ear trumpet.

cor'nice [kor'nitʃe] *sf* frame; (*fig*) setting, background.

'**corno** *sm* (*ZOOL*: *pl*(*f*) **~a**, *MUS*) horn; **fare le ~a a qn** to be unfaithful to sb; **cor'nuto, a** *ag* (*con corna*) horned; (*fam!: marito*) cuckolded // *sm* (*fam!*) cuckold; (*: insulto*) bastard (*!*).

Corno'vaglia [korno'vaʎʎa] *sf*: **la ~** Cornwall.

'**coro** *sm* chorus; (*REL*) choir.

co'rona *sf* crown; (*di fiori*) wreath; **coro'nare** *vt* to crown.

'**corpo** *sm* body; (*cadavere*) (dead) body; (*militare, diplomatico*) corps *inv*; (*di opere*) corpus; **prendere ~** to take shape; **a ~ a ~** hand-to-hand; **~ di ballo** corps de ballet; **~ di guardia** guard-room; **~ insegnante** teaching staff.

corpo'rale *ag* bodily; (*punizione*) corporal.

corpora'tura *sf* build, physique.

corporazi'one [korporat'tsjone] *sf* corporation.

corpu'lento, a *ag* stout.

corre'dare *vt*: **~ di** to provide *o* furnish with; **cor'redo** *sm* equipment; (*di sposa*) trousseau.

cor'reggere [kor'rɛddʒere] *vt* to correct; (*compiti*) to correct, mark.

cor'rente *ag* (*fiume*) flowing; (*acqua del rubinetto*) running; (*moneta, prezzo*) current; (*comune*) everyday // *sm*: **essere al ~ (di)** to be well-informed (about); **mettere al ~ (di)** to inform (of) // *sf* (*movimento di liquido*) current, stream; (*spiffero*) draught; (*ELETTR, METEOR*) current; (*fig*) trend, tendency; **la vostra lettera del 5 ~ mese** (*COMM*)

your letter of the 5th of this month; **corrente'mente** *av* commonly; **parlare una lingua correntemente** to speak a language fluently.

'**correre** *vi* to run; (*precipitarsi*) to rush; (*partecipare a una gara*) to race, run; (*fig: diffondersi*) to go round // *vt* (*SPORT: gara*) to compete in; (*rischio*) to run; (*pericolo*) to face; **~ dietro a qn** to run after sb; **corre voce che ...** it is rumoured that ....

cor'retto, a *pp di* **correggere** // *ag* (*comportamento*) correct, proper; **caffè ~ al cognac** coffee laced with brandy.

correzi'one [korret'tsjone] *sf* correction; marking; **~ di bozze** proofreading.

corri'doio *sm* corridor.

corri'dore *sm* (*SPORT*) runner; (*: su veicolo*) racer.

corri'era *sf* coach (*Brit*), bus.

corri'ere *sm* (*diplomatico, di guerra*) courier; (*posta*) mail, post; (*COMM*) carrier.

corrispet'tivo *sm* (*somma*) amount due.

corrispon'dente *ag* corresponding // *sm/f* correspondent.

corrispon'denza [korrispon'dentsa] *sf* correspondence.

corris'pondere *vi* (*equivalere*): **~ (a)** to correspond (to); (*per lettera*): **~ con** to correspond with // *vt* (*stipendio*) to pay; (*fig: amore*) to return; **cor-ris'posto, a** *pp di* **corrispondere**.

corrobo'rare *vt* to strengthen, fortify; (*fig*) to corroborate, bear out.

cor'rodere *vt*, **~rsi** *vr* to corrode.

cor'rompere *vt* to corrupt; (*comprare*) to bribe.

corrosi'one *sf* corrosion.

cor'roso, a *pp di* **corrodere**.

cor'rotto, a *pp di* **corrompere** // *ag* corrupt.

corrucci'arsi [korrut'tʃarsi] *vr* to grow angry *o* vexed.

corru'gare *vt* to wrinkle; **~ la fronte** to knit one's brows.

corruzi'one [korrut'tsjone] *sf* corruption; bribery.

'**corsa** *sf* running *q*; (*gara*) race; (*di autobus, taxi*) journey, trip; **fare una ~** to run, dash; (*SPORT*) to run a race.

cor'sia *sf* (*AUT, SPORT*) lane; (*di ospedale*) ward.

cor'sivo *sm* cursive (writing); (*TIP*) italics *pl*.

'**corso, a** *pp di* **correre** // *sm* course; (*strada cittadina*) main street; (*di unità monetaria*) circulation; (*di titoli, valori*) rate, price; **dar libero ~ a** to give free expression to; **in ~** in progress, under way; (*annata*) current; **~ d'acqua** river, stream; (*artificiale*) waterway; **~ serale** evening class.

'**corte** *sf* (court)yard; (*DIR, regale*) court; **fare la ~ a qn** to court sb; **~**

marziale court-martial.

cor'teccia, ce [kor'tettʃa] *sf* bark.

corteggi'are [korted'dʒare] *vt* to court.

cor'teo *sm* procession.

cor'tese *ag* courteous; **corte'sia** *sf* courtesy; **per cortesia** ... excuse me, please ....

cortigi'ano, a [korti'dʒano] *sm/f* courtier // *sf* courtesan.

cor'tile *sm* (court)yard.

cor'tina *sf* curtain; *(anche fig)* screen.

'corto, a *ag* short; **essere a ~ di qc** to be short of sth; **~ circuito** short-circuit.

'corvo *sm* raven.

'cosa *sf* thing; *(faccenda)* affair, matter, business *q; (che) ~? what?; (che)* **cos'è?** what is it?; **a ~ pensi?** what are you thinking about?; **a ~e fatte** when it's all over.

'coscia, sce ['kɔʃʃa] *sf* thigh; **~ di pollo** *(CUC)* chicken leg.

cosci'ente [koʃ'ʃɛnte] *ag* conscious; **~ di** conscious *o* aware of; **cosci'enza** *sf* conscience; *(consapevolezza)* consciousness; **coscienzi'oso, a** *ag* conscientious.

cosci'otto [koʃ'ʃɔtto] *sm* *(CUC)* leg.

cos'critto *sm* (MIL) conscript.

così ◆ *av* 1 *(in questo modo)* like this, (in) this way; *(in tal modo)* so; **le cose stanno ~** this is the way things stand; **non ho detto ~!** I didn't say that!; **come stai? — (e) ~** how are you? — so-so; **e ~ via and so on; per ~ dire** so to speak
2 *(tanto)* so; **~ lontano** so far away; **un ragazzo ~ intelligente** such an intelligent boy
◆ *ag inv (tale)*: **non ho mai visto un film ~** I've never seen such a film
◆ *cong (perciò)* so, therefore
2: ~ ... come as ... as; **non è ~ bravo come te** he's not as good as you; **~ ... che so ... that.**

cosid'detto, a *ag* so-called.

cos'metico, a, ci, che *ag, sm* cosmetic.

cos'pargere [kos'pardʒere] *vt*: **~ di** to sprinkle with; **cos'parso, a** *pp di* **cospargere.**

cos'petto *sm*: **al ~ di** in front of; in the presence of.

cos'picuo, a *ag* considerable, large.

cospi'rare *vi* to conspire; **cospirazi'one** *sf* conspiracy.

'costa *sf (tra terra e mare)* coast(line); *(litorale)* shore; (ANAT) rib; **la C~ Azzurra** the French Riviera.

costà *av* there.

cos'tante *ag* constant; *(persona)* steadfast // *sf* constant.

cos'tare *vi, vt* to cost; **~ caro** to be expensive, cost a lot.

cos'tata *sf* (CUC) large chop.

cos'tato *sm* (ANAT) ribs *pl.*

costeggi'are [kosted'dʒare] *vt* to be close to; to run alongside.

cos'tei *pronome vedi* **costui.**

costernazi'one [kosternat'tsjone] *sf* dismay, consternation.

costi'ero, a *ag* coastal, coast *cpd* // *sf* stretch of coast.

costitu'ire *vt (comitato, gruppo)* to set up, form; *(collezione)* to put together, build up; *(sog: elementi, parti: comporre)* to make up, constitute; *(rappresentare)* to constitute; *(DIR)* to appoint; **~rsi alla polizia** to give o.s. up to the police.

costituzio'nale [kostituttsjo'nale] *ag* constitutional.

costituzi'one [kostitut'tsjone] *sf* setting up; building up; constitution.

'costo *sm* cost; **a ogni** *o* **qualunque ~, a tutti i ~i** at all costs.

'costola *sf* (ANAT) rib.

costo'letta *sf* (CUC) cutlet.

cos'toro *pronome pl vedi* **costui.**

cos'toso, a *ag* expensive, costly.

cos'tretto, a *pp di* **costringere.**

cos'tringere [kos'trindʒere] *vt*: **~ qn a fare qc** to force sb to do sth; **cos-trizi'one** *sf* coercion.

costru'ire *vt* to construct, build; **co-struzi'one** *sf* construction, building.

cos'tui, cos'tei, *pl* **cos'toro** *pronome* *(soggetto)* he/she; *pl* they; *(complemento)* him/her; *pl* them; **si può sapere chi è ~?** *(peg)* just who is that fellow?

cos'tume *sm (uso)* custom; *(foggia di vestire, indumento)* costume; **~i** *smpl* morals, morality *sg*; **il buon ~** public morality; **~ da bagno** bathing *o* swimming costume (Brit), swimsuit; *(da uomo)* bathing *o* swimming trunks *pl.*

co'tenna *sf* bacon rind.

co'togna [ko'toɲɲa] *sf* quince.

coto'letta *sf (di maiale, montone)* chop; *(di vitello, agnello)* cutlet.

co'tone *sm* cotton; **~ idrofilo** cotton wool (Brit), absorbent cotton (US).

'cotta *sf (fam: innamoramento)* crush.

'cottimo *sm*: **lavorare a ~** to do piecework.

'cotto, a *pp di* **cuocere** // *ag* cooked; *(fam: innamorato)* head-over-heels in love.

cot'tura *sf* cooking; *(in forno)* baking; *(in umido)* stewing.

co'vare *vt* to hatch; *(fig: malattia)* to be sickening for; *(: odio, rancore)* to nurse // *vi (fuoco, fig)* to smoulder.

'covo *sm* den.

co'vone *sm* sheaf.

'cozza ['kɔttsa] *sf* mussel.

coz'zare [kot'tsare] *vi*: **~ contro** to bang into, collide with.

C.P. *abbr* = **casella postale.**

'crampo *sm* cramp.

'cranio *sm* skull.

cra'vatta *sf* tie.

cre'anza [kre'antsa] *sf* manners *pl.*

cre'are *vt* to create; **cre'ato** *sm* creation; **crea'tore**, **'trice** *ag* creative // *sm* creator; **crea'tura** *sf* creature; (*bimbo*) baby, infant; **creazi'one** *sf* creation; (*fondazione*) foundation, establishment.

cre'dente *sm/f* (REL) believer.

cre'denza [kre'dentsa] *sf* belief; (*armadio*) sideboard.

credenzi'ali [kreden'tsjali] *sfpl* credentials.

'credere *vt* to believe // *vi*: ~ **in**, ~ **a** to believe in; ~ **qn onesto** to believe sb (to be) honest; ~ **che** to believe *o* think that; ~**rsi furbo** to think one is clever.

'credito *sm* (*anche* COMM) credit; (*reputazione*) esteem, repute; **comprare a** ~ to buy on credit.

'credo *sm inv* creed.

'crema *sf* cream; (*con uova, zucchero etc*) custard; ~ **solare** sun cream.

cre'mare *vt* to cremate.

Crem'lino *sm*: **il** ~ **the** Kremlin.

'crepa *sf* crack.

cre'paccio [kre'pattʃo] *sm* large crack, fissure; (*di ghiacciaio*) crevasse.

crepacu'ore *sm* broken heart.

cre'pare *vi* (*fam: morire*) to snuff it, kick the bucket; ~ **dalle risa** to split one's sides laughing.

crepi'tare *vi* (*fuoco*) to crackle; (*pioggia*) to patter.

cre'puscolo *sm* twilight, dusk.

'crescere ['kreʃʃere] *vi* to grow // *vt* (*figli*) to raise; **'crescita** *sf* growth; **cresci'uto**, **a** *pp di* **crescere**.

'cresima *sf* (REL) confirmation.

'crespo, **a** *ag* (*capelli*) frizzy; (*tessuto*) puckered // *sm* crêpe.

'cresta *sf* crest; (*di polli, uccelli*) crest, comb.

'creta *sf* chalk; clay.

cre'tino, **a** *ag* stupid // *sm/f* idiot, fool.

cric *sm inv* (TECN) jack.

'cricca, **che** *sf* clique.

'cricco, **chi** *sm* = **cric**.

crimi'nale *ag*, *sm/f* criminal.

'crimine *sm* (DIR) crime.

'crine *sm* horsehair; **crini'era** *sf* mane.

crisan'temo *sm* chrysanthemum.

'crisi *sf inv* crisis; (MED) attack, fit; ~ **di nervi** attack *o* fit of nerves.

cristalliz'zare [kristalid'dzare] *vi*, ~**rsi** *vr* to crystallize; (*fig*) to become fossilized.

cris'tallo *sm* crystal.

cristia'nesimo *sm* Christianity.

cristi'ano, **a** *ag*, *sm/f* Christian.

'Cristo *sm* Christ.

cri'terio *sm* criterion; (*buon senso*) (common) sense.

'critica, **che** *sf vedi* **critico**.

criti'care *vt* to criticize.

'critico, **a**, **ci**, **che** *ag* critical // *sm* critic // *sf* criticism; **la** ~**a** (*attività*) criticism; (*persone*) the critics *pl.*

cri'vello *sm* riddle.

'croce ['krotʃe] *sf* cross; **in** ~ (*di traverso*) crosswise; (*fig*) on tenterhooks; **la C~ Rossa** the Red Cross.

croce'figgere [krotʃe'fiddʒere] *etc* = **crocifiggere** *etc.*

croce'via [krotʃe'via] *sm inv* crossroads *sg.*

croci'ata [kro'tʃata] *sf* crusade.

cro'cicchio [kro'tʃikkjo] *sm* crossroads *sg.*

croci'era [kro'tʃera] *sf* (*viaggio*) cruise; (ARCHIT) transept.

croci'figgere [krotʃi'fiddʒere] *vt* to crucify; **crocifissi'one** *sf* crucifixion; **croci'fisso**, **a** *pp di* **crocifiggere**.

crogi'olo, **crogiu'olo** [kro'dʒɔlo] *sm* (*fig*) melting pot.

crol'lare *vi* to collapse; **'crollo** *sm* collapse; (*di prezzi*) slump, sudden fall.

cro'mato, **a** *ag* chromium-plated.

'cromo *sm* chrome, chromium.

cromo'soma, **i** *sm* chromosome.

'cronaca, **che** *sf* chronicle; (STAMPA) news *sg*; (: *rubrica*) column; (TV, RADIO) commentary; **fatto** *o* **episodio di** ~ news item; ~ **nera** crime news *sg*; crime column.

'cronico, **a**, **ci**, **che** *ag* chronic.

cro'nista, **i** *sm* (STAMPA) reporter, columnist.

cronolo'gia [kronolo'dʒia] *sf* chronology.

cro'nometro *sm* chronometer; (*a scatto*) stopwatch.

'crosta *sf* crust.

cros'tacei [kros'tatʃei] *smpl* shellfish.

cros'tata *sf* (CUC) tart.

cros'tino *sm* (CUC) croûton; (: *da antipasto*) canapé.

'cruccio ['kruttʃo] *sm* worry, torment.

cruci'verba *sm inv* crossword (puzzle).

cru'dele *ag* cruel; **crudeltà** *sf* cruelty.

'crudo, **a** *ag* (*non cotto*) raw; (*aspro*) harsh, severe.

cru'miro *sm* (*peg*) blackleg (*Brit*), scab.

'crusca *sf* bran.

crus'cotto *sm* (AUT) dashboard.

'Cuba *sf* Cuba.

'cubico, **a**, **ci**, **che** *ag* cubic.

'cubo, **a** *ag* cubic // *sm* cube; **elevare al** ~ (MAT) to cube.

cuc'cagna [kuk'kaɲɲa] *sf*: **paese della** ~ land of plenty; **albero della** ~ greasy pole (*fig*).

cuc'cetta [kut'tʃetta] *sf* (FERR) couchette; (NAUT) berth.

cucchiai'ata [kukja'jata] *sf* spoonful.

cucchia'ino [kukkja'ino] *sm* teaspoon; coffee spoon.

cucchi'aio [kuk'kjajo] *sm* spoon.

'cuccia ['kuttʃa] *sf* dog's bed; **a** ~! down!

'cucciolo ['kuttʃolo] *sm* cub; (*di cane*) puppy.

cu'cina [ku'tʃina] *sf* (*locale*) kitchen;

(*arte culinaria*) cooking, cookery; (*le vivande*) food, cooking; (*apparecchio*) cooker; ~ **componibile** fitted kitchen; **cuci'nare** *vt* to cook.

cu'cire [ku'tʃire] *vt* to sew, stitch; **cuci'trice** *sf* stapler; **cuci'tura** *sf* sewing, stitching; (*costura*) seam.

cucù *sm inv*, **cu'culo** *sm* cuckoo.

'cuffia *sf* bonnet, cap; (*da infermiera*) cap; (*da bagno*) (bathing) cap; (*per ascoltare*) headphones *pl*, headset.

cu'gino, a [ku'dʒino] *smlf* cousin.

'cui *pronome* **1** (*nei complementi indiretti: persona*) whom; (: *oggetto, animale*) which; **la persona/le persone a** ~ **accennavi** the person/people you were referring *o* to whom you were referring; **i libri di** ~ **parlavo** the books I was talking about *o* about which I was talking; **il quartiere in** ~ **abito** the district where I live; **la ragione per** ~ the reason why

2 (*inserito tra articolo e sostantivo*) whose; **la donna i** ~ **figli sono scomparsi** the woman whose children have disappeared; **il signore, dal** ~ **figlio ho avuto il libro** the man from whose son I got the book.

culi'naria *sf* cookery.

'culla *sf* cradle.

cul'lare *vt* to rock.

culmi'nare *vi*: ~ **in** *o* **con** to culminate in.

'culmine *sm* top, summit.

'culo *sm* (*fam!*) arse (*Brit!*), ass (*US!*); (: *fig: fortuna*): **aver** ~ to have the luck of the devil.

'culto *sm* (*religione*) religion; (*adorazione*) worship, adoration; (*venerazione: anche fig*) cult.

cul'tura *sf* culture; education, learning; **cultu'rale** *ag* cultural.

cumula'tivo, a *ag* cumulative; (*prezzo*) inclusive; (*biglietto*) group (*cpd*)

'cumulo *sm* (*mucchio*) pile, heap; (*METEOR*) cumulus.

'cuneo *sm* wedge.

cu'oca *sf* vedi **cuoco**.

cu'ocere ['kwɔtʃere] *vt* (*alimenti*) to cook; (*mattoni etc*) to fire // *vi* to cook; ~ **al forno** (*pane*) to bake; (*arrosto*) to roast; **cu'oco, a, chi, che** *smlf* cook; (*di ristorante*) chef.

cu'oio *sm* leather; ~ **capelluto** scalp.

cu'ore *sm* heart; ~**i** *smpl* (*CARTE*) hearts; **avere buon** ~ to be kind-hearted; **stare a** ~ **a qn** to be important to sb.

cupi'digia [kupi'didʒa] *sf* greed, covetousness.

'cupo, a *ag* dark; (*suono*) dull; (*fig*) gloomy, dismal.

'cupola *sf* dome; cupola.

'cura *sf* care; (*MED: trattamento*) (course of) treatment; **aver** ~ **di** (*occuparsi di*) to look after; **a** ~ **di** (*li-**

bro) edited by; ~ **dimagrante** diet.

cu'rare *vt* (*malato, malattia*) to treat; (: *guarire*) to cure; (*aver cura di*) to take care of; (*testo*) to edit; ~**rsi** *vr* to take care of o.s.; (*MED*) to follow a course of treatment; ~**rsi di** to pay attention to.

cu'rato *sm* parish priest; (*protestante*) vicar, minister.

cura'tore, 'trice *smlf* (*DIR*) trustee; (*di antologia etc*) editor.

curio'sare *vi* to look round, wander round; (*tra libri*) to browse; ~ **nei negozi** to look *o* wander round the shops.

curiosità *sf inv* curiosity; (*cosa rara*) curio, curiosity.

curi'oso, a *ag* (*che vuol sapere*) curious, inquiring; (*ficcanaso*) curious, inquisitive; (*bizzarro*) strange, curious; **essere** ~ **di** to be curious about.

cur'sore *sm* (*INFORM*) cursor.

'curva *sf* curve; (*stradale*) bend, curve.

cur'vare *vt* to bend // *vi* (*veicolo*) to take a bend; (*strada*) to bend, curve; ~**rsi** *vr* to bend; (*legno*) to warp.

'curvo, a *ag* curved; (*piegato*) bent.

cusci'netto [kuʃʃi'netto] *sm* pad; (*TECN*) bearing // *ag inv*: **stato** ~ buffer state; **a sfere** ball bearing.

cu'scino [kuʃ'ʃino] *sm* cushion; (*guanciale*) pillow.

'cuspide *sf* (*ARCHIT*) spire.

cus'tode *smlf* keeper, custodian.

cus'todia *sf* care; (*DIR*) custody; (*astuccio*) case, holder.

custo'dire *vt* (*conservare*) to keep; (*assistere*) to look after, take care of; (*fare la guardia*) to guard.

'cute *sf* (*ANAT*) skin.

cu'ticola *sf* cuticle.

C.V. *abbr* (= *cavallo vapore*) h.p.

D

da *prep* (*da* + *il* = **dal**, *da* + *lo* = **dallo**, *da* + *l'* = **dall'**, *da* + *la* = **dalla**, *da* + *i* = **dai**, *da* + *gli* = **dagli**, *da* + *le* = **dalle**) **1** (*agente*) by; **dipinto** ~ **un grande artista** painted by a great artist

2 (*causa*) with; **tremare dalla paura** to tremble with fear

3 (*stato in luogo*) at; **abito** ~ **lui** I'm living at his house *o* with him; **sono dal giornalaio/**~ **Francesco** I'm at the newsagent's/Francesco's (house)

4 (*moto a luogo*) to; (*moto per luogo*) through; **vado** ~ **Pietro/dal giornalaio** I'm going to Pietro's (house)/to the newsagent's; **sono passati dalla finestra** they came in through the window

5 (*provenienza, allontanamento*) from; **arrivare/partire** ~ **Milano** to arrive/depart from Milan; **scendere dal treno/dalla macchina** to get off the train/out of the car; **si trova a 5 km** ~ **qui** it's 5 km from here

6 (*tempo: durata*) for; (*: a partire da: nel passato*) since; (*: nel futuro*) from; **vivo qui ~ un anno** I've been living here for a year; **è dalle 3 che ti aspetto** I've been waiting for you since 3 (o'clock); **~ oggi in poi** from today onwards; **~ bambino** as a child, when I (*o he etc*) was a child

7 (*modo, maniera*) like; **comportarsi ~ uomo** to behave like a man; **l'ho fatto ~ me** I did it (by) myself

8 (*descrittivo*): **una macchina ~ corsa** a racing car; **una ragazza dai capelli biondi** a girl with blonde hair; **un vestito ~ 100.000 lire** a 100,000 lire dress; **sordo ~ un orecchio** deaf in one ear.

dab'bene *ag inv* honest, decent.

dac'capo, da 'capo *av* (*di nuovo*) (once) again; (*dal principio*) all over again, from the beginning.

dacché [dak'ke] *cong* since.

'dado *sm* (*da gioco*) dice *o* die (*pl* dice); (*CUC*) stock (*Brit*) *o* bouillon (*US*) cube; (*TECN*) (screw)nut; **~i** *smpl* (game of) dice.

daf'fare, da 'fare *sm* work, toil.

'dagli ['daλλi], **'dai** *prep + det vedi* da.

'daino *sm* (fallow) deer *inv*; (*pelle*) buckskin.

dal, dall', 'dalla, 'dalle, 'dallo *prep + det vedi* da.

dal'tonico, a, ci, che *ag* colour-blind.

'dama *sf* lady; (*nei balli*) partner; (*gioco*) draughts *sg* (*Brit*), checkers *sg* (*US*).

damigi'ana [dami'dʒana] *sf* demijohn.

da'naro *sm* = **denaro**.

da'nese *ag* Danish // *sm/f* Dane // *sm* (*LING*) Danish.

Dani'marca *sf*: **la ~** Denmark.

dan'nare *vt* (*REL*) to damn; **~rsi** *vr* (*fig: tormentarsi*) to be worried to death; **far ~ qn** to drive sb mad; **dannazi'one** *sf* damnation.

danneggi'are [danned'dʒare] *vt* to damage; (*rovinare*) to spoil; (*nuocere*) to harm.

'danno *sm* damage; (*a persona*) harm, injury; **~i** *smpl* (*DIR*) damages; **dan'noso, a** *ag*: **dannoso (a, per)** harmful (to), bad (for).

Da'nubio *sm*: **il ~** the Danube.

'danza ['dantsa] *sf*: **la ~** dancing; **una ~** a dance.

dan'zare [dan'tsare] *vt, vi* to dance.

dapper'tutto *av* everywhere.

dap'poco *ag inv* inept, worthless.

dap'prima *av* at first.

'dardo *sm* dart.

'dare *sm* (*COMM*) debit // *vt* to give; (*produrre: frutti, suono*) to produce // *vi* (*guardare*): **~ su** to look (out) onto; **~rsi** *vr*: **~rsi a** to dedicate o.s. to; **~rsi al commercio** to go into business; **~rsi al**

bere to take to drink; **~ da mangiare a qn** to give sb sth to eat; **~ per certo qc** to consider sth certain; **~ per morto qn** to give sb up for dead; **~rsi per vinto** to give in.

'darsena *sf* dock; dockyard.

'data *sf* date; **~ di nascita** date of birth.

da'tare *vt* to date // *vi*: **~ da** to date from.

'dato, a *ag* (*stabilito*) given // *sm* datum; **~i** *smpl* data *pl*; **~ che** given that; **un ~ di fatto** a fact.

'dattero *sm* date.

dattilogra'fare *vt* to type; **dattilogra'fia** *sf* typing; **datti'lografo, a** *sm/f* typist.

da'vanti *av* in front; (*dirimpetto*) opposite // *ag inv* front // *sm* front; **~ a** *prep* in front of; facing, opposite; (*in presenza di*) before, in front of.

davan'zale [davan'tsale] *sm* windowsill.

da'vanzo, d'a'vanzo [da'vantso] *av* more than enough.

dav'vero *av* really, indeed.

'dazio ['dattsjo] *sm* (*somma*) duty; (*luogo*) customs *pl*.

DC *sigla f* = **Democrazia Cristiana**.

d. C. *ad abbr* (= *dopo Cristo*) A.D.

'dea *sf* goddess.

'debito, a *ag* due, proper // *sm* debt; (*COMM: dare*) debit; **a tempo ~** at the right time; **debi'tore, 'trice** *sm/f* debtor.

'debole *ag* weak, feeble; (*suono*) faint; (*luce*) dim // *sm* weakness; **debo'lezza** *sf* weakness.

debut'tare *vi* to make one's début; **de'butto** *sm* début.

deca'denza [deka'dɛntsa] *sf* decline; (*DIR*) loss, forfeiture.

decaffei'nato, a *ag* decaffeinated.

decappot'tabile *ag, sf* convertible.

dece'duto, a [detʃe'duto] *ag* deceased.

de'cennio [de'tʃɛnnjo] *sm* decade.

de'cente [de'tʃɛnte] *ag* decent, respectable, proper; (*accettabile*) satisfactory, decent.

de'cesso [de'tʃɛsso] *sm* death; **atto di ~** death certificate.

de'cidere [de'tʃidere] *vt*: **~ qc** to decide on sth; (*questione, lite*) to settle sth; **~ di fare/che** to decide to do/that; **~ di qc** (*sog: cosa*) to determine sth; **~rsi (a fare)** to decide (to do), make up one's mind (to do).

deci'frare [detʃi'frare] *vt* to decode; (*fig*) to decipher, make out.

deci'male [detʃi'male] *ag* decimal.

'decimo, a ['detʃimo] *num* tenth.

de'cina [de'tʃina] *sf* ten; (*circa dieci*): **una ~ (di)** about ten.

decisi'one [detʃi'zjone] *sf* decision; **prendere una ~** to make a decision.

de'ciso, a [de'tʃizo] *pp di* **decidere**.

declas'sare *vt* to downgrade; to lower in

status.

decli'nare *vi* (*pendio*) to slope down; (*fig: diminuire*) to decline; (*tramontare*) to set, go down // *vt* to decline; **declinazi'one** *sf* (*LING*) declension; **de'clino** *sm* decline.

decol'lare *vi* (*AER*) to take off; **de'collo** *sm* take-off.

decolo'rare *vt* to bleach.

decom'porre *vt*, **decomporsi** *vr* to decompose; **decom'posto, a** *pp di* **decomporre**.

deconge'lare [dekondʒe'lare] *vt* to defrost.

deco'rare *vt* to decorate; **decora'tore, 'trice** *sm/f* (*interior*) decorator; **decorazi'one** *sf* decoration.

de'coro *sm* decorum; **deco'roso, a** *ag* decorous, dignified.

de'correre *vi* to pass, elapse; (*avere effetto*) to run, have effect; **de'corso, a** *pp di* **decorrere** // *sm* (*evoluzione: anche MED*) course.

de'crescere [de'kreʃʃere] *vi* (*diminuire*) to decrease, diminish; (*acque*) to subside, go down; (*prezzi*) to go down; **decresci'uto, a** *pp di* **decrescere**.

de'creto *sm* decree; ~ **legge** *decree with the force of law.*

'dedalo *sm* maze, labyrinth.

'dedica, che *sf* dedication.

dedi'care *vt* to dedicate.

'dedito, a *ag*: ~ **a** (*studio etc*) dedicated *o* devoted to; (*vizio*) addicted to.

de'dotto, a *pp di* **dedurre**.

de'durre *vt* (*concludere*) to deduce; (*defalcare*) to deduct; **deduzi'one** *sf* deduction.

defal'care *vt* to deduct.

defe'rente *ag* respectful, deferential.

defe'rire *vt*: ~ **a** (*DIR*) to refer to.

defezi'one [defet'tsjone] *sf* defection, desertion.

defici'ente [defi'tʃɛnte] *ag* (*mancante*): ~ **di** deficient in; (*insufficiente*) insufficient // *sm/f* mental defective; (*peg: cretino*) idiot.

'deficit ['dɛfitʃit] *sm inv* (*ECON*) deficit.

defi'nire *vt* to define; (*risolvere*) to settle; **defini'tivo, a** *ag* definitive, final; **definizi'one** *sf* definition; settlement.

deflet'tore *sm* (*AUT*) quarter-light.

de'flusso *sm* (*della marea*) ebb.

defor'mare *vt* (*alterare*) to put out of shape; (*corpo*) to deform; (*pensiero, fatto*) to distort; ~**rsi** *vr* to lose its shape.

de'forme *ag* deformed; disfigured; **deformità** *sf inv* deformity.

defrau'dare *vt*: ~ **qn di qc** to defraud sb of sth, cheat sb out of sth.

de'funto, a *ag* late *cpd* // *sm/f* deceased.

degene'rare [dedʒene'rare] *vi* to degenerate; **de'genere** *ag* degenerate.

de'gente [de'dʒɛnte] *sm/f* bedridden

person; (*ricoverato in ospedale*) inpatient.

'degli ['deʎʎi] *prep + det vedi* **di**.

de'gnarsi [deɲ'narsi] *vr*: ~ **di fare** to deign *o* condescend to do.

'degno, a *ag* dignified; ~ **di** worthy of; ~ **di lode** praiseworthy.

degra'dare *vt* (*MIL*) to demote; (*privare della dignità*) to degrade; ~**rsi** *vr* to demean o.s.

degustazi'one [degustat'tsjone] *sf* sampling, tasting.

'dei, del *prep + det vedi* **di**.

dela'tore, 'trice *sm/f* police informer.

'delega, ghe *sf* (*procura*) proxy.

dele'gare *vt* to delegate; **dele'gato** *sm* delegate.

del'fino *sm* (*ZOOL.*) dolphin; (*STORIA*) dauphin; (*fig*) probable successor.

delibe'rare *vt* to come to a decision on // *vi* (*DIR*): ~ (**su qc**) to rule (on sth).

delica'tezza [delika'tettsa] *sf* (*anche CUC*) delicacy; frailty; thoughtfulness; tactfulness.

deli'cato, a *ag* delicate; (*salute*) delicate, frail; (*fig: gentile*) thoughtful, considerate; (*: che dimostra tatto*) tactful.

deline'are *vt* to outline; ~**rsi** *vr* to be outlined; (*fig*) to emerge.

delin'quente *sm/f* criminal, delinquent; **delin'quenza** *sf* criminality, delinquency; **delinquenza minorile** juvenile delinquency.

deli'rare *vi* to be delirious, rave; (*fig*) to rave.

de'lirio *sm* delirium; (*ragionamento insensato*) raving; (*fig*): **andare/mandare in** ~ to go/send into a frenzy.

de'litto *sm* crime.

de'lizia [de'littsja] *sf* delight; **delizi'oso, a** *ag* delightful; (*cibi*) delicious.

dell', 'della, 'delle, 'dello *prep + det vedi* **di**.

delta'plano *sm* hang-glider; **volo col** ~ hang-gliding.

de'ludere *vt* to disappoint; **delusi'one** *sf* disappointment; **de'luso, a** *pp di* **deludere**.

de'manio *sm* state property.

de'menza [de'mɛntsa] *sf* dementia; (*stupidità*) foolishness.

demo'cratico, a, ci, che *ag* democratic.

democra'zia [demokrat'tsia] *sf* democracy.

democristi'ano, a *ag, sm/f* Christian Democrat.

demo'lire *vt* to demolish.

'demone *sm* demon.

de'monio *sm* demon, devil; **il D~** the Devil.

de'naro *sm* money.

denomi'nare *vt* to name; ~**rsi** *vr* to be named *o* called; **denominazi'one** *sf* name; denomination.

densità *sf inv* density.

'denso, a *ag* thick, dense.

den'tale *ag* dental.

'dente *sm* tooth; (*di forchetta*) prong; (*GEO: cima*) jagged peak; **al ~** (*CUC: pasta*) cooked so as to be firm when eaten; **~i del giudizio** wisdom teeth; **denti'era** *sf* (set of) false teeth *pl.*

denti'fricio [denti'fritʃo] *sm* toothpaste.

den'tista, i, e *sm/f* dentist.

'dentro *av* inside; (*in casa*) indoors; (*fig: nell'intimo*) inwardly // *prep:* **~ (a)** in; **piegato in ~** folded over; **qui/là ~** in here/there; **~ di sé** (*pensare, brontolare*) to oneself.

de'nuncia, ce *o* **cie** [de'nuntʃa], **de'nunzia** [de'nuntsja] *sf* denunciation; declaration; **~ dei redditi** (income) tax return.

denunci'are [denun'tʃare], **denunzi'are** [denun'tsjare] *vt* to denounce; (*dichiarare*) to declare.

denutrizi'one [denutrit'tsjone] *sf* malnutrition.

deodo'rante *sm* deodorant.

depe'rire *vi* to waste away.

depila'torio, a *ag* hair-removing *cpd*, depilatory.

dépli'ant [depli'ã] *sm inv* leaflet; (*opuscolo*) brochure.

deplo'revole *ag* deplorable.

de'porre *vt* (*depositare*) to put down; (*rimuovere: da una carica*) to remove; (*: re*) to depose; (*DIR*) to testify.

depor'tare *vt* to deport.

deposi'tare *vt* (*gen, GEO, ECON*) to deposit; (*lasciare*) to leave; (*merci*) to store.

de'posito *sm* deposit; (*luogo*) warehouse; depot; (*: MIL*) depot; **~ bagagli** left-luggage office.

deposizi'one [depozit'tsjone] *sf* deposition; (*da una carica*) removal.

de'posto, a *pp di* **deporre.**

depra'vato, a *ag* depraved // *sm/f* degenerate.

depre'dare *vt* to rob, plunder.

depressi'one *sf* depression.

de'presso, a *pp di* **deprimere** // *ag* depressed.

deprez'zare [depret'tsare] *vt* (*ECON*) to depreciate.

de'primere *vt* to depress.

depu'rare *vt* to purify.

depu'tato, a *o* **'essa** *sm/f* (*POL*) deputy, ≈ Member of Parliament (*Brit*), ≈ Member of Congress (*US*); **deputazi'one** *sf* deputation; (*POL*) position of deputy, ≈ parliamentary seat (*Brit*), ≈ seat in Congress (*US*).

deragli'are [deraʎ'ʎare] *vi* to be derailed; **far ~** to derail.

dere'litto, a *ag* derelict.

dere'tano *sm* (*fam*) bottom, buttocks *pl.*

de'ridere *vt* to mock, deride; **de'riso, a** *pp di* **deridere.**

de'riva *sf* (*NAUT, AER*) drift; **andare alla ~** (*anche fig*) to drift.

deri'vare *vi:* **~ da** to derive from // *vt* to derive; (*corso d'acqua*) to divert; **derivazi'one** *sf* derivation; diversion.

derma'tologo, a, gi, ghe *sm/f* dermatologist.

der'rate *sfpl* commodities; **~ alimentari** foodstuffs.

deru'bare *vt* to rob.

des'critto, a *pp di* **descrivere.**

des'crivere *vt* to describe; **descrizi'one** *sf* description.

de'serto, a *ag* deserted // *sm* (*GEO*) desert; **isola ~a** desert island.

deside'rare *vt* to want, wish for; (*sessualmente*) to desire; **~ fare/che qn faccia** to want *o* wish to do/sb to do; **desidera fare una passeggiata?** would you like to go for a walk?

desi'derio *sm* wish; (*più intenso, carnale*) desire.

deside'roso, a *ag:* **~ di** longing *o* eager for.

desi'nenza [dezi'nɛntsa] *sf* (*LING*) ending, inflexion.

de'sistere *vi:* **~ da** to give up, desist from; **desis'tito, a** *pp di* **desistere.**

deso'lato, a *ag* (*paesaggio*) desolate; (*persona: spiacente*) sorry.

des'tare *vt* to wake (up); (*fig*) to awaken, arouse; **~rsi** *vr* to wake (up).

desti'nare *vt* to destine; (*assegnare*) to appoint, assign; (*indirizzare*) to address; **~ qc a qn** to intend to give sth to sb, intend sb to have sth; **destina'tario, a** *sm/f* (*di lettera*) addressee.

destinazi'one [destinat'tsjone] *sf* destination; (*uso*) purpose.

des'tino *sm* destiny, fate.

destitu'ire *vt* to dismiss, remove.

'desto, a *ag* (wide) awake.

'destra *sf vedi* **destro.**

destreggi'arsi [destred'dʒarsi] *vr* to manoeuvre (*Brit*), maneuver (*US*).

des'trezza [des'trettsa] *sf* skill, dexterity.

'destro, a *ag* right, right-hand; (*abile*) skilful, adroit // *sf* (*mano*) right hand; (*parte*) right (side); (*POL*): **la ~a** the Right; **a ~a** (*essere*) on the right; (*andare*) to the right.

dete'nere *vt* (*incarico, primato*) to hold; (*proprietà*) to have, possess; (*in prigione*) to detain, hold; **dete'nuto, a** *sm/f* prisoner; **detenzi'one** *sf* holding; possession; detention.

deter'gente [deter'dʒɛnte] *ag* detergent; (*crema, latte*) cleansing // *sm* detergent.

deterio'rare *vt* to damage; **~rsi** *vr* to deteriorate.

determi'nare *vt* to determine; **determinazi'one** *sf* determination; (*decisione*) decision.

deter'sivo *sm* detergent.

detes'tare *vt* to detest, hate.

de'trarre *vt*: ~ (da) to deduct (from), take away (from); **de'tratto, a** *pp di* **detrarre; detrazi'one** *sf* deduction; detrazione d'imposta tax allowance.

detri'mento *sm* detriment, harm; **a** ~ **di** to the detriment of.

de'trito *sm* (GEO) detritus.

dettagli'are [detta^'ʎare] *vt* to detail, give full details of.

det'taglio [det'taʎʎo] *sm* detail; (COMM): **il** ~ retail; **al** ~ (COMM) retail; separately.

det'tare *vt* to dictate; ~ **legge** (fig) to lay down the law; **det'tato** *sm* dictation; **detta'tura** *sf* dictation.

'detto, a *pp di* **dire** // *ag* (soprannominato) called, known as; (già nominato) above-mentioned // *sm* saying; ~ **fatto** no sooner said than done.

detur'pare *vt* to disfigure; (moralmente) to sully.

devas'tare *vt* to devastate; (fig) to ravage.

devi'are *vi*: ~ (da) to turn off (from) // *vt* to divert; **deviazi'one** *sf* (anche AUT) diversion.

devo'luto, a *pp di* **devolvere.**

devoluzi'one [devolut'tsjone] *sf* (DIR) devolution, transfer.

de'volvere *vt* (DIR) to transfer, devolve.

de'voto, a *ag* (REL) devout, pious; (affezionato) devoted.

devozi'one [devot'tsjone] *sf* devoutness; (anche REL) devotion.

di *prep* (di + il = **del**, di + lo = **dello**, di + l' = **dell'**, di + la = **della**, di + i = **dei**, di + gli = **degli**, di + le = **delle**) **1** (possesso, specificazione) of; (composto da, scritto da) by; **la macchina** ~ **Paolo/mio fratello** Paolo's/my brother's car; **un amico** ~ **mio fratello** a friend of my brother's, one of my brother's friends; **un quadro** ~ **Botticelli** a painting by Botticelli **2** (caratterizzazione, misura) of; **una casa** ~ **mattoni** a brick house, a house made of bricks; **un orologio d'oro** a gold watch; **un bimbo** ~ **3 anni** a child of 3, a 3-year-old child **3** (causa, mezzo, modo) with; **tremare** ~ **paura** to tremble with fear; **morire** ~ **cancro** to die of cancer; **spalmare** ~ **burro** to spread with butter **4** (argomento) about, of; **discutere** ~ **sport** to talk about sport **5** (luogo: provenienza) from; out of; **essere** ~ **Roma** to be from Rome; **uscire** ~ **casa** to come out o leave the house **6** (tempo) in; **d'estate/d'inverno** in (the) summer/winter; ~ **notte** by night, at night; ~ **mattina/sera** in the morning/evening; ~ **domenica** on Sundays

♦ *det* (una certa quantità di) some; (: negativo) any; (: interrogativo) any, some; **del pane** (some) bread; **delle caramelle** (some) sweets; **degli amici miei** some friends of mine; **vuoi del vino?** do you want some o any wine?

dia'bete *sm* diabetes sg.

di'acono *sm* (REL) deacon.

dia'dema, i *sm* diadem; (di donna) tiara.

dia'framma, i *sm* (divisione) screen; (ANAT, FOT, contraccettivo) diaphragm.

di'agnosi [di'aɲɲozi] *sf* diagnosis sg.

diago'nale *ag, sf* diagonal.

dia'gramma, i *sm* diagram.

dia'letto *sm* dialect.

di'alogo, ghi *sm* dialogue.

dia'mante *sm* diamond.

di'ametro *sm* diameter.

di'amine *escl*: **che** ~ ...? what on earth ...?

diaposi'tiva *sf* transparency, slide.

di'ario *sm* diary; ~ **degli esami** (SCOL) exam timetable.

diar'rea *sf* diarrhoea.

di'avolo *sm* devil.

di'battere *vt* to debate, discuss; **~rsi** *vr* to struggle; **di'battito** *sm* debate, discussion.

dicas'tero *sm* ministry.

di'cembre [di'tʃɛmbre] *sm* December.

dice'ria [ditʃe'ria] *sf* rumour, piece of gossip.

dichia'rare [dikja'rare] *vt* to declare; **dichiarazi'one** *sf* declaration.

dician'nove [ditʃan'nove] *num* nineteen.

dicias'sette [ditʃas'sɛtte] *num* seventeen.

dici'otto [di'tʃɔtto] *num* eighteen.

dici'tura [ditʃi'tura] *sf* words pl, wording.

di'eci ['djɛtʃi] *num* ten; **die'cina** *sf* = **decina.**

'diesel ['dizəl] *sm inv* diesel engine.

di'eta *sf* diet; **essere a** ~ to be on a diet.

di'etro *av* behind; (in fondo) at the back // *prep* behind; (tempo: dopo) after // *sm* back, rear // *ag inv* back cpd; **le zampe di** ~ the hind legs; ~ **richiesta** on demand; (scritta) on application.

di'fatti *cong* in fact, as a matter of fact.

di'fendere *vt* to defend; **difen'sivo, a** *ag* defensive // *sf*: **stare sulla difensiva** (anche fig) to be on the defensive; **difen'sore, a** *sm/f* defender; **avvocato difensore** counsel for the defence; **di'feso, a** *pp di* **difendere** // *sf* defence.

difet'tare *vi* to be defective; ~ **di** to be lacking in, lack; **difet'tivo, a** *ag* defective.

di'fetto *sm* (mancanza): ~ **di** lack of; shortage of; (di fabbricazione) fault, flaw, defect; (morale) fault, failing, defect; (fisico) defect; **far** ~ to be lacking; **in** ~ at fault; **in the wrong**; **difet'toso, a** *ag* defective, faulty.

diffa'mare *vt* to slander; to libel.

diffe'rente *ag* different.

diffe'renza [diffe'rentsa] *sf* difference; a ~ di unlike.

differenzi'are [differen'tsjare] *vt* to differentiate; ~rsi da to differentiate o.s. from; to differ from.

diffe'rire *vt* to postpone, defer // *vi* to be different.

dif'ficile [dif'fitʃile] *ag* difficult; (*persona*) hard to please, difficult (to please); (*poco probabile*): è ~ che sia libero it is unlikely that he'll be free // *sm* difficult part; difficulty; **difficoltà** *sf inv* difficulty.

dif'fida *sf* (*DIR*) warning, notice.

diffi'dare *vi*: ~ di to be suspicious o distrustful of // *vt* (*DIR*) to warn; ~ qn dal fare qc to warn sb not to do sth, caution sb against doing sth; **diffi'dente** *ag* suspicious, distrustful; **diffi'denza** *sf* suspicion, distrust.

dif'fondere *vt* (*luce, calore*) to diffuse; (*notizie*) to spread, circulate; ~rsi *vr* to spread; **diffusi'one** *sf* diffusion; spread; (*anche di giornale*) circulation; (*FISICA*) scattering; **dif'fuso, a** *pp di* **diffondere** // *ag* (*malattia, fenomeno*) widespread.

difi'lato *av* (*direttamente*) straight, directly; (*subito*) straight away.

difte'rite *sf* (*MED*) diphtheria.

'diga, ghe *sf* dam; (*portuale*) breakwater.

dige'rente [didʒe'rɛnte] *ag* (*apparato*) digestive.

dige'rire [didʒe'rire] *vt* to digest; **digesti'one** *sf* digestion; **diges'tivo, a** *ag* digestive // *sm* (after-dinner) liqueur.

digi'tale [didʒi'tale] *ag* digital; (*delle dita*) finger *cpd*, digital // *sf* (*BOT*) foxglove.

digi'tare [didʒi'tare] *vt, vi* (*INFORM*) to key (in).

digiu'nare [didʒu'nare] *vi* to starve o.s.; (*REL*) to fast; **digi'uno, a** *ag*: essere **digiuno** not to have eaten // *sm* fast; a **digiuno** on an empty stomach.

dignità [diɲɲi'ta] *sf inv* dignity; **di'gni'toso, a** *ag* dignified.

'DIGOS ['digɔs] *sigla f* (= *Divisione Investigazioni Generali e Operazioni Speciali*) police department dealing with political security.

digri'gnare [digriɲ'ɲare] *vt*: ~ i denti to grind one's teeth.

dila'gare *vi* to flood; (*fig*) to spread.

dilani'are *vt* (*preda*) to tear to pieces.

dilapi'dare *vt* to squander, waste.

dila'tare *vt* to dilate; (*gas*) to cause to expand; (*passaggio, cavità*) to open (up); ~rsi *vr* to dilate; (*FISICA*) to expand.

dilazio'nare [dilattsjo'nare] *vt* to delay, defer; **dilazi'one** *sf* delay; (*COMM: di pagamento etc*) extension; (*rinvio*) postponement.

dileggi'are [diled'dʒare] *vt* to mock, deride.

dilegu'are *vi*, ~rsi *vr* to vanish, disappear.

di'lemma, i *sm* dilemma.

dilet'tante *sm/f* dilettante; (*anche SPORT*) amateur.

dilet'tare *vt* to give pleasure to, delight; ~rsi *vr*: ~rsi di to take pleasure in, enjoy.

di'letto, a *ag* dear, beloved // *sm* pleasure, delight.

dili'gente [dili'dʒɛnte] *ag* (*scrupoloso*) diligent; (*accurato*) careful, accurate; **dili'genza** *sf* diligence; care; (*carrozza*) stagecoach.

dilu'ire *vt* to dilute.

dilun'garsi *vr* (*fig*): ~ su to talk at length on o about.

diluvi'are *vb impers* to pour (down).

di'luvio *sm* downpour; (*inondazione, fig*) flood.

dima'grire *vi* to get thinner, lose weight.

dime'nare *vt* to wave, shake; ~rsi *vr* to toss and turn; (*fig*) to struggle; ~ la coda (*sog: cane*) to wag its tail.

dimensi'one *sf* dimension; (*grandezza*) size.

dimenti'canza [dimenti'kantsa] *sf* forgetfulness; (*errore*) oversight, slip; per ~ inadvertently.

dimenti'care *vt* to forget; ~rsi di qc to forget sth.

di'messo, a *pp di* **dimettere** // *ag* (*voce*) subdued; (*uomo, abito*) modest, humble.

di'mettere *vt*: ~ qn da to dismiss sb from; (*dall'ospedale*) to discharge sb from; ~rsi (da) to resign (from).

dimez'zare [dimed'dzare] *vt* to halve.

diminu'ire *vt* to reduce, diminish; (*prezzi*) to bring down, reduce // *vi* to decrease, diminish; (*rumore*) to die down, die away; (*prezzi*) to fall, go down; **diminuzi'one** *sf* decreasing, diminishing.

dimissi'oni *sfpl* resignation *sg*; dare o presentare le ~ to resign, hand in one's resignation.

di'mora *sf* residence.

dimo'rare *vi* to reside.

dimos'trare *vt* to demonstrate, show; (*provare*) to prove, demonstrate; ~rsi *vr*: ~rsi molto abile to show o.s. o prove to be very clever; dimostra 30 anni he looks about 30 (years old); **dimostrazi'one** *sf* demonstration; proof.

di'namico, a, ci, che *ag* dynamic // *sf* dynamics *sg*.

dina'mite *sf* dynamite.

'dinamo *sf inv* dynamo.

di'nanzi [di'nantsi]: ~ a *prep* in front of.

dini'ego, ghi *sm* refusal; denial.

dinocco'lato, a *ag* lanky; camminare ~

to walk with a slouch.

din'torno *av* round, (round) about; ~i *smpl* outskirts; **nei ~i di** in the vicinity *o* neighbourhood of.

'**dio**, *pl* '**dei** *sm* god; D~ God; **gli dei** the gods; D~ **mio!** my goodness!, my God!

di'ocesi [di'ɔtʃezi] *sf inv* diocese.

dipa'nare *vt* (*lana*) to wind into a ball; (*fig*) to disentangle, sort out.

diparti'mento *sm* department.

dipen'dente *ag* dependent // *sm/f* employee; **dipen'denza** *sf* dependence; **essere alle dipendenze di qn** to be employed by sb *o* in sb's employ.

di'pendere *vi*: ~ **da** to depend on; (*finanziariamente*) to be dependent on; (*derivare*) to come from, be due to; **di'peso, a** *pp di* **dipendere**.

di'pingere [di'pindʒere] *vt* to paint; **di'pinto, a** *pp di* **dipingere** // *sm* painting.

di'ploma, i *sm* diploma.

diplo'mare *vt* to award a diploma to, graduate (*US*) // *vi* to obtain a diploma, graduate (*US*).

diplo'matico, a, ci, che *ag* diplomatic // *sm* diplomat.

diploma'zia [diplomat'tsia] *sf* diplomacy.

di'porto *sm*: **imbarcazione** *f* **da ~** pleasure craft.

dira'dare *vt* to thin (out); (*visite*) to reduce, make less frequent; ~**rsi** *vr* to dis perse; (*nebbia*) to clear (up).

dira'mare *vt* to issue // *vi*, ~**rsi** *vr* (*strade*) to branch.

'**dire** *vt* to say; (*segreto, fatto*) to tell; ~ **qc a qn** to tell sb sth; ~ **a qn di fare qc** to tell sb to do sth; ~ **di sì/no** to say yes/ no; **si dice che ...** they say that ...; **si direbbe che ...** it looks (*o* sounds) as though ...; **dica, signora?** (*in un negozio*) yes, Madam, can I help you?

diret'tissimo *sm* (*FERR*) fast (through) train.

di'retto, a *pp di* **dirigere** // *ag* direct // *sm* (*FERR*) through train.

diret'tore, 'trice *sm/f* (*di azienda*) director; manager/ess; (*di scuola elementare*) head (teacher) (*Brit*), principal (*US*); ~ **d'orchestra** conductor.

direzi'one [diret'tsjone] *sf* board of directors; management; (*senso di movimento*) direction; **in ~ di** in the direction of, towards.

diri'gente [diri'dʒɛnte] *sm/f* executive; (*POL*) leader // *ag*: **classe ~** ruling class.

di'rigere [di'ridʒere] *vt* to direct; (*impresa*) to run, manage; (*MUS*) to conduct; ~**rsi** *vr*: ~**rsi verso** *o* **a** to make *o* head for.

dirim'petto *av* opposite; ~ **a** *prep* opposite, facing.

di'ritto, a *ag* straight; (*onesto*) straight, upright // *av* straight, directly; **andare ~** to go straight on // *sm* right side;

(*TENNIS*) forehand; (*MAGLIA*) plain stitch; (*prerogativa*) right; (*leggi, scienza*): **il ~** law; ~**i** *smpl* (*tasse*) duty *sg*; **stare ~** to stand up straight; **aver ~ a qc** to be entitled to sth; ~**i d'autore** royalties.

dirit'tura *sf* (*SPORT*) straight; (*fig*) rectitude.

diroc'cato, a *ag* tumbledown, in ruins.

dirot'tare *vt* (*nave, aereo*) to change the course of; (*aereo: sotto minaccia*) to hijack; (*traffico*) to divert // *vi* (*nave, aereo*) to change course; **dirotta'tore, 'trice** *sm/f* hijacker.

di'rotto, a *ag* (*pioggia*) torrential; (*pianto*) unrestrained; **piovere a ~** to pour, rain cats and dogs; **piangere a ~** to cry one's heart out.

di'rupo *sm* crag, precipice.

disabi'tato, a *ag* uninhabited.

disabitu'arsi *vr*: ~ **a** to get out of the habit of.

disac'cordo *sm* disagreement.

disadat'tato, a *ag* (*PSIC*) maladjusted.

disa'dorno, a *ag* plain, unadorned.

disagi'ato, a [diza'dʒato] *ag* poor, needy; (*vita*) hard.

di'sagio [di'zadʒo] *sm* discomfort; (*disturbo*) inconvenience; (*fig: imbarazzo*) embarrassment; ~**i** *smpl* hardship *sg*, poverty *sg*; **essere a ~** to be ill at ease.

disappro'vare *vt* to disapprove of; **disapprovazi'one** *sf* disapproval.

disap'punto *sm* disappointment.

disar'mare *vt*, *vi* to disarm; **di'sarmo** *sm* (*MIL*) disarmament.

di'sastro *sm* disaster.

disat'tento, a *ag* inattentive; **disattenzi'one** *sf* carelessness, lack of attention.

disa'vanzo [diza'vantso] *sm* (*ECON*) deficit.

disavven'tura *sf* misadventure, mishap.

dis'brigo, ghi *sm* (*prompt*) clearing up *o* settlement.

dis'capito *sm*: **a ~ di** to the detriment of.

dis'carica, che *sf* (*di rifiuti*) rubbish tip *o* dump.

discen'dente [diʃʃen'dente] *ag* descending // *sm/f* descendant.

di'scendere [diʃ'ʃendere] *vt* to go (*o* come) down // *vi* to go (*o* come) down; (*strada*) to go down; (*smontare*) to get off; ~ **da** (*famiglia*) to be descended from; ~ **dalla macchina/dal treno** to get out of the car/out of *o* off the train; ~ **da cavallo** to dismount, get off one's horse.

di'scepolo, a [diʃ'ʃepolo] *sm/f* disciple.

di'scernere [diʃ'ʃernere] *vt* to discern.

di'sceso, a [diʃ'ʃeso] *pp di* **discendere** // *sf* descent; (*pendio*) slope; **in ~a** (*strada*) downhill *cpd*, sloping; ~**a libera** (*SCI*) downhill (race).

disci'ogliere [diʃ'ʃɔʎʎere] *vt*, ~**rsi** *vr* to

dissolve; (*fondere*) to melt; **disci'olto, a** *pp di* **disciogliere.**

disci'plina [diʃʃi'plina] *sf* discipline; **discipli'nare** *ag* disciplinary // *vt* to discipline.

'disco, schi *sm* disc; (*SPORT*) discus; (*fonografico*) record; (*INFORM*) disk; ~ **orario** (*AUT*) parking disc; ~ **rigido** (*IN-FORM*) hard disk; ~ **volante** flying saucer.

discol'pare *vt* to clear of blame.

disco'noscere [disko'noʃʃere] *vt* (*figlio*) to disown; (*meriti*) to ignore, disregard; **disconosci'uto, a** *pp di* **disconoscere**.

dis'corde *ag* conflicting, clashing; **dis'cordia** *sf* discord; (*dissidio*) disagreement, clash.

dis'correre *vi:* ~ (di) to talk (about).

dis'corso, a *pp di* **discorrere** // *sm* speech; (*conversazione*) conversation, talk.

dis'costo, a *ag* faraway, distant // *av* far away; ~ **da** *prep* far from.

disco'teca, che *sf* (*raccolta*) record library; (*luogo di ballo*) disco(thèque).

discre'panza [diskre'pantsa] *sf* disagreement.

dis'creto, a *ag* discreet; (*abbastanza buono*) reasonable, fair; **discrezi'one** *sf* discretion; (*giudizio*) judgment, discernment; **a discrezione di** at the discretion of.

discriminazi'one [diskriminat'tsjone] *sf* discrimination.

discussi'one *sf* discussion; (*litigio*) argument.

dis'cusso, a *pp di* **discutere.**

dis'cutere *vt* to discuss, debate; (*contestare*) to question // *vi* (*conversare*): ~ (di) to discuss; (*litigare*) to argue.

disde'gnare [disdeɲ'ɲare] *vt* to scorn.

dis'detto, a *pp di* **disdire** // *sf* cancellation; (*sfortuna*) bad luck.

dis'dire *vt* (*prenotazione*) to cancel; (*DIR*): ~ **un contratto d'affitto** to give notice (to quit).

dise'gnare [diseɲ'ɲare] *vt* to draw; (*progettare*) to design; (*fig*) to outline; **disegna'tore, 'trice** *sm/f* designer.

di'segno [di'seɲɲo] *sm* drawing; design; outline.

diser'bante *sm* weed-killer.

diser'tare *vt, vi* to desert; **diser'tore** *sm* (*MIL*) deserter.

dis'fare *vt* to undo; (*valigie*) to unpack; (*meccanismo*) to take to pieces; (*lavoro, paese*) to destroy; (*neve*) to melt; ~**rsi** *vr* to come undone; (*neve*) to melt; ~ **il letto** to strip the bed; ~**rsi di qn** (*liberarsi*) to get rid of sb; **dis'fatto, a** *pp di* **disfare** // *sf* (*sconfitta*) rout.

dis'gelo [diz'dʒelo] *sm* thaw.

dis'grazia [diz'grattsja] *sf* (*sventura*) misfortune; (*incidente*) accident, mishap; **disgrazi'ato, a** *ag* unfortunate // *sm/f* wretch.

disgre'gare *vt*, ~**rsi** *vr* to break up.

disgu'ido *sm:* ~ **postale** error in postal delivery.

disgus'tare *vt* to disgust; ~**rsi** *vr:* ~**rsi di** to be disgusted by.

dis'gusto *sm* disgust; **disgus'toso, a** *ag* disgusting.

disidra'tare *vt* to dehydrate.

disil'ludere *vt* to disillusion, disenchant.

disimpa'rare *vt* to forget.

disimpe'gnare [dizimpeɲ'ɲare] *vt* (*persona: da obblighi*): ~ **da** to release from; (*oggetto dato in pegno*) to redeem, get out of pawn; ~**rsi** *vr:* ~**rsi da** (*obblighi*) to release o.s. from, free o.s. from.

disinfet'tante *ag, sm* disinfectant.

disinfet'tare *vt* to disinfect.

disini'bito, a *ag* uninhibited.

disinte'grare *vt, vi* to disintegrate.

disinteres'sarsi *vr:* ~ **di** to take no interest in.

disinte'resse *sm* indifference; (*generosità*) unselfishness.

disintossi'care *vt* (*alcolizzato, drogato*) to treat for alcoholism (*o* drug addiction); ~ **l'organismo** to clear out one's system.

disin'volto, a *ag* casual, free and easy; **disinvol'tura** *sf* casualness, ease.

disles'sia *sf* dyslexia.

dislo'care *vt* to station, position.

dismi'sura *sf* excess; **a** ~ to excess, excessively.

disobbe'dire *etc* = **disubbidire** *etc*.

disoccu'pato, a *ag* unemployed // *sm/f* unemployed person; **disoccupazi'one** *sf* unemployment.

diso'nesto, a *ag* dishonest.

diso'nore *sm* dishonour, disgrace.

di'sopra *av* (*con contatto*) on top; (*senza contatto*) above; (*al piano superiore*) upstairs // *ag inv* (*superiore*) upper // *sm inv* top, upper part.

disordi'nato, a *ag* untidy; (*privo di misura*) irregular, wild.

di'sordine *sm* (*confusione*) disorder, confusion; (*sregolatezza*) debauchery.

disorien'tare *vt* to disorientate; ~**rsi** *vr* (*fig*) to get confused, lose one's bearings.

di'sotto *av* below, underneath; (*in fondo*) at the bottom; (*al piano inferiore*) downstairs // *ag inv* (*inferiore*) lower; bottom *cpd* // *sm inv* (*parte inferiore*) lower part; bottom.

dis'paccio [dis'pattʃo] *sm* dispatch.

'dispari *ag inv* odd, uneven.

dis'parte: in ~ *av* (*da lato*) aside, apart; **tenersi** *o* **starsene in** ~ to keep to o.s., hold aloof.

dispendi'oso, a *ag* expensive.

dis'pensa *sf* pantry, larder; (*mobile*) sideboard; (*DIR*) exemption; (*REL*) dispensation; (*fascicolo*) number, issue.

dispen'sare vt (elemosine, favori) to distribute; (esonerare) to exempt.

dispe'rare vi: ~ (di) to despair (of); ~rsi vr to despair; **dispe'rato, a** ag (persona) in despair; (caso, tentativo) desperate; **disperazi'one** sf despair.

dis'perdere vt (disseminare) to disperse; (MIL) to scatter, rout; (fig: consumare) to waste, squander; ~rsi vr to disperse; to scatter; **dis'perso, a** pp di **disperdere** // sm/f missing person.

dis'petto sm spite q, spitefulness q; fare un ~ a qn to play a (nasty) trick on sb; a ~ di in spite of; **dispet'toso, a** ag spiteful.

dispia'cere [dispja'tʃere] sm (rammarico) regret, sorrow; (dolore) grief; ~i smpl troubles, worries // vi: ~ a to displease // vb impers: mi dispiace (che) I am sorry (that); se non le dispiace, me ne vado adesso if you don't mind, I'll go now; **dispiaci'uto, a** pp di **dispiacere** // ag sorry.

dispo'nibile ag available.

dis'porre vt (sistemare) to arrange; (preparare) to prepare; (DIR) to order; (persuadere): ~ qn a to incline o dispose sb towards // vi (decidere) to decide; (usufruire): ~ di to use, have at one's disposal; (essere dotato): ~ di to have; **disporsi** vr (ordinarsi) to place o.s., arrange o.s.; **disporsi a fare** to get ready to do.

disposi'tivo sm (meccanismo) device.

disposizi'one [dispozit'tsjone] sf arrangement, layout; (stato d'animo) mood; (tendenza) bent, inclination; (comando) order; (DIR) provision, regulation; a ~ di qn at sb's disposal.

dis'posto, a pp di **disporre**.

disprez'zare [dispret'tsare] vt to despise.

dis'prezzo [dis'prettso] sm contempt.

'disputa sf dispute, quarrel.

dispu'tare vt (contendere) to dispute, contest; (gara) to take part in // vi to quarrel; ~ di to discuss; ~rsi qc to fight for sth.

dissan'guare vt (fig: persona) to bleed white; (: patrimonio) to suck dry; ~rsi vr (MED) to lose blood; (fig: rovinarsi) to ruin o.s.

dissec'care vt, ~rsi vr to dry up.

dissemi'nare vt to scatter; (fig: notizie) to spread.

dis'senso sm dissent; (disapprovazione) disapproval.

dissente'ria sf dysentery.

dissen'tire vi: ~ (da) to disagree (with).

dissertazi'one [dissertat'tsjone] sf dissertation.

disser'vizio [disser'vittsjo] sm inefficiency.

disses'tare vt (ECON) to ruin; **dis'sesto** sm (financial) ruin.

disse'tante ag refreshing.

dis'sidio sm disagreement.

dis'simile ag different, dissimilar.

dissimu'lare vt (fingere) to dissemble; (nascondere) to conceal.

dissi'pare vt to dissipate; (scialacquare) to squander, waste.

dis'solto, a pp di **dissolvere**.

disso'lubile ag soluble.

disso'luto, a pp di **dissolvere** // ag dissolute, licentious.

dis'solvere vt to dissolve; (neve) to melt; (fumo) to disperse; ~rsi vr to dissolve; to melt; to disperse.

dissu'adere vt: ~ qn da to dissuade sb from; **dissu'aso, a** pp di **dissuadere**.

distac'care vt to detach, separate; (SPORT) to leave behind; ~rsi vr to be detached; (fig) to stand out; ~rsi da (fig: allontanarsi) to grow away from.

dis'tacco, chi sm (separazione) separation; (fig: indifferenza) detachment; (SPORT): vincere con un ~ di ... to win by a distance of ....

dis'tante av far away // ag: ~ (da) distant (from), far away (from).

dis'tanza [dis'tantsa] sf distance.

distanzi'are [distan'tsjare] vt to space out, place at intervals; (SPORT) to outdistance; (fig: superare) to outstrip, surpass.

dis'tare vi: distiamo pochi chilometri da Roma we are only a few kilometres (away) from Rome.

dis'tendere vt (coperta) to spread out; (gambe) to stretch (out); (mettere a giacere) to lay; (rilassare: muscoli, nervi) to relax; ~rsi vr (rilassarsi) to relax; (sdraiarsi) to lie down; **distensi'one** sf stretching; relaxation; (POL) detente.

dis'teso, a pp di **distendere** // sf expanse, stretch.

distil'lare vt to distil.

distille'ria sf distillery.

dis'tinguere vt to distinguish.

dis'tinta sf (nota) note; (elenco) list.

distin'tivo, a ag distinctive; distinguishing // sm badge.

dis'tinto, a pp di **distinguere** // ag (dignitoso ed elegante) distinguished; ~i saluti (in lettera) yours faithfully.

distinzi'one [distin'tsjone] sf distinction.

dis'togliere [dis'tɔʎʎere] vt: ~ da to take away from; (fig) to dissuade from; **dis'tolto, a** pp di **distogliere**.

distorsi'one sf (MED) sprain; (FISICA, OTTICA) distortion.

dis'trarre vt to distract; (divertire) to entertain, amuse; **distrarsi** vr (non fare attenzione) to be distracted, let one's mind wander; (svagarsi) to amuse o enjoy o.s.; **dis'tratto, a** pp di **distrarre** // ag absent-minded; (disattento) inattentive; **distrazi'one** sf absent-mindedness;

inattention; (*svago*) distraction, entertainment.

dis'tretto *sm* district.

distribu'ire *vt* to distribute; (*CARTE*) to deal (out); (*consegnare: posta*) to deliver; (*lavoro*) to allocate, assign; (*ripartire*) to share out; **distribu'tore** *sm* (*di benzina*) petrol (*Brit*) o gas (*US*) pump; (*AUT, ELETTR*) distributor; (*automatico*) vending machine; **distribuzi'one** *sf* distribution; delivery.

distri'care *vt* to disentangle, unravel.

dis'truggere |dis'truddʒere| *vt* to destroy; **dis'trutto, a** *pp di* **distruggere; distruzi'one** *sf* destruction.

distur'bare *vt* to disturb, trouble; (*sonno, lezioni*) to disturb, interrupt; ~rsi *vr* to put o.s. out.

dis'turbo *sm* trouble, bother, inconvenience; (*indisposizione*) (slight) disorder, ailment; ~i *smpl* (*RADIO, TV*) static *sg*.

disubbidi'ente *ag* disobedient; **disubbidi'enza** *sf* disobedience.

disubbi'dire *vi*: ~ (**a qn**) to disobey (sb).

disugu'ale *ag* unequal; (*diverso*) different; (*irregolare*) uneven.

disu'mano, a *ag* inhuman.

di'suso *sm*: andare o cadere in ~ to fall into disuse.

'dita *fpl di* **dito.**

di'tale *sm* thimble.

'dito, *pl*(*f*) **'dita** *sm* finger; (*misura*) finger, finger's breadth; ~ (**del piede**) toe.

'ditta *sf* firm, business.

ditta'tore *sm* dictator.

ditta'tura *sf* dictatorship.

dit'tongo, ghi *sm* diphthong.

di'urno, a *ag* day *cpd*, daytime *cpd* // *sm* (*anche:* **albergo** ~) public toilets *with washing and shaving facilities etc.*

'diva *sf vedi* **divo.**

diva'gare *vi* to digress.

divam'pare *vi* to flare up, blaze up.

di'vano *sm* sofa; divan.

divari'care *vt* to open wide.

di'vario *sm* difference.

dive'nire *vi* = **diventare; dive'nuto, a** *pp di* **divenire.**

diven'tare *vi* to become; ~ famoso/professore to become famous/a teacher.

di'verbio *sm* altercation.

di'vergere |di'verdʒere| *vi* to diverge.

diversifi'care *vt* to diversify, vary; to differentiate.

diversi'one *sf* diversion.

diversità *sf inv* difference, diversity; (*varietà*) variety.

diver'sivo *sm* diversion, distraction.

di'verso, a *ag* (*differente*): ~ (**da**) different (from); ~i, **e** *det pl* several, various; (*COMM*) sundry // *pronome pl* several (people), many (people).

diver'tente *ag* amusing.

diverti'mento *sm* amusement, pleasure; (*passatempo*) pastime, recreation.

diver'tire *vt* to amuse, entertain; ~rsi *vr* to amuse o enjoy o.s.

divi'dendo *sm* dividend.

di'videre *vt* (*anche MAT*) to divide; (*distribuire, ripartire*) to divide (up), split (up); ~rsi *vr* (*separarsi*) to separate; (*strade*) to fork.

di'vieto *sm* prohibition; "~ **di sosta**" (*AUT*) "no parking".

divinco'larsi *vr* to wriggle, writhe.

divinità *sf inv* divinity.

di'vino, a *ag* divine.

di'visa *sf* (*MIL etc*) uniform; (*COMM*) foreign currency.

divisi'one *sf* division.

di'viso, a *pp di* **dividere.**

'divo, a *sm*/*f* star.

divo'rare *vt* to devour.

divorzi'are |divor'tsjare| *vi*: ~ (**da qn**) to divorce (sb); **divorzi'ato, a** *sm*/*f* divorcee.

di'vorzio |di'vortsjo| *sm* divorce.

divul'gare *vt* to divulge, disclose; (*rendere comprensibile*) to popularize; ~rsi *vr* to spread.

dizio'nario |dittsjo'narjo| *sm* dictionary.

dizi'one |dit'tsjone| *sf* diction; pronunciation.

do *sm* (*MUS*) C; (: *solfeggiando la scala*) do(h).

DOC |dɔk| *abbr* (= *denominazione di origine controllata*) label guaranteeing the quality of wine.

'doccia, ce |'dottʃa| *sf* (*bagno*) shower; (*condotto*) pipe; fare la ~ to have a shower.

do'cente |do'tʃɛnte| *ag* teaching // *sm*/*f* teacher; (*di università*) lecturer; **do'cenza** *sf* university teaching o lecturing.

'docile |'dɔtʃile| *ag* docile.

documen'tare *vt* to document; ~rsi *vr*: ~rsi (**su**) to gather information o material (about).

documen'tario *sm* documentary.

docu'mento *sm* document; ~i *smpl* (*d'identità etc*) papers.

'dodici |'doditʃi| *num* twelve.

do'gana *sf* (*ufficio*) customs *pl*; (*tassa*) (customs) duty; passare la ~ to go through customs; **doga'nale** *ag* customs *cpd*; **dogani'ere** *sm* customs officer.

'doglie |'dɔʎʎe| *sfpl* (*MED*) labour *sg*, labour pains.

'dolce |'doltʃe| *ag* sweet; (*colore*) soft; (*carattere, persona*) gentle, mild; (*fig: mite: clima*) mild; (*non ripido: pendio*) gentle // *sm* (*sapore dolce*) sweetness, sweet taste; (*CUC: portata*) sweet, dessert; (: *torta*) cake; **dol'cezza** *sf* sweetness; softness; mildness; gentleness; **dolci'umi** *smpl* sweets.

do'lente *ag* sorrowful, sad.

do'lere *vi* to be sore, hurt, ache; ~**rsi** *vr* to complain; (*essere spiacente*): ~**rsi di** to be sorry for; **mi duole la testa** my head aches, I've got a headache.

'dollaro *sm* dollar.

'dolo *sm* (*DIR*) malice.

Dolo'miti *sfpl*: **le** ~ the Dolomites.

do'lore *sm* (*fisico*) pain; (*morale*) sorrow, grief; **dolo'roso, a** *ag* painful; sorrowful, sad.

do'loso, a *ag* (*DIR*) malicious.

do'manda *sf* (*interrogazione*) question; (*richiesta*) demand; (: *cortese*) request; (*DIR*: *richiesta scritta*) application; (*ECON*): **la** ~ demand; **fare una** ~ **a qn** to ask sb a question; **fare** ~ (**per un lavoro**) to apply (for a job).

doman'dare *vt* (*per avere*) to ask for; (*per sapere*) to ask; (*esigere*) to demand; ~**rsi** *vr* to wonder; to ask o.s.; ~ **qc a qn** to ask sb for sth; to ask sb sth.

do'mani *av* tomorrow // *sm*: **il** ~ (*il futuro*) the future; (*il giorno successivo*) the next day; ~ **l'altro** the day after tomorrow.

do'mare *vt* to tame.

domat'tina *av* tomorrow morning.

do'menica, che *sf* Sunday; **di** *o* **la** ~ **on** Sundays; **domeni'cale** *ag* Sunday *cpd*.

do'mestica, che *sf vedi* **domestico.**

do'mestico, a, ci, che *ag* domestic // *sm/f* servant, domestic.

domi'cilio [domi'tʃiljo] *sm* (*DIR*) domicile, place of residence.

domi'nare *vt* to dominate; (*fig*: *sentimenti*) to control, master // *vi* to be in the dominant position; ~**rsi** *vr* (*controllarsi*) to control o.s.; ~ **su** (*fig*) to surpass, outclass; **dominazi'one** *sf* domination.

do'minio *sm* dominion; (*fig*: *campo*) field, domain.

do'nare *vt* to give, present; (*per beneficenza etc*) to donate // *vi* (*fig*): ~ **a** to suit, become; ~ **sangue** to give blood; **dona'tore, 'trice** *sm/f* donor; **donatore di sangue/di organi** blood/organ donor.

dondo'lare *vt* (*cullare*) to rock; ~**rsi** *vr* to swing, sway; **'dondolo** *sm*: **sedia/cavallo a dondolo** rocking chair/horse.

'donna *sf* woman; ~ **di casa** housewife; home-loving woman; ~ **di servizio** maid.

donnai'olo *sm* ladykiller.

don'nesco, a, schi, sche *ag* women's, woman's.

'donnola *sf* weasel.

'dono *sm* gift.

'dopo *av* (*tempo*) afterwards; (: *più tardi*) later; (*luogo*) after, next // *prep* after // *cong* (*temporale*): ~ **aver studiato** after having studied; ~ **mangiato va a dormire** after having

eaten *o* after a meal he goes for a sleep // *ag inv*: **il giorno** ~ the following day; **un anno** ~ a year later; ~ **di me/lui** after me/him.

dopo'barba *sm inv* after-shave.

dopodo'mani *av* the day after tomorrow.

dopogu'erra *sm* postwar years *pl*.

dopo'pranzo [dopo'prandzo] *av* after lunch (*o* dinner).

doposci [dopoʃ'ʃi] *sm inv* après-ski outfit.

doposcu'ola *sm inv* school club offering extra tuition and recreational facilities.

dopo'tutto *av* (*tutto considerato*) after all.

doppi'aggio [dop'pjaddʒo] *sm* (*CINEMA*) dubbing.

doppi'are *vt* (*NAUT*) to round; (*SPORT*) to lap; (*CINEMA*) to dub.

'doppio, a *ag* double; (*fig*: *falso*) double-dealing, deceitful // *sm* (*quantità*): **il** ~ (**di**) twice as much (*o* many), double the amount (*o* number) of; (*SPORT*) doubles *pl* // *av* double.

doppi'one *sm* duplicate (copy).

doppio'petto *sm* double-breasted jacket.

do'rare *vt* to gild; (*CUC*) to brown; **do'rato, a** *ag* golden; (*ricoperto d'oro*) gilt, gilded; **dora'tura** *sf* gilding.

dormicchi'are [dormik'kjarc] *vi* to doze.

dormigli'one, a [dormiʎ'ʎone] *sm/f* sleepyhead.

dor'mire *vt, vi* to sleep; **dor'mita** *sf*: **farsi una dormita** to have a good sleep.

dormi'torio *sm* dormitory.

dormi'veglia [dormi'veʎʎa] *sm* drowsiness.

'dorso *sm* back; (*di montagna*) ridge, crest; (*di libro*) spine; **a** ~ **di cavallo** on horseback.

do'sare *vt* to measure out; (*MED*) to dose.

'dose *sf* quantity, amount; (*MED*) dose.

'dosso *sm* (*rilievo*) rise; (*di strada*) bump; (*dorso*): **levarsi di** ~ **i vestiti** to take one's clothes off.

do'tare *vt*: ~ **di** to provide *o* supply with; (*fig*) to endow with; **dotazi'one** *sf* (*insieme di beni*) endowment; (*di macchine etc*) equipment.

'dote *sf* (*di sposa*) dowry; (*assegnata a un ente*) endowment; (*fig*) gift, talent.

Dott. *abbr* (= *dottore*) Dr.

'dotto, a *ag* (*colto*) learned // *sm* (*sapiente*) scholar; (*ANAT*) duct.

dotto'rato *sm* degree; ~ **di ricerca** doctorate, doctor's degree.

dot'tore, essa *sm/f* doctor.

dot'trina *sf* doctrine.

Dott.ssa *abbr* (= *dottoressa*) Dr.

'dove ♦ *av* (*gen*) where; (*in cui*) where, in which; (*dovunque*) wherever; ~ **sei?/vai?** where are you?/are you going?;

dimmi dov'è tell me where it is; di ~ sei? where are you from?; per ~ si passa? which way should we go?; la città ~ abito the town where o in which I live; siediti ~ vuoi sit wherever you like ◆ *cong* (*mentre, laddove*) whereas.

do'vere *sm* (*obbligo*) duty // *vt* (*essere debitore*): ~ **qc** (**a qn**) to owe (sb) sth // *vi* (*seguito dall'infinito: obbligo*) to have to; **rivolgersi a chi di** ~ to apply to the appropriate authority o person; **lui deve farlo** he has to do it, he must do it; **è dovuto partire** he had to leave; **ha dovuto pagare** he had to pay; (*: intenzione*): **devo partire domani** I'm (due) to leave tomorrow; (*: probabilità*) **dev'essere tardi** it must be late; **come si deve** (*lavorare, comportarsi*) properly; **una persona come si deve** a respectable person.

dove'roso, a *ag* (right and) proper.

do'vunque *av* (*in qualunque luogo*) wherever; (*dappertutto*) everywhere; ~ **io vada** wherever I go.

do'vuto, a *ag* (*causato*): ~ **a** due to.

doz'zina [dod'dzina] *sf* dozen; **una** ~ **di uova** a dozen eggs.

dozzi'nale [doddzi'nale] *ag* cheap, second-rate.

dra'gare *vt* to dredge.

'drago, ghi *sm* dragon.

'dramma, i *sm* drama; **dram'matico, a, ci, che** *ag* dramatic; **drammatiz'zare** *vt* to dramatize; **dramma'turgo, ghi** *sm* playwright, dramatist.

drappeggi'are [draped'dʒare] *vt* to drape.

drap'pello *sm* (MIL) squad; (*gruppo*) band, group.

'drastico, a, ci, che *ag* drastic.

dre'naggio [dre'naddʒo] *sm* drainage.

dre'nare *vt* to drain.

'dritto, a *ag, av* = diritto.

driz'zare [drit'tsare] *vt* (*far tornare diritto*) to straighten; (*volgere: sguardo, occhi*) to turn, direct; (*innalzare: antenna, muro*) to erect; ~**rsi** *vr*: ~**rsi (in piedi)** to stand up; ~ **le orecchie** to prick up one's ears.

'droga, ghe *sf* (*sostanza aromatica*) spice; (*stupefacente*) drug; **dro'gare** *vt* to season, spice; to drug, dope; **drogarsi** *vr* to take drugs; **dro'gato, a** *sm/f* drug addict.

droghe'ria [droge'ria] *sf* grocer's shop (*Brit*), grocery (store) (*US*).

'dubbio, a *ag* (*incerto*) doubtful, dubious; (*ambiguo*) dubious // *sm* (*incertezza*) doubt; **avere il** ~ **che** to be afraid that, suspect that; **mettere in** ~ **qc** to question sth; **dubbi'oso, a** *ag* doubtful, dubious.

dubi'tare *vi*: ~ **di** to doubt; (*risultato*) to be doubtful of.

Dub'lino *sf* Dublin.

'duca, chi *sm* duke.

du'chessa [du'kessa] *sf* duchess.

'due *num* two.

due'cento [due'tʃento] *num* two hundred // *sm*: **il D~** the thirteenth century.

due'pezzi [due'pettsi] *sm* (*costume da bagno*) two-piece swimsuit; (*abito femminile*) two-piece suit.

du'etto *sm* duet.

'dunque *cong* (*perciò*) so, therefore; (*riprendendo il discorso*) well (then) // *sm inv*: **venire al** ~ to come to the point.

du'omo *sm* cathedral.

'duplex *sm inv* (TEL) party line.

dupli'cato *sm* duplicate.

'duplice ['duplitʃe] *ag* double, twofold; **in** ~ **copia** in duplicate.

du'rante *prep* during.

du'rare *vi* to last; ~ **fatica a** to have difficulty in; **du'rata** *sf* length (of time); duration; **dura'turo, a** *ag*, **du'revole** *ag* lasting.

du'rezza [du'rettsa] *sf* hardness; stubbornness; harshness; toughness.

'duro, a *ag* (*pietra, lavoro, materasso, problema*) hard; (*persona: ostinato*) stubborn, obstinate; (*: severo*) harsh, hard; (*voce*) harsh; (*carne*) tough // *sm* hardness; (*difficoltà*) hard part; (*persona*) tough guy; **tener** ~ to stand firm, hold out; ~ **d'orecchi** hard of hearing.

du'rone *sm* hard skin.

E

e, *dav V spesso* **ed** *cong* and; ~ **lui?** what about him?; ~ **compralo!** well buy it then!

E. *abbr* (= *est*) E.

è *vb vedi* **essere**.

'ebano *sm* ebony.

eb'bene *cong* well (then).

eb'brezza [eb'brettsa] *sf* intoxication.

'ebbro, a *ag* drunk; ~ **di** (*gioia etc*) beside o.s. o wild with.

'ebete *ag* stupid, idiotic.

ebollizi'one [ebollit'tsjone] *sf* boiling; **punto di** ~ boiling point.

e'braico, a, ci, che *ag* Hebrew, Hebraic // *sm* (LING) Hebrew.

e'breo, a *ag* Jewish // *sm/f* Jew/Jewess.

'Ebridi *sfpl*: **le (isole)** ~ the Hebrides.

ecc *av abbr* (= eccetera) etc.

ecce'denza [ettʃe'dɛntsa] *sf* excess, surplus.

ec'cedere [et'tʃedere] *vt* to exceed // *vi* to go too far; ~ **nel bere/mangiare** to indulge in drink/food to excess.

eccel'lente [ettʃel'lɛnte] *ag* excellent; **eccel'lenza** *sf* excellence; (*titolo*) Excellency.

ec'cellere [et'tʃellere] *vi*: ~ **(in)** to excel

(at); **ec'celso, a** *pp di* **eccellere.**

ec'centrico, a, ci, che [et'tʃɛntriko] *ag* eccentric.

ecces'sivo, a [ettʃes'sivo] *ag* excessive.

ec'cesso [et'tʃɛsso] *sm* excess; **all'~** (*gentile, generoso*) to excess, excessively; **~ di velocità** (*AUT*) speeding.

ec'cetera [et'tʃetera] *av* et cetera, and so on.

ec'cetto [et'tʃetto] *prep* except, with the exception of; **~ che** *cong* except, other than; **~ che (non)** unless.

eccettu'are [ettʃettu'are] *vt* to except.

eccezio'nale [ettʃetsjo'nale] *ag* exceptional.

eccezi'one [ettʃet'tsjone] *sf* exception; (*DIR*) objection; **a ~ di** with the exception of, except for; **d'~** exceptional.

ec'cidio [et'tʃidjo] *sm* massacre.

ecci'tare [ettʃi'tare] *vt* (*curiosità, interesse*) to excite, arouse; (*folla*) to incite; **~rsi** *vr* to get excited; (*sessualmente*) to become aroused; **eccitazi'one** *sf* excitement.

'ecco *av* (*per dimostrare*): **~ il treno!** here's *o* here comes the train!; (*dav pronome*): **~mi!** here I am!; **~ne uno!** here's one (of them)!; (*dav pp*): **~ fatto!** there, that's it done!

echeggi'are [eked'dʒare] *vi* to echo.

e'clissi *sf* eclipse.

'eco, *pl(m)* **'echi** *sm o f* echo.

ecolo'gia [ekolo'dʒia] *sf* ecology.

econo'mia *sf* economy; (*scienza*) economics *sg*; (*risparmio: azione*) saving; **fare ~** to economize, make economies; **eco'nomico, a, ci, che** *ag* economic; (*poco costoso*) economical; **econo'mista, i** *sm* economist; **economiz'zare** *vt, vi* to save; **e'conomo, a** *ag* thrifty // *sm/f* (*INS*) bursar.

ed *cong vedi* **e.**

'edera *sf* ivy.

e'dicola *sf* newspaper kiosk o stand (*US*).

edifi'care *vt* to build; (*fig: teoria, azienda*) to establish; (*indurre al bene*) to edify.

edi'ficio [edi'fitʃo] *sm* building; (*fig*) structure.

e'dile *ag* building *cpd*; **edi'lizio, a** *ag* building *cpd* // *sf* building, building trade.

Edim'burgo *sf* Edinburgh.

edi'tore, 'trice *ag* publishing *cpd* // *sm/f* publisher; (*curatore*) editor; **edito'ria** *sf* publishing; **editori'ale** *ag* publishing *cpd* // *sm* editorial, leader.

edizi'one [edit'tsjone] *sf* edition; (*tiratura*) printing; (*di manifestazioni, feste etc*) production.

edu'care *vt* to educate; (*gusto, mente*) to train; **~ qn a fare** to train sb to do; **edu'cato, a** *ag* polite, well-mannered; **educazi'one** *sf* education; (*familiare*) upbringing; (*comportamento*) (good) manners *pl*; **educazione fisica** (*INS*) physical training *o* education.

effemi'nato, a *ag* effeminate.

effet'tivo, a *ag* (*reale*) real, actual; (*impiegato, professore*) permanent; (*MIL*) regular // *sm* (*MIL*) strength; (*di patrimonio etc*) sum total.

ef'fetto *sm* effect; (*COMM: cambiale*) bill; (*fig: impressione*) impression; **in ~i** in fact, actually; **effettu'are** *vt* to effect, carry out.

effi'cace [effi'katʃe] *ag* effective.

effici'ente [effi'tʃɛnte] *ag* efficient; **effici'enza** *sf* efficiency.

ef'fimero, a *ag* ephemeral.

E'geo [e'dʒɛo] *sm*: **l'~, il mare ~** the Aegean (Sea).

E'gitto [e'dʒitto] *sm*: **l'~** Egypt.

egizi'ano, a [edʒit'sjano] *ag, sm/f* Egyptian.

'egli ['eʎʎi] *pronome* he; **~ stesso** he himself.

ego'ismo *sm* selfishness, egoism; **ego'ista, i, e** *ag* selfish, egoistic // *sm/f* egoist.

egr. *abbr* = **egregio.**

e'gregio, a, gi, gie [e'grɛdʒo] *ag* distinguished; (*nelle lettere*): **E~ Signore** Dear Sir.

eguagli'anza [egwaʎ'ʎantsa] *etc vedi* **uguaglianza** *etc.*

E.I. *abbr* = **Esercito Italiano.**

elabo'rare *vt* (*progetto*) to work out, elaborate; (*dati*) to process; (*digerire*) to digest; **elabora'tore** *sm* (*INFORM*): **elaboratore elettronico** computer; **elaborazi'one** *sf* elaboration; digestion; **elaborazione dei dati** data processing.

e'lastico, a, ci, che *ag* elastic; (*fig: andatura*) springy; (*: decisione, vedute*) flexible // *sm* (*gommino*) rubber band; (*per il cucito*) elastic *q*.

ele'fante *sm* elephant.

ele'gante *ag* elegant.

e'leggere [e'leddʒere] *vt* to elect.

elemen'tare *ag* elementary; **le (scuole) ~i** *sfpl* primary (*Brit*) *o* grade (*US*) school.

ele'mento *sm* element; (*parte componente*) element, component, part; **~i** *smpl* (*della scienza etc*) elements, rudiments.

ele'mosina *sf* charity, alms *pl*; **chiedere l'~** to beg.

elen'care *vt* to list.

e'lenco, chi *sm* list; **~ telefonico** telephone directory.

e'letto, a *pp di* **eleggere** // *sm/f* (*nominato*) elected member; **elet'to'rale** *ag* electoral, election *cpd*; **eletto'rato** *sm* electorate; **elet'tore, 'trice** *sm/f* voter, elector.

elet'trauto *sm inv* workshop for car electrical repairs; (*tecnico*) car electrician.

elettri'cista, i [elettri'tʃista] *sm* electrician.

elettricità [elettritʃi'ta] *sf* electricity.

e'lettrico, a, ci, che *ag* electric(al).

elettriz'zare [elettrid'dzare] *vt* to electrify.

e'lettro... *prefisso:* **elettrocardio'gramma, i** *sm* electrocardiogram; **elet'trodo'mestico, a, ci, che** *ag:* **apparecchi elettrodomestici** domestic (electrical) appliances; **elet'trone** *sm* electron; **elet'tronico, a, ci, che** *ag* electronic // *sf* electronics *sg*.

ele'vare *vt* to raise; *(edificio)* to erect; *(multa)* to impose.

elezi'one [elet'tsjone] *sf* election; ~**i** *sfpl* (POL) election(s).

'elica, che *sf* propeller.

eli'cottero *sm* helicopter.

elimi'nare *vt* to eliminate; **elimina'toria** *sf* eliminating round.

'elio *sm* helium.

'ella *pronome* she; *(forma di cortesia)* you; ~ **stessa** she herself; you yourself.

el'metto *sm* helmet.

e'logio [e'lɔdʒo] *sm* (*discorso, scritto*) eulogy; *(lode)* praise *(di solito q)*.

elo'quente *ag* eloquent.

e'ludere *vt* to evade; **elu'sivo, a** *ag* evasive.

ema'nare *vt* to send out, give off; *(fig: leggi, decreti)* to issue // *vi:* ~ **da** to come from.

emanci'pare [emantʃi'pare] *vt* to emancipate; ~**rsi** *vr (fig)* to become liberated *o* emancipated.

embri'one *sm* embryo.

emenda'mento *sm* amendment.

emen'dare *vt* to amend.

emer'genza [emer'dʒɛntsa] *sf* emergency; **in caso di** ~ in an emergency.

e'mergere [e'mɛrdʒere] *vi* to emerge; *(sommergibile)* to surface; *(fig: distinguersi)* to stand out; **e'merso, a** *pp di* **emergere.**

e'messo, a *pp di* **emettere.**

e'mettere *vt (suono, luce)* to give out, emit; *(onde radio)* to send out; *(assegno, francobollo, ordine)* to issue; *(fig: giudizio)* to express, voice.

emi'crania *sf* migraine.

emi'grare *vi* to emigrate; **emigrazi'one** *sf* emigration.

emi'nente *ag* eminent, distinguished.

emis'fero *sm* hemisphere; ~ **boreale/australe** northern/southern hemisphere.

emissi'one *sf (vedi emettere)* emission; sending out; issue; *(RADIO)* broadcast.

emit'tente *ag (banca)* issuing; *(RADIO)* broadcasting, transmitting // *sf (RADIO)* transmitter.

emorra'gia, 'gie [emorra'dʒia] *sf* haemorrhage.

emo'tivo, a *ag* emotional.

emozio'nante [emottsjo'nante] *ag* exciting, thrilling.

emozio'nare [emottsjo'nare] *vt (appassionare)* to thrill, excite; *(commuovere)* to move; *(innervosire)* to upset; ~**rsi** *vr* to be excited; to be moved; to be upset.

emozi'one [emot'tsjone] *sf* emotion; *(agitazione)* excitement.

'empio, a *ag (sacrilego)* impious; *(spietato)* cruel, pitiless; *(malvagio)* wicked, evil.

emulsi'one *sf* emulsion.

enciclope'dia [entʃiklope'dia] *sf* encyclopaedia.

endove'noso, a *ag* (MED) intravenous.

'ENEL ['enel] *sigla m* (= *Ente Nazionale per l'Energia Elettrica*) ≈ C.E.G.B. (= *Central Electricity Generating Board*).

ener'gia, 'gie [ener'dʒia] *sf (FISICA)* energy; *(fig)* energy, strength, vigour; **e'nergico, a, ci, che** *ag* energetic, vigorous.

'enfasi *sf* emphasis; *(peg)* bombast, pomposity; **en'fatico, a, ci, che** *ag* emphatic; pompous.

'ENIT ['enit] *sigla m* = *Ente Nazionale Italiano per il Turismo.*

en'nesimo, a *ag* (MAT, fig) nth; per **l'~a volta** for the umpteenth time.

e'norme *ag* enormous, huge; **enormità** *sf inv* enormity, huge size; *(assurdità)* absurdity; **non dire enormità!** don't talk nonsense!

'ente *sm (istituzione)* body, board, corporation; *(FILOSOFIA)* being.

en'trambi, e *pronome pl* both (of them) // *ag pl:* ~ **i ragazzi** both boys, both of the boys.

en'trare *vi* to enter, go *(o come)* in; ~ **in** *(luogo)* to enter, go *(o come)* into; *(trovar posto, poter stare)* to fit into; *(essere ammesso a: club etc)* to join, become a member of; ~ **in automobile** to get into the car; **far** ~ **qn** *(visitatore etc)* to show sb in; **questo non c'entra** *(fig)* that's got nothing to do with it; **en'trata** *sf* entrance, entry; **entrate** *sfpl (COMM)* receipts, takings; *(ECON)* income *sg*.

'entro *prep (temporale)* within.

entusias'mare *vt* to excite, fill with enthusiasm; ~**rsi** **(per qc/qn)** to become enthusiastic (about sth/sb); **entusi'asmo** *sm* enthusiasm; **entusi'asta, i, e** *ag* enthusiastic // *sm/f* enthusiast; **entusi'astico, a, ci, che** *ag* enthusiastic.

enunci'are [enun'tʃare] *vt (teoria)* to enunciate, set out.

'epico, a, ci, che *ag* epic.

epide'mia *sf* epidemic.

epi'dermide *sf* skin, epidermis.

Epifa'nia *sf* Epiphany.

epiles'sia *sf* epilepsy.

e'pilogo, ghi sm conclusion.

epi'sodio sm episode.

e'piteto sm epithet.

'epoca, che sf (periodo storico) age, era; (tempo) time; (GEO) age.

ep'pure cong and yet, nevertheless.

epu'rare vt (POL) to purge.

equa'tore sm equator.

equazi'one [ekwat'tsjone] sf (MAT) equation.

e'questre ag equestrian.

equi'latero, a ag equilateral.

equili'brare vt to balance; **equi'librio** sm balance, equilibrium; perdere l'~ to lose one's balance.

e'quino, a ag horse cpd, equine.

equipaggi'are [ekwipad'dʒare] vt (di persone) to man; (di mezzi) to equip; **equi'paggio** sm crew.

equipa'rare vt to make equal.

equità sf equity, fairness.

equitazi'one [ekwitat'tsjone] sf (horse-) riding.

equiva'lente ag, sm equivalent; **equiva'lenza** sf equivalence.

equivo'care vi to misunderstand; **e'quivoco, a, ci, che** ag equivocal, ambiguous; (sospetto) dubious // sm misunderstanding; a scanso di equivoci to avoid any misunderstanding; giocare sull'equivoco to equivocate.

'equo, a ag fair, just.

'era sf era.

'erba sf grass; (aromatica, medicinale) herb; in ~ (fig) budding; **er'baccia, ce** sf weed.

e'rede sm/f heir; **eredità** sf (DIR) inheritance; (BIOL) heredity; lasciare qc in eredità a qn to leave o bequeath sth to sb; **eredi'tare** vt to inherit; **eredi'tario, a** ag hereditary.

ere'mita, i sm hermit.

ere'sia sf heresy; **e'retico, a, ci, che** ag heretical // sm/f heretic.

e'retto, a pp di erigere // ag erect, upright; **erezi'one** sf (FISIOL) erection.

er'gastolo sm (DIR: pena) life imprisonment.

'erica sf heather.

e'rigere [e'ridʒere] vt to erect, raise; (fig: fondare) to found.

ermel'lino sm ermine.

er'metico, a, ci, che ag hermetic.

'ernia sf (MED) hernia.

e'roe sm hero.

ero'gare vt (somme) to distribute; (: per beneficenza) to donate; (gas, servizi) to supply.

e'roico, a, ci, che ag heroic.

ero'ina sf heroine; (droga) heroin.

ero'ismo sm heroism.

erosi'one sf erosion.

e'rotico, a, ci, che ag erotic.

er'rare vi (vagare) to wander, roam; (sbagliare) to be mistaken.

er'rore sm error, mistake; (morale) error; per ~ by mistake.

'erta sf steep slope; stare all'~ to be on the alert.

erut'tare vt (sog: vulcano) to throw out, belch.

eruzi'one [erut'tsjone] sf eruption.

esacer'bare [ezatʃer'bare] vt to exacerbate.

esage'rare [ezadʒe'rare] vt to exaggerate // vi to exaggerate; (eccedere) to go too far; **esagerazi'one** sf exaggeration.

e'sagono sm hexagon.

esal'tare vt to exalt; (entusiasmare) to excite, stir; **esal'tato, a** sm/f fanatic.

e'same sm examination; (INS) exam, examination; fare o dare un ~ to sit o take an exam; ~ del sangue blood test.

esami'nare vt to examine.

e'sanime ag lifeless.

esaspe'rare vt to exasperate; to exacerbate; ~rsi vr to become annoyed o exasperated; **esasperazi'one** sf exasperation.

esatta'mente av exactly; accurately, precisely.

esat'tezza [ezat'tettsa] sf exactitude, accuracy, precision.

e'satto, a pp di esigere // ag (calcolo, ora) correct, right, exact; (preciso) accurate, precise; (puntuale) punctual.

esat'tore sm (di imposte etc) collector.

esau'dire vt to grant, fulfil.

esauri'ente ag exhaustive.

esauri'mento sm exhaustion; ~ nervoso nervous breakdown.

esau'rire vt (stancare) to exhaust, wear out; (provviste, miniera) to exhaust; ~rsi vr to exhaust o.s., wear o.s. out; (provviste) to run out; **esau'rito, a** ag exhausted; (merci) sold out; (libri) out of print; registrare il tutto esaurito (TEATRO) to have a full house; **e'sausto, a** ag exhausted.

'esca, pl esche sf bait.

escande'scenza [eskandeʃ'ʃentsa] sf: dare in ~e to lose one's temper, fly into a rage.

'esce, 'esci ['ɛʃe, 'ɛʃi] vb vedi uscire.

eschi'mese [eski'mese] ag, sm/f Eskimo.

escla'mare vi to exclaim, cry out; **esclamazi'one** sf exclamation.

es'cludere vt to exclude.

esclu'sivo, a ag exclusive // sf (DIR, COMM) exclusive o sole rights pl.

es'cluso, a pp di escludere.

'esco, 'escono vb vedi uscire.

escursi'one sf (gita) excursion, trip; (: a piedi) hike, walk; (METEOR) range.

ese'crare vt to loathe, abhor.

esecu'tivo, a ag, sm executive.

esecu'tore, 'trice sm/f (MUS) performer; (DIR) executor.

esecuzi'one [ezekut'tsjone] sf execution, carrying out; (MUS) performance; ~

capitale execution.

esegu'ire vt to carry out, execute; (MUS) to perform, execute.

e'sempio sm example; per ~ for example, for instance; fare un ~ to give an example; **esem'plare** ag exemplary // sm example; (copia) copy; **esemplifi'care** vt to exemplify.

esen'tare vt: ~ qn/qc da to exempt sb/sth from.

e'sente ag: ~ da (dispensato da) exempt from; (privo di) free from; **esenzi'one** sf exemption.

e'sequie sfpl funeral rites; funeral service sg.

eser'cente [ezer'tʃɛnte] sm/f trader, dealer; shopkeeper.

eserci'tare [ezertʃi'tare] vt (professione) to practise (Brit), practice (US); (allenare: corpo, mente) to exercise, train; (diritto) to exercise; (influenza, pressione) to exert; ~rsi vr to practise; ~rsi alla lotta to practise fighting; **esercitazi'one** sf (scolastica, militare) exercise.

e'sercito [e'zertʃito] sm army.

eser'cizio [ezer'tʃittsjo] sm practice; exercising; (fisico, di matematica) exercise; (ECON) financial year; (azienda) business, concern; in ~ (medico etc) practising.

esi'bire vt to exhibit, display; (documenti) to produce, present; ~rsi vr (attore) to perform; (fig) to show off; **esibizi'one** sf exhibition; (di documento) presentation; (spettacolo) show, performance.

esi'gente [ezi'dʒɛnte] ag demanding; **esi'genza** sf demand, requirement.

esi'gere [e'zidʒere] vt (pretendere) to demand; (richiedere) to demand, require; (imposte) to collect.

e'siguo, a ag small, slight.

'esile ag (persona) slender, slim; (stelo) thin; (voce) faint.

esili'are vt to exile; **e'silio** sm exile.

e'simere vt: ~ qn/qc da to exempt sb/sth from; ~rsi vr: ~rsi da to get out of.

esis'tenza [ezis'tɛntsa] sf existence.

esis'tere vi to exist.

esis'tito, a pp di esistere.

esi'tare vi to hesitate; **esitazi'one** sf hesitation.

'esito sm result, outcome.

'esodo sm exodus.

esone'rare vt: ~ qn da to exempt sb from.

e'sordio sm début.

esor'tare vt: ~ qn a fare to urge sb to do.

e'sotico, a, ci, che ag exotic.

es'pandere vt to expand; (confini) to extend; (influenza) to extend, spread; ~rsi vr to expand; **espansi'one** sf expansion; **espan'sivo, a** ag expansive,

communicative.

espatri'are vi to leave one's country.

espedi'ente sm expedient.

es'pellere vt to expel.

esperi'enza [espe'rjɛntsa] sf experience; (SCIENZA: prova) experiment.

esperi'mento sm experiment.

es'perto, a ag, sm expert.

espi'are vt to atone for.

espi'rare vt, vi to breathe out.

espli'care vt (attività) to carry out, perform.

es'plicito, a [es'plitʃito] ag explicit.

es'plodere vi (anche fig) to explode // vt to fire.

esplo'rare vt to explore; **esplora'tore** sm explorer; (anche: giovane esploratore) (boy) scout; (NAUT) scout (ship).

esplosi'one sf explosion; **esplo'sivo, a** ag, sm explosive; **es'ploso, a** pp di esplodere.

espo'nente sm/f (rappresentante) representative.

es'porre vt (merci) to display; (quadro) to exhibit, show; (fatti, idee) to explain, set out; (porre in pericolo, FOT) to expose.

espor'tare vt to export; **esportazi'one** sf exportation; export.

esposizi'one [espozit'tsjone] sf displaying; exhibiting; setting out; (anche FOT) exposure; (mostra) exhibition; (narrazione) explanation, exposition.

es'posto, a pp di esporre // ag: ~ a nord facing north // sm (AMM) statement, account; (: petizione) petition.

espressi'one sf expression.

espres'sivo, a ag expressive.

es'presso, a pp di esprimere // ag express // sm (lettera) express letter; (anche: treno ~) express train; (anche: caffè ~) espresso.

es'primere vt to express; ~rsi vr to express o.s.

espulsi'one sf expulsion; **es'pulso, a** pp di espellere.

'essa pronome f, **'esse** pronome fpl vedi esso.

es'senza [es'sɛntsa] sf essence; **essenzi'ale** ag essential; **l'essenziale** the main o most important thing.

'essere ♦ sm being; ~ umano human being

♦ vb copulativo 1 (con attributo, sostantivo) to be; sei giovane/simpatico you are o you're young/nice; è medico he is o he's a doctor

2 (+ di: appartenere) to be; di chi è la penna? whose pen is it?; è di Carla it is o it's Carla's, it belongs to Carla

3 (+ di: provenire) to be; è di Venezia he is o he's from Venice

4 (data, ora): è il 15 agosto/lunedì it is o it's the 15th of August/Monday; che ora è?, che ore sono? what time is it?; è

l'una it is *o* it's one o'clock; **sono le due**
it is *o* it's two o'clock
5 (*costare*): **quant'è?** how much is it?;
sono 20.000 lire it's 20,000 lire
◆ *vb ausiliare* **1** (*attivo*): ~ **arrivato/**
venuto to have arrived/come; **è già**
partita she has already left
2 (*passivo*) to be; ~ **fatto da** to be made
by; **è stata uccisa** she has been killed
3 (*riflessivo*): **si sono lavati** they
washed, they got washed
4 (+ *da* + *infinito*): **è da farsi subito** it
must be *o* is to be done immediately
◆ *vi* **1** (*esistere*, *trovarsi*) to be; **sono a**
casa I'm at home; ~ **in piedi/seduto** to
be standing/sitting
2: **esserci**: **c'è** there is; **ci sono** there
are; **che c'è?** what's the matter?, what
is it?; **ci sono!** (*fig*: *ho capito*) I get it!;
vedi anche **ci**
◆ *vb impers*: **è tardi/Pasqua** it's late/
Easter; **è possibile che venga** he may
come; **è così** that's the way it is.
'esso, a *pronome* it; (*riferito a persona*:
soggetto) he/she; (: *complemento*) him/
her; ~**i**, **e** *pronome* *pl* they;
(*complemento*) them.
est *sm* east.
'estasi *sf* ecstasy.
es'tate *sf* summer.
es'tatico, a, ci, che *ag* ecstatic.
es'tendere *vt* to extend; ~**rsi** *vr*
(*diffondersi*) to spread; (*territorio*, *con-*
fini) to extend; **estensi'one** *sf* extension; (*di superficie*) expanse; (*di voce*)
range.
esteri'ore *ag* outward, external.
es'terno, a *ag* (*porta*, *muro*) outer, outside; (*scala*) outside; (*alunno*,
impressione) external // *sm* outside,
exterior // *sm/f* (*allievo*) day pupil; **per**
uso ~ for external use only.
'estero, a *ag* foreign // *sm*: **all'~** abroad.
es'teso, a *pp di* **estendere** // *ag*
extensive, large; **scrivere per ~** to write
in full.
es'tetico, a, ci, che *ag* aesthetic // *sf*
(*disciplina*) aesthetics *sg*; (*bellezza*)
attractiveness; **este'tista, i, e** *sm/f*
beautician.
'estimo *sm* valuation; (*disciplina*)
surveying.
es'tinguere *vt* to extinguish, put out;
(*debito*) to pay off; ~**rsi** *vr* to go out;
(*specie*) to become extinct; **es'tinto, a**
pp di **estinguere**; **estin'tore** *sm* (*fire*)
extinguisher; **estinzi'one** *sf* putting out;
(*di specie*) extinction.
estir'pare *vt* (*pianta*) to uproot, pull up;
(*fig*: *vizio*) to eradicate.
es'tivo, a *ag* summer *cpd*.
es'torcere [es'tortʃere] *vt*: ~ **qc** (**a qn**) to
extort sth (from sb); **es'torto, a** *pp di*
estorcere.
estradizi'one [estradit'tsjone] *sf* extradi-

tion.
es'traneo, a *ag* foreign; (*discorso*)
extraneous, unrelated // *sm/f* stranger;
rimanere ~ a qc to take no part in sth.
es'trarre *vt* to extract; (*minerali*) to
mine; (*sorteggiare*) to draw; **es'tratto,**
a *pp di* **estrarre** // *sm* extract; (*di*
documento) abstract; **estratto conto**
statement of account; **estratto di nascita**
birth certificate; **estrazi'one** *sf* extraction; mining; drawing *q*; draw.
estremità *sf inv* extremity, end // *sfpl*
(*ANAT*) extremities.
es'tremo, a *ag* extreme; (*ultimo*: *ora*,
tentativo) final, last // *sm* extreme; (*di*
pazienza, *forze*) limit, end; ~**i** *smpl*
(*AMM*: *dati essenziali*) details, particulars; **l'~ Oriente** the Far East.
'estro *sm* (*capriccio*) whim, fancy;
(*ispirazione* *creativa*) inspiration;
es'troso, a *ag* whimsical, capricious;
inspired.
estro'verso, a *ag*, *sm* extrovert.
'esule *sm/f* exile.
età *sf inv* age; **all'~ di 8 anni** at the age
of 8, at 8 years of age; **ha la mia ~** he (*o*
she) is the same age as me *o* as I am;
raggiungere la maggiore ~ to come of
age; **essere in ~ minore** to be under age.
'etere *sm* ether; **e'tereo, a** *ag* ethereal.
eternità *sf* eternity.
e'terno, a *ag* eternal.
etero'geneo, a [etero'dʒɛneo] *ag* hetero-
geneous.
'etica *sf vedi* **etico**.
eti'chetta [eti'ketta] *sf* label; (*ce-*
rimoniale): **l'~ etiquette.**
'etico, a, ci, che *ag* ethical // *sf* ethics
sg.
etimolo'gia, 'gie [etimolo'dʒia] *sf*
etymology.
Eti'opia *sf*: **l'~ Ethiopia.**
'Etna *sm*: **l'~ Etna.**
'etnico, a, ci, che *ag* ethnic.
e'trusco, a, schi, sche *ag*, *sm/f*
Etruscan.
'ettaro *sm* hectare (= 10,000 *m²*).
'ett. *sm abbr di* **ettogrammo**.
etto'grammo *sm* hectogram(me) (=
100 *grams*).
Eucaris'tia *sf*: **l'~ the Eucharist.**
Eu'ropa *sf*: **l'~ Europe; euro'peo, a** *ag*,
sm/f European.
evacu'are *vt* to evacuate.
e'vadere *vi* (*fuggire*): ~ **da** to escape
from // *vt* (*sbrigare*) to deal with, dispatch; (*tasse*) to evade.
evan'gelico, a, ci, che [evan'dʒɛliko]
ag evangelical.
evapo'rare *vi* to evaporate;
evaporazi'one *sf* evaporation.
evasi'one *sf* (*vedi* **evadere**) escape; dispatch; ~ **fiscale** tax evasion.
eva'sivo, a *ag* evasive.
e'vaso, a *pp di* **evadere** // *sm* escapee.

eveni'enza [eve'njɛntsa] *sf*: **pronto(a) per ogni ~** ready for any eventuality.

e'vento *sm* event.

eventu'ale *ag* possible.

evi'dente *ag* evident, obvious; **evi'denza** *sf* obviousness; **mettere in evidenza** to point out, highlight.

evi'tare *vt* to avoid; **~ di fare** to avoid doing; **~ qc a qn** to spare sb sth.

'evo *sm* age, epoch.

evo'care *vt* to evoke.

evo'luto, a *pp di* **evolvere** // *ag* (*civiltà*) (highly) developed, advanced; (*persona*) independent.

evoluzi'one [evolut'tsjone] *sf* evolution.

e'volversi *vr* to evolve.

ev'viva *escl* hurrah!; **~ il re!** long live the king!, hurrah for the king!

ex *prefisso* ex, former.

'extra *ag inv* first-rate; top-quality // *sm inv* extra; **extraconiu'gale** *ag* extramarital.

F

fa *vb vedi* **fare** // *sm inv* (*MUS*) F; (*: solfeggiando la scala*) fa // *av*: **10 anni ~** 10 years ago.

fabbi'sogno [fabbi'zoɲɲo] *sm* needs *pl*, requirements *pl*.

'fabbrica *sf* factory; **fabbri'cante** *sm* manufacturer, maker; **fabbri'care** *vt* to build; (*produrre*) to manufacture, make; (*fig*) to fabricate, invent.

'fabbro *sm* (black)smith.

fac'cenda [fat't∫ɛnda] *sf* matter, affair; (*cosa da fare*) task, chore.

fac'chino [fak'kino] *sm* porter.

'faccia, ce ['fatt∫a] *sf* face; (*di moneta, medaglia*) side; **~ a ~** face to face.

facci'ata [fat't∫ata] *sf* façade; (*di pagina*) side.

'faccio ['fatt∫o] *vb vedi* **fare**.

fa'ceto, a [fa't∫eto] *ag* witty, humorous.

'facile ['fat∫ile] *ag* easy; (*affabile*) easygoing; (*disposto*): **~ a** inclined to, prone to; (*probabile*): **è ~ che piova** it's likely to rain; **facilità** *sf* easiness; (*disposizione, dono*) aptitude; **facili'tare** *vt* to make easier.

facino'roso, a [fat∫ino'roso] *ag* violent.

facoltà *sf inv* faculty; (*CHIMICA*) property; (*autorità*) power.

facolta'tivo, a *ag* optional; (*fermata d'autobus*) request *cpd*.

fac'simile *sm* facsimile.

'faggio ['fadd∫o] *sm* beech.

fagi'ano [fa'dʒano] *sm* pheasant.

fagio'lino [fadʒo'lino] *sm* French (*Brit*) *o* string bean.

fagi'olo [fa'dʒɔlo] *sm* bean.

fa'gotto *sm* bundle; (*MUS*) bassoon; **far ~** (*fig*) to pack up and go.

'fai *vb vedi* **fare**.

'falce ['falt∫e] *sf* scythe; **fal'cetto** *sm* sickle; **falci'are** *vt* to cut; (*fig*) to mow down.

'falco, chi *sm* hawk.

fal'cone *sm* falcon.

'falda *sf* layer, stratum; (*di cappello*) brim; (*di cappotto*) tails *pl*; (*di monte*) lower slope; (*di tetto*) pitch; **nevica a larghe ~e** the snow is falling in large flakes; **abito a ~e** tails *pl*.

fale'gname [faleɲ'ɲame] *sm* joiner.

fal'lace [fal'lat∫e] *ag* misleading, deceptive.

falli'mento *sm* failure; bankruptcy.

fal'lire *vi* (*non riuscire*): **~ (in)** to fail (in); (*DIR*) to go bankrupt // *vt* (*colpo, bersaglio*) to miss; **fal'lito, a** *ag* unsuccessful; bankrupt // *sm/f* bankrupt.

'fallo *sm* error, mistake; (*imperfezione*) defect, flaw; (*SPORT*) foul; fault; **senza ~** without fail.

falò *sm inv* bonfire.

fal'sare *vt* to distort, misrepresent; **fal'sario** *sm* forger; counterfeiter; **falsifi'care** *vt* to forge; (*monete*) to forge, counterfeit.

'falso, a *ag* false; (*errato*) wrong; (*falsificato*) forged; fake; (*: oro, gioielli*) imitation *cpd* // *sm* forgery; **giurare il ~** to commit perjury.

'fama *sf* fame; (*reputazione*) reputation, name.

'fame *sf* hunger; **aver ~** to be hungry; **fa'melico, a, ci, che** *ag* ravenous.

fa'miglia [fa'miʎʎa] *sf* family.

famili'are *ag* (*della famiglia*) family *cpd*; (*ben noto*) familiar; (*rapporti, atmosfera*) friendly; (*LING*) informal, colloquial // *sm/f* relative, relation; **familiarità** *sf* familiarity; friendliness; informality.

fa'moso, a *ag* famous, well-known.

fa'nale *sm* (*AUT*) light, lamp (*Brit*); (*luce stradale*, *NAUT*) light; (*di faro*) beacon.

fa'natico, a, ci, che *ag* fanatical; (*del teatro, calcio etc*): **~ di** *o* **per** mad *o* crazy about // *sm/f* fanatic; (*tifoso*) fan.

fanci'ullo, a [fan't∫ullo] *sm/f* child.

fan'donia *sf* tall story; **~e** *sfpl* nonsense *sg*.

fan'fara *sf* brass band; (*musica*) fanfare.

'fango, ghi *sm* mud; **fan'goso, a** *ag* muddy.

'fanno *vb vedi* **fare**.

fannul'lone *a* *sm/f* idler, loafer.

fantasci'enza [fanta∫'∫ɛntsa] *sf* science fiction.

fanta'sia *sf* fantasy, imagination; (*capriccio*) whim, caprice // *ag inv*: **vestito ~** patterned dress.

fan'tasma, i *sm* ghost, phantom.

fan'tastico, a, ci, che *ag* fantastic; (*potenza, ingegno*) imaginative.

'fante *sm* infantryman; (*CARTE*) jack,

knave (*Brit*); **fante'ria** *sf* infantry.

fan'toccio [fan'tɔttʃo] *sm* puppet.

fara'butto *sm* crook.

far'dello *sm* bundle; (*fig*) burden.

'fare ♦ *sm* 1 (*modo di fare*): **con ~ distratto** absent-mindedly; **ha un ~ simpatico** he has a pleasant manner
2: **sul far del giorno/della notte** at daybreak/nightfall
♦ *vt* 1 (*fabbricare, creare*) to make; (: *casa*) to build; (: *assegno*) to make out; **~ un pasto/una promessa/un film** to make a meal/a promise/a film; **~ rumore** to make a noise
2 (*effettuare: lavoro, attività, studi*) to do; (: *sport*) to play; **cosa fa?** (*adesso*) what are you doing?; (*di professione*) what do you do?; **~ psicologia/italiano** (*INS*) to do psychology/Italian; **~ un viaggio** to go on a trip *o* journey; **~ una passeggiata** to go for a walk; **~ la spesa** to do the shopping
3 (*funzione*) to be; (*TEATRO*) to play, be; **~ il medico** to be a doctor; **~ il malato** (*fingere*) to act the invalid
4 (*suscitare: sentimenti*): **~ paura a qn** to frighten sb; **mi fa rabbia** it makes me angry; **(non) fa niente** (*non importa*) it doesn't matter
5 (*ammontare*): **3 più 3 fa 6** 3 and 3 are *o* make 6; **fanno 6.000 lire** that's 6,000 lire; **Roma fa 2.000.000 di abitanti** Rome has 2,000,000 inhabitants; **che ora fai?** what time do you make it?
6 (+ *infinito*): **far ~ qc a qn** (*obbligare*) to make sb do sth; (*permettere*) to let sb do sth; **fammi vedere** let me see; **far partire il motore** to start (up) the engine; **far riparare la macchina/costruire una casa** to get *o* have the car repaired/a house built
7: **~rsi**: **~rsi una gonna** to make o.s. a skirt; **~rsi un nome** to make a name for o.s.; **~rsi la permanente** to get a perm; **~rsi tagliare i capelli** to get one's hair cut; **~rsi operare** to have an operation; **si è fatto lavare la macchina** he got somebody to wash the car
8 (*fraseologia*): **farcela** to succeed, manage; **non ce la faccio più** I can't go on; **ce la faremo** we'll make it; **me l'hanno fatta!** (*imbrogliare*) I've been done!; **lo facevo più giovane** I thought he was younger; **fare sì/no con la testa** to nod/shake one's head
♦ *vi* 1 (*agire*) to act, do; **fate come volete** do as you like; **~ presto** to be quick; **~ da** to act as; **non c'è niente da ~** it's no use; **saperci ~ con qn/qc** to know how to deal with sb/sth; **faccia pure!** go ahead!
2 (*dire*) to say; **"davvero?" fece "really?"** he said
3: **~ per** (*essere adatto*) to be suitable for; **~ per ~ qc** to be about to do sth;

fece per andarsene he made as if to leave
4: **~rsi**: **si fa così** you do it like this, this is the way it's done; **non si fa così!** (*rimprovero*) that's no way to behave!; **la festa non si fa** the party is off
5: **~ a gara con qn** to compete *o* vie with sb; **~ a pugni** to come to blows; **~ in tempo a ~** to be in time to do
♦ *vb impers*: **fa bel tempo** the weather is fine; **fa caldo/freddo** it's hot/cold; **fa notte** it's getting dark
♦ *vr*: **~rsi** 1 (*diventare*) to become; **~rsi prete** to become a priest; **~rsi grande/vecchio** to grow tall/old
2 (*spostarsi*): **~rsi avanti/indietro** to move forward/back
3 (*fam: drogarsi*) to be a junkie.

far'falla *sf* butterfly.

fa'rina *sf* flour.

farma'cia, 'cie [farma'tʃia] *sf* pharmacy; (*negozio*) chemist's (shop) (*Brit*), pharmacy; **farma'cista, i, e** *sm/f* chemist (*Brit*), pharmacist.

'farmaco, ci *o* **chi** *sm* drug, medicine.

'faro *sm* (*NAUT*) lighthouse; (*AER*) beacon; (*AUT*) headlight.

'farsa *sf* farce.

'fascia, sce ['faʃʃa] *sf* band, strip; (*MED*) bandage; (*di sindaco, ufficiale*) sash; (*parte di territorio*) strip, belt; (*di contribuenti etc*) group, band; **essere in ~sce** (*anche fig*) to be in one's infancy; **~ oraria** time band.

fasci'are [faʃ'ʃare] *vt* to bind; (*MED*) to bandage; (*bambino*) to put a nappy (*Brit*) *o* diaper (*US*) on.

fa'scicolo [faʃ'ʃikolo] *sm* (*di documenti*) file, dossier; (*di rivista*) issue, number; (*opuscolo*) booklet, pamphlet.

'fascino [faʃʃino] *sm* charm, fascination.

'fascio ['faʃʃo] *sm* bundle, sheaf; (*di fiori*) bunch; (*di luce*) beam; (*POL*): **il F~** the Fascist Party.

fa'scismo [faʃ'ʃizmo] *sm* fascism.

'fase *sf* phase; (*TECN*) stroke; **fuori ~** (*motore*) rough.

fas'tidio *sm* bother, trouble; **dare ~ a qn** to bother *o* annoy sb; **sento ~ allo stomaco** my stomach's upset; **avere ~i con la polizia** to have trouble *o* bother with the police; **fastidi'oso, a** *ag* annoying, tiresome; (*schifiltoso*) fastidious.

'fasto *sm* pomp, splendour.

'fata *sf* fairy.

fa'tale *ag* fatal; (*inevitabile*) inevitable; (*fig*) irresistible; **fatalità** *sf inv* inevitability; (*avversità*) misfortune; (*fato*) fate, destiny.

fa'tica, che *sf* hard work, toil; (*sforzo*) effort; (*di metalli*) fatigue; **a ~** with difficulty; **fare ~ a fare qc** to have a job doing sth; **fati'care** *vi* to toil; **faticare a fare qc** to have difficulty doing sth; **fati'coso, a** *ag* tiring, exhausting;

(*lavoro*) laborious.

'fato *sm* fate, destiny.

'fatto, a *pp di* **fare** // *ag*: **un uomo ~ a** grown man; **~ a mano/in casa** hand-/home-made // *sm* fact; (*azione*) deed; (*avvenimento*) event, occurrence; (*di romanzo, film*) action, story; **cogliere qn sul ~** to catch sb red-handed; **il ~ sta o è che** the fact remains o is that; **in ~ di** as for, as far as ... is concerned.

fat'tore *sm* (*AGR*) farm manager; (*MAT, elemento costitutivo*) factor.

fatto'ria *sf* farm; farmhouse.

fatto'rino *sm* errand-boy; (*di ufficio*) office-boy; (*d'albergo*) porter.

fat'tura *sf* (*COMM*) invoice; (*di abito*) tailoring; (*malia*) spell.

fattu'rare *vt* (*COMM*) to invoice; (*prodotto*) to produce; (*vino*) to adulterate.

'fatuo, a *ag* vain, fatuous.

'fauna *sf* fauna.

fau'tore, trice *sm/f* advocate, supporter.

fa'vella *sf* speech.

fa'villa *sf* spark.

'favola *sf* (*fiaba*) fairy tale; (*d'intento morale*) fable; (*fandonia*) yarn; **favo'loso, a** *ag* fabulous; (*incredibile*) incredible.

fa'vore *sm* favour; **per ~** please; **fare un ~ a qn** to do sb a favour; **favo'revole** *ag* favourable.

favo'rire *vt* to favour; (*il commercio, l'industria, le arti*) to promote, encourage; **vuole ~?** won't you help yourself?; **favorisca in salotto** please come into the sitting room; **favo'rito, a** *ag, sm/f* favourite.

fazzo'letto [fattso'letto] *sm* handkerchief; (*per la testa*) (head)scarf.

feb'braio *sm* February.

'febbre *sf* fever; **aver la ~** to have a high temperature; **~ da fieno** hay fever; **feb'brile** *ag* (*anche fig*) feverish.

'feccia, ce ['fettʃa] *sf* dregs *pl*.

'fecola *sf* potato flour.

fecondazi'one [fekondat'tsjone] *sf* fertilization; **~ artificiale** artificial insemination.

fe'condo, a *ag* fertile.

'fede *sf* (*credenza*) belief, faith; (*REL*) faith; (*fiducia*) faith, trust; (*fedeltà*) loyalty; (*anello*) wedding ring; (*attestato*) certificate; **aver ~ in qn** to have faith in sb; **in buona/cattiva ~** in good/bad faith; **"in ~"** (*DIR*) **"in witness whereof"**; **fe'dele** *ag*: **fedele (a)** faithful (to) // *sm/f* follower; **i fedeli** (*REL*) the faithful; **fedeltà** *sf* faithfulness; (*coniugale*) fidelity; **alta fedeltà** (*RADIO*) high fidelity.

'federa *sf* pillowslip, pillowcase.

fede'rale *ag* federal.

'fegato *sm* liver; (*fig*) guts *pl*, nerve.

'felce ['feltʃe] *sf* fern.

fe'lice [fe'litʃe] *ag* happy; (*fortunato*) lucky; **felicità** *sf* happiness.

felici'tarsi [felitʃi'tarsi] *vr* (*congratularsi*): **~ con qn per qc** to congratulate sb on sth.

fe'lino, a *ag, sm* feline.

'feltro *sm* felt.

'femmina *sf* (*ZOOL, TECN*) female; (*figlia*) girl, daughter; (*spesso peg*) woman; **femmi'nile** *ag* feminine; (*sesso*) female; (*lavoro, giornale, moda*) woman's // *sm* (*LING*) feminine; **femmi'nismo** *sm* feminism.

'fendere *vt* to cut through; **fendi'nebbia** *sm inv* (*AUT*) fog lamp.

fe'nomeno *sm* phenomenon.

'feretro *sm* coffin.

feri'ale *ag* working *cpd*, work *cpd*, week *cpd*; **giorno ~** weekday.

'ferie *sfpl* holidays (*Brit*), vacation *sg* (*US*); **andare in ~** to go on holiday o vacation.

fe'rire *vt* to injure; (*deliberatamente*: *MIL etc*) to wound; (*colpire*) to hurt; **fe'rito, a** *sm/f* wounded o injured man/woman // *sf* injury; wound.

'ferma *sf* (*MIL*) (period of) service; (*CACCIA*): **cane da ~** pointer.

fer'maglio [fer'maʎʎo] *sm* clasp; (*gioiello*) brooch; (*per documenti*) clip.

fer'mare *vt* to stop, halt; (*POLIZIA*) to detain, hold; (*bottone etc*) to fasten, fix // *vi* to stop; **~rsi** *vr* to stop, halt; **~rsi a fare qc** to stop to do sth.

fer'mata *sf* stop; **~ dell'autobus** bus stop.

fer'mento *sm* (*anche fig*) ferment; (*lievito*) yeast.

fer'mezza [fer'mettsa] *sf* (*fig*) firmness, steadfastness.

'fermo, a *ag* still, motionless; (*veicolo*) stationary; (*orologio*) not working; (*saldo: anche fig*) firm; (*voce, mano*) steady // *escl* stop!; keep still! // *sm* (*chiusura*) catch, lock; (*DIR*): **~ di polizia** police detention.

'fermo 'posta *av, sm inv* poste restante (*Brit*), general delivery (*US*).

fe'roce [fe'rɔtʃe] *ag* (*animale*) wild, fierce, ferocious; (*persona*) cruel, fierce; (*fame, dolore*) raging.

ferra'gosto *sm* (*festa*) feast of the Assumption; (*periodo*) August holidays *pl*.

ferra'menta *sfpl* ironmongery *sg* (*Brit*), hardware *sg*; **negozio di ~** ironmonger's (*Brit*), hardware shop o store (*US*).

fer'rato, a *ag* (*FERR*): **strada ~a** railway (*Brit*) o railroad (*US*) line; (*fig*): **essere ~ in** to be well up in.

'ferreo, a *ag* iron *cpd*.

'ferro *sm* iron; **una bistecca ai ~i** a grilled steak; **~ battuto** wrought iron; **~ da calza** knitting needle; **~ di cavallo** horseshoe; **~ da stiro** iron.

ferro'via *sf* railway (*Brit*), railroad (*US*); **ferrovi'ario, a** *ag* railway *cpd* (*Brit*), railroad *cpd* (*US*); **ferrovi'ere** *sm* railwayman (*Brit*), railroad man (*US*).

'fertile *ag* fertile; **fertiliz'zante** *sm* fertilizer.

'fervido, a *ag* fervent.

fer'vore *sm* fervour, ardour; (*punto culminante*) height.

'fesso, a *pp di* **fendere** // *ag* (*fam: sciocco*) crazy, cracked.

fes'sura *sf* crack, split; (*per gettone, moneta*) slot.

'festa *sf* (*religiosa*) feast; (*pubblica*) holiday; (*compleanno*) birthday; (*onomastico*) name day; (*ricevimento*) celebration, party; **far ~ a** to have a holiday; to live it up; **far ~ a qn** to give sb a warm welcome.

festeggi'are [fested'dʒare] *vt* to celebrate; (*persona*) to have a celebration for.

fes'tino *sm* party; (*con balli*) ball.

fes'tivo, a *ag* (*atmosfera*) festive; **giorno ~** holiday.

fes'toso, a *ag* merry, joyful.

fe'ticcio [fe'tittʃo] *sm* fetish.

'feto *sm* foetus (*Brit*), fetus (*US*).

'fetta *sf* slice.

fettuc'cine [fettut'tʃine] *sfpl* (*CUC*) ribbon-shaped pasta.

FF.SS. *abbr* = *Ferrovie dello Stato.*

fi'aba *sf* fairy tale.

fi'acca *sf* weariness; (*svogliatezza*) listlessness.

fiac'care *vt* to weaken.

fi'acco, a, chi, che *ag* (*stanco*) tired, weary; (*svogliato*) listless; (*debole*) weak; (*mercato*) slack.

fi'accola *sf* torch.

fi'ala *sf* phial.

fi'amma *sf* flame.

fiam'mante *ag* (*colore*) flaming; **nuovo ~** brand new.

fiammeggi'are [fjammed'dʒare] *vi* to blaze.

fiam'mifero *sm* match.

fiam'mingo, a, ghi, ghe *ag* Flemish // *sm/f* Fleming // *sm* (*LING*) Flemish; (*ZOOL*) flamingo; **i F~ghi** the Flemish.

fiancheggi'are [fjanked'dʒare] *vt* to border; (*fig*) to support, back (up); (*MIL*) to flank.

fi'anco, chi *sm* side; (*MIL*) flank; **di ~** sideways, from the side; **a ~ a ~** side by side.

fi'asco, schi *sm* flask; (*fig*) fiasco; **fare ~** to be a fiasco.

fi'ato *sm* breath; (*resistenza*) stamina; **avere il ~ grosso** to be out of breath; **prendere ~** to catch one's breath; **~i** *smpl* (*MUS*) wind instruments; **strumento a ~** wind instrument.

'fibbia *sf* buckle.

'fibra *sf* fibre; (*fig*) constitution.

fic'care *vt* to push, thrust, drive; **~rsi** *vr* (*andare a finire*) to get to.

'fico, chi *sm* (*pianta*) fig tree; (*frutto*) fig; **~ d'India** prickly pear; **~ secco** dried fig.

fidanza'mento [fidantsa'mento] *sm* engagement.

fidan'zarsi [fidan'tsarsi] *vr* to get engaged; **fidan'zato, a** *sm/f* fiancé/fiancée.

fi'darsi *vr*: **~ di** to trust; **fi'dato, a** *ag* reliable, trustworthy.

'fido, a *ag* faithful, loyal // *sm* (*COMM*) credit.

fi'ducia [fi'dutʃa] *sf* confidence, trust; **incarico di ~** position of trust, responsible position; **persona di ~** reliable person.

fi'ele *sm* (*MED*) bile; (*fig*) bitterness.

fie'nile *sm* barn; hayloft.

fi'eno *sm* hay.

fi'era *sf* fair.

fie'rezza [fje'rettsa] *sf* pride.

fi'ero, a *ag* proud; (*crudele*) fierce, cruel; (*audace*) bold.

'fifa *sf* (*fam*): **aver ~** to have the jitters.

'figlia [ˈfiʎʎa] *sf* daughter.

figli'astro, a [fiʎ'ʎastro] *sm/f* stepson/daughter.

'figlio [ˈfiʎʎo] *sm* son; (*senza distinzione di sesso*) child; **~ di papà** spoilt, wealthy young man; **~ unico** only child; **figli'occio, a, ci, ce** *sm/f* godchild, godson/daughter.

fi'gura *sf* figure; (*forma, aspetto esterno*) form, shape; (*illustrazione*) picture, illustration; **far ~** to look smart; **fare una brutta ~** to make a bad impression.

figu'rare *vi* to appear // *vt*: **~rsi qc** to imagine sth; **~rsi** *vr*: **figurati!** imagine that!; **ti do noia? — ma figurati!** am I disturbing you? — not at all!

figura'tivo, a *ag* figurative.

figu'rina *sf* figurine; (*cartoncino*) picture card.

'fila *sf* row, line; (*coda*) queue; (*serie*) series, string; **di ~** in succession; **fare la ~** to queue; **in ~ indiana** in single file.

filantro'pia *sf* philanthropy.

fi'lare *vt* to spin // *vi* (*baco, ragno*) to spin; (*formaggio fuso*) to go stringy; (*discorso*) to hang together; (*fam: amoreggiare*) to go steady; (*muoversi a forte velocità*) to go at full speed; (: *andarsene lestamente*) to make o.s. scarce; **~ diritto** (*fig*) to toe the line.

filas'trocca, che *sf* nursery rhyme.

filate'lia *sf* philately, stamp collecting.

fi'lato, a *ag* spun // *sm* yarn; **3 giorni ~i** 3 days running *o* on end; **fila'tura** *sf* spinning; (*luogo*) spinning mill.

fi'letto *sm* (*di vite*) thread; (*di carne*) fillet.

fili'ale *ag* filial // *sf* (*di impresa*) branch.

fili'grana *sf* (*in oreficeria*) filigree; (*su carta*) watermark.

film *sm inv* film; **fil'mare** *vt* to film.

'filo *sm* (*anche fig*) thread; (*filato*) yarn; (*metallico*) wire; (*di lama, rasoio*) edge; per ~ e per segno in detail; ~ d'erba blade of grass; ~ di perle string of pearls; ~ spinato barbed wire; con un ~ di voce in a whisper.

'filobus *sm inv* trolley bus.

filon'cino [filon'tʃino] *sm* ≈ French stick.

fi'lone *sm* (*di minerali*) seam, vein; (*pane*) ≈ Vienna loaf; (*fig*) trend.

filoso'fia *sf* philosophy; **fi'losofo, a** *sm/f* philosopher.

fil'trare *vt, vi* to filter.

'filtro *sm* filter; ~ dell'olio (*AUT*) oil filter.

'filza ['filtsa] *sf* (*anche fig*) string.

fin *av, prep* = **fino.**

fi'nale *ag* final // *sm* (*di opera*) end, ending; (: *MUS*) finale // *sf* (*SPORT*) final; **finalità** *sf* (*scopo*) aim, purpose; **final'mente** *av* finally, at last.

fi'nanza [fi'nantsa] *sf* finance; ~e *sfpl* (*di individuo, Stato*) finances; **finanzi'ario, a** *ag* financial; **finanzi'ere** *sm* financier; (*guardia di finanza: doganale*) customs officer; (: *tributaria*) inland revenue official.

finché [fin'ke] *cong* (*per tutto il tempo che*) as long as; (*fino al momento in cui*) until; aspetta ~ io (non) sia ritornato wait until I get back.

'fine *ag* (*lamina, carta*) thin; (*capelli, polvere*) fine; (*vista, udito*) keen, sharp; (*persona*): **raffinato**: refined, distinguished; (*osservazione*) subtle // *sf* end // *sm* aim, purpose; (*esito*) result, outcome; **secondo** ~ ulterior motive; in *o* alla ~ in the end, finally; ~ **settimana** *sm o f inv* weekend.

fi'nestra *sf* window; **fines'trino** *sm* (*di treno, auto*) window.

'fingere ['findʒere] *vt* to feign; (*supporre*) to imagine, suppose; ~rsi *vr*: ~rsi **ubriaco/pazzo** to pretend to be drunk/mad; ~ **di fare** to pretend to do.

fini'mondo *sm* pandemonium.

fi'nire *vt* to finish // *vi* to finish, end; ~ **di fare** (*compiere*) to finish doing; (*smettere*) to stop doing; ~ **in galera** to end up *o* finish up in prison; **fini'tura** *sf* finish.

finlan'dese *ag, sm* (*LING*) Finnish // *sm/f* Finn.

Fin'landia *sf*: la ~ Finland.

'fino, a *ag* (*capelli, seta*) fine; (*oro*) pure; (*fig: acuto*) shrewd // *av* (*spesso troncato in* fin: *pure, anche*) even // *prep* (*spesso troncato in* fin: *tempo*): fin quando? till when?; (: *luogo*): fin qui as far as here; ~ a (*tempo*) until, till; (*luogo*) as far as, (up) to; **fin da domani** from tomorrow onwards; **fin da ieri** since

yesterday; **fin dalla nascita** from *o* since birth.

fi'nocchio [fi'nɔkkjo] *sm* fennel; (*fam peg: pederasta*) queer.

fi'nora *av* up till now.

'finto, a *pp di* **fingere** // *ag* false; artificial // *sf* pretence, sham; (*SPORT*) feint; far ~a (*di fare*) to pretend (to do).

finzi'one [fin'tsjone] *sf* pretence, sham.

fi'occo, chi *sm* (*di nastro*) bow; (*di stoffa, lana*) flock; (*di neve*) flake; (*NAUT*) jib; coi ~chi (*fig*) first-rate; ~chi di granoturco cornflakes.

fi'ocina ['fjɔtʃina] *sf* harpoon.

fi'oco, a, chi, che *ag* faint, dim.

fi'onda *sf* catapult.

fio'raio, a *sm/f* florist.

fi'ore *sm* flower; ~i *smpl* (*CARTE*) clubs; a fior d'acqua on the surface of the water; avere i nervi a fior di pelle to be on edge.

fioren'tino, a *ag* Florentine.

fio'retto *sm* (*SCHERMA*) foil.

fio'rire *vi* (*rosa*) to flower; (*albero*) to blossom; (*fig*) to flourish.

Fi'renze [fi'rentse] *sf* Florence.

'firma *sf* signature; (*reputazione*) name.

fir'mare *vt* to sign.

fisar'monica, che *sf* accordion.

fis'cale *ag* fiscal, tax *cpd*; **medico** ~ doctor employed by Social Security to verify cases of sick leave.

fischi'are [fis'kjare] *vi* to whistle // *vt* to whistle; (*attore*) to boo, hiss.

'fischio ['fiskjo] *sm* whistle.

'fisco *sm* tax authorities *pl*, ≈ Inland Revenue (*Brit*), ≈ Internal Revenue Service (*US*).

'fisico, a, ci, che *ag* physical // *sm/f* physicist // *sm* physique // *sf* physics *sg*.

fisiolo'gia [fizjolo'dʒia] *sf* physiology.

fisiono'mia *sf* face, physiognomy.

fisiotera'pia *sf* physiotherapy.

fis'sare *vt* to fix, fasten; (*guardare intensamente*) to stare at; (*data, condizioni*) to fix, establish, set; (*prenotare*) to book; ~rsi su (*sog: sguardo, attenzione*) to focus on; (*fig: idea*) to become obsessed with; **fissazi'one** *sf* (*PSIC*) fixation.

'fisso, a *ag* fixed; (*stipendio, impiego*) regular // *av*: guardare ~ qc/qn to stare at sth/sb.

'fitta *sf vedi* **fitto.**

fit'tizio, a *ag* fictitious, imaginary.

'fitto, a *ag* thick, dense; (*pioggia*) heavy // *sm* depths *pl*, middle; (*affitto, pigione*) rent // *sf* sharp pain.

fi'ume *sm* river.

fiu'tare *vt* to smell, sniff; (*sog: animale*) to scent; (*fig: inganno*) to get wind of, smell; ~ **tabacco/cocaina** to take snuff/cocaine; **fi'uto** *sm* (*sense of*) smell; (*fig*) nose.

fla'gello [fla'dʒello] *sm* scourge.

fla'grante *ag* flagrant; **cogliere qn in ~** to catch sb red-handed.

fla'nella *sf* flannel.

flash [flaʃ] *sm inv* (FOT) flash; (*giornalistico*) newsflash.

'flauto *sm* flute.

'flebile *ag* faint, feeble.

'flemma *sf* (*calma*) coolness, phlegm; (MED) phlegm.

fles'sibile *ag* pliable; (*fig: che si adatta*) flexible.

'flesso, a *pp di* **flettere**.

flessu'oso, a *ag* supple, lithe; (*andatura*) flowing, graceful.

'flettere *vt* to bend.

F.lli *abbr* (= *fratelli*) Bros.

'flora *sf* flora.

'florido, a *ag* flourishing; (*fig*) glowing with health.

'floscio, a, sci, sce ['floʃʃo] *ag* (*cappello*) floppy, soft; (*muscoli*) flabby.

'flotta *sf* fleet.

'fluido, a *ag, sm* fluid.

flu'ire *vi* to flow.

flu'oro *sm* fluorine.

fluo'ruro *sm* fluoride.

'flusso *sm* flow; (FISICA, MED) flux; **~ e riflusso** ebb and flow.

fluttu'are *vi* to rise and fall; (ECON) to fluctuate.

fluvi'ale *ag* river *cpd*, fluvial.

'foca, che *sf* (ZOOL) seal.

fo'caccia, ce [fo'kattʃa] *sf* kind of pizza; (*dolce*) bun.

'foce, che *sf* (GEO) mouth.

foco'laio *sm* (MED) centre of infection; (*fig*) hotbed.

foco'lare *sm* hearth, fireside; (TECN) furnace.

'fodera *sf* (*di vestito*) lining; (*di libro, poltrona*) cover; **fode'rare** *vt* to line; to cover.

'fodero *sm* (*di spada*) scabbard; (*di pugnale*) sheath; (*di pistola*) holster.

'foga *sf* enthusiasm, ardour.

'foggia, ge ['fɔdʒa] *sf* (*maniera*) style; (*aspetto*) form, shape; (*moda*) fashion, style.

'foglia ['fɔʎʎa] *sf* leaf; **~ d'argento/d'oro** silver/gold leaf; **fogli'ame** *sm* foliage, leaves *pl*.

'foglio ['fɔʎʎo] *sm* (*di carta*) sheet (of paper); (*di metallo*) sheet; (*documento*) document; (*banconota*) (bank)note; **~ rosa** (AUT) provisional licence; **~ di via** (DIR) expulsion order; **~ volante** pamphlet.

'fogna ['foɲɲa] *sf* drain, sewer; **fogna'tura** *sf* drainage, sewerage.

folgo'rare *vt* (*sog: fulmine*) to strike down; (: *alta tensione*) to electrocute.

'folla *sf* crowd, throng.

'folle *ag* mad, insane; (TECN) idle; **in ~** (AUT) in neutral.

fol'lia *sf* folly, foolishness; foolish act;

(*pazzia*) madness, lunacy.

'folto, a *ag* thick.

fomen'tare *vt* to stir up, foment.

fondamen'tale *ag* fundamental, basic.

fonda'mento *sm* foundation; **~a** *sfpl* (EDIL) foundations.

fon'dare *vt* to found; (*fig: dar base*): **~ qc su** to base sth on; **fondazi'one** *sf* foundation.

'fondere *vt* (*neve*) to melt; (*metallo*) to fuse, melt; (*fig: colori*) to merge, blend; (: *imprese, gruppi*) to merge // *vi* to melt; **~rsi** *vr* to melt; (*fig: partiti, correnti*) to unite, merge; **fonde'ria** *sf* foundry.

'fondo, a *ag* deep // *sm* (*di recipiente, pozzo*) bottom; (*di stanza*) back; (*quantità di liquido che resta, deposito*) dregs *pl*; (*sfondo*) background; (*unità immobiliare*) property, estate; (*somma di denaro*) fund; (SPORT) long-distance race; **~i** *smpl* (*denaro*) funds; **a notte ~a** at dead of night; **in ~ a** at the bottom of; **at the back of**; (*strada*) at the end of; **andare a ~** (*nave*) to sink; **conoscere a ~** to know inside out; **dar ~ a** (*fig: provviste, soldi*) to use up; **in ~** (*fig*) after all, all things considered; **andare fino in ~ a** (*fig*) to examine thoroughly; **a ~ perduto** (COMM) without security; **~i di caffè** coffee grounds; **~i di magazzino** old o unsold stock *sg*.

fo'netica *sf* phonetics *sg*.

fon'tana *sf* fountain.

'fonte *sf* spring, source; (*fig*) source // *sm*: **~ battesimale** (REL) font.

fo'raggio [fo'raddʒo] *sm* fodder, forage.

fo'rare *vt* to pierce, make a hole in; (*pallone*) to burst; (*biglietto*) to punch; **~ una gomma** to burst a tyre (*Brit*) o tire (*US*).

'forbici ['fɔrbitʃi] *sfpl* scissors.

'forca, che *sf* (AGR) fork, pitchfork; (*patibolo*) gallows *sg*.

for'cella [for'tʃɛlla] *sf* (TECN) fork; (*di monte*) pass.

for'chetta [for'ketta] *sf* fork.

for'cina [for'tʃina] *sf* hairpin.

'forcipe ['fɔrtʃipe] *sm* forceps *pl*.

fo'resta *sf* forest.

foresti'ero, a *ag* foreign // *sm/f* foreigner.

'forfora *sf* dandruff.

'forgia, ge ['fɔrdʒa] *sf* forge; **forgi'are** *vt* to forge.

'forma *sf* form; (*aspetto esteriore*) form, shape; (DIR: *procedura*) procedure; (*per calzature*) last; (*stampo da cucina*) mould; **~e** *sfpl* (*del corpo*) figure, shape; **le ~e** (*convenzioni*) appearances; **essere in ~** to be in good shape.

formag'gino [formad'dʒino] *sm* processed cheese.

for'maggio [for'maddʒo] *sm* cheese.

for'male *ag* formal; **formalità** *sf inv*

formality.

for'mare vt to form, shape, make; (numero di telefono) to dial; (fig: carattere) to form, mould; ~rsi vr to form, take shape; **for'mato** sm format, size; **formazi'one** sf formation; (fig: educazione) training.

for'mica, che sf ant; **formi'caio** sm anthill.

formico'lare vi (gamba, braccio) to tingle; (brulicare: anche fig): ~ di to be swarming with; mi formicola la gamba I've got pins and needles in my leg, my leg's tingling; **formico'lio** sm pins and needles pl; swarming.

formi'dabile ag powerful, formidable; (straordinario) remarkable.

'formula sf formula; ~ di cortesia courtesy form.

formu'lare vt to formulate; to express.

for'nace [for'natʃe] sf (per laterizi etc) kiln; (per metalli) furnace.

for'naio sm baker.

for'nello sm (elettrico, a gas) ring; (di pipa) bowl.

for'nire vt: ~ qn di qc, ~ qc a qn to provide o supply sb with sth, to supply sth to sb.

'forno sm (di cucina) oven; (panetteria) bakery; (TECN: per calce etc) kiln; (: per metalli) furnace.

'foro sm (buco) hole; (STORIA) forum; (tribunale) (law) court.

'forse av perhaps, maybe; (circa) about; essere in ~ to be in doubt.

forsen'nato, a ag mad, insane.

'forte ag strong; (suono) loud; (spesa) considerable, great; (passione, dolore) great, deep // av strongly; (velocemente) fast; (a voce alta) loud(ly); (violentemente) hard // sm (edificio) fort; (specialità) forte, strong point; essere ~ in qc to be good at sth.

for'tezza [for'tettsa] sf (morale) strength; (luogo fortificato) fortress.

for'tuito, a ag fortuitous, chance.

for'tuna sf (destino) fortune, luck; (buona sorte) success, fortune; (eredità, averi) fortune; **per** ~ luckily, fortunately; di ~ makeshift, improvised; atterraggio di ~ emergency landing; **fortu'nato, a** ag lucky, fortunate; (coronato da successo) successful.

forvi'are vt, vi = **fuorviare**.

'forza ['fɔrtsa] sf strength; (potere) power; (FISICA) force; ~e sfpl (fisiche) strength sg; (MIL) forces // escl come on!; per ~ against one's will; (naturalmente) of course; a viva ~ by force; a ~ di by dint of; ~ maggiore circumstances beyond one's control; la ~ pubblica the police pl; le ~e armate the armed forces.

for'zare [for'tsare] vt to force; ~ qn a fare to force sb to do; **for'zato, a** ag forced // sm (DIR) prisoner sentenced to hard labour.

fos'chia [fos'kia] sf mist, haze.

'fosco, a, schi, sche ag dark, gloomy.

'fosforo sm phosphorous.

'fossa sf pit; (di cimitero) grave; ~ biologica septic tank.

fos'sato sm ditch; (di fortezza) moat.

fos'setta sf dimple.

'fossile ag, sm fossil.

'fosso sm ditch; (MIL) trench.

'foto sf photo // prefisso: **foto'copia** sf photocopy; **fotocopi'are** vt to photocopy; **fotogra'fare** vt to photograph; **fotogra'fia** sf (procedimento) photography; (immagine) photograph; **fare una fotografia** to take a photograph; **una fotografia a colori/in bianco e nero** a colour/black and white photograph; **fo'tografo, a** sm/f photographer; **fotoro'manzo** sm romantic picture story.

fra prep = **tra**.

fracas'sare vt to shatter, smash; ~rsi vr to shatter, smash; (veicolo) to crash; **fra'casso** sm smash; crash; (baccano) din, racket.

'fradicio, a, ci, ce ['fraditʃo] ag (molto bagnato) soaking (wet); ubriaco ~ blind drunk.

'fragile ['fradʒile] ag fragile; (fig: salute) delicate.

'fragola sf strawberry.

fra'gore sm roar; (di tuono) rumble.

frago'roso, a ag deafening.

fra'grante ag fragrant.

frain'tendere vt to misunderstand; **frain'teso, a** pp di **fraintendere**.

fram'mento sm fragment.

'frana sf landslide; (fig: persona): essere una ~ to be useless; **fra'nare** vi to slip, slide down.

fran'cese [fran'tʃeze] ag French // sm/f Frenchman/woman // sm (LING) French; i F~i the French.

fran'chezza [fran'kettsa] sf frankness, openness.

'Francia ['frantʃa] sf: la ~ France.

'franco, a, chi, che ag (COMM) free; (sincero) frank, open, sincere // sm (moneta) franc; **farla ~a** (fig) to get off scot-free; ~ di dogana duty-free; ~ a domicilio delivered free of charge; **prezzo ~ fabbrica** ex-works price; ~ tiratore sm sniper.

franco'bollo sm (postage) stamp.

fran'gente [fran'dʒɛnte] sm (onda) breaker; (scoglio emergente) reef; (circostanza) situation, circumstance.

'frangia, ge ['frandʒa] sf fringe.

frantu'mare vt, ~rsi vr to break into pieces, shatter.

frap'pé sm milk shake.

'frasca, sche sf (leafy) branch.

'frase sf (LING) sentence; (locuzione,

espressione, *MUS*) phrase; ~ **fatta** set phrase.

'frassino *sm* ash (tree).

frastagli'ato, a [frastaʎˈʎato] *ag* (*costa*) indented, jagged.

frastor'nare *vt* to daze; to befuddle.

frastu'ono *sm* hubbub, din.

'frate *sm* friar, monk.

fratel'lanza [fratelˈlantsa] *sf* brotherhood; (*associazione*) fraternity.

fratel'lastro *sm* stepbrother.

fra'tello *sm* brother; ~**i** *smpl* brothers; (*nel senso di fratelli e sorelle*) brothers and sisters.

fra'terno, a *ag* fraternal, brotherly.

frat'tanto *av* in the meantime, meanwhile.

frat'tempo *sm*: nel ~ in the meantime, meanwhile.

frat'tura *sf* fracture; (*fig*) split, break.

frazi'one [fratˈtsjone] *sf* fraction; (*borgata*): ~ di comune hamlet.

'freccia, ce [ˈfrettʃa] *sf* arrow; ~ di direzione (*AUT*) indicator.

fred'dare *vt* to shoot dead.

fred'dezza [fredˈdettsa] *sf* coldness.

'freddo, a *ag, sm* cold; fa ~ it's cold; aver ~ to be cold; a ~ (*fig*) deliberately; **freddo'loso, a** *ag* sensitive to the cold.

fred'dura *sf* pun.

fre'gare *vt* to rub; (*fam: truffare*) to take in, cheat; (: *rubare*) to swipe, pinch; **fregarsene** (*fam!*): chi se ne **frega?** who gives a damn (about it)?

fre'gata *sf* rub; (*fam*) swindle; (*NAUT*) frigate.

'fregio [ˈfredʒo] *sm* (*ARCHIT*) frieze, (*ornamento*) decoration.

'fremere *vi*: ~ di to tremble o quiver with; **'fremito** *sm* tremor, quiver.

fre'nare *vt* (*veicolo*) to slow down; (*cavallo*) to rein in; (*lacrime*) to restrain, hold back // *vi* to brake; ~**rsi** *vr* (*fig*) to restrain o.s., control o.s.; **fre'nata** *sf*: fare una frenata to brake.

frene'sia *sf* frenzy.

'freno *sm* brake; (*morso*) bit; ~ a disco disc brake; ~ a mano handbrake; tenere a ~ to restrain.

frequen'tare *vt* (*scuola, corso*) to attend; (*locale, bar*) to go to, frequent; (*persone*) to see (often).

fre'quente *ag* frequent; di ~ frequently; **fre'quenza** *sf* frequency; (*INS*) attendance.

fres'chezza [fresˈkettsa] *sf* freshness.

'fresco, a, schi, sche *ag* fresh; (*temperatura*) cool; (*notizia*) recent, fresh // *sm*: godere il ~ to enjoy the cool air; stare ~ (*fig*) to be in for it; mettere al ~ to put in a cool place.

'fretta *sf* hurry, haste; in ~ in a hurry; in ~ e furia in a mad rush; aver ~ to be in a hurry; **fretto'loso, a** *ag* (*persona*) in a hurry; (*lavoro etc*) hurried, rushed.

fri'abile *ag* (*terreno*) friable; (*pasta*) crumbly.

'friggere [ˈfriddʒere] *vt* to fry // *vi* (*olio etc*) to sizzle.

'frigido, a [ˈfridʒido] *ag* (*MED*) frigid.

'frigo *sm* fridge.

frigo'rifero, a *ag* refrigerating // *sm* refrigerator.

fringu'ello *sm* chaffinch.

frit'tata *sf* omelette; fare una ~ (*fig*) to make a mess of things.

frit'tella *sf* (*CUC*) pancake; (: *ripiena*) fritter.

'fritto, a *pp di* **friggere** // *ag* fried // *sm* fried food; ~ misto mixed fry.

frit'tura *sf* (*CUC*): ~ di pesce mixed fried fish.

'frivolo, a *ag* frivolous.

frizi'one [friˈtsjone] *sf* friction; (*di pelle*) rub, rub-down; (*AUT*) clutch.

friz'zante [friddʒzante] *ag* (*anche fig*) sparkling.

'frizzo [ˈfriddzo] *sm* witticism.

fro'dare *vt* to defraud, cheat.

'frode *sf* fraud; ~ fiscale tax evasion.

'frollo, a *ag* (*carne*) tender; (: *di selvaggina*) high; (*fig: persona*) soft; pasta ~**a** short(crust) pastry.

'fronda *sf* (*leafy*) branch; (*di partito politico*) internal opposition; ~**e** *sfpl* foliage *sg*.

fron'tale *ag* frontal; (*scontro*) head-on.

'fronte *sf* (*ANAT*) forehead; (*di edificio*) front, façade // *sm* (*MIL, POL, METEOR*) front; a ~, di ~ facing, opposite; di ~ a (*posizione*) opposite, facing, in front of; (*a paragone di*) compared with.

fronteggi'are [fronteddʒˈdʒare] *vt* (*avversari, difficoltà*) to face, stand up to; (*spese*) to cope with.

fronti'era *sf* border, frontier.

'fronzolo [ˈfrondzolo] *sm* frill.

'frottola *sf* fib; ~**e** *sfpl* nonsense *sg*.

fru'gare *vi* to rummage // *vt* to search.

frul'lare *vt* (*CUC*) to whisk // *vi* (*uccelli*) to flutter; **frul'lato** *sm* milk shake; fruit drink; **frulla'tore** *sm* electric mixer; **frul'lino** *sm* whisk.

fru'mento *sm* wheat.

fru'scio [fruʃˈʃio] *sm* rustle, rustling; (*di acque*) murmur.

'frusta *sf* whip; (*CUC*) whisk.

frus'tare *vt* to whip.

frus'tino *sm* riding crop.

frus'trare *vt* to frustrate.

'frutta *sf* fruit; (*portata*) dessert; ~ candita/secca candied/dried fruit.

frut'tare *vi* to bear dividends, give a return.

frut'teto *sm* orchard.

frutti'vendolo, a *sm/f* greengrocer (*Brit*), produce dealer (*US*).

'frutto *sm* fruit; (*fig: risultato*) result(s); (*ECON: interesse*) interest; (: *reddito*) income; ~**i di mare** seafood *sg*.

FS *abbr* = *Ferrovie dello Stato*.

fu *vb vedi* **essere** // *ag inv*: **il ~ Paolo Bianchi** the late Paolo Bianchi.

fuci'lare [futʃi'lare] *vt* to shoot; **fuci'lata** *sf* rifle shot.

fu'cile [fu'tʃile] *sm* rifle, gun; *(da caccia)* shotgun, gun.

fu'cina [fu'tʃina] *sf* forge.

'fuga *sf* escape, flight; *(di gas, liquidi)* leak; *(MUS)* fugue; **~ di cervelli** brain drain.

fu'gace [fu'gatʃe] *ag* fleeting, transient.

fug'gevole [fud'dʒevole] *ag* fleeting.

fuggi'asco, a, schi, sche [fud'dʒasko] *ag*, *sm/f* fugitive.

fuggi'fuggi [fuddʒi'fuddʒi] *sm* scramble, stampede.

fug'gire [fud'dʒire] *vi* to flee, run away; *(fig: passar veloce)* to fly // *vt* to avoid; **fuggi'tivo, a** *sm/f* fugitive, runaway.

ful'gore *sm* brilliance, splendour.

fu'liggine [fu'liddʒine] *sf* soot.

fulmi'nare *vt (sog: fulmine)* to strike; *(: elettricità)* to electrocute; *(con arma da fuoco)* to shoot dead; *(fig: con lo sguardo)* to look daggers at.

'fulmine *sm* thunderbolt; lightning *q*.

fumai'olo *sm (di nave)* funnel; *(di fabbrica)* chimney.

fu'mare *vi* to smoke; *(emettere vapore)* to steam // *vt* to smoke; **fu'mata** *sf* *(segnale)* smoke signal; **farsi una fumata** to have a smoke; **fuma'tore, 'trice** *sm/f* smoker.

fu'metto *sm* comic strip; **~i** *smpl* comics.

'fumo *sm* smoke; *(vapore)* steam; *(il fumare tabacco)* smoking; **~i** *smpl* fumes; **i ~i dell'alcool** the after-effects of drink; **vendere ~** to deceive, cheat; **fu'moso, a** *ag* smoky; *(fig)* muddled.

fu'nambolo, a *sm/f* tightrope walker.

'fune *sf* rope, cord; *(più grossa)* cable.

'funebre *ag (rito)* funeral; *(aspetto)* gloomy, funereal.

fune'rale *sm* funeral.

'fungere [ˈfundʒere] *vi*: **~ da** to act as.

'fungo, ghi *sm* fungus; *(commestibile)* mushroom; **~ velenoso** toadstool.

funico'lare *sf* funicular railway.

funi'via *sf* cable railway.

funzio'nare [funtsjoˈnare] *vi* to work, function; *(fungere)*: **~ da** to act as.

funzio'nario [funtsjoˈnarjo] *sm* official.

funzi'one [funˈtsjone] *sf* function; *(carica)* post, position; *(REL)* service; **in ~** *(meccanismo)* in operation; **in ~ di** *(come)* as; **fare la ~ di qn** *(farne le veci)* to take sb's place.

fu'oco, chi *sm* fire; *(fornello)* ring; *(FOT, FISICA)* focus; **dare ~ a qc** to set fire to sth; **far ~** *(sparare)* to fire; **~ d'artificio** firework.

fuorché [fwor'ke] *cong, prep* except.

fu'ori *av* outside; *(all'aperto)* outdoors, outside; *(fuori di casa, SPORT)* out; *(esclamativo)* get out! // *prep*: **~ (di)** out of, outside // *sm* outside; **lasciar ~ qc/qn** to leave sth/sb out; **far ~ qn** *(fam)* to kill sb, do sb in; **essere ~ di sé** to be beside o.s.; **~ luogo** *(inopportuno)* out of place, uncalled for; **~ mano** out of the way, remote; **~ pericolo** out of danger; **~ uso** old-fashioned; obsolete.

fu'ori... *prefisso*: **fuori'bordo** *sm inv* speedboat (with outboard motor); outboard motor; **fuori'classe** *sm/f inv* (undisputed) champion; **fuorigi'oco** *sm* offside; **fuori'legge** *sm/f inv* outlaw; **fuori'serie** *ag inv* *(auto etc)* custom-built // *sf* custom-built car; **fuori'strada** *sm* *(AUT)* cross-country vehicle; **fuoru'scito, a, fuoriu'scito, a** *sm/f* exile; **fuorvi'are** *vt* to mislead; *(fig)* to lead astray // *vi* to go astray.

'furbo, a *ag* clever, smart; *(peg)* cunning.

fu'rente *ag*: **~ (contro)** furious (with).

fur'fante *sm* rascal, scoundrel.

fur'gone *sm* van.

'furia *sf (ira)* fury, rage; *(fig: impeto)* fury, violence; *(fretta)* rush; **a ~ di** by dint of; **andare su tutte le ~e** to get into a towering rage; **furi'bondo, a** *ag* furious.

furi'oso, a *ag* furious; *(mare, vento)* raging.

fu'rore *sm* fury; *(esaltazione)* frenzy; **far ~** to be all the rage.

fur'tivo, a *ag* furtive.

'furto *sm* theft; **~ con scasso** burglary.

'fusa *sfpl*: **fare le ~** to purr.

fu'sibile *sm (ELETTR)* fuse.

fusi'one *sf (di metalli)* fusion, melting; *(colata)* casting; *(COMM)* merger; *(fig)* merging.

'fuso, a *pp di* **fondere** // *sm (FILATURA)* spindle; **~ orario** time zone.

fus'tagno [fusˈtaɲɲo] *sm* corduroy.

fus'tino *sm (di detersivo)* tub.

'fusto *sm* stem; *(ANAT, di albero)* trunk; *(recipiente)* drum, can.

fu'turo, a *ag, sm* future.

G

gab'bare *vt* to take in, dupe; **~rsi** *vr*: **~rsi di qn** to make fun of sb.

'gabbia *sf* cage; *(DIR)* dock; *(da imballaggio)* crate; **~ dell'ascensore** lift *(Brit)* o elevator *(US)* shaft; **~ toracica** *(ANAT)* rib cage.

gabbi'ano *sm* (sea)gull.

gabi'netto *sm (MED etc)* consulting room; *(POL)* ministry; *(di decenza)* toilet, lavatory; *(INS: di fisica etc)* laboratory.

'gaffe [gaf] *sf inv* blunder.

gagli'ardo, a [gaʎˈʎardo] *ag* strong,

vigorous.

'**gaio, a** *ag* cheerful, gay.

'**gala** *sf* (*sfarzo*) pomp; (*festa*) gala.

ga'**lante** *ag* gallant, courteous; (*avventura*) amorous; **galante'ria** *sf* gallantry.

galantu'**omo**, *pl* **galantu'omini** *sm* gentleman.

ga'**lassia** *sf* galaxy.

gala'**teo** *sm* (good) manners *pl*.

gale'**otto** *sm* (*remalore*) galley slave; (*carcerato*) convict.

ga'**lera** *sf* (*NAUT*) galley; (*prigione*) prison.

'**galla** *sf*: a ~ afloat; venire a ~ to surface, come to the surface; (*fig: verità*) to come out.

galleggi'**ante** [galled'dʒante] *ag* floating // *sm* (*natante*) barge; (*di pescatore, lenza, TECN*) float.

galleggi'**are** [galled'dʒare] *vi* to float.

galle'**ria** *sf* (*traforo*) tunnel; (*ARCHIT, d'arte*) gallery; (*TEATRO*) circle; (*strada coperta con negozi*) arcade.

'**Galles** *sm*: il ~ Wales; **gal'lese** *ag, sm* (*LING*) Welsh // *sm/f* Welshman/woman.

gal'**letta** *sf* cracker.

gal'**lina** *sf* hen.

'**gallo** *sm* cock.

gal'**lone** *sm* piece of braid; (*MIL*) stripe; (*unità di misura*) gallon.

galop'**pare** *vi* to gallop.

ga'**loppo** *sm* gallop; al o di ~ at a gallop.

'**gamba** *sf* leg; (*asta: di lettera*) stem; in ~ (*in buona salute*) well; (*bravo, sveglio*) bright, smart; prendere qc sotto ~ (*fig*) to treat sth too lightly.

gambe'**retto** *sm* shrimp.

gambe**ro** *sm* (*di acqua dolce*) crayfish; (*di mare*) prawn.

'**gambo** *sm* stem; (*di frutta*) stalk.

'**gamma** *sf* (*MUS*) scale; (*di colori, fig*) range.

ga'**nascia, sce** [ga'naʃʃa ʃʃ jaw; ~ooo del freno (*AUT*) brake shoes.

'**gancio** ['gantʃo] *sm* hook.

'**gangheri** ['gangeri] *smpl*: uscire dai ~ (*fig*) to fly into a temper.

'**gara** *sf* competition; (*SPORT*) competition; contest; match; (: *corsa*) race; fare a ~ to compete, vie.

ga'**rage** [ga'raʒ] *sm inv* garage.

garan'**tire** *vt* to guarantee; (*debito*) to stand surety for; (*dare per certo*) to assure.

garan'**zia** [garan'tsia] *sf* guarantee; (*pegno*) security.

gar'**bato, a** *ag* courteous, polite.

'**garbo** *sm* (*buone maniere*) politeness, courtesy; (*di vestito etc*) grace, style.

gareggi'**are** [gared'dʒare] *vi* to compete.

garga'**rismo** *sm* gargle; fare i ~i to gargle.

ga'**rofano** *sm* carnation; chiodo di ~

clove.

'**garza** ['gardza] *sf* (*per bende*) gauze.

gar'**zone** [gar'dzone] *sm* (*di negozio*) boy.

gas *sm inv* gas; a tutto ~ at full speed; dare ~ (*AUT*) to accelerate.

ga'**solio** *sm* diesel (oil).

ga's(s)**ato, a** *ag* (*bibita*) aerated, fizzy.

gas'**soso, a** *ag* gaseous; gassy // *sf* fizzy drink.

gastrono'**mia** *sf* gastronomy.

gat'**tino** *sm* kitten.

'**gatto, a** *sm/f* cat, tomcat/she-cat; ~ selvatico wildcat; ~ delle nevi (*AUT, SCI*) snowcat.

gatto'**pardo** *sm*: ~ africano serval; ~ americano ocelot.

'**gaudio** *sm* joy, happiness.

ga'**vetta** *sf* (*MIL*) mess tin; venire dalla ~ (*MIL, fig*) to rise from the ranks.

'**gazza** ['gaddza] *sf* magpie.

gaz'**zella** [gad'dzella] *sf* gazelle; (*dei carabinieri*) (high-speed) police car.

gaz'**zetta** [gad'dzetta] *sf* news sheet; G~ Ufficiale *official publication containing details of new laws*.

gel [dʒɛl] *sm inv* gel.

ge'**lare** [dʒe'lare] *vt, vi, vb impers* to freeze; (*fig*) **ge'lata** *sf* frost.

gelate'**ria** [dʒelate'ria] *sf* ice-cream shop.

gela'**tina** [dʒela'tina] *sf* gelatine; ~ esplosiva dynamite; ~ di frutta fruit jelly.

ge'**lato, a** [dʒe'lato] *ag* frozen // *sm* ice cream.

'**gelido, a** ['dʒɛlido] *ag* icy, ice-cold.

'**gelo** ['dʒɛlo] *sm* (*temperatura*) intense cold; (*brina*) frost; (*fig*) chill; **ge'lone** *sm* chilblain.

gelo'**sia** [dʒelo'sia] *sf* jealousy.

ge'**loso, a** [dʒe'loso] *ag* jealous.

'**gelso** ['dʒɛlso] *sm* mulberry (tree).

gelso'**mino** [dʒelso'mino] *sm* jasmine.

ge'**mello, a** [dʒe'mɛllo] *ag, sm/f* twin; ~i *smpl* (*di camicia*) cufflinks; (*dello zodiaco*): G~i Gemini *sg*.

'**gemere** ['dʒemere] *vi* to moan, groan; (*cigolare*) to creak; (*gocciolare*) to drip, ooze; '**gemito** *sm* moan, groan.

'**gemma** ['dʒemma] *sf* (*BOT*) bud; (*pietra preziosa*) gem.

gene'**rale** [dʒene'rale] *ag, sm* general; in ~ (*per sommi capi*) in general terms; (*di solito*) usually, in general; a ~ richiesta by popular request; **generalità** *sfpl* (*dati d'identità*) particulars; **generaliz'zare** *vt, vi* to generalize; **general'mente** *av* generally.

gene'**rare** [dʒene'rare] *vt* (*dar vita*) to give birth to; (*produrre*) to produce; (*causare*) to arouse; (*TECN*) to produce, generate; **genera'tore** *sm* (*TECN*) generator; **generazi'one** *sf* generation.

'**genere** ['dʒɛnere] *sm* kind, type, sort; (*BIOL*) genus; (*merce*) article, product; (*LING*) gender; (*ARTE, LETTERATURA*) genre; in ~ generally, as a rule; il ~ umano mankind; ~i alimentari food-stuffs.

ge'nerico, a, ci, che [dʒe'nɛriko] *ag* generic; (*vago*) vague, imprecise.

'genero ['dʒenero] *sm* son-in-law.

generosità [dʒenerosi'ta] *sf* generosity.

gene'roso, a [dʒene'roso] *ag* generous.

ge'netico, a, ci, che [dʒe'nɛtiko] *ag* genetic // *sf* genetics *sg.*

gen'giva [dʒen'dʒiva] *sf* (ANAT) gum.

geni'ale [dʒen'jale] *ag* (*persona*) of genius; (*idea*) ingenious, brilliant.

'genio ['dʒɛnjo] *sm* genius; **andare a ~ a** qn to be to sb's liking, appeal to sb.

geni'tale [dʒeni'tale] *ag* genital; ~i *smpl* genitals.

geni'tore [dʒeni'tore] *sm* parent, father *o* mother; ~i *smpl* parents.

gen'naio [dʒen'najo] *sm* January.

'Genova ['dʒenova] *sf* Genoa.

gen'taglia [dʒen'taʎʎa] *sf* (*peg*) rabble.

'gente ['dʒɛnte] *sf* people *pl.*

gen'tile [dʒen'tile] *ag* (*persona, atto*) kind; (: *garbato*) courteous, polite; (*nelle lettere*): **G~ Signore** Dear Sir; (: *sulla busta*): **G~ Signor Fernando Villa** Mr Fernando Villa; **genti'lezza** *sf* kindness; courtesy, politeness; **per gentilezza** (*per favore*) please.

gentilu'omo, *pl* **gentilu'omini** [dʒenti'lwɔmo] *sm* gentleman.

genu'ino, a [dʒenu'ino] *ag* (*prodotto*) natural; (*persona, sentimento*) genuine, sincere.

geogra'fia [dʒeogra'fia] *sf* geography.

geolo'gia [dʒeolo'dʒia] *sf* geology.

ge'ometra, i, e [dʒe'ɔmetra] *sm/f* (*professionista*) surveyor.

geome'tria [dʒeome'tria] *sf* geometry; **geo'metrico, a, ci, che** *ag* geometric(al).

ge'ranio [dʒe'ranjo] *sm* geranium.

gerar'chia [dʒerar'kia] *sf* hierarchy.

ge'rente [dʒe'rɛnte] *sm/f* manager/manageress.

'gergo, ghi ['dʒergo] *sm* jargon; slang.

geria'tria [dʒerja'tria] *sf* geriatrics *sg.*

Ger'mania [dʒer'manja] *sf*: **la ~ occidentale/orientale** West/East Germany.

'germe ['dʒerme] *sm* germ; (*fig*) seed.

germogli'are [dʒermoʎ'ʎare] *vi* to sprout; to germinate; **ger'moglio** *sm* shoot; bud.

gero'glifico, ci [dʒero'glifiko] *sm* hieroglyphic.

'gesso ['dʒesso] *sm* chalk; (SCULTURA, MED, EDIL) plaster; (*statua*) plaster figure; (*minerale*) gypsum.

gesti'one [dʒes'tjone] *sf* management.

ges'tire [dʒes'tire] *vt* to run, manage.

'gesto ['dʒesto] *sm* gesture.

ges'tore [dʒes'tore] *sm* manager.

Gesù [dʒe'zu] *sm* Jesus.

gesu'ita, i [dʒezu'ita] *sm* Jesuit.

get'tare [dʒet'tare] *vt* to throw; (*anche*: ~ **via**) to throw away *o* out; (SCULTURA) to cast; (EDIL) to lay; (*acqua*) to spout; (*grido*) to utter; ~**rsi** *vr*: ~**rsi in** (*sog: fiume*) to flow into; ~ **uno sguardo su** to take a quick look at; **get'tata** *sf* (*di cemento, gesso, metalli*) cast; (*diga*) jetty.

'getto ['dʒetto] *sm* (*di gas, liquido,* AER) jet; **a ~ continuo** uninterruptedly; **di ~** (*fig*) straight off, in one go.

get'tone [dʒet'tone] *sm* token; (*per giochi*) counter; (: *roulette etc*) chip; ~ **telefonico** telephone token.

ghiacci'aio [gjat'tʃajo] *sm* glacier.

ghiacci'are [gjat'tʃare] *vt* to freeze; (*fig*): ~ **qn** to make sb's blood run cold // *vi* to freeze, ice over; **ghiacci'ato, a** *ag* frozen; (*bevanda*) ice-cold.

ghi'accio ['gjattʃo] *sm* ice.

ghiacci'olo [gjat'tʃɔlo] *sm* icicle; (*tipo di gelato*) ice lolly (*Brit*), popsicle (*US*).

ghi'aia ['gjaja] *sf* gravel.

ghi'anda ['gjanda] *sf* (BOT) acorn.

ghi'andola ['gjandola] *sf* gland.

ghigliot'tina [giʎʎot'tina] *sf* guillotine.

ghi'gnare [gin'nare] *vi* to sneer.

ghi'otto, a ['gjotto] *ag* greedy; (*cibo*) delicious, appetizing; **ghiot'tone, a** *sm/f* glutton.

ghiri'bizzo [giri'biddzo] *sm* whim.

ghiri'goro [giri'gɔro] *sm* scribble, squiggle.

ghir'landa [gir'landa] *sf* garland, wreath.

'ghiro ['giro] *sm* dormouse.

'ghisa ['giza] *sf* cast iron.

già [dʒa] *av* already; (*ex, in precedenza*) formerly // *escl* of course!, yes indeed!

gi'acca, che ['dʒakka] *sf* jacket; ~ **a vento** windcheater (*Brit*), windbreaker (*US*).

giacché [dʒak'ke] *cong* since, as.

giac'chetta [dʒak'ketta] *sf* (light) jacket.

gia'cenza [dʒa'tʃɛntsa] *sf*: **merce in ~** goods in stock; **capitale in ~** uninvested capital; ~**e di magazzino** unsold stock.

gia'cere [dʒa'tʃere] *vi* to lie; **giaci'mento** *sm* deposit.

gia'cinto [dʒa'tʃinto] *sm* hyacinth.

gi'ada ['dʒada] *sf* jade.

giaggi'olo [dʒad'dʒɔlo] *sm* iris.

giagu'aro [dʒa'gwaro] *sm* jaguar.

gi'allo ['dʒallo] *ag* yellow; (*carnagione*) sallow // *sm* yellow; (*anche:* **romanzo ~**) detective novel; (*anche: film ~*) detective film; ~ **dell'uovo** yolk.

giam'mai [dʒam'mai] *av* never.

Giap'pone [dʒap'pone] *sm* Japan; **giappo'nese** *ag, sm/f, sm* Japanese *inv.*

gi'ara ['dʒara] *sf* jar.

giardi'naggio [dʒardi'naddʒo] *sm* gardening.

giardi'netta [dʒardi'netta] *sf* estate car (*Brit*), station wagon (*US*).

giardini'ere, a [dʒardi'njɛre] *sm/f* gardener // *sf* (*misto di sottaceti*) mixed pickles *pl*; (*automobile*) = **giardinetta.**

giar'dino [dʒar'dino] *sm* garden; ~ **d'infanzia** nursery school; ~ **pubblico** public gardens *pl*, (public) park; ~ **zoologico** zoo.

giarretti'era [dʒarret'tjɛra] *sf* garter.

giavel'lotto [dʒavel'lɔtto] *sm* javelin.

gi'gante, 'essa [dʒi'gante] *sm/f* giant // *ag* giant, gigantic; (*COMM*) giant-size; **gigan'tesco, a, schi, sche** *ag* gigantic.

'giglio ['dʒiʎʎo] *sm* lily.

gilè [dʒi'le] *sm inv* waistcoat.

gin [dʒin] *sm inv* gin.

gine'cologo, a, gi, ghe [dʒine'kɔlogo] *sm/f* gynaecologist.

gi'nepro [dʒi'nepro] *sm* juniper.

gi'nestra [dʒi'nɛstra] *sf* (*BOT*) broom.

Gi'nevra [dʒi'nevra] *sf* Geneva.

gingil'larsi [dʒindʒil'larsi] *vr* to fritter away one's time; (*giocare*): ~ **con** to fiddle with.

gin'gillo [dʒin'dʒillo] *sm* plaything.

gin'nasio [dʒin'nazjo] *sm the 4th and 5th year of secondary school in Italy.*

gin'nasta, i, e [dʒin'nasta] *sm/f* gymnast; **gin'nastica** *sf* gymnastics *sg*; (*esercizio fisico*) keep-fit exercises; (*INS*) physical education.

gi'nocchio [dʒi'nɔkkjo] *pl(m)* **gi'nocchi** *o pl(f)* **gi'nocchia** *sm* knee; **stare in** ~ to kneel, be on one's knees; **mettersi in** ~ to kneel (down); **ginocchi'oni** *av* on one's knees.

gio'care [dʒo'kare] *vt* to play; (*scommettere*) to stake, wager, bet; (*ingannare*) to take in // *vi* to play; (*a roulette etc*) to gamble; (*fig*) to play a part, be important; (*TECN: meccanismo*) to be loose; ~ **a** (*gioco, sport*) to play; (*cavalli*) to bet on; **~rsi la carriera** to put one's career at risk; **gioca'tore, 'trice** *sm/f* player; gambler.

gio'cattolo [dʒo'kattolo] *sm* toy.

gio'chetto [dʒo'ketto] *sm* (*tranello*) trick; (*fig*): **è un** ~ it's child's play.

gi'oco, chi ['dʒɔko] *sm* game; (*divertimento, TECN*) play; (*al casinò*) gambling; (*CARTE*) hand; (*insieme di pezzi etc necessari per un gioco*) set; **per** ~ for fun; **fare il doppio** ~ **con qn** to double-cross sb; ~ **d'azzardo** game of chance; ~ **della palla** football; ~ **degli scacchi** chess set; **i Giochi Olimpici** the Olympic Games.

giocoli'ere [dʒoko'ljɛre] *sm* juggler.

gio'coso, a [dʒo'koso] *ag* playful, jesting.

gi'ogo, ghi ['dʒɔgo] *sm* yoke.

gi'oia ['dʒɔja] *sf* joy, delight; (*pietra preziosa*) jewel, precious stone.

gioiel'leria [dʒojelle'ria] *sf* jeweller's craft; jeweller's (shop).

gioielli'ere, a [dʒojel'ljɛre] *sm/f* jeweller.

gioi'ello [dʒo'jɛllo] *sm* jewel, piece of jewellery; **~i** *smpl* jewellery *sg*.

gioi'oso, a [dʒo'joso] *ag* joyful.

Gior'dania [dʒor'danja] *sf*: **la** ~ Jordan.

giorna'laio, a [dʒorna'lajo] *sm/f* newsagent (*Brit*), newsdealer (*US*).

gior'nale [dʒor'nale] *sm* (news)paper; (*diario*) journal, diary; (*COMM*) journal; ~ **di bordo** log, ~ **radio** radio news *sg*.

giornali'ero, a [dʒorna'ljɛro] *ag* daily; (*che varia: umore*) changeable // *sm* day labourer.

giorna'lismo [dʒorna'lizmo] *sm* journalism.

giorna'lista, i, e [dʒorna'lista] *sm/f* journalist.

gior'nata [dʒor'nata] *sf* day; ~ **lavorativa** working day.

gi'orno ['dʒorno] *sm* day; (*opposto alla notte*) day, daytime; (*luce del* ~) daylight; **al** ~ per day; **di** ~ by day; **al** ~ **d'oggi** nowadays.

gi'ostra ['dʒɔstra] *sf* (*per bimbi*) merry-go-round; (*torneo storico*) joust.

gio'vane ['dʒovane] *ag* young; (*aspetto*) youthful // *sm/f* youth/girl, young man/woman; **i ~i** young people; **giova'nile** *ag* youthful; (*scritti*) early; (*errore*) of youth; **giova'notto** *sm* young man.

gio'vare [dʒo'vare] *vi*: ~ **a** (*essere utile*) to be useful to; (*far bene*) to be good for // *vb impers* (*essere bene, utile*) to be useful; **~rsi di qc** to make use of sth.

giovedì [dʒove'di] *sm inv* Thursday; **di** *o* **il** ~ on Thursdays.

gioventù [dʒoven'tu] *sf* (*periodo*) youth; (*i giovani*) young people *pl*, youth.

giovi'ale [dʒo'vjale] *ag* jovial, jolly.

giovi'nezza [dʒovi'nettsa] *sf* youth.

gira'dischi [dʒira'diski] *sm inv* record player.

gi'raffa [dʒi'raffa] *sf* giraffe.

gi'randola [dʒi'randola] *sf* (*fuoco d'artificio*) Catherine wheel; (*giocattolo*) toy windmill; (*banderuola*) weather vane, weathercock.

gi'rare [dʒi'rare] *vt* (*far ruotare*) to turn; (*percorrere, visitare*) to go round; (*CINEMA*) to shoot; to make; (*COMM*) to endorse // *vi* to turn; (*più veloce*) to spin; (*andare in giro*) to wander, go around; **~rsi** *vr* to turn; ~ **attorno a** to go round; to revolve round; **far** ~ **la testa a qn** to make sb dizzy; (*fig*) to turn sb's head.

girar'rosto [dʒirar'rɔsto] *sm* (*CUC*) spit.

gira'sole [dʒira'sole] *sm* sunflower.

gi'rata [dʒi'rata] *sf* (*passeggiata*) stroll; (*con veicolo*) drive; (*COMM*) endorsement.

gira'volta [dʒira'vɔlta] *sf* twirl, turn; (*curva*) sharp bend; (*fig*) about-turn.

gi'revole [dʒi'revole] *ag* revolving, turning.

gi'rino [dʒi'rino] *sm* tadpole.

'giro ['dʒiro] *sm* (*circuito, cerchio*) circle; (*di chiave, manovella*) turn; (*viaggio*) tour, excursion; (*passeggiata*) stroll, walk; (*in macchina*) drive; (*in bicicletta*) ride; (*SPORT: della pista*) lap; (*di denaro*) circulation; (*CARTE*) hand; (*TECN*) revolution; **prendere in ~ qn** (*fig*) to pull sb's leg; **fare un ~** to go for a walk (*o* a drive *o* a ride); **andare in ~** to go about, walk around; **a stretto ~ di posta** by return of post; **nel ~ di un mese** in a month's time; **essere nel ~** (*fig*) to belong to a circle (of friends); **~ d'affari** (*COMM*) turnover; **~ di parole** circumlocution; **~ di prova** (*AUT*) test drive; **~ turistico** sightseeing tour; **giro-'collo** *sm*: **a girocollo** crew-neck *cpd*.

gironzo'lare [dʒirondzo'lare] *vi* to stroll about.

'gita ['dʒita] *sf* excursion, trip; **fare una ~** to go for a trip, go on an outing.

gi'tano, a [dʒi'tano] *sm/f* gipsy.

giù [dʒu] *av* down; (*dabbasso*) downstairs; **in ~** downwards, down; **~ di lì** (*pressappoco*) thereabouts; **bambini dai 6 anni in ~** children aged 6 and under; **per: cadere ~ per le scale** to fall down the stairs; **essere ~** (*fig: di salute*) to be run down; (: *di spirito*) to be depressed.

giub'botto [dʒub'botto] *sm* jerkin; **~ antiproiettile** bulletproof vest.

gi'ubilo ['dʒubilo] *sm* rejoicing.

giudi'care [dʒudi'kare] *vt* to judge; (*accusato*) to try; (*lite*) to arbitrate in; **~ qn/qc bello** to consider sb/sth (to be) beautiful.

gi'udice ['dʒuditʃe] *sm* judge; **~ conciliatore** justice of the peace; **~ popolare** member of a jury.

giu'dizio [dʒu'dittsjo] *sm* judgment; (*opinione*) opinion; (*DIR*) judgment, sentence; (: *processo*) trial; (: *verdetto*) verdict; **aver ~** to be wise *o* prudent; **citare in ~** to summons; **giudizi'oso, a** *ag* prudent, judicious.

gi'ugno ['dʒuɲɲo] *sm* June.

giul'lare [dʒul'lare] *sm* jester.

giu'menta [dʒu'menta] *sf* mare.

gi'unco, chi ['dʒunko] *sm* rush.

gi'ungere ['dʒundʒere] *vi* to arrive // *vt* (*mani etc*) to join; **~ a** to arrive at, reach.

gi'ungla ['dʒungla] *sf* jungle.

gi'unto, a ['dʒunto] *pp di* **giungere** // *sm* (*TECN*) coupling, joint // *sf* addition; (*organo esecutivo, amministrativo*) council, board; **per ~a** into the bargain, in addition; **~a militare** military junta; **giun'tura** *sf* joint.

giuo'care [dʒwo'kare] *vt, vi* = **giocare**; **giu'oco** *sm* = **gioco**.

giura'mento [dʒura'mento] *sm* oath; **~ falso** perjury.

giu'rare [dʒu'rare] *vt* to swear // *vi* to swear, take an oath; **giu'rato, a** *ag*: **nemico giurato** sworn enemy // *sm/f* juror, juryman/woman.

giu'ria [dʒu'ria] *sf* jury.

giu'ridico, a, ci, che [dʒu'ridiko] *ag* legal.

giustifi'care [dʒustifi'kare] *vt* to justify; **giustificazi'one** *sf* justification; (*INS*) (note of) excuse.

gius'tizia [dʒus'tittsja] *sf* justice; **giustizi'are** *vt* to execute, put to death; **giustizi'ere** *sm* executioner.

gi'usto, a ['dʒusto] *ag* (*equo*) fair, just; (*vero*) true, correct; (*adatto*) right, suitable; (*preciso*) exact, correct // *av* (*esattamente*) exactly, precisely; (*per l'appunto, appena*) just; **arrivare ~** to arrive just in time; **ho ~ bisogno di te** you're just the person I need.

glaci'ale [gla'tʃale] *ag* glacial.

'glandola *sf* = **ghiandola**.

gli [ʎi] *det mpl* (*dav V, s impura, gn, pn, ps, x, z*) the // *pronome* (*a lui*) to him; (*a esso*) to it; (*in coppia con la, la, li, le, ne: a lui, a lei, a loro etc*): **gliele do** I'm giving them to him (*o* her *o* them).

gli'ela ['ʎela] *etc vedi* **gli**.

glo'bale *ag* overall.

'globo *sm* globe.

'globulo *sm* (*ANAT*): **~ rosso/bianco** red/white corpuscle.

'gloria *sf* glory; **glori'oso, a** *ag* glorious.

glos'sario *sm* glossary.

'gnocchi ['ɲɔkki] *smpl* (*CUC*) *small dumplings made of semolina pasta or potato.*

'gobba *sf* (*ANAT*) hump; (*protuberanza*) bump.

'gobbo, a *ag* hunchbacked; (*ricurvo*) round-shouldered // *sm/f* hunchback.

'goccia, ce ['gottʃa] *sf* drop; **goccio'lare** *vi, vt* to drip.

go'dere *vi* (*compiacersi*): **~ (di)** to be delighted (at), rejoice (at); (*trarre vantaggio*): **~ di** to enjoy, benefit from // *vt* to enjoy; **~rsi la vita** to enjoy life; **~sela** to have a good time, enjoy o.s.; **godi'mento** *sm* enjoyment.

'goffo, a *ag* clumsy, awkward.

'gola *sf* (*ANAT*) throat; (*golosità*) gluttony, greed; (*di camino*) flue; (*di monte*) gorge; **fare ~** (*anche fig*) to tempt.

golf *sm inv* (*SPORT*) golf; (*maglia*) cardigan.

'golfo *sm* gulf.

go'loso, a *ag* greedy.

'gomito *sm* elbow; (*di strada etc*) sharp bend.

go'mitolo *sm* ball.

'gomma *sf* rubber; (*colla*) gum; (*per cancellare*) rubber, eraser; (*di veicolo*) tyre (*Brit*), tire (*US*); **~ a terra** flat tyre (*Brit*) *o* tire (*US*); **gommapi'uma** *sf* ®

foam rubber.

'**gondola** *sf* gondola; **gondoli'ere** *sm* gondolier.

gonfa'lone *sm* banner.

gonfi'are *vt* (*pallone*) to blow up, inflate; (*dilatare*, *ingrossare*) to swell; (*fig: notizia*) to exaggerate; ~rsi *vr* to swell; (*fiume*) to rise; '**gonfio, a** *ag* swollen; (*stomaco*) bloated; (*vela*) full; **gonfi'ore** *sm* swelling.

gongo'lare *vi* to look pleased with o.s.; ~ di gioia to be overjoyed.

'**gonna** *sf* skirt; ~ pantalone culottes *pl.*

'**gonzo** ['gondzo] *sm* simpleton, fool.

gorgheggi'are [gorged'dʒare] *vi* to warble; to trill.

'**gorgo, ghi** *sm* whirlpool.

gorgogli'are [gorgoʎ'ʎare] *vi* to gurgle.

go'rilla *sm inv* gorilla; (*guardia del corpo*) bodyguard.

'**gotta** *sf* gout.

gover'nante *sm/f* ruler // *sf* (*di bambini*) governess; (*donna di servizio*) housekeeper.

gover'nare *vt* (*stato*) to govern, rule; (*pilotare, guidare*) to steer; (*bestiame*) to tend, look after; **governa'tivo, a** *ag* government *cpd*; **governa'tore** *sm* governor.

go'verno *sm* government.

gozzovigli'are [gottsoviʎ'ʎare] *vi* to make merry, carouse.

gracchi'are [grak'kjare] *vi* to caw.

graci'dare [gratʃi'dare] *vi* to croak.

'**gracile** ['gratʃile] *ag* frail, delicate.

gra'dasso *sm* boaster.

gradazi'one [gradat'tsjone] *sf* (*sfumatura*) gradation; ~ alcolica alcoholic content, strength.

gra'devole *ag* pleasant, agreeable.

gradi'mento *sm* pleasure, satisfaction; è di suo ~? is it to your liking?

gradi'nata *sf* flight of steps; (*in teatro, studio*) tiers *pl.*

gra'dino *sm* step; (*ALPINISMO*) foothold.

gra'dire *vt* (*accettare con piacere*) to accept; (*desiderare*) to wish, like; gradisce una tazza di tè? would you like a cup of tea?; **gra'dito, a** *ag* pleasing; welcome.

'**grado** *sm* (*MAT, FISICA etc*) degree; (*stadio*) degree, level; (*MIL, sociale*) rank; essere in ~ di fare to be in a position to do.

gradu'ale *ag* gradual.

gradu'are *vt* to grade; **gradu'ato, a** *ag* (*esercizi*) graded; (*scala, termometro*) graduated // *sm* (*MIL*) non-commissioned officer.

'**graffa** *sf* (*gancio*) clip; (*segno grafico*) brace.

graffi'are *vt* to scratch.

'**graffio** *sm* scratch.

gra'fia *sf* (*spelling*); (*scrittura*) handwriting.

'**grafico, a, ci, che** *ag* graphic // *sm* graph; (*persona*) graphic designer // *sf* graphic arts *pl.*

gra'migna [gra'miɲɲa] *sf* weed; couch grass.

gram'matica, che *sf* grammar; **grammati'cale** *ag* grammatical.

'**grammo** *sm* gram(me).

gran *ag vedi* grande.

'**grana** *sf* (*granello, di minerali, corpi spezzati*) grain; (*fam: seccatura*) trouble; (: *soldi*) cash // *sm inv* Parmesan (cheese).

gra'naio *sm* granary, barn.

gra'nata *sf* (*frutto*) pomegranate; (*pietra preziosa*) garnet; (*proiettile*) grenade.

Gran Bre'tagna [granbre'taɲɲa] *sf*: la ~ Great Britain.

'**granchio** ['grankjo] *sm* crab; (*fig*) blunder; prendere un ~ (*fig*) to blunder.

grandango'lare *sm* wide-angle lens *sg.*

'**grande,** *qualche volta* **gran** +*C,* **grand'** +*V ag* (*grosso, largo, vasto*) big, large; (*alto*) tall; (*lungo*) long; (*in sensi astratti*) great // *sm/f* (*persona adulta*) adult, grown-up; (*chi ha ingegno e potenza*) great man/woman; fare le cose in ~ to do things in style; una gran bella donna a very beautiful woman; non è una gran cosa *o* un gran che it's nothing special; non ne so gran che I don't know very much about it.

grandeggi'are [granded'dʒare] *vi* (*emergere per grandezza*); ~ su to tower over; (*darsi arie*) to put on airs.

gran'dezza [gran'dettsa] *sf* (*dimensione*) size; magnitude; (*fig*) greatness; in ~ naturale lifesize.

grandi'nare *vb impers* to hail.

'**grandine** *sf* hail.

gran'duca, chi *sm* grand duke.

gra'nello *sm* (*di cereali, uva*) seed; (*di frutta*) pip; (*di sabbia, sale etc*) grain.

gra'nita *sf* kind of water ice.

gra'nito *sm* granite.

'**grano** *sm* (*in quasi tutti i sensi*) grain; (*frumento*) wheat; (*di rosario, collana*) bead; ~ di pepe peppercorn.

gran'turco *sm* maize.

'**granulo** *sm* granule; (*MED*) pellet.

'**grappa** *sf* rough, strong brandy.

'**grappolo** *sm* bunch, cluster.

gras'setto *sm* (*TIP*) bold (type).

'**grasso, a** *ag* fat; (*cibo*) fatty; (*pelle*) greasy; (*terreno*) rich; (*fig: guadagno, annata*) plentiful; (: *volgare*) coarse, lewd // *sm* (*di persona, animale*) fat; (*sostanza che unge*) grease; **gras'soccio, a, ci, ce** *ag* plump.

'**grata** *sf* grating.

gra'ticola *sf* grill.

gra'tifica, che *sf* bonus.

'**gratis** *av* free, for nothing.

grati'tudine *sf* gratitude.

'grato, a *ag* grateful; (*gradito*) pleasant, agreeable.

gratta'capo *sm* worry, headache.

grattaci'elo [gratta'tʃɛlo] *sm* skyscraper.

grat'tare *vt* (*pelle*) to scratch; (*raschiare*) to scrape; (*pane, formaggio, carote*) to grate; (*fam: rubare*) to pinch // *vi* (*stridere*) to grate; (*AUT*) to grind; **~rsi** *vr* to scratch o.s.

grat'tugia, gie [grat'tudʒa] *sf* grater; **grattugi'are** *vt* to grate; **pane grattugiato** breadcrumbs *pl*.

gra'tuito, a *ag* free; (*fig*) gratuitous.

gra'vame *sm* tax; (*fig*) burden, weight.

gra'vare *vt* to burden // *vi*: **~ su** to weigh on.

'grave *ag* (*danno, pericolo, peccato etc*) grave, serious; (*responsabilità*) heavy, grave; (*contegno*) grave, solemn; (*voce, suono*) deep, low-pitched; (*LING*): **accento ~** grave accent; **un malato ~** a person who is seriously ill.

gravi'danza [gravi'dantsa] *sf* pregnancy.

'gravido, a *ag* pregnant.

gravità *sf* seriousness; (*anche FISICA*) gravity.

gra'voso, a *ag* heavy, onerous.

'grazia ['grattsja] *sf* grace; (*favore*) favour; (*DIR*) pardon; **grazi'are** *vt* (*DIR*) to pardon.

'grazie ['grattsje] *escl* thank you!; **~ mille!** *o* **tante!** *o* **infinite!** thank you very much!; **~ a** thanks to.

grazi'oso, a [grat'tsjoso] *ag* charming, delightful; (*gentile*) gracious.

'Grecia ['grɛtʃa] *sf*: **la ~** Greece; **'greco, a, ci, che** *ag, sm/f, sm* Greek.

'gregge, *pl(f)* **i** ['greddʒe] *sm* flock.

'greggio, a, gi, ge ['greddʒo] *ag* raw, unrefined; (*diamante*) rough, uncut; (*tessuto*) unbleached // *sm* (*anche*: **petrolio ~**) crude (oil).

grembi'ule *sm* apron; (*sopravveste*) overall.

'grembo *sm* lap; (*ventre della madre*) womb.

gre'mito, a *ag*: **~ (di)** packed *o* crowded (with).

'gretto, a *ag* mean, stingy; (*fig*) narrow-minded.

'greve *ag* heavy.

'grezzo, a ['greddzo] *ag* = **greggio.**

gri'dare *vi* (*per chiamare*) to shout, cry (out); (*strillare*) to scream, yell // *vt* to shout (out), yell (out); **~ aiuto** to cry *o* shout for help.

'grido, *pl(m)* **i** *o* *pl(f)* **a** *sm* shout, cry; scream, yell; (*di animale*) cry; **di ~** famous.

'grigio, a, gi, gie ['gridʒo] *ag, sm* grey.

'griglia ['griʎʎa] *sf* (*per arrostire*) grill; (*ELETTR*) grid; (*inferriata*) grating; **alla ~** (*CUC*) grilled; **grigli'ata** *sf* (*CUC*) grill.

gril'letto *sm* trigger.

'grillo *sm* (*ZOOL*) cricket; (*fig*) whim.

grimal'dello *sm* picklock.

'grinta *sf* grim ' expression; (*SPORT*) fighting spirit.

'grinza ['grintsa] *sf* crease, wrinkle; (*ruga*) wrinkle; **non fare una ~** (*fig: ragionamento*) to be faultless; **grin'zoso, a** *ag* creased; wrinkled.

grip'pare *vi* (*TECN*) to seize.

gris'sino *sm* bread-stick.

'gronda *sf* eaves *pl*.

gron'daia *sf* gutter.

gron'dare *vi* to pour; (*essere bagnato*): **~ di** to be dripping with // *vt* to drip with.

'groppa *sf* (*di animale*) back, rump; (*fam: dell'uomo*) back, shoulders *pl*.

'groppo *sm* tangle; **avere un ~ alla gola** (*fig*) to have a lump in one's throat.

gros'sezza [gros'settsa] *sf* size; thickness.

gros'sista, i, e *sm/f* (*COMM*) wholesaler.

'grosso, a *ag* big, large; (*di spessore*) thick; (*grossolano: anche fig*) coarse; (*grave, insopportabile*) serious, great; (*tempo, mare*) rough // *sm*: **il ~ di** the bulk of; **un pezzo ~** (*fig*) a VIP, a bigwig; **farla ~a** to do something very stupid; **dirle ~e** to tell tall stories; **sbagliarsi di ~** to be completely wrong.

grosso'lano, a *ag* rough, coarse; (*fig*) coarse, crude; (*: errore*) stupid.

grosso'modo *av* roughly.

'grotta *sf* cave; grotto.

grot'tesco, a, schi, sche *ag* grotesque.

grovi'era *sm o f* gruyère (cheese).

gro'viglio [gro'viʎʎo] *sm* tangle; (*fig*) muddle.

gru *sf inv* crane.

'gruccia, ce ['gruttʃa] *sf* (*per camminare*) crutch; (*per abiti*) coathanger.

gru'gnire [gruɲ'ɲire] *vi* to grunt; **gru'gnito** *sm* grunt.

'grugno ['gruɲɲo] *sm* snout; (*fam: faccia*) mug.

'grullo, a *ag* silly, stupid.

'grumo *sm* (*di sangue*) clot; (*di farina etc*) lump.

'gruppo *sm* group; **~ sanguigno** blood group.

gruvi'era *sm o f* = **groviera.**

guada'gnare [gwadaɲ'ɲare] *vt* (*ottenere*) to gain; (*soldi, stipendio*) to earn; (*vincere*) to win; (*raggiungere*) to reach.

gua'dagno [gwa'daɲɲo] *sm* earnings *pl*; (*COMM*) profit; (*vantaggio, utile*) advantage, gain; **~ lordo/netto** gross/net earnings *pl*.

gu'ado *sm* ford; **passare a ~** to ford.

gu'ai *escl*: **~ a te** (*o lui etc*)! woe betide you (*o him etc*)!

gua'ina *sf* (*fodero*) sheath; (*indumento per donna*) girdle.

gu'aio *sm* trouble, mishap; (*inconveniente*) trouble, snag.

gua'ire *vi* to whine, yelp.

gu'ancia, ce ['gwantʃa] *sf* cheek.

guanci'ale [gwan'tʃale] *sm* pillow.

gu'anto *sm* glove.

gu'arda... *prefisso:* ~'**boschi** *sm inv* forester; ~'**caccia** *sm inv* gamekeeper; ~'**coste** *sm inv* coastguard; (*nave*) coastguard patrol vessel; ~'**linee** *sm inv* (*SPORT*) linesman.

guar'dare *vt* (*con lo sguardo: osservare*) to look at; (*film, televisione*) to watch; (*custodire*) to look after, take care of // *vi* to look; (*badare*): ~ **a** to pay attention to; (*luoghi: esser orientato*): ~ **a** to face; ~**rsi** *vr* to look at o.s.; ~**rsi da** (*astenersi*) to refrain from; (*stare in guardia*) to beware of; ~**rsi da fare** to take care not to do; **guarda di non sbagliare** try not to make a mistake; ~ **a vista** qn to keep a close watch on sb.

guarda'roba *sm inv* wardrobe; (*locale*) cloakroom; **guardarobi'ere, a** *sm/f* cloakroom attendant.

gu'ardia *sf* (*individuo, corpo*) guard; (*sorveglianza*) watch; **fare la** ~ **a** qc/qn to guard sth/sb; **stare in** ~ (*fig*) to be on one's guard; **di** ~ (*medico*) on call; ~ **carceraria** (*prison*) warder; ~ **del corpo** bodyguard; ~ **di finanza** (*corpo*) customs *pl*; (*persona*) customs officer; ~ **medica** emergency doctor service.

guardi'ano, a *sm/f* (*di carcere*) warder; (*di villa etc*) caretaker; (*di museo*) custodian; (*di zoo*) keeper; ~ **notturno** night watchman.

guar'dingo, a, ghi, ghe *ag* wary, cautious.

guardi'ola *sf* porter's lodge; (*MIL*) lookout tower.

guarigi'one [gwari'dʒone] *sf* recovery.

gua'rire *vt* (*persona, malattia*) to cure; (*ferita*) to heal // *vi* to recover, be cured; to heal (up).

guarnigi'one [gwarni'dʒone] *sf* garrison.

guar'nire *vt* (*ornare: abiti*) to trim; (*CUC*) to garnish; **guarnizi'one** *sf* trimming; garnish; (*TECN*) gasket.

guasta'feste *sm/f inv* spoilsport.

guas'tare *vt* to spoil, ruin; (*meccanismo*) to break; ~**rsi** *vr* (*cibo*) to go bad; (*meccanismo*) to break down; (*tempo*) to change for the worse; (*amici*) to quarrel, fall out.

gu'asto, a *ag* (*non funzionante*) broken; (: *telefono etc*) out of order; (*andato a male*) bad, rotten; (: *dente*) decayed, bad; (*fig: corrotto*) depraved // *sm* breakdown; (*avaria*) failure; ~ **al motore** engine failure.

guazza'buglio [gwattsa'buʎʎo] *sm* muddle.

gu'ercio, a, ci, ce ['gwertʃo] *ag* cross-eyed.

gu'erra *sf* war; (*tecnica: atomica, chimica etc*) warfare; **fare la** ~ **(a)** to wage war (against); ~ **mondiale** world war; **guerreggi'are** *vi* to wage war; **guerri'ero, a** *ag* warlike // *sm* warrior; **guer'riglia** *sf* guerrilla warfare; **guerrigli'ero** *sm* guerrilla.

'gufo *sm* owl.

gu'ida *sf* guide; (*comando, direzione*) guidance, direction; (*AUT*) driving; (: *sterzo*) steering; (*tappeto, di tenda, cassetto*) runner; ~ **a destra/sinistra** (*AUT*) right-/left-hand drive; ~ **telefonica** telephone directory.

gui'dare *vt* to guide; (*condurre a capo*) to lead; (*auto*) to drive; (*aereo, nave*) to pilot; **sai** ~? can you drive?; **guida'tore, trice** *sm/f* (*conducente*) driver.

guin'zaglio [gwin'tsaʎʎo] *sm* leash, lead.

gu'isa *sf*: **a** ~ **di** like, in the manner of.

guiz'zare [gwit'tsare] *vi* to dart; to flicker; to leap; ~ **via** (*fuggire*) to slip away.

'guscio ['guʃʃo] *sm* shell.

gus'tare *vt* (*cibi*) to taste; (: *assaporare con piacere*) to enjoy, savour; (*fig*) to enjoy, appreciate // *vi*: ~ **a** to please; **non mi gusta affatto** I don't like it at all.

'gusto *sm* taste; (*sapore*) flavour; (*godimento*) enjoyment; **al** ~ **di fragola** strawberry-flavoured; **mangiare di** ~ to eat heartily; **prenderci** ~: **ci ha preso** ~ he's acquired a taste for it, he's got to like it; **gus'toso, a** *ag* tasty; (*fig*) agreeable.

H

h *abbr* = **ora, altezza.**

ha, 'hai [a, ai] *vb vedi* **avere.**

hall [hɔl] *sf inv* hall, foyer.

'handicap ['handikap] *sm inv* handicap; **handicap'pato, a** *ag* handicapped // *sm/f* handicapped person, disabled person.

'hanno ['anno] *vb vedi* **avere.**

'hascisc ['haʃiʃ] *sm* hashish.

'herpes ['ɛrpes] *sm* (*MED*) herpes *sg*; ~ **zoster** shingles *sg*.

ho [ɔ] *vb vedi* **avere.**

'hobby ['hɔbi] *sm inv* hobby.

'hockey ['hɔki] *sm* hockey; ~ **su ghiaccio** ice hockey.

'hostess ['houstis] *sf inv* air hostess (*Brit*) o stewardess.

ho'tel *sm inv* hotel.

I

i *det mpl* the.

i'ato *sm* hiatus.

ibernazi'one [ibernat'tsjone] *sf* hibernation.

'ibrido, a *ag*, *sm* hybrid.

Id'dio *sm* God.

i'dea *sf* idea; (*opinione*) opinion, view; (*ideale*) ideal; dare l'~ di to seem, look like; ~ **fissa** obsession; **neanche** *o* **neppure per ~!** certainly not!

ide'ale *ag*, *sm* ideal.

ide'are *vt* (*immaginare*) to think up, conceive; (*progettare*) to plan.

i'dentico, a, ci, che *ag* identical.

identifi'care *vt* to identify; **identificazi'one** *sf* identification.

identità *sf inv* identity.

idi'oma, i *sm* idiom, language; **idio'-matico, a, ci, che** *ag* idiomatic; **frase idiomatica** idiom.

idi'ota, i, e *ag* idiotic // *sm/f* idiot.

idola'trare *vt* to worship; (*fig*) to idolize.

'idolo *sm* idol.

idoneità *sf* suitability.

i'doneo, a *ag*: ~ **a** suitable for, fit for; (*MIL*) fit for; (*qualificato*) qualified for.

i'drante *sm* hydrant.

i'draulico, a, ci, che *ag* hydraulic // *sm* plumber // *sf* hydraulics *sg*.

idroe'lettrico, a, ci, che *ag* hydro-electric.

i'drofilo, a *ag vedi* **cotone**.

idrofo'bia *sf* rabies *sg*.

i'drogeno [i'drɔdʒeno] *sm* hydrogen.

idros'calo *sm* seaplane base.

idrovo'lante *sm* seaplane.

i'ena *sf* hyena.

i'eri *av*, *sm* yesterday; **il giornale di ~** yesterday's paper; ~ **l'altro** the day before yesterday; ~ **sera** yesterday evening.

igi'ene [i'dʒɛne] *sf* hygiene; ~ **pubblica** public health; **igi'enico, a, ci, che** *ag* hygienic; (*salubre*) healthy.

i'gnaro, a [iɲ'ɲaro] *ag*: ~ **di** unaware of, ignorant of.

i'gnobile [iɲ'ɲɔbile] *ag* despicable, vile.

igno'rante [iɲɲo'rante] *ag* ignorant.

igno'rare [iɲɲo'rare] *vt* (*non sapere, conoscere*) to be ignorant *o* unaware of, not to know; (*fingere di non vedere, sentire*) to ignore.

i'gnoto, a [iɲ'ɲɔto] *ag* unknown.

il *det m* (*pl* (m) **i**; *diventa* **lo** (*pl* **gli**) *davanti a s impura, gn, pn, ps, x, z*; *f* **la** (*pl* **le**)) **1** the; ~ **libro/lo studente/l'acqua** the book/the student/the water; **gli scolari** the pupils

2 (*astrazione*): ~ **coraggio/l'amore/la giovinezza** courage/love/youth

3 (*tempo*): ~ **mattino/la sera** in the morning/evening; ~ **venerdì** *etc* (*abitualmente*) on Fridays *etc*; (*quel giorno*) on (the) Friday *etc*; **la settimana prossima** next week

4 (*distributivo*) a, an; **2.500 lire** ~ **chilo/paio** 2,500 lire a *o* per kilo/pair; **110 km**

l'ora 110 km an *o* per hour

5 (*partitivo*) some, any; **hai messo lo zucchero?** have you added sugar?; **hai comprato** ~ **latte?** did you buy (some *o* any) milk?

6 (*possesso*): **aprire gli occhi** to open one's eyes; **rompersi la gamba** to break one's leg; **avere i capelli neri/~ naso rosso** to have dark hair/a red nose; **mettiti le scarpe** put your shoes on

7 (*con nomi propri*): ~ **Petrarca** Petrarch; ~ **Presidente Reagan** President Reagan; **dov'è la Francesca?** where's Francesca?

8 (*con nomi geografici*): ~ **Tevere** the Tiber; **l'Italia** Italy; ~ **Regno Unito** the United Kingdom; **l'Everest** Everest; **le Alpi** the Alps.

'ilare *ag* cheerful; **ilarità** *sf* hilarity, mirth.

illangui'dire *vi* to grow weak *o* feeble.

illazi'one [illat'tsjone] *sf* inference, deduction.

ille'gale *ag* illegal.

illeg'gibile [illed'dʒibile] *ag* illegible.

ille'gittimo, a [ille'dʒittimo] *ag* illegitimate.

il'leso, a *ag* unhurt, unharmed.

illette'rato, a *ag* illiterate.

illi'bato, a *ag*: **donna ~a** virgin.

illimi'tato, a *ag* boundless; unlimited.

ill.mo *abbr* = **illustrissimo**.

il'ludere *vt* to deceive, delude; ~**rsi** *vr* to deceive o.s., delude o.s.

illumi'nare *vt* to light up, illuminate; (*fig*) to enlighten; ~**rsi** *vr* to light up; ~ **a giorno** to floodlight; **illuminazi'one** *sf* lighting; illumination; floodlighting; (*fig*) flash of inspiration.

illusi'one *sf* illusion; **farsi delle ~i** to delude o.s.

illusio'nismo *sm* conjuring.

il'luso, a *pp di* **illudere**.

illus'trare *vt* to illustrate; **illustra'tivo, a** *ag* illustrative; **illustrazi'one** *sf* illustration.

il'lustre *ag* eminent, renowned; **illus'trissimo, a** *ag* (*negli indirizzi*) very revered.

imbacuc'care *vt*, ~**rsi** *vr* to wrap up.

imbal'laggio [imbal'laddʒo] *sm* packing *q*.

imbal'lare *vt* to pack; (*AUT*) to race; ~**rsi** *vr* (*AUT*) to race.

imbalsa'mare *vt* to embalm.

imbambo'lato, a *ag* (*sguardo*) vacant, blank.

imban'dire *vt*: ~ **un pranzo** to prepare a lavish meal.

imbaraz'zare [imbarat'tsare] *vt* (*mettere a disagio*) to embarrass; (*ostacolare: movimenti*) to hamper; (: *stomaco*) to lie heavily on.

imba'razzo [imba'rattso] *sm* (*disagio*) embarrassment; (*perplessità*) puzzlement, bewilderment; ~ di stomaco indigestion.

imbarca'dero *sm* landing stage.

imbar'care *vt* (*passeggeri*) to embark; (*merci*) to load; ~rsi *vr*: ~rsi su to board; ~rsi per l'America to sail for America; ~rsi in (*fig: affare etc*) to embark on.

imbarcazi'one [imbarkat'tsjone] *sf* (small) boat, (small) craft *inv*; ~ di salvataggio lifeboat.

im'barco, chi *sm* embarkation; loading; boarding; (*banchina*) landing stage.

imbas'tire *vt* (*cucire*) to tack; (*fig: abbozzare*) to sketch, outline.

im'battersi *vr*: ~ in (*incontrare*) to bump *o* run into.

imbat'tibile *ag* unbeatable, invincible.

imbavagli'are [imbavaʎ'ʎare] *vt* to gag.

imbec'cata *sf* (*TEATRO*) prompt.

imbe'cille [imbe'tʃille] *ag* idiotic // *sm/f* idiot; (*MED*) imbecile.

imbel'lire *vt* to adorn, embellish // *vi* to grow more beautiful.

im'berbe *ag* beardless.

im'bevere *vt* to soak; ~rsi *vr*: ~rsi di to soak up, absorb.

imbian'care *vt* to whiten; (*muro*) to whitewash // *vi* to become *o* turn white.

imbian'chino [imbjan'kino] *sm* (house) painter, painter and decorator.

imboc'care *vt* (*bambino*) to feed; (*entrare: strada*) to enter, turn into // *vi*: ~ in (*sog: strada*) to lead into; (: *fiume*) to flow into.

imbocca'tura *sf* mouth; (*di strada, porto*) entrance; (*MUS, del morso*) mouthpiece.

im'bocco, chi *sm* entrance.

imbos'care *vt* to hide; ~rsi *vr* (*MIL*) to evade military service.

imbos'cata *sf* ambush.

imbottigli'are [imbottiʎ'ʎare] *vt* to bottle; (*NAUT*) to blockade; (*MIL*) to hem in; ~rsi *vr* to be stuck in a traffic jam.

imbot'tire *vt* to stuff; (*giacca*) to pad; **imbot'tita** *sf* quilt; **imbotti'tura** *sf* stuffing; padding.

imbrat'tare *vt* to dirty, smear, daub.

imbrigli'are [imbriʎ'ʎare] *vt* to bridle.

imbroc'care *vt* (*fig*) to guess correctly.

imbrogli'are [imbroʎ'ʎare] *vt* to mix up; (*fig: raggirare*) to deceive, cheat; (: *confondere*) to confuse, mix up; ~rsi *vr* to get tangled; (*fig*) to become confused; **im'broglio** *sm* (*groviglio*) tangle; (*situazione confusa*) mess; (*truffa*) swindle, trick; **imbrogli'one, a** *sm/f* cheat, swindler.

imbronci'are [imbron'tʃare] *vi* (*anche*: ~rsi) to sulk; **imbronci'ato, a** *ag* sulky.

imbru'nire *vi, vb impers* to grow dark; all'~ at dusk.

imbrut'tire *vt* to make ugly // *vi* to become ugly.

imbu'care *vt* to post.

imbur'rare *vt* to butter.

im'buto *sm* funnel.

imi'tare *vt* to imitate; (*riprodurre*) to copy; (*assomigliare*) to look like; **imitazi'one** *sf* imitation.

immaco'lato, a *ag* spotless; immaculate.

immagazzi'nare [immagaddzi'nare] *vt* to store.

immagi'nare [immadʒi'nare] *vt* to imagine; (*supporre*) to suppose; (*inventare*) to invent; s'immagini! don't mention it!, not at all!; **immagi'nario, a** *ag* imaginary; **immaginazi'one** *sf* imagination; (*cosa immaginata*) fancy.

im'magine [im'madʒine] *sf* image; (*rappresentazione grafica, mentale*) picture.

imman'cabile *ag* certain; unfailing.

immangi'abile [imman'dʒabile] *ag* inedible.

immatrico'lare *vt* to register; ~rsi *vr* (*INS*) to matriculate, enrol; **immatricolazi'one** *sf* registration; matriculation, enrolment.

imma'turo, a *ag* (*frutto*) unripe; (*persona*) immature; (*prematuro*) premature.

immedesi'marsi *vr*: ~ in to identify with.

immediata'mente *av* immediately, at once.

immedi'ato, a *ag* immediate.

im'memore *ag*: ~ di forgetful of.

im'menso, a *ag* immense.

im'mergere [im'merdʒere] *vt* to immerse, plunge; ~rsi *vr* to plunge; (*sommergibile*) to dive, submerge; (*dedicarsi a*): ~rsi in to immerse o.s. in.

immeri'tato, a *ag* undeserved.

immeri'tevole *ag* undeserving, unworthy.

immersi'one *sf* immersion; (*di sommergibile*) submersion, dive; (*di palombaro*) dive.

im'merso, a *pp di* immergere.

im'mettere *vt*: ~ (in) to introduce (into); ~ dati in un computer to enter data on a computer.

immi'grato, a *sm/f* immigrant; **immigrazi'one** *sf* immigration.

immi'nente *ag* imminent.

immischi'are [immis'kjare] *vt*: ~ qn in to involve sb in; ~rsi in to interfere *o* meddle in.

immissi'one *sf* (*di aria, gas*) intake; ~ di dati (*INFORM*) data entry.

im'mobile *ag* motionless, still; (**beni**) ~i *smpl* real estate *sg*; **immobili'are** *ag* (*DIR*) property *cpd*; **immobilità** *sf* stillness; immobility.

immo'desto, a *ag* immodest.

immo'lare *vt* to sacrifice, immolate.

immon'dizia [immon'dittsja] *sf* dirt,

filth; (*spesso al pl: spazzatura, rifiuti*) rubbish q, refuse q.

im'mondo, a *ag* filthy, foul.

immo'rale *ag* immoral.

immor'tale *ag* immortal.

im'mune *ag* (*esente*) exempt; (*MED, DIR*) immune; **immunità** *sf* immunity; **immunità parlamentare** parliamentary privilege.

immu'tabile *ag* immutable; unchanging.

impacchet'tare [impakket'tare] *vt* to pack up.

impacci'are [impat'tʃare] *vt* to hinder, hamper; **impacci'ato, a** *ag* awkward, clumsy; (*imbarazzo*) embarrassed; **im'paccio** *sm* obstacle; (*imbarazzo*) embarrassment; (*situazione imbarazzante*) awkward situation.

im'pacco, chi *sm* (*MED*) compress.

impadro'nirsi *vr*: ~ di to seize, take possession of; (*fig: apprendere a fondo*) to master.

impa'gabile *ag* priceless.

impagi'nare [impadʒi'nare] *vt* (*TIP*) to paginate, page (up).

impagli'are [impaʎ'ʎare] *vt* to stuff (with straw).

impa'lato, a *ag* (*fig*) stiff as a board.

impalca'tura *sf* scaffolding.

impalli'dire *vi* to turn pale; (*fig*) to fade.

impa'nare *vt* (*CUC*) to dip in breadcrumbs.

impantа'narsi *vr* to sink (in the mud); (*fig*) to get bogged down.

impappi'narsi *vr* to stammer, falter.

impa'rare *vt* to learn.

impareggi'abile [impared'dʒabile] *ag* incomparable.

imparen'tarsi *vr*: ~ con to marry into.

'impari *ag inv* (*disuguale*) unequal; (*dispari*) odd.

impar'tire *vt* to bestow, give.

imparzi'ale [impar'tsjale] *ag* impartial, unbiased.

impas'sibile *ag* impassive.

impas'tare *vt* (*pasta*) to knead; (*colori*) to mix.

im'pasto *sm* (*l'impastare: di pane*) kneading; (: *di cemento*) mixing; (*pasta*) dough; (*anche fig*) mixture.

im'patto *sm* impact.

impau'rire *vt* to scare, frighten // *vi* (*anche*: ~rsi) to become scared o frightened.

impazi'ente [impat'tsjɛnte] *ag* impatient; **impazi'enza** *sf* impatience.

impaz'zata [impat'tsata] *sf*: all'~ (*precipitosamente*) at breakneck speed.

impaz'zire [impat'tsire] *vi* to go mad; ~ per qn/qc to be crazy about sb/sth.

impec'cabile *ag* impeccable.

impedi'mento *sm* obstacle, hindrance.

impe'dire *vt* (*vietare*): ~ a qn di fare to prevent sb from doing; (*ostruire*) to obstruct; (*impacciare*) to hamper, hinder.

impe'gnare [impeɲ'ɲare] *vt* (*dare in pegno*) to pawn; (*onore etc*) to pledge; (*prenotare*) to book, reserve; (*obbligare*) to oblige; (*occupare*) to keep busy; (*MIL: nemico*) to engage; ~rsi *vr* (*vincolarsi*): ~rsi a fare to undertake to do; (*mettersi risolutamente*): ~rsi in qc to devote o.s. to sth; ~rsi con qn (*accordarsi*) to come to an agreement with sb; **impegna'tivo, a** *ag* binding; (*lavoro*) demanding, exacting; **impe'gnato, a** *ag* (*occupato*) busy; (*fig: romanzo, autore*) committed, engagé.

im'pegno [im'peɲɲo] *sm* (*obbligo*) obligation; (*promessa*) promise, pledge; (*zelo*) diligence, zeal; (*compito, d'autore*) commitment.

impel'lente *ag* pressing, urgent.

impene'trabile *ag* impenetrable.

impen'narsi *vr* (*cavallo*) to rear up; (*AER*) to nose up; (*fig*) to bridle.

impen'sato, a *ag* unforeseen, unexpected.

impensie'rire *vt*, ~rsi *vr* to worry.

impe'rare *vi* (*anche fig*) to reign, rule.

impera'tivo, a *ag, sm* imperative.

impera'tore, 'trice *sm/f* emperor/empress.

imperdo'nabile *ag* unforgivable, unpardonable.

imper'fetto, a *ag* imperfect // *sm* (*LING*) imperfect (tense); **imperfezi'one** *sf* imperfection.

imperi'ale *ag* imperial.

imperi'oso, a *ag* (*persona*) imperious; (*motivo, esigenza*) urgent, pressing.

impe'rizia [impe'rittsja] *sf* lack of experience.

imperma'lirsi *vr* to take offence.

imperme'abile *ag* waterproof // *sm* raincoat.

imperni'are *vt*: ~ qc su to hinge sth on; (*fig*) to base sth on; ~rsi *vr* (*fig*): ~rsi su to be based on.

im'pero *sm* empire; (*forza, autorità*) rule, control.

imperscru'tabile *ag* inscrutable.

imperso'nale *ag* impersonal.

imperso'nare *vt* to personify; (*TEATRO*) to play, act (the part of).

imperter'rito, a *ag* fearless, undaunted; impassive.

imperti'nente *ag* impertinent.

imperver'sare *vi* to rage.

'impeto *sm* (*moto, forza*) force, impetus; (*assalto*) onslaught; (*fig: impulso*) impulse; (: *slancio*) transport; con ~ energetically; vehemently.

impet'tito, a *ag* stiff, erect.

impetu'oso, a *ag* (*vento*) strong, raging; (*persona*) impetuous.

impian'tare vt (motore) to install; (azienda, discussione) to establish, start.

impi'anto sm (installazione) installation; (apparecchiature) plant; (sistema) system; ~ **elettrico** wiring; ~ **sportivo** sports complex; ~i **di risalita** (SCI) ski lifts.

impias'trare, impiastricci'are [impiastrit'tʃare] vt to smear, dirty.

impi'astro sm poultice.

impic'care vt to hang; ~rsi vr to hang o.s.

impicci'are [impit'tʃare] vt to hinder, hamper; ~rsi vr to meddle, interfere; **im'piccio** sm (ostacolo) hindrance; (seccatura) trouble, bother; (affare imbrogliato) mess; **essere d'impiccio** to be in the way.

impie'gare vt (usare) to use, employ; (assumere) to employ, take on; (spendere: denaro, tempo) to spend; (investire) to invest; ~rsi vr to get a job, obtain employment; **impie'gato, a** sm/f employee.

impi'ego, ghi sm (uso) use; (occupazione) employment; (posto di lavoro) (regular) job, post; (ECON) investment.

impieto'sire vt to move to pity; ~rsi vr to be moved to pity.

impie'trire vt (fig) to petrify.

impigli'are [impiʎ'ʎare] vt to catch, entangle; ~rsi vr to get caught up o entangled.

impi'grire vt to make lazy // vi (anche: ~rsi) to grow lazy.

impli'care vt to imply; (coinvolgere) to involve; ~rsi vr: ~rsi (in) to become involved (in); **implicazl'one** sf implication.

im'plicito, a [im'plitʃito] ag implicit.

impolve'rare vt to cover with dust; ~rsi vr to get dusty.

impo'nente ag imposing, impressive.

impo'nibile ag taxable // sm taxable income.

impopo'lare ag unpopular.

im'porre vt to impose; (costringere) to force, make; (far valere) to impose, enforce; **imporsi** vr (persona) to assert o.s.; (cosa: rendersi necessario) to become necessary; (aver successo: moda, attore) to become popular; ~ **a qn di fare** to force sb to do, make sb do.

impor'tante ag important; **impor'tanza** sf importance; **dare importanza a qc** to attach importance to sth; **darsi importanza** to give o.s. airs.

impor'tare vt (introdurre dall'estero) to import // vi to matter, be important // vb impers (essere necessario) to be necessary; (interessare) to matter; **non importa!** it doesn't matter!; **non me ne importa!** I don't care!; **importazi'one** sf importation; (merci importate) imports pl.

im'porto sm (total) amount.

importu'nare vt to bother.

impor'tuno, a ag irksome, annoying.

imposizi'one [impozit'tsjone] sf imposition; order, command; (onere, imposta) tax.

imposses'sarsi vr: ~ **di** to seize, take possession of.

impos'sibile ag impossible; **fare l'~** to do one's utmost, do all one can; **impossibilità** sf impossibility; **essere nell'impossibilità di fare qc** to be unable to do sth.

im'posta sf (di finestra) shutter; (tassa) tax; ~ **sul reddito** income tax; ~ **sul valore aggiunto** (I.V.A.) value added tax (VAT) (Brit), sales tax (US).

impos'tare vt (imbucare) to post; (preparare) to plan, set out; (avviare) to begin, start off; (voce) to pitch.

im'posto, a pp di imporre.

impo'tente ag weak, powerless; (anche MED) impotent.

impove'rire vt to impoverish // vi (anche: ~rsi) to become poor.

imprati'cabile ag (strada) impassable; (campo da gioco) unplayable.

imprati'chire [imprati'kire] vt to train; ~rsi **in qc** to practise (Brit) o practice (US) sth.

impre'gnare [impreɲ'ɲare] vt: ~ **(di)** (imbevere) to soak o impregnate (with); (riempire: anche fig) to fill (with).

imprendi'tore sm (industriale) entrepreneur; (appaltatore) contractor; **piccolo ~** small businessman.

im'presa sf (iniziativa) enterprise; (azione) exploit; (azienda) firm, concern.

impre'sarlo sm (TEATRO) manager, impresario; ~ **di pompe funebri** funeral director.

imprescin'dibile [impreʃʃin'dibile] ag not to be ignored.

impressio'nante ag impressive; upsetting.

impressio'nare vt to impress; (turbare) to upset; (FOT) to expose; ~rsi vr to be easily upset.

impressi'one sf impression; (fig: sensazione) sensation, feeling; (stampa) printing; **fare ~** (colpire) to impress; (turbare) to frighten, upset; **fare buona/cattiva ~ a** to make a good/bad impression on.

im'presso, a pp di imprimere.

impres'tare vt: ~ **qc a qn** to lend sth to sb.

impreve'dibile ag unforeseeable; (persona) unpredictable.

imprevi'dente ag lacking in foresight.

impre'visto, a ag unexpected, unforeseen // sm unforeseen event; **salvo ~i** unless anything unexpected happens.

imprigio'nare [impridʒo'nare] *vt* to imprison.

im'primere *vt* (*anche fig*) to impress, stamp; (*comunicare: movimento*) to transmit, give.

impro'babile *ag* improbable, unlikely.

im'pronta *sf* imprint, impression, sign; (*di piede, mano*) print; (*fig*) mark, stamp; ~ **digitale** fingerprint.

impro'perio *sm* insult; ~**i** *smpl* abuse *sg*.

im'proprio, a *ag* improper; **arma** ~**a** offensive weapon.

improvvisa'mente *av* suddenly; unexpectedly.

improvvi'sare *vt* to improvise; ~**rsi** *vr*: ~**rsi cuoco** (to decide to) act as cook; **improvvi'sata** *sf* (pleasant) surprise.

improv'viso, a *ag* (*imprevisto*) unexpected; (*subitaneo*) sudden; **all'**~ unexpectedly; suddenly.

impru'dente *ag* unwise, rash.

impu'dico, a, chi, che *ag* immodest.

impu'gnare [impun'ɲare] *vt* to grasp, grip; (*DIR*) to contest; **impugna'tura** *sf* grip, grasp; (*manico*) handle; (: *di spada*) hilt.

impul'sivo, a *ag* impulsive.

im'pulso *sm* impulse.

impun'tarsi *vr* to stop dead, refuse to budge; (*fig*) to be obstinate.

impu'tare *vt* (*ascrivere*): ~ **qc a** to attribute sth to; (*DIR: accusare*): ~ **qn di** to charge sb with, accuse sb of; **impu'tato, a** *sm/f* (*DIR*) accused, defendant; **imputazi'one** *sf* (*DIR*) charge.

imputri'dire *vi* to rot.

in (*in + il* = **nel**, *in + lo* = **nello**, *in + l'* = **nell'**, *in + la* = **nella**, *in + i* = **nei**, *in + gli* = **negli**, *in + le* = **nelle**) *prep* **1** (*stato in luogo*) in; **vivere** ~ **Italia/città** to live in Italy/town; **essere** ~ **casa/ufficio** to be at home/the office; **se fossi** ~ **te** if I were you

2 (*moto a luogo*) to; (: *dentro*) into; **andare** ~ **Germania/città** to go to Germany/town; **andare** ~ **ufficio** to go to the office; **entrare** ~ **macchina/casa** to get into the car/go into the house

3 (*tempo*) in; **nel 1989** in 1989; ~ **giugno/estate** in June/summer

4 (*modo, maniera*) in; ~ **silenzio** in silence; ~ **abito da sera** in evening dress; ~ **guerra** at war; ~ **vacanza** on holiday; **Maria Bianchi** ~ **Rossi** Maria Rossi née Bianchi

5 (*mezzo*) by; **viaggiare** ~ **autobus/treno** to travel by bus/train

6 (*materia*) made of; ~ **marmo** made of marble, marble *cpd*; **una collana** ~ **oro** a gold necklace

7 (*misura*) in; **siamo** ~ **quattro** there are four of us; ~ **tutto** in all

8 (*fine*): **dare** ~ **dono** to give as a gift; **spende tutto** ~ **alcool** he spends all his money on drink; ~ **onore di** in honour of.

i'nabile *ag*: ~ **a** incapable of; (*fisicamente, MIL*) unfit for; **inabilità** *sf* incapacity.

inabi'tabile *ag* uninhabitable.

inacces'sibile [inattʃes'sibile] *ag* (*luogo*) inaccessible; (*persona*) unapproachable; (*mistero*) unfathomable.

inaccet'tabile [inattʃet'tabile] *ag* unacceptable.

ina'datto, a *ag*: ~ **(a)** unsuitable *o* unfit (for).

inadegu'ato, a *ag* inadequate.

inadempi'enza [inadem'pjɛntsa] *sf*: ~ **(a)** non-fulfilment (of).

inaffer'rabile *ag* elusive; (*concetto, senso*) difficult to grasp.

ina'lare *vt* to inhale.

inalbe'rare *vt* (*NAUT*) to hoist, raise; ~**rsi** *vr* (*fig*) to flare up, fly off the handle.

inalte'rabile *ag* unchangeable; (*colore*) fast, permanent; (*affetto*) constant.

inalte'rato, a *ag* unchanged.

inami'dato, a *ag* starched.

inani'mato, a *ag* inanimate; (*senza vita: corpo*) lifeless.

inappa'gabile *ag* insatiable.

inappel'labile *ag* (*decisione*) final, irrevocable; (*DIR*) final, not open to appeal.

inappe'tenza [inappe'tɛntsa] *sf* (*MED*) lack of appetite.

inappun'tabile *ag* irreproachable, flawless.

inar'care *vt* (*schiena*) to arch; (*sopracciglia*) to raise; ~**rsi** *vr* to arch.

inari'dire *vt* to make arid, dry up // *vi* (*anche*: ~**rsi**) to dry up, become arid.

inaspet'tato, a *ag* unexpected.

inas'prire *vt* (*disciplina*) to tighten up, make harsher; (*carattere*) to embitter; ~**rsi** *vr* to become harsher; to become bitter; to become worse.

inattac'cabile *ag* (*anche fig*) unassailable; (*alibi*) cast-iron.

inatten'dibile *ag* unreliable.

inat'teso, a *ag* unexpected.

inattu'abile *ag* impracticable.

inau'dito, a *ag* unheard of.

inaugu'rare *vt* to inaugurate, open; (*monumento*) to unveil.

inavve'duto, a *ag* careless, inadvertent.

inavver'tenza [inavver'tɛntsa] *sf* carelessness, inadvertence.

incagli'arsi [inkaʎ'ʎare] *vi* (*NAUT: anche:* ~**rsi**) to run aground.

incal'lito, a *ag* calloused; (*fig*) hardened, inveterate; (: *insensibile*) hard.

incal'zare [inkal'tsare] *vt* to follow *o* pursue closely; (*fig*) to press // *vi* (*urgere*) to be pressing; (*essere imminente*) to be imminent.

iname'rare vt (DIR) to expropriate.

incammi'nare vt (fig: avviare) to start up; ~rsi vr to set off.

incande'scente [inkandeʃ'ʃɛnte] ag incandescent, white-hot.

incan'tare vt to enchant, bewitch; ~rsi vr (rimanere intontito) to be spellbound; to be in a daze; (meccanismo: bloccarsi) to jam; **incanta'tore, 'trice** ag enchanting, bewitching // smlf enchanter/enchantress; **incan'tesimo** sm spell, charm; **incan'tevole** ag charming, enchanting.

in'canto sm spell, charm, enchantment; (asta) auction; **come per ~** as if by magic; **mettere all'~** to put up for auction.

incanu'tire vi to go white.

inca'pace [inka'patʃe] ag incapable; **incapacità** sf inability; (DIR) incapacity.

incapo'nirsi vr to be stubborn, be determined.

incap'pare vi: ~ **in qc/qn** (anche fig) to run into sth/sb.

incapricci'arsi [inkaprit'tʃarsi] vr: ~ **di** to take a fancy to o for.

incapsu'lare vt (dente) to crown.

incarce'rare [inkartʃe'rare] vt to imprison.

incari'care vt: ~ **qn di fare** to give sb the responsibility of doing; ~rsi **di** to take care o charge of; **incari'cato, a** ag: **incaricato (di)** in charge (of), responsible (for) // smlf delegate, representative; **professore incaricato** teacher with a temporary appointment; **incaricato d'affari** (POL) chargé d'affaires.

in'carico, chi sm task, job.

incar'nare vt to embody; ~rsi vr to be embodied; (REL) to become incarnate.

incarta'mento sm dossier, file.

incar'tare vt to wrap (in paper).

incas'sare vt (merce) to pack (in cases); (gemma: incastonare) to set; (ECON: riscuotere) to collect; (PUGILATO: colpi) to take, stand up to; **in'casso** sm cashing, encashment; (introito) takings pl.

incasto'nare vt to set; **incastona'tura** sf setting.

incas'trare vt to fit in, insert; (fig: intrappolare) to catch; ~rsi vr (combaciare) to fit together; (restare bloccato) to become stuck; **in'castro** sm slot, groove; (punto di unione) joint.

incate'nare vt to chain up.

incatra'mare vt to tar.

incatti'vire vt to make wicked; ~rsi vr to turn nasty.

in'cauto, a ag imprudent, rash.

inca'vare vt to hollow out; **inca'vato, a** ag hollow; (occhi) sunken; **in'cavo** sm hollow; (solco) groove.

incendi'are [intʃen'djare] vt to set fire to; ~rsi vr to catch fire, burst into flames.

incendi'ario, a [intʃen'djarjo] ag incendiary // smlf arsonist.

in'cendio [in'tʃendjo] sm fire.

incene'rire [intʃene'rire] vt to burn to ashes, incinerate; (cadavere) to cremate; ~rsi vr to be burnt to ashes.

in'censo [in'tʃenso] sm incense.

incensu'rato, a [intʃensu'rato] ag (DIR): **essere ~** to have a clean record.

incen'tivo [intʃen'tivo] sm incentive.

incep'pare [intʃep'pare] vt to obstruct, hamper; ~rsi vr to jam.

ince'rata [intʃe'rata] sf (tela) tarpaulin; (impermeabile) oilskins pl.

incer'tezza [intʃer'tettsa] sf uncertainty.

in'certo, a [in'tʃerto] ag uncertain; (irresoluto) undecided, hesitating // sm uncertainty.

in'cetta [in'tʃetta] sf buying up; **fare ~ di qc** to buy up sth.

inchi'esta [in'kjesta] sf investigation, inquiry.

inchi'nare [inki'nare] vt to bow; ~rsi vr to bend down; (per riverenza) to bow; (: donna) to curtsy; **in'chino** sm bow; curtsy.

inchio'dare [inkjo'dare] vt to nail (down); ~ **la macchina** (AUT) to jam on the brakes.

inchi'ostro [in'kjostro] sm ink; ~ **simpatico** invisible ink.

inciam'pare [intʃam'pare] vi to trip, stumble.

inci'ampo [in'tʃampo] sm obstacle; **essere d'~ a qn** (fig) to be in sb's way.

inciden'tale [intʃiden'tale] ag incidental.

inci'dente [intʃi'dente] sm accident; ~ **d'auto** car accident.

inci'denza [intʃi'dentsa] sf incidence; **avere una forte ~ su qc** to affect sth greatly.

in'cidere [in'tʃidere] vi: ~ **su** to bear upon, affect // vt (tagliare incavando) to cut into; (ARTE) to engrave; (: etch); (canzone) to record.

in'cinta [in'tʃinta] ag f pregnant.

incipri'are [intʃi'prjare] vt to powder.

in'circa [in'tʃirka] av: **all'~** more or less, very nearly.

incisi'one [intʃi'zjone] sf cut; (disegno) engraving; etching; (registrazione) recording; (MED) incision.

in'ciso, a [in'tʃizo] pp di **incidere** // sm: **per ~** incidentally, by the way.

inci'vile [intʃi'vile] ag uncivilized; (villano) impolite.

incivi'lire [intʃivi'lire] vt to civilize.

incl. abbr (= incluso) encl.

incli'nare vt to tilt // vi (fig): ~ **a qc/a fare** to incline towards sth/doing; to tend towards sth/to do; ~rsi vr (barca) to list; (aereo) to bank; **incli'nato, a** ag sloping; **inclinazi'one** *sf* slope; *(fig)* inclination, tendency; **in'cline** *ag*: incline a inclined to.

in'cludere *vt* to include; *(accludere)* to enclose; **inclu'sivo, a** *ag*: inclusivo di inclusive of; **in'cluso, a** *pp di* **includere** // *ag* included; enclosed.

incoe'rente *ag* incoherent; *(contraddittorio)* inconsistent.

in'cognito, a [in'kɔɲnito] *ag* unknown // *sm*: **in ~** incognito // *sf (MAT, fig)* unknown quantity.

incol'lare *vt* to glue, gum; *(unire con colla)* to stick together.

incolon'nare *vt* to draw up in columns.

inco'lore *ag* colourless.

incol'pare *vt*: **~ qn di** to charge sb with.

in'colto, a *ag (terreno)* uncultivated; *(trascurato: capelli)* neglected; *(persona)* uneducated.

in'colume *ag* safe and sound, unhurt.

in'combere *vi (sovrastare minacciando)*: **~ su** to threaten, hang over.

incominci'are [inkomin'tʃare] *vi, vt* to begin, start.

in'comodo, a *ag* uncomfortable; *(inopportuno)* inconvenient // *sm* inconvenience, bother.

incompe'tente *ag* incompetent.

incompi'uto, a *ag* unfinished, incomplete.

incom'pleto, a *ag* incomplete.

incompren'sibile *ag* incomprehensible.

incom'preso, a *ag* not understood; misunderstood.

inconce'pibile [inkontʃe'pibile] *ag* inconceivable.

inconcili'abile [inkontʃi'ljabile] *ag* irreconcilable.

inconclu'dente *ag* inconclusive; *(persona)* ineffectual.

incondizio'nato, a [inkondittsjo'nato] *ag* unconditional.

inconfu'tabile *ag* irrefutable.

incongru'ente *ag* inconsistent.

in'congruo, a *ag* incongruous.

inconsa'pevole *ag*: **~ di** unaware of, ignorant of.

in'conscio, a, sci, sce [in'kɔnʃo] *ag* unconscious // *sm (PSIC)*: **l'~** the unconscious.

inconsis'tente *ag* insubstantial; unfounded.

inconsu'eto, a *ag* unusual.

incon'sulto, a *ag* rash.

incon'trare *vt* to meet; *(difficoltà)* to meet with; **~rsi** *vr* to meet.

incontras'tabile *ag* incontrovertible, indisputable.

in'contro *av*: **~ a** *(verso)* towards // *sm* meeting; *(SPORT)* match; meeting; **~ di calcio** football match.

inconveni'ente *sm* drawback, snag.

incoraggia'mento   [inkoraddʒa'mento]

sm encouragement.

incoraggi'are [inkorad'dʒare] *vt* to encourage.

incornici'are [inkorni'tʃare] *vt* to frame.

incoro'nare *vt* to crown; **incoronazi'one** *sf* coronation.

incorpo'rare *vt* to incorporate; *(fig: annettere)* to annex.

in'correre *vi*: **~ in** to meet with, run into.

incosci'ente [inkoʃ'ʃɛnte] *ag (inconscio)* unconscious; *(irresponsabile)* reckless, thoughtless; **incosci'enza** *sf* unconsciousness; recklessness, thoughtlessness.

incre'dibile *ag* incredible, unbelievable.

in'credulo, a *ag* incredulous, disbelieving.

incremen'tare *vt* to increase; *(dar sviluppo a)* to promote.

incre'mento *sm (sviluppo)* development; *(aumento numerico)* increase, growth.

incres'parsi *vr (acqua)* to ripple; *(capelli)* to go frizzy; *(pelle, tessuto)* to wrinkle.

incrimi'nare *vt (DIR)* to charge.

incri'nare *vt* to crack; *(fig: rapporti, amicizia)* to cause to deteriorate; **~rsi** *vr* to crack; to deteriorate; **incrina'tura** *sf* crack; *(fig)* rift.

incroci'are [inkro'tʃare] *vt* to cross; *(incontrare)* to meet // *vi (NAUT, AER)* to cruise; **~rsi** *vr (strade)* to cross, intersect; *(persone, veicoli)* to pass each other; **~ le braccia/le gambe** to fold one's arms/cross one's legs; **in'crocia'tore** *sm* cruiser.

in'crocio [in'krotʃo] *sm (anche FERR)* crossing; *(di strade)* crossroads.

incros'tare *vt* to encrust.

incuba'trice [inkuba'tritʃe] *sf* incubator.

'incubo *sm* nightmare.

in'cudine *sf* anvil.

incu'rante *ag*: **~ (di)** heedless (of), careless (of).

incurio'sire *vt* to make curious; **~rsi** *vr* to become curious.

incursi'one *sf* raid.

incur'vare *vt*, **~rsi** *vr* to bend, curve.

in'cusso, a *pp di* **incutere**.

incusto'dito, a *ag* unguarded, unattended.

in'cutere *vt* to arouse; **~ timore/rispetto a qn** to strike fear into sb/command sb's respect.

'indaco *sm* indigo.

indaffa'rato, a *ag* busy.

inda'gare *vt* to investigate.

in'dagine [in'dadʒine] *sf* investigation, inquiry; *(ricerca)* research, study.

indebi'tarsi *vr* to run o get into debt.

in'debito, a *ag* undue; undeserved.

indebo'lire *vt, vi (anche:* **~rsi***)* to weaken.

inde'cente [inde'tʃɛnte] *ag* indecent; **inde'cenza** *sf* indecency.

inde'ciso, a [inde'tʃizo] *ag* indecisive; (*irresoluto*) undecided.

inde'fesso, a *ag* untiring, indefatigable.

indefi'nito, a *ag* (*anche* LING) indefinite; (*impreciso, non determinato*) undefined.

in'degno, a [in'deɲɲo] *ag* (*atto*) shameful; (*persona*) unworthy.

indelica'tezza [indelika'tettsa] *sf* tactlessness.

indemoni'ato, a *ag* possessed (by the devil).

in'denne *ag* unhurt, uninjured; **indennità** *sf inv* (*rimborso: di spese*) allowance; (: *di perdita*) compensation, indemnity; **indennità di contingenza** cost-of-living allowance; **indennità di trasferta** travel expenses *pl*.

indenniz'zare [indennid'dzare] *vt* to compensate; **inden'nizzo** *sm* (*somma*) compensation, indemnity.

indero'gabile *ag* binding.

'India *sf*: l'~ India; **indi'ano, a** *ag* Indian // *sm/f* (*d'India*) Indian; (*d'America*) Red Indian.

indiavo'lato, a *ag* possessed (by the devil); (*vivace, violento*) wild.

indi'care *vt* (*mostrare*) to show, indicate; (: *col dito*) to point to, point out; (*consigliare*) to suggest, recommend; **indica'tivo, a** *ag* indicative // *sm* (LING) indicative (mood); **indica'tore** *sm* (*elenco*) guide; directory; (TECN) gauge; indicator; **cartello indicatore** sign; **indicatore di velocità** (AUT) speedometer; **indicatore della benzina** fuel gauge; **indicazi'one** *sf* indication; (*informazione*) piece of information; **indicazioni per l'uso** instructions for use.

'indice ['inditʃe] *sm* (ANAT: *dito*) index finger, forefinger; (*lancetta*) needle, pointer; (*fig: indizio*) sign; (TECN, MAT, *nei libri*) index; ~ **di gradimento** (RADIO, TV) popularity rating.

indi'cibile [indi'tʃibile] *ag* inexpressible.

indietreggi'are [indietred'dʒare] *vi* to draw back, retreat.

indi'etro *av* back; (*guardare*) behind, back; (*andare, cadere: anche:* all'~) backwards; **rimanere** ~ to be left behind; **essere** ~ (*col lavoro*) to be behind; (*orologio*) to be slow; **rimandare qc** ~ to send sth back.

indi'feso, a *ag* (*città etc*) undefended; (*persona*) defenceless.

indiffe'rente *ag* indifferent; **indiffe'renza** *sf* indifference.

in'digeno, a [in'didʒeno] *ag* indigenous, native // *sm/f* native.

indi'gente [indi'dʒɛnte] *ag* poverty-stricken, destitute; **indi'genza** *sf* extreme poverty.

indigesti'one [indidʒes'tjone] *sf* indigestion.

indi'gesto, a [indi'dʒɛsto] *ag* indigestible.

indi'gnare [indiɲ'ɲare] *vt* to fill with indignation; ~**rsi** *vr* to be (*o* get) indignant.

indimenti'cabile *ag* unforgettable.

indipen'dente *ag* independent; **indipen'denza** *sf* independence.

in'dire *vt* (*concorso*) to announce; (*elezioni*) to call.

indi'retto, a *ag* indirect.

indiriz'zare [indirit'tsare] *vt* (*dirigere*) to direct; (*mandare*) to send; (*lettera*) to address.

indi'rizzo [indi'rittso] *sm* address; (*direzione*) direction; (*avvio*) trend, course.

indis'creto, a *ag* indiscreet.

indis'cusso, a *ag* unquestioned.

indispen'sabile *ag* indispensable, essential.

indispet'tire *vt* to irritate, annoy // *vi* (*anche:* ~**rsi**) to get irritated *o* annoyed.

in'divia *sf* endive.

individu'ale *ag* individual; **individualità** *sf* individuality.

individu'are *vt* (*dar forma distinta a*) to characterize; (*determinare*) to locate; (*riconoscere*) to single out.

indi'viduo *sm* individual.

indizi'are [indit'tsjare] *vt*: ~ **qn di qc** to cast suspicion on sb for sth; **indizi'ato, a** *ag* suspected // *sm/f* suspect.

in'dizio [in'dittsjo] *sm* (*segno*) sign, indication; (POLIZIA) clue; (DIR) piece of evidence.

'indole *sf* nature, character.

indolen'zito, a [indolen'tsito] *ag* stiff, aching; (*intorpidito*) numb.

indo'lore *ag* painless.

indo'mani *sm*: l'~ the next day, the following day.

Indo'nesia *sf*: l'~ Indonesia.

indos'sare *vt* (*mettere indosso*) to put on; (*avere indosso*) to have on; **indossa'tore, 'trice** *sm/f* model.

in'dotto, a *ag pp di* **indurre**.

indottri'nare *vt* to indoctrinate.

indovi'nare *vt* (*scoprire*) to guess; (*immaginare*) to imagine, guess; (*il futuro*) to foretell; **indovi'nato, a** *ag* successful; (*scelta*) inspired; **indovi'nello** *sm* riddle; **indo'vino, a** *sm/f* fortuneteller.

indubbia'mente *av* undoubtedly.

in'dubbio, a *ag* certain, undoubted.

indugi'are [indu'dʒare] *vi* to take one's time, delay.

in'dugio [in'dudʒo] *sm* (*ritardo*) delay; **senza** ~ without delay.

indul'gente [indul'dʒɛnte] *ag* indulgent; (*giudice*) lenient; **indul'genza** *sf* indulgence; leniency.

in'dulgere [in'duldʒere] *vi*: ~ **a** (*accondiscendere*) to comply with;

(*abbandonarsi*) to indulge in; **in'dulto, a** *pp di* **indulgere** // *sm* (*DIR*) pardon.

indu'mento *sm* article of clothing, garment; ~**i** *smpl* clothes.

indu'rire *vt* to harden // *vi* (*anche:* ~**rsi**) to harden, become hard.

in'durre *vt:* ~ **qn a fare qc** to induce *o* persuade sb to do sth; ~ **qn in errore** to mislead sb.

in'dustria *sf* industry; **industri'ale** *ag* industrial // *sm* industrialist.

industri'arsi *vr* to do one's best, try hard.

industri'oso, a *ag* industrious, hardworking.

induzi'one [indut'tsjone] *sf* induction.

inebe'tito, a *ag* dazed, stunned.

inebri'are *vt* (*anche fig*) to intoxicate; ~**rsi** *vr* to become intoxicated.

inecce'pibile [inettʃe'pibile] *ag* unexceptionable.

i'nedia *sf* starvation.

i'nedito, a *ag* unpublished.

ineffi'cace [ineffi'katʃe] *ag* ineffective.

ineffici'ente [ineffi'tʃɛnte] *ag* inefficient.

inegu'ale *ag* unequal; (*irregolare*) uneven.

ine'rente *ag:* ~ **a** concerning, regarding.

i'nerme *ag* unarmed; defenceless.

inerpi'carsi *vr:* ~ **(su)** to clamber (up).

i'nerte *ag* inert; (*inattivo*) indolent, sluggish; **i'nerzia** *sf* inertia; indolence, sluggishness.

ine'satto, a *ag* (*impreciso*) inexact; (*erroneo*) incorrect; (*AMM: non riscosso*) uncollected.

inesis'tente *ag* non-existent.

inesperi'enza [inespe'rjɛntsa] *sf* inexperience.

ines'perto, a *ag* inexperienced.

i'netto, a *ag* (*incapace*) inept; (*che non ha attitudine*): ~ **(a)** unsuited (to).

ine'vaso, a *ag* (*ordine, corrispondenza*) outstanding.

inevi'tabile *ag* inevitable.

i'nezia [i'nɛttsja] *sf* trifle, thing of no importance.

infagot'tare *vt* to bundle up, wrap up; ~**rsi** *vr* to wrap up.

infal'libile *ag* infallible.

infa'mare *vt* to defame.

in'fame *ag* infamous; (*fig: cosa, compito*) awful, dreadful.

infan'tile *ag* child *cpd*; childlike; (*adulto, azione*) childish; **letteratura** ~ children's books *pl.*

in'fanzia [in'fantsja] *sf* childhood; (*bambini*) children *pl*; **prima** ~ babyhood, infancy.

infari'nare *vt* to cover with (*o sprinkle with o dip in*) flour; ~ **di zucchero** to sprinkle with sugar; **infarina'tura** *sf* (*fig*) smattering.

in'farto *sm* (*MED*): ~ **(cardiaco)** coronary.

infasti'dire *vt* to annoy, irritate; ~**rsi** to get annoyed *o* irritated.

infati'cabile *ag* tireless, untiring.

in'fatti *cong* as a matter of fact, in fact, actually.

infatu'arsi *vr:* ~ **di** *o* **per** to become infatuated with, fall for; **infatuazi'one** *sf* infatuation.

in'fausto, a *ag* unpropitious, unfavourable.

infe'condo, a *ag* infertile.

infe'dele *ag* unfaithful; **infedeltà** *sf* infidelity.

infe'lice [infe'litʃe] *ag* unhappy; (*sfortunato*) unlucky, unfortunate; (*inopportuno*) inopportune, ill-timed; (*mal riuscito: lavoro*) bad, poor; **infelicità** *sf* unhappiness.

inferi'ore *ag* lower; (*per intelligenza, qualità*) inferior // *sm/f* inferior; ~ **a** (*numero, quantità*) less *o* smaller than; (*meno buono*) inferior to; ~ **alla media** below average; **inferiorità** *sf* inferiority.

inferme'ria *sf* infirmary; (*di scuola, nave*) sick bay.

infermi'ere, a *sm/f* nurse.

infermità *sf inv* illness; infirmity.

in'fermo, a *ag* (*ammalato*) ill; (*debole*) infirm.

infer'nale *ag* infernal; (*proposito, complotto*) diabolical.

in'ferno *sm* hell.

inferri'ata *sf* grating.

infervo'rare *vt* to arouse enthusiasm in; ~**rsi** *vr* to get excited, get carried away.

infet'tare *vt* to infect; ~**rsi** *vr* to become infected; **infet'tivo, a** *ag* infectious; **in'fetto, a** *ag* infected; (*acque*) polluted, contaminated; **infezi'one** *sf* infection.

infiac'chire [infjak'kire] *vt* to weaken // *vi* (*anche:* ~**rsi**) to grow weak.

infiam'mabile *ag* inflammable.

infiam'mare *vt* to set alight; (*fig, MED*) to inflame; ~**rsi** *vr* to catch fire; (*MED*) to become inflamed; (*fig*): ~**rsi di** to be fired with; **infiammazi'one** *sf* (*MED*) inflammation.

in'fido, a *ag* unreliable, treacherous.

infie'rire *vi:* ~ **su** (*fisicamente*) to attack furiously; (*verbalmente*) to rage at; (*epidemia*) to rage over.

in'figgere [in'fiddʒere] *vt:* ~ **qc in** to thrust *o* drive sth into.

infi'lare *vt* (*ago*) to thread; (*mettere: chiave*) to insert; (*: anello, vestito*) to slip *o* put on; (*strada*) to turn into, take; ~**rsi** *vr:* ~**rsi in** to slip into; (*indossare*) to slip on; ~ **l'uscio** to slip in; to slip out.

infil'trarsi *vr* to penetrate, seep through; (*MIL*) to infiltrate; **infiltrazi'one** *sf* infiltration.

infil'zare [infil'tsare] *vt* (*infilare*) to string together; (*trafiggere*) to pierce.

'infimo, a *ag* lowest.

in'fine av finally; (insomma) in short.

infinità sf infinity; (in quantità): **un'~ di** an infinite number of.

infi'nito, a ag infinite; (LING) infinitive // sm infinity; (LING) infinitive; **all'~** (senza fine) endlessly.

infinocchi'are [infinok'kjare] vt (fam) to hoodwink.

infischi'arsi [infis'kjarsi] vr: **~ di** not to care about.

in'fisso, a pp di **infiggere** // sm fixture; (di porta, finestra) frame.

infit'tire vt, vi (anche: ~rsi) to thicken.

inflazi'one [inflat'tsjone] sf inflation.

in'fliggere [in'fliddʒere] vt to inflict; **in'flitto, a** pp di **infliggere**.

influ'ente ag influential; **influ'enza** sf influence; (MED) influenza, flu.

influ'ire vi: **~ su** to influence.

in'flusso sm influence.

infol'tire vt, vi to thicken.

infon'dato, a ag unfounded, groundless.

in'fondere vt: **~ qc in qn** to instill sth in sb.

infor'care vt to fork (up); (bicicletta, cavallo) to get on; (occhiali) to put on.

infor'mare vt to inform, tell; ~rsi vr: ~rsi (di o su) to inquire (about).

infor'matica sf computer science.

informa'tivo, a ag informative.

informa'tore sm informer.

informazi'one [informat'tsjone] sf piece of information; ~i sfpl information sg; **chiedere un'~** to ask for (some) information.

in'forme ag shapeless.

informico'larsi, informico'lirsi vr to have pins and needles.

infor'tunio sm accident; **~ sul lavoro** industrial accident, accident at work.

infos'sarsi vr (terreno) to sink; (guance) to become hollow; **infos'sato, a** ag hollow; (occhi) deep-set; (: per malattia) sunken.

in'frangere [in'frandʒere] vt to smash; (fig: legge, patti) to break; ~rsi vr to smash, break; **infran'gibile** ag unbreakable; **in'franto, a** pp di **infrangere** // ag broken.

infrazi'one [infrat'tsjone] sf: **~ a** breaking of, violation of.

infredda'tura sf slight cold.

infreddo'lito, a ag cold, chilled.

infruttu'oso, a ag fruitless.

infu'ori av out; **all'~** outwards; **all'~ di** (eccetto) except, with the exception of.

infuri'are vi to rage; ~rsi vr to fly into a rage.

infusi'one sf infusion.

in'fuso, a pp di **infondere** // sm infusion; **~ di camomilla** camomile tea.

Ing. abbr = **ingegnere**.

ingabbi'are vt to cage.

ingaggi'are [ingad'dʒare] vt (assumere con compenso) to take on, hire; (SPORT) to sign on; (MIL) to engage; **in'gaggio** sm hiring; signing on.

ingan'nare vt to deceive; (coniuge) to be unfaithful to; (fisco) to cheat; (eludere) to dodge, elude; (fig: tempo) to while away // vi (apparenza) to be deceptive; ~rsi vr to be mistaken, be wrong; **ingan'nevole** ag deceptive.

in'ganno sm deceit, deception; (azione) trick; (menzogna, frode) cheat, swindle; (illusione) illusion.

ingarbugli'are [ingarbuʎ'ʎare] vt to tangle; (fig) to confuse, muddle; ~rsi vr to become confused o muddled.

inge'gnarsi [indʒeɲ'ɲarsi] vr to do one's best, try hard; **~ per vivere** to live by one's wits.

inge'gnere [indʒeɲ'ɲɛre] sm engineer; **~ civile/navale** civil/naval engineer; **ingegne'ria** sf engineering.

in'gegno [in'dʒeɲɲo] sm (intelligenza) intelligence, brains pl; (capacità creativa) ingenuity; (disposizione) talent; **inge'gnoso, a** ag ingenious, clever.

ingelo'sire [indʒelo'zire] vt to make jealous // vi (anche: ~rsi) to become jealous.

in'gente [in'dʒɛnte] ag huge, enormous.

ingenuità [indʒenui'ta] sf ingenuousness.

in'genuo, a [in'dʒɛnuo] ag ingenuous, naïve.

inges'sare [indʒes'sare] vt (MED) to put in plaster; **ingessa'tura** sf plaster.

Inghil'terra [ingil'tɛrra] sf: **l'~** England.

inghiot'tire [ingjot'tire] vt to swallow.

ingial'lire [indʒal'lire] vi to go yellow.

ingigan'tire [indʒigan'tire] vt to enlarge, magnify // vi to become gigantic o enormous.

inginocchi'arsi [indʒinok'kjarsi] vr to kneel (down).

ingiù [in'dʒu] av down, downwards.

ingi'uria [in'dʒurja] sf insult; (fig: danno) damage, **ingiuri'are** vt to insult, abuse; **ingiuri'oso, a** ag insulting, abusive.

ingius'tizia [indʒus'tittsja] sf injustice.

ingi'usto, a [in'dʒusto] ag unjust, unfair.

in'glese ag English // sm/f Englishman/woman // sm (LING) English; **gli I~i** the English; **andarsene o filare all'~** to take French leave.

ingoi'are vt to gulp (down); (fig) to swallow (up).

ingol'fare vt, ~rsi vr (motore) to flood.

ingom'brare vt (strada) to block; (stanza) to clutter up; **in'gombro, a** ag (strada, passaggio) blocked // sm obstacle; **essere d'ingombro** to be in the way.

in'gordo, a ag: **~ di** greedy for; (fig) greedy o avid for.

ingor'garsi vr to be blocked up, be choked up.

in'gorgo, ghi *sm* blockage, obstruction; *(anche:* ~ **stradale)** traffic jam.

ingoz'zare [ingot'tsare] *vt (animali)* to fatten; *(fig: persona)* to stuff; ~**rsi** *vr:* ~**rsi (di)** to stuff o.s. (with).

ingra'naggio [ingra'naddʒo] *sm (TECN)* gear; *(di orologio)* mechanism; **gli** ~**i della burocrazia** the bureaucratic machinery.

ingra'nare *vi* to mesh, engage // *vt* to engage; ~ **la marcia** to get into gear.

ingrandi'mento *sm* enlargement; extension.

ingran'dire *vt (anche FOT)* to enlarge; *(estendere)* to extend; *(OTTICA, fig)* to magnify // *vi (anche:* ~**rsi)** to become larger *o* bigger; *(aumentare)* to grow, increase; *(espandersi)* to expand.

ingras'sare *vt* to make fat; *(animali)* to fatten; *(AGR: terreno)* to manure; *(lubrificare)* to oil, lubricate // *vi (anche:* ~**rsi)** to get fat, put on weight.

in'grato, a *ag* ungrateful; *(lavoro)* thankless, unrewarding.

ingrazi'are [ingrat'tsjare] *vt:* ~**rsi qn** to ingratiate o.s. with sb.

ingredi'ente *sm* ingredient.

in'gresso *sm (porta)* entrance; *(atrio)* hall; *(l'entrare)* entrance, entry; *(facoltà di entrare)* admission; "~ **libero"** "admission free".

ingros'sare *vt* to increase; *(folla, livello)* to swell // *vi (anche:* ~**rsi)** to increase; to swell.

in'grosso *av:* **all'**~ *(COMM)* wholesale; *(all'incirca)* roughly, about.

ingual'cibile [ingwal'tʃibile] *ag* crease-resistant.

ingua'ribile *ag* incurable.

'inguine *sm (ANAT)* groin.

ini'bire *vt* to forbid, prohibit; *(PSIC)* to inhibit; **inibizi'one** *sf* prohibition; inhibition.

iniet'tare *vt* to inject; ~**rsi** *vr:* ~**rsi di sangue** *(occhi)* to become bloodshot; **iniezi'one** *sf* injection.

inimi'carsi *vr:* ~ **con qn** to fall out with sb.

inimi'cizia [inimi'tʃittsja] *sf* animosity.

ininter'rotto, a *ag* unbroken; uninterrupted.

iniquità *sf inv* iniquity; *(atto)* wicked action.

inizi'ale [init'tsjale] *ag, sf* initial.

inizi'are [init'tsjare] *vi, vt* to begin, start; ~ **qn a** to initiate sb into; *(pittura etc)* to introduce sb to; ~ **a fare qc** to start doing sth.

inizia'tiva [inittsja'tiva] *sf* initiative; ~ **privata** private enterprise.

i'nizio [i'nittsjo] *sm* beginning; **all'**~ at the beginning, at the start; **dare** ~ **a qc** to start sth, get sth going.

innaffi'are *etc* = **annaffiare** *etc.*

innal'zare [innal'tsare] *vt (sollevare, alzare)* to raise; *(rizzare)* to erect; ~**rsi** *vr* to rise.

innamo'rare *vt* to enchant, charm; ~**rsi** *vr:* ~**rsi (di qn)** to fall in love (with sb); **innamo'rato, a** *ag (che nutre amore):* **innamorato (di)** in love (with); *(appassionato):* **innamorato di** very fond of // *sm/f* lover; sweetheart.

in'nanzi [in'nantsi] *av (stato in luogo)* in front, ahead; *(moto a luogo)* forward, on; *(tempo: prima)* before // *prep (prima)* before; ~ **a** in front of.

in'nato, a *ag* innate.

innatu'rale *ag* unnatural.

inne'gabile *ag* undeniable.

innervo'sire *vt:* ~ **qn** to get on sb's nerves; ~**rsi** *vr* to get irritated *o* upset.

innes'care *vt* to prime; **in'nesco, schi** *sm* primer.

innes'tare *vt (BOT, MED)* to graft; *(TECN)* to engage; *(inserire: presa)* to insert; **in'nesto** *sm* graft; grafting *q*; *(TECN)* clutch; *(ELETTR)* connection.

'inno *sm* hymn; ~ **nazionale** national anthem.

inno'cente [inno'tʃɛnte] *ag* innocent; **inno'cenza** *sf* innocence.

in'nocuo, a *ag* innocuous, harmless.

inno'vare *vt* to change, make innovations in.

innume'revole *ag* innumerable.

ino'doro, a *ag* odourless.

inol'trare *vt (AMM)* to pass on, forward; ~**rsi** *vr (addentrarsi)* to advance, go forward.

i'noltre *av* besides, moreover.

inon'dare *vt* to flood; **inondazi'one** *sf* flooding *q*; flood.

inope'roso, a *ag* inactive, idle.

inoppor'tuno, a *ag* untimely, ill-timed; inappropriate; *(momento)* inopportune.

inorgo'glire [inorgoʎ'ʎire] *vt* to make proud // *vi (anche:* ~**rsi)** to become proud; ~**rsi di qc** to pride o.s. on sth.

inorri'dire *vt* to horrify // *vi* to be horrified.

inospi'tale *ag* inhospitable.

inosser'vato, a *ag (non notato)* unobserved; *(non rispettato)* not observed, not kept.

inossi'dabile *ag* stainless.

inqua'drare *vt (foto, immagine)* to frame; *(fig)* to situate, set.

inquie'tare *vt (turbare)* to disturb, worry; ~**rsi** *vr* to worry, become anxious; *(impazientirsi)* to get upset.

inqui'eto, a *ag* restless; *(preoccupato)* worried, anxious; **inquie'tudine** *sf* anxiety, worry.

inqui'lino, a *sm/f* tenant.

inquina'mento *sm* pollution.

inqui'nare *vt* to pollute.

inqui'sire *vt, vi* to investigate; **inquisi'tore, 'trice** *ag (sguardo)* inquiring; **inquisizi'one** *sf (STORIA)* inquisition.

insabbi'are vt (fig: pratica) to shelve; ~rsi vr (arenarsi: barca) to run aground; (fig: pratica) to be shelved.

insac'cati smpl (CUC) sausages.

insa'lata sf salad; ~ mista mixed salad; **insalati'era** sf salad bowl.

insa'lubre ag unhealthy.

insa'nabile ag (piaga) which cannot be healed; (situazione) irremediable; (odio) implacable.

insangui'nare vt to stain with blood.

insa'puta sf: all'~ di qn without sb knowing.

insce'nare [infe'nare] vt (TEATRO) to stage, put on; (fig) to stage.

insedi'are vt to install; ~rsi vr to take up office; (popolo, colonia) to settle.

in'segna [in'seɲɲa] sf sign; (emblema) sign, emblem; (bandiera) flag, banner; ~e sfpl (decorazioni) insignia pl.

insegna'mento [inseɲɲa'mento] sm teaching.

inse'gnante [inseɲ'ɲante] ag teaching // sm/f teacher.

inse'gnare [inseɲ'ɲare] vt, vi to teach; ~ a qn qc to teach sb sth; ~ a qn a fare qc to teach sb (how) to do sth.

insegui'mento sm pursuit, chase.

insegu'ire vt to pursue, chase.

inselvati'chire [inselvati'kire] vi (anche: ~rsi) to grow wild.

insena'tura sf inlet, creek.

insen'sato, a ag senseless, stupid.

insen'sibile ag (nervo) insensible; (persona) indifferent.

inse'rire vt to insert; (ELETTR) to connect; (allegare) to enclose; (annuncio) to put in, place; ~rsi vr (fig): ~rsi in to become part of; **in'serto** sm (pubblicazione) insert.

inservi'ente sm/f attendant.

inserzi'one [inser'tsjone] sf insertion; (avviso) advertisement; fare un'~ sul giornale to put an advertisement in the paper.

insetti'cida, i [insetti'tʃida] sm insecticide.

in'setto sm insect.

in'sidia sf snare, trap; (pericolo) hidden danger; **insidi'are** vt: ~ la vita di qn to make an attempt on sb's life.

insi'eme av together // prep: ~ a o con together with // sm whole; (MAT, servizio, assortimento) set; (MODA) ensemble, outfit; tutti ~ all together; tutto ~ all together; (in una volta) at one go; nell'~ on the whole; d'~ (veduta etc) overall.

insignifi'cante [insiɲɲifi'kante] ag insignificant.

insi'gnire [insiɲ'ɲire] vt: ~ qn di to honour o decorate sb with.

insin'cero, a [insin'tʃero] ag insincere.

insinda'cabile ag unquestionable.

insinu'are vt (introdurre): ~ qc in to slip o slide sth into; (fig) to insinuate, imply; ~rsi vr: ~rsi in to seep into; (fig) to creep into; to worm one's way into.

insis'tente ag insistent; persistent.

in'sistere vi: ~ su qc to insist on sth; ~ in qc/a fare (perseverare) to persist in sth/in doing; **insis'tito, a** pp di **insistere**.

insoddis'fatto, a ag dissatisfied.

insoffe'rente ag intolerant.

insolazi'one [insolat'tsjone] sf (MED) sunstroke.

inso'lente ag insolent; **insolen'tire** vi to grow insolent // vt to insult, be rude to.

in'solito, a ag unusual, out of the ordinary.

inso'luto, a ag (non risolto) unsolved; (non pagato) unpaid, outstanding.

insol'vibile ag insolvent.

in'somma av (in breve, in conclusione) in short; (dunque) well // escl for heaven's sake!

in'sonne ag sleepless; **in'sonnia** sf insomnia, sleeplessness.

insonno'lito, a ag sleepy, drowsy.

insoppor'tabile ag unbearable.

in'sorgere [in'sordʒere] vi (ribellarsi) to rise up, rebel; (apparire) to come up, arise.

in'sorto, a pp di **insorgere** // sm/f rebel, insurgent.

insospet'tire vt to make suspicious // vi (anche: ~rsi) to become suspicious.

inspi'rare vt to breathe in, inhale.

in'stabile ag (carico, indole) unstable; (tempo) unsettled; (equilibrio) unsteady.

instal'lare vt to install; ~rsi vr (sistemarsi): ~rsi in to settle in; **installazi'one** sf installation.

instan'cabile ag untiring, indefatigable.

instau'rare vt to introduce, institute.

instra'dare vt: ~ (verso) to direct (towards).

insuc'cesso [insut'tʃesso] sm failure, flop.

insudici'are [insudi'tʃare] vt to dirty; ~rsi vr to get dirty.

insuffici'ente [insuffi'tʃente] ag insufficient; (compito, allievo) inadequate; **insuffici'enza** sf insufficiency; inadequacy; (INS) fail.

insu'lare ag insular.

insu'lina sf insulin.

in'sulso, a ag (sciocco) inane, silly; (persona) dull, insipid.

insul'tare vt to insult, affront.

in'sulto sm insult, affront.

insussis'tente ag non-existent.

intac'care vt (fare tacche) to cut into; (corrodere) to corrode; (fig: cominciare ad usare: risparmi) to break into; (: ledere) to damage.

intagli'are [intaʎ'ʎare] *vt* to carve; **in'taglio** *sm* carving.

intan'gibile [intan'dʒibile] *ag* untouchable; inviolable.

in'tanto *av* (*nel frattempo*) meanwhile, in the meantime; (*per cominciare*) just to begin with; ~ **che** *cong* while.

in'tarsio *sm* inlaying *q*, marquetry *q*; inlay.

inta'sare *vt* to choke (up), block (up); (*AUT*) to obstruct, block; ~**rsi** *vr* to become choked *o* blocked.

intas'care *vt* to pocket.

in'tatto, a *ag* intact; (*puro*) unsullied.

intavo'lare *vt* to start, enter into.

inte'grale *ag* complete; (*pane, farina*) wholemeal (*Brit*), whole-wheat (*US*); (*MAT*): **calcolo ~** integral calculus.

inte'grante *ag*: **parte ~** integral part.

inte'grare *vt* to complete; (*MAT*) to integrate; ~**rsi** *vr* (*persona*) to become integrated.

integrità *sf* integrity.

'integro, a *ag* (*intatto, intero*) complete, whole; (*retto*) upright.

intelaia'tura *sf* frame; (*fig*) structure, framework.

intel'letto *sm* intellect; **intellettu'ale** *ag*, *sm/f* intellectual.

intelli'gente [intelli'dʒɛnte] *ag* intelligent; **intelli'genza** *sf* intelligence.

intem'perie *sfpl* bad weather *sg*.

intempes'tivo, a *ag* untimely.

inten'dente *sm*: **~ di Finanza** inland (*Brit*) *o* internal (*US*) revenue officer; **inten'denza** *sf*: **intendenza di Finanza** inland (*Brit*) *o* internal (*US*) revenue office.

in'tendere *vt* (*avere intenzione*): **~ fare qc** to intend *o* mean to do sth; (*comprendere*) to understand; (*udire*) to hear; (*significare*) to mean; ~**rsi** *vr* (*conoscere*): ~**rsi di** to know a lot about, be a connoisseur of; (*accordarsi*) to get on (well); **intendersela con qn** (*avere una relazione amorosa*) to have an affair with sb; **intendi'mento** *sm* (*intelligenza*) understanding; (*proposito*) intention; **intendi'tore, 'trice** *sm/f* connoisseur, expert.

intene'rire *vt* (*fig*) to move (to pity); ~**rsi** *vr* (*fig*) to be moved.

inten'sivo, a *ag* intensive.

in'tenso, a *ag* intense.

in'tento, a *ag* (*teso, assorto*): **~ (a)** intent (on), absorbed (in) // *sm* aim, purpose.

intenzio'nale [intentsjo'nale] *ag* intentional.

intenzi'one [inten'tsjone] *sf* intention; (*DIR*) intent; **avere ~ di fare qc** to intend to do sth, have the intention of doing sth.

interca'lare *sm* pet phrase, stock phrase // *vt* to insert.

interca'pedine *sf* gap, cavity.

intercet'tare [intertʃet'tare] *vt* to intercept.

inter'detto, a *pp di* **interdire** // *ag* forbidden, prohibited; (*sconcertato*) dumbfounded // *sm* (*REL*) interdict.

inter'dire *vt* to forbid, prohibit, ban; (*REL*) to interdict; (*DIR*) to deprive of civil rights; **interdizi'one** *sf* prohibition, ban.

interessa'mento *sm* interest.

interes'sante *ag* interesting; **essere in stato ~** to be expecting (a baby).

interes'sare *vt* to interest; (*concernere*) to concern, be of interest to; (*far intervenire*): **~ qn a** to draw sb's attention to // *vi*: **~ a** to interest, matter to; ~**rsi** *vr* (*mostrare interesse*): ~**rsi a** to take an interest in, be interested in; (*occuparsi*): ~**rsi di** to take care of.

inte'resse *sm* (*anche COMM*) interest.

inter'faccia, ce [inter'fattʃa] *sf* (*INFORM*) interface.

interfe'renza [interfe'rɛntsa] *sf* interference.

interfe'rire *vi* to interfere.

interiezi'one [interjet'tsjone] *sf* exclamation, interjection.

interi'ora *sfpl* entrails.

interi'ore *ag* interior, inner, inside, internal; (*fig*) inner.

inter'ludio *sm* (*MUS*) interlude.

inter'medio, a *ag* intermediate.

inter'mezzo [inter'mɛddzo] *sm* (*intervallo*) interval; (*breve spettacolo*) intermezzo.

inter'nare *vt* (*arrestare*) to intern; (*MED*) to commit (to a mental institution).

internazio'nale [internattsjo'nale] *ag* international.

in'terno, a *ag* (*di dentro*) internal, interior, inner; (*: mare*) inland; (*nazionale*) domestic; (*allievo*) boarding // *sm* inside, interior; (*di paese*) interior; (*fodera*) lining; (*di appartamento*) flat (number); (*TEL*) extension // *sm/f* (*INS*) boarder; ~**i** *smpl* (*CINEMA*) interior shots; **all'~** inside; **Ministero degli I~i** Ministry of the Interior, ≈ Home Office (*Brit*), Department of the Interior (*US*).

in'tero, a *ag* (*integro, intatto*) whole, entire; (*completo, totale*) complete; (*numero*) whole; (*non ridotto: biglietto*) full.

interpel'lare *vt* to consult.

inter'porre *vt* (*ostacolo*): **~ qc a qc** to put sth in the way of sth; (*influenza*) to use; **~ appello** (*DIR*) to appeal; **interporsi** *vr* to intervene; **interporsi fra** (*mettersi in mezzo*) to come between; **inter'posto, a** *pp di* **interporre**.

interpre'tare *vt* to interpret; **in'terprete** *sm/f* interpreter; (*TEATRO*) actor/actress, performer; (*MUS*) performer.

interro'gare vt to question; (INS) to test; **interroga'tivo, a** ag (occhi, sguardo) questioning, inquiring; (LING) interrogative // sm question; (fig) mystery; **interroga'torio, a** ag interrogatory, questioning // sm (DIR) questioning q; **interrogazi'one** sf questioning q; (INS) oral test.

inter'rompere vt to interrupt; (studi, trattative) to break off, interrupt; ~rsi vr to break off, stop; **inter'rotto, a** pp di **interrompere**.

interrut'tore sm switch.

interruzi'one [interrut'tsjone] sf interruption; break.

interse'care vt, ~rsi vr to intersect.

inter'stizio [inter'stittsjo] sm interstice, crack.

interur'bano, a ag inter-city; (TEL: chiamata) trunk cpd, long-distance; (: telefono) long-distance // sf trunk call, long-distance call.

inter'vallo sm interval; (spazio) space, gap.

interve'nire vi (partecipare): ~ a to take part in; (intromettersi: anche POL) to intervene; (MED: operare) to operate; **inter'vento** sm participation; (intromissione) intervention; (MED) operation; **fare un intervento nel corso di** (dibattito, programma) to take part in.

inter'vista sf interview; **intervis'tare** vt to interview.

in'teso, a pp di **intendere** // ag agreed // sf understanding; (accordo) agreement, understanding; **non darsi per ~ di** qc to take no notice of sth.

intes'tare vt (lettera) to address; (proprietà): ~ a to register in the name of; ~ un assegno a qn to make out a cheque to sb; **intestazi'one** sf heading; (su carta da lettere) letterhead; (registrazione) registration.

intes'tino, a ag (lotte) internal, civil // sm (ANAT) intestine.

inti'mare vt to order, command; **intimazi'one** sf order, command.

intimi'dire vt to intimidate // vi (anche: ~rsi) to grow shy.

intimità sf intimacy; privacy; (familiarità) familiarity.

'intimo, a ag intimate; (affetti, vita) private; (fig: profondo) inmost // sm (persona) intimate o close friend; (dell'animo) bottom, depths pl; **parti ~e** (ANAT) private parts.

intimo'rire vt to frighten; ~rsi vr to become frightened.

in'tingolo sm sauce; (pietanza) stew.

intiriz'zire [intirid'dzire] vt to numb // vi (anche: ~rsi) to go numb.

intito'lare vt to give a title to; (dedicare) to dedicate.

intolle'rabile ag intolerable.

intolle'rante ag intolerant.

in'tonaco, ci o **chi** sm plaster.

into'nare vt (canto) to start to sing; (armonizzare) to match; ~rsi vr (colori) to go together; ~rsi a (carnagione) to suit; (abito) to go with, match.

inton'tire vt to stun, daze // vi, ~rsi vr to be stunned o dazed.

in'toppo sm stumbling block, obstacle.

in'torno av around; ~ a prep (attorno a) around; (riguardo, circa) about.

intorpi'dire vt to numb; (fig) to make sluggish // vi (anche: ~rsi) to grow numb; (fig) to become sluggish.

intossi'care vt to poison; **intossicazi'one** sf poisoning.

intralci'are [intral'tʃare] vt to hamper, hold up.

intransi'tivo, a ag, sm intransitive.

intrapren'dente ag enterprising, go-ahead.

intra'prendere vt to undertake.

intrat'tabile ag intractable.

intratte'nere vt to entertain; to engage in conversation; ~rsi vr to linger; ~rsi su qc to dwell on sth.

intrave'dere vt to catch a glimpse of; (fig) to foresee.

intrecci'are [intret'tʃare] vt (capelli) to plait, braid; (intessere: anche fig) to weave, interweave, intertwine; ~rsi vr to intertwine, become interwoven; ~ le mani to clasp one's hands; **in'treccio** sm (fig: trama) plot, story.

intri'gare vi to manoeuvre (Brit), maneuver (US), scheme; **in'trigo, ghi** sm plot, intrigue.

in'trinseco, a, ci, che ag intrinsic.

in'triso, a ag: ~ (di) soaked (in).

intro'durre vt to introduce; (chiave etc): ~ qc in to insert sth into; (persone: far entrare) to show in; **introdursi** vr (moda, tecniche) to be introduced; **introdursi in** (persona: penetrare) to enter; (: entrare furtivamente) to steal o slip into; **introduzi'one** sf introduction.

in'troito sm income, revenue.

intro'mettersi vr to interfere, meddle; (interporsi) to intervene.

in'truglio [in'truʎʎo] sm concoction.

intrusi'one sf intrusion; interference.

in'truso, a sm/f intruder.

intu'ire vt to perceive by intuition; (rendersi conto) to realize; **in'tuito** sm intuition; (perspicacia) perspicacity; **intuizi'one** sf intuition.

inu'mano, a ag inhuman.

inumi'dire vt to dampen, moisten; ~rsi vr to become damp o wet.

i'nutile ag useless; (superfluo) pointless, unnecessary; **inutilità** sf uselessness; pointlessness.

inva'dente ag (fig) interfering, nosey.

in'vadere vt to invade; (affollare) to

swarm into, overrun; (sog: acque) to flood; **invadi'trice** ag vedi **invasore**.

inva'ghirsi [inva'girsi] vr: ~ di to take a fancy to.

invalidità sf infirmity; disability; (DIR) invalidity.

in'valido, a ag (infermo) infirm, invalid; (al lavoro) disabled; (DIR: nullo) invalid // sm/f invalid; disabled person.

in'vano av in vain.

invasi'one sf invasion.

in'vaso, a pp di **invadere**.

inva'sore, invadi'trice [invadi'tritʃe] ag invading // sm invader.

invecchi'are [invek'kjare] vi (persona) to grow old; (vino, popolazione) to age; (moda) to become dated // vt to age; (far apparire più vecchio) to make look older.

in'vece [in'vetʃe] av instead; (al contrario) on the contrary; ~ di prep instead of.

inve'ire vi: ~ contro to rail against.

inven'tare vt to invent; (pericoli, pettegolezzi) to make up, invent.

inven'tario sm inventory; (COMM) stocktaking q.

inven'tivo, a ag inventive // sf inventiveness.

inven'tore sm inventor.

invenzi'one [inven'tsjone] sf invention; (bugia) lie, story.

inver'nale ag winter cpd; (simile all'inverno) wintry.

in'verno sm winter.

invero'simile ag unlikely.

inversi'one sf inversion; reversal; "divieto d'~" (AUT) "no U-turns".

in'verso, a ag opposite; (MAT) inverse // sm contrary, opposite; in senso ~ in the opposite direction; in ordine ~ in reverse order.

inver'tire vt to invert, reverse; ~ la marcia (AUT) to do a U-turn; **inver'tito, a** sm/f homosexual.

investi'gare vt, vi to investigate; **investiga'tore, trice** sm/f investigator, detective; **investigazi'one** sf investigation, inquiry.

investi'mento sm (ECON) investment; (scontro, urto) crash, collision; (incidente stradale) road accident.

inves'tire vt (denaro) to invest; (sog: veicolo: pedone) to knock down; (: altro veicolo) to crash into; (apostrofare) to assail; (incaricare): ~ qn di to invest sb with.

invi'are vt to send; **invi'ato, a** sm/f envoy; (STAMPA) correspondent.

in'vidia sf envy; **invidi'are** vt: ~ qn (per qc) to envy sb for sth; ~ qc a qn to envy sb sth; **invidi'oso, a** ag envious.

in'vio, 'vii sm sending; (insieme di merci) consignment.

invipe'rito, a ag furious.

invischi'are [invis'kjare] vt (fig): ~ qn in

to involve sb in; ~**rsi** vr: ~**rsi** (con qn/in qc) to get mixed up o involved (with sb/ in sth).

invi'sibile ag invisible.

invi'tare vt to invite; ~ qn a fare to invite sb to do; **invi'tato, a** sm/f guest; **in'vito** sm invitation.

invo'care vt (chiedere: aiuto, pace) to cry out for; (appellarsi: la legge, Dio) to appeal to, invoke.

invogli'are [invoʎ'ʎare] vt: ~ qn a fare to tempt sb to do, induce sb to do.

involon'tario, a ag (errore) unintentional; (gesto) involuntary.

invol'tino sm (CUC) roulade.

in'volto sm (pacco) parcel; (fagotto) bundle.

in'volucro sm cover, wrapping.

involuzi'one [involut'tsjone] sf (di stile) convolutedness; (regresso): subire un'~ to regress.

inzacche'rare [intsakke'rare] vt to spatter with mud.

inzup'pare [intsup'pare] vt to soak; ~**rsi** vr to get soaked.

'io pronome I // sm inv: l'~ the ego, the self; ~ stesso(a) I myself.

i'odio sm iodine.

i'ogurt sm inv = **yoghurt**.

l'onio sm: lo ~, il mar ~ the Ionian (Sea).

ipermer'cato sm hypermarket.

ipertensi'one sf high blood pressure, hypertension.

ip'nosi sf hypnosis; **ipno'tismo** sm hypnotism; **ipnotiz'zare** vt to hypnotize.

ipocri'sia sf hypocrisy.

i'pocrita, i, e ag hypocritical // sm/f hypocrite.

ipo'teca, che sf mortgage; **ipote'care** vt to mortgage.

i'potesi sf inv hypothesis; **ipo'tetico, a, ci, che** ag hypothetical.

'ippico, a, ci, che ag horse cpd // sf horseracing.

ippocas'tano sm horse chestnut.

ip'podromo sm racecourse.

ippo'potamo sm hippopotamus.

'ira sf anger, wrath.

l'ran sm: l'~ Iran.

l'raq sm: l'~ Iraq.

'iride sf (arcobaleno) rainbow; (ANAT, BOT) iris.

lr'landa sf: l'~ Ireland; l'~ del Nord Northern Ireland, Ulster; **la Repubblica d'~** Eire, the Republic of Ireland; **irlan'dese** ag Irish // sm/f Irishman/ woman; **gli Irlandesi** the Irish.

iro'nia sf irony; **i'ronico, a, ci, che** ag ironic(al).

irradi'are vt to radiate; (sog: raggi di luce: illuminare) to shine on // vi (diffondersi: anche): ~**rsi** to radiate; **irradiazi'one** sf radiation.

irragio'nevole [irradʒo'nevole] ag irrational; unreasonable.

irrazio'nale [irrattsjo'nale] *ag* irrational.

irre'ale *ag* unreal.

irrecupe'rabile *ag* irretrievable; *(fig: person)* irredeemable.

irrecu'sabile *ag (offerta)* not to be refused; *(prova)* irrefutable.

irrego'lare *ag* irregular; *(terreno)* uneven.

irremo'vibile *ag (fig)* unshakeable, unyielding.

irrepa'rabile *ag* irreparable; *(fig)* inevitable.

irrepe'ribile *ag* nowhere to be found.

irrequi'eto, a *ag* restless.

irresis'tibile *ag* irresistible.

irrespon'sabile *ag* irresponsible.

irridu'cibile [irridu'tʃibile] *ag* irreducible; *(fig)* indomitable.

irri'gare *vt (annaffiare)* to irrigate; *(sog: fiume etc)* to flow through; **irrigazi'one** *sf* irrigation.

irrigi'dire [irridʒi'dire] *vt*, ~**rsi** *vr* to stiffen.

Irri'sorio, a *ag* derisory.

irri'tare *vt (mettere di malumore)* to irritate, annoy; *(MED)* to irritate; ~**rsi** *vr (stizzirsi)* to become irritated o annoyed; *(MED)* to become irritated; **irritazi'one** *sf* irritation; annoyance.

ir'rompere *vi*: ~ **in** to burst into.

irro'rare *vt* to sprinkle; *(AGR)* to spray.

irru'ente *ag (fig)* impetuous, violent.

irruzi'one [irrut'tsjone] *sf*: **fare** ~ **in** to burst into; *(sog: polizia)* to raid.

'irto, a *ag* bristly; ~ **di** bristling with.

is'critto, a *pp di* **iscrivere** // *sm/f* member; **per o in** ~ in writing.

is'crivere *vt* to register, enter; *(persona)*: ~ **(a)** to register (in), enrol (in); ~**rsi** *vr*: ~**rsi (a)** *(club, partito)* to join; *(università)* to register o enrol (at); *(esame, concorso)* to register o enter (for); **iscrizi'one** *sf (epigrafe etc)* inscription; *(a scuola, società)* enrolment, registration; *(registrazione)* registration.

Is'lam *sm*: **l'~** Islam.

Is'landa *sf*: **l'~** Iceland.

'isola *sf* island; ~ **pedonale** *(AUT)* pedestrian precinct.

isola'mento *sm* isolation; *(TECN)* insulation.

iso'lante *ag* insulating // *sm* insulator.

iso'lare *vt* to isolate; *(TECN)* to insulate; *(: acusticamente)* to soundproof; **iso'lato, a** *ag* isolated; insulated // *sm (edificio)* block.

ispetto'rato *sm* inspectorate.

ispet'tore *sm* inspector.

ispezio'nare [ispettsjo'nare] *vt* to inspect.

ispezi'one [ispet'tsjone] *sf* inspection.

'ispido, a *ag* bristly, shaggy.

ispi'rare *vt* to inspire; ~**rsi** *vr*: ~**rsi a** to

draw one's inspiration from.

Isra'ele *sm*: **l'~** Israel; **israeli'ano, a** *ag, sm/f* Israeli.

is'sare *vt* to hoist.

istan'taneo, a *ag* instantaneous // *sf (FOT)* snapshot.

is'tante *sm* instant, moment; **all'~**, **sull'~** instantly, immediately.

is'tanza [is'tantsa] *sf* petition, request.

is'terico, a, ci, che *ag* hysterical.

iste'rismo *sm* hysteria.

isti'gare *vt* to incite; **istigazi'one** *sf* incitement; **istigazione a delinquere** *(DIR)* incitement to crime.

is'tinto *sm* instinct.

istitu'ire *vt (fondare)* to institute, found; *(porre: confronto)* to establish; *(intraprendere: inchiesta)* to set up.

isti'tuto *sm* institute; *(di università)* department; *(ente, DIR)* institution; ~ **di bellezza** beauty salon.

istituzi'one [istitut'tsjone] *sf* institution.

'istmo *sm (GEO)* isthmus.

istra'dare *vt* = **instradare.**

'istrice ['istritʃe] *sm* porcupine.

istri'one *sm (peg)* ham actor.

istru'ire *vt (insegnare)* to teach; *(ammaestrare)* to train; *(informare)* to instruct, inform; *(DIR)* to prepare; **istrut'tore, 'trice** *sm/f* instructor // *ag*: **giudice istruttore** examining *(Brit)* o committing *(US)* magistrate; **istrut'toria** *sf (DIR)* (preliminary) investigation and hearing; **istruzi'one** *sf* education; training; *(direttiva)* instruction; *(DIR)* = **istruttoria**; **istruzioni per l'uso** instructions (for use).

I'talia *sf*: **l'~** Italy.

itali'ano, a *ag* Italian // *sm/f* Italian // *sm (LING)* Italian; **gli I~i** the Italians.

itine'rario *sm* itinerary.

itte'rizia [itte'rittsja] *sf (MED)* jaundice.

'ittico, a, ci, che *ag* fish *cpd*; fishing *cpd*.

Iugos'lavia *sf* = **Jugoslavia.**

iugos'lavo, a *ag, sm/f* = **jugoslavo, a.**

i'uta *sf* jute.

I.V.A. ['iva] *sigla f* = **imposta sul valore aggiunto.**

J

jazz [dʒaz] *sm* jazz.

jeans [dʒinz] *smpl* jeans.

Jugos'lavia [jugoz'lavja] *sf*: **la** ~ Yugoslavia; **jugos'lavo, a** *ag, sm/f* Yugoslav(ian).

'juta ['juta] *sf* = **iuta.**

K

K *abbr (INFORM)* K.

k *abbr (= kilo)* k.

karatè sm karate.

Kg abbr (= chilogrammo) kg.

'killer sm inv gunman, hired gun.

km abbr (= chilometro) km.

'krapfen sm inv (CUC) doughnut.

L

l' det vedi **la, lo.**

la det f (dav V **l'**) the // pronome (dav V **l'**) (oggetto: persona) her; (: cosa) it; (: forma di cortesia) you // sm inv (MUS) A; (: solfeggiando la scala) la.

là av there; di ~ (da quel luogo) from there; (in quel luogo) in there; (dall'altra parte) over there; di ~ di beyond; per di ~ that way; più in ~ further on; (tempo) later on; **fatti in ~** move up; ~ dentro/sopra/sotto in/up (o on)/under there; vedi **quello.**

'labbro sm (pl(f): **labbra**: solo nel senso ANAT) lip.

labi'rinto sm labyrinth, maze.

labora'torio sm (di ricerca) laboratory; (di arti, mestieri) workshop; ~ linguistico language laboratory.

labori'oso, a ag (faticoso) laborious; (attivo) hard-working.

labu'rista, i, e ag Labour (Brit) cpd // sm/f Labour Party member (Brit).

'lacca, che sf lacquer.

'laccio ['lattʃo] sm noose; (legaccio, tirante) lasso; (di scarpa) lace; ~ emostatico tourniquet.

lace'rare [latʃe'rare] vt to tear to shreds, lacerate; ~rsi vr to tear; **'lacero, a** ag (logoro) torn, tattered; (MED) lacerated.

'lacrima sf tear; in ~e in tears; **lacri'mare** vi to water; **lacri'mogeno, a** ag: gas lacrimogeno tear gas.

la'cuna sf (fig) gap.

'ladro sm thief; **ladro'cinio** sm theft, larceny.

laggiù [lad'dʒu] av down there; (di là) over there.

la'gnarsi [laɲ'ɲarsi] vr: ~ (di) to complain (about).

'lago, ghi sm lake.

'lagrima etc = **lacrima** etc.

la'guna sf lagoon.

'laico, a, ci, che ag (apostolato) lay; (vita) secular; (scuola) nondenominational // sm/f layman/woman // sm lay brother.

'lama sf blade // sm inv (ZOOL) llama; (REL) lama.

lambic'care vt to distil; ~rsi il cervello to rack one's brains.

lam'bire vt to lick; to lap.

la'mella sf (di metallo etc) thin sheet, thin strip; (di fungo) gill.

lamen'tare vt to lament; ~rsi vr (emettere lamenti) to moan, groan; (rammaricarsi): ~rsi (di) to complain

(about); **lamen'tela** sf complaining q; **lamen'tevole** ag (voce) complaining, plaintive; (destino) pitiful; **la'mento** sm moan, groan; wail; **lamen'toso, a** ag plaintive.

la'metta sf razor blade.

lami'era sf sheet metal.

'lamina sf (lastra sottile) thin sheet (o layer o plate); ~ d'oro gold leaf; gold foil; **lami'nare** vt to laminate; **lami'nato, a** ag laminated; (tessuto) lamé // sm laminate.

'lampada sf lamp; ~ a gas gas lamp; ~ a spirito blow lamp (Brit), blow torch (US); ~ da tavolo table lamp.

lampa'dario sm chandelier.

lampa'dina sf light bulb; ~ tascabile pocket torch (Brit) o flashlight (US).

lam'pante ag (fig: evidente) crystal clear, evident.

lampeggi'are [lamped'dʒare] vi (luce, fari) to flash // vb impers: **lampeggia** there's lightning; **lampeggia'tore** sm (AUT) indicator.

lampi'one sm street light o lamp (Brit).

'lampo sm (METEOR) flash of lightning; (di luce, fig) flash; ~i smpl lightning q // ag inv: cerniera ~ zip (fastener) (Brit), zipper (US); guerra ~ blitzkrieg.

lam'pone sm raspberry.

'lana sf wool; ~ d'acciaio steel wool; pura ~ vergine pure new wool; ~ di vetro glass wool.

lan'cetta [lan'tʃetta] sf (indice) pointer, needle; (di orologio) hand.

'lancia ['lantʃa] sf (arma) lance; (: picca) spear; (di pompa antincendio) nozzle; (imbarcazione) launch.

lanciaf'iamme [lantʃa'fjamme] sm inv flamethrower.

lanci'are [lan'tʃare] vt to throw, hurl, fling; (SPORT) to throw; (far partire: automobile) to get up to full speed; (bombe) to drop; (razzo, prodotto, moda) to launch; ~rsi vr: ~rsi contro/su to throw o hurl o fling o.s. against/on; ~rsi in (fig) to embark on.

lanci'nante [lantʃi'nante] ag (dolore) shooting, throbbing; (grido) piercing.

'lancio ['lantʃo] sm throwing q; throw; dropping q; drop; launching q; launch; ~ del peso putting the shot.

'landa sf (GEO) moor.

'languido, a ag (fiacco) languid, weak; (tenero, malinconico) languishing.

langu'ore sm weakness, languor.

lani'ficio [lani'fitʃo] sm woollen mill.

la'noso, a ag woolly.

lan'terna sf lantern; (faro) lighthouse.

la'nugine [la'nudʒine] sf down.

lapi'dare vt to stone.

lapi'dario, a ag (fig) terse.

'lapide sf (di sepolcro) tombstone; (commemorativa) plaque.

'lapis sm inv pencil.

Lap'ponia *sf* Lapland.

'lapsus *sm inv* slip.

'lardo *sm* bacon fat, lard.

lar'ghezza [lar'gettsa] *sf* width; breadth; looseness; generosity; ~ **di vedute** broad-mindedness.

'largo, a, ghi, ghe *ag* wide; broad; (*maniche*) wide; (*abito: troppo ampio*) loose; (*fig*) generous // *sm* width; breadth; (*mare aperto*): **il** ~ **the open sea** // *sf*: **stare** *o* **tenersi alla** ~**a (da qn/ qc)** to keep one's distance (from sb/sth), keep away (from sb/sth); ~ **due metri** two metres wide; ~ **di spalle** broad-shouldered; **di** ~**ghe vedute** broad-minded; **su** ~**a scala** on a large scale; **di manica** ~**a** generous, open-handed; **al** ~ **di Genova** off (the coast of) Genoa; **farsi** ~ **tra la folla** to push one's way through the crowd.

'larice ['laritʃe] *sm* (*BOT*) larch.

larin'gite [larin'dʒite] *sf* laryngitis.

'larva *sf* larva; (*fig*) shadow.

la'sagne [la'zaɲne] *sfpl* lasagna *sg*.

lasci'are [laʃ'ʃare] *vt* to leave; (*abbandonare*) to leave, abandon, give up; (*cessare di tenere*) to let go of // *vi*: ~ **fare qn** to let sb do // *vb ausiliare*: ~ **fare qn** to let sb do // *vi*: ~ **di fare** (*smettere*) to stop doing; ~**rsi andare/truffare** to let o.s. go/be cheated; ~ **andare** *o* **correre** *o* **perdere** to let things go their own way; ~ **stare qc/qn** to leave sth/sb alone.

'lascito ['laʃʃito] *sm* (*DIR*) legacy.

'laser ['lazer] *ag, sm inv*: (**raggio**) ~ laser (beam).

lassa'tivo, a *ag, sm* laxative.

'lasso *sm*: ~ **di tempo** interval, lapse of time.

lassù *av* up there.

'lastra *sf* (*di pietra*) slab; (*di metallo, FOT*) plate; (*di ghiaccio, vetro*) sheet; (*radiografica*) X-ray (plate).

lastri'care *vt* to pave; **lastri'cato** *sm*, **'lastrico, ci** *o* **chi** *sm* paving.

late'rale *ag* lateral, side *cpd*; (*uscita, ingresso etc*) side *cpd* // *sm* (*CALCIO*) half-back.

late'rizio [late'rittsjo] *sm* (perforated) brick.

lati'fondo *sm* large estate.

la'tino, a *sm* Latin; ~**-ameri'cano a** *ag* Latin-American.

lati'tante *sm/f* fugitive (from justice).

lati'tudine *sf* latitude.

'lato, a *ag* (*fig*) wide, broad // *sm* side; (*fig*) aspect, point of view; **in senso** ~ broadly speaking.

la'trare *vi* to bark.

latro'cinio [latro'tʃinjo] *sm* = **ladro-cinio**.

'latta *sf* tin (plate); (*recipiente*) tin, can.

lat'taio, a *sm/f* milkman/woman; dairyman/woman.

lat'tante *ag* unweaned.

'latte *sm* milk; ~ **detergente** cleansing milk *o* lotion; ~ **secco** *o* **in polvere** dried *o* powdered milk; ~ **scremato** skimmed milk; **'latteo, a** *ag* milky; (*dieta, prodotto*) milk *cpd*; **latte'ria** *sf* dairy; **latti'cini** *smpl* dairy products.

lat'tina *sf* (*di birra etc*) can.

lat'tuga, ghe *sf* lettuce.

'laurea *sf* degree; **laure'ando, a** *sm/f* final-year student; **laure'are** *vt* to confer a degree on; **laurearsi** *vr* to graduate; **laure'ato, a** *ag, sm/f* graduate.

'lauro *sm* laurel.

'lauto, a *ag* (*pranzo, mancia*) lavish.

'lava *sf* lava.

la'vabo *sm* washbasin.

la'vaggio [la'vaddʒo] *sm* washing *q*; ~ **del cervello** brainwashing *q*.

la'vagna [la'vaɲɲa] *sf* (*GEO*) slate; (*di scuola*) blackboard.

la'vanda *sf* (*anche MED*) wash; (*BOT*) lavender; **lavan'daia** *sf* washerwoman; **lavande'ria** *sf* laundry; **lavanderia automatica** launderette; **lavanderia a secco** dry-cleaner's; **lavan'dino** *sm* sink.

lavapi'atti *sm/f* dishwasher.

la'vare *vt* to wash; ~**rsi** *vr* to wash, have a wash; ~ **a secco** to dry-clean; ~**rsi le mani/i denti** to wash one's hands/clean one's teeth.

lava'secco *sm o f inv* drycleaner's.

lavasto'viglie [lavasto'viʎʎe] *sm o f inv* (*macchina*) dishwasher.

lava'toio *sm* (public) washhouse.

lava'trice [lava'tritʃe] *sf* washing machine.

lava'tura *sf* washing *q*; ~ **di piatti** dish-water.

lavo'rante *sm/f* worker.

lavo'rare *vi* to work; (*fig: bar, studio etc*) to do good business // *vt* to work; ~**rsi qn** (*persuaderlo*) to work on sb; ~ **a** to work on; ~ **a maglia** to knit; **lavora'tivo, a** *ag* working; **lavora'tore, 'trice** *sm/f* worker // *ag* working; **lavorazi'one** *sf* (*gen*) working; (*di legno, pietra*) carving; (*di film*) making; (*di prodotto*) manufacture; (*modo di esecuzione*) workmanship; **lavo'rio** *sm* intense activity.

la'voro *sm* work; (*occupazione*) job, work *q*; (*opera*) piece of work, job; (*ECON*) labour; ~**i forzati** hard labour *sg*; ~**i pubblici** public works.

le *det fpl* the // *pronome* (*oggetto*) them; (: *a lei, a essa*) (to) her; (: *forma di cortesia*) (to) you.

le'ale *ag* loyal; (*sincero*) sincere; (*onesto*) fair; **lealtà** *sf* loyalty; sincerity; fairness.

'lebbra *sf* leprosy.

'lecca 'lecca *sm inv* lollipop.

leccapi'edi *sm/f inv* (*peg*) toady, bootlicker.

lec'care vt to lick; (sog: gatto: latte etc) to lick o lap up; (fig) to flatter; ~rsi i baffi to lick one's lips; **lec'cata** sf lick.

'leccio ['lɛttʃo] sm holm oak, ilex.

leccor'nia sf titbit, delicacy.

'lecito, a ['lɛtʃito] ag permitted, allowed.

'ledere vt to damage, injure.

'lega, ghe sf league; (di metalli) alloy.

le'gaccio [le'gattʃo] sm string, lace.

le'gale ag legal // sm lawyer; **legaliz'zare** vt to authenticate; (regolarizzare) to legalize.

le'game sm (corda, fig: affettivo) tie, bond; (nesso logico) link, connection.

le'gare vt (prigioniero, capelli, cane) to tie (up); (libro) to bind; (CHIM) to alloy; (fig: collegare) to bind, join // vi (far lega) to unite; (fig) to get on well.

lega'tario, a smf (DIR) legatee.

le'gato sm (REL) legate; (DIR) legacy, bequest.

lega'tura sf (di libro) binding; (MUS) ligature.

le'genda [le'dʒɛnda] sf (di carta geografica etc) = **leggenda**.

'legge ['leddʒe] sf law.

leg'genda [led'dʒɛnda] sf (narrazione) legend; (di carta geografica etc) key, legend.

'leggere ['leddʒere] vt, vi to read.

legge'rezza [leddʒe'rettsa] sf lightness; thoughtlessness; fickleness.

leg'gero, a [led'dʒɛro] ag light; (agile, snello) nimble, agile, light; (tè, caffè) weak; (fig: non grave, piccolo) slight; (: spensierato) thoughtless; (: incostante) fickle; free and easy; **alla ~a** thoughtlessly.

leggi'adro, a [led'dʒadro] ag pretty, lovely; (movimento) graceful.

leg'gio, gii [led'dʒio] sm lectern; (MUS) music stand.

legisla'tura [ledʒizla'tura] sf legislature.

legislazi'one [ledʒizlat'tsjone] sf legislation.

le'gittimo, a [le'dʒittimo] ag legitimate; (fig: giustificato, lecito) justified, legitimate; **~a difesa** (DIR) self-defence.

'legna ['leɲɲa] sf firewood; **le'gname** sm wood, timber.

'legno ['leɲɲo] sm wood; (pezzo di ~) piece of wood; **di ~** wooden; **~ compensato** plywood; **le'gnoso, a** ag wooden; woody; (carne) tough.

le'gumi smpl (BOT) pulses.

'lei pronome (soggetto) she; (oggetto: per dare rilievo, con preposizione) her; (forma di cortesia: anche: **L~**) you // sm: **dare del ~ a qn** to address sb as "lei"; ~ **stessa** she herself; you yourself.

'lembo sm (di abito, strada) edge; (striscia sottile: di terra) strip.

'lemma, i sm headword.

'lemme 'lemme av (very) very slowly.

'lena sf (fig) energy, stamina.

le'nire vt to soothe.

'lente sf (OTTICA) lens sg; ~ **d'ingrandimento** magnifying glass; **~i a contatto** o **corneali** contact lenses.

len'tezza [len'tettsa] sf slowness.

len'ticchia [len'tikkja] sf (BOT) lentil.

len'tiggine [len'tiddʒine] sf freckle.

'lento, a ag slow; (molle: fune) slack; (non stretto: vite, abito) loose // sm (ballo) slow dance.

'lenza ['lentsa] sf fishing-line.

lenzu'olo [len'tswɔlo] sm sheet; **~a** sfpl pair of sheets.

le'one sm lion; (dello zodiaco): **L~** Leo.

lepo'rino, a ag: **labbro ~** harelip.

'lepre sf hare.

'lercio, a, ci, cie ['lɛrtʃo] ag filthy.

'lesbica, che sf lesbian.

lesi'nare vt to be stingy with // vi: ~ (su) to skimp (on), be stingy (with).

lesi'one sf (MED) lesion; (DIR) injury, damage; (EDIL) crack.

'leso, a pp di **ledere** // ag (offeso) injured; **parte ~a** (DIR) injured party.

les'sare vt (CUC) to boil.

'lessico, ci sm vocabulary; lexicon.

'lesso, a ag boiled // sm boiled meat.

'lesto, a ag quick; (agile) nimble; ~ **di mano** (per rubare) light-fingered; (per picchiare) free with one's fists.

le'tale ag lethal; fatal.

leta'maio sm dunghill.

le'tame sm manure, dung.

le'targo, ghi sm lethargy; (ZOOL) hibernation.

le'tizia [le'tittsja] sf joy, happiness.

'lettera sf letter; **~e** sfpl (letteratura) literature sg; (studi umanistici) arts (subjects); **alla ~** literally; **in ~e** in words, in full; **lette'rale** ag literal.

lette'rario, a ag literary.

lette'rato, a ag well-read, scholarly.

lettera'tura sf literature.

let'tiga, ghe sf (portantina) litter; (barella) stretcher.

let'tino sm cot (Brit), crib (US).

'letto, a pp di **leggere** // sm bed; **andare a ~** to go to bed; ~ **a castello** bunk beds pl; ~ **a una piazza/a due piazze** o **matrimoniale** single/double bed.

let'tore, 'trice smf reader; (INS) (foreign language) assistant (Brit), (foreign) teaching assistant (US) // sm (TECN): ~ **ottico** optical character reader.

let'tura sf reading.

leuce'mia [leutʃe'mia] sf leukaemia.

'leva sf lever; (MIL) conscription; **far ~ su qn** to work on sb; ~ **del cambio** (AUT) gear lever.

le'vante sm east; (vento) East wind; **il L~** the Levant.

le'vare vt (occhi, braccio) to raise; (sollevare, togliere: tassa, divieto) to lift; (indumenti) to take off, remove;

(*rimuovere*) to take away; (: *dal di sopra*) to take off; (: *dal di dentro*) to take out; ~**rsi** *vr* to get up; (*sole*) to rise; **le'vata** *sf* (*di posta*) collection.

leva'toio, a *ag*: ponte ~ drawbridge.

leva'tura *sf* intelligence, mental capacity.

levi'gare *vt* to smooth; (*con carta vetrata*) to sand.

levri'ere *sm* greyhound.

lezi'one [let'tsjone] *sf* lesson; (*all'università, sgridata*) lecture; fare ~ to teach; to lecture.

lezi'oso, a [let'tsjoso] *ag* affected; simpering.

'lezzo ['leddzo] *sm* stench, stink.

li *pronome pl* (*oggetto*) them.

lì *av* there; di o da ~ from there; per di ~ that way; di ~ a pochi giorni a few days later; ~ per ~ there and then; at first; essere ~ (~) per fare to be on the point of doing, be about to do; ~ dentro in there; ~ sotto under there; ~ sopra on there; up there; *vedi* **quello**.

liba'nese *ag, sm/f* Lebanese *inv*.

Li'bano *sm*: il ~ the Lebanon.

'libbra *sf* (*peso*) pound.

li'beccio [li'bettʃo] *sm* south-west wind.

li'bello *sm* libel.

li'bellula *sf* dragonfly.

libe'rale *ag, sm/f* liberal.

liberaliz'zare [liberalid'dzare] *vt* to liberalize.

libe'rare *vt* (*rendere libero: prigioniero*) to release; (: *popolo*) to free, liberate; (*sgombrare: passaggio*) to clear; (: *stanza*) to vacate; (*produrre: energia*) to release; ~**rsi** *vr*: ~**rsi** di qc/qn to get rid of sth/sb; **libera'tore, 'trice** *ag* liberating // *sm/f* liberator; **liberazi'one** *sf* liberation, freeing; release; rescuing.

'libero, a *ag* free; (*strada*) clear; (*non occupato: posto etc*) vacant; not taken; empty; not engaged; ~ di fare qc free to do sth; ~ da free from; ~ arbitrio free will; ~ professionista self employed professional person; ~ scambio free trade; **libertà** *sf inv* freedom; (*tempo disponibile*) free time // *sfpl* (*licenza*) liberties; in libertà provvisoria/vigilata released without bail/on probation; libertà di riunione right to hold meetings.

'Libia *sf*: la ~ Libya; **'libico, a, ci, che** *ag, sm/f* Libyan.

li'bidine *sf* lust.

li'braio *sm* bookseller.

li'brario, a *ag* book *cpd*.

li'brarsi *vr* to hover.

libre'ria *sf* (*bottega*) bookshop; (*stanza*) library; (*mobile*) bookcase.

li'bretto *sm* booklet; (*taccuino*) notebook; (*MUS*) libretto; ~ degli assegni cheque book; ~ di circolazione (*AUT*) logbook; ~ di risparmio (savings) bank-book, passbook; ~ universitario student's report book.

'libro *sm* book; ~ bianco (*POL*) white paper; ~ di cassa cash book; ~ mastro ledger; ~ paga payroll.

li'cenza [li'tʃentsa] *sf* (*permesso*) permission, leave; (*di pesca, caccia, circolazione*) permit, licence; (*MIL*) leave; (*INS*) school leaving certificate; (*libertà*) liberty; licentiousness; andare in ~ (*MIL*) to go on leave.

licenzia'mento [litʃentsja'mento] *sm* dismissal.

licenzi'are [litʃen'tsjare] *vt* (*impiegato*) to dismiss; (*INS*) to award a certificate to; ~**rsi** *vr* (*impiegato*) to resign, hand in one's notice; (*INS*) to obtain one's school-leaving certificate.

li'ceo [li'tʃɛo] *sm* (*INS*) secondary (*Brit*) o high (*US*) school (*for 14- to 19-year-olds*).

'lido *sm* beach, shore.

li'eto, a *ag* happy, glad; "molto ~" (*nelle presentazioni*) "pleased to meet you".

li'eve *ag* light; (*di poco conto*) slight; (*sommesso: voce*) faint, soft.

lievi'tare *vi* (*anche fig*) to rise // *vt* to leaven.

li'evito *sm* yeast; ~ di birra brewer's yeast.

'ligio, a, gi, gie ['lidʒo] *ag* faithful, loyal.

'lilla, lillà *sm inv* lilac.

'lima *sf* file.

limacci'oso, a [limat'tʃoso] *ag* slimy; muddy.

li'mare *vt* to file (down); (*fig*) to polish.

'limbo *sm* (*REL*) limbo.

li'metta *sf* nail file.

limi'tare *vt* to limit, restrict; (*circoscrivere*) to bound, surround; **limita'tivo, a** *ag* limiting, restricting; **limi'tato, a** *ag* limited, restricted.

'limite *sm* limit; (*confine*) border, boundary; ~ di velocità speed limit.

li'mitrofo, a *ag* neighbouring.

limo'nata *sf* lemonade (*Brit*), (lemon) soda (*US*); lemon squash (*Brit*), lemonade (*US*).

li'mone *sm* (*pianta*) lemon tree; (*frutto*) lemon.

'limpido, a *ag* clear; (*acqua*) limpid, clear.

'lince ['lintʃe] *sf* lynx.

linci'are *vt* to lynch.

'lindo, a *ag* tidy, spick and span; (*biancheria*) clean.

'linea *sf* line; (*di mezzi pubblici di trasporto: itinerario*) route; (: *servizio*) service; a grandi ~e in outline; mantenere la ~ to look after one's figure; di ~: aereo di ~ airliner; nave di ~ liner; volo di ~ scheduled flight; ~ aerea airline; ~ di partenza/d'arrivo

(*SPORT*) starting/finishing line; ~ **di tiro** line of fire.

linea'menti *smpl* features; (*fig*) outlines.

line'are *ag* linear; (*fig*) coherent, logical.

line'etta *sf* (*trattino*) dash; (*d'unione*) hyphen.

lin'gotto *sm* ingot, bar.

'lingua *sf* (*ANAT, CUC*) tongue; (*idioma*) language; **mostrare la ~** to stick out one's tongue; **di ~ italiana** Italian-speaking; **~ madre** mother tongue; **una ~ di terra** a spit of land.

lingu'aggio [lin'gwadd3o] *sm* language.

lingu'etta *sf* (*di strumento*) reed; (*di scarpa, TECN*) tongue; (*di busta*) flap.

lingu'istica *sf* linguistics *sg*.

'lino *sm* (*pianta*) flax; (*tessuto*) linen.

li'noleum *sm inv* linoleum, lino.

lique'fare *vt* (*render liquido*) to liquefy; (*fondere*) to melt; **~rsi** *vr* to liquefy; to melt.

liqui'dare *vt* (*società, beni; persona: uccidere*) to liquidate; (*persona: sbarazzarsene*) to get rid of; (*conto, problema*) to settle; (*COMM: merce*) to sell off, clear; **liquidazi'one** *sf* liquidation; settlement; clearance sale.

liquidità *sf* liquidity.

'liquido, a *ag, sm* liquid; **~ per freni** brake fluid.

liqui'rizia [likwi'rittsja] *sf* liquorice.

li'quore *sm* liqueur.

'lira *sf* (*unità monetaria*) lira; (*MUS*) lyre; **~ sterlina** pound sterling.

'lirico, a, ci, che *ag* lyric(al); (*MUS*) lyric // *sf* (*poesia*) lyric poetry; (*componimento poetico*) lyric; (*MUS*) opera; **cantante/teatro ~** opera singer/house.

'lisca, sche *sf* (*di pesce*) fishbone.

lisci'are [liʃ'ʃare] *vt* to smooth; (*fig*) to flatter.

'liscio, a, sci, sce ['liʃʃo] *ag* smooth; (*capelli*) straight; (*mobile*) plain; (*bevanda alcolica*) neat; (*fig*) straightforward, simple // *av*: **andare ~** to go smoothly; **passarla ~a** to get away with it.

'liso, a *ag* worn out, threadbare.

'lista *sf* (*striscia*) strip; (*elenco*) list; **~ elettorale** electoral roll; **~ delle vivande** menu.

lis'tino *sm* list; **~ dei cambi** (foreign) exchange rate; **~ dei prezzi** price list.

'lite *sf* quarrel, argument; (*DIR*) lawsuit.

liti'gare *vi* to quarrel; (*DIR*) to litigate.

li'tigio [li'tid3o] *sm* quarrel; **litigi'oso, a** *ag* quarrelsome; (*DIR*) litigious.

litogra'fia *sf* (*sistema*) lithography; (*stampa*) lithograph.

lito'rale *ag* coastal, coast *cpd* // *sm* coast.

'litro *sm* litre.

livel'lare *vt* to level, make level; **~rsi** *vr* to become level; (*fig*) to level out, balance out.

li'vello *sm* level; (*fig*) level, standard; **ad alto ~** (*fig*) high-level; **~ del mare** sea level.

'livido, a *ag* livid; (*per percosse*) bruised, black and blue; (*cielo*) leaden // *sm* bruise.

li'vore *sm* malice, spite.

Li'vorno *sf* Livorno, Leghorn.

li'vrea *sf* livery.

'lizza ['littsa] *sf* lists *pl*; **scendere in ~** (*anche fig*) to enter the lists.

lo *det m* (*dav s impura, gn, pn, ps, x, z; dav V* **l'**) *the // pronome (dav V* **l'**) (*oggetto: persona*) him; (: *cosa*) it; **~ sapevo** I knew it; **~ so** I know; **sii buono, anche se lui non ~ è** be good, even if he isn't.

lo'cale *ag* local // *sm* room; (*luogo pubblico*) premises *pl*; **~ notturno** nightclub; **località** *sf inv* locality; **localiz'zare** *vt* (*circoscrivere*) to confine, localize; (*accertare*) to locate, place.

lo'canda *sf* inn; **locandi'ere, a** *sm/f* innkeeper.

loca'tario, a *sm/f* tenant.

loca'tore, 'trice *sm/f* landlord/lady.

locazi'one [lokat'tsjone] *sf* (*da parte del locatario*) renting *q*; (*da parte del locatore*) renting out *q*, letting *q*; (*contratto di*) **~ lease**; (*canone di*) **~ rent**; **dare in ~** to rent out, let.

locomo'tiva *sf* locomotive.

locomo'tore *sm* electric locomotive.

locomozi'one [lokomot'tsjone] *sf* locomotion; **mezzi di ~** vehicles, means of transport.

lo'custa *sf* locust.

locuzi'one [lokut'tsjone] *sf* phrase, expression.

lo'dare *vt* to praise.

'lode *sf* praise; (*INS*): **laurearsi con 110 e ~** ≈ to graduate with a first-class honours degree (*Brit*), graduate summa cum laude (*US*).

'loden *sm inv* (*stoffa*) loden; (*cappotto*) loden overcoat.

lo'devole *ag* praiseworthy.

loga'ritmo *sm* logarithm.

'loggia, ge ['lɔddʒa] *sf* (*ARCHIT*) loggia; (*circolo massonico*) lodge; **loggi'one** *sm* (*di teatro*): **il loggione** the Gods *sg*.

'logico, a, ci, che ['lɔdʒiko] *ag* logical // *sf* logic.

logo'rare *vt* to wear out; (*sciupare*) to waste; **~rsi** *vr* to wear out; (*fig*) to wear o.s. out.

logo'rio *sm* wear and tear; (*fig*) strain.

lo'goro, a *ag* (*stoffa*) worn out, threadbare; (*persona*) worn out.

lom'baggine [lom'baddʒine] *sf* lumbago.

Lombar'dia *sf*: **la ~** Lombardy.

lom'bata *sf* (*taglio di carne*) loin.

'lombo *sm* (*ANAT*) loin.

lom'brico, chi sm earthworm.

londi'nese ag London cpd // sm/f Londoner.

'Londra sf London.

lon'gevo, a [lon'dʒɛvo] ag long-lived.

longi'tudine [londʒi'tudine] sf longitude.

lonta'nanza [lonta'nantsa] sf distance; absence.

lon'tano, a ag (distante) distant, faraway; (assente) absent; (vago: sospetto) slight, remote; (tempo: remoto) far-off, distant; (parente) distant, remote // av far; è ~a la casa? is it far to the house?, is the house far from here?; è ~ un chilometro it's a kilometre away o a kilometre from here; più ~ farther; da o di ~ from a distance; ~ da a long way from; alla ~a slightly, vaguely.

'lontra sf otter.

lo'quace [lo'kwatʃe] ag talkative, loquacious; (fig: gesto etc) eloquent.

'lordo, a ag dirty, filthy; (peso, stipendio) gross.

'loro pronome pl (oggetto, con preposizione) them; (complemento di termine) to them; (soggetto) they; (forma di cortesia: anche: L~) you; to you; il(la) ~, i(le) ~ det their; (forma di cortesia: anche: L~) your // pronome theirs; (forma di cortesia: anche: L~) yours; ~ stessi(e) they themselves; you yourselves.

'losco, a, schi, sche ag (fig) shady, suspicious.

'lotta sf struggle, fight; (SPORT) wrestling; ~ libera all-in wrestling; **lot'tare** vi to fight, struggle; to wrestle; **lotta'tore, trice** sm/f wrestler.

lotte'ria sf lottery; (di gara ippica) sweepstake.

'lotto sm (gioco) (state) lottery; (parte) lot; (EDIL) site.

lozi'one [lot'tsjone] sf lotion.

lubrifi'cante sm lubricant.

lubrifi'care vt to lubricate.

luc'chetto [luk'ketto] sm padlock.

lucci'care [luttʃi'kare] vi to sparkle, glitter, twinkle.

'luccio [luttʃo] sm (ZOOL) pike.

'lucciola ['luttʃola] sf (ZOOL) firefly; glowworm.

'luce ['lutʃe] sf light; (finestra) window; alla ~ di by the light of; fare ~ su qc (fig) to shed o throw light on sth; ~ del sole/della luna sun/moonlight; **lu'cente** ag shining.

lu'cerna [lu'tʃɛrna] sf oil-lamp.

lucer'nario [lutʃer'narjo] sm skylight.

lu'certola [lu'tʃertola] sf lizard.

luci'dare [lutʃi'dare] vt to polish; (ricalcare) to trace.

lucida'trice [lutʃida'tritʃe] sf floor polisher.

'lucido, a ['lutʃido] ag shining, bright; (lucidato) polished; (fig) lucid // sm shine, lustre; (per scarpe etc) polish; (disegno) tracing.

'lucro sm profit, gain; **lu'croso, a** ag lucrative, profitable.

lu'dibrio sm mockery q; (oggetto di scherno) laughing-stock.

'luglio ['luʎʎo] sm July.

'lugubre ag gloomy.

'lui pronome (soggetto) he; (oggetto: per dare rilievo, con preposizione) him; ~ stesso he himself.

lu'maca, che sf slug; (chiocciola) snail.

'lume sm light; (lampada) lamp; (fig): chiedere ~i a qn to ask sb for advice; a ~ di naso (fig) by rule of thumb.

lumi'naria sf (per feste) illuminations pl.

lumi'noso, a ag (che emette luce) luminous; (cielo, colore, stanza) bright; (sorgente) of light, light cpd; (fig: sorriso) bright, radiant.

'luna sf moon; ~ nuova/piena new/full moon; ~ di miele honeymoon.

'luna park sm inv amusement park, funfair.

lu'nare ag lunar, moon cpd.

lu'nario sm almanac; **sbarcare il ~** to make ends meet.

lu'natico, a, ci, che ag whimsical, temperamental.

lunedì sm inv Monday; di o il ~ on Mondays.

lun'gaggine [lun'gaddʒine] sf slowness; ~i della burocrazia red tape.

lun'ghezza [lun'gettsa] sf length; ~ d'onda (FISICA) wavelength.

'lungi ['lundʒi]: ~ da prep far from.

'lungo, a, ghi, ghe ag long; (lento: persona) slow; (diluito: caffè, brodo) weak, watery, thin // sm length // prep along; ~ 3 metri 3 metres long; a ~ for a long time; a ~ andare in the long run; di gran ~a (molto) by far; andare in ~ o per le lunghe to drag on; saperla ~a to know what's what; in ~ e in largo far and wide, all over; ~ il corso dei secoli throughout the centuries.

lungo'mare sm promenade.

lu'notto sm (AUT) rear o back window.

lu'ogo, ghi sm place; (posto: di incidente etc) scene, site; (punto, passo di libro) passage; in ~ di instead of; in primo ~ in the first place; aver ~ to take place; dar ~ a to give rise to; ~ comune commonplace; ~ di nascita birthplace; (AMM) place of birth; ~ di provenienza place of origin.

luogote'nente sm (MIL) lieutenant.

lu'para sf sawn-off shotgun.

'lupo, a sm/f wolf.

'luppolo sm (BOT) hop.

'lurido, a ag filthy.

lu'singa, ghe sf (spesso al pl) flattery q.

lusin'gare vt to flatter; **lusinghi'ero, a** ag flattering, gratifying.

lus'sare vt (MED) to dislocate.

Lussem'burgo sm (stato): il ~ Luxembourg // sf (città) Luxembourg.

'lusso sm luxury; di ~ luxury cpd; **lussu'oso, a** ag luxurious.

lussureggi'are [lussured'dʒare] vi to be luxuriant.

lus'suria sf lust.

lus'trare vt to polish, shine.

lustras'carpe sm/f inv shoeshine.

lus'trino sm sequin.

'lustro, a ag shiny; (pelliccia) glossy // sm shine, gloss; (fig) prestige, glory; (quinquennio) five-year period.

'lutto sm mourning; essere in/portare il ~ to be in/wear mourning; **luttu'oso, a** ag mournful, sad.

M

ma cong but; ~ insomma! for goodness sake!; ~ no! of course not!

'macabro, a ag gruesome, macabre.

macché [mak'ke] escl not at all!, certainly not!

macche'roni [makke'roni] smpl macaroni sg.

'macchia ['makkja] sf stain, spot; (chiazza di diverso colore) spot; splash, patch; (tipo di boscaglia) scrub; alla ~ (fig) in hiding; **macchi'are** vt (sporcare) to stain, mark; **macchiarsi** vr (persona) to get o.s. dirty; (stoffa) to stain; to get stained o marked.

'macchina ['makkina] sf machine; (motore, locomotiva) engine; (automobile) car; (fig: meccanismo) machinery; andare in ~ (AUT) to go by car; (STAMPA) to go to press; ~ da cucire sewing machine; ~ fotografica camera; ~ da presa cine o movie camera; ~ da scrivere typewriter; ~ a vapore steam engine.

macchi'nare [makki'nare] vt to plot.

macchi'nario [makki'narjo] sm machinery.

macchi'netta [makki'netta] sf (fam: caffettiera) percolator; (: accendino) lighter.

macchi'nista, i [makki'nista] sm (di treno) engine-driver; (di nave) engineer; (TEATRO, TV) stagehand.

macchi'noso, a [makki'noso] ag complex, complicated.

mace'donia [matʃe'dɔnja] sf fruit salad.

macel'laio [matʃel'lajo] sm butcher.

macel'lare [matʃel'lare] vt to slaughter, butcher; **macelle'ria** sf butcher's (shop); **ma'cello** sm (mattatoio) slaughterhouse, abattoir (Brit); (fig) slaughter, massacre; (: disastro) shambles sg.

mace'rare [matʃe'rare] vt to macerate; (CUC) to marinate; ~rsi vr (fig): ~rsi in to be consumed with.

ma'cerie [ma'tʃɛrje] sfpl rubble sg, debris sg.

ma'cigno [ma'tʃiɲɲo] sm (masso) rock, boulder.

maci'lento, a [matʃi'lɛnto] ag emaciated.

'macina ['matʃina] sf (pietra) millstone; (macchina) grinder; **macinacaffè** sm inv coffee grinder; **macina'pepe** sm inv peppermill.

maci'nare [matʃi'nare] vt to grind; (carne) to mince (Brit), grind (US); **maci'nato** sm meal, flour; (carne) minced (Brit) o ground (US) meat.

maci'nino [matʃi'nino] sm coffee grinder; peppermill.

'madido, a ag: ~ (di) wet o moist (with).

Ma'donna sf (REL) Our Lady.

mador'nale ag enormous, huge.

'madre sf mother; (matrice di bolletta) counterfoil // ag inv mother cpd; ragazza ~ unmarried mother; scena ~ (TEATRO) principal scene; (fig) terrible scene.

madre'lingua sf mother tongue, native language.

madre'perla sf mother-of-pearl.

ma'drina sf godmother.

maestà sf inv majesty; **maes'toso, a** ag majestic.

ma'estra sf vedi maestro.

maes'trale sm north-west wind, mistral.

maes'tranze [maes'trantse] sfpl workforce sg.

maes'tria sf mastery, skill.

ma'estro, a sm/f (INS: anche: ~ di scuola o elementare) primary (Brit) o grade school (US) teacher; (esperto) expert // sm (artigiano, fig: guida) master; (MUS) maestro // ag (principale) main; (di grande abilità) masterly, skilful; ~ a d'asilo nursery teacher; ~ di cerimonie master of ceremonies.

'mafia sf Mafia; **mafi'oso** sm member of the Mafia.

'maga sf sorceress.

ma'gagna [ma'gaɲɲa] sf defect, flaw, blemish; (noia, guaio) problem.

ma'gari escl (esprime desiderio): ~ fosse vero! if only it were true!; ti piacerebbe andare in Scozia? — ~! would you like to go to Scotland? — and how! // av (anche) even; (forse) perhaps.

magaz'zino [magad'dzino] sm warehouse; grande ~ department store.

'maggio ['maddʒo] sm May.

maggio'rana [maddʒo'rana] sf (BOT) (sweet) marjoram.

maggio'ranza [maddʒo'rantsa] sf majority.

maggio'rare [maddʒo'rare] vt to increase, raise.

maggior'domo [maddʒor'dɔmo] sm butler.

maggi'ore [mad'dʒore] ag (comparativo: più grande) bigger, larger; taller; greater; (: più vecchio: sorella, fratello) older, elder; (: di grado superiore) senior; (: più importante, MIL, MUS) major; (superlativo) biggest, largest; tallest; greatest; oldest, eldest // smlf (di grado) superior; (di età) elder; (MIL) major; (: AER) squadron leader; **la maggior parte** the majority; **andare per la ~** (cantante etc) to be very popular; **maggio'renne** ag of age // smlf person who has come of age; **maggior'mente** av much more; (con senso superlativo) most.

ma'gia [ma'dʒia] sf magic; **'magico, a, ci, che** ag magic; (fig) fascinating, charming, magical.

'magio ['madʒo] sm (REL): **i re Magi** the Magi, the Three Wise Men.

magis'tero [madʒis'tero] sm teaching; (fig: maestria) skill; (INS): **facoltà di M~** ≈ teachers' training college; **magis'trale** ag primary (Brit) o grade school (US) teachers', primary (Brit) o grade school (US) teaching cpd; skilful.

magis'trato [madʒis'trato] sm magistrate; **magistra'tura** sf magistrature; (magistrati): **la magistratura** the Bench.

'maglia ['maʎʎa] sf stitch; (lavoro ai ferri) knitting q; (tessuto, SPORT) jersey; (maglione) jersey, sweater; (di catena) link; (di rete) mesh; **~ diritta/rovescia** plain/purl; **maglie'ria** sf knitwear; (negozio) knitwear shop; **ma-gli'etta** sf (canottiera) vest; (tipo camicia) T-shirt; **magli'ficio** sm knitwear factory.

'maglio ['maʎʎo] sm mallet; (macchina) power hammer.

ma'gnete [maɲ'ɲete] sm magnet; **ma'gnetico, a, ci, che** ag magnetic.

magne'tofono [maɲɲe'tɔfono] sm tape recorder.

ma'gnifico, a, ci, che [maɲ'ɲifiko] ag magnificent, splendid; (ospite) generous.

'magno, a ['maɲɲo] ag: **aula ~a** main hall.

ma'gnolia [maɲ'ɲɔlja] sf magnolia.

'mago, ghi sm (stregone) magician, wizard; (illusionista) magician.

ma'grezza [ma'grettsa] sf thinness.

'magro, a ag (very) thin, skinny; (carne) lean; (formaggio) low-fat; (fig: scarso, misero) meagre, poor; (: meschino: scusa) poor, lame; **mangiare di ~** not to eat meat.

'mai av (nessuna volta) never; (talvolta) ever; **non ... ~** never; **~ più** never again; **come ~?** why (o how) on earth?; **chi/dove/quando ~?** whoever/wherever/whenever?

mai'ale sm (ZOOL) pig; (carne) pork.

maio'nese sf mayonnaise.

'mais sm inv maize.

mai'uscolo, a ag (lettera) capital; (fig) enormous, huge // sf capital letter.

mal av, sm vedi **male**.

malac'corto, a ag rash, careless.

mala'fede sf bad faith.

mala'mente av badly; dangerously.

malan'dato, a ag (persona: di salute) in poor health; (: di condizioni finanziarie) badly off; (trascurato) shabby.

ma'lanno sm (disgrazia) misfortune; (malattia) ailment.

mala'pena sf: **a ~** hardly, scarcely.

ma'laria sf (MED) malaria.

mala'sorte sf bad luck.

mala'ticcio, a [mala'tittʃo] ag sickly.

ma'lato, a ag ill, sick; (gamba) bad; (pianta) diseased // smlf sick person; (in ospedale) patient; **malat'tia** sf (infettiva etc) illness, disease; (cattiva salute) illness, sickness; (di pianta) disease.

malau'gurio sm bad o ill omen.

mala'vita sf underworld.

mala'voglia [mala'vɔʎʎa] sf: **di ~** unwillingly, reluctantly.

mal'concio, a, ci, ce [mal'kontʃo] ag in a sorry state.

malcon'tento sm discontent.

malcos'tume sm immorality.

mal'destro, a ag (inabile) inexpert, inexperienced; (goffo) awkward.

maldi'cenza [maldi'tʃentsa] sf malicious gossip.

maldis'posto, a ag: **~ (verso)** ill-disposed (towards).

'male av badly // sm (ciò che è ingiusto, disonesto) evil; (danno, svantaggio) harm; (sventura) misfortune; (dolore fisico, morale) pain, ache; **di ~ in peggio** from bad to worse; **sentirsi ~** to feel ill; **far ~** (dolere) to hurt; **far ~ alla salute** to be bad for one's health; **far del ~ a qn** to hurt o harm sb; **restare o rimanere ~** to be sorry; to be disappointed; to be hurt; **andare a ~** to go bad; **come va? — non c'è ~** how are you? — not bad; **mal di mare** seasickness; **avere mal di gola/testa** to have a sore throat/a headache; **aver ~ ai piedi** to have sore feet.

male'detto, a pp di **maledire** // ag cursed, damned; (fig: fam) damned, blasted.

male'dire vt to curse; **maledizi'one** sf curse; **maledizione!** damn it!

maledu'cato, a ag rude, ill-mannered.

male'fatta sf misdeed.

male'ficio [male'fitʃo] sm witchcraft.

ma'lefico, a, ci, che ag (aria, cibo) harmful, bad; (influsso, azione) evil.

ma'lessere sm indisposition, slight illness; (fig) uneasiness.

ma'levolo, a ag malevolent.

malfa'mato, a *ag* notorious.

mal'fatto, a *ag* (*persona*) deformed; (*oggetto*) badly made; (*lavoro*) badly done.

malfat'tore, 'trice *sm/f* wrongdoer.

mal'fermo, a *ag* unsteady, shaky; (*salute*) poor, delicate.

malformazi'one [malformat'tsjone] *sf* malformation.

malgo'verno *sm* maladministration.

mal'grado *prep* in spite of, despite // *cong* although; **mio** (*o* **tuo** *etc*) ~ **against** my (*o* your *etc*) will.

ma'lia *sf* spell; (*fig: fascino*) charm.

mali'gnare [malin'nare] *vi*: ~ **su** to malign, speak ill of.

ma'ligno, a [ma'linno] *ag* (*malvagio*) malicious, malignant; (*MED*) malignant.

malinco'nia *sf* melancholy, gloom; **malin'conico, a, ci, che** *ag* melancholy.

malincu'ore: **a** ~ *av* reluctantly, unwillingly.

malintenzio'nato, a [malintentsjo'nato] *ag* ill-intentioned.

malin'teso, a *ag* misunderstood; (*riguardo, senso del dovere*) mistaken, wrong // *sm* misunderstanding.

ma'lizia [ma'littsja] *sf* (*malignità*) malice; (*furbizia*) cunning; (*espediente*) trick; **malizi'oso, a** *ag* malicious; cunning; (*vivace, birichino*) mischievous.

malme'nare *vt* to beat up; (*fig*) to illtreat.

mal'messo, a *ag* shabby.

malnu'trito, a *ag* undernourished; **malnutrizi'one** *sf* malnutrition.

ma'locchio [ma'lokkjo] *sm* evil eye.

ma'lora *sf*: **andare in** ~ **to go to the dogs.**

ma'lore *sm* (sudden) illness.

mal'sano, a *ag* unhealthy.

malsi'curo, a *ag* unsafe.

'Malta *sf*: **la** ~ **Malta.**

'malta *sf* (*EDIL*) mortar.

mal'tempo *sm* bad weather.

'malto *sm* malt.

maltrat'tare *vt* to ill-treat.

malu'more *sm* bad mood; (*irritabilità*) bad temper; (*discordia*) ill feeling; **di** ~ **in a bad mood.**

mal'vagio, a, gi, gie [mal'vadʒo] *ag* wicked, evil.

malversazi'one [malversat'tsjone] *sf* (*DIR*) embezzlement.

mal'visto, a *ag*: ~ (**da**) disliked (by), unpopular (with).

malvi'vente *sm* criminal.

malvolenti'eri *av* unwillingly, reluctantly.

'mamma *sf* mummy, mum; ~ **mia!** my goodness!

mam'mella *sf* (*ANAT*) breast; (*di vacca, capra etc*) udder.

mam'mifero *sm* mammal.

'mammola *sf* (*BOT*) violet.

ma'nata *sf* (*colpo*) slap; (*quantità*) handful.

'manca *sf* left (hand); **a destra e a** ~ **left, right and centre, on all sides.**

man'canza [man'kantsa] *sf* lack; (*carenza*) shortage, scarcity; (*fallo*) fault; (*imperfezione*) failing, shortcoming; **per** ~ **di tempo** through lack of time; **in** ~ **di meglio** for lack of anything better.

man'care *vi* (*essere insufficiente*) to be lacking; (*venir meno*) to fail; (*sbagliare*) to be wrong, make a mistake; (*non esserci*) to be missing, not to be there; (*essere lontano*): ~ (**da**) to be away (from) // *vt* to miss; ~ **di** to lack; ~ **a** (*promessa*) to fail to keep; **tu mi manchi** I miss you; **mancò poco che morisse** he very nearly died; **mancano ancora 10 sterline** we're still £10 short; **manca un quarto alle 6** it's a quarter to 6; **man'cato, a** *ag* (*tentativo*) unsuccessful; (*artista*) failed.

'mancia, ce ['mantʃa] *sf* tip; ~ **competente** reward.

manci'ata [man'tʃata] *sf* handful.

man'cino, a [man'tʃino] *ag* (*braccio*) left; (*persona*) left-handed; (*fig*) underhand.

'manco *av* (*nemmeno*): ~ **per sogno** *o* **per idea!** not on your life!

man'dare *vt* to send; (*far funzionare: macchina*) to drive; (*emettere*) to send out; (*: grido*) to give, utter, let out; ~ **a chiamare qn** to send for sb; ~ **avanti** (*fig: famiglia*) to provide for; (*: fabbrica*) to run, look after; ~ **giù** to send down; (*anche fig*) to swallow; ~ **via** to send away; (*licenziare*) to fire.

manda'rino *sm* mandarin (orange); (*cinese*) mandarin.

man'data *sf* (*quantità*) lot, batch; (*di chiave*) turn; **chiudere a doppia** ~ **to double-lock.**

manda'tario *sm* (*DIR*) representative, agent.

man'dato *sm* (*incarico*) commission; (*DIR: provvedimento*) warrant; (*di deputato etc*) mandate; (*ordine di pagamento*) postal *o* money order; ~ **d'arresto** warrant for arrest.

man'dibola *sf* mandible, jaw.

'mandorla *sf* almond; **'mandorlo** *sm* almond tree.

'mandria *sf* herd.

maneggi'are [maned'dʒare] *vt* (*creta, cera*) to mould, work, fashion; (*arnesi, utensili*) to handle; (*: adoperare*) to use; (*fig: persone, denaro*) to handle, deal with; **ma'neggio** *sm* moulding; handling; use; (*intrigo*) plot, scheme; (*per cavalli*) riding school.

ma'nesco, a, schi, sche *ag* free with one's fists.

ma'nette *sfpl* handcuffs.

manga'nello *sm* club.

manga'nese *sm* manganese.

mange'reccio, a, ci, ce [mandʒe'rettʃo] *ag* edible.

mangia'dischi [mandʒa'diski] *sm inv* record player.

mangi'are [man'dʒare] *vt* to eat; (*intaccare*) to eat into o away; (*CARTE, SCACCHI etc*) to take // *vi* to eat // *sm* eating; (*cibo*) food; (*cucina*) cooking; ~rsi le parole to mumble; ~rsi le unghie to bite one's nails; **mangia'toia** *sf* feeding-trough.

man'gime [man'dʒime] *sm* fodder.

'mango, ghi *sm* mango.

ma'nia *sf* (*PSIC*) mania; (*fig*) obsession, craze; **ma'niaco, a, ci, che** *ag* suffering from a mania; **maniaco (di)** obsessed (by), crazy (about).

'manica *sf* sleeve; (*fig: gruppo*) gang, bunch; (*GEO*): **la M~, il Canale della M~** the (English) Channel; **essere di ~ larga/stretta** to be easy-going/strict; **~ a vento** (*AER*) wind sock.

mani'chino [mani'kino] *sm* (*di sarto, vetrina*) dummy.

'manico, ci *sm* handle; (*MUS*) neck.

mani'comio *sm* mental hospital; (*fig*) madhouse.

mani'cotto *sm* muff; (*TECN*) coupling; sleeve.

mani'cure *sm o f inv* manicure // *sf inv* manicurist.

mani'era *sf* way, manner; (*stile*) style, manner; ~e *sfpl* manners; **in ~ che** so that; **in ~ da** so as to; **in tutte le ~e** at all costs.

manie'rato, a *ag* affected.

manifat'tura *sf* (*lavorazione*) manufacture; (*stabilimento*) factory.

manife'stare *vt* to show, display; (*esprimere*) to express; (*rivelare*) to reveal, disclose // *vi* to demonstrate; ~rsi *vr* to show o.s.; ~rsi amico to prove o.s. (to be) a friend; **manifestazi'one** *sf* show, display; expression; (*sintomo*) sign, symptom; (*dimostrazione pubblica*) demonstration; (*cerimonia*) event.

mani'festo, a *ag* obvious, evident // *sm* poster, bill; (*scritto ideologico*) manifesto.

ma'niglia [ma'niʎʎa] *sf* handle; (*sostegno: negli autobus etc*) strap.

manipo'lare *vt* to manipulate; (*alterare: vino*) to adulterate; **manipolazi'one** *sf* manipulation; adulteration.

manis'calco, chi *sm* blacksmith.

'manna *sf* (*REL*) manna.

man'naia *sf* (*del boia*) (executioner's) axe; (*per carni*) cleaver.

man'naro: lupo ~ *sm* werewolf.

'mano, i *sf* hand; (*strato: di vernice etc*) coat; **di prima ~** (*notizia*) first-

hand; **di seconda ~** second-hand; **man ~** little by little, gradually; **man ~ che** as; **darsi o stringersi la ~** to shake hands; **mettere le ~i avanti** (*fig*) to safeguard o.s.; **restare a ~i vuote** to be left empty-handed; **venire alle ~i** to come to blows; **a ~** by hand; **~i in alto!** hands up!

mano'dopera *sf* labour.

mano'messo, a *pp di* **manomettere.**

ma'nometro *sm* gauge, manometer.

mano'mettere *vt* (*alterare*) to tamper with; (*aprire indebitamente*) to break open illegally.

ma'nopola *sf* (*dell'armatura*) gauntlet; (*guanto*) mitt; (*di impugnatura*) hand-grip; (*pomello*) knob.

manos'critto, a *ag* handwritten // *sm* manuscript.

mano'vale *sm* labourer.

mano'vella *sf* handle; (*TECN*) crank.

ma'novra *sf* manoeuvre (*Brit*), maneuver (*US*); (*FERR*) shunting; **mano'vrare** *vt* (*veicolo*) to manoeuvre (*Brit*), maneuver (*US*); (*macchina, congegno*) to operate; (*fig: persona*) to manipulate // *vi* to manoeuvre.

manro'vescio [manro'veʃʃo] *sm* slap (*with back of hand*).

man'sarda *sf* attic.

mansi'one *sf* task, duty, job.

mansu'eto, a *ag* gentle, docile.

man'tello *sm* cloak; (*fig: di neve etc*) blanket, mantle; (*TECN: involucro*) casing, shell; (*ZOOL*) coat.

mante'nere *vt* to maintain; (*adempiere: promesse*) to keep, abide by; (*provvedere a*) to support, maintain; ~rsi *vr*: ~rsi calmo/giovane to stay calm/young; **manteni'mento** *sm* maintenance.

'mantice ['mantitʃe] *sm* bellows *pl*; (*di carrozza, automobile*) hood.

'manto *sm* cloak; **~ stradale** road surface.

manu'ale *ag* manual // *sm* (*testo*) manual, handbook.

ma'nubrio *sm* handle; (*di bicicletta etc*) handlebars *pl*; (*SPORT*) dumbbell.

manu'fatto *sm* manufactured article.

manutenzi'one [manuten'tsjone] *sf* maintenance, upkeep; (*d'impianti*) maintenance, servicing.

'manzo ['mandzo] *sm* (*ZOOL*) steer; (*carne*) beef.

'mappa *sf* (*GEO*) map; **mappa'mondo** *sm* map of the world; (*globo girevole*) globe.

ma'rasma, i *sm* (*fig*) decay, decline.

mara'tona *sf* marathon.

'marca, che *sf* mark; (*bollo*) stamp; (*COMM: di prodotti*) brand; (*contrassegno, scontrino*) ticket, check; **prodotto di ~** (*di buona qualità*) high-class product; **~ da bollo** official stamp.

mar'care *vt* (*munire di contrassegno*) to

mark; (*a fuoco*) to brand; (*SPORT*: *gol*) to score; (: *avversario*) to mark; (*accentuare*) to stress; ~ **visita** (*MIL*) to report sick.

'**Marche** ['marke] *sfpl*: **le** ~ the Marches (*region of central Italy*).

mar'chese, a [mar'keze] *sm/f* marquis *o* marquess/marchioness.

marchi'are [mar'kjare] *vt* to brand; '**marchio** *sm* (*di bestiame*, *COMM*, *fig*) brand; **marchio depositato** registered trademark; **marchio di fabbrica** trademark.

'**marcia, ce** ['martʃa] *sf* (*anche MUS*, *MIL*) march; (*funzionamento*) running; (*il camminare*) walking; (*AUT*) gear; **mettere in** ~ to start; **mettersi in** ~ to get moving; **far** ~ **indietro** (*AUT*) to reverse; (*fig*) to back-pedal.

marciapi'ede [martʃa'pjɛde] *sm* (*di strada*) pavement (*Brit*), sidewalk (*US*); (*FERR*) platform.

marci'are [mar'tʃare] *vi* to march; (*andare*: *treno*, *macchina*) to go; (*funzionare*) to run, work.

'**marcio, a, ci, ce** ['martʃo] *ag* (*frutta*, *legno*) rotten, bad; (*MED*) festering; (*fig*) corrupt, rotten.

mar'cire [mar'tʃire] *vi* (*andare a male*) to go bad, rot; (*suppurare*) to fester; (*fig*) to rot, waste away.

'**marco, chi** *sm* (*unità monetaria*) mark.

'**mare** *sm* sea; **in** ~ at sea; **andare al** ~ (*in vacanza etc*) to go to the seaside; **il** M~ **del Nord** the North Sea.

ma'rea *sf* tide; **alta/bassa** ~ high/low tide.

mareggi'ata [mared'dʒata] *sf* heavy sea.

ma'remma *sf* (*GEO*) maremma, swampy coastal area.

mare'moto *sm* seaquake.

maresci'allo [mareʃ'ʃallo] *sm* (*MIL*) marshal; (: *sottufficiale*) warrant officer.

marga'rina *sf* margarine.

marghe'rita [marge'rita] *sf* (ox-eye) daisy, marguerite; (*di stampante*) daisy wheel; **margheri'tina** *sf* daisy.

'**margine** ['mardʒine] *sm* margin; (*di bosco*, *via*) edge, border.

ma'rina *sf* navy; (*costa*) coast; (*quadro*) seascape; ~ **militare/mercantile** navy/merchant navy (*Brit*) *o* marine (*US*).

mari'naio *sm* sailor.

mari'nare *vt* (*CUC*) to marinate; ~ **la scuola** to play truant; **mari'nata** *sf* marinade.

ma'rino, a *ag* sea *cpd*, marine.

mario'netta *sf* puppet.

mari'tare *vt* to marry; ~**rsi** *vr*: ~**rsi a** *o* **con qn** to marry sb, get married to sb.

ma'rito *sm* husband.

ma'rittimo, a *ag* maritime, sea *cpd*.

mar'maglia [mar'maʎʎa] *sf* mob, riffraff.

marmel'lata *sf* jam; (*di agrumi*) marmalade.

mar'mitta *sf* (*recipiente*) pot; (*AUT*) silencer.

'**marmo** *sm* marble.

mar'mocchio [mar'mɔkkjo] *sm* (*fam*) tot, kid.

mar'motta *sf* (*ZOOL*) marmot.

Ma'rocco *sm*: **il** ~ Morocco.

ma'roso *sm* breaker.

mar'rone *ag inv* brown // *sm* (*BOT*) chestnut.

mar'sala *sm inv* (*vino*) Marsala.

mar'sina *sf* tails *pl*, tail coat.

martedì *sm inv* Tuesday; **di** *o* **il** ~ on Tuesdays; ~ **grasso** Shrove Tuesday.

martel'lare *vt* to hammer // *vi* (*pulsare*) to throb; (: *cuore*) to thump.

mar'tello *sm* hammer; (*di uscio*) knocker.

marti'netto *sm* (*TECN*) jack.

'**martire** *sm/f* martyr; **mar'tirio** *sm* martyrdom; (*fig*) agony, torture.

'**martora** *sf* marten.

martori'are *vt* to torment, torture.

mar'xista, i, e *ag*, *sm/f* Marxist.

marza'pane [martsa'pane] *sm* marzipan.

'**marzo** ['martso] *sm* March.

mascal'zone [maskal'tsone] *sm* rascal, scoundrel.

ma'scella [maʃ'ʃella] *sf* (*ANAT*) jaw.

'**maschera** ['maskera] *sf* mask; (*travestimento*) disguise; (: *per un ballo etc*) fancy dress; (*TEATRO*, *CINEMA*) usher/usherette; (*personaggio del teatro*) stock character; **masche'rare** *vt* to mask; (*travestire*) to disguise; to dress up; (*fig*: *celare*) to hide, conceal; (*MIL*) to camouflage; ~**rsi da** to disguise o.s. as; to dress up as; (*fig*) to masquerade as.

mas'chile [mas'kile] *ag* masculine; (*sesso*, *popolazione*) male; (*abiti*) men's; (*per ragazzi*: *scuola*) boys'.

'**maschio, a** ['maskjo] *ag* (*BIOL*) male; (*virile*) manly // *sm* (*anche ZOOL*, *TECN*) male; (*uomo*) man; (*ragazzo*) boy; (*figlio*) son.

masco'lino, a *ag* masculine.

'**massa** *sf* mass; (*di errori etc*): **una** ~ **di** heaps of, masses of; (*di gente*) mass, multitude; (*ELETTR*) earth; **in** ~ (*COMM*) in bulk; (*tutti insieme*) en masse; **adunata in** ~ mass meeting; **di** ~ (*cultura*, *manifestazione*) mass *cpd*; **la** ~ **del popolo** the masses *pl*.

mas'sacro *sm* massacre, slaughter; (*fig*) mess, disaster.

mas'saggio [mas'saddʒo] *sm* massage.

mas'saia *sf* housewife.

masse'rizie [masse'rittsje] *sfpl* (household) furnishings.

mas'siccio, a, ci, ce [mas'sittʃo] *ag* (*oro*, *legno*) solid; (*palazzo*) massive; (*corporatura*) stout // *sm* (*GEO*) massif.

'massima sf vedi massimo.
massi'male sm maximum.
'massimo, a ag, sm maximum // sf (sentenza, regola) maxim; (METEOR) maximum temperature; al ~ at (the) most; in linea di ~a generally speaking.
'masso sm rock, boulder.
mas'sone sm freemason; massone'ria sf freemasonry.
masti'care vt to chew.
'mastice ['mastitʃe] sm mastic; (per vetri) putty.
mas'tino sm mastiff.
ma'tassa sf skein.
mate'matico, a, ci, che ag mathematical // sm/f mathematician // sf mathematics sg.
mate'rasso sm mattress; ~ a molle spring o interior-sprung mattress.
ma'teria sf (FISICA) matter; (TECN, COMM) material, matter q; (disciplina) subject; (argomento) subject matter, material; ~e prime raw materials; in ~ di (per quanto concerne) on the subject of; materi'ale ag material; (fig: grossolano) rough, rude // sm material; (insieme di strumenti etc) equipment q, materials pl.
maternità sf motherhood, maternity; (clinica) maternity hospital.
ma'terno, a ag (amore, cura etc) maternal, motherly; (nonno) maternal; (lingua, terra) mother cpd.
ma'tita sf pencil.
ma'trice [ma'tritʃe] sf matrix; (COMM) counterfoil; (fig: origine) background.
ma'tricola sf (registro) register; (numero) registration number; (nell'università) freshman, fresher.
ma'trigna [ma'triɲɲa] sf stepmother.
matrimoni'ale ag matrimonial, marriage cpd.
matri'monio sm marriage, matrimony; (durata) marriage, married life; (cerimonia) wedding.
ma'trona sf (fig) matronly woman.
mat'tina sf morning; matti'nata sf morning; (spettacolo) matinée, afternoon performance; mattini'ero, a ag: essere mattiniero to be an early riser; mat'tino sm morning.
'matto, a ag mad, crazy; (fig: falso) false, imitation; (: opaco) matt, dull // sm/f madman/woman; avere una voglia ~a di qc to be dying for sth.
mat'tone sm brick; (fig): questo libro/film è un ~ this book/film is heavy going.
matto'nella sf tile.
matu'rare vi (anche: ~rsi) (frutta, grano) to ripen; (ascesso) to come to a head; (fig: persona, idea, ECON) to mature // vt to ripen; to (make) mature.
maturità sf maturity; (di frutta) ripeness, maturity; (INS) school-leaving examination, ≈ GCE A-levels (Brit).

ma'turo, a ag mature; (frutto) ripe, mature.
'mazza ['mattsa] sf (bastone) club; (martello) sledge-hammer; (SPORT: da golf) club; (: da baseball, cricket) bat.
maz'zata [mat'tsata] sf (anche fig) heavy blow.
'mazzo ['mattso] sm (di fiori, chiavi etc) bunch; (di carte da gioco) pack.
me pronome me; ~ stesso(a) myself; sei bravo quanto ~ you are as clever as I (am) o as me.
me'andro sm meander.
M.E.C. [mɛk] sigla m (= Mercato Comune Europeo) EEC.
mec'canico, a, ci, che ag mechanical // sm mechanic // sf mechanics sg; (attinità tecnologica) mechanical engineering; (meccanismo) mechanism.
mecca'nismo sm mechanism.
me'daglia [me'daʎʎa] sf medal; medagli'one sm (ARCHIT) medallion; (gioiello) locket.
me'desimo, a ag same; (in persona): io ~ I myself.
'media sf vedi medio.
medi'ano, a ag median; (valore) mean // sm (CALCIO) half-back.
medi'ante prep by means of.
medi'are vt (fare da mediatore) to act as mediator in; (MAT) to average.
media'tore, 'trice sm/f mediator; (COMM) middle man, agent.
medica'mento sm medicine, drug.
medi'care vt to treat; (ferita) to dress; medicazi'one sf treatment, medication; dressing.
medi'cina [medi'tʃina] sf medicine; ~ legale forensic medicine; medici'nale ag medicinal // sm drug, medicine.
'medico, a, ci, che ag medical // sm doctor; ~ generico general practitioner, GP.
medie'vale ag medieval.
'medio, a ag average; (punto, ceto) middle; (altezza, statura) medium // sm (dito) middle finger // sf average; (MAT) mean; (INS: voto) end-of-term average; in ~a on average; licenza ~a leaving certificate awarded at the end of 3 years of secondary education; scuola ~a first 3 years of secondary school.
medi'ocre ag mediocre, poor.
medioe'vale ag = medievale.
medio'evo sm Middle Ages pl.
medi'tare vt to ponder over, meditate on; (progettare) to plan, think out // vi to meditate.
mediter'raneo, a ag Mediterranean; il (mare) M~ the Mediterranean (Sea).
me'dusa sf (ZOOL) jellyfish.
me'gafono sm megaphone.
'meglio ['mɛʎʎo] av, ag inv better; (con senso superlativo) best // sm (la cosa migliore): il ~ the best (thing); faresti

~ ad andartene you had better leave; alla ~ as best one can; andar di bene in ~ to get better and better; fare del proprio ~ to do one's best; per il ~ for the best; aver la ~ su qn to get the better of sb.

'mela *sf* apple; ~ cotogna quince.

mela'grana *sf* pomegranate.

melan'zana [melan'dzana] *sf* aubergine (*Brit*), eggplant (*US*).

me'lassa *sf* molasses *sg*, treacle.

me'lenso, a *ag* dull, stupid.

mel'lifluo, a *ag* (*peg*) sugary, honeyed.

'melma *sf* mud, mire.

'melo *sm* apple tree.

melo'dia *sf* melody.

me'lone *sm* (*musk*)melon.

'membra *sfpl vedi* **membro**.

'membro *sm* member; (*pl(f)* ~a: *arto*) limb.

memo'randum *sm inv* memorandum.

me'moria *sf* memory; ~e *sfpl* (*opera autobiografica*) memoirs; a ~ (*imparare, sapere*) by heart; a ~ d'uomo within living memory; **memori'ale** *sm* (*raccolta di memorie*) memoirs *pl*; (*DIR*) memorial.

mena'dito: a ~ *av* perfectly, thoroughly; **sapere qc a ~** to have sth at one's fingertips.

me'nare *vt* to lead; (*picchiare*) to hit, beat; (*dare: colpi*) to deal; ~ **la coda** (*cane*) to wag its tail.

mendi'cante *sm/f* beggar.

mendi'care *vt* to beg for // *vi* to beg.

'meno ♦ *av* **1** (*in minore misura*) less; dovresti mangiare ~ you should eat less, you shouldn't eat so much **2** (*comparativo*): ~ ... **di** not as ... as, less ... than; **sono ~ alto di te** I'm not as tall as you (are), I'm less tall than you (are); ~ ... **che** not as ... as, less ... than; ~ **che mai** less than ever; **è ~ intelligente che ricco** he's more rich than intelligent; ~ **fumo più mangio** the less I smoke the more I eat **3** (*superlativo*) least; **il ~ dotato degli studenti** the least gifted of the students; **è quello che compro ~ spesso** it's the one I buy least often **4** (*MAT*) minus; **8 ~ 5** 8 minus 5, 8 take away 5; **sono le 8 ~ un quarto** it's a quarter to 8; ~ **5 gradi** 5 degrees below zero, minus 5 degrees; **mille lire in ~** a thousand lire less **5** (*fraseologia*): **quanto ~ poteva** telefonare he could at least have phoned; **non so se accettare o ~** I don't know whether to accept or not; **fare a ~ di qc/qn** to do without sth/sb; **non potevo fare a ~ di ridere** I couldn't help laughing; ~ **male!** thank goodness!; ~ **male che sei arrivato** it's a good job that you've come **♦** *ag inv* (*tempo, denaro*) less; (*errori, persone*) fewer; **ha fatto ~ errori di tutti**

he made fewer mistakes than anyone, he made the fewest mistakes of all **♦** *sm inv* **1**: **il ~** (*il minimo*) the least; **parlare del più e del ~** to talk about this and that **2** (*MAT*) minus **♦** *prep* (*eccetto*) except (for), apart from; **a ~ che, a ~ di** unless; **a ~ che non piova** unless it rains; **non posso, a ~ di prendere ferie** I can't, unless I take some leave.

meno'mare *vt* (*danneggiare*) to maim, disable.

meno'pausa *sf* menopause.

'mensa *sf* (*locale*) canteen; (: *MIL*) mess; (: *nelle università*) refectory.

men'sile *ag* monthly // *sm* (*periodico*) monthly (magazine); (*stipendio*) monthly salary.

'mensola *sf* bracket; (*ripiano*) shelf; (*ARCHIT*) corbel.

'menta *sf* mint; (*anche:* ~ **piperita**) peppermint; (*bibita*) peppermint cordial; (*caramella*) mint, peppermint.

men'tale *ag* mental; **mentalità** *sf inv* mentality.

'mente *sf* mind; **imparare/sapere qc a ~** to learn/know sth by heart; **avere in ~ qc** to have sth in mind; **passare di ~ a qn** to slip sb's mind.

men'tire *vi* to lie.

'mento *sm* chin.

'mentolo *sm* menthol.

'mentre *cong* (*temporale*) while; (*avversativo*) whereas.

menzio'nare [mentsjo'nare] *vt* to mention.

menzi'one [men'tsjone] *sf* mention; **fare ~ di** to mention.

men'zogna [men'tsɔɲɲa] *sf* lie.

mera'viglia [mera'viʎʎa] *sf* amazement, wonder; (*persona, cosa*) marvel, wonder; **a ~** perfectly, wonderfully; **meravigli'are** *vt* to amaze, astonish; **meravigliarsi (di)** to marvel (at); (*stupirsi*) to be amazed (at), be astonished (at); **meravigli'oso, a** *ag* wonderful, marvellous.

mer'cante *sm* merchant; ~ **d'arte** art dealer; ~ **di cavalli** horse dealer; **mercanteggi'are** *vt* (*onore, voto*) to sell // *vi* to bargain, haggle; **mercan'tile** *ag* commercial, mercantile; (*nave, marina*) merchant *cpd* // *sm* (*nave*) merchantman; **mercan'zia** *sf* merchandise, goods *pl*.

mer'cato *sm* market; ~ **dei cambi** exchange market; **M~ Comune (Europeo)** (European) Common Market; ~ **nero** black market.

'merce ['mɛrtʃe] *sf* goods *pl*, merchandise; ~ **deperibile** perishable goods *pl*.

mercé [mer'tʃe] *sf* mercy.

merce'nario, a [mertʃe'narjo] *ag, sm*

mercenary.

merce'ria [mertʃe'ria] sf (articoli) haberdashery (Brit), notions pl (US); (bottega) haberdasher's shop (Brit), notions store (US).

mercoledì sm inv Wednesday; di o il ~ on Wednesdays; ~ delle Ceneri Ash Wednesday.

mer'curio sm mercury.

'merda sf (fam!) shit (!).

me'renda sf afternoon snack.

meridi'ano, a ag meridian; midday cpd, noonday // sm meridian // sf (orologio) sundial.

meridio'nale ag southern // sm/f southerner.

meridi'one sm south.

me'ringa, ghe sf (CUC) meringue.

meri'tare vt to deserve, merit // vb impers: merita andare it's worth going.

meri'tevole ag worthy.

'merito sm merit; (valore) worth; in ~ a as regards, with regard to; dare ~ a qn di to give sb credit for; finire a pari ~ to finish joint first (o second etc) to tie; **meri'torio, a** ag praiseworthy.

mer'letto sm lace.

'merlo sm (ZOOL) blackbird; (ARCHIT) battlement.

mer'luzzo [mer'luttso] sm (ZOOL) cod.

mes'chino, a [mes'kino] ag wretched; (scarso) scanty, poor; (persona: gretta) mean; (: limitata) narrow-minded, petty.

mesco'lanza [mesko'lantsa] sf mixture.

mesco'lare vt to mix; (vini, colori) to blend; (mettere in disordine) to mix up, muddle up; (carte) to shuffle; ~rsi vr to mix; to blend; to get mixed up; (fig): ~rsi in to get mixed up in, meddle in.

'mese sm month.

'messa sf (REL) mass; (il mettere): ~ in moto starting; ~ in piega set; ~ a punto (TECN) adjustment; (AUT) tuning; (fig) clarification; ~ in scena = messinscena.

messag'gero [messad'dʒero] sm messenger.

mes'saggio [mes'saddʒo] sm message.

mes'sale sm (REL) missal.

'messe sf harvest.

Mes'sia sm inv (REL): il ~ the Messiah.

'Messico sm: il ~ Mexico.

messin'scena [messin'ʃena] sf (TEATRO) production.

'messo, a pp di **mettere** // sm messenger.

mesti'ere sm (professione) job; (: manuale) trade; (: artigianale) craft; (fig: abilità nel lavoro) skill, technique; essere del ~ to know the tricks of the trade.

'mesto, a ag sad, melancholy.

'mestola sf (CUC) ladle; (EDIL) trowel.

'mestolo sm (CUC) ladle.

mestruazi'one [mestruat'tsjone] sf menstruation.

'meta sf destination; (fig) aim, goal.

metà sf inv half; (punto di mezzo) middle: **dividere qc a o per ~** to divide sth in half, halve sth; **fare a ~** (di qc con qn) to go halves (with sb in sth); **a ~ prezzo** at half price; **a ~ strada** halfway.

me'tafora sf metaphor.

me'tallico, a, ci, che ag (di metallo) metal cpd; (splendore, rumore etc) metallic.

me'tallo sm metal.

metalmec'canico, a, ci, che ag engineering cpd // sm engineering worker.

me'tano sm methane.

meteorolo'gia [meteorolo'dʒia] sf meteorology; **meteoro'logico, a, ci, che** ag meteorological, weather cpd.

me'ticcio, a, ci, ce [me'tittʃo] sm/f half-caste, half-breed.

me'todico, a, ci, che ag methodical.

'metodo sm method; (manuale) tutor (Brit), manual.

'metrico, a, ci, che ag metric; (POESIA) metrical // sf metrics sg.

'metro sm metre; (nastro) tape measure; (asta) (metre) rule.

metropoli'tano, a ag metropolitan // sf underground, subway.

'mettere vt to put; (abito) to put on; (: portare) to wear; (installare: telefono) to put in; (fig: provocare): ~ fame/ allegria a qn to make sb hungry/happy; (supporre): mettiamo che ... let's suppose o say that ... ; ~rsi vr (persona) to put o.s.; (oggetto) to go; (disporsi: faccenda) to turn out; ~rsi a sedere to sit down; ~rsi a letto to get into bed; (per malattia) to take to one's bed; ~rsi il cappello to put on one's hat; ~rsi a (cominciare) to begin to, start to; ~rsi al lavoro to set to work; ~rsi con qn (in società) to team up with sb; (in coppia) to start going out with sb; ~rci: ~rci molta cura/molto tempo to take a lot of care/a lot of time; ci ho messo 3 ore per venire it's taken me 3 hours to get here; ~rcela tutta to do one's best; ~ a tacere qn/qc to keep sb/sth quiet; ~ su casa to set up house; ~ su un negozio to start a shop; ~ via to put away.

mez'zadro [med'dzadro] sm (AGR) sharecropper.

mezza'luna [meddza'luna] sf half-moon; (dell'islamismo) crescent; (coltello) (semicircular) chopping knife.

mezza'nino [meddza'nino] sm mezzanine (floor).

mez'zano, a [med'dzano] ag (medio) average, medium; (figlio) middle cpd // sm/f (intermediario) go-between; (ruffiano) pimp.

mezza'notte [meddza'nɔtte] sf midnight.

'mezzo, a ['meddzo] *ag* half; **un ~ litro/panino** half a litre/roll // *av* half-; **~ morto** half-dead // *sm* (*metà*) half; (*parte centrale: di strada etc*) middle; (*per raggiungere un fine*) means *sg*; (*veicolo*) vehicle; (*nell'indicare l'ora*): **le nove e ~** half past nine; **mezzogiorno e ~** half past twelve // *sf*: **la ~a** half-past twelve (*in the afternoon*); **~i** *smpl* (*possibilità economiche*) means; **di ~a età** middle-aged; **un soprabito di ~a stagione** a spring (*o* autumn) coat; **di ~ middle**, in the middle; **andarci di ~** (*patir danno*) to suffer; **levarsi** *o* **togliersi di ~** to get out of the way; **in ~ a** in the middle of; **per o a ~ di** by means of; **~i di comunicazione di massa** mass media *pl*; **~i pubblici** public transport *sg*; **~i di trasporto** means of transport.

mezzogi'orno [meddzo'dʒorno] *sm* midday, noon; (*GEO*) south; **a ~** at 12 (o'clock) *o* midday *o* noon; **il ~ d'Italia** southern Italy.

mez'z'ora, mez'zora [med'dzora] *sf* half-hour, half an hour.

mi *pronome* (*dav lo, la, li, le, ne diventa me*) (*oggetto*) me; (*complemento di termine*) to me; (*riflessivo*) myself // *sm* (*MUS*) E; (*: solfeggiando la scala*) mi.

'mia *vedi* mio.

miago'lare *vi* to miaow, mew.

'mica *sf* (*CHIM*) mica // *av* (*fam*): **non ... ~** not ... at all; **non sono ~ stanco** I'm not a bit tired; **non sarà ~ partito?** he wouldn't have left, would he?; **~ male** not bad.

'miccia, ce ['mittʃa] *sf* fuse.

micidi'ale [mitʃi'djale] *ag* fatal; (*dannosissimo*) deadly.

mi'crofono *sm* microphone.

micros'copio *sm* microscope.

mi'dollo, *pl(f)* **~a** *sm* (*ANAT*) marrow.

'mie, mi'ei *vedi* mio.

mi'ele *sm* honey.

mi'etere *vt* (*AGR*) to reap, harvest; (*fig: vite*) to take, claim.

migli'aio [miʎ'ʎajo], *pl(f)* **~a** *sm* thousand; **un ~ (di)** about a thousand; **a ~a** by the thousand, in thousands.

'miglio ['miʎʎo] *sm* (*BOT*) millet; (*pl(f)* **~a**: *unità di misura*) mile; **~ marino** *o* **nautico** nautical mile.

migliora'mento [miʎʎora'mento] *sm* improvement.

miglio'rare [miʎʎo'rare] *vt, vi* to improve.

migli'ore [miʎ'ʎore] *ag* (*comparativo*) better; (*superlativo*) best // *sm*: **il ~ the best** (thing) // *sm/f*: **il(la) ~ the best** (person); **il miglior vino di questa regione** the best wine in this area.

'mignolo ['miɲɲolo] *sm* (*ANAT*) little finger, pinkie; (*: dito del piede*) little toe.

mi'grare *vi* to migrate.

'mila *pl di* mille.

Mi'lano *sf* Milan.

miliar'dario, a *sm/f* millionaire.

mili'ardo *sm* thousand million, billion (*US*).

mili'are *ag*: **pietra ~** milestone.

mili'one *sm* million; **un ~ di lire** a million lire.

mili'tante *ag, sm/f* militant.

mili'tare *vi* (*MIL*) to be a soldier, serve; (*fig: in un partito*) to be a militant // *ag* military // *sm* serviceman; **fare il ~** to do one's military service.

'milite *sm* soldier.

millanta'tore, 'trice *sm/f* boaster.

'mille *num* (*pl* **mila**) a *o* one thousand; **dieci mila** ten thousand.

mille'foglie [mille'fɔʎʎe] *sm inv* (*CUC*) cream *o* vanilla slice.

mil'lennio *sm* millennium.

millepi'edi *sm inv* centipede.

mil'lesimo, a *ag, sm* thousandth.

milli'grammo *sm* milligram(me).

mil'limetro *sm* millimetre.

'milza ['miltsa] *sf* (*ANAT*) spleen.

mimetiz'zare [mimetid'dzare] *vt* to camouflage; **~rsi** *vr* to camouflage o.s.

'mimica *sf* (*arte*) mime.

'mimo *sm* (*attore, componimento*) mime.

mi'mosa *sf* mimosa.

'mina *sf* (*esplosiva*) mine; (*di matita*) lead.

mi'naccia, ce [mi'nattʃa] *sf* threat; **minacci'are** *vt* to threaten; **minacciare qn di morte** to threaten to kill sb; **minacciare di fare qc** to threaten to do sth; **minacci'oso, a** *ag* threatening.

mi'nare *vt* (*MIL*) to mine; (*fig*) to undermine.

mina'tore *sm* miner.

mina'torio, a *ag* threatening.

mine'rale *ag, sm* mineral.

mine'rario, a *ag* (*delle miniere*) mining; (*dei minerali*) ore *cpd*.

mi'nestra *sf* soup; **~ in brodo/di verdure** noodle/vegetable soup; **mines'trone** *sm* thick vegetable and pasta soup.

mingher'lino, a [minger'lino] *ag* thin, slender.

'mini *ag inv* mini // *sf inv* miniskirt.

minia'tura *sf* miniature.

mini'era *sf* mine.

mini'gonna *sf* miniskirt.

'minimo, a *ag* minimum, least, slightest; (*piccolissimo*) very small, slight; (*il più basso*) lowest, minimum // *sm* minimum; **al ~ at least**; **girare al ~** (*AUT*) to idle.

minis'tero *sm* (*POL, REL*) ministry; (*governo*) government; **~ delle Finanze** Ministry of Finance, ≈ Treasury.

mi'nistro *sm* (*POL, REL*) minister; **~ delle Finanze** Minister of Finance, ≈ Chancellor of the Exchequer.

mino'ranza [mino'rantsa] *sf* minority.

mino'rato, a *ag* handicapped // *sm/f* physically (*o* mentally) handicapped person.

mi'nore *ag* (*comparativo*) less; (*più piccolo*) smaller; (*numero*) lower; (*inferiore*) lower, inferior; (*meno importante*) minor; (*più giovane*) younger; (*superlativo*) least; smallest; lowest; youngest // *sm/f* (*minorenne*) minor, person under age.

mino'renne *ag* under age // *sm/f* minor, person under age.

mi'nuscolo, a *ag* (*scrittura, carattere*) small; (*piccolissimo*) tiny // *sf* small letter.

mi'nuta *sf* rough copy, draft.

mi'nuto, a *ag* tiny, minute; (*pioggia*) fine; (*corporatura*) delicate, fine; (*lavoro*) detailed // *sm* (*unità di misura*) minute; **al ~** (*COMM*) retail.

'mio, 'mia, mi'ei, 'mie *det:* **il ~, la mia** *etc* my // *pronome:* **il ~, la mia** *etc* mine; **i miei** my family; **un ~ amico** a friend of mine.

'miopo *ag* short-sighted.

'mira *sf* (*anche fig*) aim; **prendere la ~** to take aim; **prendere di ~ qn** (*fig*) to pick on sb.

mi'rabile *ag* admirable, wonderful.

mi'racolo *sm* miracle.

mi'raggio [mi'raddʒo] *sm* mirage.

mi'rare *vi:* **~ a** to aim at.

mi'rino *sm* (*TECN*) sight; (*FOT*) viewer, viewfinder.

mir'tillo *sm* bilberry (*Brit*), blueberry (*US*), whortleberry.

mi'scela [miʃ'ʃela] *sf* mixture; (*di caffè*) blend.

miscel'lanea [miʃʃel'lanea] *sf* miscellany.

'mischia ['miskja] *sf* scuffle; (*RUGBY*) scrum, scrummage.

mischi'are [mis'kjare] *vt*, **~rsi** *vr* to mix, blend.

mis'cuglio [mis'kuʎʎo] *sm* mixture, hotchpotch, jumble.

mise'rabile *ag* (*infelice*) miserable, wretched; (*povero*) poverty-stricken; (*di scarso valore*) miserable.

mi'seria *sf* extreme poverty; (*infelicità*) misery; **~e** *sfpl* (*del mondo etc*) misfortunes, troubles; **porca ~!** (*fam*) blast!, damn!

miseri'cordia *sf* mercy, pity.

'misero, a *ag* miserable, wretched; (*povero*) poverty-stricken; (*insufficiente*) miserable.

mis'fatto *sm* misdeed, crime.

mi'sogino [mi'zɔdʒino] *sm* misogynist.

'missile *sm* missile.

missio'nario, a *ag, sm/f* missionary.

missi'one *sf* mission.

misteri'oso, a *ag* mysterious.

mis'tero *sm* mystery.

mistifi'care *vt* to fool, bamboozle.

'misto, a *ag* mixed; (*scuola*) mixed, coeducational // *sm* mixture.

mis'tura *sf* mixture.

mi'sura *sf* measure; (*misurazione, dimensione*) measurement; (*taglia*) size; (*provvedimento*) measure, step; (*moderazione*) moderation; (*MUS*) time; (: *divisione*) bar; (*fig: limite*) bounds *pl*, limit; **nella ~ in cui** inasmuch as, insofar as; **su ~** made to measure.

misu'rare *vt* (*ambiente, stoffa*) to measure; (*terreno*) to survey; (*abito*) to try on; (*pesare*) to weigh; (*fig: parole etc*) to weigh up; (: *spese, cibo*) to limit // *vi* to measure; **~rsi** *vr:* **~rsi con qn** to have a confrontation with sb; to compete with sb; **misu'rato, a** *ag* (*ponderato*) measured; (*prudente*) cautious; (*moderato*) moderate.

'mite *ag* mild; (*prezzo*) moderate, reasonable.

miti'gare *vt* to mitigate, lessen; (*lenire*) to soothe, relieve; **~rsi** *vr* (*odio*) to subside; (*tempo*) to become milder.

'mito *sm* myth; **mitolo'gia, 'gie** *sf* mythology.

'mitra *sf* (*REL*) mitre // *sm inv* (*arma*) sub-machine gun.

mitraglia'trice [mitraʎʎa'tritʃe] *sf* machine gun.

mit'tente *sm/f* sender.

'mobile *ag* mobile; (*parte di macchina*) moving; (*DIR: bene*) movable, personal // *sm* (*arredamento*) piece of furniture; **~i** *smpl* furniture *sg*.

mo'bilia *sf* furniture.

mobili'are *ag* (*DIR*) personal, movable.

mo'bilio *sm* = **mobilia**.

mobili'tare *vt* to mobilize.

mocas'sino *sm* moccasin.

'moccolo *sm* (*di candela*) candle-end; (*fam: bestemmia*) oath; (: *moccio*) snot; **reggere il ~** to play gooseberry (*Brit*), act as chaperon.

'moda *sf* fashion; **alla ~, di ~** fashionable, in fashion.

modalità *sf inv* formality.

mo'della *sf* model.

model'lare *vt* (*creta*) to model, shape; **~rsi** *vr:* **~rsi su** to model o.s. on.

mo'dello *sm* model; (*stampo*) mould // *ag inv* model *cpd*.

'modem *sm inv* modem.

mode'rare *vt* to moderate; **~rsi** *vr* to restrain o.s.; **mode'rato, a** *ag* moderate.

modera'tore, 'trice *sm/f* moderator.

mo'derno, a *ag* modern.

mo'destia *sf* modesty.

mo'desto, a *ag* modest.

'modico, a, ci, che *ag* reasonable, moderate.

mo'difica, che *sf* modification.

modifi'care *vt* to modify, alter; **~rsi** *vr*

to alter, change.

mo'dista *sf* milliner.

'**modo** *sm* way, manner; *(mezzo)* means, way; *(occasione)* opportunity; *(LING)* mood; *(MUS)* mode; ~**i** *smpl* manners; **a suo** ~, **a** ~ **suo** in his own way; **ad** *o* **in ogni** ~ anyway; **di** *o* **in** ~ **che** so that; **in** ~ **da** so as to; **in tutti i** ~**i** at all costs; *(comunque sia)* anyway; *(in ogni caso)* in any case; **in qualche** ~ somehow or other; ~ **di dire** turn of phrase; **per** ~ **di dire** so to speak.

modu'lare *vt* to modulate; **modulazi'one** *sf* modulation; **modulazione di frequenza** frequency modulation.

'**modulo** *sm* (*modello*) form; *(ARCHIT, lunare, di comando)* module.

'**mogano** *sm* mahogany.

'**mogio, a, gi, gie** ['mɔdʒo] *ag* down in the dumps, dejected.

'**moglie** ['moʎʎe] *sf* wife.

mo'ine *sfpl* cajolery *sg*; *(leziosità)* affectation *sg*.

'**mola** *sf* millstone; *(utensile abrasivo)* grindstone.

mo'lare *sm* (*dente*) molar.

'**mole** *sf* mass; *(dimensioni)* size; *(edificio grandioso)* massive structure.

moles'tare *vt* to bother, annoy; **mo'lestia** *sf* annoyance, bother; **recar molestia a qn** to bother sb; **mo'lesto, a** *ag* annoying.

'**molla** *sf* spring; ~**e** *sfpl* tongs.

mol'lare *vt* to release, let go; *(NAUT)* to ease; *(fig: ceffone)* to give // *vi* (*cedere*) to give in.

'**molle** *ag* soft; *(muscoli)* flabby; *(fig: debole)* weak, feeble.

mol'letta *sf* (*per capelli*) hairgrip; *(per panni stesi)* clothes peg; ~**e** *sfpl* (*per zucchero*) tongs.

'**mollica, che** *sf* crumb, soft part.

mol'lusco, schi *sm* mollusc.

'**molo** *sm* mole, breakwater; jetty.

mol'teplice [mol'teplitʃe] *ag* (*formato di più elementi*) complex; ~**i** *pl* (*svariati: interessi, attività*) numerous, various.

moltipli'care *vt* to multiply; ~**rsi** *vr* to multiply; to increase in number; **moltiplicazi'one** *sf* multiplication.

'**molto, a ◆** *det* (*quantità*) a lot of, much; *(numero)* a lot of, many; ~ **pane/carbone** a lot of bread/coal; ~**a gente** a lot of people, many people; ~**i libri** a lot of books, many books; **non ho** ~ **tempo** I haven't got much time; **per** ~ (**tempo**) for a long time

◆ *av* **1** a lot, (very) much; **viaggia** ~ **he** travels a lot; **non viaggia** ~ **he** doesn't travel much *o* a lot

2 *(intensivo: con aggettivi, avverbi)* very; (: *con participio passato*) (very) much; ~ **buono** very good; ~ **migliore,** ~ **meglio** much *o* a lot better

◆ *pronome* much, a lot; ~**i(e)** *pronome pl* many, a lot; ~**i pensano che ...** many (people) think ....

momen'taneo, a *ag* momentary, fleeting.

mo'mento *sm* moment; **da un** ~ **all'altro** at any moment; *(all'improvviso)* suddenly; **al** ~ **di fare** just as I was (*o* you were *o* he was *etc*) doing; **per il** ~ for the time being; **dal** ~ **che** ever since; *(dato che)* since; **a** ~**i** (*da un* ~ *all'altro*) any time *o* moment now; (*quasi*) nearly.

'**monaca, che** *sf* nun.

'**Monaco** *sf* Monaco; ~ (**di Baviera**) Munich.

'**monaco, ci** *sm* monk.

mo'narca, chi *sm* monarch; **monar'chia** *sf* monarchy.

monas'tero *sm* (*di monaci*) monastery; *(di monache)* convent; **mo'nastico, a, ci, che** *ag* monastic.

'**monco, a, chi, che** *ag* maimed; *(fig)* incomplete; ~ **d'un braccio** one-armed.

mon'dana *sf* prostitute.

mon'dano, a *ag* (*anche fig*) worldly; *(dell'alta società)* society *cpd*; fashionable.

mon'dare *vt* (*frutta, patate*) to peel; *(piselli)* to shell; *(pulire)* to clean.

mondi'ale *ag* (*campionato, popolazione*) world *cpd*; *(influenza)* world-wide.

'**mondo** *sm* world; (*grande quantità*): **un** ~ **di** lots of, a host of; **il bel** ~ high society.

mo'nello, a *sm/f* street urchin; *(ragazzo vivace)* scamp, imp.

mo'neta *sf* coin; *(ECON: valuta)* currency; *(denaro spicciolo)* (small) change; *(estera)* foreign currency; ~ **legale** legal tender; **mone'tario, a** *ag* monetary.

mongo'loide *ag, sm/f* (*MED*) mongol.

'**monito** *sm* warning.

'**monitor** *sm inv* (*TECN, TV*) monitor.

monoco'lore *ag* (*POL*): **governo** ~ one-party government.

mono'polio *sm* monopoly.

mo'notono, a *ag* monotonous.

monsi'gnore [monsiɲ'ɲore] *sm* (*REL: titolo*) Your (*o* His) Grace.

mon'sone *sm* monsoon.

monta'carichi [monta'kariki] *sm inv* hoist, goods lift.

mon'taggio [mon'taddʒo] *sm* (*TECN*) assembly; *(CINEMA)* editing.

mon'tagna [mon'taɲɲa] *sf* mountain; *(zona montuosa)*: **la** ~ the mountains *pl*; **andare in** ~ to go to the mountains; ~**e russe** roller coaster *sg*, big dipper *sg* (*Brit*); **monta'gnoso, a** *ag* mountainous.

monta'naro, a *ag* mountain *cpd* // *sm/f* mountain dweller.

mon'tano, a *ag* mountain *cpd*; alpine.

mon'tare *vt* to go (*o* come) up; (*cavallo*) to ride; (*apparecchiatura*) to set up, assemble; (*CUC*) to whip; (*ZOOL*) to cover; (*incastonare*) to mount, set; (*CINEMA*) to edit; (*FOT*) to mount // *vi* to go (*o* come) up; (*a cavallo*): ~ **bene/male** to ride well/badly; (*aumentare di livello, volume*) to rise; ~**rsi** *vr* to become big-headed; ~ **qc** to exaggerate sth; ~ **qn** *o* **la testa a qn** to turn sb's head; ~ **in bicicletta/macchina/treno** to get on a bicycle/into a car/on a train; ~ **a cavallo** to get on *o* mount a horse.

monta'tura *sf* assembling *q*; (*di occhiali*) frames *pl*; (*di gioiello*) mounting, setting; (*fig*): ~ **pubblicitaria** publicity stunt.

'monte *sm* mountain; **a** ~ upstream; **mandare a** ~ **qc** to upset sth, cause sth to fail; **il M~ Bianco** Mont Blanc; ~ **di pietà** pawnshop.

mon'tone *sm* (*ZOOL*) ram; **carne di** ~ mutton.

montu'oso, a *ag* mountainous.

monu'mento *sm* monument.

'mora *sf* (*del rovo*) blackberry; (*del gelso*) mulberry; (*DIR*) delay; (*: somma*) arrears *pl*.

mo'rale *ag* moral // *sf* (*scienza*) ethics *sg*, moral philosophy; (*complesso di norme*) moral standards *pl*, morality; (*condotta*) morals *pl*; (*insegnamento morale*) moral // *sm* morale; **essere giù di** ~ to be feeling down; **moralità** *sf* morality; (*condotta*) morals *pl*.

'morbido, a *ag* soft; (*pelle*) soft, smooth.

mor'billo *sm* (*MED*) measles *sg*.

'morbo *sm* disease.

mor'boso, a *ag* (*fig*) morbid.

mor'dace [mor'datʃe] *ag* biting, cutting.

mor'dente *sm* (*fig: di satira, critica*) bite; (*: di persona*) drive.

'mordere *vt* to bite; (*addentare*) to bite into; (*corrodere*) to eat into.

mori'bondo, a *ag* dying, moribund.

morige'rato, a [moridʒe'rato] *ag* of good morals.

mo'rire *vi* to die; (*abitudine, civiltà*) to die out; ~ **di fame** to die of hunger; (*fig*) to be starving; ~ **di noia/paura** to be bored/scared to death; **fa un caldo da** ~ it's terribly hot.

mormo'rare *vi* to murmur; (*brontolare*) to grumble.

'moro, a *ag* dark(-haired); dark(-complexioned); **i M~i** *smpl* (*STORIA*) the Moors.

mo'roso, a *ag* in arrears // *sm/f* (*fam: innamorato*) sweetheart.

'morsa *sf* (*TECN*) vice; (*fig: stretta*) grip.

morsi'care *vt* to nibble (at), gnaw (at); (*sog: insetto*) to bite.

'morso, a *pp di* **mordere** // *sm* bite; (*di insetto*) sting; (*parte della briglia*) bit; ~**i della fame** pangs of hunger.

mor'taio *sm* mortar.

mor'tale *ag, sm* mortal; **mortalità** *sf* mortality, death rate.

'morte *sf* death.

mortifi'care *vt* to mortify.

'morto, a *pp di* **morire** // *ag* dead // *sm/f* dead man/woman; **i** ~**i** the dead; **fare il** ~ (*nell'acqua*) to float on one's back; **il Mar M~** the Dead Sea.

mor'torio *sm* (*anche fig*) funeral.

mo'saico, ci *sm* mosaic.

'mosca, sche *sf* fly; ~ **cieca** blindman's-buff.

'Mosca *sf* Moscow.

mos'cato *sm* muscatel (wine).

mosce'rino [moʃʃe'rino] *sm* midge, gnat.

mos'chea [mos'kɛa] *sf* mosque.

mos'chetto [mos'ketto] *sm* musket.

'moscio, a, sci, sce ['mɔʃʃo] *ag* (*fig*) lifeless.

mos'cone *sm* (*ZOOL*) bluebottle; (*barca*) pedalo; (*: a remi*) kind of pedalo with oars.

'mossa *sf* movement; (*nel gioco*) move.

'mosso, a *pp di* **muovere** // *ag* (*mare*) rough; (*capelli*) wavy; (*FOT*) blurred; (*ritmo, prosa*) animated.

mos'tarda *sf* mustard.

'mostra *sf* exhibition; show; (*ostentazione*) show; **in** ~ on show; **far** ~ **di** (*fingere*) to pretend; **far** ~ **di sé** to show off.

mos'trare *vt* to show // *vi*: ~ **di fare** to pretend to do; ~**rsi** *vr* to appear.

'mostro *sm* monster; **mostru'oso, a** *ag* monstrous.

mo'tel *sm inv* motel.

moti'vare *vt* (*causare*) to cause; (*giustificare*) to justify, account for; **motivazi'one** *sf* justification; motive; (*PSIC*) motivation.

mo'tivo *sm* (*causa*) reason, cause; (*movente*) motive; (*letterario*) (central) theme; (*disegno*) motif, design, pattern; (*MUS*) motif; **per quale** ~? why?, for what reason?

'moto *sm* (*anche FISICA*) motion; (*movimento, gesto*) movement; (*esercizio fisico*) exercise; (*sommossa*) rising, revolt; (*commozione*) feeling, impulse // *sf inv* (*motocicletta*) motorbike; **mettere in** ~ to set in motion; (*AUT*) to start up.

motoci'cletta [mototʃi'kletta] *sf* motorcycle; **motoci'clismo** *sm* motorcycling, motorcycle racing; **motoci'clista, i, e** *sm/f* motorcyclist.

mo'tore, 'trice *ag* motor; (*TECN*) driving // *sm* engine, motor; **a** ~ motor *cpd*, power-driven; ~ **a combustione interna/a reazione** internal combustion/jet engine;

moto'rino *sm* moped; **motorino di avviamento** (*AUT*) starter;
motoriz'zato, a *ag* (*truppe*) motorized; (*persona*) having a car o transport.
motos'cafo *sm* motorboat.
mot'teggio [mot'teddʒo] *sm* banter.
'motto *sm* (*battuta scherzosa*) witty remark; (*frase emblematica*) motto, maxim.
mo'vente *sm* motive.
movimen'tare *vt* to liven up.
movi'mento *sm* movement; (*fig*) activity, hustle and bustle; (*MUS*) tempo, movement.
mozi'one [mot'tsjone] *sf* (*POL*) motion.
moz'zare [mot'tsare] *vt* to cut off; (*coda*) to dock; ~ **il fiato** o **il respiro a qn** (*fig*) to take sb's breath away.
mozza'rella [mottsa'rella] *sf* mozzarella (*a moist Neapolitan curd cheese*).
mozzi'cone [mottsi'kone] *sm* stub, butt, end; (*anche*: ~ **di sigaretta**) cigarette end.
'mozzo *sm* ['mɔddzo] (*MECCANICA*) hub; ['mottso] (*NAUT*) ship's boy; ~ **di stalla** stable boy.
'mucca, che *sf* cow.
'mucchio ['mukkjo] *sm* pile, heap; (*fig*): **un ~ di** lots of, heaps of.
'muco, chi *sm* mucus.
'muffa *sf* mould, mildew.
mug'gire [mud'dʒire] *vi* (*vacca*) to low, moo; (*toro*) to bellow; (*fig*) to roar; **mug'gito** *sm* low, moo; bellow; roar.
mu'ghetto [mu'getto] *sm* lily of the valley.
mu'gnaio, a [muɲ'najo] *sm/f* miller.
mugo'lare *vi* (*cane*) to whimper, whine; (*fig: persona*) to moan.
muli'nare *vi* to whirl, spin (round and round).
muli'nello *sm* (*moto vorticoso*) eddy, whirl; (*di canna da pesca*) reel; (*NAUT*) windlass.
mu'lino *sm* mill; ~ **a vento** windmill.
'mulo *sm* mule.
'multa *sf* fine; **mul'tare** *vt* to fine.
'multiplo, a *ag, sm* multiple.
'mummia *sf* mummy.
'mungere ['mundʒere] *vt* (*anche fig*) to milk.
munici'pale [munitʃi'pale] *ag* municipal; town *cpd*.
muni'cipio [muni'tʃipjo] *sm* town council, corporation; (*edificio*) town hall.
mu'nire *vt*: ~ **qc/qn di** to equip sth/sb with.
munizi'oni [munit'tsjoni] *sfpl* (*MIL*) ammunition *sg*.
'munto, a *pp di* **mungere**.
mu'overe *vt* to move; (*ruota, macchina*) to drive; (*sollevare: questione, obiezione*) to raise, bring up; (: *accusa*) to make, bring forward; **~rsi** *vr* to move; **muoviti!** hurry up!, get a move on!

'mura *sfpl vedi* **muro**.
mu'raglia [mu'raʎʎa] *sf* (high) wall.
mu'rale *ag* wall *cpd*; mural.
mu'rare *vt* (*persona, porta*) to wall up.
mura'tore *sm* mason; bricklayer.
'muro *sm* wall; ~ **di** (*cinta cittadina*) walls; **a** ~ wall *cpd*; (*armadio etc*) built-in; ~ **del suono** sound barrier; **mettere al** ~ (*fucilare*) to shoot o execute (by firing squad).
'muschio ['muskjo] *sm* (*ZOOL*) musk; (*BOT*) moss.
musco'lare *ag* muscular, muscle *cpd*.
'muscolo *sm* (*ANAT*) muscle.
mu'seo *sm* museum.
museru'ola *sf* muzzle.
'musica *sf* music; ~ **da ballo/camera** dance/chamber music; **musi'cale** *ag* musical; **musi'cista, i, e** *sm/f* musician.
'muso *sm* muzzle; (*di auto, aereo*) nose; **tenere il** ~ to sulk; **mu'sone, a** *sm/f* sulky person.
'mussola *sf* muslin.
'muta *sf* (*di animali*) moulting; (*di serpenti*) sloughing; (*per immersioni subacquee*) diving suit; (*gruppo di cani*) pack.
muta'mento *sm* change.
mu'tande *sfpl* (*da uomo*) (under)pants; **mutan'dine** *sfpl* (*da donna, bambino*) pants (*Brit*), briefs; **mutandine di plastica** plastic pants.
mu'tare *vt, vi* to change, alter; **mutazi'one** *sf* change, alteration; (*BIOL*) mutation; **mu'tevole** *ag* changeable.
muti'lare *vt* to mutilate, maim; (*fig*) to mutilate, deface; **muti'lato, a** *sm/f* disabled person (*through loss of limbs*).
mu'tismo *sm* (*MED*) mutism; (*atteggiamento*) (stubborn) silence.
'muto, a *ag* (*MED*) dumb; (*emozione, dolore, CINEMA*) silent; (*LING*) silent, mute; (*carta geografica*) blank; ~ **per lo stupore** *etc* speechless with amazement *etc*.
'mutua *sf* (*anche*: **cassa** ~) health insurance scheme.
mutu'are *vt* (*fig*) to borrow.
mutu'ato, a *sm/f* member of a health insurance scheme.
'mutuo, a *ag* (*reciproco*) mutual // *sm* (*ECON*) (long-term) loan.

N

N. *abbr* (= *nord*) N.
'nacchere ['nakkere] *sfpl* castanets.
'nafta *sf* naphtha; (*per motori diesel*) diesel oil.
nafta'lina *sf* (*CHIM*) naphthalene; (*tarmicida*) mothballs *pl*.
'naia *sf* (*ZOOL*) cobra; (*MIL*) slang term

for national service.

'nailon *sm* nylon.

'nanna *sf* (*linguaggio infantile*): **andare a ~** to go to beddy-byes.

'nano, a *ag, sm/f* dwarf.

napole'tano, a *ag, sm/f* Neapolitan.

'Napoli *sf* Naples.

'nappa *sf* tassel.

nar'ciso [nar'tʃizo] *sm* narcissus.

nar'cosi *sf* narcosis.

nar'cotico, ci *sm* narcotic.

na'rice [na'ritʃe] *sf* nostril.

nar'rare *vt* to tell the story of, recount; **narra'tivo, a** *ag* narrative // *sf* (*branca letteraria*) fiction; **narra'tore, 'trice** *sm/f* narrator; **narrazi'one** *sf* narration; (*racconto*) story, tale.

na'sale *ag* nasal.

'nascere ['naʃʃere] *vi* (*bambino*) to be born; (*pianta*) to come o spring up; (*fiume*) to rise, have its source; (*sole*) to rise; (*dente*) to come through; (*fig: derivare, conseguire*): **~ da** to arise from, be born out of; **è nata nel 1952** she was born in 1952; **'nascita** *sf* birth.

nas'condere *vt* to hide, conceal; **~rsi** *vr* to hide; **nascon'diglio** *sm* hiding place; **nascon'dino** *sm* (*gioco*) hide-and-seek; **nas'costo, a** *pp di* **nascondere** // *ag* hidden; **di nascosto** secretly.

na'sello *sm* (*ZOOL*) hake.

'naso *sm* nose.

'nastro *sm* ribbon; (*magnetico, isolante, SPORT*) tape; **~ adesivo** adhesive tape; **~ trasportatore** conveyor belt.

nas'turzio [nas'turtsjo] *sm* nasturtium.

na'tale *ag* of one's birth // *sm* (*REL*): **N~** Christmas; (*giorno della nascita*) birthday; **natalità** *sf* birth rate; **nata'lizio, a** *ag* (*del Natale*) Christmas *cpd*.

na'tante *sm* craft *inv*, boat.

'natica, che *sf* (*ANAT*) buttock.

na'tio, a, 'tii, 'tie *ag* native.

Natività *sf* (*REL*) Nativity.

na'tivo, a *ag, sm/f* native.

'nato, a *pp di* **nascere** // *ag*: **un attore ~** a born actor; **~a Pieri** née Pieri.

na'tura *sf* nature; **pagare in ~** to pay in kind; **~ morta** still life.

natu'rale *ag* natural; **natura'lezza** *sf* naturalness; **natura'lista, i, e** *sm/f* naturalist.

naturaliz'zare [naturalid'dzare] *vt* to naturalize.

natural'mente *av* naturally; (*certamente, sì*) of course.

naufra'gare *vi* (*nave*) to be wrecked; (*persona*) to be shipwrecked; (*fig*) to fall through; **nau'fragio** *sm* shipwreck; (*fig*) ruin, failure; **'naufrago, ghi** *sm* castaway, shipwreck victim.

'nausea *sf* nausea; **nausea'bondo, a** *ag* nauseating, sickening; **nause'are** *vt* to nauseate, make (feel) sick.

'nautico, a, ci, che *ag* nautical // *sf*

(*art of*) navigation.

na'vale *ag* naval.

na'vata *sf* (*anche:* **~ centrale**) nave; (*anche:* **~ laterale**) aisle.

'nave *sf* ship, vessel; **~ cisterna** tanker; **~ da guerra** warship; **~ passeggeri** passenger ship; **~ spaziale** spaceship.

na'vetta *sf* shuttle; (*servizio di collegamento*) shuttle (service).

navi'cella [navi'tʃella] *sf* (*di aerostato*) gondola.

navi'gabile *ag* navigable.

navi'gare *vi* to sail; **navigazi'one** *sf* navigation.

na'viglio [na'viʎʎo] *sm* fleet, ships *pl*; (*canale artificiale*) canal; **~ da pesca** fishing fleet.

nazio'nale [nattsjo'nale] *ag* national // *sf* (*SPORT*) national team; **naziona'lismo** *sm* nationalism; **nazionalità** *sf inv* nationality.

nazi'one [nat'tsjone] *sf* nation.

ne ◆ *pronome* **1** (*di lui, lei, loro*) of him/her/them; about him/her/them; **~ riconosco la voce** I recognize his (o her) voice

2 (*di questa, quella cosa*) of it; about it; **~ voglio ancora** I want some more (of it o them); **non parliamone più!** let's not talk about it any more!

3 (*con valore partitivo*): **hai dei libri? — sì, ~ ho** have you any books? — yes, I have (some); **hai del pane? — no, non ~ ho** have you any bread? — no, I haven't any; **quanti anni hai? — ~ ho 17** how old are you? — I'm 17

◆ *av* (*moto da luogo: da lì*) from there; **~ vengo ora** I've just come from there.

né *cong*: **~ ... ~** neither ... nor; **~ l'uno ~ l'altro lo vuole** neither of them wants it; **non parla ~ l'italiano ~ il tedesco** he speaks neither Italian nor German, he doesn't speak either Italian or German; **non piove ~ nevica** it isn't raining or snowing.

ne'anche [ne'anke] *av, cong* not even; **non ... ~** not even; **~ se volesse potrebbe venire** he couldn't come even if he wanted to; **non l'ho visto — ~ io** I didn't see him — neither did I o I didn't either; **~ per idea** o **sogno!** not on your life!

'nebbia *sf* fog; (*foschia*) mist; **nebbi'oso, a** *ag* foggy; misty.

nebu'loso, a *ag* (*atmosfera*) hazy; (*fig*) hazy, vague.

necessaria'mente [netʃessarja'mente] *av* necessarily.

neces'sario, a [netʃes'sarjo] *ag* necessary.

necessità [netʃessi'ta] *sf inv* necessity; (*povertà*) need, poverty; **necessi'tare** *vt* to require // *vi* (*aver bisogno*): **necessitare di** to need.

necro'logio [nekro'lɔdʒo] *sm* obituary notice; (*registro*) register of deaths.

ne'fando, a *ag* infamous, wicked.

ne'fasto, a *ag* inauspicious, ill-omened.

ne'gare *vt* to deny; (*rifiutare*) to deny, refuse; ~ di aver fatto/che to deny having done/that; nega'tivo, a *ag*, *sf*, *sm* negative; negazi'one *sf* negation.

ne'gletto, a [ne'gletto] *ag* (*trascurato*) neglected.

'negli ['neʎʎi] *prep + det vedi* in.

negli'gente [negli'dʒɛnte] *ag* negligent, careless; negli'genza *sf* negligence, carelessness.

negozi'ante [negot'tsjante] *sm/f* trader, dealer; (*bottegaio*) shopkeeper (*Brit*), storekeeper (*US*).

negozi'are [negot'tsjare] *vt* to negotiate // *vi*: ~ in to trade *o* deal in; negozi'ato *sm* negotiation.

ne'gozio [ne'gɔttsjo] *sm* (*locale*) shop (*Brit*), store (*US*); (*affare*) (piece of) business *q*.

'negro, a *ag*, *sm/f* Negro.

'nei, nel, nell', 'nella, 'nelle, 'nello *prep + det vedi* in.

'nembo *sm* (METEOR) nimbus.

ne'mico, a, ci, che *ag* hostile; (MIL) enemy *cpd* // *sm/f* enemy; essere ~ di to be strongly averse *o* opposed to.

nem'meno *av*, *cong* = neanche.

'nenia *sf* dirge; (*motivo monotono*) monotonous tune.

'neo *sm* mole; (*fig*) (slight) flaw.

'neo... *prefisso* neo... .

'neon *sm* (CHIM) neon.

neo'nato, a *ag* newborn // *sm/f* newborn baby.

neozelan'dese [neoddzelan'dese] *ag* New Zealand *cpd* // *sm/f* New Zealander.

nep'pure *av*, *cong* = neanche.

'nerbo *sm* lash; (*fig*) strength, backbone; nerbo'ruto, a *ag* muscular; robust.

ne'retto *sm* (TIP) bold type.

'nero, a *ag* black; (*scuro*) dark // *sm* black; il Mar N~ the Black Sea.

nerva'tura *sf* (ANAT) nervous system; (BOT) veining; (ARCHIT, TECN) rib.

'nervo *sm* (ANAT) nerve; (BOT) vein; avere i ~i to be on edge; dare sui ~i a qn to get on sb's nerves; ner'voso, a *ag* nervous; (*irritabile*) irritable // *sm* (*fam*): far venire il nervoso a qn to get on sb's nerves.

'nespola *sf* (BOT) medlar; (*fig*) blow, punch; 'nespolo *sm* medlar tree.

'nesso *sm* connection, link.

nes'suno, a *det* (*dav sm* nessun + *C*, *V*, nessuno + *s impura*, gn, pn, ps, x, z; *dav sf* nessuna + *C*, nessun' + *V*) (*non uno*) no, *espressione negativa* + any; (*qualche*) any // *pronome* (*non uno*) no one, nobody, *espressione negativa* + any(one); (: *cosa*) none, *espressione negativa* + any; (*qualcuno*) anyone, anybody; (*qualcosa*) anything; non c'è nessun libro there isn't any book, there

is no book; hai ~a obiezione? do you have any objections?; ~ è venuto, non è venuto ~ nobody came; nessun altro no one else, nobody else; nessun'altra cosa nothing else; in nessun luogo nowhere.

net'tare *vt* to clean // *sm* ['nettare] nectar.

net'tezza [net'tettsa] *sf* cleanness, cleanliness; ~ urbana cleansing department.

'netto, a *ag* (*pulito*) clean; (*chiaro*) clear, clear-cut; (*deciso*) definite; (ECON) net.

nettur'bino *sm* dustman (*Brit*), garbage collector (*US*).

neu'rosi *sf* = nevrosi.

neu'trale *ag* neutral; neutralità *sf* neutrality; neutraliz'zare *vt* to neutralize.

'neutro, a *ag* neutral; (LING) neuter // *sm* (LING) neuter.

ne'vaio *sm* snowfield.

'neve *sf* snow; nevi'care *vb impers* to snow; nevi'cata *sf* snowfall.

ne'vischio [ne'viskjo] *sm* sleet.

ne'voso, a *ag* snowy; snow-covered.

nevral'gia [nevral'dʒia] *sf* neuralgia.

nevras'tenico, a, ci, che *ag* (MED) neurasthenic; (*fig*) hot-tempered.

ne'vrosi *sf* neurosis.

'nibbio *sm* (ZOOL) kite.

'nicchia ['nikkja] *sf* niche; (*naturale*) cavity, hollow.

nicchi'are [nik'kjare] *vi* to shilly-shally, hesitate.

'nichel ['nikel] *sm* nickel.

nico'tina *sf* nicotine.

'nido *sm* nest; a ~ d'ape (*tessuto etc*) honeycomb *cpd*.

ni'ente ◆ *pronome* 1 (*nessuna cosa*) nothing; ~ può fermarlo nothing can stop him; ~ di ~ absolutely nothing; nient'altro nothing else; nient'altro che nothing but, just, only; ~ affatto not at all, not in the least; come se ~ fosse as if nothing had happened; cose da ~ trivial matters; per ~ (*gratis*, *invano*) for nothing

2 (*qualcosa*): hai bisogno di ~? do you need anything?

3: non ... ~ nothing, *espressione negativa* + anything; non ho visto ~ I saw nothing, I didn't see anything; non ho ~ da dire I have nothing *o* haven't anything to say

◆ *sm* nothing; un bel ~ absolutely nothing; basta un ~ per farla piangere the slightest thing is enough to make her cry

◆ *av* (*in nessuna misura*): non ... ~ not ... at all; non è (per) ~ buono it isn't good at all.

nientedi'meno, niente'meno *av* actually, even // *escl* really!, I say!

'Nilo *sm*: il ~ the Nile.

'ninfa *sf* nymph.

nin'fea *sf* water lily.

ninna-'nanna sf lullaby.

'**ninnolo** sm (balocco) plaything; (gingillo) knick-knack.

ni'pote sm/f (di zii) nephew/niece; (di nonni) grandson/daughter, grandchild.

'**nitido, a** ag clear; (specchio) bright.

ni'trato sm nitrate.

'**nitrico, a, ci, che** ag nitric.

ni'trire vi to neigh.

ni'trito sm (di cavallo) neighing q; neigh; (CHIM) nitrite.

nitroglice'rina [nitroglitʃe'rina] sf nitroglycerine.

'**niveo, a** ag snow-white.

no av (risposta) no; vieni o ~? are you coming or not?; perché ~? why not?; lo conosciamo? — tu ~ ma io sì do we know him? — you don't but I do; verrai, ~? you'll come, won't you?

'**nobile** ag noble // sm/f noble, nobleman/woman; **nobili'are** ag noble; **nobiltà** sf nobility; (di azione etc) nobleness.

'**nocca, che** sf (ANAT) knuckle.

nocci'ola [not'tʃɔla] ag inv (colore) hazel, light brown // sf hazelnut.

'**nocciolo** ['nɔttʃolo] sm (di frutto) stone; (fig) heart, core; [not'tʃɔlo] (albero) hazel.

'**noce** ['notʃe] sm (albero) walnut tree // sf (frutto) walnut; ~ **moscata** nutmeg.

no'civo, a [no'tʃivo] ag harmful, noxious.

'**nodo** sm (di cravatta, legname, NAUT) knot; (AUT, FERR) junction; (MED, ASTR, BOT) node; (fig: legame) bond, tie; (: punto centrale) heart, crux; **avere un ~ alla gola** to have a lump in one's throat; **no'doso, a** ag (tronco) gnarled.

'**noi** pronome (soggetto) we; (oggetto: per dare rilievo, con preposizione) us; ~ **stessi(e)** we ourselves; (oggetto) ourselves.

'**noia** sf boredom; (disturbo, impaccio) bother q, trouble q; **avere qn/qc a ~** not to like sb/sth; **mi è venuto a ~** I'm tired of it; **dare ~ a** to annoy; **avere delle ~e con qn** to have trouble with sb.

noi'altri pronome we.

noi'oso, a ag boring; (fastidioso) annoying, troublesome.

noleggi'are [noled'dʒare] vt (prendere a noleggio) to hire (Brit), rent; (dare a noleggio) to hire out (Brit), rent (out); (aereo, nave) to charter; **no'leggio** sm hire (Brit), rental; charter.

'**nolo** sm hire (Brit), rental; charter; (per trasporto merci) freight; **prendere/dare a ~ qc** to hire/hire out sth.

'**nomade** ag nomadic // sm/f nomad.

'**nome** sm name; (LING) noun; **in/a ~ di** in the name of; **di ~** (chiamato) called, named; **conoscere qn di ~** to know sb by name; ~ **d'arte** stage name; ~ **di battesimo** Christian name; ~ **depositato** trade name; ~ **di famiglia** surname.

no'mea sf notoriety.

no'mignolo [no'miɲɲolo] sm nickname.

'**nomina** sf appointment.

nomi'nale ag nominal; (LING) noun cpd.

nomi'nare vt to name; (eleggere) to appoint; (citare) to mention.

nomina'tivo, a ag (LING) nominative; (ECON) registered // sm (LING: anche: **caso** ~) nominative (case); (AMM) name.

non av not // prefisso non-; vedi **affatto, appena** etc.

nonché [non'ke] cong (tanto più, tanto meno) let alone; (e inoltre) as well as.

noncu'rante ag: ~ (**di**) careless (of), indifferent (to); **noncu'ranza** sf carelessness, indifference.

nondi'meno cong (tuttavia) however; (nonostante) nevertheless.

'**nonno, a** sm/f grandfather/mother; (in senso più familiare) grandma/grandpa; ~**i** smpl grandparents.

non'nulla sm inv: **un** ~ nothing, a trifle.

'**nono, a** ag, sm ninth.

nonos'tante prep in spite of, notwithstanding // cong although, even though.

nontiscordardimé sm inv (BOT) forget-me-not.

nord sm North // ag inv north; northern; **il Mare del N~** the North Sea; **nor'dest** sm north-east; '**nordico, a, ci, che** ag nordic, northern European; **nor'dovest** sm north-west.

'**norma** sf (principio) norm; (regola) regulation, rule; (consuetudine) custom, rule; **a** ~ **di legge** according to law, as laid down by law.

nor'male ag normal; standard cpd; **normalità** sf normality; **normaliz'zare** vt to normalize, bring back to normal.

normal'mente av normally.

norve'gese [norve'dʒese] ag, sm/f, sm Norwegian.

Nor'vegia [nor'vedʒa] sf: **la** ~ Norway.

nostal'gia [nostal'dʒia] sf (di casa, paese) homesickness; (del passato) nostalgia; **nos'talgico, a, ci, che** ag homesick; nostalgic.

nos'trano, a ag local; national; home-produced.

'**nostro, a** det: **il(la)** ~(**a**) etc our // pronome: **il(la)** ~(**a**) etc ours // sm: **il** ~ our money; our belongings; **i** ~**i** our family; our own people; **è dei** ~**i** he's one of us.

'**nota** sf (segno) mark; (comunicazione scritta, MUS) note; (fattura) bill; (elenco) list; **degno di** ~ noteworthy, worthy of note.

no'tabile ag notable; (persona) important // sm prominent citizen.

no'taio sm notary.

no'tare vt (segnare: errori) to mark;

(*registrare*) to note (down), write down; (*rilevare, osservare*) to note, notice; farsi ~ to get o.s. noticed.

notazi'one [notat'tsjone] *sf* (*MUS*) notation.

no'tevole *ag* (*talento*) notable, remarkable; (*peso*) considerable.

no'tifica, che *sf* notification.

notifi'care *vt* (*DIR*): ~ qc a qn to notify sb of sth, give sb notice of sth.

no'tizia [no'tittsja] *sf* (piece of) news *sg*; (*informazione*) piece of information; ~e *sfpl* news *sg*; information *sg*; **notizi'ario** *sm* (*RADIO, TV, STAMPA*) news *sg*.

'noto, a *ag* (well-)known.

notorietà *sf* fame; notoriety.

no'torio, a *ag* well-known; (*peg*) notorious.

not'tambulo, a *sm/f* night-bird (*fig*).

not'tata *sf* night.

'notte *sf* night; di ~ at night; (*durante la notte*) in the night, during the night; **peggio che andar di ~** worse than ever; ~ **bianca** sleepless night; **notte'tempo** *av* at night; during the night.

not'turno, a *ag* nocturnal; (*servizio, guardiano*) night *cpd*.

no'vanta *num* ninety; **novan'tesimo, a** *num* ninetieth; **novan'tina** *sf*: una novantina (di) about ninety.

'nove *num* nine.

nove'cento [nove'tʃɛnto] *num* nine hundred // *sm*: il N~ the twentieth century.

no'vella *sf* (*LETTERATURA*) short story.

novel'lino, a *ag* (*pivello*) green, inexperienced.

no'vello, a *ag* (*piante, patate*) new; (*insalata, verdura*) early; (*sposo*) newly-married.

no'vembre *sm* November.

novi'lunio *sm* (*ASTR*) new moon.

novità *sf inv* novelty; (*innovazione*) innovation; (*cosa originale, insolita*) something new; (*notizia*) (piece of) news *sg*; le ~ della moda the latest fashions.

novizi'ato [novit'tsjato] *sm* (*REL*) novitiate; (*tirocinio*) apprenticeship.

no'vizio, a [no'vittsjo] *sm/f* (*REL*) novice; (*tirocinante*) beginner, apprentice.

nozi'one [not'tsjone] *sf* notion, idea; ~i *sfpl* basic knowledge *sg*, rudiments.

'nozze ['nɔttse] *sfpl* wedding *sg*, marriage *sg*; ~ d'argento/d'oro silver/golden wedding *sg*.

ns. *abbr* (*COMM*) = **nostro**.

'nube *sf* cloud; **nubi'fragio** *sm* cloudburst.

'nubile *ag* (*donna*) unmarried, single.

'nuca *sf* nape of the neck.

nucle'are *ag* nuclear.

'nucleo *sm* nucleus; (*gruppo*) team, unit, group; (*MIL, POLIZIA*) squad; il ~ familiare the family unit.

nu'dista, i, e *sm/f* nudist.

'nudo, a *ag* (*persona*) bare, naked, nude; (*membra*) bare, naked; (*montagna*) bare // *sm* (*ARTE*) nude.

'nugolo *sm*: un ~ di a whole host of.

'nulla *pronome, av* = **niente** // *sm*: il ~ nothing.

nulla'osta *sm inv* authorization.

nullità *sf inv* nullity; (*persona*) non-entity.

'nullo, a *ag* useless, worthless; (*DIR*) null (and void); (*SPORT*): **incontro** ~ draw.

nume'rale *ag, sm* numeral.

nume'rare *vt* to number; **numerazi'one** *sf* numbering; (*araba, decimale*) notation.

nu'merico, a, ci, che *ag* numerical.

'numero *sm* number; (*romano, arabo*) numeral; (*di spettacolo*) act, turn; ~ civico house number; **nume'roso, a** *ag* numerous, many; (*con sostantivo sg: adunanza etc*) large.

'nunzio ['nuntsjo] *sm* (*REL*) nuncio.

nu'ocere ['nwɔtʃere] *vi*: ~ a to harm, damage; **nuoci'uto, a** *pp di* **nuocere**.

nu'ora *sf* daughter-in-law.

nuo'tare *vi* to swim; (*galleggiare: oggetti*) to float; **nuota'tore, 'trice** *sm/f* swimmer; **nu'oto** *sm* swimming.

nu'ova *sf vedi* **nuovo**.

nuova'mente *av* again.

Nu'ova Ze'landa [-dze'landa] *sf*: la ~ New Zealand.

nu'ovo, a *ag* new // *sf* (*notizia*) (piece of) news *sg*; di ~ again; ~ **fiammante** o **di zecca** brand-new.

nutri'ente *ag* nutritious, nourishing.

nutri'mento *sm* food, nourishment.

nu'trire *vt* to feed; (*fig: sentimenti*) to harbour, nurse; **nutri'tivo, a** *ag* nutritional; (*alimento*) nutritious; **nutrizi'one** *sf* nutrition.

'nuvola *sf* cloud; **'nuvolo, a** *ag*, **nuvo'loso, a** *ag* cloudy.

nuzi'ale [nut'tsjale] *ag* nuptial; wedding *cpd*.

O

o *cong* (*dav V spesso* **od**) or; ~ ... ~ either ... or; ~ **l'uno** ~ **l'altro** either (of them).

O. *abbr* (= *ovest*) W.

'oasi *sf inv* oasis.

obbedi'ente *etc vedi* **ubbidiente** *etc*.

obbli'gare *vt* (*costringere*): ~ qn a fare to force o oblige sb to do; (*DIR*) to bind; ~rsi *vr*: ~rsi a fare to undertake to do; **obbli'gato, a** *ag* (*costretto, grato*) obliged; (*percorso, tappa*) set, fixed; **obbliga'torio, a** *ag* compulsory, obligatory; **obbligazi'one** *sf* obligation; (*COMM*) bond, debenture; **'obbligo, ghi**

sm obligation; (*dovere*) duty; **avere l'obbligo di fare, essere nell'obbligo di fare** to be obliged to do; **essere d'obbligo** (*discorso, applauso*) to be called for.

ob'brobrio *sm* disgrace; (*fig*) mess, eyesore.

o'beso, a *ag* obese.

obiet'tare *vt*: ~ **che** to object that; ~ **su qc** to object to sth, raise objections concerning sth.

obiet'tivo, a *ag* objective // *sm* (*OTTICA, FOT*) lens *sg*, objective; (*MIL, fig*) objective.

obiet'tore *sm* objector; ~ **di coscienza** conscientious objector.

obiezi'one [objet'tsjone] *sf* objection.

obi'torio *sm* morgue, mortuary.

o'bliquo, a *ag* oblique; (*inclinato*) slanting; (*fig*) devious, underhand; **sguardo** ~ sidelong glance.

oblò *sm inv* porthole.

o'blungo, a, ghi, ghe *ag* oblong.

'oboe *sm* (*MUS*) oboe.

obsole'scenza [obsolef'fentsa] *sf* (*ECON*) obsolescence.

'oca, pl 'oche *sf* goose.

occasi'one *sf* (*caso favorevole*) opportunity; (*causa, motivo, circostanza*) occasion; (*COMM*) bargain; **d'~** (*a buon prezzo*) bargain *cpd*; (*usato*) secondhand.

occhi'aia [ok'kjaja] *sf* eye socket; ~**e** *sfpl* shadows (under the eyes).

occhi'ali [ok'kjali] *smpl* glasses, spectacles; ~ **da sole** sunglasses.

occhi'ata [ok'kjata] *sf* look, glance; **dare un'~ a** to have a look at.

occhieggi'are [okkjed'dʒare] *vi* (*apparire qua e là*) to peep (out).

occhi'ello [ok'kjello] *sm* buttonhole; (*asola*) eyelet.

'occhio ['ɔkkjo] *sm* eye; ~! careful!, watch out!; **a** ~ **nudo** with the naked eye; **a quattr'~i** privately, tête-à-tête; **dare all'~ o nell'~ a qn** to catch sb's eye; **fare l'~ a qc** to get used to sth; **tenere d'~ qn** to keep an eye on sb; **vedere di buon/mal** ~ **qc** to look favourably/unfavourably on sth.

occhio'lino [okkjo'lino] *sm*: **fare l'~ a qn** to wink at sb.

occiden'tale [ottfiden'tale] *ag* western // *sm/f* Westerner.

occi'dente [ottfi'dɛnte] *sm* west; (*POL*): **l'O~** the West; **a** ~ in the west.

oc'cipite [ot'tfipite] *sm* back of the head, occiput.

oc'cludere *vt* to block; **occlusi'one** *sf* blockage, obstruction; **oc'cluso, a** *pp di* **occludere**.

occor'rente *ag* necessary // *sm* all that is necessary.

occor'renza [okkor'rentsa] *sf* necessity, need; **all'~** in case of need.

oc'correre *vi* to be needed, be required //

vb impers: **occorre farlo** it must be done; **occorre che tu parta** you must leave, you'll have to leave; **mi occorrono i soldi** I need the money; **oc'corso, a** *pp di* **occorrere**.

occul'tare *vt* to hide, conceal.

oc'culto, a *ag* hidden, concealed; (*scienze, forze*) occult.

occu'pare *vt* to occupy; (*manodopera*) to employ; (*ingombrare*) to occupy, take up; ~**rsi** *vr* to occupy o.s., keep o.s. busy; (*impiegarsi*) to get a job; ~**rsi di** (*interessarsi*) to take an interest in; (*prendersi cura di*) to look after, take care of; **occu'pato, a** *ag* (*MIL, POL*) occupied; (*persona: affaccendato*) busy; (*posto, sedia*) taken; (*toilette, TEL*) engaged; **occupazi'one** *sf* occupation; (*impiego, lavoro*) job; (*ECON*) employment.

o'ceano [o'tfeano] *sm* ocean.

'ocra *sf* ochre.

ocu'lare *ag* ocular, eye *cpd*; **testimone** ~ eye witness.

ocu'lato, a *ag* (*attento*) cautious, prudent; (*accorto*) shrewd.

ocu'lista, i, e *sm/f* eye specialist, oculist.

'ode *sf* ode.

odi'are *vt* to hate, detest.

odi'erno, a *ag* today's, of today; (*attuale*) present.

'odio *sm* hatred; **avere in** ~ **qc/qn** to hate o detest sth/sb; **odi'oso, a** *ag* hateful, odious.

odo'rare *vt* (*annusare*) to smell; (*profumare*) to perfume, scent // *vi*: ~ (*di*) to smell (of); **odo'rato** *sm* sense of smell.

o'dore *sm* smell; **gli ~i** *smpl* (*CUC*) (aromatic) herbs; **odo'roso, a** *ag* sweet-smelling.

of'fendere *vt* to offend; (*violare*) to break, violate; (*insultare*) to insult; (*ferire*) to hurt; ~**rsi** *vr* (*con senso reciproco*) to insult one another; (*risentirsi*): ~**rsi (di)** to take offence (at), be offended (by); **offen'sivo, a** *ag*, *sf* offensive.

offe'rente *sm* (*in aste*): **al maggior** ~ to the highest bidder.

of'ferto, a *pp di* **offrire** // *sf* offer; (*donazione, anche REL*) offering; (*in gara d'appalto*) tender; (*in aste*) bid; (*ECON*) supply; "~**e d'impiego**" "situations vacant"; **fare un'~a** to make an offer; **to tender**; **to bid**.

of'feso, a *pp di* **offendere** // *ag* offended; (*fisicamente*) hurt, injured // *sm/f* offended party // *sf* insult, affront; (*MIL*) attack; (*DIR*) offence; **essere** ~ **con qn** to be annoyed with sb; **parte** ~**a** (*DIR*) plaintiff.

offi'cina [offi'tfina] *sf* workshop.

of'frire *vt* to offer; ~**rsi** *vr* (*proporsi*) to

offer (o.s.), volunteer; (occasione) to present itself; (esporsi): ~rsi a to expose o.s. to; ti offro da bere I'll buy you a drink.

offus'care vt to obscure, darken; (fig: intelletto) to dim, cloud; (: fama) to obscure, overshadow; ~rsi vr to grow dark; to cloud, grow dim; to be obscured.

of'talmico, a, ci, che ag ophthalmic.

oggettività [oddʒettivi'ta] sf objectivity.

ogget'tivo, a [oddʒet'tivo] ag objective.

og'getto [od'dʒetto] sm object; (materia, argomento) subject (matter); ~i smarriti lost property sg.

'oggi ['ɔddʒi] av, sm today; ~ a otto a week today; oggigi'orno av nowadays.

o'giva [o'dʒiva] sf ogive, pointed arch.

'ogni ['ɔɲɲi] det every, each; (tutti) all; (con valore distributivo) every; ~ uomo è mortale all men are mortal; viene ~ due giorni he comes every two days; ~ cosa everything; ad ~ costo at all costs, at any price; in ~ luogo everywhere; ~ tanto every so often; ~ volta che every time that.

Ognis'santi [oɲɲis'santi] sm All Saints' Day.

o'gnuno [oɲ'ɲuno] pronome everyone, everybody.

'ohi escl oh!; (esprimente dolore) ow!

ohimè escl oh dear!

O'landa sf: l'~ Holland; olan'dese ag Dutch // sm (LING) Dutch // sm/f Dutchman/woman; gli Olandesi the Dutch.

oleo'dotto sm oil pipeline.

ole'oso, a ag oily; (che contiene olio) oil-yielding.

ol'fatto sm sense of smell.

oli'are vt to oil.

oli'era sf oil cruet.

olim'piadi sfpl Olympic games; o'limpico, a, ci, che ag Olympic.

'olio sm oil; sott'~ (CUC) in oil; ~ di fegato di merluzzo cod liver oil; ~ d'oliva olive oil; ~ di semi vegetable oil.

o'liva sf olive; oli'vastro, a ag olive-(coloured); (carnagione) sallow; oli'veto sm olive grove; o'livo sm olive tree.

'olmo sm elm.

oltraggi'are [oltrad'dʒare] vt to outrage; to offend gravely.

ol'traggio [ol'traddʒo] sm outrage; offence, insult; ~ a pubblico ufficiale (DIR) insulting a public official; ~ al pudore (DIR) indecent behaviour; ol-traggi'oso, a ag offensive.

ol'tralpe av beyond the Alps.

ol'tranza [ol'trantsa] sf: a ~ to the last, to the bitter end.

'oltre av (più in là) further; (di più: aspettare) longer, more // prep (di là da) beyond, over, on the other side of; (più di) more than, over; (in aggiunta a) besides; (eccetto): ~ a except, apart from; oltre'mare av overseas; ol-trepas'sare vt to go beyond, exceed.

o'maggio [o'maddʒo] sm (dono) gift; (segno di rispetto) homage, tribute; ~i smpl (complimenti) respects; rendere ~ a to pay homage o tribute to; in ~ (copia, biglietto) complimentary.

ombeli'cale ag umbilical.

ombe'lico, chi sm navel.

'ombra sf (zona non assolata, fantasma) shade; (sagoma scura) shadow; sedere all'~ to sit in the shade; restare nell'~ (fig) to remain in obscurity.

ombreggi'are [ombred'dʒare] vt to shade.

om'brello sm umbrella; ombrel'lone sm beach umbrella.

om'bretto sm eyeshadow.

om'broso, a ag shady, shaded; (cavallo) nervous, skittish; (persona) touchy, easily offended.

ome'lia sf (REL) homily, sermon.

omeopa'tia sf homoeopathy.

omertà sf conspiracy of silence.

o'messo, a pp di omettere.

o'mettere vt to omit, leave out; ~ di fare o fai to omit to do.

omi'cida, i, e [omi'tʃida] ag homicidal, murderous // sm/f murderer/eress.

omi'cidio [omi'tʃidjo] sm murder; ~ colposo culpable homicide.

omissi'one sf omission; ~ di soccorso (DIR) failure to stop and give assistance.

omogeneiz'zato [omodʒeneid'dzato] sm baby food.

omo'geneo, a [omo'dʒɛneo] ag homogeneous.

omolo'gare vt to approve, recognize; to ratify.

o'monimo, a sm/f namesake // sm (LING) homonym.

omosessu'ale ag, sm/f homosexual.

'oncia, ce [ˈontʃa] sf ounce.

'onda sf wave; mettere o mandare in ~ (RADIO, TV) to broadcast; andare in ~ (RADIO, TV) to go on the air; ~e corte/medie/lunghe short/medium/long wave; on'data sf wave, billow; (fig) wave, surge; a ondate in waves; ondata di caldo heatwave.

'onde cong (affinché: con il congiuntivo) so that, in order that; (: con l'infinito) so as to, in order to.

ondeggi'are [onded'dʒare] vi (acqua) to ripple; (muoversi sulle onde: barca) to rock, roll; (fig: muoversi come le onde, barcollare) to sway; (: essere incerto) to waver.

ondula'torio, a ag undulating; (FISICA) undulatory, wave cpd.

ondulazi'one [ondulat'tsjone] sf undulation; (acconciatura) wave.

'onere sm burden; ~i fiscali taxes; one'roso, a ag (fig) heavy, onerous.

onestà *sf* honesty.

o'nesto, a *ag* (*probo, retto*) honest; (*giusto*) fair; (*casto*) chaste, virtuous.

'onice [ˈɔnitʃe] *sf* onyx.

onnipo'tente *ag* omnipotent.

onnisci'ente [onniʃˈʃɛnte] *ag* omniscient.

onniveg'gente [onnivedˈdʒɛnte] *ag* all-seeing.

ono'mastico, ci *sm* name-day.

ono'ranze [onoˈrantse] *sfpl* honours.

ono'rare *vt* to honour; (*far onore a*) to do credit to; **~rsi** *vr*: **~rsi di** to feel honoured at, be proud of.

ono'rario, a *ag* honorary // *sm* fee.

o'nore *sm* honour; **in ~ di** in honour of; **fare gli ~i di casa** to play host (*o* hostess); **fare ~ a** to honour; (*pranzo*) to do justice to; (*famiglia*) to be a credit to; **farsi ~** to distinguish o.s.; **ono'revole** *ag* honourable // *sm/f* (*POL*) ≈ Member of Parliament (*Brit*), ≈ Congressman/woman (*US*); **onorifi'cenza** *sf* honour; decoration; **ono'rifico, a, ci, che** *ag* honorary.

'onta *sf* shame, disgrace.

'O.N.U. [ˈɔnu] *sigla f* (= *Organizzazione delle Nazioni Unite*) UN, UNO.

o'paco, a, chi, che *ag* (*vetro*) opaque; (*metallo*) dull, matt.

o'pale *sm o f* opal.

'opera *sf* work; (*azione rilevante*) action, deed, work; (*MUS*) work; opus; (: *melodramma*) opera; (: *teatro*) opera house; (*ente*) institution, organization; **~ d'arte** work of art; **~ lirica** (grand) opera; **~e pubbliche** public works.

ope'raio, a *ag* working-class; workers' // *sm/f* worker; **classe ~a** working class.

ope'rare *vt* to carry out, make; (*MED*) to operate on // *vi* to operate, work; (*rimedio*) to act, work; (*MED*) to operate; **~rsi** *vr* to occur, take place; (*MED*) to have an operation; **~rsi d'appendicite** to have one's appendix out; **opera'tivo, a** *ag* operative, operating; **opera'tore, 'trice** *sm/f* operator; (*TV, CINEMA*) cameraman; **operatore economico** agent, broker; **operatore turistico** tour operator; **opera'torio, a** *ag* (*MED*) operating; **operazi'one** *sf* operation.

ope'retta *sf* (*MUS*) operetta, light opera.

ope'roso, a *ag* busy, active, hardworking.

opi'ficio [opiˈfitʃo] *sm* factory, works *pl*.

opini'one *sf* opinion.

'oppio *sm* opium.

oppo'nente *ag* opposing // *sm/f* opponent.

op'porre *vt* to oppose; **opporsi** *vr*: **opporsi (a qc)** to oppose (sth); to object (to sth); **~ resistenza/un rifiuto** to offer resistance/refuse.

opportu'nista, i, e *sm/f* opportunist.

opportunità *sf inv* opportunity; (*convenienza*) opportuneness, timeliness.

oppor'tuno, a *ag* timely, opportune.

opposi'tore, 'trice *sm/f* opposer, opponent.

opposizi'one [oppozitˈtsjone] *sf* opposition; (*DIR*) objection.

op'posto, a *pp di* **opporre** // *ag* opposite; (*opinioni*) conflicting // *sm* opposite, contrary; **all'~** on the contrary.

oppressi'one *sf* oppression.

oppres'sivo, a *ag* oppressive.

op'presso, a *pp di* **opprimere**.

oppres'sore *sm* oppressor.

op'primere *vt* (*premere, gravare*) to weigh down; (*estenuare: sog: caldo*) to suffocate, oppress; (*tiranneggiare: popolo*) to oppress.

oppu'gnare [oppuɲˈɲare] *vt* (*fig*) to refute.

op'pure *cong* or (else).

op'tare *vi*: **~ per** to opt for.

o'puscolo *sm* booklet, pamphlet.

opzi'one [opˈtsjone] *sf* option.

'ora *sf* (*60 minuti*) hour; (*momento*) time; **che ~ è?, che ~e sono?** what time is it?; **non veder l'~ di fare** to long to do, look forward to doing; **di buon'~** early; **alla buon'~!** at last!; **~ legale** *o* **estiva** summer time (*Brit*), daylight saving time (*US*); **~ locale** local time; **~ di punta** (*AUT*) rush hour // *av* (*adesso*) now; (*poco fa*): **è uscito proprio ~** he's just gone out; (*tra poco*) presently, in a minute; (*correlativo*): **~ ... ~** now ... now; **d'~ in avanti** *o* **poi** from now on; **or ~** just now, a moment ago; **5 anni** *o* **sono 5 years ago**; **~ come ~** right now, at present.

o'racolo *sm* oracle.

'orafo *sm* goldsmith.

o'rale *ag, sm* oral.

ora'mai *av* = **ormai**.

o'rario, a *ag* hourly; (*fuso, segnale*) time *cpd*; (*velocità*) per hour // *sm* timetable, schedule; (*di ufficio, visite etc*) hours *pl*, time(s *pl*).

ora'tore, 'trice *sm/f* speaker; orator

ora'torio, a *ag* oratorical // *sm* (*REL*) oratory; (*MUS*) oratorio // *sf* (*arte*) oratory.

ora'zione [oratˈtsjone] *sf* (*REL*) prayer; (*discorso*) speech, oration.

or'bene *cong* so, well (then).

'orbita *sf* (*ASTR, FISICA*) orbit; (*ANAT*) (eye-)socket.

or'chestra [orˈkɛstra] *sf* orchestra; **orches'trale** *ag* orchestral // *sm/f* orchestra player; **orches'trare** *vt* to orchestrate; (*fig*) to mount, stage-manage.

orchi'dea [orkiˈdɛa] *sf* orchid.

'orco, chi *sm* ogre.

'orda *sf* horde.

or'digno [orˈdiɲɲo] *sm* (*esplosivo*) explosive device.

ordi'nale *ag, sm* ordinal.

ordina'mento sm order, arrangement; (regolamento) regulations pl, rules pl; ~ scolastico/giuridico education/legal system.

ordi'nanza [ordi'nantsa] sf (DIR, MIL) order; (persona: MIL) orderly, batman; d'~ (MIL) regulation cpd.

ordi'nare vt (mettere in ordine) to arrange, organize; (COMM) to order; (prescrivere: medicina) to prescribe; (comandare): ~ a qn di fare qc to order o command sb to do sth; (REL) to ordain.

ordi'nario, a ag (comune) ordinary; everyday; (standard); (grossolano) coarse, common // sm ordinary; (INS: di università) full professor.

ordi'nato, a ag tidy, orderly.

ordinazi'one [ordinat'tsjone] sf (COMM) order; (REL) ordination; eseguire qc su ~ to make sth to order.

'ordine sm order; (carattere): d'~ pratico of a practical nature; all'~ (COMM: assegno) to order; di prim'~ first-class; fino a nuovo ~ until further notice; essere in ~ (documenti) to be in order; (stanza, persona) to be tidy; mettere in ~ to put in order, tidy (up); ~ del giorno (di seduta) agenda; (MIL) order of the day; ~ di pagamento (COMM) order for payment; l'~ pubblico law and order; ~i (sacri) (REL) holy orders.

or'dire vt (fig) to plot, scheme; **or'dito** sm (di tessuto) warp.

orec'chino [orek'kino] sm earring.

o'recchio [o'rekkjo], pl(f) **o'recchie** sm (ANAT) ear.

orecchi'oni [orek'kjoni] smpl (MED) mumps sg.

o'refice [o'refitʃe] sm goldsmith; jeweller; **orefice'ria** sf (arte) goldsmith's art; (negozio) jeweller's (shop).

'orfano, a ag orphan(ed) // sm/f orphan; ~ di padre/madre fatherless/motherless; **orfano'trofio** sm orphanage.

orga'netto sm barrel organ; (fam: armonica a bocca) mouth organ; (: fisarmonica) accordion.

or'ganico, a, ci, che ag organic // sm personnel, staff.

organi'gramma, i sm organization chart.

orga'nismo sm (BIOL) organism; (corpo umano) body; (AMM) body, organism.

organiz'zare [organid'dzare] vt to organize; ~rsi vr to get organized; **organizza'tore, 'trice** ag organizing // sm/f organizer; **organizzazi'one** sf organization.

'organo sm organ; (di congegno) part; (portavoce) spokesman, mouthpiece.

or'gasmo sm (FISIOL) orgasm; (fig) agitation, anxiety.

'orgia, ge ['ɔrdʒa] sf orgy.

or'goglio [or'gɔʎʎo] sm pride; **orgogli'oso, a** ag proud.

orien'tale ag oriental; eastern; east.

orienta'mento sm positioning; orientation; direction; senso di ~ sense of direction; perdere l'~ to lose one's bearings; ~ professionale careers guidance.

orien'tare vt (situare) to position; (fig) to direct, orientate; ~rsi vr to find one's bearings; (fig: tendere) to tend, lean; (: indirizzarsi): ~rsi verso to take up, go in for.

ori'ente sm east; l'O~ the East, the Orient; a ~ in the east.

o'rigano sm oregano.

origi'nale [oridʒi'nale] ag original; (bizzarro) eccentric // sm original; **originalità** sf originality; eccentricity.

origi'nare [oridʒi'nare] vt to bring about, produce // vi: ~ da to arise o spring from.

origi'nario, a [oridʒi'narjo] ag original; essere ~ di to be a native of; (provenire da) to originate from; to be native to.

o'rigine [o'ridʒine] sf origin; all'~ originally; d'~ inglese of English origin; dare ~ a to give rise to.

origli'are [oriʎ'ʎare] vi: ~ (a) to eavesdrop (on).

o'rina sf urine; **ori'nale** sm chamberpot.

ori'nare vi to urinate // vt to pass; **orina'toio** sm (public) urinal.

ori'undo, a ag: essere ~ di Milano etc to be of Milanese etc extraction o origin // sm/f person of foreign extraction o origin.

orizzon'tale [oriddzon'tale] ag horizontal.

oriz'zonte [orid'dzonte] sm horizon.

or'lare vt to hem.

'orlo sm edge, border; (di recipiente) rim, brim; (di vestito etc) hem.

'orma sf (di persona) footprint; (di animale) track; (impronta, traccia) mark, trace.

or'mai av by now, by this time; (adesso) now; (quasi) almost, nearly.

ormeggi'are [ormed'dzare] vt (NAUT) to moor; **or'meggio** sm (atto) mooring q; (luogo) moorings pl.

or'mone sm hormone.

ornamen'tale ag ornamental, decorative.

orna'mento sm ornament, decoration.

or'nare vt to adorn, decorate; ~rsi vr: ~rsi (di) to deck o.s. (out) (with); **or'nato, a** ag ornate.

ornitolo'gia [ornitolo'dʒia] sf ornithology.

'oro sm gold; d'~, in ~ gold cpd; d'~ (colore, occasione) golden; (persona) marvellous.

orologe'ria [orolodʒe'ria] sf watchmaking q; watchmaker's (shop); clock-

maker's (shop); **bomba a ~** time bomb.
orologi'aio [orolo'dʒajo] *sm* watchmaker; clockmaker.
oro'logio [oro'lɔdʒo] *sm* clock; (*da tasca, da polso*) watch; **~ da polso** wristwatch; **~ al quarzo** quartz watch; **~ a sveglia** alarm clock.
o'roscopo *sm* horoscope.
or'rendo, a *ag* (*spaventoso*) horrible, awful; (*bruttissimo*) hideous.
or'ribile *ag* horrible.
'orrido, a *ag* fearful, horrid.
orripi'lante *ag* hair-raising, horrifying.
or'rore *sm* horror; **avere in ~** qn/qc to loathe *o* detest sb/sth; **mi fanno ~** I loathe *o* detest them.
orsacchi'otto [orsak'kjɔtto] *sm* teddy bear.
'orso *sm* bear; **~ bruno/bianco** brown/polar bear.
or'taggio [or'taddʒo] *sm* vegetable.
or'tica, che *sf* (stinging) nettle.
orti'caria *sf* nettle rash.
orticol'tura *sf* horticulture.
'orto *sm* vegetable garden, kitchen garden; (*AGR*) market garden (*Brit*), truck farm (*US*).
orto'dosso, a *ag* orthodox.
ortogra'fia [ortogra'fia] *sf* spelling.
orto'lano, a *sm/f* (*venditore*) greengrocer (*Brit*), produce dealer (*US*).
ortope'dia *sf* orthopaedics *sg*; **orto'pedico, a, ci, che** *ag* orthopaedic // *sm* orthopaedic specialist.
orzai'olo [ordza'jɔlo] *sm* (*MED*) stye.
or'zata [or'dzata] *sf* barley water.
'orzo [ordzo] *sm* barley.
o'sare *vt, vi* to dare; **~ fare** to dare (to) do.
oscenità [oʃʃeni'ta] *sf inv* obscenity.
o'sceno, a [oʃ'ʃeno] *ag* obscene; (*ripugnante*) ghastly.
oscil'lare [oʃʃil'lare] *vi* (*pendolo*) to swing; (*dondolare: al vento etc*) to rock; (*variare*) to fluctuate; (*TECN*) to oscillate; (*fig*): **~ fra** to waver *o* hesitate between; **oscillazi'one** *sf* oscillation; (*di prezzi, temperatura*) fluctuation.
oscura'mento *sm* darkening; obscuring; (*in tempo di guerra*) blackout.
oscu'rare *vt* to darken, obscure; (*fig*) to obscure; **~rsi** *vr* (*cielo*) to darken, cloud over; (*persona*): **si oscurò in volto** his face clouded over.
os'curo, a *ag* dark; (*fig*) obscure; humble, lowly // *sm*: **all'~** in the dark; **tenere qn all'~ di** qc to keep sb in the dark about sth.
ospe'dale *sm* hospital; **ospedali'ero, a** *ag* hospital *cpd*.
ospi'tale *ag* hospitable; **ospitalità** *sf* hospitality.
ospi'tare *vt* to give hospitality to; (*sog: albergo*) to accommodate.
'ospite *sm/f* (*persona che ospita*) host/

hostess; (*persona ospitata*) guest.
os'pizio [os'pittsjo] *sm* (*per vecchi etc*) home.
'ossa *sfpl vedi* **osso**.
ossa'tura *sf* (*ANAT*) skeletal structure, frame; (*TECN, fig*) framework.
'osseo, a *ag* bony; (*tessuto etc*) bone *cpd*.
os'sequio, a *ag* deference, respect; **~i** *smpl* (*saluto*) respects, regards; **ossequi'oso, a** *ag* obsequious.
osser'vanza [osser'vantsa] *sf* observance.
osser'vare *vt* to observe, watch; (*esaminare*) to examine; (*notare, rilevare*) to notice, observe; (*DIR: la legge*) to observe, respect; (*mantenere: silenzio*) to keep, observe; **far ~** qc a qn to point sth out to sb; **osserva'tore, 'trice** *ag* observant, perceptive // *sm/f* observer; **osserva'torio** *sm* (*ASTR*) observatory; (*MIL*) observation post; **osservazi'one** *sf* observation; (*di legge etc*) observance; (*considerazione critica*) observation, remark; (*rimprovero*) reproof; **in osservazione** under observation.
osses'sionare *vt* to obsess, haunt; (*tormentare*) to torment, harass.
osses'sione *sf* obsession
os'sesso, a *ag* (*spiritato*) possessed.
os'sia *cong* that is, to be precise.
ossi'dare *vt*, **~rsi** *vr* to oxidize.
'ossido *sm* oxide; **~ di carbonio** carbon monoxide.
ossige'nare [ossidʒe'nare] *vt* to oxygenate; (*decolorare*) to bleach; **acqua ossigenata** hydrogen peroxide.
os'sigeno *sm* oxygen.
'osso *sm* (*pl(f)* **ossa** *nel senso ANAT*) bone; **d'~** (*bottone etc*) of bone, bone *cpd*.
osso'buco, *pl* **ossi'buchi** *sm* (*CUC*) marrowbone; (: *piatto*) stew made with knuckle of veal in tomato sauce.
os'suto, a *ag* bony.
ostaco'lare *vt* to block, obstruct.
os'tacolo *sm* obstacle; (*EQUITAZIONE*) hurdle, jump.
os'taggio [os'taddʒo] *sm* hostage.
'oste, os'tessa *sm/f* innkeeper.
osteggi'are [osted'dʒare] *vt* to oppose, be opposed to.
os'tello *sm*: **~ della gioventù** youth hostel.
osten'tare *vt* to make a show of, flaunt; **ostentazi'one** *sf* ostentation, show.
oste'ria *sf* inn.
os'tessa *sf vedi* **oste**.
os'tetrico, a, ci, che *ag* obstetric // *sm* obstetrician // *sf* midwife.
'ostia *sf* (*REL*) host; (*per medicinali*) wafer.
'ostico, a, ci, che *ag* (*fig*) harsh; hard, difficult; unpleasant.
os'tile *ag* hostile; **ostilità** *sf inv* hostility // *sfpl* (*MIL*) hostilities.

osti'narsi *vr* to insist, dig one's heels in; ~ a fare to persist (obstinately) in doing; **osti'nato, a** *ag (caparbio)* obstinate; *(tenace)* persistent, determined; **ostinazi'one** *sf* obstinacy; persistence.

ostra'cismo [ostra'tʃizmo] *sm* ostracism.

'ostrica, che *sf* oyster.

ostru'ire *vt* to obstruct; block; **ostruzi'one** *sf* obstruction, blockage.

'otre *sm (recipiente)* goatskin.

ottago'nale *ag* octagonal.

ot'tagono *sm* octagon.

ot'tanta *num* eighty; **ottan'tesimo, a** *num* eightieth; **ottan'tina** *sf*: una ottantina (di) about eighty.

ot'tavo, a *num* eighth // *sf* octave.

ottempe'rare *vi*: ~ a to comply with, obey.

ottene'brare *vt* to darken; *(fig)* to cloud.

otte'nere *vt* to obtain, get; *(risultato)* to achieve, obtain.

'ottico, a, ci, che *ag (della vista: nervo)* optic; *(dell'ottica)* optical // *sm* optician // *sf (scienza)* optics *sg*; *(FOT: lenti, prismi etc)* optics *pl.*

ottima'mente *av* excellently, very well.

otti'mismo *sm* optimism; **otti'mista, i, e** *sm/f* optimist.

'ottimo, a *ag* excellent, very good.

'otto *num* eight.

ot'tobre *sm* October.

otto'cento [otto'tʃɛnto] *num* eight hundred // *sm*: l'O~ the nineteenth century.

ot'tone *sm* brass; gli ~i *(MUS)* the brass.

ot'tundere *vt (fig)* to dull.

ottu'rare *vt* to close (up); *(dente)* to fill; **ottura'tore** *sm (FOT)* shutter; *(nelle armi)* breechblock; **otturazi'one** *sf* closing (up); *(dentaria)* filling.

ot'tuso, a *pp di* **ottundere** // *ag (MAT, fig)* obtuse; *(suono)* dull.

o'vaia *sf*, **o'vaio** *sm (ANAT)* ovary.

o'vale *ag*, *sm* oval.

o'vatta *sf* cotton wool; *(per imbottire)* padding, wadding; **ovat'tare** *vt (fig: smorzare)* to muffle.

ovazi'one [ovat'tsjone] *sf* ovation.

'ovest *sm* west.

o'vile *sm* pen, enclosure.

o'vino, a *ag* sheep *cpd*, ovine.

ovulazi'one [ovulat'tsjone] *sf* ovulation.

'ovulo *sm (FISIOL)* ovum.

o'vunque *av* = **dovunque**.

ov'vero *cong (ossia)* that is, to be precise; *(oppure)* or (else).

ovvi'are *vi*: ~ a to obviate.

'ovvio, a *ag* obvious.

ozi'are [ot'tsjare] *vi* to laze, idle.

'ozio ['ɔttsjo] *sm* idleness; *(tempo libero)* leisure; ore d'~ leisure time; stare in ~ to be idle; **ozi'oso, a** *ag* idle.

o'zono [o'dzɔno] *sm* ozone.

P

pa'cato, a *ag* quiet, calm.

pac'chetto [pak'ketto] *sm* packet; ~ azionario *(COMM)* shareholding.

'pacco, chi *sm* parcel; *(involto)* bundle.

'pace ['patʃe] *sf* peace; darsi ~ to resign o.s.

pacifi'care [patʃifi'kare] *vt (riconciliare)* to reconcile, make peace between; *(mettere in pace)* to pacify.

pa'cifico, a, ci, che [pa'tʃi:fiko] *ag (persona)* peaceable; *(vita)* peaceful; *(fig: indiscusso)* indisputable; *(: ovvio)* obvious, clear // *sm*: il P~, l'Oceano P~ the Pacific (Ocean).

paci'fista, i, e [patʃi'fista] *sm/f* pacifist.

pa'della *sf* frying pan; *(per infermi)* bedpan.

padigli'one [padiʎ'ʎone] *sm* pavilion; *(AUT)* roof.

'Padova *sf* Padua.

'padre *sm* father; ~i *smpl (antenati)* forefathers; **pa'drino** *sm* godfather.

padro'nanza [padro'nantsa] *sf* command, mastery.

pa'drone, a *sm/f* master/mistress; *(proprietario)* owner; *(datore di lavoro)* employer; essere ~ di sé to be in control of o.s.; ~ di casa master/mistress of the house; *(per gli inquilini)* landlord/lady; **padroneggi'are** *vt (fig: sentimenti)* to master, control; *(: materia)* to master, know thoroughly; **padroneggiarsi** *vr* to control o.s.

pae'saggio [pae'zaddʒo] *sm* landscape.

pae'sano, a *ag* country *cpd* // *sm/f* villager; countryman/woman.

pa'ese *sm (nazione)* country, nation; *(terra)* country, land; *(villaggio)* village; ~ di provenienza country of origin; i P~i Bassi the Netherlands.

paf'futo, a *ag* chubby, plump.

'paga, ghe *sf* pay, wages *pl.*

paga'mento *sm* payment.

pa'gano, a *ag*, *sm/f* pagan.

pa'gare *vt* to pay; *(acquisto, fig: colpa)* to pay for; *(contraccambiare)* to repay, pay back // *vi* to pay; quanto l'hai pagato? how much did you pay for it?; ~ con carta di credito to pay by credit card; ~ in contanti to pay cash.

pa'gella [pa'dʒella] *sf (INS)* report card.

'paggio ['paddʒo] *sm* page(boy).

pagherò [page'rɔ] *sm inv* acknowledgement of a debt, IOU.

'pagina ['padʒina] *sf* page.

'paglia ['paʎʎa] *sf* straw.

pagliac'cetto [paʎʎat'tʃetto] *sm (per bambini)* rompers *pl.*

pagli'accio [paʎ'ʎattʃo] *sm* clown.

pagli'etta [paʎ'ʎetta] *sf (cappello per*

uomo) (straw) boater; (_per tegami etc_) steel wool.

pa'gnotta [paɲ'nɔtta] _sf_ round loaf.

'paio, _pl_(_f_) **'paia** _sm_ pair; **un ~ di** (_alcuni_) a couple of.

pai'olo, **paiu'olo** _sm_ (copper) pot.

'pala _sf_ shovel; (_di remo, ventilatore, elica_) blade; (_di ruota_) paddle.

pa'lato _sm_ palate.

pa'lazzo [pa'lattso] _sm_ (_reggia_) palace; (_edificio_) building; **~ di giustizia** courthouse; **~ dello sport** sports stadium.

pal'chetto [pal'ketto] _sm_ shelf.

'palco, chi _sm_ (_TEATRO_) box; (_tavolato_) platform, stand; (_ripiano_) layer.

palco'scenico, ci [palko'ʃʃeniko] _sm_ (_TEATRO_) stage.

pale'sare _vt_ to reveal, disclose; **~rsi** _vr_ to reveal _o_ show o.s.

pa'lese _ag_ clear, evident.

Pales'tina _sf_: **la ~** Palestine.

pa'lestra _sf_ gymnasium; (_esercizio atletico_) exercise, training; (_fig_) training ground, school.

pa'letta _sf_ spade; (_per il focolare_) shovel; (_del capostazione_) signalling disc.

pa'letto _sm_ stake, peg; (_spranga_) bolt.

'palio _sm_ (_gara_): **il P~** horserace run at Siena; **mettere qc in ~** to offer sth as a prize.

'palla _sf_ ball; (_pallottola_) bullet; **~ canestro** _sm_ basketball; **~ nuoto** _sm_ water polo; **~ volo** _sm_ volleyball.

palleggi'are [palled'dʒare] _vi_ (_CALCIO_) to practise with the ball; (_TENNIS_) to knock up.

pallia'tivo _sm_ palliative; (_fig_) stopgap measure.

'pallido, a _ag_ pale.

pal'lina _sf_ (_bilia_) marble.

pallon'cino [pallon'tʃino] _sm_ balloon; (_lampioncino_) Chinese lantern.

pal'lone _sm_ (_palla_) ball; (_CALCIO_) football; (_aerostato_) balloon; **gioco del ~** football.

pal'lore _sm_ pallor, paleness.

pal'lottola _sf_ pellet; (_proiettile_) bullet.

'palma _sf_ (_ANAT_) = **palmo**; (_BOT, simbolo_) palm; **~ da datteri** date palm.

'palmo _sm_ (_ANAT_) palm; **restare con un ~ di naso** to be badly disappointed.

'palo _sm_ (_legno appuntito_) stake; (_sostegno_) pole; **fare da _o_ il ~** (_fig_) to act as look-out.

palom'baro _sm_ diver.

pa'lombo _sm_ (_pesce_) dogfish.

pal'pare _vt_ to feel, finger.

'palpebra _sf_ eyelid.

palpi'tare _vi_ (_cuore, polso_) to beat; (: _più forte_) to pound, throb; (_fremere_) to quiver; **'palpito** _sm_ (_del cuore_) beat; (_fig: d'amore etc_) throb.

paltò _sm inv_ overcoat.

pa'lude _sf_ marsh, swamp; **palu'doso, a**

_ag_ marshy, swampy.

pa'lustre _ag_ marsh _cpd_, swamp _cpd_.

'pampino _sm_ vine leaf.

'panca, che _sf_ bench.

pan'cetta [pan'tʃetta] _sf_ (_CUC_) bacon.

pan'chetto [pan'ketto] _sm_ stool; footstool.

pan'china [pan'kina] _sf_ garden seat; (_di giardino pubblico_) (park) bench.

'pancia, ce [''pantʃa] _sf_ belly, stomach; **mettere _o_ fare ~** to be getting a paunch; **avere mal di ~** to have stomach ache _o_ a sore stomach.

panci'otto [pan'tʃɔtto] _sm_ waistcoat.

'pancreas _sm inv_ pancreas.

'panda _sm inv_ panda.

pande'monio _sm_ pandemonium.

'pane _sm_ bread; (_pagnotta_) loaf (of bread); (_forma_): **un ~ di burro/cera** _etc_ a pat of butter/bar of wax _etc_; **guadagnarsi il ~** to earn one's living; **~ a cassetta** sliced bread; **~ integrale** wholemeal bread; **~ tostato** toast.

panette'ria (_forno_) bakery; (_negozio_) baker's (shop), bakery.

panetti'ere, a _sm/f_ baker.

panet'tone _sm a kind of spiced brioche with sultanas, eaten at Christmas._

pangrat'tato _sm_ breadcrumbs _pl_.

'panico, a, ci, che _ag, sm_ panic.

pani'ere _sm_ basket.

pani'ficio [pani'fitʃo] _sm_ (_forno_) bakery; (_negozio_) baker's (shop), bakery.

pa'nino _sm_ roll; **~ imbottito** filled roll, sandwich; **panino'teca** _sf_ sandwich bar.

'panna _sf_ (_CUC_) cream; (_TECN_) = **panne**; **~ da cucina** cooking cream; **~ montata** whipped cream.

'panne _sf inv_: **essere in ~** (_AUT_) to have broken down.

pan'nello _sm_ panel.

'panno _sm_ cloth; **~i** _smpl_ (_abiti_) clothes; **mettiti nei miei ~i** (_fig_) put yourself in my shoes.

pan'nocchia [pan'nɔkkja] _sf_ (_di mais etc_) ear.

panno'lino _sm_ (_per bambini_) nappy (_Brit_), diaper (_US_).

pano'rama, i _sm_ panorama; **pano'ramico, a, ci, che** _ag_ panoramic; **strada panoramica** scenic route.

panta'loni _smpl_ trousers (_Brit_), pants (_US_), pair _sg_ of trousers _o_ pants.

pan'tano _sm_ bog.

pan'tera _sf_ panther.

pan'tofola _sf_ slipper.

panto'mima _sf_ pantomime.

pan'zana [pan'tsana] _sf_ fib, tall story.

pao'nazzo, a [pao'nattso] _ag_ purple.

'papa, i _sm_ pope.

papà _sm inv_ dad(dy).

pa'pale _ag_ papal.

pa'pato _sm_ papacy.

pa'pavero _sm_ poppy.

'papero, a _sm/f_ (_ZOOL_) gosling // _sf_ (_fig_)

slip of the tongue, blunder.
pa'piro *sm* papyrus.
'pappa *sf* baby cereal.
pappa'gallo *sm* parrot; *(fig: uomo)* Romeo, wolf.
pappa'gorgia, ge [pappa'gɔrdʒa] *sf* double chin.
pap'pare *vt (fam: anche:* ~**rsi)** to gobble up.
'para *sf:* **suole di** ~ crepe soles.
pa'rabola *sf (MAT)* parabola; *(REL)* parable.
para'brezza [para'breddza] *sm inv (AUT)* windscreen *(Brit)*, windshield *(US)*.
paraca'dute *sm inv* parachute.
para'carro *sm* kerbstone *(Brit)*, curbstone *(US)*.
para'diso *sm* paradise.
parados'sale *ag* paradoxical.
para'dosso *sm* paradox.
para'fango, ghi *sm* mudguard.
paraf'fina *sf* paraffin, paraffin wax.
para'fulmine *sm* lightning conductor.
pa'raggi [pa'raddʒi] *smpl:* **nei** ~ **in** the vicinity, in the neighbourhood.
parago'nare *vt:* ~ **con/a** to compare with/to.
para'gone *sm* comparison; *(esempio analogo)* analogy, parallel; **reggere al** ~ to stand comparison.
pa'ragrafo *sm* paragraph.
pa'ralisi *sf* paralysis; **para'litico, a, ci, che** *ag, sm/f* paralytic.
paraliz'zare [paralid'dzare] *vt* to paralyze.
paral'lelo, a *ag* parallel // *sm (GEO)* parallel; *(comparazione):* **fare un** ~ **tra** to draw a parallel between // *sf* parallel (line); ~**e** *sfpl (attrezzo ginnico)* parallel bars.
para'lume *sm* lampshade.
pa'rametro *sm* parameter.
para'noia *sf* paranoia; **para'noico, a, ci, che** *ag, sm/f* paranoid.
para'occhi [para'ɔkki] *smpl* blinkers.
para'piglia [para'piʎʎa] *sm* commotion, uproar.
pa'rare *vt (addobbare)* to adorn, deck; *(proteggere)* to shield, protect; *(scansare: colpo)* to parry; *(CALCIO)* to save // *vi:* **dove vuole andare a** ~? what are you driving at?; ~**rsi** *vr (presentarsi)* to appear, present o.s.
para'sole *sm inv* parasol, sunshade.
paras'sita, i *sm* parasite.
pa'rata *sf (SPORT)* save; *(MIL)* review, parade.
pa'ratia *sf (di nave)* bulkhead.
para'urti *sm inv (AUT)* bumper.
para'vento *sm* folding screen; **fare da** ~ **a qn** *(fig)* to shield sb.
par'cella [par'tʃɛlla] *sf* account, fee *(of lawyer etc)*.
parcheggi'are [parked'dʒare] *vt* to park; **par'cheggio** *sm* parking *q; (luogo)* car

park; *(singolo posto)* parking space.
par'chimetro [par'kimetro] *sm* parking meter.
'parco, chi *sm* park; *(spazio per deposito)* depot; *(complesso di veicoli)* fleet.
'parco, a, chi, che *ag:* ~ **(in)** *(sobrio)* moderate (in); *(avaro)* sparing (with).
pa'recchio, a [pa'rekkjo] *det* quite a lot of; *(tempo)* quite a lot of, a long; ~**i(e)** *det pl* quite a lot of, several // *pronome* quite a lot, quite a bit; *(tempo)* quite a while, a long time; ~**i(e)** *pronome pl* quite a lot, several // *av (con ag)* quite a lot, rather; *(con vb)* quite a lot, quite a bit.
pareggi'are [pared'dʒare] *vt* to make equal; *(terreno)* to level, make level; *(bilancio, conti)* to balance // *vi (SPORT)* to draw; **pa'reggio** *sm (ECON)* balance; *(SPORT)* draw.
paren'tado *sm* relatives *pl*, relations *pl*.
pa'rente *sm/f* relative, relation.
paren'tela *sf (vincolo di sangue, fig)* relationship; *(insieme dei parenti)* relations *pl*, relatives *pl*.
pa'rentesi *sf (segno grafico)* bracket, parenthesis; *(frase incisa)* parenthesis; *(digressione)* parenthesis, digression.
pa'rere *sm (opinione)* opinion; *(consiglio)* advice, opinion; **a mio** ~ in my opinion // *vi* to seem, appear // *vb impers:* **pare che it** seems *o* appears that, they say that; **mi pare che** it seems to me that; **mi pare di sì** I think so; **fai come ti pare** do as you like; **che ti pare del mio libro?** what do you think of my book?
pa'rete *sf* wall.
'pari *ag inv (uguale)* equal, same; *(in giochi)* equal; drawn, tied; *(MAT)* even // *sm inv (POL: di Gran Bretagna)* peer // *sm/f inv* peer, equal; **copiato** ~ ~ copied word for word; **alla** ~ on the same level; **ragazza alla** ~ au pair girl; **mettersi alla** ~ **con** to place o.s. on the same level as; **mettersi in** ~ **con** to catch up with; **andare di** ~ **passo con qn** to keep pace with sb.
Pa'rigi [pa'ridʒi] *sf* Paris.
pa'riglia [pa'riʎʎa] *sf* pair; **rendere la** ~ to give tit for tat.
parità *sf* parity, equality; *(SPORT)* draw, tie.
parlamen'tare *ag* parliamentary // *sm/f* ≈ Member of Parliament *(Brit)*, ≈ Congressman/woman *(US)* // *vi* to negotiate, parley.
parla'mento *sm* parliament.
parlan'tina *sf (fam)* talkativeness; **avere una buona** ~ to have the gift of the gab.
par'lare *vi* to speak, talk; *(confidare cose segrete)* to talk // *vt* to speak; ~ **(a qn) di** to speak *o* talk (to sb) about;
parla'torio *sm (di carcere etc)* visiting

room; (REL) parlour.
parmigi'ano [parmi'dʒano] sm (grana) Parmesan (cheese).
paro'dia sf parody.
pa'rola sf word; (facoltà) speech; ~e sfpl (chiacchiere) talk sg; chiedere la ~ to ask permission to speak; prendere la ~ to take the floor; ~ d'onore word of honour; ~ d'ordine (MIL) password; ~e incrociate crossword (puzzle) sg; paro'laccia, ce sf bad word, swearword.
par'rocchia [par'rɔkkja] sf parish; parish church.
'parroco, ci sm parish priest.
par'rucca, che sf wig.
parrucchi'ere, a [parruk'kjɛre] sm/f hairdresser // sm barber.
parsi'monia sf frugality, thrift.
'parso, a pp di parere.
'parte sf part; (lato) side; (quota spettante a ciascuno) share; (direzione) direction; (POL) party; faction; (DIR) party; a ~ ag separate // av separately; scherzi a ~ joking aside; a ~ ciò apart from that; da ~ (in disparte) to one side, aside; d'altra ~ on the other hand; da ~ di (per conto di) on behalf of; da ~ mia as far as I'm concerned, as for me; da ~ a ~ right through; da ogni ~ on all sides, everywhere; (moto da luogo) from all sides; da nessuna ~ nowhere; da questa ~ (in questa direzione) this way; prendere ~ a qc to take part in sth; mettere da ~ to put aside; mettere qn a ~ di qc to inform sb of sth.
parteci'pare [partetʃi'pare] vi: ~ a to take part in, participate in; (utili etc) to share in; (spese etc) to contribute to; (dolore, successo di qn) to share (in); **partecipazi'one** sf participation; sharing; (ECON) interest; partecipazione agli utili profit-sharing; partecipazioni di nozze wedding announcement card; **par'tecipe** ag participating; essere partecipe di to take part in, participate in; to share (in); (consapevole) to be aware of.
parteggi'are [parted'dʒare] vi: ~ per to side with, be on the side of.
par'tenza [par'tɛntsa] sf departure; (SPORT) start; essere in ~ to be about to leave, be leaving.
parti'cella [parti'tʃɛlla] sf particle.
parti'cipio [parti'tʃipjo] sm participle.
partico'lare ag (specifico) particular; (proprio) personal, private; (speciale) special, particular; (caratteristico) distinctive, characteristic; (fuori dal comune) peculiar // sm detail, particular; in ~ in particular, particularly; **particolarità** sf inv particularity; detail; characteristic, feature.
partigi'ano, a [parti'dʒano] ag partisan // sm (fautore) supporter, champion;

(MIL) partisan.
par'tire vi to go, leave; (allontanarsi) to go (o drive etc) away o off; (petardo, colpo) to go off; (fig: avere inizio, SPORT) to start; sono partita da Roma alle 7 I left Rome at 7; il volo parte da Ciampino the flight leaves from Ciampino; a ~ da from.
par'tita sf (COMM) lot, consignment; (ECON: registrazione) entry, item; (CARTE, SPORT: gioco) game; (: competizione) match, game; ~ di caccia hunting party; ~ IVA VAT registration number.
par'tito sm (POL) party; (decisione) decision, resolution; (persona da maritare) match.
parti'tura sf (MUS) score.
'parto sm (MED) delivery, (child)birth; labour; **parto'rire** vt to give birth to; (fig) to produce.
parzi'ale [par'tsjale] ag (limitato) partial; (non obiettivo) biased, partial.
'pascere ['paʃʃere] vi to graze // vt (brucare) to graze on; (far pascolare) to graze, pasture; **pasci'uto, a** pp di **pascere**.
pasco'lare vt, vi to graze.
'pascolo sm pasture.
'Pasqua sf Easter; **pas'quale** ag Easter cpd.
pas'sabile ag fairly good, passable.
pas'saggio [pas'saddʒo] sm passing q, passage; (traversata) crossing q, passage; (luogo, prezzo della traversata, brano di libro etc) passage; (su veicolo altrui) lift (Brit), ride; (SPORT) pass; di ~ (persona) passing through; ~ pedonale/a livello pedestrian/level (Brit) o grade (US) crossing.
pas'sante sm/f passer-by // sm loop.
passa'porto sm passport.
pas'sare vi (andare) to go; (veicolo, pedone) to pass (by), go by; (fare una breve sosta: postino etc) to come, call; (: amico: per fare una visita) to call o drop in; (sole, aria, luce) to get through; (tr. scorrere: giorni, tempo) to pass, go by; (fig: proposta di legge) to be passed; (: dolore) to pass, go away; (CARTE) to pass // vt (attraversare) to cross; (trasmettere: messaggio): ~ qc a qn to pass sth on to sb; (dare): ~ qc a qn to pass sth to sb, give sb sth; (trascorrere: tempo) to spend; (superare: esame) to pass; (triturare: verdura) to strain; (approvare) to pass, approve; (oltrepassare, sorpassare: anche fig) to go beyond, pass; (fig: subire) to go through; ~ da ... a to pass from ... to; ~ di padre in figlio to be handed down o to pass from father to son; ~ per (anche fig) to go through; ~ per stupido/ un genio to be taken for a fool/a genius; ~ sopra (anche fig) to pass over; ~ at-

traverso (*anche fig*) to go through; ~ alla storia to pass into history; ~ a un esame to go up (o: to the next class) after an exam; ~ inosservato to go unnoticed; ~ di moda to go out of fashion; le passo il Signor X (*al telefono*) here is Mr X; I'm putting you through to Mr X; lasciar ~ qn/qc to let sb/sth through; passarsela: come te la passi? how are you getting on o along?

pas'sata sf: dare una ~ di vernice a qc to give sth a coat of paint; dare una ~ al giornale to have a look at the paper, skim through the paper.

passa'tempo sm pastime, hobby.

pas'sato, a ag past; (*sfiorito*) faded // sm past; (*LING*) past (tense); ~ prossimo (*LING*) present perfect; ~ remoto (*LING*) past historic; ~ di verdura (*CUC*) vegetable purée.

passaver'dura sm inv vegetable mill.

passeg'gero, a [passed'dʒɛro] ag passing // smf passenger.

passeggi'are [passed'dʒare] vi to go for a walk; (*in veicolo*) to go for a drive; **passeggi'ata** sf walk; drive; (*luogo*) promenade; fare una passeggiata to go for a walk (o drive); **passeg'gino** sm pushchair (*Brit*), stroller (*US*); **pas'seggio** sm walk, stroll; (*luogo*) promenade.

passe'rella sf footbridge; (*di nave, aereo*) gangway; (*pedana*) catwalk.

'passero sm sparrow.

pas'sibile ag: ~ di liable to.

passi'one sf passion.

pas'sivo, a ag passive // sm (*LING*) passive; (*ECON*) debit; (: *complesso dei debiti*) liabilities pl.

'passo sm step; (*andatura*) pace; (*rumore*) (foot)step; (*orma*) footprint; (*passaggio, fig: brano*) passage; (*valico*) pass; a ~ d'uomo at walking pace; ~ (a) ~ step by step; fare due o quattro ~i to go for a walk o a stroll; di questo ~ at this rate; "~ carraio" "vehicle entrance — keep clear".

'pasta sf (*CUC*) dough; (: *impasto per dolce*) pastry; (: *anche:* ~ alimentare) pasta; (*massa molle di materia*) paste; (*fig: indole*) nature; ~e sfpl (*pasticcini*) pastries; ~ in brodo noodle soup.

pastasci'utta [pastaʃ'ʃutta] sf pasta.

pas'tella sf batter.

pas'tello sm pastel.

pas'tetta sf (*CUC*) = **pastella**.

pas'ticca, che sf = **pastiglia**.

pasticce'ria [pastittʃe'ria] sf (*pasticcini*) pastries pl, cakes pl; (*negozio*) cake shop; (*arte*) confectionery.

pasticci'are [pastit'tʃare] vt to mess up, make a mess of // vi to make a mess.

pasticci'ere, a [pastit'tʃere] smf pastrycook; confectioner.

pas'ticcio [pas'tittʃo] sm (*CUC*) pie;

(*lavoro disordinato, imbroglio*) mess; trovarsi nei ~i to get into trouble.

pasti'ficio [pasti'fitʃo] sm pasta factory.

pas'tiglia [pas'tiʎʎa] sf pastille, lozenge.

pas'tina sf small pasta shapes used in soup.

pasti'naca, che sf parsnip.

'pasto sm meal.

pas'tore sm shepherd; (*REL*) pastor, minister; (*anche:* cane ~) sheepdog.

pastoriz'zare [pastorid'dzare] vt to pasteurize.

pas'toso, a ag doughy; pasty; (*fig: voce, colore*) mellow, soft.

pas'trano sm greatcoat.

pas'tura sf pasture.

pa'tata sf potato; ~e fritte chips (*Brit*), French fries; **pata'tine** sfpl (*potato*) crisps.

pata'trac sm (*crollo: anche fig*) crash.

pa'tella sf (*ZOOL*) limpet.

pa'tema, i sm anxiety, worry.

pa'tente sf licence; (*anche:* ~ di guida) driving licence (*Brit*), driver's license (*US*).

paternità sf paternity, fatherhood.

pa'terno, a ag (*affetto, consigli*) fatherly; (*casa, autorità*) paternal.

pa'tetico, a, ci, che ag pathetic; (*commovente*) moving, touching.

pa'tibolo sm gallows sg, scaffold.

'patina sf (*su rame etc*) patina; (*sulla lingua*) fur, coating.

pa'tire vt, vi to suffer.

pa'tito, a smf enthusiast, fan, lover.

patolo'gia [patolo'dʒia] sf pathology; **pato'logico, a, ci, che** ag pathological.

'patria sf homeland.

patri'arca, chi sm patriarch.

pa'trigno [pa'triɲɲo] sm stepfather.

patri'monio sm estate, property; (*fig*) heritage.

patri'ota, i, e smf patriot; **patri'ottico, a, ci, che** ag patriotic; **patriot'tismo** sm patriotism.

patroci'nare [patrotʃi'nare] vt (*DIR: difendere*) to defend; (*sostenere*) to sponsor, support; **patro'cinio** sm defence, support, sponsorship.

patro'nato sm patronage; (*istituzione benefica*) charitable institution o society.

pa'trono sm (*REL*) patron saint; (*socio di patronato*) patron; (*DIR*) counsel.

'patta sf flap; (*dei pantaloni*) fly.

patteggi'are [patted'dʒare] vt, vi to negotiate.

patti'naggio [patti'naddʒo] sm skating.

patti'nare vi to skate; ~ sul ghiaccio to ice-skate; **pattina'tore, 'trice** smf skater; **'pattino** sm skate; (*di slitta*) runner; (*AER*) skid; (*TECN*) sliding block; **pattini** (*da ghiaccio*) (ice) skates; pattini a rotelle roller skates; [pat'tino] (*barca*) kind of pedalo with oars.

'patto sm (*accordo*) pact, agreement;

(*condizione*) term, condition; **a ~ che** on condition that.

pat'tuglia [pat'tuʎʎa] *sf* (*MIL*) patrol.

pattu'ire *vt* to reach an agreement on.

pattumi'era *sf* (dust)bin (*Brit*), ashcan (*US*).

pa'ura *sf* fear; **aver ~ di/di fare/che** to be frightened *o* afraid of/of doing/that; **far ~ a** to frighten; **per ~ di/che** for fear of/that; **pau'roso, a** *ag* (*che fa paura*) frightening; (*che ha paura*) fearful, timorous.

'pausa *sf* (*sosta*) break; (*nel parlare, MUS*) pause.

pavi'mento *sm* floor.

pa'vone *sm* peacock; **pavoneggi'arsi** *vr* to strut about, show off.

pazien'tare [pattsjen'tare] *vi* to be patient.

pazi'ente [pat'tsjɛnte] *ag, smf* patient; **pazi'enza** *sf* patience.

paz'zesco, a, schi, sche [pat'tsesko] *ag* mad, crazy.

paz'zia [pat'tsia] *sf* (*MED*) madness, insanity; (*azione*) folly; (*di azione, decisione*) madness, folly.

'pazzo, a [pattso] *ag* (*MED*) mad, insane; (*strano*) wild, mad // *smf* madman/woman; **~ di** (*gioia, amore etc*) mad *o* crazy with; **~ per qc/qn** mad *o* crazy about sth/sb.

PCI *sigla m* = *Partito Comunista Italiano*.

'pecca, che *sf* defect, flaw, fault.

peccami'noso, a *ag* sinful.

pec'care *vi* to sin; (*fig*) to err.

pec'cato *sm* sin; **è un ~ che** it's a pity that; **che ~!** what a shame *o* pity!

pecca'tore, 'trice *smf* sinner.

'pece ['petʃe] *sf* pitch.

Pe'chino [pe'kino] *sf* Peking.

'pecora *sf* sheep; **peco'raio** *sm* shepherd; **peco'rino** *sm* sheep's milk cheese.

peculi'are *ag*: **~ di** peculiar to.

pe'daggio [pe'daddʒo] *sm* toll.

pedago'gia [pedago'dʒia] *sf* pedagogy, educational methods *pl*.

peda'lare *vi* to pedal; (*andare in bicicletta*) to cycle.

pe'dale *sm* pedal.

pe'dana *sf* footboard; (*SPORT: nel salto*) springboard; (: *nella scherma*) piste.

pe'dante *ag* pedantic // *smf* pedant.

pe'data *sf* (*impronta*) footprint; (*colpo*) kick; **prendere a ~e qn/qc** to kick sb/sth.

pede'rasta, i *sm* pederast; homosexual.

pedi'atra, i, e *smf* paediatrician; **pedia'tria** *sf* paediatrics *sg*.

pedi'cure *smf inv* chiropodist.

pe'dina *sf* (*della dama*) draughtsman (*Brit*), draftsman (*US*); (*fig*) pawn.

pedi'nare *vt* to shadow, tail.

pedo'nale *ag* pedestrian.

pe'done, a *smf* pedestrian // *sm*

(*SCACCHI*) pawn.

'peggio ['peddʒo] *av, ag inv* worse // *sm o f*: **il** *o* **la ~** the worst; **alla ~** at worst, if the worst comes to the worst; **peggiora'mento** *sm* worsening; **peggio'rare** *vt* to make worse, worsen // *vi* to grow worse, worsen; **peggiora'tivo, a** *ag* pejorative; **peggi'ore** *ag* (*comparativo*) worse; (*superlativo*) worst // *smf*: **il(la) peggiore** the worst (person).

'pegno ['peɲɲo] *sm* (*DIR*) security, pledge; (*nei giochi di società*) forfeit; (*fig*) pledge, token; **dare in ~ qc** to pawn sth.

pe'lame *sm* (*di animale*) coat, fur.

pe'lare *vt* (*spennare*) to pluck; (*spellare*) to skin; (*sbucciare*) to peel; (*fig*) to make pay through the nose; **~rsi** *vr* to go bald.

pel'lame *sm* skins *pl*, hides *pl*.

'pelle *sf* skin; (*di animale*) skin, hide; (*cuoio*) leather; **avere la ~ d'oca** to have goose pimples *o* goose flesh.

pellegri'naggio [pellegri'naddʒo] *sm* pilgrimage.

pelle'grino, a *smf* pilgrim.

pelle'rossa, pelli'rossa, pl pelli'rosse *smf* Red Indian.

pellette'ria *sf* leather goods *pl*; (*negozio*) leather goods shop.

pelli'cano *sm* pelican.

pellicce'ria [pellittʃe'ria] *sf* (*negozio*) furrier's (shop); (*quantità di pellicce*) furs *pl*.

pel'liccia, ce [pel'littʃa] *sf* (*mantello di animale*) coat, fur; (*indumento*) fur coat.

pel'licola *sf* (*membrana sottile*) film, layer; (*FOT, CINEMA*) film.

'pelo *sm* hair; (*pelame*) coat, hair; (*pelliccia*) fur; (*di tappeto*) pile; (*di liquido*) surface; **per un ~**: **per un ~ non ho perduto il treno** I very nearly missed the train; **c'è mancato un ~ che affogasse** he escaped drowning by the skin of his teeth; **pe'loso, a** *ag* hairy.

'peltro *sm* pewter.

pe'luria *sf* down.

'pena *sf* (*DIR*) sentence; (*punizione*) punishment; (*sofferenza*) sadness *q*, sorrow; (*fatica*) trouble *q*, effort; (*difficoltà*) difficulty; **far ~** to be pitiful; **mi fai ~** I feel sorry for you; **prendersi** *o* **darsi la ~ di fare** to go to the trouble of doing; **~ di morte** death sentence; **~ pecuniaria** fine; **pe'nale** *ag* penal; **penalità** *sf inv* penalty; **penaliz'zare** *vt* (*SPORT*) to penalize.

pe'nare *vi* (*patire*) to suffer; (*faticare*) to struggle.

pen'dente *ag* hanging; leaning // *sm* (*ciondolo*) pendant; (*orecchino*) drop earring; **pen'denza** *sf* slope, slant; (*grado d'inclinazione*) gradient; (*ECON*) outstanding account.

'pendere vi (essere appeso): ~ da to hang from; (essere inclinato) to lean; (fig: incombere): ~ su to hang over.

pen'dio, 'dii sm slope, slant; (luogo in pendenza) slope.

'pendola sf pendulum clock.

pendo'lare sm/f commuter.

'pendolo sm (peso) pendulum; (anche: orologio a ~) pendulum clock.

'pene sm penis.

pene'trante ag piercing, penetrating.

pene'trare vi to come o get in // vt to penetrate; ~ in to enter; (sog: proiettile) to penetrate; (: acqua, aria) to go o come into.

penicil'lina [penitʃil'lina] sf penicillin.

pe'nisola sf peninsula.

peni'tenza [peni'tɛntsa] sf penitence; (punizione) penance.

penitenzi'ario [peniten'tsjarjo] sm prison.

'penna sf (di uccello) feather; (per scrivere) pen; ~e sfpl (CUC) quills (type of pasta); ~ a feltro/ stilografica/a sfera felt-tip/fountain/ballpoint pen.

penna'rello sm felt(-tip) pen.

pennel'lare vi to paint.

pen'nello sm brush; (per dipingere) (paint)brush; a ~ (perfettamente) to perfection, perfectly; ~ per la barba shaving brush.

pen'nino sm nib.

pen'none sm (NAUT) yard; (stendardo) banner, standard.

pe'nombra sf half-light, dim light.

pe'noso, a ag painful, distressing; (faticoso) tiring, laborious.

pen'sare vi to think // vt to think; (inventare, escogitare) to think out; ~ a to think of; (amico, vacanze) to think of o about; (problema) to think about; ~ di fare qc to think of doing sth; ci penso io I'll see to o take care of it.

pensi'ero sm thought; (modo di pensare, dottrina) thinking q; (preoccupazione) worry, care, trouble; stare in ~ per qn to be worried about sb; **pensie'roso, a** ag thoughtful.

'pensile ag hanging.

pensio'nante sm/f (presso una famiglia) lodger; (di albergo) guest.

pensio'nato, a sm/f pensioner.

pensi'one sf (al prestatore di lavoro) pension; (vitto e alloggio) board and lodging; (albergo) boarding house; andare in ~ to retire; mezza ~ half board; ~ completa full board.

pen'soso, a ag thoughtful, pensive, lost in thought.

pentapar'tito sm five-party government.

Pente'coste sf Pentecost, Whit Sunday (Brit).

penti'mento sm repentance, contrition.

pen'tirsi vr: ~ di to repent of; (rammaricarsi) to regret, be sorry for.

'pentola sf pot; ~ a pressione pressure cooker.

pe'nultimo, a ag last but one (Brit), next to last, penultimate.

pe'nuria sf shortage.

penzo'lare [pendzo'lare] vi to dangle, hang loosely; **penzo'loni** av dangling, hanging down; stare penzoloni to dangle, hang down.

'pepe sm pepper; ~ macinato/in grani ground/whole pepper.

pepe'rone sm pepper, capsicum; (piccante) chili.

pe'pita sf nugget.

per prep **1** (moto attraverso luogo) through; i ladri sono passati ~ la finestra the thieves got in (o out) through the window; l'ho cercato ~ tutta la casa I've searched the whole house o all over the house for it

2 (moto a luogo) for, to; partire ~ la Germania/il mare to leave for Germany/ the sea; il treno ~ Roma the Rome train, the train for o to Rome

3 (stato in luogo): seduto/sdraiato ~ terra sitting/lying on the ground

4 (tempo) for; ~ anni/lungo tempo for years/a long time; ~ tutta l'estate throughout the summer, all summer long; lo rividi ~ Natale I saw him again at Christmas; lo faccio ~ lunedì I'll do it for Monday

5 (mezzo, maniera) by; ~ lettera/via aerea/ferrovia by letter/airmail/rail; prendere qn ~ un braccio to take sb by the arm

6 (causa, scopo) for; assente ~ malattia absent because of o through o owing to illness; ottimo ~ il mal di gola excellent for sore throats

7 (limitazione) for; è troppo difficile ~ lui it's too difficult for him; ~ quel che mi riguarda as far as I'm concerned; ~ poco che sia however little it may be; ~ questa volta ti perdono I'll forgive you this time

8 (prezzo, misura) for; (distributivo) a, per; venduto ~ 3 milioni sold for 3 million; 1000 lire ~ persona 1000 lire a o per person; uno ~ volta one at a time; uno ~ uno one by one; 5 ~ cento 5 per cent; 3 ~ 4 fa 12 3 times 4 equals 12; dividere/moltiplicare 12 ~ 4 to divide/ multiply 12 by 4

9 (in qualità di) as; (al posto di) for; avere qn ~ professore to have sb as a teacher; ti ho preso ~ Mario I mistook you for Mario, I though you were Mario; dare ~ morto qn to give sb up for dead

10 (seguito da vb: finale): ~ fare qc (so as) to do sth, in order to do sth; (: causale): ~ aver fatto qc for having done sth; (: consecutivo): è abbastanza

grande ~ andarci da solo he's big
enough to go on his own.
'**pera** *sf* pear.
pe'raltro *av* moreover, what's more.
per'bene *ag inv* respectable, decent // *av*
(*con cura*) properly, well.
percentu'ale [pertʃentu'ale] *sf* percentage.
perce'pire [pertʃe'pire] *vt* (*sentire*) to
perceive; (*ricevere*) to receive;
percezi'one *sf* perception.
perché [per'ke] ◆ *av* why; ~ no? why
not?; ~ non vuoi andarci? why don't you
want to go?; spiegami ~ l'hai fatto tell
me why you did it
◆ *cong* **1** (*causale*) because; non posso
uscire ~ ho da fare I can't go out
because o as I've a lot to do
2 (*finale*) in order that, so that; te lo do
~ tu lo legga I'm giving it to you so
(that) you can read it
3 (*consecutivo*): è troppo forte ~ si
possa batterlo he's too strong to be
beaten
◆ *sm inv* reason; il ~ di the reason for.
perciò [per'tʃɔ] *cong* so, for this (o that)
reason.
per'correre *vt* (*luogo*) to go all over; (:
paese) to travel up and down, go all
over; (*distanza*) to cover.
per'corso, a *pp di* **percorrere** // *sm*
(*tragitto*) journey; (*tratto*) route.
per'cosso, a *pp di* **percuotere** // *sf*
blow.
percu'otere *vt* to hit, strike.
percussi'one *sf* percussion; strumenti a
~ (*MUS*) percussion instruments.
'**perdere** *vt* to lose; (*lasciarsi sfuggire*)
to miss; (*sprecare: tempo, denaro*) to
waste; (*mandare in rovina: persona*) to
ruin // *vi* to lose; (*serbatoio etc.*) to leak;
~rsi *vr* (*smarrirsi*) to get lost; (*svanire*)
to disappear, vanish; saper ~ to be a
good loser; lascia ~! forget it!, never
mind!
perdigi'orno [perdi'dʒorno] *sm/f inv*
idler, waster.
'**perdita** *sf* loss; (*spreco*) waste; (*fuoriuscita*) leak; siamo in ~ (*COMM*) we
are running at a loss; a ~ d'occhio as
far as the eye can see.
perdi'tempo *sm/f inv* waster, idler.
perdo'nare *vt* to pardon, forgive;
(*scusare*) to excuse, pardon.
per'dono *sm* forgiveness; (*DIR*) pardon.
perdu'rare *vi* to go on, last; (*perseverare*) to persist.
perduta'mente *av* desperately,
passionately.
per'duto, a *pp di* **perdere**.
peregri'nare *vi* to wander, roam.
pe'renne *ag* eternal, perpetual, perennial; (*BOT*) perennial.
peren'torio, a *ag* peremptory;
(*definitivo*) final.

per'fetto, a *ag* perfect // *sm* (*LING*)
perfect (tense).
perfezio'nare [perfettsjo'nare] *vt* to
improve, perfect; ~rsi *vr* to improve.
perfezi'one [perfet'tsjone] *sf* perfection.
'**perfido, a** *ag* perfidious, treacherous.
per'fino *av* even.
perfo'rare *vt* to perforate; to punch a
hole (o holes) in; (*banda, schede*) to
punch; (*trivellare*) to drill;
perfora'tore, 'trice *sm/f* punch-card
operator o (*un utensile*) punch; (*IN-
FORM*): **perforatore di schede** card punch
// *sf* (*TECN*) boring o drilling machine;
(*INFORM*) card punch; **perforazi'one** *sf*
perforation; punching; drilling; (*IN-
FORM*) punch; (*MED*) perforation.
perga'mena *sf* parchment.
perico'lante *ag* precarious.
pe'ricolo *sm* danger; mettere in ~ to endanger, put in danger; **perico'loso, a**
ag dangerous.
perife'ria *sf* periphery; (*di città*) outskirts *pl*.
pe'rifrasi *sf* circumlocution.
pe'rimetro *sm* perimeter.
peri'odico, a, ci, che *ag* periodic(al);
(*MAT*) recurring // *sm* periodical.
pe'riodo *sm* period.
peripe'zie [peripet'tsie] *sfpl* ups and
downs, vicissitudes.
pe'rire *vi* to perish, die.
pe'rito, a *ag* expert, skilled // *sm/f*
expert; (*agronomo, navale*) surveyor;
un ~ chimico a qualified chemist.
pe'rizia [pe'rittsja] *sf* (*abilità*) ability;
(*giudizio tecnico*) expert opinion;
expert's report.
'**perla** *sf* pearl; **per'lina** *sf* bead.
perlus'trare *vt* to patrol.
perma'loso, a *ag* touchy.
perma'nente *ag* permanent // *sf*
permanent wave, perm; **perma'nenza**
sf permanence; (*soggiorno*) stay.
perma'nere *vi* to remain.
perme'are *vt* to permeate.
per'messo, a *pp di* **permettere** // *sm*
(*autorizzazione*) permission, leave; (*dato
a militare, impiegato*) leave; (*licenza*)
licence, permit; (*MIL: foglio*) pass; ~?,
è ~? (*posso entrare?*) may I come in?;
(*posso passare?*) excuse me; ~ di
lavoro/pesca work/fishing permit.
per'mettere *vt* to allow, permit; ~ a qn
qc/di fare to allow sb sth/to do; ~rsi qc/
di fare to allow o.s. sth/to do; (*avere la
possibilità*) to afford sth/to do.
per'nacchia [per'nakkja] *sf* (*fam*): fare
una ~ to blow a raspberry.
per'nice [per'nitʃe] *sf* partridge.
'**perno** *sm* pivot.
pernot'tare *vi* to spend the night, stay
overnight.
'**pero** *sm* pear tree.
però *cong* (*ma*) but; (*tuttavia*) however,

nevertheless.

pero'rare vt (DIR, fig): ~ la causa di qn to plead sb's case.

perpendico'lare ag, sf perpendicular.

perpe'trare vt to perpetrate.

perpetu'are vt to perpetuate.

per'petuo, a ag perpetual.

per'plesso, a ag perplexed; uncertain, undecided.

perqui'sire vt to search; **perquisizi'one** sf (police) search.

persecu'tore sm persecutor.

persecuzi'one [persekut'tsjone] sf persecution.

persegu'ire vt to pursue.

persegui'tare vt to persecute.

perseve'rante ag persevering.

perseve'rare vi to persevere.

'Persia sf: la ~ Persia.

persi'ano, a ag, sm/f Persian // sf shutter; ~a avvolgibile Venetian blind.

'persico, a, ci, che ag: il golfo P~ the Persian Gulf.

per'sino av = **perfino**.

persis'tente ag persistent.

per'sistere vi to persist; ~ a fare to persist in doing; **persis'tito, a** pp di **persistere**.

'perso, a pp di **perdere**.

per'sona sf person; (qualcuno): una ~ someone, somebody, espressione interrogativa + anyone o anybody; ~e sfpl people; **non c'è** ~ **che** ... there's nobody who ..., there isn't anybody who ....

perso'naggio [perso'naddʒo] sm (persona ragguardevole) personality, figure; (tipo) character, individual; (LETTERATURA) character.

perso'nale ag personal // sm staff; personnel; (figura fisica) build.

personalità sf inv personality.

personifi'care vt to personify; to embody.

perspi'cace [perspi'katʃe] ag shrewd, discerning.

persu'adere vt: ~ qn (di qc/a fare) to persuade sb (of sth/to do); **persuasi'one** sf persuasion; **persua'sivo, a** ag persuasive; **persu'aso, a** pp di **persuadere**.

per'tanto cong (quindi) so, therefore.

'pertica, che sf pole.

perti'nente ag: ~ (a) relevant (to), pertinent (to).

per'tosse sf whooping cough.

per'tugio [per'tudʒo] sm hole, opening.

pertur'bare vt to disrupt; (persona) to disturb, perturb; **perturbazi'one** sf disruption; perturbation; **perturbazione atmosferica** atmospheric disturbance.

per'vadere vt to pervade; **per'vaso, a** pp di **pervadere**.

perve'nire vi: ~ a to reach, arrive at, come to; (venire in possesso): gli pervenne una fortuna he inherited a fortune; far ~ qc a to have sth sent to; **perve'nuto, a** pp di **pervenire**.

per'verso, a ag depraved; perverse.

perver'tire vt to pervert.

p. es. abbr (= per esempio) e.g.

'pesa sf weighing q; weighbridge.

pe'sante ag heavy; (fig: noioso) dull, boring.

pe'sare vt to weigh // vi (avere un peso) to weigh; (essere pesante) to be heavy; (fig) to carry weight; ~ su (fig) to lie heavy on; to influence; to hang over; **mi pesa sgridarlo** I find it hard to scold him.

'pesca sf (pl **pesche**: frutto) peach; (il pescare) fishing; **andare a** ~ to go fishing; ~ **di beneficenza** (lotteria) lucky dip; ~ **con la lenza** angling.

pes'care vt (pesce) to fish for; to catch; (qc nell'acqua) to fish out; (fig: trovare) to get hold of, find.

pesca'tore sm fisherman; angler.

'pesce ['peʃʃe] sm fish gen inv; **P~i** (dello zodiaco) Pisces; ~ **d'aprile!** April Fool!; ~ **spada** swordfish; **pesce'cane** sm shark.

pesche'reccio [peske'rettʃo] sm fishing boat.

pesche'ria [peske'ria] sf fishmonger's (shop) (Brit), fish store (US).

peschi'era [pes'kjera] sf fishpond.

pesci'vendolo, a [peʃʃi'vendolo] sm/f fishmonger (Brit), fish merchant (US).

'pesco, schi sm peach tree.

pes'coso, a ag abounding in fish.

'peso sm weight; (SPORT) shot; **rubare sul** ~ to give short weight; **essere di** ~ **a qn** (fig) to be a burden to sb; ~ **lordo/netto** gross/net weight; ~ **piuma/mosca/gallo/medio/massimo** (PUGILATO) feather/fly/bantam/middle/heavyweight.

pessi'mismo sm pessimism; **pessi'mista, i, e** ag pessimistic // sm/f pessimist.

'pessimo, a ag very bad, awful.

pes'tare vt to tread on, trample on; (sale, pepe) to grind; (uva, aglio) to crush; (fig: picchiare): ~ **qn** to beat sb up.

'peste sf plague; (persona) nuisance, pest.

pes'tello sm pestle.

pesti'lenza [pesti'lentsa] sf pestilence; (fetore) stench.

'pesto, a ag: **c'è buio** ~ it's pitch-dark; **occhio** ~ black eye // sm (CUC) sauce made with basil, garlic, cheese and oil.

'petalo sm (BOT) petal.

pe'tardo sm firecracker, banger (Brit).

petizi'one [petit'tsjone] sf petition.

'peto sm (fam!) fart (!).

petrol'chimica [petrol'kimika] sf petrochemical industry.

petroli'era sf (nave) oil tanker.

petro'lifero, a ag oil-bearing; oil cpd.

pe'trolio sm oil, petroleum; (per lampada, fornello) paraffin.

pettego'lare vi to gossip.

pettego'lezzo [pettego'leddzo] sm gossip q; fare ~i to gossip.

pet'tegolo, a ag gossipy // sm/f gossip.

petti'nare vt to comb (the hair of); ~rsi vr to comb one's hair; **pettina'tura** sf (acconciatura) hairstyle.

'pettine sm comb; (ZOOL) scallop.

petti'rosso sm robin.

'petto sm chest; (seno) breast, bust; (CUC: di carne bovina) brisket; (: di pollo etc) breast; a doppio ~ (abito) double-breasted; **petto'ruto, a** ag broad-chested; full-breasted.

petu'lante ag insolent.

'pezza ['pettsa] sf piece of cloth; (toppa) patch; (cencio) rag, cloth.

pez'zato, a [pet'tsato] ag piebald.

pez'zente [pet'tsente] sm/f beggar.

'pezzo ['pettso] sm (gen) piece; (brandello, frammento) piece, bit; (di macchina, arnese etc) part; (STAMPA) article; (di tempo): aspettare un ~ to wait quite a while o some time; in un ~ in pieces; andare in ~i to break into pieces; un bel ~ d'uomo a fine figure of a man; abito a due ~i two-piece suit; ~ di cronaca (STAMPA) report; ~ grosso (fig) bigwig; ~ di ricambio spare part.

pia'cente [pja'tʃente] ag attractive, pleasant.

pia'cere [pja'tʃere] vi to please; una ragazza che piace a likeable girl; an attractive girl; ~ a: mi piace I like it; quei ragazzi non mi piacciono I don't like those boys; gli piacerebbe andare al cinema he would like to go to the cinema // sm pleasure; (favore) favour; "~!" (nelle presentazioni) "pleased to meet you!"; con ~ certainly, with pleasure; per ~! please; fare un ~ a qn to do sb a favour; **pia'cevole** ag pleasant, agreeable; **piaci'uto, a** pp di piacere.

pi'aga, ghe sf (lesione) sore; (ferita: anche fig) wound; (fig: flagello) scourge, curse; (: persona) pest, nuisance.

piagnis'teo [pjaɲɲis'tɛo] sm whining, whimpering.

piagnuco'lare [pjaɲɲuko'lare] vi to whimper.

pi'alla sf (arnese) plane; **pial'lare** vt to plane.

pi'ana sf stretch of level ground; (più esteso) plain.

pianeggi'ante [pjaned'dʒante] ag flat, level.

piane'rottolo sm landing.

pia'neta sm (ASTR) planet.

pi'angere ['pjandʒere] vi to cry, weep; (occhi) to water // vt to cry, weep; (lamentare) to bewail, lament; ~ la morte di qn to mourn sb's death.

pianifi'care vt to plan; **pianificazi'one**

sf planning.

pia'nista, i, e sm/f pianist.

pi'ano, a ag (piatto) flat, level; (MAT) plane; (facile) straightforward, simple; (chiaro) clear, plain // av (adagio) slowly; (a bassa voce) softly; (con cautela) slowly, carefully // sm (MAT) plane; (GEO) plain; (livello) level, plane; (di edificio) floor; (programma) plan; (MUS) piano; **pian ~** very slowly; (poco a poco) little by little; in primo/secondo ~ in the foreground/background; di primo ~ (fig) prominent, high-ranking.

piano'forte sm piano, pianoforte.

pi'anta sf (BOT) plant; (ANAT: anche: ~ del piede) sole (of the foot); (grafico) plan; (topografica) map; in ~ **stabile** on the permanent staff; **piantagi'one** sf plantation; **pian'tare** vt to plant; (conficcare) to drive o hammer in; (tenda) to put up, pitch; (fig: lasciare) to leave, desert; ~rsi vr: ~rsi davanti a qn to plant o.s. in front of sb; **piantala!** (fam) cut it out!

pianter'reno sm ground floor.

pi'anto, a pp di piangere // sm tears pl, crying.

pian'tone sm (vigilante) sentry, guard; (soldato) orderly; (AUT) steering column.

pia'nura sf plain.

pi'astra sf plate; (di pietra) slab; (di fornello) hotplate; ~ **di registrazione** tape deck; **panino alla** ~ ≈ toasted sandwich.

pias'trella sf tile.

pias'trina sf (MIL) identity disc.

piatta'forma sf (anche fig) platform.

piat'tino sm saucer.

pi'atto, a ag flat; (fig: scialbo) dull // sm (recipiente, vivanda) dish; (portata) course; (parte piana) flat (part); ~i smpl (MUS) cymbals; ~ **fondo** soup dish; ~ **forte** main course; ~ **del giorno** dish of the day, plat du jour; ~ **del giradischi** turntable; ~i **già pronti** (CULIN) ready-cooked dishes.

pi'azza ['pjattsa] sf square; (COMM) market; far ~ **pulita** to make a clean sweep; ~ **d'armi** (MIL) parade ground; **piaz'zale** sm (large) square.

piaz'zare [pjat'tsare] vt to place; (COMM) to market, sell; ~rsi vr (SPORT) to be placed.

piaz'zista, i [pjat'tsista] sm (COMM) commercial traveller.

piaz'zola [pjat'tsɔla] sf (AUT) lay-by.

'picca, che sf pike; ~che sfpl (CARTE) spades.

pic'cante ag hot, pungent; (fig) racy; biting.

pic'carsi vr: ~ **di fare** to pride o.s. on one's ability to do; ~ **per qc** to take offence at sth.

pic'chetto [pik'ketto] *sm* (*MIL, di scioperanti*) picket.

picchi'are [pik'kjare] *vt* (*persona: colpire*) to hit, strike; (: *prendere a botte*) to beat (up); (*battere*) to beat; (*sbattere*) to bang // *vi* (*bussare*) to knock; (: *con forza*) to bang; (*colpire*) to hit, strike; (*sole*) to beat down; **picchi'ata** *sf* (*percosse*) beating, thrashing; (*AER*) dive.

picchiet'tare [pikkjet'tare] *vt* (*punteggiare*) to spot, dot; (*colpire*) to tap.

'picchio ['pikkjo] *sm* woodpecker.

pic'cino, a [pit'tʃino] *ag* tiny, very small.

piccio'naia [pittʃo'naja] *sf* pigeon-loft; (*TEATRO*): **la ~** the gods *sg.*

picci'one [pit'tʃone] *sm* pigeon.

'picco, chi *sm* peak; **a ~** vertically.

'piccolo, a *ag* small; (*oggetto, mano, di età: bambino*) small, little (*dav sostantivo*); (*di breve durata: viaggio*) short; (*fig*) mean, petty // *smf* child, little one; **~i** *smpl* (*di animale*) young *pl*; **in ~** in miniature.

pic'cone *sm* pick(-axe).

pic'cozza [pik'kɔttsa] *sf* ice-axe.

pic'nic *sm inv* picnic.

pi'docchio [pi'dokkjo] *sm* louse.

pi'ede *sm* foot; (*di mobile*) leg; **in ~i** standing; **a ~i** on foot; **a ~i nudi** barefoot; **su due ~i** (*fig*) at once; **prendere ~** (*fig*) to gain ground, catch on; **sul ~ di guerra** (*MIL*) ready for action; **~ di porco** crowbar.

piedis'tallo, piedes'tallo *sm* pedestal.

pi'ega, ghe *sf* (*piegatura, GEO*) fold; (*di gonna*) pleat; (*di pantaloni*) crease; (*grinza*) wrinkle, crease; **prendere una brutta ~** (*avvenimento*) to take a turn for the worse.

pie'gare *vt* to fold; (*braccia, gambe, testa*) to bend // *vi* to bend; **~rsi** *vr* to bend; (*fig*): **~rsi (a)** to yield (to), submit (to); **pieghet'tare** *vt* to pleat; **pie'ghevole** *ag* pliable, flexible; (*porta*) folding; (*fig*) yielding, docile.

Pie'monte *sm*: **il ~** Piedmont.

pi'ena *sf vedi* **pieno.**

pi'eno, a *ag* full; (*muro, mattone*) solid // *sm* (*colmo*) height, peak; (*carico*) full load // *sf* (*di fiume*) flood, spate; (*gran folla*) crowd, throng; **~ di** full of; **in ~ giorno** in broad daylight; **fare il ~** (*di benzina*) to fill up (with petrol).

pietà *sf* pity; (*REL*) piety; **senza ~** pitiless, merciless; **avere ~ di** (*compassione*) to pity, feel sorry for; (*misericordia*) to have pity o mercy on.

pie'tanza [pje'tantsa] *sf* dish; (main) course.

pie'toso, a *ag* (*compassionevole*) pitying, compassionate; (*che desta pietà*) pitiful.

pi'etra *sf* stone; **~ preziosa** precious

stone, gem; **pie'traia** *sf* (*terreno*) stony ground; **pietrifi'care** *vt* to petrify; (*fig*) to transfix, paralyze.

'piffero *sm* (*MUS*) pipe.

pigi'ama, i [pi'dʒama] *sm* pyjamas *pl.*

'pigia 'pigia ['pidʒa'pidʒa] *sm* crowd, press.

pigi'are [pi'dʒare] *vt* to press.

pigi'one [pi'dʒone] *sf* rent.

pigli'are [piʎ'ʎare] *vt* to take, grab; (*afferrare*) to catch.

'piglio ['piʎʎo] *sm* look, expression.

pig'meo, a *smf* pygmy.

'pigna ['piɲɲa] *sf* pine cone.

pi'gnolo, a [piɲ'nolo] *ag* pernickety.

pigo'lare *vi* to cheep, chirp.

pi'grizia [pi'grittsja] *sf* laziness.

'pigro, a *ag* lazy.

'pila *sf* (*catasta, di ponte*) pile; (*ELETTR*) battery; (*fam: torcia*) torch (*Brit*), flashlight.

pi'lastro *sm* pillar.

'pillola *sf* pill; **prendere la ~** to be on the pill.

pi'lone *sm* (*di ponte*) pier; (*di linea elettrica*) pylon.

pi'lota, i, e *smf* pilot; (*AUT*) driver // *ag inv* pilot *cpd*; **~ automatico** automatic pilot; **pilo'tare** *vt* to pilot; to drive.

pi'mento *sm* pimento, allspice.

pinaco'teca, che *sf* art gallery.

pi'neta *sf* pinewood.

ping-'pong [piŋ'pɔŋ] *sm* table tennis.

'pingue *ag* fat, corpulent.

pingu'ino *sm* (*ZOOL*) penguin.

'pinna *sf* fin; (*di pinguino, spatola di gomma*) flipper.

'pino *sm* pine (tree); **pi'nolo** *sm* pine kernel.

'pinza ['pintsa] *sf* pliers *pl*; (*MED*) forceps *pl*; (*ZOOL*) pincer.

pinzette [pin'tsette] *sfpl* tweezers.

'pio, a, 'pii, 'pie *ag* pious; (*opere, istituzione*) charitable, charity *cpd*.

pi'oggia, ge ['pjɔddʒa] *sf* rain; **~ acida** acid rain.

pi'olo *sm* peg; (*di scala*) rung.

piom'bare *vi* to fall heavily; (*gettarsi con impeto*): **~ su** to fall upon, assail // *vt* (*dente*) to fill; **piomba'tura** *sf* (*di dente*) filling.

piom'bino *sm* (*sigillo*) (lead) seal; (*del filo a piombo*) plummet; (*PESCA*) sinker.

pi'ombo *sm* (*CHIM*) lead; (*sigillo*) (lead) seal; (*proiettile*) (lead) shot; **a ~** (*cadere*) straight down.

pioni'ere, a *smf* pioneer.

pi'oppo *sm* poplar.

pi'overe *vb impers* to rain // *vi* (*fig: scendere dall'alto*) to rain down; (: *affluire in gran numero*): **~ in** to pour into; **pioviggi'nare** *vb impers* to drizzle; **pio'voso, a** *ag* rainy.

pi'ovra *sf* octopus.

'pipa *sf* pipe.

pipì *sf* (*fam*): **fare ~** to have a wee (wee).

pipis'trello *sm* (ZOOL) bat.

pi'ramide *sf* pyramid.

pi'rata, i *sm* pirate; **~ della strada** hit-and-run driver.

Pire'nei *smpl*: **l ~** the Pyrenees.

'pirico, a, ci, che *ag*: **polvere ~a** gunpowder.

pi'rite *sf* pyrite.

pi'rofilo, a *ag* heat-resistant.

pi'roga, ghe *sf* dug-out canoe.

pi'romane *sm/f* pyromaniac; arsonist.

pi'roscafo *sm* steamer, steamship.

pisci'are [piʃ'ʃare] *vi* (*fam!*) to piss (!), pee (!).

pi'scina [piʃ'ʃina] *sf* (swimming) pool; (*stabilimento*) (swimming) baths *pl*.

pi'sello *sm* pea.

piso'lino *sm* nap.

'pista *sf* (*traccia*) track, trail; (*di stadio*) track; (*di pattinaggio*) rink; (*da sci*) run; (AER) runway; (*di circo*) ring; **~ da ballo** dance floor.

pis'tacchio [pis'takkjo] *sm* pistachio (tree), pistachio (nut).

pis'tola *sf* pistol, gun.

pis'tone *sm* piston.

pi'tone *sm* python.

pit'tore, 'trice *sm/f* painter; **pitto'resco, a, schi, sche** *ag* picturesque.

pit'tura *sf* painting; **pittu'rare** *vt* to paint.

più ♦ *av* **1** (*in maggiore quantità*) more; **~ del solito** more than usual; **in ~, di ~** more; **ne voglio di ~** I want some more; **ci sono 3 persone in o di ~** there are 3 more o extra people; **~ o meno** more or less; **per di ~** (*inoltre*) what's more, moreover **2** (*comparativo*) more, *aggettivo corto +* **...er;** **~ ... di/che** more ... than; **lavoro ~ di te/Paola** I work harder than you/Paola; **è ~ intelligente che ricco** he's more intelligent than rich **3** (*superlativo*) most, *aggettivo corto +* **...est;** **il ~ grande/intelligente** the biggest/most intelligent; **è quello che compro ~ spesso** that's the one I buy most often; **al ~ presto** as soon as possible; **al ~ tardi** at the latest **4** (*negazione*): **non ... ~** no more, no longer; **non ho ~ soldi** I've got no more money, I don't have any more money; **non lavoro ~** I'm no longer working, I don't work any more; **a ~ non posso** (*gridare*) at the top of one's voice; (*correre*) as fast as one can **5** (MAT) plus; **4 ~ 5 fa 9** 4 plus 5 equals 9; **~ 5 gradi** 5 degrees above freezing, plus 5 **♦** *prep* plus **♦** *av inv* **1**: **~ ... (di)** more ... (than); **~ denaro/tempo** more money/time; **~**

persone di quante ci aspettassimo more people than we expected **2** (*numerosi, diversi*) several; **l'aspettai per ~ giorni** I waited for it for several days **♦** *sm* **1** (*la maggior parte*): **il ~ è fatto** most of it is done **2** (MAT) plus (sign) **3**: **i ~** the majority.

piuccheper'fetto [pjukkepper'fetto] *sm* (LING) pluperfect, past perfect.

pi'uma *sf* feather; **~e** *sfpl* down *sg*; (*piumaggio*) plumage *sg*, feathers; **piu'maggio** *sm* plumage, feathers *pl*; **piu'mino** *sm* (eider)down; (*per letto*) eiderdown; (: *tipo danese*) duvet, continental quilt; (*giacca*) quilted jacket (*with goose-feather padding*); (*per cipria*) powder puff; (*per spolverare*) feather duster.

piut'tosto *av* rather; **~ che** (*anziché*) rather than.

pi'vello, a *sm/f* greenhorn.

'pizza ['pittsa] *sf* pizza; **pizze'ria** *sf* place where pizzas are made, sold or eaten.

pizzi'cagnolo, a [pittsi'kaɲɲolo] *sm/f* specialist grocer.

pizzi'care [pittsi'kare] *vt* (*stringere*) to nip, pinch; (*pungere*) to sting; to bite; (*MUS*) to pluck // *vi* (*prudere*) to itch, be itchy; (*cibo*) to be hot o spicy.

pizziche'ria [pittsike'ria] *sf* delicatessen (shop).

'pizzico, chi ['pittsiko] *sm* (*pizzicotto*) pinch, nip; (*piccola quantità*) pinch, dash; (*d'insetto*) sting; bite.

pizzi'cotto [pittsi'kotto] *sm* pinch, nip.

'pizzo ['pittso] *sm* (*merletto*) lace; (*barbetta*) goatee beard.

pla'care *vt* to placate, soothe; **~rsi** *vr* to calm down.

'placca, che *sf* plate; (*con iscrizione*) plaque; (*anche*: **~ dentaria**) (dental) plaque; **plac'care** *vt* to plate; **placcato in oro/argento** gold-/silver-plated.

'placido, a ['platʃido] *ag* placid, calm.

plagi'are [pla'dʒare] *vt* (*copiare*) to plagiarize; **'plagio** *sm* plagiarism.

pla'nare *vi* (AER) to glide.

'plancia, ce ['plantʃa] *sf* (NAUT) bridge.

plane'tario, a *ag* planetary // *sm* (*locale*) planetarium.

'plasma *sm* plasma.

plas'mare *vt* to mould, shape.

'plastico, a, ci, che *ag* plastic // *sm* (*rappresentazione*) relief model; (*esplosivo*): **bomba al ~** plastic bomb // *sf* (*arte*) plastic arts *pl*; (MED) plastic surgery; (*sostanza*) plastic.

plasti'lina *sf* ® plasticine ®.

'platano *sm* plane tree.

pla'tea *sf* (TEATRO) stalls *pl*.

'platino *sm* platinum.

pla'tonico, a, ci, che *ag* platonic.

plau'sibile *ag* plausible.

'**plauso** *sm* (*fig*) approval.
ple'baglia [ple'baʎʎa] *sf* (*peg*) rabble, mob.
'**plebe** *sf* common people; **ple'beo, a** *ag* plebeian; (*volgare*) coarse, common.
ple'nario, a *ag* plenary.
pleni'lunio *sm* full moon.
'**plettro** *sm* plectrum.
pleu'rite *sf* pleurisy.
'**plico, chi** *sm* (*pacco*) parcel; **in ~ a parte** (*COMM*) under separate cover.
plo'tone *sm* (*MIL*) platoon; **~ d'esecuzione** firing squad.
'**plumbeo, a** *ag* leaden.
plu'rale *ag, sm* plural; **pluralità** *sf* plurality; (*maggioranza*) majority.
plusva'lore *sm* (*ECON*) surplus.
pneu'matico, a, ci, che *ag* inflatable; pneumatic // *sm* (*AUT*) tyre (*Brit*), tire (*US*).
po' *av, sm vedi* **poco**.
'**poco, a, chi, che ◆** *ag* **1** (*quantità*) little, not much; (*numero*) few, not many; **~ pane/denaro/spazio** little *o* not much bread/money/space; **~che persone/idee** few *o* not many people/ideas; **ci vediamo tra ~** (*sottinteso: tempo*) see you soon
◆ *av* **1** (*in piccola quantità*) little, not much; (*numero limitato*) few, not many; **guadagna ~** he doesn't earn much, he earns little
2 (*con ag, av*) (a) little, not very; **sta ~ bene** he isn't very well; **è ~ più vecchia di lui** she's a little *o* slightly older than him
3 (*tempo*): **~ dopo/prima** shortly afterwards/before; **il film dura ~** the film doesn't last very long; **ci vediamo molto ~** we don't see each other very often, we hardly ever see each other
4: **un po'** a little, a bit; **è un po' corto** it's a little *o* a bit short; **arriverà fra un po'** he'll arrive shortly *o* in a little while
5: **a dir ~** to say the least; **a ~ a ~** little by little; **per ~ non cadevo** I nearly fell; **è una cosa da ~** it's nothing, it's of no importance; **una persona da ~** a worthless person
◆ *pronome* (a) little; **~chi(che)** *pronome pl* (*persone*) few (people); (*cose*) few
◆ *sm* **1** little; **vive del ~ che ha** he lives on the little he has
2: **un po'** a little; **un po' di zucchero** a little sugar; **un bel po' di denaro** quite a lot of money; **un po' per ciascuno** a bit each.
po'dere *sm* (*AGR*) farm.
pode'roso, a *ag* powerful.
podestà *sm inv* (*nel fascismo*) podesta, mayor.
'**podio** *sm* dais, platform; (*MUS*) podium.
po'dismo *sm* (*SPORT*) track events *pl*.
po'ema, i *sm* poem.

poe'sia *sf* (*arte*) poetry; (*componimento*) poem.
po'eta, 'essa *sm/f* poet/poetess; **po'etico, a, ci, che** *ag* poetic(al).
poggi'are [pod'dʒare] *vt* to lean, rest; (*posare*) to lay, place; **poggia'testa** *sm inv* (*AUT*) headrest.
'**poggio** ['pɔddʒo] *sm* hillock, knoll.
'**poi** *av* then; (*alla fine*) finally, at last; **e ~** (*inoltre*) and besides; **questa ~** (*è bella*)! (*ironico*) that's a good one!
poiché [poi'ke] *cong* since, as.
'**poker** *sm* poker.
po'lacco, a, chi, che *ag* Polish // *sm/f* Pole.
po'lare *ag* polar.
po'lemico, a, ci, che *ag* polemic(al), controversial // *sf* controversy.
po'lenta *sf* (*CUC*) sort of thick porridge made with maize flour.
poli'clinico, ci *sm* general hospital, polyclinic.
poli'estere *sm* polyester.
'**polio(mie'lite)** *sf* polio(myelitis).
'**polipo** *sm* polyp.
polisti'rolo *sm* polystyrene.
poli'tecnico, ci *sm* postgraduate technical college.
politiciz'zare [polititʃid'dzare] *vt* to politicize.
po'litico, a, ci, che *ag* political // *sm/f* politician // *sf* politics *sg*; (*linea di condotta*) policy.
poli'zia [polit'tsia] *sf* police; **~ giudiziaria** ≈ Criminal Investigation Department (CID) (*Brit*), ≈ Federal Bureau of Investigation (FBI) (*US*); **~ stradale** traffic police; **polizi'esco, a, schi, sche** *ag* police *cpd*; (*film, romanzo*) detective *cpd*; **polizi'otto** *sm* policeman; **cane poliziotto** police dog; **donna poliziotto** policewoman.
'**polizza** ['pɔlittsa] *sf* (*COMM*) bill; **~ di assicurazione** insurance policy; **~ di carico** bill of lading.
pol'laio *sm* henhouse.
pol'lame *sm* poultry.
pol'lastro *sm* (*ZOOL*) cockerel.
'**pollice** ['pɔllitʃe] *sm* thumb.
'**polline** *sm* pollen.
'**pollo** *sm* chicken.
pol'mone *sm* lung; **polmo'nite** *sf* pneumonia.
'**polo** *sm* (*GEO, FISICA*) pole; (*gioco*) polo; **il ~ sud/nord** the South/North Pole.
Po'lonia *sf*: **la ~** Poland.
'**polpa** *sf* flesh, pulp; (*carne*) lean meat.
pol'paccio [pol'pattʃo] *sm* (*ANAT*) calf.
pol'petta *sf* (*CUC*) meatball; **polpet'tone** *sm* (*CUC*) meatloaf.
'**polpo** *sm* octopus.
pol'poso, a *ag* fleshy.
pol'sino *sm* cuff.
'**polso** *sm* (*ANAT*) wrist; (*pulsazione*) pulse; (*fig: forza*) drive, vigour.

pol'tiglia [pol'tiʎʎa] sf (composto) mash, mush; (di fango e neve) slush.

pol'trire vi to laze about.

pol'trona sf armchair; (TEATRO: posto) seat in the front stalls (Brit) o orchestra (US).

pol'trone ag lazy, slothful.

'polvere sf dust; (anche: ~ da sparo) (gun)powder; (sostanza ridotta minutissima) powder, dust; **latte in ~** dried o powdered milk; **caffè in ~** instant coffee; **sapone in ~** soap powder; **polveri'era** sf powder magazine; **polveriz'zare** vt to pulverize; (nebulizzare) to atomize; (fig) to crush, pulverize; to smash; **polve'rone** sm thick cloud of dust; **polve'roso, a** ag dusty.

po'mata sf ointment, cream.

po'mello sm knob.

pomeridi'ano, a ag afternoon cpd; **nelle ore ~e** in the afternoon.

pome'riggio [pome'riddʒo] sm afternoon.

'pomice ['pɔmitʃe] sf pumice.

'pomo sm (mela) apple; (ornamentale) knob; (di sella) pommel; **~ d'Adamo** (ANAT) Adam's apple.

pomo'doro sm tomato.

'pompa sf pump; (sfarzo) pomp (and ceremony); **~e funebri** funeral parlour sg (Brit), undertaker's sg; **pom'pare** vt to pump; (trarre) to pump out; (gonfiare d'aria) to pump up.

pom'pelmo sm grapefruit.

pompi'ere sm fireman.

pom'poso, a ag pompous.

ponde'rare vt to ponder over, consider carefully.

ponde'roso, a ag (anche fig) weighty.

po'nente sm west.

'ponte sm bridge; (di nave) deck; (: anche: ~ di comando) bridge; (impalcatura) scaffold; **fare il ~** (fig) to take the extra day off (between 2 public holidays); **governo ~** interim government; **~ aereo** airlift; **~ sospeso** suspension bridge.

pon'tefice [pon'tefitʃe] sm (REL) pontiff.

pontifi'care vi (anche fig) to pontificate.

ponti'ficio, a, ci, cie [ponti'fitʃo] ag papal.

popo'lano, a ag popular, of the people.

popo'lare ag popular; (quartiere, clientela) working-class // vt (rendere abitato) to populate; **~rsi** vr to fill with people, get crowded; **popolarità** sf popularity; **popolazi'one** sf population.

'popolo sm people; **popo'loso, a** ag densely populated.

po'pone sm melon.

'poppa sf (di nave) stern; (mammella) breast.

pop'pare vt to suck.

poppa'toio sm (feeding) bottle.

porcel'lana [portʃel'lana] sf porcelain, china; piece of china.

porcel'lino, a [portʃel'lino] sm/f piglet.

porche'ria [porke'ria] sf filth, muck; (fig: oscenità) obscenity; (: azione disonesta) dirty trick; (: cosa mal fatta) rubbish.

por'cile [por'tʃile] sm pigsty.

por'cino, a [por'tʃino] ag of pigs, pork cpd // sm (fungo) type of edible mushroom.

'porco, ci sm pig; (carne) pork.

porcos'pino sm porcupine.

'porgere ['pɔrdʒere] vt to hand, give; (tendere) to hold out.

pornogra'fia sf pornography; **porno'grafico, a, ci, che** ag pornographic.

'poro sm pore; **po'roso, a** ag porous.

'porpora sf purple.

'porre vt (mettere) to put; (collocare) to place; (posare) to lay (down), put (down); (fig: supporre): **poniamo (il caso) che ...** let's suppose that ...; **porsi** vr (mettersi): **porsi a sedere/in cammino** to sit down/set off; **~ una domanda a qn** to ask sb a question, put a question to sb.

'porro sm (BOT) leek; (MED) wart.

'porta sf door; (SPORT) goal; **~e** sfpl (di città) gates; **a ~e chiuse** (DIR) in camera.

'porta... prefisso: **portaba'gagli** sm inv (facchino) porter; (AUT, FERR) luggage rack; **portabandi'era** sm inv standard bearer; **porta'cenere** sm inv ashtray; **portachi'avi** sm inv keyring; **porta'cipria** sm inv powder compact; **porta'erei** sf inv (nave) aircraft carrier // sm inv (aereo) aircraft transporter; **portafi'nestra**, pl **portefi'nestre** sf French window; **porta'foglio** sm (busta) wallet; (cartella) briefcase; (POL, BORSA) portfolio; **portafor'tuna** sm inv lucky charm; mascot; **portagi'oie** sm inv, **portagioi'elli** sm inv jewellery box.

porta'lettere sm/f inv postman/woman (Brit), mailman/woman (US).

porta'mento sm carriage, bearing.

porta'monete sm inv purse.

por'tante ag (muro etc) supporting, load-bearing.

portan'tina sf sedan chair; (per ammalati) stretcher.

por'tare vt (sostenere, sorreggere: peso, bambino, pacco) to carry; (indossare: abito, occhiali) to wear; (: capelli lunghi) to have; (avere: nome, titolo) to have, bear; (recare): **~ qc a qn** to take (o bring) sth to sb; (fig: sentimenti) to bear; **~rsi** vr (recarsi) to go; **~ avanti** (discorso, idea) to pursue; **~ via** to take away; (rubare) to take; **~ i bambini a spasso** to take the children for a walk; **~**

fortuna to bring good luck.

portasiga'rette *sm inv* cigarette case.

por'tata *sf* (*vivanda*) course; (*AUT*) carrying o loading) capacity; (*di arma*) range; (*volume d'acqua*) (rate of) flow; (*fig: limite*) scope, capability; (: *importanza*) impact, import; **alla ~ di tutti** (*conoscenza*) within everybody's capabilities; (*prezzo*) within everybody's means; **a/fuori ~ (di)** within/out of reach (of); **a ~ di mano** within (arm's) reach.

por'tatile *ag* portable.

por'tato, a *ag* (*incline*): **~ a** inclined o apt to.

porta'tore, 'trice *smf* (*anche COMM*) bearer; (*MED*) carrier.

portau'ovo *sm inv* eggcup.

porta'voce [porta'votʃe] *smf inv* spokesman/woman.

por'tento *sm* wonder, marvel.

'portico, ci *sm* portico.

porti'era *sf* (*AUT*) door.

porti'ere *sm* (*portinaio*) concierge, caretaker; (*di hotel*) porter; (*nel calcio*) goalkeeper.

porti'naio, a *smf* concierge, caretaker.

portine'ria *sf* caretaker's lodge.

'porto, a *pp di* porgere // *sm* (*NAUT*) harbour, port; (*spesa di trasporto*) carriage // *sm inv* port (wine); **~ d'armi** (*documento*) gun licence.

Porto'gallo *sm*: **il ~** Portugal; **porto'ghese** *ag*, *smf*, *sm* Portuguese *inv*.

por'tone *sm* main entrance, main door.

portu'ale *ag* harbour *cpd*, port *cpd* // *sm* dock worker.

porzi'one [por'tsjone] *sf* portion, share; (*di cibo*) portion, helping.

'posa *sf* (*FOT*) exposure; (*atteggiamento*, *di modello*) pose.

po'sare *vt* to put (down), lay (down) // *vi* (*ponte*, *edificio*, *teoria*): **~ su** to rest on; (*FOT*, *atteggiarsi*) to pose; **~rsi** *vr* (*aereo*) to land; (*uccello*) to alight; (*sguardo*) to settle.

po'sata *sf* piece of cutlery; **~e** *sfpl* cutlery *sg*.

po'sato, a *ag* serious.

pos'critto *sm* postscript.

posi'tivo, a *ag* positive.

posizi'one [pozit'tsjone] *sf* position; **prendere ~** (*fig*) to take a stand; **luci di ~** (*AUT*) sidelights.

posolo'gia, 'gie [pozolo'dʒia] *sf* dosage, directions *pl* for use.

pos'porre *vt* to place after; (*differire*) to postpone, defer; **pos'posto, a** *pp di* posporre.

posse'dere *vt* to own, possess; (*qualità*, *virtù*) to have, possess; (*conoscere a fondo: lingua etc*) to have a thorough knowledge of; (*sog: ira etc*) to possess; **possedi'mento** *sm* possession.

posses'sivo, a *ag* possessive.

pos'sesso *sm* ownership *q*; possession.

posses'sore *sm* owner.

pos'sibile *ag* possible // *sm*: **fare tutto il ~** to do everything possible; **nei limiti del ~** as far as possible; **al più tardi ~** as late as possible; **possibilità** *sf inv* possibility // *sfpl* (*mezzi*) means; **aver la possibilità di fare** to be in a position to do; to have the opportunity to do.

possi'dente *smf* landowner.

'posta *sf* (*servizio*) post, postal service; (*corrispondenza*) post, mail; (*ufficio postale*) post office; (*nei giochi d'azzardo*) stake; **~e** *sfpl* (*amministrazione*) post office; **~ aerea** airmail; **ministro delle P~e e Telecomunicazioni** Postmaster General; **posta'giro** *sm* post office cheque, postal giro (*Brit*); **pos'tale** *ag* postal, post office *cpd*.

post'bellico, a, ci, che *ag* postwar.

posteggi'are [posted'dʒare] *vt*, *vi* to park; **pos'teggio** *sm* car park (*Brit*), parking lot (*US*); (*di taxi*) rank (*Brit*), stand (*US*).

postelegra'fonico, a, ci, che *ag* postal and telecommunications *cpd*.

posteri'ore *ag* (*dietro*) back; (*dopo*) later // *sm* (*fam: sedere*) behind.

pos'ticcio, a, ci, ce [pos'tittʃo] *ag* false // *sm* hairpiece.

postici'pare [postitʃi'pare] *vt* to defer, postpone.

pos'tilla *sf* marginal note.

pos'tino *sm* postman (*Brit*), mailman (*US*).

'posto, a *pp di* porre // *sm* (*sito*, *posizione*) place; (*impiego*) job; (*spazio libero*) room, space; (*di parcheggio*) space; (*sedile: al teatro, in treno etc*) seat; (*MIL*) post; **a ~** (*in ordine*) in place, tidy; (*fig*) settled; (: *persona*) reliable; **al ~ di** in place of; **sul ~** on the spot; **mettere a ~** to tidy (up), put in order; (*faccende*) to straighten out; **~ di blocco** roadblock; **~ di polizia** police station.

pos'tribolo *sm* brothel.

'postumo, a *ag* posthumous; (*tardivo*) belated; **~i** *smpl* (*conseguenze*) aftereffects, consequences.

po'tabile *ag* drinkable; **acqua ~** drinking water.

po'tare *vt* to prune.

po'tassio *sm* potassium.

po'tente *ag* (*nazione*) strong, powerful; (*veleno*, *farmaco*) potent, strong; **po'tenza** *sf* power; (*forza*) strength.

potenzi'ale [poten'tsjale] *ag*, *sm* potential.

po'tere ♦ *sm* power; **al ~** (*partito etc*) in power; **~ d'acquisto** purchasing power **♦** *vb ausiliare* **1** (*essere in grado di*) can, be able to; **non ha potuto ripararlo** he couldn't o he wasn't able to repair it;

non è potuto venire he couldn't *o* he wasn't able to come; **spiacente di non poter aiutare** sorry not to be able to help **2** *(avere il permesso)* can, may, be allowed to; **posso entrare?** can *o* may I come in?; **si può sapere dove sei stato?** where on earth have you been?

3 *(eventualità)* may, might, could; **potrebbe essere vero** it might *o* could be true; **può aver avuto un incidente** he may *o* might *o* could have had an accident; **può darsi** perhaps; **può darsi** *o* **essere che non venga** he may *o* might not come

4 *(augurio)*: **potessi almeno parlargli!** if only I could speak to him!

5 *(suggerimento)*: **potresti almeno scusarti!** you could at least apologize!

♦ *vt* can, be able to; **può molto per noi** he can do a lot for us; **non ne posso più** *(per stanchezza)* I'm exhausted; *(per rabbia)* I can't take any more.

potestà *sf (potere)* power; *(DIR)* authority.

'povero, a *ag* poor; *(disadorno)* plain, bare *// sm/f (poor man/woman)*: **i ~i** the poor; **~ di** lacking in, having little; **povertà** *sf* poverty.

'pozza ['pottsa] *sf* pool.

poz'zanghera [pot'tsangera] *sf* puddle.

'pozzo ['pottso] *sm* well; *(cava: di carbone)* pit; *(di miniera)* shaft; **~ petrolifero** oil well.

pran'zare [pran'dzare] *vi* to dine, have dinner; to lunch, have lunch.

'pranzo ['prandzo] *sm* dinner; *(a mezzogiorno)* lunch.

'prassi *sf* usual procedure.

'pratica, che *sf* practice; *(esperienza)* experience; *(conoscenza)* knowledge, familiarity; *(tirocinio)* training, practice; *(AMM: affare)* matter, case; *(: incartamento)* file, dossier; **in ~** *(praticamente)* in practice; **mettere in ~** to put into practice.

prati'cabile *ag (progetto)* practicable, feasible; *(luogo)* passable, practicable.

prati'cante *sm/f* apprentice, trainee; *(REL)* (regular) churchgoer.

prati'care *vt* to practise; *(SPORT: tennis etc)* to play; *(: nuoto, scherma etc)* to go in for; *(eseguire: apertura, buco)* to make; **~ uno sconto** to give a discount.

'pratico, a, ci, che *ag* practical; **~ di** *(esperto)* experienced *o* skilled in; *(familiare)* familiar with.

'prato *sm* meadow; *(di giardino)* lawn.

preav'viso *sm* notice; **telefonata con ~** personal *o* person to person call.

pre'cario, a *ag* precarious; *(INS)* temporary.

precauzi'one [prekaut'tsjone] *sf* caution, care; *(misura)* precaution.

prece'dente [pretʃe'dɛnte] *ag* previous //

sm precedent; **il discorso/film ~** the previous *o* preceding speech/film; **senza ~i** unprecedented; **i penali** criminal record *sg*; **prece'denza** *sf* priority, precedence; *(AUT)* right of way.

pre'cedere [pre'tʃɛdere] *vt* to precede, go *o* come before.

pre'cetto [pre'tʃetto] *sm* precept; *(MIL)* call-up notice.

precet'tore [pretʃet'tore] *sm* (private) tutor.

precipi'tare [pretʃipi'tare] *vi (cadere)* to fall headlong; *(fig: situazione)* to get out of control // *vt (gettare dall'alto in basso)* to hurl, fling; *(fig: affrettare)* to rush; **~rsi** *vr (gettarsi)* to hurl *o* fling o.s.; *(affrettarsi)* to rush; **precipi'tazi'one** *sf (METEOR)* precipitation; *(fig)* haste; **precipi'toso, a** *ag (caduta, fuga)* headlong; *(fig: avventato)* rash, reckless; *(: affrettato)* hasty, rushed.

preci'pizio [pretʃi'pittsjo] *sm* precipice; **a ~** *(fig: correre)* headlong.

preci'sare [pretʃi'zare] *vt* to state, specify; *(spiegare)* to explain (in detail).

precisi'one [pretʃi'zjone] *sf* precision; accuracy.

pre'ciso, a [pre'tʃizo] *ag (esatto)* precise; *(accurato)* accurate, precise; *(deciso: idee)* precise, definite; *(uguale)*: **2 vestiti ~i** 2 dresses exactly the same; **sono le 9 ~e** it's exactly 9 o'clock.

pre'cludere *vt* to block, obstruct; **pre'cluso, a** *pp di* **precludere.**

pre'coce [pre'kotʃe] *ag* early; *(bambino)* precocious; *(vecchiaia)* premature.

precon'cetto [prekon'tʃetto] *sm* preconceived idea, prejudice.

precur'sore *sm* forerunner, precursor.

'preda *sf (bottino)* booty; *(animale, fig)* prey; **essere ~ di** to fall prey to; **essere in ~ a** to be prey to; **preda'tore** *sm* predator.

predeces'sore, a [predetʃes'sore] *sm/f* predecessor.

predesti'nare *vt* to predestine.

pre'detto, a *pp di* **predire.**

'predica, che *sf* sermon; *(fig)* lecture, talking-to.

predi'care *vt, vi* to preach.

predi'cato *sm (LING)* predicate.

predi'letto, a *pp di* **prediligere** // *ag, sm/f* favourite.

predilezi'one [predilet'tsjone] *sf* fondness, partiality; **avere una ~ per qc/qn** to be partial to sth/fond of sb.

predi'ligere [predi'lidʒere] *vt* to prefer, have a preference for.

pre'dire *vt* to foretell, predict.

predis'porre *vt* to get ready, prepare; **~ qn a qc** to predispose sb to sth; **predis'posto, a** *pp di* **predisporre.**

predizi'one [predit'tsjone] *sf* prediction.

predomi'nare *vi* to predominate; **predo'minio** *sm* predominance; supremacy.

prefabbri'cato, a *ag* (EDIL) prefabricated.

prefazi'one [prefat'tsjone] *sf* preface, foreword.

prefe'renza [prefe'rɛntsa] *sf* preference; **preferenzi'ale** *ag* preferential; **corsia** ~ bus and taxi lane.

prefe'rire *vt* to prefer, like better; ~ **il caffè al tè** to prefer coffee to tea, like coffee better than tea.

pre'fetto *sm* prefect; **prefet'tura** *sf* prefecture.

pre'figgersi [pre'fiddʒersi] *vr:* ~**rsi uno scopo** to set o.s. a goal.

pre'fisso, a *pp di* **prefiggere** // *sm* (LING) prefix; (TEL) dialling (Brit) *o* dial (US) code.

pre'gare *vi* to pray // *vt* (REL) to pray to; (*implorare*) to beg; (*chiedere*): ~ **qn di fare** to ask sb to do; **farsi** ~ to need coaxing *o* persuading.

pre'gevole [pre'dʒevole] *ag* valuable.

preghi'era [pre'gjɛra] *sf* (REL) prayer; (*domanda*) request.

pregi'ato, a [pre'dʒato] *ag* (*di valore*) valuable; **vino** ~ vintage wine.

'pregio ['prɛdʒo] *sm* (*stima*) esteem, regard; (*qualità*) (good) quality, merit; (*valore*) value, worth.

pregiudi'care [predʒudi'kare] *vt* to prejudice, harm, be detrimental to; **pregiudi'cato, a** *sm/f* (DIR) previous offender.

pregiu'dizio [predʒu'dittsjo] *sm* (*idea errata*) prejudice; (*danno*) harm *q*.

'pregno, a ['preɲɲo] *ag* (*gravido*) pregnant; (*saturo*): ~ **di** full of, saturated with.

'prego *escl* (*a chi ringrazia*) don't mention it!; (*invitando qn ad accomodarsi*) please sit down!; (*invitando qn ad andare prima*) after you!

pregus'tare *vt* to look forward to.

preis'torico, a, ci, che *ag* prehistoric.

pre'lato *sm* prelate.

prele'vare *vt* (*denaro*) to withdraw; (*campione*) to take; (*sog: polizia*) to take, capture.

preli'evo *sm* (MED): **fare un** ~ (**di**) to take a sample (of).

prelimi'nare *ag* preliminary; ~**i** *smpl* preliminary talks; preliminaries.

pre'ludio *sm* prelude.

pré-ma'man [prema'mã] *sm inv* maternity dress.

prema'turo, a *ag* premature.

premeditazi'one [premeditat'tsjone] *sf* (DIR) premeditation; **con** ~ *ag* premeditated // *av* with intent.

'premere *vt* to press // *vi:* ~ **su** to press down on; (*fig*) to put pressure on; ~ **a** (*fig: importare*) to matter to.

pre'messo, a *pp di* **premettere** // *sf* introductory statement, introduction.

pre'mettere *vt* to put before; (*dire prima*) to start by saying, state first.

premi'are *vt* to give a prize to; (*fig: merito, onestà*) to reward.

'premio *sm* prize; (*ricompensa*) reward; (COMM) premium; (AMM: *indennità*) bonus.

premu'nirsi *vr:* ~ **di** to provide o.s. with; ~ **contro** to protect o.s. from, guard o.s. against.

pre'mura *sf* (*fretta*) haste, hurry; (*riguardo*) attention, care; **premu'roso, a** *ag* thoughtful, considerate.

prena'tale *ag* antenatal.

'prendere *vt* to take; (*andare a prendere*) to get, fetch; (*ottenere*) to get; (*guadagnare*) to get, earn; (*catturare: ladro, pesce*) to catch; (*collaboratore, dipendente*) to take on; (*passeggero*) to pick up; (*chiedere: somma, prezzo*) to charge, ask; (*trattare: persona*) to handle // *vi* (*colla, cemento*) to set; (*pianta*) to take; (*fuoco: nel camino*) to catch; (*voltare*): ~ **a destra** to turn (to the) right; ~**rsi** *vr* (*azzuffarsi*): ~**rsi a pugni** to come to blows; **prendi qualcosa?** (*da bere, da mangiare*) would you like something to eat (*o* drink)?; **prendo un caffè** I'll have a coffee; ~ **a fare qc** to start doing sth; ~ **qn/qc per** (*scambiare*) to take sb/sth for; ~ **fuoco** to catch fire; ~ **parte a** to take part in; ~**rsi cura di qn/qc** to look after sb/sth; **prendersela** (*adirarsi*) to get annoyed; (*preoccuparsi*) to get upset, worry.

prendi'sole *sm inv* sundress.

preno'tare *vt* to book, reserve; **prenotazi'one** *sf* booking, reservation.

preoccu'pare *vt* to worry; to preoccupy; ~**rsi** *vr:* ~**rsi di qn/qc** to worry about sb/sth; ~**rsi per qn** to be anxious for sb; **preoccupazi'one** *sf* worry, anxiety.

prepa'rare *vt* to prepare; (*esame, concorso*) to prepare for; ~**rsi** *vr* (*vestirsi*) to get ready; ~**rsi a qc/a fare** to get ready *o* prepare (o.s.) for sth/to do; ~ **da mangiare** to prepare a meal; **prepa'rativi** *smpl* preparations; **prepa'rato** *sm* (*prodotto*) preparation; **preparazi'one** *sf* preparation.

preposizi'one [prepozit'tsjone] *sf* (LING) preposition.

prepo'tente *ag* (*persona*) domineering, arrogant; (*bisogno, desiderio*) overwhelming, pressing // *sm/f* bully; **prepo'tenza** *sf* arrogance; arrogant behaviour.

'presa *sf* taking *q*; catching *q*; (*di città*) capture; (*indurimento: di cemento*) setting; (*appiglio, SPORT*) hold; (*di acqua, gas*) (supply) point; (ELETTR): ~ (**di corrente**) socket; (: **al muro**) point;

(*piccola quantità: di sale etc*) pinch; (*CARTE*) trick; far ~ (*colla*) to set; far ~ sul pubblico to catch the public's imagination; ~ d'aria air inlet; essere alle ~e con qc (*fig*) to be struggling with sth.

pre'sagio [pre'zadʒo] *sm* omen.

presa'gire [preza'dʒire] *vt* to foresee.

'presbite *ag* long-sighted.

presbi'terio *sm* presbytery.

pre'scindere [preʃ'ʃindere] *vi*: ~ da to leave out of consideration; a ~ da apart from.

pres'critto, a *pp di* **prescrivere**.

pres'crivere *vt* to prescribe; **prescrizi'one** *sf* (*MED, DIR*) prescription; (*norma*) rule, regulation.

presen'tare *vt* to present; (*far conoscere*): ~ qn (a) to introduce sb (to); (*AMM: inoltrare*) to submit; ~rsi *vr* (*recarsi, farsi vedere*) to present o.s., appear; (*farsi conoscere*) to introduce o.s.; (*occasione*) to arise; ~rsi come candidato (*POL*) to stand as a candidate; ~rsi bene/male to have a good/poor appearance; **presentazi'one** *sf* presentation; introduction.

pre'sente *ag* present; (*questo*) this // *sm* present; i ~i those present; aver ~ qc/qn to remember sth/sb.

presenti'mento *sm* premonition.

pre'senza [pre'zɛntsa] *sf* presence; (*aspetto esteriore*) appearance; ~ di spirito presence of mind.

pre'sepio, pre'sepe *sm* crib.

preser'vare *vt* to protect; to save; **preserva'tivo** *sm* sheath, condom.

'preside *sm/f* (*INS*) head (teacher) (*Brit*), principal (*US*); (*di facoltà universitaria*) dean.

presi'dente *sm* (*POL*) president; (*di assemblea, COMM*) chairman; ~ del consiglio prime minister; **presi-den'tessa** *sf* president; president's wife; chairwoman; **presi'denza** *sf* presidency; office of president; chairmanship.

presidi'are *vt* to garrison; **pre'sidio** *sm* garrison.

presi'edere *vt* to preside over // *vi*: ~ a to direct, be in charge of.

'preso, a *pp di* **prendere**.

'pressa *sf* (*TECN*) press.

pressap'poco *av* about, roughly.

pres'sare *vt* to press.

pressi'one *sf* pressure; far ~ su qn to put pressure on sb; ~ sanguigna blood pressure.

'presso *av* (*vicino*) nearby, close at hand // *prep* (*vicino a*) near; (*accanto a*) beside, next to; (*in casa di*): ~ qn at sb's home; (*nelle lettere*) care of (*abbr* c/o); (*alle dipendenze di*): lavora ~ di noi he works for o with us // *smpl*: nei ~i di near, in the vicinity of.

pressuriz'zare [pressurid'dzare] *vt* to pressurize.

presta'nome *sm/f inv* (*peg*) figurehead.

pres'tante *ag* good-looking.

pres'tare *vt*: ~ (qc a qn) to lend (sb sth o sth to sb); ~rsi *vr* (*offrirsi*): ~rsi a fare to offer to do; (*essere adatto*): ~rsi a to lend itself to, be suitable for; ~ aiuto to lend a hand; ~ attenzione to pay attention; ~ fede a qc/qn to give credence to sth/sb; ~ orecchio to listen; **prestazi'one** *sf* (*TECN, SPORT*) performance; **prestazioni** *sfpl* (*di persona: servizi*) services.

prestigia'tore, 'trice [prestidʒa'tore] *sm/f* conjurer.

pres'tigio [pres'tidʒo] *sm* (*potere*) prestige; (*illusione*): gioco di ~ conjuring trick.

'prestito *sm* lending *q*; loan; dar in ~ to lend; prendere in ~ to borrow.

'presto *av* (*tra poco*) soon; (*in fretta*) quickly; (*di buon'ora*) early; a ~ see you soon; fare ~ a fare qc to hurry up and do sth; (*non costare fatica*) to have no trouble doing sth; si fa ~ a criticare it's easy to criticize.

pre'sumere *vt* to presume, assume; **pre'sunto, a** *pp di* **presumere**.

presuntu'oso, a *ag* presumptuous.

presunzi'one [prezun'tsjone] *sf* presumption.

presup'porre *vt* to suppose; to presuppose.

'prete *sm* priest.

preten'dente *sm/f* pretender // *sm* (*corteggiatore*) suitor.

pre'tendere *vt* (*esigere*) to demand, require; (*sostenere*): ~ che to claim that; pretende di aver sempre ragione he thinks he's always right.

pretenzi'oso, a [preten'tsjoso] *ag* pretentious.

pre'teso, a *pp di* **pretendere** // *sf* (*esigenza*) claim, demand; (*presunzione, sfarzo*) pretentiousness; senza ~e unpretentious.

pre'testo *sm* pretext, excuse.

pre'tore *sm* magistrate.

preva'lente *ag* prevailing; **preva'lenza** *sf* predominance.

preva'lere *vi* to prevail; **pre'valso, a** *pp di* **prevalere**.

preve'dere *vt* (*indovinare*) to foresee; (*presagire*) to foretell; (*considerare*) to make provision for.

preve'nire *vt* (*anticipare*) to forestall; to anticipate; (*evitare*) to avoid, prevent; (*avvertire*): ~ qn (di) to warn sb (of); to inform sb (of).

preven'tivo, a *ag* preventive // *sm* (*COMM*) estimate.

prevenzi'one [preven'tsjone] *sf* prevention; (*preconcetto*) prejudice.

previ'dente *ag* showing foresight;

prudent; **provi'denza** *sf* foresight; istituto di previdenza provident institution; previdenza sociale social security (*Brit*), welfare (*US*).

previsi'one *sf* forecast, prediction; ~i meteorologiche *o* del tempo weather forecast *sg*.

pre'visto, a *pp di* **prevedere** // *sm*: più/meno del ~ more/less than expected.

prezi'oso, a [pret'tsjoso] *ag* precious; invaluable // *sm* jewel; valuable.

prez'zemolo [pret'tsemolo] *sm* parsley.

'prezzo ['prettso] *sm* price; ~ d'acquisto/di vendita buying/selling price.

prigi'one [pri'dʒone] *sf* prison; **prigio'nia** *sf* imprisonment; **prigioni'ero, a** *ag* captive // *smlf* prisoner.

'prima *sf vedi* **primo** // *av* before; (*in anticipo*) in advance, beforehand; (*per l'addietro*) at one time, formerly; (*più presto*) sooner, earlier; (*in primo luogo*) first // *cong*: ~ di fare/che parta before doing/he leaves; ~ di *prep* before; ~ o poi sooner or later.

pri'mario, a *ag* primary; (*principale*) chief, leading, primary // *sm* (*MED*) chief physician.

pri'mate *sm* (*REL, ZOOL*) primate.

pri'mato *sm* supremacy; (*SPORT*) record.

prima'vera *sf* spring; **primave'rile** *ag* spring *cpd*.

primeggi'are [primed'dʒare] *vi* to excel, be one of the best.

primi'tivo, a *ag* primitive; original.

pri'mizie [pri'mittsje] *sfpl* early produce *sg*.

'primo, a *ag* first; (*fig*) initial; basic; prime // *smlf* first (one) // *sm* (*CUC*) first course; (*in date*): il ~ luglio the first of July // *sf* (*TEATRO*) first night; (*CINEMA*) première; (*AUT*) first (gear); le ~e ore del mattino the early hours of the morning; ai ~i di maggio at the beginning of May; viaggiare in ~a to travel first-class; in ~ luogo first of all, in the first place; di prim'ordine *o* ~a qualità first-class, first-rate; in un ~ tempo at first; ~a donna leading lady; (*di opera lirica*) prima donna.

primo'genito, a [primo'dʒenito] *ag, sml f* firstborn.

primordi'ale *ag* primordial.

'primula *sf* primrose.

princi'pale [printʃi'pale] *ag* main, principal // *sm* manager, boss.

princi'pato [printʃi'pato] *sm* principality.

'principe ['printʃipe] *sm* prince; ~ ereditario crown prince; **princi'pessa** *sf* princess.

principi'ante [printʃi'pjante] *smlf* beginner.

prin'cipio [prin'tʃipjo] *sm* (*inizio*) beginning, start; (*origine*) origin, cause; (*concetto, norma*) principle; al *o* in ~ at first; per ~ on principle.

pri'ore *sm* (*REL*) prior.

priorità *sf* priority.

'prisma, i *sm* prism.

pri'vare *vt*: ~ qn di to deprive sb of; ~rsi di to go *o* do without.

priva'tiva *sf* (*ECON*) monopoly.

pri'vato, a *ag* private // *smlf* private citizen; in ~ in private.

privazi'one [privat'tsjone] *sf* privation, hardship.

privilegi'are [privile'dʒare] *vt* to grant a privilege to.

privi'legio [privi'ledʒo] *sm* privilege.

'privo, a *ag*: ~ di without, lacking.

pro *prep* for, on behalf of // *sm inv* (*utilità*) advantage, benefit; a che ~? what's the use?; il ~ e il contro the pros and cons.

pro'babile *ag* probable, likely; **probabilità** *sf inv* probability.

pro'blema, i *sm* problem.

pro'boscide [pro'bɔʃʃide] *sf* (*di elefante*) trunk.

procacci'are [prokat'tʃare] *vt* to get, obtain.

pro'cedere [pro'tʃɛdere] *vi* to proceed; (*comportarsi*) to behave; (*iniziare*): ~ a to start; ~ contro (*DIR*) to start legal proceedings against; **procedi'mento** *sm* (*modo di condurre*) procedure; (*di avvenimenti*) course; (*TECN*) process; procedimento penale (*DIR*) criminal proceedings; **proce'dura** *sf* (*DIR*) procedure.

proces'sare [protʃes'sare] *vt* (*DIR*) to try.

processi'one [protʃes'sjone] *sf* procession.

pro'cesso [pro'tʃesso] *sm* (*DIR*) trial; proceedings *pl*; (*metodo*) process.

pro'cinto [pro'tʃinto] *sm*: in ~ di fare about to do, on the point of doing.

pro'clama, i *sm* proclamation.

procla'mare *vt* to proclaim.

procre'are *vt* to procreate.

pro'cura *sf* (*DIR*) proxy; power of attorney; (*ufficio*) attorney's office.

procu'rare *vt*: ~ qc a qn (*fornire*) to get *o* obtain sth for sb; (*causare: noie etc*) to bring *o* give sb sth.

procura'tore, 'trice *smlf* (*DIR*) ≈ solicitor; (*: chi ha la procura*) attorney; proxy; ~ generale (*in corte d'appello*) public prosecutor; (*in corte di cassazione*) Attorney General; ~ della Repubblica (*in corte d'assise, tribunale*) public prosecutor.

prodi'gare *vt* to be lavish with; ~rsi per qn to do all one can for sb.

pro'digio [pro'didʒo] *sm* marvel, wonder; (*persona*) prodigy; **prodigi'oso, a** *ag* prodigious; phenomenal.

'prodigo, a, ghi, ghe *ag* lavish, extravagant.
pro'dotto, a *pp di* **produrre** // *sm* product; ~i agricoli farm produce *sg*.
pro'durre *vt* to produce; **produttività** *sf* productivity; **produt'tivo, a** *ag* productive; **produt'tore, 'trice** *sm/f* producer; **produzi'one** *sf* production; (*rendimento*) output.
pro'emio *sm* introduction, preface.
Prof. *abbr* (= *professore*) Prof.
profa'nare *vt* to desecrate.
pro'fano, a *ag* (*mondano*) secular; profane; (*sacrilego*) profane.
profe'rire *vt* to utter.
profes'sare *vt* to profess; (*medicina etc*) to practise.
professio'nale *ag* professional.
professi'one *sf* profession; **professio'nista, i, e** *sm/f* professional.
profes'sore, 'essa *sm/f* (*INS*) teacher; (: *di università*) lecturer; (: *titolare di cattedra*) professor.
pro'feta, i *sm* prophet; **profe'zia** *sf* prophecy.
pro'ficuo, a *ag* useful, profitable.
profi'lare *vt* to outline; (*ornare: vestito*) to edge; ~rsi *vr* to stand out, be silhouetted; to loom up.
pro'filo *sm* profile; (*breve descrizione*) sketch, outline; di ~ in profile.
profit'tare *vi*: ~ di (*trarre profitto*) to profit by; (*approfittare*) to take advantage of.
pro'fitto *sm* advantage, profit, benefit; (*fig: progresso*) progress; (*COMM*) profit.
profondità *sf inv* depth.
pro'fondo, a *ag* deep; (*rancore, meditazione*) profound // *sm* depth(s *pl*), bottom; ~ 8 metri 8 metres deep.
'profugo, a, ghi, ghe *sm/f* refugee.
profu'mare *vt* to perfume // *vi* to be fragrant; ~rsi *vr* to put on perfume *o* scent.
profume'ria *sf* perfumery; (*negozio*) perfume shop.
pro'fumo *sm* (*prodotto*) perfume, scent; (*fragranza*) scent, fragrance.
profusi'one *sf* profusion; a ~ in plenty.
proget'tare [prod3et'tare] *vt* to plan; (*TECN: edificio*) to plan, design; **pro'getto** *sm* plan; (*idea*) plan, project; **progetto di legge** bill.
pro'gramma, i *sm* programme; (*TV, RADIO*) programmes *pl*; (*INS*) syllabus, curriculum; (*INFORM*) program; **program'mare** *vt* (*TV, RADIO*) to put on; (*INFORM*) to program; (*ECON*) to plan; **programma'tore, 'trice** *sm/f* (*INFORM*) computer programmer.
progre'dire *vi* to progress, make progress.
progres'sivo, a *ag* progressive.
pro'gresso *sm* progress *q*; fare ~i to make progress.

proi'bire *vt* to forbid, prohibit; **proibi'tivo, a** *ag* prohibitive; **proibizi'one** *sf* prohibition.
proiet'tare *vt* (*gen, GEOM, CINEMA*) to project; (: *presentare*) to show, screen; (*luce, ombra*) to throw, cast, project; **proi'ettile** *sm* projectile, bullet (*o* shell *etc*); **proiet'tore** *sm* (*CINEMA*) projector; (*AUT*) headlamp; (*MIL*) searchlight; **proiezi'one** *sf* (*CINEMA*) projection; showing.
'prole *sf* children *pl*, offspring.
prole'tario, a *ag, sm* proletarian.
prolife'rare *vi* (*fig*) to proliferate.
pro'lisso, a *ag* verbose.
'prologo, ghi *sm* prologue.
pro'lunga, ghe *sf* (*di cavo elettrico etc*) extension.
prolun'gare *vt* (*discorso, attesa*) to prolong; (*linea, termine*) to extend.
prome'moria *sm inv* memorandum.
pro'messa *sf* promise.
pro'messo, a *pp di* **promettere**.
pro'mettere *vt* to promise // *vi* to be *o* look promising; ~ a qn di fare to promise sb that one will do.
promi'nente *ag* prominent.
promiscuità *sf* promiscuousness.
promon'torio *sm* promontory, headland.
pro'mosso, a *pp di* **promuovere**.
promo'tore, trice *sm/f* promoter, organizer.
promozi'one [promot'tsjone] *sf* promotion.
promul'gare *vt* to promulgate.
promu'overe *vt* to promote.
proni'pote *sm/f* (*di nonni*) great-grandchild, great-grandson/granddaughter; (*di zii*) great-nephew/niece; ~i *smpl* (*discendenti*) descendants.
pro'nome *sm* (*LING*) pronoun.
pron'tezza [pron'tettsa] *sf* readiness; quickness, promptness.
'pronto, a *ag* ready; (*rapido*) fast, quick, prompt; ~! (*TEL*) hello!; ~ all'ira quick-tempered; ~ soccorso first aid.
prontu'ario *sm* manual, handbook.
pro'nuncia [pro'nuntfa] *etc* = **pronunzia** *etc*.
pro'nunzia [pro'nuntsja] *sf* pronunciation; **pronunzi'are** *vt* (*parola, sentenza*) to pronounce; (*dire*) to utter; (*discorso*) to deliver; **pronunziarsi** *vr* to declare one's opinion; **pronunzi'ato, a** *ag* (*spiccato*) pronounced, marked; (*sporgente*) prominent.
propa'ganda *sf* propaganda.
propa'gare *vt* (*notizia, malattia*) to spread; (*REL, BIOL*) to propagate; ~rsi *vr* to spread; (*BIOL*) to propagate; (*FISICA*) to be propagated.
pro'pendere *vi*: ~ per to favour, lean towards; **propensi'one** *sf* inclination, propensity; **pro'penso, a** *pp di*

propendere.
propi'nare *vt* to administer.
pro'pizio, a [pro'pittsjo] *ag* favourable.
pro'porre *vt* (*suggerire*): ~ qc (a qn) to suggest sth (to sb); (*candidato*) to put forward; (*legge*, *brindisi*) to propose; ~ di fare to suggest o propose doing; proporsi di fare to propose o intend to do; proporsi una meta to set o.s. a goal.
proporzio'nale [proportsjo'nale] *ag* proportional.
proporzio'nare [proportsjo'nare] *vt*: ~ qc a to proportion o adjust sth to.
proporzi'one [propor'tsjone] *sf* proportion; in ~ a in proportion to.
pro'posito *sm* (*intenzione*) intention, aim; (*argomento*) subject, matter; a ~ di regarding, with regard to; di ~ (*apposta*) deliberately, on purpose; a ~ by the way; capitare a ~ (*cosa*, *persona*) to turn up at the right time.
proposizi'one [propozit'tsjone] *sf* (*LING*) clause; (: *periodo*) sentence.
pro'posto, a *pp di* **proporre** // *sf* proposal; (*suggerimento*) suggestion; ~a di legge bill.
proprietà *sf inv* (*ciò che si possiede*) property *gen q*, estate; (*caratteristica*) property; (*correttezza*) correctness; **proprie'tario, a** *sm/f* owner; (*di albergo etc*) proprietor, owner; (*per l'inquilino*) landlord/lady.
'proprio, a *ag* (*possessivo*) own; (: *impersonale*) one's; (*esatto*) exact, correct, proper; (*senso*, *significato*) literal; (*LING*: *nome*) proper; (*particolare*): ~ di characteristic of, peculiar to // *av* (*precisamente*) just, exactly; (*davvero*) really; (*affatto*): non ... ~ not ... at all; l'ha visto con i (suoi) ~i occhi he saw it with his own eyes.
'prora *sf* (*NAUT*) bow(s *pl*), prow.
'proroga, ghe *sf* extension; postponement; **proro'gare** *vt* to extend; (*differire*) to postpone, defer.
pro'rompere *vi* to burst out; **pro'rotto, a** *pp di* **prorompere**.
'prosa *sf* prose; **pro'saico, a, ci, che** *ag* (*fig*) prosaic, mundane.
pro'sciogliere [proʃ'ʃɔʎʎere] *vt* to release; (*DIR*) to acquit; **prosci'olto, a** *pp di* **prosciogliere**.
prosciu'gare [proʃʃu'gare] *vt* (*terreni*) to drain, reclaim; ~rsi *vr* to dry up.
prosci'utto [proʃ'ʃutto] *sm* ham.
prosegui'mento *sm* continuation; buon ~! all the best!; (a chi viaggia) enjoy the rest of your journey!
prosegu'ire *vt* to carry on with, continue // *vi* to carry on, go on.
prospe'rare *vi* to thrive; **prosperità** *sf* prosperity; **'prospero, a** *ag* (*fiorente*) flourishing, thriving, prosperous; **pro-spe'roso, a** *ag* (*robusto*) hale and hearty; (: *ragazza*) buxom.

prospet'tare *vt* (*esporre*) to point out, show; ~rsi *vr* to look, appear.
prospet'tiva *sf* (*ARTE*) perspective; (*veduta*) view; (*fig*: *previsione*, *possibilità*) prospect.
pros'petto *sm* (*DISEGNO*) elevation; (*veduta*) view, prospect; (*facciata*) façade, front; (*tabella*) table; (*sommario*) summary.
prospici'ente [prospi'tʃente] *ag*: ~ qc facing o overlooking sth.
prossimità *sf* nearness, proximity; in ~ di near (to), close to.
'prossimo, a *ag* (*vicino*): ~ a near (to), close to; (*che viene subito dopo*) next; (*parente*) close // *sm* neighbour, fellow man.
prosti'tuta *sf* prostitute; **prostituzi'one** *sf* prostitution.
pros'trare *vt* (*fig*) to exhaust, wear out; ~rsi *vr* (*fig*) to humble o.s.
protago'nista, i, e *sm/f* protagonist.
pro'teggere [pro'tɛddʒere] *vt* to protect.
prote'ina *sf* protein.
pro'tendere *vt* to stretch out; **pro'teso, a** *pp di* **protendere**.
pro'testa *sf* protest.
protes'tante *ag*, *sm/f* Protestant.
protes'tare *vt*, *vi* to protest; ~rsi *vr*: ~rsi innocente *etc* to protest one's innocence o that one is innocent *etc*.
protet'tivo, a *ag* protective.
pro'tetto, a *pp di* **proteggere**.
protet'tore, 'trice *sm/f* protector; (*sostenitore*) patron.
protezi'one [protet'tsjone] *sf* protection; (*patrocinio*) patronage.
protocol'lare *vt* to register // *ag* formal, of protocol.
proto'collo *sm* protocol; (*registro*) register of documents.
pro'totipo *sm* prototype.
pro'trarre *vt* (*prolungare*) to prolong; **pro'tratto, a** *pp di* **protrarre**.
protube'ranza [protube'rantsa] *sf* protuberance, bulge.
'prova *sf* (*esperimento*, *cimento*) test, trial; (*tentativo*) attempt, try; (*MAT*, *testimonianza*, *documento etc*) proof; (*DIR*) evidence *q*, proof; (*INS*) exam, test; (*TEATRO*) rehearsal; (*di abito*) fitting; a ~ di (*in testimonianza di*) as proof of; a ~ di fuoco fireproof; fino a ~ contraria until it is proved otherwise; mettere alla ~ to put to the test; giro di ~ test o trial run; ~ generale (*TEATRO*) dress rehearsal.
pro'vare *vt* (*sperimentare*) to test; (*tentare*) to try, attempt; (*assaggiare*) to try, taste; (*sperimentare in sé*) to experience; (*sentire*) to feel; (*cimentare*) to put to the test; (*dimostrare*) to prove; (*abito*) to try on; ~rsi *vr*: ~rsi (a fare) to try o attempt (to do); ~ a fare to try o attempt to do.

proveni'enza [prove'njɛntsa] *sf* origin, source.

prove'nire *vi*: ~ **da** to come from.

pro'venti *smpl* revenue *sg*.

prove'nuto, a *pp di* **provenire**.

pro'verbio *sm* proverb.

pro'vetta *sf* test tube; **bambino in** ~ test-tube baby.

pro'vetto, a *ag* skilled, experienced.

pro'vincia, e *o* **cie** [pro'vintʃa] *sf* province; **provinci'ale** *ag* provincial; (*strada*) **provinciale** main road (*Brit*), highway (*US*).

pro'vino *sm* (*CINEMA*) screen test; (*campione*) specimen.

provo'cante *ag* (*attraente*) provocative.

provo'care *vt* (*causare*) to cause, bring about; (*eccitare: riso, pietà*) to arouse; (*irritare, sfidare*) to provoke; **provoca'torio, a** *ag* provocative; **provocazi'one** *sf* provocation.

provve'dere *vi* (*disporre*): ~ (**a**) to provide (for); (*prendere un provvedimento*) to take steps, act // *vt*: ~ **qc a qn** to supply sth to sb; **~rsi** *vr*: **~rsi di** to provide o.s. with; **provvedi'mento** *sm* measure; (*di previdenza*) precaution.

provvi'denza [provvi'dɛntsa] *sf*: **la** ~ providence; **provvidenzi'ale** *ag* providential.

provvigi'one [provvi'dʒone] *sf* (*COMM*) commission.

provvi'sorio, a *ag* temporary.

prov'vista *sf* provision, supply.

'prua *sf* (*NAUT*) = **prora**.

pru'dente *ag* cautious, prudent; (*assennato*) sensible, wise; **pru'denza** *sf* prudence, caution; wisdom.

'prudere *vi* to itch, be itchy.

'prugna ['pruɲɲa] *sf* plum; ~ **secca** prune.

prurigi'noso, a [pruridʒi'noso] *ag* itchy.

pru'rito *sm* itchiness *q*; itch.

P.S. *abbr* (= *postscriptum*) P.S.; (*POLIZIA*) = **Pubblica Sicurezza**.

pseu'donimo *sm* pseudonym.

PSI *sigla m* = *Partito Socialista Italiano*.

psicana'lista, i, e *sm/f* psychoanalyst.

'psiche ['psike] *sf* (*PSIC*) psyche.

psichi'atra, i, e [psi'kjatra] *sm/f* psychiatrist; **psichi'atrico, a, ci, che** *ag* psychiatric.

'psichico, a, ci, che ['psikiko] *ag* psychological.

psicolo'gia [psikolo'dʒia] *sf* psychology; **psico'logico, a, ci, che** *ag* psychological; **psi'cologo, a, gi, ghe** *sm/f* psychologist.

psico'patico, a, ci, che *ag* psychopathic // *sm/f* psychopath.

P.T. *abbr* = *Posta e Telegrafi*.

pubbli'care *vt* to publish.

pubblicazi'one [pubblikat'tsjone] *sf* publication; **~i** (**matrimoniali**) *sfpl* (marriage) banns.

pubbli'cista, i, e [pubbli'tʃista] *sm/f* (*STAMPA*) occasional contributor.

pubblicità [pubbliʧi'ta] *sf* (*diffusione*) publicity; (*attività*) advertising; (*annunci nei giornali*) advertisements *pl*; **pubblici'tario, a** *ag* advertising *cpd*; (*trovata, film*) publicity *cpd*.

'pubblico, a, ci, che *ag* public; (*statale: scuola etc*) state *cpd* // *sm* public; (*spettatori*) audience; **in** ~ **in** public; ~ **funzionario** civil servant; **P~ Ministero** Public Prosecutor's Office; **la P~a Sicurezza** the police.

'pube *sm* (*ANAT*) pubis.

pubertà *sf* puberty.

'pudico, a, ci, che *ag* modest.

pu'dore *sm* modesty.

puericul'tura *sf* paediatric nursing; infant care.

pue'rile *ag* childish.

pugi'lato [pudʒi'lato] *sm* boxing.

'pugile ['pudʒile] *sm* boxer.

pugna'lare [puɲɲa'lare] *vt* to stab.

pu'gnale [pun'ɲale] *sm* dagger.

'pugno ['puɲɲo] *sm* fist; (*colpo*) punch; (*quantità*) fistful.

'pulce ['pulʧe] *sf* flea.

pul'cino [pul'ʧino] *sm* chick.

pu'ledro, a *sm/f* colt/filly.

pu'leggia, ge [pu'leddʒa] *sf* pulley.

pu'lire *vt* to clean; (*lucidare*) to polish; **pu'lito, a** *ag* (*anche fig*) clean; (*ordinato*) neat, tidy // *sf* quick clean; **puli'tura** *sf* cleaning; **pulitura a secco** dry cleaning; **puli'zia** *sf* cleaning; cleanness; **fare le pulizie** to do the cleaning, do the housework.

'pullman *sm inv* coach.

pul'lover *sm inv* pullover, jumper.

pullu'lare *vi* to swarm, teem.

pul'mino *sm* minibus.

'pulpito *sm* pulpit.

pul'sante *sm* (push-)button.

pul'sare *vi* to pulsate, beat; **pulsazi'one** *sf* beat.

pul'viscolo *sm* fine dust.

'puma *sm inv* puma.

pun'gente [pun'dʒɛnte] *ag* prickly; stinging; (*anche fig*) biting.

'pungere ['pundʒere] *vt* to prick; (*sog: insetto, ortica*) to sting; (*: freddo*) to bite.

pungigli'one [pundʒiʎ'ʎone] *sm* sting.

pu'nire *vt* to punish; **punizi'one** *sf* punishment; (*SPORT*) penalty.

'punta *sf* point; (*parte terminale*) tip, end; (*di monte*) peak; (*di costa*) promontory; (*minima parte*) touch, trace; **in** ~ **di piedi** on tip-toe; **ore di** ~ peak hours; **uomo di** ~ front-rank *o* leading man.

pun'tare *vt* (*piedi a terra, gomiti sul tavolo*) to plant; (*dirigere: pistola*) to point; (*scommettere*) to bet // *vi* (*mi-*

rare): ~ a to aim at; (*avviarsi*): ~ su to head o make for; (*fig: contare*): ~ su to count o rely on.

pun'tata *sf* (*gita*) short trip; (*scommessa*) bet; (*parte di opera*) instalment; **romanzo a ~e** serial.

punteggia'tura [punteddʒa'tura] *sf* (*LING*) punctuation.

pun'teggio [pun'teddʒo] *sm* score.

puntel'lare *vt* to support.

pun'tello *sm* prop, support.

puntigli'oso, a [puntiʎ'ʎoso] *ag* punctilious.

pun'tina *sf*: ~ **da disegno** drawing pin.

pun'tino *sm* dot; **fare qc a ~** to do sth properly.

'punto, a *pp di* **pungere** // *sm* (*segno, macchiolina*) dot; (*LING*) full stop; (*MAT, momento, di punteggio, fig: argomento*) point; (*posto*) spot; (*a scuola*) mark; (*nel cucire, nella maglia, MED*) stitch // *av*: **non ... ~** not at all; **due ~i** *sm* (*LING*) colon; **sul ~ di fare** (just) about to do; **fare il ~** (*NAUT*) to take a bearing; (*fig*): **fare il ~ della situazione** to take stock of the situation; to sum up the situation; **alle 6 in ~** at 6 o'clock sharp o on the dot; **essere a buon ~** to have reached a satisfactory stage; **mettere a ~** to adjust; (*motore*) to tune; (*cannocchiale*) to focus; (*fig*) to settle; **di ~ in bianco** point-blank; **~ cardinale** point of the compass, cardinal point; **~ debole** weak point; **~ esclamativo/ interrogativo** exclamation/question mark; **~ di riferimento** landmark; (*fig*) point of reference; **~ di vendita** retail outlet; **~ e virgola** semicolon; **~ di vista** (*fig*) point of view; **~i di sospensione** suspension points.

puntu'ale *ag* punctual; **puntualità** *sf* punctuality.

pun'tura *sf* (*di ago*) prick; (*di insetto*) sting, bite; (*MED*) puncture; (: *iniezione*) injection; (*dolore*) sharp pain.

punzecchi'are [puntsek'kjare] *vt* to prick; (*fig*) to tease.

pun'zone [pun'tsone] *sm* (*per metalli*) stamp, die.

'pupa *sf* doll.

pu'pazzo [pu'pattso] *sm* puppet.

pu'pillo, a *sm/f* (*DIR*) ward; (*prediletto*) favourite, pet // *sf* (*ANAT*) pupil.

purché [pur'ke] *cong* provided that, on condition that.

'pure *cong* (*tuttavia*) and yet, nevertheless; (*anche se*) even if // *av* (*anche*) too, also; **pur di** (*al fine di*) just to; **faccia ~!** go ahead!, please do!

purè *sm*, **pu'rea** *sf* (*CUC*) purée; (: *di patate*) mashed potatoes.

pu'rezza [pu'rettsa] *sf* purity.

'purga, ghe *sf* (*MED*) purging *q*; purge; (*POL*) purge.

pur'gante *sm* (*MED*) purgative, purge.

pur'gare *vt* (*MED, POL*) to purge; (*pulire*) to clean.

purga'torio *sm* purgatory.

purifi'care *vt* to purify; (*metallo*) to refine.

puri'tano, a *ag, sm/f* puritan.

'puro, a *ag* pure; (*acqua*) clear, limpid; (*vino*) undiluted; **puro'sangue** *sm/f inv* thoroughbred.

pur'troppo *av* unfortunately.

'pustola *sf* pimple.

puti'ferio *sm* rumpus, row.

putre'fare *vi* to putrefy, rot; **pu-tre'fatto, a** *pp di* **putrefare**.

'putrido, a *ag* putrid, rotten.

put'tana *sf* (*fam!*) whore (!).

'puzza ['puttsa] *sf* = **puzzo**.

puz'zare [put'tsare] *vi* to stink.

'puzzo ['puttso] *sm* stink, foul smell.

'puzzola ['puttsola] *sf* polecat.

puzzo'lente [puttso'lɛnte] *ag* stinking.

Q

qua *av* here; **in ~** (*verso questa parte*) this way; **da un anno in ~** for a year now; **da quando in ~?** since when?; **per di ~** (*passare*) this way; **al di ~ di** (*fiume, strada*) on this side of; **~ dentro/fuori** *etc* in/out here *etc*; *vedi* **questo**.

qua'derno *sm* notebook; (*per scuola*) exercise book.

qua'drante *sm* quadrant; (*di orologio*) face.

qua'drare *vi* (*bilancio*) to balance, tally; (*descrizione*) to correspond; (*fig*): ~ a to please, be to one's liking // *vt* (*MAT*) to square; **non mi quadra** I don't like it; **qua'drato, a** *ag* square; (*fig: equili-brato*) level-headed, sensible; (: *peg*) square // *sm* (*MAT*) square; (*PUGILATO*) ring; **5 al quadrato** 5 squared.

qua'dretto *sm*: **a ~i** (*tessuto*) checked; (*foglio*) squared.

quadri'foglio [kwadri'fɔʎʎo] *sm* four-leaf clover.

'quadro *sm* (*pittura*) painting, picture; (*quadrato*) square; (*tabella*) table, chart; (*TECN*) board, panel; (*TEATRO*) scene; (*fig: scena, spettacolo*) sight; (: *descrizione*) outline, description; **~i** *smpl* (*POL*) party organizers; (*MIL*) cadres; (*COMM*) managerial staff; (*CARTE*) diamonds.

'quadruplo, a *ag, sm* quadruple.

quaggiù [kwad'dʒu] *av* down here.

'quaglia ['kwaʎʎa] *sf* quail.

'qualche ['kwalke] *det* **1** some, a few; (*in interrogative*) any; **ho comprato ~ libro** I've bought some o a few books; **~ volta** sometimes; **hai ~ sigaretta?** have you any cigarettes?

2 (*uno*): **c'è ~ medico?** is there a

doctor?; **in** ~ **modo** somehow
3 (*un certo, parecchio*) some; **un personaggio di** ~ **rilievo** a figure of some importance
4: ~ **cosa** = **qualcosa**.

qualche'duno [kwalke'duno] *pronome* = **qualcuno**.

qual'cosa *pronome* something; (*in espressioni interrogative*) anything; **qualcos'altro** something else; anything else; ~ **di nuovo** something new; anything new; ~ **da mangiare** something to eat; anything to eat; **c'è** ~ **che non va?** is there something *o* anything wrong?

qual'cuno *pronome* (*persona*) someone, somebody; (: *in espressioni interrogative*) anyone, anybody; (*alcuni*) some; ~ **è favorevole a noi** some are on our side; **qualcun altro** someone *o* somebody else; anyone *o* anybody else.

'quale (*spesso troncato in* **qual**) ♦ *det* **1** (*interrogativo*) what; (: *scegliendo tra due o più cose o persone*) which; ~ **uomo/denaro?** what man/money?; **which** man/money?; ~**i sono i tuoi programmi?** what are your plans?; ~ **stanza preferisci?** which room do you prefer?
2 (*relativo: come*): **il risultato fu** ~ **ci si aspettava** the result was as expected
3 (*esclamativo*) what; ~ **disgrazia!** what bad luck!
♦ *pronome* **1** (*interrogativo*) which; ~ **dei due scegli?** which of the two do you want?
2 (*relativo*): **il(la)** ~ (*persona: soggetto*) who; (: *oggetto, con preposizione*) whom; (*cosa*) which; (*possessivo*) whose; **suo padre, il** ~ **è avvocato,** ... his father, who is a lawyer, ...; **il signore con il** ~ **parlavo** the gentleman to whom I was speaking; **l'albergo al** ~ **ci siamo fermati** the hotel where we stayed *o* which we stayed at; **la signora della** ~ **ammiriamo la bellezza** the lady whose beauty we admire
3 (*relativo: in elenchi*) such as, like; **piante** ~**i l'edera** plants like *o* such as ivy; ~ **sindaco di questa città** as mayor of this town.

qua'lifica, che *sf* qualification; (*titolo*) title.

qualifi'care *vt* to qualify; (*definire*): ~ **qn/qc come** to describe sb/sth as; ~**rsi** *vr* (*anche SPORT*) to qualify; **qualifica'tivo, a** *ag* qualifying; **qualificazi'one** *sf* qualification; **gara di qualificazione** (*SPORT*) qualifying event.

qualità *sf inv* quality; **in** ~ **di** in one's capacity as.

qua'lora *cong* in case, if.

qual'siasi, qua'lunque *det inv* any; (*quale che sia*) whatever; (*discriminativo*) whichever; (*posposto: mediocre*) poor, indifferent; ordinary; **mettiti un vestito** ~ put on any old dress; ~ **cosa** anything; ~ **cosa accada** whatever happens; **a** ~ **costo** at any cost, whatever the cost; **l'uomo** ~ the man in the street; ~ **persona** anyone, anybody.

'quando *cong, av* when; ~ **sarò ricco** when I'm rich; **da** ~ (*dacché*) since; (*interrogativo*): **da** ~ **sei qui?** how long have you been here?; **quand'anche** even if.

quantità *sf inv* quantity; (*gran numero*): **una** ~ **di** a great deal of; a lot of; **in grande** ~ in large quantities; **quanti'tativo** *sm* (*COMM*) amount, quantity.

'quanto, a ♦ *det* **1** (*interrogativo: quantità*) how much; (: *numero*) how many; ~ **pane/denaro?** how much bread/money?; ~**i libri/ragazzi?** how many books/boys?; ~ **tempo?** how long?; ~**i anni hai?** how old are you?
2 (*esclamativo*): ~**e storie!** what a lot of nonsense!; ~ **tempo sprecato!** what a waste of time!
3 (*relativo: quantità*) as much ... as; (: *numero*) as many ... as; **ho** ~ **denaro mi occorre** I have as much money as I need; **prendi** ~**i libri vuoi** take as many books as you like
♦ *pronome* **1** (*interrogativo: quantità*) how much; (: *numero*) how many; (: *tempo*) how long; ~ **mi dai?** how much will you give me?; ~**i me ne hai portati?** how many did you bring me?; **da** ~ **sei qui?** how long have you been here?; ~**i ne abbiamo oggi?** what's the date today?
2 (*relativo: quantità*) as much as; (: *numero*) as many as; **farò** ~ **posso** I'll do as much as I can; **possono venire** ~**i sono stati invitati** all those who have been invited can come
♦ *av* **1** (*interrogativo: con ag, av*) how; (: *con vb*) how much; ~ **stanco ti sembra?** how tired did he seem to you?; ~ **corre la tua moto?** how fast can your motorbike go?; ~ **costa? how much does it cost?; quant'è?** how much is it?
2 (*esclamativo: con ag, av*) how; (: *con vb*) how much; ~ **sono felice!** how happy I am!; **sapessi** ~ **abbiamo camminato!** if you knew how far we've walked!; **studierò** ~ **posso** I'll study as much as *o* all I can; ~ **prima** as soon as possible
3: in ~ (*in qualità di*) as; (*perché, per il fatto che*) as, since; (**in**) ~ **a** (*per ciò che riguarda*) as for, as regards
4: per ~ (*nonostante, anche se*) however; **per** ~ **si sforzi, non ce la farà** try as he may, he won't manage it; **per** ~ **sia brava, fa degli errori** however good she may be, she makes mistakes; **per** ~ **io sappia** as far as I know.

quan'tunque *cong* although, though.

qua'ranta *num* forty.

quaran'tena *sf* quarantine.

quaran'tesimo, a *num* fortieth.
quaran'tina *sf*: una ~ (di) about forty.
qua'resima *sf*: la ~ Lent.
'quarta *sf vedi* quarto.
quar'tetto *sm* quartet(te).
quarti'ere *sm* district, area; (MIL) quarters *pl*; ~ **generale** headquarters *pl*, HQ.
'quarto, a *ag* fourth // *sm* fourth; (*quarta parte*) quarter // *sf* (AUT) fourth (gear); **le 6 e un** ~ a quarter past six; ~ **d'ora** quarter of an hour; **~i di finale** quarter final.
'quarzo ['kwartso] *sm* quartz.
'quasi *av* almost, nearly // *cong* (*anche*: ~ **che**) as if; (*non*) ... ~ **mai** hardly ever; ~ ~ **me ne andrei** I've half a mind to leave.
quassù *av* up here.
'quatto, a *ag* crouched, squatting; (*silenzioso*) silent; ~ ~ very quietly; stealthily.
quat'tordici [kwat'torditʃi] *num* fourteen.
quat'trini *smpl* money *sg*, cash *sg*.
'quattro *num* four; **in** ~ **e quatt'rotto** in less than no time; **quattro'cento** *num* four hundred // *sm*: **il Quattrocento** the fifteenth century; **quattro'mila** *num* four thousand.
'quello, a ◆ *det* (*dav sm* **quel** + C, **quell'** + V, **quello** + *s impura, gn, pn, ps, x, z*; *pl* **quei** + C, **quegli** + V *o s impura, gn, pn, ps, x, z*; *dav sf* **quella** + C, **quell'** + V; *pl* **quelle**) that; those *pl*; ~**a casa** that house; **quegli uomini** those men; **voglio** ~**a camicia** (lì *o* là) I want that shirt
◆ *pronome* **1** (*dimostrativo*) that (one); those (ones) *pl*; (*ciò*) that; **conosci** ~**a?** do you know that woman?; **prendo** ~ **bianco** I'll take the white one; **chi è** ~? who's that?; **prendiamo** ~ (lì *o* là) let's take that one (there)
2 (*relativo*): ~**(a) che** (*persona*) the one (who); (*cosa*) the one (which), the one (that); ~**i(e) che** (*persone*) those who; (*cose*) those which; **è lui** ~ **che non voleva venire** he's the one who didn't want to come; **ho fatto** ~ **che potevo** I did what I could.
'quercia, ce ['kwɛrtʃa] *sf* oak (tree); (*legno*) oak.
que'rela *sf* (DIR) (legal) action;
quere'lare *vt* to bring an action against.
que'sito *sm* question, query; problem.
questio'nare *vi*: ~ **di/su qc** to argue about/over sth.
questio'nario *sm* questionnaire.
questi'one *sf* problem, question; (*controversia*) issue; (*litigio*) quarrel; **in** ~ in question; **fuori di** ~ out of the question; **è** ~ **di tempo** it's a matter *o* question of time.
'questo, a ◆ *det* **1** (*dimostrativo*) this; these *pl*; ~ **libro** (qui *o* qua) this book;

io prendo ~ **cappotto, tu quello** I'll take this coat, you take that one; **quest'oggi** today; ~**a sera** this evening
2 (*enfatico*): **non fatemi più prendere di** ~**e paure** don't frighten me like that again
◆ *pronome* (*dimostrativo*) this (one); these (ones) *pl*; (*ciò*) this; **prendo** ~ (qui *o* qua) I'll take this one; **preferisci** ~**i o quelli?** do you prefer these (ones) or those (ones)?; ~ **intendevo** *io* this is what I meant; **vengono Paolo e Luca:** ~ **da Roma, quello da Palermo** Paolo and Luca are coming: the former from Palermo, the latter from Rome.
ques'tore *sm* ≈ chief constable (*Brit*), ≈ police commissioner (*US*).
'questua *sf* collection (of alms).
ques'tura *sf* police headquarters *pl*.
qui *av* here; **da** *o* **di** ~ from here; **di** ~ **in avanti** from now on; **di** ~ **a poco/una settimana** in a little while/a week's time; ~ **dentro/sopra/vicino** in/up/near here; *vedi* **questo**.
quie'tanza [kwje'tantsa] *sf* receipt.
quie'tare *vt* to calm, soothe.
qui'ete *sf* quiet, quietness; calmness; stillness; peace.
qui'eto, a *ag* quiet; (*notte*) calm, still; (*mare*) calm.
'quindi *av* then // *cong* therefore, so.
'quindici ['kwinditʃi] *num* fifteen; ~ **giorni** a fortnight (*Brit*), two weeks.
quindi'cina [kwindi'tʃina] *sf* (*serie*): **una** ~ (di) about fifteen; **fra una** ~ **di giorni** in a fortnight.
quin'quennio *sm* period of five years.
quin'tale *sm* quintal (*100 kg*).
'quinte *sfpl* (TEATRO) wings.
'quinto, a *num* fifth.
'quota *sf* (*parte*) quota, share; (AER) height, altitude; (IPPICA) odds *pl*; **prendere/perdere** ~ (AER) to gain/lose height *o* altitude; ~ **d'iscrizione** enrolment fee; (*ad un club*) membership fee.
quo'tare *vt* (BORSA) to quote; **quotazi'one** *sf* quotation.
quotidi'ano, a *ag* daily; (*banale*) everyday // *sm* (*giornale*) daily (paper).
quozi'ente [kwot'tsjɛnte] *sm* (MAT) quotient; ~ **d'intelligenza** intelligence quotient, IQ.

R

ra'barbaro *sm* rhubarb.
'rabbia *sf* (*ira*) anger, rage; (*accanimento, furia*) fury; (MED: *idrofobia*) rabies *sg*.
rab'bino *sm* rabbi.
rabbi'oso, a *ag* angry, furious; (*facile all'ira*) quick-tempered; (*forze, acqua etc*) furious, raging; (MED) rabid, mad.
rabbo'nire *vt*, **~rsi** *vr* to calm down.

rabbrivi'dire *vi* to shudder, shiver.

rabbui'arsi *vr* to grow dark.

raccapez'zarsi [rakkapet'tsarsi] *vr:* non ~ to be at a loss.

raccapricci'ante [rakkaprit'tʃante] *ag* horrifying.

raccatta'palle *sm inv* (SPORT) ballboy.

raccat'tare *vt* to pick up.

rac'chetta [rak'ketta] *sf* (per tennis) racket; (per ping-pong) bat; ~ da neve snowshoe; ~ da sci ski stick.

racchi'udere [rak'kjudere] *vt* to contain; **racchi'uso, a** *pp di* racchiudere.

rac'cogliere [rak'koʎʎere] *vt* to collect; (raccattare) to pick up; (frutti, fiori) to pick, pluck; (AGR) to harvest; (approvazione, voti) to win; (profughi) to take in; ~rsi *vr* to gather; (fig) to gather one's thoughts; to meditate; **raccogli'mento** *sm* meditation; **raccogli'tore** *sm* (cartella) folder, binder; raccoglitore a fogli mobili loose-leaf binder.

rac'colto, a *pp di* raccogliere // *ag* (persona: pensoso) thoughtful; (luogo: appartato) secluded, quiet // *sm* (AGR) crop, harvest // *sf* collecting *q*; collection; (AGR) harvesting *q*, gathering *q*; harvest, crop; (adunata) gathering.

raccoman'dare *vt* to recommend; (affidare) to entrust; (esortare): ~ a qn di non fare to tell *o* warn sb not to do; ~rsi *vr:* ~rsi a qn to commend o.s. to sb; mi raccomando! don't forget!; **raccoman'data** *sf* (anche: lettera raccomandata) recorded-delivery letter; **raccomandazi'one** *sf* recommendation.

raccon'tare *vt:* ~ (a qn) (dire) to tell (sb); (narrare) to relate (to sb), tell (sb) about; **rac'conto** *sm* telling *q*, relating *q*; (fatto raccontato) story, tale.

raccorci'are [rakkor'tʃare] *vt* to shorten.

rac'cordo *sm* (TECN: giunzione) connection, joint; (AUT: di autostrada) slip road (Brit), entrance (o exit) ramp (US); ~ anulare (AUT) ring road (Brit), beltway (US).

ra'chitico, a, ci, che [ra'kitiko] *ag* suffering from rickets; (fig) scraggy, scrawny.

racimo'lare [ratʃimo'lare] *vt* (fig) to scrape together, glean.

'rada *sf* (natural) harbour.

'radar *sm* radar.

raddol'cire [raddol'tʃire] *vt* (persona, carattere) to soften; ~rsi *vr* (tempo) to grow milder; (persona) to soften, mellow.

raddoppi'are *vt, vi* to double.

raddriz'zare [raddrit'tsare] *vt* to straighten; (fig: correggere) to put straight, correct.

'radere *vt* (barba) to shave off; (mento) to shave; (fig: rasentare) to graze; to skim; ~rsi *vr* to shave (o.s.); ~ al suolo

to raze to the ground.

radi'ale *ag* radial.

radi'are *vt* to strike off.

radia'tore *sm* radiator.

radiazi'one [radjat'tsjone] *sf* (FISICA) radiation; (cancellazione) striking off.

radi'cale *ag* radical // *sm* (LING) root.

ra'dicchio [ra'dikkjo] *sm* chicory.

ra'dice [ra'ditʃe] *sf* root.

'radio *sf inv* radio // *sm* (CHIM) radium; **radioat'tivo, a** *ag* radioactive; **radiodiffusi'one** *sf* (radio) broadcasting; **radiogra'fare** *vt* to X-ray; **radiogra'fia** *sf* radiography; (foto) X-ray photograph.

radi'oso, a *ag* radiant.

radiostazi'one [radjostat'tsjone] *sf* radio station.

radiotera'pia *sf* radiotherapy.

'rado, a *ag* (capelli) sparse, thin; (visite) infrequent; di ~ rarely.

radu'nare *vt, ~rsi* *vr* to gather, assemble.

ra'dura *sf* clearing.

'rafano *sm* horseradish.

raffazzo'nare [raffattso'nare] *vt* to patch up.

raf'fermo, a *ag* stale.

'raffica, che *sf* (METEOR) gust (of wind); (di colpi: scarica) burst of gunfire.

raffigu'rare *vt* to represent.

raffi'nare *vt* to refine; **raffina'tezza** *sf* refinement; **raffi'nato, a** *ag* refined; **raffine'ria** *sf* refinery.

raffor'zare [raffor'tsare] *vt* to reinforce.

raffredda'mento *sm* cooling.

raffred'dare *vt* to cool; (fig) to dampen, have a cooling effect on; ~rsi *vr* to grow cool *o* cold; (prendere un raffreddore) to catch a cold; (fig) to cool (off).

raffred'dato, a *ag* (MED): essere ~ to have a cold.

raffred'dore *sm* (MED) cold.

raf'fronto *sm* comparison.

'rafia *sf* (fibra) raffia.

ra'gazzo, a [ra'gattso] *sm/f* boy/girl; (fam: fidanzato) boyfriend/girlfriend.

raggi'ante [rad'dʒante] *ag* radiant, shining.

'raggio ['raddʒo] *sm* (di sole etc) ray; (MAT, distanza) radius; (di ruota etc) spoke; ~ d'azione range; ~i X X-rays.

raggi'rare [raddʒi'rare] *vt* to take in, trick; **rag'giro** *sm* trick.

raggi'ungere [rad'dʒundʒere] *vt* to reach; (persona: riprendere) to catch up (with); (bersaglio) to hit; (fig: meta) to achieve; **raggi'unto, a** *pp di* raggiungere.

raggomito'larsi *vr* to curl up.

raggranel'lare *vt* to scrape together.

raggrin'zare [raggrin'tsare] *vt, vi* (anche: ~rsi) to wrinkle.

raggrup'pare *vt* to group (together).

raggu'aglio [rag'gwaʎʎo] *sm* comparison; (*informazione, relazione*) piece of information.

ragguar'devole *ag* (*degno di riguardo*) distinguished, notable; (*notevole: somma*) considerable.

ragiona'mento [radʒona'mento] *sm* reasoning *q*; arguing *q*; argument.

ragio'nare [radʒo'nare] *vi* (*usare la ragione*) to reason; (*discorrere*): ~ (di) to argue (about).

ragi'one [ra'dʒone] *sf* reason; (*dimostrazione, prova*) argument, reason; (*diritto*) right; **aver ~** to be right; **aver ~ di qn** to get the better of sb; **dare ~ a qn** to agree with sb; to prove sb right; **perdere la ~** to become insane; (*fig*) to take leave of one's senses; **in ~ di** at the rate of; to the amount of; according to; **a o con ~** rightly, justly; **~ sociale** (*COMM*) corporate name; **a ragion veduta** after due consideration.

ragione'ria [radʒone'ria] *sf* accountancy; accounts department.

ragio'nevole [radʒo'nevole] *ag* reasonable.

ragioni'ere, a [radʒo'njere] *sm/f* accountant.

ragli'are [raʎ'ʎare] *vi* to bray.

ragna'tela [raɲɲa'tela] *sf* cobweb, spider's web.

'ragno ['raɲɲo] *sm* spider.

ragù *sm inv* (*CUC*) meat sauce; stew.

RAI-TV [raiti'vu] *sigla f* = *Radio televisione italiana.*

rallegra'menti *smpl* congratulations.

ralle'grare *vt* to cheer up; **~rsi** *vr* to cheer up; (*provare allegrezza*) to rejoice; **~rsi con qn** to congratulate sb.

rallen'tare *vt* to slow down; (*fig*) to lessen, slacken // *vi* to slow down.

raman'zina [raman'dzina] *sf* lecture, telling-off.

'rame *sm* (*CHIM*) copper.

rammari'carsi *vr*: ~ (di) (*rincrescersi*) to be sorry (about), regret; (*lamentarsi*) to complain (about); **ram'marico, chi** *sm* regret.

rammen'dare *vt* to mend; (*calza*) to darn; **ram'mendo** *sm* mending *q*; darning *q*; mend; darn.

rammen'tare *vt* to remember, recall; (*richiamare alla memoria*): ~ **qc a qn** to remind sb of sth; **~rsi** *vr*: **~rsi (di qc)** to remember (sth).

rammol'lire *vt* to soften // *vi* (*anche:* **~rsi**) to go soft.

'ramo *sm* branch.

ramo'scello [ramoʃ'ʃello] *sm* twig.

'rampa *sf* flight (of stairs); **~ di lancio** launching pad.

rampi'cante *ag* (*BOT*) climbing.

ram'pone *sm* harpoon; (*ALPINISMO*) crampon.

'rana *sf* frog.

'rancido, a ['rantʃido] *ag* rancid.

ran'core *sm* rancour, resentment.

ran'dagio, a, gi, gie *o* **ge** [ran'dadʒo] *ag* (*gatto, cane*) stray.

ran'dello *sm* club, cudgel.

'rango, ghi *sm* (*condizione sociale, MIL: riga*) rank.

rannicchi'arsi [rannik'kjarsi] *vr* to crouch, huddle.

rannuvo'larsi *vr* to cloud over, become overcast.

ra'nocchio [ra'nɔkkjo] *sm* (edible) frog.

'rantolo *sm* wheeze; (*di agonizzanti*) death rattle.

'rapa *sf* (*BOT*) turnip.

ra'pace [ra'patʃe] *ag* (*animale*) predatory; (*fig*) rapacious, grasping // *sm* bird of prey.

ra'pare *vt* (*capelli*) to crop, cut very short.

'rapida *sf vedi* **rapido.**

rapida'mente *av* quickly, rapidly.

rapidità *sf* speed.

'rapido, a *ag* fast; (*esame, occhiata*) quick, rapid // *sm* (*FERR*) express (train) // *sf* (*di fiume*) rapid.

rapi'mento *sm* kidnapping; (*fig*) rapture.

ra'pina *sf* robbery; **~ a mano armata** armed robbery; **rapi'nare** *vt* to rob; **rapina'tore, 'trice** *sm/f* robber.

ra'pire *vt* (*cose*) to steal; (*persone*) to kidnap; (*fig*) to enrapture, delight; **rapi'tore, 'trice** *sm/f* kidnapper.

rappor'tare *vt* (*confrontare*) to compare; (*riprodurre*) to reproduce.

rap'porto *sm* (*resoconto*) report; (*legame*) relationship; (*MAT, TECN*) ratio; **~i** *smpl* (*fra persone, paesi*) relations; **~i sessuali** sexual intercourse *sg*.

rap'prendersi *vr* to coagulate, clot; (*latte*) to curdle.

rappre'saglia [rappre'saʎʎa] *sf* reprisal, retaliation.

rappresen'tante *sm/f* representative; **rappresen'tanza** *sf* delegation, deputation; (*COMM: ufficio, sede*) agency.

rappresen'tare *vt* to represent; (*TEATRO*) to perform; **rappresenta'tivo, a** *ag* representative; **rappresentazi'one** *sf* representation; performing *q*; (*spettacolo*) performance.

rap'preso, a *pp di* **rapprendere.**

rapso'dia *sf* rhapsody.

rara'mente *av* seldom, rarely.

rare'fatto, a *ag* rarefied.

'raro, a *ag* rare.

ra'sare *vt* (*barba etc*) to shave off; (*siepi, erba*) to trim, cut; **~rsi** *vr* to shave (o.s.).

raschi'are [ras'kjare] *vt* to scrape; (*macchia, fango*) to scrape off // *vi* to clear one's throat.

rasen'tare *vt* (*andar rasente*) to keep

close to; (*sfiorare*) to skim along (*o over*); (*fig*) to border on.

ra'sente *prep*: ~ (a) close to, very near.

'raso, a *pp di* **radere** // *ag* (*barba*) shaved; (*capelli*) cropped; (*con misure di capacità*) level; (*pieno: bicchiere*) full to the brim // *sm* (*tessuto*) satin; ~ **terra** close to the ground; **un cucchiaio** ~ **a** level spoonful.

ra'soio *sm* razor; ~ **elettrico** electric shaver *o* razor.

ras'segna [ras'seɲɲa] *sf* (*MIL*) inspection, review; (*esame*) inspection; (*resoconto*) review, survey; (*pubblicazione letteraria etc*) review; (*mostra*) exhibition, show; **passare in** ~ (*MIL*, *fig*) to review.

rasse'gnare [rasseɲ'ɲare] *vt*: ~ **le dimissioni** to resign, hand in one's resignation; **~rsi** *vr* (*accettare*): **~rsi (a qc/a fare)** to resign o.s. (to sth/to doing); **rassegnazi'one** *sf* resignation.

rasse'narsi *vr* (*tempo*) to clear up.

rasset'tare *vt* to tidy, put in order; (*aggiustare*) to repair, mend.

rassicu'rare *vt* to reassure.

rasso'dare *vt* to harden, stiffen.

rassomigli'anza [rassomiʎ'ʎantsa] *sf* resemblance.

rassomigli'are [rassomiʎ'ʎare] *vi*: ~ **a** to resemble, look like.

rastrel'lare *vt* to rake; (*fig: perlustrare*) to comb.

rastrelli'era *sf* rack; (*per piatti*) dish rack.

ras'trello *sm* rake.

'rata *sf* (*quota*) instalment; **pagare a ~e** to pay by instalments *o* on hire purchase (*Brit*).

ratifi'care *vt* (*DIR*) to ratify.

'ratto *sm* (*DIR*) abduction; (*ZOOL*) rat.

rattop'pare *vt* to patch; **rat'toppo** *sm* patching *q*; patch.

rattrap'pire *vt* to make stiff; **~rsi** *vr* to be stiff.

rattris'tare *vt* to sadden; **~rsi** *vr* to become sad.

'rauco, a, chi, che *ag* hoarse.

rava'nello *sm* radish.

ravi'oli *smpl* ravioli *sg*.

ravve'dersi *vr* to mend one's ways.

ravvici'nare [ravvitʃi'nare] *vt* (*avvicinare*): ~ **qc a** to bring sth nearer to; (*: due tubi*) to bring closer together; (*riconciliare*) to reconcile, bring together.

ravvi'sare *vt* to recognize.

ravvi'vare *vt* to revive; (*fig*) to brighten up, enliven; **~rsi** *vr* to revive; to brighten up.

razio'cinio [ratsjo'tʃinjo] *sm* reasoning *q*; reason; (*buon senso*) common sense.

razio'nale [rattsjo'nale] *ag* rational.

razio'nare [rattsjo'nare] *vt* to ration.

razi'one [rat'tsjone] *sf* ration; (*porzione*)

portion, share.

'razza ['rattsa] *sf* race; (*ZOOL*) breed; (*discendenza, stirpe*) stock, race; (*sorta*) sort, kind.

raz'zia [rat'tsia] *sf* raid, foray.

razzi'ale [rat'tsjale] *ag* racial.

raz'zismo [rat'tsizmo] *sm* racism, racialism.

raz'zista, i, e [rat'tsista] *ag*, *sm/f* racist, racialist.

'razzo ['raddzo] *sm* rocket.

razzo'lare [rattso'lare] *vi* (*galline*) to scratch about.

re *sm inv* king; (*MUS*) D; (*: solfeggiando la scala*) re.

rea'gire [rea'dʒire] *vi* to react.

re'ale *ag* real; (*di, da re*) royal // *sm*: **il** ~ reality; **rea'lismo** *sm* realism; **rea'lista, i, e** *sm/f* realist; (*POL*) royalist.

realiz'zare [realid'dzare] *vt* (*progetto etc*) to realize, carry out; (*sogno, desiderio*) to realize, fulfil; (*scopo*) to achieve; (*COMM: titoli etc*) to realize; (*CALCIO etc*) to score; **~rsi** *vr* to be realized; **realizzazi'one** *sf* realization; fulfilment; achievement.

real'mente *av* really, actually.

realtà *sf inv* reality.

re'ato *sm* offence.

reat'tore *sm* (*FISICA*) reactor; (*AER: aereo*) jet; (*: motore*) jet engine.

reazio'nario, a [reattsjo'narjo] *ag* (*POL*) reactionary.

reazi'one [reat'tsjone] *sf* reaction.

'rebbio *sm* prong.

recapi'tare *vt* to deliver.

re'capito *sm* (*indirizzo*) address; (*consegna*) delivery.

re'care *vt* (*portare*) to bring; (*avere su di sé*) to carry, bear; (*cagionare*) to cause, bring; **~rsi** *vr* to go.

re'cedere [re'tʃedere] *vi* to withdraw.

recensi'one [retʃen'sjone] *sf* review; **recen'sire** *vt* to review.

re'cente [re'tʃente] *ag* recent; **di** ~ recently, **recente'mente** *av* recently.

recessi'one [retʃes'sjone] *sf* (*ECON*) recession.

re'cidere [re'tʃidere] *vt* to cut off, chop off.

reci'divo, a [retʃi'divo] *sm/f* (*DIR*) second (*o* habitual) offender, recidivist.

re'cinto [re'tʃinto] *sm* enclosure; (*ciò che recinge*) fence; surrounding wall.

recipi'ente [retʃi'pjɛnte] *sm* container.

re'ciproco, a, ci, che [re'tʃiproko] *ag* reciprocal.

re'ciso, a [re'tʃizo] *pp di* **recidere**.

'recita ['rɛtʃita] *sf* performance.

reci'tare [retʃi'tare] *vt* (*poesia, lezione*) to recite; (*dramma*) to perform; (*ruolo*) to play *o* act (the part of); **recitazi'one** *sf* recitation; (*di attore*) acting.

recla'mare *vi* to complain // *vt*

(richiedere) to demand.
ré'clame [re'klam] *sf inv* advertising *q*; advertisement, advert *(Brit)*, ad *(fam)*.
re'clamo *sm* complaint.
reclusi'one *sf (DIR)* imprisonment.
'recluta *sf* recruit; **reclu'tare** *vt* to recruit.
re'condito, a *ag* secluded; *(fig)* secret, hidden.
recriminazi'one [rekriminat'tsjone] *sf* recrimination.
recrude'scenza [rekrudeʃ'ʃentsa] *sf* fresh outbreak.
recupe'rare *vt* = ricuperare.
redargu'ire *vt* to rebuke.
re'datto, a *pp di* redigere; **redat'tore, 'trice** *sm/f (STAMPA)* editor; (: *di articolo)* writer; *(di dizionario etc)* compiler; **redattore capo** chief editor; **redazi'one** *sf* editing; writing; *(sede)* editorial office(s); *(personale)* editorial staff; *(versione)* version.
reddi'tizio, a [reddi'tittsjo] *ag* profitable.
'reddito *sm* income; *(dello Stato)* revenue; *(di un capitale)* yield.
re'dento, a *pp di* redimere.
redenzi'one [reden'tsjone] *sf* redemption.
re'digere [re'didʒere] *vt* to write; *(contratto)* to draw up.
re'dimere *vt* to deliver; *(REL)* to redeem.
'redini *sfpl* reins.
'reduce ['redutʃe] *ag*: ~ **da** returning from, back from // *sm/f* survivor.
refe'rendum *sm inv* referendum.
refe'renza [refe'rentsa] *sf* reference.
re'ferto *sm* medical report.
refet'torio *sm* refectory.
refrat'tario, a *ag* refractory.
refrige'rare [refridʒe'rare] *vt* to refrigerate; *(rinfrescare)* to cool, refresh.
rega'lare *vt* to give (as a present), make a present of.
re'gale *ag* regal.
re'galo *sm* gift, present.
re'gata *sf* regatta.
reg'gente [red'dʒente] *sm/f* regent.
'reggere ['reddʒere] *vt (tenere)* to hold; *(sostenere)* to support, bear, hold up; *(portare)* to carry, bear; *(resistere)* to withstand; *(dirigere: impresa)* to manage, run; *(governare)* to rule, govern; *(LING)* to take, be followed by // *vi (resistere)*: ~ **a** to stand up to, hold out against; *(sopportare)*: ~ **a** to stand; *(durare)* to last; *(fig: teoria etc)* to hold water; ~**rsi** *vr (stare ritto)* to stand; *(fig: dominarsi)* to control o.s.; ~**rsi sulle gambe o in piedi** to stand up.
'reggia, ge ['reddʒa] *sf* royal palace.
reggi'calze [reddʒi'kaltse] *sm inv* suspender belt.
reggi'mento [reddʒi'mento] *sm (MIL)* regiment.

reggi'petto [reddʒi'petto] *sm*, **reggi'seno** [reddʒi'seno] *sm* bra.
re'gia, 'gie [re'dʒia] *sf (TV, CINEMA etc)* direction.
re'gime [re'dʒime] *sm (POL)* regime; *(DIR: aureo, patrimoniale etc)* system; *(MED)* diet; *(TECN)* (engine) speed.
re'gina [re'dʒina] *sf* queen.
'regio, a, gi, gie ['redʒo] *ag* royal.
regio'nale [redʒo'nale] *ag* regional.
regi'one [re'dʒone] *sf* region; *(territorio)* region, district, area.
re'gista, i, e [re'dʒista] *sm/f (TV, CINEMA etc)* director.
regis'trare [redʒis'trare] *vt (AMM)* to register; *(COMM)* to enter; *(notare)* to note, take note of; *(canzone, conversazione, sog: strumento di misura)* to record; *(mettere a punto)* to adjust, regulate; *(bagagli)* to check in; **registra'tore** *sm (strumento)* recorder, register; *(magnetofono)* tape recorder; **registratore di cassa** cash register; **registrazi'one** *sf* recording; *(AMM)* registration; *(COMM)* entry; *(di bagagli)* check-in.
re'gistro [re'dʒistro] *sm (libro)* register; ledger; logbook; *(DIR)* registry; *(MUS, TECN)* register.
re'gnare [reɲ'ɲare] *vi* to reign, rule; *(fig)* to reign.
'regno ['reɲɲo] *sm* kingdom; *(periodo)* reign; *(fig)* realm; **il ~ animale/vegetale** the animal/vegetable kingdom; **il R~ Unito** the United Kingdom.
'regola *sf* rule; **a ~ d'arte** duly; perfectly; **in ~** in order.
regola'mento *sm (complesso di norme)* regulations *pl*; *(di debito)* settlement; ~ **di conti** *(fig)* settling of scores.
rego'lare *ag* regular; *(in regola: domanda)* in order, lawful // *vt* to regulate, control; *(apparecchio)* to adjust, regulate; *(questione, conto, debito)* to settle; ~**rsi** *vr (moderarsi)*: ~**rsi nel bere/nello spendere** to control one's drinking/spending; *(comportarsi)* to behave, act; **regolarità** *sf inv* regularity.
'regolo *sm* ruler; ~ **calcolatore** slide rule.
reinte'grare *vt (energie)* to recover; *(in una carica)* to reinstate.
rela'tivo, a *ag* relative.
relazi'one [relat'tsjone] *sf (fra cose, persone)* relation(ship); *(resoconto)* report, account; ~**i** *sfpl (conoscenze)* connections.
rele'gare *vt* to banish; *(fig)* to relegate.
religi'one [reli'dʒone] *sf* religion; **religi'oso, a** *ag* religious // *sm/f* monk/nun.
re'liquia *sf* relic.
re'litto *sm* wreck; *(fig)* down-and-out.
re'mare *vi* to row.

remini'scenze [reminiʃ'ʃɛntse] *sfpl* reminiscences.

remissi'one *sf* remission.

remis'sivo, a *ag* submissive, compliant.

'remo *sm* oar.

re'moto, a *ag* remote.

'rendere *vt* (*ridare*) to return, give back; (: *saluto etc*) to return; (*produrre*) to yield, bring in; (*esprimere, tradurre*) to render; (*far diventare*): ~ qc possibile to make sth possible; ~ grazie a qn to thank sb; ~rsi utile to make o.s. useful; ~rsi conto di qc to realize sth.

rendi'conto *sm* (*rapporto*) report, account; (*AMM, COMM*) statement of account.

rendi'mento *sm* (*reddito*) yield; (*di manodopera, TECN*) efficiency; (*capacità di produrre*) output; (*di studenti*) performance.

'rendita *sf* (*di individuo*) private *o* unearned income; (*COMM*) revenue; ~ annua annuity.

'rene *sm* kidney.

'reni *sfpl* back *sg*.

reni'tente *ag* reluctant, unwilling; ~ ai consigli di qn unwilling to follow sb's advice; essere ~ alla leva (*MIL*) to fail to report for military service.

'renna *sf* reindeer *inv*.

'Reno *sm*: il ~ the Rhine.

'reo, a *sm/f* (*DIR*) offender.

re'parto *sm* department, section; (*MIL*) detachment.

repel'lente *ag* repulsive.

repen'taglio [repen'taʎʎo] *sm*: mettere a ~ to jeopardize, risk.

repen'tino, a *ag* sudden, unexpected.

repe'rire *vt* to find, trace.

re'perto *sm* (*ARCHEOLOGIA*) find; (*MED*) report; (*DIR: anche*: ~ giudiziario) exhibit.

reper'torio *sm* (*TEATRO*) repertory; (*elenco*) index, (alphabetical) list.

'replica, che *sf* repetition; reply, answer; (*obiezione*) objection; (*TEATRO, CINEMA*) repeat performance; (*copia*) replica.

repli'care *vt* (*ripetere*) to repeat; (*rispondere*) to answer, reply.

repressi'one *sf* repression.

re'presso, a *pp di* **reprimere**.

re'primere *vt* to suppress, repress.

re'pubblica, che *sf* republic; **repubbli'cano, a** *ag, sm/f* republican.

repu'tare *vt* to consider, judge.

reputazi'one [reputat'tsjone] *sf* reputation.

'requie *sf*: senza ~ unceasingly.

requi'sire *vt* to requisition.

requi'sito *sm* requirement.

requisizi'one [rekwizit'tsjone] *sf* requisition.

'resa *sf* (*l'arrendersi*) surrender; (*re-*

stituzione, rendimento) return; ~ dei conti rendering of accounts; (*fig*) day of reckoning.

resi'dente *ag* resident; **resi'denza** *sf* residence; **residenzi'ale** *ag* residential.

re'siduo, a *ag* residual, remaining // *sm* remainder; (*CHIM*) residue.

'resina *sf* resin.

resis'tente *ag* (*che resiste*): ~ a resistant to; (*forte*) strong; (*duraturo*) long-lasting, durable; ~ al caldo heat-resistant; **resis'tenza** *sf* resistance; (*di persona: fisica*) stamina, endurance; (: *mentale*) endurance, resistance.

re'sistere *vi* to resist; ~ a (*assalto, tentazioni*) to resist; (*dolore, sog: pianta*) to withstand; (*non patir danno*) to be resistant to; **resis'tito, a** *pp di* **resistere**.

'reso, a *pp di* **rendere**.

reso'conto *sm* report, account.

res'pingere [res'pindʒere] *vt* to drive back, repel; (*rifiutare*) to reject; (*INS: bocciare*) to fail; **res'pinto, a** *pp di* **respingere**.

respi'rare *vi* to breathe; (*fig*) to get one's breath; to breathe again // *vt* to breathe (in), inhale; **respira'tore** *sm* respirator; **respirazi'one** *sf* breathing; respirazione artificiale artificial respiration; **res'piro** *sm* breathing *q*; (*singolo atto*) breath; (*fig*) respite, rest; mandare un respiro di sollievo to give a sigh of relief.

respon'sabile *ag* responsible // *sm/f* person responsible; (*capo*) person in charge; ~ di responsible for; (*DIR*) liable for; **responsabilità** *sf inv* responsibility; (*legale*) liability.

res'ponso *sm* answer.

'ressa *sf* crowd, throng.

res'tare *vi* (*rimanere*) to remain, stay; (*diventare*): ~ orfano/cieco to become *o* be left an orphan/become blind; (*trovarsi*): ~ sorpreso to be surprised; (*avanzare*) to be left, remain; ~ d'accordo to agree; non resta più niente there's nothing left; restano pochi giorni there are only a few days left.

restau'rare *vt* to restore; **restaurazi'one** *sf* (*POL*) restoration; **res'tauro** *sm* (*di edifici etc*) restoration.

res'tio, a, 'tii, 'tie *ag* restive; (*persona*): ~ a reluctant to.

restitu'ire *vt* to return, give back; (*energie, forze*) to restore.

'resto *sm* remainder, rest; (*denaro*) change; (*MAT*) remainder; ~i *smpl* leftovers; (*di città*) remains; del ~ moreover, besides; ~i mortali (mortal) remains.

res'tringere [res'trindʒere] *vt* to reduce; (*vestito*) to take in; (*stoffa*) to shrink; (*fig*) to restrict, limit; ~rsi *vr* (*strada*) to narrow; (*stoffa*) to shrink; **re-**

strizi'one sf restriction.

'**rete** sf net; (fig) trap, snare; (di recinzione) wire netting; (AUT, FERR, di spionaggio etc) network; **segnare una** ~ (CALCIO) to score a goal; ~ **del letto** (sprung) bed base.

reti'cente [reti'tʃɛnte] ag reticent.

retico'lato sm grid; (rete metallica) wire netting; (di filo spinato) barbed wire (fence).

'**retina** sf (ANAT) retina.

re'torico, a, ci, che ag rhetorical // sf rhetoric.

retribu'ire vt to pay; (premiare) to reward; **retribuzi'one** sf payment; reward.

'**retro** sm inv back // av (dietro): **vedi** ~ see over(leaf).

retro'cedere [retro'tʃɛdere] vi to withdraw // vt (CALCIO) to relegate; (MIL) to degrade.

re'trogrado, a ag (fig) reactionary, backward-looking.

retro'marcia [retro'martʃa] sf (AUT) reverse; (: dispositivo) reverse gear.

retrospet'tivo, a ag retrospective.

retrovi'sore sm (AUT) (rear-view) mirror.

'**retta** sf (MAT) straight line; (di convitto) charge for bed and board; (fig: ascolto): **dar** ~ **a** to listen to, pay attention to.

rettango'lare ag rectangular.

ret'tangolo, a ag right-angled // sm rectangle.

ret'tifica, che sf rectification, correction.

rettifi'care vt (curva) to straighten; (fig) to rectify, correct.

'**rettile** sm reptile.

retti'lineo, a ag rectilinear.

retti'tudine sf rectitude, uprightness.

'**retto, a** pp di **reggere** // ag straight; (MAT): **angolo** ~ right angle; (onesto) honest, upright; (giusto, esatto) correct, proper, right.

ret'tore sm (REL) rector; (di università) ≈ chancellor.

reuma'tismo sm rheumatism.

reve'rendo, a ag: **il** ~ **padre Belli** the Reverend Father Belli.

rever'sibile ag reversible.

revisio'nare vt (conti) to audit; (TECN) to overhaul, service; (DIR: processo) to review; (componimento) to revise.

revisi'one sf auditing q; audit; servicing q; overhaul; review; revision.

revi'sore sm: ~ **di conti/bozze** auditor/proofreader.

'**revoca** sf revocation.

revo'care vt to revoke.

re'volver sm inv revolver.

riabili'tare vt to rehabilitate; (fig) to restore to favour.

rial'zare [rial'tsare] vt to raise, lift; (alzare di più) to heighten, raise; (aumentare: prezzi) to increase, raise // vi (prezzi) to rise, increase; **ri'alzo** sm (di prezzi) increase, rise; (sporgenza) rise.

rianimazi'one [rianimat'tsjone] sf (MED) resuscitation; **centro di** ~ intensive care unit.

riap'pendere vt to rehang; (TEL) to hang up.

ria'prire vt, ~**rsi** vr to reopen, open again.

ri'armo sm (MIL) rearmament.

rias'setto sm (di stanza etc) rearrangement; (ordinamento) reorganization.

rias'sumere vt (riprendere) to resume; (impiegare di nuovo) to re-employ; (sintetizzare) to summarize; **rias'sunto, a** pp di **riassumere** // sm summary.

ria'vere vt to have again; (avere indietro) to get back; (riacquistare) to recover; ~**rsi** vr to recover.

riba'dire vt (fig) to confirm.

ri'balta sf flap; (TEATRO: proscenio) front of the stage; (: apparecchio d'illuminazione) footlights pl; (fig) limelight.

ribal'tabile ag (sedile) tip-up.

ribal'tare vt, vi (anche: ~**rsi**) to turn over, tip over.

ribas'sare vt to lower, bring down // vi to come down, fall; **ri'basso** sm reduction, fall.

ri'battere vt to return, hit back; (confutare) to refute; ~ **che** to retort that.

ribel'larsi vr: ~ **(a)** to rebel (against); **ri'belle** ag (soldati) rebel; (ragazzo) rebellious // sm/f rebel; **ribelli'one** sf rebellion.

'**ribes** sm inv currant; ~ **nero** blackcurrant; ~ **rosso** redcurrant.

ribol'lire vi (fermentare) to ferment; (fare bolle) to bubble, boil; (fig) to seethe.

ri'brezzo [ri'breddzo] sm disgust, loathing; **far** ~ **a** to disgust.

ribut'tante ag disgusting, revolting.

rica'dere vi to fall again; (scendere a terra, fig: nel peccato etc) to fall back; (vestiti, capelli etc) to hang (down); (riversarsi: fatiche, colpe): ~ **su** to fall on; **rica'duta** sf (MED) relapse.

rical'care vt (disegni) to trace; (fig) to follow faithfully.

rica'mare vt to embroider.

ricambi'are vt to change again; (contraccambiare) to repay, return; **ri'cambio** sm exchange, return; (FISIOL) metabolism; **ricambi** smpl, **pezzi di ricambio** spare parts.

ri'camo sm embroidery.

ricapito'lare vt to recapitulate, sum up.

ricari'care vt (arma, macchina fotografica) to reload; (pipa) to refill; (orologio) to rewind; (batteria) to recharge.

ricat'tare vt to blackmail; **ricatta'tore, 'trice** sm/f blackmailer; **ri'catto** sm blackmail.

rica'vare vt (estrarre) to draw out, extract; (ottenere) to obtain, gain; **ri'cavo** sm proceeds pl.

ric'chezza [rik'kettsa] sf wealth; (fig) richness; ~**e** sfpl (beni) wealth sg, riches.

'riccio, a ['rittʃo] ag curly // sm (ZOOL) hedgehog; (: anche: ~ di mare) sea urchin; **'ricciolo** sm curl; **ricci'uto, a** ag curly.

'ricco, a, chi, che ag rich; (persona, paese) rich, wealthy // sm/f rich man/woman; i ~**chi** the rich; ~ **di** full of; rich in.

ri'cerca, che [ri'tʃerka] sf search; (indagine) investigation, inquiry; (studio): la ~ research; una ~ piece of research.

ricer'care [ritʃer'kare] vt (motivi, cause) to look for, try to determine; (successo, piacere) to pursue; (onore, gloria) to seek; **ricer'cato, a** ag (apprezzato) much sought-after; (affettato) studied, affected // sm/f (POLIZIA) wanted man/woman.

ri'cetta [ri'tʃetta] sf (MED) prescription; (CUC) recipe.

ricettazi'one [ritʃettat'tsjone] sf (DIR) receiving (stolen goods).

ri'cevere [ri'tʃevere] vt to receive; (stipendio, lettera) to get, receive; (accogliere: ospite) to welcome; (vedere: cliente, rappresentante etc) to see; **ricevi'mento** sm receiving q; (trattenimento) reception; **ricevi'tore** sm (TECN) receiver; **ricevitore delle imposte** tax collector; **rice'vuta** sf receipt; **ricevuta fiscale** receipt for tax purposes; **ricezi'one** sf (RADIO, TV) reception.

richia'mare [rikja'mare] vt (chiamare indietro, ritelefonare) to call back; (ambasciatore, truppe) to recall; (rimproverare) to reprimand; (attirare) to attract, draw; ~**rsi a** (riferirsi a) to refer to; **richi'amo** sm call; recall; reprimand; attraction.

richi'edere [ri'kjɛdere] vt to ask again for; (chiedere indietro): ~ qc to ask for sth back; (chiedere: per sapere) to ask; (: per avere) to ask for; (AMM: documenti) to apply for; (esigere) to need, require; **richi'esto, a** pp di **richiedere** // sf (domanda) request; (AMM) application, request; (esigenza) demand, request; a richiesta on request.

'ricino ['ritʃino] sm: olio di ~ castor oil.

ricognizi'one [rikoɲɲit'tsjone] sf (MIL) reconnaissance; (DIR) recognition, acknowledgement.

ricominci'are [rikomin'tʃare] vt, vi to start again, begin again.

ricom'pensa sf reward.

ricompen'sare vt to reward.

riconcili'are [rikontʃi'ljare] vt to reconcile; ~**rsi** vr to be reconciled; **riconciliazi'one** sf reconciliation.

ricono'scente [rikonoʃ'ʃɛnte] ag grateful; **ricono'scenza** sf gratitude.

rico'noscere [riko'noʃʃere] vt to recognize; (DIR: figlio, debito) to acknowledge; (ammettere: errore) to admit, acknowledge; **riconosci'mento** sm recognition; acknowledgement; (identificazione) identification; **riconosci'uto, a** pp di **riconoscere**.

rico'prire vt (coprire) to cover; (occupare: carica) to hold.

ricor'dare vt to remember, recall; (richiamare alla memoria): ~ qc a qn to remind sb of sth; ~**rsi** vr: ~**rsi (di)** to remember; ~**rsi di qc/di** aver fatto to remember sth/having done.

ri'cordo sm memory; (regalo) keepsake, souvenir; (di viaggio) souvenir; ~**i** smpl (memorie) memoirs.

ricor'rente ag recurrent, recurring; **ricor'renza** sf recurrence; (festività) anniversary.

ri'correre vi (ripetersi) to recur; ~ **a** (rivolgersi) to turn to; (: DIR) to appeal to; (servirsi di) to have recourse to; **ri'corso, a** pp di **ricorrere** // sm recurrence; (DIR) appeal; far ricorso a = ricorrere a.

ricostru'ire vt (casa) to rebuild; (fatti) to reconstruct; **ricostruzi'one** sf rebuilding q; reconstruction.

ri'cotta sf soft white unsalted cheese made from sheep's milk.

ricove'rare vt to give shelter to; ~ **qn in ospedale** to admit sb to hospital.

ri'covero sm shelter, refuge; (MIL) shelter; (MED) admission (to hospital).

ricre'are vt to recreate; (rinvigorire) to restore; (fig: distrarre) to amuse.

ricreazi'one [rikreat'tsjone] sf recreation, entertainment; (INS) break.

ri'credersi vr to change one's mind.

ricupe'rare vt (rientrare in possesso di) to recover, get back; (tempo perduto) to make up for; (NAUT) to salvage; (: naufraghi) to rescue; (delinquente) to rehabilitate; ~ **lo svantaggio** (SPORT) to close the gap.

ridacchi'are [ridak'kjare] vi to snigger.

ri'dare vt to return, give back.

'ridere vi to laugh; (deridere, beffare): ~ **di** to laugh at, make fun of.

ri'detto, a pp di **ridire**.

ri'dicolo, a ag ridiculous, absurd.

ridimensio'nare vt to reorganize; (fig) to see in the right perspective.

ri'dire vt to repeat; (criticare) to find fault with; to object to; **trova sempre qualcosa da ~** he always manages to find fault.

ridon'dante ag redundant.

ri'dotto, a pp di **ridurre**.

ri'durre vt (anche CHIM, MAT) to reduce; (prezzo, spese) to cut, reduce; (accorciare: opera letteraria) to abridge; (: RADIO, TV) to adapt; **ridursi** vr (diminuirsi) to be reduced, shrink; ridursi a to be reduced to; **ridursi pelle e ossa** to be reduced to skin and bone; **riduzi'one** sf reduction; abridgement; adaptation.

riem'pire vt to fill (up); (modulo) to fill in o out; ~rsi vr to fill (up); (mangiare troppo) to stuff o.s.; ~ qc di to fill sth (up) with.

rien'tranza [rien'trantsa] sf recess; indentation.

rien'trare vi (entrare di nuovo) to go (o come) back in; (tornare) to return; (fare una rientranza) to go in, curve inwards; to be indented; (riguardare): ~ in to be included among, form part of; **ri'entro** sm (ritorno) return; (di astronave) re-entry.

riepilo'gare vt to summarize // vi to recapitulate.

ri'fare vt to do again; (ricostruire) to make again; (nodo) to tie again, do up again; (imitare) to imitate, copy; ~rsi vr (risarcirsi): ~rsi di to make up for; (vendicarsi): ~rsi di qc su qn to get one's own back on sb for sth; (riferirsi): ~rsi a to go back to; to follow; ~ il letto to make the bed; ~rsi una vita to make a new life for o.s.; **ri'fatto, a** pp di **rifare**.

riferi'mento sm reference; in o con ~ a with reference to.

rife'rire vt (riportare) to report; (ascrivere): ~ qc a to attribute sth to // vi to do a report; ~rsi vr: ~rsi a to refer to.

rifi'nire vt to finish off, put the finishing touches to; **rifini'tura** sf finishing touch; **rifiniture** sfpl (di mobile, auto) finish sg.

rifiu'tare vt to refuse; ~ di fare to refuse to do; **rifi'uto** sm refusal; **rifiuti** smpl (spazzatura) rubbish sg, refuse sg.

riflessi'one sf (FISICA, meditazione) reflection; (il pensare) thought, reflection; (osservazione) remark.

rifles'sivo, a ag (persona) thoughtful, reflective; (LING) reflexive.

ri'flesso, a pp di **riflettere** // sm (di luce, rispecchiamento) reflection; (FISIOL) reflex; **di o per** ~ indirectly.

ri'flettere vt to reflect // vi to think; ~rsi vr to be reflected; ~ su to think over.

riflet'tore sm reflector; (proiettore) floodlight; searchlight.

ri'flusso sm flowing back; (della marea) ebb; **un'epoca di** ~ an era of nostalgia.

ri'fondere vt (rimborsare) to refund, repay.

ri'forma sf reform; **la R~** (REL) the Reformation.

rifor'mare vt to re-form; (cambiare, innovare) to reform; (MIL: recluta) to declare unfit for service; (: soldato) to invalid out, discharge; **riforma'torio** sm (DIR) community home (Brit), reformatory (US).

riforni'mento sm supplying, providing; restocking; ~i smpl supplies, provisions.

rifor'nire vt (provvedere): ~ di to supply o provide with; (fornire di nuovo: casa etc) to restock.

ri'frangere [ri'frandʒere] vt to refract; **ri'fratto, a** pp di **rifrangere**; **rifrazi'one** sf refraction.

rifug'gire [rifud'dʒire] vi to escape again; (fig): ~ da to shun.

rifugi'arsi [rifu'dʒarsi] vr to take refuge; **rifugi'ato, a** sm/f refugee.

ri'fugio [ri'fudʒo] sm refuge, shelter; (in montagna) shelter; ~ antiaereo air-raid shelter.

'riga, ghe sf line; (striscia) stripe; (di persone, cose) line, row; (regolo) ruler; (scrimatura) parting; mettersi in ~ to line up; a ~ghe (foglio) lined; (vestito) striped.

ri'gagnolo [ri'gaɲɲolo] sm rivulet.

ri'gare vt (foglio) to rule // vi: ~ diritto (fig) to toe the line.

rigatti'ere sm junk dealer.

riget'tare [ridʒet'tare] vt (gettare indietro) to throw back; (fig: respingere) to reject; (vomitare) to bring o throw up; **ri'getto** sm (anche MED) rejection.

rigidità [ridʒidi'ta] sf rigidity; stiffness; severity, rigours pl; strictness.

'rigido, a ['ridʒido] ag rigid, stiff; (membra etc: indurite) stiff; (METEOR) harsh, severe; (fig) strict.

rigi'rare [ridʒi'rare] vt to turn; ~rsi vr to turn round; (nel letto) to turn over; ~ qc tra le mani to turn sth over in one's hands; ~ il discorso to change the subject.

'rigo, ghi sm line; (MUS) staff, stave.

rigogli'oso, a [rigoʎ'ʎoso] ag (pianta) luxuriant; (fig: commercio, sviluppo) thriving.

ri'gonfio, a ag swollen.

ri'gore sm (METEOR) harshness, rigours pl; (fig) severity, strictness; (anche: calcio di ~) penalty; di ~ compulsory; a rigor di termini strictly speaking; a **rigo'roso, a** ag (severo: persona, ordine) strict; (preciso) rigorous.

rigover'nare vt to wash (up).

riguar'dare vt to look at again; (considerare) to regard, consider; (concernere) to regard, concern; ~rsi vr (aver cura di sé) to look after o.s.

rigu'ardo sm (attenzione) care; (considerazione) regard, respect; ~ a concerning, with regard to; non aver ~i nell'agire/nel parlare to act/speak freely.

rilasci'are [rilaʃ'ʃare] vt (rimettere in

libertà) to release; (*AMM: documenti*) to issue; **ri'lascio** *sm* release; issue.

rilas'sare *vt* to relax; ~**rsi** *vr* to relax; (*fig: disciplina*) to become slack.

rile'gare *vt* (*libro*) to bind; **rilega'tura** *sf* binding.

ri'leggere [ri'lɛddʒere] *vt* to reread, read again; (*rivedere*) to read over.

ri'lento: *a* ~ *av* slowly.

rileva'mento *sm* (*topografico, statistico*) survey; (*NAUT*) bearing.

rile'vante *ag* considerable; important.

rile'vare *vt* (*ricavare*) to find; (*notare*) to notice; (*mettere in evidenza*) to point out; (*venire a conoscere: notizia*) to learn; (*raccogliere: dati*) to gather, collect; (*TOPOGRAFIA*) to survey; (*MIL*) to relieve; (*COMM*) to take over.

rili'evo *sm* (*ARTE, GEO*) relief; (*fig: rilevanza*) importance; (*osservazione*) point, remark; (*TOPOGRAFIA*) survey; **dar** ~ **a** *o* **mettere in** ~ **qc** (*fig*) to bring sth out, highlight sth.

rilut'tante *ag* reluctant; **rilut'tanza** *sf* reluctance.

'rima *sf* rhyme; (*verso*) verse.

riman'dare *vt* to send again; (*restituire, rinviare*) to send back, return; (*differire*): ~ **qc (a)** to postpone sth *o* put sth off (till); (*fare riferimento*): ~ **qn a** to refer sb to; **essere rimandato** (*INS*) to have to repeat one's exams; **ri'mando** *sm* (*rinvio*) return; (*dilazione*) postponement; (*riferimento*) cross-reference.

rima'nente *ag* remaining // *sm* rest, remainder; **i** ~**i** (*persone*) the rest of them, the others; **rima'nenza** *sf* rest, remainder; **rimanenze** *sfpl* (*COMM*) unsold stock *sg*.

rima'nere *vi* (*restare*) to remain, stay; (*avanzare*) to be left, remain; (*restare stupito*) to be amazed; (*restare, mancare*): **rimangono poche settimane a Pasqua** there are only a few weeks left till Easter; **rimane da vedere se** it remains to be seen whether; (*diventare*): ~ **vedovo** to be left a widower; (*trovarsi*): ~ **confuso/sorpreso** to be confused/surprised.

ri'mare *vt, vi* to rhyme.

rimargi'nare [rimardʒi'nare] *vt, vi* (*anche*: ~**rsi**) to heal.

ri'masto, a *pp di* **rimanere**.

rima'sugli [rima'suʎʎi] *smpl* leftovers.

rimbal'zare [rimbal'tsare] *vi* to bounce back, rebound; (*proiettile*) to ricochet; **rim'balzo** *sm* rebound; ricochet.

rimbam'bito, a *ag* senile, in one's dotage.

rimboc'care *vt* (*orlo*) to turn up; (*coperta*) to tuck in; (*maniche, pantaloni*) to turn *o* roll up.

rimbom'bare *vi* to resound.

rimbor'sare *vt* to pay back, repay; **rim'borso** *sm* repayment.

rimedi'are *vi*: ~ **a** to remedy // *vt* (*fam: procurarsi*) to get *o* scrape together.

ri'medio *sm* (*medicina*) medicine; (*cura, fig*) remedy, cure.

rimesco'lare *vt* to mix well, stir well; (*carte*) to shuffle; **sentirsi** ~ **il sangue** (*per paura*) to feel one's blood run cold; (*per rabbia*) to feel one's blood boil.

ri'messa *sf* (*locale: per veicoli*) garage; (: *per aerei*) hangar; (*COMM: di merce*) consignment; (: *di denaro*) remittance; (*TENNIS*) return; (*CALCIO: anche*: ~ **in gioco**) throw-in.

ri'messo, a *pp di* **rimettere**.

ri'mettere *vt* (*mettere di nuovo*) to put back; (*indossare di nuovo*): ~ **qc** to put sth back on, put sth on again; (*restituire*) to return, give back; (*affidare*) to entrust; (: *decisione*) to refer; (*condonare*) to remit; (*COMM: merci*) to deliver; (: *denaro*) to remit; (*vomitare*) to bring up; (*perdere: anche*: **rimetterci**) to lose; ~**rsi al bello** (*tempo*) to clear up; ~**rsi in salute** to get better, recover one's health.

'rimmel *sm inv* ® mascara.

rimoder'nare *vt* to modernize.

rimon'tare *vt* (*meccanismo*) to reassemble; (: *tenda*) to put up again // *vi* (*salire di nuovo*): ~ **in** (*macchina, treno*) to get back into; (*SPORT*) to close the gap.

rimorchi'are [rimor'kjare] *vt* to tow; (*fig: ragazza*) to pick up; **rimorchia'tore** *sm* (*NAUT*) tug(boat).

ri'morchio [ri'mɔrkjo] *sm* tow; (*veicolo*) trailer.

ri'morso *sm* remorse.

rimozi'one [rimot'tsjone] *sf* removal; (*da un impiego*) dismissal; (*PSIC*) repression.

rim'pasto *sm* (*POL*) reshuffle.

rimpatri'are *vi* to return home // *vt* to repatriate; **rim'patrio** *sm* repatriation.

rimpi'angere [rim'pjandʒere] *vt* to regret; (*persona*) to miss; **rimpi'anto, a** *pp di* **rimpiangere** // *sm* regret.

rimpiat'tino *sm* hide-and-seek.

rimpiaz'zare [rimpjat'tsare] *vt* to replace.

rimpiccio'lire [rimpittʃo'lire] *vt* to make smaller // *vi* (*anche*: ~**rsi**) to become smaller.

rimpin'zare [rimpin'tsare] *vt*: ~ **di** *o* cram *o* stuff with.

rimprove'rare *vt* to rebuke, reprimand; **rim'provero** *sm* rebuke, reprimand.

rimugi'nare [rimudʒi'nare] *vt* (*fig*) to turn over in one's mind.

rimunerazi'one [rimunerat'tsjone] *sf* remuneration; (*premio*) reward.

rimu'overe *vt* to remove; (*destituire*) to dismiss.

Rinasci'mento [rinaʃʃi'mento] *sm*: **il** ~ the Renaissance.

ri'nascita [ri'naʃʃita] *sf* rebirth, revival.

rincal'zare [rinkal'tsare] *vt* (*palo, albero*) to support, prop up; (*lenzuola*) to tuck in.

rinca'rare *vt* to increase the price of // *vi* to go up, become more expensive.

rinca'sare *vi* to go home.

rinchi'udere [rin'kjudere] *vt* to shut (*o* lock) up; ~rsi *vr*: ~rsi in to shut o.s. up in; ~rsi in se stesso to withdraw into o.s.; **rinchi'uso, a** *pp di* **rinchiudere.**

rin'correre *vt* to chase, run after; **rin'corso, a** *pp di* **rincorrere** // *sf* short run.

rin'crescere [rin'kreʃʃere] *vb impers*: mi rincresce che/di non poter fare I'm sorry that/I can't do, I regret that/being unable to do; **rincresci'mento** *sm* regret; **rincresci'uto, a** *pp di* **rincrescere.**

rincu'lare *vi* to draw back; (*arma*) to recoil.

rinfacci'are [rinfat'tʃare] *vt* (*fig*): ~ qc a qn to throw sth in sb's face.

rinfor'zare [rinfor'tsare] *vt* to reinforce, strengthen // *vi* (*anche*: ~rsi) to grow stronger; **rin'forzo** *sm*: mettere un rinforzo a to strengthen; di rinforzo (*asse, sbarra*) strengthening; (*esercito*) supporting; (*personale*) extra, additional; **rinforzi** *smpl* (*MIL*) reinforcements.

rinfran'care *vt* to encourage, reassure.

rinfres'care *vt* (*atmosfera, temperatura*) to cool (down); (*abito, pareti*) to freshen up // *vi* (*tempo*) to grow cooler; ~rsi *vr* (*ristorarsi*) to refresh o.s.; (*lavarsi*) to freshen up; **rin'fresco, schi** *sm* (*festa*) party; **rinfreschi** *smpl* refreshments.

rin'fusa *sf*: alla ~ in confusion, higgledy-piggledy.

ringhi'are [rin'gjare] *vi* to growl, snarl.

ringhi'era [rin'gjɛra] *sf* railing; (*delle scale*) banister(s *pl*).

ringiova'nire [rindʒova'nire] *vt* (*sog: vestito, acconciatura etc*): ~ qn to make sb look younger; (: *vacanze etc*) to rejuvenate // *vi* (*anche*: ~rsi) to become (*o* look) younger.

ringrazia'mento [ringrattsja'mento] *sm* thanks *pl*.

ringrazi'are [ringrat'tsjare] *vt* to thank; ~ qn di qc to thank sb for sth.

rinne'gare *vt* (*fede*) to renounce; (*figlio*) to disown, repudiate; **rinne'gato, a** *sm/f* renegade.

rinnova'mento *sm* renewal; (*economico*) revival.

rinno'vare *vt* to renew; (*ripetere*) to repeat, renew; ~rsi *vr* (*fenomeno*) to be repeated, recur; **rin'novo** *sm* (*di contratto*) renewal; "chiuso per rinnovo dei locali" "closed for alterations".

rinoce'ronte [rinotʃe'ronte] *sm* rhinoceros.

rino'mato, a *ag* renowned, celebrated.

rinsal'dare *vt* to strengthen.

rintoc'care *vi* (*campana*) to toll; (*orologio*) to strike.

rintracci'are [rintrat'tʃare] *vt* to track down.

rintro'nare *vi* to boom, roar // *vt* (*assordare*) to deafen; (*stordire*) to stun.

ri'nuncia [ri'nuntʃa] *etc* = **rinunzia** *etc.*

ri'nunzia [ri'nuntsja] *sf* renunciation.

rinunzi'are [rinun'tsjare] *vi*: ~ a to give up, renounce.

rinve'nire *vt* to find, recover; (*scoprire*) to discover, find out // *vi* (*riprendere i sensi*) to come round; (*riprendere l'aspetto naturale*) to revive.

rinvi'are *vt* (*rimandare indietro*) to send back, return; (*differire*): ~ qc (a) to postpone sth *o* put sth off (till); to adjourn sth (till); (*fare un rimando*): ~ qn a to refer sb to.

rinvigo'rire *vt* to strengthen.

rin'vio, 'vii *sm* (*rimando*) return; (*differimento*) postponement; (: *di seduta*) adjournment; (*in un testo*) cross-reference.

ri'one *sm* district, quarter.

riordi'nare *vt* (*rimettere in ordine*) to tidy; (*riorganizzare*) to reorganize.

riorganiz'zare [riorganid'dzare] *vt* to reorganize.

ripa'gare *vt* to repay.

ripa'rare *vt* (*proteggere*) to protect, defend; (*correggere: male, torto*) to make up for; (: *errore*) to put right; (*aggiustare*) to repair // *vi* (*mettere rimedio*): ~ a to make up for; ~rsi *vr* (*rifugiarsi*) to take refuge *o* shelter; **riparazi'one** *sf* (*di un torto*) reparation; (*di guasto, scarpe*) repairing *q*; repair; (*risarcimento*) compensation.

ri'paro *sm* (*protezione*) shelter, protection; (*rimedio*) remedy.

ripar'tire *vt* (*dividere*) to divide up; (*distribuire*) to share out // *vi* to set off again; to leave again.

ripas'sare *vi* to come (*o* go) back // *vt* (*scritto, lezione*) to go over (again).

ripen'sare *vi* to think; (*cambiare pensiero*) to change one's mind; (*tornare col pensiero*): ~ a to recall.

ripercu'otersi *vr*: ~ su (*fig*) to have repercussions on.

ripercussi'one *sf* (*fig*): avere una ~ *o* delle ~i su to have repercussions on.

ripes'care *vt* (*pesce*) to catch again; (*persona, cosa*) to fish out; (*fig: ritrovare*) to dig out.

ri'petere *vt* to repeat; (*ripassare*) to go over; **ripetizi'one** *sf* repetition; (*di lezione*) revision; **ripetizioni** *sfpl* (*INS*) private tutoring *o* coaching *sg*.

ripi'ano *sm* (*GEO*) terrace; (*di mobile*) shelf.

ri'picca *sf*: per ~ out of spite.

'ripido, a *ag* steep.

ripie'gare vt to refold; (piegare più volte) to fold (up) // vi (MIL) to retreat, fall back; (fig: accontentarsi): ~ su to make do with; ~rsi vr to bend; **ripi'ego, ghi** sm expedient.

ripi'eno, a ag full; (CUC) stuffed; (: panino) filled // sm (CUC) stuffing.

ri'porre vt (porre al suo posto) to put back, replace; (mettere via) to put away; (fiducia, speranza): ~ qc in qn to place o put sth in sb.

ripor'tare vt (portare indietro) to bring (o take) back; (riferire) to report; (citare) to quote; (ricevere) to receive, get; (vittoria) to gain; (successo) to have; (MAT) to carry; ~rsi a (anche fig) to go back to; (riferirsi a) to refer to; ~ danni to suffer damage.

ripo'sare vt (bicchiere, valigia) to put down; (dare sollievo) to rest // vi to rest; ~rsi vr to rest; **ri'poso** sm rest; (MIL): riposo! at ease!; a riposo (in pensione) retired; giorno di riposo day off.

ripos'tiglio [ripos'tiʎʎo] sm lumber-room.

ri'posto, a pp di riporre.

ri'prendere vt (prigioniero, fortezza) to recapture; (prendere indietro) to take back; (ricominciare: lavoro) to resume; (andare a prendere) to fetch, come back for; (assumere di nuovo: impiegati) to take on again, re-employ; (rimproverare) to tell off; (restringere: abito) to take in; (CINEMA) to shoot; ~rsi vr to recover; (correggersi) to correct o.s.; **ri'preso, a** pp di riprendere // sf recapture; resumption; (economica, da malattia, emozione) recovery; (AUT) acceleration q; (TEATRO, CINEMA) rerun; (CINEMA: presa) shooting q; shot; (SPORT) second half; (: PUGILATO) round; a più riprese on several occasions, several times.

ripristi'nare vt to restore.

ripro'durre vt to reproduce; riprodursi vr (BIOL) to reproduce; (riformarsi) to form again; **riprodut'tivo, a** ag reproductive; **riproduzi'one** sf reproduction, riproduzione vietata all rights reserved.

ripudi'are vt to repudiate, disown.

ripu'gnante [ripuɲ'ɲante] ag disgusting, repulsive.

ripu'gnare [ripuɲ'ɲare] vi: ~ a qn to repel o disgust sb.

ripu'lire vt to clean up; (sog: ladri) to clean out; (perfezionare) to polish, refine.

ri'quadro sm square; (ARCHIT) panel.

ri'saia sf paddy field.

risa'lire vi (ritornare in su) to go back up; ~ a (ritornare con la mente) to go back to; (datare da) to date back to, go back to.

risal'tare vi (fig: distinguersi) to stand

out; (ARCHIT) to project, jut out; **ri'salto** sm prominence; (sporgenza) projection; mettere o porre in risalto qc to make sth stand out.

risa'nare vt (guarire) to heal, cure; (palude) to reclaim; (economia) to improve; (bilancio) to reorganize.

risa'puto, a ag: è ~ che ... everyone knows that ..., it is common knowledge that ....

risarci'mento [risartʃi'mento] sm: ~ (di) compensation (for).

risar'cire [risar'tʃire] vt (cose) to pay compensation for; (persona): ~ qn di qc to compensate sb for sth.

ri'sata sf laugh.

riscalda'mento sm heating; ~ centrale central heating.

riscal'dare vt (scaldare) to heat; (: mani, persona) to warm; (minestra) to reheat; ~rsi vr to warm up.

riscat'tare vt (prigioniero) to ransom, pay a ransom for; (DIR) to redeem; ~rsi vr (da disonore) to redeem o.s.; **ris'catto** sm ransom; redemption.

rischia'rare vt (illuminare) to light up; (colore) to make lighter; ~rsi vr (tempo) to clear up; (cielo) to clear; (fig: volto) to brighten up; ~rsi la voce to clear one's throat.

rischi'are [ris'kjare] vt to risk // vi: ~ di fare qc to risk o run the risk of doing sth.

'rischio ['riskjo] sm risk; **rischi'oso, a** ag risky, dangerous.

riscia'cquare [riʃʃa'kware] vt to rinse.

riscon'trare vt (confrontare: due cose) to compare; (esaminare) to check, verify; (rilevare) to find; **ris'contro** sm comparison; check, verification; (AMM: lettera di risposta) reply.

riscossi'one sf collection.

ris'cosso, a pp di riscuotere // sf (riconquista) recovery, reconquest.

ris'cuotere vt (ritirare una somma dovuta) to collect; (: stipendio) to draw, collect; (assegno) to cash; (fig: successo etc, to win, earn; ~rsi vr: ~rsi (da) to shake o.s. (out of), rouse o.s. (from).

risenti'mento sm resentment.

risen'tire vt to hear again; (provare) to feel // vi: ~ di to feel (o show) the effects of; ~rsi vr: ~rsi di o per to take offence at, resent; **risen'tito, a** ag resentful.

ri'serbo sm reserve.

ri'serva sf reserve; (di caccia, pesca) preserve; (restrizione, di indigeni) reservation; di ~ (provviste etc) in reserve.

riser'vare vt (tenere in serbo) to keep, put aside; (prenotare) to book, reserve; ~rsi vr: ~rsi di fare qc to intend to do sth; **riser'vato, a** ag (prenotato, fig: persona) reserved; (confidenziale) confidential; **riserva'tezza** sf reserve.

risi'edere vi: ~ a o in to reside in.

'risma sf (di carta) ream; (fig) kind, sort.

'riso, a pp di ridere // sm (pl(f) ~a: il ridere): un ~ a laugh; il ~ laughter; (pianta) rice.

riso'lino sm snigger.

ri'solto, a pp di risolvere.

risolu'tezza [risolu'tettsa] sf determination.

riso'luto, a ag determined, resolute.

risoluzi'one [risolut'tsjone] sf solving q; (MAT) solution; (decisione, di immagine) resolution.

ri'solvere vt (difficoltà, controversia) to resolve; (problema) to solve; (decidere): ~ di fare to resolve to do; ~rsi vr (decidersi): ~rsi a fare to make up one's mind to do; (andare a finire): ~rsi in to end up, turn out; ~rsi in nulla to come to nothing.

riso'nanza [riso'nantsa] sf resonance; aver vasta ~ (fig: fatto etc) to be known far and wide.

riso'nare vt, vi = risuonare.

ri'sorgere [ri'sordʒere] vi to rise again; **risorgi'mento** sm revival; il Risorgimento (STORIA) the Risorgimento.

ri'sorsa sf expedient, resort; ~e sfpl (naturali, finanziarie etc) resources; persona piena di ~e resourceful person.

ri'sorto, a pp di risorgere.

ri'sotto sm (CUC) risotto.

risparmi'are vt to save; (non uccidere) to spare // vi to save; ~ qc a qn to spare sb sth.

ris'parmio sm saving q; (denaro) savings pl.

rispec'chiare [rispek'kjare] vt to reflect.

rispet'tabile ag respectable.

rispet'tare vt to respect; farsi ~ to command respect.

rispet'tivo, a ag respective.

ris'petto sm respect; ~i smpl (saluti) respects, regards; ~ a (in paragone a) compared to; (in relazione a) as regards, as for; **rispet'toso, a** ag respectful.

ris'plendere vi to shine.

ris'pondere vi to answer, reply; (freni) to respond; ~ a (domanda) to answer, reply to; (persona) to answer; (invito) to reply to; (provocazione, sog: veicolo, apparecchio) to respond to; (corrispondere a) to correspond to; (: speranze, bisogno) to answer; ~ di to answer for; **ris'posto, a** pp di rispondere // sf answer, reply; in risposta a in reply to.

'rissa sf brawl.

ristabi'lire vt to re-establish, restore; (persona: sog: riposo etc) to restore to health; ~rsi vr to recover.

rista'gnare [ristaɲ'ɲare] vi (acqua) to

become stagnant; (sangue) to cease flowing; (fig: industria) to stagnate; **ris'tagno** sm stagnation.

ris'tampa sf reprinting q; reprint.

risto'rante sm restaurant.

risto'rarsi vr to have something to eat and drink; (riposarsi) to rest, have a rest; **ris'toro** sm (bevanda, cibo) refreshment; servizio di ristoro (FERR) refreshments pl.

ristret'tezza [ristret'tettsa] sf (strettezza) narrowness; (fig: scarsezza) scarcity, lack; (: meschinità) meanness; ~e sfpl (povertà) financial straits.

ris'tretto, a pp di restringere // ag (racchiuso) enclosed, hemmed in; (angusto) narrow; (limitato) ~ o (a) stricted o limited (to); (CUC: brodo) thick; (: caffè) extra strong.

risucchi'are [risuk'kjare] vt to suck in.

risul'tare vi (dimostrarsi) to prove (to be), turn out (to be); (riuscire): ~ vincitore to emerge as the winner; ~ da (provenire) to result from, be the result of; mi risulta che ... I understand that ...; non mi risulta not as far as I know; **risul'tato** sm result.

risuo'nare vi (rimbombare) to resound.

risurrezi'one [risurret'tsjone] sf (REL) resurrection.

risusci'tare [risuʃʃi'tare] vt to resuscitate, restore to life; (fig) to revive, bring back // vi to rise (from the dead).

ris'veglio [riz'veʎʎo] sm waking up; (fig) revival.

ris'volto sm (di giacca) lapel; (di pantaloni) turn-up; (di manica) cuff; (di tasca) flap; (di libro) inside flap; (fig) implication.

ritagli'are [ritaʎ'ʎare] vt (tagliar via) to cut out; **ri'taglio** sm (di giornale) cutting, clipping; (di stoffa etc) scrap; nei ritagli di tempo in one's spare time.

ritar'dare vi (persona, treno) to be late; (orologio) to be slow // vt (rallentare) to slow down; (impedire) to delay, hold up; (differire) to postpone, delay; **ritarda'tario, a** sm/f latecomer.

ri'tardo sm delay; (di persona aspettata) lateness q; (fig: mentale) backwardness; in ~ late.

ri'tegno [ri'teɲɲo] sm restraint.

rite'nere vt (trattenere) to hold back; (: somma) to deduct; (giudicare) to consider, believe; **rite'nuta** sf (sul salario) deduction.

riti'rare vt to withdraw; (POL: richiamare) to recall; (andare a prendere: pacco etc) to collect, pick up; ~rsi vr to withdraw; (da un'attività) to retire; (stoffa) to shrink; (marea) to recede; **riti'rata** sf (MIL) retreat; (latrina) lavatory; **ri'tiro** sm withdrawal; recall; collection; (luogo appartato) retreat.

'ritmo sm rhythm; (fig) rate; (: della

vita) pace, tempo.

'**rito** *sm* rite; di ~ usual, customary.

ritoc'care *vt* (*disegno, fotografia*) to touch up; (*testo*) to alter; **ri'tocco, chi** *sm* touching up *q*; alteration.

ritor'nare *vi* to return, go (*o come*) back; (*ripresentarsi*) to recur; (*ridiventare*): ~ ricco to become rich again // *vt* (*restituire*) to return, give back.

ritor'nello *sm* refrain.

ri'torno *sm* return; essere di ~ to be back; avere un ~ di fiamma (*AUT*) to backfire; (*fig: persona*) to be back in love again.

ri'trarre *vt* (*trarre indietro, via*) to withdraw; (*distogliere: sguardo*) to turn away; (*rappresentare*) to portray, depict; (*ricavare*) to get, obtain.

ritrat'tare *vt* (*disdire*) to retract, take back; (*trattare nuovamente*) to deal with again.

ri'tratto, a *pp di* **ritrarre** // *sm* portrait.

ri'troso, a *ag* (*restio*): ~ **(a)** reluctant (to); (*schivo*) shy; andare a ~ to go backwards.

ritro'vare *vt* to find; (*salute*) to regain; (*persona*) to find; to meet again; ~rsi *vr* (*essere, capitare*) to find o.s.; (*raccapezzarsi*) to find one's way; (*con senso reciproco*) to meet (again); **ri'trovo** *sm* meeting place; **ritrovo notturno** night club.

'**ritto, a** *ag* (*in piedi*) standing, on one's feet; (*levato in alto*) erect, raised; (*: capelli*) standing on end; (*posto verticalmente*) upright.

ritu'ale *ag, sm* ritual.

riuni'one *sf* (*adunanza*) meeting; (*riconciliazione*) reunion.

riu'nire *vt* (*ricongiungere*) to join (*together*); (*riconciliare*) to reunite, bring together (again); ~rsi *vr* (*adunarsi*) to meet; (*tornare a stare insieme*) to be reunited.

riu'scire [riuʃ'ʃire] *vi* (*uscire di nuovo*) to go out again, go back out; (*aver esito: fatti, azioni*) to go, turn out; (*aver successo*) to succeed, be successful; (*essere, apparire*) to be, prove; (*raggiungere il fine*) to manage, succeed; ~ a fare qc to manage to do o succeed in doing o to be able to do sth; questo mi riesce nuovo this is new to me; **riu'scita** *sf* (*esito*) result, outcome; (*buon esito*) success.

'**riva** *sf* (*di fiume*) bank; (*di lago, mare*) shore.

ri'vale *sm/f* rival; **rivalità** *sf* rivalry.

ri'valsa *sf* (*rivincita*) revenge; (*risarcimento*) compensation.

rivalu'tare *vt* (*ECON*) to revalue.

rivan'gare *vt* (*ricordi etc*) to dig up (again).

rive'dere *vt* to see again; (*ripassare*) to

revise; (*verificare*) to check.

rive'lare *vt* to reveal; (*divulgare*) to reveal, disclose; (*dare indizio*) to reveal, show; ~rsi *vr* (*manifestarsi*) to be revealed; ~rsi onesto *etc* to prove to be honest *etc*; **rivela'tore** *sm* (*TECN*) detector; (*FOT*) developer; **rivelazi'one** *sf* revelation.

rivendi'care *vt* to claim, demand.

ri'vendita *sf* (*bottega*) retailer's (shop).

rivendi'tore, 'trice *sm/f* retailer; ~ autorizzato (*COMM*) authorized dealer.

ri'verbero *sm* (*di luce, calore*) reflection; (*di suono*) reverberation.

rive'renza [rive'rɛntsa] *sf* reverence; (*inchino*) bow; curtsey.

rive'rire *vt* (*rispettare*) to revere; (*salutare*) to pay one's respects to.

river'sare *vt* (*anche fig*) to pour; ~rsi *vr* (*fig: persone*) to pour out.

rivesti'mento *sm* covering; coating.

rives'tire *vt* to dress again; (*ricoprire*) to cover; to coat; (*fig: carica*) to hold; ~rsi *vr* to get dressed again; to change (one's clothes).

rivi'era *sf* coast; la ~ **italiana** the Italian Riviera.

ri'vincita [ri'vintʃita] *sf* (*SPORT*) return match; (*fig*) revenge.

rivis'suto, a *pp di* **rivivere**.

ri'vista *sf* review; (*periodico*) magazine, review; (*TEATRO*) revue; variety show.

ri'vivere *vi* (*riacquistare forza*) to come alive again; (*tornare in uso*) to be revived // *vt* to relive.

ri'volgere [ri'vɔldʒere] *vt* (*attenzione, sguardo*) to turn, direct; (*parole*) to address; ~rsi *vr* to turn round; (*fig: dirigersi per informazioni*): ~rsi a to go and see and speak to; (*: ufficio*) to enquire at.

ri'volta *sf* revolt, rebellion.

rivol'tare *vt* to turn over; (*con l'interno all'esterno*) to turn inside out; (*disgustare: stomaco*) to upset, turn; ~rsi *vr* (*ribellarsi*): ~rsi **(a)** to rebel (against).

rivol'tella *sf* revolver.

ri'volto, a *pp di* **rivolgere**.

rivoluzio'nare [rivoluttsjo'nare] *vt* to revolutionize.

rivoluzio'nario, a [rivoluttsjo'narjo] *ag, sm/f* revolutionary.

rivoluzi'one [rivolut'tsjone] *sf* revolution.

riz'zare [rit'tsare] *vt* to raise, erect; ~rsi *vr* to stand up; (*capelli*) to stand on end.

'**roba** *sf* stuff, things *pl*; (*possessi, beni*) belongings *pl*, things *pl*, possessions *pl*; ~ da mangiare things *pl* to eat, food; ~ da matti sheer madness *o* lunacy.

'**robot** *sm inv* robot.

ro'busto, a *ag* robust, sturdy; (*solido: catena*) strong.

'**rocca, che** *sf* fortress.

rocca'forte *sf* stronghold.

roc'chetto [rok'ketto] *sm* reel, spool.

'**roccia, ce** ['rɔttʃa] *sf* rock; **fare ~** (*SPORT*) to go rock climbing; **roc'cioso, a** *ag* rocky.

ro'daggio [ro'daddʒo] *sm* running (*Brit*) *o* breaking (*US*) in; **in ~** running (*Brit*) *o* breaking (*US*) in.

'**Rodano** *sm*: **il ~** the Rhone.

'**rodere** *vt* to gnaw (at); (*distruggere poco a poco*) to eat into.

rodi'tore *sm* (*ZOOL*) rodent.

rodo'dendro *sm* rhododendron.

'**rogna** ['rɔɲɲa] *sf* (*MED*) scabies *sg*; (*fig*) bother, nuisance.

ro'gnone [roɲ'ɲone] *sm* (*CUC*) kidney.

'**rogo, ghi** *sm* (*per cadaveri*) (funeral) pyre; (*supplizio*): **il ~** the stake.

rol'lio *sm* roll(ing).

'**Roma** *sf* Rome.

Roma'nia *sf*: **la ~** Romania.

ro'manico, a, ci, che *ag* Romanesque.

ro'mano, a *ag*, *sm/f* Roman.

romanti'cismo [romanti'tʃizmo] *sm* romanticism.

ro'mantico, a, ci, che *ag* romantic.

ro'manza [ro'mandza] *sf* (*MUS*, *LETTERATURA*) romance.

roman'zesco, a, schi, sche [roman'dzesko] *ag* (*stile*, *personaggi*) fictional; (*fig*) storybook *cpd*.

romanzi'ere [roman'dzjere] *sm* novelist.

ro'manzo, a [ro'mandzo] *ag* (*LING*) romance *cpd* // *sm* (*medievale*) romance; (*moderno*) novel; **~ d'appendice** serial (story).

rom'bare *vi* to rumble, thunder, roar.

'**rombo** *sm* rumble, thunder, roar; (*MAT*) rhombus; (*ZOOL*) turbot; brill.

ro'meno, a *ag*, *sm/f*, *sm* = **rumeno, a**.

'**rompere** *vt* to break; (*conversazione*, *fidanzamento*) to break off // *vi* to break; **~rsi** *vr* to break; **mi rompe le scatole** (*fam*) he (*o* she) is a pain in the neck; **~rsi un braccio** to break an arm; **rompi'capo** *sm* worry, headache; (*indovinello*) puzzle; (*in enigmistica*) brainteaser; **rompighi'accio** *sm* (*NAUT*) icebreaker; **rompis'catole** *sm/f inv* (*fam*) pest, pain in the neck.

'**ronda** *sf* (*MIL*) rounds *pl*, patrol.

ron'della *sf* (*TECN*) washer.

'**rondine** *sf* (*ZOOL*) swallow.

ron'done *sm* (*ZOOL*) swift.

ron'zare [ron'dzare] *vi* to buzz, hum.

ron'zino [ron'dzino] *sm* (*peg*: *cavallo*) nag.

'**rosa** *sf* rose // *ag inv*, *sm* pink; **ro'saio** *sm* (*pianta*) rosebush, rose tree; (*giardino*) rose garden; **ro'sario** *sm* (*REL*) rosary; **ro'sato, a** *ag* pink, rosy // *sm* (*vino*) rosé (wine); **ro'seo, a** *ag* (*anche fig*) rosy.

rosicchi'are [rosik'kjare] *vt* to gnaw (at); (*mangiucchiare*) to nibble (at).

rosma'rino *sm* rosemary.

'**roso, a** *pp di* **rodere**.

roso'lare *vt* (*CUC*) to brown.

roso'lia *sf* (*MED*) German measles *sg*, rubella.

ro'sone *sm* rosette; (*vetrata*) rose window.

'**rospo** *sm* (*ZOOL*) toad.

ros'setto *sm* (*per labbra*) lipstick; (*per guance*) rouge.

'**rosso, a** *ag*, *sm*, *sm/f* red; **il mar R~** the Red Sea; **~ d'uovo** egg yolk; **ros'sore** *sm* flush, blush.

rosticce'ria [rostittʃe'ria] *sf* shop selling roast meat and other cooked food.

'**rostro** *sm* rostrum; (*becco*) beak.

ro'tabile *ag* (*percorribile*): **strada ~** roadway; (*FERR*): **materiale** *m* **~** rolling stock.

ro'taia *sf* rut, track; (*FERR*) rail.

ro'tare *vt*, *vi* to rotate; **rotazi'one** *sf* rotation.

rote'are *vt*, *vi* to whirl; **~ gli occhi** to roll one's eyes.

ro'tella *sf* small wheel; (*di mobile*) castor.

roto'lare *vt*, *vi* to roll; **~rsi** *vr* to roll (about).

'**rotolo** *sm* roll; **andare a ~i** (*fig*) to go to rack and ruin.

ro'tondo, a *ag* round // *sf* rotunda.

ro'tore *sm* rotor.

'**rotta** *sf* (*AER*, *NAUT*) course, route; (*MIL*) rout; **a ~ di collo** at breakneck speed; **essere in ~ con qn** to be on bad terms with sb.

rot'tame *sm* fragment, scrap, broken bit; **~i** *smpl* (*di nave*, *aereo etc*) wreckage *sg*; **~i di ferro** scrap iron *sg*.

'**rotto, a** *pp di* **rompere** // *ag* broken; (*calzoni*) torn, split; (*persona*: *pratico*, *resistente*): **~ a** accustomed *o* inured to; **per il ~ della cuffia** by the skin of one's teeth.

rot'tura *sf* breaking *q*; break; breaking off; (*MED*) fracture, break.

rou'lotte [ru'lɔt] *sf* caravan.

ro'vente *ag* red-hot.

'**rovere** *sm* oak.

rovesci'are [roveʃ'ʃare] *vt* (*versare in giù*) to pour; (: *accidentalmente*) to spill; (*capovolgere*) to turn upside down; (*gettare a terra*) to knock down; (: *fig*: *governo*) to overthrow; (*piegare all'indietro*: *testa*) to throw back; **~rsi** *vr* (*sedia*, *macchina*) to overturn; (*barca*) to capsize; (*liquido*) to spill; (*fig*: *situazione*) to be reversed.

ro'vescio, sci [ro'veʃʃo] *sm* other side, wrong side; (*della mano*) back; (*di moneta*) reverse; (*pioggia*) sudden downpour; (*fig*) setback; (*MAGLIA*: *anche*: **punto ~**) purl (stitch); (*TENNIS*) backhand (stroke); **a ~** upside-down; inside-out; (*piegare a ~* to misunderstand sth.

ro'vina *sf* ruin; **~e** *sfpl* ruins; **andare in ~** (*andare a pezzi*) to collapse; (*fig*) to go to rack and ruin.

rovi'nare *vi* to collapse, fall down // *vt* (*far cadere giù: casa*) to demolish; (*danneggiare, fig*) to ruin; **rovi'noso, a** *ag* disastrous; damaging; violent.

rovis'tare *vt* (*casa*) to ransack; (*tasche*) to rummage in (*o* through).

'rovo *sm* (*BOT*) blackberry bush, bramble bush.

'rozzo, a ['roddzo] *ag* rough, coarse.

'ruba *sf*: **andare a ~** to sell like hot cakes.

ru'bare *vt* to steal; **~ qc a qn** to steal sth from sb.

rubi'netto *sm* tap, faucet (*US*).

ru'bino *sm* ruby.

ru'brica, che *sf* (*STAMPA*) column; (*quadernetto*) index book; address book.

rude *ag* tough, rough.

'rudere *sm* (*rovina*) ruins *pl*.

rudimen'tale *ag* rudimentary, basic.

rudi'menti *smpl* rudiments; basic principles; basic knowledge *sg*.

ruffi'ano *sm* pimp.

'ruga, ghe *sf* wrinkle.

'ruggine ['ruddʒine] *sf* rust.

rug'gire [rud'dʒire] *vi* to roar.

rugi'ada [ru'dʒada] *sf* dew.

ru'goso, a *ag* wrinkled.

rul'lare *vi* (*tamburo, nave*) to roll; (*aereo*) to taxi.

'rullo *sm* (*di tamburi*) roll; (*arnese cilindrico, TIP*) roller; **~ compressore** steam roller; **~ di pellicola** roll of film.

rum *sm* rum.

ru'meno, a *ag, sm/f, sm* Romanian.

rumi'nare *vt* (*ZOOL*) to ruminate.

ru'more *sm*: **un ~** a noise, a sound; (*fig*) a rumour; **il ~** noise; **rumo'roso, a** *ag* noisy.

ru'olo *sm* (*TEATRO, fig*) role, part; (*elenco*) roll, register, list; **di ~** permanent, on the permanent staff.

ru'ota *sf* wheel; **a ~** (*forma*) circular; **~ anteriore/posteriore** front/back wheel; **~ di scorta** spare wheel.

ruo'tare *vt, vi* = **rotare**.

'rupe *sf* cliff.

ru'rale *ag* rural, country *cpd*.

ru'scello [ruʃ'ʃello] *sm* stream.

'ruspa *sf* excavator.

rus'sare *vi* to snore.

'Russia *sf*: **la ~** Russia; **'russo, a** *ag, sm/f, sm* Russian.

'rustico, a, ci, che *ag* rustic; (*fig*) rough, unrefined.

rut'tare *vi* to belch; **'rutto** *sm* belch.

'ruvido, a *ag* rough, coarse.

ruzzo'lare [ruttso'lare] *vi* to tumble down; **ruzzo'loni** *av*: **cadere ruzzoloni** to tumble down; **fare le scale ruzzoloni** to tumble down the stairs.

S

S. *abbr* (= *sud*) S.

sa *vb vedi* **sapere.**

'sabato *sm* Saturday; **di** *o* **il ~** on Saturdays.

'sabbia *sf* sand; **~e mobili** quicksand(s); **sabbi'oso, a** *ag* sandy.

sabo'taggio [sabo'taddʒo] *sm* sabotage.

sabo'tare *vt* to sabotage.

'sacca, che *sf* bag; (*bisaccia*) haversack; (*insenatura*) inlet; **~ da viaggio** travelling bag.

sacca'rina *sf* saccharin(e).

sac'cente [sat'tʃente] *sm/f* know-all (*Brit*), know-it-all (*US*).

saccheggi'are [sakked'dʒare] *vt* to sack, plunder; **sac'cheggio** *sm* sack(ing).

sac'chetto [sak'ketto] *sm* (small) bag; (small) sack.

'sacco, chi *sm* bag; (*per carbone etc*) sack; (*ANAT, BIOL*) sac; (*tela*) sacking; (*saccheggio*) sack(ing); (*fig: grande quantità*): **un ~ di** lots of, heaps of; **~ a pelo** sleeping bag; **~ per i rifiuti** bin bag.

sacer'dote [satʃer'dote] *sm* priest; **sacer'dozio** *sm* priesthood.

sacra'mento *sm* sacrament.

sacrifi'care *vt* to sacrifice; **~rsi** *vr* to sacrifice o.s.; (*privarsi di qc*) to make sacrifices.

sacri'ficio [sakri'fitʃo] *sm* sacrifice.

sacri'legio [sakri'ledʒo] *sm* sacrilege.

'sacro, a *ag* sacred.

'sadico, a, ci, che *ag* sadistic // *sm/f* sadist.

sa'etta *sf* arrow; (*fulmine: anche fig*) thunderbolt; flash of lightning.

sa'fari *sm inv* safari.

sa'gace [sa'gatʃe] *ag* shrewd, sagacious.

sag'gezza [sad'dʒettsa] *sf* wisdom.

saggi'are [sad'dʒare] *vt* (*metalli*) to assay; (*fig*) to test.

'saggio, a, gi, ge ['saddʒo] *ag* wise // *sm* (*persona*) sage; (*operazione sperimentale*) test; (: *dell'oro*) assay; (*fig: prova*) proof; (*campione indicativo*) sample; (*ricerca, esame critico*) essay.

Sagit'tario [sadʒit'tarjo] *sm* Sagittarius.

'sagoma *sf* (*profilo*) outline, profile; (*forma*) form, shape; (*TECN*) template; (*bersaglio*) target; (*fig: persona*) character.

'sagra *sf* festival.

sagres'tano *sm* sacristan; sexton.

sagres'tia *sf* sacristy; (*culto protestante*) vestry.

Sa'hara [sa'ara] *sm*: **il (deserto del) ~** the Sahara (Desert).

'sai *vb vedi* **sapere.**

'sala *sf* hall; (*stanza*) room; **~ d'aspetto** waiting room; **~ da ballo** ballroom; **~ per concerti** concert hall; **~ da gioco**

gaming room; ~ **operatoria** operating theatre; ~ **da pranzo** dining room.

sa'lame *sm* salami *q*, salami sausage.

sala'moia *sf* (*CUC*) brine.

sa'lare *vt* to salt.

salari'ato, a *sm/f* wage-earner.

sa'lario *sm* pay, wages *pl*.

sa'lato, a *ag* (*sapore*) salty; (*CUC*) salted, salt *cpd*; (*fig: discorso etc*) biting, sharp; (: *prezzi*) steep, stiff.

sal'dare *vt* (*congiungere*) to join, bind; (*parti metalliche*) to solder; (: *con saldatura autogena*) to weld; (*conto*) to settle, pay; **salda'tura** *sf* soldering; welding; (*punto saldato*) soldered joint; weld.

sal'dezza [sal'dettsa] *sf* firmness; strength.

'saldo, a *ag* (*resistente, forte*) strong, firm; (*fermo*) firm, steady, stable; (*fig*) firm, steadfast // *sm* (*svendita*) sale; (*di conto*) settlement; (*ECON*) balance.

'sale *sm* salt; (*fig*): **ha poco ~ in zucca** he doesn't have much sense; ~ **fino/ grosso** table/cooking salt.

'salice ['salitʃe] *sm* willow; ~ **piangente** weeping willow.

sali'ente *ag* (*fig*) salient, main.

sali'era *sf* salt cellar.

sa'lino, a *ag* saline // *sf* saltworks *sg*.

sa'lire *vi* to go (*o* come) up; (*aereo etc*) to climb, go up; (*passeggero*) to get on; (*sentiero, prezzi, livello*) to go up, rise // *vt* (*scale, gradini*) to go (*o* come) up; ~ **su** to climb (up); ~ **sul treno/ sull'autobus** to board the train/the bus; ~ **in macchina** to get into the car; **sa'lita** *sf* climb, ascent; (*erta*) hill, slope; **in salita** *ag, av* uphill.

sa'liva *sf* saliva.

'salma *sf* corpse.

'salmo *sm* psalm.

sal'mone *sm* salmon.

sa'lone *sm* (*stanza*) sitting room, lounge; (*in albergo*) lounge; (*su nave*) lounge, saloon; (*mostra*) show, exhibition; ~ **di bellezza** beauty salon.

sa'lotto *sm* lounge, sitting room; (*mobilio*) lounge suite.

sal'pare *vi* (*NAUT*) to set sail; (*anche*: ~ l'ancora) to weigh anchor.

'salsa *sf* (*CUC*) sauce; ~ **di pomodoro** tomato sauce.

sal'siccia, ce [sal'sittʃa] *sf* pork sausage.

sal'tare *vi* to jump, leap; (*esplodere*) to blow up, explode; (: *valvola*) to blow; (*venir via*) to pop off; (*non aver luogo: corso etc*) to be cancelled // *vt* to jump (over), leap (over); (*fig: pranzo, capitolo*) to skip, miss (out); (*CUC*) to sauté; **far ~** to blow up; to burst open; ~ **fuori** (*fig: apparire all'improvviso*) to turn up.

saltel'lare *vi* to skip; to hop.

saltim'banco *sm* acrobat.

'salto *sm* jump; (*SPORT*) jumping; **fare un ~** to jump, leap; **fare un ~ da qn** to pop over to sb's (place); ~ **in alto/lungo** high/long jump; ~ **con l'asta** pole vaulting; ~ **mortale** somersault.

saltu'ario, a *ag* occasional, irregular.

sa'lubre *ag* healthy, salubrious.

salume'ria *sf* delicatessen.

sa'lumi *smpl* salted pork meats.

salu'tare *ag* healthy; (*fig*) salutary, beneficial // *vt* (*per dire buon giorno, fig*) to greet; (*per dire addio*) to say goodbye to; (*MIL*) to salute.

sa'lute *sf* health; ~! (*a chi starnutisce*) bless you!; (*nei brindisi*) cheers!; **bere alla ~ di qn** to drink (to) sb's health.

sa'luto *sm* (*gesto*) wave; (*parola*) greeting; (*MIL*) salute; ~**i** *smpl* greetings; **cari ~i** best regards; **vogliate gradire i nostri più distinti ~i** Yours faithfully.

salvacon'dotto *sm* (*MIL*) safe-conduct.

salva'gente [salva'dʒɛnte] *sm* (*NAUT*) lifebuoy; (*stradale*) traffic island; ~ **a ciambella** life belt; ~ **a giubbotto** lifejacket.

salvaguar'dare *vt* to safeguard.

sal'vare *vt* to save; (*trarre da un pericolo*) to rescue; (*proteggere*) to protect; ~**rsi** *vr* to save o.s.; to escape; **salva'taggio** *sm* rescue; **salva'tore, 'trice** *sm/f* saviour.

'salve *escl* (*fam*) hi!

sal'vezza [sal'vettsa] *sf* salvation; (*sicurezza*) safety.

'salvia *sf* (*BOT*) sage.

'salvo, a *ag* safe, unhurt, unharmed; (*fuori pericolo*) safe, out of danger // *sm*: **in ~** safe // *prep* (*eccetto*) except; **mettere qc in ~** to put sth in a safe place; ~ **che** *cong* (*a meno che*) unless; (*eccetto che*) except (that); ~ **imprevisti** barring accidents.

sam'buco *sm* elder (tree).

sa'nare *vt* to heal, cure; (*economia*) to put right.

san'cire [san'tʃire] *vt* to sanction.

'sandalo *sm* (*BOT*) sandalwood; (*calzatura*) sandal.

'sangue *sm* blood; **farsi cattivo ~** to fret, get in a state; ~ **freddo** (*fig*) sangfroid, calm; **a ~ freddo** in cold blood; **sangu'igno, a** *ag* blood *cpd*; (*colore*) blood-red; **sangui'nare** *vi* to bleed; **sangui'noso, a** *ag* bloody; **sangui'suga** *sf* leech.

sanità *sf* health; (*salubrità*) healthiness; **Ministero della S~** Department of Health; ~ **mentale** sanity.

sani'tario, a *ag* health *cpd*; (*condizioni*) sanitary // *sm* (*AMM*) doctor; (*impianti*) ~**i** *smpl* bathroom *o* sanitary fittings.

'sanno *vb vedi* **sapere**.

'sano, a *ag* healthy; (*denti, costituzione*) healthy, sound; (*integro*) whole, unbroken; (*fig: politica, consigli*) sound; ~

di mente sane; di ~a pianta completely, entirely; ~ e salvo safe and sound.

santifi'care vt to sanctify; (feste) to observe.

santità sf sanctity; holiness; Sua/Vostra ~ (titolo di Papa) His/Your Holiness.

'santo, a ag holy; (fig) saintly; (seguito da nome proprio: dav sm **san** + C, **sant'** + V, **santo** + s impura, gn, pn, ps, x, z; dav sf **santa** + C, **sant'** + V) saint // sm/f saint; la S~a Sede the Holy See.

santu'ario sm sanctuary.

sanzio'nare [santsjo'nare] vt to sanction.

sanzi'one [san'tsjone] sf sanction; (penale, civile) sanction, penalty.

sa'pere vt to know; (essere capace di): so nuotare I know how to swim, I can swim // vi: ~ di (aver sapore) to taste of; (aver odore) to smell of // sm knowledge; far ~ qc a qn to inform sb about sth, let sb know sth; mi sa che non sia veru I don't think that's true.

sapi'enza [sa'pjentsa] sf wisdom.

sa'pone sm soap; ~ da bucato washing soap; **sapo'netta** sf cake o bar o tablet of soap.

sa'pore sm taste, flavour; **sapo'rito, a** ag tasty.

sappi'amo vb vedi **sapere**.

saraci'nesca [sarat∫i'neska] sf (serranda) rolling shutter.

sar'casmo sm sarcasm q; sarcastic remark.

Sar'degna [sar'deɲɲa] sf: la ~ Sardinia.

sar'dina sf sardine.

'sardo, a ag, sm/f Sardinian.

'sarto, a sm/f tailor/dressmaker; **sarto'ria** sf tailor's (shop); dressmaker's (shop); (casa di moda) fashion house; (arte) couture.

'sasso sm stone; (ciottolo) pebble; (masso) rock.

sas'sofono sm saxophone.

sas'soso, a ag stony; pebbly.

'Satana sm Satan; **sa'tanico, a, ci, che** ag satanic, fiendish.

sa'tellite sm, ag satellite.

'satira sf satire.

'saturo, a ag saturated; (fig): ~ di full of.

S.A.U.B. ['saub] sigla f (= Struttura Amministrativa Unificata di Base) state welfare system.

'sauna sf sauna.

Sa'voia sf: la ~ Savoy.

savoi'ardo, a ag of Savoy, Savoyard // sm (biscotto) sponge finger.

sazi'are [sat'tsjare] vt to satisfy, satiate; ~rsi vr (riempirsi di cibo): ~rsi (di) to eat one's fill (of); (fig): ~rsi di to grow tired o weary of.

'sazio, a ag: ~ (di) sated (with), full (of); (fig: stufo) fed up (with), sick (of).

sba'dato, a ag careless, inattentive.

sbadigli'are [zbadiʎ'ʎare] vi to yawn; **sba'diglio** sm yawn.

sbagli'are [zbaʎ'ʎare] vt to make a mistake in, get wrong // vi to make a mistake, be mistaken, be wrong; (operare in modo non giusto) to err; ~rsi vr to make a mistake, be mistaken, be wrong; ~ la mira/strada to miss one's aim/take the wrong road; **'sbaglio** sm mistake, error; (morale) error; fare uno sbaglio to make a mistake.

sbal'lare vt (merce) to unpack // vi (nel fare un conto) to overestimate; (fam: gergo della droga) to get high.

sballot'tare vt to toss (about).

sbalor'dire vt to stun, amaze // vi to be stunned, be amazed; **sbalordi'tivo, a** ag amazing; (prezzo) incredible, absurd.

sbal'zare [zbal'tsare] vt to throw, hurl // vi (balzare) to bounce; (saltare) to leap, bound; **'sbalzo** sm (spostamento improvviso) jolt, jerk; a sbalzi jerkily; (fig) in fits and starts; uno sbalzo di temperatura a sudden change in temperature.

sban'dare vi (NAUT) to list; (AER) to bank; (AUT) to skid; ~rsi vr (folla) to disperse; (fig: famiglia) to break up.

sbandie'rare vt (bandiera) to wave; (fig) to parade, show off.

sbaragli'are [zbaraʎ'ʎare] vt (MIL) to rout; (in gare sportive etc) to beat, defeat.

sba'raglio [zba'raʎʎo] sm rout; defeat; gettarsi allo ~ to risk everything.

sbaraz'zarsi [zbarat'tsarsi] vr: ~ di to get rid of, rid o.s. of.

sbar'care vt (passeggeri) to disembark; (merci) to unload // vi to disembark; **'sbarco** sm disembarkation; unloading; (MIL) landing.

'sbarra sf bar; (di passaggio a livello) barrier; (DIR): presentarsi alla ~ to appear before the court.

sbarra'mento sm (stradale) barrier; (diga) dam, barrage; (MIL) barrage.

sbar'rare vt (strada etc) to block, bar; (assegno) to cross; ~ il passo to bar the way; ~ gli occhi to open one's eyes wide.

'sbattere vt (porta) to slam, bang; (tappeti, ali, CUC) to beat; (urtare) to knock, hit // vi (porta, finestra) to bang; (agitarsi: ali, vele etc) to flap; me ne sbatto! (fam) I don't give a damn!; **sbat'tuto, a** ag (viso, aria) dejected, worn out; (uovo) beaten.

sba'vare vi to dribble; (colore) to smear, smudge.

sbia'dire vi (anche: ~rsi), vt to fade; **sbia'dito, a** ag faded; (fig) colourless, dull.

sbian'care vt to whiten; (tessuto) to bleach // vi (impallidire) to grow pale o white.

sbi'eco, a, chi, che *ag* (*storto*) squint, askew; di ~: **guardare qn di ~** (*fig*) to look askance at sb; **tagliare una stoffa di ~** to cut a material on the bias.

sbigot'tire *vt* to dismay, stun // *vi* (*anche:* ~**rsi**) to be dismayed.

sbilanci'are [zbilan'tʃare] *vt* to throw off balance; ~**rsi** *vr* (*perdere l'equilibrio*) to overbalance, lose one's balance; (*fig: compromettersi*) to compromise o.s.

sbirci'are [zbir'tʃare] *vt* to cast sidelong glances at, eye.

'sbirro *sm* (*peg*) cop.

sbizzar'rirsi [zbiddzar'rirsi] *vr* to indulge one's whims.

sbloc'care *vt* to unblock, free; (*freno*) to release; (*prezzi, affitti*) to decontrol.

sboc'care *vi*: ~ **in** (*fiume*) to flow into; (*strada*) to lead into; (*persona*) to come (out) into; (*fig: concludersi*) to end (up) in.

sboc'cato, a *ag* (*persona*) foulmouthed; (*linguaggio*) foul.

sbocci'are [zbot'tʃare] *vi* (*fiore*) to bloom, open (out).

'sbocco, chi *sm* (*di fiume*) mouth; (*di strada*) end; (*di tubazione, COMM*) outlet; (*uscita: anche fig*) way out; **siamo in una situazione senza** ~**chi** there's no way out of this for us.

sbol'lire *vi* (*fig*) to cool down, calm down.

'sbornia *sf* (*fam*): **prendersi una** ~ to get plastered.

sbor'sare *vt* (*denaro*) to pay out.

sbot'tare *vi*: ~ **in una risata/per la collera** to burst out laughing/explode with anger.

sbotto'nare *vt* to unbutton, undo.

sbracci'ato, a [zbrat'tʃato] *ag* (*camicia*) sleeveless; (*persona*) bare-armed.

sbrai'tare *vi* to yell, bawl.

sbra'nare *vt* to tear to pieces.

sbricio'lare [zbritʃo'lare] *vt*, ~**rsi** *vr* to crumble.

sbri'gare *vt* to deal with, get through; (*cliente*) to attend to, deal with; ~**rsi** *vr* to hurry (up); **sbriga'tivo, a** *ag* (*persona, modo*) quick, expeditious; (*giudizio*) hasty.

sbrindel'lato, a *ag* tattered, in tatters.

sbrodo'lare *vt* to stain, dirty.

'sbronzo, a ['zbrontso] *ag* (*fam: ubriaco*) tight // *sf*: **prendersi una** ~**a** to get tight o plastered.

sbu'care *vi* to come out, emerge; (*apparire improvvisamente*) to pop out (o up).

sbucci'are [zbut'tʃare] *vt* (*arancia, patata*) to peel; (*piselli*) to shell; ~**rsi un ginocchio** to graze one's knee.

sbudel'larsi *vr*: ~ **dalle risa** to split one's sides laughing.

sbuf'fare *vi* (*persona, cavallo*) to snort; (*: ansimare*) to puff, pant; (*treno*) to

puff; **'sbuffo** *sm* (*di aria, fumo, vapore*) puff; **maniche a sbuffo** puff(ed) sleeves.

'scabbia *sf* (MED) scabies *sg*.

sca'broso, a *ag* (*fig: difficile*) difficult, thorny; (*: imbarazzante*) embarrassing; (*: sconcio*) indecent.

scacchi'era [skak'kjɛra] *sf* chessboard.

scacci'are [skat'tʃare] *vt* to chase away o out, drive away o out.

'scacco, chi *sm* (*pezzo del gioco*) chessman; (*quadretto di scacchiera*) square; (*fig*) setback, reverse; ~**chi** *smpl* (*gioco*) chess *sg*; **a** ~**chi** (*tessuto*) check(ed); **scacco'matto** *sm* checkmate.

sca'dente *ag* shoddy, of poor quality.

sca'denza [ska'dɛntsa] *sf* (*di cambiale, contratto*) maturity; (*di passaporto*) expiry date; **a breve/lunga** ~ short-/longterm; **data di** ~ expiry date.

sca'dere *vi* (*contratto etc*) to expire; (*debito*) to fall due; (*valore, forze, peso*) to decline, go down.

sca'fandro *sm* (*di palombaro*) diving suit; (*di astronauta*) space-suit.

scaf'fale *sm* shelf; (*mobile*) set of shelves.

'scafo *sm* (NAUT, AER) hull.

scagio'nare [skadʒo'nare] *vt* to exonerate, free from blame.

'scaglia ['skaʎʎa] *sf* (ZOOL) scale; (*scheggia*) chip, flake.

scagli'are [skaʎ'ʎare] *vt* (*lanciare: anche fig*) to hurl, fling; ~**rsi** *vr*: ~**rsi su** o **contro** to hurl o fling o.s. at; (*fig*) to rail at.

scaglio'nare [skaʎʎo'nare] *vt* (*pagamenti*) to space out, spread out; (MIL) to echelon; **scagli'one** *sm* echelon; (GEO) terrace; **a scaglioni** in groups.

'scala *sf* (*a gradini etc*) staircase, stairs *pl*; (*a pioli, di corda*) ladder; (MUS, GEO, di colori, valori, fig*) scale; ~**e** *sfpl* (*scalinata*) stairs; **su vasta** ~/~ **ridotta** on a large/small scale; ~ **a libretto** stepladder; ~ **mobile** escalator; (ECON) sliding scale; ~ **mobile** (*dei salari*) index-linked pay scale.

sca'lare *vt* (ALPINISMO, muro*) to climb, scale; (*debito*) to scale down, reduce; **sca'lata** *sf* scaling *q*, climbing *q*; (*arrampicata, fig*) climb; **scala'tore, 'trice** *sm/f* climber.

scalda'bagno [skalda'baɲɲo] *sm* waterheater.

scal'dare *vt* to heat; ~**rsi** *vr* to warm up, heat up; (*al fuoco, al sole*) to warm o.s.; (*fig*) to get excited.

scal'fire *vt* to scratch.

scali'nata *sf* staircase.

sca'lino *sm* (*anche fig*) step; (*di scala a pioli*) rung.

'scalo *sm* (NAUT) slipway; (*: porto d'approdo*) port of call; (AER) stopover; **fare** ~ **(a)** (NAUT) to call (at), put in (at); (AER) to land (at), make a stop (at); ~ **merci** (FERR) goods (Brit) o freight yard.

scalop'pina sf (CUC) escalope.

scal'pello sm chisel.

scal'pore sm noise, row; **far ~** (notizia) to cause a sensation o a stir.

'scaltro, a ag cunning, shrewd.

scal'zare [skal'tsare] vt (albero) to bare the roots of; (muro, fig: autorità) to undermine.

'scalzo, a ['skaltso] ag barefoot.

scambi'are vt o to exchange; (confondere): ~ **qn/qc per** to take o mistake sb/sth for; **mi hanno scambiato il cappello** they've given me the wrong hat.

scambi'evole ag mutual, reciprocal.

'scambio sm exchange; (FERR) points pl; **fare** (uno) ~ to make a swap.

scampa'gnata [skampaɲ'ɲata] sf trip to the country.

scampa'nare vi to peal.

scam'pare vt (salvare) to rescue, save; (evitare: morte, prigione) to escape // vi: ~ **(a qc)** to survive (sth), escape (sth); **scamparla bella** to have a narrow escape.

'scampo sm (salvezza) escape; (ZOOL) prawn; **cercare ~ nella fuga** to seek safety in flight.

'scampolo sm remnant.

scanala'tura sf (incavo) channel, groove.

scandagli'are [skandaʎ'ʎare] vt (NAUT) to sound; (fig) to sound out; to probe.

scandaliz'zare [skandalid'dzare] vt to shock, scandalize; **~rsi** vr to be shocked.

'scandalo sm scandal.

Scandi'navia sf: **la ~** Scandinavia; **scandi'navo, a** ag, sm/f Scandinavian.

scan'dire vt (versi) to scan; (parole) to articulate, pronounce distinctly; **~ il tempo** (MUS) to beat time.

scan'nare vt (animale) to butcher, slaughter; (persona) to cut o slit the throat of.

'scanno sm seat, bench.

scansafa'tiche [skansafa'tike] sm/f inv idler, loafer.

scan'sare vt (rimuovere) to move (aside), shift; (schivare: schiaffo) to dodge; (sfuggire) to avoid; **~rsi** vr to move aside.

scan'sia sf shelves pl; (per libri) bookcase.

'scanso sm: **a ~ di** in order to avoid, as a precaution against.

scanti'nato sm basement.

scanto'nare vi to turn the corner; (svignarsela) to sneak off.

scapes'trato, a ag dissolute.

'scapito sm (perdita) loss; (danno) damage, detriment; **a ~ di** to the detriment of.

'scapola sf shoulder blade.

'scapolo sm bachelor.

scappa'mento sm (AUT) exhaust.

scap'pare vi (fuggire) to escape; (andare via in fretta) to rush off; **lasciarsi ~ un'occasione** to let an opportunity go by; **~ di prigione** to escape from prison; **~ di mano** (oggetto) to slip out of one's hands; **~ di mente** a qn to slip sb's mind; **mi scappò detto** I let it slip; **scap'pata** sf quick visit o call; **scappa'tella** sf escapade; **scappa'toia** sf way out.

scara'beo sm beetle.

scarabocchi'are [skarabok'kjare] vt to scribble, scrawl; **scara'bocchio** sm scribble, scrawl.

scara'faggio [skara'faddʒo] sm cockroach.

scaraven'tare vt to fling, hurl.

scarce'rare vt to release (from prison).

'scarica, che sf (di più armi) volley of shots; (di sassi, pugni) hail, shower; (ELETTR) discharge; **~ di mitra** burst of machine-gun fire.

scari'care vt (merci, camion etc) to unload; (passeggeri) to set down, put off; (arma) to unload; (: sparare, ELETTR) to discharge; (sog: corso d'acqua) to empty, pour; (fig: liberare da un peso) to unburden, relieve; **~rsi** vr (orologio) to run o wind down; (batteria, accumulatore) to go flat o dead; (fig: rilassarsi) to unwind; (: sfogarsi) to let off steam; **il fulmine si scaricò su un albero** the lightning struck a tree; **scarica'tore** sm loader; (di porto) docker.

'scarico, a, chi, che ag unloaded; (orologio) run down; (accumulatore) dead, flat // sm (di merci, materiali) unloading; (di immondizie) dumping, tipping (Brit); (: luogo) rubbish dump; (TECN: deflusso) draining; (: dispositivo) drain; (AUT) exhaust.

scar'latto, a ag scarlet.

'scarno, a ag thin, bony.

'scarpa sf shoe; **~e da ginnastica/tennis** gym/tennis shoes.

scar'pata sf escarpment.

scarseggi'are [skarsed'dʒare] vi to be scarce; **~ di** to be short of, lack.

scar'sezza [skar'settsa] sf scarcity, lack.

'scarso, a ag (insufficiente) insufficient, meagre; (povero: annata) poor, lean; (INS: voto) poor; **~ di** lacking in; **3 chili ~i** just under 3 kilos, barely 3 kilos.

scarta'mento sm (FERR) gauge; **~ normale/ridotto** standard/narrow gauge.

scar'tare vt (pacco) to unwrap; (idea) to reject; (MIL) to declare unfit for military service; (carte da gioco) to discard; (CALCIO) to dodge (past) // vi to swerve.

'scarto sm (cosa scartata, anche COMM) reject; (di veicolo) swerve; (differenza) gap, difference.

scassi'nare vt to break, force.

'scasso sm vedi **furto**.

scate'nare vt (fig) to incite, stir up; ~**rsi** vr (temporale) to break; (rivolta) to break out; (persona: infuriarsi) to rage.

'scatola sf box; (di latta) tin (Brit), can; **cibi in** ~ tinned (Brit) o canned foods; ~ **cranica** cranium.

scat'tare vt (fotografia) to take // vi (congegno, molla etc) to be released; (balzare) to spring up; (SPORT) to put on a spurt; (fig: per l'ira) to fly into a rage; ~ **in piedi** to spring to one's feet.

'scatto sm (dispositivo) release; (: di arma da fuoco) trigger mechanism; (rumore) click; (balzo) jump, start; (SPORT) spurt; (fig: di ira etc) fit; (: di stipendio) increment; **di** ~ suddenly.

scatu'rire vi to gush, spring.

scaval'care vt (ostacolo) to pass (o climb) over; (fig) to get ahead of, overtake.

sca'vare vt (terreno) to dig; (legno) to hollow out; (pozzo, galleria) to bore; (città sepolta etc) to excavate.

'scavo sm excavating q; excavation.

'scegliere ['ʃeʎʎere] vt to choose, select.

sce'icco, chi [ʃe'ikko] sm sheik.

scelle'rato, a [ʃelle'rato] ag wicked, evil.

scel'lino [ʃel'lino] sm shilling.

'scelto, a ['ʃelto] pp di **scegliere** // ag (gruppo) carefully selected; (frutta, verdura) choice, top quality; (MIL: specializzato) crack cpd, highly skilled // sf choice; selection; **di prima** ~**a** top grade o quality; **frutta o formaggi a** ~**a** a choice of fruit or cheese.

sce'mare [ʃe'mare] vt, vi to diminish.

'scemo, a ['ʃemo] ag stupid, silly.

'scempio ['ʃempjo] sm slaughter, massacre; (fig) ruin; **far** ~ **di** (fig) to play havoc with, ruin.

'scena ['ʃena] sf (gen) scene; (palcoscenico) stage; **le** ~**e** (fig: teatro) the stage; **fare una** ~ to make a scene; **andare in** ~ to be staged o put on o performed; **mettere in** ~ to stage.

sce'nario [ʃe'narjo] sm scenery; (di film) scenario.

sce'nata [ʃe'nata] sf row, scene.

'scendere ['ʃendere] vi to go (o come) down; (strada, sole) to go down; (notte) to fall; (passeggero: fermarsi) to get out, alight; (fig: temperatura, prezzi) to go o come down, fall, drop // vt (scale, pendio) to go (o come) down; ~ **dalle scale** to go (o come) down the stairs; ~ **dal treno** to get off o out of the train; ~ **dalla macchina** to get out of the car; ~ **da cavallo** to dismount, get off one's horse.

'scenico, a, ci, che ['ʃeniko] ag stage cpd, scenic.

scervel'lato, a [ʃervel'lato] ag featherbrained, scatterbrained.

'sceso, a ['ʃeso] pp di **scendere**.

'scettico, a, ci, che ['ʃettiko] ag sceptical.

'scettro ['ʃettro] sm sceptre.

'scheda ['skɛda] sf (index) card; ~ **elettorale** ballot paper; ~ **perforata** punch card; **sche'dare** vt (dati) to file; (libri) to catalogue; (registrare: anche POLIZIA) to put on one's files; **sche'dario** sm file; (mobile) filing cabinet.

'scheggia, ge ['skeddʒa] sf splinter, sliver.

'scheletro ['skɛletro] sm skeleton.

'schema, i ['skema] sm (diagramma) diagram, sketch; (progetto, abbozzo) outline, plan.

'scherma ['skerma] sf fencing.

scher'maglia [sker'maʎʎa] sf (fig) skirmish.

'schermo ['skermo] sm shield, screen; (CINEMA, TV) screen.

scher'nire [sker'nire] vt to mock, sneer at; **'scherno** sm mockery, derision.

scher'zare [sker'tsare] vi to joke.

'scherzo ['skertso] sm joke; (tiro) trick; (MUS) scherzo; **è uno** ~! (una cosa facile) it's child's play!, it's easy!; **per** ~ in jest; **for a joke o a laugh; fare un brutto** ~ **a qn** to play a nasty trick on sb; **scher'zoso, a** ag (tono, gesto) playful; (osservazione) facetious; **è un tipo scherzoso** he likes a joke.

schiaccia'noci [skjattʃa'notʃi] sm inv nutcracker.

schiacci'are [skjat'tʃare] vt (dito) to crush; (noci) to crack; ~ **un pisolino** to have a nap.

schiaffeggi'are [skjaffed'dʒare] vt to slap.

schi'affo ['skjaffo] sm slap.

schiamaz'zare [skjamat'tsare] vi to squawk, cackle.

schian'tare [skjan'tare] vt to break, tear apart; ~**rsi** vr to break (up), shatter; **schi'anto** sm (rumore) crash; tearing sound; **è uno schianto!** (fam) it's (o he's o she's) terrific!; **di schianto** all of a sudden.

schia'rire [skja'rire] vt to lighten, make lighter // vi (anche: ~**rsi**) to grow lighter; (tornar sereno) to clear, brighten up; ~**rsi la voce** to clear one's throat.

schiavitù [skjavi'tu] sf slavery.

schi'avo, a ['skjavo] sm/f slave.

schi'ena ['skjɛna] sf (ANAT) back; **schie'nale** sm (di sedia) back.

schi'era ['skjɛra] sf (MIL) rank; (gruppo) group, band.

schiera'mento [skjera'mento] sm (MIL, SPORT) formation; (fig) alliance.

schie'rare [skje'rare] vt (esercito) to line up, draw up, marshal; ~**rsi** vr to line up; (fig): ~**rsi con** o **dalla parte di**/

contro qn to side with/oppose sb.

schi'etto, a ['skjetto] *ag* (*puro*) pure; (*fig*) frank, straightforward; sincere.

'schifo ['skifo] *sm* disgust; fare ~ (*essere fatto male, dare pessimi risultati*) to be awful; mi fa ~ it makes me sick, it's disgusting; **quel libro è uno ~** that book's rotten; **schi'foso, a** *ag* disgusting, revolting; (*molto scadente*) rotten, lousy.

schioc'care [skjok'kare] *vt* (*frusta*) to crack; (*dita*) to snap; (*lingua*) to click; ~ **le labbra** to smack one's lips.

schi'udere ['skjudere] *vt*, ~**rsi** *vr* to open.

schi'uma ['skjuma] *sf* foam; (*di sapone*) lather; (*di latte*) froth; (*fig: feccia*) scum; **schiu'mare** *vt* to skim // *vi* to foam.

schi'uso, a ['skjuso] *pp di* **schiudere**.

schi'vare [ski'vare] *vt* to dodge, avoid.

'schivo, a ['skivo] *ag* (*ritroso*) stand-offish, reserved; (*timido*) shy.

schiz'zare [skit'tsare] *vt* (*spruzzare*) to spurt, squirt; (*sporcare*) to splash, spatter; (*fig: abbozzare*) to sketch // *vi* to spurt, squirt; (*saltar fuori*) to dart up (o off *etc*).

schizzi'noso, a [skittsi'noso] *ag* fussy, finicky.

'schizzo ['skittso] *sm* (*di liquido*) spurt; splash, spatter; (*abbozzo*) sketch.

sci [ʃi] *sm* (*attrezzo*) ski; (*attività*) skiing; ~ **nautico** water-skiing.

'scia, *pl* **'scie** ['ʃia] *sf* (*di imbarcazione*) wake; (*di profumo*) trail.

scià [ʃa] *sm inv* shah.

sci'abola ['ʃabola] *sf* sabre.

scia'callo [ʃa'kallo] *sm* jackal.

sciac'quare [ʃak'kware] *vt* to rinse.

scia'gura [ʃa'gura] *sf* disaster, calamity; misfortune; **sciagu'rato, a** *ag* unfortunate; (*malvagio*) wicked.

scialac'quare [ʃalak'kware] *vt* to squander.

scia'lare [ʃa'lare] *vi* to lead a life of luxury.

sci'albo, a ['ʃalbo] *ag* pale, dull; (*fig*) dull, colourless.

sci'alle ['ʃalle] *sm* shawl.

scia'luppa [ʃa'luppa] *sf* (*NAUT*) sloop; (*anche*: ~ **di salvataggio**) lifeboat.

sci'ame ['ʃame] *sm* swarm.

scian'cato, a [ʃan'kato] *ag* lame; (*mobile*) rickety.

sci'are [ʃi'are] *vi* to ski.

sci'arpa ['ʃarpa] *sf* scarf; (*fascia*) sash.

scia'tore, 'trice [ʃia'tore] *sm/f* skier.

sci'atto, a ['ʃatto] *ag* (*persona: nell'aspetto*) slovenly, unkempt; (*: nel lavoro*) sloppy, careless.

scien'tifico, a, ci, che [ʃen'tifiko] *ag* scientific.

sci'enza ['ʃentsa] *sf* science; (*sapere*) knowledge; ~**e** *sfpl* (*INS*) science *sg*; ~**e**

naturali natural sciences; **scienzi'ato, a** *sm/f* scientist.

'scimmia ['ʃimmja] *sf* monkey; **scimmiot'tare** *vt* to ape, mimic.

scimpanzé [ʃimpan'tse] *sm inv* chimpanzee.

scimu'nito, a [ʃimu'nito] *ag* silly, idiotic.

'scindere ['ʃindere] *vt*, ~**rsi** *vr* to split (up).

scin'tilla [ʃin'tilla] *sf* spark; **scintil'lare** *vi* to spark; (*acqua, occhi*) to sparkle.

scioc'chezza [ʃok'kettsa] *sf* stupidity *q*; stupid o foolish thing; dire ~**e** to talk nonsense.

sci'occo, a, chi, che ['ʃokko] *ag* stupid, foolish.

sci'ogliere ['ʃɔʎʎere] *vt* (*nodo*) to untie; (*capelli*) to loosen; (*persona, animale*) to untie, release; (*fig: persona*): ~ **da** to release from; (*neve*) to melt; (*nell'acqua: zucchero etc*) to dissolve; (*fig: mistero*) to solve; (*porre fine a: contratto*) to cancel; (*: società, matrimonio*) to dissolve; (*: riunione*) to bring to an end; ~**rsi** *vr* to loosen, come untied; to melt; to dissolve; (*assemblea etc*) to break up; ~ **i muscoli** to limber up.

sciol'tezza [ʃol'tettsa] *sf* agility; suppleness; ease.

sci'olto, a ['ʃolto] *pp di* **sciogliere** // *ag* loose; (*agile*) agile, nimble; supple; (*disinvolto*) free and easy; **versi** ~**i** (*POESIA*) blank verse.

sciope'rante [ʃope'rante] *sm/f* striker.

sciope'rare [ʃope'rare] *vi* to strike, go on strike.

sci'opero ['ʃopero] *sm* strike; fare ~ to strike; ~ **bianco** work-to-rule (*Brit*), slowdown (*US*); ~ **selvaggio** wildcat strike; ~ **a singhiozzo** on-off strike.

sci'rocco [ʃi'rokko] *sm* sirocco.

sci'roppo [ʃi'roppo] *sm* syrup.

'scisma, i ['ʃizma] *sm* (*REL*) schism.

scissi'one [ʃis'sjone] *sf* (*anche fig*) split, division; (*FISICA*) fission.

'scisso, a ['ʃisso] *pp di* **scindere**.

sciu'pare [ʃu'pare] *vt* (*abito, libro, appetito*) to spoil, ruin; (*tempo, denaro*) to waste; ~**rsi** *vr* to get spoilt o ruined; (*rovinarsi la salute*) to ruin one's health.

scivo'lare [ʃivo'lare] *vi* to slide o glide along; (*involontariamente*) to slip, slide; **'scivolo** *sm* slide; (*TECN*) chute.

scle'rosi [skle'rozi] *sf* sclerosis.

scoc'care *vt* (*freccia*) to shoot // *vi* (*guizzare*) to shoot up; (*battere: ora*) to strike.

scocci'are [skot'tʃare] (*fam*) *vt* to bother, annoy; ~**rsi** *vr* to be bothered o annoyed.

sco'della [sko'della] *sf* bowl.

scodinzo'lare [skodintso'lare] *vi* to wag its tail.

scogli'era [skoʎˈʎɛra] sf reef; cliff.

'scoglio [ˈskɔʎʎo] sm (al mare) rock.

scoi'attolo sm squirrel.

sco'lare ag: età ~ school age // vt to drain // vi to drip.

scola'resca sf schoolchildren pl, pupils pl.

sco'laro, a sm/f pupil, schoolboy/girl.

sco'lastico, a, ci, che ag school cpd; scholastic.

scol'lare vt (staccare) to unstick; ~rsi vr to come unstuck.

scolla'tura sf neckline.

'scolo sm drainage.

scolo'rire vt to fade; to discolour // vi (anche: ~rsi) to fade; to become discoloured; (impallidire) to turn pale.

scol'pire vt to carve, sculpt.

scombi'nare vt to mess up, upset.

scombusso'lare vt to upset.

scom'messo, a pp di **scommettere** // sf bet, wager.

scom'mettere vt, vi to bet.

scomo'dare vt to trouble, bother; to disturb; ~rsi vr to put o.s. out; ~rsi a fare to go to the bother o trouble of doing.

'scomodo, a ag uncomfortable; (sistemazione, posto) awkward, inconvenient.

scompa'rire vi (sparire) to disappear, vanish; (fig) to be insignificant; **scom'parso, a** pp di **scomparire** // sf disappearance.

scomparti'mento sm (FERR) compartment.

scom'parto sm compartment, division.

scompigli'are [skompiʎˈʎare] vt (cassetto, capelli) to mess up, disarrange; (fig: piani) to upset; **scom'piglio** sm mess, confusion.

scom'porre vt (parola, numero) to break up; (CHIM) to decompose; scomporsi vr (fig) to get upset, lose one's composure; **scom'posto, a** pp di **scomporre** // ag (gesto) unseemly; (capelli) ruffled, dishevelled.

sco'munica sf excommunication.

scomuni'care vt to excommunicate.

sconcer'tare [skontʃerˈtare] vt to disconcert, bewilder.

'sconcio, a, ci, ce [ˈskontʃo] ag (osceno) indecent, obscene // sm (cosa riprovevole, mal fatta) disgrace.

sconfes'sare vt to renounce, disavow; to repudiate.

scon'figgere [skonˈfiddʒere] vt to defeat, overcome.

sconfi'nare vi to cross the border; (in proprietà privata) to trespass; (fig): ~ da to stray o digress from; **sconfi'nato, a** ag boundless, unlimited.

scon'fitto, a pp di **sconfiggere** // sf defeat.

scon'forto sm despondency.

scongiu'rare [skondʒuˈrare] vt (implo-

rare) to entreat, beseech, implore; (eludere: pericolo) to ward off, avert; **scongi'uro** sm entreaty; (esorcismo) exorcism; fare gli scongiuri to touch wood (Brit), knock on wood (US).

scon'nesso, a ag (fig: discorso) incoherent, rambling.

sconosci'uto, a [skonoʃˈʃuto] ag unknown; new, strange // sm/f stranger; unknown person.

sconquas'sare vt to shatter, smash.

sconside'rato, a ag thoughtless, rash.

sconsigli'are [skonsiʎˈʎare] vt: ~ qc a qn to advise sb against sth; ~ qn dal fare qc to advise sb not to do o against doing sth.

sconso'lato, a ag inconsolable; desolate.

scon'tare vt (COMM: detrarre) to deduct; (: debito) to pay off; (: cambiale) to discount; (pena) to serve; (colpa, errori) to pay for, suffer for.

scon'tato, a ag (previsto) foreseen, taken for granted; dare per ~ che to take it for granted that.

scon'tento, a ag: ~ (di) discontented o dissatisfied (with) // sm discontent, dissatisfaction.

'sconto sm discount; fare uno ~ to give a discount.

scon'trarsi vr (treni etc) to crash, collide; (venire ad uno scontro, fig) to clash; ~ con to crash into, collide with.

scon'trino sm ticket.

'scontro sm clash, encounter; crash, collision.

scon'troso, a ag sullen, surly; (permaloso) touchy.

sconveni'ente ag unseemly, improper.

scon'volgere [skonˈvɔldʒere] vt to throw into confusion, upset; (turbare) to shake, disturb, upset; **scon'volto, a** pp di **sconvolgere**.

'scopa sf broom; (CARTE) Italian card game; **sco'pare** vt to sweep.

sco'perto, a pp di **scoprire** // ag uncovered; (capo) uncovered, bare; (macchina) open; (MIL) exposed, without cover; (conto) overdrawn // sf discovery.

'scopo sm aim, purpose; a che ~? what for?

scoppi'are vi (spaccarsi) to burst; (esplodere) to explode; (fig) to break out; ~ in pianto o a piangere to burst out crying; ~ dalle risa o dal ridere to split one's sides laughing.

scoppiet'tare vi to crackle.

'scoppio sm explosion; (di tuono, arma etc) crash, bang; (fig: di risa, ira) fit, outburst; (di guerra) outbreak; a ~ ritardato delayed-action.

sco'prire vt to discover; (liberare da ciò che copre) to uncover; (: monumento) to unveil; ~rsi vr to put on lighter clothes; (fig) to give o.s. away.

scoraggi'are [skorad'dʒare] *vt* to discourage; ~**rsi** *vr* to become discouraged, lose heart.

scorcia'toia [skortʃa'toja] *sf* short cut.

'**scorcio** ['skortʃo] *sm* (*ARTE*) foreshortening; (*di secolo, periodo*) end, close.

scor'dare *vt* to forget; ~**rsi** *vr*: ~**rsi di qc/di fare** to forget sth/to do.

'**scorgere** ['skɔrdʒere] *vt* to make out, distinguish, see.

sco'ria *sf* (*di metalli*) slag; (*vulcanica*) scoria; ~**e radioattive** (*FISICA*) radioactive waste *sg*.

'**scorno** *sm* ignominy, disgrace.

scorpacci'ata [skorpat'tʃata] *sf*: **fare una ~ (di)** to stuff o.s. (with), eat one's fill (of).

scorpi'one *sm* scorpion; (*dello zodiaco*): **S~** Scorpio.

scorraz'zare [skorrat'tsare] *vi* to run about.

'**scorrere** *vt* (*giornale, lettera*) to run *o* skim through // *vi* (*liquido, fiume*) to run, flow; (*fune*) to run; (*cassetto, porta*) to slide easily; (*tempo*) to pass (by).

scor'retto, a *ag* incorrect; (*sgarbato*) impolite, (*sconveniente*) improper.

scor'revole *ag* (*porta*) sliding; (*fig: stile*) fluent, flowing.

scorri'banda *sf* (*MIL*) raid; (*escursione*) trip, excursion.

'**scorso, a** *pp di* **scorrere** // *ag* last // *sf* quick look, glance.

scor'soio, a *ag*: **nodo ~** noose.

'**scorta** *sf* (*di personalità, convoglio*) escort; (*provvista*) supply, stock; **scor'tare** *vt* to escort.

scor'tese *ag* discourteous, rude; **scorte'sia** *sf* discourtesy, rudeness; (*azione*) discourtesy.

scorti'care *vt* to skin.

'**scorto, a** *pp di* **scorgere**.

'**scorza** ['skɔrdza] *sf* (*di albero*) bark; (*di agrumi*) peel, skin.

sco'sceso, a [skoʃ'ʃeso] *ag* steep.

'**scosso, a** *pp di* **scuotere** // *ag* (*turbato*) shaken, upset // *sf* jerk, jolt, shake; (*ELETTR, fig*) shock.

scos'tante *ag* (*fig*) off-putting (*Brit*), unpleasant.

scos'tare *vt* to move (away), shift; ~**rsi** *vr* to move away.

scostu'mato, a *ag* immoral, dissolute.

scot'tare *vt* (*ustionare*) to burn; (: *con liquido bollente*) to scald // *vi* to burn; (*caffè*) to be too hot; **scotta'tura** *sf* burn; scald.

'**scotto, a** *ag* overcooked // *sm* (*fig*): **pagare lo ~ (di)** to pay the penalty (for).

sco'vare *vt* to drive out, flush out; (*fig*) to discover.

'**Scozia** ['skɔttsja] *sf*: **la ~** Scotland; **scoz'zese** *ag* Scottish // *smf* Scot.

scredi'tare *vt* to discredit.

screpo'lare *vt*, ~**rsi** *vr* to crack; **screpola'tura** *sf* cracking *q*; crack.

screzi'ato, a [skret'tsjato] *ag* streaked.

'**screzio** ['skrɛttsjo] *sm* disagreement.

scricchio'lare [skrikkjo'lare] *vi* to creak, squeak.

'**scricciolo** ['skrittʃolo] *sm* wren.

'**scrigno** ['skriɲɲo] *sm* casket.

scrimina'tura *sf* parting.

'**scritto, a** *pp di* **scrivere** // *ag* written // *sm* writing; (*lettera*) letter, note // *sf* inscription; ~**i** *smpl* (*letterari etc*) writing *sg*; **per** *o* **in ~** in writing.

scrit'toio *sm* writing desk.

scrit'tore, 'trice *sm/f* writer.

scrit'tura *sf* writing; (*COMM*) entry; (*contratto*) contract; (*REL*): **la Sacra S~** the Scriptures *pl*; ~**e** *sfpl* (*COMM*) accounts, books.

scrittu'rare *vt* (*TEATRO, CINEMA*) to sign up, engage; (*COMM*) to enter.

scriva'nia *sf* desk.

scri'vente *sm/f* writer.

'**scrivere** *vt* to write; **come si scrive?** how is it spelt?, how do you write it?

scroc'cone, a *sm/f* scrounger.

'**scrofa** *sf* (*ZOOL*) sow.

scrol'lare *vt* to shake; ~**rsi** *vr* (*anche fig*) to give o.s. a shake; ~ **le spalle/il capo** to shrug one's shoulders/shake one's head.

scrosci'are [skroʃ'ʃare] *vi* (*pioggia*) to pour down, pelt down; (*torrente, fig: applausi*) to thunder, roar; '**scroscio** *sm* pelting; thunder, roar; (*di applausi*) burst.

scros'tare *vt* (*intonaco*) to scrape off, strip; ~**rsi** *vr* to peel off, flake off.

'**scrupolo** *sm* scruple; (*meticolosità*) care, conscientiousness.

scru'tare *vt* to scrutinize; (*intenzioni, causa*) to examine, scrutinize.

scruti'nare *vt* (*voti*) to count; **scru'tinio** *sm* (*votazione*) ballot; (*insieme delle operazioni*) poll; (*INS*) (*meeting for*) assignment of marks at end of a term or year.

scu'cire [sku'tʃire] *vt* (*orlo etc*) to unpick, undo.

scude'ria *sf* stable.

scu'detto *sm* (*SPORT*) (championship) shield; (*distintivo*) badge.

'**scudo** *sm* shield.

scul'tore, 'trice *sm/f* sculptor.

scul'tura *sf* sculpture.

scu'ola *sf* school; ~ **elementare/materna/media** primary (*Brit*) *o* grade (*US*)/nursery/secondary (*Brit*) *o* high (*US*) school; ~ **guida** driving school; ~ **dell'obbligo** compulsory education; ~**e serali** evening classes, night school *sg*; ~ **tecnica** technical college.

scu'otere *vt* to shake; ~**rsi** *vr* to jump, be startled; (*fig: muoversi*) to rouse o.s., stir o.s.; (: *turbarsi*) to be shaken.

'**scure** *sf* axe.

'**scuro, a** *ag* dark; (*fig: espressione*) grim // *sm* darkness; dark colour; (*imposta*) (window) shutter; **verde/rosso** *etc* ~ dark green/red *etc*.

scur'rile *ag* scurrilous.

'**scusa** *sf* excuse; ~**e** *sfpl* apology *sg*, apologies; **chiedere** ~ **a qn (per)** to apologize to sb (for); **chiedo** ~ I'm sorry; (*disturbando etc*) excuse me.

scu'sare *vt* to excuse; ~**rsi** *vr*: ~**rsi (di)** to apologize (for); (**mi**) **scusi** I'm sorry; (*per richiamare l'attenzione*) excuse me.

sde'gnato, a [zdeɲ'ɲato] *ag* indignant, angry.

'**sdegno** ['zdeɲɲo] *sm* scorn, disdain; **sde'gnoso, a** *ag* scornful, disdainful.

sdoga'nare *vt* (*merci*) to clear through customs.

sdolci'nato, a [zdoltʃi'nato] *ag* mawkish, oversentimental.

sdoppi'are *vt* (*dividere*) to divide o split in two.

sdrai'arsi *vr* to stretch out, lie down.

'**sdraio** *sm*: **sedia a** ~ deck chair.

sdruccio'levole [zdruttʃo'levole] *ag* slippery.

se ◆ *pronome vedi* **si**
◆ *cong* **1** (*condizionale, ipotetica*) if; ~ **nevica non vengo** I won't come if it snows; **sarei rimasto** ~ **me l'avessero chiesto** I would have stayed if they'd asked me; **non puoi fare altro** ~ **non telefonare** all you can do is phone; ~ **mai** if, if ever; **siamo noi** ~ **mai che le siamo grati** it is we who should be grateful to you; ~ **no** (*altrimenti*) or (else), otherwise
2 (*in frasi dubitative, interrogative indirette*) if, whether; **non so** ~ **scrivere o telefonare** I don't know whether o if I should write or phone.

sé *pronome* (*gen*) oneself; (*esso, essa, lui, lei, loro*) itself; himself; herself; themselves; ~ **stesso(a)** *pronome* oneself; itself; himself; herself; ~ **stessi** *pronome pl* themselves.

seb'bene *cong* although, though.

sec. *abbr* (= *secolo*) c.

'**secca** *sf vedi* **secco**.

sec'care *vt* to dry; (*prosciugare*) to dry up; (*fig: importunare*) to annoy, bother // *vi* to dry; to dry up; ~**rsi** *vr* to dry; to dry up; (*fig*) to grow annoyed; **secca'tura** *sf* (*fig*) bother *q*, trouble *q*.

'**secchia** ['sekkja] *sf* bucket, pail.

'**secco, a, chi, che** *ag* dry; (*fichi, pesce*) dried; (*foglie, ramo*) withered; (*magro: persona*) thin, skinny; (*fig: risposta, modo di fare*) curt, abrupt; (: *colpo*) clean, sharp // *sm* (*siccità*) drought // *sf* (*del mare*) shallows *pl*; **restarci** ~ (*fig: morire sul colpo*) to drop dead; **mettere in** ~ (*barca*) to beach;

rimanere in *o* **a** ~ (*NAUT*) to run aground; (*fig*) to be left in the lurch.

seco'lare *ag* age-old, centuries-old; (*laico, mondano*) secular.

'**secolo** *sm* century; (*epoca*) age.

se'conda *sf vedi* **secondo**.

secon'dario, a *ag* secondary.

se'condo, a *ag* second // *sm* second; (*di pranzo*) main course // *sf* (*AUT*) second (gear) // *prep* according to; (*nel modo prescritto*) in accordance with; ~ **me** in my opinion, to my mind; **di** ~**a classe** second-class; **di** ~**a mano** second-hand; **viaggiare in** ~**a** to travel second-class; **a** ~**a di** *prep* according to; in accordance with.

'**sedano** *sm* celery.

seda'tivo, a *ag*, *sm* sedative.

'**sede** *sf* seat; (*di ditta*) head office; (*di organizzazione*) headquarters *pl*; **in** ~ **di** (*in occasione di*) during; ~ **sociale** registered office.

seden'tario, a *ag* sedentary.

se'dere *vi* to sit, be seated; ~**rsi** *vr* to sit down // *sm* (*deretano*) behind, bottom.

'**sedia** *sf* chair.

sedi'cente [sedi'tʃɛnte] *ag* self-styled.

'**sedici** ['seditʃi] *num* sixteen.

se'dile *sm* seat; (*panchina*) bench.

sedizi'one [sedit'tsjone] *sf* revolt, rebellion.

se'dotto, a *pp di* **sedurre**.

sedu'cente [sedu'tʃɛnte] *ag* seductive; (*proposta*) very attractive.

se'durre *vt* to seduce.

se'duta *sf* session, sitting; (*riunione*) meeting; ~ **spiritica** séance; ~ **stante** (*fig*) immediately.

seduzi'one [sedut'tsjone] *sf* seduction; (*fascino*) charm, appeal.

'**sega, ghe** *sf* saw.

'**segale** *sf* rye.

se'gare *vt* to saw; (*recidere*) to saw off; **sega'tura** *sf* (*residuo*) sawdust.

'**seggio** ['sɛddʒo] *sm* seat; ~ **elettorale** polling station.

'**seggiola** ['sɛddʒola] *sf* chair; **seggio'-lino** *sm* seat; (*per bambini*) child's chair; **seggio'lone** *sm* (*per bambini*) highchair.

seggio'via [sɛddʒo'via] *sf* chairlift.

seghe'ria [sege'ria] *sf* sawmill.

segna'lare [seɲɲa'lare] *vt* (*manovra etc*) to signal; to indicate; (*annunciare*) to announce; to report; (*fig: far conoscere*) to point out; (: *persona*) to single out; ~**rsi** *vr* (*distinguersi*) to distinguish o.s.

se'gnale [seɲ'ɲale] *sm* signal; (*cartello*): ~ **stradale** road sign; ~ **d'allarme** alarm; (*FERR*) communication cord; ~ **orario** (*RADIO*) time signal; **segna'le-tica** *sf* signalling, signposting; **segnale-tica stradale** road signs *pl*.

se'gnare [seɲ'ɲare] *vt* to mark; (*prendere nota*) to note; (*indicare*) to indicate, mark; (*SPORT: goal*) to score; **~rsi** *vr* (*REL*) to make the sign of the cross, cross o.s.

'segno ['seɲno] *sm* sign; (*impronta, contrassegno*) mark; (*limite*) limit, bounds *pl*; (*bersaglio*) target; **fare ~ di sì/no** to nod (one's head)/shake one's head; **fare ~ a qn di fermarsi** to motion (to) sb to stop; **cogliere** o **colpire nel ~** (*fig*) to hit the mark.

segre'gare *vt* to segregate, isolate; **segregazi'one** *sf* segregation.

segre'tario, a *sm/f* secretary; **~ comunale** town clerk; **~ di Stato** Secretary of State.

segrete'ria *sf* (*di ditta, scuola*) (secretary's) office; (*d'organizzazione internazionale*) secretariat; (*POL etc: carica*) office of Secretary; **~ telefonica** answering service.

segre'tezza [segre'tettsa] *sf* secrecy.

se'greto, a *ag* secret // *sm* secret; secrecy *q*; **in ~** in secret, secretly.

segu'ace [se'gwatʃe] *sm/f* follower, disciple.

segu'ente *ag* following, next.

segu'ire *vt* to follow; (*frequentare: corso*) to attend // *vi* to follow; (*continuare: testo*) to continue.

segui'tare *vt* to continue, carry on with // *vi* to continue, carry on.

'seguito *sm* (*scorta*) suite, retinue; (*discepoli*) followers *pl*; (*favore*) following; (*serie*) sequence, series *sg*; (*continuazione*) continuation; (*conseguenza*) result; **di ~** at a stretch, on end; **in ~** later on; **in ~ a, a ~ di** following; (*a causa di*) as a result of, owing to.

'sei *vb vedi* **essere** // *num* six.

sei'cento [sei'tʃɛnto] *num* six hundred // *sm*: **il S~** the seventeenth century.

selci'ato [sel'tʃato] *sm* cobbled surface.

selezio'nare [selettsjo'nare] *vt* to select.

selezi'one [selet'tsjone] *sf* selection.

'sella *sf* saddle; **sel'lare** *vt* to saddle.

selvag'gina [selvad'dʒina] *sf* (*animali*) game.

sel'vaggio, a, gi, ge [sel'vaddʒo] *ag* wild; (*tribù*) savage, uncivilized; (*fig*) savage, brutal // *sm/f* savage.

sel'vatico, a, ci, che *ag* wild.

se'maforo *sm* (*AUT*) traffic lights *pl*.

sem'brare *vi* to seem // *vb impers*: **sembra che** it seems that; **mi sembra che** it seems to me that; **I think (that)**; **~ di essere** to seem to be.

'seme *sm* seed; (*sperma*) semen; (*CARTE*) suit.

se'mestre *sm* half-year, six-month period.

'semi... *prefisso* semi...; **semi'cerchio** *sm* semicircle; **semifi'nale** *sf* semifinal; **semi'freddo, a** *ag* (*CUC*) chilled // *sm* ice-cream cake.

'semina *sf* (*AGR*) sowing.

semi'nare *vt* to sow.

semi'nario *sm* seminar; (*REL*) seminary.

seminter'rato *sm* basement; (*appartamento*) basement flat.

se'mitico, a, ci, che *ag* semitic.

sem'mai = **se mai**; *vedi* **se**.

'semola *sf* bran; **~ di grano duro** durum wheat.

semo'lino *sm* semolina.

'semplice ['semplitʃe] *ag* simple; (*di un solo elemento*) single; **semplice'mente** *av* simply; **semplicità** *sf* simplicity.

'sempre *av* always; (*ancora*) still; **posso ~ tentare** I can always o still try; **da ~** always; **per ~** forever; **una volta per ~** once and for all; **~ che** *cong* provided (that); **~ più** more and more; **~ meno** less and less.

sempre'verde *ag, sm* o *f* (*BOT*) evergreen.

'senape *sf* (*CUC*) mustard.

se'nato *sm* senate; **sena'tore, 'trice** *sm/f* senator.

'senno *sm* judgment, (common) sense; **col ~ di poi** with hindsight.

sennò *av* = **se no**; *vedi* **se**.

'seno *sm* (*ANAT: petto, mammella*) breast; (: *grembo, fig*) womb; (: *cavità*) sinus; (*GEO*) inlet, creek; (*MAT*) sine.

sen'sato, a *ag* sensible.

sensazio'nale [sensatsjo'nale] *ag* sensational.

sensazi'one [sensat'tsjone] *sf* feeling, sensation; **avere la ~ che** to have a feeling that; **fare ~** to cause a sensation, create a stir.

sen'sibile *ag* sensitive; (*ai sensi*) perceptible; (*rilevante, notevole*) appreciable, noticeable; **~ a** sensitive to; **sensibilità** *sf* sensitivity.

'senso *sm* (*FISIOL, istinto*) sense; (*impressione, sensazione*) feeling, sensation; (*significato*) meaning, sense; (*direzione*) direction; **~i** *smpl* (*coscienza*) consciousness *sg*; (*sensualità*) senses; **ciò non ha ~** that doesn't make sense; **fare ~ a** (*ripugnare*) to disgust, repel; **~ comune** common sense; **in ~ orario/antiorario** clockwise/anticlockwise; **a ~ unico** (*strada*) one-way; **"~ vietato"** (*AUT*) "no entry".

sensu'ale *ag* sensual; sensuous; **sensualità** *sf* sensuality; sensuousness.

sen'tenza [sen'tentsa] *sf* (*DIR*) sentence; (*massima*) maxim; **sentenzi'are** *vi* (*DIR*) to pass judgment.

senti'ero *sm* path.

sentimen'tale *ag* sentimental; (*vita, avventura*) love *cpd*.

senti'mento *sm* feeling.

senti'nella *sf* sentry.

sen'tire *vt* (*percepire al tatto, fig*) to feel; (*udire*) to hear; (*ascoltare*) to listen to; (*odore*) to smell; (*avvertire* con il gusto, assaggiare) to taste // vi: ~ di (avere sapore) to taste of; (avere odore) to smell of; ~rsi vr (uso reciproco) to be in touch; ~rsi bene/male to feel well/unwell o ill; ~rsi di fare qc (essere disposto) to feel like doing sth.

sen'tito, a ag (sincero) sincere, warm; per ~ dire by hearsay.

'senza ['sɛntsa] prep, cong without; ~ dir nulla without saying a word; fare ~ qc to do without sth; ~ di me without me; ~ che io lo sapessi without me o my knowing; senz'altro of course, certainly; ~ dubbio no doubt; ~ scrupoli unscrupulous; ~ amici friendless.

sepa'rare vt to separate; (dividere) to divide; (tenere distinto) to distinguish; ~rsi vr (coniugi) to separate, part; (amici) to part, leave each other; ~rsi da (coniuge) to separate o part from; (amico, socio) to part company with; (oggetto) to part with; **sepa'rato, a** ag (letti, conto etc) separate; (coniugi) separated; **separazi'one** sf separation.

se'polcro sm sepulchre.

se'polto, a pp di **seppellire**.

seppel'lire vt to bury.

'seppia sf cuttlefish // ag inv sepia.

se'quenza [se'kwentsa] sf sequence.

seques'trare vt (DIR) to impound; (rapire) to kidnap; (costringere in un luogo) to keep, confine; **se'questro** sm (DIR) impoundment; sequestro di persona kidnapping.

'sera sf evening; di ~ in the evening; domani ~ tomorrow evening, tomorrow night; **se'rale** ag evening cpd; **se'rata** sf evening; (ricevimento) party.

ser'bare vt to keep; (mettere da parte) to put aside; ~ rancore/odio verso qn to bear sb a grudge/hate sb.

serba'toio sm tank; (cisterna) cistern.

'serbo sm: mettere/tenere o avere in ~ qc to put/keep sth aside.

se'reno, a ag (tempo, cielo) clear; (fig) serene, calm.

ser'gente [ser'dʒɛnte] sm (MIL) sergeant.

'serie sf inv (successione) series inv; (gruppo, collezione: di chiavi etc) set; (SPORT) division; league; (COMM): modello di ~/fuori ~ standard/custombuilt model; in ~ in quick succession; (COMM) mass cpd.

serietà sf seriousness; reliability.

'serio, a ag serious; (impiegato) responsible, reliable; (ditta, cliente) reliable, dependable; sul ~ (davvero) really, truly; (seriamente) seriously, in earnest.

ser'mone sm sermon.

serpeggi'are [serped'dʒare] vi to wind; (fig) to spread.

ser'pente sm snake; ~ a sonagli rattlesnake.

'serra sf greenhouse; hothouse.

ser'randa sf roller shutter.

ser'rare vt to close, shut; (a chiave) to lock; (stringere) to tighten; (premere: nemico) to close in on; ~ i pugni/i denti to clench one's fists/teeth; ~ le file to close ranks.

serra'tura sf lock.

'serva sf vedi **servo**.

ser'vire vt to serve; (clienti: al ristorante) to wait on; (: al negozio) to serve, attend to; (fig: giovare) to aid, help; (CARTE) to deal // vi (TENNIS) to serve; (essere utile): ~ a qn to be of use to sb; ~ a qc/a fare (utensile etc) to be used for sth/for doing; ~ (a qn) da to serve as (for sb); ~rsi vr (usare): ~rsi di to use; (prendere: cibo): ~rsi (di) to help o.s. (to); (essere cliente abituale): ~rsi da to be a regular customer at, go to.

servitù sf servitude; slavery; (personale di servizio) servants pl, domestic staff.

servizi'evole [servit'tsjevole] ag obliging, willing to help.

ser'vizio [ser'vittsjo] sm service; (al ristorante: sul conto) service (charge); (STAMPA, TV, RADIO) report; (da tè, caffè etc) set, service; ~i smpl (di casa) kitchen and bathroom; (ECON) services; essere di ~ to be on duty; fuori ~ (telefono etc) out of order; ~ compreso service included; ~ militare military service; ~i segreti secret service sg.

'servo, a sm/f servant.

ses'santa num sixty; **sessan'tesimo, a** num sixtieth.

sessan'tina sf: una ~ (di) about sixty.

sessi'one sf session.

'sesso sm sex; **sessu'ale** ag sexual, sex cpd.

ses'tante sm sextant.

'sesto, a ag, sm sixth.

'seta sf silk.

'sete sf thirst; avere ~ to be thirsty.

'setola sf bristle.

'setta sf sect.

set'tanta num seventy; **settan'tesimo, a** num seventieth.

settan'tina sf: una ~ (di) about seventy.

'sette num seven.

sette'cento [sette'tʃɛnto] num seven hundred // sm: il S~ the eighteenth century.

set'tembre sm September.

settentrio'nale ag northern.

settentri'one sm north.

'settico, a, ci, che ag (MED) septic.

setti'mana sf week; **settima'nale** ag, sm weekly.

'settimo, a ag, sm seventh.

set'tore sm sector.

severità sf severity.

se'vero, a ag severe.

se'vizie [se'vittsje] sfpl torture sg;

sevizi'are vt to torture.

sezio'nare [settsjo'nare] vt to divide into sections; (MED) to dissect.

sezi'one [set'tsjone] sf section; (MED) dissection.

sfaccen'dato, a [sfattʃen'dato] ag idle.

sfacci'ato, a [sfat'tʃato] ag (maleducato) cheeky, impudent; (vistoso) gaudy.

sfa'celo [sfa'tʃɛlo] sm (fig) ruin, collapse.

sfal'darsi vr to flake (off).

'sfarzo ['sfartso] sm pomp, splendour.

sfasci'are [sfaʃ'ʃare] vt (ferita) to unbandage; (distruggere: porta) to smash, shatter; ~rsi vr (rompersi) to smash, shatter.

sfa'tare vt (leggenda) to explode.

sfavil'lare vi to spark, send out sparks; (risplendere) to sparkle.

sfavo'revole ag unfavourable.

'sfera sf sphere; **'sferico, a, ci, che** ag spherical.

sfer'rare vt (fig: colpo) to land, deal; (: attacco) to launch.

sfer'zare [sfer'tsare] vt to whip; (fig) to lash out at.

sfi'brare vt (indebolire) to exhaust, enervate.

'sfida sf challenge; **sfi'dare** vt to challenge; (fig) to defy, brave.

sfi'ducia [sfi'dutʃa] sf distrust, mistrust.

sfigu'rare vt (persona) to disfigure; (quadro, statua) to deface // vi (far cattiva figura) to make a bad impression.

sfi'lare vt (ago) to unthread; (abito, scarpe) to slip off // vi (truppe) to march past; (atleti) to parade; ~rsi vr (perle etc) to come unstrung; (orlo, tessuto) to fray; (calza) to run, ladder; **sfi'lata** sf march past; parade; sfilata di moda fashion show.

'sfinge ['sfindʒe] sf sphinx.

sfi'nito, a ag exhausted.

sfio'rare vt to brush (against); (argomento) to touch upon.

sfio'rire vi to wither, fade.

sfo'cato, a ag (FOT) out of focus.

sfoci'are [sfo'tʃare] vi: ~ in to flow into; (fig: malcontento) to develop into.

sfo'gare vt to vent, pour out; ~rsi vr (sfogare la propria rabbia) to give vent to one's anger; (confidarsi): ~rsi (con) to pour out one's feelings (to); non sfogarti su di me! don't take your bad temper out on me!

sfoggi'are [sfod'dʒare] vt, vi to show off.

'sfoglia ['sfoʎʎa] sf sheet of pasta dough; pasta ~ (CUC) puff pastry.

sfogli'are [sfoʎ'ʎare] vt (libro) to leaf through.

'sfogo, ghi sm outlet; (eruzione cutanea) rash; (fig) outburst; dare ~ a (fig) to give vent to.

sfolgo'rante ag (luce) blazing; (fig: vittoria) brilliant.

sfol'lare vt to empty, clear // vi to disperse; ~ da (città) to evacuate.

sfon'dare vt (porta) to break down; (scarpe) to wear a hole in; (cesto, scatola) to burst, knock the bottom out of; (MIL) to break through // vi (riuscire) to make a name for o.s.

'sfondo sm background.

sfor'mato sm (CUC) type of soufflé.

sfor'nito, a ag: ~ di lacking in, without; (negozio) out of.

sfor'tuna sf misfortune, ill luck q; avere ~ to be unlucky; **sfortu'nato, a** ag unlucky; (impresa, film) unsuccessful.

sfor'zare [sfor'tsare] vt to force; (voce, occhi) to strain; ~rsi vr: ~rsi di o a o per fare to try hard to do.

'sforzo ['sfortso] sm effort; (tensione eccessiva, TECN) strain; fare uno ~ to make an effort.

sfrat'tare vt to evict; **'sfratto** sm eviction.

sfrecci'are [sfret'tʃare] vi to shoot o flash past.

sfregi'are [sfre'dʒare] vt to slash, gash; (persona) to disfigure; (quadro) to deface; **'sfregio** sm gash; scar; (fig) insult.

sfre'nato, a ag (fig) unrestrained, unbridled.

sfron'tato, a ag shameless.

sfrutta'mento sm exploitation.

sfrut'tare vt (terreno) to overwork, exhaust; (miniera) to exploit, work; (fig: operai, occasione, potere) to exploit.

sfug'gire [sfud'dʒire] vi to escape; ~ a (custode) to escape (from); (morte) to escape; ~ a qn (dettaglio, nome) to escape sb; ~ di mano a qn to slip out of sb's hand (o hands); **sfug'gita: di sfuggita** ad (rapidamente, in fretta) in passing.

sfu'mare vt (colori, contorni) to soften, shade off // vi to shade (off), fade; (fig: svanire) to vanish, disappear; (: speranze) to come to nothing; **sfuma'tura** sf shading off q; (tonalità) shade, tone; (fig) touch, hint.

sturi'ata sf (scatto di collera) fit of anger; (rimprovero) sharp rebuke.

sga'bello sm stool.

sgabuz'zino [zgabud'dzino] sm lumber room.

sgambet'tare vi to kick one's legs about.

sgam'betto sm: far lo ~ a qn to trip sb up; (fig) to oust sb.

sganasci'arsi [zganaʃ'ʃarsi] vr: ~ dalle risa to roar with laughter.

sganci'are [zgan'tʃare] vt to unhook; (FERR) to uncouple; (bombe: da aereo) to release, drop; (fig: fam: soldi) to fork out; ~rsi vr (fig): ~rsi (da) to get away (from).

sganghe'rato, a [zgangc'rato] *ag*
(*porta*) off its hinges; (*auto*) ramshackle; (*risata*) wild, boisterous.

sgar'bato, a *ag* rude, impolite.

'sgarbo *sm*: fare uno ~ a qn to be rude
to sb.

sgattaio'lare *vi* to sneak away *o* off.

sge'lare [zdʒe'lare] *vi, vt* to thaw.

'sghembo, a ['zgembo] *ag* (*obliquo*)
slanting; (*storto*) crooked.

sghignaz'zare [zgiɲɲat'tsare] *vi* to laugh
scornfully.

sgob'bare *vi* (*fam: scolaro*) to swot; (:
operaio) to slog.

sgoccio'lare [zgottʃo'lare] *vt* (*vuotare*)
to drain (to the last drop) // *vi* (*acqua*)
to drip; (*recipiente*) to drain.

sgo'larsi *vr* to talk (*o* shout *o* sing) o.s.
hoarse.

sgomb(e)'rare *vt* to clear; (*andarsene
da: stanza*) to vacate; (*evacuare*) to
evacuate.

'sgombro, a *ag*: ~ (di) clear (of), free
(from) // *sm* (*ZOOL*) mackerel; (*anche:*
sgombero) clearing; vacating; evacua-
tion; (: *trasloco*) removal.

sgomen'tare *vt* to dismay; ~rsi *vr* to
be dismayed; **sgo'mento, a** *ag* dismayed // *sm* dismay, consternation.

sgonfi'are *vt* to let down, deflate; ~rsi
vr to go down.

'sgorbio *sm* blot; scribble.

sgor'gare *vi* to gush (out).

sgoz'zare [zgot'tsare] *vt* to cut the throat
of.

sgra'devole *ag* unpleasant, disagreeable.

sgra'dito, a *ag* unpleasant, unwelcome.

sgra'nare *vt* (*piselli*) to shell; ~ gli occhi to open one's eyes wide.

sgran'chirsi [zgran'kirsi] *vr* to stretch; ~
le gambe to stretch one's legs.

sgranocchi'are [zgranok'kjare] *vt* to
munch.

'sgravio *sm*: ~ fiscale tax relief.

sgrazi'ato, a [zgrat'tsjato] *ag* clumsy,
ungainly.

sgreto'lare *vt* to cause to crumble; ~rsi
vr to crumble.

sgri'dare *vt* to scold; **sgri'data** *sf* scold-
ing.

sguai'ato, a *ag* coarse, vulgar.

sgual'cire [zgwal'tʃire] *vt* to crumple
(up), crease.

sgual'drina *sf* (*peg*) slut.

sgu'ardo *sm* (*occhiata*) look, glance;
(*espressione*) look (in one's eye).

sguaz'zare [zgwat'tsare] *vi* (*nell'acqua*)
to splash about; (*nella melma*) to
wallow; ~ nell'oro to be rolling in
money.

sguinzagli'are [zgwintsaʎ'ʎare] *vt* to let
off the leash; (*fig: persona*): ~ qn dietro
a qn to set sb on sb.

sgusci'are [zguʃ'ʃare] *vt* to shell // *vi*

(*sfuggire di mano*) to slip; ~ via to slip
o slink away.

'shampoo ['ʃampo] *sm inv* shampoo.

shock [ʃɔk] *sm inv* shock.

si ◆ *sm* (*MUS*) B; (*solfeggiando la scala*)
ti

◆ *pronome* (*dav lo, la, li, le, ne diventa*
se) **1** (*riflessivo: maschile*) himself; (:
femminile) herself; (: *neutro*) itself; (:
impersonale) oneself; (: *pl*) themselves;
lavarsi to wash (oneself); ~ è tagliato he
has cut himself; ~ credono importanti
they think a lot of themselves

2 (*riflessivo: con complemento oggetto*):
lavarsi le mani to wash one's hands; ~
sta lavando i capelli he (*o* she) is washing his (*o* her) hair

3 (*reciproco*) one another, each other; ~
amano they love one another *o* each
other

4 (*passivo*): ~ ripara facilmente it is
easily repaired

5 (*impersonale*): ~ dice che ... they *o*
people say that ...; ~ vede che è vecchio
one *o* you can see that it's old

6 (*noi*) we; tra poco ~ parte we're leaving soon.

sì *av* yes; un giorno ~ e uno no every
other day.

'sia *cong*: ~ ... ~ (*o* ... *o*): ~ che lavori,
~ che non lavori whether he works *or*
not; (*tanto ... quanto*): verranno ~ Luigi
~ suo fratello both Luigi and his brother
will be coming.

si'amo *vb vedi* **essere.**

sibi'lare *vi* to hiss; (*fischiare*) to whistle;
'sibilo *sm* hiss; whistle.

si'cario *sm* hired killer.

sicché [sik'ke] *cong* (*perciò*) so (that),
therefore; (*e quindi*) (and) so.

siccità [sittʃi'ta] *sf* drought.

sic'come *cong* since, as.

Si'cilia [si'tʃilja] *sf*: la ~ Sicily;
sicili'ano, a *ag, sm/f* Sicilian.

sicu'rezza [siku'rettsa] *sf* safety;
security; (*fiducia*) confidence; (*certezza*)
certainty; di ~ safety *cpd*; la ~ stradale
road safety.

si'curo, a *ag* safe; (*ben difeso*) secure;
(*fiducioso*) confident; (*certo*) sure,
certain; (*notizia, amico*) reliable;
(*esperto*) skilled // *av* (*anche: di* ~)
certainly; essere/mettere al ~ to be
safe/put in a safe place; ~ di sé self-
confident, sure of o.s.; sentirsi ~ to feel
safe *o* secure.

siderur'gia [siderur'dʒia] *sf* iron and
steel industry.

'sidro *sm* cider.

si'epe *sf* hedge.

si'ero *sm* (*MED*) serum.

si'esta *sf* siesta, (afternoon) nap.

si'ete *vb vedi* **essere.**

si'filide *sf* syphilis.

si'fone *sm* siphon.

Sig. *abbr* (= *signore*) Mr.

siga'retta *sf* cigarette.

'sigaro *sm* cigar.

Sigg. *abbr* (= *signori*) Messrs.

sigil'lare [sidʒil'lare] *vt* to seal.

si'gillo [si'dʒillo] *sm* seal.

'sigla *sf* initials *pl*; acronym, abbreviation; ~ automobilistica *abbreviation of province on vehicle number plate*; ~ musicale signature tune.

si'glare *vt* to initial.

Sig.na *abbr* (= *signorina*) Miss.

signifi'care [siŋnifi'kare] *vt* to mean; **significa'tivo, a** *ag* significant; **significa'cato** *sm* meaning.

si'gnora [siɲ'ɲora] *sf* lady; la ~ X Mrs ['mɪsɪz] X; **buon giorno** S~/Signore/Signorina good morning; (*deferente*) good morning Madam/Sir/Madam; (*quando si conosce il nome*) good morning Mrs/Mr/Miss X; **Gentile** S~/Signore/Signorina (*in una lettera*) Dear Madam/Sir/Madam; **il signor Rossi e ~** Mr Rossi and his wife; ~**e e signori** ladies and gentlemen.

si'gnore [siɲ'ɲore] *sm* gentleman; (*padrone*) lord, master; (*REL*): **il** S~ the Lord; **il signor X** Mr ['mɪstə*] X; **i ~i Bianchi** (*coniugi*) Mr and Mrs Bianchi; *vedi anche* **signora**.

signo'rile [siɲɲo'rile] *ag* refined.

signo'rina [siɲɲo'rina] *sf* young lady; la ~ X Miss X; *vedi anche* **signora**.

Sig.ra *abbr* (= *signora*) Mrs.

silenzia'tore [silentsja'tore] *sm* silencer.

si'lenzio [si'lentsjo] *sm* silence; **fare ~** to be quiet, stop talking; **silenzi'oso, a** *ag* silent, quiet.

si'licio [si'litʃo] *sm* silicon; **piastrina di ~** silicon chip.

'sillaba *sf* syllable.

silu'rare *vt* to torpedo; (*fig: privare del comando*) to oust.

si'luro *sm* torpedo.

simboleggi'are [simboled'dʒare] *vt* to symbolize.

'simbolo *sm* symbol.

'simile *ag* (*analogo*) similar; (*di questo tipo*): **un uomo ~** such a man, a man like this; **libri ~i** such books; ~ **a** similar to; **i suoi ~i** one's fellow men; one's peers.

simme'tria *sf* symmetry.

simpa'tia *sf* (*qualità*) pleasantness; (*inclinazione*) liking; **avere ~ per qn** to like sb, have a liking for sb; **sim'patico, a, ci, che** *ag* (*persona*) nice, pleasant, likeable; (*casa, albergo etc*) nice, pleasant.

simpatiz'zare [simpatid'dzare] *vi*: ~ **con** to take a liking to.

sim'posio *sm* symposium.

simu'lare *vt* to sham, simulate; (*TECN*) to simulate; **simulazi'one** *sf* shamming; simulation.

simul'taneo, a *ag* simultaneous.

sina'goga, ghe *sf* synagogue.

sincerità [sintʃeri'ta] *sf* sincerity.

sin'cero, a [sin'tʃero] *ag* sincere; genuine; heartfelt.

'sincope *sf* syncopation; (*MED*) blackout.

sinda'cale *ag* (trade-)union *cpd*; **sindaca'lista, i, e** *sm/f* trade unionist.

sinda'cato *sm* (*di lavoratori*) (trade) union; (*AMM, ECON, DIR*) syndicate, trust, pool; ~ **dei datori di lavoro** employers' association, employers' federation.

'sindaco, ci *sm* mayor.

sinfo'nia *sf* (*MUS*) symphony.

singhioz'zare [singjot'tsare] *vi* to sob; to hiccup.

singhi'ozzo [sin'gjottso] *sm* sob; (*MED*) hiccup; **avere il ~** to have the hiccups; **a ~** (*fig*) by fits and starts.

singo'lare *ag* (*insolito*) remarkable, singular; (*LING*) singular // *sm* (*LING*) singular; (*TENNIS*): ~ **maschile**/**femminile** men's/women's singles.

'singolo, a *ag* single, individual // *sm* (*persona*) individual; (*TENNIS*) = **singolare**.

si'nistro, a *ag* left, left-hand; (*fig*) sinister // *sm* (*incidente*) accident // *sf* (*POL*) left (wing); **a ~a** on the left; (*direzione*) to the left.

'sino *prep* = **fino**.

si'nonimo, a *ag* synonymous // *sm* synonym; ~ **di** synonymous with.

sin'tassi *sf* syntax.

'sintesi *sf* synthesis; (*riassunto*) summary, résumé.

sin'tetico, a, ci, che *ag* synthetic.

sintetiz'zare [sintetid'dzare] *vt* to synthesize; (*riassumere*) to summarize.

sinto'matico, a, ci, che *ag* symptomatic.

'sintomo *sm* symptom.

sinu'oso, a *ag* (*strada*) winding.

S.I.P. *sigla f* (= *Società italiana per l'esercizio telefonico*) *Italian telephone company*.

si'pario *sm* (*TEATRO*) curtain.

si'rena *sf* (*apparecchio*) siren; (*nella mitologia, fig*) siren, mermaid.

'Siria *sf*: la ~ Syria.

si'ringa, ghe *sf* syringe.

'sismico, a, ci, che *ag* seismic.

sis'mografo *sm* seismograph.

sis'tema, i *sm* system; method, way; ~ **di vita** way of life.

siste'mare *vt* (*mettere a posto*) to tidy, put in order; (*risolvere: questione*) to sort out, settle; (*procurare un lavoro a*) to find a job for; (*dare un alloggio a*) to settle, find accommodation for; ~**rsi** *vr* (*problema*) to be settled; (*persona: trovare alloggio*) to find accommodation (*Brit*) o accommodations (*US*); (: *trovarsi un lavoro*) to get fixed up with a job; ti sistemo io! I'll soon sort you out!

siste'matico, a, ci, che *ag* systematic.

sistemazi'one [sistemat'tsjone] *sf* arrangement, order; settlement; employment; accommodation (*Brit*), accommodations (*US*).

'sito *sm* (*letterario*) place.

situ'are *vt* to site, situate; **situ'ato, a** *ag*: **situato a/su** situated at/on.

situazi'one [situat'tsjone] *sf* situation.

slacci'are [zlat'tʃare] *vt* to undo, unfasten.

slanci'arsi [zlan'tʃarsi] *vr* to dash, fling o.s.; **slanci'ato, a** *ag* slender; **'slancio** *sm* dash, leap; (*fig*) surge; **di slancio** impetuously.

sla'vato, a *ag* faded, washed out; (*fig: viso, occhi*) pale, colourless.

'slavo, a *ag* Slav(onic), Slavic.

sle'ale *ag* disloyal; (*concorrenza etc*) unfair.

sle'gare *vt* to untie.

'slitta *sf* sledge; (*trainata*) sleigh.

slit'tare *vi* to slip, slide; (*AUT*) to skid.

slo'gare *vt* (*MED*) to dislocate.

sloggi'are [zlod'dʒare] *vt* (*inquilino*) to turn out; (*nemico*) to drive out, dislodge // *vi* to move out.

smacchi'are [zmak'kjare] *vt* to remove stains from.

'smacco, chi *sm* humiliating defeat.

smagli'ante [zmaʎ'ʎante] *ag* brilliant, dazzling.

smaglia'tura [zmaʎʎa'tura] *sf* (*su maglia, calza*) ladder; (*della pelle*) stretch mark.

smalizi'ato, a [smalit'tsjato] *ag* shrewd, cunning.

smal'tare *vt* to enamel; (*ceramica*) to glaze; (*unghie*) to varnish.

smal'tire *vt* (*merce*) to sell off; (*rifiuti*) to dispose of; (*cibo*) to digest; (*peso*) to lose; (*rabbia*) to get over; **~ la sbornia** to sober up.

'smalto *sm* (*anche: di denti*) enamel; (*per ceramica*) glaze; **~ per unghie** nail varnish.

'smania *sf* agitation, restlessness; (*fig*): **~ di** thirst for, craving for; **avere la ~ addosso** to have the fidgets; **avere la ~ di fare** to be desperate to do.

smantel'lare *vt* to dismantle.

smarri'mento *sm* loss; (*fig*) bewilderment; dismay.

smar'rire *vt* to lose; (*non riuscire a trovare*) to mislay; **~rsi** *vr* (*perdersi*) to lose one's way, get lost; (*: oggetto*) to go astray; **smar'rito, a** *ag* (*sbigottito*) bewildered.

smasche'rare [zmaske'rare] *vt* to unmask.

smemo'rato, a *ag* forgetful.

smen'tire *vt* (*negare*) to deny; (*testimonianza*) to refute; (*reputazione*) to give the lie to; **~rsi** *vr* to be in-

consistent; **smen'tita** *sf* denial; retraction.

sme'raldo *sm* emerald.

smerci'are [zmer'tʃare] *vt* (*COMM*) to sell; (*: svendere*) to sell off.

sme'riglio [zme'riʎʎo] *sm* emery.

'smesso, a *pp di* **smettere**.

'smettere *vt* to stop; (*vestiti*) to stop wearing // *vi* to stop, cease; **~ di fare** to stop doing.

'smilzo, a ['zmiltso] *ag* thin, lean.

sminu'ire *vt* to diminish, lessen; (*fig*) to belittle.

sminuz'zare [zminut'tsare] *vt* to break into small pieces; to crumble.

smis'tare *vt* (*pacchi etc*) to sort; (*FERR*) to shunt.

smisu'rato, a *ag* boundless, immeasurable; (*grandissimo*) immense, enormous.

smobili'tare *vt* to demobilize.

smo'dato, a *ag* immoderate.

smoking ['smɔukiŋ] *sm inv* dinner jacket.

smon'tare *vt* (*mobile, macchina etc*) to take to pieces, dismantle; (*fig: scoraggiare*) to dishearten // *vi* (*scendere: da cavallo*) to dismount; (*: da treno*) to get off; (*terminare il lavoro*) to stop (work); **~rsi** *vr* to lose heart; to lose one's enthusiasm.

'smorfia *sf* grimace; (*atteggiamento lezioso*) simpering; **fare ~e** to make faces; to simper; **smorfi'oso, a** *ag* simpering.

'smorto, a *ag* (*viso*) pale, wan; (*colore*) dull.

smor'zare [zmor'tsare] *vt* (*suoni*) to deaden; (*colori*) to tone down; (*luce*) to dim; (*sete*) to quench; (*entusiasmo*) to dampen; **~rsi** *vr* (*suono, luce*) to fade; (*entusiasmo*) to dampen.

'smosso, a *pp di* **smuovere**.

smotta'mento *sm* landslide.

'smunto, a *ag* haggard, pinched.

smu'overe *vt* to move, shift; (*fig: commuovere*) to move; (*: dall'inerzia*) to rouse, stir; **~rsi** *vr* to move, shift.

smus'sare *vt* (*angolo*) to round off, smooth; (*lama etc*) to blunt; **~rsi** *vr* to become blunt.

snatu'rato, a *ag* inhuman, heartless.

'snello, a *ag* (*agile*) agile; (*svelto*) slender, slim.

sner'vare *vt* to enervate, wear out; **~rsi** *vr* to become enervated.

sni'dare *vt* to drive out, flush out.

snob'bare *vt* to snub.

sno'bismo *sm* snobbery.

snoccio'lare [znottʃo'lare] *vt* (*frutta*) to stone; (*fig: orazioni*) to rattle off; (*: verità*) to blab.

sno'dare *vt* (*rendere agile, mobile*) to loosen; **~rsi** *vr* to come loose; (*articolarsi*) to bend; (*strada, fiume*) to wind.

so vb vedi **sapere**.

so'ave ag sweet, gentle, soft.

sobbal'zare [sobbal'tsare] vi to jolt, jerk; (trasalire) to jump, start; **sob'balzo** sm jerk, jolt; jump, start.

sobbar'carsi vr: ~ a to take on, undertake.

sob'borgo, ghi sm suburb.

sobil'lare vt to stir up, incite.

'sobrio, a ag sober.

socchi'udere [sok'kjudere] vt (porta) to leave ajar; (occhi) to half-close; **socchi'uso, a** pp di **socchiudere**.

soc'correre vt to help, assist; **soc'corso, a** pp di **soccorrere** // sm help, aid, assistance; **soccorsi** smpl relief sg, aid sg; **soccorso stradale** breakdown service.

socialdemo'cratico, a, ci, che [sotfaldemo'kratiko] sm/f Social Democrat.

soci'ale [so'tfale] ag social; (di associazione) club cpd, association cpd.

socia'lismo [sotfa'lizmo] sm socialism; **socia'lista, i, e** ag, sm/f socialist.

società [sotfe'ta] sf inv society; (sportiva) club; (COMM) company; ~ **per azioni (S.p.A.)** limited (Brit) o incorporated (US) company, ~ **a responsabilità limitata (S.r.l.)** type of limited liability company.

soci'evole [so'tfevole] ag sociable.

'socio ['sotfo] sm (DIR, COMM) partner; (membro di associazione) member.

'soda sf (CHIM) soda; (acqua gassata) soda (water).

soda'lizio [soda'littsjo] sm association, society.

soddisfa'cente [soddisfa'tfente] ag satisfactory.

soddis'fare vt, vi: ~ a to satisfy; (impegno) to fulfil; (debito) to pay off; (richiesta) to meet, comply with; (offesa) to make amends for; **soddis'fatto, a** pp di **soddisfare** // ag satisfied; **soddisfatto di** happy o satisfied with; pleased with; **soddisfazi'one** sf satisfaction.

'sodo, a ag firm, hard // av (picchiare, lavorare) hard; **dormire** ~ to sleep soundly.

sofà sm inv sofa.

soffe'renza [soffe'rentsa] sf suffering.

sof'ferto, a pp di **soffrire**.

soffi'are vt to blow; (notizia, segreto) to whisper // vi to blow; (sbuffare) to puff (and blow); ~**rsi il naso** to blow one's nose; ~ **qc/qn a qn** (fig) to pinch o steal sth/sb from sb; ~ **via qc** to blow sth away.

'soffice ['soffitfe] ag soft.

'soffio sm (di vento) breath; (di fumo) puff; (MED) murmur.

sof'fitta sf attic.

sof'fitto sm ceiling.

soffo'care vi (anche: ~rsi) to suffocate, choke // vt to suffocate, choke; (fig) to stifle, suppress.

sof'friggere [sof'friddʒere] vt to fry lightly.

sof'frire vt to suffer, endure; (sopportare) to bear, stand // vi to suffer; to be in pain; ~ **(di) qc** (MED) to suffer from sth.

sof'fritto, a pp di **soffriggere** // sm (CUC) fried mixture of herbs, bacon and onions.

sofisti'cato, a ag sophisticated; (vino) adulterated.

sogget'tivo, a [soddʒet'tivo] ag subjective.

sog'getto, a [sod'dʒetto] ag: ~ **a** (sottomesso) subject to; (esposto: a variazioni, danni etc) subject o liable to // sm subject.

soggezi'one [soddʒet'tsjone] sf subjection; (timidezza) awe; **avere** ~ **di qn** to stand in awe of sb; to be ill at ease in sb's presence.

sogghi'gnare [soggiɲ'ɲare] vi to sneer.

soggior'nare [soddʒor'nare] vi to stay; **soggi'orno** sm (invernale, marino) stay; (stanza) living room.

sog'giungere [sod'dʒundʒere] vt to add.

'soglia ['soʎʎa] sf doorstep; (anche fig) threshold.

sogli'ola ['soʎʎola] sf (ZOOL) sole.

so'gnare [soɲ'ɲare] vt, vi to dream; ~ **a occhi aperti** to daydream; **sogna'tore, 'trice** sm/f dreamer.

'sogno ['soɲɲo] sm dream.

'soia sf (BOT) soya.

sol sm (MUS) G; (: solfeggiando la scala) so(h).

so'laio sm (soffitta) attic.

sola'mente av only, just.

so'lare ag solar, sun cpd.

'solco, chi sm (scavo, fig: ruga) furrow; (incavo) rut, track; (di disco) groove; (scia) wake.

sol'dato sm soldier; ~ **semplice** private.

'soldo sm (fig): **non avere un** ~ to be penniless; **non vale un** ~ it's not worth a penny; ~**i** smpl (denaro) money sg.

'sole sm sun; (luce) sun(light); (tempo assolato) sun(shine); **prendere il** ~ to sunbathe.

soleggi'ato, a [soled'dʒato] ag sunny.

so'lenne ag solemn; **solennità** sf solemnity; (festività) holiday, feast day.

sol'fato sm (CHIM) sulphate.

soli'dale ag: **essere** ~ **(con)** to be in agreement (with).

solidarietà sf solidarity.

'solido, a ag solid; (forte, robusto) sturdy, solid; (fig: ditta) sound, solid // sm (MAT) solid.

soli'loquio sm soliloquy.

so'lista, i, e ag solo // sm/f soloist.

solita'mente av usually, as a rule.

soli'tario, a *ag* (*senza compagnia*) solitary, lonely; (*solo, isolato*) solitary, lone; (*deserto*) lonely // *sm* (*gioiello, gioco*) solitaire.

'solito, a *ag* usual; **essere ~ fare** to be in the habit of doing; **di ~** usually; **più tardi del ~** later than usual; **come al ~** as usual.

soli'tudine *sf* solitude.

solleci'tare [solletʃi'tare] *vt* (*lavoro*) to speed up; (*persona*) to urge on; (*chiedere con insistenza*) to press for, request urgently; (*stimolare*): **~ qn a fare** to urge sb to do; (*TECN*) to stress; **sollecitazi'one** *sf* entreaty, request; (*fig*) incentive; (*TECN*) stress.

sol'lecito, a [sol'letʃito] *ag* prompt, quick // *sm* (*lettera*) reminder; **solleci'tudine** *sf* promptness, speed.

solleti'care *vt* to tickle.

sol'letico *sm* tickling; **soffrire il ~** to be ticklish.

solleva'mento *sm* raising; lifting; revolt; **~ pesi** (*SPORT*) weight-lifting.

solle'vare *vt* to lift, raise; (*fig: persona: alleggerire*): **~ (da)** to relieve (of); (: *dar conforto*) to comfort, relieve; (: *questione*) to raise; (: *far insorgere*) to stir (to revolt); **~rsi** *vr* to rise; (*fig: riprendersi*) to recover; (: *ribellarsi*) to rise up.

solli'evo *sm* relief; (*conforto*) comfort.

'solo, a *ag* alone; (*in senso spirituale: isolato*) lonely; (*unico*): **un ~ libro** only one book, a single book; (*con ag numerale*): **veniamo noi tre ~i** just o only the three of us are coming // *av* (*soltanto*) only, just; **non ~ ... ma anche** not only ... but also; **fare qc da ~** to do sth (all) by oneself; **da me ~** single-handed, on my own.

sol'tanto *av* only.

so'lubile *ag* (*sostanza*) soluble.

soluzi'one [solut'tsjone] *sf* solution.

sol'vente *ag, sm* solvent.

'soma *sf*: **bestia da ~** beast of burden.

so'maro *sm* ass, donkey.

somigli'anza [somiʎ'ʎantsa] *sf* resemblance.

somigli'are [somiʎ'ʎare] *vi*: **~ a** to be like, resemble; (*nell'aspetto fisico*) to look like; **~rsi** *vr* to be (o look) alike.

'somma *sf* (*MAT*) sum; (*di denaro*) sum (of money); (*complesso di varie cose*) whole amount, sum total.

som'mare *vt* to add up; (*aggiungere*) to add; **tutto sommato** all things considered.

som'mario, a *ag* (*racconto, indagine*) brief; (*giustizia*) summary // *sm* summary.

som'mergere [som'mɛrdʒere] *vt* to submerge.

sommer'gibile [sommer'dʒibile] *sm* submarine.

som'merso, a *pp di* **sommergere**.

som'messo, a *ag* (*voce*) soft, subdued.

somminis'trare *vt* to give, administer.

sommità *sf inv* summit, top; (*fig*) height.

'sommo, a *ag* highest; (*rispetto etc*) highest, greatest; (*poeta, artista*) great, outstanding // *sm* (*fig*) height; **per ~i capi** briefly, covering the main points.

som'mossa *sf* uprising.

so'nare *etc* = **suonare** *etc*.

son'daggio [son'daddʒo] *sm* sounding; probe; boring, drilling; (*indagine*) survey; **~ d'opinioni** opinion poll.

son'dare *vt* (*NAUT*) to sound; (*atmosfera, piaga*) to probe; (*MINERALOGIA*) to bore, drill; (*fig: opinione etc*) to survey, poll.

so'netto *sm* sonnet.

son'nambulo, a *sm/f* sleepwalker.

sonnecchi'are [sonnek'kjare] *vi* to doze, nod.

son'nifero *sm* sleeping drug (o pill).

'sonno *sm* sleep; **prendere ~** to fall asleep; **aver ~** to be sleepy.

'sono *vb vedi* **essere**.

so'noro, a *ag* (*ambiente*) resonant; (*voce*) sonorous, ringing; (*onde, film*) sound *cpd*.

sontu'oso, a *ag* sumptuous; lavish.

sopo'rifero, a *ag* soporific.

soppe'sare *vt* to weigh in one's hand(s), feel the weight of; (*fig*) to weigh up.

soppi'atto: di ~ *av* secretly; furtively.

soppor'tare *vt* (*reggere*) to support; (*subire: perdita, spese*) to bear, sustain; (*soffrire: dolore*) to bear, endure; (*sog: cosa: freddo*) to withstand; (*sog: persona: freddo, vino*) to take; (*tollerare*) to put up with, tolerate.

sop'presso, a *pp di* **sopprimere**.

sop'primere *vt* (*carica, privilegi, testimone*) to do away with; (*pubblicazione*) to suppress; (*parola, frase*) to delete.

'sopra *prep* (*gen*) on; (*al di sopra di, più in alto di*) above; over; (*riguardo a*) on, about // *av* on top; (*attaccato, scritto*) on it; (*al di sopra*) above; (*al piano superiore*) upstairs; **donne ~ i 30 anni** women over 30 (years of age); **abito di ~** I live upstairs; **dormirci ~** (*fig*) to sleep on it.

so'prabito *sm* overcoat.

soprac'ciglio [soprat'tʃiʎʎo], *pl*(*f*) **sopracciglia** *sm* eyebrow.

sopracco'perta *sf* (*di letto*) bedspread; (*di libro*) jacket.

soprad'detto, a *ag* aforesaid.

sopraf'fare *vt* to overcome, overwhelm.

sopraf'fatto, a *pp di* **sopraffare**.

sopraf'fino, a *ag* (*pranzo, vino*) excellent.

sopraggi'ungere [soprad'dʒundʒere] *vi* (*giungere all'improvviso*) to arrive (unexpectedly); (*accadere*) to occur (unexpectedly).

sopral'luogo, ghi sm (di esperti) inspection; (di polizia) on-the-spot investigation.

sopram'mobile sm ornament.

soprannatu'rale ag supernatural.

sopran'nome sm nickname.

so'prano, a sm/f (persona) soprano // sm (voce) soprano.

soprappensi'ero av lost in thought.

sopras'salto sm: di ~ with a start; suddenly.

soprasse'dere vi: ~ a to delay, put off.

soprat'tutto av (anzitutto) above all; (specialmente) especially.

soprav'vento sm: avere/prendere il ~ su to have/get the upper hand over.

sopravvis'suto, a pp di **sopravvivere**.

soprav'vivere vi to survive; (continuare a vivere): ~ (in) to live on (in); ~ a (incidente etc) to survive; (persona) to outlive.

soprinten'dente sm/f supervisor; (statale: di belle arti etc) keeper; **soprinten'denza** sf supervision; (ente): soprintendenza alle Belle Arti government department responsible for monuments and artistic treasures.

so'pruso sm abuse of power; subire un ~ to be abused.

soq'quadro sm: mettere a ~ to turn upside-down.

sor'betto sm sorbet, water ice.

sor'bire vt to sip; (fig) to put up with.

'sorcio, ci ['sortʃo] sm mouse.

'sordido, a ag sordid; (fig: gretto) stingy.

sor'dina sf: in ~ softly; (fig) on the sly.

sordità sf deafness.

'sordo, a ag deaf; (rumore) muffled; (dolore) dull; (odio, rancore) veiled // sm/f deaf person; **sordo'muto, a** ag deaf-and-dumb // sm/f deaf-mute.

so'rella sf sister; **sorel'lastra** sf stepsister.

sor'gente [sor'dʒɛnte] sf (acqua che sgorga) spring; (di fiume, FISICA, fig) source.

'sorgere ['sordʒere] vi to rise; (scaturire) to spring, rise; (fig: difficoltà) to arise.

sormon'tare vt (fig) to overcome, surmount.

sorni'one, a ag sly.

sorpas'sare vt (AUT) to overtake; (fig) to surpass; (: eccedere) to exceed, go beyond; ~ in altezza to be higher than; (persona) to be taller than.

sorpren'dente ag surprising.

sor'prendere vt (cogliere: in flagrante etc) to catch; (stupire) to surprise; ~rsi vr: ~rsi (di) to be surprised (at); **sor'preso, a** pp di **sorprendere** // sf surprise; fare una sorpresa a qn to give sb a surprise.

sor'reggere [sor'reddʒere] vt to support, hold up; (fig) to sustain; **sor'retto, a** pp di **sorreggere**.

sor'ridere vi to smile; **sor'riso, a** pp di **sorridere** // sm smile.

'sorso sm sip.

'sorta sf sort, kind; di ~ whatever, of any kind, at all.

'sorte sf (fato) fate, destiny; (evento fortuito) chance; tirare a ~ to draw lots.

sor'teggio [sor'teddʒo] sm draw.

sorti'legio [sorti'ledʒo] sm witchcraft q; (incantesimo) spell; fare un ~ a qn to cast a spell on sb.

sor'tita sf (MIL) sortie.

'sorto, a pp di **sorgere**.

sorvegli'anza [sorveʎ'ʎantsa] sf watch; supervision; (POLIZIA, MIL) surveillance.

sorvegli'are [sorveʎ'ʎare] vt (bambino, bagagli, prigioniero) to watch, keep an eye on; (malato) to watch over; (territorio, casa) to watch o keep watch over; (lavori) to supervise.

sorvo'lare vt (territorio) to fly over // vi: ~ su (fig) to skim over.

'sosia sm inv double.

sos'pendere vt (appendere) to hang (up); (interrompere, privare di una carica) to suspend; (rimandare) to defer; ~ un quadro al muro/un lampadario al soffitto to hang a picture on the wall/a chandelier from the ceiling; **sospensi'one** sf (anche CHIM, AUT) suspension; deferment; **sos'peso, a** pp di **sospendere** // ag (appeso): sospeso a hanging on (o from); (treno, autobus) cancelled; in sospeso in abeyance; (conto) outstanding; tenere in sospeso (fig) to keep in suspense.

sospet'tare vt to suspect // vi: ~ di to suspect; (diffidare) to be suspicious of.

sos'petto, a ag suspicious // sm suspicion; **sospet'toso, a** ag suspicious.

sos'pingere [sos'pindʒere] vt to drive, push; **sos'pinto, a** pp di **sospingere**.

sospi'rare vi to sigh // vt to long for, yearn for; **sos'piro** sm sigh.

'sosta sf (fermata) stop, halt; (pausa) pause, break; senza ~ non-stop, without a break.

sostan'tivo sm noun, substantive.

sos'tanza [sos'tantsa] sf substance; ~e sfpl (ricchezze) wealth sg, possessions; in ~ in short, to sum up; **sostanzi'oso, a** ag (cibo) nourishing, substantial.

sos'tare vi (fermarsi) to stop (for a while), stay; (fare una pausa) to take a break.

sos'tegno [sos'teɲɲo] sm support.

soste'nere vt to support; (prendere su di sé) to take on, bear; (resistere) to withstand, stand up to; (affermare): ~ che to maintain that; ~rsi vr to hold o.s. up, support o.s.; (fig) to keep up one's strength; ~ **gli esami** to sit exams; **sosteni'tore, 'trice** *sm/f* supporter.

sostenta'mento *sm* maintenance, support.

soste'nuto, a *ag* (*stile*) elevated; (*velocità, ritmo*) sustained; (*prezzo*) high // *sm/f*: **fare il(la) ~(a)** to be standoffish, keep one's distance.

sostitu'ire *vt* (*mettere al posto di*): **~ qn/qc a** to substitute sb/sth for; (*prendere il posto di: persona*) to substitute for; (: *cosa*) to take the place of.

sosti'tuto, a *sm/f* substitute.

sostituzi'one [sostitut'tsjone] *sf* substitution; **in ~ di** as a substitute for, in place of.

sotta'ceti [sotta'tʃeti] *smpl* pickles.

sot'tana *sf* (*sottoveste*) underskirt; (*gonna*) skirt; (*REL*) soutane, cassock.

sotter'fugio [sotter'fudʒo] *sm* subterfuge.

sotter'raneo, a *ag* underground // *sm* cellar.

sotter'rare *vt* to bury.

sottigli'ezza [sottiʎ'ʎettsa] *sf* thinness; slimness; (*fig: acutezza*) subtlety; shrewdness; **~e** *sfpl* (*pedanteria*) quibbles.

sot'tile *ag* thin; (*figura, caviglia*) thin, slim, slender; (*fine: polvere, capelli*) fine; (*fig: leggero*) light; (: *vista*) sharp, keen; (: *olfatto*) fine, discriminating; (: *mente*) subtle; shrewd // *sm*: **non andare per il ~** not to mince matters.

sottin'tendere *vt* (*intendere qc non espresso*) to understand; (*implicare*) to imply; **sottin'teso, a** *pp di* **sottintendere** // *sm* allusion; **parlare senza sottintesi** to speak plainly.

'sotto *prep* (*gen*) under; (*più in basso di*) below // *av* underneath, beneath; below; (*al piano inferiore*): **(al piano di) ~ downstairs; ~ forma di** in the form of; **~ il monte** at the foot of the mountain; **siamo ~ Natale** it's nearly Christmas; **~ la pioggia/il sole** in the rain/sun(shine); **~ terra** underground; **~ voce** in a low voice; **chiuso ~ vuoto** vacuum-packed.

sottoline'are *vt* to underline; (*fig*) to emphasize, stress.

sottoma'rino, a *ag* (*flora*) submarine; (*cavo, navigazione*) underwater // *sm* (*NAUT*) submarine.

sotto'messo, a *pp di* **sottomettere**.

sotto'mettere *vt* to subdue, subjugate; **~rsi** *vr* to submit.

sottopas'saggio [sottopas'saddʒo] *sm* (*AUT*) underpass; (*pedonale*) subway, underpass.

sotto'porre *vt* (*costringere*) to subject; (*fig: presentare*) to submit; **sottoporsi** *vr* to submit; **sottoporsi a** (*subire*) to undergo; **sotto'posto, a** *pp di* **sottoporre**.

sottos'critto, a *pp di* **sottoscrivere**.

sottos'crivere *vt* to sign // *vi*: **~ a** to

subscribe to; **sottoscrizi'one** *sf* signing; subscription.

sottosegre'tario *sm*: **~ di Stato** Under-Secretary of State (*Brit*), Assistant Secretary of State (*US*).

sotto'sopra *av* upside-down.

sotto'terra *av* underground.

sotto'titolo *sm* subtitle.

sotto'veste *sf* underskirt.

sotto'voce [sotto'votʃe] *av* in a low voice.

sot'trarre *vt* (*MAT*) to subtract, take away; **~ qn/qc a** (*togliere*) to remove sb/sth from; (*salvare*) to save o rescue sb/sth from; **~ qc a qn** (*rubare*) to steal sth from sb; **sottrarsi** *vr*: **sottrarsi a** (*sfuggire*) to escape; (*evitare*) to avoid; **sot'tratto, a** *pp di* **sottrarre**; **sottrazi'one** *sf* subtraction; removal.

sovi'etico, a, ci, che *ag* Soviet // *sm/f* Soviet citizen.

sovraccari'care *vt* to overload.

sovrannatu'rale *ag* = **soprannaturale**.

so'vrano, a *ag* sovereign; (*fig: sommo*) supreme // *sm/f* sovereign, monarch.

sovrap'porre *vt* to place on top of, put on top of.

sovras'tare *vi*: **~ a**, *vt* (*vallata, fiume*) to overhang; (*fig*) to hang over, threaten.

sovrinten'dente *sm/f* = **soprinten-dente**; **sovrinten'denza** *sf* = **soprintendenza**.

sovru'mano, a *ag* superhuman.

sovvenzi'one [sovven'tsjone] *sf* subsidy, grant.

sovver'sivo, a *ag* subversive.

'sozzo, a ['sottso] *ag* filthy, dirty.

S.p.A. *abbr* = **società per azioni**.

spac'care *vt* to split, break; (*legna*) to chop; **~rsi** *vr* to split, break; **spacca'tura** *sf* split.

spacci'are [spat'tʃare] *vt* (*vendere*) to sell (off); (*mettere in circolazione*) to circulate; (*droga*) to peddle, push; **~rsi** *vr*: **~rsi per** (*farsi credere*) to pass o.s. off as, pretend to be; **spaccia'tore, 'trice** *sm/f* (*di droga*) pusher; (*di denaro falso*) dealer; **'spaccio** *sm* (*di merce rubata, droga*): **spaccio (di)** trafficking (in); (*in denaro falso*): **spaccio (di)** passing (of); (*vendita*) sale; (*bottega*) shop.

'spacco, chi *sm* (*fenditura*) split, crack; (*strappo*) tear; (*di gonna*) slit.

spac'cone *sm/f* boaster, braggart.

'spada *sf* sword.

spae'sato, a *ag* disorientated, lost.

spa'ghetti [spa'getti] *smpl* (*CUC*) spaghetti *sg*.

'Spagna ['spaɲɲa] *sf*: **la ~** Spain; **spa'gnolo, a** *ag* Spanish // *sm/f* Spaniard // *sm* (*LING*) Spanish; **gli Spagnoli** the Spanish.

'spago, ghi sm string, twine.
spai'ato, a ag (calza, guanto) odd.
spalan'care vt, ~rsi vr to open wide.
spa'lare vt to shovel.
'spalla sf shoulder; (fig: TEATRO) stooge; ~e sfpl (dorso) back; spalleggi'are vt to back up, support.
spal'letta sf (parapetto) parapet.
spalli'era sf (di sedia etc) back; (di letto: da capo) head(board); (: da piedi) foot(board); (GINNASTICA) wall bars pl.
spal'mare vt to spread.
'spalti smpl (di stadio) terracing.
'spandere vt to spread; (versare) to pour (out); ~rsi vr to spread; 'spanto, a pp di spandere.
spa'rare vt to fire // vi (far fuoco) to fire; (tirare) to shoot; spara'tore sm gunman; spara'toria sf exchange of shots.
sparecchi'aro [sparek'kjare] vt: ~ (la tavola) to clear the table.
spa'reggio [spa'reddʒo] sm (SPORT) play-off.
'spargere ['spardʒere] vt (spargliare) lo scatter; (versare: vino) to spill; (: lacrime, sangue) to shed; (diffondere) to spread; (emanare) to give off (o out); ~rsi vr to spread; spargi'mento sm scattering, strewing; spilling; shedding; spargimento di sangue bloodshed.
spa'rire vi to disappear, vanish.
spar'lare vi: ~ di to run down, speak ill of.
'sparo sm shot.
sparpagli'are [sparpaʎ'ʎare] vt, ~rsi vr to scatter.
'sparso, a pp di spargere // ag scattered; (sciolto) loose.
spar'tire vt (eredità, bottino) to share out; (avversari) to separate.
sparti'traffico sm inv (AUT) central reservation (Brit), median (strip) (US).
spa'ruto, a ag (viso etc) haggard.
sparvi'ero sm (ZOOL) sparrowhawk.
spasi'mare vi to be in agony; ~ di fare (fig) to yearn to do; ~ per qn to be madly in love with sb.
'spasimo sm pang; 'spasmo sm (MED) spasm; spas'modico, a, ci, che ag (angoscioso) agonizing; (MED) spasmodic.
spassio'nato, a ag dispassionate, impartial.
'spasso sm (divertimento) amusement, enjoyment; andare a ~ to go out for a walk; essere a ~ (fig) to be out of work; mandare qn a ~ (fig) to give sb the sack.
spau'racchio [spau'rakkjo] sm scarecrow.
spau'rire vt to frighten, terrify.
spa'valdo, a ag arrogant, bold.
spaventa'passeri sm inv scarecrow.
spaven'tare vt to frighten, scare; ~rsi

vr to be frightened, be scared; to get a fright; spa'vento sm fear, fright; far spavento a qn to give sb a fright; spaven'toso, a ag frightening, terrible; (fig: fam) tremendous, fantastic.
spazien'tire [spattsjen'tire] vi (anche: ~rsi) to lose one's patience.
'spazio ['spattsjo] sm space; ~ aereo airspace; spazi'oso, a ag spacious.
spazzaca'mino [spattsaka'mino] sm chimney sweep.
spaz'zare [spat'tsare] vt to sweep; (foglie etc) to sweep up; (cacciare) to sweep away; spazza'tura sf sweepings pl; (immondizia) rubbish; spaz'zino sm street sweeper.
'spazzola ['spattsola] sf brush; ~ per abiti clothesbrush; ~ da capelli hairbrush; spazzo'lare vt to brush; spazzo'lino sm (small) brush; spazzolino da denti toothbrush.
specchi'arsi [spek'kjarsi] vr to look at o.s. in a mirror; (riflettersi) to be mirrored, be reflected.
'specchio ['spekkjo] sm mirror.
speci'ale [spe'tʃale] ag special; specia'lista, i, e sm/f specialist; specialità sf inv speciality; (branca di studio) special field, speciality; specializ'zarsi vr: specializzarsi (in) to specialize (in); special'mente av especially, particularly.
'specie ['spetʃe] sf inv (BIOL, BOT, ZOOL) species inv; (tipo) kind, sort // av especially, particularly; una ~ di a kind of; fare ~ a qn to surprise sb; la ~ umana mankind.
specifi'care [spetʃifi'kare] vt to specify, state.
spe'cifico, a, ci, che [spe'tʃifiko] ag specific.
specu'lare vi: ~ su (COMM) to speculate in; (sfruttare) to exploit; (meditare) to speculate on; speculazi'one sf speculation.
spe'dire vt to send; spedizi'one sf sending; (collo) consignment; (scientifica etc) expedition.
'spegnere ['speɲɲere] vt (fuoco, sigaretta) to put out, extinguish; (apparecchio elettrico) to turn o switch off; (gas) to turn off; (fig: suoni, passioni) to stifle; (debito) to extinguish; ~rsi vr to go out; to go off; (morire) to pass away.
spel'lare vt (scuoiare) to skin; (scorticare) to graze; ~rsi vr to peel.
'spendere vt to spend.
spen'nare vt to pluck.
spensie'rato a ag carefree.
'spento, a pp di spegnere // ag (suono) muffled; (colore) dull; (sigaretta) out; (civiltà, vulcano) extinct.
spe'ranza [spe'rantsa] sf hope.
spe'rare vt to hope for // vi: ~ in to trust in; ~ che/di fare to hope that/to do; lo

spero, spero di sì I hope so.

sper'duto, a *ag* (*isolato*) out-of-the-way; (*persona: smarrita, a disagio*) lost.

spergi'uro, a |sper'dʒuro| *sm/f* perjurer // *sm* perjury.

sperimen'tale *ag* experimental.

sperimen'tare *vt* to experiment with, test; (*fig*) to test, put to the test.

'sperma, i *sm* (*BIOL*) sperm.

spe'rone *sm* spur.

sperpe'rare *vt* to squander.

'spesa *sf* (*somma di denaro*) expense; (*costo*) cost; (*acquisto*) purchase; (*fam: acquisto del cibo quotidiano*) shopping; ~e *sfpl* expenses; (*COMM*) costs; charges; **fare la** ~ to do the shopping; a ~e **di** (*a carico di*) at the expense of; ~e **generali** overheads; ~e **postali** postage *sg*; ~e **di viaggio** travelling expenses.

'speso, a *pp di* **spendere**.

'spesso, a *ag* (*fitto*) thick; (*frequente*) frequent // *av* often; ~e **volte** frequently, often.

spes'sore *sm* thickness.

spet'tabile *ag* (*abbr:* **Spett.**: *in lettere*): ~ **ditta X** Messrs X and Co.

spet'tacolo *sm* (*rappresentazione*) performance, show; (*vista, scena*) sight; **dare** ~ **di sé** to make an exhibition *o* a spectacle of o.s.; **spettaco'loso, a** *ag* spectacular.

spet'tare *vi:* ~ **a** (*decisione*) to be up to; (*stipendio*) to be due to; **spetta a te decidere** it's up to you to decide.

spetta'tore, 'trice *sm/f* (*CINEMA, TEATRO*) member of the audience; (*di avvenimento*) onlooker, witness.

spetti'nare *vt:* ~ **qn** to ruffle sb's hair; ~rsi *vr* to get one's hair in a mess.

'spettro *sm* (*fantasma*) spectre; (*FISICA*) spectrum.

'spezie |'spɛttsje| *sfpl* (*CUC*) spices.

spez'zare |spet'tsare| *vt* (*rompere*) to break; (*fig: interrompere*) to break up; ~rsi *vr* to break.

spezza'tino |spettsa'tino| *sm* (*CUC*) stew.

spezzet'tare |spettset'tare| *vt* to break up (*o chop*) into small pieces.

'spia *sf* spy; (*confidente della polizia*) informer; (*ELETTR*) indicating light; warning light; (*fessura*) peep-hole; (*fig: sintomo*) sign, indication.

spia'cente |spja'tʃɛnte| *ag* sorry; **essere** ~ **di qc/di fare qc** to be sorry about sth/ for doing sth.

spia'cevole |spja'tʃevole| *ag* unpleasant, disagreeable.

spi'aggia, ge |'spjaddʒa| *sf* beach.

spia'nare *vt* (*terreno*) to level, make level; (*edificio*) to raze to the ground; (*pasta*) to roll out; (*rendere liscio*) to smooth (out).

spi'ano *sm:* **a tutto** ~ (*lavorare*) non-stop, without a break; (*spendere*) lavishly.

spian'tato, a *ag* penniless, ruined.

spi'are *vt* to spy on; (*occasione etc*) to watch *o* wait for.

spi'azzo |'spjattso| *sm* open space; (*radura*) clearing.

spic'care *vt* (*assegno, mandato di cattura*) to issue // *vi* (*risaltare*) to stand out; ~ **il volo** to fly off; (*fig*) to spread one's wings; ~ **un balzo** to leap; **spic'cato, a** *ag* (*marcato*) marked, strong; (*notevole*) remarkable.

'spicchio |'spikkjo| *sm* (*di agrumi*) segment; (*di aglio*) clove; (*parte*) piece, slice.

spicci'arsi |spit'tʃarsi| *vr* to hurry up.

'spicciolo, a |'spittʃolo| *ag:* **moneta** ~a, ~i *smpl* (small) change.

'spicco, chi *sm:* **di** ~ outstanding; (*tema*) main, principal; **fare** ~ to stand out.

spi'edo *sm* (*CUC*) spit.

spie'gare *vt* (*far capire*) to explain; (*tovaglia*) to unfold; (*vele*) to unfurl; ~rsi *vr* to explain o.s., make o.s. clear; ~ **qc a qn** to explain sth to sb; **il problema si spiega** one can understand the problem; **spiegazi'one** *sf* explanation.

spiegaz'zare |spjegat'tsare| *vt* to crease, crumple.

spie'tato, a *ag* ruthless, pitiless.

spiffe'rare *vt* (*fam*) to blurt out, blab.

'spiga, ghe *sf* (*BOT*) ear.

spigli'ato, a |spiʎ'ʎato| *ag* self-possessed, self-confident.

'spigolo *sm* corner; (*MAT*) edge.

'spilla *sf* brooch; (*da cravatta, cappello*) pin.

spil'lare *vt* (*vino, fig*) to tap; ~ **denaro/ notizie a qn** to tap sb for money/ information.

'spillo *sm* pin; (*spilla*) brooch; ~ **di sicurezza** *o* **da balia** safety pin; ~ **di sicurezza** (*MIL*) (safety) pin.

spi'lorcio, a, ci, ce |spi'lortʃo| *ag* mean, stingy.

'spina *sf* (*BOT*) thorn; (*ZOOL*) spine, prickle; (*di pesce*) bone; (*ELETTR*) plug; (*di botte*) bunghole; **birra alla** ~ draught beer; ~ **dorsale** (*ANAT*) backbone.

spi'nacio |spi'natʃo| *sm* spinach; (*CUC*): ~i spinach *sg*.

spi'nale *ag* (*ANAT*) spinal.

'spingere |'spindʒere| *vt* to push; (*condurre: anche fig*) to drive; (*stimolare*): ~ **qn a fare** to urge *o* press sb to do; ~rsi *vr* (*inoltrarsi*) to push on, carry on; ~rsi **troppo lontano** (*anche fig*) to go too far.

spi'noso, a *ag* thorny, prickly.

'spinto, a *pp di* **spingere** // *sf* (*urto*) push; (*FISICA*) thrust; (*fig: stimolo*) incentive, spur; (*: appoggio*) string-pulling *q*; **dare una** ~a **a qn** (*fig*) to pull strings for sb.

spio'naggio |spio'naddʒo| *sm* espionage,

spying.

spi'overe *vi* (*scorrere*) to flow down; (*ricadere*) to hang down, fall.

'spira *sf* coil.

spi'raglio [spi'raʎʎo] *sm* (*fessura*) chink, narrow opening; (*raggio di luce, fig*) glimmer, gleam.

spi'rale *sf* spiral; (*contraccettivo*) coil; a ~ spiral(-shaped).

spi'rare *vi* (*vento*) to blow; (*morire*) to expire, pass away.

spiri'tato, a *ag* possessed; (*fig: persona, espressione*) wild.

spiri'tismo *sm* spiritualism.

'spirito *sm* (*REL, CHIM, disposizione d'animo, di legge etc, fantasma*) spirit; (*pensieri, intelletto*) mind; (*arguzia*) wit; (*umorismo*) humour, wit; lo S~ Santo the Holy Spirit o Ghost.

spirito'saggine [spirito'saddʒine] *sf* witticism; (*peg*) wisecrack.

spiri'toso, a *ag* witty.

spiritu'ale *ag* spiritual.

'splendere *vi* to shine.

'splendido, a *ag* splendid; (*splendente*) shining; (*sfarzoso*) magnificent, splendid.

splen'dore *sm* splendour; (*luce intensa*) brilliance, brightness.

spodes'tare *vt* to deprive of power; (*sovrano*) to depose.

'spoglia ['spoʎʎa] *sf vedi* **spoglio**.

spogli'are [spoʎ'ʎare] *vt* (*svestire*) to undress; (*privare, fig: depredare*): ~ qn di qc to deprive sb of sth; (*togliere ornamenti: anche fig*): ~ qn/qc di to strip sb/sth of; ~rsi *vr* to undress, strip; ~rsi di (*ricchezze etc*) to deprive o.s. of, give up; (*pregiudizi*) to rid o.s. of; **spoglia'toio** *sm* dressing room; (*di scuola etc*) cloakroom; (*SPORT*) changing room; **'spoglio, a** *ag* (*pianta, terreno*) bare; (*privo*) spoglio di stripped of; lacking in, without // *sm* (*di voti*) counting // *sf* (*ZOOL*) skin, hide; (: *di rettile*) slough; **'spoglie** *sfpl* (*salma*) remains; (*preda*) spoils, booty *sg*.

'spola *sf* shuttle; (*bobina di filo*) cop; fare la ~ (fra) to go to and fro o shuttle (between).

spol'pare *vt* to strip the flesh off.

spolve'rare *vt* (*anche CUC*) to dust; (*con spazzola*) to brush; (*con battipanni*) to beat; (*fig*) to polish off // *vi* to dust.

'sponda *sf* (*di fiume*) bank; (*di mare, lago*) shore; (*bordo*) edge.

spon'taneo, a *ag* spontaneous; (*persona*) unaffected, natural.

spopo'lare *vt* to depopulate // *vi* (*attirare folla*) to draw the crowds; ~rsi *vr* to become depopulated.

spor'care *vt* to dirty, make dirty; (*fig*) to sully, soil; ~rsi *vr* to get dirty.

spor'cizia [spor'tʃittsja] *sf* (*stato*) dirtiness; (*sudiciume*) dirt, filth; (*cosa sporca*) dirt *q*, something dirty; (*fig: cosa oscena*) obscenity.

'sporco, a, chi, che *ag* dirty, filthy.

spor'genza [spor'dʒɛntsa] *sf* projection.

'sporgere ['spɔrdʒere] *vt* to put out, stretch out // *vi* (*venire in fuori*) to stick out; ~rsi *vr* to lean out; ~ querela contro qn (*DIR*) to take legal action against sb.

sport *sm inv* sport.

'sporta *sf* shopping bag.

spor'tello *sm* (*di treno, auto etc*) door; (*di banca, ufficio*) window, counter; ~ automatico (*BANCA*) cash dispenser, automated telling machine.

spor'tivo, a *ag* (*gara, giornale*) sports *cpd*; (*persona*) sporty; (*abito*) casual; (*spirito, atteggiamento*) sporting.

'sporto, a *pp di* **sporgere**.

'sposa *sf* bride; (*moglie*) wife.

sposa'lizio [spoza'littsjo] *sm* wedding.

spo'sare *vt* to marry; (*fig: idea, fede*) to espouse; ~rsi *vr* to get married, marry; ~rsi con qn to marry sb, get married to sb; **spo'sato, a** *ag* married.

'sposo *sm* (*bride*)groom; (*marito*) husband; gli ~i *smpl* the newlyweds.

spos'sato, a *ag* exhausted, weary.

spos'tare *vt* to move, shift; (*cambiare: orario*) to change; ~rsi *vr* to move.

'spranga, ghe *sf* (*sbarra*) bar.

'sprazzo ['sprattso] *sm* (*di sole etc*) flash; (*fig: di gioia etc*) burst.

spre'care *vt* to waste; ~rsi *vr* (*persona*) to waste one's energy; **'spreco** *sm* waste.

spre'gevole [spre'dʒevole] *ag* contemptible, despicable.

spregiudi'cato, a [spredʒudi'kato] *ag* unprejudiced, unbiased; (*peg*) unscrupulous.

'spremere *vt* to squeeze.

spre'muta *sf* fresh juice; ~ d'arancia fresh orange juice.

sprez'zante [spret'tsante] *ag* scornful, contemptuous.

sprigio'nare [spridʒo'nare] *vt* to give off, emit; ~rsi *vr* to emanate; (*uscire con impeto*) to burst out.

spriz'zare [sprit'tsare] *vt, vi* to spurt; ~ gioia/salute to be bursting with joy/health.

sprofon'dare *vi* to sink; (*casa*) to collapse; (*suolo*) to give way, subside; ~rsi *vr*: ~rsi in (*poltrona*) to sink into; (*fig*) to become immersed o absorbed in.

spro'nare *vt* to spur (on).

'sprone *sm* (*sperone, fig*) spur.

sproporzio'nato, a [sproportsjo'nato] *ag* disproportionate, out of all proportion.

sproporzi'one [spropor'tsjone] *sf* disproportion.

spropositato, a *ag* (*lettera, discorso*) full of mistakes; (*fig: costo*) excessive, enormous.

spro'posito *sm* blunder; a ~ at the wrong time; (*rispondere, parlare*) irrelevantly.

sprovve'duto, a *ag* inexperienced, naïve.

sprov'visto, a *ag* (*mancante*): ~ di lacking in, without; alla ~a unawares.

spruz'zare [sprut'tsare] *vt* (*a nebulizzazione*) to spray; (*aspergere*) to sprinkle; (*inzaccherare*) to splash; **'spruzzo** *sm* spray; splash.

'spugna ['spuɲɲa] *sf* (*ZOOL*) sponge; (*tessuto*) towelling; **spu'gnoso, a** *ag* spongy.

'spuma *sf* (*schiuma*) foam; (*bibita*) mineral water.

spu'mante *sm* sparkling wine.

spumeggi'ante [spumed'dʒante] *ag* (*birra*) foaming; (*vino, fig*) sparkling.

spu'mone *sm* (*CUC*) mousse.

spun'tare *vt* (*coltello*) to break the point of; (*capelli*) to trim // *vi* (*uscire: germogli*) to sprout; (: *capelli*) to begin to grow; (: *denti*) to come through; (*apparire*) to appear (suddenly); ~rsi *vr* to become blunt, lose its point; **spuntarla** (*fig*) to make it, win through.

spun'tino *sm* snack.

'spunto *sm* (*TEATRO, MUS*) cue; (*fig*) starting point; dare lo ~ a (*fig*) to give rise to.

spur'gare *vt* (*fogna*) to clean, clear; ~rsi *vr* (*MED*) to expectorate.

spu'tare *vt* to spit out; (*fig*) to belch (out) // *vi* to spit; **'sputo** *sm* spittle *q*, spit *q*.

'squadra *sf* (*strumento*) (set) square; (*gruppo*) team, squad; (*di operai*) gang, squad; (*MIL*) squad; (: *AER, NAUT*) squadron; (*SPORT*) team; lavoro a ~e teamwork.

squa'drare *vt* to square, make square; (*osservare*) to look at closely.

squa'driglia [skwa'driʎʎa] *sf* (*AER*) flight; (*NAUT*) squadron.

squa'drone *sm* squadron.

squagli'arsi [skwaʎ'ʎarsi] *vr* to melt; (*fig*) to sneak off.

squa'lifica *sf* disqualification.

squalifi'care *vt* to disqualify.

'squallido, a *ag* wretched, bleak.

squal'lore *sm* wretchedness, bleakness.

'squalo *sm* shark.

'squama *sf* scale; **squa'mare** *vt* to scale; squamarsi *vr* to flake *o* peel (off).

squarcia'gola [skwartʃa'gola]: a ~ *av* at the top of one's voice.

squar'tare *vt* to quarter, cut up.

squattri'nato, a *ag* penniless.

squili'brare *vt* to unbalance; **squili'brato, a** *ag* (*PSIC*) unbalanced; **squi'librio** *sm* (*differenza, sbilancio*) imbalance; (*PSIC*) unbalance.

squil'lante *ag* shrill, sharp.

squil'lare *vi* (*campanello, telefono*) to ring (out); (*tromba*) to blare; **'squillo** *sm* ring, ringing *q*; blare; **ragazza** *f* **squillo** *inv* call girl.

squi'sito, a *ag* exquisite; (*cibo*) delicious; (*persona*) delightful.

squit'tire *vi* (*uccello*) to squawk; (*topo*) to squeak.

sradi'care *vt* to uproot; (*fig*) to eradicate.

sragio'nare [zradʒo'nare] *vi* to talk nonsense, rave.

srego'lato, a *ag* (*senza ordine: vita*) disorderly; (*smodato*) immoderate; (*dissoluto*) dissolute.

S.r.l. *abbr* = **società a responsabilità limitata.**

'stabile *ag* stable, steady; (*tempo: non variabile*) settled; (*TEATRO: compagnia*) resident // *sm* (*edificio*) building.

stabili'mento *sm* (*edificio*) establishment; (*fabbrica*) plant, factory.

stabi'lire *vt* to establish; (*fissare: prezzi, data*) to fix; (*decidere*) to decide; ~rsi *vr* (*prendere dimora*) to settle.

stac'care *vt* (*levare*) to detach, remove; (*separare: anche fig*) to separate, divide; (*strappare*) to tear off (*o* out); (*scandire: parole*) to pronounce clearly; (*SPORT*) to leave behind; ~rsi *vr* (*bottone etc*) to come off; (*scostarsi*): ~rsi (*da*) to move away (from); (*fig: separarsi*): ~rsi da to leave; non ~ gli occhi da qn not to take one's eyes off sb.

'stadio *sm* (*SPORT*) stadium; (*periodo, fase*) phase, stage.

'staffa *sf* (*di sella, TECN*) stirrup; perdere le ~e (*fig*) to fly off the handle.

staf'fetta *sf* (*messo*) dispatch rider; (*SPORT*) relay race.

stagio'nale [stadʒo'nale] *ag* seasonal.

stagio'nare [stadʒo'nare] *vt* (*legno*) to season; (*formaggi, vino*) to mature.

stagi'one [sta'dʒone] *sf* season; alta/ bassa ~ high/low season.

stagli'arsi [staʎ'ʎarsi] *vr* to stand out, be silhouetted.

sta'gnare [staɲ'ɲare] *vt* (*vaso, tegame*) to tin-plate; (*barca, botte*) to make watertight; (*sangue*) to stop // *vi* to stagnate.

'stagno, a ['staɲɲo] *ag* watertight; (*a tenuta d'aria*) airtight // *sm* (*acquitrino*) pond; (*CHIM*) tin.

sta'gnola [staɲ'ɲɔla] *sf* tinfoil.

'stalla *sf* (*per bovini*) cowshed; (*per cavalli*) stable.

stal'lone *sm* stallion.

sta'mani, stamat'tina *av* this morning.

'stampa *sf* (*TIP, FOT: tecnica*) printing; (*impressione, copia fotografica*) print; (*insieme di quotidiani, giornalisti etc*) press; ~e *sfpl* printed matter.

stam'pante *sf* (*INFORM*) printer.

stam'pare *vt* to print; (*pubblicare*) to

publish; (*coniare*) to strike, coin; (*imprimere: anche fig*) to impress.

stampa'tello *sm* block letters *pl*.

stam'pella *sf* crutch.

'stampo *sm* mould; (*fig: indole*) type, kind, sort.

sta'nare *vt* to drive out.

stan'care *vt* to tire, make tired; (*annoiare*) to bore; (*infastidire*) to annoy; ~**rsi** *vr* to get tired, tire o.s. out; ~**rsi** (**di**) to grow weary (of), grow tired (of).

stan'chezza [stan'kettsa] *sf* tiredness, fatigue.

stanco, a, chi, che *ag* tired; ~ **di** tired of, fed up with.

'stanga, ghe *sm* bar; (*di carro*) shaft.

stan'gata *sf* (*colpo: anche fig*) blow; (*cattivo risultato*) poor result; (*CALCIO*) shot.

sta'notte *av* tonight; (*notte passata*) last night.

'stante *prep*: a sé ~ (*appartamento, casa*) independent, separate.

stan'tio, a, 'tii, 'tie *ag* stale; (*burro*) rancid; (*fig*) old.

stan'tuffo *sm* piston.

'stanza ['stantsa] *sf* room; (*POESIA*) stanza; ~ **da letto** bedroom.

stanzi'are [stan'tsjare] *vt* to allocate.

stap'pare *vt* to uncork; to uncap.

'stare *vi* (*restare in un luogo*) to stay, remain; (*abitare*) to stay, live; (*essere situato*) to be, be situated; (*anche: ~ in piedi*) to be, stand; (*essere, trovarsi*) to be; (*dipendere*): se stesse in me if it were up to me, if it depended on me; (*seguito da gerundio*): sta studiando he's studying; **starci** (*esserci spazio*): nel baule non ci sta più niente there's no more room in the boot; (*accettare*) to accept; ci stai? is that okay with you?; ~ a (*attenersi a*) to follow, stick to; (*seguito dall'infinito*): stiamo a discutere we're talking; (*toccare a*): sta a te giocare it's your turn to play; ~ per fare qc to be about to do sth; come sta? how are you?; io sto bene/male I'm very well/not very well; ~ a qn (*abiti etc*) to fit sb; queste scarpe mi stanno strette these shoes are tight for me; il rosso ti sta bene red suits you.

starnu'tire *vi* to sneeze; **star'nuto** *sm* sneeze.

sta'sera *av* this evening, tonight.

sta'tale *ag* state *cpd*; government *cpd* // *sm/f* state employee, local authority employee; (*nell'amministrazione*) ≈ civil servant.

sta'tista, i *sm* statesman.

sta'tistica *sf* statistics *sg*.

'stato, a *pp di* **essere, stare** // *sm* (*condizione*) state, condition; (*POL*) state; (*DIR*) status; **essere in ~ d'accusa** (*DIR*) to be committed for trial; ~ **d'assedio/**

d'emergenza state of siege/emergency; ~ **civile** (*AMM*) marital status; ~ **maggiore** (*MIL*) staff; **gli S~i Uniti (d'America)**, the United States (of America).

'statua *sf* statue.

statuni'tense *ag* United States *cpd*, of the United States.

sta'tura *sf* (*ANAT*) height, stature; (*fig*) stature.

sta'tuto *sm* (*DIR*) statute; constitution.

sta'volta *av* this time.

stazio'nario, a [stattsjo'narjo] *ag* stationary; (*fig*) unchanged.

stazi'one [stat'tsjone] *sf* station; (*balneare, termale*) resort; ~ **degli autobus** bus station; ~ **balneare** seaside resort; ~ **ferroviaria** railway (*Brit*) o railroad (*US*) station; ~ **invernale** winter sports resort; ~ **di polizia** police station (*in small town*); ~ **di servizio** service o petrol (*Brit*) o filling station.

'stecca, che *sf* stick; (*di ombrello*) rib; (*di sigarette*) carton; (*MED*) splint; (*stonatura*): **fare una ~** to sing (o play) a wrong note.

stec'cato *sm* fence.

stec'chito, a [stek'kito] *ag* dried up; (*persona*) skinny; **lasciar ~ qn** (*fig*) to leave sb flabbergasted; **morto ~** stone dead.

'stella *sf* star; ~ **alpina** (*BOT*) edelweiss; ~ **di mare** (*ZOOL*) starfish.

'stelo *sm* stem; (*asta*) rod; **lampada a ~** standard lamp.

'stemma, i *sm* coat of arms.

stempe'rare *vt* to dilute; to dissolve; (*colori*) to mix.

sten'dardo *sm* standard.

'stendere *vt* (*braccia, gambe*) to stretch (out); (*tovaglia*) to spread (out); (*bucato*) to hang out; (*mettere a giacere*) to lay (down); (*spalmare: colore*) to spread; (*mettere per iscritto*) to draw up; ~**rsi** *vr* (*coricarsi*) to stretch out, lie down; (*estendersi*) to extend, stretch.

stenodatti'lografo, a *sm/f* shorthand typist (*Brit*), stenographer (*US*).

stenogra'fare *vt* to take down in shorthand; **stenogra'fia** *sf* shorthand.

sten'tare *vi*: ~ **a fare** to find it hard to do, have difficulty doing.

'stento *sm* (*fatica*) difficulty; ~**i** *smpl* (*privazioni*) hardship *sg*, privation *sg*; **a ~** *av* with difficulty, barely.

'sterco *sm* dung.

'stereo('fonico, a, ci, che) *ag* stereo(phonic).

'sterile *ag* sterile; (*terra*) barren; (*fig*) futile, fruitless; **sterilità** *sf* sterility.

steriliz'zare [sterilid'dzare] *vt* to sterilize; **sterilizzazi'one** *sf* sterilization.

ster'lina *sf* pound (sterling).

stermi'nare *vt* to exterminate, wipe out.

stermi'nato, a *ag* immense; endless.

ster'minio *sm* extermination, destruction.

'sterno *sm* (ANAT) breastbone.

ster'zare [ster'tsare] *vt, vi* (AUT) to steer; **'sterzo** *sm* steering; (*volante*) steering wheel.

'steso, a *pp di* **stendere**.

'stesso, a *ag* same; (*rafforzativo: in persona, proprio*): **il re ~** the king himself *o* in person // *pronome:* **lo(la) ~(a)** the same (one); **i suoi ~i avversari lo ammirano** even his enemies admire him; **fa lo ~** it doesn't matter; **per me è lo ~** it's all the same to me, it doesn't matter to me; *vedi* **io, tu** *etc*.

ste'sura *sf* drafting *q*, drawing up *q*; draft.

'stigma, i *sm* stigma.

'stigmate *sfpl* (REL) stigmata.

sti'lare *vt* to draw up, draft.

'stile *sm* style; **sti'lista, i** *sm* designer.

still'lare *vi* (*trasudare*) to ooze; (*gocciolare*) to drip; **stilli'cidio** *sm* (*fig*) continual pestering (*o* moaning *etc*).

stilo'grafica, che *sf* (*anche:* **penna ~**) fountain pen.

'stima *sf* esteem; valuation; assessment, estimate.

sti'mare *vt* (*persona*) to esteem, hold in high regard; (*terreno, casa etc*) to value; (*stabilire in misura approssimativa*) to estimate, assess; (*ritenere*): **~ che** to consider that; **~rsi fortunato** to consider o.s. (to be) lucky.

stimo'lare *vt* to stimulate; (*incitare*): **~ qn (a fare)** to spur sb on (to do).

'stimolo *sm* (*anche fig*) stimulus.

'stinco, chi *sm* shin; shinbone.

'stingere ['stindʒere] *vt, vi* (*anche:* **~rsi**) to fade; **'stinto, a** *pp di* **stingere**.

sti'pare *vt* to cram, pack; **~rsi** *vr* (*accalcarsi*) to crowd, throng.

sti'pendio *sm* salary.

'stipite *sm* (*di porta, finestra*) jamb.

stipu'lare *vt* (*redigere*) to draw up.

sti'rare *vt* (*abito*) to iron; (*distendere*) to stretch; (*strappare: muscolo*) to strain; **~rsi** *vr* to stretch (o.s.); **stira'tura** *sf* ironing.

'stirpe *sf* birth, stock; descendants *pl*.

stiti'chezza [stiti'kettsa] *sf* constipation.

'stitico, a, ci, che *ag* constipated.

'stiva *sf* (*di nave*) hold.

sti'vale *sm* boot.

'stizza ['stittsa] *sf* anger, vexation; **stiz'zirsi** *vr* to lose one's temper; **stiz'zoso, a** *ag* (*persona*) quick-tempered, irascible; (*risposta*) angry.

stocca'fisso *sm* stockfish, dried cod.

stoc'cata *sf* (*colpo*) stab, thrust; (*fig*) gibe, cutting remark.

'stoffa *sf* material, fabric; (*fig*): **aver la ~ di** to have the makings of.

'stola *sf* stole.

'stolto, a *ag* stupid, foolish.

'stomaco, chi *sm* stomach; **dare di ~** to vomit, be sick.

sto'nare *vt* to sing (*o* play) out of tune // *vi* to be out of tune, sing (*o* play) out of tune; (*fig*) to be out of place, jar; (: *colori*) to clash; **stona'tura** *sf* (*suono*) false note.

stop *sm inv* (TEL) stop; (AUT: *cartello*) stop sign; (: *fanalino d'arresto*) brakelight.

'stoppa *sf* tow.

'stoppia *sf* (AGR) stubble.

stop'pino *sm* wick; (*miccia*) fuse.

'storcere ['stortʃere] *vt* to twist; **~rsi** *vr* to writhe, twist; **~ il naso** (*fig*) to turn up one's nose; **~rsi la caviglia** to twist one's ankle.

stor'dire *vt* (*intontire*) to stun, daze; **~rsi** *vr*: **~rsi col bere** to dull one's senses with drink; **stor'dito, a** *ag* stunned; (*sventato*) scatterbrained, heedless.

'storia *sf* (*scienza, avvenimenti*) history; (*racconto, bugia*) story; (*faccenda, questione*) business *q*; (*pretesto*) excuse, pretext; **~e** *sfpl* (*smancerie*) fuss *sg*; **'storico, a, ci, che** *ag* historic(al) *o* historian.

stori'one *sm* (ZOOL) sturgeon.

stor'mire *vi* to rustle.

'stormo *sm* (*di uccelli*) flock.

stor'nare *vt* (COMM) to transfer.

'storno *sm* starling.

storpi'are *vt* to cripple, maim; (*fig: parole*) to mangle; (: *significato*) to twist.

'storpio, a *ag* crippled, maimed.

'storto, a *pp di* **storcere** *ag* (*chiodo*) twisted, bent; (*gamba, quadro*) crooked; (*fig: ragionamento*) false, wrong // *sf* (*distorsione*) sprain, twist; (*recipiente*) retort.

sto'viglie [sto'viʎʎe] *sfpl* dishes *pl*, crockery.

'strabico, a, ci, che *ag* squint-eyed; (*occhi*) squint.

stra'bismo *sm* squinting.

stra'carico, a, chi, che *ag* overloaded.

stracci'are [strat'tʃare] *vt* to tear.

'straccio, a, ci, ce ['strattʃo] *ag:* **carta ~a** waste paper // *sm* rag; (*per pulire*) cloth, duster; **stracci'vendolo** *sm* ragman.

stra'cotto, a *ag* overcooked // *sm* (CUC) beef stew.

'strada *sf* road; (*di città*) street; (*cammino, via, fig*) way; **farsi ~** (*fig*) to do well for o.s.; **essere fuori ~** (*fig*) to be on the wrong track; **~ facendo** on the way; **~ senza uscita** dead end; **stra'dale** *ag* road *cpd*.

strafalci'one [strafal'tʃone] *sm* blunder, howler.

stra'fare *vi* to overdo it; **stra'fatto, a** *pp di* **strafare**.

strafot'tente *ag:* **è ~** he doesn't give a

damn, he couldn't care less.

'**strage** ['stradʒe] *sf* massacre, slaughter.

stralu'nato, a *ag* (*occhi*) rolling; (*persona*) beside o.s., very upset.

stramaz'zare [stramat'tsare] *vi* to fall heavily.

'**strambo, a** *ag* strange, queer.

strampa'lato, a *ag* odd, eccentric.

stra'nezza [stra'nettsa] *sf* strangeness.

strango'lare *vt* to strangle; ~**rsi** *vr* to choke.

strani'ero, a *ag* foreign // *sm/f* foreigner.

'**strano, a** *ag* strange, odd.

straordi'nario, a *ag* extraordinary; (*treno etc*) special // *sm* (*lavoro*) overtime.

strapaz'zare [strapat'tsare] *vt* to ill-treat; ~**rsi** *vr* to tire o.s. out, overdo things; **stra'pazzo** *sm* strain, fatigue; **da strapazzo** (*fig*) third-rate.

strapi'ombo *sm* overhanging rock; **a** ~ overhanging.

strapo'tere *sm* excessive power.

strap'pare *vt* (*gen*) to tear, rip; (*pagina etc*) to tear off, tear out; (*sradicare*) to pull up; (*togliere*): ~ **qc a qn** to snatch sth from sb; (*fig*) to wrest sth from sb; ~**rsi** *vr* (*lacerarsi*) to rip, tear; (*rompersi*) to break; ~**rsi un muscolo** to tear a muscle; '**strappo** *sm* pull, tug; tear, rip; **fare uno strappo alla regola** to make an exception to the rule; **strappo muscolare** torn muscle.

strapun'tino *sm* jump *o* foldaway seat.

strari'pare *vi* to overflow.

strasci'care [straʃʃi'kare] *vt* to trail; (*piedi*) to drag; ~ **le parole** to drawl.

'**strascico, chi** ['straʃʃiko] *sm* (*di abito*) train; (*conseguenza*) after-effect.

strata'gemma, i [strata'dʒemma] *sm* stratagem.

strate'gia, 'gie [strate'dʒia] *sf* strategy; **stra'tegico, a, ci, che** *ag* strategic.

'**strato** *sm* layer; (*rivestimento*) coat, coating; (*GEO, fig*) stratum; (*METEOR*) stratus.

stratos'fera *sf* stratosphere.

strava'gante *ag* odd, eccentric; **strava'ganza** *sf* eccentricity.

stra'vecchio, a [stra'vekkjo] *ag* very old.

stra'vizio [stra'vittsjo] *sm* excess.

stra'volgere [stra'vɔldʒere] *vt* (*volto*) to contort; (*fig: animo*) to trouble deeply; (: *verità*) to twist, distort; **stra'volto, a** *pp di* **stravolgere.**

strazi'are [strat'tsjare] *vt* to torture, torment; '**strazio** *sm* torture; (*fig: cosa fatta male*): **essere uno** ~ to be appalling.

'**strega, ghe** *sf* witch.

stre'gare *vt* to bewitch.

stre'gone *sm* (*mago*) wizard; (*di tribù*) witch doctor.

'**stregua** *sf*: **alla** ~ **di** by the same standard as.

stre'mare *vt* to exhaust.

'**stremo** *sm* very end; **essere allo** ~ to be at the end of one's tether.

'**strenna** *sf* Christmas present.

'**strenuo, a** *ag* brave, courageous.

strepi'toso, a *ag* clamorous, deafening; (*fig: successo*) resounding.

stres'sante *ag* stressful.

'**stretta** *sf vedi* **stretto.**

stretta'mente *av* tightly; (*rigorosamente*) strictly.

stret'tezza [stret'tettsa] *sf* narrowness; ~**e** *sfpl* poverty *sg*, straitened circumstances.

'**stretto, a** *pp di* **stringere** // *ag* (*corridoio, limiti*) narrow; (*gonna, scarpe, nodo, curva*) tight; (*intimo: parente, amico*) close; (*rigoroso: osservanza*) strict; (*preciso: significato*) precise, exact // *sm* (*braccio di mare*) strait // *sf* (*di mano*) grasp; (*finanziaria*) squeeze; (*fig: dolore, turbamento*) pang; **a denti** ~**i** with clenched teeth; **lo** ~ **necessario** the bare minimum; **una** ~**a di mano** a handshake; **essere allo** ~ **c** to have one's back to the wall; **stret'toia** *sf* bottleneck; (*fig*) tricky situation.

stri'ato, a *ag* streaked.

'**stridere** *vi* (*porta*) to squeak; (*animale*) to screech, shriek; (*colori*) to clash; '**strido,** *pl*(*f*) **strida** *sm* screech, shriek; **stri'dore** *sm* screeching, shrieking; '**stridulo, a** *ag* shrill.

stril'lare *vt, vi* to scream, shriek; '**strillo** *sm* scream, shriek.

stril'lone *sm* newspaper seller.

strimin'zito, a [strimin'tsito] *ag* (*misero*) shabby; (*molto magro*) skinny.

strimpel'lare *vt* (*MUS*) to strum.

'**stringa, ghe** *sf* lace.

strin'gato, a *ag* (*fig*) concise.

'**stringere** ['strindʒere] *vt* (*avvicinare due cose*) to press (together), squeeze (together); (*tenere stretto*) to hold tight, clasp, clutch; (*pugno, mascella, denti*) to clench; (*labbra*) to compress; (*avvitare*) to tighten; (*abito*) to take in; (*sog: scarpe*) to pinch, be tight for; (*fig: concludere: patto*) to make; (: *accelerare: passo, tempo*) to quicken // *vi* (*essere stretto*) to be tight; (*tempo: incalzare*) to be pressing; ~**rsi** *vr* (*accostarsi*): ~**rsi a** to press o.s. up against; ~ **la mano a qn** to shake sb's hand; ~ **gli occhi** to screw up one's eyes.

'**striscia, sce** ['striʃʃa] *sf* (*di carta, tessuto etc*) strip; (*riga*) stripe; ~**sce** (*pedonali*) zebra crossing *sg*.

strisci'are [striʃ'ʃare] *vt* (*piedi*) to drag; (*muro, macchina*) to graze // *vi* to crawl, creep.

'**striscio** ['striʃʃo] *sm* graze; (*MED*) smear; **colpire di** ~ to graze.

strito'lare *vt* to grind.

striz'zare [strit'tsare] *vt* (*arancia*) to squeeze; (*panni*) to wring (out); ~ l'occhio to wink.

'strofa *sf*, **'strofe** *sf inv* strophe.

strofi'naccio [strofi'nattʃo] *sm* duster, cloth; (*per piatti*) dishcloth; (*per pavimenti*) floorcloth.

strofi'nare *vt* to rub.

stron'care *vt* to break off; (*fig: ribellione*) to suppress, put down; (: *film, libro*) to tear to pieces.

stropicci'are [stropit'tʃare] *vt* to rub.

stroz'zare [strot'tsare] *vt* (*soffocare*) to choke, strangle; ~**rsi** *vr* to choke; **strozza'tura** *sf* (*restringimento*) narrowing; (*di strada etc*) bottleneck.

'struggere ['struddʒere] *vt* (*fig*) to consume; ~**rsi** *vr* (*fig*): ~**rsi di** to be consumed with.

strumen'tale *ag* (*MUS*) instrumental.

strumentaliz'zare [strumentalid'dzare] *vt* to exploit, use to one's own ends.

stru'mento *sm* (*arnese, fig*) instrument, tool; (*MUS*) instrument; ~ a corda *o* ad arco/a fiato stringed/wind instrument.

'strutto *sm* lard.

strut'tura *sf* structure; **struttu'rare** *vt* to structure.

'struzzo ['struttso] *sm* ostrich.

stuc'care *vt* (*muro*) to plaster; (*vetro*) to putty; (*decorare con stucchi*) to stucco.

stuc'chevole [stuk'kevole] *ag* nauseating; (*fig*) tedious, boring.

'stucco, chi *sm* plaster; (*da vetri*) putty; (*ornamentale*) stucco; **rimanere di ~** (*fig*) to be dumbfounded.

stu'dente, 'essa *sm/f* student; (*scolaro*) pupil, schoolboy/girl; **studen'tesco, a, schi, sche** *ag* student *cpd*; school *cpd*.

studi'are *vt* to study.

'studio *sm* studying; (*ricerca, saggio, stanza*) study; (*di professionista*) office; (*di artista, CINEMA, TV, RADIO*) studio; ~**i** *smpl* (*INS*) studies; ~ **medico** doctor's surgery (*Brit*) *o* office (*US*).

studi'oso, a *ag* studious, hard-working // *sm/f* scholar.

'stufa *sf* stove; ~ **elettrica** electric fire *o* heater.

stu'fare *vt* (*CUC*) to stew; (*fig: fam*) to bore; **stu'fato** *sm* (*CUC*) stew; **'stufo, a** *ag* (*fam*): **essere stufo di** to be fed up with, be sick and tired of.

stu'oia *sf* mat.

stupefa'cente [stupefa'tʃente] *ag* stunning, astounding // *sm* drug, narcotic.

stu'pendo, a *ag* marvellous, wonderful.

stupi'daggine [stupi'daddʒine] *sf* stupid thing (to do *o* say).

stupidità *sf* stupidity.

'stupido, a *ag* stupid.

stu'pire *vt* to amaze, stun // *vi* (*anche:* ~**rsi**): ~ (**di**) to be amazed (at), be stunned (by).

stu'pore *sm* amazement, astonishment.

'stupro *sm* rape.

stu'rare *vt* (*lavandino*) to clear.

stuzzica'denti [stuttsika'denti] *sm* toothpick.

stuzzi'care [stuttsi'kare] *vt* (*ferita etc*) to poke (at), prod (at); (*fig*) to tease; (: *appetito*) to whet; (: *curiosità*) to stimulate; ~ **i denti** to pick one's teeth.

su ◆ *prep* (*su + il* = **sul**, *su + lo* = **sullo**, *su + l'* = **sull'**, *su + la* = **sulla**, *su + i* = **sui**, *su + gli* = **sugli**, *su + le* = **sulle**) **1** (*gen*) on; (*moto*) on(to); (*in cima a*) on (top of); **mettilo sul tavolo** put it on the table; **un paesino sul mare** a village by the sea

2 (*argomento*) about, on; **un libro ~ Cesare** a book on *o* about Caesar

3 (*circa*) about; **costerà sui 3 milioni** it will cost about 3 million; **una ragazza sui 17 anni** a girl of about 17 (years of age)

4: ~ **misura** made to measure; ~ **richiesta** on request; **3 casi ~ dieci** 3 cases out of 10

◆ *av* **1** (*in alto, verso l'alto*) up; **vieni ~** come on up; **guarda ~** look up; ~ **le mani!** hands up!; **in ~** (*verso l'alto*) up(wards); (*in poi*) onwards; **dai 20 anni in ~** from the age of 20 onwards

2 (*addosso*) on; **cos'hai ~?** what have you got on?

◆ *escl* come on!; ~ **coraggio!** come on, cheer up!

'sua *vedi* **suo.**

su'bacqueo, a *ag* underwater // *sm* skindiver.

sub'buglio [sub'buʎʎo] *sm* confusion, turmoil.

subcosci'ente [subkoʃ'ʃente] *ag*, *sm* subconscious.

'subdolo, a *ag* underhand, sneaky.

suben'trare *vi*: ~ **a qn in qc** to take over sth from sb.

su'bire *vt* to suffer, endure.

subis'sare *vt* (*fig*): ~ **di** to overwhelm with, load with.

subi'taneo, a *ag* sudden.

'subito *av* immediately, at once, straight away.

subodo'rare *vt* (*insidia etc*) to smell, suspect.

subordi'nato, a *ag* subordinate; (*dipendente*): ~ **a** dependent on, subject to.

subur'bano, a *ag* suburban.

succe'daneo [suttʃe'daneo] *sm* substitute.

suc'cedere [sut'tʃedere] *vi* (*prendere il posto di qn*): ~ **a** to succeed; (*venire dopo*): ~ **a** to follow; (*accadere*) to happen; ~**rsi** *vr* to follow each other; ~ **al trono** to succeed to the throne; **successi'one** *sf* succession; **succes'sivo, a** *ag* successive; **suc'cesso, a** *pp di* **succedere** // *sm* (*esito*) outcome;

(buona riuscita) success; **di successo** *(libro, personaggio)* successful.

succhi'are [suk'kjare] *vt* to suck (up).

suc'cinto, a [sut'tʃinto] *ag (discorso)* succinct; *(abito)* brief.

'succo, chi *sm* juice; *(fig)* essence, gist; **~ di frutta** fruit juice; **suc'coso, a** *ag* juicy; *(fig)* pithy.

succur'sale *sf* branch (office).

sud *sm* south // *ag inv* south; *(lato)* south, southern.

Su'dafrica *sm*: **il ~** South Africa; **sudafri'cano, a** *ag, sm/f* South African.

Suda'merica *sm*: **il ~** South America; **sudameri'cano, a** *ag, sm/f* South American.

su'dare *vi* to perspire, sweat; **~ freddo** to come out in a cold sweat; **su'data** *sf* sweat; **ho fatto una bella sudata per finirlo in tempo** it was a real sweat to get it finished in time.

sud'detto, a *ag* above-mentioned.

sud'dito, a *sm/f* subject.

suddi'videre *vt* to subdivide.

su'dest *sm* south-east.

'sudicio, a, ci, ce ['suditʃo] *ag* dirty, filthy; **sudici'ume** *sm* dirt, filth.

su'dore *sm* perspiration, sweat.

su'dovest *sm* south-west.

'sue *vedi* **suo**.

suffici'ente [suffi'tʃɛnte] *ag* enough, sufficient; *(borioso)* self-important; *(INS)* satisfactory; **suffici'enza** *sf* self-importance; pass mark; **a sufficienza** *av* enough; **ne ho avuto a sufficienza!** I've had enough of this!

suf'fisso *sm (LING)* suffix.

suf'fragio [suf'fradʒo] *sm (voto)* vote; **~ universale** universal suffrage.

suggel'lare [suddʒel'lare] *vt (fig)* to seal.

suggeri'mento [suddʒeri'mento] *sm* suggestion; *(consiglio)* piece of advice, advice *q*.

sugge'rire [suddʒe'rire] *vt (risposta)* to tell; *(consigliare)* to advise; *(proporre)* to suggest; *(TEATRO)* to prompt; **suggeri'tore, 'trice** *sm/f (TEATRO)* prompter.

suggestio'nare [suddʒestjo'nare] *vt* to influence.

suggesti'one [suddʒes'tjone] *sf (PSIC)* suggestion; *(istigazione)* instigation.

sugges'tivo, a [suddʒes'tivo] *ag (paesaggio)* evocative; *(teoria)* interesting, attractive.

'sughero ['sugero] *sm* cork.

'sugli ['suʎʎi] *prep + det vedi* **su**.

'sugo, ghi *sm (succo)* juice; *(di carne)* gravy; *(condimento)* sauce; *(fig)* gist, essence.

'sui *prep + det vedi* **su**.

sui'cida, i, e [sui'tʃida] *ag* suicidal // *sm/f* suicide.

suici'darsi [suitʃi'darsi] *vr* to commit suicide.

sui'cidio [sui'tʃidjo] *sm* suicide.

su'ino, a *ag*: **carne ~a** pork // *sm* pig; **~i** *smpl* swine *pl*.

sul, sull', 'sulla, 'sulle, 'sullo *prep + det vedi* **su**.

sulta'nina *ag f*: *(uva)* **~** sultana.

sul'tano, a *sm/f* sultan/sultana.

'sunto *sm* summary.

'suo, 'sua, 'sue, su'oi *det*: **il ~, la sua** etc *(di lui)* his; *(di lei)* her; *(di esso)* its; *(con valore indefinito)* one's, his/her; *(forma di cortesia: anche:* **S~**) your // *pronome*: **il ~, la sua** etc his; hers; yours; **i suoi** *(parenti)* his *(o* her *o* one's *o* your) family.

su'ocero, a ['swɔtʃero] *sm/f* father/mother-in-law; **i ~i** *smpl* father-and mother-in-law.

su'oi *vedi* **suo**.

su'ola *sf (di scarpa)* sole.

su'olo *sm (terreno)* ground; *(terra)* soil.

suo'nare *vt (MUS)* to play; *(campana)* to ring; *(ore)* to strike; *(clacson, allarme)* to sound // *vi* to play; *(telefono, campana)* to ring; *(ore)* to strike; *(clacson, fig. parola)* to sound.

su'ono *sm* sound.

su'ora *sf (REL)* sister.

'super *sf (anche:* **benzina ~)** ≈ four-star *(petrol)* *(Brit)*, premium *(US)*.

supe'rare *vt (oltrepassare: limite)* to exceed, surpass; *(percorrere)* to cover; *(attraversare: fiume)* to cross; *(sorpassare: veicolo)* to overtake; *(fig: essere più bravo di)* to surpass, outdo; *(: difficoltà)* to overcome; *(: esame)* to get through; **~ qn in altezza/peso** to be taller/heavier than sb; **ha superato la cinquantina** he's over fifty (years of age).

su'perbia *sf* pride.

su'perbo, a *ag* proud; *(fig)* magnificent, superb.

superfici'ale [superfi'tʃale] *ag* superficial.

super'ficie, ci [super'fitʃe] *sf* surface.

su'perfluo, a *ag* superfluous.

superi'ore *ag (piano, arto, classi)* upper; *(più elevato: temperatura, livello)*: **~** (a) higher (than); *(migliore)*: **~** (a) superior (to); **~, a** *sm/f (anche REL)* superior; **superiorità** *sf* superiority.

superla'tivo, a *ag, sm* superlative.

supermer'cato *sm* supermarket.

su'perstite *ag* surviving // *sm/f* survivor.

superstizi'one [superstit'tsjone] *sf* superstition; **superstizi'oso, a** *ag* superstitious.

su'pino, a *ag* supine.

suppel'lettile *sf* furnishings *pl*.

suppergiù [supper'dʒu] *av* more or less, roughly.

supplemen'tare *ag* extra; *(treno)* relief *cpd*; *(entrate)* additional.

supple'mento *sm* supplement.

sup'plente *ag* temporary; *(insegnante)* supply *cpd (Brit)*, substitute *cpd (US)* // *smlf* temporary member of staff; supply *(o substitute)* teacher.

'supplica, che *sf (preghiera)* plea; *(domanda scritta)* petition, request.

suppli'care *vt* to implore, beseech.

sup'plire *vi:* ~ **a** to make up for, compensate for.

sup'plizio [sup'plittsjo] *sm* torture.

sup'porre *vt* to suppose.

sup'porto *sm (sostegno)* support.

sup'posta *sf (MED)* suppository.

sup'posto, a *pp di* **supporre.**

su'premo, a *ag* supreme.

surge'lare [surdʒe'lare] *vt* to (deep-) freeze; **surge'lati** *smpl* frozen food *sg.*

sur'plus *sm inv (ECON)* surplus.

surriscal'dare *vt* to overheat.

surro'gato *sm* substitute.

suscet'tibile [suʃʃet'tibile] *ag (sensibile)* touchy, sensitive; *(soggetto):* ~ **di miglioramento** that can be improved, open to improvement.

susci'tare [suʃʃi'tare] *vt* to provoke, arouse.

su'sina *sf* plum; **su'sino** *sm* plum (tree).

sussegu'ire *vt* to follow; ~**rsi** *vr* to follow one another.

sussidi'ario, a *ag* subsidiary; auxiliary.

sus'sidio *sm* subsidy.

sussis'tenza [sussis'tɛntsa] *sf* subsistence.

sus'sistere *vi* to exist; *(essere fondato)* to be valid *o* sound.

sussul'tare *vi* to shudder.

sussur'rare *vt, vi* to whisper, murmur; **sus'surro** *sm* whisper, murmur.

sutu'rare *vt (MED)* to stitch up, suture.

sva'gare *vt (distrarre)* to distract; *(divertire)* to amuse; ~**rsi** *vr* to amuse o.s.; to enjoy o.s.

'svago, ghi *sm (riposo)* relaxation; *(ricreazione)* amusement; *(passatempo)* pastime.

svaligi'are [zvali'dʒare] *vt* to rob, burgle *(Brit)*, burglarize *(US)*.

svalu'tare *vt (ECON)* to devalue; *(fig)* to belittle; ~**rsi** *vr (ECON)* to be devalued; **svalutazi'one** *sf* devaluation.

sva'nire *vi* to disappear, vanish.

svan'taggio [zvan'taddʒo] *sm* disadvantage; *(inconveniente)* drawback, disadvantage.

svapo'rare *vi* to evaporate.

svari'ato, a *ag* varied; various.

'svastica *sf* swastika.

sve'dese *ag* Swedish // *smlf* Swede // *sm (LING)* Swedish.

'sveglia ['zveʎʎa] *sf* waking up; *(orologio)* alarm (clock); **suonare la** ~ *(MIL)* to sound the reveille.

svegli'are [zveʎ'ʎare] *vt* to wake up; *(fig)* to awaken, arouse; ~**rsi** *vr* to wake

up; *(fig)* to be revived, reawaken.

'sveglio, a ['zveʎʎo] *ag* awake; *(fig)* quick-witted.

sve'lare *vt* to reveal.

'svelto, a *ag (passo)* quick; *(mente)* quick, alert; *(linea)* slim, slender; **alla** ~**a** *av* quickly.

'svendita *sf (COMM)* (clearance) sale.

sveni'mento *sm* fainting fit, faint.

sve'nire *vi* to faint.

sven'tare *vt* to foil, thwart.

sven'tato, a *ag (distratto)* scatterbrained; *(imprudente)* rash.

svento'lare *vt, vi* to wave, flutter.

sven'trare *vt* to disembowel.

sven'tura *sf* misfortune; **sventu'rato, a** *ag* unlucky, unfortunate.

sve'nuto, a *pp di* **svenire.**

svergo'gnato, a [zvergoɲ'ɲato] *ag* shameless.

sver'nare *vi* to spend the winter.

sves'tire *vt* to undress; ~**rsi** *vr* to get undressed.

'Svezia ['zvɛttsja] *sf:* **la** ~ Sweden.

svez'zare [zvet'tsare] *vt* to wean.

svi'are *vt* to divert; *(fig)* to lead astray; ~**rsi** *vr* to go astray.

svi'gnarsela [zviɲ'narsela] *vr* to slip away, sneak off.

svilup'pare *vt,* ~**rsi** *vr* to develop.

svi'luppo *sm* development.

'svincolo *sm (COMM)* clearance; *(stradale)* motorway *(Brit)* o expressway *(US)* intersection.

svisce'rare [zviʃʃe'rare] *vt (fig: argomento)* to examine in depth; **svisce'rato, a** *ag (amore)* passionate; *(lodi)* obsequious.

'svista *sf* oversight.

svi'tare *vt* to unscrew.

'Svizzera ['zvittsera] *sf:* **la** ~ Switzerland.

'svizzero, a ['zvittsero] *ag, smlf* Swiss.

svogli'ato, a *ag* [zvoʎ'ʎato] *ag* listless; *(pigro)* lazy.

svolaz'zare [zvolat'tsare] *vi* to flutter.

'svolgere ['zvoldʒere] *vt* to unwind; *(srotolare)* to unroll; *(fig: argomento)* to develop; *(: piano, programma)* to carry out; ~**rsi** *vr* to unwind; to unroll; *(fig: aver luogo)* to take place; *(: procedere)* to go on; **svolgi'mento** *sm* development; carrying out; *(andamento)* course.

'svolta *sf (atto)* turning *q; (curva)* turn, bend; *(fig)* turning-point.

svol'tare *vi* to turn.

'svolto, a *pp di* **svolgere.**

svuo'tare *vt* to empty (out).

T

tabac'caio, a *smlf* tobacconist.

tabacche'ria [tabakke'ria] *sf* tobacconist's (shop).

ta'bacco, chi *sm* tobacco.

ta'bella *sf* (*tavola*) table; (*elenco*) list.

taber'nacolo *sm* tabernacle.

tabu'lato *sm* (*INFORM*) printout.

'tacca, che *sf* notch, nick; **di mezza ~** (*fig*) mediocre.

tac'cagno, a [tak'kappo] *ag* mean, stingy.

tac'cheggio [tak'keddʒo] *sm* shoplifting.

tac'chino [tak'kino] *sm* turkey.

tacci'are [tat'tʃare] *vt*: **~ qn di** to accuse sb of.

'tacco, chi *sm* heel.

taccu'ino *sm* notebook.

ta'cere [ta'tʃere] *vi* to be silent *o* quiet; (*smettere di parlare*) to fall silent // *vt* to keep to oneself, say nothing about; **far ~ qn** to make sb be quiet; (*fig*) to silence sb.

ta'chimetro [ta'kimetro] *sm* speedometer.

'tacito, a ['tatʃito] *ag* silent; (*sottinteso*) tacit, unspoken.

ta'fano *sm* horsefly.

taffe'ruglio [taffe'ruʎʎo] *sm* brawl, scuffle.

taffettà *sm* taffeta.

'taglia ['taʎʎa] *sf* (*statura*) height; (*misura*) size; (*riscatto*) ransom; (*ricompensa*) reward.

taglia'carte [taʎʎa'karte] *sm inv* paperknife.

tagli'ando [taʎ'ʎando] *sm* coupon.

tagli'are [taʎ'ʎare] *vt* to cut; (*recidere, interrompere*) to cut off; (*intersecare*) to cut across, intersect; (*carne*) to carve; (*vini*) to blend // *vi* to cut; (*prendere una scorciatoia*) to take a short-cut: **~ corto** (*fig*) to cut short.

taglia'telle [taʎʎa'telle] *sfpl* tagliatelle *pl*.

tagli'ente [taʎ'ʎɛnte] *ag* sharp.

'taglio ['taʎʎo] *sm* cutting *q*; cut; (*parte tagliente*) cutting edge; (*di abito*) cut, style; (*di stoffa: lunghezza*) length; (*di vini*) blending; **di ~** on edge, edgeways; **banconote di piccolo/grosso ~** notes of small/large denomination.

tagli'ola [taʎ'ʎola] *sf* trap, snare.

taglluz'zare [taʎʎut'tsare] *vt* to cut into small pieces.

'talco *sm* talcum powder.

'tale ♦ *det* **1** (*simile, così grande*) such; **un(a) ~ ... such (a) ...; non accetto ~i discorsi** I won't allow such talk; **è di una ~ arroganza** he is so arrogant; **fa una ~ confusione!** he makes such a mess!

2 (*persona o cosa indeterminata*) such-and-such; **il giorno ~ all'ora ~** on such-and-such a day at such-and-such a time; **la tal persona** that person; **ha telefonato una ~ Giovanna** somebody called Giovanna phoned

3 (*nelle similitudini*): **~ ... ~** like ...

like; **~ padre ~ figlio** like father, like son; **hai il vestito ~ quale il mio** your dress is just *o* exactly like mine

♦ *pronome* (*indefinito: persona*): **un(a) ~** someone; **quel (o quella) ~** that person, that man (*o* woman); **il tal dei ~i** what's-his-name.

ta'lento *sm* talent.

talis'mano *sm* talisman.

tallon'cino [tallon'tʃino] *sm* counterfoil.

tal'lone *sm* heel.

tal'mente *av* so.

ta'lora *av* = **talvolta**.

'talpa *sf* (*ZOOL*) mole.

tal'volta *av* sometimes, at times.

tambu'rello *sm* tambourine.

tam'buro *sm* drum.

Ta'migi [ta'midʒi] *sm*: **il ~** the Thames.

tampo'nare *vt* (*otturare*) to plug; (*urtare: macchina*) to crash *o* ram into.

tam'pone *sm* (*MED*) wad, pad; (*per timbri*) ink-pad; (*respingente*) buffer; **~ assorbente** tampon.

'tana *sf* lair, den.

'tanfo *sm* stench; musty smell.

tan'gente [tan'dʒɛnte] *ag* (*MAT*): **~ a** tangential to // *sf* tangent; (*quota*) share.

tan'tino: **un ~** *av* a little, a bit.

'tanto, a ♦ *det* **1** (*molto: quantità*) a lot of, much; (: *numero*) a lot of, many; (*così ~: quantità*) so much, such a lot of; (: *numero*) so many, such a lot of; **~e volte** so many times, so often; **~i auguri!** all the best!; **~e grazie** many thanks; **~ tempo** so long, such a long time; **ogni ~i chilometri** every so many kilometres

2: **~ ... quanto** (*quantità*) as much ... as; (*numero*) as many ... as; **ho ~a pazienza quanta ne hai tu** I have as much patience as you have *o* as you; **ha ~i amici quanti nemici** he has as many friends as he has enemies

3 (*rafforzativo*) such; **ho aspettato per ~ tempo** I waited so long *o* for such a long time

♦ *pronome* **1** (*molto*) much, a lot; (*così ~*) so much, such a lot; **~i(e)** many, a lot; so many, such a lot; **credevo ce ne fosse ~** I thought there was (such) a lot, I thought there was plenty

2: **~ quanto** (*denaro*) as much as; (*cioccolatini*) as many as; **ne ho ~ quanto basta** I have as much as I need; **due volte ~** twice as much

3 (*indeterminato*) so much; **~ per l'affitto, ~ per il gas** so much for the rent, so much for the gas; **costa un ~ al metro** it costs so much per metre; **di ~ in ~, ogni ~ so** often; **~ vale che ... I (*o* we *etc*) may as well ...; **~ meglio!** so much the better!; **~ peggio per lui!** so much the worse for him!

♦ *av* **1** (*molto*) very; **vengo ~ volentieri** I'd be very glad to come; **non ci vuole ~**

a capirlo it doesn't take much to understand it

2 (così ~: con ag, av) so; (: con vb) so much, such a lot; **è ~ bella!** she's so beautiful!; **non urlare ~** don't shout so much; **sto ~ meglio adesso** I'm so much better now; **~ ... che so ... (that)**; **~ ... da so ... as**

3: **~ ... quanto as ... as**; **conosco ~ Carlo quanto suo padre** I know both Carlo and his father; **non è poi ~ complicato quanto sembri** it's not as difficult as it seems; **~ più insisti, ~ più non mollerà** the more you insist, the more stubborn he'll be; **quanto più ... ~ meno** the more ... the less

4 (solamente) just; **~ per cambiare/ scherzare** just for a change/a joke; **una volta ~** for once

5 (a lungo) (for) long

◆ cong after all.

'tappa sf (luogo di sosta, fermata) stop, halt; (parte di un percorso) stage, leg; (SPORT) lap; **a ~e** in stages.

tap'pare vt to plug, stop up; (bottiglia) to cork.

tap'peto sm carpet; (anche: tappettino) rug; (di tavolo) cloth; (SPORT): **andare al ~** to go down for the count; **mettere sul ~** (fig) to bring up for discussion.

tappez'zare [tappet'tsare] vt (con carta) to paper; (rivestire): **~ qc (di)** to cover sth (with); **tappezze'ria** sf (tessuto) tapestry; (carta da parato) wallpaper; (arte) upholstery; **far da tappezzeria** (fig) to be a wallflower; **tappezzi'ere** sm upholsterer.

'tappo sm stopper; (in sughero) cork.

tarchi'ato, a [tar'kjato] ag stocky, thickset.

tar'dare vi to be late // vt to delay; **~ a fare** to delay doing.

'tardi av late; **più ~** later (on); **al più ~** at the latest; **sul ~** (verso sera) late in the day; **far ~** to be late; (restare alzato) to stay up late.

tar'divo, a ag (primavera) late; (rimedio) belated, tardy; (fig: bambino) retarded.

'tardo, a ag (lento, fig: ottuso) slow; (tempo: avanzato) late.

'targa, ghe sf plate; (AUT) number (Brit) o license (US) plate.

ta'riffa sf (gen) rate, tariff; (di trasporti) fare; (elenco) price list; tariff.

'tarlo sm woodworm.

'tarma sf moth.

ta'rocco, chi sm tarot card; **~chi** smpl (gioco) tarot sg.

tartagli'are [tartaʎ'ʎare] vi to stutter, stammer.

'tartaro, a ag, sm (in tutti i sensi) tartar.

tarta'ruga, ghe sf tortoise; (di mare) turtle; (materiale) tortoiseshell.

tar'tina sf canapé.

tar'tufo sm (BOT) truffle.

'tasca, sche sf pocket; **tas'cabile** ag (libro) pocket cpd; **tasca'pane** sm haversack; **tas'chino** sm breast pocket.

'tassa sf (imposta) tax; (doganale) duty; (per iscrizione: a scuola etc) fee; **~ di circolazione/di soggiorno** road/tourist tax.

tas'sametro sm taximeter.

tas'sare vt to tax; to levy a duty on.

tassa'tivo, a ag peremptory.

tassazi'one [tassat'tsjone] sf taxation.

tas'sello sm plug; wedge.

tassi sm inv = **taxi**; **tas'sista, i, e** sm/f taxi driver.

'tasso sm (di natalità, d'interesse etc) rate; (BOT) yew; (ZOOL) badger; **~ di cambio/d'interesse** rate of exchange/ interest.

tas'tare vt to feel; **~ il terreno** (fig) to see how the land lies.

tasti'era sf keyboard.

'tasto sm key; (tatto) touch, feel.

tas'toni av: **procedere (a) ~** to grope one's way forward.

'tattico, a, ci, che ag tactical // sf tactics pl.

'tatto sm (senso) touch; (fig) tact; **duro al ~** hard to the touch; **aver ~** to be tactful, have tact.

tatu'aggio [tatu'addʒo] sm tattooing; (disegno) tattoo.

tatu'are vt to tattoo.

'tavola sf table; (asse) plank, board; (lastra) tablet; (quadro) panel (painting); (illustrazione) plate; **~ calda** snack bar; **~ pieghevole** folding table.

tavo'lato sm boarding; (pavimento) wooden floor.

tavo'letta sf tablet, bar; **a ~** (AUT) flat out.

tavo'lino sm small table; (scrivania) desk.

'tavolo sm table.

tavo'lozza [tavo'lɔttsa] sf (ARTE) palette.

'taxi sm inv taxi.

'tazza ['tattsa] sf cup; **~ da caffè/tè** coffee/tea cup; **una ~ di caffè/tè** a cup of coffee/tea.

te pronome (soggetto: in forme comparative, oggetto) you.

tè sm inv tea; (trattenimento) tea party.

tea'trale ag theatrical.

te'atro sm theatre.

'tecnico, a, ci, che ag technical // sm/f technician // sf technique; (tecnologia) technology.

tecnolo'gia [teknolo'dʒia] sf technology.

te'desco, a, schi, sche ag, sm/f, sm German.

'tedio sm tedium, boredom.

te'game sm (CUC) pan.

'tegola sf tile.

tei'era sf teapot.

'tela sf (tessuto) cloth; (per vele, quadri)

canvas; (*dipinto*) canvas, painting; di ~ (*calzoni*) (heavy) cotton *cpd*; (*scarpe, borsa*) canvas *cpd*; ~ **cerata** oilcloth; (*copertone*) tarpaulin.

te'laio *sm* (*apparecchio*) loom; (*struttura*) frame.

tele'camera *sf* television camera.

tele'cronaca *sf* television report.

tele'ferica, che *sf* cableway.

telefo'nare *vi* to telephone, ring; to make a phone call // *vt* to telephone; ~ a to phone up, ring up, call up.

telefo'nata *sf* (telephone) call; ~ a carico del destinatario reverse charge (*Brit*) *o* collect (*US*) call.

tele'fonico, a, ci, che *ag* (tele)phone *cpd*.

telefo'nista, i, e *sm/f* telephonist; (*d'impresa*) switchboard operator.

te'lefono *sm* telephone; ~ a gettoni ~ pay phone.

telegior'nale [teledʒor'nale] *sm* television news (programme).

te'legrafo *sm* telegraph; (*ufficio*) telegraph office.

tele'gramma, i *sm* telegram.

tele'matica *sf* data transmission; telematics *sg*.

telepa'tia *sf* telepathy.

teles'copio *sm* telescope.

teleselezi'one [teleselet'tsjone] *sf* direct dialling.

telespetta'tore, 'trice *sm/f* (television) viewer.

televisi'one *sf* television.

televi'sore *sm* television set.

'telex *sm inv* telex.

'tema, i *sm* theme; (*INS*) essay, composition.

teme'rario, a *ag* rash, reckless.

te'mere *vt* to fear, be afraid of; (*essere sensibile a: freddo, calore*) to be sensitive to // *vi* to be afraid; (*essere preoccupato*): ~ per to worry about, fear for; ~ di/che to be afraid of/that.

temperama'tite *sm inv* pencil sharpener.

tempera'mento *sm* temperament.

tempe'rare *vt* (*aguzzare*) to sharpen; (*fig*) to moderate, control, temper.

tempe'rato, a *ag* moderate, temperate; (*clima*) temperate.

tempera'tura *sf* temperature.

tempe'rino *sm* penknife.

tem'pesta *sf* storm; ~ di sabbia/neve sand/snowstorm.

tempes'tare *vt*: ~ qn di domande to bombard sb with questions; ~ qn di colpi to rain blows on sb.

tempes'tivo, a *ag* timely.

tempes'toso, a *ag* stormy.

'tempia *sf* (*ANAT*) temple.

'tempio *sm* (*edificio*) temple.

'tempo *sm* (*METEOR*) weather; (*cronologico*) time; (*epoca*) time, times

pl; (*di film, gioco: parte*) part; (*MUS*) time; (: *battuta*) beat; (*LING*) tense; un ~ once; ~ fa some time ago; al ~ stesso *o* a un ~ at the same time; per ~ early; aver fatto il suo ~ to have had its (*o* his *etc*) day; primo/secondo ~ (*TEATRO*) first/second part; (*SPORT*) first/second half; in ~ utile in due time *o* course.

tempo'rale *ag* temporal // *sm* (*METEOR*) (thunder)storm.

tempo'raneo, a *ag* temporary.

temporeggi'are [tempored'dʒare] *vi* to play for time, temporize.

tem'prare *vt* to temper.

te'nace [te'natʃe] *ag* strong, tough; (*fig*) tenacious; **te'nacia** *sf* tenacity.

te'naglie [te'naʎʎe] *sfpl* pincers *pl*.

'tenda *sf* (*riparo*) awning; (*di finestra*) curtain; (*per campeggio etc*) tent.

ten'denza [ten'dɛntsa] *sf* tendency; (*orientamento*) trend; avere ~ a *o* per qc to have a bent for sth.

'tendere *vt* (*allungare al massimo*) to stretch, draw tight; (*porgere: mano*) to hold out; (*fig: trappola*) to lay, set // *vi*: ~ a qc/a fare to tend towards sth/to do; ~ l'orecchio to prick up one's ears; il tempo tende al caldo the weather is getting hot; un blu che tende al verde a greenish blue.

ten'dina *sf* curtain.

'tendine *sm* tendon, sinew.

ten'done *sm* (*da circo*) tent.

'tenebre *sfpl* darkness *sg*; **tene'broso, a** *ag* dark, gloomy.

te'nente *sm* lieutenant.

te'nere *vt* to hold; (*conservare, mantenere*) to keep; (*ritenere, considerare*) to consider; (*spazio: occupare*) to take up, occupy; (*seguire: strada*) to keep to // *vi* to hold; (*colori*) to be fast; (*dare importanza*): ~ a to care about; ~ a fare to want to do, be keen to do; ~rsi *vr* (*stare in una determinata posizione*) to stand; (*stimarsi*) to consider o.s.; (*aggrapparsi*): ~rsi a to hold on to; (*attenersi*): ~rsi a to stick to; ~ una conferenza to give a lecture; ~ conto di qc to take sth into consideration; ~ presente qc to bear sth in mind.

'tenero, a *ag* tender; (*pietra, cera, colore*) soft; (*fig*) tender, loving.

'tenia *sf* tapeworm.

'tennis *sm* tennis.

te'nore *sm* (*tono*) tone; (*MUS*) tenor; ~ di vita way of life; (*livello*) standard of living.

tensi'one *sf* tension.

ten'tare *vt* (*indurre*) to tempt; (*provare*): ~ qc/di fare to attempt *o* try sth/to do; **tenta'tivo** *sm* attempt; **tentazi'one** *sf* temptation.

tenten'nare *vi* to shake, be unsteady; (*fig*) to hesitate, waver // *vt*: ~ il capo to shake one's head.

ten'toni *av*: andare a ~ *(anche fig)* to grope one's way.

'tenue *ag (sottile)* fine; *(colore)* soft; *(fig)* slender, slight.

te'nuta *sf (capacità)* capacity; *(divisa)* uniform; *(abito)* dress; *(AGR)* estate; a ~ d'aria airtight; ~ di strada roadholding power.

teolo'gia [teolo'dʒia] *sf* theology; **te'ologo, gi** *sm* theologian.

teo'rema, i *sm* theorem.

teo'ria *sf* theory; **te'orico, a, ci, che** *ag* theoretic(al).

'tepido, a *ag* = tiepido.

te'pore *sm* warmth.

'teppa *sf* mob, hooligans *pl*; **tep'pismo** *sm* hooliganism; **tep'pista, i** *sm* hooligan.

tera'pia *sf* therapy.

tergicris'tallo [terdʒikris'tallo] *sm* windscreen *(Brit)* o windshield *(US)* wiper.

tergiver'sare [terdʒiver'sare] *vi* to shilly-shally.

'tergo *sm*: a ~ behind; vedi a ~ please turn over.

ter'male *ag* thermal; stazione *f* ~ spa.

'terme *sfpl* thermal baths.

'termico, a, ci, che *ag* thermic; *(unità)* thermal.

termi'nale *ag, sm* terminal.

termi'nare *vt* to end; *(lavoro)* to finish // *vi* to end.

'termine *sm* term; *(fine, estremità)* end; *(di territorio)* boundary, limit; contratto a ~ *(COMM)* forward contract; a breve/lungo ~ short-/long-term; parlare senza mezzi ~i to talk frankly, not to mince one's words.

ter'mometro *sm* thermometer.

termonucle'are *ag* thermonuclear.

'termos *sm inv* = thermos.

termosi'fone *sm* radiator; (riscaldamento a) ~ central heating.

ter'mostato *sm* thermostat.

'terra *sf (gen, ELETTR)* earth; *(sostanza)* soil, earth; *(opposto al mare)* land *q*; *(regione, paese)* land; *(argilla)* clay; ~e *sfpl (possedimento)* lands, land *sg*; a o per ~ *(stato)* on the ground (o floor); *(moto)* to the ground, down; mettere a ~ *(ELETTR)* to earth.

terra'cotta *sf* terracotta; vasellame *m* di ~ earthenware.

terra'ferma *sf* dry land, terra firma; *(continente)* mainland.

terrapi'eno *sm* embankment, bank.

ter'razza [ter'rattsa] *sf*, **ter'razzo** [ter'rattso] *sm* terrace.

terre'moto *sm* earthquake.

ter'reno, a *ag (vita, beni)* earthly // *sm (suolo, fig)* ground; *(COMM)* land *q*, plot (of land); site; *(SPORT, MIL)* field.

ter'restre *ag (superficie)* of the earth, earth's; *(di terra: battaglia, animale)* land *cpd*; *(REL)* earthly, worldly.

ter'ribile *ag* terrible, dreadful.

terrifi'cante *ag* terrifying.

territori'ale *ag* territorial.

terri'torio *sm* territory.

ter'rore *sm* terror; **terro'rismo** *sm* terrorism; **terro'rista, i, e** *sm/f* terrorist.

'terso, a *ag* clear.

'terzo, a ['tɛrtso] *ag* third // *sm (frazione)* third; *(DIR)* third party; ~i *smpl (altri)* others, other people; la ~a pagina *(STAMPA)* the Arts page.

'tesa *sf* brim.

'teschio ['tɛskjo] *sm* skull.

'tesi *sf* thesis.

'teso, a *pp di* tendere // *ag (tirato)* taut, tight; *(fig)* tense.

tesore'ria *sf* treasury.

tesori'ere *sm* treasurer.

te'soro *sm* treasure; il Ministero del T~ the Treasury.

'tessera *sf (documento)* card.

'tessere *vt* to weave; **'tessile** *ag, sm* textile; **tessi'tore, 'trice** *sm/f* weaver; **tessi'tura** *sf* weaving.

tes'suto *sm* fabric, material; *(BIOL)* tissue; *(fig)* web.

'testa *sf* head; *(di cose: estremità, parte anteriore)* head, front; di ~ *ag (vettura etc)* front; tenere ~ a qn *(nemico etc)* to stand up to sb; fare di ~ propria to go one's own way; in ~ *(SPORT)* in the lead; ~ o croce? heads or tails?; avere la ~ dura to be stubborn; ~ di serie *(TENNIS)* seed, seeded player.

testa'mento *sm (atto)* will; l'Antico/il Nuovo T~ *(REL)* the Old/New Testament.

tes'tardo, a *ag* stubborn, pig-headed.

tes'tata *sf (parte anteriore)* head; *(intestazione)* heading.

'teste *sm/f* witness.

tes'ticolo *sm* testicle.

testi'mone *sm/f (DIR)* witness.

testimoni'anza [testimo'njantsa] *sf* testimony.

testimoni'are *vt* to testify; *(fig)* to bear witness to, testify to // *vi* to give evidence, testify.

'testo *sm* text; fare ~ *(opera, autore)* to be authoritative; questo libro non fa ~ this book is not essential reading; **te-stu'ale** *ag* textual; literal, word for word.

tes'tuggine [tes'tuddʒine] *sf* tortoise; *(di mare)* turtle.

'tetano *sm (MED)* tetanus.

'tetro, a *ag* gloomy.

'tetto *sm* roof; **tet'toia** *sf* roofing; canopy.

'Tevere *sm*: il ~ the Tiber.

Tg. *abbr* = telegiornale.

'thermos ® ['tɛrmos] *sm inv* vacuum o Thermos ® flask.

ti *pronome (dav lo, la, li, le, ne diventa te) (oggetto)* you; *(complemento di* *termine*) (to) you; (*riflessivo*) yourself.

ti'ara *sf* (*REL*) tiara.

'tibia *sf* tibia, shinbone.

tic *sm inv* tic, (nervous) twitch; (*fig*) mannerism.

ticchet'tio [tikket'tio] *sm* (*di macchina da scrivere*) clatter; (*di orologio*) ticking; (*della pioggia*) patter.

'ticchio ['tikkjo] *sm* (*ghiribizzo*) whim; (*tic*) tic, (nervous) twitch.

ti'epido, a *ag* lukewarm, tepid.

ti'fare *vi*: ~ **per** to be a fan of; (*parteggiare*) to side with.

'tifo *sm* (*MED*) typhus; (*fig*): **fare il** ~ **per** to be a fan of.

tifoi'dea *sf* typhoid.

ti'fone *sm* typhoon.

ti'foso, a *sm/f* (*SPORT etc*) fan.

'tiglio ['tiʎʎo] *sm* lime (tree), linden (tree).

'tigre *sf* tiger.

tim'ballo *sm* (*strumento*) kettledrum; (*CUC*) timbale.

'timbro *sm* stamp; (*MUS*) timbre, tone.

'timido, a *ag* shy; timid.

'timo *sm* thyme.

ti'mone *sm* (*NAUT*) rudder; **timoni'ere** *sm* helmsman.

ti'more *sm* (*paura*) fear; (*rispetto*) awe; **timo'roso, a** *ag* timid, timorous.

'timpano *sm* (*ANAT*) eardrum; (*MUS*): ~**i** *smpl* kettledrums, timpani.

'tingere ['tindʒere] *vt* to dye.

'tino *sm* vat.

ti'nozza [ti'nɔttsa] *sf* tub.

'tinta *sf* (*materia colorante*) dye; (*colore*) colour, shade; **tinta'rella** *sf* (*fam*) (sun)tan.

tintin'nare *vi* to tinkle.

'tinto, a *pp di* **tingere**.

tinto'ria *sf* (*officina*) dyeworks *sg*, (*lavasecco*) dry cleaner's (shop).

tin'tura *sf* (*operazione*) dyeing; (*colorante*) dye; ~ **di iodio** tincture of iodine.

'tipico, a, ci, che *ag* typical.

'tipo *sm* type; (*genere*) kind, type; (*fam*) chap, fellow.

tipogra'fia *sf* typography; (*procedimento*) letterpress (printing); (*officina*) printing house; **tipo'grafico, a, ci, che** *ag* typographic(al); letterpress *cpd*; **ti'pografo** *sm* typographer.

ti'ranno, a *ag* tyrannical // *sm* tyrant.

ti'rante *sm* (*per tenda*) guy.

ti'rare *vt* (*gen*) to pull; (*estrarre*): ~ **qc da** to take o pull sth out of; to get sth out of; to extract sth from; (*chiudere: tenda etc*) to draw, pull; (*tracciare, disegnare*) to draw, trace; (*lanciare: sasso, palla*) to throw; (*stampare*) to print; (*pistola, freccia*) to fire // *vi* (*pipa, camino*) to draw; (*vento*) to blow; (*abito*) to be tight; (*fare fuoco*) to fire; (*fare del tiro, CALCIO*) to shoot; ~ **avanti** *vi* to struggle on // *vt* to keep going; ~ **fuori** *vt*

(*estrarre*) to take out, pull out; ~ **giù** *vt* (*abbassare*) to bring down; ~ **su** *vt* to pull up; (*capelli*) to put up; (*fig: bambino*) to bring up; ~**rsi indietro** to move back.

tira'tore *sm* gunman; **un buon** ~ a good shot; ~ **scelto** marksman.

tira'tura *sf* (*azione*) printing; (*di libro*) (print) run; (*di giornale*) circulation.

'tirchio ['tirkjo] *ag* mean, stingy.

'tiro *sm* shooting *q*, firing *q*; (*colpo, sparo*) shot; (*di palla: lancio*) throwing *q*; throw; (*fig*) trick; **cavallo da** ~ draught (*Brit*) o draft (*US*) horse; ~ **a segno** target shooting; (*luogo*) shooting range.

tiro'cinio [tiro'tʃinjo] *sm* apprenticeship; (*professionale*) training.

ti'roide *sf* thyroid (gland).

Tir'reno *sm*: **il** (*mar*) ~ the Tyrrhenian Sea.

ti'sana *sf* herb tea.

tito'lare *ag* appointed; (*sovrano*) titular // *sm/f* incumbent; (*proprietario*) owner; (*CALCIO*) regular player.

'titolo *sm* title; (*di giornale*) headline; (*diploma*) qualification; (*COMM*) security; (*: azione*) share; **a che** ~? for what reason?; **a** ~ **di amicizia** out of friendship; **a** ~ **di premio** as a prize; ~ **di credito** share; ~ **di proprietà** title deed.

titu'bante *ag* hesitant, irresolute.

'tizio, a ['tittsjo] *sm/f* fellow, chap.

tiz'zone [tit'tsone] *sm* brand.

toc'cante *ag* touching.

toc'care *vt* to touch; (*tastare*) to feel; (*fig: riguardare*) to concern; (*: commuovere*) to touch, move; (*: pungere*) to hurt, wound; (*: far cenno a: argomento*) to touch on, mention // *vi*: ~ **a** (*accadere*) to happen to; (*spettare*) to be up to; ~ **(il fondo)** (*in acqua*) to touch the bottom; **tocca a te difenderci** it's up to you to defend us; **a chi tocca?** whose turn is it?; **mi toccò pagare** I had to pay.

'tocco, chi *sm* touch; (*ARTE*) stroke, touch.

'toga, ghe *sf* toga; (*di magistrato, professore*) gown.

'togliere ['tɔʎʎere] *vt* (*rimuovere*) to take away (o off), remove; (*riprendere, non concedere più*) to take away, remove; (*MAT*) to take away, subtract; (*liberare*) to free; ~ **qc a qn** to take sth (away) from sb; **ciò non toglie che** nevertheless, be that as it may; ~**rsi il cappello** to take off one's hat.

toi'lette [twa'lɛt] *sf inv*, **to'letta** *sf* toilet; (*mobile*) dressing table.

tolle'ranza [tolle'rantsa] *sf* tolerance.

tolle'rare *vt* to tolerate.

'tolto, a *pp di* **togliere**.

to'maia *sf* (*di scarpa*) upper.

'tomba *sf* tomb.

tom'bino *sm* manhole cover.

'tombola *sf* (*gioco*) tombola; (*ruzzolone*) tumble.

'tomo *sm* volume.

'tonaca, che *sf* (*REL*) habit.

to'nare *vi* = **tuonare.**

'tondo, a *ag* round.

'tonfo *sm* splash; (*rumore sordo*) thud; (*caduta*): **fare un ~** to take a tumble.

'tonico, a, ci, che *ag, sm* tonic.

tonifi'care *vt* (*muscoli, pelle*) to tone up; (*irrobustire*) to invigorate, brace.

tonnel'laggio [tonnel'laddʒo] *sm* (*NAUT*) tonnage.

tonnel'lata *sf* ton.

'tonno *sm* tuna (fish).

'tono *sm* (*gen*) tone; (*MUS: di pezzo*) key; (*di colore*) shade, tone.

ton'silla *sf* tonsil; **tonsil'lite** *sf* tonsillitis.

'tonto, a *ag* dull, stupid.

to'pazio [to'pattsjo] *sm* topaz.

'topo *sm* mouse.

topogra'fia *sf* topography.

'toppa *sf* (*serratura*) keyhole; (*pezza*) patch.

to'race [to'ratʃe] *sm* chest.

'torba *sf* peat.

'torbido, a *ag* (*liquido*) cloudy; (: *fiume*) muddy; (*fig*) dark; troubled // *sm*: **pescare nel ~** (*fig*) to fish in troubled water.

'torcere ['tɔrtʃere] *vt* to twist; (*biancheria*) to wring (out); **~rsi** *vr* to twist, writhe.

torchi'are [tor'kjare] *vt* to press; **'torchio** *sm* press; **torchio tipografico** printing press.

'torcia, ce ['tɔrtʃa] *sf* torch; **~ elettrica** torch (*Brit*), flashlight (*US*).

torci'collo [tortʃi'kɔllo] *sm* stiff neck.

'tordo *sm* thrush.

To'rino *sf* Turin.

tor'menta *sf* snowstorm.

tormen'tare *vt* to torment; **~rsi** *vr* to fret, worry o.s.; **tor'mento** *sm* torment.

torna'conto *sm* advantage, benefit.

tor'nado *sm* tornado.

tor'nante *sm* hairpin bend.

tor'nare *vi* to return, go (*o* come) back; (*ridiventare: anche fig*) to become (again); (*riuscire giusto, esatto: conto*) to work out; (*risultare*) to turn out (to be), prove (to be); **~ utile** to prove *o* turn out (to be) useful; **~ a casa** to go (*o* come) home.

torna'sole *sm inv* litmus.

tor'neo *sm* tournament.

'tornio *sm* lathe.

'toro *sm* bull; (*dello zodiaco*): **T~** Taurus.

tor'pedine *sf* torpedo; **torpedini'era** *sf* torpedo boat.

'torre *sf* tower; (*SCACCHI*) rook, castle;

~ di controllo (*AER*) control tower.

torrefazi'one [torrefat'tsjone] *sf* roasting.

tor'rente *sm* torrent.

tor'retta *sf* turret.

torri'one *sm* keep.

tor'rone *sm* nougat.

torsi'one *sf* twisting; torsion.

'torso *sm* torso, trunk; (*ARTE*) torso.

'torsolo *sm* (*di cavolo etc*) stump; (*di frutta*) core.

'torta *sf* cake.

'torto, a *pp di* **torcere** // *ag* (*ritorto*) twisted; (*storto*) twisted, crooked // *sm* (*ingiustizia*) wrong; (*colpa*) fault; **a ~** wrongly; **aver ~** to be wrong.

'tortora *sf* turtle dove.

tortu'oso, a *ag* (*strada*) twisting; (*fig*) tortuous.

tor'tura *sf* torture; **tortu'rare** *vt* to torture.

'torvo, a *ag* menacing, grim.

tosa'erba *sm o f inv* (lawn)mower.

to'sare *vt* (*pecora*) to shear; (*siepe*) to clip, trim.

Tos'cana *sf*: **la ~** Tuscany; **tos'cano, a** *ag, sm/f* Tuscan // *sm* (*sigaro*) strong Italian cigar.

'tosse *sf* cough.

'tossico, a, ci, che *ag* toxic.

tossicodipen'dente, tossi'comane *sm/f* drug addict.

tos'sire *vi* to cough.

tosta'pane *sm inv* toaster.

tos'tare *vt* to toast; (*caffè*) to roast.

'tosto, a *ag*: **faccia ~a** cheek.

to'tale *ag, sm* total; **totalità** *sf*: **la totalità di** all of, the total amount (*o* number) of; **the whole + *sg*; totaliz'zare** *vt* to total; (*SPORT: punti*) to score.

toto'calcio [toto'kaltʃo] *sm* gambling pool betting on football results, ≈ (football) pools *pl* (*Brit*).

to'vaglia [to'vaʎʎa] *sf* tablecloth; **tova-gli'olo** *sm* napkin.

'tozzo, a ['tɔttso] *ag* squat // *sm*: **~ di pane** crust of bread.

tra *prep* (*di due persone, cose*) between; (*di più persone, cose*) among(st); (*tempo: entro*) within, in; **~ 5 giorni** in 5 days' time; **sia detto ~ noi** ... between you and me ...; **litigano ~** (*di*) **loro** they're fighting amongst themselves; **~ breve** soon; **~ sé e sé** (*parlare etc*) to oneself.

trabal'lare *vi* to stagger, totter.

traboc'care *vi* to overflow.

traboc'chetto [trabok'ketto] *sm* (*fig*) trap.

tracan'nare *vt* to gulp down.

'traccia, ce ['trattʃa] *sf* (*segno, striscia*) trail, track; (*orma*) tracks *pl*; (*residuo, testimonianza*) trace, sign; (*abbozzo*) outline.

tracci'are [trat'tʃare] *vt* to trace, mark

(out); (*disegnare*) to draw; (*fig:* *abbozzare*) to outline; **tracci'ato** *sm* (*grafico*) layout, plan.

tra'chea [tra'kɛa] *sf* windpipe, trachea.

tra'colla *sf* shoulder strap; **borsa a ~** shoulder bag.

tra'collo *sm* (*fig*) collapse, crash.

traco'tante *ag* overbearing, arrogant.

tradi'mento *sm* betrayal; (*DIR*, *MIL*) treason.

tra'dire *vt* to betray; (*coniuge*) to be unfaithful to; (*doveri: mancare*) to fail in; (*rivelare*) to give away, reveal; **tradi'tore, 'trice** *sm/f* traitor.

tradizio'nale [tradittsjo'nale] *ag* traditional.

tradizi'one [tradit'tsjone] *sf* tradition.

tra'dotto, a *pp di* **tradurre**.

tra'durre *vt* to translate; (*spiegare*) to render, convey; **tradut'tore, 'trice** *sm/f* translator; **traduzi'one** *sf* translation.

tra'ente *sm/f* (*ECON*) drawer.

trafe'lato, a *ag* out of breath.

traffi'cante *sm/f* dealer; (*peg*) trafficker.

traffi'care *vi* (*commerciare*): ~ (**in**) to trade (in), deal (in); (*affaccendarsi*) to busy o.s. // *vt* (*peg*) to traffic in.

'traffico, ci *sm* traffic; (*commercio*) trade, traffic.

tra'figgere [tra'fiddʒere] *vt* to run through, stab; (*fig*) to pierce; **tra'fitto, a** *pp di* **trafiggere**.

trafo'rare *vt* to bore, drill; **tra'foro** *sm* (*azione*) boring, drilling; (*galleria*) tunnel.

tra'gedia [tra'dʒɛdja] *sf* tragedy.

tra'ghetto [tra'gɛtto] *sm* crossing; (*barca*) ferry(boat).

'tragico, a, ci, che ['tradʒiko] *ag* tragic.

tra'gitto [tra'dʒitto] *sm* (*passaggio*) crossing; (*viaggio*) journey.

tragu'ardo *sm* (*SPORT*) finishing line; (*fig*) goal, aim.

traiet'toria *sf* trajectory.

trai'nare *vt* to drag, haul; (*rimorchiare*) to tow; **'traino** *sm* (*carro*) wagon; (*slitta*) sledge; (*carico*) load.

tralasci'are [tralaʃ'ʃare] *vt* (*studi*) to neglect; (*dettagli*) to leave out, omit.

'tralcio ['traltʃo] *sm* (*BOT*) shoot.

tra'liccio [tra'littʃo] *sm* (*tela*) ticking; (*struttura*) trellis; (*ELETTR*) pylon.

tram *sm inv* tram.

'trama *sf* (*filo*) weft, woof; (*fig:* *argomento, maneggio*) plot.

traman'dare *vt* to pass on, hand down.

tra'mare *vt* (*fig*) to scheme, plot.

tram'busto *sm* turmoil.

trames'tio *sm* bustle.

tramez'zino [tramed'dzino] *sm* sandwich.

tra'mezzo [tra'mɛddzo] *sm* (*EDIL*) partition.

'tramite *prep* through.

tramon'tare *vi* to set, go down; **tra'monto** *sm* setting; (*del sole*) sunset.

tramor'tire *vi* to faint // *vt* to stun.

trampo'lino *sm* (*per tuffi*) springboard, diving board; (*per lo sci*) ski-jump.

'trampolo *sm* stilt.

tramu'tare *vt*: ~ **in** to change into, turn into.

tra'nello *sm* trap.

trangugi'are [trangu'dʒare] *vt* to gulp down.

'tranne *prep* except (for), but (for); ~ **che** *cong* unless.

tranquil'lante *sm* (*MED*) tranquillizer.

tranquillità *sf* calm, stillness; quietness; peace of mind.

tranquilliz'zare [trankwillid'dzare] *vt* to reassure.

tran'quillo, a *ag* calm, quiet; (*bambino, scolaro*) quiet; (*sereno*) with one's mind at rest; **sta' ~** don't worry.

transat'lantico, a, ci, che *ag* transatlantic // *sm* transatlantic liner.

tran'satto, a *pp di* **transigere**.

transazi'one [transat'tsjone] *sf* compromise; (*DIR*) settlement; (*COMM*) transaction, deal.

tran'senna *sf* barrier.

tran'sigere [tran'sidʒere] *vi* (*DIR*) to reach a settlement; (*venire a patti*) to compromise, come to an agreement.

tran'sistor *sm*, **transis'tore** *sm* transistor.

transi'tabile *ag* passable.

transi'tare *vi* to pass.

transi'tivo, a *ag* transitive.

'transito *sm* transit; **di ~** (*merci*) in transit; (*stazione*) transit *cpd*; "**divieto di ~**" "no entry".

transi'torio, a *ag* transitory, transient; (*provvisorio*) provisional.

tran'via *sf* tramway (*Brit*), streetcar line (*US*).

'trapano *sm* (*utensile*) drill; (: *MED*) trepan.

trapas'sare *vt* to pierce.

tra'passo *sm* passage.

trape'lare *vi* to leak, drip; (*fig*) to leak out.

tra'pezio [tra'pɛttsjo] *sm* (*MAT*) trapezium; (*attrezzo ginnico*) trapeze.

trapian'tare *vt* to transplant; **trapi'anto** *sm* transplanting; (*MED*) transplant.

'trappola *sf* trap.

tra'punta *sf* quilt.

'trarre *vt* to draw, pull; (*portare*) to take; (*prendere, tirare fuori*) to take (out), draw; (*derivare*) to obtain; ~ **origine da qc** to have its origins o originate in sth.

trasa'lire *vi* to start, jump.

trasan'dato, a *ag* shabby.

trasbor'dare *vt* to transfer; (*NAUT*) to tran(s)ship // *vi* (*NAUT*) to change ship;

(AER) to change plane; (FERR) to change (trains).

trasci'nare [traʃʃi'nare] vt to drag; ~**rsi** vr to drag o.s. along; (fig) to drag on.

tras'correre vt (tempo) to spend, pass // vi to pass; **tras'corso, a** pp di **trascorrere**.

tras'critto, a pp di **trascrivere**.

tras'crivere vt to transcribe.

trascu'rare vt to neglect; (non considerare) to disregard; **trascura'tezza** sf carelessness, negligence; **trascu'rato, a** ag (casa) neglected; (persona) careless, negligent.

traseco'lato, a ag astounded, amazed.

trasferi'mento sm transfer; (trasloco) removal, move.

trasfe'rire vt to transfer; ~**rsi** vr to move; **tras'ferta** sf transfer; (indennità) travelling expenses pl; (SPORT) away game.

trasfigu'rare vt to transfigure.

trasfor'mare vt to transform, change.

trasfusi'one sf (MED) transfusion.

trasgre'dire vt to disobey, contravene.

tras'lato, a ag metaphorical, figurative.

traslo'care vt to move, transfer; ~**rsi** vr to move; **tras'loco, chi** sm removal.

tras'messo, a pp di **trasmettere**.

tras'mettere vt (passare): ~ qc a qn to pass sth on to sb; (mandare) to send; (TECN, TEL, MED) to transmit; (TV, RADIO) to broadcast; **trasmetti'tore** sm transmitter; **trasmissi'one** sf (gen, FISICA, TECN) transmission; (passaggio) transmission, passing on; (TV, RADIO) broadcast; **trasmit'tente** sf transmitting o broadcasting station.

traso'gnato, a [trasoɲ'ɲato] ag dreamy.

traspa'rente ag transparent.

traspa'rire vi to show (through).

traspi'rare vi to perspire; (fig) to come to light, leak out; **traspirazi'one** sf perspiration.

traspor'tare vt to carry, move; (merce) to transport, convey; lasciarsi ~ (da qc) (fig) to let o.s. be carried away (by sth); **tras'porto** sm transport.

trastul'lare vt to amuse; ~**rsi** vr to amuse o.s.

trasu'dare vi (filtrare) to ooze; (sudare) to sweat // vt to ooze with.

trasver'sale ag transverse, cross(-); running at right angles.

trasvo'lare vt to fly over.

'**tratta** sf (ECON) draft; (di persone): la ~ delle bianche the white slave trade.

tratta'mento sm treatment; (servizio) service.

trat'tare vt (gen) to treat; (commerciare) to deal in; (svolgere: argomento) to discuss, deal with; (negoziare) to negotiate // vi: ~ di to deal with; ~ con (persona) to deal with; si tratta di ... it's about ...; **tratta'tive**

sfpl negotiations; **trat'tato** sm (testo) treatise; (accordo) treaty; **trattazi'one** sf treatment.

tratteggi'are [tratted'dʒare] vt (disegnare: a tratti) to sketch, outline; (: col tratteggio) to hatch.

tratte'nere vt (far rimanere: persona) to detain; (intrattenere: ospiti) to entertain; (tenere, frenare, reprimere) to hold back, keep back; (astenersi dal consegnare) to hold, keep; (detrarre: somma) to deduct; ~**rsi** vr (astenersi) to restrain o.s., stop o.s.; (soffermarsi) to stay, remain.

tratteni'mento sm entertainment; (festa) party.

tratte'nuta sf deduction.

trat'tino sm dash; (in parole composte) hyphen.

'**tratto, a** pp di **trarre** // sm (di penna, matita) stroke; (parte) part, piece; (di strada) stretch; (di mare, cielo) expanse; (di tempo) period (of time); ~**i** smpl (caratteristiche) features; (modo di fare) ways, manners; a un ~, d'un ~ suddenly.

trat'tore sm tractor.

tratto'ria sf restaurant.

'**trauma, i** sm trauma; **trau'matico, a, ci, che** ag traumatic.

tra'vaglio [tra'vaʎʎo] sm (angoscia) pain, suffering; (MED) pains pl; ~ di parto labour pains.

trava'sare vt to decant.

'**trave** sf beam.

tra'versa sf (trave) crosspiece; (via) sidestreet; (FERR) sleeper (Brit), (railroad) tie (US); (CALCIO) crossbar.

traver'sare vt to cross; **traver'sata** sf crossing; (AER) flight, trip.

traver'sie sfpl mishaps, misfortunes.

traver'sina sf (FERR) sleeper (Brit), (railroad) tie (US).

tra'verso, a ag oblique; di ~ ag askew // av sideways; andare di ~ (cibo) to go down the wrong way; guardare di ~ to look askance at.

travesti'mento sm disguise.

traves'tire vt to disguise; ~**rsi** vr to disguise o.s.

travi'are vt (fig) to lead astray.

travi'sare vt (fig) to distort, misrepresent.

tra'volgere [tra'vɔldʒere] vt to sweep away, carry away; (fig) to overwhelm; **tra'volto, a** pp di **travolgere**.

tre num three.

trebbi'are vt to thresh.

'**treccia, ce** ['trettʃa] sf plait, braid.

tre'cento num three hundred // sm: il T~ the fourteenth century.

'**tredici** ['treditʃi] num thirteen.

'**tregua** sf truce; (fig) respite.

tre'mare vi: ~ di (freddo etc) to shiver o tremble with; (paura, rabbia) to shake

o tremble with.
tre'mendo, a *ag* terrible, awful.
tre'mila *num* three thousand.
'tremito *sm* trembling *q*; shaking *q*; shivering *q*.
tremo'lare *vi* to tremble; *(luce)* to flicker; *(foglie)* to quiver.
tre'more *sm* tremor.
'treno *sm* train; ~ **di gomme** set of tyres *(Brit)* o tires *(US)*; ~ **merci** goods *(Brit)* o freight train; ~ **viaggiatori** passenger train.
'trenta *num* thirty; **tren'tesimo, a** *num* thirtieth; **tren'tina** *sf:* **una trentina (di)** thirty or so, about thirty.
'trepido, a *ag* anxious.
treppi'ede *sm* tripod; *(CUC)* trivet.
'tresca, sche *sf* *(fig)* intrigue; *(relazione amorosa)* affair.
'trespolo *sm* trestle.
tri'angolo *sm* triangle.
tribù *sf inv* tribe.
tri'buna *sf* *(podio)* platform; *(in aule etc)* gallery; *(di stadio)* stand.
tribu'nale *sm* court.
tribu'tare *vt* to bestow.
tri'buto *sm* tax; *(fig)* tribute.
tri'checo, chi [tri'kɛko] *sm* *(ZOOL)* walrus.
tri'ciclo [tri'tʃiklo] *sm* tricycle.
trico'lore *ag* three-coloured // *sm* tricolour; *(bandiera italiana)* Italian flag.
tri'dente *sm* trident.
tri'foglio [tri'fɔʎʎo] *sm* clover.
tri'glia ['triʎʎa] *sf* red mullet.
tril'lare *vi* *(MUS)* to trill.
tri'mestre *sm* period of three months; *(INS)* term, quarter *(US)*; *(COMM)* quarter.
'trina *sf* lace.
trin'cea [trin'tʃɛa] *sf* trench; **trince'rare** *vt* to entrench.
trinci'are [trin'tʃare] *vt* to cut up.
trion'fare *vi* to triumph, win; ~ **su** to triumph over, overcome; **tri'onfo** *sm* triumph.
tripli'care *vt* to triple.
'triplice ['triplitʃe] *ag* triple; **in ~ copia** in triplicate.
'triplo, a *ag* triple; treble // *sm:* **il ~ (di)** three times as much (as); **la spesa è ~a** it costs three times as much.
'tripode *sm* tripod.
'trippa *sf* *(CUC)* tripe.
'triste *ag* sad; *(luogo)* dreary, gloomy; **tris'tezza** *sf* sadness; gloominess.
trita'carne *sm inv* mincer, grinder *(US)*.
tri'tare *vt* to mince, grind *(US)*.
'trito, a *ag* *(tritato)* minced, ground *(US)*; ~ **e ritrito** *(fig)* trite, hackneyed.
'trittico, ci *sm* *(ARTE)* triptych.
trivel'lare *vt* to drill.
trivi'ale *ag* vulgar, low.
tro'feo *sm* trophy.

'trogolo *sm* *(per maiali)* trough.
'tromba *sf* *(MUS)* trumpet; *(AUT)* horn; ~ **d'aria** whirlwind; ~ **delle scale** stairwell.
trom'bone *sm* trombone.
trom'bosi *sf* thrombosis.
tron'care *vt* to cut off; *(spezzare)* to break off.
'tronco, a, chi, che *ag* cut off; broken off; *(LING)* truncated; *(fig)* cut short // *sm* *(BOT, ANAT)* trunk; *(fig: tratto)* section; *(: pezzo: di lancia)* stump; **licenziare qn in ~** to fire sb on the spot.
troneggi'are [troned'dʒare] *vi:* ~ **(su)** to tower (over).
'tronfio, a *ag* conceited.
'trono *sm* throne.
tropi'cale *ag* tropical.
'tropico, ci *sm* tropic; **~ci** *smpl* tropics.
'troppo, a ◆ *det* *(in eccesso: quantità)* too much; *(: numero)* too many; **c'era ~a gente** there were too many people; **fa ~ caldo** it's too hot
◆ *pronome* *(in eccesso: quantità)* too much; *(: numero)* too many; **ne hai messo ~** you've put in too much; **meglio ~i che pochi** better too many than too few
◆ *av* *(eccessivamente: con ag, av)* too; *(: con vb)* too much; ~ **amaro/tardi** too bitter/late; **lavora ~** he works too much; **di ~** too much; too many; **qualche tazza di ~** a few cups too many; **3000 lire di ~** 3000 lire too much; **essere di ~** to be in the way.
'trota *sf* trout.
trot'tare *vi* to trot; **trotterel'lare** *vi* to trot along; *(bambino)* to toddle; **'trotto** *sm* trot.
'trottola *sf* spinning top.
tro'vare *vt* to find; *(giudicare)*: **trovo che I** find o think that; **~rsi** *vr* *(reciproco: incontrarsi)* to meet; *(essere, stare)* to be; *(arrivare, capitare)* to find o.s.; **andare a ~ qn** to go and see sb; ~ **qn colpevole** to find sb guilty; **~rsi bene** *(in un luogo, con qn)* to get on well; **tro'vata** *sf* good idea.
truc'care *vt* *(falsare)* to fake; *(attore etc)* to make up; *(travestire)* to disguise; *(SPORT)* to fix; *(AUT)* to soup up; **~rsi** *vr* to make up (one's face); **trucca'tore, 'trice** *sm/f* *(CINEMA, TEATRO)* make-up artist.
'trucco, chi *sm* trick; *(cosmesi)* make-up.
'truce ['trutʃe] *ag* fierce.
truci'dare [trutʃi'dare] *vt* to slaughter.
truci'olo ['trutʃolo] *sm* shaving.
'truffa *sf* fraud, swindle; **truf'fare** *vt* to swindle, cheat.
'truppa *sf* troop.
tu *pronome* you; ~ **stesso(a)** you yourself; **dare del ~ a qn** to address sb as "tu".

'tua vedi **tuo**.

'tuba sf (MUS) tuba; (cappello) top hat.

tu'bare vi to coo.

tuba'tura sf, **tubazi'one** [tubat'tsjone] sf piping q, pipes pl.

tu'betto sm tube.

'tubo sm tube; pipe; ~ **digerente** (ANAT) alimentary canal, digestive tract; ~ **di scappamento** (AUT) exhaust pipe.

'tue vedi **tuo**.

tuf'fare vt to plunge, dip; ~**rsi** vr to plunge, dive; **'tuffo** sm dive; (breve bagno) dip.

tu'gurio sm hovel.

tuli'pano sm tulip.

tume'farsi vr (MED) to swell.

'tumido, a ag swollen.

tu'more sm (MED) tumour.

tu'multo sm uproar, commotion; (sommossa) riot; (fig) turmoil; **tumul-tu'oso, a** ag rowdy, unruly; (fig) turbulent, stormy.

'tunica, che sf tunic.

Tuni'sia sf: **la** ~ Tunisia.

'tuo, 'tua, tu'oi, 'tue det: **il** ~, **la tua** etc your // pronome: **il** ~, **la tua** etc yours.

tuo'nare vi to thunder; **tuona** it is thundering, there's some thunder.

tu'ono sm thunder.

tu'orlo sm yolk.

tu'racciolo [tu'rattʃolo] sm cap, top; (di sughero) cork.

tu'rare vt to stop, plug; (con sughero) to cork; ~**rsi il naso** to hold one's nose.

turba'mento sm disturbance; (di animo) anxiety, agitation.

tur'bante sm turban.

tur'bare vt to disturb, trouble.

turbi'nare vi to whirl.

'turbine sm whirlwind; ~ **di neve** swirl of snow; ~ **di polvere/sabbia** dust/sandstorm.

turbo'lento, a ag turbulent; (ragazzo) boisterous, unruly.

turbo'lenza [turbo'lentsa] sf turbulence.

tur'chese [tur'kese] sf turquoise.

Tur'chia [tur'kia] sf: **la** ~ Turkey.

tur'chino, a [tur'kino] ag deep blue.

'turco, a, chi, che ag Turkish // sm/f Turk/Turkish woman // sm (LING) Turkish; **parlare** ~ (fig) to talk double-dutch.

tu'rismo sm tourism; tourist industry; **tu'rista, i, e** sm/f tourist; **tu'ristico, a, ci, che** ag tourist cpd.

'turno sm turn; (di lavoro) shift; **di** ~ (soldato, medico, custode) on duty; **a** ~ (rispondere) in turn; (lavorare) in shifts; **fare a** ~ **a fare qc** to take turns to do sth; **è il suo** ~ it's your (o his etc) turn.

'turpe ag filthy, vile; **turpi'loquio** sm obscene language.

'tuta sf overalls pl; (SPORT) tracksuit.

tu'tela sf (DIR: di minore) guardianship; (: protezione) protection; (difesa) defence; **tute'lare** vt to protect, defend.

tu'tore, 'trice sm/f (DIR) guardian.

tutta'via cong nevertheless, yet.

'tutto, a ♦ det **1** (intero) all; ~ **il latte** all the milk; ~**a la notte** all night; the whole night; ~ **il libro** the whole book; ~**a una bottiglia** a whole bottle

2 (pl, collettivo) all; every; ~**i i libri** all the books; ~**e le notti** every night; ~**i i venerdì** every Friday; ~**i gli uomini** all the men; (collettivo) all men; ~**i e due** both o each of us (o them o you); ~**i e cinque** all five of us (o them o you)

3 (completamente): **era** ~**a sporca** she was all dirty; **tremava** ~ he was trembling all over; **è** ~**a sua madre** she's just o exactly like her mother

4: a tutt'oggi so far, up till now; **a** ~**a velocità** at full o top speed

♦ pronome **1** (ogni cosa) everything, all; (qualsiasi cosa) anything; **ha mangiato** ~ he's eaten everything; ~ **considerato** all things considered; **in** ~: **10.000 lire in** ~ 10,000 lire in all; **in** ~ **eravamo 50** there were 50 of us in all

2: ~**i(e)** (ognuno) all, everybody; **vengono** ~**i** they are all coming, everybody's coming; ~**i quanti** all and sundry

♦ av (completamente) entirely, quite; **è** ~ **il contrario** it's quite o exactly the opposite; **tutt'al più: saranno stati tutt'al più una cinquantina** there were about fifty of them at (the very) most; **tutt'al più possiamo prendere un treno** if the worst comes to the worst we can take a train; **tutt'altro** on the contrary; **è tutt'altro che felice** he's anything but happy; **tutt'a un tratto** suddenly

♦ sm: **il** ~ the whole lot, all of it.

tutto'fare ag inv: **domestica** ~ general maid; **ragazzo** ~ office boy // sm/f handyman/woman.

tut'tora av still.

U

ubbidi'ente ag obedient; **ubbidi'enza** sf obedience.

ubbi'dire vi to obey; ~ **a** to obey; (sog: veicolo, macchina) to respond to.

ubiquità sf: **non ho il dono dell'**~ I can't be everywhere at once.

ubria'care vt: ~ **qn** to get sb drunk; (sog: alcool) to make sb drunk; (fig) to make sb's head spin o reel; ~**rsi** vr to get drunk; ~**rsi di** (fig) to become intoxicated with.

ubri'aco, a, chi, che ag, sm/f drunk.

uccelli'era [uttʃel'ljera] sf aviary.

uccel'lino [uttʃel'lino] sm baby bird, chick.

uc'cello [ut'tʃello] sm bird.

uc'cidere [ut'tʃidere] vt to kill; ~**rsi** vr

(*suicidarsi*) to kill o.s.; (*perdere la vita*) to be killed; **uccisi'one** *sf* killing; **uc'ciso, a** *pp* di **uccidere**; **ucci'sore, uccidi'trice** *sm/f* killer.

udi'enza [u'djɛntsa] *sf* audience; (*DIR*) hearing; **dare ~ (a)** to grant an audience (to).

u'dire *vt* to hear; **udi'tivo, a** *ag* auditory; **udi'to** *sm* (sense of) hearing; **udi'tore, 'trice** *sm/f* listener; (*INS*) unregistered student (*attending lectures*); **udi'torio** *sm* (*persone*) audience.

uffa *escl* tut!

uffici'ale [uffi'tʃale] *ag* official // *sm* (*AMM*) official, officer; (*MIL*) officer; ~ **di stato civile** registrar.

uf'ficio [uf'fitʃo] *sm* (*gen*) office; (*dovere*) duty; (*mansione*) task, function, job; (*agenzia*) agency, bureau; (*REL*) service; **d'~** *ag* official // *av* officially; ~ **di collocamento** employment office; ~ **informazioni** information bureau; ~ **oggetti smarriti** lost property office (*Brit*), lost and found (*US*); ~ **postale** post office.

uffici'oso, a [uffi'tʃoso] *ag* unofficial.

'ufo: a ~ *av* free, for nothing.

uggi'oso, a [ud'dʒoso] *ag* tiresome; (*tempo*) dull.

uguagli'anza [ugwaʎ'ʎantsa] *sf* equality.

uguagli'are [ugwaʎ'ʎare] *vt* to make equal; (*essere uguale*) to equal, be equal to; (*livellare*) to level; ~**rsi a** *o* **con qn** (*paragonarsi*) to compare o.s. to sb.

ugu'ale *ag* equal; (*identico*) identical, the same; (*uniforme*) level, even // *av*: **costano ~** they cost the same; **sono bravi ~** they're equally good; **ugual'mente** *av* equally; (*lo stesso*) all the same.

'ulcera ['ultʃera] *sf* ulcer.

u'liva *etc* = **oliva** *etc*.

ulteri'ore [ulteri'ore] *ag* further.

ulti'mare *vt* to finish, complete.

'ultimo, a *ag* (*finale*) last; (*estremo*) farthest, utmost; (*recente: notizia, moda*) latest; (*fig: sommo, fondamentale*) ultimate // *sm/f* last (one); **fino all'~** to the last, until the end; **da ~, in ~** in the end; **abitare all'~ piano** to live on the top floor; **per ~** (*entrare, arrivare*) last.

ulu'lare *vi* to howl; **ulu'lato** *sm* howling *q*; howl.

umanità *sf* humanity; **umani'tario, a** *ag* humanitarian.

u'mano, a *ag* human; (*comprensivo*) humane.

umbi'lico *sm* = **ombelico**.

umet'tare *vt* to dampen, moisten.

umidità *sf* dampness; humidity.

'umido, a *ag* damp; (*mano, occhi*) moist; (*clima*) humid // *sm* dampness, damp; **carne in ~** stew.

'umile *ag* humble.

umili'are *vt* to humiliate; ~**rsi** *vr* to

humble o.s.; **umiliazi'one** *sf* humiliation.

umiltà *sf* humility, humbleness.

u'more *sm* (*disposizione d'animo*) mood; (*carattere*) temper; **di buon/cattivo ~** in a good/bad mood.

umo'rismo *sm* humour; **avere il senso dell'~** to have a sense of humour; **umo'rista, i,** e *sm/f* humorist; **umo'ristico, a, ci, che** *ag* humorous, funny.

un, un', una *vedi* **uno**.

u'nanime *ag* unanimous; **unanimità** *sf* unanimity; **all'unanimità** unanimously.

unci'netto [untʃi'netto] *sm* crochet hook.

un'cino [un'tʃino] *sm* hook.

'undici ['unditʃi] *num* eleven.

'ungere ['undʒere] *vt* to grease, oil; (*REL*) to anoint; (*fig*) to flatter, butter up; ~**rsi** *vr* (*sporcarsi*) to get covered in grease; ~**rsi con la crema** to put on cream.

unghe'rese [unge'rese] *ag, sm/f, sm* Hungarian.

Unghe'ria [unge'ria] *sf*: **l'~** Hungary.

'unghia ['ungja] *sf* (*ANAT*) nail; (*di animale*) claw; (*di rapace*) talon; (*di cavallo*) hoof; **unghi'ata** *sf* (*graffio*) scratch.

ungu'ento *sm* ointment.

'unico, a, ci, che *ag* (*solo*) only; (*ineguagliabile*) unique; (*singolo: binario*) single; **figlio(a) ~(a)** only son/daughter, only child.

unifi'care *vt* to unite, unify; (*sistemi*) to standardize; **unificazi'one** *sf* uniting; unification; standardization.

uni'forme *ag* uniform; (*superficie*) even // *sf* (*divisa*) uniform.

unilate'rale *ag* one-sided; (*DIR*) unilateral.

uni'one *sf* union; (*fig: concordia*) unity, harmony; **l'U~ Sovietica** the Soviet Union.

u'nire *vt* to unite; (*congiungere*) to join, connect; (: *ingredienti, colori*) to combine; (*in matrimonio*) to unite, join together; ~**rsi** *vr* to unite; (*in matrimonio*) to be joined together; ~ **qc a** to unite sth with; to join *o* connect sth with; to combine sth with; ~**rsi a** (*gruppo, società*) to join.

unità *sf inv* (*unione, concordia*) unity; (*MAT, MIL, COMM, di misura*) unit; **uni'tario, a** *ag* unitary; **prezzo unitario** price per unit.

u'nito, a *ag* (*paese*) united; (*amici, famiglia*) close; **in tinta ~a** plain, self-coloured.

univer'sale *ag* universal; general.

università *sf inv* university; **universi'tario, a** *ag* university *cpd* // *sm/f* (*studente*) university student; (*insegnante*) academic, university lecturer.

uni'verso *sm* universe.

'uno, a (*dav sm* **un** + *C, V,* **uno** + *s impura, gn, pn, ps, x, z; dav sf* **un'** + *V,* **una** + *C*) ◆ *articolo indefinito* **1** a; (*dav vocale*) an; **un bambino** a child; **~a strada** a street; **~ zingaro** a gypsy

2 (*intensivo*): **ho avuto ~a paura!** I got such a fright!

◆ *pronome* **1** one; **prendine ~** take one (of them); **l'~ o l'altro** either (of them); **l'~ e l'altro** both (of them); **aiutarsi l'un l'altro** to help one another *o* each other; **sono entrati l'~ dopo l'altro** they came in one after the other

2 (*un tale*) someone, somebody

3 (*con valore impersonale*) one, you; **se ~ vuole** if one wants, if you want

◆ *num* one; **~a mela e due pere** one apple and two pears; **~ più ~ fa due** one plus one equals two, one and one are two ◆ *sf*: **è l'~a** it's one (o'clock).

'unto, a *pp di* **ungere** // *ag* greasy, oily // *sm* grease; **untu'oso, a** *ag* greasy, oily.

u'omo, *pl* **u'omini** *sm* man; **da ~** (*abito, scarpe*) men's, for men; **~ d'affari** businessman; **~ di paglia** stooge; **~ rana** frogman.

u'opo *sm*: **all'~** if necessary.

u'ovo, *pl(f)* **u'ova** *sm* egg; **~ affogato** poached egg; **~ bazzotto/sodo** soft-/hard-boiled egg; **~ alla coque** boiled egg; **~ di Pasqua** Easter egg; **uova strapazzate** scrambled eggs.

ura'gano *sm* hurricane.

urba'nistica *sf* town planning.

ur'bano, a *ag* urban, city *cpd*, town *cpd*; (*TEL: chiamata*) local; (*fig*) urbane.

ur'gente [ur'dʒɛnte] *ag* urgent; **ur'genza** *sf* urgency; **in caso d'urgenza** in (case of) an emergency; **d'urgenza** *ag* emergency // *av* urgently, as a matter of urgency.

'urgere ['urdʒere] *vi* to be urgent; to be needed urgently.

u'rina *sf* = **orina**.

ur'lare *vi* (*persona*) to scream, yell; (*animale, vento*) to howl // *vt* to scream, yell.

'urlo, *pl(m)* **'urli,** *pl(f)* **'urla** *sm* scream, yell; howl.

'urna *sf* urn; (*elettorale*) ballot-box; **andare alle ~e** to go to the polls.

urrà *escl* hurrah!

U.R.S.S. *abbr f*: **l'~** the USSR.

ur'tare *vt* to bump into, knock against; (*fig: irritare*) to annoy // *vi*: **~ contro** *o* **in** to bump into, knock against, crash into; (*fig: imbattersi*) to come up against; **~rsi** *vr* (*reciproco: scontrarsi*) to collide; (*: fig*) to clash; (*irritarsi*) to get annoyed; **'urto** *sm* (*colpo*) knock, bump; (*scontro*) crash, collision; (*fig*) clash.

U.S.A. ['uza] *smpl*: **gli ~** the USA.

u'sanza [u'zantsa] *sf* custom; (*moda*) fashion.

u'sare *vt* to use, employ // *vi* (*servirsi*): **~ di** to use; (*: diritto*) to exercise; (*essere di moda*) to be fashionable; (*essere solito*): **~ fare** to be in the habit of doing, be accustomed to doing // *vb impersonale*: **qui usa così** it's the custom round here; **u'sato, a** *ag* used; (*consumato*) worn; (*di seconda mano*) used, second-hand // *sm* second-hand goods *pl*.

usci'ere [uʃ'ʃere] *sm* usher.

'uscio ['uʃʃo] *sm* door.

u'scire [uʃ'ʃire] *vi* (*gen*) to come out; (*partire, andare a passeggio, a uno spettacolo etc*) to go out; (*essere sorteggiato: numero*) to come up; **~ da** (*gen*) to leave; (*posto*) to go (*o* come) out of, leave; (*solco, vasca etc*) to come out of; (*muro*) to stick out of; (*competenza etc*) to be outside; (*infanzia, adolescenza*) to leave behind; (*famiglia nobile etc*) to come from; **~ da** *o* **di casa** to go out; (*fig*) to leave home; **~ in automobile** to go out in the car, go for a drive; **~ di strada** (*AUT*) to go off *o* leave the road.

u'scita [uʃ'ʃita] *sf* (*passaggio, varco*) exit, way out; (*per divertimento*) outing; (*ECON: somma*) expenditure; (*TEATRO*) entrance; (*fig: battuta*) witty remark; **~ di sicurezza** emergency exit.

usi'gnolo [uziɲ'ɲɔlo] *sm* nightingale.

U.S.L. [uzl] *sigla f* (= *unità sanitaria locale*) local health centre.

'uso *sm* (*utilizzazione*) use; (*esercizio*) practice; (*abitudine*) custom; **a ~ di** for (the use of); **d'~** (*corrente*) in use; **fuori ~** out of use.

usti'one *sf* burn.

usu'ale *ag* common, everyday.

u'sura *sf* usury; (*logoramento*) wear (and tear).

uten'sile *sm* tool, implement; **~i da cucina** kitchen utensils.

u'tente *sm/f* user.

'utero *sm* uterus.

'utile *ag* useful // *sm* (*vantaggio*) advantage, benefit; (*ECON: profitto*) profit; **utilità** *sf* usefulness *q*; use; (*vantaggio*) benefit; **utili'tario, a** *ag* utilitarian // *sf* (*AUT*) economy car.

utiliz'zare [utilid'dzare] *vt* to use, make use of, utilize.

'uva *sf* grapes *pl*; **~ passa** raisins *pl*; **~ spina** gooseberry.

V

v. *abbr* (= *vedi*) v.

va *vb vedi* **andare**.

va'cante *ag* vacant.

va'canza [va'kantsa] *sf* (*l'essere vacante*) vacancy; (*riposo, ferie*) holiday(s *pl*)

(*Brit*), vacation (*US*); (*giorno di permesso*) day off, holiday; ~e *sfpl* (*periodo di ferie*) holidays (*Brit*), vacation *sg* (*US*); essere/andare in ~ to be/go on holiday *o* vacation; ~e estive summer holiday(s) *o* vacation.

'**vacca**, **che** *sf* cow.

vacci'nare [vattʃi'nare] *vt* to vaccinate.

vacil'lare [vatʃil'lare] *vi* to sway, wobble; (*luce*) to flicker; (*fig: memoria, coraggio*) to be failing, falter.

'**vacuo**, **a** *ag* (*fig*) empty, vacuous // *sm* vacuum.

'**vado** *vb vedi* **andare**.

vaga'bondo, **a** *sm/f* tramp, vagrant; (*fannullone*) idler, loafer.

va'gare *vi* to wander.

vagheggi'are [vaged'dʒare] *vt* to long for, dream of.

va'gina [va'dʒina] *sf* vagina.

va'gire [va'dʒire] *vi* to whimper.

'**vaglia** ['vaʎʎa] *sm inv* money order; ~ postale postal order.

vagli'are [vaʎ'ʎare] *vt* to sift; (*fig*) to weigh up; '**vaglio** *sm* sieve.

'**vago**, **a**, **ghi**, **ghe** *ag* vague.

va'gone *sm* (*FERR: per passeggeri*) coach; (: *per merci*) truck, wagon; ~ letto sleeper, sleeping car; ~ ristorante dining *o* restaurant car.

'**vai** *vb vedi* **andare**.

vai'olo *sm* smallpox.

va'langa, **ghe** *sf* avalanche.

va'lente *ag* able, talented.

va'lere *vi* (*avere forza, potenza*) to have influence; (*essere valido*) to be valid; (*avere vigore, autorità*) to hold, apply; (*essere capace: poeta, studente*) to be good, be able // *vt* (*prezzo, sforzo*) to be worth; (*corrispondere*) to correspond to; (*procurare*): ~ qc a qn to earn sb sth; ~rsi di to make use of, take advantage of; far ~ (*autorità etc*) to assert; vale a dire that is to say; ~ la pena to be worth the effort *o* worth it.

va'levole *ag* valid.

vali'care *vt* to cross.

'**valico**, **chi** *sm* (*passo*) pass.

'**valido**, **a** *ag* valid; (*rimedio*) effective; (*aiuto*) real; (*persona*) worthwhile.

valige'ria [validʒe'ria] *sf* leather goods *pl*; leather goods factory; leather goods shop.

va'ligia, **gie** *o* **ge** [va'lidʒa] *sf* (*suit*)case; fare le ~gie to pack (up); ~ diplomatica diplomatic bag.

val'lata *sf* valley.

'**valle** *sf* valley; a ~ (*di fiume*) downstream; scendere a ~ to go downhill.

val'letto *sm* valet.

va'lore *sm* (*gen*) value; (*merito*) merit, worth; (*coraggio*) valour, courage; (*COMM: titolo*) security; ~i *smpl* (*oggetti preziosi*) valuables.

valoriz'zare [valorid'dzare] *vt* (*terreno*)

to develop; (*fig*) to make the most of.

'**valso**, **a** *pp di* **valere**.

va'luta *sf* currency, money; (*BANCA*): ~ 15 gennaio interest to run from January 15th.

valu'tare *vt* (*casa, gioiello, fig*) to value; (*stabilire: peso, entrate, fig*) to estimate; **valutazi'one** *sf* valuation; estimate.

'**valvola** *sf* (*TECN, ANAT*) valve; (*ELETTR*) fuse.

'**valzer** ['valtser] *sm inv* waltz.

vam'pata *sf* (*di fiamma*) blaze; (*di calore*) blast; (: *al viso*) flush.

vam'piro *sm* vampire.

vanda'lismo *sm* vandalism.

'**vandalo** *sm* vandal.

vaneggi'are [vaned'dʒare] *vi* to rave.

'**vanga**, **ghe** *sf* spade; **van'gare** *vt* to dig.

van'gelo [van'dʒelo] *sm* gospel.

va'niglia [va'niʎʎa] *sf* vanilla.

vani'tà *sf* vanity; (*di promessa*) emptiness; (*di sforzo*) futility; **vani'toso, a** *ag* vain, conceited.

'**vanno** *vb vedi* **andare**.

'**vano**, **a** *ag* vain // *sm* (*spazio*) space; (*apertura*) opening; (*stanza*) room.

van'taggio [van'taddʒo] *sm* advantage; essere/portarsi in ~ (*SPORT*) to be in/ take the lead; **vantaggi'oso, a** *ag* advantageous; favourable.

van'tare *vt* to praise, speak highly of; ~rsi *vr*: ~rsi (**di/di aver fatto**) to boast *o* brag (about/about having done); **vante'ria** *sf* boasting; '**vanto** *sm* boasting; (*merito*) virtue, merit; (*gloria*) pride.

'**vanvera** *sf*: a ~ haphazardly; parlare a ~ to talk nonsense.

va'pore *sm* vapour; (*anche:* ~ acqueo) steam; (*nave*) steamer; a ~ (*turbina etc*) steam *cpd*; al ~ (*CUC*) steamed; **vapo'retto** *sm* steamer; **vapori'era** *sf* (*FERR*) steam engine; **vaporiz'zare** *vt* to vaporize; **vapo'roso, a** *ag* (*tessuto*) filmy; (*capelli*) soft and full.

va'rare *vt* (*NAUT, fig*) to launch; (*DIR*) to pass.

var'care *vt* to cross.

'**varco**, **chi** *sm* passage; aprirsi un ~ tra la folla to push one's way through the crowd.

vari'abile *ag* variable; (*tempo, umore*) changeable, variable // *sf* (*MAT*) variable.

vari'are *vt*, *vi* to vary; ~ di opinione to change one's mind; **variazi'one** *sf* variation; change.

va'rice [va'ritʃe] *sf* varicose vein.

vari'cella [vari'tʃɛlla] *sf* chickenpox.

vari'coso, a *ag* varicose.

varie'gato, a *ag* variegated.

varie'tà *sf inv* variety // *sm inv* variety show.

'**vario**, **a** *ag* varied; (*parecchi:* col so-

stantivo al pl) various; (*mutevole: umore*) changeable; **vario'pinto, a** *ag* multicoloured.

'**varo** *sm* (*NAUT, fig*) launch; (*di leggi*) passing.

va'**saio** *sm* potter.

'**vasca, sche** *sf* basin; (*anche: ~ da bagno*) bathtub, bath.

va'**scello** [vaʃˈʃɛllo] *sm* (*NAUT*) vessel, ship.

vase'lina *sf* vaseline.

vasel'lame *sm* (*stoviglie*) crockery; (: *di porcellana*) china; ~ **d'oro/d'argento** gold/silver plate.

'**vaso** *sm* (*recipiente*) pot; (: *barattolo*) jar; (: *decorativo*) vase; (*ANAT*) vessel; ~ **da fiori** vase; (*per piante*) flowerpot.

vas'**soio** *sm* tray.

'**vasto, a** *ag* vast, immense.

Vati'**cano** *sm*: il ~ the Vatican.

ve *pronome, av vedi* **vi**.

vecchi'**aia** [vekˈkjaja] *sf* old age.

'**vecchio, a** ['vɛkkjo] *ag* old // *sm/f* old man/woman; **i ~i** the old.

'**vece** ['vetʃe] *sf*: **in ~ di** in the place of, for; **fare le ~i di qn** to take sb's place.

ve'**dere** *vt, vi* to see; ~**rsi** *vr* to meet, see one another; **avere a che ~ con** to have something to do with; **far ~ qc a qn** to show sb sth; **farsi ~** to show o.s.; (*farsi vivo*) to show one's face; **vedi di non farlo** make sure o see you don't do it; **non (ci) si vede** (*è buio etc*) you can't see a thing; **non lo posso ~** (*fig*) I can't stand him.

ve'**detta** *sf* (*sentinella, posto*) look-out; (*NAUT*) patrol boat.

'**vedovo, a** *sm/f* widower/widow.

ve'**duta** *sf* view.

vee'**mente** *ag* vehement; violent.

vege'**tale** [vedʒeˈtale] *ag, sm* vegetable.

vegetari'**ano, a** [vedʒetaˈrjano] *ag, sm/f* vegetarian.

'**vegeto, a** ['vɛdʒeto] *ag* (*pianta*) thriving; (*persona*) strong, vigorous.

'**veglia** ['veʎʎa] *sf* wakefulness; (*sorveglianza*) watch; (*trattenimento*) evening gathering; **fare la ~ a un malato** to watch over a sick person.

vegli'**are** [veʎˈʎare] *vi* to be awake; to stay o sit up; (*stare vigile*) to watch; to keep watch // *vt* (*malato, morto*) to watch over, sit up with.

ve'**icolo** *sm* vehicle; ~ **spaziale** spacecraft *inv*.

'**vela** *sf* (*NAUT: tela*) sail; (*sport*) sailing.

ve'**lare** *vt* to veil; ~**rsi** *vr* (*occhi, luna*) to mist over; (*voce*) to become husky; ~**rsi il viso** to cover one's face (with a veil); **ve'lato, a** *ag* veiled.

veleggi'**are** [veledˈdʒare] *vi* to sail; (*AER*) to glide.

ve'**leno** *sm* poison; **vele'noso, a** *ag* poisonous.

veli'**ero** *sm* sailing ship.

ve'**lina** *sf* (*anche:* **carta ~**: *per imballare*) tissue paper; (: *per copie*) flimsy paper; (*copia*) carbon copy.

ve'**livolo** *sm* aircraft.

velleità *sf inv* vain ambition, vain desire.

'**vello** *sm* fleece.

vel'**luto** *sm* velvet; ~ **a coste** cord.

'**velo** *sm* veil; (*tessuto*) voile.

ve'**loce** [veˈlotʃe] *ag* fast, quick // *av* fast, quickly; **velo'cista, i, e** *sm/f* (*SPORT*) sprinter; **velocità** *sf* speed; **a forte velocità** at high speed; **velocità di crociera** cruising speed.

ve'**lodromo** *sm* velodrome.

'**vena** *sf* (*gen*) vein; (*filone*) vein, seam; (*fig: ispirazione*) inspiration; (: *umore*) mood; **essere in ~ di qc** to be in the mood for sth.

ve'**nale** *ag* (*prezzo, valore*) market *cpd*; (*fig*) venal; mercenary.

ven'**demmia** *sf* (*raccolta*) grape harvest; (*quantità d'uva*) grape crop, grapes *pl*; (*vino ottenuto*) vintage; **vendemmi'are** *vt* to harvest // *vi* to harvest the grapes.

'**vendere** *vt* to sell; "**vendesi**" "for sale".

ven'**detta** *sf* revenge.

vendi'**care** *vt* to avenge; ~**rsi** *vr*: ~**rsi (di)** to avenge o.s. (for); (*per rancore*) to take one's revenge (for); ~**rsi su qn** to revenge o.s. on sb; **vendica'tivo, a** *ag* vindictive.

'**vendita** *sf* sale; **la ~** (*attività*) selling; (*smercio*) sales *pl*; **in ~** on sale; ~ **all'asta** sale by auction; **vendi'tore** *sm* seller, vendor; (*gestore di negozio*) trader, dealer.

vene'**fico, a, ci, che** *dg* poisonous.

vene'**rabile** *ag*, **vene'rando, a** *ag* venerable.

vene'**rare** *vt* to venerate.

vener'**dì** *sm inv* Friday; **di** *o* **il ~** on Fridays; **V~ Santo** Good Friday.

ve'**nereo, a** *ag* venereal.

'**veneto, a** *ag, sm/f* Venetian.

Ve'**nezia** [veˈnɛttsja] *sf* Venice; **venezi'ano, a** *ag, sm/f* Venetian.

veni'**ale** *ag* venial.

ve'**nire** *vi* to come; (*riuscire: dolce, fotografia*) to turn out; (*come ausiliare: essere*): **viene ammirato da tutti** he is admired by everyone; ~ **da** to come from; **quanto viene?** how much does it cost?; **far ~** (*mandare a chiamare*) to send for; ~ **giù** to come down; ~ **meno** (*svenire*) to faint; ~ **meno a qc** not to fulfil sth; ~ **su** to come up; ~ **a trovare qn** to come and see sb; ~ **via** to come away.

ven'**taglio** [venˈtaʎʎo] *sm* fan.

ven'**tata** *sf* gust (of wind).

ven'**tenne** *ag*: **una ragazza ~** a twenty-year-old girl, a girl of twenty.

ven'**tesimo, a** *num* twentieth.

'venti num twenty.

venti'lare vt (stanza) to air, ventilate; (fig: idea, proposta) to air; **ventila'tore** sm ventilator, fan.

ven'tina sf: una ~ (di) around twenty, twenty or so.

venti'sette num twenty-seven; il ~ (giorno di paga) (monthly) pay day.

'vento sm wind.

'ventola sf (AUT, TECN) fan.

ven'tosa sf (ZOOL) sucker; (di gomma) suction pad.

ven'toso, a ag windy.

'ventre sm stomach.

ven'tura sf: andare alla ~ to trust to luck; soldato di ~ mercenary.

ven'turo, a ag next, coming.

ve'nuto, a pp di **venire** // sf coming, arrival.

vera'mente av really.

ver'bale ag verbal // sm (di riunione) minutes pl.

'verbo sm (LING) verb; (parola) word; (REL): il V~ the Word.

'verde ag, sm green; essere al ~ to be broke; ~ bottiglia/oliva ag inv bottle/ olive green.

verde'rame sm verdigris.

ver'detto sm verdict.

ver'dura sf vegetables pl.

vere'condo, a ag modest.

'verga, ghe sf rod.

ver'gato a ag (foglio) ruled.

'vergine ['vɛrdʒine] sf virgin; (dello zodiaco): V~ Virgo // ag virgin; (ragazza): essere ~ to be a virgin.

ver'gogna [ver'goɲɲa] sf shame; (timidezza) shyness, embarrassment; vergo'gnarsi vr: vergognarsi (di) to be o feel ashamed (of); to be shy (about); be embarrassed (about); **vergo'gnoso, a** ag ashamed; (timido) shy, embarrassed; (causa di vergogna: azione) shameful.

ve'rifica, che sf checking q, check.

verifi'care vt (controllare) to check; (confermare) to confirm, bear out

verità sf inv truth.

veriti'ero, a ag (che dice la verità) truthful; (conforme a verità) true.

'verme sm worm.

vermi'celli [vermi'tʃɛlli] smpl vermicelli sg.

ver'miglio [ver'miʎʎo] sm vermilion, scarlet.

'vermut sm inv vermouth.

ver'nice [ver'nitʃe] sf (colorazione) paint; (trasparente) varnish; (pelle) patent leather; "~ fresca" "wet paint"; **vernici'are** vt to paint; to varnish.

'vero, a ag (veridico): fatti, testimonianza) true; (autentico) real // sm (verità) truth; (realtà) (real) life; un ~ e proprio delinquente a real criminal, an out and out criminal.

vero'simile ag likely, probable.

ver'ruca, che sf wart.

versa'mento sm (pagamento) payment; (deposito di denaro) deposit.

ver'sante sm slopes pl, side.

ver'sare vt (fare uscire: vino, farina) to pour (out), (spargere: lacrime, sangue) to shed; (rovesciare) to spill; (ECON) to pay; (: depositare) to deposit, pay in; ~rsi vr (rovesciarsi) to spill; (fiume, folla): ~rsi (in) to pour (into).

versa'tile ag versatile.

ver'setto sm (REL) verse.

versi'one sf version; (traduzione) translation.

'verso sm (di poesia) verse, line; (di animale, uccello, venditore ambulante) cry; (direzione) direction; (modo) way; (di foglio di carta) verso; (di moneta) reverse; ~i smpl (poesia) verse sg; non c'è ~ di persuaderlo there's no way of persuading him, he can't be persuaded // prep (in direzione di) toward(s); (nei pressi di) near, around (about); (in senso temporale) about, around; (nei confronti di) for; ~ di me towards me; ~ sera towards evening.

verti'cale ag, sf vertical.

'vertice ['vɛrtitʃe] sm summit, top; (MAT) vertex; conferenza al ~ (POL) summit conference.

ver'tigine [ver'tidʒine] sf dizziness q; dizzy spell; (MED) vertigo; avere le ~i to feel dizzy; **vertigi'noso, a** ag (altezza) dizzy; (fig) breathtakingly high (o deep etc).

ve'scica, che [veʃ'ʃika] sf (ANAT) bladder; (MED) blister.

'vescovo sm bishop.

'vespa sf wasp.

'vespro sm (REL) vespers pl.

ves'sillo sm standard; (bandiera) flag.

ves'taglia [ves'taʎʎa] sf dressing gown.

'veste sf garment; (rivestimento) covering; (qualità, facoltà) capacity; ~i sfpl clothes, clothing sg; in ~ ufficiale (fig) in an official capacity; in ~ di in the guise of, as; **vesti'ario** sm wardrobe, clothes pl.

ves'tibolo sm (entrance) hall.

ves'tire vt (bambino, malato) to dress; (avere indosso) to have on, wear; ~rsi vr to dress, get dressed; **ves'tito, a** ag dressed // sm garment; (da donna) dress; (da uomo) suit; vestiti smpl clothes; vestito di bianco dressed in white.

Ve'suvio sm: il ~ Vesuvius.

vete'rano, a ag, sm/f veteran.

veteri'nario, a ag veterinary // sm veterinary surgeon (Brit), veterinarian (US), vet // sf veterinary medicine.

'veto sm inv veto.

ve'traio sm glassmaker; glazier.

ve'trato, a ag (porta, finestra) glazed;

(che contiene vetro) glass *cpd // sf* glass door *(o* window); *(di chiesa)* stained glass window.

vetre'ria *sf (stabilimento)* glassworks *sg; (oggetti di vetro)* glassware.

ve'trina *sf (di negozio)* (shop) window; *(armadio)* display cabinet; **vetri'nista, i, e** *sm/f* window dresser.

vetri'olo *sm* vitriol.

'vetro *sm* glass; *(per finestra, porta)* pane (of glass).

'vetta *sf* peak, summit, top.

vet'tore *sm (MAT, FISICA)* vector; *(chi trasporta)* carrier.

vetto'vaglie [vetto'vaʎʎe] *sfpl* supplies.

vet'tura *sf (carrozza)* carriage; *(FERR)* carriage *(Brit),* car *(US); (auto)* car *(Brit),* automobile *(US).*

vezzeggi'are [vettsed'dʒare] *vt* to fondle, caress; **vezzeggia'tivo** *sm (LING)* term of endearment.

'vezzo ['vettso] *sm* habit; **~i** *smpl (smancerie)* affected ways; *(leggiadria)* charms; **vez'zoso, a** *ag (grazioso)* charming, pretty; *(lezioso)* affected.

vi, *(dav* lo, la, li, le, ne *diventa* **ve** *pronome (oggetto)* you; *(complemento di termine)* (to) you; *(riflessivo)* yourselves; *(reciproco)* each other *// av (lì)* there; *(qui)* here; *(per questo/quel luogo)* through here/there; **~ è/sono** there is/ are.

'via *sf (gen)* way; *(strada)* street; *(sentiero, pista)* path, track; *(AMM: procedimento)* channels *pl // prep (passando per)* via, by way of *// av* away *// escl* go away!; *(suvvia)* come on!; *(SPORT)* go! *// sm (SPORT)* starting signal; **in ~ di guarigione** on the road to recovery; **per ~ di** *(a causa di)* because of, on account of; **in** *o* **per ~** on the way; **per ~ aerea** by air; *(lettere)* by airmail; **andare/essere ~** to go/be away; **~ ~ che** *(a mano a mano)* as; **dare il ~** *(SPORT)* to give the starting signal; **dare il ~ a** *(fig)* to start; **V~ lattea** *(ASTR)* Milky Way; **~ di mezzo** middle course; **in ~ provvisoria** provisionally.

viabilità *sf (di strada)* practicability; *(rete stradale)* roads *pl,* road network.

via'dotto *sm* viaduct.

viaggi'are [viad'dʒare] *vi* to travel; **viaggia'tore, 'trice** *ag* travelling *// sm* traveller; *(passeggero)* passenger.

vi'aggio ['vjaddʒo] *sm* travel(ling); *(tragitto)* journey, trip; **buon ~!** have a good trip!; **~ di nozze** honeymoon.

vi'ale *sm* avenue.

via'vai *sm* coming and going, bustle.

vi'brare *vi* to vibrate; *(agitarsi):* **~ (di)** to quiver (with).

vi'cario *sm (apostolico o)* vicar.

'vice ['vitʃe] *sm/f* deputy *// prefisso:* **~'console** *sm* vice-consul; **~diret'tore** *sm* assistant manager.

vi'cenda [vi'tʃenda] *sf* event; **a ~ in** turn; **vicen'devole** *ag* mutual, reciprocal.

vice'versa [vitʃe'vɛrsa] *av* vice versa; **da Roma a Pisa e ~** from Rome to Pisa and back.

vici'nanza [vitʃi'nantsa] *sf* nearness, closeness; **~e** *sfpl* neighbourhood, vicinity.

vici'nato [vitʃi'nato] *sm* neighbourhood; *(vicini)* neighbours *pl.*

vi'cino, a [vi'tʃino] *ag (gen)* near; *(nello spazio)* near, nearby; *(accanto)* next; *(nel tempo)* near, close at hand *// sm/f* neighbour *// av* near, close; **da ~** *(guardare)* close up; *(esaminare, seguire)* closely; *(conoscere)* well, intimately; **~ a** *prep* near (to), close to; *(accanto a)* beside; **~ di casa** neighbour.

'vicolo *sm* alley; **~ cieco** blind alley.

'video *sm inv (TV: schermo)* screen; **~cas'setta** *sf* videocassette; **~regi-stra'tore** *sm* video (recorder).

vie'tare *vt* to forbid; *(AMM)* to prohibit; **~ a qn di fare** to forbid sb to do; to prohibit sb from doing; **"vietato fumare/ l'ingresso"** "no smoking/admittance".

Viet'nam *sm:* **il ~** Vietnam; **vietna'mita, i, e** *ag, sm/f, sm* Vietnamese *inv.*

vi'gente [vi'dʒɛnte] *ag* in force.

vigi'lante [vidʒi'lante] *ag* vigilant, watchful.

vigi'lare [vidʒi'lare] *vt* to watch over, keep an eye on; **~ che** to make sure that, see to it that.

'vigile ['vidʒile] *ag* watchful *// sm (anche:* **~ urbano)** policeman *(in towns);* **~ del fuoco** fireman.

vi'gilia [vi'dʒilja] *sf (giorno antecedente)* eve; **la ~ di Natale** Christmas Eve.

vigli'acco, a, chi, che [viʎ'ʎakko] *ag* cowardly *// sm/f* coward.

'vigna ['viɲɲa] *sf,* **vi'gneto** [viɲ'ɲeto] *sm* vineyard.

vi'gnetta [viɲ'ɲetta] *sf* cartoon.

vi'gore *sm* vigour; *(DIR):* **essere/entrare in ~** to be in/come into force; **vigo'roso, a** *ag* vigorous.

'vile *ag (spregevole)* low, mean, base; *(codardo)* cowardly.

vili'pendio *sm* contempt, scorn; public insult.

'villa *sf* villa.

vil'laggio [vil'laddʒo] *sm* village.

villa'nia *sf* rudeness, lack of manners; **fare** *(o* **dire) una ~ a qn** to be rude to sb.

vil'lano, a *ag* rude, ill-mannered *// sm* boor.

villeggia'tura [villeddʒa'tura] *sf* holiday(s *pl) (Brit),* vacation *(US).*

vil'lino *sm* small house (with a garden), cottage.

vil'loso, a *ag* hairy.

viltà *sf* cowardice *q*; cowardly act.

'vimine *sm* wicker; **mobili di ~i** wicker furniture *sg.*

'vincere ['vintʃere] *vt* (*in guerra, al gioco, a una gara*) to defeat, beat; (*premio, guerra, partita*) to win; (*fig*) to overcome, conquer // *vi* to win; ~ **qn in bellezza** to be better-looking than sb; **'vincita** *sf* win; (*denaro vinto*) winnings *pl*; **vinci'tore** *sm* winner; (*MIL*) victor.

vinco'lare *vt* to bind; (*COMM: denaro*) to tie up; **'vincolo** *sm* (*fig*) bond, tie; (*DIR: servitù*) obligation.

vi'nicolo, a *ag* wine *cpd.*

'vino *sm* wine; ~ **bianco/rosso** white/red wine.

'vinto, a *pp di* **vincere.**

vi'ola *sf* (*BOT*) violet; (*MUS*) viola // *ag, sm inv* (*colore*) purple.

vio'lare *vt* (*chiesa*) to desecrate, violate; (*giuramento, legge*) to violate.

violen'tare *vt* to use violence on; (*donna*) to rape.

vio'lento, a *ag* violent; **vio'lenza** *sf* violence; **violenza carnale** rape.

vio'letto, a *ag, sm* (*colore*) violet // *sf* (*BOT*) violet.

violi'nista, i, e *sm/f* violinist.

vio'lino *sm* violin.

violon'cello [violon'tʃello] *sm* cello.

vi'ottolo *sm* path, track.

'vipera *sf* viper, adder.

vi'raggio [vi'raddʒo] *sm* (*NAUT, AER*) turn; (*FOT*) toning.

vi'rare *vt* (*NAUT*) to haul (in), heave (in) // *vi* (*NAUT, AER*) to turn; (*FOT*) to tone; ~ **di bordo** (*NAUT*) to tack.

'virgola *sf* (*LING*) comma; (*MAT*) point; **virgo'lette** *sfpl* inverted commas, quotation marks.

vi'rile *ag* (*proprio dell'uomo*) masculine; (*non puerile, da uomo*) manly, virile.

virtù *sf inv* virtue; **in o per** ~ **di** by virtue of, by.

virtu'ale *ag* virtual.

virtu'oso, a *ag* virtuous // *sm/f* (*MUS etc*) virtuoso.

'virus *sm inv* virus.

'viscere ['viʃʃere] *sm* (*ANAT*) internal organ // *sfpl* (*di animale*) entrails *pl*; (*fig*) bowels *pl.*

'vischio ['viskjo] *sm* (*BOT*) mistletoe; (*pania*) birdlime; **vischi'oso, a** *ag* sticky.

'viscido, a ['viʃʃido] *ag* slimy.

vi'sibile *ag* visible.

visi'bilio *sm*: **andare in** ~ to go into raptures.

visibilità *sf* visibility.

visi'era *sf* (*di elmo*) visor; (*di berretto*) peak.

visi'one *sf* vision; **prendere** ~ **di qc** to examine sth, look sth over; **prima/seconda** ~ (*CINEMA*) first/second showing.

'visita *sf* visit; (*MED*) visit, call; (: *esame*) examination; **visi'tare** *vt* to visit; (*MED*) to visit, call on; (: *esaminare*) to examine; **visita'tore, 'trice** *sm/f* visitor.

vi'sivo, a *ag* visual.

'viso *sm* face.

vi'sone *sm* mink.

'vispo, a *ag* quick, lively.

vis'suto, a *pp di* **vivere** // *ag* (*aria, modo di fare*) experienced.

'vista *sf* (*facoltà*) (eye)sight; (*fatto di vedere*): **la** ~ **di** the sight of; (*veduta*) view; **sparare a** ~ to shoot on sight; **in** ~ in sight; **perdere qn di** ~ to lose sight of sb; (*fig*) to lose touch with sb; **a** ~ **d'occhio** as far as the eye can see; (*fig*) before one's very eyes; **far** ~ **di fare** to pretend to do.

'visto, a *pp di* **vedere** // *sm* visa; ~ **che** *cong* seeing (that).

vis'toso, a *ag* gaudy, garish; (*ingente*) considerable.

visu'ale *ag* visual; **visualizza'tore** *sm* (*INFORM*) visual display unit, VDU.

'vita *sf* life; (*ANAT*) waist; **a** ~ for life.

vi'tale *ag* vital; **vita'lizio, a** *ag* life *cpd* // *sm* life annuity.

vita'mina *sf* vitamin.

'vite *sf* (*BOT*) vine; (*TECN*) screw.

vi'tello *sm* (*ZOOL*) calf; (*carne*) veal; (*pelle*) calfskin.

vi'ticcio [vi'tittʃo] *sm* (*BOT*) tendril.

viticol'tore *sm* wine grower; **viticol'tura** *sf* wine growing.

'vitreo, a *ag* vitreous; (*occhio, sguardo*) glassy.

'vittima *sf* victim.

'vitto *sm* food; (*in un albergo etc*) board; ~ **e alloggio** board and lodging.

vit'toria *sf* victory.

'viva *escl*: ~ **il re!** long live the king!

vi'vace [vi'vatʃe] *ag* (*vivo, animato*) lively; (: *mente*) lively, sharp; (*colore*) bright; **vivacità** *sf* vivacity; liveliness; brightness.

vi'vaio *sm* (*di pesci*) hatchery; (*AGR*) nursery.

vi'vanda *sf* food; (*piatto*) dish.

vi'vente *ag* living, alive; **i** ~**i** the living.

'vivere *vi* to live // *vt* to live; (*passare: brutto momento*) to live through, go through; (*sentire: gioie, pene di qn*) to share // *sm* life; (*anche: modo di ~*) way of life; ~**i** *smpl* food *sg*, provisions; ~ **di** to live on.

'vivido, a *ag* (*colore*) vivid, bright.

'vivo, a *ag* (*vivente*) alive, living; (: *animale*) live; (*fig*) lively; (: *colore*) bright, brilliant; **i** ~**i** the living; ~ **e vegeto** hale and hearty; **farsi** ~ to show one's face; to be heard from; **ritrarre dal** ~ to paint from life; **pungere qn nel** ~ (*fig*) to cut sb to the quick.

vizi'are [vit'tsjare] *vt* (*bambino*) to spoil;

(*corrompere moralmente*) to corrupt; **vizi'ato, a** *ag* spoilt; (*aria, acqua*) polluted.

vizio ['vittsjo] *sm* (*morale*) vice; (*cattiva abitudine*) bad habit; (*imperfezione*) flaw, defect; (*errore*) fault, mistake; **vizi'oso, a** *ag* depraved; defective; (*inesatto*) incorrect, wrong.

vocabo'lario *sm* (*dizionario*) dictionary; (*lessico*) vocabulary.

vo'cabolo *sm* word.

vo'cale *ag* vocal // *sf* vowel.

vocazi'one [vokat'tsjone] *sf* vocation; (*fig*) natural bent.

'voce ['votʃe] *sf* voice; (*diceria*) rumour; (*di un elenco, in bilancio*) item; **aver ~ in capitolo** (*fig*) to have a say in the matter.

voci'are [vo'tʃare] *vi* to shout, yell.

'voga *sf* (*NAUT*) rowing; (*usanza*): **essere in ~** to be in fashion *o* in vogue.

vo'gare *vi* to row.

'voglia ['vɔʎʎa] *sf* desire, wish; (*macchia*) birthmark; **aver ~ di qc/di fare** to feel like sth/like doing; (*più forte*) to want sth/to do.

'voi *pronome* you; **voi'altri** *pronome* you.

vo'lano *sm* (*SPORT*) shuttlecock; (*TECN*) flywheel.

vo'lante *ag* flying // *sm* (steering) wheel.

volan'tino *sm* leaflet.

vo'lare *vi* (*uccello, aereo, fig*) to fly; (*cappello*) to blow away *o* off, fly away *o* off; **~ via** to fly away *o* off.

vo'latile *ag* (*CHIM*) volatile // *sm* (*ZOOL*) bird.

volente'roso, a *ag* willing.

volenti'eri *av* willingly; "**~**" "with pleasure", "I'd be glad to".

vo'lere ♦ *sm* will, wish(es); **contro il ~ di** against the wishes of; **per ~ di qn** in obedience to sb's will *o* wishes

♦ *vt* **1** (*esigere, desiderare*) to want; **voler fare/che qn faccia** to want to do/sb to do; **volete del caffè?** would you like *o* do you want some coffee?; **vorrei questo/fare** I would *o* I'd like this/to do; **come vuoi** as you like; **senza ~** (*inavvertitamente*) without meaning to, unintentionally

2 (*consentire*): **vogliate attendere, per piacere** please wait; **vogliamo andare?** shall we go?; **vuole essere così gentile da ...?** would you be so kind as to ...?; **non ha voluto ricevermi** he wouldn't see me

3: **volerci** (*essere necessario: materiale, attenzione*) to need; (*: tempo*) to take; **quanta farina ci vuole per questa torta?** how much flour do you need for this cake?; **ci vuole un'ora per arrivare a Venezia** it takes an hour to get to Venice **4**: **voler bene a qn** (*amore*) to love sb; (*affetto*) to be fond of sb, like sb very much; **voler male a qn** to dislike sb;

volerne a qn to bear sb a grudge; **voler dire** to mean.

vol'gare *ag* vulgar; **volgariz'zare** *vt* to popularize.

'volgere ['vɔldʒere] *vt* to turn // *vi* to turn; (*tendere*): **~ a: il tempo volge al brutto** the weather is breaking; **un rosso che volge al viola** a red verging on purple; **~rsi** *vr* to turn; **~ al peggio** to take a turn for the worse; **~ al termine** to draw to an end.

'volgo *sm* common people.

voli'era *sf* aviary.

voli'tivo, a *ag* strong-willed.

'volo *sm* flight; **al ~**: **colpire qc al ~** to hit sth as it flies past; **capire al ~** to understand straight away.

volontà *sf* will; **a ~** (*mangiare, bere*) as much as one likes; **buona/cattiva ~** goodwill/lack of goodwill.

volon'tario, a *ag* voluntary // *sm* (*MIL*) volunteer.

'volpe *sf* fox.

'volta *sf* (*momento, circostanza*) time; (*turno, giro*) turn; (*curva*) turn, bend; (*ARCHIT*) vault; (*direzione*): **partire alla ~ di** to set off for; **a mia** (*o tua etc*) **~ in** turn; **una ~ once**; **una ~ sola** only once; **due ~e** twice; **una cosa per ~** one thing at a time; **una ~ per tutte** once and for all; **a ~e** at times, sometimes; **una ~ che** (*temporale*) once; (*causale*) since; **3 ~e 4** 3 times 4.

volta'faccia [volta'fattʃa] *sm inv* (*fig*) volte-face.

vol'taggio [vol'taddʒo] *sm* (*ELETTR*) voltage.

vol'tare *vt* to turn; (*girare: moneta*) to turn over; (*rigirare*) to turn round // *vi* to turn; **~rsi** *vr* to turn; to turn over; to turn round.

volteggi'are [volted'dʒare] *vi* (*volare*) to circle; (*in equitazione*) to do trick riding; (*in ginnastica*) to vault; to perform acrobatics.

'volto, a *pp di* **volgere** // *sm* face.

vo'lubile *ag* changeable, fickle.

vo'lume *sm* volume; **volumi'noso, a** *ag* voluminous, bulky.

voluttà *sf* sensual pleasure *o* delight; **voluttu'oso, a** *ag* voluptuous.

vomi'tare *vt, vi* to vomit; **'vomito** *sm* vomiting *q*; vomit.

'vongola *sf* clam.

vo'race [vo'ratʃe] *ag* voracious, greedy.

vo'ragine [vo'radʒine] *sf* abyss, chasm.

'vortice ['vortitʃe] *sm* whirlwind; whirlpool; (*fig*) whirl.

'vostro, a *det*: **il(la) ~(a)** *etc* your // *pronome*: **il(la) ~(a)** *etc* yours.

vo'tante *sm/f* voter.

vo'tare *vi* to vote // *vt* (*sottoporre a votazione*) to take a vote on; (*approvare*) to vote for; (*REL*): **~ qc a** to dedicate sth to; **votazi'one** *sf* vote, voting; **votazioni** *sfpl* (*POL*) votes; (*INS*) marks.

'voto *sm* (*POL*) vote; (*INS*) mark; (*REL*) vow; (: *offerta*) votive offering; **aver ~i belli/brutti** (*INS*) to get good/bad marks.

vs. *abbr* (*COMM*) = **vostro.**

vul'cano *sm* volcano.

vulne'rabile *ag* vulnerable.

vuo'tare *vt*, **~rsi** *vr* to empty.

vu'oto, a *ag* empty; (*fig: privo*): ~ **di** (*senso etc*) devoid of // *sm* empty space, gap; (*spazio in bianco*) blank; (*FISICA*) vacuum; (*fig: mancanza*) gap, void; **a mani ~e** empty-handed; ~ **d'aria** air pocket; ~ **a rendere** returnable bottle.

W X Y

watt [vat] *sm inv* watt.

'weekend ['wi:kend] *sm inv* weekend.

'whisky ['wiski] *sm inv* whisky.

'xeres ['ksɛres] *sm inv* sherry.

xero'copia [ksero'kɔpja] *sf* xerox ®, photocopy.

xi'lofono [ksi'lɔfono] *sm* xylophone.

yacht [jɔt] *sm inv* yacht.

'yoghurt ['jɔgurt] *sm inv* yoghurt.

Z

zabai'one [dzaba'jone] *sm dessert made of egg yolks, sugar and marsala.*

zaf'fata [tsaf'fata] *sf* (*tanfo*) stench.

zaffe'rano [dzaffe'rano] *sm* saffron.

zaf'firo [dzaf'firo] *sm* sapphire.

'zaino ['dzaino] *sm* rucksack.

'zampa ['tsampa] *sf* (*di animale: gamba*) leg; (: *piede*) paw; **a quattro ~e** on all fours.

zampil'lare [tsampil'lare] *vi* to gush, spurt; **zam'pillo** *sm* gush, spurt.

zam'pogna [tsam'poɲɲa] *sf instrument similar to bagpipes.*

'zanna ['tsanna] *sf* (*di elefante*) tusk; (*di carnivori*) fang.

zan'zara [dzan'dzara] *sf* mosquito; **zanzari'era** *sf* mosquito net.

'zappa ['tsappa] *sf* hoe; **zap'pare** *vt* to hoe.

zar, za'rina [tsar, tsa'rina] *sm/f* tsar/tsarina.

'zattera ['dzattera] *sf* raft.

za'vorra [dza'vɔrra] *sf* ballast.

'zazzera ['tsattsera] *sf* shock of hair.

'zebra ['dzebra] *sf* zebra; **~e** *sfpl* (*AUT*) zebra crossing *sg* (*Brit*), crosswalk *sg* (*US*).

'zecca, che ['tsekka] *sf* (*ZOOL*) tick; (*officina di monete*) mint.

'zelo ['dzɛlo] *sm* zeal.

'zenit ['dzenit] *sm* zenith.

'zenzero ['dzendzero] *sm* ginger.

'zeppa ['tseppa] *sf* wedge.

'zeppo, a ['tseppo] *ag:* ~ **di** crammed *o* packed with.

zer'bino [dzer'bino] *sm* doormat.

'zero ['dzɛro] *sm* zero, nought; **vincere per tre a** ~ (*SPORT*) to win three-nil.

'zeta ['dzeta] *sm o f* zed, (the letter) z.

'zia ['tsia] *sf* aunt.

zibel'lino [dzibel'lino] *sm* sable.

'zigomo ['dzigomo] *sm* cheekbone.

zig'zag [dzig'dzag] *sm inv* zigzag; **andare a** ~ to zigzag.

zim'bello [dzim'bɛllo] *sm* (*oggetto di burle*) laughing-stock.

'zinco ['dzinko] *sm* zinc.

'zingaro, a ['dzingaro] *sm/f* gipsy.

'zio ['tsio], *pl* **'zii** *sm* uncle; **zii** *smpl* (*zio e zia*) uncle and aunt.

zi'tella [dzi'tɛlla] *sf* spinster; (*peg*) old maid.

'zitto, a ['tsitto] *ag* quiet, silent; **sta' ~!** be quiet!

ziz'zania [dzid'dzanja] *sf* (*fig*): **gettare** *o* **seminare** ~ to sow discord.

'zoccolo ['tsɔkkolo] *sm* (*calzatura*) clog; (*di cavallo etc*) hoof; (*basamento*) base; plinth.

zo'diaco [dzo'diako] *sm* zodiac.

'zolfo ['tsolfo] *sm* sulphur.

'zolla ['dzɔlla] *sf* clod (of earth).

zol'letta [dzol'letta] *sf* sugar lump.

'zona ['dzɔna] *sf* zone, area; ~ **di depressione** (*METEOR*) trough of low pressure; ~ **pedonale** pedestrian precinct; ~ **verde** (*di abitato*) green area.

'zonzo ['dzondzo]: **a ~** *av:* **andare a ~** to wander about, stroll about.

zoo ['dzɔo] *sm inv* zoo.

zoolo'gia [dzoolo'dʒia] *sf* zoology.

zoppi'care [tsoppi'kare] *vi* to limp; **to be shaky, rickety.**

'zoppo, a ['tsɔppo] *ag* lame; (*fig: mobile*) shaky, rickety.

zoti'cone [dzoti'kone] *sm* lout.

'zucca, che ['tsukka] *sf* (*BOT*) marrow; pumpkin.

zucche'rare [tsukke'rare] *vt* to put sugar in; **zucche'rato, a** *ag* sweet, sweetened.

zuccheri'era [tsukke'rjɛra] *sf* sugar bowl.

zuccheri'ficio [tsukkeri'fitʃo] *sm* sugar refinery.

zucche'rino, a [tsukke'rino] *ag* sugary, sweet.

'zucchero ['tsukkero] *sm* sugar.

zuc'china [tsuk'kina] *sf*, **zuc'chino** [tsuk'kino] *sm* courgette (*Brit*), zucchini (*US*).

'zuffa ['tsuffa] *sf* brawl.

'zuppa ['tsuppa] *sf* soup; (*fig*) mixture, muddle; ~ **inglese** (*CUC*) dessert made with sponge cake, custard and chocolate, ≈ trifle (*Brit*); **zuppi'era** *sf* soup tureen.

'zuppo, a ['tsuppo] *ag:* ~ (**di**) drenched (with), soaked (with).

ENGLISH - ITALIAN
INGLESE - ITALIANO

A

A [eɪ] n (MUS) la m; (AUT): ~ **road** ≈ strada statale.

a indefinite article (before vowel or silent h: an) [eɪ, ə, æn, ən, n] **1** un (uno + s impure, gn, pn, ps, x, z), f una (un' + vowel); ~ **book** un libro; ~ **mirror** uno specchio; **an apple** una mela; **she's** ~ **doctor** è medico
2 (instead of the number 'one') un(o), f una; ~ **year ago** un anno fa; ~ **hundred/thousand** etc **pounds** cento/mille etc sterline
3 (in expressing ratios, prices etc) a, per; **3** ~ **day/week** 3 al giorno/alla settimana; **10 km an hour** 10 km all'ora; **£5** ~ **person** 5 sterline a persona or per persona.

A.A. n abbr (= Alcoholics Anonymous) AA; (Brit: = Automobile Association) ≈ A.C.I. m.

A.A.A. n abbr (US: = American Automobile Association) ≈ A.C.I. m.

aback [ə'bæk] ad: **to be taken** ~ essere sbalordito(a).

abandon [ə'bændən] vt abbandonare // n abbandono; **with** ~ sfrenatamente, spensieratamente.

abashed [ə'bæʃt] a imbarazzato(a).

abate [ə'beɪt] vi calmarsi.

abattoir ['æbətwɑ:*] n (Brit) mattatoio.

abbey ['æbɪ] n abbazia, badia.

abbot ['æbət] n abate m.

abbreviation [əbri:vɪ'eɪʃən] n abbreviazione f.

abdicate ['æbdɪkeɪt] vt abdicare a // vi abdicare.

abdomen ['æbdəmən] n addome m.

abduct [æb'dʌkt] vt rapire.

aberration [æbə'reɪʃən] n aberrazione f.

abet [ə'bet] vt see **aid**.

abeyance [ə'beɪəns] n: **in** ~ (law) in disuso; (matter) in sospeso.

abide [ə'baɪd] vt: **I can't** ~ **it/him** non lo posso soffrire or sopportare; **to** ~ **by** vt fus conformarsi a.

ability [ə'bɪlɪtɪ] n abilità f inv.

abject ['æbdʒekt] a (poverty) abietto(a); (apology) umiliante.

ablaze [ə'bleɪz] a in fiamme.

able ['eɪbl] a capace; **to be** ~ **to do sth** essere capace di fare qc, poter fare qc; **ably** ad abilmente.

abnormal [æb'nɔ:məl] a anormale.

aboard [ə'bɔ:d] ad a bordo // prep a bordo di.

abode [ə'bəud] n: **of no fixed** ~ senza fissa dimora.

abolish [ə'bɔlɪʃ] vt abolire.

abominable [ə'bɔmɪnəbl] a abominevole.

aborigine [æbə'rɪdʒɪnɪ] n aborigeno/a.

abort [ə'bɔ:t] vt abortire; ~**ion** [ə'bɔ:ʃən] n aborto; **to have an** ~**ion** abortire; ~**ive** a abortivo(a).

abound [ə'baund] vi abbondare; **to** ~ **in** abbondare di.

about [ə'baut] ◆ ad **1** (approximately) circa, quasi; ~ **a hundred/thousand** etc un centinaio/migliaio etc, circa cento/mille etc; **it takes** ~ **10 hours** ci vogliono circa 10 ore; **at** ~ **2 o'clock** verso le 2; **I've just** ~ **finished** ho quasi finito
2 (referring to place) qua e là, in giro; **to leave things lying** ~ lasciare delle cose in giro; **to run** ~ correre qua e là; **to walk** ~ camminare
3: to be ~ **to do sth** stare per fare qc
◆ prep **1** (relating to) su, di; **a book** ~ **London** un libro su Londra; **what is it** ~? di che si tratta?; (book, film etc) di cosa tratta?; (book, film etc) di cosa tratta?; **we talked** ~ **it** ne abbiamo parlato; **what or how** ~ **doing this?** che ne dici di fare questo?
2 (referring to place): **to walk** ~ **the town** camminare per la città; **her clothes were scattered** ~ **the room** i suoi vestiti erano sparsi or in giro per tutta la stanza.

about-face [ə'baut'feɪs] n, **about-turn** [ə'baut'tə:n] n dietro front m inv.

above [ə'bʌv] ad, prep sopra; **mentioned** ~ suddetto; ~ **all** soprattutto; ~**board** a aperto(a); onesto(a).

abrasive [ə'breɪzɪv] a abrasivo(a); (fig) caustico(a).

abreast [ə'brest] ad di fianco; **to keep** ~ **of** tenersi aggiornato su.

abridge [ə'brɪdʒ] vt ridurre.

abroad [ə'brɔ:d] ad all'estero.

abrupt [ə'brʌpt] a (steep) erto(a); (sudden) improvviso(a); (gruff, blunt) brusco(a).

abscess ['æbsɪs] n ascesso.

abscond [əb'skɔnd] vi scappare.

absence ['æbsəns] n assenza.

absent ['æbsənt] a assente; ~**ee** [-'ti:] n assente m/f; ~**-minded** a distratto(a).

absolute ['æbsəlu:t] a assoluto(a); ~**ly** [-'lu:tlɪ] ad assolutamente.

absolve [əb'zɔlv] vt: **to** ~ **sb** (**from**) (sin) assolvere qn (da); (oath) sciogliere qn (da).

absorb [əb'zɔ:b] vt assorbire; **to be** ~**ed**

in a book essere immerso in un libro; ~ent cotton n (US) cotone m idrofilo.

absorption [ab'sɔ:pʃən] n assorbimento.

abstain [ab'stein] vi: to ~ (from) astenersi (da).

abstemious [ab'sti:mɪəs] a astemio(a).

abstract ['æbstrækt] a astratto(a).

absurd [ab'sɔ:d] a assurdo(a).

abuse n [a'bju:s] abuso; (insults) ingiurie fpl // vt [a'bju:z] abusare di; **abusive** a ingiurioso(a).

abysmal [a'bɪzməl] a spaventoso(a).

abyss [a'bɪs] n abisso.

AC abbr (= alternating current) c.a.

academic [ækə'dɛmɪk] a accademico(a); (pej: issue) puramente formale // n universitario/a.

academy [a'kædəmɪ] n (learned body) accademia; (school) scuola privata; ~ of music conservatorio.

accelerate [æk'sɛləreɪt] vt, vi accelerare; **accelerator** n acceleratore m.

accent ['æksɛnt] n accento.

accept [ək'sɛpt] vt accettare; ~able a accettabile; ~ance n accettazione f.

access ['æksɛs] n accesso; ~ible [æk'sɛsəbl] a accessibile.

accessory [æk'sɛsərɪ] n accessorio; toilet accessories npl articoli mpl da toilette.

accident ['æksɪdənt] n incidente m; (chance) caso; by ~ per caso; ~al [-'dɛntl] a accidentale; ~ally [-'dɛntəlɪ] ad per caso; ~-prone a: he's very ~-prone è un vero passaguai.

acclaim [a'kleɪm] vt acclamare // n acclamazione f.

accommodate [a'kɔmədeɪt] vt alloggiare; (oblige, help) favorire.

accommodating [a'kɔmədeɪtɪŋ] a compiacente.

accommodation [əkɔmə'deɪʃən] n (US: ~s) alloggio.

accompany [a'kʌmpənɪ] vt accompagnare.

accomplice [a'kʌmplɪs] n complice m/f.

accomplish [a'kʌmplɪʃ] vt compiere; ~ed a (person) esperto(a); ~ment n compimento; realizzazione f; ~ments npl doti fpl.

accord [a'kɔ:d] n accordo // vt accordare; of his own ~ di propria iniziativa; ~ance n: in ~ance with in conformità con; ~ing to prep secondo; ~ingly ad in conformità.

accordion [a'kɔ:dɪən] n fisarmonica.

accost [a'kɔst] vt avvicinare.

account [a'kaunt] n (COMM) conto; (report) descrizione f; ~s npl (COMM) conti mpl; of little ~ di poca importanza; on ~ in acconto; on no ~ per nessun motivo; on ~ of a causa di; to take into ~, take ~ of tener conto di; to ~ for spiegare; giustificare; ~able a responsabile.

accountancy [a'kauntənsɪ] n ragioneria.

accountant [a'kauntənt] n ragioniere/a.

account number n numero di conto.

accumulate [a'kju:mjuleɪt] vt accumulare // vi accumularsi.

accuracy ['ækjurəsɪ] n precisione f.

accurate ['ækjurɪt] a preciso(a); ~ly ad precisamente.

accusation [ækju'zeɪʃən] n accusa.

accuse [a'kju:z] vt accusare; ~d n accusato/a.

accustom [a'kʌstəm] vt abituare; ~ed a (usual) abituale; ~ed to abituato(a) a.

ace [eɪs] n asso.

ache [eɪk] n male m, dolore m // vi (be sore) far male, dolere; my head ~s mi fa male la testa.

achieve [a'tʃi:v] vt (aim) raggiungere; (victory, success) ottenere; (task) compiere; ~ment n compimento; successo.

acid ['æsɪd] a acido(a) // n acido; ~ rain n pioggia acida.

acknowledge [ək'nɔlɪdʒ] vt (letter: also: ~ receipt of) confermare la ricevuta di; (fact) riconoscere; ~ment n conferma; riconoscimento.

acne ['æknɪ] n acne f.

acorn ['eɪkɔ:n] n ghianda.

acoustic [a'ku:stɪk] a acustico(a); ~s n, npl acustica.

acquaint [a'kweɪnt] vt: to ~ sb with sth far sapere qc a qn; to be ~ed with (person) conoscere; ~ance n conoscenza; (person) conoscente m/f.

acquiesce [ækwɪ'ɛs] vi: to ~ (in) acconsentire (a).

acquire [a'kwaɪə*] vt acquistare.

acquisition [ækwɪ'zɪʃən] n acquisto.

acquit [a'kwɪt] vt assolvere; to ~ o.s. well comportarsi bene; ~tal n assoluzione f.

acre ['eɪkə*] n acro (= 4047 m²).

acrid ['ækrɪd] a acre; pungente.

acrimonious [ækrɪ'məunɪəs] a astioso(a).

acrobat ['ækrəbæt] n acrobata m/f.

across [a'krɔs] prep (on the other side) dall'altra parte di; (crosswise) attraverso // ad dall'altra parte; in larghezza; to walk ~ (the road) attraversare (la strada); ~ from di fronte a.

acrylic [a'krɪlɪk] a acrilico(a) // n acrilico.

act [ækt] n atto; (in music-hall etc) numero; (LAW) decreto // vi agire; (THEATRE) recitare; (pretend) fingere // vt (part) recitare; to ~ as agire da; ~ing a che fa le funzioni di // n (of actor) recitazione f; (activity): to do some ~ing fare del teatro (or del cinema).

action ['ækʃən] n azione f; (MIL) combattimento; (LAW) processo; out of ~ fuori combattimento; fuori servizio; to take ~ agire; ~ replay n (TV) replay m *inv.*

activate ['æktɪveɪt] *vt* (*mechanism*) fare funzionare; (*CHEM, PHYSICS*) rendere attivo(a).

active ['æktɪv] *a* attivo(a); ~**ly** *ad* (*participate*) attivamente; (*discourage, dislike*) vivamente.

activity [æk'tɪvɪtɪ] *n* attività *f inv.*

actor ['æktə*] *n* attore *m.*

actress ['æktrɪs] *n* attrice *f.*

actual ['æktjuəl] *a* reale, vero(a); ~**ly** *ad* veramente; (*even*) addirittura.

acumen ['ækjumən] *n* acume *m.*

acute [ə'kju:t] *a* acuto(a); (*mind, person*) perspicace.

ad [æd] *n abbr* = **advertisement**.

A.D. *ad abbr* (= *Anno Domini*) d.C.

adamant ['ædəmənt] *a* irremovibile.

adapt [ə'dæpt] *vt* adattare // *vi*: to ~ (to) adattarsi (a); ~**able** *a* (*device*) adattabile; (*person*) che sa adattarsi; ~**er** *or* ~**or** *n* (*ELEC*) adattatore *m.*

add [æd] *vt* aggiungere; (*figures: also*: to ~ up) addizionare // *vi*: to ~ to (*increase*) aumentare; it doesn't ~ up (*fig*) non quadra, non ha senso.

adder ['ædə*] *n* vipera.

addict ['ædɪkt] *n* tossicomane *m/f*; (*fig*) fanatico/a; ~**ed** [ə'dɪktɪd] *a*: to be ~**ed** to (*drink etc*) essere dedito a; (*fig: football etc*) essere tifoso di; ~**ion** [ə'dɪkʃən] *n* (*MED*) tossicomania; ~**ive** [ə'dɪktɪv] *a* che dà assuefazione.

addition [ə'dɪʃən] *n* addizione *f*; in ~ inoltre; in ~ to oltre; ~**al** *a* supplementare.

additive ['ædɪtɪv] *n* additivo.

address [ə'dres] *n* indirizzo; (*talk*) discorso // *vt* indirizzare; (*speak to*) fare un discorso a.

adept ['ædept] *a*: ~ at esperto(a) in

adequate ['ædɪkwɪt] *a* adeguato(a); sufficiente.

adhere [əd'hɪə*] *vi*: to ~ to aderire a; (*fig: rule, decision*) seguire.

adhesion [əd'hi:ʒən] *n* adesione *f.*

adhesive [əd'hi:zɪv] *a* adesivo(a) // *n* adesivo; ~ **tape** *n* (*Brit: for parcels etc*) nastro adesivo; (*US: MED*) cerotto adesivo.

adjective ['ædʒektɪv] *n* aggettivo.

adjoining [ə'dʒɔɪnɪŋ] *a* accanto *inv*, adiacente.

adjourn [ə'dʒə:n] *vt* rimandare // *vi* essere aggiornato(a); (*go*) spostarsi.

adjudicate [ə'dʒu:dɪkeɪt] *vt* (*contest*) giudicare; (*claim*) decidere su.

adjust [ə'dʒʌst] *vt* aggiustare; (*COMM*) rettificare // *vi*: to ~ (to) adattarsi (a); ~**able** *a* regolabile.

ad-lib [æd'lɪb] *vt, vi* improvvisare // *ad*: ad lib a piacere, a volontà.

administer [əd'mɪnɪstə*] *vt* amministrare; (*justice*) somministrare.

administration [ədmɪnɪs'treɪʃən] *n*

amministrazione *f.*

administrative [əd'mɪnɪstrətɪv] *a* amministrativo(a).

admiral ['ædmərəl] *n* ammiraglio; **A~ty** *n* (*Brit: also*: A~ty Board) Ministero della Marina.

admiration [ædmə'reɪʃən] *n* ammirazione *f.*

admire [əd'maɪə*] *vt* ammirare.

admission [əd'mɪʃən] *n* ammissione *f*; (*to exhibition, night club etc*) ingresso; (*confession*) confessione *f.*

admit [əd'mɪt] *vt* ammettere; far entrare; (*agree*) riconoscere; to ~ to riconoscere; ~**tance** *n* ingresso; ~**tedly** *ad* bisogna pur riconoscere (che).

admonish [əd'mɔnɪʃ] *vt* ammonire.

ad nauseam [æd'nɔ:sɪæm] *ad* fino alla nausea, a non finire.

ado [ə'du:] *n*: without (any) more ~ senza più indugi.

adolescence [ædəu'lɛsns] *n* adolescenza.

adolescent [ædəu'lɛsnt] *a, n* adolescente (*m/f*).

adopt [ə'dɔpt] *vt* adottare; ~**ed** *a* adottivo(a); ~**ion** [ə'dɔpʃən] *n* adozione *f.*

adore [ə'dɔ:*] *vt* adorare.

Adriatic (Sea) [eɪdrɪ'ætɪk('si:)] *n* Adriatico.

adrift [ə'drɪft] *ad* alla deriva.

adroit [ə'drɔɪt] *a* abile, destro(a).

adult ['ædʌlt] *n* adulto/a.

adultery [ə'dʌltərɪ] *n* adulterio.

advance [əd'vɑ:ns] *n* avanzamento; (*money*) anticipo // *vt* avanzare; (*date, money*) anticipare // *vi* avanzare; in ~ in anticipo; ~**d** *a* avanzato(a); (*SCOL: studies*) superiore.

advantage [əd'vɑ:ntɪdʒ] *n* (*also TENNIS*) vantaggio; to take ~ of approfittarsi di.

advent ['ædvənt] *n* avvento; A~ Avvento.

adventure [əd'vɛntʃə*] *n* avventura.

adverb ['ædvə:b] *n* avverbio.

adverse ['ædvə:s] *a* avverso(a); ~ to contrario(a) a.

advert ['ædvə:t] *n abbr* (*Brit*) = **advertisement.**

advertise ['ædvətaɪz] *vi* (*vt*) fare pubblicità *or* réclame (a); fare un'inserzione (per vendere); to ~ for (*staff*) mettere un annuncio sul giornale per trovare.

advertisement [əd'və:tɪsmənt] *n* (*COMM*) réclame *f inv*, pubblicità *f inv*; (*in classified ads*) inserzione *f.*

advertiser ['ædvətaɪzə*] *n* (*in newspaper etc*) inserzionista *m/f.*

advertising ['ædvətaɪzɪŋ] *n* pubblicità.

advice [əd'vaɪs] *n* consigli *mpl*; (*notification*) avviso; **piece of** ~ consiglio; to take legal ~ consultare un avvocato.

advisable [əd'vaɪzəbl] *a* consigliabile.

advise [əd'vaɪz] *vt* consigliare; to ~ **sb of sth** informare qn di qc; to ~ **sb against**

sth/doing sth sconsigliare qc a qn/a qn di fare qc; **~dly** [-ədlɪ] *ad* (*deliberately*) di proposito; **~r** *n* consigliere/a; **advisory** [-ərɪ] *a* consultivo(a).

advocate *n* ['ædvəkɪt] (*upholder*) sostenitore/trice; (*LAW*) avvocato (difensore) // *vt* ['ædvəkeɪt] propugnare; **to be an ~ of** essere a favore di.

aerial ['ɛərɪəl] *n* antenna // *a* aereo(a).

aerobics [ɛə'rəubɪks] *n* aerobica.

aeroplane ['ɛərəpleɪn] *n* (*Brit*) aeroplano.

aerosol ['ɛərəsɔl] *n* (*Brit*) aerosol *m inv*.

aesthetic [ɪs'θetɪk] *a* estetico(a).

afar [ə'fɑ:°] *ad*: **from ~** da lontano.

affair [ə'fɛə°] *n* affare *m*; (*also*: love ~) relazione *f* amorosa.

affect [ə'fɛkt] *vt* toccare; (*feign*) fingere; **~ed** *a* affettato(a).

affection [ə'fɛkʃən] *n* affezione *f*; **~ate** *a* affettuoso(a).

affirmation [æfə'meɪʃən] *n* affermazione *f*.

affix [ə'fɪks] *vt* apporre; attaccare.

afflict [ə'flɪkt] *vt* affliggere.

affluence ['æfluəns] *n* abbondanza; opulenza.

affluent ['æfluənt] *a* abbondante; opulente; (*person*) ricco(a).

afford [ə'fɔ:d] *vt* permettersi; (*provide*) fornire.

afield [ə'fi:ld] *ad*: **far ~** lontano.

afloat [ə'fləut] *a*, *ad* a galla.

afoot [ə'fut] *ad*: **there is something ~** si sta preparando qualcosa.

afraid [ə'freɪd] *a* impaurito(a); **to be ~ of** *or* **to** aver paura di; **I am ~ that I'll be late** mi dispiace, ma farò tardi.

afresh [ə'frɛʃ] *ad* di nuovo.

Africa ['æfrɪkə] *n* Africa; **~n** *a*, *n* africano(a).

aft [ɑ:ft] *ad* a poppa, verso poppa.

after ['ɑ:ftə°] *prep*, *ad* dopo // *cj* dopo che; **what/who are you ~?** che/chi cerca?; **~ he left/having done** dopo che se ne fu andato/dopo aver fatto; **~ all** dopo tutto; **~ you!** dopo di lei!; **~-effects** *npl* conseguenze *fpl*; (*of illness*) postumi *mpl*; **~life** *n* vita dell'al di là; **~math** *n* conseguenze *fpl*; **in the ~math of** nel periodo dopo; **~noon** *n* pomeriggio; **~s** *n* (*col*: *dessert*) dessert *m inv*; **~-sales service** *n* (*Brit*) servizio assistenza clienti; **~-shave (lotion)** *n* dopobarba *m inv*; **~thought** *n*: **as an ~thought** come aggiunta; **~wards** *ad* dopo.

again [ə'gɛn] *ad* di nuovo; **to begin/ see ~** ricominciare/rivedere; **not ... ~** non ... più; **~ and ~** ripetutamente.

against [ə'gɛnst] *prep* contro; **~ a blue background** su uno sfondo azzurro.

age [eɪdʒ] *n* età *f inv* // *vt*, *vi* invecchiare; **it's been ~s since** sono secoli che; **he is 20 years of ~** ha 20 anni; **to**

come of ~ diventare maggiorenne; **~d 10** di 10 anni; **the ~d** ['eɪdʒɪd] gli anziani; **~ group** *n* generazione *f*; **~ limit** *n* limite *m* d'età.

agency ['eɪdʒənsɪ] *n* agenzia; **through** *or* **by the ~ of** grazie a.

agenda [ə'dʒɛndə] *n* ordine *m* del giorno.

agent ['eɪdʒənt] *n* agente *m*.

aggregate ['ægrɪgeɪt] *n* aggregato.

aggressive [ə'grɛsɪv] *a* aggressivo(a).

aggrieved [ə'gri:vd] *a* addolorato(a).

aghast [ə'gɑ:st] *a* sbigottito(a).

agitate ['ædʒɪteɪt] *vt* turbare; agitare; **to ~ for** agitarsi per.

ago [ə'gəu] *ad*: **2 days ~** 2 giorni fa; **not long ~** poco tempo fa; **how long ~?** quanto tempo fa?

agog [ə'gɔg] *a* ansioso(a), emozionato(a).

agonizing ['ægənaɪzɪŋ] *a* straziante.

agony ['ægənɪ] *n* agonia.

agree [ə'gri:] *vt* (*price*) pattuire // *vi*: **~ (with)** essere d'accordo (con); (*LING*) concordare (con); **to ~ to sth/to do sth** accettare qc/di fare qc; **to ~ that** (*admit*) ammettere che; **to ~ on sth** accordarsi su qc; **garlic doesn't ~ with me** l'aglio non mi va; **~able** *a* gradevole; (*willing*) disposto(a); **are you ~able to this?** è d'accordo con questo?; **~d** *a* (*time*, *place*) stabilito(a); **~ment** *n* accordo; **in ~ment** d'accordo.

agricultural [ægrɪ'kʌltʃərəl] *a* agricolo(a).

agriculture ['ægrɪkʌltʃə°] *n* agricoltura.

aground [ə'graund] *ad*: **to run ~** arenarsi.

ahead [ə'hɛd] *ad* avanti; davanti; **~ of** davanti a; (*fig*: *schedule etc*) in anticipo su; **~ of time** in anticipo; **go right** *or* **straight ~** tiri diritto; **they were (right) ~ of us** erano (proprio) davanti a noi.

aid [eɪd] *n* aiuto // *vt* aiutare; **in ~ of** a favore di; **to ~ and abet** (*LAW*) essere complice di.

aide [eɪd] *n* (*person*) aiutante *m*.

AIDS [eɪdz] *n abbr* (= *acquired immune deficiency syndrome*) AIDS *m*.

ailing ['eɪlɪŋ] *a* sofferente.

ailment ['eɪlmənt] *n* indisposizione *f*.

aim [eɪm] *vt*: **to ~ sth at** (*such as gun*) mirare qc a, puntare qc a; (*camera*, *remark*) rivolgere qc a; (*missile*) lanciare qc contro; (*blow etc*) tirare qc a // *vi* (*also*: **to take ~**) prendere la mira // *n* mira; **to ~ at** mirare a; **to ~ to do** aver l'intenzione di fare; **~less** *a* senza scopo.

ain't [eɪnt] (*col*) = **am not**; **aren't**; **isn't**.

air [ɛə°] *n* aria // *vt* aerare; (*grievances*, *ideas*) esprimere pubblicamente // *cpd* (*currents*) d'aria; (*attack*) aereo(a); **to throw sth into the ~** lanciare qc in aria; **by ~** (*travel*) in aereo; **on the ~** (*RADIO*, *TV*) in onda; **~bed** *n* (*Brit*) materassino; **~borne** a in volo; aerotra-sportato(a); **~ conditioning** n condizionamento d'aria; **~craft** n (pl inv) apparecchio; **~craft carrier** n portaerei f inv; **~field** n campo d'aviazione; **A~ Force** n aviazione f militare; **~ freshener** n deodorante m per ambienti; **~gun** n fucile m ad aria compressa; **~ hostess** n (Brit) hostess f inv; **~ letter** n (Brit) aerogramma m; **~lift** n ponte m aereo; **~line** n linea aerea; **~liner** n aereo di linea; **~lock** n cassa d'aria; **~mail** n: by **~mail** per via aerea; **~ mattress** n materassino; **~plane** n (US) aeroplano; **~port** n aeroporto; **~ raid** n incursione f aerea; **~sick** a che ha il mal d'aereo; **~space** n spazio aereo; **~strip** n pista d'atterraggio; **~ terminal** n air-terminal m inv; **~tight** a ermetico(a); **~ traffic controller** n controllore m del traffico aereo; **~y** a arioso(a); (manners) noncurante.

aisle [aɪl] n (of church) navata laterale; navata centrale; (of plane) corridoio.

ajar [ə'dʒɑ:ʳ] a socchiuso(a).

akin [ə'kɪn] a: **~ to** simile a.

alacrity [ə'lækrɪtɪ] n: **with ~** con prontezza.

alarm [ə'lɑ:m] n allarme m // vt allarmare; **~ clock** n sveglia.

alas [ə'læs] excl ohimè!, ahimè!

albeit [ɔ:l'bi:ɪt] cj sebbene+ sub, benché + sub.

album ['ælbəm] n album m inv; (L.P.) 33 giri m inv, L.P. m inv.

alcohol ['ælkəhɔl] n alcool m; **~ic** [-'hɔlɪk] a alcolico(a) // n alcolizzato/a.

alderman ['ɔ:ldəmən] n consigliere m comunale.

ale [eɪl] n birra.

alert [ə'lə:t] a vivo(a); (watchful) vigile // n allarme m // vt avvertire; mettere in guardia; **on the ~** all'erta.

algebra ['ældʒɪbrə] n algebra.

alias ['eɪlɪəs] ad alias // n pseudonimo, falso nome m.

alibi ['ælɪbaɪ] n alibi m inv.

alien ['eɪlɪən] n straniero/a // a: **~ (to)** estraneo(a) (a); **~ate** vt alienare.

alight [ə'laɪt] a acceso(a) // vi scendere; (bird) posarsi.

align [ə'laɪn] vt allineare.

alike [ə'laɪk] a simile // ad sia ... sia; **to look ~** assomigliarsi.

alimony ['ælɪmənɪ] n (payment) alimenti mpl.

alive [ə'laɪv] a vivo(a); (active) attivo(a).

all [ɔ:l] ◆ a tutto(a); **~ day** tutto il giorno; **~ night** tutta la notte; **~ men** tutti gli uomini; **~ five came** sono venuti tutti e cinque; **~ the books** tutti i libri; **~ the food** tutto il cibo; **~ the time** sempre; tutto tempo; **~ his life** tutta la vita

◆ pronoun **1** tutto(a); **I ate it ~**, I ate **~ of it** l'ho mangiato tutto; **~ of us went** tutti noi siamo andati; **~ of the boys went** tutti i ragazzi sono andati

2 (in phrases): **above ~** soprattutto; **after ~** dopotutto; **at ~:** not at **~** (in answer to question) niente affatto; (in answer to thanks) prego!, di niente!, s'immagini!; **I'm not at ~ tired** non sono affatto stanco(a); **anything at ~ will do** andrà bene qualsiasi cosa; **~ in ~** tutto sommato

◆ ad: **~ alone** tutto(a) solo(a); **it's not as hard as ~ that** non è poi così difficile; **~ the more/the better** tanto più/meglio; **~ but** quasi; **the score is two ~** il punteggio è di due a due.

allay [ə'leɪ] vt (fears) dissipare.

all clear n (also fig) segnale m di cessato allarme.

allegation [ælɪ'geɪʃən] n asserzione f.

allege [ə'ledʒ] vt asserire; **~dly** [ə'ledʒɪdlɪ] ad secondo quanto si asseri-sce.

allegiance [ə'li:dʒəns] n fedeltà.

allergic [ə'lə:dʒɪk] a: **~ to** allergico(a) a.

allergy ['ælədʒɪ] n allergia.

alleviate [ə'li:vɪeɪt] vt sollevare.

alley ['ælɪ] n vicolo; (in garden) vialetto.

alliance [ə'laɪəns] n alleanza.

allied ['ælaɪd] a alleato(a).

all-in ['ɔ:lɪn] a (Brit: also ad: charge) tutto compreso; **~ wrestling** n lotta americana.

all-night ['ɔ:l'naɪt] a aperto(a) (or che dura) tutta la notte.

allocate ['æləkeɪt] vt (share out) di-stribuire; (duties, sum, time): to **~ sth to** assegnare qc a; to **~ sth for** stanziare qc per.

allot [ə'lɔt] vt (share out) spartire; to **~ sth to** (time) dare qc a; (duties) asse-gnare qc a; **~ment** n (share) spartizione f; (garden) lotto di terra.

all-out ['ɔ:laut] a (effort etc) totale // ad: **to go all out for** mettercela tutta per.

allow [ə'lau] vt (practice, behaviour) permettere; (sum to spend etc) accordare; (sum, time estimated) dare; (concede): to **~ that** ammettere che; to **~ sb to do** permettere a qn di fare; **he is ~ed to do** lo può fare; to **~ for** vt fus tener conto di; **~ance** n (money received) assegno; indennità f inv; (TAX) detrazione f di imposta; **to make ~ances for** tener conto di.

alloy ['ælɔɪ] n lega.

all right ad (feel, work) bene; (as answer) va bene.

all-round ['ɔ:l'raund] a completo(a).

all-time ['ɔ:l'taɪm] a (record) assoluto(a).

allude [ə'lu:d] vi: to **~ to** alludere a.

alluring [ə'ljuərɪŋ] a seducente.

ally ['ælaɪ] n alleato.

almighty [ɔːl'maɪtɪ] a onnipotente.

almond ['ɑːmənd] n mandorla.

almost ['ɔːlməust] ad quasi.

alms [ɑːmz] npl elemosina sg.

aloft [ə'lɔft] ad in alto; (NAUT) sull'alberatura.

alone [ə'ləun] a, ad solo(a); to leave sb ~ lasciare qn in pace; to leave sth ~ lasciare stare qc; let ~ ... figuriamoci poi ..., tanto meno ... .

along [ə'lɔŋ] prep lungo // ad: is he coming ~? viene con noi?; he was hopping/limping ~ veniva saltellando/zoppicando; ~ with insieme con; all ~ (all the time) sempre, fin dall'inizio; **~side** prep accanto a; lungo // ad accanto.

aloof [ə'luːf] a distaccato(a) // ad: to stand ~ tenersi a distanza or in disparte.

aloud [ə'laud] ad ad alta voce.

alphabet ['ælfəbet] n alfabeto.

alpine ['ælpaɪn] a alpino(a).

Alps [ælps] npl: the ~ le Alpi.

already [ɔːl'redɪ] ad già.

alright ['ɔːl'raɪt] ad (Brit) = **all right**.

Alsatian [æl'seɪʃən] n (Brit: dog) pastore m tedesco, (cane m) lupo.

also ['ɔːlsəu] ad anche.

altar ['ɔltə*] n altare m.

alter ['ɔltə*] vt, vi alterare.

alternate a [ɔl'tɜːnɪt] alterno(a) // vb ['ɔltə:neɪt] vi: to ~ (with) alternarsi (a) // vt alternare; on ~ days ogni due giorni; **alternating** a (current) alternato(a).

alternative [ɔl'tɜːnətɪv] a (solutions) alternativo(a); (solution) altro(a) // n (choice) alternativa; (other possibility) altra possibilità; **~ly** ad alternativamente.

alternator ['ɔltə:neɪtə*] n (AUT) alternatore m.

although [ɔːl'ðəu] cj benché + sub, sebbene + sub.

altitude ['æltɪtjuːd] n altitudine f.

alto ['æltəu] n contralto; (male) contraltino.

altogether [ɔːltə'geðə*] ad del tutto, completamente; (on the whole) tutto considerato; (in all) in tutto.

aluminium [æljuˈmɪnɪəm], (US) **aluminum** [ə'luːmɪnəm] n alluminio.

always ['ɔːlweɪz] ad sempre.

am [æm] vb see **be**.

a.m. ad abbr (= ante meridiem) della mattina.

amalgamate [ə'mælgəmeɪt] vt amalgamare // vi amalgamarsi.

amateur ['æmətə*] n dilettante m/f // a (SPORT) dilettante; **~ish** a (pej) da dilettante.

amaze [ə'meɪz] vt stupire; to be ~d (at) essere sbalordito (da); **~ment** n stupore m; **amazing** a sorprendente, sbalorditivo(a); (bargain) sensazionale.

ambassador [æm'bæsədə*] n ambasciatore/trice.

amber ['æmbə*] n ambra; at ~ (Brit AUT) giallo.

ambiguous [æm'bɪgjuəs] a ambiguo(a).

ambition [æm'bɪʃən] n ambizione f.

ambitious [æm'bɪʃəs] a ambizioso(a).

amble ['æmbl] vi (gen: to ~ along) camminare tranquillamente.

ambulance ['æmbjuləns] n ambulanza.

ambush ['æmbuʃ] n imboscata // vt fare un'imboscata a.

amenable [ə'miːnəbl] a: ~ to (advice etc) ben disposto(a) a.

amend [ə'mend] vt (law) emendare; (text) correggere // vi emendarsi; to make ~s fare ammenda.

amenities [ə'miːnɪtɪz] npl attrezzature fpl ricreative e culturali.

America [ə'merɪkə] n America; **~n** a, n americano(a).

amiable ['eɪmɪəbl] a amabile, gentile.

amicable ['æmɪkəbl] a amichevole.

amid(st) [ə'mɪd(st)] prep fra, tra, in mezzo a.

amiss [ə'mɪs] a, ad: there's something ~ c'è qualcosa che non va bene; don't take it ~ non prendertela (a male).

ammonia [ə'məunɪə] n ammoniaca.

ammunition [æmjuˈnɪʃən] n munizioni fpl.

amok [ə'mɔk] ad: to run ~ diventare pazzo(a) furioso(a).

among(st) [ə'mʌŋ(st)] prep fra, tra, in mezzo a.

amorous ['æmərəs] a amoroso(a).

amount [ə'maunt] n somma; ammontare m; quantità f inv // vi: to ~ to (total) ammontare a; (be same as) essere come.

amp(ère) ['æmp(eə*)] n ampère m inv.

ample ['æmpl] a ampio(a); spazioso(a); (enough): this is ~ questo è più che sufficiente; to have ~ time/room avere assai tempo/posto.

amplifier ['æmplɪfaɪə*] n amplificatore m.

amuck [ə'mʌk] ad = **amok**.

amuse [ə'mjuːz] vt divertire; **~ment** n divertimento; **~ment arcade** n sala giochi.

an [æn, ən, n] indefinite article see **a**.

anaemic [ə'niːmɪk] a anemico(a).

anaesthetic [ænɪs'θetɪk] a anestetico(a) // n anestetico.

analog(ue) ['ænəlɔg] a (watch, computer) analogico(a).

analyse ['ænəlaɪz] vt (Brit) analizzare.

analysis, pl **analyses** [ə'nælsɪs, -siːz] n analisi f inv.

analyst ['ænəlɪst] n (POL etc) analista m/f; (US) (psic)analista m/f.

analyze ['ænəlaɪz] vt (US) = **analyse**.

anarchist ['ænəkɪst] a, n anarchico(a).

anarchy ['ænəkɪ] n anarchia.

anathema [ə'næθimə] *n*: that is ~ to him non vuole nemmeno sentirne parlare.

anatomy [ə'nætəmi] *n* anatomia.

ancestor ['ænsistə*] *n* antenato/a.

ancestral [æn'sestrəl] *a* avito(a).

anchor ['æŋkə*] *n* ancora // *vi* (*also*: to drop ~) gettare l'ancora // *vt* ancorare; to weigh ~ salpare *or* levare l'ancora.

anchovy ['æntʃəvi] *n* acciuga.

ancient ['einʃənt] *a* antico(a); (*fig*) anziano(a).

ancillary [æn'siləri] *a* ausiliario(a).

and [ænd] *cj* e (*often* ed *before vowel*); ~ so on e così via; try ~ come cerca di venire; he talked ~ talked non la finiva di parlare; better ~ better sempre meglio.

anew [ə'nju:] *ad* di nuovo.

angel ['eindʒəl] *n* angelo.

anger ['æŋgə*] *n* rabbia // *vt* arrabbiare.

angina [æn'dʒainə] *n* angina pectoris.

angle ['æŋgl] *n* angolo; from their ~ dal loro punto di vista; ~r *n* pescatore *m* con la lenza.

Anglican ['æŋglikən] *a*, *n* anglicano(a).

angling ['æŋgliŋ] *n* pesca con la lenza.

Anglo- ['æŋgləu] *prefix* anglo....

angry ['æŋgri] *a* arrabbiato(a), furioso(a); to be ~ with sb/at sth essere in collera con qn/per qc; to get ~ arrabbiarsi; to make sb ~ fare arrabbiare qn.

anguish ['æŋgwiʃ] *n* angoscia.

animal ['æniməl] *a*, *n* animale (*m*).

animate *vt* ['ænimeit] animare // *a* ['ænimit] animato(a); ~d *a* animato(a).

aniseed ['ænisi:d] *n* semi *mpl* di anice.

ankle ['æŋkl] *n* caviglia; ~ sock *n* calzino.

annex *n* ['ænɛks] (*also*: Brit: annexe) edificio annesso // *vt* [ə'nɛks] annettere.

annihilate [ə'naiəleit] *vt* annientare.

anniversary [æni'və:səri] *n* anniversario.

announce [ə'nauns] *vt* annunciare; ~ment *n* annuncio; (*letter*, *card*) partecipazione *f*; ~r *n* (*RADIO*, *TV*, *between programmes*) annunciatore/ trice; (: *in a programme*) presentatore/ trice.

annoy [ə'nɔi] *vt* dare fastidio a; don't get ~ed! non irritarti!; ~ance *n* fastidio; (*cause of* ~ance) noia; ~ing *a* noioso(a).

annual ['ænjuəl] *a* annuale // *n* (*BOT*) pianta annua; (*book*) annuario.

annul [ə'nʌl] *vt* annullare; (*law*) rescindere.

annum ['ænəm] *n see* per.

anonymous [ə'nɔniməs] *a* anonimo(a).

anorak ['ænəræk] *n* giacca a vento.

another [ə'nʌðə*] *a*: ~ book (*one more*) un altro libro, ancora un libro; (*a different one*) un altro libro // *pronoun* un altro(un'altra), ancora uno(a); *see also* one.

answer ['ɑ:nsə*] *n* risposta; soluzione *f* // *vi* rispondere // *vt* (*reply to*) rispondere a; (*problem*) risolvere; (*prayer*) esaudire; to ~ the phone rispondere (al telefono); in ~ to your letter in risposta alla sua lettera; to ~ the bell rispondere al campanello; to ~ the door aprire la porta; to ~ back *vi* ribattere; to ~ for *vt fus* essere responsabile di; to ~ to *vt fus* (*description*) corrispondere a; ~able *a*: ~able (to sb/for sth) responsabile (verso qn/di qc); ~ing machine *n* segreteria (telefonica) automatica.

ant [ænt] *n* formica.

antagonism [æn'tægənizəm] *n* antagonismo.

antagonize [æn'tægənaiz] *vt* provocare l'ostilità di.

Antarctic [ænt'ɑ:ktik] *n*: the ~ l'Antartide *f* // *a* antartico(a).

antenatal ['ænti'neitl] *a* prenatale; ~ clinic *n* assistenza medica preparto.

anthem ['ænθəm] *n* antifona; national ~ inno nazionale.

anthology [æn'θɔlədʒi] *n* antologia.

antibiotic ['æntibai'ɔtik] *a* antibiotico(a) // *n* antibiotico.

antibody ['æntibɔdi] *n* anticorpo.

anticipate [æn'tisipeit] *vt* prevedere; pregustare; (*wishes*, *request*) prevenire.

anticipation [æntisi'peiʃən] *n* anticipazione *f*; (*expectation*) aspettative *fpl*.

anticlimax ['ænti'klaimæks] *n*: it was an ~ fu una completa delusione.

anticlockwise ['ænti'klɔkwaiz] *a*, *ad* in senso antiorario.

antics ['æntiks] *npl* buffonerie *fpl*.

antifreeze ['ænti'fri:z] *n* anticongelante *m*.

antihistamine [ænti'histəmin] *n* antistaminico.

antiquated ['æntikweitid] *a* antiquato(a).

antique [æn'ti:k] *n* antichità *f inv* // *a* antico(a); ~ shop *n* negozio d'antichità.

antiquity [æn'tikwiti] *n* antichità *f inv*.

anti-Semitism ['ænti'semitizəm] *n* antisemitismo.

antiseptic [ænti'septik] *a* antisettico(a) // *n* antisettico.

antisocial ['ænti'səufəl] *a* asociale; (*against society*) antisociale.

antlers ['æntləz] *npl* palchi *mpl*.

anvil ['ænvil] *n* incudine *f*.

anxiety [æŋ'zaiəti] *n* ansia; (*keenness*): ~ to do smania di fare.

anxious ['æŋkʃəs] *a* ansioso(a), inquieto(a); (*keen*): ~ to do/that impaziente di fare/che + *sub*.

any ['ɛni] ♦ *a* **1** (*in questions etc*): have you ~ butter? hai del burro?, hai un po' di burro?; have you ~ children? hai bambini?; if there are ~ tickets left se ci sono ancora (dei) biglietti, se c'è ancora

qualche biglietto
2 (with negative): I haven't ~ money/
books non ho soldi/libri
3 (no matter which) qualsiasi,
qualunque; choose ~ book you like scegli
un libro qualsiasi
4 (in phrases): in ~ case in ogni caso;
~ day now da un giorno all'altro; at ~
moment in qualsiasi momento, da un
momento all'altro; at ~ rate ad ogni
modo
♦ pronoun **1** (in questions, with
negative): have you got ~? ne hai?; can
~ of you sing? qualcuno di voi sa
cantare?; I haven't ~ (of them) non ne
ho
2 (no matter which one(s)): take ~ of
those books (you like) prendi uno
qualsiasi di quei libri
♦ ad **1** (in questions etc): do you want
~ more soup/sandwiches? vuoi ancora un
po' di minestra/degli altri panini?; are
you feeling ~ better? ti senti meglio?
2 (with negative): I can't hear him ~
more non lo sento più; don't wait ~ longer non aspettare più.
anybody ['ɛnɪbədɪ] pronoun (in questions
etc) qualcuno, nessuno; (with negative)
nessuno; (no matter who) chiunque; can
you see ~? vedi qualcuno or nessuno?; if
~ should phone ... se telefona qualcuno
...; I can't see ~ non vedo nessuno; ~
could do it chiunque potrebbe farlo.
anyhow ['ɛnɪhau] ad (at any rate) ad
ogni modo, comunque; (haphazard): do
it ~ you like fallo come ti pare; I shall
go ~ ci andrò lo stesso or comunque; she
leaves things just ~ lascia tutto come
capita.
anyone ['ɛnɪwʌn] pronoun = **anybody**.
anything ['ɛnɪθɪŋ] pronoun (in question
etc) qualcosa, niente; (with negative)
niente; (no matter what): you can say ~
you like puoi dire quello che ti pare; can
you see ~? vedi niente or qualcosa?; if
~ happens to me ... se mi dovesse
succedere qualcosa ...; I can't see ~ non
vedo niente; ~ will do va bene qualsiasi
cosa or tutto.
anyway ['ɛnɪweɪ] ad (at any rate) ad
ogni modo, comunque; (besides) ad ogni
modo.
anywhere ['ɛnɪwɛə*] ad (in questions
etc) da qualche parte; (with negative)
da nessuna parte; (no matter where) da
qualsiasi or qualunque parte, dovunque;
can you see him ~? lo vedi da qualche
parte?; I can't see him ~ non lo vedo da
nessuna parte; ~ in the world dovunque
nel mondo.
apart [ə'pɑːt] ad (to one side) a parte;
(separately) separatamente; with one's
legs ~ con le gambe divaricate; 10 miles
~ a 10 miglia di distanza (l'uno dall'altro); to take ~ smontare; ~ from prep a

parte, eccetto.
apartheid [ə'pɑːteɪt] n apartheid f.
apartment [ə'pɑːtmənt] n (US)
appartamento; ~ **building** n (US)
stabile m, caseggiato.
apathetic [æpə'θɛtɪk] a apatico(a).
ape [eɪp] n scimmia // vt scimmiottare.
aperture ['æpətsjuə*] n apertura.
apex ['eɪpɛks] n apice m.
apiece [ə'piːs] ad ciascuno(a).
apologetic [əpɔlə'dʒɛtɪk] a (tone, letter)
di scusa.
apologize [ə'pɔlədʒaɪz] vi: to ~ (for sth
to sb) scusarsi (di qc a qn), chiedere
scusa (a qn per qc).
apology [ə'pɔlədʒɪ] n scuse fpl.
apostle [ə'pɔsl] n apostolo.
apostrophe [ə'pɔstrəfɪ] n (sign) apo-
strofo.
appalling [ə'pɔːlɪŋ] a spaventoso(a).
apparatus [æpə'reɪtəs] n apparato; (in
gymnasium) attrezzatura.
apparel [ə'pærl] n (US) abbigliamento,
confezioni fpl.
apparent [ə'pærənt] a evidente; ~ly
evidentemente.
apparition [æpə'rɪʃən] n apparizione f.
appeal [ə'piːl] vi (LAW) appellarsi alla
legge // n (LAW) appello; (request) richiesta; (charm) attrattiva; to ~ for
chiedere (con insistenza); to ~ to (subj:
person) appellarsi a; (subj: thing)
piacere a; to ~ to sb for mercy chiedere
pietà a qn; it doesn't ~ to me mi dice
poco; ~ing a (nice) attraente; (touching) commovente.
appear [ə'pɪə*] vi apparire; (LAW)
comparire; (publication) essere pub-
blicato(a); (seem) sembrare; it would ~
that sembra che; to ~ in Hamlet
recitare nell'Amleto; to ~ on TV
presentarsi in televisione; ~ance n
apparizione f; apparenza; (look, aspect)
aspetto.
appease [ə'piːz] vt calmare, appagare.
appendage [ə'pɛndɪdʒ] n aggiunta.
appendicitis [əpɛndɪ'saɪtɪs] n appendicite
f.
appendix, pl **appendices** [ə'pɛndɪks,
-siːz] n appendice f.
appetite ['æpɪtaɪt] n appetito.
appetizer ['æpɪtaɪzə*] n stuzzichino.
applaud [ə'plɔːd] vt, vi applaudire.
applause [ə'plɔːz] n applauso.
apple ['æpl] n mela; ~ **tree** n melo.
appliance [ə'plaɪəns] n apparecchio.
applicant ['æplɪkənt] n candidato/a.
application [æplɪ'keɪʃən] n applicazione
f; (for a job, a grant etc) domanda; ~
form n modulo per la domanda.
applied [ə'plaɪd] a applicato(a).
apply [ə'plaɪ] vt: to ~ (to) (paint,
ointment) dare (a); (theory, technique)
applicare (a) // vi: to ~ to (ask)
rivolgersi a; (be suitable for, relevant

to) riguardare, riferirsi a; **to ~ (for)**
(*permit, grant, job*) fare domanda
(per); **to ~ the brakes** frenare; **to ~ o.s.
to** dedicarsi a.

appoint [ə'pɔint] *vt* nominare; **~ment** *n*
nomina; (*arrangement to meet*)
appuntamento; **to make an ~ment**
(**with**) prendere un appuntamento (con).

appraisal [ə'preizl] *n* valutazione *f.*

appreciate [ə'priːʃieit] *vt* (*like*) apprezzare; (*be grateful for*) essere riconoscente di; (*be aware of*) rendersi conto
di // *vi* (FINANCE) aumentare.

appreciation [əpriːʃi'eiʃən] *n* ap-
prezzamento; (FINANCE) aumento del
valore.

appreciative [ə'priːʃiətiv] *a* (*person*)
sensibile; (*comment*) elogiativo(a).

apprehend [æpri'hend] *vt* (*arrest*) arrestare.

apprehension [æpri'henʃən] *n* (*fear*)
inquietudine *f.*

apprehensive [æpri'hensiv] *a* ap-
prensivo(a).

apprentice [ə'prentis] *n* apprendista *m/f*;
~ship *n* apprendistato.

approach [ə'prəutʃ] *vi* avvicinarsi // *vt*
(*come near*) avvicinarsi a; (*ask, apply
to*) rivolgersi a; (*subject, passer-by*)
avvicinare // *n* approccio; accesso; (*to
problem*) modo di affrontare; **~able** *a*
accessibile.

appropriate *a* [ə'prəupriit] appro-
priato(a); adatto(a) // *vt* [ə'prəuprieit]
(*take*) appropriarsi.

approval [ə'pruːvəl] *n* approvazione *f*; **on
~** (COMM) in prova, in esame.

approve [ə'pruːv] *vt, vi* approvare; **to ~
of** *vt fus* approvare; **~d school** *n* (*Brit*)
riformatorio.

approximate [ə'prɔksimit] *a* ap-
prossimativo(a); **~ly** *ad* circa.

apricot ['eiprikɔt] *n* albicocca.

April ['eiprəl] *n* aprile *m*; **~ fool!** pesce
d'aprile!

apron ['eiprən] *n* grembiule *m.*

apt [æpt] *a* (*suitable*) adatto(a); (*able*)
capace; (*likely*): **to be ~ to do** avere
tendenza a fare.

aptitude ['æptitjuːd] *n* abilità *f inv.*

aqualung ['ækwəlʌŋ] *n* autorespiratore
m.

aquarium [ə'kwɛəriəm] *n* acquario.

Aquarius [ə'kwɛəriəs] *n* Acquario.

Arab ['ærəb] *n* arabo/a.

Arabian [ə'reibiən] *a* arabo(a).

Arabic ['ærəbik] *a* arabico(a) // *n* arabo;
~ numerals numeri *mpl* arabi,
numerazione *f* araba.

arbitrary ['ɑːbitrəri] *a* arbitrario(a).

arbitration [ɑːbi'treiʃən] *n* (LAW) arbi-
trato; (INDUSTRY) arbitraggio.

arcade [ɑː'keid] *n* portico, (*passage with
shops*) galleria.

arch [ɑːtʃ] *n* arco; (*of foot*) arco plantare

// *vt* inarcare // *a* malizioso(a).

archaeologist [ɑːki'ɔlədʒist] *n*
archeologo/a.

archaeology [ɑːki'ɔlədʒi] *n* archeologia.

archbishop [ɑːtʃ'biʃəp] *n* arcivescovo.

arch-enemy ['ɑːtʃ'enəmi] *n* arcinemico/
a.

archeology [ɑːki'ɔlədʒi] *etc* = **archaeology** *etc.*

archer ['ɑːtʃə*] *n* arciere *m*; **~y** *n* tiro
all'arco.

architect ['ɑːkitekt] *n* architetto; **~ure**
['ɑːkitektʃə*] *n* architettura.

archives ['ɑːkaivz] *npl* archivi *mpl.*

archway ['ɑːtʃwei] *n* arco.

Arctic ['ɑːktik] *a* artico(a) // *n*: **the ~**
l'Artico.

ardent ['ɑːdənt] *a* ardente.

are [ɑː*] *vb see* **be**.

area ['ɛəriə] *n* (GEOM) area; (*zone*)
zona, (: *smaller*) settore *m.*

aren't [ɑːnt] = **are not**.

Argentina [ɑːdʒən'tiːnə] *n* Argentina;
Argentinian [-'tiniən] *a, n* argentino(a).

arguably ['ɑːgjuəbli] *ad*: **it is ~** ... si può
sostenere che sia ....

argue ['ɑːgjuː] *vi* (*quarrel*) litigare;
(*reason*) ragionare; **to ~ that** sostenere
che.

argument ['ɑːgjumənt] *n* (*reasons*)
argomento; (*quarrel*) lite *f*; (*debate*) discussione *f*; **~ative** [ɑːgju'mentətiv] *a*
litigioso(a).

Aries ['ɛəriz] *n* Ariete *m.*

arise, *pt* **arose**, *pp* **arisen** [ə'raiz, -'rəuz,
-'rizn] *vi* alzarsi; (*opportunity, problem*)
presentarsi; **to ~ from** risultare da.

aristocrat ['æristəkræt] *n* aristocratico/a.

arithmetic [ə'riθmətik] *n* aritmetica.

ark [ɑːk] *n*: Noah's A~ l'arca di Noè.

arm [ɑːm] *n* braccio // *vt* armare; **~s** *npl*
(*weapons*) armi *fpl*; **~ in ~** a braccetto.

armaments ['ɑːməmənts] *npl* armamenti
mpl.

arm: ~chair *n* poltrona; **~ed** *a*
armato(a); **~ed robbery** *n* rapina a
mano armata.

armour, (*US*) **armor** ['ɑːmə*] *n*
armatura; (*also*: **~-plating**) corazza,
blindatura; (MIL: *tanks*) mezzi *mpl*
blindati; **~ed car** *n* autoblinda *f inv*; **~y**
n arsenale *m.*

armpit ['ɑːmpit] *n* ascella.

armrest ['ɑːmrest] *n* bracciolo.

army ['ɑːmi] *n* esercito.

aroma [ə'rəumə] *n* aroma.

arose [ə'rəuz] *pt of* **arise**.

around [ə'raund] *ad* attorno, intorno //
prep intorno a; (*fig: about*): **~ £5/3
o'clock** circa 5 sterline/le 3; **is he ~?** è in
giro?

arouse [ə'rauz] *vt* (*sleeper*) svegliare;
(*curiosity, passions*) suscitare.

arrange [ə'reindʒ] *vt* sistemare; (*programme*) preparare; **to ~ to do sth**

mettersi d'accordo per fare qc; ~ment *n* sistemazione *f*; (*plans etc*): ~ments progetti *mpl*, piani *mpl*.

array [ə'reɪ] *n*: ~ of fila di.

arrears [ə'rɪəz] *npl* arretrati *mpl*; to be in ~ with one's rent essere in arretrato con l'affitto.

arrest [ə'rɛst] *vt* arrestare; (*sb's attention*) attirare // *n* arresto; under ~ in arresto.

arrival [ə'raɪvəl] *n* arrivo; (*person*) arrivato/a; a new ~ un nuovo venuto; (*baby*) un neonato.

arrive [ə'raɪv] *vi* arrivare; to ~ at *vt fus* (*fig*) raggiungere.

arrogant ['ærəgənt] *a* arrogante.

arrow ['ærəu] *n* freccia.

arse [ɑːs] *n* (*col!*) culo (!).

arson ['ɑːsn] *n* incendio doloso.

art [ɑːt] *n* arte *f*; (*craft*) mestiere *m*; A~s *npl* (SCOL) Lettere *fpl*.

artefact ['ɑːtɪfækt] *n* manufatto.

artery ['ɑːtərɪ] *n* arteria.

art gallery *n* galleria d'arte.

arthritis [ɑː'θraɪtɪs] *n* artrite *f*.

artichoke ['ɑːtɪtʃəuk] *n* carciofo; Jerusalem ~ topinambur *m inv*.

article ['ɑːtɪkl] *n* articolo; (*Brit* LAW: *training*): ~s *npl* contratto di tirocinio; ~ of clothing capo di vestiario.

articulate *a* [ɑː'tɪkjulɪt] (*person*) che si esprime forbitamente; (*speech*) articolato(a) // *vi* [ɑː'tɪkjuleɪt] articolare; ~d lorry *n* (*Brit*) autotreno.

artificial [ɑːtɪ'fɪʃl] *a* artificiale; ~ respiration *n* respirazione *f* artificiale.

artillery [ɑː'tɪlərɪ] *n* artiglieria.

artisan ['ɑːtɪzæn] *n* artigiano/a.

artist ['ɑːtɪst] *n* artista *m/f*; ~ic [ɑː'tɪstɪk] *a* artistico(a); ~ry *n* arte *f*.

artless ['ɑːtlɪs] *a* semplice, ingenuo(a).

art school *n* scuola d'arte.

as [æz] ♦ *cj* **1** (*referring to time*) mentre; ~ the years went by col passare degli anni; he came in ~ I was leaving arrivò mentre stavo uscendo; ~ from tomorrow da domani

2 (*in comparisons*): ~ big ~ grande come; twice ~ big ~ due volte più grande di; ~ much/many ~ tanto quanto/tanti quanti; ~ soon ~ possible prima possibile

3 (*since, because*) dal momento che, siccome

4 (*referring to manner, way*) come; do ~ you wish fa' come vuoi; ~ she said come ha detto lei

5 (*concerning*): ~ for *or* to that per quanto riguarda *or* quanto a quello

6: ~ if *or* though come se; he looked ~ if he was ill sembrava stare male; *see also* **long, such, well**

♦ *prep*: he works ~ a driver fa l'autista; ~ chairman of the company, he ... come presidente della compagnia, lui ...;

he gave me it ~ a present me lo ha regalato.

a.s.a.p. *abbr* (= *as soon as possible*) prima possibile.

ascend [ə'sɛnd] *vt* salire.

ascent [ə'sɛnt] *n* salita.

ascertain [æsə'teɪn] *vt* accertare.

ash [æʃ] *n* (*dust*) cenere *f*; (*also*: ~ tree) frassino.

ashamed [ə'ʃeɪmd] *a* vergognoso(a); to be ~ of vergognarsi di.

ashen ['æʃn] *a* (*pale*) livido(a).

ashore [ə'ʃɔː*] *ad* a terra.

ashtray ['æʃtreɪ] *n* portacenere *m*.

Ash Wednesday *n* mercoledì *m inv* delle Ceneri.

Asia ['eɪʃə] *n* Asia; ~n *a*, *n* asiatico(a).

aside [ə'saɪd] *ad* da parte // *n* a parte *m*.

ask [ɑːsk] *vt* (*request*) chiedere; (*question*) domandare; (*invite*) invitare; to ~ sb sth/sb to do sth chiedere qc a qn/a qn di fare qc; to ~ sb about sth chiedere a qn di qc; to ~ (sb) a question fare una domanda (a qn); to ~ sb out to dinner invitare qn a mangiare fuori; to ~ after *vt fus* chiedere di; to ~ for *vt fus* chiedere.

askance [ə'skɑːns] *ad*: to look ~ at sb guardare qn di traverso.

askew [ə'skjuː] *ad* di traverso, storto.

asleep [ə'sliːp] *a* addormentato(a); to be ~ dormire; to fall ~ addormentarsi.

asparagus [əs'pærəgəs] *n* asparagi *mpl*.

aspect ['æspɛkt] *n* aspetto.

aspersions [əs'pəːʃənz] *npl*: to cast ~ on diffamare.

asphyxiation [æsfɪksɪ'eɪʃən] *n* asfissia.

aspire [əs'paɪə*] *vi*: to ~ to aspirare a.

aspirin ['æsprɪn] *n* aspirina.

ass [æs] *n* asino; (*col*) scemo/a; (*US col*) culo (!).

assailant [ə'seɪlənt] *n* assalitore *m*.

assassinate [ə'sæsɪneɪt] *vt* assassinare; **assassination** [əsæsɪ'neɪʃən] *n* assassinio.

assault [ə'sɔːlt] *n* (MIL) assalto; (*gen*: *attack*) aggressione *f* // *vt* assaltare; aggredire; (*sexually*) violentare.

assemble [ə'sɛmbl] *vt* riunire; (TECH) montare // *vi* riunirsi.

assembly [ə'sɛmblɪ] *n* (*meeting*) assemblea; (*construction*) montaggio; ~ line *n* catena di montaggio.

assent [ə'sɛnt] *n* assenso, consenso.

assert [ə'səːt] *vt* asserire; (*insist on*) far valere.

assess [ə'sɛs] *vt* valutare; ~ment *n* valutazione *f*.

asset ['æsɛt] *n* vantaggio; ~s *npl* beni *mpl*; disponibilità *fpl*; attivo.

assign [ə'saɪn] *vt*: to ~ (to) (*task*) assegnare (a); (*resources*) riservare (a); (*cause, meaning*) attribuire (a); to ~ a date to sth fissare la data di qc; ~ment *n* compito.

assist [ə'sɪst] *vt* assistere, aiutare; **~ance** *n* assistenza, aiuto; **~ant** *n* assistente *m/f*; (*Brit: also:* **shop ~ant**) commesso/a.

associate [ə'səuʃɪɪt] *a* associato(a); (*member*) aggiunto(a) // *n* collega *m/f*; (*in business*) socio/a // *vb* [ə'səuʃɪeɪt] *vt* associare // *vi:* **to ~ with sb** frequentare qn.

association [əsəusɪ'eɪʃən] *n* associazione *f*.

assorted [ə'sɔ:tɪd] *a* assortito(a).

assortment [ə'sɔ:tmənt] *n* assortimento.

assume [ə'sju:m] *vt* supporre; (*responsibilities etc*) assumere; (*attitude, name*) prendere; **~d name** *n* nome *m* falso.

assumption [ə'sʌmpʃən] *n* supposizione *f*, ipotesi *f inv*.

assurance [ə'ʃuərəns] *n* assicurazione *f*; (*self-confidence*) fiducia in se stesso.

assure [ə'ʃuə*] *vt* assicurare.

astern [ə'stə:n] *ad* a poppa.

asthma ['æsmə] *n* asma.

astonish [ə'stɔnɪʃ] *vt* stupire; **~ment** *n* stupore *m*.

astound [ə'staund] *vt* stupire.

astray [ə'streɪ] *ad:* **to go ~** smarrirsi; (*fig*) traviarsi.

astride [ə'straɪd] *prep* a cavalcioni di.

astrology [əs'trɔlədʒɪ] *n* astrologia.

astronaut ['æstrənɔ:t] *n* astronauta *m/f*.

astronomy [əs'trɔnəmɪ] *n* astronomia.

astute [əs'tju:t] *a* astuto(a).

asylum [ə'saɪləm] *n* asilo; (*building*) manicomio.

at [æt] *prep* **1** (*referring to position, direction*) a; **~ the top** in cima; **~ the desk** al banco, alla scrivania; **~ home/ school** a casa/scuola; **~ the baker's** dal panettiere; (*to look ~ sth* guardare qc; **to throw sth ~ sb** lanciare qc a qn
2 (*referring to time*) a; **~ 4 o'clock** alle 4; **~ night** di notte; **~ Christmas** a Natale; **~ times** a volte
3 (*referring to rates, speed etc*) a; **~ £1 a kilo** a 1 sterlina al chilo; **two ~ a time** due alla volta, due per volta; **~ 50 km/h** a 50 km/h
4 (*referring to manner*): **~ a stroke** d'un solo colpo; **~ peace** in pace
5 (*referring to activity*): **to be ~ work** essere al lavoro; **to play ~ cowboys** giocare ai cowboy; **to be good ~ sth/ doing sth** essere bravo in qc/a fare qc
6 (*referring to cause*): **shocked/ surprised/annoyed ~ sth** colpito da/ sorpreso da/arrabbiato per qc; **I went ~ his suggestion** ci sono andato dietro suo consiglio.

ate [eɪt] *pt of* **eat**.

atheist ['eɪθɪɪst] *n* ateo/a.

Athens ['æθɪnz] *n* Atene *f*.

athlete ['æθli:t] *n* atleta *m/f*.

athletic [æθ'letɪk] *a* atletico(a); **~s** *n*

atletica.

Atlantic [ət'læntɪk] *a* atlantico(a) // *n:* **the ~** (**Ocean**) l'Atlantico, l'Oceano Atlantico.

atlas ['ætləs] *n* atlante *m*.

atmosphere ['ætməsfɪə*] *n* atmosfera.

atom ['ætəm] *n* atomo; **~ic** [ə'tɔmɪk] *a* atomico(a); **~(ic) bomb** *n* bomba atomica; **~izer** ['ætəmaɪzə*] *n* atomizzatore *m*.

atone [ə'təun] *vi:* **to ~ for** espiare.

atrocious [ə'trəuʃəs] *a* pessimo(a), atroce.

attach [ə'tætʃ] *vt* attaccare; (*document, letter*) allegare; (*MIL: troops*) assegnare; **to be ~ed to sb/ sth** (*to like*) essere affezionato(a) a qn/qc.

attaché case [ə'tæʃeɪ-] *n* valigetta per documenti.

attachment [ə'tætʃmənt] *n* (*tool*) accessorio; (*love*): **~ (to)** affetto (per).

attack [ə'tæk] *vt* attaccare; (*task etc*) iniziare; (*problem*) affrontare // *n* attacco; (*also:* **heart ~**) infarto.

attain [ə'teɪn] *vt* (*also:* **to ~ to**) arrivare a, raggiungere; **~ments** *npl* cognizioni *fpl*.

attempt [ə'tempt] *n* tentativo // *vt* tentare; **to make an ~ on sb's life** attentare alla vita di qn.

attend [ə'tend] *vt* frequentare; (*meeting, talk*) andare a; (*patient*) assistere; **to ~ to** *vt fus* (*needs, affairs etc*) prendersi cura di; (*customer*) occuparsi di; **~ance** *n* (*being present*) presenza; (*people present*) gente *f* presente; **~ant** *n* custode *m/f*; persona di servizio // *a* concomitante.

attention [ə'tenʃən] *n* attenzione *f*; **~!** (*MIL*) attenti!; **for the ~ of** (*ADMIN*) per l'attenzione di.

attentive [ə'tentɪv] *a* attento(a); (*kind*) premuroso(a).

attic ['ætɪk] *n* soffitta.

attitude ['ætɪtju:d] *n* atteggiamento; posa.

attorney [ə'tə:nɪ] *n* (*lawyer*) avvocato; (*having proxy*) mandatario; **A~ General** *n* (*Brit*) Procuratore *m* Generale; (*US*) Ministro della Giustizia.

attract [ə'trækt] *vt* attirare; **~ion** [ə'trækʃən] *n* (*gen pl: pleasant things*) attrattiva; (*PHYSICS, fig: towards sth*) attrazione *f*; **~ive** *a* attraente.

attribute *n* ['ætrɪbju:t] attributo // *vt* [ə'trɪbju:t]: **to ~ sth to** attribuire qc a.

attrition [ə'trɪʃən] *n:* **war of ~** guerra di logoramento.

aubergine ['əubəʒi:n] *n* melanzana.

auburn ['ɔ:bən] *a* tizianesco(a).

auction ['ɔ:kʃən] *n* (*also:* **sale by ~**) asta // *vt* (*also:* **to sell by ~**) vendere all'asta; (*also:* **to put up for ~**) mettere all'asta; **~eer** [-'ɪə*] *n* banditore *m*.

audible ['ɔ:dɪbl] *a* udibile.

audience ['ɔ:dɪəns] n (people) pubblico; spettatori mpl; ascoltatori mpl; (interview) udienza.

audio-typist ['ɔ:dɪəu'taɪpɪst] n dattilografo/a che trascrive da nastro.

audio-visual [ɔ:dɪəu'vɪzjuəl] a audiovisivo(a); ~ **aid** n sussidio audiovisivo.

audit ['ɔ:dɪt] vt rivedere, verificare.

audition [ɔ:'dɪʃən] n audizione f.

auditor ['ɔ:dɪtə*] n revisore m.

augment [ɔ:g'ment] vt, vi aumentare.

augur ['ɔ:gə*] vi: it ~s well promette bene.

August ['ɔ:gəst] n agosto.

aunt [ɑ:nt] n zia; ~**ie**, ~**y** n zietta.

au pair ['əu'pɛə*] n (also: ~ **girl**) (ragazza f) alla pari inv.

aura ['ɔ:rə] n aura.

auspicious [ɔ:s'pɪʃəs] a propizio(a).

austerity [ɔs'terɪtɪ] n austerità.

Australia [ɔs'treɪlɪə] n Australia; ~**n** a, n australiano(a).

Austria ['ɔstrɪə] n Austria; ~**n** a, n austriaco(a).

authentic [ɔ:'θentɪk] a autentico(a).

author ['ɔ:θə*] n autore/trice.

authoritarian [ɔ:θɔrɪ'tɛərɪən] a autoritario(a).

authoritative [ɔ:'θɔrɪtətɪv] a (account etc) autorevole; (manner) autoritario(a).

authority [ɔ:'θɔrɪtɪ] n autorità f inv; (permission) autorizzazione f; the authorities npl le autorità.

authorize ['ɔ:θəraɪz] vt autorizzare.

auto ['ɔ:təu] n (US) auto f inv.

autobiography [ɔ:təbaɪ'ɔgrəfɪ] n autobiografia.

autograph ['ɔ:təgrɑ:f] n autografo // vt firmare.

automatic [ɔ:tə'mætɪk] a automatico(a) // n (gun) arma automatica; (Brit AUT) automobile f con cambio automatico; ~**ally** ad automaticamente.

automation [ɔ:tə'meɪʃən] n automazione f.

automaton, pl automata [ɔ:'tɔmətən, -tə] n automa m.

automobile ['ɔ:təməbi:l] n (US) automobile f.

autonomy [ɔ:'tɔnəmɪ] n autonomia.

autumn ['ɔ:təm] n autunno.

auxiliary [ɔ:g'zɪlɪərɪ] a ausiliario(a) // n ausiliare m/f.

Av. abbr = **avenue.**

avail [ə'veɪl] vt: to ~ o.s. of servirsi di; approfittarsi di // n: to no ~ inutilmente.

available [ə'veɪləbl] a disponibile.

avalanche ['ævəlɑ:nʃ] n valanga.

avant-garde ['ævɑ̃'gɑ:d] a d'avanguardia.

Ave. abbr = **avenue.**

avenge [ə'vendʒ] vt vendicare.

avenue ['ævənju:] n viale m.

average ['ævərɪdʒ] n media // a medio(a) // vt (a certain figure) fare di or in media; on ~ in media; to ~ out vi: to ~ out at aggirarsi in media su, essere in media di.

averse [ə'vɜ:s] a: to be ~ to sth/doing essere contrario a qc/a fare.

avert [ə'vɜ:t] vt evitare, prevenire; (one's eyes) distogliere.

aviary ['eɪvɪərɪ] n voliera, uccelliera.

avocado [ævə'kɑ:dəu] n (also: Brit: ~ pear) avocado m inv.

avoid [ə'vɔɪd] vt evitare.

await [ə'weɪt] vt aspettare.

awake [ə'weɪk] a sveglio(a) // vb (pt awoke, pp awoken, awaked) vt svegliare // vi svegliarsi; ~**ning** [ə'weɪknɪŋ] n risveglio.

award [ə'wɔ:d] n premio; (LAW) decreto // vt assegnare; (LAW: damages) decretare.

aware [ə'wɛə*] a: ~ of (conscious) conscio(a) di; (informed) informato(a) di; to become ~ of accorgersi di; ~**ness** n consapevolezza.

awash [ə'wɔʃ] a: ~ (with) inondato(a) (da).

away [ə'weɪ] a, ad via; lontano(a); two kilometres ~ a due chilometri di distanza; two hours ~ by car a due ore di distanza in macchina; the holiday was two weeks ~ mancavano due settimane alle vacanze; ~ from lontano da; he's ~ for a week è andato via per una settimana; he was working/pedalling etc ~ la particella indica la continuità e l'energia dell'azione: lavorava/pedalava etc più che poteva; to fade/wither etc ~ la particella rinforza l'idea della diminuzione; ~ game n (SPORT) partita fuori casa.

awe [ɔ:] n timore m; ~**-inspiring**, ~**some** a imponente.

awful ['ɔ:fəl] a terribile; ~**ly** ad (very) terribilmente.

awhile [ə'waɪl] ad (per) un po'.

awkward ['ɔ:kwəd] a (clumsy) goffo(a); (inconvenient) scomodo(a); (embarrassing) imbarazzante.

awning ['ɔ:nɪŋ] n (of shop, hotel etc) tenda.

awoke, awoken [ə'wəuk, -kən] pt, pp of **awake.**

awry [ə'raɪ] ad di traverso // a storto(a); to go ~ andare a monte.

axe, (US) ax [æks] n scure f // vt (project etc) abolire; (jobs) sopprimere.

axis, pl axes ['æksɪs, -sɪ:z] n asse m.

axle ['æksl] n (also: ~-tree) asse m.

ay(e) [aɪ] excl (yes) sì.

B

B [bi:] *n* (*MUS*) si *m*.

B.A. *n abbr* = **Bachelor of Arts**.

baby ['beɪbɪ] *n* bambino/a; ~ **carriage** *n* (*US*) carrozzina; ~**-sit** *vi* fare il (*or* la) babysitter; ~**-sitter** *n* baby-sitter *m/f inv*.

bachelor ['bætʃələ*] *n* scapolo; B~ of Arts/Science (B.A./B.Sc.) ≈ laureato/a in lettere/scienze.

back [bæk] *n* (*of person, horse*) dorso, schiena; (*of hand*) dorso; (*of house, car*) didietro; (*of train*) coda; (*of chair*) schienale *m*; (*of page*) rovescio; (*FOOTBALL*) difensore *m* // *vt* (*candidate: also:* ~ up) appoggiare; (*horse: at races*) puntare su; (*car*) guidare a marcia indietro // *vi* indietreggiare; (*cur etc*) fare marcia indietro // *a* (*in compounds*) posteriore, di dietro; ~ seats/wheels (*AUT*) sedili *mpl*/ruote *fpl* posteriori; ~ **payments** arretrati *mpl* // *ad* (*not forward*) indietro; (*returned*): he's ~ è tornato; he ran ~ tornò indietro di corsa; (*restitution*): **throw the ball** ~ ritira la palla; **can I have it** ~? posso riaverlo?; (*again*): **he called** ~ ha richiamato; **to** ~ **down** *vi* fare marcia indietro; **to** ~ **out** *vi* (*of promise*) tirarsi indietro; **to** ~ **up** *vt* (*support*) appoggiare, sostenere; (*COMPUT*) fare una copia di riserva di; ~**bencher** *n* (*Brit*) membro del Parlamento senza potere amministrativo; ~**bone** *n* spina dorsale; ~**cloth** *n* scena di sfondo; ~**date** *vt* (*letter*) retrodatare; ~**dated pay rise** aumento retroattivo; ~**drop** *n* = ~**cloth**; ~**fire** *vi* (*AUT*) dar ritorni di fiamma; (*plans*) fallire; ~**ground** *n* sfondo; (*of events*) background *m inv*; (*basic knowledge*) base *f*; (*experience*) esperienza; **family** ~**ground** ambiente *m* familiare; ~**hand** *n* (*TENNIS: also:* ~**hand stroke**) rovescio; ~**handed** *a* (*fig*) ambiguo(a); ~**hander** *n* (*Brit: bribe*) bustarella; ~**ing** *n* (*fig*) appoggio; ~**lash** *n* contraccolpo, ripercussione *f*; ~**log** *n*: ~**log of work** lavoro arretrato; ~ **number** *n* (*of magazine etc*) numero arretrato; ~**pack** *n* zaino; ~ **pay** *n* arretrato di paga; ~**side** *n* (*col*) sedere *m*; ~**stage** *ad* nel retroscena; ~**stroke** *n* nuoto sul dorso; ~**up** *a* (*train, plane*) supplementare; (*COMPUT*) di riserva // *n* (*support*) appoggio, sostegno; (*also:* ~**up file**) file *m inv* di riserva; ~**ward** *a* (*movement*) indietro *inv*; (*person*) tardivo(a); (*country*) arretrato(a); ~**wards** *ad* indietro; (*fall, walk*) all'indietro; ~**water** *n* (*fig*) posto morto; ~**yard** *n* cortile *m* dietro la casa.

bacon ['beɪkən] *n* pancetta.

bad [bæd] *a* cattivo(a); (*child*) cattivello(a); (*meat, food*) andato(a) a male; **his** ~ **leg** la sua gamba malata; **to go** ~ andare a male.

bade [bæd] *pt of* **bid**.

badge [bædʒ] *n* insegna; (*of policeman*) stemma *m*.

badger ['bædʒə*] *n* tasso.

badly ['bædlɪ] *ad* (*work, dress etc*) male; ~ **wounded** gravemente ferito; **he needs it** ~ ne ha gran bisogno; ~ **off** *a* povero(a).

badminton ['bædmɪntən] *n* badminton *m*.

bad-tempered ['bæd'tempəd] *a* irritabile; di malumore.

baffle ['bæfl] *vt* (*puzzle*) confondere.

bag [bæg] *n* sacco; (*handbag etc*) borsa; (*of hunter*) carniere *m*; bottino // *vt* (*col: take*) mettersi in tasca; prendersi; ~**s of** (*col: lots of*) un sacco di; ~**gage** *n* bagagli *mpl*; ~**gy** *a* largo(a), sformato(a); ~**pipes** *npl* cornamusa.

ball [beɪl] *n* cauzione *f* // *vt* (*prisoner: also:* **grant** ~ **to**) concedere la libertà provvisoria su cauzione a; (*boat: also:* ~ **out**) aggottare; **on** ~ (*accused person*) in libertà provvisoria su cauzione; **to** ~ **out** *vt* (*prisoner*) ottenere la libertà provvisoria su cauzione di; *see also* **bale**.

bailiff ['beɪlɪf] *n* usciere *m*; fattore *m*.

bait [beɪt] *n* esca // *vt* (*fig*) tormentare.

bake [beɪk] *vt* cuocere al forno // *vi* cuocersi al forno; ~**d beans** *npl* fagioli *mpl* all'uccelletto; ~**r** *n* fornaio/a, panettiere/a; ~**ry** *n* panetteria; **baking** *n* cottura (al forno).

balance ['bæləns] *n* equilibrio; (*COMM: sum*) bilancio; (*scales*) bilancia // *vt* tenere in equilibrio; (*pros and cons*) soppesare; (*budget*) far quadrare; (*account*) pareggiare; (*compensate*) contrappesare; ~ **of** trade/payments bilancia commerciale/dei pagamenti; ~**d** *a* (*personality, diet*) equilibrato(a); ~ **sheet** *n* bilancio.

balcony ['bælkənɪ] *n* balcone *m*.

bald [bɔːld] *a* calvo(a).

bale [beɪl] *n* balla; **to** ~ **out** *vi* (*of a plane*) gettarsi col paracadute.

baleful ['beɪlful] *a* funesto(a).

ball [bɔːl] *n* palla; (*football*) pallone *m*; (*for golf*) pallina; (*dance*) ballo.

ballast ['bæləst] *n* zavorra.

ball bearings *npl* cuscinetti a sfere.

ballerina [bælə'riːnə] *n* ballerina.

ballet ['bæleɪ] *n* balletto; (*art*) danza classica.

balloon [bə'luːn] *n* pallone *m*; (*in comic strip*) fumetto.

ballot ['bælət] *n* scrutinio.

ball-point pen ['bɔːlpɔɪnt-] *n* penna a sfera.

ballroom ['bɔːlrum] n sala da ballo.

balm [baːm] n balsamo.

ban [bæn] n interdizione f // vt interdire.

banana [bə'naːnə] n banana.

band [bænd] n banda; (at a dance) orchestra; (MIL) fanfara; **to ~ together** vi collegarsi.

bandage ['bændɪdʒ] n benda.

bandaid ['bændeɪd] n (US) cerotto.

bandwagon ['bændwægən] n: **to jump on the ~** (fig) seguire la corrente.

bandy ['bændɪ] vt (jokes, insults) scambiare.

bandy-legged ['bændɪ'legɪd] a dalle gambe storte.

bang [bæŋ] n botta; (of door) lo sbattere; (blow) colpo // vt battere (violentemente); (door) sbattere // vi scoppiare; sbattere.

bangle ['bæŋgl] n braccialetto.

bangs [bæŋz] npl (US: fringe) frangia, frangetta.

banish ['bænɪʃ] vt bandire.

banister(s) ['bænɪstə(z)] n(pl) ringhiera.

bank [bæŋk] n banca, banco; (of river, lake) riva, sponda; (of earth) banco // vi inclinarsi in virata; **to ~ on** vt fus contare su; **~ account** n conto in banca; **~ card** n carta assegni; **~er** n banchiere m; **~er's card** n (Brit) = **~ card**; **B~ holiday** n (Brit) giorno di festa (in cui le banche sono chiuse); **~ing** n attività bancaria; professione f di banchiere; **~note** n banconota; **~ rate** n tasso bancario.

bankrupt ['bæŋkrʌpt] a fallito(a); **to go ~** fallire; **~cy** n fallimento.

bank statement n estratto conto.

banner ['bænə*] n bandiera.

banns [bænz] npl pubblicazioni fpl di matrimonio.

baptism ['bæptɪzəm] n battesimo.

bar [baː*] n barra; (of window etc) sbarra; (of chocolate) tavoletta; (fig) ostacolo; restrizione f; (pub) bar m inv; (counter: in pub) banco; (MUS) battuta // vt (road, window) sbarrare; (person) escludere; (activity) interdire; **~ of soap** saponetta; **the B~** (LAW) l'Ordine m degli avvocati; **behind ~s** (prisoner) dietro le sbarre; **~ none** senza eccezione.

barbaric [baː'bærɪk] a barbarico(a).

barbecue ['baːbɪkjuː] n barbecue m inv.

barbed wire ['baːbd-] n filo spinato.

barber ['baːbə*] n barbiere m.

bar code n (on goods) codice n a barre.

bare [bɛə*] a nudo(a) // vt scoprire, denudare; (teeth) mostrare; **~back** ad senza sella; **~faced** a sfacciato(a); **~foot** a, ad scalzo(a); **~ly** ad appena.

bargain ['baːgɪn] n (transaction) contratto; (good buy) affare m // vi trattare; **into the ~** per giunta; **to ~ for** vt fus: **he got more than he ~ed for** gli è andata peggio di quel che si aspettasse

or che avesse calcolato.

barge [baːdʒ] n chiatta; **to ~ in** vi (walk in) piombare dentro; (interrupt talk) intromettersi a sproposito; **to ~ into** vt fus urtare contro.

bark [baːk] n (of tree) corteccia; (of dog) abbaio // vi abbaiare.

barley ['baːlɪ] n orzo.

barmaid ['baːmeɪd] n cameriera al banco.

barman ['baːmən] n barista m.

barn [baːn] n granaio.

barometer [bə'rɒmɪtə*] n barometro.

baron ['bærən] n barone m; **~ess** n baronessa.

barracks ['bærəks] npl caserma.

barrage ['bæraːʒ] n (MIL, dam) sbarramento; (fig) fiume m.

barrel ['bærəl] n barile m; (of gun) canna.

barren ['bærən] a sterile; (soil) arido(a).

barricade [bærɪ'keɪd] n barricata.

barrier ['bærɪə*] n barriera.

barring ['baːrɪŋ] prep salvo.

barrister ['bærɪstə*] n (Brit) avvocato/essa (con diritto di parlare davanti a tutte le corti).

barrow ['bærəu] n (cart) carriola.

bartender ['baːtɛndə*] n (US) barista m.

barter ['baːtə*] n baratto // vt: **to ~ sth for** barattare qc con.

base [beɪs] n base f // vt: **to ~ sth on** basare qc su // a vile.

baseball ['beɪsbɔːl] n baseball m.

basement ['beɪsmənt] n seminterrato; (of shop) interrato.

bases ['beɪsiːz] npl of **basis**; ['beɪsɪz] npl of **base**.

bash [bæʃ] vt (col) picchiare.

bashful ['bæʃful] a timido(a).

basic ['beɪsɪk] a rudimentale; essenziale; **~ally** [-lɪ] ad fondamentalmente; sostanzialmente.

basil ['bæzl] n basilico.

basin ['beɪsn] n (vessel, also GEO) bacino; (also: wash~) lavabo.

basis, pl **bases** ['beɪsɪs, -siːz] n base f.

bask [baːsk] vi: **to ~ in the sun** crogiolarsi al sole.

basket ['baːskɪt] n cesta; (smaller) cestino; (with handle) paniere m; **~ball** n pallacanestro f.

bass [beɪs] n (MUS) basso.

bassoon [bə'suːn] n fagotto.

bastard ['baːstəd] n bastardo/a; (col!) stronzo (!).

bat [bæt] n pipistrello; (for baseball etc) mazza; (Brit: for table tennis) racchetta // vt: **he didn't ~ an eyelid** non battè ciglio.

batch [bætʃ] n (of bread) infornata; (of papers) cumulo.

bated ['beɪtɪd] a: **with ~ breath** col fiato sospeso.

bath [baːθ, pl baːðz] n (see also **baths**)

bagno; (*bathtub*) vasca da bagno // *vt* far fare il bagno a; **to have a ~** fare un bagno.

bathe [beɪð] *vi* fare il bagno // *vt* bagnare.

bathing ['beɪðɪŋ] *n* bagni *mpl*; **~ cap** *n* cuffia da bagno; **~ costume**, (*US*) **~ suit** *n* costume *m* da bagno.

bath: ~robe *n* accappatoio; **~room** *n* stanza da bagno.

baths [bɑːðz] *npl* bagni *mpl* pubblici.

bath towel *n* asciugamano da bagno.

baton ['bætən] *n* (*MUS*) bacchetta; (*club*) manganello.

batter ['bætə*] *vt* battere // *n* pastetta; **~ed** *a* (*hat*) sformato(a); (*pan*) ammaccato(a).

battery ['bætərɪ] *n* batteria; (*of torch*) pila.

battle ['bætl] *n* battaglia // *vi* battagliare, lottare; **~field** *n* campo di battaglia; **~ship** *n* nave *f* da guerra.

bawdy ['bɔːdɪ] *a* piccante.

bawl [bɔːl] *vi* urlare.

bay [beɪ] *n* (*of sea*) baia; **to hold sb at ~** tenere qn a bada.

bay window *n* bovindo.

bazaar [bə'zɑː*] *n* bazar *m inv*; vendita di beneficenza.

b. & b., B. & B. *abbr* = **bed and breakfast**.

BBC *n abbr* (= *British Broadcasting Corporation*) rete nazionale di radio-televisione in Gran Bretagna.

B.C. *ad abbr* (= *before Christ*) a.C.

be [biː], *pt* **was, were**, *pp* **been** ♦ *auxiliary vb* **1** (*with present participle: forming continuous tenses*): **what are you doing?** che fa?, che sta facendo?; **they're coming tomorrow** vengono domani; **I've been waiting for her for hours** sono ore che l'aspetto

2 (*with pp: forming passives*) essere; **to ~ killed** essere *or* venire ucciso(a); **the box had been opened** la scatola era stata aperta; **the thief was nowhere to ~ seen** il ladro non si trovava da nessuna parte

3 (*in tag questions*): **it was fun, wasn't it?** è stato divertente, no?; **he's good-looking, isn't he?** è un bell'uomo, vero?; **she's back, is she?** così è tornata, eh?

4 (+ *to* + *infinitive*): **the house is to ~ sold** abbiamo (*or* hanno *etc*) intenzione di vendere casa; **you're to ~ congratulated for all your work** dovremo farvi i complimenti per tutto il vostro lavoro; **he's not to open it** non deve aprirlo

♦ *vb* + *complement* **1** (*gen*) essere; **I'm English** sono inglese; **I'm tired** sono stanco(a); **I'm hot/cold** ho caldo/freddo; **he's a doctor** è medico; **2 and 2 are 4** 2 più 2 fa 4; **~ careful!** sta attento(a)!; **~ good** sii buono(a)

2 (*of health*) stare; **how are you?** come

sta?; **he's very ill** sta molto male

3 (*of age*): **how old are you?** quanti anni hai?; **I'm sixteen (years old)** ho sedici anni

4 (*cost*) costare; **how much was the meal?** quant'era *or* quanto costava il pranzo?; **that'll ~ £5, please** (fa) 5 sterline, per favore

♦ *vi* **1** (*exist, occur etc*) essere, esistere; **the best singer that ever was** il migliore cantante mai esistito *or* di tutti tempi; **~ that as it may** comunque sia, sia come sia; **so ~ it** sia pure, e sia

2 (*referring to place*) essere, trovarsi; **I won't ~ here tomorrow** non ci sarò domani; **Edinburgh is in Scotland** Edimburgo si trova in Scozia

3 (*referring to movement*): **where have you been?** dov'è stato?; **I've been to China** sono stato in Cina

♦ *impersonal vb* **1** (*referring to time, distance*) essere; **it's 5 o'clock** sono le 5; **it's the 28th of April** è il 28 aprile; **it's 10 km to the village** di qui al paese sono 10 km

2 (*referring to the weather*) fare; **it's too hot/cold** fa troppo caldo/freddo; **it's windy** c'è vento

3 (*emphatic*): **it's me** sono io; **it was Maria who paid the bill** è stata Maria che ha pagato il conto.

beach [biːtʃ] *n* spiaggia // *vt* tirare in secco.

beacon ['biːkən] *n* (*lighthouse*) faro; (*marker*) segnale *m*.

bead [biːd] *n* perlina.

beak [biːk] *n* becco.

beaker ['biːkə*] *n* coppa.

beam [biːm] *n* trave *f*; (*of light*) raggio // *vi* brillare.

bean [biːn] *n* fagiolo; (*of coffee*) chicco; **runner ~** fagiolino; **broad ~** fava; **~sprouts** *npl* germogli *mpl* di soia.

bear [bɛə*] *n* orso // *vb* (*pt* **bore**, *pp* **borne**) *vt* portare; (*endure*) sopportare // *vi*: **to ~ right/left** piegare a destra/sinistra; **to ~ out** *vt* (*suspicions*) confermare, convalidare; (*person*) dare il proprio appoggio a; **to ~ up** *vi* (*person*) fare buon viso a cattiva sorte.

beard [bɪəd] *n* barba.

bearer ['bɛərə*] *n* portatore *m*.

bearing ['bɛərɪŋ] *n* portamento; (*connection*) rapporto; **~s** *npl* (*also*: **ball ~s**) cuscinetti *mpl* a sfere; **to take a ~** fare un rilevamento; **to find one's ~s** orientarsi.

beast [biːst] *n* bestia; **~ly** *a* meschino(a); (*weather*) da cani.

beat [biːt] *n* colpo; (*of heart*) battito; (*MUS*) tempo, battuta; (*of policeman*) giro // *vt* (*pt* **beat**, *pp* **beaten**) battere; **off the ~en track** fuori mano; **to ~ time** battere il tempo; **~ it!** (*col*) fila!, fuori dai piedi!; **to ~ off** *vt* respingere; **to ~**

up vt (col: person) picchiare; (eggs) sbattere; ~**ing** n bastonata.

beautiful ['bju:tiful] a bello(a); ~**ly** ad splendidamente.

beauty ['bju:tɪ] n bellezza; ~ **salon** n istituto di bellezza; ~ **spot** n neo; (Brit: TOURISM) luogo pittoresco.

beaver ['bi:və*] n castoro.

became [bɪ'keɪm] pt of **become**.

because [bɪ'kɔz] cj perché; ~ **of** prep a causa di.

beck [bɛk] n: to be at sb's ~ and call essere a completa disposizione di qn.

beckon ['bɛkən] vt (also: ~ to) chiamare con un cenno.

become [bɪ'kʌm] vt (irg: like come) diventare; to ~ fat/thin ingrassarsi/dimagrire; what has ~ of him? che gli è successo?

becoming [bɪ'kʌmɪŋ] a (behaviour) che si conviene; (clothes) grazioso(a).

bed [bɛd] n letto; (of flowers) aiuola; (of coal, clay) strato; single/double ~ letto a una piazza/a due piazze or matrimoniale; ~ **and breakfast (b. & b.)** n (place) ≈ pensione f familiare; (terms) camera con colazione; ~**clothes** npl biancheria e coperte fpl da letto; ~**ding** n coperte e lenzuola fpl.

bedlam ['bɛdləm] n baraonda.

bedraggled [bɪ'drægld] a fradicio(a).

bed: ~**ridden** a costretto(a) a letto; ~**room** n camera da letto; ~**side** n: at sb's ~**side** al capezzale di qn; ~**sit(ter)** n (Brit) monolocale m; ~**spread** n copriletto; ~**time** n: it's ~**time** è ora di andare a letto.

bee [bi:] n ape f.

beech [bi:tʃ] n faggio.

beef [bi:f] n manzo; roast ~ arrosto di manzo; ~**burger** n hamburger m inv; ~**eater** n guardia della Torre di Londra.

beehive ['bi:haɪv] n alveare m.

beeline ['bi:laɪn] n: to make a ~ for buttarsi a capo fitto verso.

been [bi:n] pp of **be**.

beer [bɪə*] n birra.

beetle ['bi:tl] n scarafaggio; coleottero.

beetroot ['bi:tru:t] n (Brit) barbabietola.

before [bɪ'fɔ:*] prep (in time) prima di; (in space) davanti a // cj prima che + sub; prima di // ad prima; ~ going prima di andare; ~ she goes prima che vada; the week ~ la settimana prima; I've seen it ~ l'ho già visto; I've never seen it ~ è la prima volta che lo vedo; ~**hand** ad in anticipo.

beg [bɛg] vi chiedere l'elemosina // vt chiedere in elemosina; (favour) chiedere; (entreat) pregare.

began [bɪ'gæn] pt of **begin**.

beggar ['bɛgə*] n mendicante m/f.

begin [bɪ'gɪn], pt **began**, pp **begun** vt, vi cominciare; to ~ doing or to do sth incominciare or iniziare a fare qc; ~**ner**

n principiante m/f; ~**ning** n inizio, principio.

begun [bɪ'gʌn] pp of **begin**.

behalf [bɪ'hɑ:f] n: on ~ of per conto di; a nome di.

behave [bɪ'heɪv] vi comportarsi; (well: also: ~ o.s.) comportarsi bene.

behaviour, (US) **behavior** [bɪ'heɪvjə*] n comportamento, condotta.

behead [bɪ'hɛd] vt decapitare.

beheld [bɪ'hɛld] pt, pp of **behold**.

behind [bɪ'haɪnd] prep dietro; (followed by pronoun) dietro di; (time) in ritardo con // ad dietro; in ritardo // n didietro; to be ~ (schedule) essere in ritardo rispetto al programma; ~ the scenes (fig) dietro le quinte.

behold [bɪ'həuld] vt (irg: like hold) vedere, scorgere.

beige [beɪʒ] a beige inv.

being ['bi:ɪŋ] n essere m; to come into ~ cominciare ad esistere.

belated [bɪ'leɪtɪd] a tardo(a).

belch [bɛltʃ] vi ruttare // vt (gen: ~ out: smoke etc) eruttare.

belfry ['bɛlfrɪ] n campanile m.

Belgian ['bɛldʒən] a, n belga (m/f).

Belgium ['bɛldʒəm] n Belgio.

belie [bɪ'laɪ] vt smentire.

belief [bɪ'li:f] n (opinion) opinione f, convinzione f; (trust, faith) fede f; (acceptance as true) credenza.

believe [bɪ'li:v] vt, vi credere; to ~ in (God) credere in; (ghosts) credere a; (method) avere fiducia in; ~**r** n (REL) credente m/f; (in idea, activity): to be a ~**r** in credere in.

belittle [bɪ'lɪtl] vt sminuire.

bell [bɛl] n campana; (small, on door, electric) campanello.

bellow ['bɛləu] vi muggire.

bellows ['bɛləuz] npl soffietto.

belly ['bɛlɪ] n pancia.

belong [bɪ'lɔŋ] vi: to ~ to appartenere a; (club etc) essere socio di; this book ~**s** here questo libro va qui; ~**ings** npl cose fpl, roba.

beloved [bɪ'lʌvɪd] a adorato(a).

below [bɪ'ləu] prep sotto, al di sotto di // ad sotto, di sotto; giù; see ~ vedi sotto or oltre.

belt [bɛlt] n cintura; (TECH) cinghia // vt (thrash) picchiare // vi (col) filarsela; ~**way** n (US AUT: ring road) circonvallazione f; (: motorway) autostrada.

bemused [bɪ'mju:zd] a perplesso(a), stupito(a).

bench [bɛntʃ] n panca; (in workshop) banco; the B~ (LAW) la Corte.

bend [bɛnd] vb (pt, pp **bent**) vt curvare; (leg, arm) piegare // vi curvarsi; piegarsi // n (Brit: in road) curva; (in pipe, river) gomito; to ~ **down** vi chinarsi; to ~ **over** vi piegarsi.

beneath [bɪ'ni:θ] *prep* sotto, al di sotto di; (*unworthy of*) indegno(a) di // *ad* sotto, di sotto.

benefactor ['bɛnɪfæktə*] *n* benefattore *m*.

beneficial [bɛnɪ'fɪʃəl] *a* che fa bene; vantaggioso(a).

benefit ['bɛnɪfɪt] *n* beneficio, vantaggio; (*allowance of money*) indennità *f inv* // *vt* far bene a // *vi*: he'll ~ **from** it ne trarrà beneficio *or* profitto.

benevolent [bɪ'nɛvələnt] *a* benevolo(a).

benign [bɪ'naɪn] *a* (*person, smile*) benevolo(a); (*MED*) benigno(a).

bent [bɛnt] *pt, pp of* **bend** // *n* inclinazione *f* // *a* (*col: dishonest*) losco(a); **to be ~ on** essere deciso(a) a.

bequest [bɪ'kwɛst] *n* lascito.

bereaved [bɪ'ri:vd] *n*: **the ~** i familiari in lutto.

beret ['bɛreɪ] *n* berretto.

berm [bə:m] *n* (*US AUT*) corsia d'emergenza.

berry ['bɛrɪ] *n* bacca.

berserk [bə'sə:k] *a*: **to go ~** montare su tutte le furie.

berth [bə:θ] *n* (*bed*) cuccetta; (*for ship*) ormeggio // *vi* (*in harbour*) entrare in porto; (*at anchor*) gettare l'ancora.

beseech [bɪ'si:tʃ], *pt, pp* **besought** *vt* implorare.

beset, *pt, pp* **beset** [bɪ'sɛt] *vt* assalire.

beside [bɪ'saɪd] *prep* accanto a; **to be ~ o.s.** (**with anger**) essere fuori di sé; **that's ~ the point** non c'entra.

besides [bɪ'saɪdz] *ad* inoltre, per di più // *prep* oltre a; a parte.

besiege [bɪ'si:dʒ] *vt* (*town*) assediare; (*fig*) tempestare.

besought [bɪ'sɔ:t] *pt, pp of* **beseech**.

best [bɛst] *a* migliore // *ad* meglio; **the ~ part of** (*quantity*) la maggior parte di; **at ~** tutt'al più; **to make the ~ of sth** cavare il meglio possibile da qc; **to do one's ~** fare del proprio meglio; **to the ~ of my knowledge** per quel che ne so; **to the ~ of my ability** al massimo delle mie capacità; **~ man** *n* testimone *m* dello sposo.

bestow [bɪ'stəʊ] *vt* accordare; (*title*) conferire.

bet [bɛt] *n* scommessa // *vt, vi* (*pt, pp* **bet** *or* **betted**) scommettere.

betray [bɪ'treɪ] *vt* tradire; **~al** *n* tradimento.

better ['bɛtə*] *a* migliore // *ad* meglio // *vt* migliorare // *n*: **to get the ~ of** avere la meglio su; **you had ~ do it** è meglio che lo faccia; **he thought ~ of it** cambiò idea; **to get ~** migliorare; **~ off** *a* più ricco(a); (*fig*): **you'd be ~ off this way** starebbe meglio così.

betting ['bɛtɪŋ] *n* scommesse *fpl*; **~ shop** *n* (*Brit*) ufficio dell'allibratore.

between [bɪ'twi:n] *prep* tra // *ad* in mezzo, nel mezzo.

beverage ['bɛvərɪdʒ] *n* bevanda.

bevy ['bɛvɪ] *n* banda.

beware [bɪ'wɛə*] *vt, vi*: **to ~ (of)** stare attento(a) (a).

bewildered [bɪ'wɪldəd] *a* sconcertato(a), confuso(a).

bewitching [bɪ'wɪtʃɪŋ] *a* affascinante.

beyond [bɪ'jɔnd] *prep* (*in space*) oltre; (*exceeding*) al di sopra di // *ad* di là; **~ doubt** senza dubbio.

bias ['baɪəs] *n* (*prejudice*) pregiudizio; (*preference*) preferenza; **~(s)ed** *a* parziale.

bib [bɪb] *n* bavaglino.

Bible ['baɪbl] *n* Bibbia.

bicarbonate of soda [baɪ'kɑ:bənɪt-] *n* bicarbonato (di sodio).

bicker ['bɪkə*] *vi* bisticciare.

bicycle ['baɪsɪkl] *n* bicicletta.

bid [bɪd] *n* offerta; (*attempt*) tentativo // *vb* (*pt* **bade** [bæd] *or* **bid**, *pp* **bidden** ['bɪdn] *or* **bid**) *vi* fare un'offerta // *vt* fare un'offerta di; **to ~ sb good day** dire buon giorno a qn; **~der** *n*: **the highest ~der** il maggior offerente; **~ding** *n* offerte *fpl*.

bide [baɪd] *vt*: **to ~ one's time** aspettare il momento giusto.

bier [bɪə*] *n* bara.

bifocals [baɪ'fəʊklz] *npl* occhiali *mpl* bifocali.

big [bɪg] *a* grande; grosso(a).

big dipper [-'dɪpə*] *n* montagne *fpl* russe, otto *m inv* volante.

bigheaded ['bɪg'hɛdɪd] *a* presuntuoso(a).

bigot ['bɪgət] *n* persona gretta; **~ed** *a* gretto(a); **~ry** *n* grettezza.

big top *n* tendone *m* del circo.

bike [baɪk] *n* bici *f inv*.

bikini [bɪ'ki:nɪ] *n* bikini *m inv*.

bilingual [baɪ'lɪŋgwəl] *a* bilingue.

bill [bɪl] *n* conto; (*POL*) atto; (*US: banknote*) banconota; (*of bird*) becco; **"post no ~s"** "divieto di affissione"; **to fit** *or* **fill the ~** (*fig*) fare al caso; **~board** *n* tabellone *m*.

billet ['bɪlɪt] *n* alloggio.

billfold ['bɪlfəʊld] *n* (*US*) portafoglio.

billiards ['bɪljədz] *n* biliardo.

billion ['bɪljən] *n* (*Brit*) bilione *m*; (*US*) miliardo.

bin [bɪn] *n* (*for coal, rubbish*) bidone *m*; (*for bread*) cassetta; (*dust~*) pattumiera; (*litter ~*) cestino.

bind [baɪnd], *pt, pp* **bound** *vt* legare; (*oblige*) obbligare; **~ing** *n* (*of book*) legatura // *a* (*contract*) vincolante.

binge [bɪndʒ] *n* (*col*): **to go on a ~** fare baldoria.

bingo ['bɪŋgəʊ] *n* gioco simile alla tombola.

binoculars [bɪ'nɔkjʊləz] *npl* binocolo.

bio... [baɪə'...] *prefix*: **~chemistry** *n* biochimica; **~graphy** [baɪ'ɔgrəfɪ] *n* biografia; **~logical** *a* biologico(a); **~logy** [baɪˈɒlədʒɪ] *n* biologia.

birch [bəːtʃ] *n* betulla.

bird [bəːd] *n* uccello; (*Brit: col: girl*) bambola; **~'s eye view** *n* vista panoramica; **~ watcher** *n* ornitologo/a dilettante.

Biro [ˈbaɪrəu] *n* ® biro *f inv* ®.

birth [bəːθ] *n* nascita; **~ certificate** *n* certificato di nascita; **~ control** *n* controllo delle nascite; contraccezione *f*; **~day** *n* compleanno; **~ rate** *n* indice *m* di natalità.

biscuit [ˈbɪskɪt] *n* (*Brit*) biscotto.

bisect [baɪˈsɛkt] *vt* tagliare in due (parti).

bishop [ˈbɪʃəp] *n* vescovo.

bit [bɪt] *pt of* **bite** // *n* pezzo; (*of tool*) punta; (*COMPUT*) bit *m inv*; (*of horse*) morso; a **~** of un po' di; a **~** mad un po' matto; **~ by ~** a poco a poco.

bitch [bɪtʃ] *n* (*dog*) cagna; (*col!*) vacca.

bite [baɪt] *vt, vi* (*pt* bit [bɪt], *pp* bitten [ˈbɪtn]) mordere // *n* morso; (*insect ~*) puntura; (*mouthful*) boccone *m*; let's have a **~** (to eat) mangiamo un boccone; to **~** one's nails mangiarsi le unghie.

bitter [ˈbɪtə*] *a* amaro(a); (*wind, criticism*) pungente // *n* (*Brit: beer*) birra amara; **~ness** *n* amarezza; gusto amaro.

blab [blæb] *vi* parlare troppo.

black [blæk] *a* nero(a) // *n* nero; (*person*): **B~** negro/a // *vt* (*Brit INDUSTRY*) boicottare; to give sb a **~** eye fare un occhio nero a qn; in the **~** (*bank account*) in attivo; **~ and blue** *a* tutto(a) pesto(a); **~berry** *n* mora; **~bird** *n* merlo; **~board** *n* lavagna; **~currant** *n* ribes *m inv*; **~en** *vt* annerire; **~ ice** *n* strato trasparente di ghiaccio; **~leg** *n* (*Brit*) crumiro; **~list** *n* lista nera; **~mail** *n* ricatto // *vt* ricattare; **~ market** *n* mercato nero; **~out** *n* oscuramento; (*fainting*) svenimento; the **B~ Sea** *n* il Mar Nero; **~ sheep** *n* pecora nera; **~smith** *n* fabbro ferraio; **~ spot** *n* (*AUT*) luogo famigerato per gli incidenti; (*for unemployment etc*) zona critica.

bladder [ˈblædə*] *n* vescica.

blade [bleɪd] *n* lama; (*of oar*) pala; **~ of** grass filo d'erba.

blame [bleɪm] *n* colpa // *vt*: to **~** sb/sth for sth dare la colpa di qc a qn/qc; who's to **~**? chi è colpevole?

bland [blænd] *a* mite; (*taste*) blando(a).

blank [blæŋk] *a* bianco(a); (*look*) distratto(a) // *n* spazio vuoto; (*cartridge*) cartuccia a salve; **~ cheque** *n* assegno in bianco.

blanket [ˈblæŋkɪt] *n* coperta.

blare [blɛə*] *vi* strombettare.

blasphemy [ˈblæsfɪmɪ] *n* bestemmia.

blast [blɑːst] *n* raffica di vento; esplosione *f* // *vt* far saltare; **~-off** *n* (*SPACE*) lancio.

blatant [ˈbleɪtənt] *a* flagrante.

blaze [bleɪz] *n* (*fire*) incendio; (*fig*) vampata // *vi* (*fire*) ardere, fiammeggiare; (*fig*) infiammarsi // *vt*: to **~** a trail (*fig*) tracciare una via nuova.

blazer [ˈbleɪzə*] *n* blazer *m inv*.

bleach [bliːtʃ] *n* (*also*: **household ~**) varechina // *vt* (*material*) candeggiare; **~ed** *a* (*hair*) decolorato(a); **~ers** *npl* (*US SPORT*) posti *mpl* di gradinata.

bleak [bliːk] *a* tetro(a).

bleary-eyed [ˈblɪərɪˈaɪd] *a* dagli occhi offuscati.

bleat [bliːt] *vi* belare.

bleed, *pt*, *pp* **bled** [bliːd, blɛd] *vt* dissanguare // *vi* sanguinare; my nose is **~ing** mi viene fuori sangue dal naso.

bleeper [ˈbliːpə*] *n* (*device*) cicalino.

blemish [ˈblɛmɪʃ] *n* macchia.

blend [blɛnd] *n* miscela // *vt* mescolare // *vi* (*colours etc*) armonizzare.

bless, *pt*, *pp* **blessed** *or* **blest** [blɛs, blɛst] *vt* benedire; **~ing** *n* benedizione *f*; fortuna.

blew [bluː] *pt of* **blow**.

blight [blaɪt] *n* (*of plants*) golpe *f* // *vt* (*hopes etc*) rovinare.

blimey [ˈblaɪmɪ] *excl* (*Brit col*) accidenti!

blind [blaɪnd] *a* cieco(a) // *n* (*for window*) avvolgibile *m*; (*Venetian ~*) veneziana // *vt* accecare; **~ alley** *n* vicolo cieco; **~ corner** *n* (*Brit*) svolta cieca; **~fold** *n* benda // *a, ad* bendato(a) // *vt* bendare gli occhi a; **~ly** *ad* ciecamente; **~ness** *n* cecità; **~ spot** *n* (*AUT etc*) punto cieco; (*fig*) punto debole.

blink [blɪŋk] *vi* battere gli occhi; (*light*) lampeggiare; **~ers** *npl* paraocchi *mpl*.

bliss [blɪs] *n* estasi *f*.

blister [ˈblɪstə*] *n* (*on skin*) vescica; (*on paintwork*) bolla // *vi* (*paint*) coprirsi di bolle.

blithely [ˈblaɪðlɪ] *ad* allegramente.

blizzard [ˈblɪzəd] *n* bufera di neve.

bloated [ˈbləutɪd] *a* gonfio(a).

blob [blɒb] *n* (*drop*) goccia; (*stain, spot*) macchia.

bloc [blɒk] *n* (*POL*) blocco.

block [blɒk] *n* blocco; (*in pipes*) ingombro; (*toy*) cubo; (*of buildings*) isolato // *vt* bloccare; **~ade** [-ˈkeɪd] *n* blocco // *vt* assediare; **~age** *n* ostacolo; **~buster** *n* (*film, book*) grande successo; **~ of flats** *n* (*Brit*) caseggiato; **~ letters** *npl* stampatello.

bloke [bləuk] *n* (*Brit col*) tizio.

blonde [blɒnd] *a, n* biondo(a).

blood [blʌd] *n* sangue *m*; **~ donor** *n* donatore/trice di sangue; **~ group** *n* gruppo sanguigno; **~hound** *n* segugio; **~ poisoning** *n* setticemia; **~ pressure** *n* pressione *f* sanguigna; **~shed** *n* spargimento di sangue; ~**shot** a: ~**shot eyes** occhi iniettati di sangue; ~**stream** n flusso del sangue; ~ **test** n analisi f inv del sangue; ~**thirsty** a assetato(a) di sangue; ~**y** a sanguinoso(a); (Brit col!): this ~**y** ... questo maledetto ... ; ~**y awful/good** (col!) veramente terribile/ forte; ~**y-minded** a (Brit col) indisponente.

bloom [blu:m] n fiore m // vi essere in fiore.

blossom ['blɔsəm] n fiore m; (with pl sense) fiori mpl // vi essere in fiore.

blot [blɔt] n macchia // vt macchiare; **to ~ out** vt (memories) cancellare; (view) nascondere; (nation, city) annientare.

blotchy ['blɔtʃɪ] a (complexion) coperto(a) di macchie.

blotting paper ['blɔtɪŋ-] n carta assorbente.

blouse [blauz] n (feminine garment) camicetta.

blow [bləu] n colpo // vb (pt **blew**, pp **blown** [blu:, bləun]) vi soffiare // vt (fuse) far saltare; **to ~ one's nose** soffiarsi il naso; **to ~ a whistle** fischiare; **to ~ away** vt portare via; **to ~ down** vt abbattere; **to ~ off** vt far volare via; **to ~ out** vi scoppiare; **to ~ over** vi calmarsi; **to ~ up** vi saltare in aria // vt far saltare in aria; (tyre) gonfiare; (PHOT) ingrandire; ~**dry** n messa in piega a föhn; ~**lamp** n (Brit) lampada a benzina per saldare; ~**out** n (of tyre) scoppio; ~**torch** n = ~**lamp**.

blue [blu:] a azzurro(a); ~ **film/joke** film/barzelletta pornografico/a; **out of the ~** (fig) all'improvviso; **to have the ~s** essere depresso(a); ~**bottle** n moscone m; ~ **jeans** npl blue-jeans mpl; ~**print** n (fig): ~**print (for)** formula (di).

bluff [blʌf] vi bluffare // n bluff m inv // a (person) brusco(a); **to call sb's ~** mettere alla prova il bluff di qn.

blunder ['blʌndə*] n abbaglio // vi prendere un abbaglio.

blunt [blʌnt] a smussato(a); spuntato(a); (person) brusco(a) // vt smussare; spuntare.

blur [blə:*] n cosa offuscata // vt offuscare.

blurb [blə:b] n trafiletto pubblicitario.

blurt [blə:t]: **to ~ out** vt lasciarsi sfuggire.

blush [blʌʃ] vi arrossire // n rossore m.

blustery ['blʌstərɪ] a (weather) burrascoso(a).

boar [bɔ:*] n cinghiale m.

board [bɔ:d] n tavola; (on wall) tabellone m; (committee) consiglio, comitato; (in firm) consiglio d'amministrazione // vt (ship) salire a bordo di; (train) salire su; (NAUT, AVIAT): **on ~** a bordo; **full ~** (Brit) pensione completa;

half ~ (Brit) mezza pensione; ~ **and lodging** vitto e alloggio; **which goes by the ~** (fig) che viene abbandonato; **to ~ up** vt (door) chiudere con assi; ~**er** n pensionante m/f; (SCOL) convittore/trice; ~**ing card** n (AVIAT, NAUT) carta d'imbarco; ~**ing house** n pensione f; ~**ing school** n collegio; ~ **room** n sala del consiglio.

boast [bəust] vi: **to ~ (about or of)** vantarsi (di) // vt vantare // n vanteria; vanto.

boat [bəut] n nave f; (small) barca; ~**er** n (hat) paglietta; ~**swain** ['bəusn] n nostromo.

bob [bɔb] vi (boat, cork on water: also: ~ **up and down**) andare su e giù // n (Brit col) = **shilling**; **to ~ up** vi saltare fuori.

bobby ['bɔbɪ] n (Brit col) poliziotto.

bobsleigh ['bɔbsleɪ] n bob m inv.

bode [bəud] vi: **to ~ well/ill (for)** essere di buon/cattivo auspicio (per).

bodily ['bɔdɪlɪ] a fisico(a), corporale // ad corporalmente; interamente; in persona.

body ['bɔdɪ] n corpo; (of car) carrozzeria; (of plane) fusoliera; (fig: quantity) quantità f inv; **a wine with ~** un vino corposo; ~**building** n culturismo; ~**guard** n guardia del corpo; ~**work** n carrozzeria.

bog [bɔg] n palude f // vt: **to get ~ged down** (fig) impantanarsi.

boggle ['bɔgl] vi: **the mind ~s** è incredibile.

bogus ['bəugəs] a falso(a); finto(a).

boil [bɔɪl] vt, vi bollire // n (MED) foruncolo; **to come to the (Brit) or a (US) ~** raggiungere l'ebollizione; **to ~ down** vi (fig): **to ~ down to** ridursi a; **to ~ over** vi traboccare (bollendo); ~**ed egg** n uovo alla coque; ~**ed potatoes** npl patate fpl bollite or lesse; ~**er** n caldaia; ~**er suit** n (Brit) tuta; ~**ing point** n punto di ebollizione.

boisterous ['bɔɪstərəs] a chiassoso(a).

bold [bəuld] a audace; (child) impudente; (outline) chiaro(a); (colour) deciso(a).

bollard ['bɔləd] n (Brit AUT) colonnina luminosa.

bolster ['bəulstə*] n capezzale m; **to ~ up** vt sostenere.

bolt [bəult] n chiavistello; (with nut) bullone m // ad: ~ **upright** diritto(a) come un fuso // vt serrare; (food) mangiare in fretta // vi scappare via.

bomb [bɔm] n bomba // vt bombardare; ~ **disposal unit** n corpo degli artificieri; ~**er** n (AVIAT) bombardiere m; ~**shell** n (fig) notizia bomba.

bona fide ['bəunə'faɪdɪ] a sincero(a); (offer) onesto(a).

bond [bɔnd] n legame m; (binding

promise, FINANCE) obbligazione f; (COMM): in ~ in attesa di sdoganamento.

bondage ['bɔndidʒ] n schiavitù f.

bone [bəun] n osso; (of fish) spina, lisca // vt disossare; togliere le spine a; ~ **idle**, ~ **lazy** a pigrissimo(a).

bonfire ['bɔnfaɪə*] n falò m inv.

bonnet ['bɔnɪt] n cuffia; (Brit: of car) cofano.

bonus ['bəunəs] n premio.

bony ['bəunɪ] a (arm, face, MED: tissue) osseo(a); (meat) pieno(a) di ossi; (fish) pieno(a) di spine.

boo [bu:] excl ba! // vt fischiare // n fischio.

booby trap ['bu:bɪ-] n trappola.

book [buk] n libro; (of stamps etc) blocchetto // vt (ticket, seat, room) prenotare; (driver) multare; (football player) ammonire; ~s npl (COMM) conti mpl; ~**case** n scaffale m inv; ~**ing office** n (Brit RAIL) biglietteria; (: THEATRE) botteghino; ~**-keeping** n contabilità; ~**let** n libricino; ~**maker** n allibratore m; ~**seller** n libraio; ~**shop**, ~ **store** n libreria.

boom [bu:m] n (noise) rimbombo; (busy period) boom m inv // vi rimbombare; andare a gonfie vele.

boon [bu:n] n vantaggio.

boost [bu:st] n spinta // vt spingere; ~**er** n (MED) richiamo.

boot [bu:t] n stivale m; (for hiking) scarpone m da montagna; (for football etc) scarpa; (Brit: of car) portabagagli m inv // vt (COMPUT) inizializzare; to ~ (in addition) per giunta, in più.

booth [bu:ð] n (at fair) baraccone m; (of cinema, telephone, voting ~) cabina.

booty ['bu:tɪ] n bottino.

booze [bu:z] n (col) alcool m.

border ['bɔ:də*] n orlo; margine m; (of a country) frontiera; the B~s la zona di confine tra l'Inghilterra e la Scozia; to ~ **on** vt fus confinare con; ~**line** n (fig) linea di demarcazione; ~**line case** n caso limite.

bore [bɔ:*] pt of **bear** // vt (hole) perforare; (person) annoiare // n (person) seccatore/trice; (of gun) calibro; to be ~d annoiarsi; ~**dom** n noia; **boring** a noioso(a).

born [bɔ:n] a: to be ~ nascere; I was ~ in 1960 sono nato nel 1960.

borne [bɔ:n] pp of **bear**.

borough ['bʌrə] n comune m.

borrow ['bɔrəu] vt: to ~ sth (from sb) prendere in prestito qc (da qn).

bosom ['buzəm] n petto; (fig) seno.

boss [bɔs] n capo // vt comandare; ~**y** a prepotente.

bosun ['bəusn] n nostromo.

botany ['bɔtənɪ] n botanica.

botch [bɔtʃ] vt (also: ~ up) fare un pa-

sticcio di.

both [bəuθ] a entrambi(e), tutt'e due // pronoun: ~ (of them) entrambi(e); ~ of us went, we ~ went ci siamo andati tutt'e due // ad: they sell ~ meat and poultry vendono insieme la carne ed il pollame.

bother ['bɔðə*] vt (worry) preoccupare; (annoy) infastidire // vi (gen: ~ o.s.) preoccuparsi // n: it is a ~ to have to do è una seccatura dover fare; it was no ~ non c'era problema; to ~ **doing** sth darsi la pena di fare qc.

bottle ['bɔtl] n bottiglia; (baby's) biberon m inv // vt imbottigliare; to ~ **up** vt contenere; ~**neck** n ingorgo; ~**-opener** n apribottiglie m inv.

bottom ['bɔtəm] n fondo; (buttocks) sedere m // a più basso(a); ultimo(a); at the ~ of in fondo a.

bough [bau] n ramo.

bought [bɔ:t] pt, pp of **buy**.

boulder ['bəuldə*] n masso (tondeggiante).

bounce [bauns] vi (ball) rimbalzare; (cheque) essere restituito(a) // vt far rimbalzare // n (rebound) rimbalzo; ~**r** n (col) buttafuori m inv.

bound [baund] pt, pp of **bind** // n (gen pl) limite m; (leap) salto // vi (leap) saltare; (limit) delimitare // a: to be ~ to do sth (obliged) essere costretto(a) a fare qc; he's ~ to fail (likely) è certo di fallire; ~ **for** diretto(a) a; out of ~s il cui accesso è vietato.

boundary ['baundrɪ] n confine m.

bourgeois ['buəʒwɑ:] a, n borghese (m/f).

bout [baut] n periodo; (of malaria etc) attacco; (BOXING etc) incontro.

bow n [bəu] nodo; (weapon) arco; (MUS) archetto; [bau] (with body) inchino; (NAUT: also: ~s) prua // vi [bau] inchinarsi; (yield): to ~ to or before sottomettersi a.

bowels ['bauəlz] npl intestini mpl; (fig) viscere fpl.

bowl [bəul] n (for eating) scodella; (for washing) bacino; (ball) boccia; (of pipe) fornello // vi (CRICKET) servire (la palla); ~**s** n gioco delle bocce.

bow-legged ['bəu'lɛgɪd] a dalle gambe storte.

bowler ['bəulə*] n giocatore m di bocce; (CRICKET) giocatore che serve la palla; (Brit: also: ~ **hat**) bombetta.

bowling ['bəulɪŋ] n (game) gioco delle bocce; ~ **alley** n pista da bowling; ~ **green** n campo di bocce.

bow tie n cravatta a farfalla.

box [bɔks] n scatola; (also: **cardboard** ~) cartone m; (THEATRE) palco // vi fare del pugilato; ~**er** n (person) pugile m; ~**ing** n (SPORT) pugilato; **B~ing Day** n (Brit) Santo Stefano; ~**ing gloves** npl guantoni *mpl* da pugile; ~**ing ring** *n* ring *m inv*; ~ **office** *n* biglietteria; ~ **room** *n* ripostiglio.

boy [bɔɪ] *n* ragazzo.

boycott ['bɔɪkɔt] *n* boicottaggio // *vt* boicottare.

boyfriend ['bɔɪfrend] *n* ragazzo.

B.R. *abbr* = **British Rail**.

bra [braː] *n* reggipetto, reggiseno.

brace [breɪs] *n* sostegno; (*on teeth*) apparecchio correttore; (*tool*) trapano // *vt* rinforzare, sostenere; ~**s** *npl* (*Brit*) bretelle *fpl*; to ~ o.s. (*fig*) farsi coraggio.

bracelet ['breɪslɪt] *n* braccialetto.

bracing ['breɪsɪŋ] *a* invigorante.

bracken ['brækən] *n* felce *f*.

bracket ['brækɪt] *n* (*TECH*) mensola; (*group*) gruppo; (*TYP*) parentesi *f inv* // *vt* mettere fra parentesi.

brag [bræg] *vi* vantarsi.

braid [breɪd] *n* (*trimming*) passamano; (*of hair*) treccia.

brain [breɪn] *n* cervello; ~**s** *npl* cervella *fpl*; he's got ~**s** è intelligente; ~**child** *n* creatura, creazione *f*; ~**wash** *vt* fare un lavaggio di cervello a; ~**wave** *n* lampo di genio; ~**y** *a* intelligente.

braise [breɪz] *vt* brasare.

brake [breɪk] *n* (*on vehicle*) freno // *vt*, *vi* frenare; ~ **fluid** *n* liquido dei freni; ~ **light** *n* (fanalino dello) stop *m inv*.

bramble ['bræmbl] *n* rovo.

bran [bræn] *n* crusca.

branch [braːntʃ] *n* ramo; (*COMM*) succursale *f* // *vi* diramarsi.

brand [brænd] *n* marca // *vt* (*cattle*) marcare (a ferro rovente).

brand-new ['brænd'njuː] *a* nuovo(a) di zecca.

brandy ['brændɪ] *n* brandy *m inv*.

brash [bræʃ] *a* sfacciato(a).

brass [braːs] *n* ottone *m*; the ~ (*MUS*) gli ottoni; ~ **band** *n* fanfara.

brassière ['bræsɪə*] *n* reggipetto, reggiseno.

brat [bræt] *n* (*pej*) marmocchio, monello/a.

bravado [brə'vaːdəu] *n* spavalderia.

brave [breɪv] *a* coraggioso(a) // *n* guerriero *m* pelle rossa *inv* // *vt* affrontare; ~**ry** *n* coraggio.

brawl [brɔːl] *n* rissa.

brawn [brɔːn] *n* muscolo; (*meat*) carne *f* di testa di maiale.

bray [breɪ] *vi* ragliare.

brazen ['breɪzn] *a* svergognato(a) // *vt*: to ~ it out fare lo sfacciato.

brazier ['breɪzɪə*] *n* braciere *m*.

Brazil [brə'zɪl] *n* Brasile *m*.

breach [briːtʃ] *vt* aprire una breccia in // *n* (*gap*) breccia, varco; (*breaking*): ~ of contract rottura di contratto; ~ of the peace violazione *f* dell'ordine pubblico.

bread [bred] *n* pane *m*; ~ **and butter** *n* pane e burro; (*fig*) mezzi *mpl* di sussi-

stenza; ~**bin**, (*US*) ~**box** *n* cassetta *f* portapane *inv*; ~**crumbs** *npl* briciole *fpl*; (*CULIN*) pangrattato; ~**line** *n*: to be on the ~line avere appena denaro per vivere.

breadth [bretθ] *n* larghezza.

breadwinner ['bredwɪnə*] *n* chi guadagna il pane per tutta la famiglia.

break [breɪk] *vb* (*pt* **broke** [brəuk], *pp* **broken** ['brəukən]) *vt* rompere; (*law*) violare // *vi* rompersi; (*weather*) cambiare // *n* (*gap*) breccia; (*fracture*) rottura; (*rest, also SCOL*) intervallo; (: *short*) pausa; (*chance*) possibilità *f inv*; to ~ one's leg *etc* rompersi la gamba *etc*; to ~ a record battere un primato; to ~ the news to sb comunicare per primo la notizia a qn; to ~ **down** *vt* (*figures, data*) analizzare // *vi* crollare; (*MED*) avere un esaurimento (nervoso); (*AUT*) guastarsi; to ~ **even** *vi* coprire le spese; to ~ **free** *or* **loose** *vi* spezzare i legami; to ~ **in** *vt* (*horse etc*) domare // *vi* (*burglar*) fare irruzione; to ~ **into** *vt fus* (*house*) fare irruzione in; to ~ **off** *vi* (*speaker*) interrompersi; (*branch*) troncarsi; to ~ **open** *vt* (*door etc*) sfondare; to ~ **out** *vi* evadere; to ~ **out in spots** coprirsi di macchie; to ~ **up** *vi* (*partnership*) sciogliersi; (*friends*) separarsi // *vt* fare in pezzi, spaccare; (*fight etc*) interrompere, far cessare; ~**age** *n* rottura; ~**down** *n* (*AUT*) guasto; (*in communications*) interruzione *f*; (*MED*: *also*: **nervous** ~**down**) esaurimento nervoso; ~**down van** *n* (*Brit*) carro *m* attrezzi *inv*; ~**er** *n* frangente *m*.

breakfast ['brekfəst] *n* colazione *f*.

break: ~-**in** *n* irruzione *f*; ~**ing and entering** *n* (*LAW*) violazione *f* di domicilio con scasso; ~**through** *n* (*MIL*) breccia; (*fig*) passo avanti; ~**water** *n* frangiflutti *m inv*.

breast [brest] *n* (*of woman*) seno; (*chest*) petto; ~-**feed** *vt*, *vi* (*irg*: *like* feed) allattare (al seno); ~-**stroke** *n* nuoto a rana.

breath [breθ] *n* fiato; out of ~ senza fiato.

Breathalyser ['breθəlaɪzə*] *n* ® (*Brit*) alcoltest *m inv*.

breathe [briːð] *vt*, *vi* respirare; to ~ **in** *vt* inspirare // *vi* inspirare; to ~ **out** *vt*, *vi* espirare; ~**r** *n* attimo di respiro.

breathing *n* respiro, respirazione *f*.

breathless ['breθlɪs] *a* senza fiato.

breath-taking ['breθteɪkɪŋ] *a* sbalorditivo(a).

breed [briːd] *vb* (*pt*, *pp* **bred** [bred]) *vt* allevare // *vi* riprodursi // *n* razza, varietà *f inv*; ~**ing** *n* riproduzione *f*; allevamento; (*upbringing*) educazione *f*.

breeze [briːz] *n* brezza.

breezy ['briːzɪ] *a* arioso(a); allegro(a).

brew [bru:] vt (tea) fare un infuso di; (beer) fare; (plot) tramare // vi (tea) essere in infusione; (beer) essere in fermentazione; (fig) bollire in pentola; ~er n birraio; ~ery n fabbrica di birra.

bribe [braɪb] n bustarella // vt comprare; ~ry n corruzione f.

brick [brɪk] n mattone m; ~layer n muratore m.

bridal ['braɪdl] a nuziale.

bride [braɪd] n sposa; ~groom n sposo; ~smaid n damigella d'onore.

bridge [brɪdʒ] n ponte m; (NAUT) ponte di comando; (of nose) dorso; (CARDS, DENTISTRY) bridge m inv // vt (river) fare un ponte sopra; (gap) colmare.

bridle ['braɪdl] n briglia // vt tenere a freno; (horse) mettere la briglia a; ~ path n sentiero (per cavalli).

brief [bri:f] a breve // n (LAW) comparsa // vt dare istruzioni a; ~s npl mutande fpl; ~case n cartella; ~ing n istruzioni fpl; ~ly ad (glance) di sfuggita; (explain, say) brevemente.

bright [braɪt] a luminoso(a); (person) sveglio(a); (colour) vivace; ~en (also: ~en up) vt (room) rendere luminoso(a); ornare // vi schiarirsi; (person) rallegrarsi.

brilliance ['brɪljəns] n splendore m.

brilliant ['brɪljənt] a splendente.

brim [brɪm] n orlo.

brine [braɪn] n acqua salmastra; (CULIN) salamoia.

bring [brɪŋ], pt, pp **brought** vt portare; **to ~ about** vt causare; **to ~ back** vt riportare; **to ~ down** vt portare giù; abbattere; **to ~ forward** vt portare avanti; (in time) anticipare; **to ~ off** vt (task, plan) portare a compimento; **to ~ out** vt (meaning) mettere in evidenza; **to ~ round** or **to** vt (unconscious person) far rinvenire; **to ~ up** vt allevare; (question) introdurre; (food: vomit) rimettere, rigurgitare.

brink [brɪŋk] n orlo.

brisk [brɪsk] a vivace.

bristle ['brɪsl] n setola // vi rizzarsi; bristling with irto(a) di.

Britain ['brɪtən] n (also: Great ~) Gran Bretagna.

British ['brɪtɪʃ] a britannico(a); **the ~** npl i Britannici; **the ~ Isles** npl le Isole Britanniche; **~ Rail (B.R.)** n compagnia ferroviaria britannica, ≈ Ferrovie fpl dello Stato (F.S.).

Briton ['brɪtən] n britannico/a.

brittle ['brɪtl] a fragile.

broach [brəutʃ] vt (subject) affrontare.

broad [brɔ:d] a largo(a); (distinction) generale; (accent) spiccato(a); **in ~ daylight** in pieno giorno; ~cast n trasmissione f // vb (pt, pp ~cast) vt trasmettere per radio (or per televisione) // vi fare una trasmissione; ~en vt

allargare // vi allargarsi; ~ly ad (fig) in generale; ~-minded a di mente aperta.

broccoli ['brɔkəlɪ] n broccoli mpl.

brochure ['brəufjuə*] n dépliant m inv.

broil [brɔɪl] vt cuocere a fuoco vivo.

broke [brəuk] pt of **break** // a (col) squattrinato(a).

broken ['brəukn] pp of **break** // a: ~ **leg** etc gamba etc rotta; **in ~ English** in un inglese stentato; ~-**hearted** a: **to be ~-hearted** avere il cuore spezzato.

broker ['brəukə*] n agente m.

brolly ['brɔlɪ] n (Brit col) ombrello.

bronchitis [brɔŋ'kaɪtɪs] n bronchite f.

bronze [brɔnz] n bronzo.

brooch [brəutʃ] n spilla.

brood [bru:d] n covata // vi (hen) covare; (person) rimuginare.

brook [bruk] n ruscello.

broom [brum] n scopa; ~stick n manico di scopa.

Bros. abbr (= Brothers) F.lli.

broth [brɔθ] n brodo.

brothel ['brɔθl] n bordello.

brother ['brʌðə*] n fratello; ~-in-law n cognato.

brought [brɔ:t] pt, pp of **bring**.

brow [brau] n fronte f; (rare, gen: eye~) sopracciglio; (of hill) cima.

brown [braun] a bruno(a), marrone // n (colour) color m bruno or marrone // vt (CULIN) rosolare; ~ **bread** n pane m integrale, pane nero.

brownie ['braunɪ] n giovane esploratrice f.

brown paper n carta da pacchi or da imballaggio.

brown sugar n zucchero greggio.

browse [brauz] vi (among books) curiosare fra i libri.

bruise [bru:z] n ammaccatura // vt ammaccare.

brunette [bru:'nɛt] n bruna.

brunt [brʌnt] n: **the ~ of** (attack, criticism etc) il peso maggiore di.

brush [brʌʃ] n spazzola; (quarrel) schermaglia // vt spazzolare; (gen: ~ past, ~ against) sfiorare; **to ~ aside** vt scostare; **to ~ up** vt (knowledge) rinfrescare; ~wood n macchia.

Brussels ['brʌslz] n Bruxelles f; ~ **sprout** n cavolo di Bruxelles.

brutal ['bru:tl] a brutale.

brute [bru:t] n bestia // a: **by ~ force** con la forza, a viva forza.

B.Sc. n abbr = **Bachelor of Science**.

bubble ['bʌbl] n bolla // vi ribollire; (sparkle, fig) essere effervescente; ~ **bath** n bagnoschiuma m inv.

buck [bʌk] n maschio (di camoscio, caprone, coniglio etc); (US col) dollaro // vi sgropparе; **to pass the ~ (to sb)** scaricare (su di qn) la propria responsabilità; **to ~ up** vi (cheer up) rianimarsi.

bucket ['bʌkɪt] n secchio.

buckle ['bʌkl] n fibbia // vt affibbiare; (warp) deformare.

bud [bʌd] n gemma; (of flower) boccio // vi germogliare; (flower) sbocciare.

Buddhism ['budɪzəm] n buddismo.

budding ['bʌdɪŋ] a (poet etc) in erba.

buddy ['bʌdɪ] n (US) compagno.

budge [bʌdʒ] vt scostare // vi spostarsi.

budgerigar ['bʌdʒərɪgɑ:*] n pappagallino.

budget ['bʌdʒɪt] n bilancio preventivo // vi: to ~ for sth fare il bilancio per qc.

budgie ['bʌdʒɪ] n = **budgerigar**.

buff [bʌf] a color camoscio // n (enthusiast) appassionato/a.

buffalo, pl ~ or ~es ['bʌfələu] n bufalo; (US) bisonte m.

buffer ['bʌfə*] n respingente m; (COMPUT) memoria tampone, buffer m inv.

buffet n ['bufeɪ] (food, Brit: bar) buffet m inv // vt ['bʌfɪt] schiaffeggiare; scuotere; urtare; ~ car n (Brit RAIL) ≈ servizio ristoro.

bug [bʌg] n (insect) cimice f; (: gen) insetto; (fig: germ) virus m inv; (spy device) microfono spia // vt mettere sotto controllo; ~bear n spauracchio.

bugle ['bju:gl] n tromba.

build [bɪld] n (of person) corporatura // vt (pt, pp built) costruire; to ~ up vt accumulare; aumentare; ~er n costruttore m; ~ing n costruzione f; edificio; (also: ~ing trade) edilizia; ~ing society n (Brit) società f inv immobiliare.

built [bɪlt] pt, pp of **build**; ~-in a (cupboard) a muro; (device) incorporato(a); ~-up area n abitato.

bulb [bʌlb] n (BOT) bulbo; (ELEC) lampadina.

bulge [bʌldʒ] n rigonfiamento // vi essere protuberante or rigonfio(a); to be bulging with essere pieno(a) or zeppo(a) di.

bulk [bʌlk] n massa, volume m; in ~ a pacchi (or casselle etc); (COMM) all'ingrosso; the ~ of il grosso di; ~y a grosso(a); voluminoso(a).

bull [bul] n toro; ~dog n bulldog m inv.

bulldozer ['buldəuzə*] n bulldozer m inv.

bullet ['bulɪt] n pallottola.

bulletin ['bulɪtɪn] n bollettino.

bulletproof ['bulɪtpru:f] a (car) blindato(a); (vest etc) antiproiettile inv.

bullfight ['bulfaɪt] n corrida; ~er n torero; ~ing n tauromachia.

bullion ['buljən] n oro or argento in lingotti.

bullock ['bulək] n giovenco.

bullring ['bulrɪŋ] n arena (per corride).

bull's-eye ['bulzaɪ] n centro del bersaglio.

bully ['bulɪ] n prepotente m // vt angariare; (frighten) intimidire.

bum [bʌm] n (col: backside) culo; (tramp) vagabondo/a.

bumblebee ['bʌmblbi:] n bombo.

bump [bʌmp] n (blow) colpo; (jolt) scossa; (on road etc) protuberanza; (on head) bernoccolo // vt battere; to ~ into vt fus scontrarsi con; ~er n paraurti m inv // a: ~er harvest raccolto eccezionale.

bumptious ['bʌmpʃəs] a presuntuoso(a).

bumpy ['bʌmpɪ] a (road) dissestato(a).

bun [bʌn] n focaccia; (of hair) crocchia.

bunch [bʌntʃ] n (of flowers, keys) mazzo; (of bananas) ciuffo; (of people) gruppo; ~ of grapes grappolo d'uva.

bundle ['bʌndl] n fascio // vt (also: ~ up) legare in un fascio; (put): to ~ sth/sb into spingere qc/qn in.

bungalow ['bʌngələu] n bungalow m inv.

bungle ['bʌngl] vt abborracciare.

bunion ['bʌnjən] n callo (al piede).

bunk [bʌŋk] n cuccetta; ~ beds npl letti mpl a castello.

bunker ['bʌŋkə*] n (coal store) ripostiglio per il carbone; (MIL, GOLF) bunker m inv.

bunny ['bʌnɪ] n (also: ~ rabbit) coniglietto.

bunting ['bʌntɪŋ] n pavesi mpl, bandierine fpl.

buoy [bɔɪ] n boa; to ~ up vt tenere a galla; (fig) sostenere; ~ant a galleggiante; (fig) vivace.

burden ['bə:dn] n carico, fardello // vt caricare; (oppress) opprimere.

bureau, pl ~x [bjuə'rəu, -z] n (Brit: writing desk) scrivania; (US: chest of drawers) cassettone m; (office) ufficio, agenzia.

bureaucracy [bjuə'rɔkrəsɪ] n burocrazia.

burglar ['bə:glə*] n scassinatore m; ~ alarm n campanello antifurto; ~y n furto con scasso.

burial ['berɪəl] n sepoltura.

burly ['bə:lɪ] a robusto(a).

Burma ['bə:mə] n Birmania.

burn [bə:n] vt, vi (pt, pp burned or burnt) bruciare // n bruciatura, scottatura; to ~ down vt distruggere col fuoco; ~er n (on cooker) fornello; (TECH) bruciatore m, becco (a gas).

burnt [bə:nt] pt, pp of **burn**.

burrow ['bʌrəu] n tana // vt scavare.

bursar ['bə:sə*] n economo/a; (Brit: student) borsista m/f; ~y n (Brit) borsa di studio.

burst [bə:st] vb (pt, pp burst) vt far scoppiare (or esplodere) // vi esplodere; (tyre) scoppiare // n scoppio; (also: ~ pipe) rottura nel tubo, perdita; to ~ into flames/tears scoppiare in fiamme/lacrime; to ~ out laughing scoppiare a ridere; to be ~ing with essere pronto a scoppiare di; to ~ into vt fus (room etc) irrompere in; to ~ open vi aprirsi improvvisamente; (*door*) spalancarsi.

bury ['berɪ] *vt* seppellire.

bus, **~es** [bʌs, 'bʌsɪz] *n* autobus *m inv*.

bush [buʃ] *n* cespuglio; (*scrub land*) macchia; **to beat about the ~** menare il cane per l'aia.

bushy ['buʃɪ] *a* cespuglioso(a).

busily ['bɪzɪlɪ] *ad* con impegno, alacremente.

business ['bɪznɪs] *n* (*matter*) affare *m*; (*trading*) affari *mpl*; (*firm*) azienda; (*job, duty*) lavoro; **to be away on ~** essere andato via per affari; **it's none of my ~** questo non mi riguarda; **he means ~** non scherza; **~like** *a* serio(a); efficiente; **~man/woman** *n* uomo/donna d'affari; **~ trip** *n* viaggio d'affari.

busker ['bʌskə*] *n* (*Brit*) suonatore/trice ambulante.

bus-stop ['bʌsstɔp] *n* fermata d'autobus.

bust [bʌst] *n* busto; (ANAT) seno // *a* (*col: broken*) rotto(a); **to go ~** fallire.

bustle ['bʌsl] *n* movimento, attività // *vi* darsi da fare; **bustling** *a* (*person*) indaffarato(a); (*town*) animato(a).

busy ['bɪzɪ] *a* occupato(a); (*shop, street*) molto frequentato(a) // *vt*: **to ~ o.s. with** darsi da fare; **~body** *n* ficcanaso; **~ signal** *n* (US TEL) segnale *m* di occupato.

but [bʌt] ♦ *cj* ma; **I'd love to come, ~ I'm busy** vorrei tanto venire, ma ho da fare

♦ *prep* (*apart from, except*) eccetto, tranne, meno; **he was nothing ~ trouble** non dava altro che guai; **no-one ~ him can do it** nessuno può farlo tranne lui; **~ for you/your help** se non fosse per te/per il tuo aiuto; **anything ~ that** tutto ma non questo

♦ *ad* (*just, only*) solo, soltanto; **she's ~ a child** è solo una bambina; **had I ~ known** se solo avessi saputo; **I can ~ try** tentar non nuoce; **all ~ finished** quasi finito.

butcher ['butʃə*] *n* macellaio // *vt* macellare.

butler ['bʌtlə*] *n* maggiordomo.

butt [bʌt] *n* (*cask*) grossa botte *f*; (*thick end*) estremità *f inv* più grossa; (*of gun*) calcio; (*of cigarette*) mozzicone *m*; (*Brit fig: target*) oggetto // *vt* cozzare; **to ~ in** *vi* (*interrupt*) intrompere.

butter ['bʌtə*] *n* burro // *vt* imburrare; **~cup** *n* ranuncolo.

butterfly ['bʌtəflaɪ] *n* farfalla; (SWIMMING: *also:* **~ stroke**) (nuoto a) farfalla.

buttocks ['bʌtəks] *npl* natiche *fpl*.

button ['bʌtn] *n* bottone *m* // *vt* (*also:* **~ up**) abbottonare // *vi* abbottonarsi.

buttress ['bʌtrɪs] *n* contrafforte *f*.

buxom ['bʌksəm] *a* formoso(a).

buy [baɪ], *pt, pp* **bought** *vt* comprare; **to ~ sb sth/sth from sb** comprare qc per

qn/qc da qn; **to ~ sb a drink** offrire da bere a qn; **~er** *n* compratore/trice.

buzz [bʌz] *n* ronzio; (*col: phone call*) colpo di telefono // *vi* ronzare.

buzzer ['bʌzə*] *n* cicalino.

buzz word *n* (*col*) termine *m* di gran moda.

by [baɪ] ♦ *prep* **1** (*referring to cause, agent*) da; **killed ~ lightning** ucciso da un fulmine; **surrounded ~ a fence** circondato da uno steccato; **a painting ~ Picasso** un quadro di Picasso

2 (*referring to method, manner, means*): **~ bus/car/train** in autobus/macchina/treno, con l'autobus/la macchina/il treno; **to pay ~ cheque** pagare con (un) assegno; **~ moonlight** al chiaro di luna; **~ saving hard, he ...** risparmiando molto, lui ...

3 (*via, through*) per; **we came ~ Dover** siamo venuti via Dover

4 (*close to, past*) accanto a; **the house ~ the river** la casa sul fiume; **a holiday ~ the sea** una vacanza al mare; **she sat ~ his bed** si sedette accanto al suo letto; **she rushed ~ me** mi è passata accanto correndo; **I go ~ the post office every day** passo davanti all'ufficio postale ogni giorno

5 (*not later than*) per, entro; **~ 4 o'clock** per *or* entro le 4; **~ this time tomorrow** domani a quest'ora; **~ the time I got here it was too late** quando sono arrivato era ormai troppo tardi

6 (*during*): **~ day/night** di giorno/notte

7 (*amount*) a; **~ the kilo/metre** a chili/metri; **paid ~ the hour** pagato all'ora; **one ~ one** uno per uno; **little ~ little** a poco a poco

8 (MATH, *measure*): **to divide/multiply ~ 3** dividere/moltiplicare per 3; **it's broader ~ a metre** è un metro più largo, è più largo di un metro

9 (*according to*) per; **to play ~ the rules** attenersi alle regole; **it's all right ~ me** per me va bene

10: (all) **~ oneself** *etc* (tutto(a)) solo(a); **he did it (all) ~ himself** lo ha fatto (tutto) da solo

11: **~ the way** a proposito; **this wasn't my idea ~ the way** tra l'altro l'idea non è stata mia

♦ *ad* **1** *see* **go, pass** *etc*

2: **~ and ~** (*in past*) poco dopo; (*in future*) fra breve; **~ and large** nel complesso.

bye(-bye) ['baɪ'baɪ] *excl* ciao!, arrivederci!

bye(-)law ['baɪlɔ:] *n* legge *f* locale.

by-election ['baɪɪlekʃən] *n* (*Brit*) elezione *f* straordinaria.

bygone ['baɪgɔn] *a* passato(a) // *n*: **let ~s be ~s** mettiamoci una pietra sopra.

bypass ['baɪpɑ:s] *n* circonvallazione *f*; (MED) by-pass *m inv* // *vt* fare una deviazione intorno a.

by-product ['baɪprɔdʌkt] n sottoprodotto; (fig) conseguenza secondaria.

bystander ['baɪstændə*] n spettatore/trice.

byte [baɪt] n (COMPUT) byte m inv, bicarattere m.

byword ['baɪwɔːd] n: to be a ~ for essere sinonimo di.

by-your-leave ['baɪjɔː'liːv] n: without so much as a ~ senza nemmeno chiedere il permesso.

C

C [siː] n (MUS) do.
C.A. n abbr = **chartered accountant**.
cab [kæb] n taxi m inv; (of train, truck) cabina; (horse-drawn) carrozza.
cabaret ['kæbəreɪ] n cabaret m inv.
cabbage ['kæbɪdʒ] n cavolo.
cabin ['kæbɪn] n capanna; (on ship) cabina.
cabinet ['kæbɪnɪt] n (POL) consiglio dei ministri; (furniture) armadietto; (also: display ~) vetrinetta; **~-maker** n stipettaio.
cable ['keɪbl] n cavo; fune f; (TEL) cablogramma m // vt telegrafare; **~-car** n funivia; ~ **television** n televisione f via cavo.
cache [kæʃ] n: a ~ of food etc un deposito segreto di viveri etc.
cackle ['kækl] vi schiamazzare.
cactus, pl **cacti** ['kæktəs, -taɪ] n cactus m inv.
cadet [kə'dɛt] n (MIL) cadetto.
cadge [kædʒ] vt (col) scroccare.
café ['kæfeɪ] n caffè m inv.
cafeteria [kæfɪ'tɪərɪə] n self-service m inv.
cage [keɪdʒ] n gabbia.
cagey ['keɪdʒɪ] a (col) chiuso(a); guardingo(a).
cagoule [kə'guːl] n K-way m inv ®.
cajole [kə'dʒəul] vt allettare.
cake [keɪk] n torta; ~ of soap saponetta; **~d** a: **~d** with incrostato(a) di.
calculate ['kælkjuleɪt] vt calcolare; **calculation** [-'leɪʃən] n calcolo; **calculator** n calcolatrice f.
calendar ['kæləndə*] n calendario; ~ **year** n anno civile.
calf [kɑːf], pl **calves** n (of cow) vitello; (of other animals) piccolo; (also: **~skin**) (pelle f di) vitello; (ANAT) polpaccio.
calibre, (US) **caliber** ['kælɪbə*] n calibro.
call [kɔːl] vt (gen, also TEL) chiamare // vi chiamare; (visit: also: ~ **in**, ~ **round**): to ~ (for) passare (a prendere) // n (shout) grido, urlo; (visit) visita; (also: telephone ~) telefonata; to be **~ed** (person, object) chiamarsi; to be on ~

essere a disposizione; to ~ **back** vi (return) ritornare; (TEL) ritelefonare, richiamare; to ~ **for** vt fus richiedere; to ~ **off** vt disdire; to ~ **on** vt fus (visit) passare da; (request): to ~ **on sb** to do chiedere a qn di fare; to ~ **out** vi (in pain) urlare; (to person) chiamare; to ~ **up** vt (MIL) richiamare; **~box** n (Brit) cabina telefonica; **~er** n persona che chiama; visitatore/trice; ~ **girl** n ragazza f squillo inv; **~-in** n (US: phone-in) trasmissione f a filo diretto con gli ascoltatori; **~ing** n vocazione f; **~ing card** n (US) biglietto da visita.
callous ['kæləs] a indurito(a), insensibile.
calm [kɑːm] a calmo(a) // n calma // vt calmare; to ~ **down** vi calmarsi // vt calmare.
Calor gas ['kælə*-] n ® butano.
calorie ['kælərɪ] n caloria.
calves [kɑːvz] npl of **calf**.
camber ['kæmbə*] n (of road) bombatura.
Cambodia [kæm'bəudjə] n Cambogia.
came [keɪm] pt of **come**.
camel ['kæməl] n cammello.
camera ['kæmərə] n macchina fotografica; (also: cine~, movie ~) cinepresa; in ~ a porte chiuse; **~man** n cameraman m inv.
camouflage ['kæməflɑːʒ] n camuffamento; (MIL) mimetizzazione f // vt camuffare; mimetizzare.
camp [kæmp] n campeggio; (MIL) campo // vi campeggiare; accamparsi.
campaign [kæm'peɪn] n (MIL, POL etc) campagna // vi (also fig) fare una campagna.
campbed ['kæmp'bɛd] n (Brit) brandina.
camper ['kæmpə*] n campeggiatore/trice.
camping ['kæmpɪŋ] n campeggio; to go ~ andare in campeggio.
campsite ['kæmpsaɪt] n campeggio.
campus ['kæmpəs] n campus m inv.
can [kæn] auxiliary vb see next headword // n (of milk) scatola; (of oil) bidone m; (of water) tanica; (tin) scatola // vt mettere in scatola.
can [kæn] ♦ n, vt see previous headword
♦ auxiliary vb (negative **cannot**, **can't**; conditional and pt **could**) 1 (be able to) potere; I ~'t go any further non posso andare oltre; you ~ do it if you try sei in grado di farlo — basta provarci; I'll help you all I ~ ti aiuterò come potrò; I ~'t see you non ti vedo
2 (know how to) sapere, essere capace di; I ~ swim so nuotare; ~ you speak French? parla francese?
3 (may) potere; could I have a word with you? posso parlarle un momento?
4 (expressing disbelief, puzzlement etc): it ~'t be true! non può essere vero!; what CAN he want? cosa può mai volere?

5 (*expressing possibility, suggestion etc*): **he could be in the library** può darsi che sia in biblioteca; **she could have been delayed** può aver avuto un contrattempo.

Canada ['kænədə] *n* Canada *m*.

Canadian [kə'neɪdɪən] *a, n* canadese (*m/f*).

canal [kə'næl] *n* canale *m*.

canary [kə'neərɪ] *n* canarino.

cancel ['kænsəl] *vt* annullare; (*train*) sopprimere; (*cross out*) cancellare; **~lation** [-'leɪʃən] *n* annullamento; soppressione *f*; cancellazione *f*; (*TOURISM*) prenotazione *f* annullata.

cancer ['kænsə*] *n* cancro; **C~** (*sign*) Cancro.

candid ['kændɪd] *a* onesto(a).

candidate ['kændɪdeɪt] *n* candidato/a.

candle ['kændl] *n* candela; (*in church*) cero; **by ~light** a lume di candela; **~stick** *n* (*also:* **~ holder**) bugia; (*bigger, ornate*) candeliere *m*.

candour, (*US*) **candor** ['kændə*] *n* sincerità.

candy ['kændɪ] *n* zucchero candito; (*US*) caramella; caramelle *fpl*; **~-floss** *n* (*Brit*) zucchero filato.

cane [keɪn] *n* canna; (*SCOL*) verga // *vt* (*Brit SCOL*) punire a colpi di verga.

canister ['kænɪstə*] *n* scatola metallica.

cannabis ['kænəbɪs] *n* canapa indiana.

canned ['kænd] *a* (*food*) in scatola.

cannon, *pl* **~** *or* **~s** ['kænən] *n* (*gun*) cannone *m*.

cannot ['kænɔt] = **can not.**

canny ['kænɪ] *a* furbo(a).

canoe [kə'nuː] *n* canoa; (*SPORT*) canotto.

canon ['kænən] *n* (*clergyman*) canonico; (*standard*) canone *m*.

can opener [-'əupnə*] *n* apriscatole *m inv*.

canopy ['kænəpɪ] *n* baldacchino.

can't [kænt] = **can not.**

cantankerous [kæn'tæŋkərəs] *a* stizzoso(a).

canteen [kæn'tiːn] *n* mensa; (*Brit: of cutlery*) portaposate *m inv*.

canter ['kæntə*] *n* piccolo galoppo.

canvas ['kænvəs] *n* tela.

canvassing ['kænvəsɪŋ] *n* (*POL*) sollecitazione *f*; (*COMM*) indagine *f* di mercato.

canyon ['kænjən] *n* canyon *m inv*.

cap [kæp] *n* (*also Brit FOOTBALL*) berretto; (*of pen*) coperchio; (*of bottle*) tappo // *vt* tappare; (*outdo*) superare.

capability [keɪpə'bɪlɪtɪ] *n* capacità *f inv*, abilità *f inv*.

capable ['keɪpəbl] *a* capace.

capacity [kə'pæsɪtɪ] *n* capacità *f inv*; (*of lift etc*) capienza.

cape [keɪp] *n* (*garment*) cappa; (*GEO*) capo.

capital ['kæpɪtl] *n* (*also:* **~ city**) capitale *f*; (*money*) capitale *m*; (*also:* **~ letter**) (*lettera*) maiuscola; (*also:* **~ gains tax** *n* imposta sulla plusvalenza; **~ism** *n* capitalismo; **~ist** *a, n* capitalista (*m/f*); **~ize: to ~ize on** *vt fus* trarre vantaggio da; **~ punishment** *n* pena capitale.

Capricorn ['kæprɪkɔːn] *n* Capricorno.

capsize [kæp'saɪz] *vt* capovolgere // *vi* capovolgersi.

capsule ['kæpsjuːl] *n* capsula.

captain ['kæptɪn] *n* capitano.

caption ['kæpʃən] *n* leggenda.

captivate ['kæptɪveɪt] *vt* avvincere.

captive ['kæptɪv] *a, n* prigioniero(a).

captivity [kæp'tɪvɪtɪ] *n* prigionia; **in ~** (*animal*) in cattività.

capture ['kæptʃə*] *vt* catturare, prendere; (*attention*) attirare // *n* cattura; (*data* ~) registrazione *f or* rilevazione *f* di dati.

car [kɑː*] *n* macchina, automobile *f*.

carafe [kə'ræf] *n* caraffa.

caramel ['kærəməl] *n* caramello.

caravan ['kærəvæn] *n* (*Brit*) roulotte *f inv*; (*of camels*) carovana; **~ site** *n* (*Brit*) campeggio per roulotte.

carbohydrates [kɑːbəu'haɪdreɪts] *npl* (*foods*) carboidrati *mpl*.

carbon ['kɑːbən] *n* carbonio; **~ paper** *n* carta carbone.

carburettor, (*US*) **carburetor** [kɑːbju'retə*] *n* carburatore *m*.

card [kɑːd] *n* carta; (*visiting* ~ *etc*) biglietto; (*Christmas* ~ *etc*) cartolina; **~board** *n* cartone *m*; **~ game** *n* gioco di carte.

cardiac ['kɑːdɪæk] *a* cardiaco(a).

cardigan ['kɑːdɪgən] *n* cardigan *m inv*.

cardinal ['kɑːdɪnl] *a, n* cardinale (*m*).

card index *n* schedario.

care [keə*] *n* cura, attenzione *f*; (*worry*) preoccupazione *f* // *vi*: **to ~ about** interessarsi di; **~ of** (*c/o*) presso (*c/o*); **in sb's ~** alle cure di qn; **to take ~** (**to do**) fare attenzione (a fare); **to take ~ of** curarsi di; **I don't ~** non me ne importa; **to ~ for** *vt fus* aver cura di; (*like*) volere bene a.

career [kə'rɪə*] *n* carriera // *vi* (*also:* **~ along**) andare di (gran) carriera.

carefree ['keəfriː] *a* sgombro(a) di preoccupazioni.

careful ['keəful] *a* attento(a); (*cautious*) cauto(a); (**be**) **~!** attenzione!; **~ly** *ad* con cura; cautamente.

careless ['keəlɪs] *a* negligente; (*heedless*) spensierato(a).

caress [kə'rɛs] *n* carezza // *vt* accarezzare.

caretaker ['keəteɪkə*] *n* custode *m*.

car-ferry [kɑː'fɛrɪ] *n* traghetto.

cargo, *pl* **~es** ['kɑːgəu] *n* carico.

car hire *n* autonoleggio.

Caribbean [kærɪ'biːən] *a*: **the ~** (**Sea**) il Mar dei Caraibi.

caring ['kεərıŋ] *a* (*person*) premuroso(a); (*society, organization*) umanitario(a).

carnage ['ka:nıdʒ] *n* carneficina.

carnation [ka:'neıʃən] *n* garofano.

carnival ['ka:nıvəl] *n* (*public celebration*) carnevale *m*; (*US: funfair*) luna park *m inv*.

carol ['kærəl] *n*: (**Christmas**) ~ canto di Natale.

carp [ka:p] *n* (*fish*) carpa; **to** ~ **at** *vt fus* trovare a ridire su.

car park *n* (*Brit*) parcheggio.

carpenter ['ka:pıntə*] *n* carpentiere *m*.

carpentry ['ka:pıntrı] *n* carpenteria.

carpet ['ka:pıt] *n* tappeto // *vt* coprire con tappeto; ~ **slippers** *npl* pantofole *fpl*; ~ **sweeper** *n* scopatappeti *m inv*.

carriage ['kærıdʒ] *n* vettura; (*of goods*) trasporto; (*of typewriter*) carrello; (*bearing*) portamento; ~ **return** *n* (*on typewriter etc*) leva (*or* tasto) del ritorno a capo; ~**way** *n* (*Brit: part of road*) carreggiata.

carrier ['kærıə*] *n* (*of disease*) portatore/trice; (*COMM*) impresa di trasporti; (*NAUT*) portaerei *f inv*; (*on car, bicycle*) portabagagli *m inv*; ~ **bag** *n* (*Brit*) sacchetto.

carrot ['kærət] *n* carota.

carry ['kærı] *vt* (*subj: person*) portare; (: *vehicle*) trasportare; (*a motion, bill*) far passare; (*involve: responsibilities etc*) comportare // *vi* (*sound*) farsi sentire; **to be** *or* **get carried away** (*fig*) entusiasmarsi; **to** ~ **on** *vi*: **to** ~ **on with sth/doing** continuare qc/a fare // *vt* mandare avanti; **to** ~ **out** *vt* (*orders*) eseguire; (*investigation*) svolgere; ~**cot** *n* culla portabile; ~**on** *n* (*col: fuss*) casino, confusione *f*.

cart [ka:t] *n* carro // *vt* (*col*) trascinare.

carton ['ka:tən] *n* (*box*) scatola di cartone; (*of yogurt*) cartone *m*; (*of cigarettes*) stecca.

cartoon [ka:'tu:n] *n* (*PRESS*) disegno umoristico; (*satirical*) caricatura; (*comic strip*) fumetto; (*CINEMA*) disegno animato.

cartridge ['ka:trıdʒ] *n* (*for gun, pen*) cartuccia; (*for camera*) caricatore *m*; (*music tape*) cassetta.

carve [ka:v] *vt* (*meat*) trinciare; (*wood, stone*) intagliare; **to** ~ **up** *vt* (*meat*) tagliare; (*fig: country*) suddividere; **carving** *n* (*in wood etc*) scultura; **carving knife** *n* trinciante *m*.

car wash *n* lavaggio auto.

case [keıs] *n* caso; (*LAW*) causa, processo; (*box*) scatola; (*Brit: also:* suit~) valigia; **he hasn't put forward his** ~ **very well** non ha dimostrato bene il suo caso; **in** ~ **of** in caso di; **in** ~ **he** caso mai lui; **just in** ~ in caso di bisogno.

cash [kæʃ] *n* denaro; (*coins, notes*) denaro liquido // *vt* incassare; **to pay** (**in**) ~ pagare in contanti; ~ **on delivery** (**C.O.D.**) (*COMM*) pagamento alla consegna; ~**book** *n* giornale *m* di cassa; ~ **card** *n* tesserino di prelievo; ~ **desk** *n* (*Brit*) cassa; ~ **dispenser** *n* sportello automatico.

cashew [kæ'ʃu:] *n* (*also:* ~ **nut**) anacardio.

cashier [kæ'ʃıə*] *n* cassiere/a.

cashmere ['kæʃmıə*] *n* cachemire *m*.

cash register *n* registratore *m* di cassa.

casing ['keısıŋ] *n* rivestimento.

casino [kə'si:nəu] *n* casinò *m inv*.

cask [ka:sk] *n* botte *f*.

casket ['ka:skıt] *n* cofanetto; (*US: coffin*) bara.

casserole ['kæsərəul] *n* casseruola; (*food*): **chicken** ~ pollo in casseruola.

cassette [kæ'set] *n* cassetta; ~ **player** *n* riproduttore *m* a cassette; ~ **recorder** *n* registratore *m* a cassette.

cast [ka:st] *vt* (*pt, pp* **cast**) (*throw*) gettare; (*shed*) perdere; spogliarsi di; (*metal*) gettare, fondere; (*THEATRE*): **to** ~ **sb as Hamlet** scegliere qn per la parte di Amleto // *n* (*THEATRE*) complesso di attori; (*mould*) forma; (*also:* **plaster** ~) ingessatura; **to** ~ **one's vote** votare, dare il voto; **to** ~ **off** *vi* (*NAUT*) salpare.

castaway ['ka:stəwəı] *n* naufrago/a.

caster sugar ['ka:stə*-] *n* (*Brit*) zucchero semolato.

casting ['ka:stıŋ] *a*: ~ **vote** (*Brit*) voto decisivo.

cast iron *n* ghisa.

castle ['ka:sl] *n* castello; (*fortified*) rocca.

castor ['ka:stə*] *n* (*wheel*) rotella; ~ **oil** *n* olio di ricino.

castrate [kæs'treıt] *vt* castrare.

casual ['kæʒjul] *a* (*by chance*) casuale, fortuito(a); (*irregular: work etc*) avventizio(a); (*unconcerned*) noncurante, indifferente; ~ **wear** casual *m*; ~**ly** *ad* con disinvoltura; casualmente.

casualty ['kæʒjultı] *n* ferito/a; (*dead*) morto/a, vittima.

cat [kæt] *n* gatto.

catalogue, (*US*) **catalog** ['kætələg] *n* catalogo // *vt* catalogare.

catalyst ['kætəlıst] *n* catalizzatore *m*.

catapult ['kætəpʌlt] *n* catapulta; fionda.

cataract ['kætərækt] *n* (*also MED*) cateratta.

catarrh [kə'ta:*] *n* catarro.

catastrophe [kə'tæstrəfı] *n* catastrofe *f*.

catch [kætʃ] *vb* (*pt, pp* **caught**) *vt* (*train, thief, cold*) acchiappare; (*ball*) afferrare; (*person: by surprise*) sorprendere; (*understand*) comprendere; (*get entangled*) impigliare // *vi* (*fire*) prendere // *n* (*fish etc caught*) retata, presa; (*trick*) inganno; (*TECH*) gancio; to ~ sb's attention *or* eye attirare l'attenzione di qn; to ~ fire prendere fuoco; to ~ sight of scorgere; to ~ on *vi* capire; (*become popular*) affermarsi, far presa; to ~ up *vi* mettersi in pari // *vt* (*also*: ~ up with) raggiungere.

catching ['kætʃɪŋ] *a* (*MED*) contagioso(a).

catchment area ['kætʃmənt-] *n* (*Brit SCOL*) circoscrizione *f* scolare; (*GEO*) bacino pluviale.

catch phrase *n* slogan *m inv*; frase *f* fatta.

catchy ['kætʃɪ] *a* orecchiabile.

category ['kætɪgərɪ] *n* categoria.

cater ['keɪtə*] *vi* (*gen*: ~ for) provvedere da mangiare (per); to ~ for *vt fus* (*Brit*: *needs*) provvedere a; (: *readers*, *consumers*) incontrare i gusti di; ~er *n* fornitore *m*; ~ing *n* approvvigionamento.

caterpillar ['kætəpɪlə*] *n* bruco; ~ track *n* catena a cingoli.

cathedral [kə'θi:drəl] *n* cattedrale *f*, duomo.

catholic ['kæθəlɪk] *a* universale; aperto(a); eclettico(a); C~ *a*, *n* (*REL*) cattolico(a).

cat's-eye [kæts'aɪ] *n* (*Brit AUT*) catarifrangente *m*.

cattle ['kætl] *npl* bestiame *m*, bestie *fpl*.

catty ['kætɪ] *a* maligno(a), dispettoso(a).

caucus ['kɔ:kəs] *n* (*POL*: *group*) comitato di dirigenti; (: *US*) (riunione *f* del) comitato elettorale.

caught [kɔ:t] *pt*, *pp* of **catch**.

cauliflower ['kɔlɪflauə*] *n* cavolfiore *m*.

cause [kɔ:z] *n* causa // *vt* causare.

caution ['kɔ:ʃən] *n* prudenza; (*warning*) avvertimento // *vt* avvertire; ammonire.

cautious ['kɔ:ʃəs] *a* cauto(a), prudente.

cavalry ['kævəlrɪ] *n* cavalleria.

cave [keɪv] *n* caverna, grotta; to ~ in *vi* (*roof etc*) crollare; ~man *n* uomo delle caverne.

caviar(e) ['kævɪɑ:*] *n* caviale *m*.

cavort [kə'vɔ:t] *vi* far capriole.

CB *n abbr* (= *Citizens' Band* (*Radio*)): ~ radio *n* baracchino.

CBI *n abbr* (= *Confederation of British Industries*) ≈ Confindustria.

cc *abbr* = *cubic centimetres*; *carbon copy*.

cease [si:s] *vt*, *vi* cessare; ~fire *n* cessate il fuoco *m inv*; ~less *a* incessante, continuo(a).

cedar ['si:də*] *n* cedro.

ceiling ['si:lɪŋ] *n* soffitto.

celebrate ['sɛlɪbreɪt] *vt*, *vi* celebrare; ~d *a* celebre; **celebration** [-'breɪʃən] *n* celebrazione *f*.

celery ['sɛlərɪ] *n* sedano.

cell [sɛl] *n* cella; (*BIOL*) cellula; (*ELEC*) elemento (di batteria).

cellar ['sɛlə*] *n* sottosuolo, cantina.

'cello ['tʃɛləu] *n* violoncello.

Celt [kɛlt, sɛlt] *n* celta *m/f*.

Celtic ['kɛltɪk, 'sɛltɪk] *a* celtico(a).

cement [sə'mɛnt] *n* cemento // *vt* cementare; ~ mixer *n* betoniera.

cemetery ['sɛmɪtrɪ] *n* cimitero.

censor ['sɛnsə*] *n* censore *m* // *vt* censurare; ~ship *n* censura.

censure ['sɛnʃə*] *vt* riprovare, censurare.

census ['sɛnsəs] *n* censimento.

cent [sɛnt] *n* (*US*: *coin*) centesimo (= 1:100 di un dollaro); *see also* **per**.

centenary [sɛn'ti:nərɪ] *n* centenario.

center ['sɛntə*] *n*, *vt* (*US*) = **centre**.

centi... ['sɛntɪ] *prefix*: ~grade *a* centigrado(a); ~metre, (*US*) ~meter *n* centimetro.

centipede ['sɛntɪpi:d] *n* centopiedi *m inv*.

central ['sɛntrəl] *a* centrale; C~ America *n* America centrale; ~ heating *n* riscaldamento centrale; ~ize *vt* accentrare.

centre, (*US*) **center** ['sɛntə*] *n* centro // *vt* centrare; ~-forward *n* (*SPORT*) centroavanti *m inv*; ~-half *n* (*SPORT*) centromediano.

century ['sɛntjurɪ] *n* secolo; 20th ~ ventesimo secolo.

ceramic [sɪ'ræmɪk] *a* ceramico(a); ~s *npl* ceramica.

cereal ['si:rɪəl] *n* cereale *m*.

ceremony ['sɛrɪmənɪ] *n* cerimonia; to stand on ~ fare complimenti.

certain ['sə:tən] *a* certo(a); to make ~ of assicurarsi di; for ~ per certo, di sicuro; ~ly *ad* certamente, certo; ~ty *n* certezza.

certificate [sə'tɪfɪkɪt] *n* certificato; diploma *m*.

certified ['sə:tɪfaɪd]: ~ mail *n* (*US*) posta raccomandata con ricevuta di ritorno; ~ public accountant (CPA) *n* (*US*) ≈ commercialista *m/f*.

cervical ['sə:vɪkl] *a*: ~ cancer cancro della cervice; ~ smear Pap-test *m inv*.

cervix ['sə:vɪks] *n* cervice *f*.

cesspit ['sɛspɪt], **cesspool** ['sɛspu:l] *n* pozzo nero.

cf. *abbr* (= *compare*) cfr.

ch. *abbr* (= *chapter*) cap.

chafe [tʃeɪf] *vt* fregare, irritare.

chaffinch ['tʃæfɪntʃ] *n* fringuello.

chain [tʃeɪn] *n* catena // *vt* (*also*: ~ up) incatenare; ~ reaction *n* reazione *f* a catena; ~ smoke *vi* fumare una sigaretta dopo l'altra; ~ store *n* negozio a catena.

chair [tʃeə*] *n* sedia; (*armchair*) poltrona; (*of university*) cattedra // *vt* (*meeting*) presiedere; ~lift *n* seggiovia; ~man *n* presidente *m*.

chalice ['tʃælɪs] *n* calice *m*.

chalk [tʃɔ:k] *n* gesso.

challenge [ˈtʃælɪndʒ] n sfida // vt sfidare; (statement, right) mettere in dubbio; to ~ sb to do sfidare qn a fare; **challenging** a sfidante; provocatorio(a).

chamber [ˈtʃeɪmbə*] n camera; ~ **of commerce** n camera di commercio; ~**maid** n cameriera; ~ **music** n musica da camera.

chamois [ˈʃæmwɑ:] n camoscio; ~ **leather** [ˈʃæmɪ-] n pelle f di camoscio.

champagne [ʃæmˈpeɪn] n champagne m inv.

champion [ˈtʃæmpɪən] n campione/essa; ~**ship** n campionato.

chance [tʃɑ:ns] n caso; (opportunity) occasione f; (likelihood) possibilità f inv // vt: to ~ it rischiare, provarci // fortuito(a); to take a ~ rischiarlo; by ~ per caso.

chancellor [ˈtʃɑ:nsələ*] n cancelliere m; C~ **of the Exchequer** n (Brit) Cancelliere dello Scacchiere.

chandelier [ʃændəˈlɪə*] n lampadario.

change [tʃeɪndʒ] vt cambiare; (transform): to ~ sb into trasformare qn in // vi cambiarsi; (be transformed): to ~ into trasformarsi in // n cambiamento; (money) resto; to ~ one's mind cambiare idea; a ~ of clothes un cambio (di vestiti); for a ~ tanto per cambiare; small ~ spiccioli mpl, moneta; ~**able** a (weather) variabile; ~ **machine** n distributore automatico di monete; ~**over** n cambiamento, passaggio.

changing [ˈtʃeɪndʒɪŋ] a che cambia; (colours) cangiante; ~ **room** n (Brit: in shop) camerino; (: SPORT) spogliatoio.

channel [ˈtʃænl] n canale m; (of river, sea) alveo // vt canalizzare; **through the usual** ~s per le solite vie; **the (English) C~** la Manica; **the C~ Islands** npl le Isole Normanne.

chant [tʃɑ:nt] n canto; salmodia // vt cantare; salmodiare.

chaos [ˈkeɪɔs] n caos m.

chaotic [keɪˈɔtɪk] a caotico(a).

chap [tʃæp] n (Brit col: man) tipo.

chapel [ˈtʃæpəl] n cappella.

chaperon [ˈʃæpərəun] n accompagnatrice f // vt accompagnare.

chaplain [ˈtʃæplɪn] n cappellano.

chapped [tʃæpt] a (skin, lips) screpolato(a).

chapter [ˈtʃæptə*] n capitolo.

char [tʃɑ:*] vt (burn) carbonizzare // n (Brit) = **charlady**.

character [ˈkærɪktə*] n carattere m; (in novel, film) personaggio; (eccentric) originale m; ~**istic** [-ˈrɪstɪk] a caratteristico(a) // n caratteristica.

charade [ʃəˈrɑ:d] n sciarada.

charcoal [ˈtʃɑ:kəul] n carbone m di legna.

charge [tʃɑ:dʒ] n accusa; (cost) prezzo; (of gun, battery, MIL: attack) carica // vt

(gun, battery, MIL: enemy) caricare; (customer) fare pagare a; (sum) fare pagare; (LAW): to ~ sb (with) accusare qn (di) // vi (gen with: up, along etc) lanciarsi; ~s npl: bank ~s commissioni fpl bancarie; **is there a** ~? c'è da pagare?; **to reverse the** ~s (TEL) fare una telefonata a carico del destinatario; **to take** ~ **of** incaricarsi di; **to be in** ~ **of** essere responsabile per; **to** ~ **an expense (up) to sb** addebitare una spesa a qn; ~ **card** n carta f clienti inv.

chariot [ˈtʃærɪət] n carro.

charitable [ˈtʃærɪtəbl] a caritatevole.

charity [ˈtʃærɪtɪ] n carità; (organization) opera pia.

charlady [ˈtʃɑ:leɪdɪ] n (Brit) domestica a ore.

charlatan [ˈʃɑ:lətən] n ciarlatano.

charm [tʃɑ:m] n fascino; (on bracelet) ciondolo // vt affascinare, incantare; ~**ing** a affascinante.

chart [tʃɑ:t] n tabella; grafico; (map) carta nautica // vt fare una carta nautica di.

charter [ˈtʃɑ:tə*] vt (plane) noleggiare // n (document) carta; ~**ed accountant (C.A.)** n (Brit) ragioniere/a professionista; ~ **flight** n volo m charter inv.

chase [tʃeɪs] vt inseguire; (away) cacciare // n caccia.

chasm [ˈkæzəm] n abisso.

chassis [ˈʃæsɪ] n telaio.

chastity [ˈtʃæstɪtɪ] n castità.

chat [tʃæt] vi (also: **have a** ~) chiacchierare // n chiacchierata; ~ **show** n (Brit) talk show m inv.

chatter [ˈtʃætə*] vi (person) ciarlare // n ciarle fpl; **her teeth were** ~**ing** batteva i denti; ~**box** n chiacchierone/a.

chatty [ˈtʃætɪ] a (style) familiare; (person) chiacchierino(a).

chauffeur [ˈʃəufə*] n autista m.

chauvinist [ˈʃəuvɪnɪst] n (male ~) maschilista m; (nationalist) sciovinista m/f.

cheap [tʃi:p] a a buon mercato; (joke) grossolano(a); (poor quality) di cattiva qualità // ad a buon mercato; ~**en** vt ribassare; (fig) avvilire; ~**er** a meno caro(a); ~**ly** ad a buon prezzo, a buon mercato.

cheat [tʃi:t] vi imbrogliare; (at school) copiare // vt ingannare; (rob) defraudare // n imbroglione m; copione m; (trick) inganno.

check [tʃek] vt verificare; (passport, ticket) controllare; (halt) fermare; (restrain) contenere // n verifica; controllo; (curb) freno; (bill) conto; (pattern: gen pl) quadretti mpl; (US) = **cheque** // a (also: ~**ed**: pattern, cloth) a quadretti; **to** ~ **in** vi (in hotel) registrare; (at airport) presentarsi all'accettazione // vt (luggage) depositare; **to** ~ **out** vi (in hotel) saldare il conto // vt (luggage) ritirare; **to ~ up** *vi*: to ~ up (on sth) investigare (qc); to ~ up on sb informarsi sul conto di qn; **~ered** *a* (*US*) = **chequered**; **~ers** *n* (*US*) dama; **~-in (desk)** *n* check-in *m inv*, accettazione *f* (bagagli *inv*); **~ing account** *n* (*US*) conto corrente; **~mate** *n* scaccomatto; **~out** *n* (*in supermarket*) cassa; **~point** *n* posto di blocco; **~room** *n* (*US*) deposito *m* bagagli *inv*; **~up** *n* (*MED*) controllo medico.

cheek [tʃi:k] *n* guancia; (*impudence*) faccia tosta; **~bone** *n* zigomo; **~y** *a* sfacciato(a).

cheep [tʃi:p] *vi* pigolare.

cheer [tʃiə*] *vt* applaudire; (*gladden*) rallegrare // *vi* applaudire // *n* (*gen pl*) applausi *mpl*; evviva *mpl*; **~s!** salute!; **to ~ up** *vi* rallegrarsi, farsi animo // *vt* rallegrare; **~ful** *a* allegro(a).

cheerio ['tʃiərɪ'əu] *excl* (*Brit*) ciao!

cheese [tʃi:z] *n* formaggio; **~board** *n* piatto del (*or* per il) formaggio.

cheetah ['tʃi:tə] *n* ghepardo.

chef [ʃef] *n* capocuoco.

chemical ['kemikəl] *a* chimico(a) // *n* prodotto chimico.

chemist ['kemist] *n* (*Brit: pharmacist*) farmacista *m/f*; (*scientist*) chimico/a; **~ry** *n* chimica; **~'s (shop)** *n* (*Brit*) farmacia.

cheque [tʃek] *n* (*Brit*) assegno; **~book** *n* libretto degli assegni; **~ card** *n* carta *f* assegni *inv*.

chequered ['tʃɛkəd] *a* (*fig*) movimentato(a).

cherish ['tʃerɪʃ] *vt* aver caro; (*hope etc*) nutrire.

cherry ['tʃerɪ] *n* ciliegia.

chess [tʃes] *n* scacchi *mpl*; **~board** *n* scacchiera; **~man** *n* pezzo degli scacchi.

chest [tʃest] *n* petto; (*box*) cassa; **~ of drawers** *n* cassettone *m*.

chestnut ['tʃesnʌt] *n* castagna; (*also: ~ tree*) castagno.

chew [tʃu:] *vt* masticare; **~ing gum** *n* chewing gum *m*.

chic [ʃi:k] *a* elegante.

chick [tʃik] *n* pulcino; (*US col*) pollastrella.

chicken ['tʃikɪn] *n* pollo; **to ~ out** *vi* (*col*) avere fifa; **~pox** *n* varicella.

chicory ['tʃikərɪ] *n* cicoria.

chief [tʃi:f] *n* capo // *a* principale; **~ constable** *n* (*Brit*) ≈ questore *m*; **~ executive** *n* direttore *m* generale; **~ly** *ad* per lo più, soprattutto.

chilblain ['tʃilblein] *n* gelone *m*.

child, *pl* **~ren** [tʃaild, 'tʃildrən] *n* bambino/a; **~birth** *n* parto; **~hood** *n* infanzia; **~ish** *a* puerile; **~like** *a* fanciullesco(a); **~ minder** *n* (*Brit*) bambinaia.

Chile ['tʃilɪ] *n* Cile *m*.

chill [tʃil] *n* freddo; (*MED*) infreddatura // *a* freddo(a), gelido(a) // *vt* raffreddare.

chil(l)i ['tʃilɪ] *n* peperoncino.

chilly ['tʃilɪ] *a* freddo(a), fresco(a); **to feel ~** sentirsi infreddolito(a).

chime [tʃaim] *n* carillon *m inv* // *vi* suonare, scampanare.

chimney ['tʃimnɪ] *n* camino; **~ sweep** *n* spazzacamino.

chimpanzee [tʃimpæn'zi:] *n* scimpanzé *m inv*.

chin [tʃin] *n* mento.

China ['tʃainə] *n* Cina.

china ['tʃainə] *n* porcellana.

Chinese [tʃai'ni:z] *a* cinese // *n* (*pl inv*) cinese *m/f*; (*LING*) cinese *m*.

chink [tʃiŋk] *n* (*opening*) fessura; (*noise*) tintinnio.

chip [tʃip] *n* (*gen pl: CULIN*) patatina fritta; (: *US: also:* **potato ~**) patatina; (*of wood, glass, stone*) scheggia; (*also: micro~*) chip *m inv* // *vt* (*cup, plate*) scheggiare; **to ~ in** *vi* (*col: contribute*) contribuire; (: *interrupt*) intromettersi.

chiropodist [ki'rɔpədist] *n* (*Brit*) pedicure *m/f inv*.

chirp [tʃə:p] *vi* cinguettare.

chisel ['tʃizl] *n* cesello.

chit [tʃit] *n* biglietto.

chivalry ['ʃivəlrɪ] *n* cavalleria; cortesia.

chives [tʃaivz] *npl* erba cipollina.

chock [tʃɔk] *n* zeppa; **~-a-block, ~-full** *a* pieno(a) zeppo(a).

chocolate ['tʃɔklɪt] *n* (*substance*) cioccolato, cioccolata; (*drink*) cioccolata; (*a sweet*) cioccolatino.

choice [tʃɔis] *n* scelta // *a* scelto(a).

choir ['kwaiə*] *n* coro; **~boy** *n* corista *m* fanciullo.

choke [tʃəuk] *vi* soffocare // *vt* soffocare; (*block*) ingombrare // *n* (*AUT*) valvola dell'aria.

cholera ['kɔlərə] *n* colera *m*.

cholesterol [kə'lestərɔl] *n* colesterolo.

choose [tʃu:z], *pt* **chose**, *pp* **chosen** *vt* scegliere; **to ~ to do** decidere di fare; preferire fare.

choosy ['tʃu:zɪ] *a* schizzinoso(a).

chop [tʃɔp] *vt* (*wood*) spaccare; (*CULIN: also: ~ up*) tritare // *n* colpo netto; (*CULIN*) costoletta; **~s** *npl* (*jaws*) mascelle *fpl*.

chopper ['tʃɔpə*] *n* (*helicopter*) elicottero.

choppy ['tʃɔpɪ] *a* (*sea*) mosso(a).

chopsticks ['tʃɔpstiks] *npl* bastoncini *mpl* cinesi.

choral ['kɔ:rəl] *a* corale.

chord [kɔ:d] *n* (*MUS*) accordo.

chore [tʃɔ:*] *n* faccenda; **household ~s** faccende *fpl* domestiche.

choreographer [kɔri'ɔgrəfə*] *n* coreografo/a.

chorister ['kɔristə*] *n* corista *m/f*.

chortle ['tʃɔ:tl] *vi* ridacchiare.

chorus ['kɔːrəs] n coro; (repeated part of song, also fig) ritornello.

chose [tʃəuz] pt of **choose**.

chosen ['tʃəuzn] pp of **choose**.

Christ [kraist] n Cristo.

christen ['krɪsn] vt battezzare.

Christian ['krɪstɪən] a, n cristiano(a); **~ity** [-'ænɪtɪ] n cristianesimo; **~ name** n nome m (di battesimo).

Christmas ['krɪsməs] n Natale m; Merry ~! Buon Natale!; ~ **card** n cartolina di Natale; **~ Day** n il giorno di Natale; **~ Eve** n la vigilia di Natale; **~ tree** n albero di Natale.

chrome [krəum], **chromium** ['krəumɪəm] n cromo.

chronic ['krɔnɪk] a cronico(a).

chronicle ['krɔnɪkl] n cronaca.

chronological [krɔnə'lɔdʒɪkəl] a cronologico(a).

chrysanthemum [krɪ'sænθəməm] n crisantemo.

chubby ['tʃʌbɪ] a paffuto(a).

chuck [tʃʌk] vt buttare, gettare; **to ~ out** vt buttar fuori; **to ~ (up)** vt (Brit) piantare.

chuckle ['tʃʌkl] vi ridere sommessamente.

chug [tʃʌg] vi fare ciuf ciuf.

chum [tʃʌm] n compagno/a.

chunk [tʃʌŋk] n pezzo; (of bread) tocco.

church [tʃəːtʃ] n chiesa; **~yard** n sagrato.

churlish ['tʃəːlɪʃ] a rozzo(a), sgarbato(a).

churn [tʃəːn] n (for butter) zangola; (for transport: also: **milk ~**) bidone m; **to ~ out** vt sfornare.

chute [ʃuːt] n cascata; (also: **rubbish ~**) canale m di scarico; (Brit: children's slide) scivolo.

chutney ['tʃʌtnɪ] n salsa piccante (di frutta, zucchero e spezie).

CIA n abbr (US: = Central Intelligence Agency) CIA f.

CID n abbr (Brit: = Criminal Investigation Department) ≈ polizia giudiziaria.

cider ['saɪdə*] n sidro.

cigar [sɪ'gaː*] n sigaro.

cigarette [sɪgə'rɛt] n sigaretta; **~ case** n portasigarette m inv; **~ end** n mozzicone m.

cinder ['sɪndə*] n cenere f.

Cinderella [sɪndə'relə] n Cenerentola.

cine ['sɪnɪ]: **~-camera** n (Brit) cinepresa; **~-film** n (Brit) pellicola.

cinema ['sɪnəmə] n cinema m inv.

cinnamon ['sɪnəmən] n cannella.

cipher ['saɪfə*] n cifra; (fig: faceless employee etc) persona di nessun conto.

circle ['səːkl] n cerchio; (of friends etc) circolo; (in cinema) galleria // vi girare in circolo // vt (surround) circondare; (move round) girare intorno a.

circuit ['səːkɪt] n circuito; **~ous** [səː'kjuɪtəs] a indiretto(a).

circular ['səːkjulə*] a, n circolare (f).

circulate ['səːkjuleɪt] vi circolare // vt far circolare; **circulation** [-'leɪʃən] n circolazione f; (of newspaper) tiratura.

circumstances ['səːkəmstənsɪz] npl circostanze fpl; (financial condition) condizioni fpl finanziarie.

circumvent [səːkəm'vɛnt] vt aggirare.

circus ['səːkəs] n circo.

cistern ['sɪstən] n cisterna; (in toilet) serbatoio d'acqua.

citizen ['sɪtɪzn] n cittadino/a; (resident): the **~s of this town** gli abitanti di questa città; **~ship** n cittadinanza.

citrus fruit ['sɪtrəs-] n agrume m.

city ['sɪtɪ] n città f inv; the **C~** la Città di Londra (centro commerciale).

civic ['sɪvɪk] a civico(a); **~ centre** n (Brit) centro civico.

civil ['sɪvɪl] a civile; **~ engineer** n ingegnere m civile; **~ian** [sɪ'vɪlɪən] a, n borghese (m/f).

civilization [sɪvɪlaɪ'zeɪʃən] n civiltà f inv.

civilized ['sɪvɪlaɪzd] a civilizzato(a); (fig) cortese.

civil: **~ law** n codice m civile; (study) diritto civile; **~ servant** n impiegato/a statale; **C~ Service** n amministrazione f statale; **~ war** n guerra civile.

clad [klæd] a: **~ (in)** vestito(a) (di).

claim [kleɪm] vt rivendicare; sostenere, pretendere; (damages) richiedere // vi (for insurance) fare una domanda d'indennizzo // n rivendicazione f; pretesa; (right) diritto; (insurance) ~ domanda d'indennizzo; **~ant** n (ADMIN, LAW) richiedente m/f.

clairvoyant [klɛə'vɔɪənt] n chiaroveggente m/f.

clam [klæm] n vongola.

clamber ['klæmbə*] vi arrampicarsi.

clammy ['klæmɪ] a (weather) caldo(a) umido(a); (hands) viscido(a).

clamour, (US) **clamor** ['klæmə*] vi: **to ~ for** chiedere a gran voce.

clamp [klæmp] n pinza; morsa // vt ammorsare; **to ~ down on** vt fus dare un giro di vite a.

clan [klæn] n clan m inv.

clang [klæŋ] n fragore m, suono metallico.

clap [klæp] vi applaudire; **~ping** n applausi mpl.

claret ['klærət] n vino di Bordeaux.

clarify ['klærɪfaɪ] vt chiarificare, chiarire.

clarinet [klærɪ'nɛt] n clarinetto.

clarity ['klærɪtɪ] n chiarità f.

clash [klæʃ] n frastuono; (fig) scontro // vi scontrarsi; cozzare.

clasp [klɑːsp] n fermaglio, fibbia // vt stringere.

class [klɑːs] n classe f // vt classificare.

classic ['klæsɪk] *a* classico(a) // *n* classico; ~**al** *a* classico(a).

classified ['klæsɪfaɪd] *a* (*information*) segreto(a), riservato(a); ~ **advertisement**, ~ **ad** *n* annuncio economico.

classmate ['klɑ:smeɪt] *n* compagno/a di classe.

classroom ['klɑ:srum] *n* aula.

clatter ['klætə*] *n* acciottolio; scalpitio // *vi* acciottolare; scalpitare.

clause [klɔ:z] *n* clausola; (*LING*) proposizione *f*.

claw [klɔ:] *n* tenaglia; (*of bird of prey*) artiglio; (*of lobster*) pinza // *vt* (*also:* ~ **at**) graffiare; afferrare.

clay [kleɪ] *n* argilla.

clean [kli:n] *a* pulito(a); (*clear, smooth*) liscio(a) // *vt* pulire; **to** ~ **out** *vt* ripulire; **to** ~ **up** *vi* far pulizia // *vt* (*also fig*) ripulire; ~**er** *n* (*person*) donna delle pulizie; (*also:* dry ~**er**) tintore/a; (*product*) smacchiatore *m*; ~**ing** *n* pulizia; ~**liness** ['klɛnlɪnɪs] *n* pulizia.

cleanse [klɛnz] *vt* pulire; purificare; ~**r** *n* detergente *m*.

clean-shaven   ['kli:n'ʃeɪvn]   *a* sbarbato(a).

cleansing department ['klɛnzɪŋ-] *n* (*Brit*) nettezza urbana.

clear [klɪə*] *a* chiaro(a); (*road, way*) libero(a) // *vt* sgombrare; liberare; (*table*) sparecchiare; (*COMM: goods*) liquidare; (: *debt*) liquidare, saldare; (: *cheque*) fare la compensazione di; (*LAW: suspect*) discolpare; (*obstacle*) superare // *vi* (*weather*) rasserenarsi; (*fog*) andarsene // *ad:* ~ of distante da; **to** ~ **up** *vi* schiarirsi // *vt* mettere in ordine; (*mystery*) risolvere; ~**ance** *n* (*removal*) sgombro; (*free space*) spazio; (*permission*) autorizzazione *f*, permesso; ~**-cut** *a* ben delineato(a), distinto(a); ~**ing** *n* radura; ~**ing bank** *n* (*Brit*) banca (che fa uso della camera di compensazione); ~**ly** *ad* chiaramente; ~**way** *n* (*Brit*) strada con divieto di sosta.

cleaver ['kli:və*] *n* mannaia.

clef [klɛf] *n* (*MUS*) chiave *f*.

cleft [klɛft] *n* (*in rock*) crepa, fenditura.

clench [klɛntʃ] *vt* stringere.

clergy ['klə:dʒɪ] *n* clero; ~**man** *n* ecclesiastico.

clerical ['klɛrɪkəl] *a* d'impiegato; (*REL*) clericale.

clerk [klɑ:k, (*US*) klə:rk] *n* impiegato/a; (*US: sales person*) commesso/a.

clever ['klɛvə*] *a* (*mentally*) intelligente; (*deft, skilful*) abile; (*device, arrangement*) ingegnoso(a).

click [klɪk] *vi* scattare // *vt* (*heels etc*) battere; (*tongue*) far schioccare.

client ['klaɪənt] *n* cliente *m/f*.

cliff [klɪf] *n* scogliera scoscesa, rupe *f*.

climate ['klaɪmɪt] *n* clima *m*.

climax ['klaɪmæks] *n* culmine *m*.

climb [klaɪm] *vi* salire; (*clamber*) arrampicarsi // *vt* salire; (*CLIMBING*) scalare // *n* salita; arrampicata; scalata; ~**-down** *n* marcia indietro; ~**er** *n* (*also:* rock ~**er**) rocciatore/trice; alpinista *m/f*; ~**ing** *n* (*also:* rock ~**ing**) alpinismo.

clinch [klɪntʃ] *vt* (*deal*) concludere.

cling [klɪŋ], *pt*, *pp* **clung** *vi:* **to** ~ (**to**) tenersi stretto(a) (a); (*of clothes*) aderire strettamente (a).

clinic ['klɪnɪk] *n* clinica.

clink [klɪŋk] *vi* tintinnare.

clip [klɪp] *n* (*for hair*) forcina; (*also:* **paper** ~) graffetta; (*holding hose etc*) anello d'attacco // *vt* (*also:* ~ **together**: *papers*) attaccare insieme; (*hair, nails*) tagliare; (*hedge*) tosare; ~**pers** *npl* macchinetta per capelli; (*also:* nail ~**pers**) forbicine *fpl* per le unghie; ~**ping** *n* (*from newspaper*) ritaglio.

clique [kli:k] *n* cricca.

cloak [kləuk] *n* mantello // *vt* avvolgere; ~**room** *n* (*for coats etc*) guardaroba *m* *inv*; (*Brit: W.C.*) gabinetti *mpl*.

clock [klɔk] *n* orologio; **to** ~ **in** *or* **on** *vi* timbrare il cartellino (all'entrata); **to** ~ **off** *or* **out** *vi* timbrare il cartellino (all'uscita); ~**wise** *ad* in senso orario; ~**work** *n* movimento *or* meccanismo a orologeria // *a* a molla.

clog [klɔg] *n* zoccolo // *vt* intasare // *vi* intasarsi, bloccarsi.

cloister ['klɔɪstə*] *n* chiostro.

clone [kləun] *n* clone *m*.

close *a, ad and derivatives* [kləus] *a:* ~ (**to**) vicino(a) (a); (*writing, texture*) fitto(a); (*watch*) stretto(a); (*examination*) attento(a); (*weather*) afoso(a) // *ad* vicino, dappresso; ~ to *prep* vicino a; ~ **by**, ~ **at hand** *a, ad* vicino; **a** ~ **friend** un amico intimo; **to have a** ~ **shave** (*fig*) scamparla bella // *vb and derivatives* [kləuz] *vt* chiudere // *vi* (*shop etc*) chiudere; (*lid, door etc*) chiudersi; (*end*) finire // *n* (*end*) fine *f*; **to** ~ **down** *vt* chiudere (definitivamente) // *vi* cessare (definitivamente); ~**d** *a* chiuso(a); ~**d shop** *n* azienda *o* fabbrica che impiega solo aderenti ai sindacati; ~**-knit** *a* (*family, community*) molto unito(a); ~**ly** *ad* (*examine, watch*) da vicino.

closet ['klɔzɪt] *n* (*cupboard*) armadio.

close-up ['kləusʌp] *n* primo piano.

closure ['kləuʒə*] *n* chiusura.

clot [klɔt] *n* (*also:* blood ~) coagulo; (*col: idiot*) scemo/a // *vi* coagularsi.

cloth [klɔθ] *n* (*material*) tessuto, stoffa; (*also:* tea~) strofinaccio.

clothe [kləuð] *vt* vestire; ~**s** *npl* abiti *mpl*, vestiti *mpl*; ~**s brush** *n* spazzola per abiti; ~**s line** *n* corda (per stendere

il bucato); **~s peg**, *(US)* **~s pin** *n*
molletta.
clothing ['kləʊðɪŋ] *n* = **clothes.**
cloud [klaud] *n* nuvola; **~y** *a*
nuvoloso(a); *(liquid)* torbido(a).
clout [klaut] *vt* dare un colpo a.
clove [kləʊv] *n* chiodo di garofano; **~ of**
garlic spicchio d'aglio.
clover ['kləʊvə*] *n* trifoglio.
clown [klaun] *n* pagliaccio // *vi (also: ~
about, ~ around)* fare il pagliaccio.
cloying ['klɔɪɪŋ] *a (taste, smell)*
nauseabondo(a).
club [klʌb] *n (society)* club *m inv,*
circolo; *(weapon, GOLF)* mazza // *vt* bastonare // *vi:* **to ~ together** associarsi;
~s *npl (CARDS)* fiori *mpl;* **~ car** *n (US
RAIL)* vagone *m* ristorante; **~house** *n*
sede *f* del circolo.
cluck [klʌk] *vi* chiocciare.
clue [klu:] *n* indizio; *(in crosswords)*
definizione *f;* **I haven't a ~** non ho la
minima idea.
clump [klʌmp] *n:* **~ of trees** folto
d'alberi.
clumsy ['klʌmzɪ] *a (person)* goffo(a),
maldestro(a); *(object)* malfatto(a), mal
costruito(a).
clung [klʌŋ] *pt, pp of* **cling.**
cluster ['klʌstə*] *n* gruppo // *vi* raggrupparsi.
clutch [klʌtʃ] *n (grip, grasp)* presa,
stretta; *(AUT)* frizione *f* // *vt* afferrare,
stringere forte; **to ~ at** aggrapparsi a.
clutter ['klʌtə*] *vt* ingombrare.
CND *n abbr = Campaign for Nuclear
Disarmament.*
Co. *abbr* = **county; company.**
c/o *abbr* (= *care of)* presso.
coach [kəʊtʃ] *n (bus)* pullman *m inv;
(horse-drawn, of train)* carrozza;
(SPORT) allenatore/trice // *vt* allenare; **~
trip** *n* viaggio in pullman.
coagulate [kəʊ'ægjuleɪt] *vi* coagularsi.
coal [kəʊl] *n* carbone *m;* **~ face** *n* fronte
f; **~field** *n* bacino carbonifero.
coalition [kəʊə'lɪʃən] *n* coalizione *f.*
coalman, coal merchant ['kəʊlmən,
'kəʊlmə:tʃənt] *n* negoziante *m* di carbone.
coalmine ['kəʊlmaɪn] *n* miniera di
carbone.
coarse [kɔ:s] *a (salt, sand etc)*
grosso(a); *(cloth, person)* rozzo(a).
coast [kəʊst] *n* costa // *vi (with cycle etc)*
scendere a ruota libera; **~al** *a* co-
stiero(a); **~guard** *n* guardia costiera;
~line *n* linea costiera.
coat [kəʊt] *n* cappotto; *(of animal)* pelo;
(of paint) mano *f* // *vt* coprire; **~ of
arms** *n* stemma *m;* **~ hanger** *n*
attaccapanni *m inv;* **~ing** *n* rivestimento.
coax [kəʊks] *vt* indurre (con moine).
cob [kɔb] *n see* **corn.**
cobbler ['kɔblə*] *n* calzolaio.

cobbles, cobblestones ['kɔblz,
'kɔblstəunz] *npl* ciottoli *mpl.*
cobweb ['kɔbweb] *n* ragnatela.
cocaine [kə'keɪn] *n* cocaina.
cock [kɔk] *n (rooster)* gallo; *(male bird)*
maschio // *vt (gun)* armare; **~erel** *n*
galletto; **~-eyed** *a (fig)* storto(a);
strampalato(a).
cockle ['kɔkl] *n* cardio.
cockney ['kɔknɪ] *n* cockney *m/f inv
(abitante dei quartieri popolari dell'East
End di Londra).*
cockpit ['kɔkpɪt] *n (in aircraft)*
abitacolo.
cockroach ['kɔkrəʊtʃ] *n* blatta.
cocktail ['kɔkteɪl] *n* cocktail *m inv;* **~
cabinet** *n* mobile *m* bar *inv;* **~ party** *n*
cocktail *m inv.*
cocoa ['kəʊkəʊ] *n* cacao.
coconut ['kəʊkənʌt] *n* noce *f* di cocco.
cocoon [kə'ku:n] *n* bozzolo.
cod [kɔd] *n* merluzzo.
C.O.D. *abbr = cash on delivery.*
code [kəʊd] *n* codice *m.*
cod-liver oil ['kɔdlɪvə*-] *n* olio di fegato
di merluzzo.
coercion [kəʊ'ə:ʃən] *n* coercizione *f.*
coffee ['kɔfɪ] *n* caffè *m inv;* **~ bar** *n
(Brit)* caffè *m inv;* **~ break** *n* pausa
per il caffè; **~pot** *n* caffettiera; **~
table** *n* tavolino.
coffin ['kɔfɪn] *n* bara.
cog [kɔg] *n* dente *m.*
cogent ['kəʊdʒənt] *a* convincente.
coherent [kəʊ'hɪərənt] *a* coerente.
coil [kɔɪl] *n* rotolo; *(one loop)* anello;
(contraceptive) spirale *f* // *vt* avvolgere.
coin [kɔɪn] *n* moneta // *vt (word)* coniare;
~age *n* sistema *m* monetario; **~-box** *n
(Brit)* telefono a gettoni.
coincide [kəʊɪn'saɪd] *vi* coincidere;
~nce [kəʊ'ɪnsɪdəns] *n* combinazione *f.*
coke [kəʊk] *n* coke *m.*
colander ['kɔləndə*] *n* colino.
cold [kəʊld] *a* freddo(a) // *n* freddo;
(MED) raffreddore *m;* **it's ~** fa freddo;
to be ~ aver freddo; **to catch ~** prendere
freddo; **to catch a ~** prendere un raffreddore; **in ~ blood** a sangue freddo; **~
sore** *n* erpete *m.*
coleslaw ['kəʊlslɔ:] *n* insalata di cavolo
bianco.
colic ['kɔlɪk] *n* colica.
collapse [kə'læps] *vi* crollare // *n* crollo;
(MED) collasso.
collapsible [kə'læpsəbl] *a* pieghevole.
collar ['kɔlə*] *n (of coat, shirt)* colletto;
~bone *n* clavicola.
collateral [kə'lætərl] *n* garanzia.
colleague ['kɔli:g] *n* collega *m/f.*
collect [kə'lekt] *vt (gen)* raccogliere; *(as
a hobby)* fare collezione di; *(Brit: call
and pick up)* prendere; *(money owed,
pension)* riscuotere; *(donations, sub-
scriptions)* fare una colletta di // *vi*

adunarsi, riunirsi; ammucchiarsi; **to call ~** (US TEL) fare una chiamata a carico del destinatario; **~ion** [kə'lɛkʃən] n collezione f; raccolta; (for money) colletta.

collector [kə'lɛktə*] n collezionista m/f; (of taxes) esattore m.

college ['kɔlɪdʒ] n (Brit, US SCOL) college m inv; (of technology etc) istituto superiore; (body) collegio.

collide [kə'laɪd] vi: **to ~ (with)** scontrarsi (con).

collie ['kɔlɪ] n (dog) collie m inv.

colliery ['kɔlɪərɪ] n (Brit) miniera di carbone.

collision [kə'lɪʒən] n collisione f, scontro.

colloquial [kə'ləukwɪəl] a familiare.

colon ['kəulən] n (sign) due punti mpl; (MED) colon m inv.

colonel ['kə:nl] n colonnello.

colonial [kə'ləunɪəl] a coloniale.

colony ['kɔlənɪ] n colonia.

colour, (US) **color** ['kʌlə*] n colore m // vt colorare; (tint, dye) tingere; (fig: affect) influenzare // vi (blush: also: ~ up) arrossire; **~s** npl (of party, club) emblemi mpl; **~ bar** n discriminazione f razziale (in locali etc); **~-blind** a daltonico(a); **~ed** a colorato(a); (photo) a colori // n: **~eds** gente f di colore; **~ film** n (for camera) pellicola a colori; **~ful** a pieno(a) di colore, a vivaci colori; (personality) colorato(a); **~ing** n colorazione f; (substance) colorante m; (complexion) colorito; **~ scheme** n combinazione f di colori; **~ television** n televisione f a colori.

colt [kəult] n puledro.

column ['kɔləm] n colonna; **~ist** ['kɔləmnɪst] n articolista m/f.

coma ['kəumə] n coma m inv.

comb [kəum] n pettine m // vt (hair) pettinare; (area) battere a tappeto.

combat ['kɔmbæt] n combattimento // vt combattere, lottare contro.

combination [kɔmbɪ'neɪʃən] n combinazione f.

combine vb [kəm'baɪn] vt: **to ~ (with)** combinare (con); (one quality with another) unire (a) // vi unirsi; (CHEM) combinarsi // n ['kɔmbaɪn] lega; (ECON) associazione f; **~ (harvester)** n mietitrebbia.

come [kʌm], pt **came**, pp **come** vi venire; arrivare; **to ~** (decision etc) raggiungere; **to ~ undone** slacciarsi; **to ~ loose** allentarsi; **to ~ about** vi succedere; **to ~ across** vt fus trovare per caso; **to ~ along** vi = **to come on; to ~ away** vi venire via; staccarsi; **to ~ back** vi ritornare; **to ~ by** vt fus (acquire) ottenere; procurarsi; **to ~ down** vi scendere; (prices) calare; (buildings) essere demolito(a); **to ~ forward** vi farsi avanti;

presentarsi; **to ~ from** vt fus venire da; provenire da; **to ~ in** vi entrare; **to ~ in for** vt fus (criticism etc) ricevere; **to ~ into** vt fus (money) ereditare; **to ~ off** vi (button) staccarsi; (stain) andar via; (attempt) riuscire; **to ~ on** vi (pupil, work, project) fare progressi; (lights) accendersi; (electricity) entrare in funzione; **~ on!** avanti!, andiamo!, forza!; **to ~ out** vi uscire; (strike) entrare in sciopero; **to ~ round** vi (after faint, operation) riprendere conoscenza, rinvenire; **to ~ to** vi rinvenire; **to ~ up** vi venire su; **to ~ up against** vt fus (resistance, difficulties) urtare contro; **to ~ up with** vt fus: he came up with an idea venne fuori con un'idea; **to ~ upon** vt fus trovare per caso; **~back** n (THEATRE etc) ritorno.

comedian [kə'mi:dɪən] n comico.

comedown ['kʌmdaun] n rovescio.

comedy ['kɔmɪdɪ] n commedia.

comeuppance [kʌm'ʌpəns] n: **to get one's ~** ricevere ciò che si merita.

comfort ['kʌmfət] n comodità f inv, benessere m; (solace) consolazione f, conforto // vt consolare, confortare; **~s** npl comodità fpl; **~able** a comodo(a); **~ably** ad (sit etc) comodamente; (live) bene; **~ station** n (US) gabinetti mpl.

comic ['kɔmɪk] a (also: **~al**) comico(a) // n comico; (magazine) giornaletto; **~ strip** n fumetto.

coming ['kʌmɪŋ] n arrivo // a (next) prossimo(a); (future) futuro(a); **~(s) and going(s)** n(pl) andirivieni m inv.

comma ['kɔmə] n virgola.

command [kə'mɑ:nd] n ordine m, comando; (MIL: authority) comando; (mastery) padronanza // vt comandare; **to ~ sb to do** ordinare a qn di fare; **~eer** [kɔmən'dɪə*] vt requisire; **~er** n capo; (MIL) comandante m.

commando [kə'mɑ:ndəu] n commando m inv; membro di un commando.

commemorate [kə'mɛməreɪt] vt commemorare.

commence [kə'mɛns] vt, vi cominciare.

commend [kə'mɛnd] vt lodare; raccomandare.

commensurate [kə'mɛnʃərɪt] a: **~ with** proporzionato(a) a.

comment ['kɔmɛnt] n commento // vi: **to ~ (on)** fare commenti (su); **~ary** ['kɔməntərɪ] n commentario; (SPORT) radiocronaca; telecronaca; **~ator** ['kɔmənteɪtə*] n commentatore/trice; radiocronista m/f; telecronista m/f.

commerce ['kɔmə:s] n commercio.

commercial [kə'mə:ʃəl] a commerciale // n (TV: also: **~ break**) pubblicità f inv.

commiserate [kə'mɪzəreɪt] vi: **to ~ with** condolersi con.

commission [kə'mɪʃən] n commissione f

// *vt* (*MIL*) nominare (al comando); (*work of art*) commissionare; **out of** ~ (*NAUT*) in disarmo; **~aire** [kɔmiʃə'neə*] *n* (*Brit: at shop, cinema etc*) portiere *m* in livrea; **~er** *n* commissionario; (*POLICE*) questore *m*.

commit [kə'mɪt] *vt* (*act*) commettere; (*to sb's care*) affidare; **to** ~ **o.s.** (**to do**) impegnarsi (a fare); **to** ~ **suicide** suicidarsi; **~ment** *n* impegno; promessa.

committee [kə'mɪtɪ] *n* comitato.

commodity [kə'mɔdɪtɪ] *n* prodotto, articolo; (*food*) derrata.

common ['kɔmən] *a* comune; (*pej*) volgare; (*usual*) normale // *n* terreno comune; **the C~s** *npl* (*Brit*) la Camera dei Comuni; **in** ~ in comune; **~er** *n* cittadino/a (non nobile); ~ **ground** *n* (*fig*) terreno comune; ~ **law** *n* diritto consuetudinario; **~ly** *ad* comunemente, usualmente; **C~ Market** *n* Mercato Comune; **~place** *a* banale, ordinario(a); **~room** *n* sala di riunione; (*SCOL*) sala dei professori; ~ **sense** *n* buon senso; **the C~wealth** *n* il Commonwealth.

commotion [kə'məuʃən] *n* confusione *f*, tumulto.

communal ['kɔmjuːnl] *a* (*life*) comunale; (*for common use*) pubblico(a).

commune *n* ['kɔmjuːn] (*group*) comune *f* // *vi* [kə'mjuːn]: **to** ~ **with** mettersi in comunione con.

communicate [kə'mjuːnɪkeɪt] *vt* comunicare, trasmettere // *vi*: **to** ~ (**with**) comunicare (con).

communication [kəmjuːnɪ'keɪʃən] *n* comunicazione *f*; ~ **cord** *n* (*Brit*) segnale *m* d'allarme.

communion [kə'mjuːnɪən] *n* (*also*: Holy C~) comunione *f*.

communiqué [kə'mjuːnɪkeɪ] *n* comunicato.

communism ['kɔmjunɪzəm] *n* comunismo; **communist** *a, n* comunista (*m/f*).

community [kə'mjuːnɪtɪ] *n* comunità *f inv*; ~ **centre** *n* circolo ricreativo; ~ **chest** *n* (*US*) fondo di beneficenza.

commutation ticket [kɔmjuː'teɪʃən-] *n* (*US*) biglietto di abbonamento.

commute [kə'mjuːt] *vi* fare il pendolare // *vt* (*LAW*) commutare; **~r** *n* pendolare *m/f*.

compact *a* [kəm'pækt] compatto(a) // *n* ['kɔmpækt] (*also*: **powder** ~) portacipria *m inv*; ~ **disk** *n* compact disc *m inv*.

companion [kəm'pænɪən] *n* compagno/a; **~ship** *n* compagnia.

company ['kʌmpənɪ] *n* (*also* COMM, MIL, THEATRE) compagnia; **to keep sb** ~ tenere compagnia a qn; ~ **secretary** *n* (*Brit*) segretario/a generale.

comparative [kəm'pærətɪv] *a*

relativo(a); (*adjective etc*) comparativo(a); **~ly** *ad* relativamente.

compare [kəm'peə*] *vt*: **to** ~ **sth/sb with/to** confrontare qc/qn con/a // *vi*: **to** ~ (**with**) reggere il confronto (con); **comparison** [-'pærɪsn] *n* confronto.

compartment [kəm'pɑːtmənt] *n* compartimento; (*RAIL*) scompartimento.

compass ['kʌmpəs] *n* bussola; **~es** *npl* compasso.

compassion [kəm'pæʃən] *n* compassione *f*.

compatible [kəm'pætɪbl] *a* compatibile.

compel [kəm'pel] *vt* costringere, obbligare; **~ling** *a* (*fig: argument*) irresistibile.

compendium [kəm'pendɪəm] *n* compendio.

compensate ['kɔmpənseɪt] *vt* risarcire // *vi*: **to** ~ **for** compensare; **compensation** [-'seɪʃən] *n* compensazione *f*; (*money*) risarcimento.

compère ['kɔmpeə*] *n* presentatore/trice.

compete [kəm'piːt] *vi* (*take part*) concorrere; (*vie*): **to** ~ (**with**) fare concorrenza (a).

competence ['kɔmpɪtəns] *n* competenza.

competent ['kɔmpɪtənt] *a* competente.

competition [kɔmpɪ'tɪʃən] *n* gara; concorso; (*ECON*) concorrenza.

competitive [kəm'petɪtɪv] *a* (*ECON*) concorrenziale; (*sport*) agonistico(a); (*person*) che ha spirito di competizione; che ha spirito agonistico; ~ **exam** concorso.

competitor [kəm'petɪtə*] *n* concorrente *m/f*.

complacency [kəm'pleɪsnsɪ] *n* compiacenza di sé.

complain [kəm'pleɪn] *vi*: **to** ~ (**about**) lagnarsi (di); (*in shop etc*) reclamare (per); **~t** *n* lamento; reclamo; (*MED*) malattia.

complement *n* ['kɔmplɪmənt] complemento; (*especially of ship's crew etc*) effettivo // *vt* ['kɔmplɪmənt] (*enhance*) accompagnarsi bene a; **~ary** [kɔmplɪ'mentərɪ] *a* complementare.

complete [kəm'pliːt] *a* completo(a) // *vt* completare; (*a form*) riempire; **~ly** *ad* completamente; **completion** *n* completamento.

complex ['kɔmpleks] *a* complesso(a) // *n* (*PSYCH, buildings etc*) complesso.

complexion [kəm'plekʃən] *n* (*of face*) carnagione *f*; (*of event etc*) aspetto.

compliance [kəm'plaɪəns] *n* acquiescenza; **in** ~ **with** (*orders, wishes etc*) in conformità con.

complicate ['kɔmplɪkeɪt] *vt* complicare; **~d** *a* complicato(a); **complication** [-'keɪʃən] *n* complicazione *f*.

compliment *n* ['kɔmplɪmənt] complimento // *vt* ['kɔmplɪmənt] fare un complimento a; **~s** *npl* complimenti *mpl*; rispetti *mpl*; **to pay sb a ~** fare un complimento a qn; **~ary** [-'mɛntəri] *a* complimentoso(a), elogiativo(a); *(free)* in omaggio; **~ary ticket** *n* biglietto d'omaggio.

comply [kəm'plaɪ] *vi*: **to ~ with** assentire a; conformarsi a.

component [kəm'pəunənt] *n* componente *m*.

compose [kəm'pəuz] *vt* comporre; **to ~ o.s.** ricomporsi; **~d** *a* calmo(a); **~r** *n* *(MUS)* compositore/trice.

composition [kɔmpə'zɪʃən] *n* composizione *f*.

composure [kəm'pəuʒə*] *n* calma.

compound ['kɔmpaund] *n* *(CHEM, LING)* composto; *(enclosure)* recinto // *a* composto(a); **~ fracture** *n* frattura esposta.

comprehend [kɔmprɪ'hɛnd] *vt* comprendere, capire; **comprehension** [-'hɛnʃən] *n* comprensione *f*.

comprehensive [kɔmprɪ'hɛnsɪv] *a* comprensivo(a); **~ policy** *n* *(INSURANCE)* polizza che copre tutti i rischi; **~ (school)** *n* *(Brit)* scuola secondaria aperta a tutti.

compress *vt* [kəm'prɛs] comprimere // *n* ['kɔmprɛs] *(MED)* compressa.

comprise [kəm'praɪz] *vt* *(also:* **be ~d of)** comprendere.

compromise ['kɔmprəmaɪz] *n* compromesso // *vt* compromettere // *vi* venire a un compromesso.

compulsion [kəm'pʌlʃən] *n* costrizione *f*.

compulsive [kəm'pʌlsɪv] *a* *(PSYCH)* incontrollabile.

compulsory [kəm'pʌlsəri] *a* obbligatorio(a).

computer [kəm'pjuːtə*] *n* computer *m inv*, elaboratore *m* elettronico; **~ize** *vt* computerizzare; **~ programmer** *n* programmatore/trice; **~ programming** *n* programmazione *f* di computer; **~ science, computing** *n* informatica.

comrade ['kɔmrɪd] *n* compagno/a.

con [kɔn] *vt* *(col)* truffare // *n* truffa.

conceal [kən'siːl] *vt* nascondere.

conceit [kən'siːt] *n* presunzione *f*, vanità; **~ed** *a* presuntuoso(a), vanitoso(a).

conceive [kən'siːv] *vt* concepire // *vi* concepire un bambino.

concentrate ['kɔnsəntreɪt] *vi* concentrarsi // *vt* concentrare.

concentration [kɔnsən'treɪʃən] *n* concentrazione *f*; **~ camp** *n* campo di concentramento.

concept ['kɔnsɛpt] *n* concetto.

conception [kən'sɛpʃən] *n* concezione *f*.

concern [kən'səːn] *n* affare *m*; *(COMM)* azienda, ditta; *(anxiety)* preoccupazione *f* // *vt* riguardare; **to be ~ed (about)** preoccuparsi (di); **~ing** *prep* riguardo a, circa.

concert ['kɔnsət] *n* concerto; **~ed**

[kən'səːtɪd] *a* concertato(a); **~ hall** *n* sala da concerti.

concertina [kɔnsə'tiːnə] *n* piccola fisarmonica // *vi* ridursi come una fisarmonica.

concerto [kən'tʃəːtəu] *n* concerto.

conclude [kən'kluːd] *vt* concludere; **conclusion** [-'kluːʒən] *n* conclusione *f*; **conclusive** [-'kluːsɪv] *a* conclusivo(a).

concoct [kən'kɔkt] *vt* inventare; **~ion** [-'kɔkʃən] *n* miscuglio.

concourse ['kɔŋkɔːs] *n* *(hall)* atrio.

concrete ['kɔŋkriːt] *n* calcestruzzo // *a* concreto(a); di calcestruzzo.

concur [kən'kəː*] *vi* concordare.

concurrently [kən'kʌrntlɪ] *ad* simultaneamente.

concussion [kən'kʌʃən] *n* commozione *f* cerebrale.

condemn [kən'dɛm] *vt* condannare; **~ation** [kɔndɛm'neɪʃən] *n* condanna.

condensation [kɔndɛn'seɪʃən] *n* condensazione *f*.

condense [kən'dɛns] *vi* condensarsi // *vt* condensare; **~d milk** *n* latte *m* condensato.

condition [kən'dɪʃən] *n* condizione *f* // *vt* condizionare, regolare; **on ~ that** *a* condizione che (+ *sub*, a condizione di; **~al** *a* condizionale; **~er** *n* *(for hair)* balsamo.

condolences [kən'dəulənsɪz] *npl* condoglianze *fpl*.

condom ['kɔndəm] *n* preservativo.

condominium [kɔndə'mɪnɪəm] *n* *(US)* condominio.

condone [kən'dəun] *vt* condonare.

conducive [kən'djuːsɪv] *a*: **~ to** favorevole a.

conduct *n* ['kɔndʌkt] condotta // *vt* [kən'dʌkt] condurre; *(manage)* dirigere; amministrare; *(MUS)* dirigere; **to ~ o.s.** comportarsi; **~ed tour** *n* gita accompagnata; **~or** *n* *(of orchestra)* direttore *m* d'orchestra; *(on bus)* bigliettaio; *(US: on train)* controllore *m*; *(ELEC)* conduttore *m*; **~ress** *n* *(on bus)* bigliettaia.

conduit ['kɔndɪt] *n* condotto; tubo.

cone [kəun] *n* cono; *(BOT)* pigna.

confectioner [kən'fɛkʃənə*] *n* pasticciere *m*; **~'s (shop)** *n* ≈ pasticceria; **~y** *n* dolciumi *mpl*.

confer [kən'fəː*] *vt*: **to ~ sth on** conferire qc a // *vi* conferire.

conference ['kɔnfərns] *n* congresso.

confess [kən'fɛs] *vt* confessare, ammettere // *vi* confessarsi; **~ion** [-'fɛʃən] *n* confessione *f*.

confetti [kən'fɛtɪ] *n* coriandoli *mpl*.

confide [kən'faɪd] *vi*: **to ~ in** confidarsi con.

confidence ['kɔnfɪdns] *n* confidenza; *(trust)* fiducia; *(also:* self~) sicurezza di sé; **in ~** *(speak, write)* in confidenza,

confidenzialmente; ~ **trick** *n* truffa;
confident *a* sicuro(a); sicuro(a) di sé;
confidential [kɔnfɪ'dɛnʃəl] *a* riservato(a).
confine [kən'faɪn] *vt* limitare; (*shut up*)
rinchiudere; ~**s** ['kɔnfaɪnz] *npl* confini
mpl; ~**d** *a* (*space*) ristretto(a); ~**ment**
n prigionia; (*MIL*) consegna; (*MED*)
parto.
confirm [kən'fə:m] *vt* confermare; (*REL*)
cresimare; ~**ation** [kɔnfə'meɪʃən] *n*
conferma; cresima; ~**ed** *a*
inveterato(a).
confiscate ['kɔnfɪskeɪt] *vt* confiscare.
conflict *n* ['kɔnflɪkt] conflitto // *vi*
[kən'flɪkt] essere in conflitto; ~**ing** *a*
contrastante.
conform [kən'fɔ:m] *vi*: to ~ (to)
conformarsi (a).
confound [kən'faund] *vt* confondere.
confront [kən'frʌnt] *vt* confrontare;
(*enemy, danger*) affrontare; ~**ation**
[kɔnfrən'teɪʃən] *n* confronto.
confuse [kən'fju:z] *vt* imbrogliare; (*one
thing with another*) confondere; ~**d** *a*
confuso(a); **confusing** *a* che fa
confondere; **confusion** [-'fju:ʒən] *n*
confusione *f*.
congeal [kən'dʒi:l] *vi* (*blood*) congelarsi.
congenial [kən'dʒi:nɪəl] *a* (*person*)
simpatico(a); (*thing*) congeniale.
congested [kən'dʒɛstɪd] *a* congestionato(a).
congestion [kən'dʒɛstʃən] *n* congestione
f.
congratulate [kən'grætjuleɪt] *vt*: to ~ sb
(on) congratularsi con qn (per *or* di);
congratulations [-'leɪʃənz] *npl* auguri
mpl; (*on success*) complimenti *mpl*.
congregate ['kɔngrɪgeɪt] *vi* congregarsi,
riunirsi.
congress ['kɔngrɛs] *n* congresso; ~**man**
n (*US*) membro del Congresso.
conjecture [kən'dʒɛktʃə*] *n* congettura.
conjunction [kən'dʒʌŋkʃən] *n*
congiunzione *f*.
conjunctivitis [kəndʒʌŋktɪ'vaɪtɪs] *n*
congiuntivite *f*.
conjure ['kʌndʒə*] *vi* fare giochi di prestigio; to ~ **up** *vt* (*ghost, spirit*)
evocare; (*memories*) rievocare; ~**r** *n*
prestidigitatore/trice, prestigiatore/trice.
conk out [kɔŋk-] *vi* (*col*) andare in
panne.
conman ['kɔnmæn] *n* truffatore *m*.
connect [kə'nɛkt] *vt* connettere,
collegare; (*ELEC*) collegare; (*fig*)
associare // *vi* (*train*): to ~ **with** essere
in coincidenza con; **to be ~ed with**
(*associated*) aver rapporti con; (*by
birth, marriage*) essere imparentato
con; ~**ion** [-ʃən] *n* relazione *f*, rapporto;
(*ELEC*) connessione *f*; (*TEL*)
collegamento; **in ~ion with** con
riferimento a.

connive [kə'naɪv] *vi*: to ~ **at** essere
connivente in.
connoisseur [kɔnɪ'sə*] *n* conoscitore/
trice.
conquer ['kɔŋkə*] *vt* conquistare;
(*feelings*) vincere.
conquest ['kɔŋkwɛst] *n* conquista.
cons [kɔnz] *npl* see **convenience, pro.**
conscience ['kɔnʃəns] *n* coscienza.
conscientious [kɔnʃɪ'ɛnʃəs] *a* coscienzioso(a).
conscious ['kɔnʃəs] *a* consapevole;
(*MED*) conscio(a); ~**ness** *n*
consapevolezza; coscienza.
conscript ['kɔnskrɪpt] *n* coscritto.
consent [kən'sɛnt] *n* consenso // *vi*: to ~
(to) acconsentire (a).
consequence ['kɔnsɪkwəns] *n*
conseguenza, risultato; importanza.
consequently ['kɔnsɪkwəntlɪ] *ad* di
conseguenza, dunque.
conservation [kɔnsə'veɪʃən] *n*
conservazione *f*.
conservative [kən'sə:vətɪv] *a*
conservatore(trice); (*cautious*) cauto(a);
C~ *a, n* (*Brit POL*) conservatore(trice).
conservatory [kən'sə:vətrɪ] *n*
(*greenhouse*) serra.
conserve [kən'sə:v] *vt* conservare // *n*
conserva.
consider [kən'sɪdə*] *vt* considerare;
(*take into account*) tener conto di; to ~
doing sth considerare la possibilità di
fare qc.
considerable [kən'sɪdərəbl] *a*
considerevole, notevole; **considerably**
ad notevolmente, decisamente.
considerate [kən'sɪdərɪt] *a*
premuroso(a).
consideration [kənsɪdə'reɪʃən] *n*
considerazione *f*; (*reward*)
rimunerazione *f*.
considering [kən'sɪdərɪŋ] *prep* in
considerazione di.
consign [kən'saɪn] *vt* consegnare; (*send:
goods*) spedire; ~**ment** *n* consegna;
spedizione *f*.
consist [kən'sɪst] *vi*: to ~ **of** constare di,
essere composto(a) di.
consistency [kən'sɪstənsɪ] *n* consistenza;
(*fig*) coerenza.
consistent [kən'sɪstənt] *a* coerente; (*constant*) costante; ~ **with** compatibile con.
consolation [kɔnsə'leɪʃən] *n* consolazione
f.
console *vt* [kən'səul] consolare // *n*
['kɔnsəul] quadro di comando.
consonant ['kɔnsənənt] *n* consonante *f*.
consortium [kən'sɔ:tɪəm] *n* consorzio.
conspicuous [kən'spɪkjuəs] *a* cospicuo(a).
conspiracy [kən'spɪrəsɪ] *n* congiura, cospirazione *f*.
constable ['kʌnstəbl] *n* (*Brit*) ≈
poliziotto, agente *m* di polizia.

constabulary [kən'stæbjulərɪ] n forze fpl dell'ordine.

constant ['kɔnstənt] a costante; continuo(a); **~ly** ad costantemente; continuamente.

constipated ['kɔnstɪpeɪtɪd] a stitico(a).

constipation [kɔnstɪ'peɪʃən] n stitichezza.

constituency [kən'stɪtjuənsɪ] n collegio elettorale.

constituent [kən'stɪtjuənt] n elettore/trice; (part) elemento componente.

constitution [kɔnstɪ'tju:ʃən] n costituzione f; **~al** a costituzionale.

constraint [kən'streɪnt] n costrizione f.

construct [kən'strʌkt] vt costruire; **~ion** [-ʃən] n costruzione f; **~ive** a costruttivo(a).

construe [kən'stru:] vt interpretare.

consul ['kɔnsl] n console m; **~ate** ['kɔnsjulɪt] n consolato.

consult [kən'sʌlt] vt consultare // vi consultarsi; **~ant** n (MED) consulente m medico; (other specialist) consulente; **~ing room** n (Brit) ambulatorio.

consume [kən'sju:m] vt consumare; **~r** n consumatore/trice; **~r goods** npl beni mpl di consumo; **~r society** n società dei consumi.

consummate ['kɔnsʌmeɪt] vt consumare.

consumption [kən'sʌmpʃən] n consumo; (MED) consunzione f.

cont. abbr = continued.

contact ['kɔntækt] n contatto; (person) conoscenza // vt mettersi in contatto con; **~ lenses** npl lenti fpl a contatto.

contagious [kən'teɪdʒəs] a contagioso(a).

contain [kən'teɪn] vt contenere; to ~ o.s. contenersi; **~er** n recipiente m; (for shipping etc) container m.

contaminate [kən'tæmɪneɪt] vt contaminare.

cont'd abbr = continued.

contemplate ['kɔntəmpleɪt] vt contemplare; (consider) pensare a (or di).

contemporary [kən'tempərərɪ] a contemporaneo(a); (design) moderno(a) // n contemporaneo/a.

contempt [kən'tempt] n disprezzo; ~ of court (LAW) oltraggio alla Corte; **~uous** a sdegnoso(a).

contend [kən'tend] vt: to ~ that sostenere che // vi: to ~ with lottare contro; **~er** n contendente m/f; concorrente m/f.

content [kən'tent] a contento(a), soddisfatto(a) // vt contentare, soddisfare // n ['kɔntent] contenuto; **~s** npl contenuto; (of barrel etc: capacity) capacità f inv; (table of) **~s** indice m; **~ed** a contento(a), soddisfatto(a).

contention [kən'tenʃən] n contesa; (assertion) tesi f inv.

contentment [kən'tentmənt] n contentezza.

contest n ['kɔntest] lotta; (competition) gara, concorso // vt [kən'test] contestare; impugnare; (compete for) contendere; **~ant** [kən'testənt] n concorrente m/f; (in fight) avversario/a.

context ['kɔntekst] n contesto.

continent ['kɔntɪnənt] n continente m; the C~ (Brit) l'Europa continentale; **~al** [-'nentl] a continentale // n abitante m/f dell'Europa continentale; **~al quilt** n (Brit) piumino.

contingency [kən'tɪndʒənsɪ] n eventualità f inv; ~ plan n misura d'emergenza.

continual [kən'tɪnjuəl] a continuo(a).

continuation [kəntɪnju'eɪʃən] n continuazione f; (after interruption) ripresa; (of story) seguito.

continue [kən'tɪnju:] vi continuare // vt continuare; (start again) riprendere.

continuous [kən'tɪnjuəs] a continuo(a), ininterrotto(a); ~ stationery n carta a moduli continui.

contort [kən'tɔ:t] vt contorcere.

contour ['kɔntuə*] n contorno, profilo; (also: ~ line) curva di livello.

contraband ['kɔntrəbænd] n contrabbando.

contraceptive [kɔntrə'septɪv] a contraccettivo(a) // n contraccettivo.

contract n ['kɔntrækt] contratto // vi [kən'trækt] (become smaller) contrarsi; (COMM): to ~ to do sth fare un contratto per fare qc; **~ion** [-ʃən] n contrazione f; **~or** n imprenditore m.

contradict [kɔntrə'dɪkt] vt contraddire.

contraption [kən'træpʃən] n (pej) aggeggio.

contrary ['kɔntrərɪ] a contrario(a); (unfavourable) avverso(a), contrario(a); [kən'treərɪ] (perverse) bisbetico(a) // n contrario; on the ~ al contrario; unless you hear to the ~ a meno che non si disdica.

contrast n ['kɔntrɑ:st] contrasto // vt [kən'trɑ:st] mettere in contrasto.

contribute [kən'trɪbju:t] vi contribuire // vt: to ~ £10/an article to dare 10 sterline/un articolo a; to ~ to contribuire a; (newspaper) scrivere per; **contribution** [kɔntrɪ'bju:ʃən] n contribuzione f; **contributor** n (to newspaper) collaboratore/trice.

contrivance [kən'traɪvəns] n congegno; espediente m.

contrive [kən'traɪv] vt inventare; escogitare // vi: to ~ to do fare in modo di fare.

control [kən'trəul] vt dominare; (firm, operation etc) dirigere; (check) controllare // n controllo; **~s** npl comandi mpl; under ~ sotto controllo; to be in ~ of aver autorità su; essere responsabile di; controllare; **to go out of ~** (*car*) non rispondere ai comandi; (*situation*) sfuggire di mano; **~ panel** *n* quadro dei comandi; **~ room** *n* (*NAUT, MIL*) sala di comando; (*RADIO, TV*) sala di regia; **~ tower** *n* (*AVIAT*) torre *f* di controllo.

controversial [kɔntrə'və:ʃl] *a* controverso(a), polemico(a).

controversy ['kɔntrəvə:sɪ] *n* controversia, polemica.

convalesce [kɔnvə'lɛs] *vi* rimettersi in salute.

convene [kən'vi:n] *vt* convocare // *vi* convenire, adunarsi.

convenience [kən'vi:nɪəns] *n* comodità *f* *inv*; **at your ~** a suo comodo; **all modern ~s**, (*Brit*) **all mod cons** tutte le comodità moderne.

convenient [kən'vi:nɪənt] *a* conveniente, comodo(a).

convent ['kɔnvənt] *n* convento.

convention [kən'venʃən] *n* convenzione *f*; (*meeting*) convegno; **~al** *a* convenzionale.

conversant [kən'və:snt] *a*: **to be ~ with** essere al corrente di; essere pratico(a) di.

conversation [kɔnvə'seɪʃən] *n* conversazione *f*; **~al** *a* non formale.

converse *n* ['kɔnvə:s] contrario, opposto // *vi* [kən'və:s] conversare; **~ly** [-'və:slɪ] *ad* al contrario, per contro.

convert *vt* [kən'və:t] (*REL, COMM*) convertire; (*alter*) trasformare // *n* ['kɔnvə:t] convertito/a; **~ible** *a* (*currency*) convertibile // *n* macchina decappottabile.

convex ['kɔnvɛks] *a* convesso(a).

convey [kən'veɪ] *vt* trasportare; (*thanks*) comunicare; (*idea*) dare; **~or belt** *n* nastro trasportatore.

convict *vt* [kən'vɪkt] dichiarare colpevole // *n* ['kɔnvɪkt] carcerato/a; **~ion** [-ʃən] *n* condanna; (*belief*) convinzione *f*.

convince [kən'vɪns] *vt* convincere, persuadere; **convincing** *a* convincente.

convivial [kən'vɪvɪəl] *a* allegro(a).

convoluted [kɔnvə'lu:tɪd] *a* (*argument etc*) involuto(a).

convoy ['kɔnvɔɪ] *n* convoglio.

convulse [kən'vʌls] *vt* sconvolgere; **to be ~d with laughter** contorcersi dalle risa.

coo [ku:] *vi* tubare.

cook [kuk] *vt* cucinare, cuocere // *vi* cuocere; (*person*) cucinare // *n* cuoco/a; **~book** *n* libro di cucina; **~er** *n* fornello, cucina; **~ery** *n* cucina; **~ery book** *n* (*Brit*) = **~book**; **~ie** *n* (*US*) biscotto; **~ing** *n* cucina.

cool [ku:l] *a* fresco(a); (*not afraid*) calmo(a); (*unfriendly*) freddo(a); (*impertinent*) sfacciato(a) // *vt* raffreddare, rinfrescare // *vi* raffreddarsi, rinfrescarsi.

coop [ku:p] *n* stia // *vt*: **to ~ up** (*fig*) rinchiudere.

cooperate [kəu'ɔpəreɪt] *vi* cooperare, collaborare; **cooperation** [-'reɪʃən] *n* cooperazione *f*, collaborazione *f*.

cooperative [kəu'ɔpərətɪv] *a* cooperativo(a) // *n* cooperativa.

coordinate *vt* [kəu'ɔ:dɪneɪt] coordinare // *n* [kəu'ɔ:dɪnət] (*MATH*) coordinata; **~s** *npl* (*clothes*) coordinati *mpl*.

cop [kɔp] *n* (*col*) sbirro.

cope [kəup] *vi* farcela; **to ~ with** (*problems*) far fronte a.

copper ['kɔpə*] *n* rame *m*; (*col: policeman*) sbirro; **~s** *npl* spiccioli *mpl*.

coppice ['kɔpɪs] *n*, **copse** [kɔps] *n* bosco ceduo.

copulate ['kɔpjuleɪt] *vi* accoppiarsi.

copy ['kɔpɪ] *n* copia; (*book etc*) esemplare *m* // *vt* copiare; **~right** *n* diritto d'autore.

coral ['kɔrəl] *n* corallo.

cord [kɔ:d] *n* corda; (*fabric*) velluto a coste.

cordial ['kɔ:dɪəl] *a*, *n* cordiale (*m*).

cordon ['kɔ:dn] *n* cordone *m*; **to ~ off** *vt* fare cordone a.

corduroy ['kɔ:dərɔɪ] *n* fustagno.

core [kɔ:*] *n* (*of fruit*) torsolo; (*TECH*) centro // *vt* estrarre il torsolo da.

cork [kɔ:k] *n* sughero; (*of bottle*) tappo; **~screw** *n* cavatappi *m inv*.

corn [kɔ:n] *n* (*Brit: wheat*) grano; (*US: maize*) granturco; (*on foot*) callo; **~ on the cob** (*CULIN*) pannocchia cotta.

corned beef ['kɔ:nd-] *n* carne *f* di manzo in scatola.

corner ['kɔ:nə*] *n* angolo; (*AUT*) curva // *vt* intrappolare; mettere con le spalle al muro; (*COMM: market*) accaparrare // *vi* prendere una curva; **~stone** *n* pietra angolare.

cornet ['kɔ:nɪt] *n* (*MUS*) cornetta; (*Brit: of ice-cream*) cono.

cornflakes ['kɔ:nfleɪks] *npl* fiocchi *mpl* di granturco.

cornflour ['kɔ:nflauə*] *n* (*Brit*) farina finissima di granturco.

cornstarch ['kɔ:nstɑ:tʃ] *n* (*US*) = **cornflour**.

Cornwall ['kɔ:nwəl] *n* Cornovaglia.

corny ['kɔ:nɪ] *a* (*col*) trito(a).

coronary ['kɔrənərɪ] *n*: **~ (thrombosis)** trombosi *f* coronaria.

coronation [kɔrə'neɪʃən] *n* incoronazione *f*.

coroner ['kɔrənə*] *n* magistrato incaricato di indagare la causa di morte in circostanze sospette.

coronet ['kɔrənɪt] *n* diadema *m*.

corporal ['kɔ:pərl] *n* caporalmaggiore *m* // *a*: **~ punishment** pena corporale.

corporate ['kɔ:pərɪt] *a* costituito(a) (in corporazione); comune.

corporation [kɔ:pə'reɪʃən] *n* (*of town*) consiglio comunale; (*COMM*) ente *m*.

corps [kɔ:*], pl **corps** [kɔ:z] n corpo.

corpse [kɔ:ps] n cadavere m.

corral [kə'rɑ:l] n recinto.

correct [kə'rɛkt] a (accurate) corretto(a), esatto(a); (proper) corretto(a) // vt correggere; **~ion** [-ʃən] n correzione f.

correspond [kɔrɪs'pɔnd] vi corrispondere; **~ence** n corrispondenza; **~ence course** n corso per corrispondenza; **~ent** n corrispondente m/f.

corridor ['kɔrɪdɔ:*] n corridoio.

corrode [kə'rəud] vt corrodere // vi corrodersi.

corrugated ['kɔrəgeɪtɪd] a increspato(a); ondulato(a); **~ iron** n lamiera di ferro ondulata.

corrupt [kə'rʌpt] a corrotto(a) // vt corrompere; **~ion** [-ʃən] n corruzione f.

corset ['kɔ:sɪt] n busto.

cortège [kɔ:'teɪʒ] n corteo.

cosh [kɔʃ] n (Brit) randello (corto).

cosmetic [kɔz'metɪk] n cosmetico.

cosset ['kɔsɪt] vt vezzeggiare.

cost [kɔst] n costo // vb (pt, pp **cost**) vi costare // vt stabilire il prezzo di; **~s** npl (LAW) spese fpl; it's ~ £5/too much costa 5 sterline/troppo; at all **~s** a ogni costo.

co-star ['kəusta:*] n attore/trice della stessa importanza del protagonista.

cost-effective [kɔstɪ'fektɪv] a conveniente.

costly ['kɔstlɪ] a costoso(a), caro(a).

cost-of-living [kɔstəv'lɪvɪŋ] a: **~ allowance** indennità f inv di contingenza; **~ index** indice m della scala mobile.

cost price n (Brit) prezzo all'ingrosso.

costume ['kɔstju:m] n costume m; (lady's suit) tailleur m inv; (Brit: also: **swimming ~**) costume da bagno; **~ jewellery** n bigiotteria.

cosy, (US) **cozy** ['kəuzɪ] a intimo(a).

cot [kɔt] n (Brit: child's) lettino; (US: campbed) brandina.

cottage ['kɔtɪdʒ] n cottage m inv; **~ cheese** n fiocchi mpl di latte magro; **~ industry** n industria artigianale basata sul lavoro a cottimo; **~ pie** n piatto a base di carne macinata in sugo e purè di patate.

cotton ['kɔtn] n cotone m; **to ~ on to** vt fus (col) afferrare; **~ candy** n (US) zucchero filato; **~ wool** n (Brit) cotone idrofilo.

couch [kautʃ] n sofà m inv // vt esprimere.

couchette [ku:'ʃet] n (on train, boat) cuccetta.

cough [kɔf] vi tossire // n tosse f; **~ drop** n pasticca per la tosse.

could [kud] pt of **can**; **~n't** = **could not**.

council ['kaunsl] n consiglio; city or town **~** consiglio comunale; **~ estate** n (Brit) quartiere m di case popolari; **~**

house n (Brit) casa popolare; **~lor** n consigliere/a.

counsel ['kaunsl] n avvocato; consultazione f; **~lor** n consigliere/a.

count [kaunt] vt, vi contare // n conto; (nobleman) conte m; **to ~ on** vt fus contare su; **~down** n conto alla rovescia.

countenance ['kauntɪnəns] n volto, aspetto // vt approvare.

counter ['kauntə*] n banco // vt opporsi a; (blow) parare // ad: **~ to** contro; in opposizione a; **to act ~** agire in opposizione a; (poison etc) annullare gli effetti di; **~-espionage** n controspionaggio.

counterfeit ['kauntəfɪt] n contraffazione f, falso // vt contraffare, falsificare // a falso(a).

counterfoil ['kauntəfɔɪl] n matrice f.

countermand [kauntə'ma:nd] vt annullare.

counterpart ['kauntəpa:t] n (of document etc) copia; (of person) corrispondente m/f.

counter-productive [kauntəprə'dʌktɪv] a controproducente.

countersign ['kauntəsaɪn] vt controfirmare.

countess ['kauntɪs] n contessa.

countless ['kauntlɪs] a innumerevole.

country ['kʌntrɪ] n paese m; (native land) patria; (as opposed to town) campagna; (region) regione f; **~ dancing** n (Brit) danza popolare; **~ house** n villa in campagna; **~man** n (national) compatriota m; (rural) contadino; **~side** n campagna.

county ['kauntɪ] n contea.

coup, **~s** [ku:, -z] n colpo; (also: **~ d'état**) colpo di Stato.

couple ['kʌpl] n coppia // vt (carriages) agganciare; (TECH) accoppiare; (ideas, names) associare; **a ~ of** un paio di.

coupon ['ku:pɔn] n buono; (COMM) coupon m inv.

courage ['kʌrɪdʒ] n coraggio.

courgette [kuə'ʒet] n (Brit) zucchina.

courier ['kurɪə*] n corriere m; (for tourists) guida.

course [kɔ:s] n corso; (of ship) rotta; (for golf) campo; (part of meal) piatto; **first ~** primo piatto; **of ~** ad senz'altro, naturalmente; **~ of action** modo d'agire; **~ of lectures** corso di lezioni; **a ~ of treatment** (MED) una cura.

court [kɔ:t] n corte f; (TENNIS) campo // vt (woman) fare la corte a; **to take to ~** citare in tribunale.

courteous ['kə:tɪəs] a cortese.

courtesan [kɔ:tɪ'zæn] n cortigiana.

courtesy ['kə:təsɪ] n cortesia; **by ~ of** per gentile concessione di.

court-house ['kɔ:thaus] n (US) palazzo di giustizia.

courtier ['kɔːtɪə*] n cortigiano/a.
court-martial, pl **courts-martial**
['kɔːt'mɑːʃəl] n corte f marziale.
courtroom ['kɔːtrum] n tribunale m.
courtyard ['kɔːtjɑːd] n cortile m.
cousin ['kʌzn] n cugino/a; **first ~** cugino
di primo grado.
cove [kəuv] n piccola baia.
covenant ['kʌvənənt] n accordo.
cover ['kʌvə*] vt coprire // n (of pan)
coperchio; (over furniture) fodera; (of
book) copertina; (shelter) riparo;
(COMM, INSURANCE) copertura; **to take
~** (shelter) ripararsi; **under ~** al riparo;
under ~ of darkness protetto
dall'oscurità; **under separate ~** (COMM)
a parte, in plico separato; **to ~ up for sb**
coprire qn; **~age** n (PRESS, TV, RADIO):
to give full ~age to sth fare un ampio
servizio su qc; **~ charge** n coperto;
~ing n copertura; **~ing letter,** (US) **~
letter** n lettera d'accompagnamento; **~
note** n (INSURANCE) polizza (di
assicurazione) provvisoria.
covert ['kʌvət] a (hidden) nascosto(a);
(glance) furtivo(a).
cover-up ['kʌvərʌp] n occultamento (di
informazioni).
covet ['kʌvɪt] vt bramare.
cow [kau] n vacca // vt (person)
intimidire.
coward ['kauəd] n vigliacco/a; **~ice** [-ɪs]
n vigliaccheria; **~ly** a vigliacco(a).
cowboy ['kaubɔɪ] n cow-boy m inv.
cower ['kauə*] vi acquattarsi.
coxswain ['kɔksn] n (abbr: cox)
timoniere m.
coy [kɔɪ] a falsamente timido(a).
cozy ['kəuzɪ] a (US) = **cosy.**
CPA n abbr (US) = **certified public
accountant.**
crab [kræb] n granchio; **~ apple** n mela
selvatica.
crack [kræk] n fessura, crepa; incrinatura; (noise) schiocco; (: of gun)
scoppio; (joke) battuta; (col: attempt):
to have a ~ at sth tentare qc // vt
spaccare; incrinare; (whip) schioccare;
(nut) schiacciare // a (troops) fuori
classe; **to ~ down on** vt fus porre
freno a; **to ~ up** vi crollare; **~er** n
cracker m inv; petardo.
crackle ['krækl] vi crepitare.
cradle ['kreɪdl] n culla.
craft [krɑːft] n mestiere m; (cunning)
astuzia; (boat) naviglio; **~sman** n
artigiano; **~smanship** n abilità; **~y** a
furbo(a), astuto(a).
crag [kræg] n roccia.
cram [kræm] vt (fill): **to ~ sth with**
riempire qc di; (put): **to ~ sth into**
stipare qc in // vi (for exams) prepararsi
(in gran fretta).
cramp [kræmp] n crampo; **~ed** a ri-
stretto(a).

crampon ['kræmpən] n (CLIMBING)
rampone m.
cranberry ['krænbərɪ] n mirtillo.
crane [kreɪn] n gru f inv.
crank [kræŋk] n manovella; (person)
persona stramba; **~shaft** n albero a
gomiti.
cranny ['krænɪ] n see **nook.**
crash [kræʃ] n fragore m; (of car)
incidente m; (of plane) caduta // vt
fracassare // vi (plane) fracassarsi;
(car) avere un incidente; (two cars)
scontrarsi; (fig) fallire, andare in
rovina; **to ~ into** scontrarsi con; **~
course** n corso intensivo; **~ helmet** n
casco; **~ landing** n atterraggio di
fortuna.
crate [kreɪt] n gabbia.
cravat(e) [krə'væt] n fazzoletto da collo.
crave [kreɪv] vt, vi: **to ~ (for)** desiderare
ardentemente.
crawl [krɔːl] vi strisciare carponi; (vehicle) avanzare lentamente // n
(SWIMMING) crawl m.
crayfish ['kreɪfɪʃ] n (pl inv) (freshwater)
gambero (d'acqua dolce); (saltwater)
gambero.
crayon ['kreɪən] n matita colorata.
craze [kreɪz] n mania.
crazy ['kreɪzɪ] a matto(a); **~ paving** n
lastricato a mosaico irregolare.
creak [kriːk] vi cigolare, scricchiolare.
cream [kriːm] n crema; (fresh) panna //
a (colour) color crema inv; **~ cake** n
torta alla panna; **~ cheese** n formaggio
fresco; **~y** a cremoso(a).
crease [kriːs] n grinza; (deliberate) piega
// vt sgualcire.
create [kriː'eɪt] vt creare; **creation**
[-ʃən] n creazione f; **creative** a
creativo(a).
creature ['kriːtʃə*] n creatura.
crèche, creche [kreʃ] n asilo infantile.
credence ['kriːdns] n: **to lend** or **give ~**
to prestare fede a.
credentials [krɪ'denʃlz] npl (papers)
credenziali fpl.
credit ['kredɪt] n credito; onore m // vt
(COMM) accreditare; (believe: also:
give ~ to) credere, prestar fede a; **~s**
npl (CINEMA) titoli mpl; **to ~ sb with**
(fig) attribuire a qn; **to be in ~** (person)
essere creditore(trice); (bank account)
essere coperto(a); **~ card** n carta di
credito; **~or** n creditore/trice.
creed [kriːd] n credo; dottrina.
creek [kriːk] n insenatura; (US) piccolo
fiume m.
creep [kriːp], pt, pp **crept** vi avanzare
furtivamente (or pian piano); (plant)
arrampicarsi; **~er** n pianta rampicante;
~y a (frightening) che fa accapponare
la pelle.
cremate [krɪ'meɪt] vt cremare.
crematorium, pl **crematoria**

[kremə'tɔːrɪəm, -'tɔːrɪə] *n* forno crematorio.

crêpe [kreɪp] *n* crespo; ~ **bandage** *n* (*Brit*) fascia elastica.

crept [krɛpt] *pt, pp* of **creep.**

crescent ['krɛsnt] *n* (*shape*) mezzaluna; (*street*) strada semicircolare.

cress [krɛs] *n* crescione *m*.

crest [krɛst] *n* cresta; (*of helmet*) pennacchiera; (*of coat of arms*) cimiero; ~**fallen** *a* mortificato(a).

crevasse [krɪ'væs] *n* crepaccio.

crevice ['krɛvɪs] *n* fessura, crepa.

crew [kruː] *n* equipaggio; **to have a** ~-**cut** avere i capelli a spazzola; ~-**neck** *n* girocollo.

crib [krɪb] *n* culla; (*REL*) presepio // *vt* (*col*) copiare.

crick [krɪk] *n* crampo.

cricket ['krɪkɪt] *n* (*insect*) grillo; (*game*) cricket *m*.

crime [kraɪm] *n* crimine *m*; **criminal** ['krɪmɪnl] *a, n* criminale (*m/f*).

crimson ['krɪmzn] *a* color cremisi *inv*.

cringe [krɪndʒ] *vi* acquattarsi; (*fig*) essere servile.

crinkle ['krɪŋkl] *vt* arricciare, increspare.

cripple ['krɪpl] *n* zoppo/a // *vt* azzoppare.

crisis, *pl* **crises** ['kraɪsɪs, -siːz] *n* crisi *f inv*.

crisp [krɪsp] *a* croccante; (*fig*) frizzante; vivace; deciso(a); ~**s** *npl* (*Brit*) patatine *fpl*.

criss-cross ['krɪskrɔs] *a* incrociato(a).

criterion, *pl* **criteria** [kraɪ'tɪərɪən, -'tɪərɪə] *n* criterio.

critic ['krɪtɪk] *n* critico; ~**al** *a* critico(a); ~**ally** *ad* (*speak etc*) criticamente; ~**ally ill** gravemente malato; ~**ism** ['krɪtɪsɪzm] *n* critica; ~**ize** ['krɪtɪsaɪz] *vt* criticare.

croak [krəuk] *vi* gracchiare; (*frog*) gracidare.

crochet ['krəuʃeɪ] *n* lavoro all'uncinetto.

crockery ['krɔkərɪ] *n* vasellame *m*.

crocodile ['krɔkədaɪl] *n* coccodrillo.

crocus ['krəukəs] *n* croco.

croft [krɔft] *n* (*Brit*) piccolo podere *m*.

crony ['krəunɪ] *n* (*col*) amicone/a.

crook [kruk] *n* truffatore *m*; (*of shepherd*) bastone *m*; ~**ed** ['krukɪd] *a* curvo(a), storto(a); (*action*) disonesto(a).

crop [krɔp] *n* (*produce*) coltivazione *f*; (*amount produced*) raccolto; (*riding* ~) frustino; **to** ~ **up** *vi* presentarsi.

croquette [krə'kɛt] *n* crocchetta.

cross [krɔs] *n* croce *f*; (*BIOL*) incrocio // *vt* (*street etc*) attraversare; (*arms, legs, BIOL*) incrociare; (*cheque*) sbarrare // *a* di cattivo umore; **to** ~ **o.s.** fare il segno della croce, segnarsi; **to** ~ **out** *vt* cancellare; **to** ~ **over** *vi* attraversare; ~**bar** *n* traversa; ~**country (race)** *n* cross-country *m inv*; ~**examine** *vt*

(*LAW*) interrogare in contraddittorio; ~**-eyed** *a* strabico(a); ~**fire** *n* fuoco incrociato; ~**ing** *n* incrocio; (*sea passage*) traversata; (*also*: pedestrian ~**ing**) passaggio pedonale; ~**ing guard** *n* (*US*) *dipendente comunale che aiuta i bambini ad attraversare la strada*; ~ **purposes** *npl*: **to be at** ~ **purposes** non parlare della stessa cosa; ~**-reference** *n* rinvio, rimando; ~**roads** *n* incrocio; ~ **section** *n* (*BIOL*) sezione *f* trasversale; (*in population*) settore *m* rappresentativo; ~**walk** *n* (*US*) strisce *fpl* pedonali, passaggio pedonale; ~**wind** *n* vento di traverso; ~**wise** *ad* di traverso; ~**word** *n* cruciverba *m inv*.

crotch [krɔtʃ] *n* (*of garment*) pattina.

crotchety ['krɔtʃɪtɪ] *a* (*person*) burbero(a).

crouch [krautʃ] *vi* acquattarsi; rannicchiarsi.

crouton ['kruːtɔn] *n* crostino.

crow [krəu] *n* (*bird*) cornacchia; (*of cock*) canto del gallo // *vi* (*cock*) cantare; (*fig*) vantarsi; cantar vittoria.

crowbar ['krəubɑː*] *n* piede *m* di porco.

crowd [kraud] *n* folla // *vt* affollare, stipare // *vi* affollarsi; ~**ed** *a* affollato(a); ~**ed with** stipato(a) di.

crown [kraun] *n* corona; (*of head*) calotta cranica; (*of hat*) cocuzzolo; (*of hill*) cima // *vt* incoronare; ~ **jewels** *npl* gioielli *mpl* della Corona; ~ **prince** *n* principe *m* ereditario.

crow's feet *npl* zampe *fpl* di gallina.

crucial ['kruːʃl] *a* cruciale, decisivo(a).

crucifix ['kruːsɪfɪks] *n* crocifisso; ~**ion** [-'fɪkʃən] *n* crocifissione *f*.

crude [kruːd] *a* (*materials*) greggio(a); non raffinato(a); (*fig: basic*) crudo(a), primitivo(a); (: *vulgar*) rozzo(a), grossolano(a); ~ (**oil**) *n* (petrolio) greggio.

cruel ['kruəl] *a* crudele; ~**ty** *n* crudeltà *f inv*.

cruet ['kruːɪt] *n* ampolla.

cruise [kruːz] *n* crociera // *vi* andare a velocità di crociera; (*taxi*) circolare; ~**r** *n* incrociatore *m*.

crumb [krʌm] *n* briciola.

crumble ['krʌmbl] *vt* sbriciolare // *vi* sbriciolarsi; (*plaster etc*) sgretolarsi; (*land, earth*) franare; (*building, fig*) crollare; **crumbly** *a* friabile.

crumpet ['krʌmpɪt] *n* specie di frittella.

crumple ['krʌmpl] *vt* raggrinzare, spiegazzare.

crunch [krʌntʃ] *vt* sgranocchiare; (*underfoot*) scricchiolare // *n* (*fig*) punto *or* momento cruciale; ~**y** *a* croccante.

crusade [kruː'seɪd] *n* crociata.

crush [krʌʃ] *n* folla // *vt* schiacciare; (*crumple*) sgualcire.

crust [krʌst] *n* crosta.

crutch [krʌtʃ] *n* gruccia.

crux [krʌks] n nodo.
cry [kraɪ] vi piangere; (shout: also: ~ out) urlare // n urlo, grido; **to ~ off** vi ritirarsi.
cryptic ['krɪptɪk] a ermetico(a).
crystal ['krɪstl] n cristallo; **~-clear** a cristallino(a).
cub [kʌb] n cucciolo; (also: ~ scout) lupetto.
Cuba ['kju:bə] n Cuba.
cubbyhole ['kʌbɪhəul] n angolino.
cube [kju:b] n cubo // vt (MATH) elevare al cubo; **cubic** a cubico(a); (metre, foot) cubo(a); **cubic capacity** n cilindrata.
cubicle ['kju:bɪkl] n scompartimento separato; cabina.
cuckoo ['kuku:] n cucù m inv; ~ **clock** n orologio a cucù.
cucumber ['kju:kʌmbə*] n cetriolo.
cuddle ['kʌdl] vt abbracciare, coccolare // vi abbracciarsi.
cue [kju:] n (snooker ~) stecca; (THEATRE etc) segnale m.
cuff [kʌf] n (Brit: of shirt, coat etc) polsino; (US: of trousers) risvolto; **off the ~** ad improvvisando; **~link** n gemello.
cuisine [kwɪ'zi:n] n cucina.
cul-de-sac ['kʌldəsæk] n vicolo cieco.
culminate ['kʌlmɪneɪt] vi: **to ~ in** culminare con; **culmination** [-'neɪʃən] n culmine m.
culottes [kju:'lɒts] npl gonna f pantalone inv.
culpable ['kʌlpəbl] a colpevole.
culprit ['kʌlprɪt] n colpevole m/f.
cult [kʌlt] n culto.
cultivate ['kʌltɪveɪt] vt (also fig) coltivare; **cultivation** [-'veɪʃən] n coltivazione f.
cultural ['kʌltʃərəl] a culturale.
culture ['kʌltʃə*] n (also fig) cultura; **~d** a colto(a).
cumbersome ['kʌmbəsəm] a ingombrante.
cunning ['kʌnɪŋ] n astuzia, furberia // a astuto(a), furbo(a).
cup [kʌp] n tazza; (prize) coppa.
cupboard ['kʌbəd] n armadio.
cup-tie ['kʌptaɪ] n (Brit) partita di coppa.
curate ['kjuərɪt] n cappellano.
curator [kjuə'reɪtə*] n direttore m (di museo etc).
curb [kə:b] vt tenere a freno // n freno; (US) = **kerb**.
curdle ['kə:dl] vi cagliare.
cure [kjuə*] vt guarire; (CULIN) trattare; affumicare; essiccare // n rimedio.
curfew ['kə:fju:] n coprifuoco.
curio ['kjuərɪəu] n curiosità f inv.
curiosity [kjuərɪ'ɒsɪtɪ] n curiosità.
curious ['kjuərɪəs] a curioso(a).
curl [kə:l] n riccio // vt ondulare; (tightly)

arricciare // vi arricciarsi; **to ~ up** vi avvolgersi a spirale; rannicchiarsi; **~er** n bigodino.
curly ['kə:lɪ] a ricciuto(a).
currant ['kʌrnt] n uva passa.
currency ['kʌrnsɪ] n moneta; **to gain ~** (fig) acquistare larga diffusione.
current ['kʌrnt] a, n corrente (f); ~ **account** n (Brit) conto corrente; ~ **affairs** npl attualità fpl; **~ly** ad attualmente.
curriculum, pl **~s** or **curricula** [kə'rɪkjuləm, -lə] n curriculum m inv; ~ **vitae (CV)** n curriculum vitae m inv.
curry ['kʌrɪ] n curry m inv // vt: **to ~ favour with** cercare di attirarsi i favori di.
curse [kə:s] vt maledire // vi bestemmiare // n maledizione f; bestemmia.
cursor ['kə:sə*] n (COMPUT) cursore m.
cursory ['kə:sərɪ] a superficiale.
curt [kə:t] a secco(a).
curtail [kə:'teɪl] vt (visit etc) accorciare; (expenses etc) ridurre, decurtare.
curtain ['kə:tn] n tenda.
curts(e)y ['kə:tsɪ] n inchino, riverenza // vi fare un inchino or una riverenza.
curve [kə:v] n curva // vi curvarsi.
cushion ['kuʃən] n cuscino // vt (shock) fare da cuscinetto a.
custard ['kʌstəd] n (for pouring) crema.
custodian [kʌs'təudɪən] n custode m/f.
custody ['kʌstədɪ] n (of child) tutela; (for offenders) arresto.
custom ['kʌstəm] n costume m, usanza; (LAW) consuetudine f; (COMM) clientela; **~ary** a consueto(a).
customer ['kʌstəmə*] n cliente m/f.
customized ['kʌstəmaɪzd] a (car etc) fuoriserie inv.
custom-made ['kʌstəm'meɪd] a (clothes) fatto(a) su misura; (other goods) fatto(a) su ordinazione.
customs ['kʌstəmz] npl dogana; ~ **officer** n doganiere m.
cut [kʌt] vb (pt, pp **cut**) vt tagliare; (shape, make) intagliare; (reduce) ridurre // vi tagliare; (intersect) tagliarsi // n taglio; (in salary etc) riduzione f; **to ~ a tooth** mettere un dente; **to ~ down** vt (tree etc) abbattere // vt fus (also: ~ **down on**) ridurre; **to ~ off** vt tagliare; (fig) isolare; **to ~ out** vt tagliare fuori; eliminare; ritagliare; **to ~ up** vt (paper, meat) tagliare a pezzi; **~back** n riduzione f.
cute [kju:t] a grazioso(a); (clever) astuto(a).
cuticle ['kju:tɪkl] n (on nail) pellicina, cuticola.
cutlery ['kʌtlərɪ] n posate fpl.
cutlet ['kʌtlɪt] n costoletta.
cut: **~out** n interruttore m; (cardboard

~) ritaglio; **~-price**, (US) **~-rate** a a prezzo ridotto; **~throat** n assassino // a (razor) da barbiere; (competition) spietato(a).

cutting ['kʌtɪŋ] a tagliente; (fig) pungente // n (Brit: from newspaper) ritaglio (di giornale).

CV n abbr = **curriculum vitae**.

cwt abbr = **hundredweight(s)**.

cyanide ['saɪənaɪd] n cianuro.

cycle ['saɪkl] n ciclo; (bicycle) bicicletta // vi andare in bicicletta.

cycling ['saɪklɪŋ] n ciclismo.

cyclist ['saɪklɪst] n ciclista m/f.

cygnet ['sɪgnɪt] n cigno giovane.

cylinder ['sɪlɪndə*] n cilindro; **~-head gasket** n guarnizione f della testata del cilindro.

cymbals ['sɪmblz] npl cembali mpl.

cynic ['sɪnɪk] n cinico/a; **~al** a cinico(a); **~ism** ['sɪnɪsɪzəm] n cinismo.

Cypriot ['sɪprɪət] a, n cipriota (m/f).

Cyprus ['saɪprəs] n Cipro.

cyst [sɪst] n cisti f inv.

cystitis [sɪs'taɪtɪs] n cistite f.

czar [zɑ:*] n zar m inv.

Czech [tʃɛk] a ceco(a) // n ceco/a; (LING) ceco.

Czechoslovakia [tʃɛkəslə'vækɪə] n Cecoslovacchia; **~n** a, n cecoslovacco(a).

D

D [di:] n (MUS) re m.

dab [dæb] vt (eyes, wound) tamponare; (paint, cream) applicare (con leggeri colpetti).

dabble ['dæbl] vi: to ~ in occuparsi (da dilettante) di.

dad, daddy [dæd, 'dædɪ] n babbo, papà m inv.

daffodil ['dæfədɪl] n trombone m, giunchiglia.

daft [dɑ:ft] a sciocco(a).

dagger ['dægə*] n pugnale m.

daily ['deɪlɪ] a quotidiano(a), giornaliero(a) // n quotidiano // ad tutti i giorni.

dainty ['deɪntɪ] a delicato(a), grazioso(a).

dairy ['dɛərɪ] n (shop) latteria; (on farm) caseificio // a caseario(a); ~ **produce** n latticini mpl.

dais ['deɪɪs] n pedana, palco.

daisy ['deɪzɪ] n margherita; ~ **wheel** n (on printer) margherita.

dale [deɪl] n valle f.

dam [dæm] n diga // vt sbarrare; costruire dighe su.

damage ['dæmɪdʒ] n danno, danni mpl; (fig) danno // vt danneggiare; (fig) recar danno a; **~s** npl (LAW) danni.

damn [dæm] vt condannare; (curse) maledire // n (col): **I don't give a ~** non

me ne importa un fico // a (col: also: ~ed): **this ~** ... questo maledetto ...; ~ (it)! accidenti!

damp [dæmp] a umido(a) // n umidità, umido // vt (also: ~en: cloth, rag) inumidire, bagnare; (enthusiasm etc) spegnere.

damson ['dæmzən] n susina damaschina.

dance [dɑ:ns] n danza, ballo; (ball) ballo // vi ballare; ~ **hall** n dancing m inv, sala da ballo; **~r** n danzatore/trice; (professional) ballerino/a.

dancing ['dɑ:nsɪŋ] n danza, ballo.

dandelion ['dændɪlaɪən] n dente m di leone.

dandruff ['dændrəf] n forfora.

Dane [deɪn] n danese m/f.

danger ['deɪndʒə*] n pericolo; **there is a ~ of fire** c'è pericolo di incendio; **in ~** in pericolo; **he was in ~ of falling** rischiava di cadere; **~ous** a pericoloso(a).

dangle ['dæŋgl] vt dondolare; (fig) far balenare // vi pendolare.

Danish ['deɪnɪʃ] a danese // n (LING) danese m.

dapper ['dæpə*] a lindo(a).

dare [dɛə*] vt: to ~ **sb** to do sfidare qn a fare // vi: to ~ (to) do sth osare fare qc; **I ~ say** (I suppose) immagino (che); **~devil** n scavezzacollo m/f; **daring** a audace, ardito(a) // n audacia.

dark [dɑ:k] a (night, room) buio(a), scuro(a); (colour, complexion) scuro(a); (fig) cupo(a), tetro(a), nero(a) // n: in the ~ al buio; in the ~ about (fig) all'oscuro di; after ~ a notte fatta; **~en** vt (room) oscurare; (photo, painting) far scuro(a) // vi oscurarsi; imbrunirsi; ~ **glasses** npl occhiali mpl scuri; **~ness** n oscurità, buio; ~ **room** n camera oscura.

darling ['dɑ:lɪŋ] a caro(a) // n tesoro.

darn [dɑ:n] vt rammendare.

dart [dɑ:t] n freccetta // vi: to ~ **towards** precipitarsi verso; to ~ **away** guizzare via; **~s** n tiro al bersaglio (con freccette); **~board** n bersaglio (per freccette).

dash [dæʃ] n (sign) lineetta; (small quantity) punta // vt (missile) gettare; (hopes) infrangere // vi: to ~ **towards** precipitarsi verso; to ~ **away** or **off** vi scappare via.

dashboard ['dæʃbɔ:d] n (AUT) cruscotto.

dashing ['dæʃɪŋ] a ardito(a).

data ['deɪtə] npl dati mpl; **~base** n base f di dati, data base m inv; ~ **processing** n elaborazione f (elettronica) dei dati.

date [deɪt] n data; appuntamento; (fruit) dattero // vt datare; ~ **of birth** data di nascita; to ~ ad fino a oggi; **out of ~** scaduto(a); (old-fashioned) passato(a) di moda; **~d** a passato(a) di moda.

daub [dɔ:b] vt imbrattare.

daughter ['dɔ:tə*] n figlia; ~-in-law n nuora.

daunt [dɔ:nt] vt intimidire; ~ing a non invidiabile.

dawdle ['dɔ:dl] vi bighellonare.

dawn [dɔ:n] n alba // vi (day) spuntare; (fig) venire in mente; it ~ed on him that ... gli è venuto in mente che ...

day [deɪ] n giorno; (as duration) giornata; (period of time, age) tempo, epoca; the ~ before il giorno avanti or prima; the ~ after, the following ~ il giorno dopo or seguente; the ~ after tomorrow dopodomani; the ~ before yesterday l'altroieri; by ~ di giorno; ~break n spuntar m del giorno; ~dream vi sognare a occhi aperti; ~light n luce f del giorno; ~ return n (Brit) biglietto giornaliero di andata e ritorno; ~time n giorno; ~-to- a (life, organization) quotidiano(a).

daze [deɪz] vt (subject: drug) inebetire; (: blow) stordire // n: in a ~ inebetito(a); stordito(a).

dazzle ['dæzl] vt abbagliare.

DC abbr (= direct current) c.c.

deacon ['di:kən] n diacono.

dead [dɛd] a morto(a); (numb) intirizzito(a) // ad assolutamente, perfettamente; he was shot ~ fu colpito a morte; ~ on time in perfetto orario; ~ tired stanco(a) morto(a); to stop ~ fermarsi in tronco; the ~ i morti; ~en vt (blow, sound) ammortire; (make numb) intirizzire; ~ end n vicolo cieco; ~ heat n (SPORT): to finish in a ~ heat finire alla pari; ~line n scadenza; ~lock n punto morto; ~ loss n: to be a ~ loss (col: person, thing) non valere niente; ~ly a mortale; (weapon, poison) micidiale; ~pan a a faccia impassibile.

deaf [dɛf] a sordo(a); ~en vt assordare; ~-mute n sordomuto/a; ~ness n sordità.

deal [di:l] n accordo; (business ~) affare m // vt (pt, pp dealt [dɛlt]) (blow, cards) dare; a great ~ (of) molto(a); to ~ in vt fus occuparsi di; to ~ with vt fus (COMM) fare affari con, trattare con; (handle) occuparsi di; (be about: book etc) trattare di; ~er n commerciante m/f; ~ings npl (COMM) relazioni fpl; (relations) rapporti mpl.

dean [di:n] n (REL) decano; (SCOL) preside m di facoltà (or di collegio).

dear [dɪə*] a caro(a) // n: my ~ caro mio/cara mia; ~ me! Dio mio!; D~ Sir/Madam (in letter) Egregio Signore/Egregia Signora; D~ Mr/Mrs X Gentile Signor/Signora X; ~ly ad (love) moltissimo; (pay) a caro prezzo.

death [dɛθ] n morte f; (ADMIN) decesso; ~ certificate n atto di decesso; ~ duties npl (Brit) imposta or tassa di successione; ~ly a di morte; ~ penalty n pena di morte; ~ rate n indice m di mortalità.

debacle [dɪ'bækl] n fiasco.

debar [dɪ'bɑ:*] vt: to ~ sb from doing impedire a qn di fare.

debase [dɪ'beɪs] vt (currency) adulterare; (person) degradare.

debatable [dɪ'beɪtəbl] a discutibile.

debate [dɪ'beɪt] n dibattito // vt dibattere; discutere.

debauchery [dɪ'bɔːtʃərɪ] n dissolutezza.

debit ['dɛbɪt] n debito // vt: to ~ a sum to sb or to sb's account addebitare una somma a qn.

debris ['dɛbri:] n detriti mpl.

debt [dɛt] n debito; to be in ~ essere indebitato(a); ~or n debitore/trice.

debunk [di:'bʌŋk] vt (theory, claim) smentire.

début ['deɪbju:] n debutto.

decade ['dɛkeɪd] n decennio.

decadence ['dɛkədəns] n decadenza.

decaffeinated [dɪ'kæfɪneɪtɪd] a decaffeinato(a).

decanter [dɪ'kæntə*] n caraffa.

decay [dɪ'keɪ] n decadimento; imputridimento; (fig) rovina; (also: tooth ~) carie f // vi (rot) imputridire; (fig) andare in rovina.

deceased [dɪ'si:st] n defunto/a.

deceit [dɪ'si:t] n inganno; ~ful a ingannevole, perfido(a).

deceive [dɪ'si:v] vt ingannare.

December [dɪ'sɛmbə*] n dicembre m.

decent ['di:sənt] a decente; they were very ~ about it si sono comportati da signori riguardo a ciò.

deception [dɪ'sɛpʃən] n inganno.

deceptive [dɪ'sɛptɪv] a ingannevole.

decide [dɪ'saɪd] vt (person) far prendere una decisione a; (question, argument) risolvere, decidere // vi decidere, decidersi; to ~ to do/that decidere di fare/che; to ~ on decidere per; ~d a (resolute) deciso(a); (clear, definite) netto(a), chiaro(a); ~dly [-dɪdlɪ] ad indubbiamente; decisamente.

decimal ['dɛsɪməl] a, n decimale (m); ~ point n ~ virgola.

decipher [dɪ'saɪfə*] vt decifrare.

decision [dɪ'sɪʒən] n decisione f.

decisive [dɪ'saɪsɪv] a decisivo(a).

deck [dɛk] n (NAUT) ponte m; (of bus): top ~ imperiale m; (of cards) mazzo; ~chair n sedia a sdraio.

declaration [dɛklə'reɪʃən] n dichiarazione f.

declare [dɪ'klɛə*] vt dichiarare.

decline [dɪ'klaɪn] n (decay) declino; (lessening) ribasso // vt declinare; rifiutare // vi declinare; diminuire.

decode [di:'kəʊd] vt decifrare.

decompose [di:kəm'pəʊz] vi decomporre.

décor ['deɪkɔ:*] n decorazione f.

decorate ['dɛkəreɪt] vt (adorn, give a medal to) decorare; (paint and paper) tinteggiare e tappezzare; **decoration** [-'reɪʃən] n (medal etc, adornment) decorazione f; **decorator** n decoratore m.

decorum [dɪ'kɔ:rəm] n decoro.

decoy ['di:kɔɪ] n zimbello.

decrease n ['di:kri:s] diminuzione f // vt, vi [di:'kri:s] diminuire.

decree [dɪ'kri:] n decreto; ~ **nisi** [-'naɪsaɪ] n sentenza provvisoria di divorzio.

dedicate ['dedɪkeɪt] vt consacrare; (book etc) dedicare.

dedication [dedɪ'keɪʃən] n (devotion) dedizione f.

deduce [dɪ'dju:s] vt dedurre.

deduct [dɪ'dʌkt] vt: to ~ sth (from) dedurre qc (da); (from wage etc) trattenere qc (da); ~**ion** [dɪ'dʌkʃən] n (deducting) deduzione f; (from wage etc) trattenuta; (deducing) deduzione f, conclusione f.

deed [di:d] n azione f, atto; (LAW) atto.

deep [di:p] a profondo(a); **4 metres** ~ profondo(a) 4 metri // ad: **spectators stood 20** ~ c'erano 20 file di spettatori; ~**en** vt (hole) approfondire // vi approfondirsi; (darkness) farsi più buio; ~**-freeze** n congelatore m // vt congelare; ~**-fry** vt friggere in olio abbondante; ~**ly** ad profondamente; ~**sea diving** n immersione f in alto mare.

deer [dɪə*] n (pl inv): the ~ i cervidi; (red) ~ cervo; (fallow) ~ daino; (roe) ~ capriolo.

deface [dɪ'feɪs] vt imbrattare.

default [dɪ'fɔ:lt] vi (LAW) essere contumace; (gen) essere inadempiente // n (COMPUT: also: ~ **value**) default m inv; **by** ~ (LAW) in contumacia; (SPORT) per abbandono.

defeat [dɪ'fi:t] n sconfitta // vt (team, opponents) sconfiggere; (fig: plans, efforts) frustrare; ~**ist** a, n disfattista (m/f).

defect n ['di:fɛkt] difetto // vi [dɪ'fɛkt]: to ~ **to the enemy** passare al nemico; ~**ive** [dɪ'fɛktɪv] a difettoso(a).

defence, (US) **defense** [dɪ'fɛns] n difesa; **in** ~ **of** in difesa di; ~**less** a senza difesa.

defend [dɪ'fɛnd] vt difendere; ~**ant** n imputato/a; ~**er** n difensore m.

defense [dɪ'fɛns] n (US) = **defence**.

defer [dɪ'fɜ:*] vt (postpone) differire, rinviare // vi: to ~ **to** rimettersi a.

defiance [dɪ'faɪəns] n sfida; **in** ~ **of** a dispetto di.

defiant [dɪ'faɪənt] a (attitude) di sfida; (person) ribelle.

deficiency [dɪ'fɪʃənsɪ] n deficienza; carenza.

deficit ['dɛfɪsɪt] n disavanzo.

defile vb [dɪ'faɪl] vt contaminare // vi sfilare // n ['di:faɪl] gola, stretta.

define [dɪ'faɪn] vt definire.

definite ['dɛfɪnɪt] a (fixed) definito(a), preciso(a); (clear, obvious) ben definito(a), esatto(a); (LING) determinativo(a); **he was** ~ **about it** ne era sicuro; ~**ly** ad indubbiamente.

definition [dɛfɪ'nɪʃən] n definizione f.

deflate [di:'fleɪt] vt sgonfiare.

deflect [dɪ'flɛkt] vt deflettere, deviare.

deformed [dɪ'fɔ:md] a deforme.

defraud [dɪ'frɔ:d] vt defraudare.

defray [dɪ'freɪ] vt: to ~ **sb's expenses** sostenere le spese di qn.

defrost [di:'frɒst] vt (fridge) disgelare; ~**er** n (US: demister) sbrinatore m.

deft [dɛft] a svelto(a), destro(a).

defunct [dɪ'fʌŋkt] a defunto(a).

defuse [di:'fju:z] vt disinnescare.

defy [dɪ'faɪ] vt sfidare; (efforts etc) resistere a.

degenerate vi [dɪ'dʒɛnəreɪt] degenerare // a [dɪ'dʒɛnərɪt] degenere.

degree [dɪ'gri:] n grado; (SCOL) laurea (universitaria); **a** (first) ~ **in maths** una laurea in matematica; **by** ~**s** (gradually) gradualmente, a poco a poco; **to some** ~ fino a un certo punto, in certa misura.

dehydrated [di:haɪ'dreɪtɪd] a disidratato(a); (milk, eggs) in polvere.

de-ice [di:'aɪs] vt (windscreen) disgelare.

deign [deɪn] vi: to ~ **to do** degnarsi di fare.

deity ['di:ɪtɪ] n divinità f inv.

dejected [dɪ'dʒɛktɪd] a abbattuto(a), avvilito(a).

delay [dɪ'leɪ] vt (journey, operation) ritardare, rinviare; (travellers, trains) ritardare // vi: to ~ (in doing sth) ritardare (a fare qc) // n ritardo.

delectable [dɪ'lɛktəbl] a (person, food) delizioso(a).

delegate n ['dɛlɪgɪt] delegato/a // vt ['dɛlɪgeɪt] delegare.

delete [dɪ'li:t] vt cancellare.

deliberate a [dɪ'lɪbərɪt] (intentional) intenzionale; (slow) misurato(a) // vi [dɪ'lɪbəreɪt] deliberare, riflettere; ~**ly** ad (on purpose) deliberatamente.

delicacy ['dɛlɪkəsɪ] n delicatezza.

delicate ['dɛlɪkɪt] a delicato(a).

delicatessen [dɛlɪkə'tɛsn] n ≈ salumeria.

delicious [dɪ'lɪʃəs] a delizioso(a), squisito(a).

delight [dɪ'laɪt] n delizia, gran piacere m // vt dilettare; ~**ed** a: ~**ed** (at or with) contentissimo(a) (di), felice (di); ~**ed to do** felice di fare; ~**ful** a delizioso(a); incantevole.

delinquent [dɪ'lɪŋkwənt] a, n delinquente (m/f).

delirious [dɪ'lɪrɪəs] a: to be ~ delirare.

deliver [dɪ'lɪvə*] vt (mail) distribuire;

(goods) consegnare; *(speech)* pronunciare; *(free)* liberare; *(MED)* far partorire; **~y** *n* distribuzione *f*; consegna; *(of speaker)* dizione *f*; *(MED)* parto.

delude [dɪ'lu:d] *vt* deludere, illudere.

deluge ['dɛljuːdʒ] *n* diluvio.

delusion [dɪ'lu:ʒən] *n* illusione *f*.

delve [dɛlv] *vi*: to ~ into frugare in; *(subject)* far ricerche in.

demand [dɪ'mɑːnd] *vt* richiedere // *n* domanda; *(ECON, claim)* richiesta; in ~ ricercato(a), richiesto(a); on ~ a richiesta; **~ing** *a* *(boss)* esigente; *(work)* impegnativo(a).

demean [dɪ'miːn] *vt*: to ~ o.s. umiliarsi.

demeanour, *(US)* **demeanor** [dɪ'miːnə*] *n* comportamento; contegno.

demented [dɪ'mɛntɪd] *a* demente, impazzito(a).

demise [dɪ'maɪz] *n* decesso.

demister [diː'mɪstə*] *n* *(AUT)* sbrinatore *m*.

demo ['dɛməu] *n* *abbr* *(col*: = *demonstration)* manifestazione *f*.

demobilize [diː'məubɪlaɪz] *vt* smobilitare.

democracy [dɪ'mɔkrəsɪ] *n* democrazia.

democrat ['dɛməkræt] *n* democratico/a; **~ic** [dɛmə'krætɪk] *a* democratico(a).

demolish [dɪ'mɔlɪʃ] *vt* demolire.

demonstrate ['dɛmənstreɪt] *vt* dimostrare, provare // *vi*: to ~ *(for/against)* dimostrare (per/contro), manifestare (per/contro); **demonstration** [-'streɪʃən] *n* dimostrazione *f*; *(POL)* manifestazione *f*, dimostrazione; **demonstrator** *n* *(POL)* dimostrante *m/f*.

demote [dɪ'məut] *vt* far retrocedere.

demure [dɪ'mjuə*] *a* contegnoso(a).

den [dɛn] *n* tana, covo.

denatured alcohol [diː'neɪtʃəd-] *n* *(US)* alcool *m* *inv* denaturato.

denial [dɪ'naɪəl] *n* diniego; rifiuto.

denim ['dɛnɪm] *n* tessuto di cotone ritorto; **~s** *npl* blue jeans *mpl*.

Denmark ['dɛnmɑːk] *n* Danimarca.

denomination [dɪnɔmɪ'neɪʃən] *n* *(money)* valore *m*; *(REL)* confessione *f*.

denounce [dɪ'nauns] *vt* denunciare.

dense [dɛns] *a* fitto(a); *(stupid)* ottuso(a), duro(a).

density ['dɛnsɪtɪ] *n* densità *f inv*.

dent [dɛnt] *n* ammaccatura // *vt* *(also*: make a ~ in) ammaccare.

dental ['dɛntl] *a* dentale; ~ **surgeon** *n* medico/a dentista.

dentist ['dɛntɪst] *n* dentista *m/f*; **~ry** *n* odontoiatria.

denture(s) ['dɛntʃə(z)] *n(pl)* dentiera.

deny [dɪ'naɪ] *vt* negare; *(refuse)* rifiutare.

deodorant [diː'əudərənt] *n* deodorante *m*.

depart [dɪ'pɑːt] *vi* partire; to ~ from

(fig) deviare da.

department [dɪ'pɑːtmənt] *n* *(COMM)* reparto; *(SCOL)* sezione *f*, dipartimento; *(POL)* ministero; ~ **store** *n* grande magazzino.

departure [dɪ'pɑːtʃə*] *n* partenza; *(fig)*: ~ **from** deviazione *f* da; a new ~ una svolta (decisiva); ~ **lounge** *n* *(at airport)* sala d'attesa.

depend [dɪ'pɛnd] *vi*: to ~ on dipendere da; *(rely on)* contare su; it ~s dipende; ~ing on the result ... a seconda del risultato ...; **~able** *a* fidato(a); *(car etc)* affidabile; **~ant** *n* persona a carico; **~ent** *a*: to be **~ent** on dipendere da; *(child, relative)* essere a carico di // *n* = **~ant**.

depict [dɪ'pɪkt] *vt* *(in picture)* dipingere; *(in words)* descrivere.

depleted [dɪ'pliːtɪd] *a* diminuito(a).

deploy [dɪ'plɔɪ] *vt* dispiegare.

depopulation ['diːpɔpju'leɪʃən] *n* spopolamento.

deport [dɪ'pɔːt] *vt* deportare; espellere.

deportment [dɪ'pɔːtmənt] *n* portamento.

depose [dɪ'pəuz] *vt* deporre.

deposit [dɪ'pɔzɪt] *n* *(COMM, GEO)* deposito; *(of ore, oil)* giacimento; *(CHEM)* sedimento; *(part payment)* acconto; *(for hired goods etc)* cauzione *f* // *vt* depositare; dare in acconto; mettere *or* lasciare in deposito; ~ **account** *n* conto vincolato.

depot ['dɛpəu] *n* deposito.

depreciate [dɪ'priːʃɪeɪt] *vt* svalutare // *vi* svalutarsi.

depress [dɪ'prɛs] *vt* deprimere; *(press down)* premere; **~ed** *a* *(person)* depresso(a), abbattuto(a); *(area)* depresso(a); **~ing** *a* deprimente; **~ion** [dɪ'prɛʃən] *n* depressione *f*.

deprivation [dɛprɪ'veɪʃən] *n* privazione *f*; *(loss)* perdita.

deprive [dɪ'praɪv] *vt*: to ~ sb of privare qn di; **~d** *a* disgraziato(a).

depth [dɛpθ] *n* profondità *f inv*; in the ~s of nel profondo di; nel cuore di; in the ~s of winter in pieno inverno.

deputize ['dɛpjutaɪz] *vi*: to ~ for svolgere le funzioni di.

deputy ['dɛpjutɪ] *a*: ~ **head** *(SCOL)* vice-preside *m/f* // *n* *(replacement)* supplente *m/f*; *(second in command)* vice *m/f*.

derail [dɪ'reɪl] *vt* far deragliare; to be **~ed** deragliare.

deranged [dɪ'reɪndʒd] *a*: to be (mentally) ~ essere pazzo(a).

derby ['dəːbɪ] *n* *(US: bowler hat)* bombetta.

derelict ['dɛrɪlɪkt] *a* abbandonato(a).

deride [dɪ'raɪd] *vt* deridere.

derisory [dɪ'raɪsərɪ] *a* *(sum)* irrisorio(a); *(laughter, person)* beffardo(a).

derive [dɪ'raɪv] *vt*: to ~ sth from derivare qc da; trarre qc da // *vi*: to ~

from derivare da.

derogatory [dɪ'rɔgətərɪ] a denigratorio(a).

derrick ['derɪk] n gru f inv; (for oil) derrick m inv.

derv [də:v] n (Brit) gasolio.

descend [dɪ'send] vt, vi discendere, scendere; **to ~ from** discendere da; **~ant** n discendente m/f.

descent [dɪ'sent] n discesa; (origin) discendenza, famiglia.

describe [dɪs'kraɪb] vt descrivere; **description** [-'krɪpʃən] n descrizione f; (sort) genere m, specie f.

desecrate ['desɪkreɪt] vt profanare.

desert n ['dezət] deserto // vb [dɪ'zə:t] vt lasciare, abbandonare // vi (MIL) disertare; **~er** n disertore m; **~ island** n isola deserta; **~s** [dɪ'zə:ts] npl: **to get one's just ~s** avere ciò che si merita.

deserve [dɪ'zə:v] vt meritare; **deserving** a (person) meritevole, degno(a); (cause) meritorio(a).

design [dɪ'zaɪn] n (sketch) disegno; (layout, shape) linea; (pattern) fantasia; (COMM) disegno tecnico; (intention) intenzione f // vt disegnare; progettare; **to have ~s on** aver mire su.

designer [dɪ'zaɪnə*] n (ART, TECH) disegnatore/trice; (of fashion) modellista m/f.

desire [dɪ'zaɪə*] n desiderio, voglia // vt desiderare, volere.

desk [desk] n (in office) scrivania; (for pupil) banco; (Brit: in shop, restaurant) cassa; (in hotel) ricevimento; (at airport) accettazione f.

desolate ['desəlɪt] a desolato(a).

despair [dɪs'peə*] n disperazione f // vi: **to ~ of** disperare di.

despatch [dɪs'pætʃ] n, vt = dispatch.

desperate ['despərɪt] a disperato(a); (fugitive) capace di tutto; **~ly** ad disperatamente; (very) terribilmente, estremamente.

desperation [despə'reɪʃən] n disperazione f.

despicable [dɪs'pɪkəbl] a disprezzabile.

despise [dɪs'paɪz] vt disprezzare, sdegnare.

despite [dɪs'paɪt] prep malgrado, a dispetto di, nonostante.

despondent [dɪs'pɔndənt] a abbattuto(a), scoraggiato(a).

dessert [dɪ'zə:t] n dolce m; frutta; **~spoon** n cucchiaio da dolci.

destination [destɪ'neɪʃən] n destinazione f.

destiny ['destɪnɪ] n destino.

destitute ['destɪtju:t] a indigente, bisognoso(a).

destroy [dɪs'trɔɪ] vt distruggere; **~er** n (NAUT) cacciatorpediniere m.

destruction [dɪs'trʌkʃən] n distruzione f.

detach [dɪ'tætʃ] vt staccare, distaccare;

~ed a (attitude) distante; **~ed house** n villa; **~ment** n (MIL) distaccamento; (fig) distacco.

detail ['di:teɪl] n particolare m, dettaglio // vt dettagliare, particolareggiare; **in ~** nei particolari; **~ed** a particolareggiato(a).

detain [dɪ'teɪn] vt trattenere; (in captivity) detenere.

detect [dɪ'tekt] vt scoprire, scorgere; (MED, POLICE, RADAR etc) individuare; **~ion** [dɪ'tekʃən] n scoperta; individuazione f; **~ive** n investigatore/trice; **private ~ive** investigatore m privato; **~ive story** n giallo.

detention [dɪ'tenʃən] n detenzione f; (SCOL) permanenza forzata per punizione.

deter [dɪ'tə:*] vt dissuadere.

detergent [dɪ'tə:dʒənt] n detersivo.

deteriorate [dɪ'tɪərɪəreɪt] vi deteriorarsi.

determine [dɪ'tə:mɪn] vt determinare; **to ~ to do** decidere da fare; **~d** a (person) risoluto(a), deciso(a).

detour ['di:tuə*] n deviazione f // vt (US: traffic) deviare.

detract [dɪ'trækt] vt: **to ~ from** detrarre da.

detriment ['detrɪmənt] n: **to the ~ of** a detrimento di; **~al** [detrɪ'mentl] a: **~al to** dannoso(a) a, nocivo(a) a.

devaluation [dɪvælju'eɪʃən] n svalutazione f.

devastating ['devəsteɪtɪŋ] a devastatore(trice).

develop [dɪ'veləp] vt sviluppare; (habit) prendere (gradualmente) // vi svilupparsi; (facts, symptoms: appear) manifestarsi, rivelarsi; **~ing country** paese m in via di sviluppo; **~ment** n sviluppo.

device [dɪ'vaɪs] n (apparatus) congegno.

devil ['devl] n diavolo; demonio.

devious ['di:vɪəs] a (means) indiretto(a), tortuoso(a); (person) subdolo(a).

devise [dɪ'vaɪz] vt escogitare, concepire.

devoid [dɪ'vɔɪd] a: **~ of** privo(a) di.

devolution [di:və'lu:ʃən] n (POL) decentramento.

devote [dɪ'vəut] vt: **to ~ sth to** dedicare qc a; **~d** a devoto(a); **to be ~d to** essere molto affezionato(a) a; **~e** [devəu'ti:] n (MUS, SPORT) appassionato/a.

devotion [dɪ'vəuʃən] n devozione f, attaccamento; (REL) atto di devozione, preghiera.

devour [dɪ'vauə*] vt divorare.

devout [dɪ'vaut] a pio(a), devoto(a).

dew [dju:] n rugiada.

dexterity [deks'terɪtɪ] n destrezza.

DHSS n abbr (= Department of Health and Social Security) ≈ ministero della Sanità e della Previdenza sociale.

diabetes [daɪə'bi:ti:z] n diabete m; dia-

betic [-'betɪk] *a*, *n* diabetico(a).

diabolical [daɪə'bɔlɪkl] *a* (*col: weather, behaviour*) orribile.

diagnosis, *pl* **diagnoses** [daɪəg'nəusɪs, -siːz] *n* diagnosi *f inv*.

diagonal [daɪ'ægənl] *a*, *n* diagonale (*f*).

diagram [daɪəgræm] *n* diagramma *m*.

dial ['daɪəl] *n* quadrante *m*; (*on telephone*) disco combinatore // *vt* (*number*) fare.

dialect ['daɪəlɛkt] *n* dialetto.

dialling ['daɪəlɪŋ]: ~ **code**, (*US*) **dial code** *n* prefisso; ~ **tone**, (*US*) **dial tone** *n* segnale *m* di linea libera.

dialogue ['daɪəlɔg] *n* dialogo.

diameter [daɪ'æmɪtə*] *n* diametro.

diamond ['daɪəmənd] *n* diamante *m*; (*shape*) rombo; ~s *npl* (*CARDS*) quadri *mpl*.

diaper ['daɪəpə*] *n* (*US*) pannolino.

diaphragm ['daɪəfræm] *n* diaframma *m*.

diarrhoea, (*US*) **diarrhea** [daɪə'riːə] *n* diarrea.

diary ['daɪərɪ] *n* (*daily account*) diario; (*book*) agenda.

dice [daɪs] *n* (*pl inv*) dado // *vt* (*CULIN*) tagliare a dadini.

Dictaphone ['dɪktəfəun] *n* ® dittafono ®.

dictate *vt* [dɪk'teɪt] dettare // *n* ['dɪkteɪt] dettame *m*.

dictation [dɪk'teɪʃən] *n* dettato.

dictator [dɪk'teɪtə*] *n* dittatore *m*; ~**ship** *n* dittatura.

dictionary ['dɪkʃənrɪ] *n* dizionario.

did [dɪd] *pt of* **do**.

didn't = **did not**.

die [daɪ] *n* (*pl* **dies**) conio; matrice *f*; stampo // *vi* morire; to be dying for sth/ to do sth morire dalla voglia di qc/di fare qc; to ~ **away** *vi* spegnersi a poco a poco; to ~ **down** *vi* abbassarsi; to ~ **out** *vi* estinguersi.

diehard ['daɪhɑːd] *n* reazionario/a.

Diesel ['diːzəl]: ~ **engine** *n* motore *m* diesel *inv*; ~ (**oil**) *n* gasolio (per motori diesel).

diet ['daɪət] *n* alimentazione *f*; (*restricted food*) dieta // *vi* (*also:* **be on a** ~) stare a dieta.

differ ['dɪfə*] *vi*: to ~ **from sth** differire da qc; essere diverso(a) da qc; to ~ **from sb over sth** essere in disaccordo con qn su qc; ~**ence** *n* differenza; (*quarrel*) screzio; ~**ent** *a* diverso(a); ~**entiate** [-'rɛnʃɪeɪt] *vi* differenziarsi; to ~**entiate between** discriminare *or* fare differenza fra.

difficult ['dɪfɪkəlt] *a* difficile; ~**y** *n* difficoltà *f inv*.

diffident ['dɪfɪdənt] *a* sfiduciato(a).

dig [dɪg] *vt* (*pt, pp* **dug**) (*hole*) scavare; (*garden*) vangare // *n* (*prod*) gomitata; (*fig*) frecciata; to ~ **in** *vi* (*MIL: also:* ~ o.s. **in**) trincerarsi; (*col: eat*) attaccare

a mangiare; to ~ **into** *vt fus* (*snow, soil*) scavare; to ~ **one's nails into** conficcare le unghie in; to ~ **up** *vt* scavare; (*tree etc*) sradicare.

digest [daɪ'dʒɛst] *vt* digerire; ~**ion** [dɪ'dʒɛstʃən] *n* digestione *f*; ~**ive** *a* (*juices, system*) digerente.

digit ['dɪdʒɪt] *n* cifra; (*finger*) dito; ~**al** *a* digitale.

dignified ['dɪgnɪfaɪd] *a* dignitoso(a).

dignity ['dɪgnɪtɪ] *n* dignità.

digress [daɪ'grɛs] *vi*: to ~ **from** divagare da.

digs [dɪgz] *npl* (*Brit col*) camera ammobiliata.

dilapidated [dɪ'læpɪdeɪtɪd] *a* cadente.

dilemma [daɪ'lɛmə] *n* dilemma *m*.

diligent ['dɪlɪdʒənt] *a* diligente.

dilute [daɪ'luːt] *vt* diluire; (*with water*) annacquare.

dim [dɪm] *a* (*light, eyesight*) debole; (*memory, outline*) vago(a); (*stupid*) lento(a) d'ingegno // *vt* (*light*) abbassare.

dime [daɪm] *n* (*US*) = 10 cents.

dimension [daɪ'mɛnʃən] *n* dimensione *f*.

diminish [dɪ'mɪnɪʃ] *vt*, *vi* diminuire.

diminutive [dɪ'mɪnjutɪv] *a* minuscolo(a) // *n* (*LING*) diminutivo.

dimmers ['dɪməz] *npl* (*US AUT*) anabbaglianti *mpl*; luci *fpl* di posizione.

dimple ['dɪmpl] *n* fossetta.

din [dɪn] *n* chiasso, fracasso.

dine [daɪn] *vi* pranzare.

dinghy ['dɪŋgɪ] *n* battello pneumatico; (*also:* **rubber** ~) gommone *m*; (*also:* **sailing** ~) dinghy *m inv*.

dingy ['dɪndʒɪ] *a* grigio(a).

dining ['daɪnɪŋ] *cpd*: ~ **car** *n* (*Brit*) vagone *m* ristorante; ~ **room** *n* sala da pranzo.

dinner ['dɪnə*] *n* (*lunch*) pranzo; (*evening meal*) cena; (*public*) banchetto; ~'s **ready!** a tavola!; ~ **jacket** *n* smoking *m inv*; ~ **party** *n* cena; ~ **time** *n* ora di pranzo (*or* cena).

dint [dɪnt] *n*: by ~ of a forza di.

dip [dɪp] *n* discesa; (*in sea*) bagno // *vt* immergere; bagnare; (*Brit AUT: lights*) abbassare // *vi* abbassarsi.

diphthong ['dɪfθɔŋ] *n* dittongo.

diploma [dɪ'pləumə] *n* diploma *m*.

diplomacy [dɪ'pləuməsɪ] *n* diplomazia.

diplomat ['dɪpləmæt] *n* diplomatico; ~**ic** [dɪplə'mætɪk] *a* diplomatico(a).

dipstick ['dɪpstɪk] *n* (*AUT*) indicatore *m* di livello dell'olio.

dire [daɪə*] *a* terribile; estremo(a).

direct [daɪ'rɛkt] *a* diretto(a) // *vt* dirigere; can you ~ me to ...? mi può indicare la strada per ...?

direction [dɪ'rɛkʃən] *n* direzione *f*; sense of ~ senso dell'orientamento; ~s *npl* (*advice*) chiarimenti *mpl*; ~s for use istruzioni *fpl*.

directly [dɪ'rɛktlɪ] *ad* (*in straight line*) direttamente; (*at once*) subito.

director [dɪ'rɛktə*] *n* direttore/trice; amministratore/trice; (*THEATRE, CINEMA*) regista *m/f*.

directory [dɪ'rɛktərɪ] *n* elenco.

dirt [dɜːt] *n* sporcizia; immondizia; ~-**cheap** *a* da due soldi; ~**y** *a* sporco(a) // *vt* sporcare; ~**y trick** *n* brutto scherzo.

disability [dɪsə'bɪlɪtɪ] *n* invalidità *f inv*; (*LAW*) incapacità *f inv*.

disabled [dɪs'eɪbld] *a* invalido(a); (*maimed*) mutilato(a); (*through illness, old age*) inabile.

disadvantage [dɪsəd'vɑːntɪdʒ] *n* svantaggio.

disagree [dɪsə'griː] *vi* (*differ*) discordare; (*be against, think otherwise*): **to ~ (with)** essere in disaccordo (con); dissentire (da); ~**able** *a* sgradevole; (*person*) antipatico(a); ~**ment** *n* disaccordo.

disappear [dɪsə'pɪə*] *vi* scomparire; ~**ance** *n* scomparsa.

disappoint [dɪsə'pɔɪnt] *vt* deludere; ~**ed** *a* deluso(a); ~**ing** *a* deludente; ~**ment** *n* delusione *f*.

disapproval [dɪsə'pruːvəl] *n* disapprovazione *f*.

disapprove [dɪsə'pruːv] *vi*: **to ~ of** disapprovare.

disarm [dɪs'ɑːm] *vt* disarmare; ~**ament** *n* disarmo.

disarray [dɪsə'reɪ] *n*: **in ~** (*army*) in rotta; (*organization*) in uno stato di confusione; (*clothes, hair*) in disordine.

disaster [dɪ'zɑːstə*]*n* disastro.

disband [dɪs'bænd] *vt* sbandare; (*MIL*) congedare // *vi* sciogliersi.

disbelief [ˈdɪsbə'liːf] *n* incredulità.

disc [dɪsk] *n* disco; (*COMPUT*) = **disk**.

discard [dɪs'kɑːd] *vt* (*old things*) scartare; (*fig*) abbandonare.

discern [dɪ'sɜːn] *vt* discernere, distinguere; ~**ing** *a* perspicace.

discharge *vt* [dɪs'tʃɑːdʒ] (*duties*) compiere; (*ELEC, waste etc*) scaricare; (*MED*) emettere; (*patient*) dimettere; (*employee*) licenziare; (*soldier*) congedare; (*defendant*) liberare // *n* ['dɪstʃɑːdʒ] (*ELEC*) scarica; (*MED*) emissione *f*; (*dismissal*) licenziamento; congedo; liberazione *f*.

disciple [dɪ'saɪpl] *n* discepolo.

discipline ['dɪsɪplɪn] *n* disciplina // *vt* disciplinare; (*punish*) punire.

disc jockey *n* disc jockey *m inv*.

disclaim [dɪs'kleɪm] *vt* negare, smentire.

disclose [dɪs'kləuz] *vt* rivelare, svelare; **disclosure** [-'kləuʒə*] *n* rivelazione *f*.

disco ['dɪskəu] *n abbr* = **discothèque**.

discoloured, (*US*) **discolored** [dɪs'kʌləd] *a* scolorito(a); ingiallito(a).

discomfort [dɪs'kʌmfət] *n* disagio; (*lack of comfort*) scomodità *f inv*.

disconcert [dɪskən'sɜːt] *vt* sconcertare.

disconnect [dɪskə'nɛkt] *vt* sconnettere, staccare; (*ELEC, RADIO*) staccare; (*gas, water*) chiudere.

disconsolate [dɪs'kɔnsəlɪt] *a* sconsolato(a).

discontent [dɪskən'tɛnt] *n* scontentezza; ~**ed** *a* scontento(a).

discontinue [dɪskən'tɪnjuː] *vt* smettere, cessare.

discord ['dɪskɔːd] *n* disaccordo; (*MUS*) dissonanza.

discothèque ['dɪskəutɛk] *n* discoteca.

discount *n* ['dɪskaunt] sconto // *vt* [dɪs'kaunt] scontare.

discourage [dɪs'kʌrɪdʒ] *vt* scoraggiare.

discourteous [dɪs'kɜːtɪəs] *a* scortese.

discover [dɪs'kʌvə*] *vt* scoprire; ~**y** *n* scoperta.

discredit [dɪs'krɛdɪt] *vt* screditare; mettere in dubbio.

discreet [dɪ'skriːt] *a* discreto(a).

discrepancy [dɪ'skrɛpənsɪ] *n* discrepanza.

discriminate [dɪ'skrɪmɪneɪt] *vi*: **to ~ between** distinguere tra; **to ~ against** discriminare contro; **discriminating** *a* fine, giudizioso(a); **discrimination** [-'neɪʃən] *n* discriminazione *f*; (*judgment*) discernimento.

discuss [dɪ'skʌs] *vt* discutere; (*debate*) dibattere; ~**ion** [dɪ'skʌʃən] *n* discussione *f*.

disdain [dɪs'deɪn] *n* disdegno.

disease [dɪ'ziːz] *n* malattia.

disembark [dɪsɪm'bɑːk] *vt, vi* sbarcare.

disengage [dɪsɪn'geɪdʒ] *vt* disimpegnare; (*TECH*) distaccare; (*AUT: clutch*) disinnestare.

disfigure [dɪs'fɪgə*] *vt* sfigurare.

disgrace [dɪs'greɪs] *n* vergogna; (*disfavour*) disgrazia // *vt* disonorare, far cadere in disgrazia; ~**ful** *a* scandaloso(a), vergognoso(a).

disgruntled [dɪs'grʌntld] *a* scontento(a), di cattivo umore.

disguise [dɪs'gaɪz] *n* travestimento // *vt* travestire; **in ~** travestito(a).

disgust [dɪs'gʌst] *n* disgusto, nausea // *vt* disgustare, far schifo a; ~**ing** *a* disgustoso(a); ripugnante.

dish [dɪʃ] *n* piatto; **to do** *or* **wash the ~es** fare i piatti; **to ~ up** *vt* servire; (*facts, statistics*) presentare; ~**cloth** *n* strofinaccio.

dishearten [dɪs'hɑːtn] *vt* scoraggiare.

dishevelled [dɪ'ʃɛvəld] *a* arruffato(a); scapigliato(a).

dishonest [dɪs'ɔnɪst] *a* disonesto(a).

dishonour, (*US*) **dishonor** [dɪs'ɔnə*] *n* disonore *m*; ~**able** *a* disonorevole.

dish towel *n* (*US*) strofinaccio dei piatti.

dishwasher ['dɪʃwɔʃə*] *n* lavastoviglie *f inv*; (*person*) sguattero/a.

disillusion [dɪsɪ'lu:ʒən] *vt* disilludere, disingannare // *n* disillusione *f*.

disincentive [dɪsɪn'sɛntɪv] *n*: to be a ~ essere demotivante; to be a ~ to sb demotivare qn.

disinfect [dɪsɪn'fɛkt] *vt* disinfettare; ~ant *n* disinfettante *m*.

disintegrate [dɪs'ɪntɪɡreɪt] *vi* disintegrarsi.

disinterested [dɪs'ɪntrəstɪd] *a* disinteressato(a).

disjointed [dɪs'dʒɔɪntɪd] *a* sconnesso(a).

disk [dɪsk] *n* (COMPUT) disco: single-/double-sided ~ disco a facciata singola/doppia; ~ drive *n* lettore *m*; ~ette *n* (US) = **disk**.

dislike [dɪs'laɪk] *n* antipatia, avversione *f* // *vt*: he ~s it non gli piace.

dislocate ['dɪsləkeɪt] *vt* slogare; disorganizzare.

dislodge [dɪs'lɔdʒ] *vt* rimuovere, staccare; (enemy) sloggiare.

disloyal [dɪs'lɔɪəl] *a* sleale.

dismal ['dɪzml] *a* triste, cupo(a).

dismantle [dɪs'mæntl] *vt* smantellare, smontare; (fort, warship) disarmare.

dismay [dɪs'meɪ] *n* costernazione *f* // *vt* sgomentare.

dismiss [dɪs'mɪs] *vt* congedare; (employee) licenziare; (idea) scacciare; (LAW) respingere; ~al *n* congedo; licenziamento.

dismount [dɪs'maunt] *vi* scendere.

disobedience [dɪsə'bi:dɪəns] *n* disubbidienza.

disobedient [dɪsə'bi:dɪənt] *a* disubbidiente.

disobey [dɪsə'beɪ] *vt* disubbidire.

disorder [dɪs'ɔ:də*] *n* disordine *m*; (rioting) tumulto; (MED) disturbo; ~ly *a* disordinato(a); tumultuoso(a).

disorientated [dɪs'ɔ:rɪənteɪtɪd] *a* disorientato(a).

disown [dɪs'əun] *vt* ripudiare.

disparaging [dɪs'pærɪdʒɪŋ] *a* spregiativo(a), sprezzante.

dispassionate [dɪs'pæʃənət] *a* calmo(a), freddo(a); imparziale.

dispatch [dɪs'pætʃ] *vt* spedire, inviare // *n* spedizione *f*, invio; (MIL, PRESS) dispaccio.

dispel [dɪs'pɛl] *vt* dissipare, scacciare.

dispensary [dɪs'pɛnsərɪ] *n* farmacia; (in chemist's) dispensario.

dispense [dɪs'pɛns] *vt* distribuire, amministrare; to ~ with *vt fus* fare a meno di; ~r *n* (container) distributore *m*; dispensing chemist *n* (Brit) farmacista *m/f*.

disperse [dɪs'pɜ:s] *vt* disperdere; (knowledge) disseminare // *vi* disperdersi.

dispirited [dɪs'pɪrɪtɪd] *a* scoraggiato(a), abbattuto(a).

displace [dɪs'pleɪs] *vt* spostare; ~d

person *n* (POL) profugo/a.

display [dɪs'pleɪ] *n* mostra; esposizione *f*; (of feeling etc) manifestazione *f*; (screen) schermo; (pej) ostentazione *f* // *vt* mostrare; (goods) esporre; (results) affiggere; (departure times) indicare.

displease [dɪs'pli:z] *vt* dispiacere a, scontentare; ~d with scontento di; displeasure [-'plɛʒə*] *n* dispiacere *m*.

disposable [dɪs'pəuzəbl] *a* (pack etc) a perdere; (income) disponibile; ~ nappy *n* pannolino di carta.

disposal [dɪs'pəuzl] *n* (of rubbish) evacuazione *f*; distruzione *f*; at one's ~ alla sua disposizione.

dispose [dɪs'pəuz] *vt* disporre; to ~ of *vt* (time, money) disporre di; (unwanted goods) sbarazzarsi di; (problem) eliminare; ~d *a*: ~d to do disposto(a) a fare; disposition [-'zɪʃən] *n* disposizione *f*; (temperament) carattere *m*.

disproportionate [dɪsprə'pɔ:ʃənət] *a* sproporzionato(a).

disprove [dɪs'pru:v] *vt* confutare.

dispute [dɪs'pju:t] *n* disputa; (also: industrial ~) controversia (sindacale) // *vt* contestare; (matter) discutere; (victory) disputare.

disqualify [dɪs'kwɔlɪfaɪ] *vt* (SPORT) squalificare; to ~ sb from sth/from doing rendere qn incapace a qc/a fare; squalificare qn da qc/da fare; to ~ sb from driving ritirare la patente a qn.

disquiet [dɪs'kwaɪət] *n* inquietudine *f*

disregard [dɪsrɪ'ɡɑ:d] *vt* non far caso a, non badare a.

disrepair [dɪsrɪ'pɛə*] *n* cattivo stato; to fall into ~ (building) andare in rovina; (street) deteriorarsi.

disreputable [dɪs'rɛpjutəbl] *a* (person) di cattiva fama.

disrupt [dɪs'rʌpt] *vt* mettere in disordine.

dissatisfaction [dɪssætɪs'fækʃən] *n* scontentezza, insoddisfazione *f*.

dissect [dɪ'sɛkt] *vt* sezionare.

dissent [dɪ'sɛnt] *n* dissenso.

dissertation [dɪsə'teɪʃən] *n* tesi *f inv*, dissertazione *f*.

disservice [dɪs'sɜ:vɪs] *n*: to do sb a ~ fare un cattivo servizio a qn.

dissimilar [dɪ'sɪmɪlə*] *a*: ~ (to) dissimile or diverso(a) (da).

dissipate ['dɪsɪpeɪt] *vt* dissipare; ~d *a* dissipato(a).

dissolute ['dɪsəlu:t] *a* dissoluto(a), licenzioso(a).

dissolution [dɪsə'lu:ʃən] *n* (of organization, marriage, POL) scioglimento.

dissolve [dɪ'zɔlv] *vt* dissolvere, sciogliere; (POL, marriage etc) sciogliere // *vi* dissolversi, sciogliersi; (fig) svanire.

distance ['dɪstns] *n* distanza; in the ~ in lontananza.

distant ['dɪstnt] *a* lontano(a), distante;

(manner) riservato(a), freddo(a).

distaste [dɪs'teɪst] *n* ripugnanza; **~ful** *a* ripugnante, sgradevole.

distended [dɪs'tɛndɪd] *a* *(stomach)* dilatato(a).

distil [dɪs'tɪl] *vt* distillare; **~lery** *n* distilleria.

distinct [dɪs'tɪŋkt] *a* distinto(a); *(preference, progress)* definito(a); as ~ from a differenza di; **~ion** [dɪs'tɪŋkʃən] *n* distinzione *f*; *(in exam)* lode *f*; **~ive** *a* distintivo(a).

distinguish [dɪs'tɪŋgwɪʃ] *vt* distinguere; discernere; **~ed** *a* *(eminent)* eminente; **~ing** *a* *(feature)* distinto(a), caratteristico(a).

distort [dɪs'tɔ:t] *vt* distorcere; *(TECH)* deformare.

distract [dɪs'trækt] *vt* distrarre; **~ed** *a* distratto(a); **~ion** [dɪs'trækʃən] *n* distrazione *f*.

distraught [dɪs'trɔ:t] *a* stravolto(a).

distress [dɪs'trɛs] *n* angoscia; *(pain)* dolore *m* // *vt* affliggere; **~ing** *a* doloroso(a).

distribute [dɪs'trɪbju:t] *vt* distribuire; **distribution** [-'bju:ʃən] *n* distribuzione *f*; **distributor** *n* distributore *m*.

district ['dɪstrɪkt] *n* *(of country)* regione *f*; *(of town)* quartiere *m*; *(ADMIN)* distretto; ~ **attorney** *n* *(US)* ≈ sostituto procuratore *m* della Repubblica; ~ **nurse** *n* *(Brit)* infermiera di quartiere.

distrust [dɪs'trʌst] *n* diffidenza, sfiducia // *vt* non aver fiducia in.

disturb [dɪs'tə:b] *vt* disturbare; *(inconvenience)* scomodare; **~ance** *n* disturbo; *(political etc)* tumulto; *(by drunks etc)* disordini *mpl*; **~ed** *a* *(worried, upset)* turbato(a); emotionally **~ed** con turbe emotive; **~ing** *a* sconvolgente.

disuse [dɪs'ju:s] *n*: to fall into ~ cadere in disuso.

disused [dɪs'ju:zd] *a* abbandonato(a).

ditch [dɪtʃ] *n* fossa // *vt* *(col)* piantare in asso.

dither ['dɪðə*] *vi* vacillare.

ditto ['dɪtəu] *ad* idem.

dive [daɪv] *n* tuffo; *(of submarine)* immersione *f*; *(AVIAT)* picchiata; *(pej)* buco // *vi* tuffarsi; **~r** *n* tuffatore/trice; palombaro.

diverse [daɪ'və:s] *a* vario(a).

diversion [daɪ'və:ʃən] *n* *(Brit AUT)* deviazione *f*; *(distraction)* divertimento.

divert [daɪ'və:t] *vt* deviare; *(amuse)* divertire.

divide [dɪ'vaɪd] *vt* dividere; *(separate)* separare // *vi* dividersi; **~d highway** *n* *(US)* strada a doppia carreggiata.

dividend ['dɪvɪdɛnd] *n* dividendo.

divine [dɪ'vaɪn] *a* divino(a).

diving ['daɪvɪŋ] *n* tuffo; ~ **board** *n* trampolino.

divinity [dɪ'vɪnɪtɪ] *n* divinità *f* *inv*; teologia.

division [dɪ'vɪʒən] *n* divisione *f*; separazione *f*.

divorce [dɪ'vɔ:s] *n* divorzio // *vt* divorziare da; **~d** *a* divorziato(a); **~e** [-'si:] *n* divorziato/a.

D.I.Y. *n abbr (Brit)* = **do-it-yourself**.

dizzy ['dɪzɪ] *a* *(height)* vertiginoso(a); to feel ~ avere il capogiro; to make sb ~ far venire il capogiro a qn.

DJ *n abbr* = **disc jockey**.

do [du:] ◆ *n* *(col: party etc)* festa; it was rather a grand ~ è stato un ricevimento piuttosto importante

◆ *vb (pt did, pp done)* **1** *(in negative constructions)* non tradotto; I **don't** understand non capisco

2 *(to form questions)* non tradotto; **didn't** you know? non lo sapevi?; why didn't you come? perché non sei venuto?

3 *(for emphasis, in polite expressions)*: she does seem rather late sembra essere piuttosto in ritardo; ~ sit down si accomodi la prego, prego si sieda; ~ take care! mi raccomando, sta attento!

4 *(used to avoid repeating vb)*: she swims better than I ~ lei nuota meglio di me; ~ you agree? — yes, I ~/no, I don't sei d'accordo? — sì/no; she lives in Glasgow — so ~ I lei vive a Glasgow — anch'io; he asked me to help him and I did mi ha chiesto di aiutarlo ed io l'ho fatto

5 *(in question tags)*: you like him, don't you? ti piace, vero?; I don't know him, ~ I? non lo conosco, vero?

◆ *vt (gen, carry out, perform etc)* fare; what are you ~ing tonight? che fa stasera?; to ~ the cooking cucinare; to ~ the washing-up fare i piatti; to ~ one's teeth lavarsi i denti; to ~ one's hair/nails farsi i capelli/le unghie; the car was ~ing 100 la macchina faceva i 100 all'ora

◆ *vi* **1** *(act, behave)* fare; ~ as I ~ faccia come me, faccia come faccio io

2 *(get on, fare)* andare; he's ~ing well/badly at school va bene/male a scuola; how ~ you ~? piacere!

3 *(suit)* andare bene; this room will ~ questa stanza va bene

4 *(be sufficient)* bastare; will £10 ~? basteranno 10 sterline?; that'll ~ basta così; that'll ~! *(in annoyance)* ora basta!; to make ~ *(with)* arrangiarsi (con)

to do away with *vt fus (kill)* far fuori; *(abolish)* abolire

to do up *vt (laces)* allacciare; *(dress, buttons)* abbottonare; *(renovate: room, house)* rimettere a nuovo, rifare

to do with *vt fus (need)* aver bisogno di; *(be connected)*: what has it got to ~ with you? e tu che c'entri?; I won't have anything to ~ with it non voglio avere niente a che farci; it **has to ~ with** money si tratta di soldi

to do without *vi* fare senza ◆ *vt fus* fare a meno di.

dock [dɔk] *n* bacino; (*LAW*) banco degli imputati // *vi* entrare in bacino; **~er** *n* scaricatore *m*; **~yard** *n* cantiere *m* (navale).

doctor ['dɔktə*] *n* medico/a; (*Ph.D. etc*) dottore/essa // *vt* (*fig*) alterare, manipolare; (*drink etc*) adulterare; **D~ of Philosophy (Ph.D.)** *n* dottorato di ricerca; (*person*) titolare *m/f* di un dottorato di ricerca.

doctrine ['dɔktrɪn] *n* dottrina.

document ['dɔkjumənt] *n* documento; **~ary** [-'mentərɪ] *a* documentario(a); (*evidence*) documentato(a) // *n* documentario.

dodge [dɔdʒ] *n* trucco; schivata // *vt* schivare, eludere.

doe [dəu] *n* (*deer*) femmina di daino; (*rabbit*) coniglia.

does [dʌz] *vb see* do; **doesn't** = does not.

dog [dɔg] *n* cane *m* // *vt* (*follow closely*) pedinare; (*fig*: *memory etc*) perseguitare; **~ collar** *n* collare *m* di cane; (*fig*) collarino; **~-eared** *a* (*book*) con orecchie.

dogged ['dɔgɪd] *a* ostinato(a), tenace.

dogsbody ['dɔgzbɔdɪ] *n* factotum *m inv.*

doings ['duɪŋz] *npl* attività *fpl.*

do-it-yourself [du:ɪtjɔ:'self] *n* il far da sé.

doldrums ['dɔldrəmz] *npl* (*fig*): **to be in the ~** essere giù.

dole [dəul] *n* (*Brit*) sussidio di disoccupazione; **to be on the ~** vivere del sussidio; **to ~ out** *vt* distribuire.

doleful ['dəulful] *a* triste, doloroso(a).

doll [dɔl] *n* bambola; **to ~ o.s. up** farsi bello(a).

dollar ['dɔlə*] *n* dollaro.

dolphin ['dɔlfɪn] *n* delfino.

domain [də'meɪn] *n* dominio.

dome [dəum] *n* cupola.

domestic [də'mestɪk] *a* (*duty, happiness, animal*) domestico(a); (*policy, affairs, flights*) nazionale; **~ated** *a* addomesticato(a).

dominate ['dɔmɪneɪt] *vt* dominare.

domineering [dɔmɪ'nɪərɪŋ] *a* dispotico(a), autoritario(a).

dominion [də'mɪnɪən] *n* dominio; sovranità; dominion *m inv.*

domino, ~es ['dɔmɪnəu] *n* domino; **~es** *n* (*game*) gioco del domino.

don [dɔn] *n* (*Brit*) docente *m/f* universitario(a).

donate [də'neɪt] *vt* donare.

done [dʌn] *pp of* do.

donkey ['dɔŋkɪ] *n* asino.

donor ['dəunə*] *n* donatore/trice.

don't [dəunt] *vb* = do not.

doodle ['du:dl] *vi* scarabocchiare.

doom [du:m] *n* destino; rovina // *vt*: **to be ~ed (to failure)** essere predestinato(a) (a fallire); **~sday** *n* il giorno del Giudizio.

door [dɔ:*] *n* porta; **~bell** *n* campanello; **~man** *n* (*in hotel*) portiere *m* in livrea; (*in block of flats*) portinaio; **~mat** *n* stuoia della porta; **~step** *n* gradino della porta; **~way** *n* porta.

dope [dəup] *n* (*col*: *drugs*) roba // *vt* (*horse etc*) drogare.

dopey ['dəupɪ] *a* (*col*) inebetito(a).

dormant ['dɔ:mənt] *a* inattivo(a); (*fig*) latente.

dormitory ['dɔ:mɪtrɪ] *n* dormitorio.

dose [dəus] *n* dose *f*; (*bout*) attacco.

doss house ['dɔs-] *n* (*Brit*) asilo notturno.

dot [dɔt] *n* punto; macchiolina; **~ted with** punteggiato(a) di; **on the ~** in punto.

dote [dəut]: **to ~ on** *vt fus* essere infatuato(a) di.

dot-matrix printer [dɔt'meɪtrɪks-] *n* stampante *f* a matrice a punti.

dotted line ['dɔtɪd-] *n* linea punteggiata.

double ['dʌbl] *a* doppio(a) // *ad* (*fold*) in due, doppio; (*twice*): **to cost ~** (sth) costare il doppio (di qc) // *n* sosia *m inv*; (*CINEMA*) controfigura // *vt* raddoppiare; (*fold*) piegare doppio *or* in due // *vi* raddoppiarsi; **on the ~**, (*Brit*) **at the ~** a passo di corsa; **~s** *n* (*TENNIS*) doppio; **~ bass** *n* contrabbasso; **~ bed** *n* letto matrimoniale; **~-breasted** *a* a doppio petto; **~cross** *vt* fare il doppio gioco con; **~decker** *n* autobus *m inv* a due piani; **~ glazing** *n* (*Brit*) doppi vetri *mpl*; **~ room** *n*. camera per due; **doubly** *ad* doppiamente.

doubt [daut] *n* dubbio // *vt* dubitare di; **to ~ that** dubitare che + *sub*; **~ful** *a* dubbioso(a), incerto(a); (*person*) equivoco(a); **~less** *ad* indubbiamente.

dough [dəu] *n* pasta, impasto; **~nut** *n* bombolone *m.*

douse [dauz] *vt* (*drench*) inzuppare; (*extinguish*) spegnere.

dove [dʌv] *n* colombo/a.

dovetail ['dʌvteɪl] *vi* (*fig*) combaciare.

dowdy ['daudɪ] *a* trasandato(a); malvestito(a).

down [daun] *n* (*fluff*) piumino // *ad* giù, di sotto // *prep* giù per // *vt* (*col*: *drink*) scolarsi; **~ with X!** abbasso X!; **~-and-out** *n* barbone *m*; **~-at-heel** *a* scalcagnato(a); (*fig*) trasandato(a); **~cast** *a* abbattuto(a); **~fall** *n* caduta; rovina; **~hearted** *a* scoraggiato(a); **~hill** *ad*: **to go ~hill** andare in discesa // *n* (*SKI*: *also*: **~hill race**) discesa libera; **~ payment** *n* acconto; **~pour** *n* scroscio di pioggia; **~right** *a* franco(a); (*refusal*) assoluto(a); **~stairs** *ad* di sotto; al piano inferiore; **~stream** *ad* a valle; **~-to-earth** *a* pratico(a); **~town** *ad* in città; **~ under** *ad* (*Australia etc*) agli antipodi; **~ward** ['daunwəd] *a*, *ad*, **~wards** ['daunwədz] *ad* in giù, in discesa.

dowry ['dauri] *n* dote *f*.

doz. *abbr* = **dozen.**

doze [dəuz] *vi* sonnecchiare; **to ~ off** *vi* appisolarsi.

dozen ['dʌzn] *n* dozzina; **a ~ books** una dozzina di libri; **~s of** decine *fpl* di.

Dr. *abbr* = **doctor; drive** (*n*).

drab [dræb] *a* tetro(a), grigio(a).

draft [drɑːft] *n* abbozzo; (*COMM*) tratta; (*US MIL*) contingente *m*; (: *call-up*) leva // *vt* abbozzare; *see also* **draught.**

draftsman ['drɑːftsmən] *n* (*US*) = **draughtsman.**

drag [dræg] *vt* trascinare; (*river*) dragare // *vi* trascinarsi // *n* (*col*) noioso/a; noia, fatica; (*women's clothing*): **in ~** travestito (da donna); **to ~ on** *vi* tirar avanti lentamente.

dragon ['drægən] *n* drago.

dragonfly ['drægənflai] *n* libellula.

drain [drein] *n* canale *m* di scolo; (*for sewage*) fogna; (*on resources*) salasso // *vt* (*land, marshes*) prosciugare; (*vegetables*) scolare; (*reservoir etc*) vuotare // *vi* (*water*) defluire (via); **~age** *n* prosciugamento; fognatura; **~ing board,** (*US*) **~board** *n* piano del lavello; **~pipe** *n* tubo di scarico.

dram [dræm] *n* bicchierino.

drama ['drɑːmə] *n* (*art*) dramma *m*, teatro; (*play*) commedia; (*event*) dramma; **~tic** [drə'mætik] *a* drammatico(a); **~tist** ['dræmətist] *n* drammaturgo/a; **~tize** *vt* (*events*) drammatizzare; (*adapt: for TV/cinema*) ridurre *or* adattare per la televisione/lo schermo.

drank [dræŋk] *pt of* **drink.**

drape [dreip] *vt* drappeggiare; **~s** *npl* (*US*) tende *fpl*; **~r** *n* (*Brit*) negoziante *m/f* di stoffe.

drastic ['dræstik] *a* drastico(a).

draught, (*US*) **draft** [drɑːft] *n* corrente *f* d'aria; (*NAUT*) pescaggio; **~s** *n* (*Brit*) (*gioco della*) dama; **on ~** (*beer*) alla spina; **~board** *n* (*Brit*) scacchiera.

draughtsman, (*US*) **draftsman** ['drɑːftsmən] *n* disegnatore *m*.

draw [drɔː] *vb* (*pt* **drew,** *pp* **drawn**) *vt* tirare; (*attract*) attirare; (*picture*) disegnare; (*line, circle*) tracciare; (*money*) ritirare // *vi* (*SPORT*) pareggiare // *n* pareggio; (*in lottery*) estrazione *f*; (*attraction*) attrazione *f*; **to ~ near** *vi* avvicinarsi; **to ~ out** *vi* (*lengthen*) allungarsi // *vt* (*money*) ritirare; **to ~ up** *vi* (*stop*) arrestarsi, fermarsi // *vt* (*document*) compilare; **~back** *n* svantaggio, inconveniente *m*; **~bridge** *n* ponte *m* levatoio.

drawer [drɔː*] *n* cassetto; ['drɔːə*] (*of*

cheque) traente *m/f*.

drawing ['drɔːiŋ] *n* disegno; **~ board** *n* tavola da disegno; **~ pin** *n* (*Brit*) puntina da disegno; **~ room** *n* salotto.

drawl [drɔːl] *n* pronuncia strascicata.

drawn [drɔːn] *pp of* **draw.**

dread [dred] *n* terrore *m* // *vt* tremare all'idea di; **~ful** *a* terribile.

dream [driːm] *n* sogno // *vt*, *vi* (*pt*, *pp* **dreamed** *or* **dreamt** [dremt]) sognare; **~y** *a* sognante.

dreary ['driəri] *a* tetro(a); monotono(a).

dredge [dredʒ] *vt* dragare.

dregs [dregz] *npl* feccia.

drench [drentʃ] *vt* inzuppare.

dress [dres] *n* vestito; (*clothing*) abbigliamento // *vt* vestire; (*wound*) fasciare; (*food*) condire; preparare // *vi* vestirsi; **to get ~ed** vestirsi; **to ~ up** *vi* vestirsi a festa; (*in fancy dress*) vestirsi in costume; **~ circle** *n* (*Brit*) prima galleria; **~er** *n* (*THEATRE*) assistente *m/f* del camerino; (*furniture*) credenza; **~ing** *n* (*MED*) benda; (*CULIN*) condimento; **~ing gown** *n* (*Brit*) vestaglia; **~ing room** *n* (*THEATRE*) camerino; (*SPORT*) spogliatoio; **~ing table** *n* toilette *f inv*; **~maker** *n* sarta; **~ rehearsal** *n* prova generale; **~y** *a* (*col*) elegante.

drew [druː] *pt of* **draw.**

dribble ['dribl] *vi* gocciolare; (*baby*) sbavare; (*FOOTBALL*) dribblare.

dried [draid] *a* (*fruit, beans*) secco(a); (*eggs, milk*) in polvere.

drier ['draiə*] *n* = **dryer.**

drift [drift] *n* (*of current etc*) direzione *f*; forza; (*of sand etc*) turbine *m*; (*of snow*) cumulo; turbine; (*general meaning*) senso // *vi* (*boat*) essere trasportato(a) dalla corrente; (*sand, snow*) ammucchiarsi; **~wood** *n* resti *mpl* della mareggiata.

drill [dril] *n* trapano; (*MIL*) esercitazione *f* // *vt* trapanare // *vi* (*for oil*) fare trivellazioni.

drink [driŋk] *n* bevanda, bibita // *vt*, *vi* (*pt* **drank,** *pp* **drunk**) bere; **to have a ~** bere qualcosa; **a ~ of water** un po' d'acqua; **~er** *n* bevitore/trice; **~ing water** *n* acqua potabile.

drip [drip] *n* goccia; gocciolamento; (*MED*) fleboclisi *f inv* // *vi* gocciolare; (*washing*) sgocciolare; (*wall*) trasudare; **~-dry** *a* (*shirt*) che non si stira; **~ping** *n* grasso d'arrosto.

drive [draiv] *n* passeggiata *or* giro in macchina; (*also*: **~way**) viale *m* d'accesso; (*energy*) energia; (*PSYCH*) impulso; bisogno; (*push*) sforzo eccezionale; campagna; (*SPORT*) drive *m inv*; (*TECH*) trasmissione *f*; propulsione *f*; presa; (*also*: **disk ~**) lettore *m* // *vb* (*pt* **drove,** *pp* **driven**) *vt* guidare; (*nail*) piantare; (*push*) cacciare, spingere; (*TECH: motor*) azionare; far funzionare // *vi* (*AUT: at controls*) guidare; (: *travel*) andare in macchina; **left-/right-hand** ~ guida a sinistra/destra; **to** ~ **sb mad** far impazzire qn.

drivel ['drɪvl] *n* idiozie *fpl*.

driven ['drɪvn] *pp of* **drive**.

driver ['draɪvə*] *n* conducente *m/f*; (*of taxi*) tassista *m*; (*of bus*) autista *m*; ~'s **license** *n* (*US*) patente *f* di guida.

driveway ['draɪvweɪ] *n* viale *m* d'accesso.

driving ['draɪvɪŋ] *a*: ~ **rain** pioggia sferzante // *n* guida; ~ **instructor** *n* istruttore/trice di scuola guida; ~ **lesson** *n* lezione *f* di guida; ~ **licence** *n* (*Brit*) patente *f* di guida; ~ **mirror** *n* specchietto retrovisore; ~ **school** *n* scuola *f* guida *inv*; ~ **test** *n* esame *m* di guida.

drizzle ['drɪzl] *n* pioggerella.

droll [drəul] *a* buffo(a).

drone [drəun] *n* ronzio; (*male bee*) fuco.

drool [dru:l] *vi* sbavare.

droop [dru:p] *vi* abbassarsi; languire.

drop [drɔp] *n* goccia; (*fall*) caduta; (*also*: **parachute** ~) lancio; (*steep in cline*) salto // *vt* lasciare cadere; (*voice, eyes, price*) abbassare; (*set down from car*) far scendere // *vi* cascare; ~s *npl* (*MED*) gocce *fpl*; **to** ~ **off** *vi* (*sleep*) addormentarsi; **to** ~ **out** *vi* (*withdraw*) ritirarsi; (*student etc*) smettere di studiare; ~-**out** *n* (*from society/from university*) chi ha abbandonato (la società/gli studi); ~**pings** *npl* sterco.

drought [draut] *n* siccità *f inv*.

drove [drəuv] *pt of* **drive**.

drown [draun] *vt* affogare // *vi* affogarsi.

drowsy ['drauzɪ] *a* sonnolento(a), assonnato(a).

drudgery ['drʌdʒərɪ] *n* lavoro faticoso.

drug [drʌg] *n* farmaco; (*narcotic*) droga // *vt* drogare; ~ **addict** *n* tossicomane *m/f*; ~**gist** *n* (*US*) persona che gestisce un *drugstore*; ~**store** *n* (*US*) drugstore *m inv*.

drum [drʌm] *n* tamburo; (*for oil, petrol*) fusto // *vi* tamburellare; ~s *npl* batteria; ~**mer** *n* batterista *m/f*.

drunk [drʌŋk] *pp of* **drink** // *a* ubriaco(a); ebbro(a) // *n* (*also*: ~**ard**) ubriacone/a; ~**en** *a* ubriaco(a); da ubriaco.

dry [draɪ] *a* secco(a); (*day, clothes*) asciutto(a) // *vt* seccare; (*clothes, hair, hands*) asciugare // *vi* asciugarsi; **to** ~ **up** *vi* seccarsi; ~-**cleaner's** *n* lavasecco *m inv*; ~**er** *n* (*for hair*) föhn *m inv*, asciugacapelli *m inv*; (*for clothes*) asciugabiancheria; (*US: spin-dryer*) centrifuga; ~ **goods store** *n* (*US*) negozio di stoffe; ~ **rot** *n* fungo del legno.

dual ['djuəl] *a* doppio(a); ~ **carriage-**

way *n* (*Brit*) strada a doppia carreggiata.

dubbed [dʌbd] *a* (*CINEMA*) doppiato(a); (*nicknamed*) soprannominato(a).

dubious ['dju:bɪəs] *a* dubbio(a).

Dublin ['dʌblɪn] *n* Dublino *f*.

duchess ['dʌtʃɪs] *n* duchessa.

duck [dʌk] *n* anatra // *vi* abbassare la testa; ~**ling** *n* anatroccolo.

duct [dʌkt] *n* condotto; (*ANAT*) canale *m*.

dud [dʌd] *n* (*shell*) proiettile *m* che fa cilecca; (*object, tool*): **it's a** ~ è inutile, non funziona // *a* (*Brit: cheque*) a vuoto; (: *note, coin*) falso(a).

due [dju:] *a* dovuto(a); (*expected*) atteso(a); (*fitting*) giusto(a) // *n* dovuto // *ad*: ~ **north** diritto verso nord; ~s *npl* (*for club, union*) quota; (*in harbour*) diritti *mpl* di porto; **in** ~ **course** a tempo debito; **finalmente**; ~ **to** dovuto a; a causa di; **to be** ~ **to do** dover fare.

duet [dju:'et] *n* duetto.

duffel [dʌfl] *a*: ~ **bag** sacca da viaggio di tela; ~ **coat** montgomery *m inv*.

dug [dʌg] *pt, pp of* **dig**.

duke [dju:k] *n* duca *m*.

dull [dʌl] *a* (*boring*) noioso(a); (*slow-witted*) ottuso(a); (*sound, pain*) sordo(a); (*weather, day*) fosco(a), scuro(a); (*blade*) smussato(a) // *vt* (*pain, grief*) attutire; (*mind, senses*) intorpidire.

duly ['dju:lɪ] *ad* (*on time*) a tempo debito; (*as expected*) debitamente.

dumb [dʌm] *a* muto(a); (*stupid*) stupido(a); **dumbfounded** [dʌm-'faundɪd] *a* stupito(a), stordito(a).

dummy ['dʌmɪ] *n* (*tailor's model*) manichino; (*SPORT*) finto; (*Brit: for baby*) tettarella // *a* falso(a), finto(a).

dump [dʌmp] *n* mucchio di rifiuti; (*place*) immondezzaio; (*MIL*) deposito // *vt* (*put down*) scaricare; mettere giù; (*get rid of*) buttar via; ~**ing** *n* (*ECON*) dumping *m*; (*of rubbish*): "**no** ~**ing**" "vietato lo scarico".

dumpling ['dʌmplɪŋ] *n* specie di gnocco.

dumpy ['dʌmpɪ] *a* tracagnotto(a).

dung [dʌŋ] *n* concime *m*.

dungarees [dʌŋgə'ri:z] *npl* tuta.

dungeon ['dʌndʒən] *n* prigione *f* sotterranea.

dupe [dju:p] *vt* gabbare, ingannare.

duplex ['dju:pleks] *n* (*US: house*) casa con muro divisorio in comune con un'altra; (: *apartment*) appartamento su due piani.

duplicate *n* ['dju:plɪkət] doppio // *vt* ['dju:plɪkeɪt] raddoppiare; (*on machine*) ciclostilare.

durable ['djuərəbl] *a* durevole; (*clothes, metal*) resistente.

duration [djuə'reɪʃən] *n* durata.

duress [djuə'rɛs] *n*: **under** ~ sotto costrizione.

during ['djuəriŋ] *prep* durante, nel corso di.

dusk [dʌsk] *n* crepuscolo.

dust [dʌst] *n* polvere *f* // *vt* (*furniture*) spolverare; (*cake etc*): **to ~ with** cospargere con; **~bin** *n* (*Brit*) pattumiera; **~er** *n* straccio per la polvere; **~ jacket** *n* sopraccoperta; **~man** *n* (*Brit*) netturbino; **~y** *a* polveroso(a).

Dutch [dʌtʃ] *a* olandese // *n* (*LING*) olandese *m*; **the ~** *npl* gli Olandesi; **to go ~** fare alla romana; **~man/woman** *n* olandese *m/f*.

dutiful ['dju:tiful] *a* (*child*) rispettoso(a).

duty ['dju:ti] *n* dovere *m*; (*tax*) dazio, tassa; **duties** *npl* mansioni *fpl*; **on ~** di servizio; **off ~** libero(a), fuori servizio; **~-free** *a* esente da dazio.

duvet ['du:vei] *n* (*Brit*) piumino, piumone *m*.

dwarf [dwɔ:f] *n* nano/a // *vt* far apparire piccolo.

dwell, *pt*, *pp* **dwelt** [dwɛl, dwɛlt] *vi* dimorare; **to ~ on** *vt fus* indugiare su; **~ing** *n* dimora.

dwindle ['dwindl] *vi* diminuire, decrescere.

dye [dai] *n* tinta // *vt* tingere.

dying ['daiiŋ] *a* morente, moribondo(a).

dyke [daik] *n* (*Brit*) diga.

dynamic [dai'næmik] *a* dinamico(a).

dynamite ['dainəmait] *n* dinamite *f*.

dynamo ['dainəməu] *n* dinamo *f inv*.

dysentery ['disintri] *n* dissenteria.

dyslexia [dis'lɛksiə] *n* dislessia.

E

E [i:] *n* (*MUS*) mi *m*.

each [i:tʃ] *a* ogni, ciascuno(a) // *pronoun* ciascuno(a), ognuno(a); **~ one** ognuno(a); **~ other** si (*or ci etc*); **they hate ~ other** si odiano (l'un l'altro); **you are jealous of ~ other** siete gelosi l'uno dell'altro; **they have 2 books ~** hanno 2 libri ciascuno.

eager ['i:gə*] *a* impaziente; desideroso(a); ardente; **to be ~ for** essere desideroso di, aver gran voglia di.

eagle ['i:gl] *n* aquila.

ear [iə*] *n* orecchio; (*of corn*) pannocchia; **~ache** *n* mal *m* d'orecchi; **~drum** *n* timpano.

earl [ə:l] *n* conte *m*.

earlier ['ə:liə*] *a* precedente // *ad* prima.

early ['ə:li] *ad* presto, di buon'ora; (*ahead of time*) in anticipo // *a* precoce; anticipato(a); che si fa vedere di buon'ora; **to have an ~ night** andare a letto presto; **in the ~ or ~ in the spring/ 19th century** all'inizio della primavera/ dell'Ottocento; **~ retirement** *n* ritiro anticipato.

earmark ['iəmɑ:k] *vt*: **to ~ sth for** destinare qc a.

earn [ə:n] *vt* guadagnare; (*rest, reward*) meritare.

earnest ['ə:nist] *a* serio(a); **in ~** *ad* sul serio.

earnings ['ə:niŋz] *npl* guadagni *mpl*; (*salary*) stipendio.

earphones ['iəfəunz] *npl* cuffia.

earring ['iəriŋ] *n* orecchino.

earshot ['iəʃɔt] *n*: **out of/within ~** fuori portata/a portata d'orecchio.

earth [ə:θ] *n* (*gen, also Brit ELEC*) terra; (*of fox etc*) tana // *vt* (*Brit ELEC*) mettere a terra; **~enware** *n* terracotta; stoviglie *fpl* di terracotta // *a* di terracotta; **~quake** *n* terremoto; **~y** *a* (*fig*) grossolano(a).

ease [i:z] *n* agio, comodo // *vt* (*soothe*) calmare; (*loosen*) allentare; **to ~ sth out/in** tirare fuori/infilare qc con delicatezza; facilitare l'uscita/l'entrata di qc; **at ~** a proprio agio; (*MIL*) a riposo; **to ~ off** *or* **up** *vi* diminuire; (*slow down*) rallentarsi; (*fig*) rilassarsi.

easel ['i:zl] *n* cavalletto.

east [i:st] *n* est *m* // *a* dell'est // *ad* a oriente; **the E~** l'Oriente *m*.

Easter ['i:stə*] *n* Pasqua; **~ egg** *n* uovo di Pasqua.

easterly ['i:stəli] *a* dall'est, d'oriente.

eastern ['i:stən] *a* orientale, d'oriente.

East Germany *n* Germania dell'Est.

eastward(s) ['i:stwəd(z)] *ad* verso est, verso levante.

easy ['i:zi] *a* facile; (*manner*) disinvolto(a) // *ad*: **to take it** *or* **things ~** prendersela con calma; **~ chair** *n* poltrona; **~-going** *a* accomodante.

eat, *pt* **ate**, *pp* **eaten** [i:t, eit, 'i:tn] *vt*, *vi* mangiare; **to ~ into, to ~ away at** *vt fus* rodere.

eaves [i:vz] *npl* gronda.

eavesdrop ['i:vzdrɔp] *vi*: **to ~ (on a conversation)** origliare (una conversazione).

ebb [ɛb] *n* riflusso // *vi* rifluire; (*fig: also*: **~ away**) declinare.

ebony ['ɛbəni] *n* ebano.

eccentric [ik'sɛntrik] *a*, *n* eccentrico(a).

echo, **~es** ['ɛkəu] *n* eco *m or f* // *vt* ripetere; fare eco a // *vi* echeggiare; dare un eco.

eclipse [i'klips] *n* eclissi *f inv* // *vt* eclissare.

ecology [i'kɔlədʒi] *n* ecologia.

economic [i:kə'nɔmik] *a* economico(a); **~al** *a* economico(a); (*person*) economo(a); **~s** *n* economia.

economize [i'kɔnəmaiz] *vi* risparmiare, fare economia.

economy [i'kɔnəmi] *n* economia.

ecstasy ['ɛkstəsi] *n* estasi *f inv*.

eczema ['ɛksimə] *n* eczema *m*.

edge [ɛdʒ] *n* margine *m*; (*of table, plate,*

cup) orlo; (*of knife etc*) taglio // *vt* bordare; **on ~** (*fig*) = **edgy; to ~ away from** sgattaiolare da; **~ways** *ad* di fianco; **he couldn't get a word in ~ways** non riuscì a dire una parola.

edgy ['edʒɪ] *a* nervoso(a).

edible ['edɪbl] *a* commestibile; (*meal*) mangiabile.

edict ['i:dɪkt] *n* editto.

Edinburgh ['edɪnbərə] *n* Edimburgo *f*.

edit ['edɪt] *vt* curare; **~ion** ['ɪdɪʃən] *n* edizione *f*; **~or** *n* (*in newspaper*) redattore/trice; redattore/trice capo; (*of sb's work*) curatore/trice; **~orial** [-'tɔ:rɪəl] *a* redazionale, editoriale // *n* editoriale *m*.

educate ['edjukeɪt] *vt* istruire; educare.

education [edju'keɪʃən] *n* educazione *f*; (*schooling*) istruzione *f*; **~al** *a* pedagogico(a); scolastico(a); istruttivo(a).

EEC *n abbr* (= *European Economic Community*) C.E.E. *f* (= *Comunità Economica Europea*).

eel [i:l] *n* anguilla.

eerie ['ɪərɪ] *a* che fa accapponare la pelle.

effect [ɪ'fekt] *n* effetto // *vt* effettuare; **~s** *npl* (*THEATRE*) effetti *mpl* scenici; **to take ~** (*law*) entrare in vigore; (*drug*) fare effetto; **in ~** effettivamente; **~ive** *a* efficace; **~ively** *ad* efficacemente; (*in reality*) effettivamente; **~iveness** *n* efficacia.

effeminate [ɪ'femɪnɪt] *a* effeminato(a).

efficiency [ɪ'fɪʃənsɪ] *n* efficienza; rendimento effettivo.

efficient [ɪ'fɪʃənt] *a* efficiente.

effort ['efət] *n* sforzo.

effrontery [ɪ'frʌntərɪ] *n* sfrontatezza.

effusive [ɪ'fju:sɪv] *a* (*person*) espansivo(a); (*welcome, letter*) caloroso(a); (*thanks, apologies*) interminabile.

e.g. *ad abbr* (= *exempli gratia*) per esempio, p.es.

egg [eg] *n* uovo; **to ~ on** *vt* incitare; **~cup** *n* portauovo *m inv*; **~plant** *n* (*especially US*) melanzana; **~shell** *n* guscio d'uovo.

ego ['i:gəu] *n* ego *m inv*.

egotism ['egəutɪzəm] *n* egotismo.

egotist ['egəutɪst] *n* egotista *m/f*.

Egypt ['i:dʒɪpt] *n* Egitto; **~ian** [ɪ'dʒɪpʃən] *a*, *n* egiziano(a).

eiderdown ['aɪdədaun] *n* piumino.

eight [eɪt] *num* otto; **~een** *num* diciotto; **~eighth** [eɪtθ] *num* ottavo(a); **~y** *num* ottanta.

Eire ['ɛərə] *n* Repubblica d'Irlanda.

either ['aɪðə*] *a* l'uno(a) o l'altro(a); (*both, each*) ciascuno(a); **on ~ side** su ciascun lato // *pronoun:* ~ (*of them*) (o) l'uno(a) o l'altro(a); **I don't like ~** non mi piace né l'uno né l'altro // *ad* nean-

che; **no, I don't ~** no, neanch'io // *cj:* **~ good or bad** o buono o cattivo.

eject [ɪ'dʒekt] *vt* espellere; lanciare.

eke [i:k]: **to ~ out** *vt* far durare; aumentare.

elaborate *a* [ɪ'læbərɪt] elaborato(a), minuzioso(a) // *vb* [ɪ'læbəreɪt] *vt* elaborare // *vi* fornire i particolari.

elapse [ɪ'læps] *vi* trascorrere, passare.

elastic [ɪ'læstɪk] *a* elastico(a) // *n* elastico; **~ band** (*Brit*) elastico.

elated [ɪ'leɪtɪd] *a* pieno(a) di gioia.

elbow ['elbəu] *n* gomito.

elder ['eldə*] *a* maggiore, più vecchio(a) // *n* (*tree*) sambuco; **one's ~s** i più anziani; **~ly** *a* anziano(a) // *npl:* **the ~ly** gli anziani.

eldest ['eldɪst] *a*, *n:* **the ~** (*child*) il(la) maggiore (dei bambini).

elect [ɪ'lekt] *vt* eleggere; **to ~ to do** decidere di fare // *a:* **the president ~** il presidente designato; **~ion** [ɪ'lekʃən] *n* elezione *f*; **~ioneering** [ɪlekʃə'nɪərɪŋ] *n* propaganda elettorale; **~or** *n* elettore/trice; **~orate** *n* elettorato.

electric [ɪ'lektrɪk] *a* elettrico(a); **~al** *a* elettrico(a); **~ blanket** *n* coperta elettrica; **~ fire** *n* stufa elettrica.

electrician [ɪlek'trɪʃən] *n* elettricista *m*.

electricity [ɪlek'trɪsɪtɪ] *n* elettricità.

electrify [ɪ'lektrɪfaɪ] *vt* (*RAIL*) elettrificare; (*audience*) elettrizzare.

electrocute [ɪ'lektrəukju:t] *vt* fulminare.

electronic [ɪlek'trɒnɪk] *a* elettronico(a); **~ mail** *n* posta elettronica; **~s** *n* elettronica.

elegant ['elɪgənt] *a* elegante.

element ['elɪmənt] *n* elemento; (*of heater, kettle etc*) resistenza; **~ary** [-'mentərɪ] *a* elementare.

elephant ['elɪfənt] *n* elefante/essa.

elevate ['elɪveɪt] *vt* elevare.

elevator ['elɪveɪtə*] *n* elevatore *m*; (*US: lift*) ascensore *m*.

eleven [ɪ'levn] *num* undici; **~ses** *npl* (*Brit*) caffè *m* a metà mattina; **~th** *a* undicesimo(a).

elicit [ɪ'lɪsɪt] *vt:* **to ~ (from)** trarre (da), cavare fuori (da).

eligible ['elɪdʒəbl] *a* eleggibile; (*for membership*) che ha i requisiti.

ellipse [ɪ'lɪps] *n* ellisse *f*.

elm [elm] *n* olmo.

elongated ['i:lɒŋgeɪtɪd] *a* allungato(a).

elope [ɪ'ləup] *vi* (*lovers*) scappare.

eloquent ['eləkwənt] *a* eloquente.

else [els] *ad* altro; **something ~** qualcos'altro; **somewhere ~** altrove; **everywhere ~** in qualsiasi altro luogo; **nobody ~** nessun altro; **where ~?** in quale altro luogo?; **little ~** poco altro; **~where** *ad* altrove.

elucidate [ɪ'lu:sɪdeɪt] *vt* delucidare.

elude [ɪ'lu:d] *vt* eludere.

elusive [ɪ'lu:sɪv] *a* elusivo(a).

emaciated [ɪ'meɪsɪeɪtɪd] a emaciato(a).

emancipate [ɪ'mænsɪpeɪt] vt emancipare.

embankment [ɪm'bæŋkmənt] n (of road, railway) terrapieno; (riverside) argine m; (dyke) diga.

embark [ɪm'bɑːk] vi: to ~ (on) imbarcarsi (su) // vt imbarcare; to ~ on (fig) imbarcarsi in; ~ation [ɛmbɑː'keɪʃən] n imbarco.

embarrass [ɪm'bærəs] vt imbarazzare; ~ed a imbarazzato(a); ~ing a imbarazzante; ~ment n imbarazzo.

embassy ['ɛmbəsɪ] n ambasciata.

embed [ɪm'bɛd] vt conficcare, incastrare.

embellish [ɪm'bɛlɪʃ] vt abbellire.

embers ['ɛmbəz] npl braci fpl.

embezzle [ɪm'bɛzl] vt appropriarsi indebitamente di.

embitter [ɪm'bɪtə*] vt amareggiare; inasprire.

embody [ɪm'bɔdɪ] vt (features) racchiudere, comprendere; (ideas) dar forma concreta a, esprimere.

embossed [ɪm'bɔst] a in rilievo; goffrato(a).

embrace [ɪm'breɪs] vt abbracciare // vi abbracciarsi // n abbraccio.

embroider [ɪm'brɔɪdə*] vt ricamare; (fig: story) abbellire; ~y n ricamo.

embryo ['ɛmbrɪəu] n (also fig) embrione m.

emerald ['ɛmərəld] n smeraldo.

emerge [ɪ'mɜːdʒ] vi apparire, sorgere.

emergence [ɪ'mɜːdʒəns] n apparizione f.

emergency [ɪ'mɜːdʒənsɪ] n emergenza; in an ~ in caso di emergenza; ~ cord n (US) segnale m d'allarme; ~ exit n uscita di sicurezza; ~ landing n atterraggio forzato; the ~ services npl (fire, police, ambulance) servizi mpl di pronto intervento.

emery board ['ɛmərɪ-] n limetta di carta smerigliata.

emigrate ['ɛmɪgreɪt] vi emigrare.

eminent ['ɛmɪnənt] a eminente.

emit [ɪ'mɪt] vt emettere.

emotion [ɪ'məuʃən] n emozione f; ~al a (person) emotivo(a); (scene) commovente; (tone, speech) carico(a) d'emozione.

emperor ['ɛmpərə*] n imperatore m.

emphasis, pl -ases ['ɛmfəsɪs, -siːz] n enfasi f inv; importanza.

emphasize ['ɛmfəsaɪz] vt (word, point) sottolineare; (feature) mettere in evidenza.

emphatic [ɛm'fætɪk] a (strong) vigoroso(a); (unambiguous, clear) netto(a); ~ally ad vigorosamente; nettamente.

empire ['ɛmpaɪə*] n impero.

employ [ɪm'plɔɪ] vt impiegare; ~ee [-'iː] n impiegato/a; ~er n principale m/f, datore m di lavoro; ~ment n impiego;

~ment agency n agenzia di collocamento.

empower [ɪm'pauə*] vt: to ~ sb to do concedere autorità a qn di fare.

empress ['ɛmprɪs] n imperatrice f.

emptiness ['ɛmptɪnɪs] n vuoto.

empty ['ɛmptɪ] a vuoto(a); (threat, promise) vano(a) // vt vuotare // vi vuotarsi; (liquid) scaricarsi // (bottle) vuoto; ~-handed a a mani vuote.

emulate ['ɛmjuleɪt] vt emulare.

emulsion [ɪ'mʌlʃən] n emulsione f; ~ (paint) n colore m a tempera.

enable [ɪ'neɪbl] vt: to ~ sb to do permettere a qn di fare.

enact [ɪn'ækt] vt (law) emanare; (play, scene) rappresentare.

enamel [ɪ'næməl] n smalto.

encased [ɪn'keɪst] a: ~ in racchiuso(a) in; rivestito(a).

enchant [ɪn'tʃɑːnt] vt incantare; (subj: magic spell) catturare; ~ing a incantevole, affascinante.

encircle [ɪn'sɜːkl] vt accerchiare.

encl. abbr (= enclosed) all.

enclave ['ɛnkleɪv] n enclave f.

enclose [ɪn'kləuz] vt (land) circondare, recingere; (letter etc): to ~ (with) allegare (con); please find ~d trovi qui accluso.

enclosure [ɪn'kləuʒə*] n recinto; (COMM) allegato.

encompass [ɪn'kʌmpəs] vt comprendere.

encore [ɔŋ'kɔː*] excl, n bis (m inv).

encounter [ɪn'kauntə*] n incontro // vt incontrare.

encourage [ɪn'kʌrɪdʒ] vt incoraggiare; ~ment n incoraggiamento.

encroach [ɪn'krəutʃ] vi: to ~ (up)on (rights) usurpare; (time) abusare di; (land) oltrepassare i limiti di.

encyclop(a)edia [ɛnsaɪkləu'piːdɪə] n enciclopedia.

end [ɛnd] n fine f; (aim) fine m; (of table) bordo estremo // vt finire; (also: bring to an ~, put an ~ to) mettere fine a // vi finire; in the ~ alla fine; on ~ (object) ritto(a); to stand on ~ (hair) rizzarsi; for 5 hours on ~ per 5 ore di fila; to ~ up vi: to ~ up in finire in.

endanger [ɪn'deɪndʒə*] vt mettere in pericolo.

endearing [ɪn'dɪərɪŋ] a accattivante.

endeavour, (US) **endeavor** [ɪn'dɛvə*] n sforzo, tentativo // vi: to ~ to do cercare or sforzarsi di fare.

ending ['ɛndɪŋ] n fine f, conclusione f; (LING) desinenza.

endive ['ɛndaɪv] n (curly) indivia (riccia); (smooth, flat) indivia belga.

endless ['ɛndlɪs] a senza fine; (patience, resources) infinito(a).

endorse [ɪn'dɔːs] vt (cheque) girare; (approve) approvare, appoggiare; ~ment n (on driving licence) con-

travvenzione registrata sulla patente.

endow [ɪn'dau] *vt* (*provide with money*) devolvere denaro a; (*equip*): to ~ with fornire di, dotare di.

endurance [ɪn'djuərəns] *n* resistenza; pazienza.

endure [ɪn'djuə*] *vt* sopportare, resistere a // *vi* durare.

enemy ['enəmɪ] *a*, *n* nemico(a).

energetic [enə'dʒetɪk] *a* energico(a); attivo(a).

energy ['enədʒɪ] *n* energia.

enforce [ɪn'fɔːs] *vt* (*LAW*) applicare, far osservare; ~d *a* forzato(a).

engage [ɪn'geɪdʒ] *vt* (*hire*) assumere; (*lawyer*) incaricare; (*attention*, *interest*) assorbire; (*MIL*) attaccare; (*TECH*): to ~ gear/the clutch innestare la marcia/la frizione // *vi* (*TECH*) ingranare; to ~ in impegnarsi in; ~d *a* (*Brit: busy, in use*) occupato(a); (*betrothed*) fidanzato(a); to get ~d fidanzarsi; ~d tone *n* (*Brit TEL*) segnale *m* di occupato; ~ment *n* impegno, obbligo; appuntamento; (*to marry*) fidanzamento; (*MIL*) combattimento; ~ment ring *n* anello di fidanzamento.

engaging [ɪn'geɪdʒɪŋ] *a* attraente.

engender [ɪn'dʒendə*] *vt* produrre, causare.

engine ['endʒɪn] *n* (*AUT*) motore *m*; (*RAIL*) locomotiva; ~ driver *n* (*of train*) macchinista *m*.

engineer [endʒɪ'nɪə*] *n* ingegnere *m*; (*US RAIL*) macchinista *m*; ~ing *n* ingegneria.

England ['ɪŋglənd] *n* Inghilterra.

English ['ɪŋglɪʃ] *a* inglese // *n* (*LING*) inglese *m*; the ~ *npl* gli Inglesi; the ~ Channel *n* la Manica; ~man/woman *n* inglese *m/f*.

engraving [ɪn'greɪvɪŋ] *n* incisione *f*.

engrossed [ɪn'grəust] *a*: ~ in assorbito(a) da, preso(a) da.

engulf [ɪn'gʌlf] *vt* inghiottire.

enhance [ɪn'hɑːns] *vt* accrescere.

enjoy [ɪn'dʒɔɪ] *vt* godere; (*have: success, fortune*) avere; to ~ o.s. godersela, divertirsi; ~able *a* piacevole; ~ment *n* piacere *m*, godimento.

enlarge [ɪn'lɑːdʒ] *vt* ingrandire // *vi*: to ~ on (*subject*) dilungarsi su.

enlighten [ɪn'laɪtn] *vt* illuminare; dare schiarimenti a; ~ed *a* illuminato(a); ~ment *n*: the E~ment (*HISTORY*) l'Illuminismo.

enlist [ɪn'lɪst] *vt* arruolare; (*support*) procurare // *vi* arruolarsi.

enmity ['enmɪtɪ] *n* inimicizia.

enormous [ɪ'nɔːməs] *a* enorme.

enough [ɪ'nʌf] *a*, *n*: ~ time/books assai tempo/libri; have you got ~? ne ha abbastanza *or* a sufficienza? // *ad*: big ~ abbastanza grande; he has not worked ~ non ha lavorato abbastanza; ~! basta!; that's ~, thanks basta così, grazie; I've

had ~ of him ne ho abbastanza di lui; ... which, funnily ~ ... che, strano a dirsi.

enquire [ɪn'kwaɪə*] *vt*, *vi* = **inquire**.

enrage [ɪn'reɪdʒ] *vt* fare arrabbiare.

enrich [ɪn'rɪtʃ] *vt* arricchire.

enrol [ɪn'rəul] *vt* iscrivere // *vi* iscriversi; ~ment *n* iscrizione *f*.

ensign *n* (*NAUT*) ['ensən] bandiera; (*MIL*) ['ensaɪn] portabandiera *m inv*.

ensue [ɪn'sjuː] *vi* seguire, risultare.

ensure [ɪn'ʃuə*] *vt* assicurare; garantire; to ~ that assicurarsi che.

entail [ɪn'teɪl] *vt* comportare.

entangle [ɪn'tæŋgl] *vt* impigliare.

enter ['entə*] *vt* (*room*) entrare in; (*club*) associarsi a; (*army*) arruolarsi in; (*competition*) partecipare a; (*sb for a competition*) iscrivere; (*write down*) registrare; (*COMPUT*) inserire // *vi* entrare; to ~ for *vt fus* iscriversi a; to ~ into *vt fus* (*explanation*) cominciare a dare; (*debate*) partecipare a; (*agreement*) concludere; to ~ (up)on *vt fus* cominciare.

enterprise ['entəpraɪz] *n* (*undertaking, company*) impresa; (*spirit*) iniziativa; free ~ liberalismo economico; private ~ iniziativa privata.

enterprising ['entəpraɪzɪŋ] *a* intraprendente.

entertain [entə'teɪn] *vt* divertire; (*invite*) ricevere; (*idea, plan*) nutrire; ~er *n* comico/a; ~ing *a* divertente; ~ment *n* (*amusement*) divertimento; (*show*) spettacolo.

enthralled [ɪn'θrɔːld] *a* affascinato(a).

enthusiasm [ɪn'θuːzɪæzəm] *n* entusiasmo.

enthusiast [ɪn'θuːzɪæst] *n* entusiasta *m/f*; ~ic [-'æstɪk] *a* entusiasta, entusiastico(a); to be ~ic about sth/sb essere appassionato di qc/entusiasta di qn.

entice [ɪn'taɪs] *vt* allettare, sedurre.

entire [ɪn'taɪə*] *a* intero(a); ~ly *ad* completamente, interamente; ~ty [ɪn'taɪərətɪ] *n*: in its ~ty nel suo complesso.

entitle [ɪn'taɪtl] *vt* (*give right*): to ~ sb to sth/to do dare diritto a qn a qc/a fare; ~d *a* (*book*) che si intitola; to be ~d to do avere il diritto di fare.

entrails ['entreɪlz] *npl* interiora *fpl*.

entrance *n* ['entrns] entrata, ingresso; (*of person*) entrata // *vt* [ɪn'trɑːns] incantare, rapire; to gain ~ to (*university etc*) essere ammesso a; ~ examination *n* esame *m* di ammissione; ~ fee *n* tassa d'iscrizione; (*to museum etc*) prezzo d'ingresso; ~ ramp *n* (*US AUT*) rampa di accesso.

entrant ['entrnt] *n* partecipante *m/f*; concorrente *m/f*.

entreat [en'triːt] *vt* supplicare.

entrenched [en'trentʃt] *a* radicato(a).

entrepreneur [ɒntrəprə'nəː*] *n* imprenditore *m*.

entrust [ɪn'trʌst] *vt*: to ~ sth to affidare qc a.

entry ['ɛntrɪ] *n* entrata; (*way in*) entrata, ingresso; (*item: on list*) iscrizione *f*; (*in dictionary*) voce *f*; **no** ~ vietato l'ingresso; (*AUT*) divieto di accesso; ~ **form** *n* modulo d'iscrizione; ~ **phone** *n* citofono.

envelop [ɪn'vɛləp] *vt* avvolgere, avviluppare.

envelope ['ɛnvələup] *n* busta.

envious ['ɛnvɪəs] *a* invidioso(a).

environment [ɪn'vaɪərnmənt] *n* ambiente *m*; ~**al** [-'mɛntl] *a* ecologico(a); ambientale.

envisage [ɪn'vɪzɪdʒ] *vt* immaginare; prevedere.

envoy ['ɛnvɔɪ] *n* inviato/a.

envy ['ɛnvɪ] *n* invidia // *vt* invidiare; to ~ sb sth invidiare qn per qc.

epic ['ɛpɪk] *n* poema *m* epico // *a* epico(a).

epidemic [ɛpɪ'dɛmɪk] *n* epidemia.

epilepsy ['ɛpɪlɛpsɪ] *n* epilessia.

episode ['ɛpɪsəud] *n* episodio.

epistle [ɪ'pɪsl] *n* epistola.

epitome [ɪ'pɪtəmɪ] *n* epitome *f*; quintessenza; **epitomize** *vt* (*fig*) incarnare.

equable ['ɛkwəbl] *a* uniforme; equilibrato(a).

equal ['i:kwl] *a, n* uguale (*m/f*) // *vt* uguagliare; ~ to (*task*) all'altezza di; ~**ity** [i:'kwɔlɪtɪ] *n* uguaglianza; ~**ize** *vt, vi* pareggiare; ~**izer** *n* pareggio; ~**ly** *ad* ugualmente.

equanimity [ɛkwə'nɪmɪtɪ] *n* serenità.

equate [ɪ'kweɪt] *vt*: to ~ sth with considerare qc uguale a; (*compare*) paragonare qc con; **equation** [ɪ'kweɪʃən] *n* (*MATH*) equazione *f*.

equator [ɪ'kweɪtə*] *n* equatore *m*.

equilibrium [i:kwɪ'lɪbrɪəm] *n* equilibrio.

equip [ɪ'kwɪp] *vt* equipaggiare, attrezzare; to ~ sb/sth with fornire qn/qc di; to be well ~**ped** (*office etc*) essere ben attrezzato(a); he is well ~**ped** for the job ha i requisiti necessari per quel lavoro; ~**ment** *n* attrezzatura; (*electrical etc*) apparecchiatura.

equitable ['ɛkwɪtəbl] *a* equo(a), giusto(a).

equities ['ɛkwɪtɪz] *npl* (*Brit COMM*) azioni *fpl* ordinarie.

equivalent [ɪ'kwɪvələnt] *a, n* equivalente (*m*); to be ~ to equivalere a.

equivocal [ɪ'kwɪvəkl] *a* equivoco(a); (*open to suspicion*) dubbio(a).

era ['ɪərə] *n* era, età *f inv*.

eradicate [ɪ'rædɪkeɪt] *vt* sradicare.

erase [ɪ'reɪz] *vt* cancellare; ~**r** *n* gomma.

erect [ɪ'rɛkt] *a* eretto(a) // *vt* costruire; (*monument, tent*) alzare; ~**ion**

[ɪ'rɛkʃən] *n* erezione *f*.

ermine ['ə:mɪn] *n* ermellino.

erode [ɪ'rəud] *vt* erodere; (*metal*) corrodere.

erotic [ɪ'rɔtɪk] *a* erotico(a).

err [ə:*] *vi* errare; (*REL*) peccare.

errand ['ɛrnd] *n* commissione *f*.

erratic [ɪ'rætɪk] *a* imprevedibile; (*person, mood*) incostante.

error ['ɛrə*] *n* errore *m*.

erupt [ɪ'rʌpt] *vi* erompere; (*volcano*) mettersi (*or* essere) in eruzione; ~**ion** [ɪ'rʌpʃən] *n* eruzione *f*.

escalate ['ɛskəleɪt] *vi* intensificarsi.

escalator ['ɛskəleɪtə*] *n* scala mobile.

escapade [ɛskə'peɪd] *n* scappatella; avventura.

escape [ɪ'skeɪp] *n* evasione *f*; fuga; (*of gas etc*) fuga, fuoriuscita // *vi* fuggire; (*from jail*) evadere, scappare; (*fig*) sfuggire; (*leak*) uscire // *vt* sfuggire a; to ~ from sb sfuggire a qn; **escapism** *n* evasione *f* (dalla realtà).

escort *n* ['ɛskɔ:t] scorta; (*male companion*) cavaliere *m* // *vt* [ɪ'skɔ:t] scortare; accompagnare.

Eskimo ['ɛskɪməu] *n* eschimese *m/f*.

especially [ɪ'spɛʃlɪ] *ad* specialmente; soprattutto; espressamente.

espionage ['ɛspɪəna:ʒ] *n* spionaggio.

Esquire [ɪ'skwaɪə*] *n* (*abbr* Esq.): J. Brown, ~ Signor J. Brown.

essay ['ɛseɪ] *n* (*SCOL*) composizione *f*; (*LITERATURE*) saggio.

essence ['ɛsns] *n* essenza.

essential [ɪ'sɛnʃl] *a* essenziale; (*basic*) fondamentale // *n* elemento essenziale; ~**ly** *ad* essenzialmente.

establish [ɪ'stæblɪʃ] *vt* stabilire; (*business*) mettere su; (*one's power etc*) confermare; ~**ment** *n* stabilimento; the E~ment la classe dirigente, l'establishment *m*.

estate [ɪ'steɪt] *n* proprietà *f inv*; beni *mpl*, patrimonio; ~ **agent** *n* (*Brit*) agente *m* immobiliare; ~ **car** *n* (*Brit*) giardiniera.

esteem [ɪ'sti:m] *n* stima // *vt* (*think highly of*) stimare; (*consider*) considerare.

esthetic [ɪs'θɛtɪk] *a* (*US*) = **aesthetic**.

estimate *n* ['ɛstɪmət] stima; (*COMM*) preventivo // *vt* ['ɛstɪmeɪt] stimare, valutare; **estimation** [-'meɪʃən] *n* stima; opinione *f*.

estranged [ɪ'streɪndʒd] *a* separato(a).

etc *abbr* (= *et cetera*) etc, ecc.

etching ['ɛtʃɪŋ] *n* acquaforte *f*.

eternal [ɪ'tə:nl] *a* eterno(a).

eternity [ɪ'tə:nɪtɪ] *n* eternità.

ether ['i:θə*] *n* etere *m*.

ethical ['ɛθɪkl] *a* etico(a), morale.

ethics ['ɛθɪks] *n* etica // *npl* morale *f*.

Ethiopia [i:θɪ'əupɪə] *n* Etiopia.

ethnic ['ɛθnɪk] *a* etnico(a).

ethos ['i:θɔs] *n* norma di vita.

etiquette [ˈɛtɪkɛt] n etichetta.

Eurocheque [ˈjuərəutʃɛk] n eurochèque m inv.

Europe [ˈjuərəp] n Europa; **~an** [-ˈpiːən] a, n europeo(a).

evacuate [ɪˈvækjueɪt] vt evacuare.

evade [ɪˈveɪd] vt eludere; (duties etc) sottrarsi a.

evaluate [ɪˈvæljueɪt] vt valutare.

evaporate [ɪˈvæpəreɪt] vi evaporare // vt far evaporare; **~d milk** n latte m concentrato.

evasion [ɪˈveɪʒən] n evasione f.

evasive [ɪˈveɪsɪv] a evasivo(a).

eve [iːv] n: on the **~ of** alla vigilia di.

even [ˈiːvn] a regolare; (number) pari inv // ad anche, perfino; **~ if, ~ though** anche se; **~ more** ancora di più; **~ so** ciò nonostante; **not ~** nemmeno; **to get ~ with sb** dare la pari a qn; **to ~ out** vi pareggiare.

evening [ˈiːvnɪŋ] n sera; (as duration, event) serata; **in the ~** la sera; **~ class** n corso serale; **~ dress** n (woman's) abito da sera; **in ~ dress** (man) in abito scuro; (woman) in abito lungo.

event [ɪˈvent] n avvenimento; (SPORT) gara; **in the ~ of** in caso di; **~ful** a denso(a) di eventi.

eventual [ɪˈventʃuəl] a finale; **~ity** [-ˈælɪtɪ] n possibilità f inv, eventualità f inv; **~ly** ad finalmente.

ever [ˈɛvə*] ad mai; (at all times) sempre; **the best ~** il migliore che ci sia mai stato; **have you ~ seen it?** l'ha mai visto?; **~ since** ad da allora // cj sin da quando; **~ so pretty** così bello(a); **~green** n sempreverde m; **~lasting** a eterno(a).

every [ˈɛvrɪ] a ogni; **~ day** tutti i giorni, ogni giorno; **~ other/third day** ogni due/tre giorni; **~ other car** una macchina su due; **~ now and then** ogni tanto, di quando in quando; **~body** pronoun ognuno, tutti pl; **~day** a quotidiano(a); di ogni giorno; **~one** = **~body**; **~thing** pronoun tutto, ogni cosa; **~where** ad (gen) dappertutto; (wherever) ovunque.

evict [ɪˈvɪkt] vt sfrattare.

evidence [ˈɛvɪdns] n (proof) prova; (of witness) testimonianza; (sign): **to show ~ of** dare segni di; **to give ~** deporre.

evident [ˈɛvɪdnt] a evidente; **~ly** ad evidentemente.

evil [ˈiːvl] a cattivo(a), maligno(a) // n male m.

evoke [ɪˈvəuk] vt evocare.

evolution [iːvəˈluːʃən] n evoluzione f.

evolve [ɪˈvɒlv] vt elaborare // vi svilupparsi, evolversi.

ewe [juː] n pecora.

ex- [ɛks] prefix ex.

exacerbate [ɛksˈæsəbeɪt] vt aggravare.

exact [ɪgˈzækt] a esatto(a) // vt: **to ~ sth**

(from) estorcere qc (da); esigere qc (da); **~ing** a esigente; (work) faticoso(a); **~itude** n esattezza, precisione f; **~ly** ad esattamente.

exaggerate [ɪgˈzædʒəreɪt] vt, vi esagerare; **exaggeration** [-ˈreɪʃən] n esagerazione f.

exalted [ɪgˈzɔːltɪd] a esaltato(a); elevato(a).

exam [ɪgˈzæm] n abbr (SCOL) = **examination**.

examination [ɪgzæmɪˈneɪʃən] n (SCOL) esame m; (MED) controllo.

examine [ɪgˈzæmɪn] vt esaminare; (LAW: person) interrogare; **~r** n esaminatore/trice.

example [ɪgˈzɑːmpl] n esempio; **for ~** ad or per esempio.

exasperate [ɪgˈzɑːspəreɪt] vt esasperare; **exasperating** a esasperante; **exasperation** [-ˈreɪʃən] n esasperazione f.

excavate [ˈɛkskəveɪt] vt scavare.

exceed [ɪkˈsiːd] vt superare; (one's powers, time limit) oltrepassare; **~ingly** ad eccessivamente.

excellent [ˈɛksələnt] a eccellente.

except [ɪkˈsept] prep (also: **~ for, ~ing**) salvo, all'infuori di, eccetto // vt escludere; **~ if/when** salvo se/quando; **~ that** salvo che; **~ion** [ɪkˈsepʃən] n eccezione f; **to take ~ion to** trovare a ridire su; **~ional** [ɪkˈsepʃənl] a eccezionale.

excerpt [ˈɛksəːpt] n estratto.

excess [ɪkˈsɛs] n eccesso; **~ baggage** n bagaglio in eccedenza; **~ fare** n supplemento; **~ive** a eccessivo(a).

exchange [ɪksˈtʃeɪndʒ] n scambio; (also: **telephone ~**) centralino // vt: **to ~** (for) scambiare (con); **~ rate** n tasso di cambio.

Exchequer [ɪksˈtʃekə*] n: **the ~** (Brit) lo Scacchiere, ≈ il ministero delle Finanze.

excise [ˈɛksaɪz] n imposta, dazio.

excite [ɪkˈsaɪt] vt eccitare; **to get ~d** eccitarsi; **~ment** n eccitazione f; agitazione f; **exciting** a avventuroso(a); (film, book) appassionante.

exclaim [ɪkˈskleɪm] vi esclamare; **exclamation** [ɛkskləˈmeɪʃən] n esclamazione f; **exclamation mark** n punto esclamativo.

exclude [ɪkˈskluːd] vt escludere.

exclusive [ɪkˈskluːsɪv] a esclusivo(a); (club) selettivo(a); (district) snob inv; **~ of VAT** I.V.A. esclusa.

excommunicate [ɛkskəˈmjuːnɪkeɪt] vt scomunicare.

excruciating [ɪkˈskruːʃɪeɪtɪŋ] a straziante, atroce.

excursion [ɪkˈskəːʃən] n escursione f, gita.

excuse n [ɪkˈskjuːs] scusa // vt [ɪkˈskjuːz] scusare; **to ~ sb from** (activity) dispensare qn da; **~ me!** mi scusi!; **now,**

if you will ~ me ... ora, mi scusi ma ...
ex-directory ['eksdɪ'rektərɪ] a (Brit
TEL): to be ~ non essere sull'elenco.
execute ['eksɪkjuːt] vt (prisoner) giu-
stiziare; (plan etc) eseguire.
execution [eksɪ'kjuːʃən] n esecuzione f;
~er n boia m inv.
executive [ɪg'zekjutɪv] n (COMM)
dirigente m; (POL) esecutivo // a
esecutivo(a).
exemplify [ɪg'zemplɪfaɪ] vt esemplificare.
exempt [ɪg'zempt] a esentato(a) // vt: to
~ sb from esentare qn da; ~ion
[ɪg'zempʃən] n esenzione f.
exercise ['eksəsaɪz] n esercizio // vt
esercitare; (dog) portar fuori // vi fare
del movimento or moto; ~ book n
quaderno.
exert [ɪg'zɜːt] vt esercitare; to ~ o.s.
sforzarsi; ~ion n [-ʃən] n sforzo.
exhaust [ɪg'zɔːst] n (also: ~ fumes)
scappamento; (also: ~ pipe) tubo di
scappamento // vt esaurire; ~ed a
esaurito(a); ~ion [ɪg'zɔːstʃən] n
esaurimento; nervous ~ion so-
vraffaticamento mentale; ~ive a
esauriente.
exhibit [ɪg'zɪbɪt] n (ART) oggetto esposto;
(LAW) documento or oggetto esibito // vt
esporre; (courage, skill) dimostrare;
~ion [eksɪ'bɪʃən] n mostra, esposizione
f.
exhilarating [ɪg'zɪləreɪtɪŋ] a esilarante;
stimolante.
exhort [ɪg'zɔːt] vt esortare.
exile ['eksaɪl] n esilio; (person) esiliato/a
// vt esiliare.
exist [ɪg'zɪst] vi esistere; ~ence n esistenza; to be in ~ence esistere; ~ing a
esistente.
exit ['eksɪt] n uscita // vi (THEATRE,
COMPUT) uscire; ~ ramp n (US AUT)
rampa di uscita.
exodus ['eksədəs] n esodo.
exonerate [ɪg'zɒnəreɪt] vt: to ~ from discolpare da.
exotic [ɪg'zɒtɪk] a esotico(a).
expand [ɪk'spænd] vt espandere;
estendere; allargare // vi (trade etc)
svilupparsi, ampliarsi; espandersi; (gas)
espandersi; (metal) dilatarsi.
expanse [ɪk'spæns] n distesa, estensione
f.
expansion [ɪk'spænʃən] n (gen)
espansione f; (of town, economy)
sviluppo; (of metal) dilatazione f.
expect [ɪk'spekt] vt (anticipate)
prevedere, aspettarsi, prevedere or
aspettarsi che + sub; (count on) contare
su; (hope for) sperare; (require) richiedere, esigere; (suppose) supporre;
(await, also baby) aspettare // vi: to be
~ing in stato interessante; to ~
sb to do aspettarsi che qn faccia; ~ancy
n (anticipation) attesa; life ~ancy

probabilità fpl di vita; ~ant mother n
gestante f; ~ation [ekspek'teɪʃən] n
aspettativa; speranza.
expedience, expediency [ɪk'spiːdɪəns,
ɪk'spiːdɪənsɪ] n convenienza.
expedient [ɪk'spiːdɪənt] a conveniente;
vantaggioso(a) // n espediente m.
expedite ['ekspədaɪt] vt sbrigare;
facilitare.
expedition [ekspə'dɪʃən] n spedizione f.
expel [ɪk'spel] vt espellere.
expend [ɪk'spend] vt spendere; (use up)
consumare; ~able a sacrificabile;
~iture [ɪk'spendɪtʃə*] n spesa.
expense [ɪk'spens] n spesa; (high cost)
costo; ~s npl (COMM) spese fpl,
indennità fpl; at the ~ of a spese di; ~
account n conto m spese inv.
expensive [ɪk'spensɪv] a caro(a), co-
stoso(a).
experience [ɪk'spɪərɪəns] n esperienza //
vt (pleasure) provare; (hardship) soffrire; ~d a esperto(a).
experiment n [ɪk'sperɪmənt]
esperimento, esperienza // vi
[ɪk'sperɪment] fare esperimenti; to ~
with sperimentare.
expert ['ekspɜːt] a, n esperto(a); ~ise
[-'tiːz] n competenza.
expire [ɪk'spaɪə*] vi (period of time,
licence) scadere; expiry n scadenza.
explain [ɪk'spleɪn] vt spiegare; explanation [eksplə'neɪʃən] n spiegazione f;
explanatory [ɪk'splænətrɪ] a espli-
cativo(a).
explicit [ɪk'splɪsɪt] a esplicito(a);
(definite) netto(a).
explode [ɪk'spləud] vi esplodere.
exploit n ['eksplɔɪt] impresa // vt
[ɪk'splɔɪt] sfruttare; ~ation [-'teɪʃən] n
sfruttamento.
exploratory [ɪk'splɒrətrɪ] a (fig: talks)
esplorativo(a).
explore [ɪk'splɔː*] vt esplorare;
(possibilities) esaminare; ~r n
esploratore/trice.
explosion [ɪk'spləuʒən] n esplosione f.
explosive [ɪk'spləusɪv] a esplosivo(a) //
n esplosivo.
exponent [ɪk'spəunənt] n esponente m/f.
export vt [ek'spɔːt] esportare // n
['ekspɔːt] esportazione f; articolo di
esportazione // cpd d'esportazione; ~er n
esportatore m.
expose [ɪk'spəuz] vt esporre; (unmask)
smascherare; ~d a (position) espo-
sto(a).
exposure [ɪk'spəuʒə*] n esposizione f;
(PHOT) posa; (MED) assideramento; ~
meter n esposimetro.
expound [ɪk'spaund] vt esporre.
express [ɪk'spres] a (definite) chiaro(a),
espresso(a); (Brit: letter etc) espresso
inv // n (train) espresso // ad (send)
espresso // vt esprimere; ~ion

[ɪk'spreʃən] *n* espressione *f*; ~**ive** *a* espressivo(a); ~**ly** *ad* espressamente; ~**way** *n* (*US: urban motorway*) autostrada che attraversa la città.

exquisite [ɛk'skwɪzɪt] *a* squisito(a).

oxtend [ɪk'stɛnd] *vt* (*visit*) protrarre; (*road, deadline*) prolungare; (*building*) ampliare; (*offer*) offrire, porgere // *vi* (*land*) estendersi.

extension [ɪk'stɛnʃən] *n* (*of road, term*) prolungamento; (*of contract, deadline*) proroga; (*building*) annesso; (*to wire, table*) prolunga; (*telephone*) interno; (: *in private house*) apparecchio supplementare.

extensive [ɪk'stɛnsɪv] *a* esteso(a), ampio(a); (*damage*) su larga scala; (*alterations*) notevole; (*inquiries*) esauriente; (*use*) grande; ~**ly** *ad*: he's travelled ~ly ha viaggiato molto.

extent [ɪk'stɛnt] *n* estensione *f*; to some ~ fino a un certo punto; to what ~? fino a che punto?; to the ~ of ... fino al punto di ...

extenuating [ɪks'tɛnjueɪtɪŋ] *a*: ~ circumstances attenuanti *fpl*.

exterior [ɛk'stɪərɪə*] *a* esteriore, esterno(a) // *n* esteriore *m*, esterno; aspetto (esteriore).

exterminate [ɪk'stə:mɪneɪt] *vt* sterminare.

external [ɛk'stə:nl] *a* esterno(a), esteriore.

extinct [ɪk'stɪŋkt] *a* estinto(a).

extinguish [ɪk'stɪŋgwɪʃ] *vt* estinguere; ~**er** *n* estintore *m*.

extort [ɪk'stɔ:t] *vt*: to ~ sth (from) estorcere qc (da); ~**ionate** [ɪk'stɔ:ʃnət] *a* esorbitante.

extra ['ɛkstrə] *a* extra *inv*, supplementare // *ad* (*in addition*) di più // *n* supplemento; (*THEATRE*) comparso.

extra... ['ɛkstrə] *prefix* extra... .

extract *vt* [ɪk'strækt] estrarre; (*money, promise*) strappare // *n* ['ɛkstrækt] estratto; (*passage*) brano.

extracurricular ['ɛkstrəkə'rɪkjulə*] *a* parascolastico(a).

extradite ['ɛkstrədaɪt] *vt* estradare.

extramarital [ɛkstrə'mærɪtl] *a* extraconiugale.

extramural [ɛkstrə'mjuərl] *a* fuori dell'università.

extraordinary [ɪk'strɔ:dnrɪ] *a* straordinario(a).

extravagance [ɪk'strævəgəns] *n* sperpero; stravaganza.

extravagant [ɪk'strævəgənt] *a* stravagante; (*in spending*) dispendioso(a).

extreme [ɪk'stri:m] *a* estremo(a) // *n* estremo; ~**ly** *ad* estremamente.

extricate ['ɛkstrɪkeɪt] *vt*: to ~ sth (from) districare qc (da).

extrovert ['ɛkstrəvə:t] *n* estroverso/a.

exude [ɪg'zju:d] *vt* trasudare; (*fig*) emanare.

eye [aɪ] *n* occhio; (*of needle*) cruna // *vt* osservare; **to keep an ~ on** tenere d'occhio; ~**ball** *n* globo dell'occhio; ~**bath** *n* occhino; ~**brow** *n* sopracciglio; ~**brow pencil** *n* matita per le sopracciglia; ~**drops** *npl* gocce *fpl* oculari, collirio; ~**lash** *n* ciglio; ~**lid** *n* palpebra; ~ **liner** *n* eye-liner *m inv*; ~**opener** *n* rivelazione *f*; ~**shadow** *n* ombretto; ~**sight** *n* vista; ~**sore** *n* pugno nell'occhio; ~ **witness** *n* testimone *m/f* oculare.

F

F [ɛf] *n* (*MUS*) fa *m*.

fable ['feɪbl] *n* favola.

fabric ['fæbrɪk] *n* stoffa, tessuto.

fabrication [fæbrɪ'keɪʃən] *n* fabbricazione *f*; falsificazione *f*.

fabulous ['fæbjuləs] *a* favoloso(a); (*col: super*) favoloso(a), fantastico(a).

façade [fə'sɑ:d] *n* facciata.

face [feɪs] *n* faccia, viso, volto; (*expression*) faccia, (*grimace*) smorfia; (*of clock*) quadrante *m*; (*of building*) facciata; (*side, surface*) faccia // *vt* essere di fronte a; (*fig*) affrontare; ~ **down** a faccia in giù; to make *or* pull a ~ fare una smorfia; **in the** ~ **of** (*difficulties etc*) di fronte a; **on the** ~ **of** it a prima vista; ~ **to** ~ faccia a faccia; **to** ~ **up to** *vt fus* affrontare, far fronte a; ~ **cloth** *n* (*Brit*) guanto di spugna; ~ **cream** *n* crema per il viso; ~ **lift** *n* lifting *m inv*; (*of façade etc*) ripulita.

facet ['fæsɪt] *n* faccetta, sfaccettatura; (*fig*) sfaccettatura.

facetious [fə'si:ʃəs] *a* faceto(a).

face value *n* (*of coin*) valore *m* facciale *or* nominale; **to take sth at** ~ (*fig*) giudicare qc dalle apparenze.

facilities [fə'sɪlɪtɪz] *npl* attrezzature *fpl*; **credit** ~ facilitazioni *fpl* di credito.

facing ['feɪsɪŋ] *prep* di fronte a // *n* (*of wall etc*) rivestimento; (*SEWING*) paramontura.

facsimile [fæk'sɪmɪlɪ] *n* facsimile *m inv*; ~ **machine** *n* telecopiatrice *f*.

fact [fækt] *n* fatto; **in** ~ infatti.

factor ['fæktə*] *n* fattore *m*.

factory ['fæktərɪ] *n* fabbrica, stabilimento.

factual ['fæktjuəl] *a* che si attiene ai fatti.

faculty ['fækəltɪ] *n* facoltà *f inv*.

fad [fæd] *n* mania; capriccio.

fade [feɪd] *vi* sbiadire, sbiadirsi; (*light, sound, hope*) attenuarsi, affievolirsi; (*flower*) appassire.

fag [fæg] *n* (*col: cigarette*) cicca.

fail [feɪl] *vt* (*exam*) non superare; (*candidate*) bocciare; (*subj: courage,* *memory*) mancare a // *vi* fallire; (*student*) essere respinto(a); (*supplies*) mancare; (*eyesight, health, light*) venire a mancare; **to ~ to do sth** (*neglect*) mancare di fare qc; (*be unable*) non riuscire a fare qc; **without ~** senza fallo; certamente; **~ing** *n* difetto // *prep* in mancanza di; **~ure** ['feiljə*] *n* fallimento; (*person*) fallito/a; (*mechanical etc*) guasto.

faint [feint] *a* debole; (*recollection*) vago(a); (*mark*) indistinto(a) // *vi* svenire; to feel ~ sentirsi svenire.

fair [fɛə*] *a* (*person, decision*) giusto(a), equo(a); (*hair etc*) biondo(a); (*skin, complexion*) bianco(a); (*weather*) bello(a), clemente; (*good enough*) assai buono(a); (*sizeable*) bello(a) // *ad* (*play*) lealmente // *n* fiera; (*Brit: funfair*) luna park *m inv*; **~ly** *ad* equamente; (*quite*) abbastanza; **~ness** *n* equità, giustizia; **~ play** *n* correttezza.

fairy ['fɛəri] *n* fata; **~ tale** *n* fiaba.

faith [feiθ] *n* fede *f*; (*trust*) fiducia; (*sect*) religione *f*, fede *f*; **~ful** *a* fedele; **~fully** *ad* fedelmente; **yours ~fully** (*Brit: in letters*) distinti saluti.

fake [feik] *n* imitazione *f*; (*picture*) falso; (*person*) impostore/a // *a* falso(a) // *vt* (*accounts*) falsificare; (*illness*) fingere; (*painting*) contraffare.

falcon ['fɔːlkən] *n* falco, falcone *m*.

fall [fɔːl] *n* caduta; (*in temperature*) abbassamento; (*in price*) ribasso; (*US: autumn*) autunno // *vi* (*pt* **fell**, *pp* **fallen**) cadere; (*temperature, price*) abbassare; **~s** *npl* (*waterfall*) cascate *fpl*; **to ~ flat** *vi* (*on one's face*) cadere bocconi; (*joke*) fare cilecca; (*plan*) fallire; **to ~ back** *vi* (*retreat*) indietreggiare; (*MIL*) ritirarsi; **to ~ back on** *vt fus* (*remedy etc*) ripiegare su; **to ~ behind** *vi* rimanere indietro; **to ~ down** *vi* (*person*) cadere; (*building*) crollare; **to ~ for** *vt fus* (*person*) prendere una cotta per; **to ~ for a trick** (*or a story etc*) cascarci; **to ~ in** *vi* crollare; (*MIL*) mettersi in riga; **to ~ off** *vi* cadere; (*diminish*) diminuire, abbassarsi; **to ~ out** *vi* (*friends etc*) litigare; **to ~ through** *vi* (*plan, project*) fallire.

fallacy ['fæləsi] *n* errore *m*.

fallen ['fɔːlən] *pp of* **fall**.

fallout ['fɔːlaut] *n* fall-out *m*; **~ shelter** *n* rifugio antiatomico.

fallow ['fæləu] *a* incolto(a), a maggese.

false [fɔːls] *a* falso(a); **under ~ pretences** con l'inganno; **~ teeth** *npl* (*Brit*) denti *mpl* finti.

falter ['fɔːltə*] *vi* esitare, vacillare.

fame [feim] *n* fama, celebrità.

familiar [fə'miliə*] *a* familiare; (*common*) comune; (*close*) intimo(a); **to be ~ with** (*subject*) conoscere; **~ity** [fəmili'æriti] *n* familiarità; intimità;

~ize [fə'miliəraiz] *vt*: **to ~ize sb with sth** far conoscere qc a qn.

family ['fæmili] *n* famiglia.

famine ['fæmin] *n* carestia.

famished ['fæmiʃt] *a* affamato(a).

famous ['feiməs] *a* famoso(a); **~ly** *ad* (*get on*) a meraviglia.

fan [fæn] *n* (*folding*) ventaglio; (*ELEC*) ventilatore *m*; (*person*) ammiratore/trice; tifoso/a // *vt* far vento a; (*fire, quarrel*) alimentare; **to ~ out** *vi* spargersi (a ventaglio).

fanatic [fə'nætik] *n* fanatico/a.

fan belt *n* cinghia del ventilatore.

fanciful ['fænsiful] *a* fantasioso(a); (*object*) di fantasia.

fancy ['fænsi] *n* immaginazione *f*, fantasia; (*whim*) capriccio // *a* (di) fantasia *inv* // *vt* (*feel like, want*) aver voglia di; **to take a ~ to** incapricciarsi di; **~ dress** *n* costume *m* (per mascera); **~-dress ball** *n* ballo in maschera.

fang [fæŋ] *n* zanna; (*of snake*) dente *m*.

fantastic [fæn'tæstik] *a* fantastico(a).

fantasy ['fæntəsi] *n* fantasia, immaginazione *f*; fantasticheria; chimera.

far [faː*] *a*: **the ~** side/end l'altra parte/ l'altro capo // *ad* lontano; **~ away**, **~ off** lontano, distante; **~ better** assai migliore; **~ from** lontano da; **by ~** di gran lunga; **go as ~ as the farm** vada fino alla fattoria; **as ~ as I know** per quel che so; **~away** *a* lontano(a).

farce [faːs] *n* farsa.

farcical ['faːsikəl] *a* farsesco(a).

fare [fɛə*] *n* (*on trains, buses*) tariffa; (*in taxi*) prezzo della corsa; (*food*) vitto, cibo // *vi* passarsela; **half ~** metà tariffa; **full ~** tariffa intera.

Far East *n*: **the ~** l'Estremo Oriente *m*.

farewell [fɛə'wel] *excl, n* addio.

farm [faːm] *n* fattoria, podere *m* // *vt* coltivare; **~er** *n* coltivatore/trice; agricoltore/trice; **~hand** *n* bracciante *m* agricolo; **~house** *n* fattoria; **~ing** *n* agricoltura; **~ worker** *n* = **~hand**; **~yard** *n* aia.

far-reaching ['faː'riːtʃiŋ] *a* di vasta portata.

fart [faːt] (*col!*) *n* scoreggia(!) // *vi* scoreggiare (!).

farther ['faːðə*] *ad* più lontano // *a* più lontano(a).

farthest ['faːðist] *superlative of* **far**.

fascinate ['fæsineit] *vt* affascinare; **fascinating** *a* affascinante; **fascination** [-'neiʃən] *n* fascino.

fascism ['fæʃizəm] *n* fascismo.

fascist ['fæʃist] *a, n* fascista (*m/f*).

fashion ['fæʃən] *n* moda; (*manner*) maniera, modo // *vt* foggiare, formare; **in ~** alla moda; **out of ~** passato(a) di moda; **~able** *a* alla moda, di moda; **~**

show n sfilata di moda.

fast [fɑːst] a rapido(a), svelto(a), veloce; (clock): **to be ~** andare avanti; (dye, colour) solido(a) // ad rapidamente; (stuck, held) saldamente // n digiuno // vi digiunare; **~ asleep** profondamente addormentato.

fasten ['fɑːsn] vt chiudere, fissare; (coat) abbottonare, allacciare // vi chiudersi, fissarsi; **~er**, **~ing** n fermaglio, chiusura.

fast food n fast food m.

fastidious [fæs'tɪdɪəs] a esigente, difficile.

fat [fæt] a grasso(a) // n grasso.

fatal ['feɪtl] a fatale; mortale; disastroso(a); **~ity** [fə'tælɪtɪ] n (road death etc) morto/a, vittima; **~ly** ad a morte.

fate [feɪt] n destino; (of person) sorte f; **~ful** a fatidico(a).

father ['fɑːðə*] n padre m; **~-in-law** n suocero; **~ly** a paterno(a).

fathom ['fæðəm] n braccio (= 1828 mm) // vt (mystery) penetrare, sondare.

fatigue [fə'tiːg] n stanchezza; (MIL) corvé f.

fatten ['fætn] vt, vi ingrassare.

fatty ['fætɪ] a (food) grasso(a) // n (col) ciccione/a.

fatuous ['fætjuəs] a fatuo(a).

faucet ['fɔːsɪt] n (US) rubinetto.

fault [fɔːlt] n colpa; (TENNIS) fallo; (defect) difetto; (GEO) faglia // vt criticare; it's my **~** è colpa mia; to **find ~ with** trovare da ridire su; at **~** in fallo; to **a ~** eccessivamente; **~less** a perfetto(a); senza difetto; impeccabile; **~y** a difettoso(a).

fauna ['fɔːnə] n fauna.

faux pas ['fəʊ'pɑː] n gaffe f inv.

favour, (US) **favor** ['feɪvə*] n favore m, cortesia, piacere m // vt (proposition) favorire, essere favorevole a; (pupil etc) favorire; (team, horse) dare per vincente; to **do sb a ~** fare un favore or una cortesia a qn; to **find ~ with** (subj: person) entrare nelle buone grazie di; (: suggestion) avere l'approvazione di; in **~ of** in favore di; **~able** a favorevole; **~ite** [-rɪt] a, n favorito/a.

fawn [fɔːn] n daino // a (also: **~-coloured**) marrone chiaro inv // vi: to **~ (up)on** adulare servilmente.

fax [fæks] n (document) facsimile m inv, telecopia; (machine) telecopiatrice f.

FBI n abbr (US: = Federal Bureau of Investigation) F.B.I. f.

fear [fɪə*] n paura, timore m // vt aver paura di, temere; **for ~ of** per paura di; **~ful** a pauroso(a); (sight, noise) terribile, spaventoso(a).

feasibility [fiːzə'bɪlɪtɪ] n praticabilità.

feasible ['fiːzəbl] a possibile, realizzabile.

feast [fiːst] n festa, banchetto; (REL: also: **~ day**) festa // vi banchettare.

feat [fiːt] n impresa, fatto insigne.

feather ['fɛðə*] n penna.

feature ['fiːtʃə*] n caratteristica; (article) articolo // vt (subj: film) avere come protagonista // vi figurare; **~s** npl (of face) fisionomia; **~ film** n film m inv principale.

February ['fɛbruərɪ] n febbraio.

fed [fɛd] pt, pp of **feed**.

federal ['fɛdərəl] a federale.

fed-up [fɛd'ʌp] a: to **be ~** essere stufo(a).

fee [fiː] n pagamento; (of doctor, lawyer) onorario; (for examination) tassa d'esame; **school ~s** tasse fpl scolastiche.

feeble ['fiːbl] a debole.

feed [fiːd] n (of baby) pappa; (of animal) mangime m; (on printer) meccanismo di alimentazione // vt (pt, pp **fed**) nutrire; (Brit: baby) allattare; (horse etc) dare da mangiare a; (fire, machine) alimentare; to **~ material into** introdurre materiale in; to **~ data/information into** inserire dati/informazioni in; to **~ on** vt fus nutrirsi di; **~back** n feed-back m; **~ing bottle** n (Brit) biberon m inv.

feel [fiːl] n (sense of touch) tatto; (of substance) consistenza // vt (pt, pp **felt**) toccare; palpare; tastare; (cold, pain, anger) sentire; (grief) provare; (think, believe): to **~ (that)** pensare che; to **~ hungry/cold** aver fame/freddo; to **~ lonely/better** sentirsi solo/meglio; I **don't ~ well** non mi sento bene; to **~ like** (want) aver voglia di; to **~ about** or **around** for cercare a tastoni; **~er** n (of insect) antenna; to **put out ~ers** (fig) fare un sondaggio; **~ing** n sensazione f; sentimento.

feign [feɪn] vt fingere, simulare.

fell [fɛl] pt of **fall** // vt (tree) abbattere.

fellow ['fɛləʊ] n individuo, tipo; compagno; (of learned society) membro // cpd: **~ countryman** n compatriota m; **~ men** npl simili mpl; **~ship** n associazione f; compagnia; specie di borsa di studio universitaria.

felony ['fɛlənɪ] n reato, crimine m.

felt [fɛlt] pt, pp of **feel** // n feltro; **~-tip pen** n pennarello.

female ['fiːmeɪl] n (ZOOL) femmina; (pej: woman) donna, femmina // a femminile; (BIOL, ELEC) femmina inv; (sex, character) femminile; (vote etc) di donne.

feminine ['fɛmɪnɪn] a, n femminile (m).

feminist ['fɛmɪnɪst] n femminista m/f.

fence [fɛns] n recinto; (col: person) ricettatore/trice // vt (also: **~ in**) recingere // vi schermire; **fencing** n (SPORT) scherma.

fend [fɛnd] vi: to **~ for o.s.** arrangiarsi; to **~ off** vt (attack, attacker) respingere, difendersi da; (questions) eludere.

fender ['fɛndə*] n parafuoco; (US) parafango; paraurti m inv.

ferment vi [fə'mɛnt] fermentare // n ['fə:mɛnt] agitazione f, eccitazione f.

fern [fə:n] n felce f.

ferocious [fə'rəuʃəs] a feroce.

ferret ['fɛrɪt] n furetto.

ferry ['fɛrɪ] n (small) traghetto; (large: also: ~**boat**) nave f traghetto inv // vt traghettare.

fertile ['fə:taɪl] a fertile; (BIOL) fecondo(a); **fertilizer** ['fə:tɪlaɪzə*] n fertilizzante m.

fester ['fɛstə*] vi suppurare.

festival ['fɛstɪvəl] n (REL) festa; (ART, MUS) festival m inv.

festive ['fɛstɪv] a di festa; the ~ season (Brit: Christmas) il periodo delle feste.

festivities [fɛs'tɪvɪtɪz] npl festeggiamenti mpl.

festoon [fɛs'tu:n] vt: to ~ with ornare di.

fetch [fɛtʃ] vt andare a prendere; (sell for) essere venduto(a) per.

fetching ['fɛtʃɪŋ] a attraente.

fête [feɪt] n festa.

fetish ['fɛtɪʃ] n feticcio.

fetus ['fi:təs] n (US) = **foetus**.

feud [fju:d] n contesa, lotta // vi essere in lotta.

feudal ['fju:dl] a feudale.

fever ['fi:və*] n febbre f; ~**ish** a febbrile.

few [fju:] a pochi(e); they were ~ erano pochi; a ~ a qualche inv // pronoun alcuni(e); ~**er** a meno inv; meno numerosi(e); ~**est** a il minor numero di.

fiancé [fɪ'ɑ̃:ŋseɪ] n fidanzato; ~**e** n fidanzata.

fib [fɪb] n piccola bugia.

fibre, (US) **fiber** ['faɪbə*] n fibra; ~**glass** n fibra di vetro.

fickle ['fɪkl] a incostante, capriccioso(a).

fiction ['fɪkʃən] n narrativa, romanzi mpl; (sth made up) finzione f; ~**al** a immaginario(a).

fictitious [fɪk'tɪʃəs] a fittizio(a).

fiddle ['fɪdl] n (MUS) violino; (cheating) imbroglio; truffa // vt (Brit: accounts) falsificare, falsare; **to ~ with** vt fus gingillarsi con.

fidelity [fɪ'dɛlɪtɪ] n fedeltà; (accuracy) esattezza.

fidget ['fɪdʒɪt] vi agitarsi.

field [fi:ld] n campo; ~ **marshal** n feldmaresciallo; ~**work** n ricerche fpl esterne.

fiend [fi:nd] n demonio.

fierce [fɪəs] a (look, fighting) fiero(a); (wind) furioso(a); (attack) feroce; (enemy) acerrimo(a).

fiery ['faɪərɪ] a ardente; infocato(a).

fifteen [fɪf'ti:n] num quindici.

fifth [fɪfθ] num quinto(a).

fifty ['fɪftɪ] num cinquanta; ~-~ a: a ~-

~ **chance** una possibilità su due // ad fifty-fifty, metà per ciascuno.

fig [fɪg] n fico.

fight [faɪt] n zuffa, rissa; (MIL) battaglia, combattimento; (against cancer etc) lotta // vb (pt, pp **fought**) vt picchiare; combattere; (cancer, alcoholism) lottare contro, combattere // vi battersi, combattere; ~**er** n combattente m; (plane) aeroplano da caccia; ~**ing** n combattimento.

figment ['fɪgmənt] n: a ~ of the imagination un parto della fantasia.

figurative ['fɪgjurətɪv] a figurato(a).

figure ['fɪgə*] n (DRAWING, GEOM) figura; (number, cipher) cifra; (body, outline) forma // vi (appear) figurare; (US: make sense) spiegarsi; **to ~ out** vt riuscire a capire; calcolare; ~**head** n (NAUT) polena; (pej) prestanome m/f inv; ~ **of speech** n figura retorica.

file [faɪl] n (tool) lima; (dossier) incartamento; (folder) cartellina; (for loose leaf) raccoglitore m; (COMPUT) archivio; (row) fila // vt (nails, wood) limare; (papers) archiviare; (LAW: claim) presentare; passare agli atti; **to ~ in/out** vi entrare/uscire in fila; **to ~ past** vt fus marciare in fila davanti a.

filing ['faɪlɪŋ] n archiviare m; ~ **cabinet** n casellario.

fill [fɪl] vt riempire; (tooth) otturare; (job) coprire // n: **to eat one's ~** mangiare a sazietà; **to ~ in** vt (hole) riempire; (form) compilare; **to ~ up** vt riempire // vi (AUT) fare il pieno; ~ **it up, please** (AUT) mi faccia il pieno, per piacere.

fillet ['fɪlɪt] n filetto; ~ **steak** n bistecca di filetto.

filling ['fɪlɪŋ] n (CULIN) impasto, ripieno; (for tooth) otturazione f; ~ **station** n stazione f di rifornimento.

film [fɪlm] n (CINEMA) film m inv; (PHOT) pellicola; (thin layer) velo // vt (scene) filmare; ~ **star** n divo/a dello schermo; ~ **strip** n filmina.

filter ['fɪltə*] n filtro // vt filtrare; ~ **lane** n (Brit AUT) corsia di svincolo; ~-**tipped** a con filtro.

filth [fɪlθ] n sporcizia; (fig) oscenità; ~**y** a lordo(a), sozzo(a); (language) osceno(a).

fin [fɪn] n (of fish) pinna.

final ['faɪnl] a finale, ultimo(a); definitivo(a) // n (SPORT) finale f; ~**s** npl (SCOL) esami mpl finali; ~**e** [fɪ'nɑ:lɪ] n finale m; ~**ize** vt mettere a punto; ~**ly** ad (lastly) alla fine; (eventually) finalmente.

finance [faɪ'næns] n finanza // vt finanziare; ~**s** npl finanze fpl.

financial [faɪ'nænʃəl] a finanziario(a).

financier [faɪ'nænsɪə*] n finanziatore m.

find [faɪnd] vt (pt, pp **found**) trovare;

(lost object) ritrovare // n trovata, scoperta; **to ~ sb guilty** *(LAW)* giudicare qn colpevole; **to ~ out** vt informarsi di; *(truth, secret)* scoprire; *(person)* cogliere in fallo; **to ~ out about** informarsi di; *(by chance)* scoprire; **~ings** npl *(LAW)* sentenza, conclusioni fpl; *(of report)* conclusioni.

fine [faɪn] a bello(a); ottimo(a); *(thin, subtle)* fine // ad *(well)* molto bene; *(small)* finemente // n *(LAW)* multa // vt *(LAW)* multare; **to be ~** *(weather)* far bello; **~ arts** npl belle arti fpl.

finery ['faɪnərɪ] n abiti mpl eleganti.

finger ['fɪŋgə*] n dito // vt toccare, tastare; **little/index ~** mignolo/(dito) indice m; **~nail** n unghia; **~print** n impronta digitale; **~tip** n punta del dito.

finicky ['fɪnɪkɪ] a esigente, pignolo(a); minuzioso(a).

finish ['fɪnɪʃ] n fine f; *(polish etc)* finitura // vt finire; *(use up)* esaurire // vi finire; *(session)* terminare; **to ~ doing sth** finire di fare qc; **to ~ third** arrivare terzo(a); **to ~ off** vt compiere; *(kill)* uccidere; **to ~ up** vi, vt finire; **~ing line** n linea d'arrivo; **~ing school** n scuola privata di perfezionamento *(per signorine)*.

finite ['faɪnaɪt] a limitato(a); *(verb)* finito(a).

Finland ['fɪnlənd] n Finlandia.

Finn [fɪn] n finlandese m/f; **~ish** a finlandese // n *(LING)* finlandese m.

fir [fə:*] n abete m.

fire [faɪə*] n fuoco; incendio // vt *(discharge)*: **to ~ a gun** scaricare un fucile; *(fig)* infiammare; *(dismiss)* licenziare // vi sparare, far fuoco; **on ~** in fiamme; **~ alarm** n allarme m d'incendio; **~arm** n arma da fuoco; **~ brigade**, *(US)* **~ department** n *(corpo dei)* pompieri mpl; **~ engine** n autopompa; **~ escape** n scala di sicurezza; **~ extinguisher** n estintore m; **~man** n pompiere m; **~place** n focolare m; **~side** n angolo del focolare; **~ station** n caserma dei pompieri; **~wood** n legna; **~work** n fuoco d'artificio; **~works display** n spettacolo pirotecnico.

firing ['faɪərɪŋ] n *(MIL)* spari mpl, tiro; **~ squad** n plotone m d'esecuzione.

firm [fə:m] a fermo(a) // n ditta, azienda; **~ly** ad fermamente.

first [fə:st] a primo(a) // ad *(before others)* il primo, la prima; *(before other things)* per primo; *(when listing reasons etc)* per prima cosa // n *(person: in race)* primo/a; *(SCOL)* laurea con lode; *(AUT)* prima; **at ~** dapprima, all'inizio; **~ of all** prima di tutto; **~ aid** n pronto soccorso; **~-aid kit** n cassetta pronto soccorso; **~-class** a di prima classe; **~-hand** a di prima mano; **~ lady** n *(US)* moglie f del presidente; **~ly** ad in

primo luogo; **~ name** n prenome m; **~-rate** a di prima qualità, ottimo(a).

fish [fɪʃ] n *(pl inv)* pesce m // vi pescare; **to go ~ing** andare a pesca; **~erman** n pescatore m; **~ farm** n vivaio; **~ fingers** npl *(Brit)* bastoncini mpl di pesce *(surgelati)*; **~ing boat** n barca da pesca; **~ing line** n lenza; **~ing rod** n canna da pesca; **~monger** n pescivendolo; **~monger's (shop)** n pescheria; **~ sticks** npl *(US)* = **~ fingers**; **~y** a *(fig)* sospetto(a).

fist [fɪst] n pugno.

fit [fɪt] a *(MED, SPORT)* in forma; *(proper)* adatto(a), appropriato(a); conveniente // vt *(subj: clothes)* stare bene a; *(adjust)* aggiustare; *(put in, attach)* mettere; installare; *(equip)* fornire, equipaggiare // vi *(clothes)* stare bene; *(parts)* andare bene, adattarsi; *(in space, gap)* entrare // n *(MED)* accesso, attacco; **~ to** in grado di; **~ for** adatto(a) a; degno(a) di; **a ~ of anger** un accesso d'ira; **this dress is a tight/good ~** questo vestito è stretto/sta bene; **by ~s and starts** a sbalzi; **to ~ in** vi accordarsi; adattarsi; **to ~ out** vt *(Brit: also: ~ up)* equipaggiare; **~ful** a saltuario(a); **~ment** n componibile m; **~ness** n *(MED)* forma fisica; *(of remark)* appropriatezza; **~ted carpet** n moquette f; **~ted kitchen** n cucina componibile; **~ter** n aggiustatore m or montatore m meccanico; *(DRESSMAKING)* sarto/a; **~ting** a appropriato(a) // n *(of dress)* prova; *(of piece of equipment)* montaggio, aggiustaggio; **~ting room** n camerino; **~tings** npl impianti mpl.

five [faɪv] num cinque; **~r** n *(col. Brit)* biglietto da cinque sterline; (: *US)* biglietto da cinque dollari.

fix [fɪks] vt fissare; mettere in ordine; *(mend)* riparare // n: **to be in a ~** essere nei guai; **to ~ up** vt *(meeting)* fissare; **to ~ sb up with sth** procurare qc a qn; **~ation** n fissazione f; **~ed** [fɪkst] a *(prices etc)* fisso(a); **~ture** ['fɪkstʃə*] n impianto *(fisso)*; *(SPORT)* incontro *(del calendario sportivo)*.

fizz [fɪz] vi frizzare.

fizzle ['fɪzl] vi frizzare; **to ~ out** vi finire in nulla.

fizzy ['fɪzɪ] a frizzante; gassato(a).

flabbergasted ['flæbəgɑːstɪd] a sbalordito(a).

flabby ['flæbɪ] a flaccido(a).

flag [flæg] n bandiera; *(also: ~stone)* pietra da lastricare // vi stancarsi; affievolirsi; **to ~ down** vt fare segno *(di fermarsi)* a.

flagpole ['flægpəul] n albero.

flair [flɛə*] n *(for business etc)* fiuto; *(for languages etc)* facilità.

flak [flæk] n *(MIL)* fuoco d'artiglieria;

(col: criticism) critiche *fpl*.

flake [fleɪk] *n (of rust, paint)* scaglia; *(of snow, soap powder)* fiocco // *vi (also: ~ off)* sfaldarsi.

flamboyant [flæm'bɔɪənt] *a* sgargiante.

flame [fleɪm] *n* fiamma.

flamingo [flə'mɪŋgəu] *n* fenicottero, fiammingo.

flammable ['flæməbl] *a* infiammabile.

flan [flæn] *n (Brit)* flan *m inv*.

flank [flæŋk] *n* fianco.

flannel ['flænl] *n (Brit: also:* **face ~**) guanto di spugna; *(fabric)* flanella; **~s** *npl* pantaloni *mpl* di flanella.

flap [flæp] *n (of pocket)* patta; *(of envelope)* lembo // *vt (wings)* battere // *vi (sail, flag)* sbattere; *(col: also:* **be in a ~**) essere in agitazione.

flare [flɛə*] *n* razzo; *(in skirt etc)* svasatura; **to ~ up** *vi* andare in fiamme; *(fig: person)* infiammarsi di rabbia; *(: revolt)* scoppiare.

flash [flæʃ] *n* vampata; *(also: news ~)* notizia *f* lampo *inv*; *(PHOT)* flash *m inv* // *vt* accendere e spegnere; *(send: message)* trasmettere // *vi* brillare; *(light on ambulance, eyes etc)* lampeggiare; **in a ~** in un lampo; **to ~ one's headlights** lampeggiare; **he ~ed** by or past ci passò davanti come un lampo; **~bulb** *n* cubo *m* flash *inv*; **~cube** *n* flash *m inv*; **~light** *n* lampadina tascabile.

flashy ['flæʃɪ] *a (pej)* vistoso(a).

flask [flɑːsk] *n* fiasco; *(CHEM)* beuta; *(also:* **vacuum ~**) thermos *m inv* ®.

flat [flæt] *a* piatto(a); *(tyre)* sgonfio(a), a terra; *(denial)* netto(a); *(MUS)* bemolle *inv*; *(: voice)* stonato(a) // *n (Brit: rooms)* appartamento; *(AUT)* pneumatico sgonfio; *(MUS)* bemolle *m*; **to work ~ out** lavorare a più non posso; **~ly** *ad* categoricamente; **~ten** *vt (also:* **~ten out**) appiattire.

flatter ['flætə*] *vt* lusingare; **~ing** *a* lusinghiero(a); **~y** *n* adulazione *f*.

flaunt [flɔːnt] *vt* fare mostra di.

flavour, *(US)* **flavor** ['fleɪvə*] *n* gusto, sapore *m* // *vt* insaporire, aggiungere sapore a; **vanilla-~ed** al gusto di vaniglia; **~ing** *n* essenza (artificiale).

flaw [flɔː] *n* difetto.

flax [flæks] *n* lino; **~en** *a* biondo(a).

flea [fliː] *n* pulce *f*.

fleck [flɛk] *n (mark)* macchiolina; *(pattern)* screziatura.

flee, *pt, pp* **fled** [fliː, flɛd] *vt* fuggire da // *vi* fuggire, scappare.

fleece [fliːs] *n* vello // *vt (col)* pelare.

fleet [fliːt] *n* flotta; *(of lorries etc)* convoglio; parco.

fleeting ['fliːtɪŋ] *a* fugace, fuggitivo(a); *(visit)* volante.

Flemish ['flɛmɪʃ] *a* fiammingo(a) // *n (LING)* fiammingo.

flesh [flɛʃ] *n* carne *f*; *(of fruit)* polpa; **~ wound** *n* ferita superficiale.

flew [fluː] *pt of* **fly**.

flex [flɛks] *n* filo (flessibile) // *vt* flettere; *(muscles)* contrarre; **~ible** *a* flessibile.

flick [flɪk] *n* colpetto; scarto; **to ~ through** *vt fus* sfogliare.

flicker ['flɪkə*] *vi* tremolare // *n* tremolio.

flier ['flaɪə*] *n* aviatore *m*.

flight [flaɪt] *n* volo; *(escape)* fuga; *(also: ~ of steps)* scalinata; **~ attendant** *n (US)* steward *m inv*, hostess *f inv*; **~ deck** *n (AVIAT)* cabina di controllo; *(NAUT)* ponte *m* di comando.

flimsy ['flɪmzɪ] *a (fabric)* inconsistente; *(excuse)* meschino(a).

flinch [flɪntʃ] *vi* ritirarsi; **to ~ from** tirarsi indietro di fronte a.

fling [flɪŋ], *pt, pp* **flung** *vt* lanciare, gettare.

flint [flɪnt] *n* selce *f*; *(in lighter)* pietrina.

flip [flɪp] *n* colpetto.

flippant ['flɪpənt] *a* senza rispetto, irriverente.

flipper ['flɪpə*] *n* pinna.

flirt [flɜːt] *vi* flirtare // *n* civetta.

flit [flɪt] *vi* svolazzare.

float [fləut] *n* galleggiante *m*; *(in procession)* carro; *(money)* somma // *vi* galleggiare // *vt* far galleggiare; *(loan, business)* lanciare.

flock [flɔk] *n* gregge *m*; *(of people)* folla.

flog [flɔg] *vt* flagellare.

flood [flʌd] *n* alluvione *m*; *(of words, tears etc)* diluvio // *vt* allagare; **~ing** *n* inondazione *f*; **~light** *n* riflettore *m* // *vt* illuminare a giorno.

floor [flɔː*] *n* pavimento; *(storey)* piano; *(fig: at meeting):* **the ~** il pubblico // *vt* pavimentare; *(knock down)* atterrare; **on the ~** per terra; **ground ~**, *(US)* **first ~** pianterreno; **first ~,** *(US)* **second ~** primo piano; **~board** *n* tavellone *m* di legno; **~ show** *n* spettacolo di varietà.

flop [flɔp] *n* fiasco.

floppy ['flɔpɪ] *a* floscio(a), molle; **~ (disk)** *n (COMPUT)* floppy disk *m inv*.

flora ['flɔːrə] *n* flora.

Florence ['flɔrəns] *n* Firenze *f*; **Florentine** ['flɔrəntaɪn] *a* fiorentino(a).

florid ['flɔrɪd] *a (complexion)* florido(a); *(style)* fiorito(a).

florist ['flɔrɪst] *n* fioraio/a.

flounce [flauns] *n* balzo.

flounder ['flaundə*] *vi* annaspare // *n (ZOOL)* passera di mare.

flour ['flauə*] *n* farina.

flourish ['flʌrɪʃ] *vi* fiorire // *vt* brandire // *n* abbellimento; svolazzo; *(of trumpets)* fanfara.

flout [flaut] *vt (order)* contravvenire a; *(convention)* sfidare.

flow [fləu] *n* flusso; circolazione *f* // *vi* fluire; *(traffic, blood in veins)* circolare; *(hair)* scendere; **~ chart** *n* schema *m* di flusso.

flower ['flauə*] *n* fiore *m* // *vi* fiorire; ~
bed *n* aiuola; ~**pot** *n* vaso da fiori; ~**y**
a fiorito(a).

flown [fləun] *pp of* **fly**.

flu [flu:] *n* influenza.

fluctuate ['flʌktjueɪt] *vi* fluttuare,
oscillare.

fluency ['flu:ənsɪ] *n* facilità, scioltezza;
his ~ in English la sua scioltezza nel
parlare l'inglese.

fluent ['flu:ənt] *a* (*speech*) facile,
sciolto(a); corrente; he speaks ~ Italian
parla l'italiano correntemente.

fluff [flʌf] *n* lanugine *f*; ~**y** *a*
lanuginoso(a); (*toy*) di peluche.

fluid ['flu:ɪd] *a* fluido(a) // *n* fluido.

fluke [flu:k] *n* (*col*) colpo di fortuna.

flung [flʌŋ] *pt*, *pp of* **fling**.

fluoride ['fluəraɪd] *n* fluoruro.

flurry ['flʌrɪ] *n* (*of snow*) tempesta; a ~
of activity/excitement una febbre di
attività/improvvisa agitazione.

flush [flʌʃ] *n* rossore *m*; (*fig*) ebbrezza;
(: *of youth, beauty etc*) rigoglio, pieno
vigore // *vt* ripulire con un getto d'acqua
// *vi* arrossire // *a*: ~ **with** a livello di,
pari a; to ~ the toilet tirare l'acqua; to
~ **out** *vt* (*birds*) far alzare in volo;
(*animals, fig*) stanare; ~**ed** *a* tutto(a)
rosso(a).

flustered ['flʌstəd] *a* sconvolto(a).

flute [flu:t] *n* flauto.

flutter ['flʌtə*] *n* agitazione *f*; (*of wings*)
frullìo // *vi* (*bird*) battere le ali.

flux [flʌks] *n*: in a state of ~ in continuo
mutamento.

fly [flaɪ] *n* (*insect*) mosca; (*on trousers*:
also: flies) bracchetta // *vb* (*pt* **flew**, *pp*
flown) *vt* pilotare, (*passengers, cargo*)
trasportare (in aereo); (*distances*)
percorrere // *vi* volare; (*passengers*)
andare in aereo; (*escape*) fuggire; (*flag*)
sventolare; to ~ **away** *or* **off** *vi* volare
via; ~**ing** *n* (*activity*) aviazione *f*;
(*action*) volo // *a*: ~**ing** **visit** visita
volante; **with** ~**ing colours** con risultati
brillanti; ~**ing saucer** *n* disco volante;
~**ing start** *n*: to get off to a ~**ing start**
partire come un razzo; ~**over** *n* (*Brit*:
bridge) cavalcavia *m inv*; ~**sheet** *n*
(*for tent*) soprattetto.

foal [fəul] *n* puledro.

foam [fəum] *n* schiuma // *vi* schiumare;
~ **rubber** *n* gommapiuma ®.

fob [fɔb] *vt*: to ~ **sb off** with appioppare
qn con; sbarazzarsi di qn con.

focus ['fəukəs] *n* (*pl* ~**es**) fuoco; (*of
interest*) centro // *vt* (*field glasses etc*)
mettere a fuoco // *vi*: to ~ **on** (*with
camera*) mettere a fuoco; (*person*)
fissare lo sguardo su; **in** ~ a fuoco; **out
of** ~ sfocato(a).

fodder ['fɔdə*] *n* foraggio.

foe [fəu] *n* nemico.

foetus, (*US*) **fetus** ['fi:təs] *n* feto.

fog [fɔg] *n* nebbia; ~**gy** *a* nebbioso(a);
it's ~**gy** c'è nebbia; ~ **lamp** *n* (*AUT*)
faro *m* antinebbia *inv*.

foil [fɔɪl] *vt* confondere, frustrare // *n*
lamina di metallo; (*kitchen* ~) foglio di
alluminio; (*FENCING*) fioretto.

fold [fəuld] *n* (*bend, crease*) piega;
(*AGR*) ovile *m*; (*fig*) gregge *m* // *vt*
piegare; to ~ **up** *vi* (*business*) crollare
// *vt* (*map etc*) piegare, ripiegare; ~**er** *n*
(*for papers*) cartella; cartellina; (*brochure*) dépliant *m inv*; ~**ing** *a* (*chair,
bed*) pieghevole.

foliage ['fəulɪdʒ] *n* fogliame *m*.

folk [fəuk] *npl* gente *f* // *a* popolare; ~**s**
npl famiglia; ~**lore** ['fəuklɔ:*] *n* folclore
m; ~ **song** *n* canto popolare.

follow ['fɔləu] *vt* seguire // *vi* seguire;
(*result*) conseguire, risultare; he ~**ed**
suit lui ha fatto lo stesso; to ~ **up** *vt*
(*victory*) sfruttare; (*letter, offer*) fare
seguito a; (*case*) seguire; ~**er** *n*
seguace *m/f*, discepolo/a; ~**ing** *a*
seguente, successivo(a) // *n* seguito, discepoli *mpl*.

folly ['fɔlɪ] *n* pazzia, follia.

fond [fɔnd] *a* (*memory, look*) tenero(a),
affettuoso(a); to be ~ **of** volere bene a.

fondle ['fɔndl] *vt* accarezzare.

food [fu:d] *n* cibo; ~ **mixer** *n* frullatore
m; ~ **poisoning** *n* intossicazione *f*; ~
processor *n* tritatutto *m inv* elettrico;
~**stuffs** *npl* generi *fpl* alimentari.

fool [fu:l] *n* sciocco/a; (*HISTORY: of king*)
buffone *m*; (*CULIN*) frullato // *vt*
ingannare // *vi* (*gen*: ~ **around**) fare lo
sciocco; ~**hardy** *a* avventato(a); ~**ish**
a scemo(a), stupido(a); imprudente;
~**proof** *a* (*plan etc*) sicurissimo(a).

foot [fut] *n* (*pl* **feet**) piede *m*; (*measure*)
piede (= 304 *mm*; 12 *inches*); (*of
animal*) zampa // *vt* (*bill*) pagare; **on** ~
a piedi; ~**age** *n* (*CINEMA*: *length*) ≈
metraggio; (: *material*) sequenza;
~**ball** *n* pallone *m*; (*sport*: *Brit*) calcio;
(: *US*) football *m* americano; ~**baller** *n*
(*Brit*) = ~**ball player**; ~**ball ground**
n campo di calcio; ~**ball player** *n*
(*Brit*) calciatore *m*; (*US*) giocatore *m* di
football americano; ~**brake** *n* freno a
pedale; ~**bridge** *n* passerella; ~**hills**
npl contrafforti *fpl*; ~**hold** *n* punto
d'appoggio; ~**ing** *n* (*fig*) posizione *f*; to
lose one's ~ mettere un piede in fallo;
~**lights** *npl* luci *fpl* della ribalta; ~**man**
n lacchè *m inv*; ~**note** *n* nota (a piè di
pagina); ~**path** *n* sentiero; (*in street*)
marciapiede *m*; ~**print** *n* orma, impronta; ~**step** *n* passo; ~**wear** *n*
calzatura.

for [fɔ:*] ◆ *prep* **1** (*indicating destination, intention, purpose*) per; the
train ~ London il treno per Londra; he
went ~ the paper è andato a prendere il

giornale; it's time ~ lunch è ora di pranzo; what's it ~? a che serve?; what ~? (why) perché?
2 (on behalf of, representing) per; to work ~ sb/sth lavorare per qn/qc; I'll ask him ~ you glielo chiederò a nome tuo; G ~ George G come George
3 (because of) per, a causa di; ~ this reason per questo motivo
4 (with regard to) per; it's cold ~ July è freddo per luglio; ~ everyone who voted yes, 50 voted no per ogni voto a favore ce n'erano 50 contro
5 (in exchange for) per; I sold it ~ £5 l'ho venduto per 5 sterline
6 (in favour of) per, a favore di; are you ~ or against us? è con noi o contro di noi?; I'm all ~ it sono completamente a favore
7 (referring to distance, time) per; there are roadworks ~ 5 km ci sono lavori in corso per 5 km; he was away ~ 2 years è stato via per 2 anni; she will be away ~ a month starà via un mese; it hasn't rained ~ 3 weeks non piove da 3 settimane; can you do it ~ tomorrow? può farlo per domani?
8 (with infinitive clauses): it is not ~ me to decide non sta a me decidere; it would be best ~ you to leave sarebbe meglio che lei se ne andasse; there is still time ~ you to do it ha ancora tempo per farlo; ~ this to be possible ... perché ciò sia possibile ...
9 (in spite of) nonostante; ~ all his complaints, he's very fond of her nonostante tutte le sue lamentele, le vuole molto bene
◆ cj (since, as: rather formal) dal momento che, poiché.

forage ['fɔrɪdʒ] vi foraggiare.
foray ['fɔreɪ] n incursione f.
forbid, pt **forbad(e)**, pp **forbidden** [fə'bɪd, -'bæd, -'bɪdn] vt vietare, interdire; to ~ sb to do sth proibire a qn di fare qc; ~**den** a vietato(a); ~**ding** a arcigno(a), d'aspetto minaccioso.
force [fɔːs] n forza // vt forzare; the F~s npl (Brit) le forze armate; to ~ o.s. to do costringersi a fare; in ~ (in large numbers) in gran numero; (law) in vigore; to come into ~ entrare in vigore; ~**-feed** vt (animal, prisoner) sottoporre ad alimentazione forzata; ~**ful** a forte, vigoroso(a).
forceps ['fɔːsɛps] npl forcipe m.
forcibly ['fɔːsəblɪ] ad con la forza; (vigorously) vigorosamente.
ford [fɔːd] n guado m // vt guadare.
fore [fɔː*] n: to the ~ in prima linea; to come to the ~ mettersi in evidenza.
forearm ['fɔːrɑːm] n avambraccio.
foreboding [fɔː'bəudɪŋ] n presagio di male.
forecast ['fɔːkɑːst] n previsione f // vt

(irg: like **cast**) prevedere.
forecourt ['fɔːkɔːt] n (of garage) corte f esterna.
forefathers ['fɔːfɑːðəz] npl antenati mpl, avi mpl.
forefinger ['fɔːfɪŋgə*] n (dito) indice m.
forefront ['fɔːfrʌnt] n: in the ~ of all'avanguardia in.
forego [fɔː'gəu] vt = **forgo**.
foregone ['fɔːgɔn] a: it's a ~ conclusion è una conclusione scontata.
foreground ['fɔːgraund] n primo piano.
forehead ['fɔrɪd] n fronte f.
foreign ['fɔrɪn] a straniero(a); (trade) estero(a); ~ **body** n corpo estraneo; ~**er** n straniero/a; F~ **Office** n (Brit) Ministero degli Esteri; ~ **secretary** n (Brit) ministro degli Affari esteri.
foreleg ['fɔːlɛg] n zampa anteriore.
foreman ['fɔːmən] n caposquadra m.
foremost ['fɔːməust] a principale; più in vista // ad: first and ~ innanzitutto.
forensic [fə'rɛnsɪk] a: ~ **medicine** medicina legale.
forerunner ['fɔːrʌnə*] n precursore m.
foresee, pt **foresaw**, pp **foreseen** [fɔː'siː, -'sɔː, -'siːn] vt prevedere; ~**able** a prevedibile.
foreshadow [fɔː'ʃædəu] vt presagire, far prevedere.
foresight ['fɔːsaɪt] n previdenza f.
forest ['fɔrɪst] n foresta.
forestall [fɔː'stɔːl] vt prevenire.
forestry ['fɔrɪstrɪ] n silvicoltura.
foretaste ['fɔːteɪst] n pregustazione f.
foretell, pt, pp **foretold** [fɔː'tɛl, -'təuld] vt predire.
forever [fə'rɛvə*] ad per sempre; (fig) sempre, di continuo.
foreword ['fɔːwəːd] n prefazione f.
forfeit ['fɔːfɪt] n ammenda, pena // vt perdere; (one's happiness, health) giocarsi.
forgave [fə'geɪv] pt of **forgive**.
forge [fɔːdʒ] n fucina // vt (signature, Brit: money) contraffare, falsificare; (wrought iron) fucinare, foggiare; to ~ **ahead** vi tirare avanti; ~**r** n contraffattore m; ~**ry** n falso; (activity) contraffazione f.
forget [fə'gɛt], pt **forgot**, pp **forgotten** vt, vi dimenticare; ~**ful** a di corta memoria; ~**ful of** dimentico(a) di; ~-**me-not** n nontiscordardimé m inv.
forgive [fə'gɪv], pt **forgave**, pp **forgiven** vt perdonare; to ~ sb for sth perdonare qc a qn; ~**ness** n perdono.
forgo [fɔː'gəu], pt **forwent**, pp **forgone** vt rinunciare a.
forgot [fə'gɔt] pt of **forget**.
forgotten [fə'gɔtn] pp of **forget**.
fork [fɔːk] n (for eating) forchetta; (for gardening) forca; (of roads) bivio; (of railways) inforcazione f // vi (road) biforcarsi; to ~ **out** (col: pay) vt

sborsare // vi pagare; ~-**lift truck** n carrello elevatore.

forlorn [fə'lɔ:n] a (person) sconsolato(a); (place) abbandonato(a); (attempt) disperato(a); (hope) vano(a).

form [fɔ:m] n forma; (SCOL) classe f; (questionnaire) scheda // vt formare; in top ~ in gran forma.

formal ['fɔ:məl] a (offer, receipt) vero(a) e proprio(a); (person) cerimonioso(a); (occasion, dinner) formale, ufficiale; (ART, PHILOSOPHY) formale; ~**ly** ad ufficialmente; formalmente; cerimoniosamente.

format ['fɔ:mæt] n formato // vt (COMPUT) formattare.

formation [fɔ:'meɪʃən] n formazione f.

formative ['fɔ:mətɪv] a: ~ **years** anni mpl formativi.

former ['fɔ:mə*] a vecchio(a) (before n), ex inv (before n); the ~ ... the latter quello ... questo; ~**ly** ad in passato.

formula ['fɔ:mjulə] n formula.

forsake, pt **forsook**, pp **forsaken** [fə'seɪk, -'suk, -'seɪkən] vt abbandonare.

fort [fɔ:t] n forte m.

forth [fɔ:θ] ad in avanti; to go back and ~ andare avanti e indietro; and so ~ e così via; ~**coming** a prossimo(a); (character) aperto(a), comunicativo(a); ~**right** a franco(a), schietto(a); ~**with** ad immediatamente, subito.

fortify ['fɔ:tɪfaɪ] vt fortificare; **fortified wine** n vino ad alta gradazione alcolica.

fortnight ['fɔ:tnaɪt] n quindici giorni mpl, due settimane fpl; ~**ly** a bimensile // ad ogni quindici giorni.

fortress ['fɔ:trɪs] n fortezza, rocca.

fortunate ['fɔ:tʃənɪt] a fortunato(a); it is ~ that è una fortuna che; ~**ly** ad fortunatamente.

fortune ['fɔ:tʃən] n fortuna; ~**teller** n indovino/a.

forty ['fɔ:tɪ] num quaranta.

forum ['fɔ:rəm] n foro.

forward ['fɔ:wəd] a (ahead of schedule) in anticipo; (movement, position) in avanti; (not shy) aperto(a); diretto(a); sfacciato(a) // n (SPORT) avanti m inv // vt (letter) inoltrare; (parcel, goods) spedire; (fig) promuovere, appoggiare; to move ~ avanzare; ~(**s**) ad avanti.

forwent [fɔ:'went] pt of **forgo**.

fossil ['fɔsl] a, n fossile (m).

foster ['fɔstə*] vt incoraggiare, nutrire; (child) avere in affidamento; ~ **child** n bambino(a) preso(a) in affidamento; ~ **mother** n madre f affidataria.

fought [fɔ:t] pt, pp of **fight**.

foul [faul] a (smell, food) cattivo(a); (weather) brutto(a); (language) osceno(a); (deed) infame // n (FOOTBALL) fallo // vt sporcare; (football player) commettere un fallo su.

found [faund] pt, pp of **find** // vt (es-

tablish) fondare; ~**ation** [-'deɪʃən] n (act) fondazione f; (base) base f; (also: ~**ation cream**) fondo tinta; ~**ations** npl (of building) fondamenta fpl.

founder ['faundə*] n fondatore/trice // vi affondare.

foundry ['faundrɪ] n fonderia.

fount [faunt] n fonte f.

fountain ['fauntɪn] n fontana; ~ **pen** n penna stilografica.

four [fɔ:*] num quattro; on all ~**s** a carponi; ~-**poster** n (also: ~-**poster bed**) letto a quattro colonne; ~**some** ['fɔ:səm] n partita a quattro; uscita in quattro; ~**teen** num quattordici; ~**th** num quarto(a).

fowl [faul] n pollame m; volatile m.

fox [fɔks] n volpe f // vt confondere.

foyer ['fɔɪeɪ] n atrio; (THEATRE) ridotto.

fraction ['frækʃən] n frazione f.

fracture ['fræktʃə*] n frattura.

fragile ['frædʒaɪl] a fragile.

fragment ['frægmənt] n frammento.

fragrant ['freɪgrənt] a fragrante, profumato(a).

frail [freɪl] a debole, delicato(a).

frame [freɪm] n (of building) armatura; (of human, animal) ossatura, corpo; (of picture) cornice f; (of door, window) telaio; (of spectacles: also: ~**s**) montatura; ~ **of mind** n stato d'animo; ~**work** n struttura.

France [frɑ:ns] n Francia.

franchise ['fræntʃaɪz] n (POL) diritto di voto; (COMM) concessione f.

frank [fræŋk] a franco(a), aperto(a) // vt (letter) affrancare; ~**ly** ad francamente, sinceramente.

frantic ['fræntɪk] a frenetico(a).

fraternity [frə'tɜ:nɪtɪ] n (club) associazione f; (spirit) fratellanza.

fraud [frɔ:d] n truffa; (LAW) frode f; (person) impostore/a.

fraught [frɔ:t] a: ~ **with** pieno(a) di, intriso(a) da.

fray [freɪ] n baruffa // vt logorare // vi logorarsi; her nerves were ~ed aveva i nervi a pezzi.

freak [fri:k] n fenomeno, mostro // cpd fenomenale.

freckle ['frekl] n lentiggine f.

free [fri:] a libero(a); (gratis) gratuito(a); (liberal) generoso(a) // vt (prisoner, jammed person) liberare; (jammed object) districare; ~ (of charge), for ~ ad gratuitamente; ~**dom** ['fri:dəm] n libertà; ~-**for-all** n parapiglia m generale; ~ **gift** n regalo, omaggio; ~**hold** n proprietà assoluta; ~ **kick** n calcio libero; ~**lance** a indipendente; ~**ly** ad liberamente; (liberally) liberalmente; ~**mason** n massone m; ~**post** n affrancatura a carico del destinatario; ~-**range** a (hen) ruspante; (eggs) di gallina ru-

spante; ~ **trade** n libero scambio;
~**way** n (US) superstrada; ~**wheel** vi
andare a ruota libera; ~ **will** n libero
arbitrio; of one's own ~ **will** di
spontanea volontà.

freeze [fri:z] vb (pt **froze**, pp **frozen**) vi
gelare // vt gelare; (food) congelare;
(prices, salaries) bloccare // n gelo;
blocco; ~**-dried** a liofilizzato(a); ~**r** n
congelatore m.

freezing ['fri:zɪŋ] a: **I'm** ~ mi sto
congelando // n (also: ~ **point**) punto di
congelamento; **3 degrees below** ~ 3 gradi
sotto zero.

freight [freɪt] n (goods) merce f, merci
fpl; (money charged) spese fpl di trasporto; ~ **train** n (US) treno m merci
inv.

French [frɛntʃ] a francese // n (LING)
francese m; the ~ npl i Francesi; ~
bean n fagiolino; ~ **fried potatoes**,
(US) ~ **fries** npl patate fpl fritte;
~**man** n francese m; ~ **window** n
portafinestra; ~**woman** n francese f.

frenzy ['frɛnzɪ] n frenesia.

frequent a ['fri:kwənt] frequente // vt
[frɪ'kwɛnt] frequentare; ~**ly** ad
frequentemente, spesso.

fresco ['frɛskəu] n affresco.

fresh [frɛʃ] a fresco(a); (new) nuovo(a);
(cheeky) sfacciato(a); ~**en** vi (wind,
air) rinfrescare; **to** ~**en up** vi rinfrescarsi; ~**er** n (Brit SCOL: col) ma-
tricola; ~**ly** ad di recente, di fresco;
~**man** n (US) = ~**er**; ~**ness** n fre-
schezza; ~**water** a (fish) d'acqua dolce.

fret [frɛt] vi agitarsi, affliggersi.

friar ['fraɪə*] n frate m.

friction ['frɪkʃən] n frizione f, attrito.

Friday ['fraɪdɪ] n venerdì m inv.

fridge [frɪdʒ] n (Brit) frigo, frigorifero.

fried [fraɪd] pt, pp of **fry** // a fritto(a).

friend [frɛnd] n amico/a; ~**ly** a amichevole; ~**ship** n amicizia.

frieze [fri:z] n fregio.

fright [fraɪt] n paura, spavento; **to take** ~
spaventarsi; ~**en** vt spaventare, far
paura a; ~**ened** a spaventato(a);
~**ening** a spaventoso(a), pauroso(a);
~**ful** a orribile.

frigid ['frɪdʒɪd] a (woman) frigido(a).

frill [frɪl] n balza.

fringe [frɪndʒ] n (Brit: of hair) frangia;
(edge: of forest etc) margine m; (fig):
on the ~ al margine; ~ **benefits** npl
vantaggi mpl.

frisk [frɪsk] vt perquisire.

frisky ['frɪskɪ] a vivace, vispo(a).

fritter ['frɪtə*] n frittella; **to** ~ **away** vt
sprecare.

frivolity [frɪ'vɔlɪtɪ] n frivolezza.

frivolous ['frɪvələs] a frivolo(a).

frizzy ['frɪzɪ] a crespo(a).

fro [frəu] ad: **to and** ~ avanti e indietro.

frock [frɔk] n vestito.

frog [frɔg] n rana; ~**man** n uomo m
rana inv.

frolic ['frɔlɪk] vi sgambettare.

from [frɔm] prep **1** (indicating starting
place, origin etc) da; **where do you come**
~?, **where are you** ~? da dove viene?, di
dov'è?; ~ **London to Glasgow** da Londra
a Glasgow; **a letter** ~ **my sister** una
lettera da mia sorella; **tell him** ~ **me**
that ... gli dica da parte mia che ...
2 (indicating time) da; ~ **one o'clock to**
or **until** or **till two** dall'una alle due; ~
January (on) da gennaio, a partire da
gennaio
3 (indicating distance) da; **the hotel is 1**
km ~ **the beach** l'albergo è a 1 km dalla
spiaggia
4 (indicating price, number etc) da;
prices range ~ **£10 to £50** i prezzi vanno
dalle 10 alle 50 sterline
5 (indicating difference) da; **he can't**
tell red ~ **green** non sa distinguere il
rosso dal verde
6 (because of, on the basis of): ~ **what**
he says da quanto dice lui; **weak** ~
hunger debole per la fame.

front [frʌnt] n (of house, dress) davanti
m inv; (of train) testa; (of book)
copertina; (promenade: also: sea ~)
lungomare m; (MIL, POL, METEOR)
fronte m; (fig: appearances) fronte f //
a primo(a); anteriore, davanti inv; **in** ~
of davanti a; ~ **door** n porta d'entrata;
(of car) sportello anteriore; ~**ier**
['frʌntɪə*] n frontiera; ~ **page** n prima
pagina; ~ **room** n (Brit) salotto; ~**-**
wheel drive n trasmissione f anteriore.

frost [frɔst] n gelo; (also: hoar~) brina;
~**bite** n congelamento; ~**ed** a (glass)
smerigliato(a); ~**y** a (window)
coperto(a) di ghiaccio; (welcome)
gelido(a).

froth ['frɔθ] n spuma; schiuma.

frown [fraun] n cipiglio // vi accigliarsi.

froze [frəuz] pt of **freeze**; ~**n** pp of
freeze // a (food) congelato(a).

fruit [fru:t] n (pl inv) frutto;
(collectively) frutta; ~**erer** n
fruttivendolo; ~**erer's (shop)** n: **at the**
~**erer's (shop)** dal fruttivendolo; ~**ful** a
fruttuoso(a); (plant) fruttifero(a); (soil)
fertile; ~**ion** [fru:'ɪʃən] n: **to come to**
~**ion** realizzarsi; ~ **juice** n succo di
frutta; ~ **machine** n (Brit) macchina f
mangiasoldi inv; ~ **salad** n macedonia.

frustrate [frʌs'treɪt] vt frustrare; ~**d** a
frustrato(a).

fry [fraɪ], pt, pp **fried** vt friggere; **the**
small ~ i pesci piccoli; ~**ing pan** n
padella.

ft. abbr = **foot**, **feet**.

fuddy-duddy ['fʌdɪdʌdɪ] n matusa.

fudge [fʌdʒ] n (CULIN) specie di caramella a base di latte, burro e zucchero.

fuel [fjuəl] n (for heating) combustibile

m; (for propelling) carburante m; ~ **tank** n deposito m nafta inv; (on vehicle) serbatoio (della benzina).

fugitive ['fju:dʒɪtɪv] n fuggitivo/a, profugo/a.

fulfil [ful'fɪl] vt (function) compiere; (order) eseguire; (wish, desire) soddisfare, appagare; ~ment n (of wishes) soddisfazione f, appagamento.

full [ful] a pieno(a); (details, skirt) ampio(a) // ad: to know ~ well that sapere benissimo che; I'm ~ (up) sono pieno; ~ employment piena occupazione; a ~ two hours due ore intere; at ~ speed a tutta velocità; in ~ per intero; to pay in ~ pagare tutto; ~ moon n luna piena; ~-scale a (attack, war) su larga scala; (model) in grandezza naturale; ~ stop n punto; ~-time a, ad (work) a tempo pieno // n (SPORT) fine f partita; ~y ad interamente, pienamente, completamente; ~y-fledged a (teacher, member etc) a tutti gli effetti.

fulsome ['fulsəm] a (pej: praise, gratitude) esagerato(a).

fumble ['fʌmbl] vi brancolare, andare a tentoni; **to ~ with** vt fus trafficare.

fume [fju:m] vi essere furioso(a); ~s npl esalazioni fpl, vapori mpl.

fumigate ['fju:mɪgeɪt] vt suffumicare.

fun [fʌn] n divertimento, spasso; **to have ~** divertirsi; **for ~** per scherzo; **to make ~ of** vt fus prendersi gioco di.

function ['fʌŋkʃən] n funzione f; cerimonia, ricevimento // vi funzionare; ~al a funzionale.

fund [fʌnd] n fondo, cassa; (source) fondo; (store) riserva; ~s npl (money) fondi mpl.

fundamental [fʌndə'mentl] a fondamentale.

funeral ['fju:nərəl] n funerale m; ~ **parlour** n impresa di pompe funebri; ~ **service** n ufficio funebre.

fun fair n (Brit) luna park m inv.

fungus, pl **fungi** ['fʌŋgəs, -gaɪ] n fungo; (mould) muffa.

funnel ['fʌnl] n imbuto; (of ship) ciminiera.

funny ['fʌnɪ] a divertente, buffo(a); (strange) strano(a), bizzarro(a).

fur [fə:*] n pelo; pelliccia; (Brit: in kettle etc) deposito calcare; ~ **coat** n pelliccia.

furious ['fjuərɪəs] a furioso(a); (effort) accanito(a).

furlong ['fə:lɔŋ] n = 201.17 m (termine ippico).

furlough ['fə:ləu] n congedo, permesso.

furnace ['fə:nɪs] n fornace f.

furnish ['fə:nɪʃ] vt ammobiliare; (supply) fornire; ~ings npl mobili mpl, mobilia.

furniture ['fə:nɪtʃə*] n mobili mpl; **piece of ~** mobile m.

furrow ['fʌrəu] n solco.

furry ['fə:rɪ] a (animal) peloso(a).

further ['fə:ðə*] a supplementare, altro(a); nuovo(a); più lontano(a) // ad più lontano; (more) di più; (moreover) inoltre // vt favorire, promuovere; ~ **college of education** n istituto statale con corsi specializzati (di formazione professionale, aggiornamento professionale etc); ~**more** [fə:ðə'mɔ:*] ad inoltre, per di più.

furthest ['fə:ðɪst] superlative of **far**.

fury ['fjuərɪ] n furore m.

fuse [fju:z] n fusibile m; (for bomb etc) miccia, spoletta // vt fondere; (Brit ELEC): **to ~ the lights** far saltare i fusibili // vi fondersi; ~ **box** n cassetta dei fusibili.

fuselage ['fju:zəla:ʒ] n fusoliera.

fuss [fʌs] n chiasso, trambusto, confusione f; (complaining) storie fpl; **to make a ~** fare delle storie; ~**y** a (person) puntiglioso(a), esigente; **che fa le storie**; (dress) carico(a) di fronzoli; (style) elaborato(a).

future ['fju:tʃə*] a futuro(a) // n futuro, avvenire m; (LING) futuro; **in ~** in futuro.

fuze [fju:z] (US) = **fuse**.

fuzzy ['fʌzɪ] a (PHOT) indistinto(a), sfocato(a); (hair) crespo(a).

G

G [dʒi:] n (MUS) sol m.

gabble ['gæbl] vi borbottare; farfugliare.

gable ['geɪbl] n frontone m.

gadget ['gædʒɪt] n aggeggio.

Gaelic ['geɪlɪk] a gaelico(a) // n (LING) gaelico.

gag [gæg] n bavaglio; (joke) facezia, scherzo // vt imbavagliare.

gaiety ['geɪɪtɪ] n gaiezza.

gaily ['geɪlɪ] ad allegramente.

gain [geɪn] n guadagno, profitto // vt guadagnare // vi (watch) andare avanti; **to ~ in/by** aumentare di/con; **to ~ 3lbs (in weight)** aumentare di 3 libbre.

gait [geɪt] n andatura.

gal. abbr = **gallon**.

galaxy ['gæləksɪ] n galassia.

gale [geɪl] n vento forte; burrasca.

gallant ['gælənt] a valoroso(a); (towards ladies) galante, cortese.

gall bladder ['gɔ:l-] n cistifellea.

gallery ['gælərɪ] n galleria.

galley ['gælɪ] n (ship's kitchen) cambusa; (ship) galea.

gallon ['gælən] n gallone m (= 8 pints; Brit = 4.543l; US = 3.785l).

gallop ['gæləp] n galoppo // vi galoppare.

gallows ['gæləuz] n forca.

gallstone ['gɔ:lstəun] n calcolo biliare.

galore [gə'lɔ:*] ad a iosa, a profusione.

galvanize ['gælvənaiz] *vt* galvanizzare.
gambit ['gæmbit] *n* (*fig*): (opening) ~ prima mossa.
gamble ['gæmbl] *n* azzardo, rischio calcolato // *vt*, *vi* giocare; **to ~ on** (*fig*) giocare su; **~r** *n* giocatore/trice d'azzardo; **gambling** *n* gioco d'azzardo.
game [geim] *n* gioco; (*event*) partita; (*HUNTING*) selvaggina // *a* coraggioso(a); (*ready*): **to be ~** (for sth/to do) essere pronto(a) (a qc/a fare); **big ~** *n* selvaggina grossa; **~keeper** *n* guardacaccia *m inv*.
gammon ['gæmən] *n* (*bacon*) quarto di maiale; (*ham*) prosciutto affumicato.
gamut ['gæmət] *n* gamma.
gang [gæŋ] *n* banda, squadra // *vi*: **to ~ up on sb** far combutta contro qn.
gangrene ['gæŋgri:n] *n* cancrena.
gangster ['gæŋstə*] *n* gangster *m inv*.
gangway ['gæŋwei] *n* passerella; (*Brit*: *of bus*) corridoio.
gaol [dʒeil] *n*, *vt* (*Brit*) = **jail**.
gap [gæp] *n* buco; (*in time*) intervallo; (*fig*) lacuna; vuoto.
gape [geip] *vi* restare a bocca aperta; **gaping** *a* (*hole*) squarciato(a).
garage ['gærɑ:ʒ] *n* garage *m inv*.
garbage ['gɑ:bidʒ] *n* immondizie *fpl*, rifiuti *mpl*; **~ can** *n* (*US*) bidone *m* della spazzatura.
garbled ['gɑ:bld] *a* deformato(a); ingarbugliato(a).
garden ['gɑ:dn] *n* giardino // *vi* lavorare nel giardino; **~er** *n* giardiniere/a; **~ing** *n* giardinaggio.
gargle ['gɑ:gl] *vi* fare gargarismi // *n* gargarismo.
gargoyle ['gɑ:goil] *n* gargouille *f inv*.
garish ['gɛəriʃ] *a* vistoso(a).
garland ['gɑ:lənd] *n* ghirlanda; corona.
garlic ['gɑ:lik] *n* aglio.
garment ['gɑ:mənt] *n* indumento.
garrison ['gærisn] *n* guarnigione *f*.
garrulous ['gærjuləs] *a* ciarliero(a), loquace.
garter ['gɑ:tə*] *n* giarrettiera.
gas [gæs] *n* gas *m inv*; (*US*: *gasoline*) benzina // *vt* asfissiare con il gas; (*MIL*) gasare; **~ cooker** *n* (*Brit*) cucina a gas; **~ cylinder** *n* bombola del gas; **~ fire** *n* radiatore *m* a gas.
gash [gæʃ] *n* sfregio // *vt* sfregiare.
gasket ['gæskit] *n* (*AUT*) guarnizione *f*.
gas mask *n* maschera *f* antigas *inv*.
gas meter *n* contatore *m* del gas.
gasoline ['gæsəli:n] *n* (*US*) benzina.
gasp [gɑ:sp] *vi* ansare, boccheggiare; (*in surprise*) restare senza fiato; **to ~ out** *vt* dire affannosamente.
gas ring *n* fornello a gas.
gassy ['gæsi] *a* gassoso(a).
gas tap *n* rubinetto del gas.
gate [geit] *n* cancello; **~crash** *vt* (*Brit*) partecipare senza invito a; **~way** *n*

porta.
gather ['gæðə*] *vt* (*flowers*, *fruit*) cogliere; (*pick up*) raccogliere; (*assemble*) radunare; raccogliere; (*understand*) capire // *vi* (*assemble*) radunarsi; **to ~ speed** acquistare velocità; **~ing** *n* adunanza.
gauche [gəuʃ] *a* goffo(a), maldestro(a).
gaudy ['gɔ:di] *a* vistoso(a).
gauge [geidʒ] *n* (*standard measure*) calibro; (*RAIL*) scartamento; (*instrument*) indicatore *m* // *vt* misurare.
gaunt [gɔ:nt] *a* scarno(a); (*grim*, *desolate*) desolato(a).
gauntlet ['gɔ:ntlit] *n* (*fig*): **to run the ~ through an angry crowd** passare sotto il fuoco di una folla ostile; **to throw down the ~** gettare il guanto.
gauze [gɔ:z] *n* garza.
gave [geiv] *pt* of **give**.
gay [gei] *a* (*person*) gaio(a), allegro(a); (*colour*) vivace, vivo(a); (*col*) omosessuale.
gaze [geiz] *n* sguardo fisso // *vi*: **to ~ at** guardare fisso.
GB *abbr* = **Great Britain**.
GCE *n abbr* (*Brit*: = *General Certificate of Education*) ≈ maturità.
GCSE *n abbr* (*Brit*) = *General Certificate of Secondary Education*.
gear [giə*] *n* attrezzi *mpl*, equipaggiamento; (*belongings*) roba; (*TECH*) ingranaggio; (*AUT*) marcia *f* // *vt* (*fig*: *adapt*): **to ~ sth to** adattare qc a; **in top** or (*US*) **high/low/bottom ~** in quarta (or quinta)/seconda/prima; **in ~** in marcia; **~ box** *n* scatola del cambio; **~ lever**, (*US*) **~ shift** *n* leva del cambio.
geese [gi:s] *npl* of **goose**.
gel [dʒel] *n* gel *m inv*.
gelignite ['dʒelignait] *n* nitroglicerina.
gem [dʒem] *n* gemma.
Gemini ['dʒeminai] *n* Gemelli *mpl*.
gender ['dʒendə*] *n* genere *m*.
general ['dʒenərl] *n* generale *m* // *a* generale; **in ~** in genere; **~ delivery** *n* (*US*) fermo posta *m*; **~ election** *n* elezioni *fpl* generali; **~ize** *vi* generalizzare; **~ly** *ad* generalmente; **~ practitioner (G.P.)** *n* medico generico.
generate ['dʒenəreit] *vt* generare.
generation [dʒenə'reiʃən] *n* generazione *f*.
generator ['dʒenəreitə*] *n* generatore *m*.
generosity [dʒenə'rositi] *n* generosità.
generous ['dʒenərəs] *a* generoso(a); (*copious*) abbondante.
genetic [dʒi'netik] *a* genetico(a).
Geneva [dʒi'ni:və] *n* Ginevra.
genial ['dʒi:niəl] *a* geniale, cordiale.
genitals ['dʒenitlz] *npl* genitali *mpl*.
genius ['dʒi:niəs] *n* genio.
Genoa ['dʒenəuə] *n* Genova.
gent [dʒent] *n abbr* = **gentleman**.

genteel [dʒɛn'tiːl] *a* raffinato(a), distinto(a).

gentle ['dʒɛntl] *a* delicato(a); (*persona*) dolce.

gentleman ['dʒɛntlmən] *n* signore *m*; (*well-bred man*) gentiluomo.

gently ['dʒɛntlɪ] *ad* delicatamente.

gentry ['dʒɛntrɪ] *n* nobiltà minore.

gents [dʒɛnts] *n* W.C. *m* (per signori).

genuine ['dʒɛnjuɪn] *a* autentico(a); sincero(a).

geography [dʒɪ'ɔgrəfɪ] *n* geografia.

geology [dʒɪ'ɔlədʒɪ] *n* geologia.

geometric(al) [dʒɪə'mɛtrɪk(l)] *a* geometrico(a).

geometry [dʒɪ'ɔmɛtrɪ] *n* geometria.

geranium [dʒɪ'reɪnjəm] *n* geranio.

geriatric [dʒɛrɪ'ætrɪk] *a* geriatrico(a).

germ [dʒə:m] *n* (*MED*) microbo; (*BIOL*, *fig*) germe *m*.

German ['dʒə:mən] *a* tedesco(a) // *n* tedesco/a; (*LING*) tedesco; ~ **measles** *n* rosolia.

Germany ['dʒə:mənɪ] *n* Germania.

gesture ['dʒɛstjə*] *n* gesto.

get [gɛt], *pt*, *pp* **got**, *pp* **gotten** (*US*) ◆ *vi* **1** (*become*, *be*) diventare, farsi; to ~ old invecchiare; to ~ **tired** stancarsi; to ~ **drunk** ubriacarsi; to ~ **killed** venire *or* rimanere ucciso(a); **when do I ~ paid?** quando mi pagate?; **it's ~ting late** si sta facendo tardi

2 (*go*): to ~ **to/from** andare a/da; to ~ **home** arrivare *or* tornare a casa; **how did you ~ here?** come sei venuto?

3 (*begin*) mettersi a, cominciare a; to ~ **to know sb** incominciare a conoscere qn; **let's ~ going** *or* **started** muoviamoci

4 (*modal auxiliary vb*): **you've got to do it** devi farlo

◆ *vt* **1**: to ~ **sth done** (*do*) fare qc; (*have done*) far fare qc; to ~ **one's hair cut** farsi tagliare i capelli; to ~ **sb to do sth** far fare qc a qn

2 (*obtain*: *money*, *permission*, *results*) ottenere; (*find*: *job*, *flat*) trovare; (*fetch*: *person*, *doctor*) chiamare; (*: object*) prendere; to ~ **sth for sb** prendere *or* procurare qc a qn; ~ **me Mr Jones, please** (*TEL*) mi passi il signor Jones, per favore; **can I ~ you a drink?** le posso offrire da bere?

3 (*receive*: *present*, *letter*, *prize*) ricevere; (*acquire*: *reputation*) farsi; **how much did you ~ for the painting?** quanto le hanno dato per il quadro?

4 (*catch*) prendere; (*hit*: *target etc*) colpire; to ~ **sb by the arm/throat** afferrare qn per un braccio/alla gola; ~ **him!** prendetelo!

5 (*take*, *move*) portare; to ~ **sth to sb** far avere qc a qn; **do you think we'll ~ it through the door?** pensi che riusciremo a farlo passare per la porta?

6 (*catch*, *take*: *plane*, *bus etc*) prendere

7 (*understand*) afferrare; (*hear*) sentire; **I've got it!** ci sono arrivato!, ci sono!; **I'm sorry, I didn't ~ your name** scusi, non ho capito (*or* sentito) il suo nome

8 (*have*, *possess*): **to have got** avere; **how many have you got?** quanti ne ha?

to get about *vi* muoversi; (*news*) diffondersi

to get along *vi* (*agree*) andare d'accordo; (*depart*) andarsene; (*manage*) = **to get by**

to get at *vt fus* (*attack*) prendersela con; (*reach*) raggiungere, arrivare a

to get away *vi* partire, andarsene; (*escape*) scappare

to get away with *vt fus* cavarsela; farla franca

to get back *vi* (*return*) ritornare, tornare ◆ *vt* riottenere, riavere

to get by *vi* (*pass*) passare; (*manage*) farcela

to get down *vi*, *vt fus* scendere ◆ *vt* far scendere; (*depress*) buttare giù

to get down to *vt fus* (*work*) mettersi a (fare)

to get in *vi* entrare; (*train*) arrivare; (*arrive home*) ritornare, tornare

to get into *vt fus* entrare in; to ~ **into a rage** incavolarsi

to get off *vi* (*from train etc*) scendere; (*depart*: *person*, *car*) andare via; (*escape*) cavarsela ◆ *vt* (*remove*: *clothes*, *stain*) levare ◆ *vt fus* (*train*, *bus*) scendere da

to get on *vi* (*at exam etc*) andare; (*agree*): to ~ **on** (**with**) andare d'accordo (con) ◆ *vt fus* montare in; (*horse*) montare su

to get out *vi* uscire; (*of vehicle*) scendere ◆ *vt* tirar fuori, far uscire

to get out of *vt fus* uscire da; (*duty etc*) evitare

to get over *vt fus* (*illness*) riaversi da

to get round *vt fus* aggirare; (*fig*: *person*) rigirare

to get through *vi* (*TEL*) avere la linea

to get through to *vt fus* (*TEL*) parlare a

to get together *vi* riunirsi ◆ *vt* raccogliere; (*people*) adunare

to get up *vi* (*rise*) alzarsi ◆ *vt fus* salire su per

to get up to *vt fus* (*reach*) raggiungere; (*prank etc*) fare.

getaway ['gɛtəweɪ] *n* fuga.

geyser ['giːzə*] *n* scaldabagno; (*GEO*) geyser *m inv*.

Ghana ['gɑːnə] *n* Ghana *m*.

ghastly ['gɑːstlɪ] *a* orribile, orrendo(a).

gherkin ['gə:kɪn] *n* cetriolino.

ghost [gəust] *n* fantasma *m*, spettro.

giant ['dʒaɪənt] *n* gigante/essa // *a* gigante, enorme.

gibberish ['dʒɪbərɪʃ] *n* parole *fpl* senza

senso.

gibe [dʒaɪb] *n* frecciata.

giblets ['dʒɪblɪts] *npl* frattaglie *fpl*.

Gibraltar [dʒɪ'brɔːltə*] *n* Gibilterra.

giddy ['gɪdɪ] *a* (*dizzy*): **to be ~** aver le vertigini; (*height*) vertiginoso(a).

gift [gɪft] *n* regalo; (*donation, ability*) dono; **~ed** *a* dotato(a); **~ token** *or* **voucher** *n* buono *m* omaggio *inv*.

gigantic [dʒaɪ'gæntɪk] *a* gigantesco(a).

giggle ['gɪgl] *vi* ridere scioccamente.

gill [dʒɪl] *n* (*measure*) = 0.25 pints (*Brit = 0.148l, US = 0.118l*).

gills [gɪlz] *npl* (*of fish*) branchie *fpl*.

gilt [gɪlt] *n* doratura // *a* dorato(a); **~- edged** *a* (*COMM*) della massima sicurezza.

gimmick ['gɪmɪk] *n* trucco.

gin [dʒɪn] *n* (*liquor*) gin *m inv*.

ginger ['dʒɪndʒə*] *n* zenzero; **~ ale, ~ beer** *n* bibita gassosa allo zenzero; **~bread** *n* pan *m* di zenzero.

gingerly ['dʒɪndʒəlɪ] *ad* cautamente.

gipsy ['dʒɪpsɪ] *n* zingaro/a.

giraffe [dʒɪ'rɑːf] *n* giraffa.

girder ['gəːdə*] *n* trave *f*.

girdle ['gəːdl] *n* (*corset*) guaina.

girl [gəːl] *n* ragazza; (*young unmarried woman*) signorina; (*daughter*) figlia, figliola; **~friend** *n* (*of girl*) amica; (*of boy*) ragazza; **~ish** *a* da ragazza.

giro ['dʒaɪrəʊ] *n* (*bank ~*) versamento bancario; (*post office ~*) postagiro.

girth [gəːθ] *n* circonferenza; (*of horse*) cinghia.

gist [dʒɪst] *n* succo.

give [gɪv] *vb* (*pt* **gave**, *pp* **given**) *vt* dare // *vi* cedere; **to ~ sb sth, ~ sth to sb** dare qc a qn; **to ~ a cry/sigh** mettere un grido/sospiro; **to ~ away** *vt* dare via; (*give free*) fare dono di; (*betray*) tradire; (*disclose*) rivelare; (*bride*) condurre all'altare; **to ~ back** *vt* rendere; **to ~ in** *vi* cedere // *vt* consegnare; **to ~ off** *vt* emettere; **to ~ out** *vt* distribuire; annunciare; **to ~ up** *vi* rinunciare // *vt* rinunciare a; **to ~ up smoking** smettere di fumare; **to ~ o.s. up** arrendersi; **to ~ way** *vi* cedere; (*Brit AUT*) dare la precedenza.

glacier ['glæsɪə*] *n* ghiacciaio.

glad [glæd] *a* lieto(a), contento(a).

gladly ['glædlɪ] *ad* volentieri.

glamorous ['glæmərəs] *a* affascinante, seducente.

glamour ['glæmə*] *n* fascino.

glance [glɑːns] *n* occhiata, sguardo // *vi*: **to ~ at** dare un'occhiata a; **to ~ off** (*bullet*) rimbalzare su; **glancing** *a* (*blow*) che colpisce di striscio.

gland [glænd] *n* ghiandola.

glare [glɛə*] *n* riverbero, luce *f* abbagliante; (*look*) sguardo furioso // *vi* abbagliare; **to ~ at** guardare male; **glaring** *a* (*mistake*) madornale.

glass [glɑːs] *n* (*substance*) vetro; (*tumbler*) bicchiere *m*; (*also*: **looking ~**) specchio; **~es** *npl* (*spectacles*) occhiali *mpl*; **~ware** *n* vetrame *m*; **~y** *a* (*eyes*) vitreo(a).

glaze [gleɪz] *vt* (*door*) fornire di vetri; (*pottery*) smaltare // *n* smalto.

glazier ['gleɪzɪə*] *n* vetraio.

gleam [gliːm] *n* barlume *m*; raggio // *vi* luccicare; **~ing** *a* lucente.

glean [gliːn] *vt* (*information*) racimolare.

glee [gliː] *n* allegrezza, gioia.

glen [glɛn] *n* valletta.

glib [glɪb] *a* dalla parola facile; facile.

glide [glaɪd] *vi* scivolare; (*AVIAT, birds*) planare; **~r** *n* (*AVIAT*) aliante *m*; **gliding** *n* (*AVIAT*) volo a vela.

glimmer ['glɪmə*] *vi* luccicare // *n* barlume *m*.

glimpse [glɪmps] *n* impressione *f* fugace // *vt* vedere al volo.

glint [glɪnt] *n* luccichio // *vi* luccicare.

glisten ['glɪsn] *vi* luccicare.

glitter ['glɪtə*] *vi* scintillare // *n* scintillio.

gloat [gləʊt] *vi*: **to ~ (over)** gongolare di piacere (per).

global ['gləʊbl] *a* globale.

globe [gləʊb] *n* globo, sfera.

gloom [gluːm] *n* oscurità, buio; (*sadness*) tristezza, malinconia; **~y** *a* fosco(a), triste.

glorious ['glɔːrɪəs] *a* glorioso(a); magnifico(a).

glory ['glɔːrɪ] *n* gloria; splendore *m* // *vi*: **to ~ in** gloriarsi di *or* in.

gloss [glɔs] *n* (*shine*) lucentezza; **to ~ over** *vt fus* scivolare su.

glossary ['glɔsərɪ] *n* glossario.

glossy ['glɔsɪ] *a* lucente.

glove [glʌv] *n* guanto; **~ compartment** *n* (*AUT*) vano portaoggetti.

glow [gləʊ] *vi* ardere; (*face*) essere luminoso(a) // *n* bagliore *m*; (*of face*) colorito acceso.

glower ['glaʊə*] *vi*: **to ~ (at sb)** guardare (qn) in cagnesco.

glue [gluː] *n* colla // *vt* incollare.

glum [glʌm] *a* abbattuto(a).

glut [glʌt] *n* eccesso // *vt* saziare; (*market*) saturare.

glutton ['glʌtn] *n* ghiottone/a; **a ~ for work** un(a) patito(a) del lavoro.

gnarled [nɑːld] *a* nodoso(a).

gnat [næt] *n* moscerino.

gnaw [nɔː] *vt* rodere.

go [gəʊ] *vb* (*pt* **went**, *pp* **gone**) *vi* andare; (*depart*) partire, andarsene; (*work*) funzionare; (*break etc*) cedere; (*be sold*): **to ~ for £10** essere venduto per 10 sterline; (*fit, suit*): **to ~ with** andare bene con; (*become*): **to ~ pale** diventare pallido(a); **to ~ mouldy** ammuffire // *n* (*pl* **~es**): **to have a ~ (at)** provare; **to be on the ~** essere in moto; **whose ~ is it?** a chi tocca?; **he's**

going to do sta per fare; **to ~ for a walk** andare a fare una passeggiata; **to ~ dancing/shopping** andare a ballare/fare la spesa; **how did it ~?** com'è andato?; **to ~ round the back/by the shop** passare da dietro/davanti al negozio; **to ~ about** vi (*rumour*) correre, circolare // vt fus: **how do I ~ about this?** qual'è la prassi per questo?; **to ~ ahead** vi andare avanti; **~ ahead!** faccia pure!; **to ~ along** vi andare, avanzare // vt fus percorrere; **to ~ away** vi partire, andarsene; **to ~ back** vi tornare, ritornare; (*go again*) andare di nuovo; **to ~ back on** vt fus (*promise*) non mantenere; **to ~ by** vi (*years, time*) scorrere // vt fus attenersi a, seguire (alla lettera); prestar fede a; **to ~ down** vi scendere; (*ship*) affondare; (*sun*) tramontare // vt fus scendere; **to ~ for** vt fus (*fetch*) andare a prendere; (*col: like*) andar matto/a per; (*attack*) attaccare; saltare addosso a; **to ~ in** vi entrare; **to ~ in for** vt fus (*competition*) iscriversi a; (*be interested in*) interessarsi di; **to ~ into** vt fus entrare in; (*investigate*) indagare, esaminare; (*embark on*) lanciarsi in; **to ~ off** vi partire, andar via; (*food*) guastarsi; (*explode*) esplodere, scoppiare; (*event*) passare // vt fus: **I've gone off chocolate** la cioccolata non mi piace più; **the gun went off** il fucile si scaricò; **to ~ on** vi continuare; (*happen*) succedere; **to ~ on doing** continuare a fare; **to ~ out** vi uscire; (*fire, light*) spegnersi; **to ~ over** vi (*ship*) ribaltarsi // vt fus (*check*) esaminare; **to ~ through** vt fus (*town etc*) attraversare; **to ~ up** vi salire // vt fus salire su per; **to ~ without** vt fus fare a meno di.

goad [gəud] vt spronare.

go-ahead ['gəuəhɛd] a intraprendente // n via m.

goal [gəul] n (SPORT) gol m, rete f; (: place) porta; (fig: aim) fine m, scopo; **~keeper** n portiere m; **~-post** n palo (della porta).

goat [gəut] n capra.

gobble ['gɔbl] vt (also: ~ **down**, ~ **up**) ingoiare.

goblet ['gɔblɪt] n calice m, coppa.

god [gɔd] n dio; **G~** n Dio; **~child** n figlioccio/a; **~daughter** n figlioccia; **~dess** n dea; **~father** n padrino; **~forsaken** a desolato(a), sperduto(a); **~mother** n madrina; **~send** n dono del cielo; **~son** n figlioccio.

goggles ['gɔglz] npl occhiali mpl (di protezione).

going ['gəuɪŋ] n (conditions) andare m, stato del terreno // a: **the ~ rate** la tariffa in vigore.

gold [gəuld] n oro // a d'oro; **~en** a

(made of gold) d'oro; (gold in colour) dorato(a); **~fish** n pesce m dorato or rosso; **~-plated** a placcato(a) oro inv; **~smith** n orefice m, orafo.

golf [gɔlf] n golf m; **~ ball** n (for game) pallina da golf; (on typewriter) pallina; **~ club** n circolo di golf; (stick) bastone m or mazza da golf; **~ course** n campo di golf; **~er** n giocatore/trice di golf.

gondola ['gɔndələ] n gondola.

gone [gɔn] pp of **go** // a partito(a).

gong [gɔŋ] n gong m inv.

good [gud] a buono(a); (kind) buono(a), gentile; (child) bravo(a) // n bene m; **~s** npl (COMM etc) beni mpl; merci fpl; **~!** bene!, ottimo!; **to be ~ at** essere bravo(a) in; **to be ~ for** andare bene per; **it's ~ for you** fa bene; **would you be ~ enough to ...?** avrebbe la gentilezza di ...?; **a ~ deal (of)** molto(a), una buona quantità (di); **a ~ many** molti(e); **to make ~** vi (succeed) aver successo // vt (deficit) colmare; (losses) compensare; **it's no ~ complaining** brontolare non serve a niente; **for ~** per sempre, definitivamente; **~ morning!** buon giorno!; **~ afternoon/evening!** buona sera!; **~ night!** buona notte!; **~bye** excl arrivederci!; **G~ Friday** n Venerdì Santo; **~-looking** a bello(a); **~-natured** a affabile; (discussion) amichevole, cordiale; **~ness** n (of person) bontà; **for ~ness sake!** per amor di Dio!; **~ness gracious!** santo cielo!, mamma mia!; **~s train** n (Brit) treno m merci inv; **~will** n amicizia, benevolenza; (COMM) avviamento.

goose [guːs], pl **geese** n oca.

gooseberry ['guzbəri] n uva spina; **to play ~** tenere la candela.

gooseflesh ['guːsflɛʃ] n, **goose pimples** npl pelle f d'oca.

gore [gɔː*] vt incornare // n sangue m (coagulato).

gorge [gɔːdʒ] n gola // vt: **to ~ o.s.** (on) ingozzarsi (di).

gorgeous ['gɔːdʒəs] a magnifico(a).

gorilla [gə'rɪlə] n gorilla m inv.

gorse [gɔːs] n ginestrone m.

gory ['gɔːrɪ] a sanguinoso(a).

go-slow ['gəu'sləu] n (Brit) rallentamento dei lavori (per agitazione sindacale).

gospel ['gɔspl] n vangelo.

gossip ['gɔsɪp] n chiacchiere fpl; pettegolezzi mpl; (person) pettegolo/a // vi chiacchierare; (maliciously) pettegolare.

got [gɔt] pt, pp of **get**; **~ten** (US) pp of **get**.

gout [gaut] n gotta.

govern ['gʌvən] vt governare; (LING) reggere.

governess ['gʌvənɪs] n governante f.

government ['gʌvnmənt] n governo.

governor ['gʌvənə⁰] n (of state, bank) governatore m; (of school, hospital) amministratore m.

gown [gaun] n vestito lungo; (of teacher, Brit: of judge) toga.

G.P. n abbr = **general practitioner**.

grab [græb] vt afferrare, arraffare; (property, power) impadronirsi di.

grace [greɪs] n grazia // vt onorare; 5 days' ~ dilazione f di 5 giorni; to say ~ dire il benedicite; ~**ful** a elegante, aggraziato(a); **gracious** ['greɪʃəs] a grazioso(a); misericordioso(a).

grade [greɪd] n (COMM) qualità f inv; classe f; categoria; (in hierarchy) grado; (US: SCOL) voto; classe // vt classificare; ordinare; graduare; ~ **crossing** n (US) passaggio a livello; ~ **school** n (US) scuola elementare.

gradient ['greɪdɪənt] n pendenza, inclinazione f.

gradual ['grædjuəl] a graduale; ~**ly** ad man mano, a poco a poco.

graduate n ['grædjuɪt] laureato/a // vi ['grædjueɪt] laurearsi; **graduation** [-'eɪʃən] n cerimonia del conferimento della laurea.

graffiti [grə'fiːtɪ] npl graffiti mpl.

graft [graːft] n (AGR, MED) innesto // vt innestare; **hard** ~ n (col): by sheer hard ~ lavorando da matti.

grain [greɪn] n grano; (of sand) granello; (of wood) venatura.

gram [græm] n grammo.

grammar ['græmə⁰] n grammatica; ~ **school** n (Brit) ≈ liceo.

grammatical [grə'mætɪkl] a grammaticale.

gramme [græm] n = **gram**.

grand [grænd] a grande, magnifico(a); grandioso(a); ~**children** npl nipoti mpl; ~**dad** n (col) nonno; ~**daughter** n nipote f; ~**father** n nonno; ~**ma** n (col) nonna; ~**mother** n nonna; ~**pa** n (col) = ~**dad**; ~**parents** npl nonni mpl; ~ **piano** n pianoforte m a coda; ~**son** n nipote m; ~**stand** n (SPORT) tribuna.

granite ['grænɪt] n granito.

granny ['grænɪ] n (col) nonna.

grant [graːnt] vt accordare; (a request) accogliere; (admit) ammettere, concedere // n (SCOL) borsa; (ADMIN) sussidio, sovvenzione f; to take sth for ~ed dare qc per scontato.

granulated ['grænjuleɪtɪd] a: ~ sugar zucchero cristallizzato.

grape [greɪp] n chicco d'uva, acino.

grapefruit ['greɪpfruːt] n pompelmo.

graph [graːf] n grafico; ~**ic** a grafico(a); (vivid) vivido(a); ~**ics** n grafica // npl illustrazioni fpl.

grapple ['græpl] vi: to ~ with essere alle prese con.

grasp [graːsp] vt afferrare // n (grip) presa; (fig) potere m; comprensione f;

~**ing** a avido(a).

grass [graːs] n erba; ~**hopper** n cavalletta; ~-**roots** a di base; ~ **snake** n natrice f.

grate [greɪt] n graticola (del focolare) // vi cigolare, stridere // vt (CULIN) grattugiare.

grateful ['greɪtful] a grato(a), riconoscente; ~**ly** ad con gratitudine.

grater ['greɪtə⁰] n grattugia.

gratify ['grætɪfaɪ] vt appagare; (whim) soddisfare.

grating ['greɪtɪŋ] n (iron bars) grata // a (noise) stridente, stridulo(a).

gratitude ['grætɪtjuːd] n gratitudine f.

gratuity [grə'tjuːɪtɪ] n mancia.

grave [greɪv] n tomba // a grave, serio(a).

gravel ['grævl] n ghiaia.

gravestone ['greɪvstəun] n pietra tombale.

graveyard ['greɪvjɑːd] n cimitero.

gravity ['grævɪtɪ] n (PHYSICS) gravità; pesantezza; (seriousness) gravità, serietà.

gravy ['greɪvɪ] n intingolo della carne; salsa.

gray [greɪ] a = **grey**.

graze [greɪz] vi pascolare, pascere // vt (touch lightly) sfiorare; (scrape) escoriare // n (MED) escoriazione f.

grease [griːs] n (fat) grasso; (lubricant) lubrificante m // vt ingrassare; lubrificare; ~**proof paper** n (Brit) carta oleata; **greasy** a grasso(a), untuoso(a).

great [greɪt] a grande; (col) magnifico(a), meraviglioso(a); **G~ Britain** n Gran Bretagna; ~**grandfather** n bisnonno; ~**grandmother** n bisnonna; ~**ly** ad molto; ~**ness** n grandezza.

Greece [griːs] n Grecia.

greed [griːd] n (also: ~**iness**) avarizia; (for food) golosità, ghiottoneria; ~**y** a avido(a); goloso(a), ghiotto(a).

Greek [griːk] a greco(a) // n greco/a; (LING) greco.

green [griːn] a verde; (inexperienced) inesperto(a), ingenuo(a) // n verde m; (stretch of grass) prato; (also: village ~) ≈ piazza del paese; ~s npl (vegetables) verdura; ~ **belt** n (round town) cintura di verde; ~ **card** n (AUT) carta verde; ~**ery** n verde m; ~**gage** n susina Regina Claudia; ~**grocer** n (Brit) fruttivendolo/a, erbivendolo/a; ~**house** n serra.

Greenland ['griːnlənd] n Groenlandia.

greet [griːt] vt salutare; ~**ing** n saluto; ~**ing(s) card** n cartolina d'auguri.

grenade [grə'neɪd] n granata.

grew [gruː] pt of **grow**.

grey [greɪ] a grigio(a); ~**hound** n levriere m.

grid [grɪd] n grata; (ELEC) rete f.

grief [griːf] n dolore m.

grievance ['gri:vəns] n doglianza, lagnanza.

grieve [gri:v] vi addolorarsi; rattristarsi // vt addolorare; **to ~ for sb** (dead person) piangere qn.

grievous ['gri:vəs] a: **~ bodily harm** (LAW) aggressione f.

grill [grɪl] n (on cooker) griglia // vt (Brit) cuocere ai ferri; (question) interrogare senza sosta.

grille [grɪl] n grata; (AUT) griglia.

grim [grɪm] a sinistro(a), brutto(a).

grimace [grɪ'meɪs] n smorfia // vi fare smorfie; fare boccacce.

grime [graɪm] n sudiciume m.

grimy ['graɪmɪ] a sudicio(a).

grin [grɪn] n sorriso smagliante // vi fare un gran sorriso.

grind [graɪnd] vt (pt, pp **ground**) macinare; (make sharp) arrotare // n (work) sgobbata; **to ~ one's teeth** digrignare i denti.

grip [grɪp] n impugnatura; presa; (holdall) borsa da viaggio // vt impugnare; afferrare; **to come to ~s with** affrontare; cercare di risolvere.

gripping ['grɪpɪŋ] a avvincente.

grisly ['grɪzlɪ] a macabro(a), orrido(a).

gristle ['grɪsl] n cartilagine f.

grit [grɪt] n ghiaia; (courage) fegato // vt (road) coprire di sabbia; **to ~ one's teeth** stringere i denti.

groan [grəun] n gemito // vi gemere.

grocer ['grəusə*] n negoziante m di generi alimentari; **~ies** npl provviste fpl.

groggy ['grɔgɪ] a barcollante.

groin [grɔɪn] n inguine m.

groom [gru:m] n palafreniere m; (also: bride~) sposo // vt (horse) strigliare; (fig): **to ~ sb for** avviare qn a.

groove [gru:v] n scanalatura, solco.

grope [grəup] vi andare a tentoni; **to ~ for** vt fus cercare a tastoni.

gross [grəus] a grossolano(a); (COMM) lordo(a) // n (pl inv) (twelve dozen) grossa; **~ly** ad (greatly) molto.

grotesque [grəu'tesk] a grottesco(a).

grotto ['grɔtəu] n grotta.

ground [graund] pt, pp of **grind** // n suolo, terra; (land) terreno; (SPORT) campo; (reason: gen pl) ragione f; (US: also: ~ **wire**) terra // vt (plane) tenere a terra // vi (ship) arenarsi; **~s** npl (of coffee etc) fondi mpl; (gardens etc) terreno, giardini mpl; **on/to the ~** per/a terra; **to gain/lose ~** guadagnare/perdere terreno; **~ cloth** n (US) = **~sheet**; **~ing** n (in education) basi fpl; **~less** a infondato(a); **~sheet** n (Brit) telone m impermeabile; **~ staff** n personale m di terra; **~ swell** n maremoto; (fig) movimento d'opinione; **~work** n preparazione f.

group [gru:p] n gruppo // vt (also: ~

together) raggruppare // vi (also: ~ together) raggrupparsi.

grouse [graus] n (pl inv) (bird) tetraone m // vi (complain) brontolare.

grove [grəuv] n boschetto.

grovel ['grɔvl] vi (fig): **to ~** (before) strisciare (di fronte a).

grow [grəu], pt **grew**, pp **grown** vi crescere; (increase) aumentare; (become): **to ~ rich/weak** arricchirsi/indebolirsi // vt coltivare, far crescere; **to ~ up** vi farsi grande, crescere; **~er** n coltivatore/trice; **~ing** a (fear, amount) crescente.

growl [graul] vi ringhiare.

grown [grəun] pp of **grow** // a adulto(a), maturo(a); **~-up** n adulto/a, grande m/f.

growth [grəuθ] n crescita, sviluppo; (what has grown) crescita; (MED) escrescenza, tumore m.

grub [grʌb] n larva; (col: food) roba (da mangiare).

grubby ['grʌbɪ] a sporco(a).

grudge [grʌdʒ] n rancore m // vt: **to ~ sb** sth dare qc a qn di malavoglia; invidiare qc a qn; **to bear sb a ~ (for)** serbar rancore a qn (per).

gruelling ['gruəlɪŋ] a estenuante.

gruesome ['gru:səm] a orribile.

gruff [grʌf] a rozzo(a).

grumble ['grʌmbl] vi brontolare, lagnarsi.

grumpy ['grʌmpɪ] a stizzito(a).

grunt [grʌnt] vi grugnire // n grugnito.

G-string ['dʒi:strɪŋ] n tanga m inv.

guarantee [gærən'ti:] n garanzia // vt garantire.

guard [ga:d] n guardia; (BOXING) difesa; (one man) guardia, sentinella; (Brit RAIL) capotreno // vt fare la guardia a; **~ed** a (fig) cauto(a), guardingo(a); **~ian** n custode m; (of minor) tutore/trice; **~'s van** n (Brit RAIL) vagone m di servizio.

guerrilla [gə'rɪlə] n guerrigliero; **~ warfare** n guerriglia.

guess [ges] vi indovinare // vt indovinare; (US) credere, pensare // n congettura; **~work** n: **I got the answer by ~work** ho azzeccato la risposta.

guest [gest] n ospite m/f; (in hotel) cliente m/f; **~-house** n pensione f; **~ room** n camera degli ospiti.

guffaw [gʌ'fɔ:] vi scoppiare in una risata sonora.

guidance ['gaɪdəns] n guida, direzione f.

guide [gaɪd] n (person, book etc) guida; (also: girl ~) giovane esploratrice f // vt guidare; **~book** n guida; **~ dog** n cane m guida inv; **~lines** npl (fig) indicazioni fpl, linee fpl direttive.

guild [gɪld] n arte f, corporazione f; associazione f.

guile [gaɪl] n astuzia.

guillotine ['gɪləti:n] n ghigliottina.

guilt [gɪlt] n colpevolezza; **~y** a

colpevole.
guinea pig ['gɪnɪ-] *n* cavia.
guise [gaɪz] *n* maschera.
guitar [gɪ'tɑ:*] *n* chitarra.
gulf [gʌlf] *n* golfo; (*abyss*) abisso.
gull [gʌl] *n* gabbiano.
gullet ['gʌlɪt] *n* gola.
gullible ['gʌlɪbl] *a* credulo(a).
gully ['gʌlɪ] *n* burrone *m*; gola; canale *m*.
gulp [gʌlp] *vi* deglutire; (*from emotion*) avere il nodo in gola // *vt* (*also*: ~ **down**) tracannare, inghiottire.
gum [gʌm] *n* (ANAT) gengiva; (*glue*) colla; (*sweet*) gelatina di frutta; (*also*: *chewing-~*) chewing-gum *m* // *vt* incollare; ~**boots** *npl* (*Brit*) stivali *mpl* di gomma.
gun [gʌn] *n* fucile *m*; (*small*) pistola, rivoltella; (*rifle*) carabina; (*shotgun*) fucile da caccia; (*cannon*) cannone *m*; ~**boat** *n* cannoniera; ~**fire** *n* spari *mpl*; ~**man** *n* bandito armato; ~**ner** *n* artigliere *m*; ~**point** *n*: at ~**point** sotto minaccia di fucile; ~**powder** *n* polvere *f* da sparo; ~**shot** *n* sparo; ~**smith** *n* armaiolo.
gurgle ['gə:gl] *vi* gorgogliare.
guru ['guru:] *n* guru *m inv*.
gush [gʌʃ] *vi* sgorgare; (*fig*) abbandonarsi ad effusioni.
gusset ['gʌsɪt] *n* gherone *m*.
gust [gʌst] *n* (*of wind*) raffica; (*of smoke*) buffata.
gusto ['gʌstəu] *n* entusiasmo.
gut [gʌt] *n* intestino, budello; (MUS etc) minugia; ~s *npl* (*courage*) fegato.
gutter ['gʌtə*] *n* (*of roof*) grondaia; (*in street*) cunetta.
guy [gaɪ] *n* (*also*: ~**rope**) cavo *or* corda di fissaggio; (*col*: *man*) tipo, elemento; (*figure*) effigie di Guy Fawkes.
guzzle ['gʌzl] *vi* gozzovigliare // *vt* trangugiare.
gym [dʒɪm] *n* (*also*: **gymnasium**) palestra; (*also*: **gymnastics**) ginnastica.
gymnast ['dʒɪmnæst] *n* ginnasta *m/f*; ~**ics** [-'næstɪks] *n, npl* ginnastica.
gym shoes *npl* scarpe *fpl* da ginnastica.
gym slip *n* (*Brit*) grembiule *m* da scuola (*per ragazze*).
gynaecologist, (US) **gynecologist** [gaɪnɪ'kɒlədʒɪst] *n* ginecologo/a.
gypsy ['dʒɪpsɪ] *n* = **gipsy**.
gyrate [dʒaɪ'reɪt] *vi* girare.

H

haberdashery ['hæbə'dæʃərɪ] *n* (*Brit*) merceria.
habit ['hæbɪt] *n* abitudine *f*; (*costume*) abito; (REL) tonaca.
habitation [hæbɪ'teɪʃən] *n* abitazione *f*.
habitual [hə'bɪtjuəl] *a* abituale; (*drinker, liar*) inveterato(a); ~**ly** *ad* abitualmente, di solito.
hack [hæk] *vt* tagliare, fare a pezzi // *n* (*cut*) taglio; (*blow*) colpo; (*pej*: *writer*) negro.
hackneyed ['hæknɪd] *a* comune, trito(a).
had [hæd] *pt, pp of* **have.**
haddock, *pl* ~ *or* ~**s** ['hædək] *n* eglefino.
hadn't ['hædnt] = **had not.**
haemorrhage, (US) **hemorrhage** ['hemərɪdʒ] *n* emorragia.
haemorrhoids, (US) **hemorrhoids** ['hemərɔɪdz] *npl* emorroidi *fpl*.
haggard ['hægəd] *a* smunto(a).
haggle ['hægl] *vi* mercanteggiare.
Hague [heɪg] *n*: The ~ L'Aia.
hail [heɪl] *n* grandine *f* // *vt* (*call*) chiamare; (*greet*) salutare // *vi* grandinare; ~**stone** *n* chicco di grandine.
hair [heə*] *n* capelli *mpl*; (*single hair*: *on head*) capello; (: *on body*) pelo; **to do one's ~** pettinarsi; ~**brush** *n* spazzola per capelli; ~**cut** *n* taglio di capelli; ~**do** ['heədu:] *n* acconciatura, pettinatura; ~**dresser** *n* parrucchiere/a; ~**dryer** *n* asciugacapelli *m inv*; ~ **grip** *n* forcina; ~**pin** *n* forcina; ~**pin bend,** (US) ~**pin curve** *n* tornante *m*; ~**raising** *a* orripilante; ~ **remover** *n* crema depilatoria; ~ **spray** *n* lacca per capelli; ~**style** *n* pettinatura, acconciatura; ~**y** *a* irsuto(a); peloso(a); (*col*: *frightening*) spavento-so(a).
hake, *pl* ~ *or* ~**s** [heɪk] *n* nasello.
half [hɑ:f] *n* (*pl* **halves**) mezzo, metà *f inv* // *a* mezzo(a) // *ad* a mezzo, a metà; ~ **an hour** mezz'ora; ~ **a dozen** mezza dozzina; ~ **a pound** mezza libbra; **two and a ~** due e mezzo; **a week and a ~** una settimana e mezza; ~ (*of it*) la metà; ~ (*of*) la metà di; **to cut sth in ~** tagliare qc in due; ~ **asleep** mezzo(a) addormentato(a); ~**back** *n* (SPORT) mediano; ~**breed,** ~**caste** *n* meticcio/a; ~**hearted** *a* tiepido(a); ~**hour** *n* mezz'ora; ~**mast** *n*: at ~**mast** (*flag*) a mezz'asta; ~**penny** ['heɪpnɪ] *n* (*Brit*) mezzo penny *m inv*; ~**price** *a, ad* a metà prezzo; ~ **term** *n* (*Brit SCOL*) vacanza a *or* di metà trimestre; ~**time** *n* (SPORT) intervallo; ~**way** *ad* a metà strada.
halibut ['hælɪbət] *n* (*pl inv*) ippoglosso.
hall [hɔ:l] *n* sala, salone *m*; (*entrance way*) entrata; (*corridor*) corridoio; (*mansion*) grande villa, maniero; ~ **of residence** *n* (*Brit*) casa dello studente.
hallmark ['hɔ:lmɑ:k] *n* marchio di garanzia; (*fig*) caratteristica.
hallo [hə'ləu] *excl* = **hello.**
Hallowe'en [hæləu'i:n] *n* vigilia d'Ognissanti.
hallucination [həlu:sɪ'neɪʃən] *n*

allucinazione f.

hallway ['hɔ:lweɪ] n corridoio; (*entrance*) ingresso.

halo ['heɪləʊ] n (*of saint etc*) aureola; (*of sun*) alone m.

halt [hɔ:lt] n fermata // vt fermare // vi fermarsi.

halve [hɑ:v] vt (*apple etc*) dividere a metà; (*expense*) ridurre di metà.

halves [hɑ:vz] npl of **half**.

ham [hæm] n prosciutto.

hamburger ['hæmbə:gə*] n hamburger m inv.

hamlet ['hæmlɪt] n paesetto.

hammer ['hæmə*] n martello // vt martellare; (*fig*) sconfiggere duramente // vi: to ~ on or at the door picchiare alla porta.

hammock ['hæmək] n amaca.

hamper ['hæmpə*] vt impedire // n cesta.

hamster ['hæmstə*] n criceto.

hand [hænd] n mano f; (*of clock*) lancetta; (*handwriting*) scrittura; (*at cards*) mano; (: *game*) partita; (*worker*) operaio/a // vt dare, passare; to give sb a ~ dare una mano a qn; at ~ a portata di mano; in ~ a disposizione; (*work*) in corso; on ~ (*person*) disponibile; (*services*) pronto(a) a intervenire; to ~ (*information etc*) a portata di mano; on the one ~ ..., on the other ~ da un lato ..., dall'altro; to ~ in vt consegnare; to ~ out vt distribuire; to ~ over vt passare; cedere; ~bag n borsetta; ~book n manuale m; ~brake n freno a mano; ~cuffs npl manette fpl; ~ful n manciata, pugno.

handicap ['hændɪkæp] n handicap m inv // vt handicappare; to be physically ~ped essere handicappato(a); to be mentally ~ped essere un(a) handicappato(a) mentale.

handicraft ['hændɪkrɑ:ft] n lavoro d'artigiano.

handiwork ['hændɪwə:k] n opera.

handkerchief ['hæŋkətʃɪf] n fazzoletto.

handle ['hændl] n (*of door etc*) maniglia; (*of cup etc*) ansa; (*of knife etc*) impugnatura; (*of saucepan*) manico; (*for winding*) manovella // vt toccare, maneggiare; (*deal with*) occuparsi di; (*treat: people*) trattare; "~ with care" "fragile"; to fly off the ~ (*fig*) perdere le staffe, uscire dai gangheri; ~bar(s) n(pl) manubrio.

hand: ~ **luggage** n bagagli mpl a mano; ~**made** a fatto(a) a mano; ~**out** n (*leaflet*) volantino; (*at lecture*) prospetto; ~**rail** n corrimano; ~**shake** n stretta di mano.

handsome ['hænsəm] a bello(a); (*reward*) generoso(a); (*profit, fortune*) considerevole.

handwriting ['hændraɪtɪŋ] n scrittura.

handy ['hændɪ] a (*person*) bravo(a);

(*close at hand*) a portata di mano; (*convenient*) comodo(a); ~**man** n tuttofare m inv.

hang [hæŋ], pt, pp **hung** vt appendere; (*criminal*: pt, pp **hanged**) impiccare // vi pendere; (*hair*) scendere; (*drapery*) cadere; to get the ~ of sth (*col*) capire come qc funziona; to ~ **about** vi bighellonare, ciondolare; to ~ **on** vi (*wait*) aspettare; to ~ **up** vi (*TEL*) riattaccare // vt appendere.

hangar ['hæŋə*] n hangar m inv.

hanger ['hæŋə*] n gruccia.

hanger-on [hæŋər'ɔn] n parassita m.

hang-gliding ['hæŋglaɪdɪŋ] n volo col deltaplano.

hangover ['hæŋəʊvə*] n (*after drinking*) postumi mpl di sbornia.

hang-up ['hæŋʌp] n complesso.

hanker ['hæŋkə*] vi: to ~ after bramare.

hankie, hanky ['hæŋkɪ] n abbr = **handkerchief**.

haphazard [hæp'hæzəd] a a casaccio, alla carlona.

happen ['hæpən] vi accadere, succedere; as it ~s guarda caso; ~**ing** n avvenimento.

happily ['hæpɪlɪ] ad felicemente; fortunatamente.

happiness ['hæpɪnɪs] n felicità, contentezza.

happy ['hæpɪ] a felice, contento(a); ~ **with** (*arrangements etc*) soddisfatto(a) di; ~ **birthday!** buon compleanno!; ~-**go-lucky** a spensierato(a).

harangue [hə'ræŋ] vt arringare.

harass ['hærəs] vt molestare; ~**ment** n molestia.

harbour, (US) harbor ['hɑ:bə*] n porto // vt dare rifugio a.

hard [hɑ:d] a duro(a) // ad (*work*) sodo; (*think, try*) bene; to look ~ at guardare fissamente; esaminare attentamente; no ~ feelings! senza rancore!; to be ~ of hearing essere duro(a) d'orecchio; to be ~ done by essere trattato(a) ingiustamente; ~**back** n libro rilegato; ~ **cash** n denaro in contanti; ~ **disk** n (*COMPUT*) disco rigido; ~**en** vt, vi indurire; ~-**headed** a pratico(a); ~ **labour** n lavori forzati mpl.

hardly ['hɑ:dlɪ] ad (*scarcely*) appena; it's ~ the case non è proprio il caso; that can ~ be true non può essere vero; ~ anyone/anywhere quasi nessuno/a nessuna parte; ~ ever quasi mai.

hardship ['hɑ:dʃɪp] n avversità f inv; privazioni fpl.

hard-up [hɑ:d'ʌp] a (*col*) al verde.

hardware ['hɑ:dwɛə*] n ferramenta fpl; (*COMPUT*) hardware m; ~ **shop** n (negozio di) ferramenta fpl.

hard-wearing [hɑ:d'wɛərɪŋ] a resistente; (*shoes*) robusto(a).

hard-working [hɑ:d'wə:kɪŋ] a

lavoratore(trice).

hardy ['hɑːdɪ] a robusto(a); (plant) resistente al gelo.

hare [heə*] n lepre f; ~-**brained** a folle; scervellato(a).

harm [hɑːm] n male m; (wrong) danno // vt (person) fare male a; (thing) danneggiare; out of ~'s way al sicuro; ~**ful** a dannoso(a); ~**less** a innocuo(a); inoffensivo(a).

harmonica [hɑːˈmɒnɪkə] n armonica.

harmonious [hɑːˈməunɪəs] a armonioso(a).

harmony ['hɑːmənɪ] n armonia.

harness ['hɑːnɪs] n bardatura, finimenti mpl // vt (horse) bardare; (resources) sfruttare.

harp [hɑːp] n arpa // vi: to ~ on about insistere tediosamente su.

harpoon [hɑːˈpuːn] n arpione m.

harrowing ['hærəuɪŋ] a straziante.

harsh [hɑːʃ] a (hard) duro(a); (severe) severo(a); (unpleasant: sound) rauco(a); (: colour) chiassoso(a); violento(a); ~**ly** ad duramente; severamente.

harvest ['hɑːvɪst] n raccolto; (of grapes) vendemmia // vt fare il raccolto di, raccogliere; vendemmiare.

has [hæz] vb see **have**.

hash [hæʃ] n (CULIN) specie di spezzatino fatto con carne già cotta; (fig: mess) pasticcio.

hashish ['hæʃɪʃ] n hascisc m.

hasn't ['hæznt] = **has not**.

hassle ['hæsl] n (col) sacco di problemi.

haste [heɪst] n fretta; precipitazione f; ~**n** ['heɪsn] vt affrettare // vi affrettarsi; **hastily** ad in fretta; precipitosamente; **hasty** a affrettato(a); precipitoso(a).

hat [hæt] n cappello.

hatch [hætʃ] n (NAUT: also: ~**way**) boccaporto; (also: **service** ~) portello di servizio // vi schiudersi // vt covare.

hatchback ['hætʃbæk] n (AUT) tre (or cinque) porte f inv.

hatchet ['hætʃɪt] n accetta.

hate [heɪt] vt odiare, detestare // n odio; ~**ful** a odioso(a), detestabile.

hatred ['heɪtrɪd] n odio.

hat trick n: to get a ~ segnare tre punti consecutivi (or vincere per tre volte consecutive).

haughty ['hɔːtɪ] a altero(a), arrogante.

haul [hɔːl] vt trascinare, tirare // n (of fish) pescata; (of stolen goods etc) bottino; ~**age** n trasporto; autotrasporto; ~**ier**, (US) ~**er** n trasportatore m.

haunch [hɔːntʃ] n anca.

haunt [hɔːnt] vt (subj: fear) pervadere; (: person) frequentare // n rifugio; a ghost ~s this house questa casa è abitata da un fantasma.

have [hæv], pt, pp **had** ♦ auxiliary vb **1**

(gen) avere; essere; to ~ arrived/gone essere arrivato(a)/andato(a); to ~ eaten/slept avere mangiato/dormito; he has been kind/promoted è stato gentile/promosso; having finished or when he had finished, he left dopo aver finito, se n'è andato

2 (in tag questions): you've done it, ~n't you? l'ha fatto, (non è) vero?; he hasn't done it, has he? non l'ha fatto, vero?

3 (in short answers and questions): you've made a mistake — no I ~n't/so I ~ ha fatto un errore — ma no, niente affatto/sì, è vero; we ~n't paid — yes we ~! non abbiamo pagato — ma sì che abbiamo pagato!; I've been there before, ~ you? ci sono già stato, e lei?

♦ modal auxiliary vb (be obliged): to ~ (got) to do sth dover fare qc; I ~n't got or I don't ~ to wear glasses non ho bisogno di portare gli occhiali

♦ vt **1** (possess, obtain) avere; he has (got) blue eyes/dark hair ha gli occhi azzurri/i capelli scuri; do you ~ or ~ you got a car/phone? ha la macchina/il telefono?; may I ~ your address? potrebbe darmi il suo indirizzo?; you can ~ it for £5 te lo lascio per 5 sterline

2 (+ noun: take, hold etc): to ~ breakfast/a swim/a bath fare colazione/una nuotata/un bagno; to ~ lunch pranzare; to ~ dinner cenare; to ~ a drink bere qualcosa; to ~ a cigarette fumare una sigaretta

3: to ~ sth done far fare qc; to ~ one's hair cut farsi tagliare i capelli; to ~ sb do sth far fare qc a qn

4 (experience, suffer) avere; to ~ a cold/flu avere il raffreddore/l'influenza; she had her bag stolen le hanno rubato la borsa

5 (col: dupe): you've been had! ci sei cascato!

to have out vt: to ~ it out with sb (settle a problem etc) mettere le cose in chiaro con qn.

haven ['heɪvn] n porto; (fig) rifugio.

haven't ['hævnt] = **have not**.

haversack ['hævəsæk] n zaino.

havoc ['hævək] n caos m.

hawk [hɔːk] n falco.

hay [heɪ] n fieno; ~ **fever** n febbre f da fieno; ~**stack** n pagliaio.

haywire ['heɪwaɪə*] a (col): to go ~ perdere la testa; impazzire.

hazard ['hæzəd] n azzardo, ventura; pericolo, rischio; ~ **(warning) lights** npl (AUT) luci fpl di emergenza.

haze [heɪz] n foschia.

hazelnut ['heɪzlnʌt] n nocciola.

hazy ['heɪzɪ] a fosco(a); (idea) vago(a); (photograph) indistinto(a).

he [hiː] pronoun lui, egli; it is ~ who ... è lui che ....

head [hed] n testa, capo; (leader) capo //

vt (*list*) essere in testa a; (*group*) essere a capo di; ~s (or tails) testa (o croce), pari (o dispari); ~ first a capofitto, di testa; ~ over heels in love pazzamente innamorato(a); to ~ the ball dare di testa alla palla; to ~ for *vt fus* dirigersi verso; ~ache n mal m di testa; ~dress n (*of Indian etc*) copricapo; (*of bride*) acconciatura; ~ing n titolo; intestazione *f*; ~lamp n (*Brit*) = ~light; ~land n promontorio; ~light n fanale m; ~line n titolo; ~long ad (*fall*) a capofitto; (*rush*) precipitosamente; ~master n preside m; ~mistress n preside f; ~ office n sede f (centrale); ~-on a (*collision*) frontale; ~phones npl cuffia; ~quarters (HQ) npl ufficio centrale; (*MIL*) quartiere m generale; ~rest n poggiacapo; ~room n (*in car*) altezza dell'abitacolo; (*under bridge*) altezza limite; ~scarf n foulard m inv; ~strong a testardo(a); ~ waiter n capocameriere m; ~way n: to make ~way fare progressi; ~wind n controvento, ~y a (*experience, period*) inebriante.

heal [hi:l] *vt, vi* guarire.

health [hɛlθ] n salute f; ~ food(s) n(pl) alimenti mpl integrali; the H~ Service n (*Brit*) ≈ il Servizio Sanitario Statale; ~y a (*person*) in buona salute; (*climate*) salubre; (*food*) salutare; (*attitude etc*) sano(a).

heap [hi:p] n mucchio // *vt* ammucchiare.

hear, *pt, pp* **heard** [hɪə*, hə:d] *vt* sentire; (*news*) ascoltare; (*lecture*) assistere a // *vi* sentire; to ~ about avere notizie di; sentire parlare di; to ~ from sb ricevere notizie da qn; ~ing n (*sense*) udito; (*of witnesses*) audizione f; (*of a case*) udienza; ~ing aid n apparecchio acustico; ~say n dicerie fpl, chiacchiere fpl.

hearse [hə:s] n carro funebre.

heart [ha:t] n cuore m; ~s npl (*CARDS*) cuori mpl; at ~ in fondo; by ~ (*learn, know*) a memoria; ~ attack n attacco di cuore; ~beat n battito del cuore; ~broken a: to be ~broken avere il cuore spezzato; ~burn n bruciore m di stomaco; ~ failure n arresto cardiaco; ~felt a sincero(a).

hearth [ha:θ] n focolare m.

heartily ['ha:tɪlɪ] ad (*laugh*) di cuore; (*eat*) di buon appetito; (*agree*) in pieno, completamente.

hearty ['ha:tɪ] a caloroso(a); robusto(a), sano(a); vigoroso(a).

heat [hi:t] n calore m; (*fig*) ardore m; fuoco; (*SPORT*: also: qualifying ~) prova eliminatoria // *vt* scaldare; to ~ up *vi* (*liquids*) scaldarsi; (*room*) riscaldarsi // *vt* riscaldare; ~ed a riscaldato(a); (*fig*) appassionato(a), acceso(a), eccitato(a); ~er n stufa; radiatore m.

heath [hi:θ] n (*Brit*) landa.

heathen ['hi:ðn] a, n pagano(a).

heather ['hɛðə*] n erica.

heating ['hi:tɪŋ] n riscaldamento.

heatstroke ['hi:tstrəuk] n colpo di sole.

heatwave ['hi:tweɪv] n ondata di caldo.

heave [hi:v] *vt* sollevare (con forza) // *vi* sollevarsi; (*retch*) aver conati di vomito // n (*push*) grande spinta.

heaven ['hɛvn] n paradiso, cielo; ~ly a divino(a), celeste.

heavily ['hɛvɪlɪ] ad pesantemente; (*drink, smoke*) molto.

heavy ['hɛvɪ] a pesante; (*sea*) grosso(a); (*rain*) forte; (*drinker, smoker*) gran (*before noun*); ~ goods vehicle (HGV) n veicolo per trasporti pesanti; ~weight n (*SPORT*) peso massimo.

Hebrew ['hi:bru:] a ebreo(a) // n (*LING*) ebraico.

Hebrides ['hɛbrɪdiːz] npl: the ~ le Ebridi.

heckle ['hɛkl] *vt* interpellare e dare noia a (*un oratore*).

hectic ['hɛktɪk] a movimentato(a).

he'd [hi:d] = he would, he had.

hedge [hɛdʒ] n siepe f // *vi* essere clusivo(a); to ~ one's bets (*fig*) coprirsi dai rischi.

hedgehog ['hɛdʒhɔg] n riccio.

heed [hi:d] *vt* (*also:* take ~ of) badare a, far conto di; ~less a sbadato(a).

heel [hi:l] n (*ANAT*) calcagno; (*of shoe*) tacco // *vt* (*shoe*) rifare i tacchi a.

hefty ['hɛftɪ] a (*person*) solido(a); (*parcel*) pesante; (*piece, price*) grosso(a).

heifer ['hɛfə*] n giovenca.

height [haɪt] n altezza; (*high ground*) altura; (*fig: of glory*) apice m; (: *of stupidity*) colmo; ~en *vt* innalzare; (*fig*) accrescere.

heir [ɛə*] n erede m; ~ess n erede f; ~loom n mobile m (or gioiello or quadro) di famiglia.

held [hɛld] *pt, pp* of hold.

helicopter ['hɛlɪkɔptə*] n elicottero.

heliport ['hɛlɪpɔ:t] n eliporto.

helium ['hi:lɪəm] n elio.

hell [hɛl] n inferno; ~! (*col*) porca miseria!, accidenti!

he'll [hi:l] = he will, he shall.

hellish ['hɛlɪʃ] a infernale.

hello [hə'ləu] *excl* buon giorno!; ciao! (*to sb one addresses as "tu"*); (*surprise*) ma guarda!

helm [hɛlm] n (*NAUT*) timone m.

helmet ['hɛlmɪt] n casco.

help [hɛlp] n aiuto; (*charwoman*) donna di servizio; (*assistant etc*) impiegato/a // *vt* aiutare; ~! aiuto!; ~ yourself (*to bread*) si serva (del pane); he can't ~ it non ci può far niente; ~er n aiutante m/f, assistente m/f; ~ful a di grande aiuto; (*useful*) utile; ~ing n porzione f;

~less *a* impotente; debole.
hem [hɛm] *n* orlo // *vt* fare l'orlo a; **to ~ in** *vt* cingere.
he-man ['hi:mæn] *n* fusto.
hemisphere ['hɛmɪsfɪə*] *n* emisfero.
hemorrhage ['hɛmərɪdʒ] *n* (*US*) = **haemorrhage**.
hemorrhoids ['hɛmərɔɪdz] *npl* (*US*) = **haemorroids**.
hen [hɛn] *n* gallina.
hence [hɛns] *ad* (*therefore*) dunque; 2 years ~ di qui a 2 anni; **~forth** *ad* d'ora in poi.
henchman ['hɛntʃmən] *n* (*pej*) caudatario.
henpecked ['hɛnpɛkt] *a* dominato dalla moglie.
hepatitis [hɛpə'taɪtɪs] *n* epatite *f*.
her [hə:*] *pronoun* (*direct*) la, l' + *vowel*; (*indirect*) le; (*stressed, after prep*) lei; *see note at* **she** // *a* il(la) suo(a), i(le) suoi(sue); *see also* **me, my.**
herald ['hɛrəld] *n* araldo // *vt* annunciare.
heraldry ['hɛrəldrɪ] *n* araldica.
herb [hə:b] *n* erba.
herd [hə:d] *n* mandria.
here [hɪə*] *ad* qui, qua // *excl* ehi!; **~!** (*at roll call*) presente!; **~ is/are** ecco; **~'s** my sister ecco mia sorella; **~ he/she** is eccolo/eccola; **~ she** comes eccola che viene; **~after** *ad* in futuro; dopo questo // *n*: **the ~after** l'al di là *m*; **~by** *ad* (*in letter*) con la presente.
hereditary [hɪ'rɛdɪtrɪ] *a* ereditario(a).
heresy ['hɛrəsɪ] *n* eresia.
heretic ['hɛrətɪk] *n* eretico/a.
heritage ['hɛrɪtɪdʒ] *n* eredità; (*fig*) retaggio.
hermetically [hə:'mɛtɪklɪ] *ad*: **~ sealed** ermeticamente chiuso(a).
hermit ['hə:mɪt] *n* eremita *m*.
hernia ['hə:nɪə] *n* ernia.
hero, ~es ['hɪərəu] *n* eroe *m*.
heroin ['hɛrəuɪn] *n* eroina.
heroine ['hɛrəuɪn] *n* eroina.
heron ['hɛrən] *n* airone *m*.
herring ['hɛrɪŋ] *n* aringa.
hers [hə:z] *pronoun* il(la) suo(a), i(le) suoi(sue); *see also* **mine.**
herself [hə:'sɛlf] *pronoun* (*reflexive*) si; (*emphatic*) lei stessa; (*after prep*) se stessa, sé; *see also* **oneself.**
he's [hi:z] = **he is, he has.**
hesitant ['hɛzɪtənt] *a* esitante, indeciso(a).
hesitate ['hɛzɪteɪt] *vi*: **to ~** (*about/to do*) esitare (su/a fare); **hesitation** [-'teɪʃən] *n* esitazione *f*.
heterosexual ['hɛtərəu'sɛksjuəl] *a*, *n* eterosessuale (*m/f*).
hexagon ['hɛksəgən] *n* esagono.
heyday ['heɪdeɪ] *n*: **the ~** of i bei giorni di, l'età d'oro di.
HGV *n abbr* = **heavy goods vehicle.**
hi [haɪ] *excl* ciao!

hiatus [haɪ'eɪtəs] *n* vuoto; (*LING*) iato.
hibernate ['haɪbəneɪt] *vi* ibernare.
hiccough, hiccup ['hɪkʌp] *vi* singhiozzare // *n* singhiozzo.
hide [haɪd] *n* (*skin*) pelle *f* // *vb* (*pt* **hid**, *pp* **hidden** [hɪd, 'hɪdn]) *vt*: **to ~** *sth* (from sb) nascondere qc (a qn) // *vi*: **to ~** (from sb) nascondersi (da qn); **~and-seek** *n* rimpiattino; **~away** *n* nascondiglio.
hideous ['hɪdɪəs] *a* laido(a); orribile.
hiding ['haɪdɪŋ] *n* (*beating*) bastonata; **to be in ~** (*concealed*) tenersi nascosto(a).
hierarchy ['haɪərɑːkɪ] *n* gerarchia.
hi-fi ['haɪfaɪ] *n* stereo // *a* ad alta fedeltà, hi-fi *inv*.
high [haɪ] *a* alto(a); (*speed, respect, number*) grande; (*wind*) forte // *a* alto, in alto; 20m ~ alto(a) 20m; **~boy** *n* (*US: tallboy*) cassettone *m*; **~brow** *a, n* intellettuale (*m/f*); **~chair** *n* seggiolone *m*; **~er education** *n* studi *mpl* superiori; **~handed** *a* prepotente; **~jack** *vt* = **hijack**; **~ jump** *n* (*SPORT*) salto in alto; **the H~lands** *npl* le Highlands scozzesi; **~light** *n* (*fig: of event*) momento culminante // *vt* mettere in evidenza; **~ly** *ad* molto; **~ly strung** *a* teso(a) di nervi, eccitabile; **~ness** *n* altezza; Her H~ness Sua Altezza; **~pitched** *a* acuto(a); **~rise block** *n* palazzone *m*; **~ school** *n* scuola secondaria; (*US*) istituto superiore d'istruzione; **~ season** *n* (*Brit*) alta stagione; **~ street** *n* (*Brit*) strada principale.
highway ['haɪweɪ] *n* strada maestra; H~ Code *n* (*Brit*) codice *m* della strada.
hijack ['haɪdʒæk] *vt* dirottare; **~er** *n* dirottatore/trice.
hike [haɪk] *vi* fare un'escursione a piedi // *n* escursione *f* a piedi; (*in prices*) aumento; **~r** *n* escursionista *m/f*.
hilarious [hɪ'lɛərɪəs] *a* (*behaviour, event*) che fa schiantare dal ridere.
hilarity [hɪ'lærɪtɪ] *n* ilarità.
hill [hɪl] *n* collina, colle *m*; (*fairly high*) montagna; (*on road*) salita; **~side** *n* fianco della collina; **~y** *a* collinoso(a); montagnoso(a).
hilt [hɪlt] *n* (*of sword*) elsa; **to the ~** (*fig: support*) fino in fondo.
him [hɪm] *pronoun* (*direct*) lo, l' + *vowel*; (*indirect*) gli; (*stressed, after prep*) lui; *see also* **me**; **~self** *pronoun* (*reflexive*) si; (*emphatic*) lui stesso; (*after prep*) se stesso, sé; *see also* **oneself.**
hind [haɪnd] *a* posteriore // *n* cerva.
hinder ['hɪndə*] *vt* ostacolare; (*delay*) tardare; (*prevent*): **to ~** sb **from** doing impedire a qn di fare; **hindrance** ['hɪndrəns] *n* ostacolo, impedimento.
hindsight ['haɪndsaɪt] *n*: **with ~** con il

senno di poi.

Hindu ['hindu:] n indù m/f inv.

hinge [hindʒ] n cardine m // vi (fig): to ~ on dipendere da.

hint [hint] n accenno, allusione f; (advice) consiglio // vt: to ~ that lasciar capire che // vi: to ~ at accennare a.

hip [hip] n anca, fianco.

hippopotamus, pl ~es or **hippopotami** [hipə'pɔtəməs, -'pɔtəmai] n ippopotamo.

hire ['haiə*] vt (Brit: car, equipment) noleggiare; (worker) assumere, dare lavoro a // n nolo, noleggio; **for ~** da nolo; (taxi) libero(a); ~ **purchase (H.P.)** n (Brit) acquisto (or vendita) rateale.

his [hiz] a, pronoun il(la) suo(sua), i(le) suoi(sue); see also **my, mine.**

hiss [his] vi fischiare; (cat, snake) sibilare // n fischio, sibilo.

historic(al) [hi'stɔrik(l)] a storico(a).

history ['histəri] n storia.

hit [hit] vt (pt, pp hit) colpire, picchiare; (knock against) battere; (reach: target) raggiungere; (collide with: car) urtare contro; (fig: affect) colpire; (find: problem etc) incontrare // n colpo; (success, song) successo; to ~ **it off** with sb andare molto d'accordo con qn; ~ **and-run driver** n pirata m della strada.

hitch [hitʃ] vt (fasten) attaccare; (also: ~ up) tirare su // n (difficulty) intoppo, difficoltà f inv; to ~ **a lift** fare l'autostop.

hitch-hike ['hitʃhaik] vi fare l'autostop; ~**r** n autostoppista m/f.

hi-tech ['hai'tɛk] a di alta tecnologia // n alta tecnologia.

hitherto [hiðə'tu:] ad in precedenza.

hive [haiv] n alveare m; to ~ **off** vt separare.

H.M.S. abbr = His (Her) Majesty's Ship.

hoard [hɔ:d] n (of food) provviste fpl; (of money) gruzzolo // vt ammassare.

hoarding ['hɔ:diŋ] n (Brit: for posters) tabellone m per affissioni.

hoarfrost ['hɔ:frɔst] n brina.

hoarse [hɔ:s] a rauco(a).

hoax [həuks] n scherzo; falso allarme.

hob [hɔb] n piastra (con fornelli).

hobble ['hɔbl] vi zoppicare.

hobby ['hɔbi] n hobby m inv, passatempo; ~**-horse** n (fig) chiodo fisso.

hobo ['həubəu] n (US) vagabondo.

hockey ['hɔki] n hockey m.

hoe [həu] n zappa.

hog [hɔg] n maiale m // vt (fig) arraffare; to go the whole ~ farlo fino in fondo.

hoist [hɔist] n paranco // vt issare.

hold [həuld] vb (pt, pp held) vt tenere; (contain) contenere; (keep back) trattenere; (believe) mantenere;

considerare; (possess) avere, possedere; detenere // vi (withstand pressure) tenere; (be valid) essere valido(a) // n presa; (fig) potere m; (NAUT) stiva; ~ **the line!** (TEL) resti in linea!; to ~ **one's own** (fig) difendersi bene; **to catch** or **get** (a) ~ **of** afferrare; **to get** ~ **of** (fig) trovare; **to** ~ **back** vt trattenere; (secret) tenere celato(a); **to** ~ **down** vt (person) tenere a terra; (job) tenere; **to** ~ **off** vt tener lontano; **to** ~ **on** vi tener fermo; (wait) aspettare; ~ **on!** (TEL) resti in linea!; **to** ~ **on to** vt fus tenersi stretto(a) a; (keep) conservare; **to** ~ **out** vt offrire // vi (resist) resistere; **to** ~ **up** vt (raise) alzare; (support) sostenere; (delay) ritardare; ~**all** n (Brit) borsone m; ~**er** n (of ticket, title) possessore/posseditrice; (of office etc) incaricato/a; (of record) detentore/trice; ~**ing** n (share) azioni fpl, titoli mpl; (farm) podere m, tenuta; ~**up** n (robbery) rapina a mano armata; (delay) ritardo; (Brit. in traffic) blocco.

hole [həul] n buco, buca // vt bucare.

holiday ['hɔlədi] n vacanza; (day off) giorno di vacanza; (public) giorno festivo; on ~ in vacanza; ~ **camp** n (for children) colonia (di villeggiatura); (also: ~ **centre**) = villaggio (di vacanze); ~**-maker** n (Brit) villeggiante m/f; ~ **resort** n luogo di villeggiatura.

holiness ['həulinis] n santità.

Holland ['hɔlənd] n Olanda.

hollow ['hɔləu] a cavo(a), vuoto(a); (fig) falso(a); vano(a) // n cavità f inv; (in land) valletta, depressione f // vt: to ~ **out** scavare.

holly ['hɔli] n agrifoglio.

holocaust ['hɔləkɔ:st] n olocausto.

holster ['həulstə*] n fondina (di pistola).

holy ['həuli] a santo(a); (bread) benedetto(a), consacrato(a); (ground) consacrato(a); **H~ Ghost** or **Spirit** n Spirito Santo; ~ **orders** npl ordini mpl (sacri).

homage ['hɔmidʒ] n omaggio; **to pay ~ to** rendere omaggio a.

home [həum] n casa; (country) patria; (institution) casa, ricovero // a familiare; (cooking etc) casalingo(a); (ECON, POL) nazionale, interno(a) // ad a casa; in patria; (right in: nail etc) fino in fondo; at ~ a casa; **to go** (or **come**) ~ tornare a casa (or in patria); **make yourself at** ~ si metta a suo agio; ~ **address** n indirizzo di casa; ~ **computer** n home computer m inv; ~**land** n patria; ~**less** a senza tetto; spatriato(a); ~**ly** a semplice, alla buona; accogliente; ~**-made** a casalingo(a); **H~ Office** n (Brit) ministero degli Interni; ~ **rule** n autogoverno; **H~ Secretary** n (Brit) ministro degli Interni; **~sick** a: to be ~sick avere la nostalgia; **~ town** n città f inv natale; **~ward** ['həumwəd] a (journey) di ritorno; **~work** n compiti mpl (per casa).

homicide ['hɒmɪsaɪd] n (US) omicidio.

homoeopathy [həumɪ'ɒpəθɪ] n omeopatia.

homogeneous [hɔməu'dʒi:nɪəs] a omogeneo(a).

homosexual [hɔməu'sɛksjuəl] a, n omosessuale (m/f).

honest ['ɒnɪst] a onesto(a); sincero(a); **~ly** ad onestamente; sinceramente; **~y** n onestà.

honey ['hʌnɪ] n miele m; **~comb** n favo; **~moon** n luna di miele, viaggio di nozze; **~suckle** n (BOT) caprifoglio.

honk [hɒŋk] vi suonare il clacson.

honorary ['ɒnərərɪ] a onorario(a); (duty, title) onorifico(a).

honour, (US **honor** ['ɒnə*]) vt onorare // n onore m; **~able** a onorevole; **~s degree** n (SCOL) laurea specializzata.

hood [hud] n cappuccio; (Brit AUT) capote f; (US AUT) cofano.

hoodlum ['hu:dləm] n teppista m/f.

hoodwink ['hudwɪŋk] vt infinocchiare.

hoof [hu:f], pl **~s** or **hooves** n zoccolo.

hook [huk] n gancio; (for fishing) amo // vt uncinare; (dress) agganciare.

hooligan ['hu:lɪgən] n giovinastro, teppista m.

hoop [hu:p] n cerchio.

hoot [hu:t] vi (AUT) suonare il clacson; **~er** n (Brit AUT) clacson m inv; (NAUT) sirena.

hoover ['hu:və*] ® (Brit) n aspirapolvere m inv // vt pulire con l'aspirapolvere.

hooves [hu:vz] npl of **hoof**.

hop [hɒp] vi saltellare, saltare; (on one foot) saltare su una gamba // n salto.

hope [həup] vt, vi sperare // n speranza; I ~ so/not spero di sì/no; **~ful** a (person) pieno(a) di speranza; (situation) promettente; **~fully** ad con speranza; **~fully he will recover** speriamo che si riprenda; **~less** a senza speranza, disperato(a); (useless) inutile.

hops [hɒps] npl luppoli mpl.

horde [hɔ:d] n orda.

horizon [hə'raɪzn] n orizzonte m; **~tal** [hɔrɪ'zɒntl] a orizzontale.

hormone ['hɔ:məun] n ormone m.

horn [hɔ:n] n (ZOOL, MUS) corno; (AUT) clacson m inv.

hornet ['hɔ:nɪt] n calabrone m.

horny ['hɔ:nɪ] a corneo(a); (hands) calloso(a); (col) arrapato(a).

horoscope ['hɔrəskəup] n oroscopo.

horrendous [hə'rɛndəs] a orrendo(a).

horrible ['hɒrɪbl] a orribile, tremendo(a).

horrid ['hɒrɪd] a orrido(a); (person)

antipatico(a).

horrify ['hɒrɪfaɪ] vt scandalizzare.

horror ['hɒrə*] n orrore m; **~ film** n film m inv dell'orrore.

hors d'œuvre [ɔː'dəːvrə] n antipasto.

horse [hɔ:s] n cavallo; **~ back**: on ~back a cavallo; **~ chestnut** n ippocastano; **~man** n cavaliere m; **~power (h.p.)** n cavallo (vapore); **~racing** n ippica; **~radish** n rafano; **~shoe** n ferro di cavallo; **~woman** n amazzone f.

horticulture ['hɔ:tɪkʌltʃə*] n orticoltura.

hose [həuz] n (also: ~pipe) tubo; (also: garden ~) tubo per annaffiare.

hospice ['hɒspɪs] n ricovero, ospizio.

hospitable [hɒs'pɪtəbl] a ospitale.

hospital ['hɒspɪtl] n ospedale m.

hospitality [hɒspɪ'tælɪtɪ] n ospitalità.

host [həust] n ospite m; (REL) ostia; (large number): **a ~ of** una schiera di.

hostage ['hɒstɪdʒ] n ostaggio/a.

hostel ['hɒstl] n ostello; (also: **youth ~**) ostello della gioventù.

hostess ['həustɪs] n ospite f; (Brit: air ~) hostess f inv; (in nightclub) entraîneuse f inv.

hostile ['hɒstaɪl] a ostile.

hostility [hɒ'stɪlɪtɪ] n ostilità f inv.

hot [hɒt] a caldo(a); (as opposed to only warm) molto caldo(a); (spicy) piccante; (fig) accanito(a); ardente; violento(a), focoso(a); **to be ~** (person) aver caldo; (object) essere caldo(a); (weather) far caldo; **~bed** n (fig) focolaio; **~ dog** n hot dog m inv.

hotel [həu'tɛl] n albergo; **~ier** n albergatore/trice.

hot: **~headed** a focoso(a), eccitabile; **~house** n serra; **~ line** n (POL) telefono rosso; **~ly** ad violentemente; **~plate** n (on cooker) piastra riscaldante; **~-water bottle** n borsa dell'acqua calda.

hound [haund] vt perseguitare // n segugio.

hour ['auə*] n ora; **~ly** a all'ora // ad ogni ora; **~ly paid** a pagato(a) a ore.

house n [haus] (pl **~s** ['hauzɪz]) (also: firm) casa; (POL) camera; (THEATRE) sala; pubblico; spettacolo // vt [hauz] (person) ospitare, alloggiare; **on the ~** (fig) offerto(a) dalla casa; **~boat** n house boat f inv; **~breaking** n furto con scasso; **~coat** n vestaglia; **~hold** n famiglia; casa; **~keeper** n governante f; **~keeping** n (work) governo della casa; **~keeping (money)** soldi mpl per le spese di casa; **~warming party** n festa per inaugurare la casa nuova; **~wife** n massaia, casalinga; **~work** n faccende fpl domestiche.

housing ['hauzɪŋ] n alloggio; **~ development**, (Brit) **~ estate** n zona residenziale con case popolari e/o *private.*

hovel ['hɒvl] *n* casupola.

hover ['hɔvə*] *vi* (*bird*) librarsi; (*helicopter*) volare a punto fisso; ~**craft** *n* hovercraft *m inv*.

how [hau] *ad* come; ~ **are you?** come sta?; ~ **do you do?** piacere!; ~ **far is it to the river?** quanto è lontano il fiume?; ~ **long have you been here?** da quando è qui?; ~ **lovely!/awful!** che bello!/ orrore!; ~ **many?** quanti(e)?; ~ **much?** quanto(a)?; ~ **much milk?** quanto latte?; ~ **many people?** quante persone?; ~ **old are you?** quanti anni ha?; ~**ever** *ad* in qualsiasi modo *or* maniera che; (+ *adjective*) per quanto + *sub*; (*in questions*) come // *cj* comunque, però.

howl [haul] *n* ululato // *vi* ululare.

h.p., H.P. *abbr* = **hire purchase, horsepower.**

HQ *n abbr* = **headquarters.**

hub [hʌb] *n* (*of wheel*) mozzo; (*fig*) ful-cro.

hubbub ['hʌbʌb] *n* baccano.

hub cap *n* coprimozzo.

huddle ['hʌdl] *vi*: to ~ **together** rannic-chiarsi l'uno contro l'altro.

hue [hju:] *n* tinta; ~ **and cry** *n* clamore *m.*

huff [hʌf] *n*: in a ~ stizzito(a).

hug [hʌg] *vt* abbracciare; (*shore, kerb*) stringere // *n* abbraccio, stretta.

huge [hju:dʒ] *a* enorme, immenso(a).

hulk [hʌlk] *n* (*ship*) nave *f* in disarmo; (*building, car*) carcassa; (*person*) ma-stodonte *m.*

hull [hʌl] *n* (*of ship*) scafo.

hullo [hə'ləu] *excl* = **hello.**

hum [hʌm] *vt* (*tune*) canticchiare // *vi* canticchiare; (*insect, plane, tool*) ronzare.

human ['hju:mən] *a* umano(a) // *n* essere *m* umano.

humane [hju:'meɪn] *a* umanitario(a).

humanitarian [hju:mænɪ'tɛərɪən] *a* umanitario(a).

humanity [hju:'mænɪtɪ] *n* umanità.

humble ['hʌmbl] *a* umile, modesto(a) // *vt* umiliare.

humbug ['hʌmbʌg] *n* inganno; scioc-chezze *fpl.*

humdrum ['hʌmdrʌm] *a* monotono(a), tedioso(a).

humid ['hju:mɪd] *a* umido(a).

humiliate [hju:'mɪlɪeɪt] *vt* umiliare; **humiliation** [-'eɪʃən] *n* umiliazione *f.*

humility [hju:'mɪlɪtɪ] *n* umiltà.

humorous ['hju:mərəs] *a* umoristico(a); (*person*) buffo(a).

humour, (*US*) **humor** ['hju:mə*] *n* umore *m* // *vt* (*person*) compiacere; (*sb's whims*) assecondare.

hump [hʌmp] *n* gobba.

hunch [hʌntʃ] *n* gobba; (*premonition*)

intuizione *f*; ~**back** *n* gobbo/a; ~**ed** *a* incurvato(a).

hundred ['hʌndrəd] *num* cento; ~**s of** centinaia *fpl* di; ~**weight** *n* (*Brit*) = 50.8 kg; 112 lb; (*US*) = 45.3 kg; 100 lb.

hung [hʌŋ] *pt, pp of* **hang.**

Hungary ['hʌŋgərɪ] *n* Ungheria.

hunger ['hʌŋgə*] *n* fame *f* // *vi*: to ~ **for** desiderare ardentemente.

hungry ['hʌŋgrɪ] *a* affamato(a); to be ~ aver fame.

hunk [hʌŋk] *n* (*of bread etc*) bel pezzo.

hunt [hʌnt] *vt* (*seek*) cercare; (*SPORT*) cacciare // *vi* andare a caccia // *n* caccia; ~**er** *n* cacciatore *m*; ~**ing** *n* caccia.

hurdle ['hə:dl] *n* (*SPORT, fig*) ostacolo.

hurl [hə:l] *vt* lanciare con violenza.

hurrah, hurray [hu'rɑ:, hu'reɪ] *excl* urrà!, evviva!

hurricane ['hʌrɪkən] *n* uragano.

hurried ['hʌrɪd] *a* affrettato(a); (*work*) fatto(a) in fretta; ~**ly** *ad* in fretta.

hurry ['hʌrɪ] *n* fretta // *vb* (*also*: ~ **up**) *vi* affrettarsi // *vt* (*person*) affrettare; (*work*) far in fretta; to be in a ~ aver fretta; to do sth in a ~ fare qc in fretta; to ~ in/out entrare/uscire in fretta.

hurt [hə:t] *vb* (*pt, pp* **hurt**) *vt* (*cause pain to*) far male a; (*injure, fig*) ferire // *vi* far male // *a* ferito(a); ~**ful** *a* (*remark*) che ferisce.

hurtle ['hə:tl] *vt* scagliare // *vi*: to ~ past/down passare/scendere a razzo.

husband ['hʌzbənd] *n* marito.

hush [hʌʃ] *n* silenzio, calma // *vt* zittire; ~**!** zitto(a)!

husk [hʌsk] *n* (*of wheat*) cartoccio; (*of rice, maize*) buccia.

husky ['hʌskɪ] *a* roco(a) // *n* cane *m* eschimese.

hustle ['hʌsl] *vt* spingere, incalzare // *n* pigia pigia *m inv*; ~ **and bustle** *n* trambusto.

hut [hʌt] *n* rifugio; (*shed*) ripostiglio.

hutch [hʌtʃ] *n* gabbia.

hyacinth ['haɪəsɪnθ] *n* giacinto.

hybrid ['haɪbrɪd] *a* ibrido(a) // *n* ibrido.

hydrant ['haɪdrənt] *n* (*also*: **fire** ~) idrante *m.*

hydraulic [haɪ'drɔ:lɪk] *a* idraulico(a).

hydroelectric [haɪdrəʊɪ'lɛktrɪk] *a* idroelettrico(a).

hydrofoil ['haɪdrəʊfɔɪl] *n* aliscafo.

hydrogen ['haɪdrədʒən] *n* idrogeno.

hyena [haɪ'i:nə] *n* iena.

hygiene ['haɪdʒi:n] *n* igiene *f.*

hymn [hɪm] *n* inno; cantica.

hype [haɪp] *n* (*col*) campagna pub-blicitaria.

hypermarket ['haɪpəmɑ:kɪt] *n* ipermercato.

hyphen ['haɪfn] *n* trattino.

hypnotism ['hɪpnətɪzm] *n* ipnotismo.

hypnotize ['hɪpnətaɪz] *vt* ipnotizzare.

hypocrisy [hɪ'pɔkrɪsɪ] *n* ipocrisia.
hypocrite ['hɪpəkrɪt] *n* ipocrita *m/f*;
hypocritical [-'krɪtɪkl] *a* ipocrita.
hypothermia [haɪpəu'θə:mɪə] *n*
ipotermia.
hypothesis, *pl* **hypotheses** [haɪ'pɔθɪsɪs,
-si:z] *n* ipotesi *f inv*.
hypothetical [haɪpəu'θetɪkl] *a*
ipotetico(a).
hysterical [hɪ'sterɪkl] *a* isterico(a).
hysterics [hɪ'sterɪks] *npl* accesso di
isteria; (*laughter*) attacco di riso.

I

I [aɪ] *pronoun* io.
ice [aɪs] *n* ghiaccio; (*on road*) gelo // *vt*
(*cake*) glassare; (*drink*) mettere in fresco // *vi* (*also:* ~ **over**) ghiacciare;
(*also:* ~ **up**) gelare; ~ **axe** *n* piccozza
da ghiaccio; ~**berg** *n* iceberg *m inv*;
~**box** *n* (*US*) frigorifero; (*Brit*) reparto
ghiaccio; (*insulated box*) frigo portatile;
~ **cream** *n* gelato; ~ **hockey** *n* hockey
m su ghiaccio.
Iceland ['aɪslənd] *n* Islanda.
ice: ~ **lolly** *n* (*Brit*) ghiacciolo; ~ **rink**
n pista di pattinaggio; ~ **skating** *n*
pattinaggio sul ghiaccio.
icicle ['aɪsɪkl] *n* ghiacciolo.
icing ['aɪsɪŋ] *n* (*AVIAT etc*) patina di
ghiaccio; (*CULIN*) glassa; ~ **sugar** *n*
(*Brit*) zucchero a velo.
icy ['aɪsɪ] *a* ghiacciato(a); (*weather,
temperature*) gelido(a).
I'd [aɪd] = **I would, I had**.
idea [aɪ'dɪə] *n* idea.
ideal [aɪ'dɪəl] *a, n* ideale (*m*).
identical [aɪ'dentɪkl] *a* identico(a).
identification [aɪdentɪfɪ'keɪʃən] *n*
identificazione *f*; **means of** ~ carta
d'identità.
identify [aɪ'dentɪfaɪ] *vt* identificare.
identikit picture [aɪ'dentɪkɪt-] *n*
identikit *m inv*.
identity [aɪ'dentɪtɪ] *n* identità *f inv*; ~
card *n* carta d'identità.
idiom ['ɪdɪəm] *n* idioma *m*; (*phrase*)
espressione *f* idiomatica.
idiot ['ɪdɪət] *n* idiota *m/f*; ~**ic** [-'ɔtɪk] *a*
idiota.
idle ['aɪdl] *a* inattivo(a); (*lazy*) pigro(a),
ozioso(a); (*unemployed*) disoccupato(a);
(*question, pleasures*) ozioso(a); **to lie** ~
stare fermo, non funzionare; **to** ~
away *vt* (*time*) sprecare, buttar via.
idol ['aɪdl] *n* idolo; ~**ize** *vt* idoleggiare.
i.e. *ad abbr* (= *that is*) cioè.
if [ɪf] *cj* se; ~ **I were you** ... se fossi in te
..., **io al tuo posto** ...; ~ **so** se è così; ~
not se no; ~ **only** se solo *or* soltanto.
ignite [ɪg'naɪt] *vt* accendere // *vi*
accendersi.
ignition [ɪg'nɪʃən] *n* (*AUT*) accensione *f*;

to switch on/off the ~ accendere/
spegnere il motore; ~ **key** *n* (*AUT*)
chiave *f* dell'accensione.
ignorant ['ɪgnərənt] *a* ignorante; **to be** ~
of (*subject*) essere ignorante in; (*events*)
essere ignaro(a) di.
ignore [ɪg'nɔ:*] *vt* non tener conto di;
(*person, fact*) ignorare.
I'll [aɪl] = **I will, I shall**.
ill [ɪl] *a* (*sick*) malato(a); (*bad*)
cattivo(a) // *n* male *m* // *ad*: **to speak** *etc*
~ **of sb** parlare *etc* male di qn; **to take**
or **be taken** ~ ammalarsi; ~**-advised** *a*
(*decision*) poco giudizioso(a); (*person*)
mal consigliato(a); ~**-at-ease** *a* a
disagio.
illegal [ɪ'li:gl] *a* illegale.
illegible [ɪ'ledʒɪbl] *a* illeggibile.
illegitimate [ɪlɪ'dʒɪtɪmət] *a*
illegittimo(a).
ill-fated [ɪl'feɪtɪd] *a* nefasto(a).
ill feeling *n* rancore *m*.
illiterate [ɪ'lɪtərət] *a* analfabeta,
illetterato(a); (*letter*) scorretto(a).
illness ['ɪlnɪs] *n* malattia.
ill-treat [ɪl'tri:t] *vt* maltrattare.
illuminate [ɪ'lu:mɪneɪt] *vt* illuminare;
illumination [-'neɪʃən] *n* illuminazione *f*.
illusion [ɪ'lu:ʒən] *n* illusione *f*; **to be**
under the ~ **that** avere l'impressione
che.
illustrate ['ɪləstreɪt] *vt* illustrare;
illustration [-'streɪʃən] *n* illustrazione *f*.
ill will *n* cattiva volontà.
I'm [aɪm] = **I am**.
image ['ɪmɪdʒ] *n* immagine *f*; (*public
face*) immagine (pubblica); ~**ry** *n*
immagini *fpl*.
imaginary [ɪ'mædʒɪnərɪ] *a* immagina-
rio(a).
imagination [ɪmædʒɪ'neɪʃən] *n* immaginazione *f*, fantasia.
imaginative [ɪ'mædʒɪnətɪv] *a* immagino-
so(a).
imagine [ɪ'mædʒɪn] *vt* immaginare.
imbalance [ɪm'bæləns] *n* squilibrio.
imitate ['ɪmɪteɪt] *vt* imitare; **imitation**
[-'teɪʃən] *n* imitazione *f*.
immaculate [ɪ'mækjulət] *a*
immacolato(a); (*dress, appearance*)
impeccabile.
immaterial [ɪmə'tɪərɪəl] *a* immateriale,
indifferente.
immature [ɪmə'tjuə*] *a* immaturo(a).
immediate [ɪ'mi:dɪət] *a* immediato(a);
~**ly** *ad* (*at once*) subito,
immediatamente; ~**ly next to** proprio
accanto a.
immense [ɪ'mens] *a* immenso(a);
enorme.
immerse [ɪ'mə:s] *vt* immergere.
immersion heater [ɪ'mə:ʃən-] *n* (*Brit*)
scaldaacqua *m inv* a immersione.
immigrant ['ɪmɪgrənt] *n* immigrante *m/
f*; immigrato/a.

immigration [ɪmɪ'greɪʃən] *n* immigrazione *f*.
imminent ['ɪmɪnənt] *a* imminente.
immoral [ɪ'mɒrl] *a* immorale.
immortal [ɪ'mɔːtl] *a, n* immortale (*m/f*).
immune [ɪ'mjuːn] *a*: ~ (**to**) immune (da).
immunity [ɪ'mjuːnɪtɪ] *n* immunità.
imp [ɪmp] *n* folletto, diavoletto; (*child*) diavoletto.
impact ['ɪmpækt] *n* impatto.
impair [ɪm'pɛə*] *vt* danneggiare.
impart [ɪm'pɑːt] *vt* (*make known*) comunicare; (*bestow*) impartire.
impartial [ɪm'pɑːʃl] *a* imparziale.
impassable [ɪm'pɑːsəbl] *a* insuperabile; (*road*) impraticabile.
impassive [ɪm'pæsɪv] *a* impassibile.
impatience [ɪm'peɪʃəns] *n* impazienza.
impatient [ɪm'peɪʃənt] *a* impaziente; to get *or* grow ~ perdere la pazienza.
impeccable [ɪm'pɛkəbl] *a* impeccabile.
impede [ɪm'piːd] *vt* impedire.
impediment [ɪm'pedɪmənt] *n* impedimento; (*also*: speech ~) difetto di pronuncia.
impending [ɪm'pendɪŋ] *a* imminente.
imperative [ɪm'perətɪv] *a* imperativo(a); necessario(a), urgente; (*voice*) imperioso(a) // *n* (*LING*) imperativo.
imperfect [ɪm'pɔːfɪkt] *a* imperfetto(a); (*goods etc*) difettoso(a).
imperial [ɪm'pɪərɪəl] *a* imperiale; (*measure*) legale.
impersonal [ɪm'pɔːsənl] *a* impersonale.
impersonate [ɪm'pɔːsəneɪt] *vt* impersonare; (*THEATRE*) fare la mimica di.
impertinent [ɪm'pɔːtɪnənt] *a* insolente, impertinente.
impervious [ɪm'pɔːvɪəs] *a* impermeabile; (*fig*): ~ to insensibile a; impassibile di fronte a.
impetuous [ɪm'petjuəs] *a* impetuoso(a), precipitoso(a).
impetus ['ɪmpətəs] *n* impeto.
impinge [ɪm'pɪndʒ]: to ~ on *vt fus* (*person*) colpire; (*rights*) ledere.
implement *n* ['ɪmplɪmənt] attrezzo; (*for cooking*) utensile *m* // *vt* ['ɪmplɪmənt] effettuare.
implicit [ɪm'plɪsɪt] *a* implicito(a); (*complete*) completo(a).
imply [ɪm'plaɪ] *vt* insinuare; suggerire.
impolite [ɪmpə'laɪt] *a* scortese.
import *vt* [ɪm'pɔːt] importare // *n* ['ɪmpɔːt] (*COMM*) importazione *f*; (*meaning*) significato, senso.
importance [ɪm'pɔːtns] *n* importanza.
important [ɪm'pɔːtnt] *a* importante; it's not ~ non ha importanza.
importer [ɪm'pɔːtə*] *n* importatore/trice.
impose [ɪm'pəʊz] *vt* imporre // *vi*: to ~ on sb sfruttare la bontà di qn.
imposing [ɪm'pəʊzɪŋ] *a* imponente.

imposition [ɪmpə'zɪʃən] *n* (*of tax etc*) imposizione *f*; to be an ~ on (*person*) abusare della gentilezza di.
impossibility [ɪmpɒsə'bɪlɪtɪ] *n* impossibilità.
impossible [ɪm'pɒsɪbl] *a* impossibile.
impotent ['ɪmpətnt] *a* impotente.
impound [ɪm'paʊnd] *vt* confiscare.
impoverished [ɪm'pɒvərɪʃt] *a* impoverito(a).
impractical [ɪm'præktɪkl] *a* non pratico(a).
impregnable [ɪm'pregnəbl] *a* (*fortress*) inespugnabile; (*fig*) inoppugnabile; irrefutabile.
impress [ɪm'pres] *vt* impressionare; (*mark*) imprimere, stampare; to ~ sth on sb far capire qc a qn.
impression [ɪm'preʃən] *n* impressione *f*; to be under the ~ that avere l'impressione che.
impressive [ɪm'presɪv] *a* impressionante.
imprint ['ɪmprɪnt] *n* (*PUBLISHING*) sigla editoriale.
imprison [ɪm'prɪzn] *vt* imprigionare; ~ment *n* imprigionamento.
improbable [ɪm'prɒbəbl] *a* improbabile; (*excuse*) inverosimile.
impromptu [ɪm'prɒmptjuː] *a* improvviso(a).
improper [ɪm'prɒpə*] *a* scorretto(a); (*unsuitable*) inadatto(a), improprio(a); sconveniente, indecente.
improve [ɪm'pruːv] *vt* migliorare // *vi* migliorare; (*pupil etc*) fare progressi; ~ment *n* miglioramento; progresso.
improvise ['ɪmprəvaɪz] *vt, vi* improvvisare.
impudent ['ɪmpjudnt] *a* impudente, sfacciato(a).
impulse ['ɪmpʌls] *n* impulso; on ~ d'impulso, impulsivamente.
impulsive [ɪm'pʌlsɪv] *a* impulsivo(a).
in [ɪn] ◆ *prep* 1 (*indicating place, position*) in; ~ **the house/garden** in casa/ giardino; ~ **the box** nella scatola; ~ **the fridge** nel frigorifero; **I have it** ~ **my hand** ce l'ho in mano; ~ **town/the country** in città/campagna; ~ **school** a scuola; ~ **here/there** qui/lì dentro
2 (*with place names: of town, region, country*): ~ **London** a Londra; ~ **England** in Inghilterra; ~ **the United States** negli Stati Uniti; ~ **Yorkshire** nello Yorkshire
3 (*indicating time: during, in the space of*) in; ~ **spring/summer** in primavera/ estate; ~ **1988** nel 1988; ~ **May** in *or* a maggio; **I'll see you** ~ **July** ci vediamo a luglio; ~ **the afternoon** nel pomeriggio; **at 4 o'clock** ~ **the afternoon** alle 4 del pomeriggio; **I did it** ~ **3 hours/days** l'ho fatto in 3 ore/giorni; **I'll see you** ~ **2 weeks** *or* ~ **2 weeks' time** ci vediamo tra 2 settimane

4 (*indicating manner etc*) a; ~ a loud/soft voice a voce alta/bassa; ~ pencil a matita; ~ English/French in inglese/francese; the boy ~ the blue shirt il ragazzo con la camicia blu
5 (*indicating circumstances*): ~ the sun al sole; ~ the shade all'ombra; ~ the rain sotto la pioggia; a rise ~ prices un aumento dei prezzi
6 (*indicating mood, state*): ~ tears in lacrime; ~ anger per la rabbia; ~ despair disperato(a); ~ good condition in buono stato, in buone condizioni; to live ~ luxury vivere nel lusso
7 (*with ratios, numbers*): 1 ~ 10 1 su 10; 20 pence ~ the pound 20 pence per sterlina; they lined up ~ twos si misero in fila a due a due
8 (*referring to people, works*) in; the disease is common ~ children la malattia è comune nei bambini; ~ (the works of) Dickens in Dickens
9 (*indicating profession etc*) in; to be ~ teaching fare l'insegnante, insegnare; to be ~ publishing essere nell'editoria
10 (*after superlative*) di; the best ~ the class il migliore della classe
11 (*with present participle*): ~ saying this dicendo questo, nel dire questo
♦ *ad*: to be ~ (*person: at home, work*) esserci; (*train, ship, plane*) essere arrivato(a); (*in fashion*) essere di moda; to ask sb ~ invitare qn ad entrare; to run/limp *etc* ~ entrare di corsa/zoppicando *etc*
♦ *n*: the ~s and outs of the problem tutti i particolari del problema.

in., ins *abbr* = **inch(es).**

inability [ɪnə'bɪlɪtɪ] *n* inabilità, incapacità.

inaccurate [ɪn'ækjurət] *a* inesatto(a), impreciso(a).

inadequate [ɪn'ædɪkwət] *a* insufficiente.

inadvertently [ɪnəd'və:tntlɪ] *ad* senza volerlo.

inane [ɪ'neɪn] *a* vacuo(a), stupido(a).

inanimate [ɪn'ænɪmət] *a* inanimato(a).

inappropriate [ɪnə'prəuprɪət] *a* disadatto(a); (*word, expression*) improprio(a).

inarticulate [ɪnɑ:'tɪkjulət] *a* (*person*) che si esprime male; (*speech*) inarticolato(a).

inasmuch as [ɪnəz'mʌtʃæz] *ad* in quanto che; (*seeing that*) poiché.

inaudible [ɪn'ɔ:dɪbl] *a* che non si riesce a sentire.

inauguration [ɪnɔ:gju'reɪʃən] *n* inaugurazione *f*; insediamento in carica.

in-between [ɪnbɪ'twi:n] *a* fra i (*or* le) due.

inborn [ɪn'bɔ:n] *a* (*feeling*) innato(a); (*defect*) congenito(a).

inbred [ɪn'brɛd] *a* innato(a); (*family*) connaturato(a).

Inc. *abbr* = **incorporated.**

incapable [ɪn'keɪpəbl] *a* incapace.

incapacitate [ɪnkə'pæsɪteɪt] *vt*: to ~ sb from doing rendere qn incapace di fare.

incense *n* ['ɪnsɛns] incenso // *vt* [ɪn'sɛns] (*anger*) infuriare.

incentive [ɪn'sɛntɪv] *n* incentivo.

incessant [ɪn'sɛsnt] *a* incessante; ~ly *ad* di continuo, senza sosta.

inch [ɪntʃ] *n* pollice *m* (= 25 mm; 12 in a foot); within an ~ of a un pelo da; he didn't give an ~ non ha ceduto di un millimetro; to ~ forward *vi* avanzare pian piano.

incidence ['ɪnsɪdns] *n* (*of crime, disease*) incidenza.

incident ['ɪnsɪdnt] *n* incidente *m*; (*in book*) episodio.

incidental [ɪnsɪ'dɛntl] *a* accessorio(a), d'accompagnamento; (*unplanned*) incidentale; ~ to marginale a; ~ly [-'dɛntəlɪ] *ad* (*by the way*) a proposito.

inclination [ɪnklɪ'neɪʃən] *n* inclinazione *f*.

incline *n* ['ɪnklaɪn] pendenza, pendio // *vb* [ɪn'klaɪn] *vt* inclinare // *vi*: to ~ to tendere a; to be ~d to do tendere a fare; essere propenso(a) a fare.

include [ɪn'klu:d] *vt* includere, comprendere; **including** *prep* compreso(a), incluso(a).

inclusive [ɪn'klu:sɪv] *a* incluso(a), compreso(a) // *ad*: ~ of tax *etc* tasse *etc* comprese.

incoherent [ɪnkəu'hɪərənt] *a* incoerente.

income ['ɪnkʌm] *n* reddito; ~ tax *n* imposta sul reddito.

incompetent [ɪn'kɔmpɪtnt] *a* incompetente, incapace.

incomplete [ɪnkəm'pli:t] *a* incompleto(a).

incongruous [ɪn'kɔŋgruəs] *a* poco appropriato(a); (*remark, act*) incongruo(a).

inconsiderate [ɪnkən'sɪdərət] *a* sconsiderato(a).

inconsistency [ɪnkən'sɪstənsɪ] *n* (*of actions, statement*) incoerenza; (*of work*) irregolarità.

inconspicuous [ɪnkən'spɪkjuəs] *a* incospicuo(a); (*colour*) poco appariscente; (*dress*) dimesso(a).

inconvenience [ɪnkən'vi:njəns] *n* inconveniente *m*; (*trouble*) disturbo // *vt* disturbare.

inconvenient [ɪnkən'vi:njənt] *a* scomodo(a).

incorporate [ɪn'kɔ:pəreɪt] *vt* incorporare; (*contain*) contenere; ~d *a*: ~d company (*US*: *abbr* **Inc.**) società *f inv* anonima (S.A.).

incorrect [ɪnkə'rɛkt] *a* scorretto(a); (*statement*) impreciso(a).

increase *n* ['ɪnkri:s] aumento // *vi, vt* [ɪn'kri:s] aumentare.

increasing [ɪn'kri:sɪŋ] *a* (*number*) crescente; ~ly *ad* sempre più.

incredible [ɪn'krɛdɪbl] *a* incredibile.

incredulous [ɪn'krɛdjuləs] *a* incredulo(a).

increment ['ɪnkrɪmənt] *n* aumento, incremento.

incriminate [ɪn'krɪmɪneɪt] *vt* compromettere.

incubator ['ɪnkjubeɪtə*] *n* incubatrice *f*.

incumbent [ɪn'kʌmbənt] *n* titolare *m/f* // *a*: to be ~ on sb spettare a qn.

incur [ɪn'kə:*] *vt* (*expenses*) incorrere; (*anger, risk*) esporsi a; (*debt*) contrarre; (*loss*) subire.

indebted [ɪn'dɛtɪd] *a*: to be ~ to sb (for) essere obbligato(a) verso qn (per).

indecent [ɪn'di:snt] *a* indecente; ~ **assault** *n* (*Brit*) aggressione *f* a scopo di violenza sessuale; ~ **exposure** *n* atti *mpl* osceni in luogo pubblico.

indecisive [ɪndɪ'saɪsɪv] *a* indeciso(a); (*discussion*) non decisivo(a).

indeed [ɪn'di:d] *ad* infatti; veramente; yes ~! certamente!

indefinite [ɪn'dɛfɪnɪt] *a* indefinito(a); (*answer*) vago(a); (*period, number*) indeterminato(a); ~**ly** *ad* (*wait*) indefinitamente.

indemnity [ɪn'dɛmnɪtɪ] *n* (*insurance*) assicurazione *f*; (*compensation*) indennità, indennizzo.

independence [ɪndɪ'pɛndns] *n* indipendenza.

independent [ɪndɪ'pɛndnt] *a* indipendente.

index ['ɪndɛks] *n* (*pl* ~**es**: *in book*) indice *m*; (: *in library etc*) catalogo; (*pl* **indices**: *ratio, sign*) indice *m*; ~ **card** *n* scheda; ~ **finger** *n* (dito) indice *m*; ~**-linked**, (*US*) ~**ed** *a* legato(a) al costo della vita.

India ['ɪndɪə] *n* India; ~**n** *a*, *n* indiano(a); Red ~n pellerossa *m/f*.

indicate ['ɪndɪkeɪt] *vt* indicare; **indication** [-'keɪʃən] *n* indicazione *f*, segno.

indicative [ɪn'dɪkətɪv] *a*: ~ of indicativo(a) di // *n* (*LING*) indicativo.

indicator ['ɪndɪkeɪtə*] *n* indicatore *m*.

indices ['ɪndɪsi:z] *npl of* **index**.

indictment [ɪn'daɪtmənt] *n* accusa.

indifference [ɪn'dɪfrəns] *n* indifferenza.

indifferent [ɪn'dɪfrənt] *a* indifferente; (*poor*) mediocre.

indigenous [ɪn'dɪdʒɪnəs] *a* indigeno(a).

indigestible [ɪndɪ'dʒɛstɪbl] *a* indigeribile.

indigestion [ɪndɪ'dʒɛstʃən] *n* indigestione *f*.

indignant [ɪn'dɪgnənt] *a*: ~ (at sth/with sb) indignato(a) (per qc/contro qn).

indignity [ɪn'dɪgnɪtɪ] *n* umiliazione *f*.

indirect [ɪndɪ'rɛkt] *a* indiretto(a).

indiscreet [ɪndɪ'skri:t] *a* indiscreto(a); (*rash*) imprudente.

indiscriminate [ɪndɪ'skrɪmɪnət] *a* (*person*) che non sa discernere; (*admiration*) cieco(a); (*killings*) indiscriminato(a).

indisputable [ɪndɪ'spju:təbl] *a* incontestabile, indiscutibile.

individual [ɪndɪ'vɪdjuəl] *n* individuo // *a* individuale; (*characteristic*) particolare, originale; ~**ist** *n* individualista *m/f*; ~**ity** [-'ælɪtɪ] *n* individualità.

indoctrination [ɪndɒktrɪ'neɪʃən] *n* indottrinamento.

Indonesia [ɪndə'ni:zɪə] *n* Indonesia.

indoor ['ɪndɔ:*] *a* da interno; (*plant*) d'appartamento; (*swimming pool*) coperto(a); (*sport, games*) fatto(a) al coperto; ~**s** [ɪn'dɔ:z] *ad* all'interno; (*at home*) in casa.

induce [ɪn'dju:s] *vt* persuadere; (*bring about*) provocare; ~**ment** *n* incitamento; (*incentive*) stimolo, incentivo.

induction [ɪn'dʌkʃən] *n* (*MED*: *of birth*) parto indotto; ~ **course** *n* (*Brit*) corso di avviamento.

indulge [ɪn'dʌldʒ] *vt* (*whim*) compiacere, soddisfare; (*child*) viziare // *vi*: to ~ in sth concedersi qc; abbandonarsi a qc; ~**nce** *n* lusso (che uno si permette); (*leniency*) indulgenza; ~**nt** *a* indulgente.

industrial [ɪn'dʌstrɪəl] *a* industriale; (*injury*) sul lavoro; (*dispute*) di lavoro; ~ **action** *n* azione *f* rivendicativa; ~ **estate** *n* (*Brit*) zona industriale; ~**ist** *n* industriale *m*; ~ **park** *n* (*US*) = ~ **estate**.

industrious [ɪn'dʌstrɪəs] *a* industrioso(a), assiduo(a).

industry ['ɪndəstrɪ] *n* industria; (*diligence*) operosità.

inebriated [ɪ'ni:brɪeɪtɪd] *a* ubriaco(a).

inedible [ɪn'ɛdɪbl] *a* immangiabile.

ineffective [ɪnɪ'fɛktɪv], **ineffectual** [ɪnɪ'fɛktʃuəl] *a* inefficace; incompetente.

inefficiency [ɪnɪ'fɪʃənsɪ] *n* inefficienza.

inefficient [ɪnɪ'fɪʃənt] *a* inefficiente.

inept [ɪ'nɛpt] *a* inetto(a).

inequality [ɪnɪ'kwɒlɪtɪ] *n* ineguaglianza.

inescapable [ɪnɪ'skeɪpəbl] *a* inevitabile.

inevitable [ɪn'ɛvɪtəbl] *a* inevitabile; **inevitably** *ad* inevitabilmente.

inexact [ɪnɪg'zækt] *a* inesatto(a).

inexpensive [ɪnɪk'spɛnsɪv] *a* poco costoso(a).

inexperienced [ɪnɪks'pɪərɪənst] *a* inesperto(a), senza esperienza.

infallible [ɪn'fælɪbl] *a* infallibile.

infamous ['ɪnfəməs] *a* infame.

infancy ['ɪnfənsɪ] *n* infanzia.

infant ['ɪnfənt] *n* bambino/a; ~ **school** *n* (*Brit*) scuola elementare (*per bambini dall'età di 5 a 7 anni*).

infantry ['ɪnfəntrɪ] *n* fanteria.

infatuated [ɪn'fætjueɪtɪd] *a*: ~ with infatuato(a) di.

infatuation [ɪnfætju'eɪʃən] *n* infatuazione *f*.

infect [ɪn'fɛkt] *vt* infettare; ~**ion**

[ɪn'fɛkʃən] **[ɪn'fɛkʃəs]** *n* infezione *f*; **~ious** *a* (*disease*) infettivo(a), contagioso(a); (*person, laughter*) contagioso(a).

infer [ɪn'fə:*] *vt* inferire, dedurre.

inferior [ɪn'fɪərɪə*] *a* inferiore; (*goods*) di qualità scadente // in inferiore *m/f*; (*in rank*) subalterno/a; **~ity** [ɪnfɪərɪ'orətɪ] *n* inferiorità; **~ity complex** *n* complesso di inferiorità.

infertile [ɪn'fə:taɪl] *a* sterile.

in-fighting ['ɪnfaɪtɪŋ] *n* lotte *fpl* intestine.

infinite ['ɪnfɪnɪt] *a* infinito(a).

infinitive [ɪn'fɪnɪtɪv] *n* infinito.

infinity [ɪn'fɪnɪtɪ] *n* infinità; (*also MATH*) infinito.

infirmary [ɪn'fə:mərɪ] *n* ospedale *m*; (*in school, factory*) infermeria *f*.

infirmity [ɪn'fə:mɪtɪ] *n* infermità *f inv*.

inflamed [ɪn'fleɪmd] *a* infiammato(a).

inflammable [ɪn'flæməbl] *a* (*Brit*) infiammabile.

inflammation [ɪnflə'meɪʃən] *n* infiammazione *f*.

inflatable [ɪn'fleɪtəbl] *a* gonfiabile.

inflate [ɪn'fleɪt] *vt* (*tyre, balloon*) gonfiare; (*fig*) esagerare; gonfiare; **~flation** [ɪn'fleɪʃən] *n* (*ECON*) inflazione *f*; **~flationary** [ɪn'fleɪʃnərɪ] *a* inflazionistico(a).

inflict [ɪn'flɪkt] *vt*: **to ~ on** infliggere a.

influence ['ɪnfluəns] *n* influenza // *vt* influenzare; **under the ~ of** sotto l'influenza di.

influential [ɪnflu'ɛnʃl] *a* influente.

influenza [ɪnflu'ɛnzə] *n* (*MED*) influenza.

influx ['ɪnflʌks] *n* afflusso.

inform [ɪn'fɔ:m] *vt*: **to ~ sb (of)** informare qn (di) // *vi*: **to ~ on sb** denunciare qn; **to ~ sb about** mettere qn al corrente di.

informal [ɪn'fɔ:ml] *a* (*person, manner*) alla buona, semplice; (*visit, discussion*) informale; (*announcement, invitation*) non ufficiale; **~ity** [-'mælɪtɪ] *n* semplicità, informalità; carattere *m* non ufficiale.

informant [ɪn'fɔ:mənt] *n* informatore/trice.

information [ɪnfə'meɪʃən] *n* informazioni *fpl*; particolari *mpl*; **a piece of ~** un'informazione; **~ office** *n* ufficio *m* informazioni *inv*.

informative [ɪn'fɔ:mətɪv] *a* istruttivo(a).

informer [ɪn'fɔ:mə*] *n* informatore/trice; **to turn ~** (*POLICE*) denunciare i complici.

infringe [ɪn'frɪndʒ] *vt* infrangere // *vi*: **to ~ on** calpestare; **~ment** *n*: **~ment (of)** infrazione *f* (di).

infuriating [ɪn'fjuərɪeɪtɪŋ] *a* molto irritante.

ingenious [ɪn'dʒi:njəs] *a* ingegnoso(a).

ingenuity [ɪndʒɪ'nju:ɪtɪ] *n* ingegnosità.

ingenuous [ɪn'dʒɛnjuəs] *a* ingenuo(a).

ingot ['ɪŋgət] *n* lingotto.

ingrained [ɪn'greɪnd] *a* radicato(a).

ingratiate [ɪn'greɪʃɪeɪt] *vt*: **to ~ o.s. with sb** ingraziarsi qn.

ingredient [ɪn'gri:dɪənt] *n* ingrediente *m*; elemento.

inhabit [ɪn'hæbɪt] *vt* abitare.

inhabitant [ɪn'hæbɪtnt] *n* abitante *m/f*.

inhale [ɪn'heɪl] *vt* inalare // *vi* (*in smoking*) aspirare.

inherent [ɪn'hɪərənt] *a*: **~ (in or to)** inerente (a).

inherit [ɪn'hɛrɪt] *vt* ereditare; **~ance** *n* eredità.

inhibit [ɪn'hɪbɪt] *vt* (*PSYCH*) inibire; **to ~ sb from doing** impedire a qn di fare; **~ion** [-'bɪʃən] *n* inibizione *f*.

inhospitable [ɪnhɔs'pɪtəbl] *a* inospitale.

inhuman [ɪn'hju:mən] *a* inumano(a).

initial [ɪ'nɪʃl] *a* iniziale // *n* iniziale *f* // *vt* siglare; **~s** *npl* iniziali *fpl*; (*as signature*) sigla; **~ly** *ad* inizialmente, all'inizio.

initiate [ɪ'nɪʃɪeɪt] *vt* (*start*) avviare; intraprendere; iniziare; (*person*) iniziare.

initiative [ɪ'nɪʃɪətɪv] *n* iniziativa.

inject [ɪn'dʒɛkt] *vt* (*liquid*) iniettare; (*person*) fare una puntura a; **~ion** [ɪn'dʒɛkʃən] *n* iniezione *f*, puntura.

injure ['ɪndʒə*] *vt* ferire; (*wrong*) fare male *or* torto a; (*damage: reputation etc*) nuocere a; **~d** *a* (*person, arm*) ferito(a).

injury ['ɪndʒərɪ] *n* ferita; (*wrong*) torto; **~ time** *n* (*SPORT*) tempo di ricupero.

injustice [ɪn'dʒʌstɪs] *n* ingiustizia.

ink [ɪŋk] *n* inchiostro.

inkling ['ɪŋklɪŋ] *n* sentore *m*, vaga idea.

inlaid ['ɪnleɪd] *a* incrostato(a); (*table etc*) intarsiato(a).

inland *a* ['ɪnlənd] interno(a) // *ad* [ɪn'lænd] all'interno; **I~ Revenue** *n* (*Brit*) Fisco.

in-laws ['ɪnlɔ:z] *npl* suoceri *mpl*; famiglia del marito (*or* della moglie).

inlet ['ɪnlet] *n* (*GEO*) insenatura, baia.

inmate ['ɪnmeɪt] *n* (*in prison*) carcerato/a; (*in asylum*) ricoverato/a.

inn [ɪn] *n* locanda.

innate [ɪ'neɪt] *a* innato(a).

inner ['ɪnə*] *a* interno(a), interiore; **~ city** *n* centro di una zona urbana; **~ tube** *n* camera d'aria.

innings ['ɪnɪŋz] *n* (*CRICKET*) turno di battuta.

innocence ['ɪnəsns] *n* innocenza.

innocent ['ɪnəsnt] *a* innocente.

innocuous [ɪ'nɔkjuəs] *a* innocuo(a).

innuendo, **~es** [ɪnju'ɛndəu] *n* insinuazione *f*.

innumerable [ɪ'nju:mrəbl] *a* innumerevole.

inordinately [ɪ'nɔ:dɪnətlɪ] *ad* smoderatamente.

in-patient ['ɪnpeɪʃənt] *n* ricoverato/a.

input ['ɪnput] n (ELEC) energia, potenza; (of machine) alimentazione f; (of computer) input m.

inquest ['ɪnkwest] n inchiesta.

inquire [ɪn'kwaɪə*] vi informarsi // vt domandare, informarsi su; **to ~ about** vt fus informarsi di or su; **to ~ into** vt fus fare indagini su; **inquiry** n domanda; (LAW) indagine f, investigazione f; **inquiry office** n (Brit) ufficio m informazioni inv.

inquisitive [ɪn'kwɪzɪtɪv] a curioso(a).

inroad ['ɪnrəud] n incursione f.

insane [ɪn'seɪn] a matto(a), pazzo(a); (MED) alienato(a).

insanity [ɪn'sænɪtɪ] n follia; (MED) alienazione f mentale.

inscription [ɪn'skrɪpʃən] n iscrizione f; dedica.

inscrutable [ɪn'skru:təbl] a imperscrutabile.

insect ['ɪnsɛkt] n insetto; **~icide** [ɪn'sɛktɪsaɪd] n insetticida m.

insecure [ɪnsɪ'kjuə*] a malsicuro(a); (person) insicuro(a).

insemination [ɪnsɛmɪ'neɪʃən] n: artificial ~ fecondazione f artificiale.

insensible [ɪn'sensɪbl] a insensibile; (unconscious) privo(a) di sensi.

insensitive [ɪn'sensɪtɪv] a insensibile.

insert vt [ɪn'sə:t] inserire, introdurre // n ['ɪnsə:t] inserto; **~ion** [ɪn'sə:ʃən] n inserzione f.

in-service [ɪn'sə:vɪs] a (training, course) durante l'orario di lavoro.

inshore [ɪn'ʃɔ:*] a costiero(a) // ad presso la riva; verso la riva.

inside ['ɪnsaɪd] n interno, parte f interiore // a interno(a), interiore // ad dentro, all'interno // prep dentro, all'interno di; (of time): ~ **10 minutes** entro 10 minuti; **~s** npl (col) ventre m; ~ **forward** n (SPORT) mezzala, interno; ~ **lane** n (AUT) corsia di marcia; ~ **out** ad (turn) a rovescio; (know) a fondo; **to turn sth ~ out** rivoltare qc.

insight ['ɪnsaɪt] n acume m, perspicacia; (glimpse, idea) percezione f.

insignia [ɪn'sɪgnɪə] npl insegne fpl.

insignificant [ɪnsɪg'nɪfɪkənt] a insignificante.

insincere [ɪnsɪn'sɪə*] a insincero(a).

insinuate [ɪn'sɪnjueɪt] vt insinuare.

insist [ɪn'sɪst] vi insistere; **to ~ on doing** insistere per fare; **to ~ that** insistere perché + sub; (claim) sostenere che; **~ent** a insistente.

insole ['ɪnsəul] n soletta.

insolent ['ɪnsələnt] a insolente.

insomnia [ɪn'sɒmnɪə] n insonnia.

inspect [ɪn'spɛkt] vt ispezionare; (ticket) controllare; **~ion** [ɪn'spɛkʃən] n ispezione f; controllo; **~or** n ispettore/trice; (Brit: on buses, trains) controllore m.

inspire [ɪn'spaɪə*] vt ispirare.

install [ɪn'stɔ:l] vt installare; **~ation** [ɪnstə'leɪʃən] n installazione f.

instalment, (US) **installment** [ɪn'stɔ:lmənt] n rata; (of TV serial etc) puntata; in **~s** (pay) a rate; (receive) una parte per volta; (: publication) a fascicoli.

instance ['ɪnstəns] n esempio, caso; **for** ~ per or ad esempio; in many **~s** in molti casi; in the first ~ in primo luogo.

instant ['ɪnstənt] n istante m, attimo // a immediato(a); urgente; (coffee, food) in polvere; **~ly** ad immediatamente, subito.

instead [ɪn'stɛd] ad invece; ~ **of** invece di; ~ **of sb** al posto di qn.

instep ['ɪnstɛp] n collo del piede; (of shoe) collo della scarpa.

instil [ɪn'stɪl] vt: **to ~ (into)** inculcare (in).

instinct ['ɪnstɪŋkt] n istinto.

institute ['ɪnstɪtju:t] n istituto // vt istituire, stabilire; (inquiry) avviare; (proceedings) iniziare.

institution [ɪnstɪ'tju:ʃən] n istituzione f; istituto (d'istruzione); istituto (psichiatrico).

instruct [ɪn'strʌkt] vt istruire; **to ~ sb in sth** insegnare qc a qn; **to ~ sb to do** dare ordini a qn di fare; **~ion** [ɪn'strʌkʃən] n istruzione f; **~ions (for use)** istruzioni per l'uso; **~or** n istruttore/trice; (for skiing) maestro/a.

instrument ['ɪnstrəmənt] n strumento; **~al** [-'mɛntl] a (MUS) strumentale; **to be ~al in** essere d'aiuto in; ~ **panel** n quadro m portastrumenti inv.

insufficient [ɪnsə'fɪʃənt] a insufficiente.

insular ['ɪnsjulə*] a insulare; (person) di mente ristretta.

insulate ['ɪnsjuleɪt] vt isolare; **insulating tape** n nastro isolante; **insulation** [-'leɪʃən] n isolamento.

insulin ['ɪnsjulɪn] n insulina.

insult n ['ɪnsʌlt] insulto, affronto // vt [ɪn'sʌlt] insultare; **~ing** a offensivo(a), ingiurioso(a).

insuperable [ɪn'sju:prəbl] a insormontabile, insuperabile.

insurance [ɪn'ʃuərəns] n assicurazione f; **fire/life** ~ assicurazione contro gli incendi/sulla vita; ~ **policy** n polizza d'assicurazione.

insure [ɪn'ʃuə*] vt assicurare.

intact [ɪn'tækt] a intatto(a).

intake ['ɪnteɪk] n (TECH) immissione f; (of food) consumo; (Brit: of pupils etc) afflusso.

integral ['ɪntɪgrəl] a integrale; (part) integrante.

integrate ['ɪntɪgreɪt] vt integrare.

integrity [ɪn'tegrɪtɪ] n integrità.

intellect ['ɪntəlɛkt] n intelletto; **~ual** [-'lɛktjuəl] a, n intellettuale (m/f).

intelligence [ɪn'tɛlɪdʒəns] n intelligenza; (MIL etc) informazioni fpl.

intelligent [ɪn'tɛlɪdʒənt] a intelligente.

intend [ɪn'tɛnd] vt (gift etc): to ~ sth for destinare qc a; to ~ to do aver l'intenzione di fare; **~ed** a (effect) voluto(a).

intense [ɪn'tɛns] a intenso(a); (person) di forti sentimenti; **~ly** ad intensamente; profondamente.

intensive [ɪn'tɛnsɪv] a intensivo(a); ~ **care unit** n reparto terapia intensiva.

intent [ɪn'tɛnt] n intenzione f // a: ~ (on) intento(a) (a), immerso(a) (in); to all ~s and purposes a tutti gli effetti; to be ~ on doing sth essere deciso a fare qc.

intention [ɪn'tɛnʃən] n intenzione f; **~al** a intenzionale, deliberato(a); **~ally** ad apposta.

intently [ɪn'tɛntlɪ] ad attentamente.

inter [ɪn'tə:*] vt sotterrare.

interact [ɪntər'ækt] vi agire reciprocamente, interagire.

interchange n ['ɪntətʃeɪndʒ] (exchange) scambio; (on motorway) incrocio pluridirezionale // vt [ɪntə'tʃeɪndʒ] scambiare; sostituire l'uno(a) per l'altro(a); **~able** a intercambiabile.

intercom ['ɪntəkəm] n interfono.

intercourse ['ɪntəkɔ:s] n rapporti mpl.

interest ['ɪntrɪst] n interesse m; (COMM: stake, share) interessi mpl // vt interessare; **~ed** a interessato(a); to be ~ed in interessarsi di; **~ing** a interessante; ~ **rate** n tasso di interesse.

interface ['ɪntəfeɪs] n (COMPUT) interfaccia.

interfere [ɪntə'fɪə*] vi: to ~ in (quarrel, other people's business) immischiarsi in; to ~ with (object) toccare; (plans) ostacolare; (duty) interferire con.

interference [ɪntə'fɪərəns] n interferenza.

interim ['ɪntərɪm] a provvisorio(a) // n: in the ~ nel frattempo.

interior [ɪn'tɪərɪə*] n interno; (of country) entroterra // a interiore, interno(a); ~ **designer** n arredatore/trice.

interlock [ɪntə'lɔk] vi ingranarsi // vt ingranare.

interloper ['ɪntələupə*] n intruso/a.

interlude ['ɪntəlu:d] n intervallo; (THEATRE) intermezzo.

intermediate [ɪntə'mi:dɪət] a intermedio(a); (SCOL: course, level) medio(a).

intermission [ɪntə'mɪʃən] n pausa; (THEATRE, CINEMA) intermissione f, intervallo.

intern vt [ɪn'tə:n] internare // n ['ɪntə:n] (US) medico interno.

internal [ɪn'tə:nl] a interno(a); **~ly** ad all'interno; "not to be taken ~ly" "per uso esterno"; **I~ Revenue Service (IRS)** n (US) Fisco.

international [ɪntə'næʃnl] a internazionale.

interplay ['ɪntəpleɪ] n azione e reazione f.

interpret [ɪn'tə:prɪt] vt interpretare // vi fare da interprete; **~er** n interprete m/f.

interrelated [ɪntərɪ'leɪtɪd] a correlato(a).

interrogate [ɪn'tɛrəugeɪt] vt interrogare; **interrogation** [-'geɪʃən] n interrogazione f; (of suspect etc) interrogatorio; **interrogative** [ɪntə'rɔgətɪv] a interrogativo(a).

interrupt [ɪntə'rʌpt] vt interrompere; **~ion** [-'rʌpʃən] n interruzione f.

intersect [ɪntə'sɛkt] vt intersecare // vi (roads) intersecarsi; **~ion** [-'sɛkʃən] n intersezione f; (of roads) incrocio.

intersperse [ɪntə'spə:s] vt: to ~ with costellare di.

intertwine [ɪntə'twaɪn] vt intrecciare // vi intrecciarsi.

interval ['ɪntəvl] n intervallo; at ~s a intervalli.

intervene [ɪntə'vi:n] vi (time) intercorrere; (event, person) intervenire; **intervention** [-'vɛnʃən] n intervento.

interview ['ɪntəvju:] n (RADIO, TV etc) intervista; (for job) colloquio // vt intervistare; avere un colloquio con; **~er** n intervistatore/trice.

intestine [ɪn'tɛstɪn] n intestino.

intimacy ['ɪntɪməsɪ] n intimità.

intimate a ['ɪntɪmət] intimo(a); (knowledge) profondo(a) // vt ['ɪntɪmeɪt] lasciar capire.

into ['ɪntu:] prep dentro, in; come ~ the house vieni dentro la casa; ~ Italian in italiano.

intolerable [ɪn'tɔlərəbl] a intollerabile.

intolerance [ɪn'tɔlərns] n intolleranza.

intolerant [ɪn'tɔlərnt] a: ~ of intollerante di.

intoxicate [ɪn'tɔksɪkeɪt] vt inebriare; **~d** a inebriato(a); **intoxication** [-'keɪʃən] n ebbrezza.

intractable [ɪn'træktəbl] a intrattabile.

intransitive [ɪn'trænsɪtɪv] a intransitivo(a).

intravenous [ɪntrə'vi:nəs] a endovenoso(a).

in-tray ['ɪntreɪ] n contenitore m per la corrispondenza in arrivo.

intricate ['ɪntrɪkət] a intricato(a), complicato(a).

intrigue [ɪn'tri:g] n intrigo // vt affascinare // vi complottare, tramare; **intriguing** a affascinante.

intrinsic [ɪn'trɪnsɪk] a intrinseco(a).

introduce [ɪntrə'dju:s] vt introdurre; to ~ sb (to sb) presentare qn (a qn); to ~ sb to (pastime, technique) iniziare qn a; **introduction** [-'dʌkʃən] n introduzione f; (of person) presentazione f; **introductory** a introduttivo(a).

intrude [ɪn'tru:d] vi (person): to ~ (on)

intromettersi (in); **am I intruding?** disturbo?; **~r** n intruso/a.

intuition [ɪntjuːˈɪʃən] n intuizione f.

inundate [ˈɪnʌndeɪt] vt: **to ~ with** inondare di.

invade [ɪnˈveɪd] vt invadere.

invalid n [ˈɪnvəlɪd] malato/a; (with disability) invalido/a // a [ɪnˈvælɪd] (not valid) invalido(a), non valido(a).

invaluable [ɪnˈvæljuəbl] a prezioso(a); inestimabile.

invariably [ɪnˈvɛərɪəblɪ] ad invariabilmente; sempre.

invasion [ɪnˈveɪʒən] n invasione f.

invent [ɪnˈvɛnt] vt inventare; **~ion** [ɪnˈvɛnʃən] n invenzione f; **~ive** a inventivo(a); **~or** n inventore m.

inventory [ˈɪnvəntrɪ] n inventario.

invert [ɪnˈvəːt] vt invertire; (cup, object) rovesciare; **~ed commas** npl (Brit) virgolette fpl.

invest [ɪnˈvɛst] vt investire // vi fare investimenti.

investigate [ɪnˈvɛstɪgeɪt] vt investigare, indagare; (crime) fare indagini su; **investigation** [-ˈgeɪʃən] n investigazione f; (of crime) indagine f.

investment [ɪnˈvɛstmənt] n investimento.

investor [ɪnˈvɛstə*] n investitore/trice; azionista m/f.

invidious [ɪnˈvɪdɪəs] a odioso(a); (task) spiacevole.

invigilate [ɪnˈvɪdʒɪleɪt] vt, vi (in exam) sorvegliare.

invigorating [ɪnˈvɪgəreɪtɪŋ] a stimolante; vivificante.

invisible [ɪnˈvɪzɪbl] a invisibile; **~ ink** n inchiostro simpatico.

invitation [ɪnvɪˈteɪʃən] n invito.

invite [ɪnˈvaɪt] vt invitare; (opinions etc) sollecitare; (trouble) provocare; **inviting** a invitante, attraente.

invoice [ˈɪnvɔɪs] n fattura.

involuntary [ɪnˈvɔləntrɪ] a involontario(a).

involve [ɪnˈvɔlv] vt (entail) richiedere, comportare; (associate): **to ~ sb (in)** implicare qn (in); coinvolgere qn (in); **~d** a involuto(a), complesso(a); **to feel ~d** sentirsi coinvolto(a); **~ment (in)** implicazione f; coinvolgimento; **~ment (in)** impegno (in); partecipazione f (in).

inward [ˈɪnwəd] a (movement) verso l'interno; (thought, feeling) interiore, intimo(a); **~(s)** ad verso l'interno.

I/O abbr (COMPUT: = input/output) I/O.

iodine [ˈaɪədiːn] n iodio.

iota [aɪˈəʊtə] n (fig) briciolo.

IOU n abbr (= I owe you) pagherò m inv.

IQ n abbr (= intelligence quotient) quoziente m d'intelligenza.

IRA n abbr (= Irish Republican Army) IRA f.

Iran [ɪˈrɑːn] n Iran m.

Iraq [ɪˈrɑːk] n Iraq m.

Ireland [ˈaɪələnd] n Irlanda.

iris, **~es** [ˈaɪrɪs, -ɪz] n iride f; (BOT) giaggiolo, iride.

Irish [ˈaɪrɪʃ] a irlandese // npl: **the ~** gli Irlandesi; **~man** n irlandese m; **~ Sea** n Mar m d'Irlanda; **~woman** n irlandese f.

irksome [ˈəːksəm] a seccante.

iron [ˈaɪən] n ferro; (for clothes) ferro da stiro // a di or in ferro // vt (clothes) stirare; **to ~ out** vt (crease) appianare; (fig) spianare; far sparire; **the I~ Curtain** n la cortina di ferro.

ironic(al) [aɪˈrɔnɪk(l)] a ironico(a).

ironing [ˈaɪənɪŋ] n (act) stirare m; (clothes) roba da stirare; **~ board** n asse f da stiro.

ironmonger [ˈaɪənmʌŋgə*] n (Brit) negoziante m in ferramenta; **~'s (shop)** n negozio di ferramenta.

ironworks [ˈaɪənwəːks] n ferriera.

irony [ˈaɪrənɪ] n ironia.

irrational [ɪˈræʃənl] a irrazionale; irragionevole; illogico(a).

irregular [ɪˈrɛgjulə*] a irregolare.

irrelevant [ɪˈrɛləvənt] a non pertinente.

irreplaceable [ɪrɪˈpleɪsəbl] a insostituibile.

irrepressible [ɪrɪˈprɛsəbl] a irrefrenabile.

irresistible [ɪrɪˈzɪstɪbl] a irresistibile.

irrespective [ɪrɪˈspɛktɪv]: **~ of** prep senza riguardo a.

irresponsible [ɪrɪˈspɔnsɪbl] a irresponsabile.

irrigate [ˈɪrɪgeɪt] vt irrigare; **irrigation** [-ˈgeɪʃən] n irrigazione f.

irritable [ˈɪrɪtəbl] a irritabile.

irritate [ˈɪrɪteɪt] vt irritare; **irritating** a (person, sound etc) irritante; **irritation** [-ˈteɪʃən] n irritazione f.

IRS n abbr = **Internal Revenue Service**.

is [ɪz] vb see be.

Islam [ˈɪzlɑːm] n Islam m.

island [ˈaɪlənd] n isola; (also: traffic ~) salvagente m; **~er** n isolano/a.

isle [aɪl] n isola.

isn't [ˈɪznt] = is not.

isolate [ˈaɪsəleɪt] vt isolare; **~d** a isolato(a); **isolation** [-ˈleɪʃən] n isolamento.

Israel [ˈɪzreɪl] n Israele m; **~i** [ɪzˈreɪlɪ] a, n israeliano(a).

issue [ˈɪʃjuː] n questione f, problema m; (outcome) esito, risultato; (of banknotes etc) emissione f; (of newspaper etc) numero; (offspring) discendenza // vt (rations, equipment) distribuire; (orders) dare; (book) pubblicare; (banknotes, cheques, stamps) emettere; **at ~** in gioco, in discussione; **to take ~ with sb (over sth)** prendere posizione contro qn (riguardo a qc).

isthmus [ˈɪsməs] n istmo.

it [ɪt] *pronoun* **1** (*specific: subject*) esso(a); (: *direct object*) lo(la), l'; (: *indirect object*) gli(le); where's my book? — ~'s on the table dov'è il mio libro? — è sulla tavola; I can't find ~ non lo (*or* la) trovo; give ~ to me dammelo (*or* dammela); about/from/of ~ ne; I spoke to him about ~ gliene ho parlato; what did you learn from ~? quale insegnamento ne hai tratto?; I'm proud of ~ ne sono fiero; did you go to ~? ci sei andato?; put the book in ~ mettici il libro

2 (*impersonal*): ~'s raining piove; ~'s Friday tomorrow domani è venerdì; ~'s 6 o'clock sono le 6; who is ~? — ~'s me chi è? — sono io.

Italian [ɪ'tæljən] *a* italiano(a) // *n* italiano/a; (*LING*) italiano; the ~s gli Italiani.

italic [ɪ'tælɪk] *a* corsivo(a); ~s *npl* corsivo.

Italy [ˈɪtəlɪ] *n* Italia.

itch [ɪtʃ] *n* prurito // *vi* (*person*) avere il prurito; (*part of body*) prudere; to be ~ing to do sth aver una gran voglia di fare qc; ~y *a* che prude; to be ~y = to ~.

it'd [ˈɪtd] = it would; it had.

item [ˈaɪtəm] *n* articolo; (*on agenda*) punto; (*in programme*) numero; (*also:* news ~) notizia; ~ize *vt* specificare, dettagliare.

itinerant [ɪ'tɪnərənt] *a* ambulante.

itinerary [aɪ'tɪnərərɪ] *n* itinerario.

it'll [ˈɪtl] = it will, it shall.

its [ɪts] *a* il(la) suo(a), i(le) suoi(sue).

it's [ɪts] = it is; it has.

itself [ɪt'sɛlf] *pronoun* (*emphatic*) esso(a) stesso(a); (*reflexive*) si.

ITV *n abbr* (*Brit:* = Independent Television) rete televisiva in concorrenza con la BBC.

I.U.D. *n abbr* (= intra-uterine device) spirale *f*.

I've [aɪv] = I have.

ivory [ˈaɪvərɪ] *n* avorio.

ivy [ˈaɪvɪ] *n* edera.

J

jab [dʒæb] *vt*: to ~ sth into affondare *or* piantare qc dentro // *n* colpo; (*MED:* col) puntura.

jack [dʒæk] *n* (*AUT*) cricco; (*CARDS*) fante *m*; to ~ up *vt* sollevare sul cricco.

jackal [ˈdʒækl] *n* sciacallo.

jackdaw [ˈdʒækdɔ:] *n* taccola.

jacket [ˈdʒækɪt] *n* giacca; (*of book*) copertura.

jack-knife [ˈdʒæknaɪf] *vi*: the lorry ~d l'autotreno si è piegato su se stesso.

jack plug *n* (*ELEC*) jack *m inv*.

jackpot [ˈdʒækpɔt] *n* primo premio (in denaro).

jade [dʒeɪd] *n* (*stone*) giada.

jaded [ˈdʒeɪdɪd] *a* sfinito(a), spossato(a).

jagged [ˈdʒægɪd] *a* sbocconcellato(a); (*cliffs etc*) frastagliato(a).

jail [dʒeɪl] *n* prigione *f* // *vt* mandare in prigione; ~er *n* custode *m* del carcere.

jam [dʒæm] *n* marmellata; (*of shoppers etc*) ressa; (*also:* traffic ~) ingorgo // *vt* (*passage etc*) ingombrare, ostacolare; (*mechanism, drawer etc*) bloccare; (*RADIO*) disturbare con interferenze // *vi* (*mechanism, sliding part*) incepparsi, bloccarsi; (*gun*) incepparsi; to ~ sth into forzare qc dentro; infilare qc a forza dentro.

Jamaica [dʒə'meɪkə] *n* Giamaica.

jangle [ˈdʒæŋgl] *vi* risuonare; (*bracelet*) tintinnare.

janitor [ˈdʒænɪtə*] *n* (*caretaker*) portiere *m*; (: *SCOL*) bidello.

January [ˈdʒænjuərɪ] *n* gennaio.

Japan [dʒə'pæn] *n* Giappone *m*; ~ese [dʒæpə'ni:z] *a* giapponese // *n* (*pl inv*) giapponese *m/f*; (*LING*) giapponese *m*.

jar [dʒɑ:*] *n* (*glass*) barattolo, vasetto // *vi* (*sound*) stridere; (*colours etc*) stonare.

jargon [ˈdʒɑ:gən] *n* gergo.

jasmin(e) [ˈdʒæzmɪn] *n* gelsomino.

jaundice [ˈdʒɔ:ndɪs] *n* itterizia; ~d *a* (*fig*) invidioso(a) e critico(a).

jaunt [dʒɔ:nt] *n* gita; ~y *a* vivace; disinvolto(a).

javelin [ˈdʒævlɪn] *n* giavellotto.

jaw [dʒɔ:] *n* mascella.

jay [dʒeɪ] *n* ghiandaia.

jaywalker [ˈdʒeɪwɔ:kə*] *n* pedone(a) indisciplinato(a).

jazz [dʒæz] *n* jazz *m*; to ~ up *vt* rendere vivace.

jealous [ˈdʒɛləs] *a* geloso(a); ~y *n* gelosia.

jeans [dʒi:nz] *npl* (blue-)jeans *mpl*.

jeer [dʒɪə*] *vi*: to ~ (at) fischiare; beffeggiare.

jelly [ˈdʒɛlɪ] *n* gelatina; ~fish *n* medusa.

jeopardy [ˈdʒɛpədɪ] *n*: in ~ in pericolo.

jerk [dʒə:k] *n* sobbalzo, scossa; sussulto // *vt* dare una scossa a // *vi* (*vehicles*) sobbalzare.

jerkin [ˈdʒə:kɪn] *n* giubbotto.

jersey [ˈdʒə:zɪ] *n* maglia.

jest [dʒɛst] *n* scherzo.

Jesus [ˈdʒi:zəs] *n* Gesù *m*.

jet [dʒɛt] *n* (*of gas, liquid*) getto; (*AVIAT*) aviogetto; ~-black *a* nero(a) come l'ebano, corvino(a); ~ engine *n* motore *m* a reazione; ~ lag *n* (problemi *mpl* dovuti allo) sbalzo dei fusi orari.

jettison [ˈdʒɛtɪsn] *vt* gettare in mare.

jetty [ˈdʒɛtɪ] *n* molo.

Jew [dʒu:] *n* ebreo.

jewel [ˈdʒu:əl] *n* gioiello; ~ler *n* orefice

m, gioielliere/a; **~ler's (shop)** *n* oreficeria, gioielleria; **~lery** *n* gioielli *mpl.*

Jewess [dʒu:ɪs] *n* ebrea.

Jewish ['dʒu:ɪʃ] *a* ebreo(a), ebraico(a).

jib [dʒɪb] *n* (NAUT) fiocco; (of crane) braccio.

jibe [dʒaɪb] *n* beffa.

jiffy ['dʒɪfɪ] *n* (col): **in a ~** in un batter d'occhio.

jig [dʒɪg] *n* giga.

jigsaw ['dʒɪgsɔ:] *n* (also: **~ puzzle**) puzzle *m inv.*

jilt [dʒɪlt] *vt* piantare in asso.

jingle ['dʒɪŋgl] *n* (advert) sigla pubblicitaria // *vi* tintinnare, scampanellare.

jinx [dʒɪŋks] *n* (col) iettatura; (person) iettatore/trice.

jitters ['dʒɪtəz] *npl* (col): **to get the ~** aver fifa.

job [dʒɔb] *n* lavoro; (employment) impiego, posto; **it's a good ~ that ...** meno male che ...; **just the ~!** proprio quello che ci vuole; **~ centre** *n* (Brit) ufficio di collocamento; **~-less** *a* senza lavoro, disoccupato(a).

jockey ['dʒɔkɪ] *n* fantino, jockey *m inv* // *vi*: **to ~ for position** manovrare per una posizione di vantaggio.

jocular ['dʒɔkjulə*] *a* gioviale; scherzoso(a).

jog [dʒɔg] *vt* urtare // *vi* (SPORT) fare footing, fare jogging; **to ~ along** trottare; (fig) andare avanti piano piano; **~ging** *n* footing *m*, jogging *m.*

join [dʒɔɪn] *vt* unire, congiungere; (become member of) iscriversi a; (meet) raggiungere; riunirsi a // *vi* (roads, rivers) confluire // *n* giuntura; **to ~ in** *vi* partecipare // *vt fus* unirsi a; **to ~ up** *vi* arruolarsi.

joiner ['dʒɔɪnə*] *n* falegname *m*; **~y** *n* falegnameria.

joint [dʒɔɪnt] *n* (TECH) giuntura; giunto; (ANAT) articolazione *f*, giuntura; (Brit CULIN) arrosto; (col: place) locale *m* // *a* comune; **~ account** *n* (at bank etc) conto in comune, conto comune; **~ly** *ad* in comune, insieme.

joist [dʒɔɪst] *n* trave *f.*

joke [dʒəuk] *n* scherzo; (funny story) barzelletta; (also: **practical ~**) beffa // *vi* scherzare; **to play a ~ on sb** fare uno scherzo a qn; **~r** *n* buffone/a, burlone/a; (CARDS) matta, jolly *m inv.*

jolly ['dʒɔlɪ] *a* allegro(a), gioioso(a) // *ad* (col) veramente, proprio.

jolt [dʒəult] *n* scossa, sobbalzo // *vt* urtare.

Jordan ['dʒɔ:dən] *n* (country) Giordania; (river) Giordano.

jostle ['dʒɔsl] *vt* spingere coi gomiti // *vi* farsi spazio coi gomiti.

jot [dʒɔt] *n*: **not one ~** nemmeno un po'; **to ~ down** *vt* annotare in fretta,

buttare giù; **~ter** *n* (Brit) blocco.

journal ['dʒə:nl] *n* giornale *m*; rivista; diario; **~ism** *n* giornalismo; **~ist** *n* giornalista *m/f.*

journey ['dʒə:nɪ] *n* viaggio; (distance covered) tragitto // *vi* viaggiare.

joy [dʒɔɪ] *n* gioia; **~ful, ~ous** *a* gioioso(a), allegro(a); **~ ride** *n* gita in automobile (specialmente rubata); **~stick** *n* (AVIAT) barra di comando; (COMPUT) joystick *m inv.*

J.P. *n abbr* = **Justice of the Peace.**

Jr, Jun., Junr *abbr* = **junior.**

jubilant ['dʒu:bɪlnt] *a* giubilante; trionfante.

jubilee ['dʒu:bɪli:] *n* giubileo; **silver ~** venticinquesimo anniversario.

judge [dʒʌdʒ] *n* giudice *m/f* // *vt* giudicare; **judg(e)ment** *n* giudizio; (punishment) punizione *f.*

judicial [dʒu:'dɪʃl] *a* giudiziale, giudiziario(a).

judiciary [dʒu:'dɪʃɪərɪ] *n* magistratura.

judo ['dʒu:dəu] *n* judo.

jug [dʒʌg] *n* brocca, bricco.

juggernaut ['dʒʌgənɔ:t] *n* (Brit: huge truck) bestione *m.*

juggle ['dʒʌgl] *vi* fare giochi di destrezza; **~r** *n* giocoliere/a.

Jugoslav ['ju:gəuslɑ:v] *etc* = **Yugoslav** *etc.*

juice [dʒu:s] *n* succo.

juicy ['dʒu:sɪ] *a* succoso(a).

jukebox ['dʒu:kbɔks] *n* juke-box *m inv.*

July [dʒu:'laɪ] *n* luglio.

jumble ['dʒʌmbl] *n* miscuglio // *vt* (also: **~ up**) mischiare; **~ sale** *n* (Brit) vendita di oggetti per beneficenza.

jumbo (jet) ['dʒʌmbəu-] *n* jumbo-jet *m inv.*

jump [dʒʌmp] *vi* saltare, balzare; (start) sobbalzare; (increase) rincarare // *vt* saltare // *n* salto, balzo; sobbalzo.

jumper ['dʒʌmpə*] *n* (Brit: pullover) maglione *m*, pullover *m inv*; (US: dress) scamiciato; **~ cables** *npl* (US) = **jump leads.**

jump leads *npl* (Brit) cavi *mpl* per batteria.

jumpy ['dʒʌmpɪ] *a* nervoso(a), agitato(a).

junction ['dʒʌŋkʃən] *n* (Brit: of roads) incrocio; (of rails) nodo ferroviario.

juncture ['dʒʌŋktʃə*] *n*: **at this ~** in questa congiuntura.

June [dʒu:n] *n* giugno.

jungle ['dʒʌŋgl] *n* giungla.

junior ['dʒu:nɪə*] *a, n*: **he's ~ to me (by 2 years), he's my ~ (by 2 years)** è più giovane di me (di 2 anni); **he's ~ to me (seniority)** è al di sotto di me, ho più anzianità di lui; **~ school** *n* (Brit) scuola elementare (da 8 a 11 anni).

junk [dʒʌŋk] *n* (rubbish) chincaglia; (ship) giunca; **~ food** *n* porcherie *fpl*;

~ **shop** n chincaglieria.
juror ['dʒuərə*] n giurato/a.
jury ['dʒuəri] n giuria.
just [dʒʌst] a giusto(a) // ad: he's ~ done
it/left lo ha appena fatto/è appena
partito; ~ **as I expected** proprio come
me lo aspettavo; ~ **right** proprio giusto;
~ **2 o'clock** le 2 precise; she's ~ **as
clever as you** è in gamba proprio quanto
te; it's ~ **as well that** ... meno male
che ...; ~ **as I arrived** proprio mentre
arrivavo; it was ~ **before/enough/here**
era poco prima/appena assai/proprio qui;
it's ~ **me** sono solo io; it's ~ **a mistake**
non è che uno sbaglio; ~ **missed/caught**
appena perso/preso; ~ **listen to this!**
senta un po' questo!
justice ['dʒʌstis] n giustizia; **J~ of the
Peace (J.P.)** n giudice m conciliatore.
justify ['dʒʌstifai] vt giustificare.
jut [dʒʌt] vi (also: ~ out) sporgersi.
juvenile ['dʒu:vənail] a giovane,
giovanile; (court) dei minorenni;
(books) per ragazzi // n giovane m/f,
minorenne m/f.
juxtapose ['dʒʌkstəpəuz] vt giu-
stapporre.

K

K abbr (= one thousand) mille; (=
kilobyte) K.
kangaroo [kæŋgə'ru:] n canguro.
karate [kə'rɑːti] n karatè m.
kebab [kə'bæb] n spiedino.
keel [ki:l] n chiglia; **on an even** ~ (fig) in
uno stato normale.
keen [ki:n] a (interest, desire) vivo(a);
(eye, intelligence) acuto(a);
(competition) serrato(a); (edge) af-
filato(a); (eager) entusiasta; **to be** ~ **to
do** or **on doing sth** avere una gran voglia
di fare qc; **to be** ~ **on sth** essere
appassionato(a) di qc; **to be** ~ **on sb**
avere un debole per qn.
keep [ki:p] vb (pt, pp **kept**) vt tenere;
(hold back) trattenere; (feed: one's
family etc) mantenere, sostentare; (a
promise) mantenere; (chickens, bees,
pigs etc) allevare // vi (food)
mantenersi; (remain: in a certain state
or place) restare // n (of castle) maschio; (food etc): **enough for his** ~ abbastanza per vitto e alloggio; (col): **for ~s**
per sempre; **to** ~ **doing sth** continuare a
fare qc; fare qc di continuo; **to** ~ **sb
from doing/sth happening** impedire
a qn di fare/che qc succeda; **to** ~ **sb
busy/a place tidy** tenere qn occupato(a)/
un luogo in ordine; **to** ~ **sth to o.s.** tenere
qc per sé; **to** ~ **sth (back) from sb**
celare qc a qn; **to** ~ **time** (clock) andar
bene; **to** ~ **on** vi continuare; **to** ~ **on
doing** continuare a fare; **to** ~ **out** vt

tener fuori; **"~ out"** "vietato l'accesso";
to ~ **up** vi mantenersi // vt continuare,
mantenere; **to** ~ **up with** tener dietro a,
andare di pari passo con; (work etc)
farcela a seguire; **~er** n custode m/f,
guardiano/a; **~-fit** n ginnastica; **~ing** n
(care) custodia; **in ~ing with** in armonia
con; in accordo con; **~sake** n ricordo.
keg [kɛg] n barilotto.
kennel ['kɛnl] n canile m.
kept [kɛpt] pt, pp of **keep**.
kerb [kə:b] n (Brit) orlo del marciapiede.
kernel ['kə:nl] n nocciolo.
kettle ['kɛtl] n bollitore m.
kettle drums npl timpano.
key [ki:] n (gen, MUS) chiave f; (of piano,
typewriter) tasto // vt (also: ~ **in**)
digitare; **~board** n tastiera; **~ed up** a
(person) agitato(a); **~hole** n buco della
serratura; **~note** n (MUS) tonica; (fig)
nota dominante; ~ **ring** n portachiavi m
inv.
khaki ['kɑːki] a, n cachi (m).
kick [kik] vt calciare, dare calci a // vi
(horse) tirar calci // n calcio; (of rifle)
contraccolpo; (thrill): **he does it for ~s**
lo fa giusto per il piacere di farlo; **to** ~
off vi (SPORT) dare il primo calcio.
kid [kid] n (col: child) ragazzino/a;
(animal, leather) capretto // vi (col)
scherzare // vt (col) prendere in giro.
kidnap ['kidnæp] vt rapire, sequestrare;
~per n rapitore/trice; **~ping** n sequestro (di persona).
kidney ['kidni] n (ANAT) rene m;
(CULIN) rognone m.
kill [kil] vt uccidere, ammazzare; (fig)
sopprimere; sopraffare; ammazzare // n
uccisione f; **~er** n uccisore m, killer m
inv; assassino/a; **~ing** n assassinio;
(massacre) strage f; **~joy** n guastafeste
m/f inv.
kiln [kiln] n forno.
kilo ['ki:ləu] n chilo; **~byte** n (COMPUT)
kilobyte m inv; **~gram(me)**
['kiləugræm] n chilogrammo; **~metre**,
(US) **~meter** ['kiləmi:tə*] n chilometro;
~watt ['kiləuwɔt] n chilowatt m inv.
kilt [kilt] n gonnellino scozzese.
kin [kin] n see **next, kith**.
kind [kaind] a gentile, buono(a) // n sorta,
specie f; (species) genere m; **to be two
of a** ~ essere molto simili; **in** ~ (COMM)
in natura.
kindergarten ['kindəgɑːtn] n giardino
d'infanzia.
kind-hearted [kaind'hɑːtid] a di buon
cuore.
kindle ['kindl] vt accendere, infiammare.
kindly ['kaindli] a pieno(a) di bontà,
benevolo(a) // ad con bontà, gentilmente;
will you ~... vuole ... per favore.
kindness ['kaindnis] n bontà, gentilezza.
kindred ['kindrəd] a imparentato(a); ~
spirit n spirito affine.

king [kɪŋ] n re m inv; **~dom** n regno, reame m; **~fisher** n martin m inv pescatore; **~size** a super inv; gigante.

kinky [ˈkɪŋkɪ] a (fig) eccentrico(a); dai gusti particolari.

kiosk [ˈkiːɔsk] n edicola, chiosco; (Brit TEL) cabina (telefonica).

kipper [ˈkɪpə*] n aringa affumicata.

kiss [kɪs] n bacio // vt baciare; **to ~ (each other)** baciarsi.

kit [kɪt] n equipaggiamento, corredo; (set of tools etc) attrezzi mpl; (for assembly) scatola di montaggio.

kitchen [ˈkɪtʃɪn] n cucina; **~ sink** n acquaio.

kite [kaɪt] n (toy) aquilone m; (ZOOL) nibbio.

kith [kɪθ] n: **~ and kin** amici e parenti mpl.

kitten [ˈkɪtn] n gattino/a, micino/a.

kitty [ˈkɪtɪ] n (money) fondo comune.

knack [næk] n: **to have the ~ of** avere l'abilità di; **there's a ~ to doing this** c'è un trucco per fare questo.

knapsack [ˈnæpsæk] n zaino, sacco da montagna.

knead [niːd] vt impastare.

knee [niː] n ginocchio; **~cap** n rotula.

kneel, pl, pp **knelt** [niːl, nɛlt] vi (also: **~ down**) inginocchiarsi.

knell [nɛl] n rintocco.

knew [njuː] pt of **know**.

knickers [ˈnɪkəz] npl (Brit) mutandine fpl.

knife [naɪf] n (pl **knives**) coltello // vt accoltellare, dare una coltellata a.

knight [naɪt] n cavaliere m; (CHESS) cavallo; **~hood** n (title): **to get a ~hood** essere fatto cavaliere.

knit [nɪt] vt fare a maglia; (fig): **to ~ together** unire // vi lavorare a maglia; (broken bones) saldarsi; **~ting** n lavoro a maglia; **~ting needle** n ferro (da calza); **~wear** n maglieria.

knives [naɪvz] npl of **knife**.

knob [nɔb] n bottone m; manopola.

knock [nɔk] vt colpire; urtare; (fig: col) criticare // vi (engine) battere; (at door etc): **to ~ at/on** bussare a // n bussata; colpo, botta; **to ~ down** vt abbattere; **to ~ off** vi (col: finish) smettere (di lavorare); **to ~ out** vt stendere; (BOXING) mettere K.O.; **to ~ over** vt (person) investire; (object) far cadere; **~er** n (on door) battente m; **~-kneed** a che ha le gambe ad x; **~out** n (BOXING) knock out m inv.

knot [nɔt] n nodo // vt annodare; **~ty** a (fig) spinoso(a).

know [nəu] vt (pt **knew**, pp **known**) sapere; (person, author, place) conoscere; **to ~ how to do** sapere fare; **to ~ about** or **of sth/sb** conoscere qc/qn; **~-all** n sapientone/a; **~-how** n tecnica; pratica; **~ing** a (look etc) d'in-

tesa; **~ingly** ad (purposely) consapevolmente; (smile, look) con aria d'intesa.

knowledge [ˈnɔlɪdʒ] n consapevolezza; (learning) conoscenza, sapere m; **~able** a ben informato(a).

known [nəun] pp of **know**.

knuckle [ˈnʌkl] n nocca.

Koran [kɔˈrɑːn] n Corano.

Korea [kəˈrɪə] n Corea.

kosher [ˈkəuʃə*] a kasher inv.

L

lab [læb] n abbr (= laboratory) laboratorio.

label [ˈleɪbl] n etichetta, cartellino; (brand: of record) casa // vt etichettare.

laboratory [ləˈbɔrətərɪ] n laboratorio.

labour, (US) **labor** [ˈleɪbə*] n (task) lavoro; (workmen) manodopera; (MED) travaglio del parto, doglie fpl // vi: **to ~ (at)** lavorare duro (a); **in ~** (MED) in travaglio; **L~**, the **L~ party** (Brit) il partito laburista, i laburisti; **~ed** a (breathing) affannoso(a); (style) pesante; **~er** n manovale m; (on farm) lavoratore m agricolo.

lace [leɪs] n merletto, pizzo; (of shoe etc) laccio // vt (shoe) allacciare.

lack [læk] n mancanza // vt mancare di; **through** or **for ~ of** per mancanza di; **to be ~ing** mancare; **to be ~ing in** mancare di.

lackadaisical [lækəˈdeɪzɪkl] a disinteressato(a), noncurante.

lacquer [ˈlækə*] n lacca.

lad [læd] n ragazzo, giovanotto.

ladder [ˈlædə*] n scala; (Brit: in tights) smagliatura // vt smagliare // vi smagliarsi.

laden [ˈleɪdn] a: **~ (with)** carico(a) or caricato(a) (di).

ladle [ˈleɪdl] n mestolo.

lady [ˈleɪdɪ] n signora; dama; **L~** Smith lady Smith; **the ladies' (room)** i gabinetti per signore; **~bird**, (US) **~bug** n coccinella; **~-in-waiting** n dama di compagnia; **~like** a da signora, distinto(a); **~ship** n: **your ~ship** signora contessa (or baronessa etc).

lag [læg] vi (also: **~ behind**) trascinarsi // vt (pipes) rivestire di materiale isolante.

lager [ˈlɑːgə*] n lager m inv.

lagoon [ləˈguːn] n laguna.

laid [leɪd] pt, pp of **lay**; **~ back** a (col) rilassato(a), tranquillo(a).

lain [leɪn] pp of **lie**.

lair [lɛə*] n covo, tana.

laity [ˈleɪətɪ] n laici mpl.

lake [leɪk] n lago.

lamb [læm] n agnello.

lame [leɪm] a zoppo(a).

lament [ləˈmɛnt] n lamento // vt

lamentare, piangere.

laminated ['læmɪneɪtɪd] *a* laminato(a).

lamp [læmp] *n* lampada.

lampoon [læm'puːn] *n* satira.

lamp: ~**post** *n* (*Brit*) lampione *m*; ~**shade** *n* paralume *m*.

lance [lɑːns] *n* lancia // *vt* (*MED*) incidere; ~ **corporal** *n* (*Brit*) caporale *m*.

land [lænd] *n* (*as opposed to sea*) terra (ferma); (*country*) paese *m*; (*soil*) terreno; suolo; (*estate*) terreni *mpl*, terre *fpl* // *vi* (*from ship*) sbarcare; (*AVIAT*) atterrare; (*fig: fall*) cadere // *vt* (*obtain*) acchiappare; (*passengers*) sbarcare; (*goods*) scaricare; **to ~ up** *vi* andare a finire; ~**ing** *n* sbarco; atterraggio; (*of staircase*) pianerottolo; ~**ing stage** *n* (*Brit*) pontile *m* da sbarco; ~**lady** *n* padrona *or* proprietaria di casa; ~**lord** *n* padrone *m or* proprietario di casa; (*of pub etc*) oste *m*; ~**mark** *n* punto di riferimento; (*fig*) pietra miliare; ~**owner** *n* proprietario(a) terriero(a).

landscape ['lænskeɪp] *n* paesaggio.

landslide ['lændslaɪd] *n* (*GEO*) frana; (*fig: POL*) valanga.

lane [leɪn] *n* (*in country*) viottolo; (*in town*) stradetta; (*AUT, in race*) corsia.

language ['læŋgwɪdʒ] *n* lingua; (*way one speaks*) linguaggio; **bad ~** linguaggio volgare; ~ **laboratory** *n* laboratorio linguistico.

languid ['læŋgwɪd] *a* languente; languido(a).

lank [læŋk] *a* (*hair*) liscio(a) e opaco(a).

lanky ['læŋkɪ] *a* allampanato(a).

lantern ['læntn] *n* lanterna.

lap [læp] *n* (*of track*) giro; (*of body*): **in or on one's ~** in grembo // *vt* (*also:* ~ **up**) papparsi, leccare // *vi* (*waves*) sciabordare.

lapel [lə'pɛl] *n* risvolto.

Lapland ['læplænd] *n* Lapponia.

lapse [læps] *n* lapsus *m inv*; (*longer*) caduta // *vi* (*law, act*) cadere; (*ticket, passport*) scadere; **to ~ into bad habits** pigliare cattive abitudini; ~ **of time** spazio di tempo.

larceny ['lɑːsənɪ] *n* furto.

lard [lɑːd] *n* lardo.

larder ['lɑːdə*] *n* dispensa.

large [lɑːdʒ] *a* grande; (*person, animal*) grosso(a); **at ~** (*free*) in libertà; (*generally*) in generale; nell'insieme; ~**ly** *ad* in gran parte.

largesse [lɑː'ʒɛs] *n* generosità.

lark [lɑːk] *n* (*bird*) allodola; (*joke*) scherzo, gioco; **to ~ about** *vi* fare lo stupido.

laryngitis [lærɪn'dʒaɪtɪs] *n* laringite *f*.

laser ['leɪzə*] *n* laser *m*; ~ **printer** *n* stampante *f* laser *inv*.

lash [læʃ] *n* frustata; (*also:* eye~) ciglio

// *vt* frustare; (*tie*) assicurare con una corda; **to ~ out** *vi*: **to ~ out** (at *or* against sb/sth) attaccare violentemente (qn/qc); **to ~ out** (on sth) (*col: spend*) spendere un sacco di soldi (per qc).

lass [læs] *n* ragazza.

lasso [læ'suː] *n* laccio.

last [lɑːst] *a* ultimo(a); (*week, month, year*) scorso(a), passato(a) // *ad* per ultimo // *vi* durare; ~ **week** la settimana scorsa; ~ **night** ieri sera, la notte scorsa; **at ~** finalmente, alla fine; ~ **but one** penultimo(a); ~**-ditch** *a* (*attempt*) estremo(a); ~**ing** *a* durevole; ~**ly** *ad* infine, per finire; ~**-minute** *a* fatto(a) (*or* preso(a) *etc*) all'ultimo momento.

latch [lætʃ] *n* serratura a scatto.

late [leɪt] *a* (*not on time*) in ritardo; (*far on in day etc*) tardi *inv*; tardo(a); (*recent*) recente, ultimo(a); (*former*) ex; (*dead*) defunto(a) // *ad* tardi; (*behind time, schedule*) in ritardo; **of ~** di recente; **in the ~ afternoon** nel tardo pomeriggio; **in ~ May** verso la fine di maggio; ~**comer** *n* ritardatario/a; ~**ly** *ad* recentemente.

later ['leɪtə*] *a* (*date etc*) posteriore; (*version etc*) successivo(a) // *ad* più tardi; ~ **on** più avanti.

lateral ['lætərl] *a* laterale.

latest ['leɪtɪst] *a* ultimo(a), più recente; **at the ~** al più tardi.

lathe [leɪð] *n* tornio.

lather ['lɑːðə*] *n* schiuma di sapone // *vt* insaponare.

Latin ['lætɪn] *n* latino // *a* latino(a); ~ **America** *n* America Latina; ~**-American** *a* sudamericano(a).

latitude ['lætɪtjuːd] *n* latitudine *f*.

latter ['lætə*] *a* secondo(a); più recente // *n*: **the ~** quest'ultimo, il secondo; ~**ly** *ad* recentemente, negli ultimi tempi.

lattice ['lætɪs] *n* traliccio; graticolato.

laudable ['lɔːdəbl] *a* lodevole.

laugh [lɑːf] *n* risata // *vi* ridere; **to ~ at** *vt fus* (*misfortune etc*) ridere di; **to ~ off** *vt* prendere alla leggera; ~**able** *a* ridicolo(a); ~**ing stock** *n*: **the** ~**ing stock of** lo zimbello di; ~**ter** *n* riso; risate *fpl*.

launch [lɔːntʃ] *n* (*of rocket etc*) lancio; (*of new ship*) varo; (*boat*) scialuppa; (*also:* **motor ~**) lancia // *vt* (*rocket*) lanciare; (*ship, plan*) varare; ~**(ing) pad** *n* rampa di lancio.

launder ['lɔːndə*] *vt* lavare e stirare.

launderette [lɔːn'drɛt], (*US*) **laundromat** ['lɔːndrəmæt] *n* lavanderia (automatica).

laundry ['lɔːndrɪ] *n* lavanderia; (*clothes*) biancheria.

laureate ['lɔːrɪət] *a see* **poet**.

laurel ['lɔːrl] *n* lauro.

lava ['lɑːvə] *n* lava.

lavatory ['lævətərɪ] *n* gabinetto.

lavender ['lævəndə*] n lavanda.

lavish ['lævɪʃ] a copioso(a); abbondante; (giving freely): ~ **with** prodigo(a) di, largo(a) in // vt: to ~ **on** sb/sth (care) profondere a qn/qc.

law [lɔ:] n legge f; civil/criminal ~ diritto civile/penale; ~**abiding** a ubbidiente alla legge; ~ **and order** n l'ordine m pubblico; ~ **court** n tribunale m, corte f di giustizia; ~**ful** a legale; lecito(a).

lawn [lɔ:n] n tappeto erboso; ~**mower** n tosaerba m or f inv; ~ **tennis** n tennis m su prato.

law school n facoltà f inv di legge.

lawsuit ['lɔ:su:t] n processo, causa.

lawyer ['lɔ:jə*] n (consultant, with company) giurista m/f; (for sales, wills etc) ≈ notaio; (partner, in court) ≈ avvocato/essa.

lax [læks] a rilassato(a); negligente.

laxative ['læksətɪv] n lassativo.

laxity ['læksɪtɪ] n rilassatezza; negligenza.

lay [leɪ] pt of **lie** // a laico(a); secolare // vt (pt, pp **laid**) posare, mettere; (eggs) fare; (trap) tendere; (plans) fare, elaborare; to ~ **the table** apparecchiare la tavola; to ~ **aside** or **by** vt mettere da parte; to ~ **down** vt mettere giù; to ~ **down the law** dettar legge; to ~ **off** vt (workers) licenziare; to ~ **on** vt (water, gas) installare, mettere; (provide) fornire; (paint) applicare; to ~ **out** vt (design) progettare; (display) presentare; (spend) sborsare; to ~ **up** vt (to store) accumulare; (ship) mettere in disarmo; (subj: illness) costringere a letto; ~**about** n sfaccendato/a, fannullone/a; ~**by** n (Brit) piazzola (di sosta).

layer ['leɪə*] n strato.

layman ['leɪmən] n laico; profano.

layout ['leɪaut] n lay-out m inv, disposizione f; (PRESS) impaginazione f.

laze [leɪz] vi oziare.

lazy ['leɪzɪ] a pigro(a).

lb. abbr = **pound** (weight).

lead [li:d] n (front position) posizione f di testa; (distance, time ahead) vantaggio; (clue) indizio; (ELEC) filo (elettrico); (for dog) guinzaglio; (THEATRE) parte f principale; [led] (metal) piombo; (in pencil) mina // vb (pt, pp **led**) vt menare, guidare, condurre; (induce) indurre; (be leader of) essere a capo di; (SPORT) essere in testa a // vi condurre, essere in testa; to ~ **astray** vt sviare; to ~ **away** vt condurre via; to ~ **back** vt: to ~ **back to** ricondurre a; to ~ **on** vt (tease) tenere sulla corda; to ~ **on to** vt (induce) portare a; to ~ **to** vt fus condurre a; portare a; to ~ **up to** vt fus portare a.

leaden ['ledn] a (sky, sea) plumbeo(a); (heavy: footsteps) pesante.

leader ['li:də*] n capo; leader m inv; (in newspaper) articolo di fondo; ~**ship** n direzione f; capacità di comando.

leading ['li:dɪŋ] a primo(a); principale; ~ **man/lady** n (THEATRE) primo attore/prima attrice; ~ **light** n (person) personaggio di primo piano.

leaf [li:f] n (pl **leaves**) foglia; (of table) ribalta // vi: to ~ **through** sth sfogliare qc; to **turn over a new** ~ cambiar vita.

leaflet ['li:flɪt] n dépliant m inv; (POL, REL) volantino.

league [li:g] n lega; (FOOTBALL) campionato; to be in ~ **with** essere in lega con.

leak [li:k] n (out, also fig) fuga; (in) infiltrazione f // vi (roof, bucket) perdere; (liquid) uscire; (shoes) lasciar passare l'acqua // vt (liquid) spandere; (information) divulgare; to ~ **out** vi uscire; (information) trapelare.

lean [li:n] a magro(a) // vb (pt, pp **leaned** or **leant** [lɛnt]) vt: to ~ **sth on** sth appoggiare qc su qc // vi (slope) pendere; (rest): to ~ **against** appoggiarsi contro, essere appoggiato(a) a; to ~ **on** appoggiarsi a; to ~ **back/forward** vi sporgersi in avanti/indietro; to ~ **out** vi sporgersi; to ~ **over** vi inclinarsi; ~**ing** n: ~**ing** (towards) propensione f (per); ~**to** n (roof) tettoia; (shed) capanno con tetto a una falda.

leap [li:p] n salto, balzo // vi (pt, pp **leaped** or **leapt** [lɛpt]) saltare, balzare; ~**frog** n gioco della cavallina; ~ **year** n anno bisestile.

learn, pt, pp **learned** or **learnt** [lə:n, -t] vt, vi imparare; to ~ **how to do** sth imparare a fare qc; ~**ed** ['lə:nɪd] a erudito(a), dotto(a); ~**er** n principiante m/f; apprendista m/f; (Brit: also: ~**er driver**) guidatore/trice principiante; ~**ing** n erudizione f, sapienza.

lease [li:s] n contratto d'affitto // vt affittare.

leash [li:ʃ] n guinzaglio.

least [li:st] a: the ~ + noun il(la) più piccolo(a), il(la) minimo(a); (smallest amount of) il(la) meno; the ~ + adjective: the ~ **beautiful girl** la ragazza meno bella; the ~ **expensive** il(la) meno caro(a); I **have the** ~ **money** ho meno denaro di tutti; at ~ almeno; not in the ~ affatto, per nulla.

leather ['lɛðə*] n cuoio // cpd di cuoio.

leave [li:v] vb (pt, pp **left**) vt lasciare; (go away from) partire da // vi partire, andarsene // n (time off) congedo; (MIL, also: consent) licenza; to be **left** rimanere; there's some **milk left over** c'è rimasto del latte; on ~ in congedo; to ~ **behind** vt (person, object) lasciare indietro; (: forget) dimenticare; to ~ **out** vt omettere, tralasciare; ~ **of absence** n congedo.

leaves [li:vz] *npl of* **leaf**.

Lebanon ['lɛbənən] *n* Libano.

lecherous ['lɛtʃərəs] *a* lascivo(a), lubrico(a).

lecture ['lɛktʃə*] *n* conferenza; (*SCOL*) lezione *f* // *vi* fare conferenze; fare lezioni // *vt* (*scold*) rimproverare, fare una ramanzina a; to ~ on fare una conferenza su; to give a ~ on tenere una conferenza su.

lecturer ['lɛktʃərə*] *n* (*speaker*) conferenziere/a; (*Brit: at university*) professore/essa, docente *m/f*.

led [lɛd] *pt, pp of* **lead**.

ledge [lɛdʒ] *n* (*of window*) davanzale *m*; (*on wall etc*) sporgenza; (*of mountain*) cornice *f*, cengia.

ledger ['lɛdʒə*] *n* libro maestro, registro.

lee [li:] *n* lato sottovento.

leech [li:tʃ] *n* sanguisuga.

leek [li:k] *n* porro.

leer [lɪə*] *vi*: to ~ at sb gettare uno sguardo voglioso (*or* maligno) su qn.

leeway ['li:weɪ] *n* (*fig*): to have some ~ avere una certa libertà di agire.

left [lɛft] *pt, pp of* **leave** // *a* sinistro(a) // *ad* a sinistra // *n* sinistra; **on the** ~, to the ~ a sinistra; the L~ (*POL*) la sinistra; ~-handed *a* mancino(a); ~-hand side *n* lato *or* fianco sinistro; ~ luggage (office) *n* (*Brit*) deposito *m* bagagli *inv*; ~-overs *npl* avanzi *mpl*, resti *mpl*; ~-wing *a* (*POL*) di sinistra.

leg [lɛg] *n* gamba; (*of animal*) zampa; (*of furniture*) piede *m*; (*CULIN: of chicken*) coscia; (*of journey*) tappa; lst/2nd ~ (*SPORT*) partita di andata/ritorno.

legacy ['lɛgəsɪ] *n* eredità *f inv*.

legal ['li:gl] *a* legale; ~ holiday *n* (*US*) giorno festivo, festa nazionale; ~ tender *n* moneta legale.

legend ['lɛdʒənd] *n* leggenda.

legible ['lɛdʒəbl] *a* leggibile.

legislation [lɛdʒɪs'leɪʃən] *n* legislazione *f*; **legislature** ['lɛdʒɪslətʃə*] *n* corpo legislativo.

legitimate [lɪ'dʒɪtɪmət] *a* legittimo(a).

leg-room ['lɛgru:m] *n* spazio per le gambe.

leisure ['lɛʒə*] *n* agio, tempo libero; ricreazioni *fpl*; at ~ all'agio; a proprio comodo; ~ centre *n* centro di ricreazione; ~ly *a* tranquillo(a); fatto(a) con comodo *or* senza fretta.

lemon ['lɛmən] *n* limone *m*; ~ade [-'neɪd] *n* limonata; ~ tea *n* tè *m inv* al limone.

lend [lɛnd], *pt, pp* **lent** *vt*: to ~ sth (to sb) prestare qc (a qn).

length [lɛŋθ] *n* lunghezza; (*section: of road, pipe etc*) pezzo, tratto; at ~ (*at last*) finalmente, alla fine; (*lengthily*) a lungo; ~en *vt* allungare, prolungare // *vi* allungarsi; ~ways *ad* per il lungo; ~y *a* molto lungo(a).

lenient ['li:nɪənt] *a* indulgente, clemente.

lens [lɛnz] *n* lente *f*; (*of camera*) obiettivo.

Lent [lɛnt] *n* Quaresima.

lent [lɛnt] *pt, pp of* **lend**.

lentil ['lɛntl] *n* lenticchia.

Leo ['li:əu] *n* Leone *m*.

leotard ['li:əta:d] *n* calzamaglia.

leper ['lɛpə*] *n* lebbroso/a.

leprosy ['lɛprəsɪ] *n* lebbra.

lesbian ['lɛzbɪən] *n* lesbica.

less [lɛs] *a, pronoun, ad* meno; ~ than you/ever meno di lei/che mai; ~ than half meno della metà; ~ and ~ sempre meno; the ~ he works ... meno lavora ... .

lessen ['lɛsn] *vi* diminuire, attenuarsi // *vt* diminuire, ridurre.

lesser ['lɛsə*] *a* minore, più piccolo(a); to a ~ extent in grado *or* misura minore.

lesson ['lɛsn] *n* lezione *f*.

lest [lɛst] *cj* per paura di + *infinitive*, per paura che + *sub*.

let, *pt, pp* **let** [lɛt] *vt* lasciare; (*Brit: lease*) dare in affitto; to ~ sb do sth lasciar fare qc a qn, lasciare che qn faccia qc; to ~ sb know sth far sapere qc a qn; he ~ me go mi ha lasciato andare; ~'s go andiamo; ~ him come to lasci venire; "to ~" "affittasi"; to ~ down *vt* (*lower*) abbassare; (*dress*) allungare; (*hair*) sciogliere; (*disappoint*) deludere; to ~ go *vt, vi* mollare; to ~ in *vt* lasciare entrare; (*visitor etc*) far entrare; to ~ off *vt* (*allow to go*) lasciare andare; (*firework etc*) far partire; (*smell etc*) emettere; to ~ on *vi* (*col*) dire; to ~ out *vt* lasciare uscire; (*dress*) allargare; (*scream*) emettere; to ~ up *vi* diminuire.

lethal ['li:θl] *a* letale, mortale.

lethargy ['lɛθədʒɪ] *n* letargia.

letter ['lɛtə*] *n* lettera; ~ bomb *n* lettera esplosiva; ~box *n* (*Brit*) buca delle lettere; ~ing *n* iscrizione *f*; caratteri *mpl*.

lettuce ['lɛtɪs] *n* lattuga, insalata.

leukaemia, (US) leukemia [lu:'ki:mɪə] *n* leucemia.

level ['lɛvl] *a* piatto(a), piano(a); orizzontale // *n* livello; (*also*: spirit ~) livella (a bolla d'aria) // *vt* livellare, spianare; to be ~ with essere alla pari di; A ~s *npl* (*Brit*) ≈ esami *mpl* di maturità; O ~s *npl* (*Brit*) esami fatti in Inghilterra all'età di 16 anni; on the ~ piatto(a); (*fig*) onesto(a); to ~ off or out *vi* (*prices etc*) stabilizzarsi; ~ crossing *n* (*Brit*) passaggio a livello; ~-headed *a* equilibrato(a).

lever ['li:və*] *n* leva // *vt*: to ~ up/out sollevare/estrarre con una leva; ~age *n*: ~age (on *or* with) ascendente *m* (su).

levy ['lɛvɪ] *n* tassa, imposta // *vt* imporre.

lewd [lu:d] *a* osceno(a), lascivo(a).

liability [laɪə'bɪlətɪ] n responsabilità f inv; (handicap) peso; **liabilities** npl debiti mpl; (on balance sheet) passivo.

liable ['laɪəbl] a (subject): ~ **to** soggetto(a) a; passibile di; (responsible): ~ **(for)** responsabile (di); (likely): ~ **to do** propenso(a) a fare.

liaison [liː'eɪzɒn] n relazione f; (MIL) collegamento.

liar ['laɪə*] n bugiardo/a.

libel ['laɪbl] n libello, diffamazione f // vt diffamare.

liberal ['lɪbərl] a liberale; (generous): to be ~ **with** distribuire liberalmente.

liberty ['lɪbətɪ] n libertà f inv; at ~ **to do** libero(a) di fare.

Libra ['liːbrə] n Bilancia.

librarian [laɪ'brɛərɪən] n bibliotecario/a.

library ['laɪbrərɪ] n biblioteca.

Libya ['lɪbɪə] n Libia.

lice [laɪs] npl of **louse.**

licence, (US) **license** ['laɪsns] n autorizzazione f, permesso; (COMM) licenza; (RADIO, TV) canone m, abbonamento; (also: driving ~, (US) driver's ~) patente f di guida; (excessive freedom) licenza; ~ **number** n numero di targa; ~ **plate** n targa.

license ['laɪsns] n (US) = **licence** // vt dare una licenza a; ~**d** a (for alcohol) che ha la licenza di vendere bibite alcoliche.

lick [lɪk] vt leccare.

licorice ['lɪkərɪs] n = **liquorice.**

lid [lɪd] n coperchio.

lie [laɪ] n bugia, menzogna // vi mentire, dire bugie; (pt **lay,** pp **lain**) (rest) giacere, star disteso(a); (in grave) giacere, riposare; (of object: be situated) trovarsi, essere; to ~ **low** (fig) latitare; to ~ **about** vi (things) essere in giro; (person) bighellonare; ~**down** n (Brit): to have a ~**down** sdraiarsi, riposarsi; ~**in** n (Brit): to have a ~**in** rimanere a letto.

lieutenant [lɛf'tɛnənt, (US) luː'tɛnənt] n tenente m.

life [laɪf] n (pl **lives**) vita // cpd di vita; della vita; a vita; ~ **assurance** n (Brit) assicurazione f sulla vita; ~**belt** n (Brit) salvagente m; ~**boat** n scialuppa di salvataggio; ~**guard** n bagnino; ~ **insurance** n = ~ **assurance;** ~ **jacket** n giubbotto di salvataggio; ~**less** a senza vita; ~**like** a verosimile; rassomigliante; ~**long** a per tutta la vita; ~ **preserver** n (US) salvagente m; giubbotto di salvataggio; ~**saver** n bagnino; ~ **sentence** n ergastolo; ~**sized** a a grandezza naturale; ~ **span** n (durata della) vita; ~**style** n stile m di vita; ~ **support system** n respiratore m automatico; ~**time** n: in his ~time durante la sua vita; once in a ~time una volta nella vita.

lift [lɪft] vt sollevare, levare; (steal) prendere, rubare // vi (fog) alzarsi // n (Brit: elevator) ascensore m; to give sb a ~ (Brit) dare un passaggio a qn; ~ **off** n decollo.

light [laɪt] n luce f, lume m; (daylight) luce f, giorno; (lamp) lampada; (AUT: rear ~) luce f di posizione; (: headlamp) fanale m; (for cigarette etc): have you got a ~? ha da accendere? // vt (pt, pp **lighted** or **lit**) (candle, cigarette, fire) accendere; (room) illuminare // a (room, colour) chiaro(a); (not heavy, also fig) leggero(a); ~**s** npl (AUT: traffic ~s) semaforo; to come to ~ venire alla luce, emergere; to ~ **up** vi illuminarsi // vt illuminare; ~ **bulb** n lampadina; ~**en** vi schiarirsi // vt (give light to) illuminare; (make lighter) schiarire; (make less heavy) alleggerire; ~**er** n (also: cigarette ~er) accendino; (boat) chiatta; ~**-headed** a stordito(a); ~**-hearted** a gioioso(a), gaio(a); ~**house** n faro; ~**ing** n illuminazione f; ~**ly** ad leggermente; to get off ~ly cavarsela a buon mercato; ~**ness** n chiarezza; (in weight) leggerezza.

lightning ['laɪtnɪŋ] n lampo, fulmine m; ~ **conductor,** (US) ~ **rod** n parafulmine m.

light pen n penna ottica.

lightweight ['laɪtweɪt] a (suit) leggero(a); (boxer) peso leggero inv // n (BOXING) peso leggero.

like [laɪk] vt (person) volere bene a; (activity, object, food): I ~ **swimming/ that book/chocolate** mi piace nuotare/ quel libro/il cioccolato // prep come // a simile, uguale // n: the ~ uno(a) uguale; his ~**s and dislikes** i suoi gusti, I would ~, I'd ~ mi piacerebbe, vorrei; would you ~ a coffee? gradirebbe un caffè?; be/look ~ sb/sth somigliare a qn/qc; that's just ~ **him** è proprio da lui; do it ~ **this** fallo così; it is nothing ~ ... non è affatto come ...; ~**able** a simpatico(a).

likelihood ['laɪklɪhʊd] n probabilità f.

likely ['laɪklɪ] a probabile; plausibile; he's ~ **to leave** probabilmente partirà, è probabile che parta; not ~! neanche per sogno!

likeness ['laɪknɪs] n somiglianza.

likewise ['laɪkwaɪz] ad similmente, nello stesso modo.

liking ['laɪkɪŋ] n: ~ **(for)** debole m (per).

lilac ['laɪlək] n lilla m inv // a lilla inv.

lily ['lɪlɪ] n giglio; ~ **of the valley** n mughetto.

limb [lɪm] n membro.

limber ['lɪmbə*]: to ~ **up** vi riscaldarsi i muscoli.

limbo ['lɪmbəʊ] n: to be in ~ (fig) essere lasciato(a) nel dimenticatoio.

lime [laɪm] n (tree) tiglio; (fruit) limetta; (GEO) calce f.

limelight ['laɪmlaɪt] *n*: in the ~ *(fig)* alla ribalta, in vista.

limerick ['lɪmərɪk] *n* poesiola umoristica di 5 versi.

limestone ['laɪmstəun] *n* pietra calcarea; *(GEO)* calcare *m*.

limit ['lɪmɪt] *n* limite *m* // *vt* limitare; ~**ed** *a* limitato(a), ristretto(a); to be ~**ed** to limitarsi a; ~**ed (liability) company (Ltd)** *n (Brit)* ≈ società *f inv* a responsabilità limitata (S.r.l.).

limp [lɪmp] *n*: to have a ~ zoppicare // *vi* zoppicare // *a* floscio(a), fiacco(a).

limpet ['lɪmpɪt] *n* patella.

line [laɪn] *n* linea; *(rope)* corda; *(wire)* filo; *(of poem)* verso; *(row, series)* fila, riga; coda // *vt (clothes)*: to ~ **(with)** foderare (di); *(box)*: to ~ **(with)** rivestire *or* foderare (di); *(subj: trees, crowd)* fiancheggiare; ~ **of business** settore *m or* ramo d'attività; in ~ **with** in linea con; **to** ~ **up** *vi* allinearsi, mettersi in fila // *vt* mettere in fila.

lined [laɪnd] *a (face)* rugoso(a); *(paper)* a righe, rigato(a).

linen ['lɪnɪn] *n* biancheria, panni *mpl*; *(cloth)* tela di lino.

liner ['laɪnə*] *n* nave *f* di linea.

linesman ['laɪnzmən] *n* guardalinee *m inv*.

line-up ['laɪnʌp] *n* allineamento, fila; *(SPORT)* formazione *f* di gioco.

linger ['lɪŋɡə*] *vi* attardarsi; indugiare; *(smell, tradition)* persistere.

lingo, ~**es** ['lɪŋɡəu] *n (pej)* gergo.

linguistics [lɪŋ'gwɪstɪks] *n* linguistica.

lining ['laɪnɪŋ] *n* fodera.

link [lɪŋk] *n (of a chain)* anello; *(connection)* legame *m*, collegamento // *vt* collegare, unire, congiungere; ~**s** *npl (GOLF)* pista *or* terreno da golf; **to** ~ **up** *vt* collegare, unire // *vi* riunirsi; associarsi.

lino ['laɪnəu], **linoleum** [lɪ'nəuliəm] *n* linoleum *m inv*.

lion ['laɪən] *n* leone *m*; ~**ess** *n* leonessa.

lip [lɪp] *n* labbro; *(of cup etc)* orlo; *(insolence)* sfacciataggine *f*; ~**read** *vi* leggere sulle labbra; ~ **salve** *n* burro di cacao; ~ **service** *n*: to pay ~ service to sth essere favorevole a qc solo a parole; ~**stick** *n* rossetto.

liqueur [lɪ'kjuə*] *n* liquore *m*.

liquid ['lɪkwɪd] *n* liquido // *a* liquido(a).

liquidize ['lɪkwɪdaɪz] *vt (CULIN)* passare al frullatore; ~**r** *n* frullatore *m* (a brocca).

liquor ['lɪkə*] *n* alcool *m*.

liquorice ['lɪkərɪs] *n* liquirizia.

liquor store *n (US)* negozio di liquori.

lisp [lɪsp] *n* difetto nel pronunciare le sibilanti.

list [lɪst] *n* lista, elenco; *(of ship)* sbandamento // *vt (write down)* mettere in lista; fare una lista di; *(enumerate)*

elencare // *vi (ship)* sbandare.

listen ['lɪsn] *vi* ascoltare; **to** ~ **to** ascoltare; ~**er** *n* ascoltatore/trice.

listless ['lɪstlɪs] *a* apatico(a).

lit [lɪt] *pt, pp of* **light**.

liter ['li:tə*] *n (US)* = **litre**.

literacy ['lɪtərəsɪ] *n* il sapere leggere e scrivere.

literal ['lɪtərl] *a* letterale.

literary ['lɪtərərɪ] *a* letterario(a).

literate ['lɪtərət] *a* che sa leggere e scrivere.

literature ['lɪtərɪtʃə*] *n* letteratura; *(brochures etc)* materiale *m*.

lithe [laɪð] *a* agile, snello(a).

litigation [lɪtɪ'geɪʃən] *n* causa.

litre, (US) liter ['li:tə*] *n* litro.

litter ['lɪtə*] *n (rubbish)* rifiuti *mpl*; *(young animals)* figliata // *vt* sparagliare; lasciare rifiuti in; ~ **bin** *n (Brit)* cestino per rifiuti; ~**ed** *a*: ~**ed with** coperto(a) di.

little ['lɪtl] *a (small)* piccolo(a); *(not much)* poco(a) // *ad* poco; **a** ~ **un po'** (di); **a** ~ **milk** un po' di latte; ~ **by** ~ a poco a poco.

live *vi* [lɪv] vivere; *(reside)* vivere, abitare // *a* [laɪv] *(animal)* vivo(a); *(wire)* sotto tensione; *(broadcast)* diretto(a); **to** ~ **down** *vt* far dimenticare (alla gente); **to** ~ **on** *vt fus (food)* vivere di // *vi* sopravvivere, continuare a vivere; **to** ~ **together** *vi* vivere insieme, convivere; **to** ~ **up to** *vt fus* tener fede a, non venir meno a.

livelihood ['laɪvlɪhud] *n* mezzi *mpl* di sostentamento.

lively ['laɪvlɪ] *a* vivace, vivo(a).

liven up ['laɪvnʌp] *vt (discussion, evening)* animare.

liver ['lɪvə*] *n* fegato.

livery ['lɪvərɪ] *n* livrea.

lives [laɪvz] *npl of* **life**.

livestock ['laɪvstɔk] *n* bestiame *m*.

livid ['lɪvɪd] *a* livido(a); *(furious)* livido(a) di rabbia, furibondo(a).

living ['lɪvɪŋ] *a* vivo(a), vivente // *n*: to earn *or* make a ~ guadagnarsi la vita; ~ **conditions** *npl* condizioni *fpl* di vita; ~ **room** *n* soggiorno; ~ **wage** *n* salario sufficiente per vivere.

lizard ['lɪzəd] *n* lucertola.

load [ləud] *n (weight)* peso; *(ELEC, TECH, thing carried)* carico // *vt (also:* ~ up)*: to* ~ **(with)** *(lorry, ship)* caricare (di); *(gun, camera, COMPUT)* caricare (con); **a** ~ **of**, ~**s of** *(fig)* un sacco di; ~**ed** *a (dice)* falsato(a); *(question)* capzioso(a); *(col: rich)* carico(a); di soldi; *(: drunk)* ubriaco(a); ~**ing bay** *n* piazzola di carico.

loaf [ləuf] *n (pl* **loaves**) pane *m*, pagnotta // *vi (also:* ~ **about**, ~ **around**) bighellonare.

loan [ləun] *n* prestito // *vt* dare in prestito; on ~ in prestito.

loath [ləʊθ] a: to be ~ to do essere restio(a) a fare.

loathe [ləʊð] vt detestare, aborrire.

loaves [ləʊvz] npl of **loaf**.

lobby ['lɔbɪ] n atrio, vestibolo; (POL: pressure group) gruppo di pressione // vt fare pressione su.

lobster ['lɔbstə*] n aragosta.

local ['ləʊkl] a locale // n (Brit: pub) ≈ bar m inv all'angolo; the ~s npl la gente della zona; ~ **call** n (TEL) telefonata urbana; ~ **government** n amministrazione f locale.

locality [ləʊ'kælɪtɪ] n località f inv; (position) posto, luogo.

locally ['ləʊkəlɪ] ad da queste parti; nel vicinato.

locate [ləʊ'keɪt] vt (find) trovare; (situate) collocare.

location [ləʊ'keɪʃən] n posizione f; on ~ (CINEMA) all'esterno.

loch [lɔx] n lago.

lock [lɔk] n (of door, box) serratura; (of canal) chiusa; (of hair) ciocca, riccio // vt (with key) chiudere a chiave; (immobilize) bloccare // vi (door etc) chiudersi; (wheels) bloccarsi, incepparsi.

locker ['lɔkə*] n armadietto.

locket ['lɔkɪt] n medaglione m.

locksmith ['lɔksmɪθ] n magnano.

lock-up ['lɔkʌp] n (garage) box m inv.

locomotive [ləʊkə'məʊtɪv] n locomotiva.

locum ['ləʊkəm] n (MED) medico sostituto.

locust ['ləʊkəst] n locusta.

lodge [lɔdʒ] n casetta, portineria // vi (person): to ~ (with) essere a pensione (presso or da) // vt (appeal etc) presentare, fare; to ~ a complaint presentare un reclamo; ~r n affittuario/a; (with room and meals) pensionante m/f.

lodgings ['lɔdʒɪŋz] npl camera d'affitto; camera ammobiliata.

loft [lɔft] n solaio, soffitta; (AGR) granaio.

lofty ['lɔftɪ] a alto(a); (haughty) altezzoso(a).

log [lɔg] n (of wood) ceppo; (book) = **logbook**.

logbook ['lɔgbuk] n (NAUT, AVIAT) diario di bordo; (AUT) libretto di circolazione; (of lorry driver) registro di viaggio; (of events, movement of goods etc) registro.

loggerheads ['lɔgəhedz] npl: at ~ (with) ai ferri corti (con).

logic ['lɔdʒɪk] n logica; ~al a logico(a).

loin [lɔɪn] n (CULIN) lombata.

loiter ['lɔɪtə*] vi attardarsi; to ~ (about) indugiare, bighellonare.

loll [lɔl] vi (also: ~ about) essere stravaccato(a).

lollipop ['lɔlɪpɔp] n lecca lecca m inv; ~ **man/lady** n (Brit) impiegato/a che aiuta i bambini ad attraversare la strada in vicinanza di scuole.

London ['lʌndən] n Londra; ~**er** n londinese m/f.

lone [ləʊn] a solitario(a).

loneliness ['ləʊnlɪnɪs] n solitudine f, isolamento.

lonely ['ləʊnlɪ] a solo(a); solitario(a), isolato(a).

long [lɔŋ] a lungo(a) // ad a lungo, per molto tempo // vi: to ~ **for sth/to do** desiderare qc/di fare; non veder l'ora di aver qc/di fare; **so** or **as** ~ **as** (while) finché; (provided that) sempre che + sub; **don't be** ~! fai presto!; **how** ~ **is this river/course?** quanto è lungo questo fiume/corso?; **6 metres** ~ lungo 6 metri; **6 months** ~ che dura 6 mesi, di 6 mesi; **all night** ~ tutta la notte; **he no** ~**er comes** non viene più; ~ **before** molto tempo prima; **before** ~ (+ future) presto, fra poco; (+ past) poco tempo dopo; **at** ~ **last** finalmente; ~-**distance** a (race) di fondo; (call) interurbano(a); ~ **hand** n scrittura normale, ~**ing** n desiderio, voglia, brama // a di desiderio; (fig) di nostalgia.

longitude ['lɔŋgɪtjuːd] n longitudine f.

long: ~ **jump** n salto in lungo; ~-**playing record (L.P.)** n (disco) 33 giri m inv; ~-**range** a a lunga portata; ~-**sighted** a presbite; (fig) lungimirante; ~-**standing** a di vecchia data; ~-**suffering** a estremamente paziente; infinitamente tollerante; ~-**term** a a lungo termine; ~ **wave** n onde fpl lunghe; ~-**winded** a prolisso(a), interminabile.

loo [luː] n (Brit col) W.C. m inv, cesso.

look [luk] vi guardare; (seem) sembrare, parere; (building etc): to ~ **south/on to the sea** dare a sud/sul mare // n sguardo; (appearance) aspetto, aria; ~s npl aspetto; bellezza; **to** ~ **after** vt fus occuparsi di, prendere cura di; (keep an eye on) guardare, badare a; **to** ~ **at** vt fus guardare; **to** ~ **back** vi: to ~ **back at** voltarsi a guardare; **to** ~ **back on** (event etc) ripensare a; **to** ~ **down on** vt fus (fig) guardare dall'alto, disprezzare; **to** ~ **for** vt fus cercare; **to** ~ **forward to** vt fus non veder l'ora di; (in letters): **we** ~ **forward to hearing from you** in attesa di una vostra gentile risposta; **to** ~ **into** vt fus esaminare; **to** ~ **on** vi fare da spettatore; **to** ~ **out** vi (beware): to ~ **out (for)** stare in guardia (per); **to** ~ **out for sb/sth** cercare; (watch for): to ~ **out for sb/sth** guardare se arriva qn/qc; **to** ~ **round** vi (turn) girarsi, voltarsi; (in shop) dare un'occhiata; **to** ~ **to** vt fus stare attento(a) a; (rely on) contare su; **to** ~

up vi alzare gli occhi; (improve) migliorare // vt (word) cercare; (friend) andare a trovare; **to ~ up to** vt fus avere rispetto per; **~out** n posto d'osservazione; guardia; **to be on the ~out (for)** stare in guardia (per).

loom [lu:m] n telaio // vi sorgere; (fig) minacciare.

loony ['lu:nɪ] a (col) pazzo/a.

loop [lu:p] n cappio; **~hole** n via d'uscita; scappatoia.

loose [lu:s] a (knot) sciolto(a); (screw) allentato(a); (stone) cadente; (clothes) ampio(a), largo(a); (animal) in libertà, scappato(a); (life, morals) dissoluto(a); (discipline) allentato(a); (thinking) poco rigoroso(a), vago(a); **~ change** n spiccioli mpl, moneta; **~ chippings** npl (on road) ghiaino; **~ end** n: **to be at a ~ end** or (US) **at ~ ends** non saper che fare; **~ly** ad lentamente; approssimativamente; **~n** vt sciogliere.

loot [lu:t] n bottino // vt saccheggiare.

lop [lɔp] vt (also: **~ off**) tagliare via, recidere.

lop-sided ['lɔp'saɪdɪd] a non equilibrato(a), asimmetrico(a).

lord [lɔ:d] n signore m; **L~** Smith lord Smith; **the L~** il Signore; **the (House of) L~s** (Brit) la Camera dei Lord; **~ship** n: **your L~ship** Sua Eccellenza.

lore [lɔ:*] n tradizioni fpl.

lorry ['lɔrɪ] n (Brit) camion m inv; **~ driver** n (Brit) camionista m.

lose [lu:z], pt, pp **lost** vt perdere; (pursuers) distanziare // vi perdere; **to ~** (time) (clock) ritardare; **to get lost** vi perdersi, smarrirsi; **~r** n perdente m/f.

loss [lɔs] n perdita; **to be at a ~** essere perplesso(a).

lost [lɔst] pt, pp of **lose** // a perduto(a); **~ property**, (US) **~ and found** n oggetti mpl smarriti.

lot [lɔt] n (at auctions) lotto; (destiny) destino, sorte f; **the ~** tutto(a) quanto(a); tutti(e) quanti(e); **a ~** molto; **a ~ of** una gran quantità di, un sacco di; **~s of** molto(a); **to draw ~s (for sth)** tirare a sorte (per qc).

lotion ['ləʊʃən] n lozione f.

lottery ['lɔtərɪ] n lotteria.

loud [laud] a forte, alto(a); (gaudy) vistoso(a), sgargiante // ad (speak etc) forte; **~hailer** n (Brit) portavoce m inv; **~ly** ad fortemente, ad alta voce; **~speaker** n altoparlante m.

lounge [laundʒ] n salotto, soggiorno // vi oziare; starsene colle mani in mano; **~ suit** n (Brit) completo da uomo.

louse [laus], pl **lice** n pidocchio.

lousy ['lauzɪ] a (fig) orrendo(a), schifoso(a).

lout [laut] n zoticone m.

louvre, (US) **louver** ['lu:və*] a (door, window) con apertura a gelosia.

lovable ['lʌvəbl] a simpatico(a), carino(a); amabile.

love [lʌv] n amore m // vt amare; voler bene a; **to ~ to do: I ~ to do** mi piace fare; **to be in ~ with** essere innamorato(a) di; **to make ~** fare l'amore; "**15 ~**" (TENNIS) "15 a zero"; **~ affair** n relazione f; **~ life** n vita sentimentale.

lovely ['lʌvlɪ] a bello(a); (delicious: smell, meal) buono(a).

lover ['lʌvə*] n amante m/f; (amateur): **a ~ of** un(un')amante di; un(un')appassionato(a) di.

loving ['lʌvɪŋ] a affettuoso(a), amoroso(a), tenero(a).

low [ləʊ] a basso(a) // ad in basso // n (METEOR) depressione f // vi (cow) muggire; **to feel ~** sentirsi giù; **to turn (down) ~** vt abbassare; **~cut** a (dress) scollato(a); **~er** vt calare; (reduce) abbassare; **~fat** a magro(a); **~lands** npl (GEO) pianura; **~ly** a umile, modesto(a); **~lying** a a basso livello.

loyal ['lɔɪəl] a fedele, leale; **~ty** n fedeltà, lealtà.

lozenge ['lɔzɪndʒ] n (MED) pastiglia; (GEOM) losanga.

L.P. n abbr = **long-playing record.**

L-plates ['elpleɪts] npl (Brit) cartelli sui veicoli dei guidatori principianti.

Ltd abbr = **limited.**

lubricant ['lu:brɪkənt] n lubrificante m.

lubricate ['lu:brɪkeɪt] vt lubrificare.

luck [lʌk] n fortuna, sorte f; **bad ~** sfortuna, mala sorte; **good ~!** buona fortuna!; **~ily** ad fortunatamente, per fortuna; **~y** a fortunato(a); (number etc) che porta fortuna.

ludicrous ['lu:dɪkrəs] a ridicolo(a), assurdo(a).

lug [lʌg] vt trascinare.

luggage ['lʌgɪdʒ] n bagagli mpl; **~ rack** n portabagagli m inv.

lukewarm ['lu:kwɔ:m] a tiepido(a).

lull [lʌl] n intervallo di calma // vt (child) cullare; (person, fear) acquietare, calmare.

lullaby ['lʌləbaɪ] n ninnananna.

lumbago [lʌm'beɪgəʊ] n lombaggine f.

lumber ['lʌmbə*] n roba vecchia; **~jack** n boscaiolo.

luminous ['lu:mɪnəs] a luminoso(a).

lump [lʌmp] n pezzo; (in sauce) grumo; (swelling) gonfiore m // vt (also: **~ together**) riunire, mettere insieme; **a ~ sum** una somma globale.

lunacy ['lu:nəsɪ] n demenza, follia, pazzia.

lunar ['lu:nə*] a lunare.

lunatic ['lu:nətɪk] a, n pazzo(a), matto(a).

lunch [lʌntʃ] n pranzo, colazione f.

luncheon ['lʌntʃən] n pranzo; **~ meat** n

≈ mortadella; ~ **voucher** n buono m pasto inv.

lung [lʌŋ] n polmone m.

lunge [lʌndʒ] vi (also: ~ **forward**) fare un balzo in avanti; to ~ at balzare su.

lurch [ləːtʃ] vi vacillare, barcollare // n scatto improvviso; to leave sb in the ~ piantare in asso qn.

lure [luə*] n richiamo; lusinga // vt attirare (con l'inganno).

lurid ['luərɪd] a sgargiante; (details etc) impressionante.

lurk [ləːk] vi stare in agguato.

luscious ['lʌʃəs] a succulento(a); delizioso(a).

lush [lʌʃ] a lussureggiante.

lust [lʌst] n lussuria; cupidigia; desiderio; (fig); ~ **for** sete f di; **to** ~ **after** vt fus bramare, desiderare.

lusty ['lʌstɪ] a vigoroso(a), robusto(a).

Luxembourg ['lʌksəmbəːg] n (state) Lussemburgo m; (city) Lussemburgo f.

luxuriant [lʌg'zjuərɪənt] a lussureggiante.

luxurious [lʌg'zjuərɪəs] a sontuoso(a), di lusso.

luxury ['lʌkʃərɪ] n lusso // cpd di lusso.

lying ['laɪɪŋ] n bugie fpl, menzogne fpl.

lynch [lɪntʃ] vt linciare.

lynx [lɪnks] n lince f.

lyric ['lɪrɪk] a lirico(a); ~s npl (of song) parole fpl; ~al a lirico(a).

M

m. abbr = **metre, mile, million.**

M.A. abbr = **Master of Arts.**

mac [mæk] n (Brit) impermeabile m.

macaroni [mækə'rəunɪ] n maccheroni mpl.

mace [meɪs] n mazza; (spice) macis m or f.

machine [mə'ʃiːn] n macchina // vt (dress etc) cucire a macchina; ~ **gun** n mitragliatrice f; ~**ry** n macchinario, macchine fpl; (fig) macchina.

mackerel ['mækrl] n (pl inv) sgombro.

mackintosh ['mækɪntɒʃ] n (Brit) impermeabile m.

mad [mæd] a matto(a), pazzo(a); (foolish) sciocco(a); (angry) furioso(a).

madam ['mædəm] n signora.

madden ['mædn] vt fare infuriare.

made [meɪd] pt, pp of **make.**

Madeira [mə'dɪərə] n (GEO) Madera; (wine) madera.

made-to-measure ['meɪdtə'meʒə*] a (Brit) fatto(a) su misura.

madly ['mædlɪ] ad follemente; (love) alla follia.

madman ['mædmən] n pazzo, alienato.

madness ['mædnɪs] n pazzia.

magazine [mægə'ziːn] n (PRESS) rivista; (MIL: store) magazzino, deposito; (of firearm) caricatore m.

maggot ['mægət] n baco, verme m.

magic ['mædʒɪk] n magia // a magico(a); ~**al** a magico(a); ~**ian** [mə'dʒɪʃən] n mago/a.

magistrate ['mædʒɪstreɪt] n magistrato; giudice m/f.

magnet ['mægnɪt] n magnete m, calamita; ~**ic** [-'nɛtɪk] a magnetico(a).

magnificent [mæg'nɪfɪsnt] a magnifico(a).

magnify ['mægnɪfaɪ] vt ingrandire; ~**ing glass** n lente f d'ingrandimento.

magnitude ['mægnɪtjuːd] n grandezza; importanza.

magpie ['mægpaɪ] n gazza.

mahogany [mə'hɒgənɪ] n mogano // cpd di or in mogano.

maid [meɪd] n domestica; (in hotel) cameriera; old ~ (pej) vecchia zitella.

maiden ['meɪdn] n fanciulla // a (aunt etc) nubile; (speech, voyage) inaugurale; ~ **name** n nome m nubile or da ragazza.

mail [meɪl] n posta // vt spedire (per posta); ~**box** n (US) cassetta delle lettere; ~**ing list** n elenco d'indirizzi; ~**order** n vendita (or acquisto) per corrispondenza.

maim [meɪm] vt mutilare.

main [meɪn] a principale // n (pipe) conduttura principale; the ~s (ELEC) la linea principale; in the ~ nel complesso, nell'insieme; ~**frame** n (COMPUT) mainframe m inv; ~**land** n continente m; ~**ly** ad principalmente, soprattutto; ~ **road** n strada principale; ~**stay** n (fig) sostegno principale; ~**stream** n (fig) corrente f principale.

maintain [meɪn'teɪn] vt mantenere; (affirm) sostenere; **maintenance** ['meɪntənəns] n manutenzione f; (alimony) alimenti mpl.

maize [meɪz] n granturco, mais m.

majestic [mə'dʒɛstɪk] a maestoso(a).

majesty ['mædʒɪstɪ] n maestà f inv.

major ['meɪdʒə*] n (MIL) maggiore m // a (greater, MUS) maggiore; (in importance) principale, importante.

Majorca [mə'jɔːkə] n Maiorca.

majority [mə'dʒɔrɪtɪ] n maggioranza.

make [meɪk] vt (pt, pp **made**) fare; (manufacture) fare, fabbricare; (cause to be): to ~ sb sad etc rendere qn triste etc; (force): to ~ sb do sth costringere qn a fare qc, far fare qc a qn; (equal): 2 and 2 ~ 4 2 più 2 fa 4 // n fabbricazione f; (brand) marca; to ~ a fool of sb far fare a qn la figura dello scemo; to ~ a profit realizzare un profitto; to ~ a loss subire una perdita; to ~ it (arrive) arrivare; (achieve sth) farcela; what time do you ~ it? che ora fai?; to ~ do with arrangiarsi con; **to** ~ **for** vt fus (place) avviarsi verso; **to** ~ **out** vt (write out) scrivere; (: cheque) emettere; (*understand*) capire; (*see*) distinguere; (: *numbers*) decifrare; **to ~ up** vt (*invent*) inventare; (*parcel*) fare // vi conciliarsi; (*with cosmetics*) truccarsi; **to ~ up for** vt fus compensare; ricuperare; **~-believe** n: a world of ~-believe un mondo di favole; it's just ~-believe è tutta un'invenzione; **~r** n fabbricante m; creatore/trice, autore/trice; **~shift** a improvvisato(a); **~-up** n trucco; **~-up remover** n struccatore m.

making ['meɪkɪŋ] n (*fig*): **in the ~** in formazione; **to have the ~s of** (*actor, athlete etc*) avere la stoffa di.

maladjusted [mælə'dʒʌstɪd] a disadattato(a).

malaria [mə'lɛərɪə] n malaria.

Malaya [mə'leɪə] n Malesia.

male [meɪl] n (*BIOL, ELEC*) maschio // a maschile; maschio(a).

malevolent [mə'lɛvələnt] a malevolo(a).

malfunction [mæl'fʌŋkʃən] n funzione f difettosa.

malice ['mælɪs] n malevolenza; **malicious** [mə'lɪʃəs] a malevolo(a); (*LAW*) doloso(a).

malign [mə'laɪn] vt malignare su; calunniare.

malignant [mə'lɪgnənt] a (*MED*) maligno(a).

mall [mɔːl] n (*also*: **shopping ~**) centro commerciale.

mallet ['mælɪt] n maglio.

malnutrition [mælnjuː'trɪʃən] n denutrizione f.

malpractice [mæl'præktɪs] n prevaricazione f; negligenza.

malt [mɔːlt] n malto.

Malta ['mɔːltə] n Malta.

mammal ['mæml] n mammifero.

mammoth ['mæməθ] n mammut m inv // a enorme, gigantesco(a).

man [mæn] n (pl **men**) uomo; (*CHESS*) pezzo; (*DRAUGHTS*) pedina // vt fornire d'uomini; stare a; essere di servizio a; **an old ~** un vecchio; **~ and wife** marito e moglie.

manage ['mænɪdʒ] vi farcela // vt (*be in charge of*) occuparsi di; gestire; **to ~ to do sth** riuscire a far qc; **~able** a maneggevole; fattibile; **~ment** n amministrazione f, direzione f; **~r** n direttore m; (*of shop, restaurant*) gerente m; (*of artist*) manager m inv; **~ress** [-ə'rɛs] n direttrice f; gerente f; **~rial** [-ə'dʒɪərɪəl] a dirigenziale; **managing** a: managing director amministratore m delegato.

mandarin ['mændərɪn] n (*person, fruit*) mandarino.

mandatory ['mændətərɪ] a obbligatorio(a); ingiuntivo(a).

mane [meɪn] n criniera.

maneuver [mə'nuːvə*] etc (*US*) =

manoeuvre etc.

manfully ['mænfəlɪ] ad valorosamente.

mangle ['mæŋgl] vt straziare; mutilare // n strizzatoio.

mango, **~es** [ˈmæŋgəʊ] n mango.

mangy ['meɪndʒɪ] a rognoso(a).

manhandle [mæn'hændl] vt malmenare.

manhole ['mænhəʊl] n botola stradale.

manhood ['mænhud] n età virile; virilità.

man-hour ['mæn'auə*] n ora di lavoro.

manhunt ['mænhʌnt] n caccia all'uomo.

mania ['meɪnɪə] n mania; **~c** ['meɪnɪæk] n maniaco/a.

manic ['mænɪk] a (*behaviour, activity*) maniacale.

manicure ['mænɪkjuə*] n manicure f inv; **~ set** n trousse f inv della manicure.

manifest ['mænɪfɛst] vt manifestare // a manifesto(a), palese.

manifesto [mænɪ'fɛstəu] n manifesto.

manipulate [mə'nɪpjuleɪt] vt manipolare.

mankind [mæn'kaɪnd] n umanità, genere m umano.

manly ['mænlɪ] a virile; coraggioso(a).

man-made ['mæn'meɪd] a sintetico(a); artificiale.

manner ['mænə*] n maniera, modo; **~s** npl maniere fpl; **~ism** n vezzo, tic m inv.

manoeuvre, (*US*) **maneuver** [mə'nuː'və*] vt manovrare // vi far manovre // n manovra.

manor ['mænə*] n (*also*: **~ house**) maniero.

manpower ['mænpauə*] n manodopera.

mansion ['mænʃən] n casa signorile.

manslaughter ['mænslɔ:tə*] n omicidio preterintenzionale.

mantelpiece ['mæntlpi:s] n mensola del caminetto.

Mantua ['mæntjuə] n Mantova.

manual ['mænjuəl] a manuale // n manuale m.

manufacture [mænju'fæktʃə*] vt fabbricare // n fabbricazione f, manifattura; **~r** n fabbricante m.

manure [mə'njuə*] n concime m.

manuscript ['mænjuskrɪpt] n manoscritto.

many ['mɛnɪ] a molti(e) // pronoun molti(e), un gran numero; **a great ~** moltissimi(e), un gran numero (di); **~ a ...** molti(e) ..., più di un(a) ... .

map [mæp] n carta (geografica) // vt fare una carta di; **to ~ out** vt tracciare un piano di.

maple ['meɪpl] n acero.

mar [mɑ:*] vt sciupare.

marathon ['mærəθən] n maratona.

marauder [mə'rɔːdə*] n saccheggiatore m; predatore m.

marble ['mɑːbl] n marmo; (*toy*) pallina, bilia; **~s** n (*game*) palline, bilie.

March [mɑːtʃ] n marzo.

march [mɑ:tʃ] *vi* marciare; sfilare // *n* marcia; (*demonstration*) dimostrazione *f*.

mare [mɛə*] *n* giumenta.

margarine [mɑ:dʒə'ri:n] *n* margarina.

margin ['mɑ:dʒɪn] *n* margine *m*; **~al (seat)** *n* (*POL*) seggio elettorale ottenuto con una stretta maggioranza.

marigold ['mærɪgəʊld] *n* calendola.

marijuana [mærɪ'wɑ:nə] *n* marijuana.

marine [mə'ri:n] *a* (*animal*, *plant*) marino(a); (*forces*, *engineering*) marittimo(a) // *n* fante *m* di marina; (*US*) marine *m inv*.

marital ['mærɪtl] *a* maritale, coniugale; **~ status** stato coniugale.

mark [mɑ:k] *n* segno; (*stain*) macchia; (*of skid etc*) traccia; (*Brit SCOL*) voto; (*SPORT*) bersaglio; (*currency*) marco // *vt* segnare; (*stain*) macchiare; (*Brit SCOL*) dare un voto a; correggere; **to ~ time** segnare il passo; **to ~ out** *vt* delimitare; **~ed** *a* spiccato(a), chiaro(a); **~er** *n* (*sign*) segno; (*bookmark*) segnalibro.

market ['mɑ:kɪt] *n* mercato // *vt* (*COMM*) mettere in vendita; **~ garden** *n* (*Brit*) orto industriale; **~ing** *n* marketing *m*; **~ place** *n* piazza del mercato; (*COMM*) piazza, mercato; **~ research** *n* indagine *f or* ricerca di mercato; **~ value** *n* valore *m* di mercato.

marksman ['mɑ:ksmən] *n* tiratore *m* scelto.

marmalade ['mɑ:məleɪd] *n* marmellata d'arance.

maroon [mə'ru:n] *vt* (*fig*): to be **~ed** (in *or* at) essere abbandonato(a) (in) // *a* bordeaux *inv*.

marquee [mɑ:'ki:] *n* padiglione *m*.

marquess, marquis ['mɑ:kwɪs] *n* marchese *m*.

marriage ['mærɪdʒ] *n* matrimonio; **~ bureau** *n* agenzia matrimoniale; **~ certificate** *n* certificato di matrimonio.

married ['mærɪd] *a* sposato(a); (*life, love*) coniugale, matrimoniale.

marrow ['mærəʊ] *n* midollo; (*vegetable*) zucca.

marry ['mærɪ] *vt* sposare, sposarsi con; (*subj: father, priest etc*) dare in matrimonio // *vi* (*also*: **get married**) sposarsi.

Mars [mɑ:z] *n* (*planet*) Marte *m*.

marsh [mɑ:ʃ] *n* palude *f*.

marshal ['mɑ:ʃl] *n* maresciallo; (*US*: *fire*) capo; (*: police*) capitano // *vt* adunare.

martyr ['mɑ:tə*] *n* martire *m/f* // *vt* martirizzare; **~dom** *n* martirio.

marvel ['mɑ:vl] *n* meraviglia // *vi*: to **~** (at) meravigliarsi (di); **~lous**, (*US*) **~ous** *a* meraviglioso(a).

Marxist ['mɑ:ksɪst] *a, n* marxista (*m/f*).

marzipan ['mɑ:zɪpæn] *n* marzapane *m*.

mascara [mæs'kɑ:rə] *n* mascara *m*.

masculine ['mæskjʊlɪn] *a* maschile // *n* genere *m* maschile.

mashed [mæʃt] *a*: **~ potatoes** purè *m* di patate.

mask [mɑ:sk] *n* maschera // *vt* mascherare.

mason ['meɪsn] *n* (*also*: **stone~**) scalpellino; (*also*: **free~**) massone *m*; **~ry** *n* muratura.

masquerade [mæskə'reɪd] *n* ballo in maschera; (*fig*) mascherata // *vi*: to **~** as farsi passare per.

mass [mæs] *n* moltitudine *f*, massa; (*PHYSICS*) massa; (*REL*) messa // *vi* ammassarsi; **the ~es** le masse.

massacre ['mæsəkə*] *n* massacro.

massage ['mæsɑ:ʒ] *n* massaggio.

masseur [mæ'sə:*] *n* massaggiatore *m*; **masseuse** [-'sə:z] *n* massaggiatrice *f*.

massive ['mæsɪv] *a* enorme, massiccio(a).

mass media *npl* mass media *mpl*.

mass-produce ['mæsprə'dju:s] *vt* produrre in serie.

mast [mɑ:st] *n* albero.

master ['mɑ:stə*] *n* padrone *m*, (*ART etc, teacher*: *in primary school*) maestro; (*: in secondary school*) professore *m*; (*title for boys*): M~ X Signorino X // *vt* domare; (*learn*) imparare a fondo; (*understand*) conoscere a fondo; **~ key** *n* chiave *f* maestra; **~ly** *a* magistrale; **~mind** *n* mente *f* superiore // *vt* essere il cervello di; **M~ of Arts/Science (M.A./M.Sc.)** *n* Master *m inv* in lettere/ scienze; **~piece** *n* capolavoro; **~y** *n* dominio; padronanza.

mat [mæt] *n* stuoia; (*also*: **door~**) stoino, zerbino // *a* = **matt**.

match [mætʃ] *n* fiammifero; (*game*) partita, incontro; (*fig*) uguale *m/f*; matrimonio; partito // *vt* intonare; (*go well with*) andare benissimo con; (*equal*) uguagliare // *vi* combaciare; **to be a good ~** andare bene; **~box** *n* scatola per fiammiferi; **~ing** *a* ben assortito(a).

mate [meɪt] *n* compagno/a di lavoro; (*col*: *friend*) amico/a; (*animal*) compagno/a; (*in merchant navy*) secondo // *vi* accoppiarsi // *vt* accoppiare.

material [mə'tɪərɪəl] *n* (*substance*) materiale *m*, materia; (*cloth*) stoffa // *a* materiale; (*important*) essenziale; **~s** *npl* materiali *mpl*.

maternal [mə'tə:nl] *a* materno(a).

maternity [mə'tə:nɪtɪ] *n* maternità; **~ dress** *n* vestito *m* pre-maman *inv*; **~ hospital** *n* ≈ clinica ostetrica.

math [mæθ] *n* (*US*) = **maths**.

mathematical [mæθə'mætɪkl] *a* matematico(a).

mathematics [mæθə'mætɪks] *n* matematica.

maths [mæθs], (US) **math** [mæθ] n matematica.

matinée ['mætɪneɪ] n matinée f inv.

mating ['meɪtɪŋ] n accoppiamento.

matriculation [mətrɪkju'leɪʃən] n immatricolazione f.

matrimonial [mætrɪ'məunɪəl] a matrimoniale, coniugale.

matrimony ['mætrɪmənɪ] n matrimonio.

matron ['meɪtrən] n (in hospital) capoinfermiera; (in school) infermiera; ~**ly** a da matrona.

mat(t) [mæt] a opaco(a).

matted ['mætɪd] a ingarbugliato(a).

matter ['mætə*] n questione f; (PHYSICS) materia, sostanza; (content) contenuto; (MED: pus) pus m // vi importare; it doesn't ~ non importa; (I don't mind) non fa niente; what's the ~? che cosa c'è?; no ~ what qualsiasi cosa accada; as a ~ of course come cosa naturale; as a ~ of fact in verità; ~-**of-fact** a prosaico(a).

mattress ['mætrɪs] n materasso.

mature [mə'tjuə*] a maturo(a); (cheese) stagionato(a) // vi maturare; stagionare; (COMM) scadere.

maul [mɔ:l] vt lacerare.

mauve [məuv] a malva inv.

maxim ['mæksɪm] n massima.

maximum ['mæksɪməm] a massimo(a) // n (pl **maxima** ['mæksɪmə]) massimo.

May [meɪ] n maggio.

may [meɪ] vi (conditional: **might**) (indicating possibility): he ~ come può darsi che venga; (be allowed to): ~ I smoke? posso fumare?; (wishes): ~ God bless you! Dio la benedica!

maybe ['meɪbɪ] ad forse, può darsi; ~ he'll ... può darsi che lui ... +sub, forse lui ....

May Day n il primo maggio.

mayhem ['meɪhem] n cagnara.

mayonnaise [meɪə'neɪz] n maionese f.

mayor [meə*] n sindaco; ~**ess** n sindaco (donna); moglie f del sindaco.

maze [meɪz] n labirinto, dedalo.

M.D. abbr = Doctor of Medicine.

me [mi:] pronoun mi, m' + vowel or silent 'h'; (stressed, after prep) me; he heard ~ mi ha or m'ha sentito; give ~ a book dammi (or mi dia) un libro; it's ~ sono io; with ~ con me; without ~ senza di me.

meadow ['medəu] n prato.

meagre, (US) **meager** ['mi:gə*] a magro(a).

meal [mi:l] n pasto; (flour) farina; ~**time** n l'ora di mangiare.

mean [mi:n] a (with money) avaro(a), gretto(a); (unkind) meschino(a), maligno(a); (average) medio(a) // vt (pt, pp **meant**) (signify) significare, voler dire; (intend): to ~ to do aver l'intenzione di fare // n mezzo; (MATH) media; ~**s** npl

mezzi mpl; by ~**s** of per mezzo di; (person) a mezzo di; by all ~**s** ma certo, prego; to be meant for essere destinato(a) a; do you ~ it? dice sul serio?; what do you ~? che cosa vuol dire?

meander [mɪ'ændə*] vi far meandri; (fig) divagare.

meaning ['mi:nɪŋ] n significato, senso; ~**ful** a significativo(a); ~**less** a senza senso.

meant [ment] pt, pp of **mean**.

meantime ['mi:ntaɪm] ad, **meanwhile** ['mi:nwaɪl] ad (also: **in the** ~) nel frattempo.

measles ['mi:zlz] n morbillo.

measly ['mi:zlɪ] a (col) miserabile.

measure ['meʒə*] vt, vi misurare // n misura; (ruler) metro; ~**ments** npl misure fpl; chest/hip ~ment giro petto/fianchi.

meat [mi:t] n carne f; ~**ball** n polpetta di carne; ~**y** a che sa di carne; (fig) sostanzioso(a).

Mecca ['mekə] n Mecca.

mechanic [mɪ'kænɪk] n meccanico; ~**al** a meccanico(a); ~**s** n meccanica // npl meccanismo.

mechanism ['mekənɪzəm] n meccanismo.

medal ['medl] n medaglia; ~**lion** [mɪ'dælɪən] n medaglione m.

meddle ['medl] vi: to ~ in immischiarsi in, mettere le mani in; to ~ with toccare.

media ['mi:dɪə] npl media mpl.

mediaeval [medɪ'i:vl] a = **medieval**.

median ['mi:dɪən] n mediana; (US: also: ~ **strip**) banchina f spartitraffico.

mediate ['mi:dɪeɪt] vi interporsi; fare da mediatore/trice.

Medicaid ['medɪkeɪd] n (US) assistenza medica ai poveri.

medical ['medɪkl] a medico(a).

Medicare ['medɪkeə*] n (US) assistenza medica agli anziani.

medication [medɪ'keɪʃən] n medicinali mpl, farmaci mpl.

medicine ['medsɪn] n medicina.

medieval [medɪ'i:vl] a medievale.

mediocre [mi:dɪ'əukə*] a mediocre.

meditate ['medɪteɪt] vi: to ~ (on) meditare (su).

Mediterranean [medɪtə'reɪnɪən] a mediterraneo(a); the ~ (Sea) il (mare) Mediterraneo.

medium ['mi:dɪəm] a medio(a) // n (pl **media**: means) mezzo; (pl **mediums**: person) medium m inv; the happy ~ una giusta via di mezzo; ~ **wave** n onde fpl medie.

medley ['medlɪ] n selezione f.

meek [mi:k] a dolce, umile.

meet [mi:t], pt, pp **met** vt incontrare; (for the first time) fare la conoscenza di;

(*fig*) affrontare; soddisfare; raggiungere // *vi* incontrarsi; (*in session*) riunirsi; (*join: objects*) unirsi; **I'll ~ you at the station** verrò a prenderla alla stazione; **to ~ with** *vt fus* incontrare; **~ing** *n* incontro; (*session: of club etc*) riunione *f*; (*interview*) intervista; **she's at a ~ing** (*COMM*) è in riunione.

megabyte ['mɛgəbaɪt] *n* (*COMPUT*) megabyte *m inv*.

megaphone ['mɛgəfəʊn] *n* megafono.

melancholy ['mɛlənkəlɪ] *n* malinconia // *a* malinconico(a).

mellow ['mɛləʊ] *a* (*wine, sound*) ricco(a); (*person, light*) dolce; (*colour*) caldo(a); (*fruit*) maturo(a) // *vi* (*person*) addolcirsi.

melody ['mɛlədɪ] *n* melodia.

melon ['mɛlən] *n* melone *m*.

melt [mɛlt] *vi* (*gen*) sciogliersi, struggersi; (*metals*) fondersi; (*fig*) intenerirsi // *vt* sciogliere, struggere; fondere; (*person*) commuovere; **to ~ away** *vi* sciogliersi completamente; **to ~ down** *vt* fondere; **~down** *n* (*in nuclear reactor*) fusione *f* (dovuta a surriscaldamento); **~ing pot** *n* (*fig*) crogiolo.

member ['mɛmbə*] *n* membro; **M~ of the European Parliament (MEP)** *n* (*Brit*) eurodeputato; **M~ of Parliament (MP)** *n* (*Brit*) deputato; **~ship** *n* iscrizione *f*; (*numero d'*)iscritti *mpl*, membri *mpl*; **~ship card** *n* tessera (di iscrizione).

memento [mə'mɛntəʊ] *n* ricordo, souvenir *m inv*.

memo ['mɛməʊ] *n* appunto; (*COMM etc*) comunicazione *f* di servizio.

memoirs ['mɛmwɑ:z] *npl* memorie *fpl*, ricordi *mpl*.

memorandum, *pl* **memoranda** [mɛmə'rændəm, -də] *n* appunto; (*COMM etc*) comunicazione *f* di servizio; (*DIPLOMACY*) memorandum *m inv*.

memorial [mɪ'mɔ:rɪəl] *n* monumento commemorativo // *a* commemorativo(a).

memorize ['mɛmɔraɪz] *vt* imparare a memoria.

memory ['mɛmɔrɪ] *n* (*also COMPUT*) memoria; (*recollection*) ricordo.

men [mɛn] *npl of* **man**.

menace ['mɛnɔs] *n* minaccia // *vt* minacciare.

menagerie [mɪ'nædʒərɪ] *n* serraglio.

mend [mɛnd] *vt* aggiustare, riparare; (*darn*) rammendare // *n* rammendo; **on the ~** in via di guarigione.

menial ['mi:nɪəl] *a* da servo, domestico(a); umile.

meningitis [mɛnɪn'dʒaɪtɪs] *n* meningite *f*.

menopause ['mɛnəʊpɔ:z] *n* menopausa.

menstruation [mɛnstru'eɪʃən] *n* mestruazione *f*.

mental ['mɛntl] *a* mentale.

mentality [mɛn'tælɪt] *n* mentalità *f inv*.

menthol ['mɛnθɒl] *n* mentolo.

mention ['mɛnʃən] *n* menzione *f* // *vt* menzionare, far menzione di; **don't ~ it!** non c'è di che!, prego!

menu ['mɛnju:] *n* (*set ~, COMPUT*) menù *m inv*; (*printed*) carta.

MEP *n abbr* = **Member of the European Parliament.**

mercenary ['mɔ:sɪnərɪ] *a* venale // *n* mercenario.

merchandise ['mɔ:tʃəndaɪz] *n* merci *fpl*.

merchant ['mɔ:tʃənt] *n* mercante *m*, commerciante *m*; **~ bank** *n* (*Brit*) banca d'affari; **~ navy,** (*US*) **~ marine** *n* marina mercantile.

merciful ['mɔ:sɪful] *a* pietoso(a), clemente.

merciless ['mɔ:sɪlɪs] *a* spietato(a).

mercury ['mɔ:kjurɪ] *n* mercurio.

mercy ['mɔ:sɪ] *n* pietà; (*REL*) misericordia; **at the ~ of** alla mercè di.

mere [mɪə*] *a* semplice; **by a ~ chance** per mero caso; **~ly** *ad* semplicemente, non ... che.

merge [mɔ:dʒ] *vt* unire // *vi* fondersi, unirsi; (*COMM*) fondersi; **~r** *n* (*COMM*) fusione *f*.

meringue [mə'ræŋ] *n* meringa.

merit ['mɛrɪt] *n* merito, valore *m* // *vt* meritare.

mermaid ['mɔ:meɪd] *n* sirena.

merry ['mɛrɪ] *a* gaio(a), allegro(a); **M~ Christmas!** Buon Natale!; **~-go-round** *n* carosello.

mesh [mɛʃ] *n* maglia; rete *f*.

mesmerize ['mɛzmɔraɪz] *vt* ipnotizzare; affascinare.

mess [mɛs] *n* confusione *f*, disordine *m*; (*fig*) pasticcio; (*MIL*) mensa; **to ~ about** *or* **around** *vi* (*col*) trastullarsi; **to ~ about** *or* **around with** *vt fus* (*col*) gingillarsi con; (: *plans*) fare un pasticcio di; **to ~ up** *vt* sporcare; fare un pasticcio di; rovinare.

message ['mɛsɪdʒ] *n* messaggio.

messenger ['mɛsɪndʒə*] *n* messaggero/a.

Messrs ['mɛsəz] *abbr* (*on letters*) Spett.

messy ['mɛsɪ] *a* sporco(a); disordinato(a).

met [mɛt] *pt, pp of* **meet**.

metal ['mɛtl] *n* metallo; **~lic** [-'tælɪk] *a* metallico(a).

metaphor ['mɛtəfə*] *n* metafora.

mete [mi:t]: **to ~ out** *vt fus* infliggere.

meteorology [mi:tɪə'rɔlədʒɪ] *n* meteorologia.

meter ['mi:tə*] *n* (*instrument*) contatore *m*; (*US: unit*) = **metre**.

method ['mɛθəd] *n* metodo; **~ical** [mɪ'θɔdɪkl] *a* metodico(a).

Methodist ['mɛθədɪst] *a, n* metodista (*m/f*).

methylated spirit ['mɛθɪleɪtɪd-] *n* (*Brit*:

also: meths) alcool *m* denaturato.

metre, (*US*) **meter** ['mi:tə*] *n* metro.

metric ['mɛtrɪk] *a* metrico(a).

metropolitan [mɛtrə'pɒlɪtən] *a* metropolitano(a); **the M~ Police** *n* (*Brit*) la polizia di Londra.

mettle ['mɛtl] *n* coraggio.

mew [mju:] *vi* (*cat*) miagolare.

mews [mju:z] *n*: ~ **cottage** (*Brit*) villetta ricavata da un'antica scuderia.

Mexico ['mɛksɪkəu] *n* Messico.

miaow [mi:'au] *vi* miagolare.

mice [maɪs] *npl of* **mouse**.

micro ['maɪkrəu] *n* (*also*: ~-**computer**) microcomputer *m inv*.

microchip ['maɪkrəutʃɪp] *n* microcircuito integrato.

microfilm ['maɪkrəufɪlm] *n* microfilm *m inv* // *vt* microfilmare.

microphone ['maɪkrəfəun] *n* microfono.

microscope ['maɪkrəskəup] *n* microscopio.

microwave ['maɪkrəuweɪv] *n* (*also*: ~ **oven**) forno a microonde.

mid [mɪd] *a*: ~ **May** metà maggio; ~ **afternoon** metà pomeriggio; in ~ **air** a mezz'aria; ~**day** *n* mezzogiorno.

middle ['mɪdl] *n* mezzo; centro; (*waist*) vita // *a* di mezzo; in the ~ of the night nel bel mezzo della notte; ~-**aged** *a* di mezza età; **the M~ Ages** *npl* il Medioevo; ~-**class** *a* ≈ borghese; the ~ **class(es)** *n*(*pl*) ≈ la borghesia; **M~ East** *n* Medio Oriente *m*; ~**man** *n* intermediario; agente *m* rivenditore; ~**name** *n* secondo nome *m*; ~**weight** *n* (*BOXING*) peso medio.

middling ['mɪdlɪŋ] *a* medio(a).

midge [mɪdʒ] *n* moscerino.

midget ['mɪdʒɪt] *n* nano/a.

Midlands ['mɪdləndz] *npl* contee del centro dell'Inghilterra.

midnight ['mɪdnaɪt] *n* mezzanotte *f*.

midriff ['mɪdrɪf] *n* diaframma *m*.

midst [mɪdst] *n*: in the ~ of in mezzo a.

midsummer [mɪd'sʌmə*] *n* mezza o piena estate *f*.

midway [mɪd'weɪ] *a*, *ad*: ~ (**between**) a mezza strada (fra).

midweek [mɪd'wi:k] *a*, *ad* a metà settimana.

midwife, *pl* **midwives** ['mɪdwaɪf, -vz] *n* levatrice *f*; ~**ry** [-wɪfərɪ] *n* ostetrica.

might [maɪt] *vb see* **may** // *n* potere *m*, forza; ~**y** *a* forte, potente.

migraine ['mi:greɪn] *n* emicrania.

migrant ['maɪgrənt] *a* (*bird*) migratore(trice); (*person*) nomade; (*worker*) emigrato(a).

migrate [maɪ'greɪt] *vi* migrare.

mike [maɪk] *n abbr* (= *microphone*) microfono.

Milan [mɪ'læn] *n* Milano *f*.

mild [maɪld] *a* mite; (*person, voice*) dolce; (*flavour*) delicato(a); (*illness*)

leggero(a) // *n* birra leggera.

mildew ['mɪldju:] *n* muffa.

mildly ['maɪldlɪ] *ad* mitemente; dolcemente; delicatamente; leggermente; **to put it** ~ a dire poco.

mile [maɪl] *n* miglio; ~**age** *n* distanza in miglia, ≈ chilometraggio; ~**stone** *n* pietra miliare.

milieu ['mi:ljə:] *n* ambiente *m*.

militant ['mɪlɪtnt] *a*, *n* militante (*m/f*).

military ['mɪlɪtərɪ] *a* militare.

militate ['mɪlɪteɪt] *vi*: **to** ~ **against** essere d'ostacolo a.

milk [mɪlk] *n* latte *m* // *vt* (*cow*) mungere; (*fig*) sfruttare; ~ **chocolate** *n* cioccolato al latte; ~**man** *n* lattaio; ~ **shake** *n* frappé *m inv*; ~**y** *a* lattiginoso(a); (*colour*) latteo(a); **M~y Way** *n* Via Lattea.

mill [mɪl] *n* mulino; (*small: for coffee, pepper etc*) macinino; (*factory*) fabbrica; (*spinning* ~) filatura // *vt* macinare // *vi* (*also*: ~ **about**) formicolare.

millennium, *pl* ~**s** *or* **millennia** [mɪ'lɛnɪəm, -'lɛnɪə] *n* millennio.

miller ['mɪlə*] *n* mugnaio.

millet ['mɪlɪt] *n* miglio.

milli... ['mɪlɪ] *prefix*: ~**gram(me)** *n* milligrammo; ~**metre,** (*US*) ~**meter** *n* millimetro.

millinery ['mɪlɪnərɪ] *n* modisteria.

million ['mɪljən] *n* milione *m*; ~**aire** *n* milionario, ≈ miliardario.

millstone ['mɪlstəun] *n* macina.

milometer [maɪ'lɒmɪtə*] *n* ≈ contachilometri *m inv*.

mime [maɪm] *n* mimo // *vt*, *vi* mimare.

mimic ['mɪmɪk] *n* imitatore/trice // *vt* fare la mimica di; ~**ry** *n* mimica; (*ZOOL*) mimetismo.

min. *abbr* = **minute(s)**, **minimum**.

mince [mɪns] *vt* tritare, macinare // *vi* (*in walking*) camminare a passettini // *n* (*Brit CULIN*) carne *f* tritata *or* macinata; ~**meat** *n* frutta secca tritata per uso in pasticceria; ~ **pie** *n* specie di torta con frutta secca; ~**r** *n* tritacarne *m inv*.

mind [maɪnd] *n* mente *f* // *vt* (*attend to, look after*) badare a, occuparsi di; (*be careful*) fare attenzione a; **I don't** ~ **the noise** il rumore non mi dà alcun fastidio; **I don't** ~ non m'importa; it is on my ~ mi preoccupa; **to my** ~ secondo me, a mio parere; **to be out of one's** ~ essere uscito(a) di mente; **to keep** *or* **bear sth in** ~ non dimenticare qc; **to make up one's** ~ decidersi; ~ **you,** ... sì, però va detto che ...; **never** ~ non importa, non fa niente; "~ **the step**" "attenzione allo scalino"; ~**er** *n* (*child* ~*er*) bambinaia; (*bodyguard*) guardia del corpo; ~**ful** *a*: ~**ful of** attento(a) a; memore di; ~**less**

a idiota.

mine [main] *pronoun* il(la) mio(a), *pl* i(le) miei(mie); *that book is ~* quel libro è mio; *yours is red, ~ is green* il tuo è rosso, il mio è verde; *a friend of ~* un mio amico // *n* miniera; *(explosive)* mina // *vt (coal)* estrarre; *(ship, beach)* minare.

miner ['mainə*] *n* minatore *m*.

mineral ['minərəl] *a* minerale // *n* minerale *m*; *~s npl (Brit: soft drinks)* bevande *fpl* gasate; *~ water n* acqua minerale.

minesweeper ['mainswi:pə*] *n* dragamine *m inv*.

mingle ['mingl] *vi*: *to ~ with* mescolarsi a, mischiarsi con.

miniature ['minətʃə*] *a* in miniatura // *n* miniatura.

minibus ['minibʌs] *n* minibus *m inv*.

minim ['minim] *n (MUS)* minima.

minimum ['miniməm] *n (pl minima* ['minimə]) minimo // *a* minimo(a).

mining ['mainiŋ] *n* industria mineraria // *a* minerario(a); di minatori.

miniskirt ['miniskə:t] *n* minigonna.

minister ['ministə*] *n (Brit POL)* ministro; *(REL)* pastore *m* // *vi*: *to ~ to* sb assistere qn; *to ~ to* sb's needs provvedere ai bisogni di qn; *~ial* [-'tiəriəl] *a (Brit POL)* ministeriale.

ministry ['ministri] *n (Brit POL)* ministero; *(REL)*: *to go into the ~* diventare pastore.

mink [miŋk] *n* visone *m*.

minnow ['minəu] *n* pesciolino d'acqua dolce.

minor ['mainə*] *a* minore, di poca importanza; *(MUS)* minore // *n (LAW)* minorenne *m/f*.

minority [mai'nɔriti] *n* minoranza.

mint [mint] *n (plant)* menta; *(sweet)* pasticca di menta // *vt (coins)* battere; *the (Royal) M~, (US) the (US) M~* la Zecca; *in ~ condition* come nuovo(a) di zecca.

minus ['mainəs] *n (also: ~ sign)* segno meno // *prep* meno.

minute *a* [mai'nju:t] minuscolo(a); *(detail)* minuzioso(a) // *n* ['minit] minuto; *(official record)* processo verbale, resoconto sommario; *~s npl* verbale *m*, verbali *mpl*.

miracle ['mirəkl] *n* miracolo.

mirage ['mira:ʒ] *n* miraggio.

mire ['maiə*] *n* pantano, melma.

mirror ['mirə*] *n* specchio // *vt* rispecchiare, riflettere.

mirth [mə:θ] *n* gaiezza.

misadventure [misəd'ventʃə*] *n* disavventura; *death by ~* morte *f* accidentale.

misapprehension ['misæpri'henʃən] *n* malinteso.

misbehave [misbi'heiv] *vi* comportarsi

male.

miscarriage ['miskæridʒ] *n (MED)* aborto spontaneo; *~ of justice* errore *m* giudiziario.

miscellaneous [misi'leiniəs] *a (items)* vario(a); *(selection)* misto(a).

mischief ['mistʃif] *n (naughtiness)* birichineria; *(harm)* male *m*, danno; *(maliciousness)* malizia; **mischievous** *a (naughty)* birichino(a); *(harmful)* dannoso(a).

misconception ['miskən'sepʃən] *n* idea sbagliata.

misconduct [mis'kɔndʌkt] *n* cattiva condotta; *professional ~* reato professionale.

misconstrue [miskən'stru:] *vt* interpretare male.

misdeed [mis'di:d] *n* misfatto.

misdemeanour, (US) misdemeanor [misdi'mi:nə*] *n* misfatto; infrazione *f.*

miser ['maizə*] *n* avaro.

miserable ['mizərəbl] *a* infelice; *(wretched)* miserabile.

miserly ['maizəli] *a* avaro(a).

misery ['mizəri] *n (unhappiness)* tristezza; *(pain)* sofferenza; *(wretchedness)* miseria.

misfire [mis'faiə*] *vi* far cilecca; *(car engine)* perdere colpi.

misfit ['misfit] *n (person)* spostato/a.

misfortune [mis'fɔ:tʃən] *n* sfortuna.

misgiving(s) [mis'giviŋ(z)] *n(pl)* dubbi *mpl*, sospetti *mpl*.

misguided [mis'gaidid] *a* sbagliato(a); poco giudizioso(a).

mishandle [mis'hændl] *vt (treat roughly)* maltrattare; *(mismanage)* trattare male.

mishap ['mishæp] *n* disgrazia.

misinterpret [misin'tə:prit] *vt* interpretare male.

misjudge [mis'dʒʌdʒ] *vt* giudicare male.

mislay [mis'lei] *vt irg* smarrire.

mislead [mis'li:d] *vt irg* sviare; *~ing a* ingannevole.

misnomer [mis'nəumə*] *n* termine *m* sbagliato *or* improprio.

misplace [mis'pleis] *vt* smarrire; collocare fuori posto.

misprint ['misprint] *n* errore *m* di stampa.

Miss [mis] *n* Signorina.

miss [mis] *vt (fail to get)* perdere; *(regret the absence of)*: *I ~ him/it* sento la sua mancanza, lui/esso mi manca // *vi* mancare // *n (shot)* colpo mancato; *to ~ out vt (Brit)* omettere.

misshapen [mis'ʃeipən] *a* deforme.

missile ['misail] *n (AVIAT)* missile *m*; *(object thrown)* proiettile *m*.

missing ['misiŋ] *a* perso(a), smarrito(a); *(person)* scomparso(a); *(: after disaster, MIL)* disperso(a); *to be ~* mancare.

mission ['mɪʃən] n missione f; ~**ary** n missionario/a.

misspent ['mɪs'spent] a: his ~ youth la sua gioventù sciupata.

mist [mɪst] n nebbia, foschia // vi (also: ~ over, ~ up) annebbiarsi; (: Brit: windows) appannarsi.

mistake [mɪs'teɪk] n sbaglio, errore m // vt (irg: like **take**) sbagliarsi di; fraintendere; **to make a ~** fare uno sbaglio, sbagliare; **by ~** per sbaglio; **to ~ for** prendere per; ~**n** a (idea etc) sbagliato(a); **to be ~n** sbagliarsi.

mister ['mɪstə*] n (col) signore m; see **Mr.**

mistletoe ['mɪsltəu] n vischio.

mistook [mɪs'tuk] pt of **mistake.**

mistress ['mɪstrɪs] n padrona; (lover) amante f; (Brit SCOL) insegnante f; see **Mrs.**

mistrust [mɪs'trʌst] vt diffidare di.

misty ['mɪstɪ] a nebbioso(a), brumoso(a).

misunderstand [mɪsʌndə'stænd] vt, vi irg capire male, fraintendere; ~**ing** n malinteso, equivoco.

misuse n [mɪs'juːs] cattivo uso; (of power) abuso // vt [mɪs'juːz] far cattivo uso di; abusare di.

mitigate ['mɪtɪgeɪt] vt mitigare.

mitt(en) ['mɪt(n)] n mezzo guanto; manopola.

mix [mɪks] vt mescolare // vi mescolarsi // n mescolanza; preparato; **to ~ up** vt mescolare; (confuse) confondere; ~**ed** a misto(a); ~**ed grill** n misto alla griglia; ~**ed-up** a (confused) confuso(a); ~**er** n (for food: electric) frullatore m; (: hand) frullino; (person): **he is a good ~er** è molto socievole; ~**ture** n mescolanza; (blend: of tobacco etc) miscela; (MED) sciroppo; ~**-up** n confusione f.

moan [məun] n gemito // vi gemere; (col: complain): **to ~ (about)** lamentarsi (di); ~**ing** n gemiti mpl.

moat [məut] n fossato.

mob [mɔb] n folla; (disorderly) calca; (pej): **the ~** la plebaglia // vt accalcarsi intorno a.

mobile ['məubaɪl] a mobile; ~ **home** n grande roulotte f inv (utilizzata come domicilio).

mock [mɔk] vt deridere, burlarsi di // a falso(a); ~**ery** n derisione f.

mod [mɔd] a see **convenience.**

mode [məud] n modo.

model ['mɔdl] n modello; (person: for fashion) indossatore/trice; (: for artist) modello/a // vt modellare // vi fare l'indossatore (or l'indossatrice) // a (small-scale: railway etc) in miniatura; (child, factory) modello inv; **to ~ clothes** presentare degli abiti.

modem ['məudem] n modem m inv.

moderate a, n ['mɔdərət] moderato(a) // vb ['mɔdəreɪt] vi moderarsi, placarsi // vt moderare.

modern ['mɔdən] a moderno(a); ~**ize** vt modernizzare.

modest ['mɔdɪst] a modesto(a); ~**y** n modestia.

modicum ['mɔdɪkəm] n: **a ~ of** un minimo di.

modify ['mɔdɪfaɪ] vt modificare.

mogul ['məugl] n (fig) magnate m, pezzo grosso.

mohair ['məuheə*] n mohair m.

moist [mɔɪst] a umido(a); ~**en** ['mɔɪsn] vt inumidire; ~**ure** ['mɔɪstʃə*] n umidità; (on glass) goccioline fpl di vapore; ~**urizer** ['mɔɪstʃəraɪzə*] n idratante f.

molar ['məulə*] n molare m.

molasses [məu'læsɪz] n molassa.

mold [məuld] n, vt (US) = **mould.**

mole [məul] n (animal) talpa; (spot) neo.

molest [məu'lest] vt molestare.

mollycoddle ['mɔlɪkɔdl] vt coccolare, vezzeggiare.

molt [məult] vi (US) = **moult.**

molten ['məultən] a fuso(a).

mom [mɔm] n (US) = **mum.**

moment ['məumənt] n momento, istante m; importanza; **at the ~** al momento, in questo momento; ~**ary** a momentaneo(a), passeggero(a); ~**ous** [-'mentəs] a di grande importanza.

momentum [məu'mentəm] n velocità acquista, slancio; (PHYSICS) momento; **to gather ~** aumentare di velocità.

mommy ['mɔmɪ] n (US) = **mummy.**

Monaco ['mɔnəkəu] n Principato di Monaco.

monarch ['mɔnək] n monarca m; ~**y** n monarchia.

monastery ['mɔnəstərɪ] n monastero.

monastic [mə'næstɪk] a monastico(a).

Monday ['mʌndɪ] n lunedì m inv.

monetary ['mʌnɪtərɪ] a monetario(a).

money ['mʌnɪ] n denaro, soldi mpl; ~**lender** n prestatore m di denaro; ~ **order** n vaglia m inv; ~**-spinner** n (col) miniera d'oro (fig).

mongol ['mɔngəl] a, n (MED) mongoloide (m/f).

mongrel ['mʌngrəl] n (dog) cane m bastardo.

monitor ['mɔnɪtə*] n (SCOL) capoclasse m/f; (TV, COMPUT) monitor m inv // vt controllare.

monk [mʌnk] n monaco.

monkey ['mʌnkɪ] n scimmia; ~ **nut** n (Brit) nocciolina americana; ~ **wrench** n chiave f a rullino.

mono... ['mɔnəu] prefix: ~**chrome** a monocromo(a).

monopoly [mə'nɔpəlɪ] n monopolio.

monotone ['mɔnətəun] n pronunzia (or voce f) monotona.

monotonous [mə'nɔtənəs]   *a* monotono(a).

monsoon [mɔn'suːn] *n* monsone *m*.

monster ['mɔnstə*] *n* mostro.

monstrous ['mɔnstrəs] *a* mostruoso(a).

montage [mɔn'tɑːʒ] *n* montaggio.

month [mʌnθ] *n* mese *m*; **~ly** *a* mensile // *ad* al mese; ogni mese // *n* (*magazine*) rivista mensile.

monument ['mɔnjumənt] *n* monumento.

moo [muː] *vi* muggire, mugghiare.

mood [muːd] *n* umore *m*; **to be in a good/bad ~** essere di buon/cattivo umore; **~y** *a* (*variable*) capriccioso(a), lunatico(a); (*sullen*) imbronciato(a).

moon [muːn] *n* luna; **~light** *n* chiaro di luna; **~lighting** *n* lavoro nero; **~lit** *a*: **a ~lit night** una notte rischiarata dalla luna.

moor [muə*] *n* brughiera // *vt* (*ship*) ormeggiare // *vi* ormeggiarsi.

moorland ['muələnd] *n* brughiera.

moose [muːs] *n* (*pl inv*) alce *m*.

mop [mɔp] *n* lavapavimenti *m inv*; (*also*: **~ of hair**) zazzera // *vt* lavare con lo straccio; **to ~ up** *vt* asciugare con uno straccio.

mope [məup] *vi* fare il broncio.

moped ['məuped] *n* ciclomotore *m*.

moral ['mɔrl] *a* morale // *n* morale *f*; **~s** *npl* moralità.

morale [mɔ'rɑːl] *n* morale *m*.

morality [mə'rælıtı] *n* moralità.

morass [mə'ræs] *n* palude *f*, pantano.

morbid ['mɔːbıd] *a* morboso(a).

more [mɔː*] ◆ *a* **1** (*greater in number etc*) più; **~ people/letters than we expected** più persone/lettere di quante ne aspettavamo; **I have ~ wine/money than you** ho più vino/soldi di te; **I have ~ wine than beer** ho più vino che birra **2** (*additional*) altro(a), ancora; **do you want (some) ~ tea?** vuole dell'altro tè?, vuole ancora del tè?; **I have no or I don't have any ~ money** non ho più soldi ◆ *pronoun* **1** (*greater amount*) più; **~ than 10** più di 10; **it cost ~ than we expected** ha costato più di quanto ci aspettavamo **2** (*further or additional amount*) ancora; **is there any ~?** ce n'è ancora?; **there's no ~** non ce n'è più; **a little ~** ancora un po'; **many/much ~** molti(e)/molto(a) di più ◆ *ad*: **~ dangerous/easily (than)** più pericoloso/facilmente (di); **~ and ~** sempre di più; **~ and ~ difficult** sempre più difficile; **~ or less** più o meno; **~ than ever** più che mai.

moreover [mɔː'rəuvə*] *ad* inoltre, di più.

morgue [mɔːg] *n* obitorio.

morning ['mɔːnıŋ] *n* mattina, mattino; (*duration*) mattinata; **in the ~** la mattina; **7 o'clock in the ~** le 7 di or della mattina.

Morocco [mə'rɔkəu] *n* Marocco.

moron ['mɔːrɔn] *n* deficiente *m/f*.

morose [mə'rəus] *a* cupo(a), tetro(a).

Morse [mɔːs] *n* (*also*: **~ code**) alfabeto Morse.

morsel ['mɔːsl] *n* boccone *m*.

mortal ['mɔːtl] *a*, *n* mortale (*m*); **~ity** [-'tælıtı] *n* mortalità.

mortar ['mɔːtə*] *n* (*CONSTR*) malta; (*dish*) mortaio.

mortgage ['mɔːgıdʒ] *n* ipoteca; (*loan*) prestito ipotecario // *vt* ipotecare; **~ company** *n* (*US*) società *f inv* di credito immobiliare.

mortified ['mɔːtıfaıd] *a* umiliato(a).

mortuary ['mɔːtjuərı] *n* camera mortuaria; obitorio.

mosaic [məu'zeık] *n* mosaico.

Moscow ['mɔskəu] *n* Mosca.

Moslem ['mɔzləm] *a*, *n* = **Muslim**.

mosque [mɔsk] *n* moschea.

mosquito [mɔs'kiːtəu] *n* (*~es*) zanzara.

moss [mɔs] *n* muschio.

most [məust] ◆ *a* la maggior parte di; il più di // *pronoun* la maggior parte // *ad* più; (*work, sleep etc*) di più; (*very*) molto, estremamente; **the ~** (*also*: **+** *adjective*) il(la) più; **~ of** la maggior parte di; **~ of them** quasi tutti; **I saw (the) ~** ho visto più io; **at the (very) ~** al massimo; **to make the ~ of** trarre il massimo vantaggio da; **a ~ interesting book** un libro estremamente interessante; **~ly** *ad* per lo più.

MOT *n abbr* (*Brit*: = Ministry of Transport*): **the ~** (*test*) revisione annuale obbligatoria degli autoveicoli.

motel [məu'tɛl] *n* motel *m inv*.

moth [mɔθ] *n* farfalla notturna; tarma; **~ball** *n* pallina di naftalina.

mother ['mʌðə*] *n* madre *f* // *vt* (*care for*) fare da madre a; **~hood** *n* maternità; **~-in-law** *n* suocera; **~ly** *a* materno(a); **~-of-pearl** *n* madreperla; **~-to-be** *n* futura mamma; **~ tongue** *n* madrelingua.

motion ['məuʃən] *n* movimento, moto; (*gesture*) gesto; (*at meeting*) mozione *f* // *vt, vi*: **~ (to) sb to do fare** cenno a qn di fare; **~less** *a* immobile; **~ picture** *n* film *m inv*.

motivated ['məutıveıtıd] *a* motivato(a).

motive ['məutıv] *n* motivo.

motley ['mɔtlı] *a* eterogeneo(a), molto vario(a).

motor ['məutə*] *n* motore *m*; (*Brit col: vehicle*) macchina // *a* motore(trice); **~bike** *n* moto *f inv*; **~boat** *n* motoscafo; **~car** *n* (*Brit*) automobile *f*; **~cycle** *n* motocicletta; **~cyclist** *n* motociclista *m/f*; **~ing** *n* (*Brit*) turismo automobilistico; **~ist** *n* automobilista *m/f*; **~ racing** *n* (*Brit*) corse *fpl* automobilistiche; **~way** *n* (*Brit*) autostrada.

mottled ['mɔtld] a chiazzato(a), marezzato(a).

motto, ~es ['mɔtəu] n motto.

mould, (US) **mold** [məuld] n forma, stampo; (mildew) muffa // vt formare; (fig) foggiare; **~er** vi (decay) ammuffire; **~y** a ammuffito(a).

moult, (US) **molt** [məult] vi far la muta.

mound [maund] n rialzo, collinetta.

mount [maunt] n monte m, montagna; (horse) cavalcatura; (for jewel etc) montatura // vt montare; (horse) montare a // vi salire, montare; (also: ~ up) aumentare.

mountain ['mauntin] n montagna // cpd di montagna; **~eer** [-'niə*] n alpinista m/f; **~eering** [-'niəriŋ] n alpinismo; **~ous** a montagnoso(a); **~side** n fianco della montagna.

mourn [mɔ:n] vt piangere, lamentare // vi: to ~ (for sb) piangere (la morte di qn); **~er** n parente m/f or amico/a del defunto; persona venuta a rendere omaggio al defunto; **~ful** a triste, lugubre; **~ing** n lutto // cpd (dress) da lutto; in ~ing in lutto.

mouse [maus], pl **mice** n topo; (COMPUT) mouse m inv; **~trap** n trappola per i topi.

mousse [mu:s] n mousse f inv.

moustache [məs'tɑ:ʃ] n baffi mpl.

mousy ['mausi] a (person) timido(a); (hair) né chiaro(a) né scuro(a).

mouth, ~s [mauθ, -ðz] n bocca; (of river) bocca, foce f; (opening) orifizio; **~ful** n boccata; ~ **organ** n armonica; **~piece** n (of musical instrument) imboccatura, bocchino; (spokesman) portavoce m/f inv; **~wash** n collutorio; **~-watering** a che fa venire l'acquolina in bocca.

movable ['mu:vəbl] a mobile.

move [mu:v] n (movement) movimento; (in game) mossa; (: turn to play) turno; (change of house) trasloco // vt muovere, spostare; (emotionally) commuovere; (POL: resolution etc) proporre // vi (gen) muoversi, spostarsi; (traffic) circolare; (also: ~ **house**) cambiar casa, traslocare; **to ~ towards** andare verso; to ~ sb to do sth indurre or spingere qn a fare qc; **to get a ~ on** affrettarsi, sbrigarsi; **to ~ about** or **around** vi (fidget) agitarsi; (travel) viaggiare; **to ~ along** vi muoversi avanti; **to ~ away** vi allontanarsi, andarsene; **to ~ back** vi indietreggiare; (return) ritornare; **to ~ forward** vi avanzare // vt avanzare, spostare in avanti; (people) far avanzare; **to ~ in** vi (to a house) entrare (in una nuova casa); **to ~ on** vi riprendere la strada // vt (onlookers) far circolare; **to ~ out** vi (of house) sgombrare; **to ~ over** vi spostarsi; **to ~ up** vi avanzare.

movement ['mu:vmənt] n (gen) movimento; (gesture) gesto; (of stars, water, physical) moto.

movie ['mu:vi] n film m inv; **the ~s** il cinema; ~ **camera** n cinepresa.

moving ['mu:viŋ] a mobile; (causing emotion) commovente.

mow, pt **mowed,** pp **mowed** or **mown** [məu, -n] vt falciare; (lawn) mietere; **to ~ down** vt falciare; **~er** n (also: lawnmower) tagliaerba m inv.

MP n abbr = **Member of Parliament.**

m.p.h. abbr = miles per hour (60 m.p.h. = 96 km/h).

Mr, Mr. ['mistə*] n: ~ X Signor X, Sig. X.

Mrs, Mrs. ['misiz] n: ~ X Signora X, Sig.ra X.

Ms, Ms. [miz] n (= Miss or Mrs): ~ X ≈ Signora X, Sig.ra X.

M.Sc. abbr = **Master of Science.**

much [mʌtʃ] a molto(a) // ad, n or pronoun molto; **how ~ is it?** quanto costa?; **too ~** troppo.

muck [mʌk] n (mud) fango; (dirt) sporcizia; **to ~ about** or **around** vi (col) fare lo stupido; (: waste time) gingillarsi; **to ~ up** vt (col: ruin) rovinare.

mud [mʌd] n fango.

muddle ['mʌdl] n confusione f, disordine m; pasticcio // vt (also: ~ **up**) impasticciare; **to be in a ~** (person) non riuscire a raccapezzarsi; **to ~ through** vi cavarsela alla meno peggio.

muddy ['mʌdi] a fangoso(a).

mudguard ['mʌdgɑ:d] n parafango.

mudslinging ['mʌdsliŋiŋ] n (fig) denigrazione f.

muff [mʌf] n manicotto // vt (shot, catch etc) mancare, sbagliare.

muffin ['mʌfin] n specie di pasticcino soffice da tè.

muffle ['mʌfl] vt (sound) smorzare, attutire; (against cold) imbacuccare.

muffler ['mʌflə*] n (US AUT) marmitta; (: on motorbike) silenziatore m.

mug [mʌg] n (cup) tazzone m; (for beer) boccale m; (col: face) muso; (: fool) scemo/a // vt (assault) assalire; **~ging** n assalto.

muggy ['mʌgi] a afoso(a).

mule [mju:l] n mulo.

mull [mʌl]: **to ~ over** vt rimuginare.

mulled [mʌld] a: ~ **wine** vino caldo.

multi-level ['mʌltilevl] a (US) = **multistorey.**

multiple ['mʌltipl] a multiplo(a); molteplice // n multiplo; ~ **sclerosis** n sclerosi f a placche.

multiplication [mʌltipli'keiʃən] n moltiplicazione f.

multiply ['mʌltiplai] vt moltiplicare // vi moltiplicarsi.

multistorey ['mʌlti'stɔ:ri] a (Brit:

building, car park) a più piani.
mum [mʌm] n (Brit) mamma // a: to keep ~ non aprire bocca.
mumble ['mʌmbl] vt, vi borbottare.
mummy ['mʌmɪ] n (Brit: mother) mamma; (embalmed) mummia.
mumps [mʌmps] n orecchioni mpl.
munch [mʌntʃ] vt, vi sgranocchiare.
mundane [mʌn'deɪn] a terra a terra inv.
municipal [mju:'nɪsɪpl] a municipale; ~ity [-'pælɪtɪ] n municipio.
mural ['mjuərl] n dipinto murale.
murder ['mə:də*] n assassinio, omicidio // vt assassinare; ~er n omicida m, assassino; ~ous a micidiale.
murky ['mə:kɪ] a tenebroso(a), buio(a).
murmur ['mə:mə*] n mormorio // vt, vi mormorare.
muscle ['mʌsl] n muscolo; to ~ in vi immischiarsi.
muscular ['mʌskjulə*] a muscolare; (person, arm) muscoloso(a).
muse [mju:z] vi meditare, sognare // n musa.
museum [mju:'zɪəm] n museo.
mushroom ['mʌʃrum] n fungo.
music ['mju:zɪk] n musica; ~al a musicale // n (show) commedia musicale; ~al box n carillon m inv; ~al instrument n strumento musicale; ~ hall n teatro di varietà; ~ian [-'zɪʃən] n musicista m/f.
musk [mʌsk] n muschio.
Muslim ['mʌzlɪm] a, n musulmano(a).
muslin ['mʌzlɪn] n mussola.
mussel ['mʌsl] n cozza.
must [mʌst] auxiliary vb (obligation): I ~ do it devo farlo; (probability): he ~ be there by now dovrebbe essere arrivato ormai; I ~ have made a mistake devo essermi sbagliato // n cosa da non mancare; cosa d'obbligo.
mustard ['mʌstəd] n senape f, mostarda.
muster ['mʌstə*] vt radunare.
mustn't ['mʌsnt] = must not.
musty ['mʌstɪ] a che sa di muffa o di rinchiuso.
mutation [mju:'teɪʃən] n mutazione f.
mute [mju:t] a, n muto(a).
muted ['mju:tɪd] a (noise) attutito(a), smorzato(a); (criticism) attenuato(a).
mutiny ['mju:tɪnɪ] n ammutinamento.
mutter ['mʌtə*] vt, vi borbottare, brontolare.
mutton ['mʌtn] n carne f di montone.
mutual ['mju:tʃuəl] a mutuo(a), reciproco(a).
muzzle ['mʌzl] n muso; (protective device) museruola; (of gun) bocca // vt mettere la museruola a.
my [maɪ] a il(la) mio(a), pl i(le) miei(mie); ~ house la mia casa; ~ books i miei libri; ~ brother mio fratello; I've washed ~ hair/cut ~ finger mi sono lavato i capelli/tagliato il dito.

myself [maɪ'sɛlf] pronoun (reflexive) mi; (emphatic) io stesso(a); (after prep) me; see also oneself.
mysterious [mɪs'tɪərɪəs] a misterioso(a).
mystery ['mɪstərɪ] n mistero.
mystify ['mɪstɪfaɪ] vt mistificare; (puzzle) confondere.
mystique [mɪs'ti:k] n fascino.
myth [mɪθ] n mito; ~ology [mɪ'θɔlədʒɪ] n mitologia.

N

n/a abbr = not applicable.
nab [næb] vt (col) beccare, acchiappare.
nag [næg] n (pej: horse) ronzino; (: person) brontolone/a // vt tormentare // vi brontolare in continuazione; ~ging a (doubt, pain) persistente.
nail [neɪl] n (human) unghia; (metal) chiodo // vt inchiodare; to ~ sb down to a date/price costringere qn .a un appuntamento/ad accettare un prezzo; ~brush n spazzolino da or per unghie; ~file n lima da or per unghie; ~ polish n smalto da or per unghie; ~ polish remover n acetone m, solvente m; ~ scissors npl forbici fpl da or per unghie; ~ varnish n (Brit) = ~ polish.
naïve [naɪ'i:v] a ingenuo(a).
naked ['neɪkɪd] a nudo(a).
name [neɪm] n nome m; (reputation) nome, reputazione f // vt (baby etc) chiamare; (plant, illness) nominare; (person, object) identificare; (price, date) fissare; by ~ di nome; she knows them all by ~ li conosce tutti per nome; ~less a senza nome; ~ly ad cioè; ~sake n omonimo.
nanny ['nænɪ] n bambinaia.
nap [næp] n (sleep) pisolino; (of cloth) peluria; to be caught ~ping essere preso alla sprovvista.
nape [neɪp] n: ~ of the neck nuca.
napkin ['næpkɪn] n (also: table ~) tovagliolo.
nappy ['næpɪ] n (Brit) pannolino; ~ rash n arrossamento (causato dal pannolino).
narcissus, pl **narcissi** [nɑ:'sɪsəs, -saɪ] n narciso.
narcotic [nɑ:'kɔtɪk] n narcotico // a narcotico(a).
narrative ['nærətɪv] n narrativa // a narrativo(a).
narrow ['nærəu] a stretto(a); (fig) limitato(a), ristretto(a) // vi restringersi; to have a ~ escape farcela per un pelo; to ~ sth down to ridurre qc a; ~ly ad per un pelo; (time) per poco; ~-minded a meschino(a).
nasty ['nɑ:stɪ] a (person, remark) cattivo(a); (smell, wound, situation) brutto(a).

nation ['neɪʃən] n nazione f.

national ['næʃənl] a nazionale // n cittadino/a; ~ **dress** n costume m nazionale; **N~ Health Service (NHS)** n (Brit) servizio nazionale di assistenza sanitaria, ≈ S.A.U.B. f; **N~ Insurance** n (Brit) ≈ Previdenza Sociale; ~**ism** n nazionalismo; ~**ity** [-'nælɪtɪ] n nazionalità f inv; ~**ize** vt nazionalizzare; ~**ly** ad a livello nazionale.

nation-wide ['neɪʃənwaɪd] a diffuso(a) in tutto il paese // ad in tutto il paese.

native ['neɪtɪv] n abitante m/f del paese; (in colonies) indigeno/a // a indigeno(a); (country) natio(a); (ability) innato(a); a ~ **of Russia** un nativo della Russia; a ~ **speaker of French** una persona di madrelingua francese; ~ **language** n madrelingua.

NATO ['neɪtəu] n abbr (= North Atlantic Treaty Organization) N.A.T.O. f.

natural ['nætʃrəl] a naturale; (ability) innato(a); (manner) semplice; ~ **gas** n gas m metano; ~**ize** vt naturalizzare; **to become ~ized** (person) naturalizzarsi; ~**ly** ad naturalmente; (by nature: gifted) di natura.

nature ['neɪtʃə*] n natura; (character) natura, indole f; **by** ~ di natura.

naught [nɔ:t] n = nought.

naughty ['nɔ:tɪ] a (child) birichino(a), cattivello(a); (story, film) spinto(a).

nausea ['nɔ:sɪə] n (MED) nausea; (fig: disgust) schifo; ~**te** ['nɔ:sɪeɪt] vt nauseare; far schifo a.

nautical ['nɔ:tɪkl] a nautico(a).

naval ['neɪvl] a navale; ~ **officer** n ufficiale m di marina.

nave [neɪv] n navata centrale.

navel ['neɪvl] n ombelico.

navigate ['nævɪgeɪt] vt percorrere navigando // vi navigare; (AUT) fare da navigatore; **navigation** [-'geɪʃən] n navigazione f; **navigator** n (NAUT, AVIAT) ufficiale m di rotta; (explorer) navigatore m; (AUT) copilota m/f.

navvy ['nævɪ] n (Brit) manovale m.

navy ['neɪvɪ] n marina; ~**(-blue)** a blu scuro inv.

Nazi ['nɑ:tsɪ] n nazista m/f.

NB abbr (= nota bene) N.B.

near [nɪə*] a vicino(a); (relation) prossimo(a) // ad vicino // prep (also: ~ **to**) vicino a, presso; (: time) verso // vt avvicinarsi a; ~**by** [nɪə'baɪ] a vicino(a) // ad vicino; ~**ly** ad quasi; I ~**ly fell** per poco non sono caduto; (: **miss** n: that was a ~ miss c'è mancato poco; ~**side** n (AUT: in Britain) lato sinistro; (: in Italy etc) lato destro; ~**-sighted** a miope.

neat [ni:t] a (person, room) ordinato(a); (work) pulito(a); (solution, plan) ben indovinato(a), azzeccato(a); (spirits) li-scio(a); ~**ly** ad con ordine; (skilfully) abilmente.

necessarily ['nesɪsrɪlɪ] ad necessariamente.

necessary ['nesɪsrɪ] a necessario(a).

necessity [nɪ'sesɪtɪ] n necessità f inv.

neck [nek] n collo; (of garment) colletto // vi (col) pomiciare, sbaciucchiarsi; ~ **and** ~ testa a testa.

necklace ['neklɪs] n collana.

neckline ['neklaɪn] n scollatura.

necktie ['nektaɪ] n cravatta.

née [neɪ] a: ~ **Scott** nata Scott.

need [ni:d] n bisogno // vt aver bisogno di; **to** ~ **to do** dover fare; aver bisogno di fare; **you don't** ~ **to go** non devi andare, non c'è bisogno che tu vada.

needle ['ni:dl] n ago // vt punzecchiare.

needless ['ni:dlɪs] a inutile.

needlework ['ni:dlwə:k] n cucito.

needn't ['ni:dnt] = **need not**.

needy ['ni:dɪ] a bisognoso(a).

negative ['negətɪv] n (answer) risposta negativa; (LING) negazione f; (PHOT) negativo // a negativo(a).

neglect [nɪ'glekt] vt trascurare // n (of person, duty) negligenza; **state of** ~ stato di abbandono.

negligee ['neglɪʒeɪ] n négligé m inv.

negligence ['neglɪdʒəns] n negligenza.

negligible ['neglɪdʒɪbl] a insignificante, trascurabile.

negotiate [nɪ'gəuʃɪeɪt] vi: **to** ~ **(with)** negoziare (con) // vt (COMM) negoziare; (obstacle) superare; **negotiation** [-'eɪʃən] n negoziato, trattativa.

Negro ['ni:grəu] a, n (pl ~**es**) negro(a).

neigh [neɪ] vi nitrire.

neighbour, (US) **neighbor** ['neɪbə*] n vicino/a; ~**hood** n vicinato; ~**ing** a vicino(a); ~**ly** a: **he is a** ~**ly person** è un buon vicino.

neither ['naɪðə*] a, pronoun né l'uno(a) né l'altro(a), nessuno(a) dei(delle) due // cj neanche, nemmeno, neppure // ad: ~ **good nor bad** né buono né cattivo; **I didn't move and** ~ **did Claude** io non mi mossi e nemmeno Claude; ..., ~ **did I refuse** ..., ma non ho nemmeno rifiutato.

neon ['ni:ɔn] n neon m; ~ **light** n luce f al neon.

nephew ['nevju:] n nipote m.

nerve [nə:v] n nervo; (fig) coraggio; (impudence) faccia tosta; **a fit of** ~**s** una crisi di nervi; ~**-racking** a che spezza i nervi.

nervous ['nə:vəs] a nervoso(a); (anxious) agitato(a), in apprensione; ~ **breakdown** n esaurimento nervoso.

nest [nest] n nido // vi fare il nido, nidificare; ~ **egg** n (fig) gruzzolo.

nestle ['nesl] vi accoccolarsi.

net [net] n rete f // a netto(a) // vt (fish etc) prendere con la rete; (profit) ricavare un utile netto di; ~**ball** n *specie di pallacanestro;* ~ **curtains** *npl* tende *fpl* di tulle.

Netherlands ['nɛðələndz] *npl:* the ~ i Paesi Bassi.

nett [nɛt] *a* = **net**.

netting ['nɛtɪŋ] *n (for fence etc)* reticolato.

nettle ['nɛtl] *n* ortica.

network ['nɛtwɔːk] *n* rete *f*.

neurotic [njuə'rɔtɪk] *a, n* nevrotico(a).

neuter ['njuːtə*] *a* neutro(a) // *n* neutro // *vt (cat etc)* castrare.

neutral ['njuːtrəl] *a* neutro(a); *(persòn, nation)* neutrale // *n (AUT):* in ~ in folle; ~**ize** *vt* neutralizzare.

never ['nɛvə*] *ad* (non...) mai; ~ **again** mai più; I'll ~ go there again non ci vado più; ~ in my life mai in vita mia; *see also* **mind**; ~**-ending** *a* interminabile; ~**theless** [nɛvəðə'lɛs] *ad* tuttavia, ciò nonostante, ciò nondimeno.

new [njuː] *a* nuovo(a); *(brand new)* nuovo(a) di zecca; ~**born** *a* neonato(a); ~**comer** ['njuːkʌmə*] *n* nuovo(a) venuto(a); ~**fangled** ['njuːfæŋgld] *a (pej)* stramoderno(a); ~**found** *a* nuovo(a); ~**ly** *ad* di recente; ~**ly-weds** *npl* sposini *mpl*, sposi *mpl* novelli.

news [njuːz] *n* notizie *fpl*; *(RADIO)* giornale *m* radio; *(TV)* telegiornale *m*; a **piece of** ~ una notizia; ~ **agency** *n* agenzia di stampa; ~**agent** *n (Brit)* giornalaio; ~**caster** *n (RADIO, TV)* annunciatore/trice; ~**dealer** *n (US)* = ~**agent**; ~ **flash** *n* notizia *f* lampo *inv*; ~**letter** *n* bollettino; ~**paper** *n* giornale *m*; ~**print** *n* carta da giornale; ~**reader** *n* = ~**caster**; ~**reel** *n* cinegiornale *m*; ~ **stand** *n* edicola.

newt [njuːt] *n* tritone *m*.

New Year *n* Anno Nuovo; ~**'s Day** *n* il Capodanno; ~**'s Eve** *n* la vigilia di Capodanno.

New Zealand [-'ziːlənd] *n* Nuova Zelanda; ~**er** *n* neozelandese *m/f*.

next [nɛkst] *a* prossimo(a) // *ad* accanto; *(in time)* dopo; the ~ day il giorno dopo, l'indomani, ~ **year** l'anno prossimo; when do we meet ~? quando ci rincontriamo?; ~ **door** *ad* accanto; ~**-of-kin** *n* parente *m/f* prossimo(a); ~ **to** *prep* accanto a; ~ **to nothing** quasi niente.

NHS *n abbr* = **National Health Service**.

nib [nɪb] *n (of pen)* pennino.

nibble ['nɪbl] *vt* mordicchiare.

Nicaragua [nɪkə'rægjuə] *n* Nicaragua *m*.

nice [naɪs] *a (holiday, trip)* piacevole; *(flat, picture)* bello(a); *(person)* simpatico(a), gentile; *(distinction, point)* sottile; ~**-looking** *a* bello(a); ~**ly** *ad* bene.

niceties ['naɪsɪtɪz] *npl* finezze *fpl*.

niche [niːʃ] *n* nicchia; *(fig):* to find a ~ for o.s. trovare la propria strada.

nick [nɪk] *n* tacca // *vt (col)* rubare; in the ~ of time appena in tempo.

nickel ['nɪkl] *n* nichel *m*; *(US) moneta da cinque centesimi di dollaro*.

nickname ['nɪkneɪm] *n* soprannome *m* // *vt* soprannominare.

niece [niːs] *n* nipote *f*.

Nigeria [naɪ'dʒɪərɪə] *n* Nigeria.

nigger ['nɪgə*] *n (col!: highly offensive)* negro/a.

niggling ['nɪglɪŋ] *a* pignolo(a).

night [naɪt] *n* notte *f*; *(evening)* sera; at ~ la sera; by ~ di notte; the ~ before last l'altro ieri notte *(or sera)*; ~**cap** *n* bicchierino prima di andare a letto; ~ **club** *n* locale *m* notturno; ~**dress** *n* camicia da notte; ~**fall** *n* crepuscolo; ~**gown** *n*, ~**ie** ['naɪtɪ] *n* camicia da notte.

nightingale ['naɪtɪŋgeɪl] *n* usignolo.

night life *n* vita notturna.

nightly ['naɪtlɪ] *a* di ogni notte *or* sera; *(by night)* notturno(a) // *ad* ogni notte *or* sera.

nightmare ['naɪtmɛə*] *n* incubo.

night: ~ porter *n* portiere *m* di notte; ~ **school** *n* scuola serale; ~ **shift** *n* turno di notte; ~**-time** *n* notte *f*.

nil [nɪl] *n* nulla *m*; *(Brit SPORT)* zero.

Nile [naɪl] *n:* the ~ il Nilo.

nimble ['nɪmbl] *a* agile.

nine [naɪn] *num* nove; ~**teen** *num* diciannove; ~**ty** *num* novanta.

ninth [naɪnθ] *a* nono(a).

nip [nɪp] *vt* pizzicare.

nipple ['nɪpl] *n (ANAT)* capezzolo.

nitrogen ['naɪtrədʒən] *n* azoto.

no [nəu] ♦ *ad (opposite of "yes")* no; are you coming? — ~ (I'm not) viene? — no (non vengo); would you like some more? — ~ thank you ne vuole ancora un po'? — no, grazie

♦ *a (not any)* nessuno(a); I have ~ money/time/books non ho soldi/tempo/ libri; ~ student would have done it nessuno studente lo avrebbe fatto; "~ parking" "divieto di sosta"; "~ smoking" "vietato fumare"

♦ *n (pl* ~**es)** no *m inv*.

nobility [nəu'bɪlɪtɪ] *n* nobiltà.

noble ['nəubl] *a, n* nobile (*m*).

nobody ['nəubədɪ] *pronoun* nessuno.

nod [nɔd] *vi* accennare col capo, fare un cenno; *(sleep)* sonnecchiare // *vt:* to ~ one's head fare di sì col capo // *n* cenno; to ~ off *vi* assopirsi.

noise [nɔɪz] *n* rumore *m*; *(din, racket)* chiasso; **noisy** *a (street, car)* rumoroso(a); *(person)* chiassoso(a).

no man's land ['nəumænzlænd] *n* terra di nessuno.

nominal ['nɔmɪnl] *a* nominale.

nominate ['nɔmɪneɪt] *vt (propose)* proporre come candidato; *(elect)* nominare.

nominee [nɔmɪ'ni:] *n* persona nominata; candidato/a.

non... [nɔn] *prefix* non...; **~-alcoholic** *a* analcolico(a); **~-committal** ['nɔnkə'mɪtl] *a* evasivo(a).

nondescript ['nɔndɪskrɪpt] *a* qualunque *inv*.

none [nʌn] *pronoun* (*not one thing*) niente; (*not one person*) nessuno(a); **~** of you nessuno(a) di voi; I've **~** left non ne ho più; he's **~** the worse for it non ne ha risentito.

nonentity [nɔ'nɛntɪtɪ] *n* persona insignificante.

nonetheless [nʌnðə'lɛs] *ad* nondimeno.

non: **~-existent** *a* inesistente; **~-fiction** *n* saggistica.

nonplussed [nɔn'plʌst] *a* sconcertato(a).

nonsense ['nɔnsəns] *n* sciocchezze *fpl*.

non: **~-smoker** *n* non fumatore/trice; **~-stick** *a* antiaderente, antiadesivo(a); **~-stop** *a* continuo(a); (*train, bus*) direttissimo(a) // *ad* senza sosta.

noodles ['nu:dlz] *npl* taglierini *mpl*.

nook [nuk] *n:* **~s and crannies** angoli *mpl*.

noon [nu:n] *n* mezzogiorno.

no one ['nəuwʌn] *pronoun* = **nobody.**

noose [nu:s] *n* nodo scorsoio; (*hangman's*) cappio.

nor [nɔ:*] *cj* = **neither** // *ad see* **neither.**

norm [nɔ:m] *n* norma.

normal ['nɔ:ml] *a* normale; **~ly** *ad* normalmente.

north [nɔ:θ] *n* nord *m*, settentrione *m* // *a* nord *inv*, del nord, settentrionale // *ad* verso nord; **N~ America** *n* America del Nord; **~-east** *n* nord-est *m*; **~erly** ['nɔ:ðəlɪ] *a* (*point, direction*) verso nord; **~ern** ['nɔ:ðən] *a* del nord, settentrionale; **N~ern Ireland** *n* Irlanda del Nord; **N~ Pole** *n* Polo Nord; **N~ Sea** *n* Mare *m* del Nord; **~ward(s)** ['nɔ:θwəd(z)] *ad* verso nord; **~-west** *n* nord-ovest *m*.

Norway ['nɔ:weɪ] *n* Norvegia.

Norwegian [nɔ:'wi:dʒən] *a* norvegese // *n* norvegese *m/f*; (*LING*) norvegese *m*.

nose [nəuz] *n* naso; (*of animal*) muso // *vi:* to **~** about aggirarsi; **~bleed** *n* emorragia nasale; **~-dive** *n* picchiata; **~y** *a* = **nosy.**

nostalgia [nɔs'tældʒɪə] *n* nostalgia.

nostril ['nɔstrɪl] *n* narice *f*; (*of horse*) frogia.

nosy ['nəuzɪ] *a* curioso(a).

not [nɔt] *ad* non; he is **~** or isn't here non è qui, non c'è; you must **~** or you mustn't do that non devi fare quello; it's too late, isn't it or is it **~**? è troppo tardi, vero?; **~** that I don't like him non che (lui) non mi piaccia; **~** yet/now non ancora/ora; *see also* **all, only.**

notably ['nəutəblɪ] *ad* (*markedly*)

notevolmente; (*particularly*) in particolare.

notary ['nəutərɪ] *n* (*also:* **~ public**) notaio.

notch [nɔtʃ] *n* tacca.

note [nəut] *n* nota; (*letter, banknote*) biglietto // *vt* (*also:* **~ down**) prendere nota di; to take **~s** prendere appunti; **~book** *n* taccuino; **~d** ['nəutɪd] *a* celebre; **~pad** *n* bloc-notes *m inv*; **~paper** *n* carta da lettere.

nothing ['nʌθɪŋ] *n* nulla *m*, niente *m*; (*zero*) zero; he does **~** non fa niente; **~** new niente di nuovo; for **~** per niente.

notice ['nəutɪs] *n* avviso; (*of leaving*) preavviso // *vt* notare, accorgersi di; to take **~** of fare attenzione a; to bring sth to sb's **~** far notare qc a qn; at short **~** con un breve preavviso; until further **~** fino a nuovo avviso; to hand in one's **~** licenziarsi; **~able** *a* evidente; **~ board** *n* (*Brit*) tabellone *m* per affissi.

notify ['nəutɪfaɪ] *vt:* to **~** sth to sb far sapere qc a qn; to **~** sb of sth avvisare qn di qc.

notion ['nəuʃən] *n* idea; (*concept*) nozione *f*.

notorious [nəu'tɔ:rɪəs] *a* famigerato(a).

notwithstanding [nɔtwɪθ'stændɪŋ] *ad* nondimeno // *prep* nonostante, malgrado.

nougat ['nu:ga:] *n* torrone *m*.

nought [nɔ:t] *n* zero.

noun [naun] *n* nome *m*, sostantivo.

nourish ['nʌrɪʃ] *vt* nutrire; **~ing** *a* nutriente; **~ment** *n* nutrimento.

novel ['nɔvl] *n* romanzo // *a* nuovo(a); **~ist** *n* romanziere/a; **~ty** *n* novità *f inv*.

November [nəu'vɛmbə*] *n* novembre *m*.

novice ['nɔvɪs] *n* principiante *m/f*; (*REL*) novizio/a.

now [nau] *ad* ora, adesso // *cj:* **~** (that) adesso che, ora che; by **~** ormai; just **~** proprio ora; right **~** subito, immediatamente; **~ and then**, **~ and again** ogni tanto; from **~ on** da ora in poi; **~adays** ['nauədeɪz] *ad* oggidì.

nowhere ['nəuwɛə*] *ad* in nessun luogo, da nessuna parte.

nozzle ['nɔzl] *n* (*of hose etc*) boccaglio; (*of fire extinguisher*) lancia.

nuance ['nju:ɑ̃:ns] *n* sfumatura.

nuclear ['nju:klɪə*] *a* nucleare.

nucleus, *pl* **nuclei** ['nju:klɪəs, 'nju:klɪaɪ] *n* nucleo.

nude [nju:d] *a* nudo(a) // *n* (*ART*) nudo; in the **~** tutto(a) nudo(a).

nudge [nʌdʒ] *vt* dare una gomitata a.

nudist ['nju:dɪst] *n* nudista *m/f*.

nuisance ['nju:sns] *n:* it's a **~** è una seccatura; he's a **~** è uno scocciatore; what a **~**! che seccatura!

null [nʌl] *a:* **~ and void** nullo(a).

numb [nʌm] *a* intorpidito(a); **~ with cold** intirizzito(a) (dal freddo).

number ['nʌmbə*] *n* numero // *vt*

numerare; (include) contare; a ~ of un certo numero di; to be ~ed among venire annoverato(a) tra; they were 10 in ~ erano in tutto 10; ~ **plate** n (Brit AUT) targa.

numeral ['nju:mərəl] n numero, cifra.

numerate ['nju:mərɪt] a: to be ~ avere nozioni di aritmetica.

numerical [nju:'mɛrɪkl] a numerico(a).

numerous ['nju:mərəs] a numeroso(a).

nun [nʌn] n suora, monaca.

nurse [nə:s] n infermiere/a // vt (patient, cold) curare; (baby: Brit) cullare; (: US) allattare, dare il latte a; (hope) nutrire.

nursery ['nə:sərɪ] n (room) camera dei bambini; (institution) asilo; (for plants) vivaio; ~ **rhyme** n filastrocca; ~ **school** n scuola materna; ~ **slope** n (Brit SKI) pista per principianti.

nursing ['nə:sɪŋ] n (profession) professione f di infermiere (or di infermiera); ~ **home** n casa di cura.

nurture ['nə:tʃə*] vt allevare; nutrire.

nut [nʌt] n (of metal) dado; (fruit) noce f; he's ~ (col) è matto; ~**crackers** npl schiaccianoci m inv.

nutmeg ['nʌtmɛg] n noce f moscata.

nutritious [nju:'trɪʃəs] a nutriente.

nutshell ['nʌtʃɛl] n guscio di noce; in a ~ in poche parole.

nylon ['naɪlɔn] n nailon m // a di nailon.

nymph [nɪmf] n ninfa.

O

oak [əuk] n quercia // a di quercia.

O.A.P. abbr = old age pensioner.

oar [ɔ:*] n remo.

oasis, pl **oases** [əu'eɪsɪs] n oasi f inv.

oath [əuθ] n giuramento; (swear word) bestemmia.

oatmeal ['əutmi:l] n farina d'avena.

oats [əuts] npl avena.

obedience [ə'bi:dɪəns] n ubbidienza.

obedient [ə'bi:dɪənt] a ubbidiente.

obey [ə'beɪ] vt ubbidire a; (instructions, regulations) osservare // vi ubbidire.

obituary [ə'bɪtjuərɪ] n necrologia.

object n ['ɔbdʒɪkt] oggetto; (purpose) scopo, intento; (LING) complemento oggetto // vi [əb'dʒɛkt]: to ~ to (attitude) disapprovare; (proposal) protestare contro, sollevare delle obiezioni contro; expense is no ~ non si bada a spese; I ~! mi oppongo!; **he ~ed that** ... he obiettò che ...; ~**ion** [əb'dʒɛkʃən] n obiezione f; (drawback) inconveniente m; ~**ionable** [əb'dʒɛkʃənəbl] a antipatico(a); (smell) sgradevole; (language) scostumato(a); ~**ive** n obiettivo // a obiettivo(a).

obligation [ɔblɪ'geɪʃən] n obbligo, dovere m; (debt) obbligo (di riconoscenza); without ~ senza impegno.

oblige [ə'blaɪdʒ] vt (force): to ~ sb to do costringere qn a fare; (do a favour) fare una cortesia a; to be ~d to sb for sth essere grato a qn per qc; **obliging** a servizievole, compiacente.

oblique [ə'bli:k] a obliquo(a); (allusion) indiretto(a).

obliterate [ə'blɪtəreɪt] vt cancellare.

oblivion [ə'blɪvɪən] n oblio.

oblivious [ə'blɪvɪəs] a: ~ of incurante di; inconscio(a) di.

oblong ['ɔblɔŋ] a oblungo(a) // n rettangolo.

obnoxious [əb'nɔkʃəs] a odioso(a); (smell) disgustoso(a), ripugnante.

oboe ['əubəu] n oboe m.

obscene [əb'si:n] a osceno(a).

obscure [əb'skjuə*] a oscuro(a) // vt oscurare; (hide: sun) nascondere.

observant [əb'zə:vnt] a attento(a).

observation [ɔbzə'veɪʃən] n osservazione f; (by police etc) sorveglianza.

observatory [əb'zə:vətrɪ] n osservatorio.

observe [əb'zə:v] vt osservare; (remark) fare osservare; ~**r** n osservatore/trice.

obsess [əb'sɛs] vt ossessionare; ~**ive** a ossessivo(a).

obsolescence [ɔbsə'lɛsns] n obsolescenza.

obsolete ['ɔbsəli:t] a obsoleto(a); (word) desueto(a).

obstacle ['ɔbstəkl] n ostacolo.

obstinate ['ɔbstɪnɪt] a ostinato(a).

obstruct [əb'strʌkt] vt (block) ostruire, ostacolare; (halt) fermare; (hinder) impedire.

obtain [əb'teɪn] vt ottenere // vi essere in uso; ~**able** a ottenibile.

obtrusive [əb'tru:sɪv] a (person) importuno(a); (smell) invadente; (building etc) imponente e invadente.

obtuse [əb'tju:s] a ottuso(a).

obvious ['ɔbvɪəs] a ovvio(a), evidente; ~**ly** ad ovviamente; certo.

occasion [ə'keɪʒən] n occasione f; (event) avvenimento // vt cagionare; ~**al** a occasionale; ~**ally** ad ogni tanto.

occupation [ɔkju'peɪʃən] n occupazione f; (job) mestiere m, professione f; ~**al hazard** n rischio del mestiere.

occupier ['ɔkjupaɪə*] n occupante m/f.

occupy ['ɔkjupaɪ] vt occupare; to ~ o.s. with or by doing occuparsi a fare.

occur [ə'kə:*] vi accadere; (difficulty, opportunity) capitare; (phenomenon, error) trovarsi; to ~ to sb venire in mente a qn; ~**rence** n caso, fatto; presenza.

ocean ['əuʃən] n oceano; ~~**going** a d'alto mare.

o'clock [ə'klɔk] ad: it is 5 ~ sono le 5.

OCR n abbr = optical character recognition/reader.

octave ['ɔktɪv] n ottavo.

October [ɔk'təubə*] n ottobre m.

octopus ['ɔktəpəs] *n* polpo, piovra.

odd [ɔd] ` *a* (*strange*) strano(a), bizzarro(a); (*number*) dispari *inv*; (*left over*) in più; (*not of a set*) spaiato(a); 60-~ 60 e oltre; at ~ times di tanto in tanto; the ~ one out l'eccezione *f*; ~**s and ends** npl avanzi mpl; ~**ity** *n* bizzarria; (*person*) originale *m*; ~ **jobs** npl lavori mpl occasionali; ~**ly** ad stranamente; ~**ments** npl (COMM) rimanenze fpl; ~**s** npl (*in betting*) quota; it makes no ~s non importa; at ~s in contesa.

odometer [ɔ'dɔmitə*] *n* odometro.

odour, (US) **odor** ['əudə*] *n* odore *m*.

of [ɔv, əv] prep **1** (gen) di; a boy ~ 10 un ragazzo di 10 anni; a friend ~ **ours** un nostro amico; that was kind ~ **you** è stato molto gentile da parte sua
2 (*expressing quantity, amount, dates etc*) di; a kilo ~ **flour** un chilo di farina; how much ~ **this do you need**? quanto gliene serve?; there were 3 ~ **them** (*people*) erano in 3; (*objects*) ce n'erano 3; 3 ~ **us went** 3 di noi sono andati; the 5th ~ **July** il 5 luglio
3 (*from, out of*) di, in; made ~ **wood** (*fatto*) di *or* in legno.

off [ɔf] a, ad (*engine*) spento(a); (*tap*) chiuso(a); (*Brit: food: bad*) andato(a) a male; (*absent*) assente; (*cancelled*) sospeso(a) // prep da; a poca distanza di; to be ~ (*to leave*) partire, andarsene; to be ~ **sick** essere assente per malattia; a day ~ un giorno di vacanza; to have an ~ **day** non essere in forma; he had his coat ~ si era tolto il cappotto; 10% ~ (COMM) con uno sconto di 10%; ~ **the coast** al largo della costa; I'm ~ **meat** la carne non mi va più; (*no longer eat it*) non mangio più la carne; **on the** ~ **chance** a caso.

offal ['ɔfl] *n* (CULIN) frattaglie fpl.

offbeat ['ɔfbiːt] a eccentrico(a).

off-colour ['ɔf'kʌlə*] a (*Brit: ill*) malato(a), indisposto(a).

offence, (US) **offense** [ə'fɛns] *n* (LAW) contravvenzione *f*; (: *more serious*) reato; to take ~ at offendersi per.

offend [ə'fɛnd] vt (*person*) offendere; ~**er** *n* delinquente m/f; (*against regulations*) contravventore/trice.

offensive [ə'fɛnsɪv] a offensivo(a); (*smell etc*) sgradevole, ripugnante // *n* (MIL) offensiva.

offer ['ɔfə*] *n* offerta, proposta // vt offrire; "on ~" (COMM) "in offerta speciale"; ~**ing** *n* offerta.

offhand [ɔf'hænd] a disinvolto(a), noncurante // ad all'improvviso.

office ['ɔfis] *n* (*place*) ufficio; (*position*) carica; doctor's ~ (US) studio; to take ~ entrare in carica; ~ **automation** *n* automazione *f* d'ufficio; burotica; ~ **block**, (US) ~ **building** *n* complesso di uffici; ~ **hours** npl orario d'ufficio; (US MED) orario di visite.

officer ['ɔfisə*] *n* (MIL etc) ufficiale *m*; (*of organization*) funzionario; (*also*: **police** ~) agente *m* di polizia.

office worker *n* impiegato/a d'ufficio.

official [ə'fiʃl] a (*authorized*) ufficiale // *n* ufficiale *m*; (*civil servant*) impiegato/a statale; funzionario; ~**dom** *n* burocrazia.

officiate [ə'fiʃieɪt] vi presenziare; to ~ at a marriage celebrare un matrimonio.

officious [ə'fiʃəs] a invadente.

offing ['ɔfiŋ] *n*: in the ~ (*fig*) in vista.

off: ~-licence *n* (*Brit: shop*) spaccio di bevande alcoliche; ~**-line** a, ad (COMPUT) off-line *inv*, fuori linea; (: *switched off*) spento(a); ~**-peak** a (*ticket etc*) a tariffa ridotta; (*time*) non di punta; ~**-putting** a (*Brit*) sgradevole, antipatico(a); ~**-season** a, ad fuori stagione.

offset ['ɔfsɛt] vt irg (*counteract*) controbilanciare, compensare.

offshoot ['ɔfʃuːt] *n* (*fig*) diramazione *f*.

offshore [ɔf'ʃɔ:*] a (*breeze*) di terra; (*island*) vicino alla costa; (*fishing*) costiero(a).

offside ['ɔf'said] a (SPORT) fuori gioco; (AUT: in Britain) destro(a); (: in Italy etc) sinistro(a) // *n* (AUT) lato destro; lato sinistro.

offspring ['ɔfspriŋ] *n* prole *f*, discendenza.

off: ~stage ad dietro le quinte; ~**-the-peg**, (US) ~**-the-rack** ad prêt-à-porter; ~**-white** a bianco sporco *inv*.

often ['ɔfn] ad spesso; how ~ do you go? quanto spesso vai?

ogle ['əugl] vt occhieggiare.

oh [əu] excl oh!

oil [ɔil] *n* olio; (*petroleum*) petrolio; (*for central heating*) nafta // vt (*machine*) lubrificare; ~**can** *n* oliatore m a mano; (*for storing*) latta da olio; ~**field** *n* giacimento petrolifero; ~ **filter** *n* (AUT) filtro dell'olio; ~ **fired** a a nafta; ~ **level** *n* livello dell'olio; ~ **painting** *n* quadro a olio; ~ **refinery** *n* raffineria di petrolio; ~ **rig** *n* derrick m *inv*; (*at sea*) piattaforma per trivellazioni subacquee; ~**skins** npl indumenti mpl di tela cerata; ~ **tanker** *n* petroliera; ~ **well** *n* pozzo petrolifero; ~**y** a unto(a), oleoso(a); (*food*) untuoso(a).

ointment ['ɔintmənt] *n* unguento.

O.K., okay ['əu'kei] excl d'accordo! // vt approvare; is it ~?, are you ~? tutto bene?

old [əuld] a vecchio(a); (*ancient*) antico(a), vecchio(a); (*person*) vecchio(a), anziano(a); how ~ are you? quanti anni ha?; he's 10 years ~ ha 10 anni; ~**er brother/sister** fratello/sorella maggiore; ~ **age** *n* vecchiaia; ~ **age**

pensioner (O.A.P.) *n* (*Brit*) pensionato/a; **~-fashioned** *a* antiquato(a), fuori moda; (*person*) all'antica.

olive ['ɔlɪv] *n* (*fruit*) oliva; (*tree*) olivo // *a* (*also*: **~-green**) verde oliva *inv*; **~ oil** *n* olio d'oliva.

Olympic [əu'lɪmpɪk] *a* olimpico(a); the **~ Games**, the **~s** i giochi olimpici, le Olimpiadi.

omelet(te) ['ɔmlɪt] *n* omelette *f inv*.

omen ['əumən] *n* presagio, augurio.

ominous ['ɔmɪnəs] *a* minaccioso(a); (*event*) di malaugurio.

omit [əu'mɪt] *vt* omettere.

on [ɔn] ◆ *prep* 1 (*indicating position*) su; **~ the wall** sulla parete; **~ the left** a *or* sulla sinistra

2 (*indicating means, method, condition etc*): **~ foot** a piedi; **~ the train/plane** in treno/aereo; **~ the telephone** al telefono; **~ the radio/television** alla radio/televisione; **to be ~ drugs** drogarsi; **~ holiday** in vacanza

3 (*referring to time*): **~ Friday** venerdì; **~ Fridays** il *or* di venerdì; **~ June 20th** il 20 giugno; **~ Friday, June 20th** venerdì, 20 giugno; **a week ~ Friday** venerdì a otto; **~ his arrival** al suo arrivo; **~ seeing this** vedendo ciò

4 (*about, concerning*) su, di; **information ~ train services** informazioni sui collegamenti ferroviari; **a book ~ Goldoni/physics** un libro su Goldoni/di *or* sulla fisica

◆ *ad* 1 (*referring to dress, covering*): **to have one's coat ~** avere indosso il cappotto; **to put one's coat ~** mettersi il cappotto; **what's she got ~?** cosa indossa?; **she put her boots/gloves/hat ~** si mise gli stivali/i guanti/il cappello; **screw the lid ~** tightly avvita bene il coperchio

2 (*further, continuously*): **to walk ~, go ~ etc** continuare, proseguire *etc*; **to read ~** continuare a leggere; **~ and off** ogni tanto

◆ *a* 1 (*in operation: machine, TV, light*) acceso(a); (: *tap*) aperto(a); (: *brake*) inserito(a); **is the meeting still ~?** (*in progress*) la riunione è ancora in corso?; (*not cancelled*) è confermato l'incontro?; **there's a good film ~ at the cinema** danno un buon film al cinema

2 (*col*): **that's not ~!** (*not acceptable*) non si fa così!; (*not possible*) non se ne parla neanche!

once [wʌns] *ad* una volta // *cj* non appena, quando; **~ he had left/it was done** dopo che se n'era andato/fu fatto; **at ~** subito; (*simultaneously*) a un tempo; **~ more** ancora una volta; **~ and for all** una volta per sempre; **~ upon a time** c'era una volta.

oncoming ['ɔnkʌmɪŋ] *a* (*traffic*) che viene in senso opposto.

one [wʌn] ◆ *num* uno(a); **~ hundred and fifty** centocinquanta; **~ day** un giorno

◆ *a* 1 (*sole*) unico(a); **the ~ book which** l'unico libro che; **the ~ man who** l'unico che

2 (*same*) stesso(a); **they came in the ~ car** sono venuti nella stessa macchina

◆ *pronoun* 1: **this ~** questo/a; **that ~** quello/a; **I've already got ~/a red ~** ne ho già uno/uno rosso; **~ by ~** uno per uno

2: **~ another** l'un l'altro; **to look at ~ another** guardarsi

3 (*impersonal*) si; **~ never knows** non si sa mai; **to cut ~'s finger** tagliarsi un dito; **~ needs to eat** bisogna mangiare.

one: **~-armed bandit** *n* slot-machine *f inv*; **~-day excursion** *n* (*US*) biglietto giornaliero di andata e ritorno; **~-man** *a* (*business*) diretto(a) *etc* da un solo uomo; **~-man band** *n* suonatore ambulante con vari strumenti; **~-off** *n* (*Brit col*) fatto eccezionale.

oneself [wʌn'sɛlf] *pronoun* (*reflexive*) si; (*after prep*) se stesso(a), sé; **to do sth (by) ~** fare qc da sé; **to hurt ~** farsi male; **to keep sth for ~** tenere qc per sé; **to talk to ~** parlare da solo.

one: **~-sided** *a* (*argument*) unilaterale; **~-to-~** *a* (*relationship*) univoco(a); **~-upmanship** [-'ʌpmənʃɪp] *n* l'arte di fare sempre meglio degli altri; **~-way** *a* (*street, traffic*) a senso unico.

ongoing ['ɔngəuɪŋ] *a* in corso; in attuazione.

onion ['ʌnjən] *n* cipolla.

on-line ['ɔnlaɪn] *a*, *ad* (*COMPUT*) on-line *inv*.

onlooker ['ɔnlukə*] *n* spettatore/trice.

only ['əunlɪ] *ad* solo, soltanto // *a* solo(a), unico(a) // *cj* solo che, ma; **an ~ child** un figlio unico; **not ~ ... but also** non solo ... ma anche; **I ~ took one** ne ho preso soltanto uno, non ne ho preso che uno.

onset ['ɔnset] *n* inizio; (*of winter, old age*) approssimarsi *m*.

onshore ['ɔnʃɔ:*] *a* (*wind*) di mare.

onslaught ['ɔnslɔ:t] *n* attacco, assalto.

onto ['ɔntu] *prep* su, sopra.

onus ['əunəs] *n* onere *m*, peso.

onward(s) ['ɔnwəd(z)] *ad* (*move*) in avanti.

onyx ['ɔnɪks] *n* onice *f*.

ooze [u:z] *vi* stillare.

opaque [əu'peɪk] *a* opaco(a).

OPEC ['əupek] *n abbr* (= *Organization of Petroleum-Exporting Countries*) O.P.E.C. *f*.

open ['əupn] *a* aperto(a); (*road*) libero(a); (*meeting*) pubblico(a); (*admiration*) evidente, franco(a); (*question*) insoluto(a); (*enemy*) dichiarato(a) // *vt* aprire // *vi* (*eyes, door, debate*) aprirsi; (*flower*) sbocciare; (*shop, bank, museum*) aprire; (*book etc*:

commence) cominciare; in the ~ (air) all'aperto; to ~ on to *vt fus* (*subj: room, door*) dare su; to ~ up *vt* aprire; (*blocked road*) sgombrare // *vi* aprirsi; ~ing *n* apertura; (*opportunity*) occasione *f*, opportunità *f inv*; sbocco; (*job*) posto vacante; ~ly *ad* apertamente; ~-minded *a* che ha la mente aperta; ~-plan *a* senza pareti divisorie.

opera ['ɔpərə] *n* opera; ~ house *n* opera.

operate ['ɔpəreit] *vt* (*machine*) azionare, far funzionare; (*system*) usare // *vi* funzionare; (*drug*) essere efficace; to ~ on sb (for) (*MED*) operare qn (di).

operatic [ɔpə'rætik] *a* dell'opera, lirico(a).

operating ['ɔpəreitiŋ] *a*: ~ table tavolo operatorio; ~ theatre sala operatoria.

operation [ɔpə'reiʃən] *n* operazione *f*; to be in ~ (*machine*) essere in azione *or* funzionamento; (*system*) essere in vigore; to have an ~ (*MED*) subire un'operazione; ~al *a* in funzione; d'esercizio.

operative ['ɔpərətiv] *a* (*measure*) operativo(a).

operator ['ɔpəreitə*] *n* (*of machine*) operatore/trice; (*TEL*) centralinista *m/f*.

opinion [ə'pinjən] *n* opinione *f*, parere *m*; in my ~ secondo me, a mio avviso; ~ated *a* dogmatico(a); ~ poll *n* sondaggio di opinioni.

opium ['əupiəm] *n* oppio.

opponent [ə'pəunənt] *n* avversario/a.

opportunist [ɔpə'tju:nist] *n* opportunista *m/f*.

opportunity [ɔpə'tju:niti] *n* opportunità *f inv*, occasione *f*; to take the ~ of doing cogliere l'occasione per fare.

oppose [ə'pəuz] *vt* opporsi a; ~d to a contrario(a) a; as ~d to in contrasto con; **opposing** *a* opposto(a); (*team*) avversario(a).

opposite ['ɔpəzit] *a* opposto(a); (*house etc*) di fronte // *ad* di fronte, dirimpetto // *prep* di fronte a // *n* opposto, contrario; (*of word*) contrario.

opposition [ɔpə'ziʃən] *n* opposizione *f*.

oppress [ə'prɛs] *vt* opprimere.

opt [ɔpt] *vi*: to ~ for optare per; to ~ to do scegliere di fare; to ~ out of ritirarsi da.

optical ['ɔptikl] *a* ottico(a); ~ **character recognition** (**OCR**) *n* lettura ottica; ~ **character reader** (**OCR**) *n* lettore ottico.

optician [ɔp'tiʃən] *n* ottico.

optimist ['ɔptimist] *n* ottimista *m/f*; ~ic [-'mistik] *a* ottimistico(a).

optimum ['ɔptiməm] *a* ottimale.

option ['ɔpʃən] *n* scelta; (*SCOL*) materia facoltativa; (*COMM*) opzione *f*; ~al *a* facoltativo(a); (*COMM*) a scelta.

or [ɔ:*] *cj* o, oppure; (*with negative*): he hasn't seen ~ heard anything non ha visto né sentito niente; ~ else se no, altrimenti; oppure.

oral ['ɔ:rəl] *a* orale // *n* esame *m* orale.

orange ['ɔrindʒ] *n* (*fruit*) arancia // *a* arancione.

orator ['ɔrətə*] *n* oratore/trice.

orbit ['ɔ:bit] *n* orbita.

orchard ['ɔ:tʃəd] *n* frutteto.

orchestra ['ɔ:kistrə] *n* orchestra; (*US: seating*) platea; ~l [-'kɛstrəl] *a* orchestrale; (*concert*) sinfonico(a).

orchid ['ɔ:kid] *n* orchidea.

ordain [ɔ:'dein] *vt* (*REL*) ordinare; (*decide*) decretare.

ordeal [ɔ:'di:l] *n* prova, travaglio.

order ['ɔ:də*] *n* ordine *m*; (*COMM*) ordinazione *f* // *vt* ordinare; in ~ in ordine; (*of document*) in regola; in (working) ~ funzionante; in ~ of size in ordine di grandezza; in ~ to do per fare; in ~ that affinché +*sub*; on ~ (*COMM*) in ordinazione; to ~ sb to do ordinare a qn di fare; the lower ~s (*pej*) i ceti inferiori; ~ **form** *n* modulo d'ordinazione; ~ly *n* (*MIL*) attendente *m* // *a* (*room*) in ordine; (*mind*) metodico(a); (*person*) ordinato(a), metodico(a).

ordinary ['ɔ:dnri] *a* normale, comune; (*pej*) mediocre; out of the ~ diverso dal solito, fuori dell'ordinario.

ore [ɔ:*] *n* minerale *m* grezzo.

organ ['ɔ:gən] *n* organo; ~ic [ɔ:'gænik] *a* organico(a).

organization [ɔ:gənai'zeiʃən] *n* organizzazione *f*.

organize ['ɔ:gənaiz] *vt* organizzare; ~r *n* organizzatore/trice.

orgasm ['ɔ:gæzəm] *n* orgasmo.

orgy ['ɔ:dʒi] *n* orgia.

Orient ['ɔ:riənt] *n*: the ~ l'Oriente *m*; **oriental** [-'ɛntl] *a, n* orientale (*m/f*).

origin ['ɔridʒin] *n* origine *f*.

original [ə'ridʒinl] *a* originale; (*earliest*) originario(a) // *n* originale *m*; ~ly *ad* (*at first*) all'inizio.

originate [ə'ridʒineit] *vi*: to ~ from essere originario(a) di; (*suggestion*) provenire da; to ~ in avere origine in.

Orkneys ['ɔ:kniz] *npl*: the ~ (*also*: the **Orkney Islands**) le Orcadi.

ornament ['ɔ:nəmənt] *n* ornamento; (*trinket*) ninnolo; ~al [-'mɛntl] *a* ornamentale.

ornate [ɔ:'neit] *a* molto ornato(a).

orphan ['ɔ:fn] *n* orfano/a // *vt*: to be ~ed diventare orfano; ~age *n* orfanotrofio.

orthodox ['ɔ:θədɔks] *a* ortodosso(a).

orthopaedic, (*US*) **orthopedic** [ɔ:θə'pi:dik] *a* ortopedico(a).

ostensibly [ɔs'tensibli] *ad* all'apparenza.

ostentatious [ɔstɛn'teiʃəs] *a* pretenzioso(a); ostentato(a).

ostrich ['ɒstrɪtʃ] n struzzo.

other ['ʌðə*] a altro(a) // pronoun: the ~ (one) l'altro(a); ~s (~ people) altri mpl; ~ than altro che; a parte; ~wise ad, cj altrimenti.

otter ['ɒtə*] n lontra.

ouch [autʃ] excl ohi!, ahi!

ought, pt ought [ɔːt] auxiliary vb: I ~ to do it dovrei farlo; this ~ to have been corrected questo avrebbe dovuto essere corretto; he ~ to win dovrebbe vincere.

ounce [auns] n oncia (= 28.35 g; 16 in a pound).

our ['auə*] a il(la) nostro(a), pl i(le) nostri(e); see also **my**; ~s pronoun il(la) nostro(a), pl i(le) nostri(e); see also **mine**; ~selves pronoun pl (reflexive) ci; (after preposition) noi; (emphatic) noi stessi(e); see also **oneself**.

oust [aust] vt cacciare, espellere.

out [aut] ad fuori; (published, not at home etc) uscito(a); (light, fire) spento(a); ~ here qui fuori; ~ there là fuori; he's ~ è uscito; (unconscious) ha perso conoscenza; to be ~ in one's calculations essersi sbagliato nei calcoli; to **run/back** etc ~ uscire di corsa/a marcia indietro etc; ~ loud ad ad alta voce; ~ of (outside) fuori di; (because of: anger etc) per; (from among): ~ of 10 su 10; (without): ~ of petrol senza benzina, a corto di benzina; ~ of order (machine etc) guasto(a); ~-and-~ a (liar, thief etc) vero(a) e proprio(a).

outback ['autbæk] n (in Australia) interno, entroterra.

outboard ['autbɔːd] n: ~ (motor) (motore m) fuoribordo.

outbreak ['autbreɪk] n scoppio; epidemia.

outburst ['autbəːst] n scoppio.

outcast ['autkɑːst] n esule m/f; (socially) paria m inv.

outcome ['autkʌm] n esito, risultato.

outcrop ['autkrɒp] n (of rock) affioramento.

outcry ['autkraɪ] n protesta, clamore m.

outdated [aut'deɪtɪd] a (custom, clothes) fuori moda; (idea) sorpassato(a).

outdo [aut'duː] vt irg sorpassare.

outdoor [aut'dɔː*] a all'aperto; ~s ad fuori; all'aria aperta.

outer ['autə*] a esteriore; ~ space n spazio cosmico.

outfit ['autfɪt] n equipaggiamento; (clothes) abito; "~ter's" (Brit) "confezioni da uomo".

outgoing ['autgəuɪŋ] a (character) socievole; ~s npl (Brit: expenses) spese fpl, uscite fpl.

outgrow [aut'grəu] vt irg (clothes) diventare troppo grande per.

outhouse ['authaus] n costruzione f annessa.

outing ['autɪŋ] n gita; escursione f.

outlandish [aut'lændɪʃ] a strano(a).

outlaw ['autlɔː] n fuorilegge m/f.

outlay ['autleɪ] n spese fpl; (investment) sborsa, spesa.

outlet ['autlet] n (for liquid etc) sbocco, scarico; (US ELEC) presa di corrente; (for emotion) sfogo; (for goods) sbocco; (also: retail ~) punto di vendita.

outline ['autlaɪn] n contorno, profilo; (summary) abbozzo, grandi linee fpl.

outlive [aut'lɪv] vt sopravvivere a.

outlook ['autluk] n prospettiva, vista.

outlying ['autlaɪɪŋ] a periferico(a).

outmoded [aut'məudɪd] a passato(a) di moda; antiquato(a).

outnumber [aut'nʌmbə*] vt superare in numero.

out-of-date [autəv'deɪt] a (passport) scaduto(a); (clothes) fuori moda inv.

out-of-the-way ['autəvðə'weɪ] a (place) fuori mano inv.

outpatient ['autpeɪʃənt] n paziente m/f esterno(a).

outpost ['autpəust] n avamposto.

output ['autput] n produzione f; (COMPUT) output m inv.

outrage ['autreɪdʒ] n oltraggio; scandalo // vt oltraggiare; ~ous [-'reɪdʒəs] a oltraggioso(a); scandaloso(a).

outright ad [aut'raɪt] completamente; schiettamente; apertamente; sul colpo // a ['autraɪt] completo(a); schietto(a) e netto(a).

outset ['autset] n inizio.

outside [aut'saɪd] n esterno, esteriore m // a esterno(a), esteriore // ad fuori, all'esterno // prep fuori di, all'esterno di; at the ~ (fig) al massimo; ~ lane n (AUT) corsia di sorpasso; ~-left/-right n (FOOTBALL) ala sinistra/destra; ~ line n (TEL) linea esterna; ~r n (in race etc) outsider m inv; (stranger) straniero/a.

outsize ['autsaɪz] a enorme; (clothes) per taglie forti.

outskirts ['autskəːts] npl sobborghi mpl.

outspoken [aut'spəukən] a molto franco(a).

outstanding [aut'stændɪŋ] a eccezionale, di rilievo; (unfinished) non completo(a); non evaso(a); non regolato(a).

outstay [aut'steɪ] vt: to ~ one's welcome diventare un ospite sgradito.

outstretched [aut'stretʃt] a (hand) teso(a); (body) disteso(a).

outstrip [aut'strɪp] vt (competitors, demand) superare.

out-tray ['auttreɪ] n contenitore m per la corrispondenza in partenza.

outward ['autwəd] a (sign, appearances) esteriore; (journey) d'andata; ~ly ad esteriormente; in apparenza.

outweigh [aut'weɪ] vt avere maggior peso di.

outwit [aut'wɪt] vt superare in astuzia.

oval ['əʊvl] *a, n* ovale (*m*).

ovary ['əʊvərɪ] *n* ovaia.

oven ['ʌvn] *n* forno; **~proof** *a* da forno.

over ['əʊvə*] *ad* al di sopra // *a* (*or ad*) (*finished*) finito(a), terminato(a); (*too*) troppo; (*remaining*) che avanza // *prep* su; sopra; (*above*) al di sopra di; (*on the other side of*) di là di; (*more than*) più di; (*during*) durante; **~ here** qui; **~ there** là; **all ~** (*everywhere*) dappertutto; (*finished*) tutto(a) finito(a); **~ and ~** (*again*) più e più volte; **~ and above** oltre (a); **to ask sb ~** invitare qn (a passare).

overall *a, n* ['əʊvərɔːl] *a* totale // *n* (*Brit*) grembiule *m* // *ad* [əʊvər'ɔːl] nell'insieme, complessivamente; **~s** *npl* tuta (da lavoro).

overawe [əʊvər'ɔː] *vt* intimidire.

overbalance [əʊvə'bæləns] *vi* perdere l'equilibrio.

overbearing [əʊvə'bɛərɪŋ] *a* imperioso(a), prepotente.

overboard ['əʊvəbɔːd] *ad* (*NAUT*) fuori bordo, in mare.

overbook [əʊvə'buk] *vt*: **the hotel was ~ed** le prenotazioni all'albergo superavano i posti disponibili.

overcast ['əʊvəkɑːst] *a* coperto(a).

overcharge [əʊvə'tʃɑːdʒ] *vt*: **to ~ sb for sth** far pagare troppo caro a qn per qc.

overcoat ['əʊvəkəʊt] *n* soprabito, cappotto.

overcome [əʊvə'kʌm] *vt irg* superare; sopraffare.

overcrowded [əʊvə'kraudɪd] *a* sovraffollato(a).

overdo [əʊvə'duː] *vt irg* esagerare; (*overcook*) cuocere troppo.

overdose ['əʊvədəʊs] *n* dose *f* eccessiva.

overdraft ['əʊvədrɑːft] *n* scoperto (di conto).

overdrawn [əʊvə'drɔːn] *a* (*account*) scoperto(a).

overdue [əʊvə'djuː] *a* in ritardo; (*recognition*) tardivo(a).

overestimate [əʊvər'ɛstɪmeɪt] *vt* sopravvalutare.

overflow *vi* [əʊvə'fləʊ] traboccare // *n* ['əʊvəfləʊ] troppopieno.

overgrown [əʊvə'grəʊn] *a* (*garden*) ricoperto(a) di vegetazione.

overhaul *vt* [əʊvə'hɔːl] revisionare // *n* ['əʊvəhɔːl] revisione *f*.

overhead *ad* [əʊvə'hɛd] di sopra // *a* ['əʊvəhɛd] aereo(a); (*lighting*) verticale; **~s** *npl*, (*US*) **~** *n* spese *fpl* generali.

overhear [əʊvə'hɪə*] *vt irg* sentire (per caso).

overheat [əʊvə'hiːt] *vi* (*engine*) surriscaldare.

overjoyed [əʊvə'dʒɔɪd] *a* pazzo(a) di gioia.

overkill ['əʊvəkɪl] *n* (*fig*) eccessi *mpl*.

overlap [əʊvə'læp] *vi* sovrapporsi.

overleaf [əʊvə'liːf] *ad* a tergo.

overload [əʊvə'ləʊd] *vt* sovraccaricare.

overlook [əʊvə'luk] *vt* (*have view of*) dare su; (*miss*) trascurare; (*forgive*) passare sopra a.

overnight [əʊvə'naɪt] *ad* (*happen*) durante la notte; (*fig*) tutto ad un tratto // *a* di notte; fulmineo(a); **he stayed there ~** ci ha passato la notte.

overpower [əʊvə'pauə*] *vt* sopraffare; **~ing** *a* irresistibile; (*heat, stench*) soffocante.

overrate [əʊvə'reɪt] *vt* sopravvalutare.

override [əʊvə'raɪd] *vt* (*irg: like* ride) (*order, objection*) passar sopra a; (*decision*) annullare; **overriding** *a* preponderante.

overrule [əʊvə'ruːl] *vt* (*decision*) annullare; (*claim*) respingere.

overrun [əʊvə'rʌn] *vt* (*irg: like* run) (*country*) invadere; (*time limit*) superare.

overseas [əʊvə'siːz] *ad* oltremare; (*abroad*) all'estero // *a* (*trade*) estero(a); (*visitor*) straniero(a).

overseer ['əʊvəsɪə*] *n* (*in factory*) caposquadra *m*.

overshadow [əʊvə'ʃædəʊ] *vt* (*fig*) eclissare.

overshoot [əʊvə'ʃuːt] *vt irg* superare.

oversight ['əʊvəsaɪt] *n* omissione *f*, svista.

oversleep [əʊvə'sliːp] *vi irg* dormire troppo a lungo.

overstep [əʊvə'stɛp] *vt*: **to ~ the mark** superare ogni limite.

overt [əʊ'vɜːt] *a* palese.

overtake [əʊvə'teɪk] *vt irg* sorpassare.

overthrow [əʊvə'θrəʊ] *vt irg* (*government*) rovesciare.

overtime ['əʊvətaɪm] *n* (lavoro) straordinario.

overtone ['əʊvətəʊn] *n* (*also*: **~s**) sfumatura.

overture ['əʊvətʃuə*] *n* (*MUS*) ouverture *f inv*; (*fig*) approccio.

overturn [əʊvə'tɜːn] *vt* rovesciare // *vi* rovesciarsi.

overweight [əʊvə'weɪt] *a* (*person*) troppo grasso(a); (*luggage*) troppo pesante.

overwhelm [əʊvə'wɛlm] *vt* sopraffare; sommergere; schiacciare; **~ing** *a* (*victory, defeat*) schiacciante; (*desire*) irresistibile.

overwork [əʊvə'wɜːk] *vt* far lavorare troppo // *vi* lavorare troppo, strapazzarsi.

overwrought [əʊvə'rɔːt] *a* molto agitato(a).

owe [əʊ] *vt* dovere; **to ~ sb sth, to ~ sth to sb** dovere qc a qn.

owing to ['əʊɪŋtuː] *prep* a causa di.

owl [aul] *n* gufo.

own [əʊn] *vt* possedere // *a* proprio(a); **a room of my ~** la mia propria camera; **to**

get one's ~ back vendicarsi; on one's ~ tutto(a) solo(a); **to ~ up** vi confessare; **~er** n proprietario/a; **~ership** n possesso.

ox, pl **oxen** [ɔks, 'ɔksn] n bue m.

oxtail ['ɔksteɪl] n: ~ **soup** minestra di coda di bue.

oxygen ['ɔksɪdʒən] n ossigeno; ~ **mask** n maschera ad ossigeno.

oyster ['ɔɪstə*] n ostrica.

oz. abbr = **ounce(s)**.

ozone ['əuzəun] n ozono.

P

p [piː] abbr = **penny, pence**.

pa [paː] n (col) papà m inv, babbo.

P.A. n abbr = **personal assistant, public address system**.

p.a. abbr = **per annum**.

pace [peɪs] n passo; (speed) passo; velocità // vi: to ~ **up and down** camminare su e giù; to **keep** ~ **with** camminare di pari passo a; (events) tenersi al corrente di; **~maker** n (MED) segnapasso.

pacific [pə'sɪfɪk] n: the P~ (Ocean) il Pacifico, l'Oceano Pacifico.

pack [pæk] n pacco; balla; (of hounds) muta; (of thieves etc) banda; (of cards) mazzo // vt (goods) impaccare, imballare; (in suitcase etc) mettere; (box) riempire; (cram) stipare, pigiare; (press down) tamponare; turare; to ~ (one's bags) fare la valigia; **to ~ off** vt (person) spedire.

package ['pækɪdʒ] n pacco; balla; (also: ~ **deal**) pacchetto; forfait m inv; ~ **tour** n viaggio organizzato.

packed lunch n pranzo al sacco.

packet ['pækɪt] n pacchetto.

packing ['pækɪŋ] n imballaggio; ~ **case** n cassa da imballaggio.

pact [pækt] n patto, accordo; trattato.

pad [pæd] n blocco; (for inking) tampone m; (col: flat) appartamentino // vt imbottire; **~ding** n imbottitura; (fig) riempitivo.

paddle ['pædl] n (oar) pagaia; (US: for table tennis) racchetta da ping-pong // vi sguazzare // vt: to ~ **a canoe** etc vogare con la pagaia; ~ **steamer** n battello a ruote; **paddling pool** n (Brit) piscina per bambini.

paddy field ['pædɪ-] n risaia.

padlock ['pædlɔk] n lucchetto.

paediatrics, (US) **pediatrics** [piːdɪ'ætrɪks] n pediatria.

pagan ['peɪgən] a, n pagano(a).

page [peɪdʒ] n pagina; (also: ~ **boy**) fattorino; (at wedding) paggio // vt (in hotel etc) (far) chiamare.

pageant ['pædʒənt] n spettacolo storico; grande cerimonia; **~ry** n pompa.

paid [peɪd] pt, pp of **pay** // a (work, official) rimunerato(a); **to put** ~ **to** (Brit) mettere fine a.

pail [peɪl] n secchio.

pain [peɪn] n dolore m; **to be in** ~ soffrire, aver male; **to take ~s to do** mettercela tutta per fare; **~ed** a addolorato(a), afflitto(a); **~ful** a doloroso(a), che fa male; difficile, penoso(a); **~fully** ad (fig: very) fin troppo; **~killer** n antalgico, antidolorifico; **~less** a indolore.

painstaking ['peɪnzteɪkɪŋ] a (person) sollecito(a); (work) accurato(a).

paint [peɪnt] n vernice f, colore m // vt dipingere; (walls, door etc) verniciare; to ~ **the door blue** verniciare la porta di azzurro; **~brush** n pennello; **~er** n (artist) pittore m; (decorator) imbianchino; **~ing** n pittura; verniciatura; (picture) dipinto, quadro; **~work** n tinta; (of car) vernice f.

pair [peə*] n (of shoes, gloves etc) paio; (of people) coppia; duo m inv; **a** ~ **of scissors/trousers** un paio di forbici/ pantaloni.

pajamas [pɪ'dʒɑːməz] npl (US) pigiama m.

Pakistan [paːkɪ'stuːn] n Pakistan m; **~i** a, n pakistano(a).

pal [pæl] n (col) amico/a, compagno/a.

palace ['pæləs] n palazzo.

palatable ['pælɪtəbl] a gustoso(a).

palate ['pælɪt] n palato.

palatial [pə'leɪʃəl] a sontuoso(a), sfarzoso(a).

palaver [pə'lɑːvə*] n chiacchiere fpl; storie fpl.

pale [peɪl] a pallido(a) // n: **to be beyond the** ~ aver oltrepassato ogni limite; **to grow** ~ diventare pallido, impallidire.

Palestine ['pælɪstaɪn] n Palestina; **Palestinian** [-'tɪnɪən] a, n palestinese (m/f).

palette ['pælɪt] n tavolozza.

paling ['peɪlɪŋ] n (stake) palo; (fence) palizzata.

pall [pɔːl] n (of smoke) cappa // vi: to ~ (on) diventare noioso(a) (a).

pallet ['pælɪt] n (for goods) paletta.

pallid ['pælɪd] a pallido(a), smorto(a).

pallor ['pælə*] n pallore m.

palm [paːm] n (ANAT) palma, palmo; (also: ~ **tree**) palma // vt: to ~ **sth off on sb** (col) rifilare qc a qn; P~ **Sunday** n Domenica delle Palme.

palpable ['pælpəbl] a palpabile.

paltry ['pɔːltrɪ] a derisorio(a); insignificante.

pamper ['pæmpə*] vt viziare, accarezzare.

pamphlet ['pæmflət] n dépliant m inv.

pan [pæn] n (also: **sauce~**) casseruola; (also: **frying** ~) padella // vi (CINEMA) fare una panoramica.

panache [pə'næʃ] *n* stile *m*.

pancake ['pænkeɪk] *n* frittella.

pancreas ['pæŋkrɪəs] *n* pancreas *m inv*.

panda ['pændə] *n* panda *m inv*; ~ **car** *n* (*Brit*) auto *f* della polizia.

pandemonium [pændɪ'məʊnɪəm] *n* pandemonio.

pander ['pændə*] *vi*: to ~ to lusingare; concedere tutto a.

pane [peɪn] *n* vetro.

panel ['pænl] *n* (*of wood, cloth etc*) pannello; (*RADIO, TV*) giuria; ~**ling**, (*US*) ~**ing** *n* rivestimento a pannelli.

pang [pæŋ] *n*: ~s of hunger spasimi *mpl* della fame; ~s of conscience morsi *mpl* di coscienza.

panic ['pænɪk] *n* panico // *vi* perdere il sangue freddo; ~**ky** *a* (*person*) pauroso(a); ~-**stricken** *a* (*person*) preso(a) dal panico, in preda al panico; (*look*) terrorizzato(a).

pansy ['pænzɪ] *n* (*BOT*) viola del pensiero, pensée *f inv*; (*col*) femminuccia.

pant [pænt] *vi* ansare.

panther ['pænθə*] *n* pantera.

panties [pæntɪz] *npl* slip *m*, mutandine *fpl*.

pantihose ['pæntɪhəʊz] *n* (*US*) collant *m inv*.

pantomime ['pæntəmaɪm] *n* (*Brit*) pantomima.

pantry ['pæntrɪ] *n* dispensa.

pants [pænts] *npl* mutande *fpl*, slip *m*; (*US*: *trousers*) pantaloni *mpl*.

papal ['peɪpəl] *a* papale, pontificio(a).

paper ['peɪpə*] *n* carta; (*also*: wall~) carta da parati, tappezzeria; (*also*: news~) giornale *m*; (*study, article*) saggio; (*exam*) prova scritta // *a* di carta // *vt* tappezzare; ~s *npl* (*also*: identity ~s) carte *fpl*, documenti *mpl*; ~**back** *n* tascabile *m*; edizione *f* economica; ~ **clip** *n* graffetta, clip *f inv*; ~ **hankie** *n* fazzolettino di carta; ~ **mill** *n* cartiera; ~**weight** *n* fermacarte *m inv*; ~**work** *n* lavoro amministrativo.

papier-mâché ['pæpɪeɪ'mæʃeɪ] *n* cartapesta.

par [pɑ:*] *n* parità, pari *f*; (*GOLF*) norma; on a ~ with alla pari con.

parable ['pærəbl] *n* parabola.

parachute ['pærəʃu:t] *n* paracadute *m inv*.

parade [pə'reɪd] *n* parata; (*inspection*) rivista, rassegna // *vt* (*fig*) fare sfoggio di // *vi* sfilare in parata.

paradise ['pærədaɪs] *n* paradiso.

paradox ['pærədɒks] *n* paradosso; ~**ically** [-'dɒksɪklɪ] *ad* paradossalmente.

paraffin ['pærəfɪn] *n* (*Brit*): ~ (oil) paraffina.

paragon ['pærəgən] *n* modello di perfezione *or* di virtù.

paragraph ['pærəgrɑ:f] *n* paragrafo.

parallel ['pærəlɛl] *a* parallelo(a); (*fig*) analogo(a) // *n* (*line*) parallela; (*fig, GEO*) parallelo.

paralysis [pə'rælɪsɪs] *n* paralisi *f inv*.

paralyze ['pærəlaɪz] *vt* paralizzare.

paramount ['pærəmaʊnt] *a*: of ~ importance di capitale importanza.

paranoid ['pærənɔɪd] *a* paranoico(a).

paraphernalia [pærəfə'neɪlɪə] *n* attrezzi *mpl*, roba.

parasol ['pærəsɒl] *n* parasole *m*.

paratrooper ['pærətru:pə*] *n* paracadutista *m* (*soldato*).

parcel ['pɑ:sl] *n* pacco, pacchetto // *vt* (*also*: ~ up) impaccare.

parch [pɑ:tʃ] *vt* riardere; ~**ed** *a* (*person*) assetato(a).

parchment ['pɑ:tʃmənt] *n* pergamena.

pardon ['pɑ:dn] *n* perdono; grazia // *vt* perdonare; (*LAW*) graziare; ~ me! mi scusi!; I beg your ~! scusi!; I beg your ~?, (*US*) ~ me? prego?

parent ['peərənt] *n* genitore *m*; ~s *npl* genitori *mpl*; ~**al** [pə'rɛntl] *a* dei genitori.

parenthesis, *pl* **parentheses** [pə'rɛnθɪsɪs, -sɪ:z] *n* parentesi *f inv*.

Paris ['pærɪs] *n* Parigi *f*.

parish ['pærɪʃ] *n* parrocchia; (*civil*) ≈ municipio // *a* parrocchiale.

park [pɑ:k] *n* parco // *vt, vi* parcheggiare.

parka ['pɑ:kə] *n* eskimo.

parking ['pɑ:kɪŋ] *n* parcheggio; "no ~" "sosta vietata"; ~ **lot** *n* (*US*) posteggio, parcheggio; ~ **meter** *n* parchimetro; ~ **ticket** *n* multa per sosta vietata.

parlance ['pɑ:ləns] *n* gergo.

parliament ['pɑ:ləmənt] *n* parlamento; ~**ary** [-'mɛntərɪ] *a* parlamentare.

parlour, (*US*) **parlor** ['pɑ:lə*] *n* salotto.

parochial [pə'rəʊkɪəl] *a* parrocchiale; (*pej*) provinciale.

parody ['pærədɪ] *n* parodia.

parole [pə'rəʊl] *n*: on ~ in libertà per buona condotta.

parrot ['pærət] *n* pappagallo.

parry ['pærɪ] *vt* parare.

parsley ['pɑ:slɪ] *n* prezzemolo.

parsnip ['pɑ:snɪp] *n* pastinaca.

parson ['pɑ:sn] *n* prete *m*; (*Church of England*) parroco.

part [pɑ:t] *n* parte *f*; (*of machine*) pezzo; (*MUS*) voce *f*; parte; (*US*: *in hair*) scriminatura // *a* in parte // *ad* = **partly** // *vt* separare *vi* (*people*) separarsi; (*roads*) dividersi; to take ~ in prendere parte a; for my ~ per parte mia; to take sth in good ~ prendere bene qc; to take sb's ~ parteggiare per *or* prendere le parti di qn; for the most ~ in generale; nella maggior parte dei casi; to ~ with *vt fus* separarsi da; rinunciare a; ~ **exchange** *n* (*Brit*): in ~ exchange in pagamento parziale.

partial ['pɑ:ʃl] *a* parziale; to be ~ to

avere un debole per.

participate [pɑ:'tɪsɪpeɪt] *vi*: to ~ (in) prendere parte (a), partecipare (a); **participation** [-'peɪʃən] *n* partecipazione *f*.

participle ['pɑ:tɪsɪpl] *n* participio.

particle ['pɑ:tɪkl] *n* particella.

particular [pə'tɪkjulə*] *a* particolare; speciale; (*fussy*) difficile; meticoloso(a); ~**s** *npl* particolari *mpl*, dettagli *mpl*; (*information*) informazioni *fpl*; **in** ~ in particolare, particolarmente; ~**ly** *ad* particolarmente; in particolare.

parting ['pɑ:tɪŋ] *n* separazione *f*; (*Brit: in hair*) scriminatura // *a* d'addio.

partisan [pɑ:tɪ'zæn] *n* partigiano/a // *a* partigiano(a); di parte.

partition [pɑ:'tɪʃən] *n* (*POL*) partizione *f*; (*wall*) tramezzo.

partly ['pɑ:tlɪ] *ad* parzialmente; in parte.

partner ['pɑ:tnə*] *n* (*COMM*) socio/a; (*SPORT*) compagno/a; (*at dance*) cavaliere/dama; ~**ship** *n* associazione *f*; (*COMM*) società *f inv*.

partridge ['pɑ:trɪdʒ] *n* pernice *f*.

part-time ['pɑ:t'taɪm] *a, ad* a orario ridotto.

party ['pɑ:tɪ] *n* (*POL*) partito; (*team*) squadra; gruppo; (*LAW*) parte *f*; (*celebration*) ricevimento; serata; festa // *cpd* (*POL*) del partito, di partito; (*dress, finery*) della festa; ~ **line** *n* (*TEL*) duplex *m inv*.

pass [pɑ:s] *vt* (*gen*) passare; (*place*) passare davanti a; (*exam*) passare, superare; (*candidate*) promuovere; (*overtake, surpass*) sorpassare, superare; (*approve*) approvare // *vi* passare // *n* (*permit*) lasciapassare *m inv*; permesso; (*in mountains*) passo, gola; (*SPORT*) passaggio; (*SCOL: also*: ~ **mark**): **to get a** ~ prendere la sufficienza; **to** ~ **sth through a hole** *etc* far passare qc attraverso un buco *etc*; **to make a** ~ **at sb** (*col*) fare delle proposte *or* delle avances a qn; **to** ~ **away** *vi* morire; **to** ~ **by** *vi* passare // *vt* trascurare; **to** ~ **on** *vt* passare; **to** ~ **out** *vi* svenire; **to** ~ **up** *vt* (*opportunity*) lasciarsi sfuggire, perdere; ~**able** *a* (*road*) praticabile; (*work*) accettabile.

passage ['pæsɪdʒ] *n* (*gen*) passaggio; (*also*: ~**way**) corridoio; (*in book*) brano, passo; (*by boat*) traversata.

passbook ['pɑ:sbuk] *n* libretto di risparmio.

passenger ['pæsɪndʒə*] *n* passeggero/a.

passer-by ['pɑ:sə'baɪ] *n* passante *m/f*.

passing ['pɑ:sɪŋ] *a* (*fig*) fuggevole; **to mention sth in** ~ accennare a qc di sfuggita; ~ **place** *n* (*AUT*) piazzola di sosta.

passion ['pæʃən] *n* passione *f*; amore *m*; ~**ate** *a* appassionato(a).

passive ['pæsɪv] *a* (*also LING*)

passivo(a).

Passover ['pɑ:səuvə*] *n* Pasqua ebraica.

passport ['pɑ:spɔ:t] *n* passaporto; ~ **control** *n* controllo *m* passaporti *inv*.

password ['pɑ:swɔ:d] *n* parola d'ordine.

past [pɑ:st] *prep* (*further than*) oltre, di là di; dopo; (*later than*) dopo // *a* passato(a); (*president etc*) ex *inv* // *n* passato; **he's** ~ **forty** ha più di quarant'anni; **for the** ~ **few days** da qualche giorno; in questi ultimi giorni; **to run** ~ passare di corsa.

pasta ['pæstə] *n* pasta.

paste [peɪst] *n* (*glue*) colla; (*CULIN*) pâté *m inv*; pasta // *vt* collare.

pastel ['pæstl] *a* pastello *inv*.

pasteurized ['pæstəraɪzd] *a* pastorizzato(a).

pastille ['pæstl] *n* pastiglia.

pastime ['pɑ:staɪm] *n* passatempo.

pastor ['pɑ:stə*] *n* pastore *m*.

pastry ['peɪstrɪ] *n* pasta.

pasture ['pɑ:stʃə*] *n* pascolo.

pasty *n* ['pæstɪ] pasticcio di carne // *a* ['peɪstɪ] pastoso(a); (*complexion*) pallido(a).

pat [pæt] *vt* accarezzare, dare un colpetto (affettuoso) a.

patch [pætʃ] *n* (*of material*) toppa; (*spot*) macchia; (*of land*) pezzo // *vt* (*clothes*) rattoppare; (**to go through**) **a bad** ~ (attraversare) un brutto periodo; **to** ~ **up** *vt* rappezzare; ~**y** *a* irregolare.

pâté ['pætɪ] *n* pâté *m inv*.

patent ['peɪtnt] *n* brevetto // *vt* brevettare // *a* patente, manifesto(a); ~ **leather** *n* cuoio verniciato.

paternal [pə'tə:nl] *a* paterno(a).

path [pɑ:θ] *n* sentiero, viottolo; viale *m*; (*fig*) via, strada; (*of planet, missile*) traiettoria.

pathetic [pə'θetɪk] *a* (*pitiful*) patetico(a); (*very bad*) penoso(a).

pathological [pæθə'lɔdʒɪkl] *a* patologico(a).

patience ['peɪʃns] *n* pazienza; (*Brit CARDS*) solitario.

patient ['peɪʃnt] *n* paziente *m/f*; malato/a // *a* paziente.

patio ['pætɪəu] *n* terrazza.

patriot ['peɪtrɪət] *n* patriota *m/f*; ~**ic** [pætrɪ'ɔtɪk] *a* patriottico(a); ~**ism** *n* patriottismo.

patrol [pə'trəul] *n* pattuglia // *vt* pattugliare; ~ **car** *n* autoradio *f inv* (della polizia); ~**man** *n* (*US*) poliziotto.

patron ['peɪtrən] *n* (*in shop*) cliente *m/f*; (*of charity*) benefattore/trice; ~ **of the arts** mecenate *m/f*; ~**ize** ['pætrənaɪz] *vt* essere cliente abituale di; (*fig*) trattare con condiscendenza.

patter ['pætə*] *n* picchiettio; (*sales talk*) propaganda di vendita.

pattern ['pætən] *n* modello; (*design*)

disegno, motivo; (*sample*) campione *m*.
paunch [pɔ:ntʃ] *n* pancione *m*.
pauper ['pɔ:pə*] *n* indigente *m/f*.
pause [pɔ:z] *n* pausa // *vi* fare una pausa, arrestarsi.
pave [peɪv] *vt* pavimentare; to ~ the way for aprire la via a.
pavement ['peɪvmənt] *n* (*Brit*) marciapiede *m*.
pavilion [pə'vɪlɪən] *n* padiglione *m*; tendone *m*.
paving ['peɪvɪŋ] *n* pavimentazione *f*; ~ stone *n* lastra di pietra.
paw [pɔ:] *n* zampa // *vt* dare una zampata a; (*subj: person: pej*) palpare.
pawn [pɔ:n] *n* pegno; (*CHESS*) pedone *m*; (*fig*) pedina // *vt* dare in pegno; ~broker *n* prestatore *m* su pegno; ~shop *n* monte *m* di pietà.
pay [peɪ] *n* stipendio; paga // *vb* (*pt, pp* paid) *vt* pagare // *vi* pagare; (*be profit-able*) rendere; to ~ attention (to) fare attenzione (a); to ~ back *vt* rimborsare; to ~ for *vt fus* pagare; to ~ in *vt* versare; to ~ off *vt* (*debt*) saldare; (*person*) pagare; (*employee*) pagare e licenziare // *vi* (*scheme, decision*) dare dei frutti; to ~ up *vt* saldare; ~able *a* pagabile; ~ee *n* beneficiario/a; ~ envelope *n* (*US*) = ~ packet; ~ment *n* pagamento; versamento; saldamento; advance ~ment (*part sum*) anticipo, acconto; (*total sum*) pagamento anticipato; ~ packet *n* (*Brit*) busta *f* paga *inv*; ~ phone *n* cabina telefonica; ~roll *n* ruolo (organico); ~ slip *n* foglio *m* paga *inv*.
PC *n abbr* = **personal computer**.
p.c. *abbr* = **per cent**.
pea [pi:] *n* pisello.
peace [pi:s] *n* pace *f*; (*calm*) calma, tranquillità; ~able *a* pacifico(a); ~ful *a* pacifico(a), calmo(a).
peach [pi:tʃ] *n* pesca.
peacock ['pi:kɔk] *n* pavone *m*.
peak [pi:k] *n* (*of mountain*) cima, vetta; (*mountain itself*) picco; (*fig*) massimo; (: *of career*) acme *f*; ~ hours *npl* ore *fpl* di punta.
peal [pi:l] *n* (*of bells*) scampanio, carillon *m inv*; ~s of laughter scoppi *mpl* di risa.
peanut ['pi:nʌt] *n* arachide *f*, nocciolina americana.
pear [pɛə*] *n* pera.
pearl [pə:l] *n* perla.
peasant ['pɛznt] *n* contadino/a.
peat [pi:t] *n* torba.
pebble ['pɛbl] *n* ciottolo.
peck [pɛk] *vt* (*also*: ~ at) beccare; (*food*) mangiucchiare // *n* colpo di becco; (*kiss*) bacetto; ~ing order *n* ordine *m* gerarchico; ~ish *a* (*Brit col*): I feel ~ish ho un languorino.
peculiar [pɪ'kju:lɪə*] *a* strano(a),

bizzarro(a); peculiare; ~ to peculiare di.
pedal ['pɛdl] *n* pedale *m* // *vi* pedalare.
pedantic [pɪ'dæntɪk] *a* pedantesco(a).
peddler ['pɛdlə*] *n* (*US*) = **pedlar**.
pedestal ['pɛdəstl] *n* piedestallo.
pedestrian [pɪ'dɛstrɪən] *n* pedone/a // *a* pedonale; (*fig*) prosaico(a), pedestre; ~ crossing *n* (*Brit*) passaggio pedonale.
pediatrics [pi:dɪ'ætrɪks] *n* (*US*) = **paediatrics**.
pedigree ['pɛdɪgri:] *n* stirpe *f*; (*of animal*) pedigree *m inv* // *cpd* (*animal*) di razza.
pedlar ['pɛdlə*] *n* venditore *m* ambulante.
pee [pi:] *vi* (*col*) pisciare.
peek [pi:k] *vi* guardare furtivamente.
peel [pi:l] *n* buccia; (*of orange, lemon*) scorza // *vt* sbucciare // *vi* (*paint etc*) staccarsi.
peep [pi:p] *n* (*Brit: look*) sguardo furtivo, sbirciata; (*sound*) pigolio // *vi* (*Brit*) guardare furtivamente; to ~ out *vi* mostrarsi furtivamente; ~hole *n* spioncino.
peer [pɪə*] *vi*: to ~ at scrutare // *n* (*no-ble*) pari *m inv*; (*equal*) pari *m/f inv*, uguale *m/f*; ~age *n* dignità di pari; pari *mpl*.
peeved [pi:vd] *a* stizzito(a).
peevish ['pi:vɪʃ] *a* stizzoso(a).
peg [pɛg] *n* caviglia; (*for coat etc*) attaccapanni *m inv*; (*Brit: also*: clothes ~) molletta // *vt* (*prices*) fissare, stabilizzare.
Peking [pi:'kɪŋ] *n* Pechino *f*.
pelican ['pɛlɪkən] *n* pellicano; ~ crossing *n* (*Brit AUT*) attraversamento pedonale con semaforo a controllo manuale.
pellet ['pɛlɪt] *n* pallottola, pallina.
pelmet ['pɛlmɪt] *n* mantovana; cassonetto.
pelt [pɛlt] *vt*: to ~ sb (with) bombardare qn (con) // *vi* (*rain*) piovere a dirotto // *n* pelle *f*.
pelvis ['pɛlvɪs] *n* pelvi *f inv*, bacino.
pen [pɛn] *n* penna; (*for sheep*) recinto.
penal ['pi:nl] *a* penale; ~ize *vt* punire; (*SPORT*) penalizzare; (*fig*) svantaggiare.
penalty ['pɛnltɪ] *n* penalità *f inv*; sanzione *f* penale; (*fine*) ammenda; (*SPORT*) penalizzazione *f*; ~ (kick) *n* (*FOOTBALL*) calcio di rigore.
penance ['pɛnəns] *n* penitenza.
pence [pɛns] *npl of* **penny**.
pencil ['pɛnsl] *n* matita; ~ case *n* astuccio per matite; ~ sharpener *n* temperamatite *m inv*.
pendant ['pɛndnt] *n* pendaglio.
pending ['pɛndɪŋ] *prep* in attesa di // *a* in sospeso.
pendulum ['pɛndjuləm] *n* pendolo.
penetrate ['pɛnɪtreɪt] *vt* penetrare.
penfriend ['pɛnfrɛnd] *n* (*Brit*) corri-

spondente *m/f*.

penguin ['pɛŋgwɪn] *n* pinguino.

penicillin [pɛnɪ'sɪlɪn] *n* penicillina.

peninsula [pə'nɪnsjulə] *n* penisola.

penis ['pi:nɪs] *n* pene *m*.

penitent ['pɛnɪtnt] *a* penitente.

penitentiary [pɛnɪ'tɛnʃərɪ] *n* (*US*) carcere *m*.

penknife ['pɛnnaɪf] *n* temperino.

pen name *n* pseudonimo.

penniless ['pɛnɪlɪs] *a* senza un soldo.

penny, *pl* **pennies** *or* (*Brit*) **pence** ['pɛnɪ, 'pɛnɪz, pɛns] *n* penny *m* (*pl* pence); (*US*) centesimo.

penpal ['pɛnpæl] *n* corrispondente *m/f*.

pension ['pɛnʃən] *n* pensione *f*; **~er** *n* (*Brit*) pensionato/a.

pensive ['pɛnsɪv] *a* pensoso(a).

penthouse ['pɛnthaus] *n* appartamento (di lusso) nell'attico.

pent-up ['pɛntʌp] *a* (*feelings*) represso(a).

people ['pi:pl] *npl* gente *f*; persone *fpl*; (*citizens*) popolo // *n* (*nation, race*) popolo // *vt* popolare; **4/several ~ came** 4/parecchie persone sono venute; **the room was full of ~** la stanza era piena di gente.

pep [pɛp] *n* (*col*) dinamismo; **to ~ up** *vt* vivacizzare; (*food*) rendere più gustoso(a).

pepper ['pɛpə*] *n* pepe *m*; (*vegetable*) peperone *m* // *vt* pepare; **~mint** *n* (*plant*) menta peperita; (*sweet*) pasticca di menta.

peptalk ['pɛptɔːk] *n* (*col*) discorso di incoraggiamento.

per [pə:*] *prep* per; a; **~ hour** all'ora; **~ kilo** *etc* il chilo *etc*; **~ day** al giorno; **~ annum** *ad* all'anno; **~ capita** *a* pro capite *inv*.

perceive [pə'si:v] *vt* percepire; (*notice*) accorgersi di.

per cent [pə:'sɛnt] *ad* per cento.

percentage [pə'sɛntɪdʒ] *n* percentuale *f*.

perception [pə'sɛpʃən] *n* percezione *f*; sensibilità; perspicacia.

perceptive [pə'sɛptɪv] *a* percettivo(a); perspicace.

perch [pə:tʃ] *n* (*fish*) pesce *m* persico; (*for bird*) sostegno, ramo // *vi* appollaiarsi.

percolator ['pə:kəleɪtə*] *n* caffettiera a pressione; caffettiera elettrica.

percussion [pə'kʌʃən] *n* percussione *f*; (*MUS*) strumenti *mpl* a percussione.

peremptory [pə'rɛmptərɪ] *a* perentorio(a).

perennial [pə'rɛnɪəl] *a* perenne // *n* pianta perenne.

perfect *a, n* ['pə:fɪkt] *a* perfetto(a) // *n* (*also:* **~ tense**) perfetto, passato prossimo // *vt* [pə'fɛkt] perfezionare; mettere a punto; **~ly** *ad* perfettamente, alla perfezione.

perforate ['pə:fəreɪt] *vt* perforare; **perforation** [-'reɪʃən] *n* perforazione *f*; (*line of holes*) dentellatura.

perform [pə'fɔ:m] *vt* (*carry out*) eseguire, fare; (*symphony etc*) suonare; (*play, ballet*) dare; (*opera*) fare // *vi* suonare; recitare; **~ance** *n* esecuzione *f*; (*at theatre etc*) rappresentazione *f*, spettacolo; (*of an artist*) interpretazione *f*; (*of player etc*) performance *f*; (*of car, engine*) prestazione *f*; **~er** *n* artista *m/f*; **~ing** *a* (*animal*) ammaestrato(a).

perfume ['pə:fju:m] *n* profumo.

perfunctory [pə'fʌŋktərɪ] *a* superficiale, per la forma.

perhaps [pə'hæps] *ad* forse.

peril ['pɛrɪl] *n* pericolo.

perimeter [pə'rɪmɪtə*] *n* perimetro; **~ wall** *n* muro di cinta.

period ['pɪərɪəd] *n* periodo; (*HISTORY*) epoca; (*SCOL*) lezione *f*; (*full stop*) punto; (*MED*) mestruazioni *fpl* // *a* (*costume, furniture*) d'epoca; **~ic** [-'ɔdɪk] *a* periodico(a); **~ical** [-'ɔdɪkl] *a* periodico(a) // *n* periodico.

peripheral [pə'rɪfərəl] *a* periferico(a) // *n* (*COMPUT*) unità *f inv* periferica.

perish ['pɛrɪʃ] *vi* perire, morire; (*decay*) deteriorarsi; **~able** *a* deperibile.

perjury ['pə:dʒərɪ] *n* spergiuro.

perk [pə:k] *n* vantaggio; **to ~ up** *vi* (*cheer up*) rianimarsi; **~y** *a* (*cheerful*) vivace, allegro(a).

perm [pə:m] *n* (*for hair*) permanente *f*.

permanent ['pə:mənənt] *a* permanente.

permeate ['pə:mɪeɪt] *vi* penetrare // *vt* permeare.

permissible [pə'mɪsɪbl] *a* permissibile, ammissibile.

permission [pə'mɪʃən] *n* permesso.

permissive [pə'mɪsɪv] *a* tollerante; **the ~ society** la società permissiva.

permit *n* ['pə:mɪt] permesso // *vt* [pə'mɪt] permettere; **to ~ sb to do** permettere a qn di fare; dare il permesso a qn di fare.

perpendicular [pə:pən'dɪkjulə*] *a, n* perpendicolare (*f*).

perplex [pə'plɛks] *vt* lasciare perplesso(a).

persecute ['pə:sɪkju:t] *vt* perseguitare.

persevere [pə:sɪ'vɪə*] *vi* perseverare.

Persian ['pə:ʃən] *a* persiano(a) // *n* (*LING*) persiano; **the (~) Gulf** *n* il Golfo Persico.

persist [pə'sɪst] *vi*: **to ~ (in doing)** persistere (nel fare); ostinarsi (a fare); **~ent** *a* persistente; ostinato(a).

person ['pə:sn] *n* persona; **in ~** di *or* in persona, personalmente; **~able** *a* di bell'aspetto; **~al** *a* personale; individuale; **~al assistant (P.A.)** *n* segretaria personale; **~ computer (PC)** *n* personal computer *m inv*; **~ality** [-'nælɪtɪ] *n* personalità *f inv*; **~ally** *ad* personalmente.

personnel [pɜːsə'nɛl] n personale m.

perspective [pə'spɛktɪv] n prospettiva.

perspiration [pɜːspɪ'reɪʃən] n traspirazione f, sudore m.

persuade [pə'sweɪd] vt: to ~ sb to do sth persuadere qn a fare qc.

pert [pɜːt] a (bold) sfacciato(a), impertinente.

pertaining [pə'teɪnɪŋ]: ~ to prep che riguarda.

perturb [pə'tɜːb] vt turbare.

peruse [pə'ruːz] vt leggere.

pervade [pə'veɪd] vt pervadere.

perverse [pə'vɜːs] a perverso(a).

pervert n ['pɜːvɜːt] pervertito/a // vt [pə'vɜːt] pervertire.

pessimism ['pɛsɪmɪzəm] n pessimismo.

pessimist ['pɛsɪmɪst] n pessimista m/f; ~ic [-'mɪstɪk] a pessimistico(a).

pest [pɛst] n animale m (or insetto) pestifero; (fig) peste f.

pester ['pɛstə*] vt tormentare, molestare.

pet [pɛt] n animale m domestico; (favourite) favorito/a // vt accarezzare // vi (col) fare il petting.

petal ['pɛtl] n petalo.

peter ['piːtə*]: to ~ out vi esaurirsi; - estinguersi.

petite [pə'tiːt] a piccolo(a) e aggraziato(a).

petition [pə'tɪʃən] n petizione f.

petrified ['pɛtrɪfaɪd] a (fig) morto(a) di paura.

petrol ['pɛtrəl] n (Brit) benzina; two/four-star ~ ≈ benzina normale/super; ~ can n tanica per benzina.

petroleum [pə'trəʊlɪəm] n petrolio.

petrol: ~ **pump** n (Brit: in car, at garage) pompa di benzina; ~ **station** n (Brit) stazione f di rifornimento; ~ **tank** n (Brit) serbatoio della benzina.

petticoat ['pɛtɪkəʊt] n sottana.

petty ['pɛtɪ] a (mean) meschino(a); (unimportant) insignificante; ~ **cash** n piccola cassa; ~ **officer** n sottufficiale m di marina.

petulant ['pɛtjʊlənt] a irritabile.

pew [pjuː] n panca (di chiesa).

pewter ['pjuːtə*] n peltro.

phallic ['fælɪk] a fallico(a).

phantom ['fæntəm] n fantasma m.

pharmaceutical [fɑːmə'sjuːtɪkl] a farmaceutico(a).

pharmacy ['fɑːməsɪ] n farmacia.

phase [feɪz] n fase f, periodo // vt: to ~ sth in/out introdurre/eliminare qc progressivamente.

Ph.D. n abbr = **Doctor of Philosophy**.

pheasant ['fɛznt] n fagiano.

phenomenon, pl **phenomena** [fə'nɒmɪnən, -nə] n fenomeno.

philanthropist [fɪ'lænθrəpɪst] n filantropo.

philately [fɪ'lætəlɪ] n filatelia.

philosophical [fɪlə'sɒfɪkl] a filosofico(a).

philosophy [fɪ'lɒsəfɪ] n filosofia.

phlegmatic [flɛg'mætɪk] a flemmatico(a).

phobia ['fəʊbjə] n fobia.

phone [fəʊn] n telefono // vt telefonare; to be on the ~ avere il telefono; (be calling) essere al telefono; to ~ **back** vt, vi richiamare; to ~ **up** vt telefonare a // vi telefonare; ~ **book** n guida del telefono, elenco telefonico; ~ **box** or **booth** n cabina telefonica; ~ **call** n telefonata; ~-**in** n (Brit RADIO, TV) trasmissione f a filo diretto con gli ascoltatori.

phonetics [fə'nɛtɪks] n fonetica.

phoney ['fəʊnɪ] a falso(a), fasullo(a) // n (person) ciarlatano.

phonograph ['fəʊnəgrɑːf] n (US) giradischi m inv.

phony ['fəʊnɪ] a = **phoney**.

phosphate ['fɒsfeɪt] n fosfato.

phosphorus ['fɒsfərəs] n fosforo.

photo ['fəʊtəʊ] n foto f inv.

photo... ['fəʊtəʊ] prefix: ~**copier** n fotocopiatrice f; ~**copy** n fotocopia // vt fotocopiare; ~**graph** n fotografia // vt fotografare; ~**grapher** [fə'tɒgrəfə*] n fotografo; ~**graphy** [fə'tɒgrəfɪ] n fotografia.

phrase [freɪz] n espressione f; (LING) locuzione f; (MUS) frase f // vt esprimere; ~ **book** n vocabolarietto.

physical ['fɪzɪkl] a fisico(a); ~ **education** n educazione f fisica; ~**ly** ad fisicamente.

physician [fɪ'zɪʃən] n medico.

physicist ['fɪzɪsɪst] n fisico.

physics ['fɪzɪks] n fisica.

physiology [fɪzɪ'ɒlədʒɪ] n fisiologia.

physique [fɪ'ziːk] n fisico; costituzione f.

pianist ['piːənɪst] n pianista m/f.

piano [pɪ'ænəʊ] n pianoforte m.

piccolo ['pɪkələʊ] n ottavino.

pick [pɪk] n (tool: also: ~-axe) piccone m // vt scegliere; (gather) cogliere; **take your** ~ scelga; the ~ of il fior fiore di; to ~ **off** vt (kill) abbattere (uno dopo l'altro); to ~ **on** vt fus (person) avercela con; to ~ **out** vt scegliere; (distinguish) distinguere; to ~ **up** vi (improve) migliorarsi // vt raccogliere; (collect) passare a prendere; (AUT: give lift to) far salire; (learn) imparare; to ~ up speed acquistare velocità; to ~ o.s. up rialzarsi.

picket ['pɪkɪt] n (in strike) scioperante m/f che fa parte di un picchetto; picchetto // vt picchettare.

pickle ['pɪkl] n (also: ~s: as condiment) sottaceti mpl // vt mettere sottaceto; mettere in salamoia.

pickpocket ['pɪkpɒkɪt] n borsaiolo.

pickup ['pɪkʌp] n (Brit: on record player) pick-up m inv; (small truck) camioncino.

picnic ['pɪknɪk] *n* picnic *m inv*.

pictorial [pɪk'tɔːrɪəl] *a* illustrato(a).

picture ['pɪktʃə*] *n* quadro; (*painting*) pittura; (*photograph*) foto(grafia); (*drawing*) disegno; (*film*) film *m inv* // *vt* raffigurarsi; **the ~s** (*Brit*) il cinema; **~ book** *n* libro illustrato.

picturesque [pɪktʃə'rɛsk] *a* pittoresco(a).

pidgin English ['pɪdʒɪn-] *n* inglese semplificato misto ad elementi indigeni.

pie [paɪ] *n* torta; (*of meat*) pasticcio.

piece [piːs] *n* pezzo; (*of land*) appezzamento; (*item*): **a ~ of furniture/advice** un mobile/consiglio // *vt*: **to ~ together** mettere insieme; **to take to ~s** smontare; **~meal** *ad* pezzo a pezzo, a spizzico; **~work** *n* (lavoro a) cottimo.

pie chart *n* grafico a torta.

pier [pɪə*] *n* molo; (*of bridge etc*) pila.

pierce [pɪəs] *vt* forare; (*with arrow etc*) trafiggere.

piercing ['pɪəsɪŋ] *a* (*cry*) acuto(a).

pig [pɪg] *n* maiale *m*, porco.

pigeon ['pɪdʒən] *n* piccione *m*; **~hole** *n* casella.

piggy bank ['pɪgɪ-] *n* salvadanaro.

pigheaded ['pɪg'hɛdɪd] *a* caparbio(a), cocciuto(a).

piglet ['pɪglɪt] *n* porcellino.

pigskin ['pɪgskɪn] *n* cinghiale *m*.

pigsty ['pɪgstaɪ] *n* porcile *m*.

pigtail ['pɪgteɪl] *n* treccina.

pike [paɪk] *n* (*spear*) picca; (*fish*) luccio.

pilchard ['pɪltʃəd] *n* specie di sardina.

pile [paɪl] *n* (*pillar, of books*) pila; (*heap*) mucchio; (*of carpet*) pelo // *vb* (*also*: **~ up**) *vt* ammucchiare // *vi* ammucchiarsi; **to ~ into** (*car*) stiparsi *or* ammucchiarsi in.

piles [paɪlz] *npl* emorroidi *fpl*.

pileup ['paɪlʌp] *n* (*AUT*) tamponamento a catena.

pilfering ['pɪlfərɪŋ] *n* rubacchiare *m*.

pilgrim ['pɪlgrɪm] *n* pellegrino/a; **~age** *n* pellegrinaggio.

pill [pɪl] *n* pillola; **the ~** la pillola.

pillage ['pɪlɪdʒ] *vt* saccheggiare.

pillar ['pɪlə*] *n* colonna; **~ box** *n* (*Brit*) cassetta postale.

pillion ['pɪljən] *n* (*of motor cycle*) sellino posteriore.

pillory ['pɪlərɪ] *vt* mettere alla berlina.

pillow ['pɪləu] *n* guanciale *m*; **~case** *n* federa.

pilot ['paɪlət] *n* pilota *m/f* // *cpd* (*scheme etc*) pilota *inv* // *vt* pilotare; **~ light** *n* fiamma pilota.

pimp [pɪmp] *n* mezzano.

pimple ['pɪmpl] *n* foruncolo.

pin [pɪn] *n* spillo; (*TECH*) perno // *vt* attaccare con uno spillo; **~s and needles** formicolio; **to ~ sb down** (*fig*) obbligare qn a pronunziarsi; **to ~ sth on sb** (*fig*)

addossare la colpa di qc a qn.

pinafore ['pɪnəfɔː*] *n* grembiule *m* (senza maniche).

pinball ['pɪnbɔːl] *n* (*also*: **~ machine**) flipper *m inv*.

pincers ['pɪnsəz] *npl* pinzette *fpl*.

pinch [pɪntʃ] *n* pizzicotto, pizzico // *vt* pizzicare; (*col: steal*) grattare // *vi* (*shoe*) stringere; **at a ~** in caso di bisogno.

pincushion ['pɪnkuʃən] *n* puntaspilli *m inv*.

pine [paɪn] *n* (*also*: **~ tree**) pino // *vi*: **to ~ for** struggersi dal desiderio di; **to ~ away** *vi* languire.

pineapple ['paɪnæpl] *n* ananas *m inv*.

ping [pɪŋ] *n* (*noise*) tintinnio; **~-pong** *n* ® ping-pong *m* ®.

pink [pɪŋk] *a* rosa *inv* // *n* (*colour*) rosa *m inv*; (*BOT*) garofano.

pinpoint ['pɪnpɔɪnt] *vt* indicare con precisione.

pint [paɪnt] *n* pinta (*Brit* = 0.57*l*; *US* = 0.47*l*); (*Brit col*) ≈ birra da mezzo.

pioneer [paɪə'nɪə*] *n* pioniere/a.

pious ['paɪəs] *a* pio(a).

pip [pɪp] *n* (*seed*) seme *m*; (*Brit: time signal on radio*) segnale *m* orario.

pipe [paɪp] *n* tubo; (*for smoking*) pipa; (*MUS*) piffero // *vt* portare per mezzo di tubazione; **~s** *npl* (*also*: **bag~s**) cornamusa (scozzese); **to ~ down** *vi* (*col*) calmarsi; **~ cleaner** *n* scovolino; **~ dream** *n* vana speranza; **~line** *n* conduttura; (*for oil*) oleodotto; **~r** *n* piffero; suonatore/trice di cornamusa.

piping ['paɪpɪŋ] *ad*: **~ hot** caldo bollente.

pique [piːk] *n* picca.

pirate ['paɪərət] *n* pirata *m*.

Pisces ['paɪsiːz] *n* Pesci *mpl*.

piss [pɪs] *n* (*col*) pisciare; **~ed** *a* (*col: drunk*) ubriaco(a) fradicio(a).

pistol ['pɪstl] *n* pistola.

piston ['pɪstən] *n* pistone *m*.

pit [pɪt] *n* buca, fossa; (*also*: **coal ~**) miniera; (*also*: **orchestra ~**) orchestra // *vt*: **to ~ sb against sb** opporre qn a qn; **~s** *npl* (*AUT*) box *m*.

pitch [pɪtʃ] *n* (*throw*) lancia; (*MUS*) tono; (*of voice*) altezza; (*Brit SPORT*) campo; (*NAUT*) beccheggio; (*tar*) pece *f* // *vt* (*throw*) lanciare // *vi* (*fall*) cascare; (*NAUT*) beccheggiare; **to ~ a tent** piantare una tenda; **~ed battle** *n* battaglia campale.

pitcher ['pɪtʃə*] *n* brocca.

pitchfork ['pɪtʃfɔːk] *n* forcone *m*.

piteous ['pɪtɪəs] *a* pietoso(a).

pitfall ['pɪtfɔːl] *n* trappola.

pith [pɪθ] *n* (*of plant*) midollo; (*of orange*) parte *f* interna della scorza; (*fig*) essenza, succo; vigore *m*.

pithy ['pɪθɪ] *a* conciso(a); vigoroso(a).

pitiful ['pɪtɪful] *a* (*touching*) pietoso(a); (*contemptible*) miserabile.

pitiless ['pɪtɪlɪs] *a* spietato(a).

pittance ['pɪtns] *n* miseria, magro salario.

pity ['pɪtɪ] *n* pietà // *vt* aver pietà di; what a ~! che peccato!

pivot ['pɪvət] *n* perno.

pizza ['piːtsə] *n* pizza.

placard ['plækɑːd] *n* affisso.

placate [plə'keɪt] *vt* placare, calmare.

place [pleɪs] *n* posto, luogo; (*proper position, rank, seat*) posto; (*house*) casa, alloggio; (*home*): at/to his ~ a casa sua // *vt* (*object*) posare, mettere; (*identify*) riconoscere; individuare; to take ~ aver luogo; succedere; to change ~s with sb scambiare il posto con qn; out of ~ (*not suitable*) inopportuno(a); in the first ~ in primo luogo; to ~ an order dare un'ordinazione.

placid ['plæsɪd] *a* placido(a), calmo(a).

plagiarism ['pleɪdʒərɪzm] *n* plagio.

plague [pleɪg] *n* peste *f* // *vt* tormentare.

plaice [pleɪs] *n* (*pl inv*) pianuzza.

plaid [plæd] *n* plaid *m inv*.

plain [pleɪn] *a* (*clear*) chiaro(a), palese; (*simple*) semplice; (*frank*) franco(a), aperto(a); (*not handsome*) bruttino(a); (*without seasoning etc*) scondito(a); naturale; (*in one colour*) tinta unita *inv* // *ad* francamente, chiaramente // *n* pianura; ~ **chocolate** *n* cioccolato fondente; ~ **clothes** *npl*: in ~ **clothes** (*police*) in borghese; ~**ly** *ad* chiaramente; (*frankly*) francamente.

plaintiff ['pleɪntɪf] *n* attore/trice.

plaintive ['pleɪntɪv] *a* (*cry, voice*) dolente, lamentoso(a).

plait [plæt] *n* treccia.

plan [plæn] *n* pianta; (*scheme*) progetto, piano // *vt* (*think in advance*) progettare; (*prepare*) organizzare // *vi* far piani *or* progetti.

plane [pleɪn] *n* (*AVIAT*) aereo; (*tree*) platano; (*tool*) pialla; (*ART, MATH etc*) piano // *a* piano(a), piatto(a) // *vt* (*with tool*) piallare.

planet ['plænɪt] *n* pianeta *m*.

plank [plæŋk] *n* tavola, asse *f*.

planner ['plænə*] *n* pianificatore/trice.

planning ['plænɪŋ] *n* progettazione *f*; family ~ pianificazione *f* delle nascite; ~ **permission** *n* permesso di costruzione.

plant [plɑːnt] *n* pianta; (*machinery*) impianto; (*factory*) fabbrica // *vt* piantare; (*bomb*) mettere.

plantation [plæn'teɪʃən] *n* piantagione *f*.

plaque [plæk] *n* placca.

plaster ['plɑːstə*] *n* intonaco; (*also*: ~ of Paris) gesso; (*Brit: also:* sticking ~) cerotto // *vt* intonacare; ingessare; (*cover*): to ~ with coprire di; in ~ (*leg etc*) ingessato(a); ~**ed** *a* (*col*) ubriaco(a) fradicio(a).

plastic ['plæstɪk] *n* plastica // *a* (*made of plastic*) di *or* in plastica; (*flexible*) pla-

stico(a), malleabile; (*art*) plastico(a); ~ **bag** *n* sacchetto di plastica.

plasticine ['plæstɪsiːn] *n* ® plastilina ®.

plastic surgery *n* chirurgia plastica.

plate [pleɪt] *n* (*dish*) piatto; (*sheet of metal*) lamiera; (*PHOT*) lastra; (*in book*) tavola.

plateau, ~**s** *or* ~**x** ['plætəu, -z] *n* altipiano.

plate glass *n* vetro piano.

platform ['plætfɔːm] *n* (*stage, at meeting*) palco; (*RAIL*) marciapiede *m*; (*Brit: of bus*) piattaforma; ~ **ticket** *n* (*Brit*) biglietto d'ingresso ai binari.

platinum ['plætɪnəm] *n* platino.

platitude ['plætɪtjuːd] *n* luogo comune.

platoon [plə'tuːn] *n* plotone *m*.

platter ['plætə*] *n* piatto.

plausible ['plɔːzɪbl] *a* plausibile, credibile; (*person*) convincente.

play [pleɪ] *n* gioco; (*THEATRE*) commedia // *vt* (*game*) giocare a; (*team, opponent*) giocare contro; (*instrument, piece of music*) suonare; (*play, part*) interpretare // *vi* giocare; suonare; recitare; to ~ safe giocare sul sicuro; to ~ down *vt* minimizzare; to ~ up *vi* (*cause trouble*) fare i capricci; ~**boy** *n* playboy *m inv*; ~**er** *n* giocatore/trice; (*THEATRE*) attore/trice; (*MUS*) musicista *m/f*; ~**ful** *a* giocoso(a); ~**ground** *n* (*in school*) cortile *m* per la ricreazione; (*in park*) parco *m* giochi *inv*; ~**group** *n* giardino d'infanzia; ~**ing card** *n* carta da gioco; ~**ing field** *n* campo sportivo; ~**mate** *n* compagno/a di gioco; ~**off** *n* (*SPORT*) bella; ~**pen** *n* box *m inv*; ~**school** = ~**group**; ~**thing** *n* giocattolo; ~**wright** *n* drammaturgo/a.

plc *abbr* (= *public limited company*) *società per azioni a responsabilità limitata quotata in borsa.*

plea [pliː] *n* (*request*) preghiera, domanda; (*excuse*) scusa; (*LAW*) (argomento di) difesa.

plead [pliːd] *vt* patrocinare; (*give as excuse*) addurre a pretesto // *vi* (*LAW*) perorare la causa; (*beg*): to ~ with sb implorare qn.

pleasant ['plɛznt] *a* piacevole, gradevole; ~**ries** *npl* (*polite remarks*): to exchange ~**ries** scambiarsi i convenevoli.

please [pliːz] *vt* piacere a // *vi* (*think fit*): do as you ~ faccia come le pare; ~! per piacere!; ~ **yourself!** come ti (*or* le) pare!; ~**d** *a*: ~**d** (*with*) contento(a) (di); ~**d to meet you!** piacere!; **pleasing** *a* piacevole, che fa piacere.

pleasure ['plɛʒə*] *n* piacere *m*; "it's a ~" "prego".

pleat [pliːt] *n* piega.

plectrum ['plɛktrəm] *n* plettro.

pledge [plɛdʒ] *n* pegno; (*promise*) promessa // *vt* impegnare; promettere.

plentiful ['plɛntɪful] *a* abbondante, copioso(a).

plenty ['plɛntɪ] *n* abbondanza; ~ **of** tanto(a), molto(a); un'abbondanza di.

pleurisy ['pluərɪsɪ] *n* pleurite *f*.

pliable ['plaɪəbl] *a* flessibile; *(person)* malleabile.

pliers ['plaɪəz] *npl* pinza.

plight [plaɪt] *n* situazione *f* critica.

plimsolls ['plɪmsəlz] *npl* (*Brit*) scarpe *fpl* da tennis.

plinth [plɪnθ] *n* plinto; piedistallo.

plod [plɒd] *vi* camminare a stento; *(fig)* sgobbare; **~der** *n* sgobbone *m*.

plonk [plɒŋk] (*col*) *n* (*Brit*: *wine*) vino da poco // *vt*: **to ~ sth down** buttare giù qc bruscamente.

plot [plɒt] *n* congiura, cospirazione *f*; *(of story, play)* trama; *(of land)* lotto // *vt* *(mark out)* fare la pianta di; rilevare; (: *diagram etc*) tracciare; *(conspire)* congiurare, cospirare // *vi* congiurare; **~ter** *n* (*instrument*) plotter *m inv*.

plough, (*US*) **plow** [plaʊ] *n* aratro // *vt* *(earth)* arare; **to ~ back** *vt* (*COMM*) reinvestire; **to ~ through** *vt fus* (*snow etc*) procedere a fatica in.

ploy [plɔɪ] *n* stratagemma *m*.

pluck [plʌk] *vt* (*fruit*) cogliere; (*musical instrument*) pizzicare; (*bird*) spennare // *n* coraggio, fegato; **to ~ up courage** farsi coraggio; **~y** *a* coraggioso(a).

plug [plʌg] *n* tappo; (*ELEC*) spina; (*AUT*: *also*: **spark(ing) ~**) candela // *vt* (*hole*) tappare; (*col*: *advertise*) spingere; **to ~ in** *vt* (*ELEC*) attaccare a una presa.

plum [plʌm] *n* (*fruit*) susina // *cpd*: ~ **job** (*col*) impiego ottimo or favoloso.

plumb [plʌm] *a* verticale // *n* piombo // *ad* (*exactly*) esattamente // *vt* sondare.

plumber ['plʌmə*] *n* idraulico.

plumbing ['plʌmɪŋ] *n* (*trade*) lavoro di idraulico; (*piping*) tubature *fpl*.

plume [pluːm] *n* piuma, penna; (*decorative*) pennacchio.

plummet ['plʌmɪt] *vi* cadere a piombo.

plump [plʌmp] *a* grassoccio(a) // *vt*: **to ~ sth (down)** on lasciar cadere qc di peso su; **to ~ for** *vt fus* (*col*: *choose*) decidersi per.

plunder ['plʌndə*] *n* saccheggio // *vt* saccheggiare.

plunge [plʌndʒ] *n* tuffo // *vt* immergere // *vi* (*fall*) cadere, precipitare; **to take the ~** saltare il fosso; **~r** *n* sturalavandini *m inv*; **plunging** *a* (*neckline*) profondo(a).

pluperfect [pluː'pəːfɪkt] *n* piuccheperfetto.

plural ['pluərl] *a*, *n* plurale (*m*).

plus [plʌs] *n* (*also*: ~ **sign**) segno più // *prep* più; **ten/twenty ~** più di dieci/venti.

plush [plʌʃ] *a* lussuoso(a).

ply [plaɪ] *n* (*of wool*) capo; (*of wood*) strato // *vt* (*tool*) maneggiare; (*a trade*) esercitare // *vi* (*ship*) fare il servizio; **to ~ sb with drink** dare da bere continuamente a qn; **~wood** *n* legno compensato.

P.M. *n abbr* = **prime minister.**

p.m. *ad abbr* (= *post meridiem*) del pomeriggio.

pneumatic drill [njuː'mætɪk-] *n* martello pneumatico.

pneumonia [njuː'məʊnɪə] *n* polmonite *f*.

poach [pəʊtʃ] *vt* (*cook*) affogare; (*steal*) cacciare (*or* pescare) di frodo // *vi* fare il bracconiere; **~er** *n* bracconiere *m*.

P.O. Box *n abbr* = **Post Office Box.**

pocket ['pɒkɪt] *n* tasca // *vt* intascare; **to be out of ~** (*Brit*) rimetterci; **~book** *n* (*wallet*) portafoglio; (*notebook*) taccuino; ~ **knife** *n* temperino; ~ **money** *n* paghetta, settimana.

pod [pɒd] *n* guscio // *vt* sgusciare.

podgy ['pɒdʒɪ] *a* grassoccio(a).

podiatrist [pɒ'diːətrɪst] *n* (*US*) callista *m/f*, pedicure *m/f*.

poem ['pəʊɪm] *n* poesia.

poet ['pəʊɪt] *n* poeta/essa; **~ic** [-'ɛtɪk] *a* poetico(a); ~ **laureate** *n* poeta *m* laureato (*nominato dalla Corte Reale*); **~ry** *n* poesia.

poignant ['pɔɪnjənt] *a* struggente.

point [pɔɪnt] *n* (*gen*) punto; (*tip: of needle etc*) punta; (*in time*) punto, momento; (*SCOL*) voto; (*main idea, important part*) nocciolo; (*also*: **decimal ~**): **2 ~ 3 (2.3)** 2 virgola 3 (2,3) // *vt* (*show*) indicare; (*gun etc*): **to ~ sth at** puntare qc contro // *vi* mostrare a dito; **~s** *npl* (*AUT*) puntine *fpl*; (*RAIL*) scambio; **to be on the ~ of doing sth** essere sul punto di *or* stare per fare qc; **to make a ~** fare un'osservazione; **to get the ~** capire; **to come to the ~** venire al fatto; **there's no ~** (**in doing**) è inutile (fare); **to ~ out** *vt* far notare; **to ~ to** *vt fus* indicare; (*fig*) dimostrare; **~-blank** *ad* (*also*: **at ~-blank range**) a bruciapelo; (*fig*) categoricamente; **~ed** *a* (*shape*) aguzzo(a), appuntito(a); (*remark*) specifico(a); **~edly** *ad* in maniera inequivocabile; **~er** *n* (*stick*) bacchetta; (*needle*) lancetta; (*dog*) pointer *m*, cane *m* da punta; **~less** *a* inutile, vano(a); ~ **of view** *n* punto di vista.

poise [pɔɪz] *n* (*balance*) equilibrio; (*of head, body*) portamento; (*calmness*) calma // *vt* tenere in equilibrio.

poison ['pɔɪzn] *n* veleno // *vt* avvelenare; **~ing** *n* avvelenamento; **~ous** *a* velenoso(a).

poke [pəʊk] *vt* (*fire*) attizzare; (*jab with finger, stick etc*) punzecchiare; (*put*): **to ~ sth in(to)** spingere qc dentro; **to ~ about** *vi* frugare.

poker ['pəʊkə*] *n* attizzatoio; (*CARDS*) poker *m*; **~-faced** *a* dal viso impassibile.

poky ['pəukɪ] a piccolo(a) e stretto(a).

Poland ['pəulənd] n Polonia.

polar ['pəulə*] a polare; ~ **bear** n orso bianco.

Pole [pəul] n polacco/a.

pole [pəul] n (of wood) palo; (ELEC, GEO) polo; ~ **bean** n (US: runner bean) fagiolino; ~ **vault** n salto con l'asta.

police [pə'li:s] n polizia // vt mantenere l'ordine in; ~ **car** n macchina della polizia; ~**man** n- poliziotto, agente m di polizia; ~ **station** n posto di polizia; ~**woman** n donna f poliziotto inv.

policy ['pɔlɪsɪ] n politica; (also: insurance ~) polizza (d'assicurazione).

polio ['pəulɪəu] n polio f.

Polish ['pəulɪʃ] a polacco(a) // n (LING) polacco.

polish ['pɔlɪʃ] n (for shoes) lucido; (for floor) cera; (for nails) smalto; (shine) lucentezza, lustro; (fig: refinement) raffinatezza // vt lucidare; (fig: improve) raffinare; **to ~ off** vt (work) sbrigare; (food) mangiarsi; ~**ed** a (fig) raffinato(a).

polite [pə'laɪt] a cortese; ~**ness** n cortesia.

politic ['pɔlɪtɪk] a diplomatico(a); ~**al** [pə'lɪtɪkl] a politico(a); ~**ally** ad politicamente; ~**ian** [-'tɪʃən] n politico; ~**s** npl politica.

polka ['pɔlkə] n polca; ~ **dot** n pois m inv.

poll [pəul] n scrutinio; (votes cast) voti mpl; (also: opinion ~) sondaggio (d'opinioni) // vt ottenere.

pollen ['pɔlən] n polline m.

pollination [pɔlɪ'neɪʃən] n impollinazione f.

polling ['pəulɪŋ] (Brit): ~ **booth** n cabina elettorale; ~ **day** n giorno delle elezioni; ~ **station** n sezione f elettorale.

pollute [pə'lu:t] vt inquinare.

pollution [pə'lu:ʃən] n inquinamento.

polo ['pəuləu] n polo; ~-**neck** a a collo alto risvoltato.

polyester [pɔlɪ'ɛstə*] n poliestere m.

polystyrene [pɔlɪ'staɪri:n] n polistirolo.

polytechnic [pɔlɪ'teknɪk] n (college) istituto superiore ad indirizzo tecnologico.

polythene ['pɔlɪθi:n] n politene m; ~ **bag** n sacco di plastica.

pomegranate ['pɔmɪgrænɪt] n melagrana.

pomp [pɔmp] n pompa, fasto.

pompom ['pɔmpɔm], **pompon** ['pɔmpɔn] n pompon m inv.

pompous ['pɔmpəs] a pomposo(a).

pond [pɔnd] n pozza; stagno.

ponder ['pɔndə*] vt ponderare, riflettere su; ~**ous** a ponderoso(a), pesante.

pong [pɔŋ] n (Brit col) puzzo.

pontiff ['pɔntɪf] n pontefice m.

pony ['pəunɪ] n pony m inv; ~**tail** n coda di cavallo; ~ **trekking** n (Brit) escursione f a cavallo.

poodle ['pu:dl] n barboncino, barbone m.

pool [pu:l] n (of rain) pozza; (pond) stagno; (artificial) vasca; (also: swimming ~) piscina; (sth shared) fondo comune; (billiards) specie di biliardo a buca // vt mettere in comune; **typing ~** servizio comune di dattilografia; (football) ~**s** ≈ totocalcio.

poor [puə*] a povero(a); (mediocre) mediocre, cattivo(a) // npl: **the ~** i poveri; ~**ly** ad poveramente; male // a indisposto(a), malato(a).

pop [pɔp] n (noise) schiocco; (MUS) musica pop; (US col: father) babbo // vt (put) mettere (in fretta) // vi scoppiare; (cork) schioccare; **to ~ in** vi passare; **to ~ out** vi fare un salto fuori; **to ~ up** vi apparire, sorgere; ~ **concert** n concerto m pop inv; ~**corn** n pop-corn m.

pope [pəup] n papa m.

poplar ['pɔplə*] n pioppo.

poppy ['pɔpɪ] n papavero.

popsicle ['pɔpsɪkl] n (US: ice lolly) ghiacciolo.

popular ['pɔpjulə*] a popolare; (fashionable) in voga; ~**ity** [-'lærɪtɪ] n popolarità; ~**ize** vt divulgare; (science) volgarizzare.

population [pɔpju'leɪʃən] n popolazione f.

porcelain ['pɔ:slɪn] n porcellana.

porch [pɔ:tʃ] n veranda.

porcupine ['pɔ:kjupaɪn] n porcospino.

pore [pɔ:*] n poro // vi: **to ~ over** essere immerso(a) in.

pork [pɔ:k] n carne f di maiale.

pornographic [pɔ:nə'græfɪk] a pornografico(a).

pornography [pɔ:'nɔgrəfɪ] n pornografia.

porpoise ['pɔ:pəs] n focena.

porridge ['pɔrɪdʒ] n porridge m.

port [pɔ:t] n porto; (opening in ship) portello; (NAUT: left side) babordo; (wine) porto; ~ **of call** (porto di) scalo.

portable ['pɔ:təbl] a portatile.

portent ['pɔ:tent] n presagio.

porter ['pɔ:tə*] n (for luggage) facchino, portabagagli m inv; (doorkeeper) portiere m, portinaio.

portfolio [pɔ:t'fəulɪəu] n (case) cartella; (POL, FINANCE) portafoglio; (of artist) raccolta dei propri lavori.

porthole ['pɔ:thəul] n oblò m inv.

portion ['pɔ:ʃən] n porzione f.

portly ['pɔ:tlɪ] a corpulento(a).

portrait ['pɔ:treɪt] n ritratto.

portray [pɔ:'treɪ] vt fare il ritratto di; (character on stage) rappresentare; (in writing) ritrarre.

Portugal ['pɔ:tjugl] n Portogallo.
Portuguese [pɔ:tju'gi:z] a portoghese // n (pl inv) portoghese m/f; (LING) portoghese m.
pose [pəuz] n posa // vi posare; (pretend): to ~ as atteggiarsi a, posare a // vt porre.
posh [pɔʃ] a (col) elegante; (family) per bene.
position [pə'zɪʃən] n posizione f; (job) posto.
positive ['pɔzɪtɪv] a positivo(a); (certain) sicuro(a), certo(a); (definite) preciso(a); definitivo(a).
posse ['pɔsɪ] n (US) drappello.
possess [pə'zɛs] vt possedere; ~ion [pə'zɛʃən] n possesso; (object) bene m; ~ive a possessivo(a).
possibility [pɔsɪ'bɪlɪtɪ] n possibilità f inv.
possible ['pɔsɪbl] a possibile; as big as ~ il più grande possibile.
possibly ['pɔsɪblɪ] ad (perhaps) forse; if you ~ can se le è possibile; I cannot ~ come proprio non posso venire.
post [pəust] n (Brit) posta; (: collection) levata; (job, situation) posto; (pole) palo // vt (Brit: send by post) impostare; (MIL) appostare; (notice) affiggere; (Brit: appoint): to ~ to assegnare a; ~age n affrancatura; ~al order n vaglia m inv postale; ~box n (Brit) cassetta postale; ~card n cartolina; ~ code n (Brit) codice m (di avviamento) postale.
poster ['pəustə*] n manifesto, affisso.
poste restante [pəust'rɛstã:nt] n (Brit) fermo posta m.
postgraduate ['pəust'grædjuət] n laureato/a che continua gli studi.
posthumous ['pɔstjuməs] a postumo(a).
postman ['pəustmən] n postino.
postmark ['pəustmɑ:k] n bollo or timbro postale.
postmaster ['pəustmɑ:stə*] n direttore m d'un ufficio postale.
post-mortem [pəust'mɔ:təm] n autopsia.
post office n (building) ufficio postale; (organization): the Post Office ≈ le Poste e Telecomunicazioni; Post Office Box (P.O. Box) n casella postale (C.P.).
postpone [pəs'pəun] vt rinviare.
postscript ['pəustskrɪpt] n poscritto.
posture ['pɔstʃə*] n portamento; (pose) posa, atteggiamento // vi posare.
postwar ['pəust'wɔ:*] a del dopoguerra.
posy ['pəuzɪ] n mazzetto di fiori.
pot [pɔt] n (for cooking) pentola; casseruola; (for plants, jam) vaso; (col: marijuana) erba // vt (plant) piantare in vaso; to go to ~ (col: work, performance) andare in malora.
potato, ~es [pə'teɪtəu] n patata; ~ peeler n sbucciapatate m inv.
potent ['pəutnt] a potente, forte.

potential [pə'tɛnʃl] a potenziale // n possibilità fpl; ~ly ad potenzialmente.
pothole ['pɔthəul] n (in road) buca; (Brit: underground) caverna; **potholing** n (Brit): to go potholing fare la speleologia.
potluck [pɔt'lʌk] n: to take ~ tentare la sorte.
potshot ['pɔtʃɔt] n: to take ~s or a ~ at tirare a vanvera contro.
potted ['pɔtɪd] a (food) in conserva; (plant) in vaso.
potter ['pɔtə*] n vasaio // vi: to ~ around, ~ about lavoracchiare; ~y n ceramiche fpl.
potty ['pɔtɪ] a (col: mad) tocco(a) // n (child's) vasino.
pouch [pautʃ] n borsa; (ZOOL) marsupio.
poultry ['pəultrɪ] n pollame m.
pounce [pauns] vi: to ~ (on) balzare addosso a, piombare su // n balzo.
pound [paund] n (weight) libbra; (money) (lira) sterlina; (for dogs) canile m municipale // vt (beat) battere; (crush) pestare, polverizzare // vi (beat) battere, martellare.
pour [pɔ:*] vt versare // vi riversarsi; (rain) piovere a dirotto; to ~ away or off vt vuotare; to ~ in vi (people) entrare a fiotti; to ~ out vt vuotare; versare; (serve: a drink) mescere; ~ing a: ~ing rain pioggia torrenziale.
pout [paut] vi sporgere le labbra; fare il broncio.
poverty ['pɔvətɪ] n povertà, miseria; ~-stricken a molto povero(a), misero(a).
powder ['paudə*] n polvere f // vt spolverizzare; (face) incipriare; to ~ one's nose incipriarsi il naso, ~ compact n portacipria m inv; ~ed milk n latte m in polvere; ~ puff n piumino di cipria; ~ room n toilette f inv (per signore).
power ['pauə*] n (strength) potenza, forza; (ability, POL: of party, leader) potere m; (MATH) potenza; (ELEC) corrente f // vt fornire di energia; to be in ~ (POL etc) essere al potere; ~ cut n (Brit) interruzione f or mancanza di corrente; ~ failure n interruzione f della corrente elettrica; ~ful a potente, forte; ~less a impotente, senza potere; ~ point n (Brit) presa di corrente; ~ station n centrale f elettrica.
p.p. abbr (= per procurationem): ~ J. Smith per J. Smith.
PR abbr = **public relations**.
practicable ['præktɪkəbl] a (scheme) praticabile.
practical ['præktɪkl] a pratico(a); ~ity [-'kælɪtɪ] n (no pl) (of situation etc) lato pratico; ~ joke n beffa; ~ly ad (almost) quasi.
practice ['præktɪs] n pratica; (of

profession) esercizio; (*at football etc*) allenamento; (*business*) gabinetto; clientela // *vt, vi* (*US*) = **practise**; in ~ (*in reality*) in pratica; out of ~ fuori esercizio.

practise, (*US*) **practice** ['præktɪs] *vt* (*work at: piano, one's backhand etc*) esercitarsi a; (*train for: skiing, running etc*) allenarsi a; (*a sport, religion*) praticare; (*method*) usare; (*profession*) esercitare // *vi* esercitarsi; (*train*) allenarsi; **practising** *a* (*Christian etc*) praticante; (*lawyer*) che esercita la professione.

practitioner [præk'tɪʃənə*] *n* professionista *m/f*.

pragmatic [præg'mætɪk] *a* prammatico(a).

prairie ['prɛərɪ] *n* prateria.

praise [preɪz] *n* elogio, lode *f* // *vt* elogiare, lodare; ~**worthy** *a* lodevole.

pram [præm] *n* (*Brit*) carrozzina.

prance [prɑːns] *vi* (*horse*) impennarsi.

prank [præŋk] *n* burla.

prawn [prɔːn] *n* gamberetto.

pray [preɪ] *vi* pregare.

prayer [prɛə*] *n* preghiera.

preach [priːtʃ] *vt, vi* predicare.

precarious [prɪ'kɛərɪəs] *a* precario(a).

precaution [prɪ'kɔːʃən] *n* precauzione *f*.

precede [prɪ'siːd] *vt, vi* precedere.

precedence ['prɛsɪdəns] *n* precedenza.

precedent ['prɛsɪdənt] *n* precedente *m*.

precept ['priːsɛpt] *n* precetto.

precinct ['priːsɪŋkt] *n* (*round cathedral*) recinto; ~**s** *npl* (*neighbourhood*) dintorni *mpl*, vicinanze *fpl*; **pedestrian** ~ (*Brit*) zona pedonale.

precious ['prɛʃəs] *a* prezioso(a).

precipitate [prɪ'sɪpɪtɪt] *a* (*hasty*) precipitoso(a).

précis, *pl* **précis** ['preɪsiː, -z] *n* riassunto.

precise [prɪ'saɪs] *a* preciso(a); ~**ly** *ad* precisamente.

preclude [prɪ'kluːd] *vt* precludere, impedire.

precocious [prɪ'kəʊʃəs] *a* precoce.

precondition [priːkən'dɪʃən] *n* condizione *f* necessaria.

predecessor ['priːdɪsɛsə*] *n* predecessore/a.

predicament [prɪ'dɪkəmənt] *n* situazione *f* difficile.

predict [prɪ'dɪkt] *vt* predire; ~**able** *a* prevedibile.

predominantly [prɪ'dɒmɪnəntlɪ] *ad* in maggior parte; soprattutto.

predominate [prɪ'dɒmɪneɪt] *vi* predominare.

preen [priːn] *vt*: to ~ itself (*bird*) lisciarsi le penne; to ~ o.s. agghindarsi.

prefab ['priːfæb] *n* casa prefabbricata.

preface ['prɛfəs] *n* prefazione *f*.

prefect ['priːfɛkt] *n* (*Brit: in school*) studente/essa con funzioni disciplinari;

(*in Italy*) prefetto.

prefer [prɪ'fəː*] *vt* preferire; ~**ably** ['prɛfrəblɪ] *ad* preferibilmente; ~**ence** ['prɛfrəns] *n* preferenza; ~**ential** [prɛfə'rɛnʃəl] *a* preferenziale.

prefix ['priːfɪks] *n* prefisso.

pregnancy ['prɛgnənsɪ] *n* gravidanza.

pregnant ['prɛgnənt] *a* incinta *af*.

prehistoric ['priːhɪs'tɒrɪk] *a* preistorico(a).

prejudice ['prɛdʒudɪs] *n* pregiudizio; (*harm*) torto, danno // *vt* pregiudicare, ledere; ~**d** *a* (*person*) pieno(a) di pregiudizi; (*view*) prevenuto(a).

preliminary [prɪ'lɪmɪnərɪ] *a* preliminare; **preliminaries** *npl* preliminari *mpl*.

premarital ['priː'mærɪtl] *a* prematrimoniale.

premature ['prɛmətʃuə*] *a* prematuro(a).

premier ['prɛmɪə*] *a* primo(a) // *n* (*POL*) primo ministro.

première ['prɛmɪɛə*] *n* prima.

premise ['prɛmɪs] *n* premessa; ~**s** *npl* locale *m*; on the ~**s** sul posto.

premium ['priːmɪəm] *n* premio; to be at a ~ essere ricercatissimo; ~ **bond** *n* (*Brit*) obbligazione *f* a premio.

premonition [prɛmə'nɪʃən] *n* premonizione *f*.

preoccupied [priː'ɒkjupaɪd] *a* preoccupato(a).

prep [prep] *n* (*SCOL: study*) studio; ~ **school** *n* = **preparatory school**.

prepaid [priː'peɪd] *a* pagato(a) in anticipo.

preparation [prɛpə'reɪʃən] *n* preparazione *f*; ~**s** *npl* (*for trip, war*) preparativi *mpl*.

preparatory [prɪ'pærətərɪ] *a* preparatorio(a); ~ **school** *n* scuola elementare privata.

prepare [prɪ'pɛə*] *vt* preparare // *vi*: to ~ for prepararsi a; ~**d** to pronto(a) a.

preposition [prɛpə'zɪʃən] *n* preposizione *f*.

preposterous [prɪ'pɒstərəs] *a* assurdo(a).

prerequisite [priː'rɛkwɪzɪt] *n* requisito indispensabile.

prescribe [prɪ'skraɪb] *vt* prescrivere; (*MED*) ordinare.

prescription [prɪ'skrɪpʃən] *n* prescrizione *f*; (*MED*) ricetta.

presence ['prɛzns] *n* presenza; ~ **of mind** presenza di spirito.

present ['prɛznt] *a* presente; (*wife, residence, job*) attuale // *n* regalo; (*also:* ~ **tense**) tempo presente // *vt* [prɪ'zɛnt] presentare; (*give*): to ~ sb with sth offrire qc a qn; to give sb a ~ fare un regalo a qn; at ~ al momento; ~**ation** [-'teɪʃən] *n* presentazione *f*; (*gift*) regalo, dono; (*ceremony*) consegna ufficiale; ~-**day** *a* attuale, d'oggigiorno; ~**er** *n*

(RADIO, TV) presentatore/trice; **~ly** ad (soon) fra poco, presto; (at present) al momento.

preservative [prɪ'zə:vətɪv] n conservante m.

preserve [prɪ'zə:v] vt (keep safe) preservare, proteggere; (maintain) conservare; (food) mettere in conserva // n (for game, fish) riserva; (often pl: jam) marmellata; (: fruit) frutta sciroppata.

preside [prɪ'zaɪd] vi presiedere.

president ['prezɪdənt] n presidente m; **~ial** [-'denʃl] a presidenziale.

press [pres] n (tool, machine) pressa; (for wine) torchio; (newspapers) stampa; (crowd) folla // vt (push) premere, pigiare; (squeeze) spremere; (: hand) stringere; (clothes: iron) stirare; (pursue) incalzare; (insist): to ~ sth on sb far accettare qc da qn // vi premere, accalcare; we are ~ed for time ci manca il tempo; to ~ for sth insistere per avere qc; **to ~ on** vi continuare; ~ **conference** n conferenza stampa; **~ing** a urgente // n stiratura; ~ **stud** n (Brit) bottone m a pressione; **~-up** n (Brit) flessione f sulle braccia.

pressure ['preʃə*] n pressione f; ~ **cooker** n pentola a pressione; ~ **gauge** n manometro; ~ **group** n gruppo di pressione.

prestige [pres'ti:ʒ] n prestigio.

presumably [prɪ'zju:məblɪ] ad presumibilmente.

presume [prɪ'zju:m] vt supporre; to ~ to do (dare) permettersi di fare.

presumption [prɪ'zʌmpʃən] n presunzione f; (boldness) audacia.

presumptuous [prɪ'zʌmpʃəs] a presuntuoso(a).

pretence, (US) **pretense** [prɪ'tens] n (claim) pretesa; to make a ~ of doing far finta di fare.

pretend [prɪ'tend] vt (feign) fingere // vi (feign) far finta; (claim): to ~ to sth pretendere a qc; to ~ to do far finta di fare.

pretense [prɪ'tens] n (US) = **pretence**.

pretension [prɪ'tenʃən] n (claim) pretesa.

pretentious [prɪ'tenʃəs] a pretenzioso(a).

pretext ['pri:tekst] n pretesto.

pretty ['prɪtɪ] a grazioso(a), carino(a) // ad abbastanza, assai.

prevail [prɪ'veɪl] vi (win, be usual) prevalere; (persuade): to ~ (up)on sb to do persuadere qn a fare; **~ing** a dominante.

prevalent ['prevələnt] a (belief) predominante; (customs) diffuso(a); (fashion) corrente; (disease) comune.

prevent [prɪ'vent] vt prevenire; to ~ sb from doing impedire a qn di fare; **~ion**

[-'venʃən] n prevenzione f; **~ive** a preventivo(a).

preview ['pri:vju:] n (of film) anteprima.

previous ['pri:vɪəs] a precedente; anteriore; **~ly** ad prima.

prewar ['pri:'wɔ:*] a anteguerra inv.

prey [preɪ] n preda // vi: to ~ on far preda di.

price [praɪs] n prezzo // vt (goods) fissare il prezzo di; valutare; **~less** a inapprezzabile; ~ **list** n listino (dei) prezzi.

prick [prɪk] n puntura // vt pungere; to ~ up one's ears drizzare gli orecchi.

prickle ['prɪkl] n (of plant) spina; (sensation) pizzicore m.

prickly ['prɪklɪ] a spinoso(a); (fig: person) permaloso(a); ~ **heat** n sudamina.

pride [praɪd] n orgoglio; superbia // vt: to ~ o.s. on essere orgoglioso(a) di; vantarsi di.

priest [pri:st] n prete m, sacerdote m; **~hood** n sacerdozio.

prig [prɪg] n: he's a ~ è compiaciuto di se stesso.

prim [prɪm] a pudico(a); contegnoso(a).

primarily ['praɪmərɪlɪ] ad principalmente, essenzialmente.

primary ['praɪmərɪ] a primario(a); (first in importance) primo(a); ~ **school** n (Brit) scuola elementare.

prime [praɪm] a primario(a), fondamentale; (excellent) di prima qualità // vt (gun) innescare; (pump) adescare; (fig) mettere al corrente; in the ~ of life nel fiore della vita; **P~ Minister (P.M.)** n primo ministro.

primer ['praɪmə*] n (book) testo elementare.

primeval [praɪ'mi:vl] a primitivo(a).

primitive ['prɪmɪtɪv] a primitivo(a).

primrose ['prɪmrəuz] n primavera.

primus (stove) ['praɪməs(stəuv)] n ® (Brit) fornello a petrolio.

prince [prɪns] n principe m.

princess [prɪn'ses] n principessa.

principal ['prɪnsɪpl] a principale // n (headmaster) preside m.

principle ['prɪnsɪpl] n principio; in ~ in linea di principio; on ~ per principio.

print [prɪnt] n (mark) impronta; (letters) caratteri mpl; (fabric) tessuto stampato; (ART, PHOT) stampa // vt imprimere; (publish) stampare, pubblicare; (write in capitals) scrivere in stampatello; out of ~ esaurito(a); **~ed matter** n stampe fpl; **~er** n tipografo; (machine) stampante f; **~ing** n stampa; **~-out** n (COMPUT) tabulato.

prior ['praɪə*] a precedente // n priore m; ~ **to doing** prima di fare.

priority [praɪ'ɒrɪtɪ] n priorità f inv; precedenza.

priory ['praɪərɪ] n monastero.

prise [praɪz] vt: to ~ open forzare.

prison ['prɪzn] n prigione f // cpd (system) carcerario(a); (conditions, food) nelle or delle prigioni; ~**er** n prigioniero/a.

pristine ['prɪstiːn] a immacolato(a).

privacy ['prɪvəsɪ] n solitudine f, intimità.

private ['praɪvɪt] a privato(a); personale // n soldato semplice; "~" (on envelope) "riservata"; in ~ in privato; ~ **enterprise** n iniziativa privata; ~ **eye** n investigatore m privato; ~**ly** ad in privato; (within oneself) dentro di sé; ~ **property** n proprietà privata; **privatize** vt privatizzare.

privet ['prɪvɪt] n ligustro.

privilege ['prɪvɪlɪdʒ] n privilegio.

privy ['prɪvɪ] a: to be ~ to essere al corrente di; ~ **council** n Consiglio della Corona.

prize [praɪz] n premio // a (example, idiot) perfetto(a); (bull, novel) premiato(a) // vt apprezzare, pregiare; ~ **giving** n premiazione f; ~**winner** n premiato/a.

pro [prəʊ] n (SPORT) professionista m/f; the ~**s and cons** il pro e il contro.

probability [prɔbə'bɪlɪtɪ] n probabilità f inv.

probable ['prɔbəbl] a probabile; **probably** ad probabilmente.

probation [prə'beɪʃən] n (in employment) periodo di prova; (LAW) libertà vigilata; **on** ~ (employee) in prova; (LAW) in libertà vigilata.

probe [prəʊb] n (MED, SPACE) sonda; (enquiry) indagine f, investigazione f // vt sondare, esplorare; indagare.

problem ['prɔbləm] n problema m.

procedure [prə'siːdʒə*] n (ADMIN, LAW) procedura; (method) metodo, procedimento.

proceed [prə'siːd] vi (go forward) avanzare, andare avanti; (go about it) procedere; (continue): to ~ (with) continuare; to ~ to andare a; passare a; to ~ to do mettersi a fare; ~**ings** npl misure fpl; (LAW) procedimento; (meeting) riunione f; (records) rendiconti mpl; atti mpl; ~**s** ['prəʊsiːdz] npl profitto, incasso.

process ['prəʊses] n processo; (method) metodo, sistema m // vt trattare; (information) elaborare; ~**ing** n trattamento; elaborazione f.

procession [prə'seʃən] n processione f, corteo; **funeral** ~ corteo funebre.

proclaim [prə'kleɪm] vt proclamare, dichiarare.

procrastinate [prəʊ'kræstɪneɪt] vi procrastinare.

prod [prɔd] vt dare un colpetto a; pungolare.

prodigal ['prɔdɪgl] a prodigo(a).

prodigy ['prɔdɪdʒɪ] n prodigio.

produce n ['prɔdjuːs] (AGR) prodotto, prodotti mpl // vt [prə'djuːs] produrre; (to show) esibire, mostrare; (cause) cagionare, causare; (THEATRE) mettere in scena; ~**r** n (THEATRE) direttore/trice; (AGR, CINEMA) produttore m.

product ['prɔdʌkt] n prodotto.

production [prə'dʌkʃən] n produzione f; (THEATRE) messa in scena; ~ **line** n catena di lavorazione.

productivity [prɔdʌk'tɪvɪtɪ] n produttività.

profane [prə'feɪn] a profano(a); (language) empio(a).

profession [prə'feʃən] n professione f; ~**al** n (SPORT) professionista m/f // a professionale; (work) da professionista; ~**alism** n professionismo.

professor [prə'fesə*] n professore m (titolare di una cattedra).

proficiency [prə'fɪʃənsɪ] n competenza, abilità.

profile ['prəʊfaɪl] n profilo.

profit ['prɔfɪt] n profitto; beneficio // vi: to ~ (by or from) approfittare (di); ~**ability** [-'bɪlɪtɪ] n redditività; ~**able** a redditizio(a).

profiteering [prɔfɪ'tɪərɪŋ] n (pej) affarismo.

profound [prə'faʊnd] a profondo(a).

profusely [prə'fjuːslɪ] ad con grande effusione.

progeny ['prɔdʒɪnɪ] n progenie f; discendenti mpl.

programme, (US) **program** ['prəʊgræm] n programma m // vt programmare; ~**r**, (US) **programer** n programmatore/trice.

progress n ['prəʊgres] progresso // vi [prə'gres] avanzare, procedere; **in** ~ in corso; **to make** ~ far progressi; ~**ive** [-'gresɪv] a progressivo(a); (person) progressista m/f.

prohibit [prə'hɪbɪt] vt proibire, vietare; ~**ion** [prəʊɪ'bɪʃən] n (US) proibizionismo, ~**ive** a (price etc) proibitivo(a).

project n ['prɔdʒekt] (plan) piano; (venture) progetto; (SCOL) studio // vb [prə'dʒekt] vt proiettare // vi (stick out) sporgere.

projectile [prə'dʒektaɪl] n proiettile m.

projector [prə'dʒektə*] n proiettore m.

prolong [prə'lɔŋ] vt prolungare.

prom [prɔm] n abbr = **promenade**; (US: ball) ballo studentesco.

promenade [prɔmə'nɑːd] n (by sea) lungomare m; ~ **concert** n concerto di musica classica.

prominent ['prɔmɪnənt] a (standing out) prominente; (important) importante.

promiscuous [prə'mɪskjuəs] a (sexually) di facili costumi.

promise ['prɔmɪs] n promessa // vt, vi promettere; **promising** a promettente.

promote [prə'məʊt] vt promuovere; (venture, event) organizzare; ~**r** n (of

sporting event) organizzatore/trice;
promotion [-'məʊʃən] *n* promozione *f*.

prompt [prɒmpt] *a* rapido(a), svelto(a);
puntuale; *(reply)* sollecito(a) // *ad*
(punctually) in punto // *n (COMPUT)*
prompt *m* // *vt* incitare; provocare;
(THEATRE) suggerire a; **~ly** *ad*
prontamente; puntualmente; **~ness** *n*
prontezza; puntualità.

prone [prəʊn] *a (lying)* prono(a); ~ **to**
propenso(a) a, incline a.

prong [prɒŋ] *n* rebbio, punta.

pronoun ['prəʊnaʊn] *n* pronome *m*.

pronounce [prə'naʊns] *vt* pronunziare //
vi: **to** ~ **(up)on** pronunziare su.

pronunciation [prənʌnsɪ'eɪʃən] *n*
pronunzia.

proof [pru:f] *n* prova; *(of book)* bozza;
(PHOT) provino; *(of alcohol)* grado // *a*:
~ **against** a prova di.

prop [prɒp] *n* sostegno, appoggio // *vt*
(also: ~ **up)** sostenere, appoggiare;
(lean): **to** ~ **sth against** appoggiare qc
contro or a.

propaganda [prɒpə'gændə] *n*
propaganda.

propel [prə'pɛl] *vt* spingere (in avanti),
muovere; **~ler** *n* elica; **~ling pencil** *n*
(Brit) matita a mina.

propensity [prə'pɛnsɪtɪ] *n* tendenza.

proper ['prɒpə*] *a (suited, right)*
adatto(a), appropriato(a); *(seemly)*
decente; *(authentic)* vero(a); *(col: real)*
noun + vero(a) e proprio(a); **~ly** *ad*
(eat, study) bene; *(behave)* come si
deve; ~ **noun** *n* nome *m* proprio.

property ['prɒpətɪ] *n (things owned)* beni
mpl; *(land, building)* proprietà *f inv*;
(CHEM etc: quality) proprietà; ~
owner *n* proprietario/a.

prophecy ['prɒfɪsɪ] *n* profezia.

prophesy ['prɒfɪsaɪ] *vt* predire.

prophet ['prɒfɪt] *n* profeta *m*.

proportion [prə'pɔ:ʃən] *n* proporzione *f*;
(share) parte *f* // *vt* proporzionare,
commisurare; **~al** *a* proporzionale;
~ate *a* proporzionato(a).

proposal [prə'pəʊzl] *n* proposta; *(plan)*
progetto; *(of marriage)* proposta di matrimonio.

propose [prə'pəʊz] *vt* proporre,
suggerire // *vi* fare una proposta di matrimonio; **to** ~ **to do** proporsi di fare,
aver l'intenzione di fare.

proposition [prɒpə'zɪʃən] *n* proposizione
f.

proprietor [prə'praɪətə*] *n* proprietario/
a.

propriety [prə'praɪətɪ] *n (seemliness)*
decoro, rispetto delle convenienze sociali.

prose [prəʊz] *n* prosa; *(SCOL: translation)* traduzione *f* dalla madrelingua.

prosecute ['prɒsɪkju:t] *vt* processare;
prosecution [-'kju:ʃən] *n* processo;
(accusing side) accusa; **prosecutor** *n*

(also: **public prosecutor)** ≈ procuratore
m della Repubblica.

prospect *n* ['prɒspɛkt] prospettiva;
(hope) speranza // *vb* [prə'spɛkt] *vt* fare
assaggi in // *vi* fare assaggi; **~s** *npl (for
work etc)* prospettive *fpl*; **prospective**
[-'spɛktɪv] *a* possibile; futuro(a).

prospectus [prə'spɛktəs] *n* prospetto,
programma *m*.

prosperity [prɒ'spɛrɪtɪ] *n* prosperità.

prostitute ['prɒstɪtju:t] *n* prostituta.

protect [prə'tɛkt] *vt* proteggere,
salvaguardare; **~ion** *n* protezione *f*;
~ive *a* protettivo(a).

protégé ['prəʊtəʒeɪ] *n* protetto; **~e** *n*
protetta.

protein ['prəʊti:n] *n* proteina.

protest *n* ['prəʊtest] protesta // *vt, vi*
[prə'test] protestare.

Protestant ['prɒtɪstənt] *a, n* protestante
(m/f).

protester [prə'tɛstə*] *n* dimostrante *m/f*.

prototype ['prəʊtətaɪp] *n* prototipo.

protracted [prə'træktɪd] *a* tirato(a) per
le lunghe.

protrude [prə'tru:d] *vi* sporgere.

protuberance [prə'tju:bərəns] *n*
sporgenza.

proud [praʊd] *a* fiero(a), orgoglioso(a);
(pej) superbo(a).

prove [pru:v] *vt* provare, dimostrare //
vi: **to** ~ **correct** *etc* risultare vero(a)
etc; **to** ~ **o.s.** mostrare le proprie
capacità.

proverb ['prɒvə:b] *n* proverbio.

provide [prə'vaɪd] *vt* fornire,
provvedere; **to** ~ **sb with sth** fornire or
provvedere qn di qc; **to** ~ **for** *vt fus*
provvedere a; **~d (that)** *cj* purché +
sub, a condizione che + *sub*.

providing [prə'vaɪdɪŋ] *cj* purché + *sub*, a
condizione che + *sub*.

province ['prɒvɪns] *n* provincia;
provincial [prə'vɪnʃəl] *a* provinciale.

provision [prə'vɪʒən] *n (supply)* riserva;
(supplying) provvista; rifornimento;
(stipulation) condizione *f*; **~s** *npl (food)*
provviste *fpl*; **~al** *a* provvisorio(a).

proviso [prə'vaɪzəʊ] *n* condizione *f*.

provocative [prə'vɒkətɪv] *a (aggressive)*
provocatorio(a); *(thought-provoking)*
stimolante; *(seductive)* provocante.

provoke [prə'vəʊk] *vt* provocare;
incitare.

prow [praʊ] *n* prua.

prowess ['praʊɪs] *n* prodezza.

prowl [praʊl] *vi (also:* ~ **about,** ~
around) aggirarsi; **~er** *n* tipo sospetto
*(che s'aggira con l'intenzione di rubare,
aggredire etc)*.

proximity [prɒk'sɪmɪtɪ] *n* prossimità.

proxy ['prɒksɪ] *n* procura.

prudent ['pru:dnt] *a* prudente.

prudish ['pru:dɪʃ] *a* puritano(a).

prune [pru:n] *n* prugna secca // *vt* potare.

pry [praɪ] *vi*: to ~ **into** ficcare il naso in.
PS *abbr* (= *postscript*) P.S.
psalm [sɑ:m] *n* salmo.
pseudo- ['sju:dəʊ] *prefix* pseudo...
pseudonym ['sju:dənɪm] *n* pseudonimo.
psyche ['saɪkɪ] *n* psiche *f*.
psychiatric [saɪkɪ'ætrɪk] *a* psichia-trico(a).
psychiatrist [saɪ'kaɪətrɪst] *n* psichiatra *m/f*.
psychic ['saɪkɪk] *a* (*also*: ~al) psi-chico(a); (*person*) dotato(a) di qualità telepatiche.
psychoanalyst [saɪkəʊ'ænəlɪst] *n* psica-nalista *m/f*.
psychological [saɪkə'lɒdʒɪkl] *a* psico-logico(a).
psychologist [saɪ'kɒlədʒɪst] *n* psicologo/a.
psychology [saɪ'kɒlədʒɪ] *n* psicologia.
psychopath ['saɪkəʊpæθ] *n* psicopatico/a.
P.T.O. *abbr* (= *please turn over*) v.r.
pub [pʌb] *n abbr* (= *public house*) pub *m inv*.
pubic ['pju:bɪk] *a* pubico(a), del pube.
public ['pʌblɪk] *a* pubblico(a) // *n* pub-blico; **in** ~ in pubblico; ~ **address system (P.A.)** *n* impianto di am-plificazione.
publican ['pʌblɪkən] *n* proprietario di un pub.
publication [pʌblɪ'keɪʃən] *n* pub-blicazione *f*.
public: ~ **company** *n* società *f inv* per azioni (*costituita tramite pubblica sotto-scrizione*); ~ **convenience** *n* (*Brit*) gabinetti *mpl*; ~ **holiday** *n* giorno fe-stivo, festa nazionale; ~ **house** *n* (*Brit*) pub *m inv*.
publicity [pʌb'lɪsɪtɪ] *n* pubblicità.
publicize ['pʌblɪsaɪz] *vt* rendere pub-blico(a).
publicly ['pʌblɪklɪ] *ad* pubblicamente.
public: ~ **opinion** *n* opinione *f* pub-blica; ~ **relations (PR)** *n* pubbliche relazioni *fpl*; ~ **school** *n* (*Brit*) scuola privata; (*US*) scuola statale; ~-**spirited** *a* che ha senso civico; ~ **transport** *n* mezzi *mpl* pubblici.
publish ['pʌblɪʃ] *vt* pubblicare; ~**er** *n* editore *m*; ~**ing** *n* (*industry*) editoria; (*of a book*) pubblicazione *f*.
puck [pʌk] *n* (*ICE HOCKEY*) disco.
pucker ['pʌkə*] *vt* corrugare.
pudding ['pʊdɪŋ] *n* budino; (*Brit*: *dessert*) dolce *m*; **black** ~ sanguinaccio.
puddle ['pʌdl] *n* pozza, pozzanghera.
puff [pʌf] *n* sbuffo // *vt*: to ~ **one's pipe** tirare sboccate di fumo // *vi* uscire a sbuffi; (*pant*) ansare; to ~ **out smoke** mandar fuori sbuffi di fumo; ~**ed** *a* (*col*: *out of breath*) senza fiato; ~ **pastry** *n* pasta sfoglia; ~**y** *a* gonfio(a).
pull [pʊl] *n* (*tug*): **to give sth a** ~ tirare su qc; (*fig*) influenza //· *vt* tirare; (*mus-*)

cle) strappare // *vi* tirare; **to** ~ **to pieces** fare a pezzi; **to** ~ **one's punches** (*BOXING*) risparmiare l'avversario; **to** ~ **one's weight** dare il proprio contributo; **to** ~ **o.s. together** ricomporsi, ri-prendersi; **to** ~ **sb's leg** prendere in giro qn; **to** ~ **apart** *vt* (*break*) fare a pezzi; **to** ~ **down** *vt* (*house*) demolire; (*tree*) abbattere; **to** ~ **in** *vi* (*AUT*: *at the kerb*) accostarsi; (*RAIL*) entrare in stazione; **to** ~ **off** *vt* (*deal etc*) portare a compimento; **to** ~ **out** *vi* partire; (*AUT*: *come out of line*) spostarsi sulla mezzeria // *vt* staccare; far uscire; (*withdraw*) ritirare; **to** ~ **over** *vi* (*AUT*) accostare; **to** ~ **through** *vi* farcela; **to** ~ **up** *vi* (*stop*) fermarsi // *vt* (*uproot*) sradicare; (*stop*) fermare.
pulley ['pʊlɪ] *n* puleggia, carrucola.
pullover ['pʊləʊvə*] *n* pullover *m inv*.
pulp [pʌlp] *n* (*of fruit*) polpa; (*for paper*) pasta per carta.
pulpit ['pʊlpɪt] *n* pulpito.
pulsate [pʌl'seɪt] *vi* battere, palpitare.
pulse [pʌls] *n* polso.
pummel ['pʌml] *vt* dare pugni a.
pump [pʌmp] *n* pompa; (*shoe*) scarpetta // *vt* pompare; (*fig*: *col*) far parlare; **to** ~ **up** *vt* gonfiare.
pumpkin ['pʌmpkɪn] *n* zucca.
pun [pʌn] *n* gioco di parole.
punch [pʌntʃ] *n* (*blow*) pugno; (*fig*: *force*) forza; (*tool*) punzone *m*; (*drink*) ponce *m* // *vt* (*hit*): **to** ~ **sb/sth** dare un pugno a qn/qc; **to** ~ **a hole (in)** fare un buco (in); ~ **line** *n* (*of joke*) battuta finale; ~-**up** *n* (*Brit col*) rissa.
punctual ['pʌŋktjʊəl] *a* puntuale; ~**ity** [-'ælɪtɪ] *n* puntualità.
punctuation [pʌŋktjʊ'eɪʃən] *n* interpunzione *f*, punteggiatura.
puncture ['pʌŋktʃə*] *n* foratura // *vt* forare.
pundit ['pʌndɪt] *n* sapientone/a.
pungent ['pʌndʒənt] *a* piccante; (*fig*) mordace, caustico(a).
punish ['pʌnɪʃ] *vt* punire; ~**ment** *n* punizione *f*.
punk [pʌŋk] *n* (*also*: ~ **rocker**) punk *m/f inv*; (*also*: ~ **rock**) musica punk, punk rock *m*; (*US col*: *hoodlum*) teppista *m*.
punt [pʌnt] *n* (*boat*) barchino; (*FOOTBALL*) colpo a volo.
punter ['pʌntə*] *n* (*Brit*: *gambler*) scommettitore/trice.
puny ['pju:nɪ] *a* gracile.
pup [pʌp] *n* cucciolo/a.
pupil ['pju:pl] *n* allievo/a; (*ANAT*) pupilla.
puppet ['pʌpɪt] *n* burattino.
puppy ['pʌpɪ] *n* cucciolo/a, cagnolino/a.
purchase ['pə:tʃɪs] *n* acquisto, compera // *vt* comprare; ~**r** *n* compratore/trice.
pure [pjʊə*] *a* puro(a).
purely ['pjʊəlɪ] *ad* puramente.
purge [pə:dʒ] *n* (*MED*) purga; (*POL*)

epurazione f // vt purgare; (fig) epurare.

puritan ['pjuərɪtən] a, n puritano(a).

purl [pə:l] n punto rovescio.

purple ['pə:pl] a di porpora; viola inv.

purport [pə:'pɔ:t] vi: to ~ to be/do pretendere di essere/fare.

purpose ['pə:pəs] n intenzione f, scopo; **on** ~ apposta; **~ful** a deciso(a), risoluto(a).

purr [pə:*] vi fare le fusa.

purse [pə:s] n borsellino // vt contrarre.

purser ['pə:sə*] n (NAUT) commissario di bordo.

pursue [pə'sju:] vt inseguire.

pursuit [pə'sju:t] n inseguimento; (occupation) occupazione f, attività f inv.

purveyor [pə'veɪə*] n fornitore/trice.

push [puʃ] n spinta; (effort) grande sforzo; (drive) energia // vt spingere; (button) premere; (thrust): to ~ sth (into) ficcare qc (in); (fig) fare pubblicità a // vi spingere; premere; **to ~ aside** vt scostare; **to ~ off** vi (col) filare; **to ~ on** vi (continue) continuare; **to ~ through** vt (measure) far approvare; **to ~ up** vt (total, prices) far salire; **~chair** n (Brit) passeggino; **~er** n (drug ~er) spacciatore/trice; **~over** n (col): it's a **~over** è un lavoro da bambini; **~-up** n (US: press-up) flessione f sulle braccia; **~y** a (pej) opportunista.

puss, pussy(-cat) [pus, 'pusɪ(kæt)] n micio.

put, pt, pp **put** [put] vt mettere, porre; (say) dire, esprimere; (a question) fare; (estimate) stimare; **to ~ about** vi (NAUT) virare di bordo // vt (rumour) diffondere; **to ~ across** vt (ideas etc) comunicare; far capire; **to ~ away** vt (return) mettere a posto; **to ~ back** vt (replace) rimettere (a posto); (postpone) rinviare; (delay) ritardare; **to ~ by** vt (money) mettere da parte; **to ~ down** vt (parcel etc) posare, mettere giù; (pay) versare; (in writing) mettere per iscritto; (suppress: revolt etc) reprimere, sopprimere; (attribute) attribuire; **to ~ forward** vt (ideas) avanzare, proporre; (date) anticipare; **to ~ in** vt (application, complaint) presentare; **to ~ off** vt (postpone) rimandare, rinviare; (discourage) dissuadere; **to ~ on** vt (clothes, lipstick etc) mettere; (light etc) accendere; (play etc) mettere in scena; (food, meal) servire; (brake) mettere; **to ~ on weight** ingrassare; **to ~ on airs** darsi delle arie; **to ~ out** vt mettere fuori; (one's hand) porgere; (light etc) spegnere; (person: inconvenience) scomodare; **to ~ up** vt (raise) sollevare, alzare; (pin up) affiggere; (hang) appendere; (build) costruire, erigere; (increase) aumentare;

(accommodate) alloggiare; **to ~ up with** vt fus sopportare.

putt [pʌt] vt (ball) colpire leggermente // n colpo leggero; **~ing green** n green m inv; campo da putting.

putty ['pʌtɪ] n stucco.

puzzle ['pʌzl] n enigma m, mistero; (jigsaw) puzzle m; (also: crossword ~) parole fpl incrociate, cruciverba m inv // vt confondere, rendere perplesso(a) // vi scervellarsi.

pyjamas [pɪ'dʒɑ:məz] npl (Brit) pigiama m.

pylon ['paɪlən] n pilone m.

pyramid ['pɪrəmɪd] n piramide f.

Pyrenees [pɪrɪ'ni:z] npl: the ~ i Pirenei.

Q

quack [kwæk] n (of duck) qua qua m inv; (pej: doctor) dottoruccio/a.

quad [kwɔd] n abbr = **quadrangle, quadruplet.**

quadrangle ['kwɔdræŋgl] n (MATH) quadrilatero, (courtyard) cortile m.

quadruple [kwɔ'drupl] vt quadruplicare // vi quadruplicarsi.

quadruplet [kwɔ'dru:plɪt] n uno/a di quattro gemelli.

quagmire ['kwægmaɪə*] n pantano.

quail [kweɪl] n (ZOOL) quaglia // vi (person) perdersi d'animo.

quaint [kweɪnt] a bizzarro(a); (old-fashioned) antiquato(a); grazioso(a), pittoresco(a).

quake [kweɪk] vi tremare // n abbr = **earthquake.**

Quaker ['kweɪkə*] n quacchero/a.

qualification [kwɔlɪfɪ'keɪʃən] n (degree etc) qualifica, titolo; (ability) competenza, qualificazione f; (limitation) riserva, restrizione f.

qualified ['kwɔlɪfaɪd] a qualificato(a); (able) competente, qualificato(a); (limited) condizionato(a).

qualify ['kwɔlɪfaɪ] vt abilitare; (limit: statement) modificare, precisare // vi: to ~ (as) qualificarsi (come); to ~ (for) acquistare i requisiti necessari (per); (SPORT) qualificarsi (per or a).

quality ['kwɔlɪtɪ] n qualità f inv.

qualm [kwɑ:m] n dubbio; scrupolo.

quandary ['kwɔndrɪ] n: in a ~ in un dilemma.

quantity ['kwɔntɪtɪ] n quantità f inv; **~ surveyor** n geometra m (specializzato nel calcolare la quantità e il costo del materiale da costruzione).

quarantine ['kwɔrnti:n] n quarantena.

quarrel ['kwɔrl] n lite f, disputa // vi litigare; **~some** a litigioso(a).

quarry ['kwɔrɪ] n (for stone) cava; (animal) preda // vt (marble etc) estrarre.

quart [kwɔ:t] n ≈ litro.
quarter ['kwɔ:tə*] n quarto; (of year) trimestre m; (district) quartiere m // vt dividere in quattro; (MIL) alloggiare; ~s npl alloggio; (MIL) alloggi mpl, quadrato; a ~ of an hour un quarto d'ora; ~ **final** n quarto di finale; ~**ly** a trimestrale // ad trimestralmente; ~**master** n (MIL) furiere m.
quartet(te) [kwɔ:'tɛt] n quartetto.
quartz [kwɔ:ts] n quarzo; ~ **watch** n orologio al quarzo.
quash [kwɔʃ] vt (verdict) annullare.
quaver ['kweɪvə*] n (Brit MUS) croma // vi tremolare.
quay [ki:] n (also: ~**side**) banchina.
queasy ['kwi:zɪ] a (stomach) delicato(a); to feel ~ aver la nausea.
queen [kwi:n] n (gen) regina; (CARDS etc) regina, donna; ~ **mother** n regina madre.
queer [kwɪə*] a strano(a), curioso(a); (suspicious) dubbio(a), sospetto(a); (sick): I feel ~ mi sento poco bene // n (col) finocchio.
quell [kwɛl] vt domare.
quench [kwɛntʃ] vt (flames) spegnere; to ~ one's thirst dissetarsi.
querulous ['kwɛruləs] a querulo(a).
query ['kwɪərɪ] n domanda, questione f; (doubt) dubbio // vt mettere in questione.
quest [kwɛst] n cerca, ricerca.
question ['kwɛstʃən] n domanda, questione f // vt (person) interrogare; (plan, idea) mettere in questione or in dubbio; it's a ~ of doing si tratta di fare; beyond ~ fuori di dubbio; out of the ~ fuori discussione, impossibile; ~**able** a discutibile; ~ **mark** n punto interrogativo.
questionnaire [kwɛstʃə'nɛə*] n questionario.
queue [kju:] n (Brit) coda, fila // vi fare la coda.
quibble ['kwɪbl] vi cavillare.
quick [kwɪk] a rapido(a), veloce; (reply) pronto(a); (mind) pronto(a), acuto(a) // ad rapidamente, presto // n: cut to the ~ (fig) toccato(a) sul vivo; be ~! fa presto!; ~**en** vt accelerare, affrettare; (rouse) animare, stimolare // vi accelerare, affrettarsi; ~**ly** ad rapidamente, velocemente; ~**sand** n sabbie fpl mobili; ~-**witted** a pronto(a) d'ingegno.
quid [kwɪd] n (pl inv) (Brit col) sterlina.
quiet ['kwaɪət] a tranquillo(a), quieto(a); (ceremony) semplice; (colour) discreto(a) // n tranquillità, calma // vt, vi (US) = ~**en**; keep ~! sta zitto!; ~**en** (also: ~**en down**) vi calmarsi, chetarsi // vt calmare, chetare; ~**ly** ad tranquillamente, calmamente, sommessamente, discretamente.
quilt [kwɪlt] n trapunta; (continental ~) piumino.

quin [kwɪn] n abbr = **quintuplet.**
quinine [kwɪ'ni:n] n chinino.
quintuplet [kwɪn'tju:plɪt] n uno/a di cinque gemelli.
quip [kwɪp] n frizzo.
quirk [kwə:k] n ghiribizzo.
quit, pt, pp quit or quitted [kwɪt] vt lasciare, partire da // vi (give up) mollare; (resign) dimettersi; notice to ~ preavviso (dato all'inquilino).
quite [kwaɪt] ad (rather) assai; (entirely) completamente, del tutto; ~ understand capisco perfettamente; ~ a few of them non pochi di loro; ~ (so)! esatto!
quits [kwɪts] a: ~ (with) pari (con); let's call it ~ adesso siamo pari.
quiver ['kwɪvə*] vi tremare, fremere // n (for arrows) faretra.
quiz [kwɪz] n (game) quiz m inv; indovinello // vt interrogare; ~**zical** a enigmatico(a).
quota ['kwəutə] n quota.
quotation [kwəu'teɪʃən] n citazione f; (of shares etc) quotazione f; (estimate) preventivo; ~ **marks** npl virgolette fpl.
quote [kwəut] n citazione f // vt (sentence) citare; (price) dare, fissare; (shares) quotare // vi: to ~ from citare.

R

rabbi ['ræbaɪ] n rabbino.
rabbit ['ræbɪt] n coniglio; ~ **hutch** n conigliera.
rabble ['ræbl] n (pej) canaglia, plebaglia.
rabies ['reɪbi:z] n rabbia.
RAC n abbr (Brit) = Royal Automobile Club.
race [reɪs] n razza; (competition, rush) corsa // vt (person) gareggiare (in corsa) con; (horse) far correre; (engine) imballare // vi correre; ~ **car** n (US) = **racing car**; ~ **car driver** n (US) = **racing driver**; ~**course** n campo di corse, ippodromo; ~**horse** n cavallo da corsa; ~ **relations** npl rapporti mpl razziali; ~**track** n pista.
racial ['reɪʃl] a razziale; ~**ist** a, n razzista (m/f).
racing ['reɪsɪŋ] n corsa; ~ **car** n (Brit) macchina da corsa; ~ **driver** n (Brit) corridore m automobilista.
racism ['reɪsɪzəm] n razzismo; **racist** a, n razzista (m/f).
rack [ræk] n rastrelliera; (also: luggage ~) rete f, portabagagli m inv; (also: roof ~) portabagagli // vt torturare, tormentare; to ~ one's brains scervellarsi.
racket ['rækɪt] n (for tennis) racchetta; (noise) fracasso; baccano; (swindle) imbroglio, truffa; (organized crime) racket m inv.

racquet ['rækɪt] n racchetta.
racy ['reɪsɪ] a brioso(a); piccante.
radar ['reɪdɑ:*] n radar m // cpd radar inv.
radial5.5 ['reɪdɪəl] a (also: ~-ply) radiale.
radiant ['reɪdɪənt] a raggiante; (PHYSICS) radiante.
radiate ['reɪdɪeɪt] vt (heat) irraggiare, irradiare // vi (lines) irradiarsi.
radiation [reɪdɪ'eɪʃən] n irradiamento; (radioactive) radiazione f.
radiator ['reɪdɪeɪtə*] n radiatore m.
radical ['rædɪkl] a radicale.
radii ['reɪdɪaɪ] npl of **radius**.
radio ['reɪdɪəu] n radio f inv; on the ~ alla radio.
radioactive [reɪdɪəu'æktɪv] a radioattivo(a).
radio station n stazione f radio inv.
radish ['rædɪʃ] n ravanello.
radium ['reɪdɪəm] n radio.
radius ['reɪdɪəs], pl **radii** n raggio; (ANAT) radio.
RAF n abbr = **Royal Air Force**.
raffle ['ræfl] n lotteria.
raft [rɑ:ft] n zattera; (also: life ~) zattera di salvataggio.
rafter ['rɑ:ftə*] n trave f.
rag [ræg] n straccio, cencio; (pej: newspaper) giornalaccio, bandiera; (for charity) iniziativa studentesca a scopo benefico // vt (Brit) prendere in giro; ~s npl stracci mpl, brandelli mpl; ~-and-bone man n (Brit) = **ragman**; ~ doll n bambola di pezza.
rage [reɪdʒ] n (fury) collera, furia // vi (person) andare su tutte le furie; (storm) infuriare; it's all the ~ fa furore.
ragged ['rægɪd] a (edge) irregolare; (cuff) logoro(a); (appearance) pezzente.
ragman ['rægmæn] n straccivendolo.
raid [reɪd] n (MIL) incursione f; (criminal) rapina; (by police) irruzione f // vt fare un'incursione in; rapinare; fare irruzione in.
rail [reɪl] n (on stair) ringhiera; (on bridge, balcony) parapetto; (of ship) battagliola; (for train) rotaia; ~s npl binario, rotaie fpl; by ~ per ferrovia; ~ing(s) n(pl) ringhiere fpl; ~road n (US) = ~way; ~way n (Brit) ferrovia; ~way line n (Brit) linea ferroviaria; ~wayman n (Brit) ferroviere m; ~way station n (Brit) stazione f ferroviaria.
rain [reɪn] n pioggia // vi piovere; in the ~ sotto la pioggia; it's ~ing piove; ~bow n arcobaleno; ~coat n impermeabile m; ~drop n goccia di pioggia; ~fall n pioggia; (measurement) piovosità; ~y a piovoso(a).
raise [reɪz] n aumento // vt (lift) alzare; sollevare; (build) erigere; (increase) aumentare; (a protest, doubt, question) sollevare; (cattle, family) allevare; (crop) coltivare; (army, funds) raccogliere; (loan) ottenere; to ~ one's voice alzare la voce.
raisin ['reɪzn] n uva secca.
rajah ['rɑ:dʒə] n ragia m inv.
rake [reɪk] n (tool) rastrello; (person) libertino // vt (garden) rastrellare; (with machine gun) spazzare.
rally ['rælɪ] n (POL etc) riunione f; (AUT) rally m inv; (TENNIS) scambio // vt riunire, radunare // vi raccogliersi, radunarsi; (sick person, Stock Exchange) riprendersi; to ~ round vt fus raggrupparsi intorno a; venire in aiuto di.
RAM [ræm] n abbr (= random access memory) memoria ad accesso casuale.
ram [ræm] n montone m, ariete m; (device) ariete // vt conficcare; (crash into) cozzare, sbattere contro; percuotere; speronare.
ramble ['ræmbl] n escursione f // vi (pej: also: ~ on) divagare; ~r n escursionista m/f; (BOT) rosa rampicante; **rambling** a (speech) sconnesso(a); (BOT) rampicante.
ramp [ræmp] n rampa; on/off ~ (US AUT) raccordo di entrata/uscita.
rampage [ræm'peɪdʒ] n: to go on the ~ scatenarsi in modo violento.
rampant ['ræmpənt] a (disease etc) che infierisce.
rampart ['ræmpɑ:t] n bastione m.
ramshackle ['ræmʃækl] a (house) cadente; (car etc) sgangherato(a).
ran [ræn] pt of **run**.
ranch [rɑ:ntʃ] n ranch m inv; ~er n proprietario di un ranch; cowboy m inv.
rancid ['rænsɪd] a rancido(a).
rancour, (US) **rancor** ['rænkə*] n rancore m.
random ['rændəm] a fatto(a) or detto(a) per caso // n: at ~ a casaccio; ~ access n (COMPUT) accesso casuale.
randy ['rændɪ] a (Brit col) arrapato(a); lascivo(a).
rang [ræŋ] pt of **ring**.
range [reɪndʒ] n (of mountains) catena; (of missile, voice) portata; (of products) gamma; (MIL: also: shooting ~) campo di tiro; (also: kitchen ~) fornello, cucina economica // vi: to ~ over coprire; to ~ from ... to andare da ... a.
ranger ['reɪndʒə*] n guardia forestale.
rank [ræŋk] n fila; (MIL) grado; (Brit: also: taxi ~) posteggio di taxi // vi: to ~ among essere nel numero di // a puzzolente; vero(a) e proprio(a); the ~s (MIL) la truppa; the ~ and file (fig) la gran massa.
rankle ['ræŋkl] vi bruciare.
ransack ['rænsæk] vt rovistare; (plunder) saccheggiare.

ransom ['rænsəm] n riscatto; **to hold sb to ~** (fig) esercitare pressione su qn.

rant [rænt] vi vociare.

rap [ræp] vt bussare a; picchiare su.

rape [reɪp] n violenza carnale, stupro; (BOT) ravizzone m // vt violentare; **~(seed) oil** n olio di ravizzone.

rapid ['ræpɪd] a rapido(a); **~s** npl (GEO) rapida; **~ly** ad rapidamente.

rapist ['reɪpɪst] n violentatore m.

rapport [ræ'pɔː*] n rapporto.

rapture ['ræptʃə*] n estasi f inv.

rare [rɛə*] a raro(a); (CULIN: steak) al sangue.

rarefied ['rɛərɪfaɪd] a (air, atmosphere) rarefatto(a).

rarely ['rɛəlɪ] ad raramente.

raring ['rɛərɪŋ] a: **to be ~ to go** (col) non veder l'ora di cominciare.

rascal ['rɑːskl] n mascalzone m.

rash [ræʃ] a imprudente, sconsiderato(a) // n (MED) eruzione f.

rasher ['ræʃə*] n fetta sottile (di lardo or prosciutto).

raspberry ['rɑːzbərɪ] n lampone m.

rasping ['rɑːspɪŋ] a stridulo(a).

rat [ræt] n ratto.

rate [reɪt] n (proportion) tasso, percentuale f; (speed) velocità f inv; (price) tariffa // vt giudicare; stimare; **to ~ sb/sth as** valutare qn/qc come; **~s** npl (Brit) imposte fpl comunali; (fees) tariffe fpl; **~able value** n (Brit) valore m imponibile or locativo (di una proprietà); **~payer** n (Brit) contribuente m/f (che paga le imposte comunali).

rather ['rɑːðə*] ad piuttosto; **it's ~ expensive** è piuttosto caro; (too much) è un po' caro; **there's ~ a lot** ce n'è parecchio; **I would** or **I'd ~ go** preferirei andare.

ratify ['rætɪfaɪ] vt ratificare.

rating ['reɪtɪŋ] n classificazione f; punteggio di merito; (NAUT: category) classe f; (: Brit: sailor) marinaio semplice.

ratio ['reɪʃɪəu] n proporzione f.

ration ['ræʃən] n (gen pl) razioni fpl // vt razionare.

rational ['ræʃənl] a razionale, ragionevole; (solution, reasoning) logico(a); **~e** [-'nɑːl] n fondamento logico; giustificazione f; **~ize** vt razionalizzare.

rat race n carrierismo, corsa al successo.

rattle ['rætl] n tintinnio; (louder) strepito; (object: of baby) sonaglino; (: of sports fan) raganella // vi risuonare, tintinnare; fare un rumore di ferraglia // vt scuotere (con strepito); **~snake** n serpente m a sonagli.

raucous ['rɔːkəs] a rauco(a).

ravage ['rævɪdʒ] vt devastare; **~s** npl danni mpl.

rave [reɪv] vi (in anger) infuriarsi; (with enthusiasm) andare in estasi; (MED) delirare.

raven ['reɪvən] n corvo.

ravenous ['rævənəs] a affamato(a).

ravine [rə'viːn] n burrone m.

raving ['reɪvɪŋ] a: **~ lunatic** pazzo(a) furioso(a).

ravioli [rævɪ'əulɪ] n ravioli mpl.

ravishing ['rævɪʃɪŋ] a incantevole.

raw [rɔː] a (uncooked) crudo(a); (not processed) greggio(a); (sore) vivo(a); (inexperienced) inesperto(a); **~ deal** n (col) bidonata; **~ material** n materia prima.

ray [reɪ] n raggio; **a ~ of hope** un barlume di speranza.

rayon ['reɪɔn] n raion m.

raze [reɪz] vt radere, distruggere.

razor ['reɪzə*] n rasoio; **~ blade** n lama di rasoio.

Rd abbr = road.

re [riː] prep con riferimento a.

reach [riːtʃ] n portata; (of river etc) tratto // vt raggiungere; arrivare a // vi stendersi; **out of/within ~** fuori/a portata di mano; **to ~ out** vi: **to ~ out for** stendere la mano per prendere.

react [riː'ækt] vi reagire; **~ion** [-'ækʃən] n reazione f.

reactor [riː'æktə*] n reattore m.

read, pt, pp **read** [riːd, rɛd] vi leggere // vt leggere; (understand) intendere, interpretare; (study) studiare; **to ~ out** vt leggere ad alta voce; **~able** a (writing) leggibile; (book etc) che si legge volentieri; **~er** n lettore/trice; (book) libro di lettura; (Brit: at university) professore con funzioni preminenti di ricerca; **~ership** n (of paper etc) numero di lettori.

readily ['rɛdɪlɪ] ad volentieri; (easily) facilmente.

readiness ['rɛdɪnɪs] n prontezza; **in ~** (prepared) pronto(a).

reading ['riːdɪŋ] n lettura; (understanding) interpretazione f; (on instrument) indicazione f.

ready ['rɛdɪ] a pronto(a); (willing) pronto(a), disposto(a); (quick) rapido(a); (available) disponibile // ad: **~-cooked** già cotto(a) // n: **at the ~** (MIL) pronto a sparare; (fig) tutto(a) pronto(a); **to get ~** vi prepararsi // vt preparare; **~-made** a prefabbricato(a); (clothes) confezionato(a); **~ money** n denaro contante, contanti mpl; **~ reckoner** n prontuario di calcolo; **~-to-wear** a prêt-à-porter inv.

real [rɪəl] a reale; vero(a); **in ~ terms** in realtà; **~ estate** n beni mpl immobili; **~ism** n (also ART) realismo; **~ist** n realista m/f; **~istic** [-'lɪstɪk] a realistico(a).

reality [riː'ælɪtɪ] n realtà f inv.

realization [rɪəlaɪˈzeɪʃən] *n* presa di coscienza; realizzazione *f*.

realize [ˈrɪəlaɪz] *vt* (*understand*) rendersi conto di; (*a project*, COMM: *asset*) realizzare.

really [ˈrɪəlɪ] *ad* veramente, davvero.

realm [rɛlm] *n* reame *m*, regno.

realtor [ˈrɪəltɔ:*] *n* (US) agente *m* immobiliare.

reap [ri:p] *vt* mietere; (*fig*) raccogliere.

reappear [ri:əˈpɪə*] *vi* ricomparire, riapparire.

rear [rɪə*] *a* di dietro; (AUT: *wheel etc*) posteriore // *n* didietro, parte *f* posteriore // *vt* (*cattle, family*) allevare // *vi* (*also:* ~ *up: animal*) impennarsi.

rearmament [ri:ˈɑ:məmənt] *n* riarmo.

rearrange [ri:əˈreɪndʒ] *vt* riordinare.

rear-view mirror [ˈrɪəvju:-] *n* (AUT) specchio retrovisore.

reason [ˈri:zn] *n* ragione *f*; (*cause, motive*) ragione, motivo // *vi*: to ~ with sb far ragionare qn; to have ~ to think avere motivo per pensare; it stands to ~ that è ovvio che; ~able *a* ragionevole; (*not bad*) accettabile; ~ably *ad* ragionevolmente; ~ing *n* ragionamento.

reassurance [ri:əˈʃuərəns] *n* rassicurazione *f*.

reassure [ri:əˈʃuə*] *vt* rassicurare; to ~ sb of rassicurare qn di *or* su.

rebate [ˈri:beɪt] *n* (*on product*) ribasso; (*on tax etc*) sgravio; (*repayment*) rimborso.

rebel *n* [ˈrɛbl] ribelle *m/f* // *vi* [rɪˈbɛl] ribellarsi; ~lion *n* ribellione *f*; ~lious *a* ribelle.

rebound *vi* [rɪˈbaund] (*ball*) rimbalzare // *n* [ˈri:baund] rimbalzo.

rebuff [rɪˈbʌf] *n* secco rifiuto.

rebuke [rɪˈbju:k] *vt* rimproverare.

rebut [rɪˈbʌt] *vt* rifiutare.

recall [rɪˈkɔ:l] *vt* richiamare; (*remember*) ricordare, richiamare alla mente // *n* richiamo.

recant [rɪˈkænt] *vi* ritrattarsi; (REL) fare abiura.

recap [ˈri:kæp] *vt* ricapitolare // *vi* riassumere.

recapitulate [ri:kəˈpɪtjuleɪt] *vt, vi* = **recap.**

rec'd *abbr* = **received.**

recede [rɪˈsi:d] *vi* allontanarsi; ritirarsi; calare; **receding** *a* (*forehead, chin*) sfuggente; he's got a receding hairline sta stempiando.

receipt [rɪˈsi:t] *n* (*document*) ricevuta; (*act of receiving*) ricevimento; ~s *npl* (COMM) introiti *mpl*.

receive [rɪˈsi:v] *vt* ricevere; (*guest*) ricevere, accogliere.

receiver [rɪˈsi:və*] *n* (TEL) ricevitore *m*; (*of stolen goods*) ricettatore/trice; (LAW) curatore *m* fallimentare.

recent [ˈri:snt] *a* recente; ~ly *ad* recentemente.

receptacle [rɪˈsɛptɪkl] *n* recipiente *m*.

reception [rɪˈsɛpʃən] *n* ricevimento; (*welcome*) accoglienza; (TV *etc*) ricezione *f*; ~ **desk** *n* (*in hotel*) reception *f inv*; (*in hospital, at doctor's*) accettazione *f*; (*in offices etc*) portineria; ~ist *n* receptionist *m/f inv*.

receptive [rɪˈsɛptɪv] *a* ricettivo(a).

recess [rɪˈsɛs] *n* (*in room*) alcova; (POL *etc: holiday*) vacanze *fpl*; ~ion [-ˈsɛʃən] *n* recessione *f*.

recharge [ri:ˈtʃɑ:dʒ] *vt* (*battery*) ricaricare.

recipe [ˈrɛsɪpɪ] *n* ricetta.

recipient [rɪˈsɪpɪənt] *n* beneficiario/a; (*of letter*) destinatario/a.

recital [rɪˈsaɪtl] *n* recital *m inv*.

recite [rɪˈsaɪt] *vt* (*poem*) recitare.

reckless [ˈrɛkləs] *a* (*driver etc*) spericolato(a).

reckon [ˈrɛkən] *vt* (*count*) calcolare; (*consider*) considerare, stimare; (*think*): I ~ that ... penso che ...; to ~ on *vt fus* contare su; ~ing *n* conto; stima.

reclaim [rɪˈkleɪm] *vt* (*land*) bonificare; (*demand back*) richiedere, reclamare.

recline [rɪˈklaɪn] *vi* stare sdraiato(a); **reclining** *a* (*seat*) ribaltabile.

recluse [rɪˈklu:s] *n* eremita *m*, appartato/a.

recognition [rɛkəgˈnɪʃən] *n* riconoscimento; to gain ~ essere riconosciuto(a); transformed beyond ~ irriconoscibile.

recognize [ˈrɛkəgnaɪz] *vt*: to ~ (by/as) riconoscere (a *or* da/come).

recoil [rɪˈkɔɪl] *vi* (*person*): to ~ (from) indietreggiare (davanti a) // *n* (*of gun*) rinculo.

recollect [rɛkəˈlɛkt] *vt* ricordare; ~ion [-ˈlɛkʃən] *n* ricordo.

recommend [rɛkəˈmɛnd] *vt* raccomandare; (*advise*) consigliare.

reconcile [ˈrɛkənsaɪl] *vt* (*two people*) riconciliare; (*two facts*) conciliare, quadrare; to ~ o.s. to rassegnarsi a.

recondition [ri:kənˈdɪʃən] *vt* rimettere a nuovo.

reconnaissance [rɪˈkɒnɪsns] *n* (MIL) ricognizione *f*.

reconnoitre, (US) **reconnoiter** [rɛkəˈnɔɪtə*] (MIL) *vt* fare una ricognizione di // *vi* fare una ricognizione.

reconstruct [ri:kənˈstrʌkt] *vt* ricostruire.

record *n* [ˈrɛkɔ:d] ricordo, documento; (*of meeting etc*) nota, verbale *m*; (*register*) registro; (*file*) pratica, dossier *m inv*; (*also: police* ~) fedina penale sporca; (MUS: *disc*) disco; (SPORT) record *m inv*, primato // *vt* [rɪˈkɔ:d] (*set down*) prendere nota di, registrare; (*relate*) raccontare; (MUS: *song etc*) registrare; in ~ time a tempo di record; to keep a ~ of tener nota di; off the ~ *a* ufficioso(a) // *ad* ufficiosamente; **~ card** *n* (*in file*) scheda; **~ed delivery** *n* (*Brit POST*): **~ed delivery letter** *etc* lettera *etc* raccomandata; **~er** *n* (*LAW*) avvocato *che funge da giudice*; (*MUS*) flauto diritto; **~ holder** *n* (*SPORT*) primatista *m/f*; **~ing** *n* (*MUS*) registrazione *f*; **~ player** *n* giradischi *m inv*.

recount [rɪ'kaunt] *vt* raccontare, narrare.

re-count *n* ['ri:kaunt] (*POL: of votes*) nuovo computo // *vt* [ri:'kaunt] ricontare.

recoup [rɪ'ku:p] *vt* ricuperare.

recourse [rɪ'kɔ:s] *n* ricorso; rimedio.

recover [rɪ'kʌvə*] *vt* ricuperare // *vi* (*from illness*) rimettersi (in salute), ristabilirsi; (*country, person: from shock*) riprendersi.

recovery [rɪ'kʌvərɪ] *n* ricupero; ristabilimento; ripresa.

recreation [rɛkrɪ'eɪʃən] *n* ricreazione *f*; svago; **~al** *a* ricreativo(a).

recrimination [rɪkrɪmɪ'neɪʃən] *n* recriminazione *f*.

recruit [rɪ'kru:t] *n* recluta // *vt* reclutare.

rectangle ['rɛktæŋgl] *n* rettangolo; **rectangular** [-'tæŋgjulə*] *a* rettangolare.

rectify ['rɛktɪfaɪ] *vt* (*error*) rettificare; (*omission*) riparare.

rector ['rɛktə*] *n* (*REL*) parroco (*anglicano*); **rectory** *n* presbiterio.

recuperate [rɪ'kju:pəreɪt] *vi* ristabilirsi.

recur [rɪ'kə:*] *vi* riaccadere, (*idea, opportunity*) riapparire; (*symptoms*) ripresentarsi; **~rent** *a* ricorrente, periodico(a).

red [rɛd] *n* rosso; (*POL: pej*) rosso/a // *a* rosso(a); **in the ~** (*account*) scoperto; (*business*) in deficit; **~ carpet treatment** *n* cerimonia col gran pavese; **R~ Cross** *n* Croce *f* Rossa; **~currant** *n* ribes *m inv*; **~den** *vt* arrossare // *vi* arrossire; **~dish** *a* rossiccio(a).

redeem [rɪ'di:m] *vt* (*debt*) riscattare; (*sth in pawn*) ritirare; (*fig, also REL*) redimere; **~ing** *a* (*feature*) che salva.

redeploy [ri:dɪ'plɔɪ] *vt* (*resources*) riorganizzare.

red-haired [rɛd'hɛəd] *a* dai capelli rossi.

red-handed [rɛd'hændɪd] *a*: **to be caught ~** essere preso(a) in flagrante *or* con le mani nel sacco.

redhead ['rɛdhɛd] *n* rosso/a.

red herring *n* (*fig*) falsa pista.

red-hot [rɛd'hɔt] *a* arroventato(a).

redirect [ri:daɪ'rɛkt] *vt* (*mail*) far seguire.

redistribute [ri:dɪ'strɪbju:t] *vt* ridistribuire.

red light *n*: **to go through a ~** (*AUT*) passare col rosso; **red-light district** *n* quartiere *m* luce rossa *inv*.

redo [ri:'du:] *vt irg* rifare.

redolent ['rɛdələnt] *a*: **~ of** che sa di; (*fig*) che ricorda.

redouble [rɪ'dʌbl] *vt*: **to ~ one's efforts** raddoppiare gli sforzi.

redress [rɪ'drɛs] *n* riparazione *f* // *vt* riparare.

Red Sea *n*: **the ~** il Mar Rosso.

redskin ['rɛdskɪn] *n* pellerossa *m/f*.

red tape *n* (*fig*) burocrazia.

reduce [rɪ'dju:s] *vt* ridurre; (*lower*) ridurre, abbassare; **"~ speed now"** (*AUT*) "rallentare"; **reduction** [rɪ'dʌkʃən] *n* riduzione *f*; (*of price*) ribasso; (*discount*) sconto.

redundancy [rɪ'dʌndənsɪ] *n* licenziamento.

redundant [rɪ'dʌndnt] *a* (*worker*) licenziato(a); (*detail, object*) superfluo(a); **to be made ~** essere licenziato (*per eccesso di personale*).

reed [ri:d] *n* (*BOT*) canna; (*MUS: of clarinet etc*) ancia.

reef [ri:f] *n* (*at sea*) scogliera.

reek [ri:k] *vi*: **to ~ (of)** puzzare (di).

reel [ri:l] *n* bobina, rocchetto; (*TECH*) aspo; (*FISHING*) mulinello; (*CINEMA*) rotolo // *vt* (*TECH*) annaspare; (*also: ~ up*) avvolgere // *vi* (*sway*) barcollare.

ref [rɛf] *n abbr* (*col: = referee*) arbitro.

refectory [rɪ'fɛktərɪ] *n* refettorio.

refer [rɪ'fə:*] *vt*: **to ~ sth to** (*dispute, decision*) deferire qc a; **to ~ sb to** (*inquirer: for information*) indirizzare qn a; (*reader: to text*) rimandare qn a; **to ~ to** *vt fus* (*allude to*) accennare a; (*apply to*) riferire a; (*consult*) rivolgersi a.

referee [rɛfə'ri:] *n* arbitro; (*Brit: for job application*) referenza // *vt* arbitrare.

reference ['rɛfrəns] *n* riferimento; (*mention*) menzione *f*, allusione *f*; (*for job application: letter*) referenza; lettera di raccomandazione; (*: person*) referenza; **with ~ to** riguardo a; (*COMM: in letter*) in or con riferimento a; **~ book** *n* libro di consultazione; **~ number** *n* numero di riferimento.

referendum, *pl* **referenda** [rɛfə'rɛndəm, -də] *n* referendum *m inv*.

refill *vt* [ri:'fɪl] riempire di nuovo; (*pen, lighter etc*) ricaricare // *n* ['ri:fɪl] (*for pen etc*) ricambio.

refine [rɪ'faɪn] *vt* raffinare; **~d** *a* (*person, taste*) raffinato(a).

reflect [rɪ'flɛkt] *vt* (*light, image*) riflettere; (*fig*) rispecchiare // *vi* (*think*) riflettere, considerare; **to ~ on** *vt fus* (*discredit*) rispecchiarsi su; **~ion** [-'flɛkʃən] *n* riflessione *f*; (*image*) riflesso; (*criticism*): **~ion on** giudizio su; attacco a; **on ~ion** pensandoci sopra.

reflex ['ri:flɛks] *a* riflesso(a) // *n* riflesso; **~ive** [rɪ'flɛksɪv] *a* (*LING*) riflessivo(a).

reform [rɪ'fɔ:m] *n* riforma // *vt* riformare; **the R~ation** [rɛfə'meɪʃən] *n* la Riforma; **~atory** *n* (*US*) riformatorio.

refrain [rɪ'freɪn] vi: to ~ from doing trattenersi dal fare // n ritornello.

refresh [rɪ'fref] vt rinfrescare; (subj: food, sleep) ristorare; ~er course n (Brit) corso di aggiornamento; ~ing a (drink) rinfrescante; (sleep) riposante, ristoratore(trice); ~ments npl rinfreschi mpl.

refrigerator [rɪ'frɪdʒəreɪtə*] n frigorifero.

refuel [riː'fjuəl] vi far rifornimento (di carburante).

refuge ['refjuːdʒ] n rifugio; to take ~ in rifugiarsi in.

refugee [refjuˈdʒiː] n rifugiato/a, profugo/a.

refund n ['riːfʌnd] rimborso // vt [rɪ'fʌnd] rimborsare.

refurbish [riːˈfɔːbɪʃ] vt rimettere a nuovo.

refusal [rɪ'fjuːzəl] n rifiuto; to have first ~ on avere il diritto d'opzione su.

refuse n ['refjuːs] rifiuti mpl // vt, vi [rɪ'fjuːz] rifiutare; to ~ to do rifiutare di fare; ~ collection n raccolta di rifiuti.

refute [rɪ'fjuːt] vt confutare.

regain [rɪ'geɪn] vt riguadagnare; riacquistare, ricuperare.

regal ['riːgl] a regio(a); ~ia [rɪ'geɪlɪə] n insegne fpl regie.

regard [rɪ'gɑːd] n riguardo, stima // vt considerare, stimare; to give one's ~s to porgere i suoi saluti a; "with kindest ~s" "cordiali saluti"; ~ing, as ~s, with ~ to riguardo a; ~less ad lo stesso; ~less of a dispetto di, nonostante.

regenerate [rɪ'dʒenəreɪt] vt rigenerare.

régime [reɪ'ʒiːm] n regime m.

regiment n ['redʒɪmənt] reggimento // vt ['redʒɪment] irreggimentare; ~al [-'mentl] a reggimentale.

region ['riːdʒən] n regione f; in the ~ of (fig) all'incirca di; ~al a regionale.

register ['redʒɪstə*] n registro; (also: electoral ~) lista elettorale // vt registrare; (vehicle) immatricolare; (luggage) spedire assicurato(a); (letter) assicurare; (subj: instrument) segnare // vi iscriversi; (at hotel) firmare il registro; (make impression) entrare in testa; ~ed a (design) depositato(a); (Brit: letter) assicurato(a); ~ed trademark n marchio depositato.

registrar ['redʒɪstrɑː*] n ufficiale m di stato civile; segretario.

registration [redʒɪs'treɪʃən] n (act) registrazione f; iscrizione f; (AUT: also: ~ number) numero di targa.

registry ['redʒɪstrɪ] n ufficio del registro; ~ office n (Brit) anagrafe f; to get married in a ~ office ≈ sposarsi in municipio.

regret [rɪ'gret] n rimpianto, rincrescimento // vt rimpiangere; ~fully ad con rincrescimento; ~table a de-

plorevole.

regular ['regjulə*] a regolare; (usual) abituale, normale; (soldier) dell'esercito regolare; (COMM: size) normale // n (client etc) cliente m/f abituale; ~ly ad regolarmente.

regulate ['regjuleɪt] vt regolare; **regulation** [-'leɪʃən] n (rule) regola, regolamento; (adjustment) regolazione f.

rehabilitation ['riːhəbɪlɪ'teɪʃən] n (of offender) riabilitazione f; (of disabled) riadattamento.

rehearsal [rɪ'həːsəl] n prova.

rehearse [rɪ'həːs] vt provare.

reign [reɪn] n regno // vi regnare.

reimburse [riːɪm'bəːs] vt rimborsare.

rein [reɪn] n (for horse) briglia.

reindeer ['reɪndɪə*] n (pl inv) renna.

reinforce [riːɪn'fɔːs] vt rinforzare; ~d concrete n cemento armato; ~ments npl (MIL) rinforzi mpl.

reinstate [riːɪn'steɪt] vt reintegrare.

reiterate [riːˈɪtəreɪt] vt reiterare, ripetere.

reject n ['riːdʒekt] (COMM) scarto // vt [rɪ'dʒekt] rifiutare, respingere; (COMM: goods) scartare; ~ion [rɪ'dʒekʃən] n rifiuto.

rejoice [rɪ'dʒɔɪs] vi: to ~ (at or over) provare diletto in.

rejuvenate [rɪ'dʒuːvəneɪt] vt ringiovanire.

relapse [rɪ'læps] n (MED) ricaduta.

relate [rɪ'leɪt] vt (tell) raccontare; (connect) collegare // vi: to ~ to (connect) riferirsi a; (get on with) stabilire un rapporto con; ~d a imparentato(a); collegato(a), connesso(a); **relating to** prep che riguarda, rispetto a.

relation [rɪ'leɪʃən] n (person) parente m/ f; (link) rapporto, relazione f; ~ship n rapporto; (personal ties) rapporti mpl, relazioni fpl; (also: family ~ship) legami mpl di parentela.

relative ['relətɪv] n parente m/f // a relativo(a); (respective) rispettivo(a).

relax [rɪ'læks] vi rilasciarsi; (person: unwind) rilassarsi // vt rilasciare; (mind, person) rilassare; ~ation [riːlæk'seɪʃən] n rilasciamento; rilassamento; (entertainment) ricreazione f, svago; ~ed a rilasciato(a); rilassato(a); ~ing a rilassante.

relay ['riːleɪ] n (SPORT) corsa a staffetta // vt (message) trasmettere.

release [rɪ'liːs] n (from prison) rilascio; (from obligation) liberazione f; (of gas etc) emissione f; (of film etc) distribuzione f; (record) disco; (device) disinnesto // vt (prisoner) rilasciare; (from obligation, wreckage etc) liberare; (book, film) fare uscire; (news) rendere pubblico(a); (gas etc) emettere; (TECH: catch, spring etc) disinnestare; (let go) rilasciare; lasciar andare; sciogliere.

relegate ['rcləgeit] *vt* relegare; (*SPORT*): to be ~d essere retrocesso(a).

relent [rɪ'lɛnt] *vi* cedere; **~less** *a* implacabile.

relevant ['rɛləvənt] *a* pertinente; (*chapter*) in questione; ~ **to** pertinente a.

reliability [rɪlaɪə'bɪlɪtɪ] *n* (*of person*) serietà; (*of machine*) affidabilità.

reliable [rɪ'laɪəbl] *a* (*person, firm*) fidato(a), che dà affidamento; (*method*) sicuro(a); (*machine*) affidabile; **reliably** *ad*: to be reliably informed sapere da fonti sicure.

reliance [rɪ'laɪəns] *n*: ~ (on) fiducia (in); bisogno (di).

relic ['rɛlɪk] *n* (*REL*) reliquia; (*of the past*) resto.

relief [rɪ'li:f] *n* (*from pain, anxiety*) sollievo; (*help, supplies*) soccorsi *mpl*; (*of guard*) cambio; (*ART, GEO*) rilievo.

relieve [rɪ'li:v] *vt* (*pain, patient*) sollevare; (*bring help*) soccorrere; (*take over from: gen*) sostituire; (: *guard*) rilevare; **to** ~ **sb of sth** (*load*) alleggerire qn di qc; **to** ~ **o.s.** fare i propri bisogni.

religion [rɪ'lɪdʒən] *n* religione *f*; **religious** *a* religioso(a).

relinquish [rɪ'lɪŋkwɪʃ] *vt* abbandonare; (*plan, habit*) rinunziare a.

relish ['rɛlɪʃ] *n* (*CULIN*) condimento; (*enjoyment*) gran piacere *m* // *vt* (*food etc*) godere; **to** ~ **doing** adorare fare.

relocate ['ri:ləu'keit] *vt* trasferire // *vi* trasferirsi.

reluctance [rɪ'lʌktəns] *n* riluttanza.

reluctant [rɪ'lʌktənt] *a* riluttante, mal disposto(a); **~ly** *ad* di mala voglia, a malincuore.

rely [rɪ'laɪ]: **to** ~ **on** *vt fus* contare su; (*be dependent*) dipendere da.

remain [rɪ'meɪn] *vi* restare, rimanere; **~der** *n* resto; (*COMM*) rimanenza; **~ing** *a* che rimane; **~s** *npl* resti *mpl*.

remand [rɪ'mɑ:nd] *n*: on ~ in detenzione preventiva // *vt*: to ~ in custody rinviare in carcere; trattenere a disposizione della legge; ~ **home** *n* (*Brit*) riformatorio, casa di correzione.

remark [rɪ'mɑ:k] *n* osservazione *f* // *vt* osservare, dire; (*notice*) notare; **~able** *a* notevole; eccezionale.

remedial [rɪ'mi:dɪəl] *a* (*tuition, classes*) di riparazione.

remedy ['rɛmədɪ] *n*: ~ (for) rimedio (per) // *vt* rimediare a.

remember [rɪ'mɛmbə*] *vt* ricordare, ricordarsi di; **remembrance** *n* memoria; ricordo.

remind [rɪ'maɪnd] *vt*: to ~ **sb of sth** ricordare qc a qn; to ~ **sb to do** ricordare a qn di fare; **~er** *n* richiamo; (*note etc*) promemoria *m inv*.

reminisce [rɛmɪ'nɪs] *vi*: to ~ (about) abbandonarsi ai ricordi (di).

reminiscent [rɛmɪ'nɪsnt] *a*: ~ of che fa pensare a, che richiama.

remiss [rɪ'mɪs] *a* negligente.

remission [rɪ'mɪʃən] *n* remissione *f*; (*of fee*) esonero.

remit [rɪ'mɪt] *vt* (*send: money*) rimettere; **~tance** *n* rimessa.

remnant ['rɛmnənt] *n* resto, avanzo; **~s** *npl* (*COMM*) scampoli *mpl*; fine *f* serie.

remorse [rɪ'mɔ:s] *n* rimorso; **~ful** *a* pieno(a) di rimorsi; **~less** *a* (*fig*) spietato(a).

remote [rɪ'məut] *a* remoto(a), lontano(a); (*person*) distaccato(a); ~ **control** *n* telecomando; **~ly** *ad* remotamente; (*slightly*) vagamente.

remould ['ri:məuld] *n* (*Brit: tyre*) gomma rivestita.

removable [rɪ'mu:vəbl] *a* (*detachable*) staccabile.

removal [rɪ'mu:vəl] *n* (*taking away*) rimozione *f*; soppressione *f*; (*Brit: from house*) trasloco; (*from office: dismissal*) destituzione *f*; (*MED*) ablazione *f*; ~ **van** *n* (*Brit*) furgone *m* per traslochi.

remove [rɪ'mu:v] *vt* togliere, rimuovere; (*employee*) destituire; (*stain*) far sparire; (*doubt, abuse*) sopprimere, eliminare; **~rs** *npl* (*Brit: company*) ditta *or* impresa di traslochi.

Renaissance [rɪ'neɪsɑ:ns] *n*: **the** ~ il Rinascimento.

render ['rɛndə*] *vt* rendere; (*CULIN: fat*) struggere; **~ing** *n* (*MUS etc*) interpretazione *f*.

rendez-vous ['rɔndɪvu:] *n* appuntamento; (*place*) luogo d'incontro; (*meeting*) incontro.

renegade ['rɛnɪgeɪd] *n* rinnegato/a.

renew [rɪ'nju:] *vt* rinnovare; (*negotiations*) riprendere; **~al** *n* rinnovamento; ripresa.

renounce [rɪ'nauns] *vt* rinunziare a; (*disown*) ripudiare.

renovate ['rɛnəveɪt] *vt* rinnovare; (*art work*) restaurare; **renovation** [-'veɪʃən] *n* rinnovamento; restauro.

renown [rɪ'naun] *n* rinomanza; **~ed** *a* rinomato(a).

rent [rɛnt] *n* affitto // *vt* (*take for rent*) prendere in affitto; (*also:* ~ **out**) dare in affitto; **~al** *n* (*for television, car*) fitto.

renunciation [rɪnʌnsɪ'eɪʃən] *n* rinnegamento; (*self-denial*) rinunzia.

rep [rɛp] *n abbr* (*COMM:* = *representative*) rappresentante *m/f*; (*THEATRE:* = *repertory*) teatro di repertorio.

repair [rɪ'pɛə*] *n* riparazione *f* // *vt* riparare; **in good/bad** ~ in buona/cattiva condizione; ~ **kit** *n* corredo per riparazioni; ~ **shop** *n* (*AUT etc*) officina.

repartee [rɛpɑ:'ti:] *n* risposta pronta.

repatriate [ri:'pætrɪeɪt] *vt* rimpatriare.

repay [ri:'peɪ] *vt irg* (*money, creditor*) rimborsare, ripagare; (*sb's efforts*) ricompensare; ~**ment** *n* rimborsamento; ricompensa.

repeal [rɪ'pi:l] *n* (*of law*) abrogazione *f*; (*of sentence*) annullamento // *vt* abrogare; annullare.

repeat [rɪ'pi:t] *n* (*RADIO, TV*) replica // *vt* ripetere; (*pattern*) riprodurre; (*promise, attack, also COMM: order*) rinnovare // *vi* ripetere; ~**edly** *ad* ripetutamente, spesso.

repel [rɪ'pɛl] *vt* respingere; ~**lent** *a* repellente // *n*: **insect** ~**lent** prodotto *m* anti-insetti *inv*.

repent [rɪ'pɛnt] *vi*: **to** ~ (**of**) pentirsi (di); ~**ance** *n* pentimento.

repertoire ['rɛpətwa:*] *n* repertorio.

repertory ['rɛpətərɪ] *n* (*also*: ~ **theatre**) teatro di repertorio.

repetition [rɛpɪ'tɪʃən] *n* ripetizione *f*; (*COMM: of order etc*) rinnovo.

repetitive [rɪ'pɛtɪtɪv] *a* (*movement*) che si ripete; (*work*) monotono(a); (*speech*) pieno(a) di ripetizioni.

replace [rɪ'pleɪs] *vt* (*put back*) rimettere a posto; (*take the place of*) sostituire; ~**ment** *n* rimessa; sostituzione *f*; (*person*) sostituto/a.

replay ['ri:pleɪ] *n* (*of match*) partita ripetuta; (*of tape, film*) replay *m inv*.

replenish [rɪ'plɛnɪʃ] *vt* (*glass*) riempire; (*stock etc*) rifornire.

replete [rɪ'pli:t] *a* ripieno(a); (*well-fed*) sazio(a).

replica ['rɛplɪkə] *n* replica, copia.

reply [rɪ'plaɪ] *n* risposta // *vi* rispondere; ~ **coupon** *n* buono di risposta.

report [rɪ'pɔ:t] *n* rapporto; (*PRESS etc*) cronaca; (*Brit: also*: **school** ~) pagella // *vt* riportare; (*PRESS etc*) fare una cronaca su; (*bring to notice: occurrence*) segnalare; (: *person*) denunciare // *vi* (*make a report*) fare un rapporto (*or* una cronaca); (*present o.s.*): **to** ~ (**to sb**) presentarsi (a qn); ~ **card** *n* (*US, Scottish*) pagella; ~**edly** *ad* stando a quanto si dice; **he** ~**edly told them to ...** avrebbe detto loro di ...; ~**er** *n* reporter *m inv*.

repose [rɪ'pəuz] *n*: **in** ~ (*face, mouth*) in riposo.

reprehensible [rɛprɪ'hɛnsɪbl] *a* riprensibile.

represent [rɛprɪ'zɛnt] *vt* rappresentare; ~**ation** [-'teɪʃən] *n* rappresentazione *f*; ~**ations** *npl* (*protest*) protesta; ~**ative** *n* rappresentativo/a; (*US POL*) deputato/a // *a* rappresentativo(a), caratteristico(a).

repress [rɪ'prɛs] *vt* reprimere; ~**ion** [-'prɛʃən] *n* repressione *f*.

reprieve [rɪ'pri:v] *n* (*LAW*) sospensione *f* dell'esecuzione della condanna; (*fig*) dilazione *f*.

reprimand ['rɛprɪma:nd] *n* rimprovero // *vt* rimproverare.

reprisal [rɪ'praɪzl] *n* rappresaglia.

reproach [rɪ'prəutʃ] *n* rimprovero // *vt*: **to** ~ **sb with sth** rimproverare qn di qc; ~**ful** *a* di rimprovero.

reproduce [rɪ:prə'dju:s] *vt* riprodurre // *vi* riprodursi; **reproduction** [-'dʌkʃən] *n* riproduzione *f*.

reproof [rɪ'pru:f] *n* riprovazione *f*.

reprove [rɪ'pru:v] *vt* (*action*) disapprovare; (*person*): **to** ~ (**for**) biasimare (per).

reptile ['rɛptaɪl] *n* rettile *m*.

republic [rɪ'pʌblɪk] *n* repubblica; ~**an** *a*, *n* repubblicano(a).

repulse [rɪ'pʌls] *vt* respingere.

repulsive [rɪ'pʌlsɪv] *a* ripugnante, ripulsivo(a).

reputable ['rɛpjutəbl] *a* di buona reputazione; (*occupation*) rispettabile.

reputation [rɛpju'teɪʃən] *n* reputazione *f*.

repute [rɪ'pju:t] *n* reputazione *f*; ~**d** *a* reputato(a); ~**dly** *ad* secondo quanto si dice.

request [rɪ'kwɛst] *n* domanda; (*formal*) richiesta // *vt*: **to** ~ (**of** *or* **from sb**) chiedere (a qn); ~ **stop** *n* (*Brit: for bus*) fermata facoltativa *or* a richiesta.

require [rɪ'kwaɪə*] *vt* (*need: subj: person*) aver bisogno di; (: *thing, situation*) richiedere; (*want*) volere; esigere; (*order*) obbligare; ~**ment** *n* esigenza; bisogno; requisito.

requisite ['rɛkwɪzɪt] *n* cosa necessaria // *a* necessario(a).

requisition [rɛkwɪ'zɪʃən] *n*: ~ (**for**) richiesta (di) // *vt* (*MIL*) requisire.

rescue ['rɛskju:] *n* salvataggio; (*help*) soccorso // *vt* salvare; ~ **party** *n* squadra di salvataggio; ~**r** *n* salvatore/trice.

research [rɪ'sɜ:tʃ] *n* ricerca, ricerche *fpl* // *vt* fare ricerche su.

resemblance [rɪ'zɛmbləns] *n* somiglianza.

resemble [rɪ'zɛmbl] *vt* assomigliare a.

resent [rɪ'zɛnt] *vt* risentirsi di; ~**ful** *a* pieno(a) di risentimento; ~**ment** *n* risentimento.

reservation [rɛzə'veɪʃən] *n* (*booking*) prenotazione *f*; (*doubt*) dubbio; (*protected area*) riserva; (*Brit: on road: also*: **central** ~) spartitraffico *m inv*; **to make a** ~ (**in an hotel/a restaurant/on a plane**) prenotare (una camera/una tavola/un posto).

reserve [rɪ'zɜ:v] *n* riserva // *vt* (*seats etc*) prenotare; ~**s** *npl* (*MIL*) riserve *fpl*; **in** ~ in serbo; ~**d** *a* (*shy*) riservato(a); (*seat*) prenotato(a).

reservoir ['rɛzəvwa:*] *n* serbatoio.

reshuffle [ri:'ʃʌfl] *n*: **Cabinet** ~ (*POL*) rimpasto governativo.

reside [rɪ'zaɪd] *vi* risiedere.

residence ['rɛzɪdəns] *n* residenza; ~

permit n (Brit) permesso di soggiorno.

resident ['rezɪdənt] n residente m/f; (in hotel) cliente m/f fisso(a) // a residente; **~ial** [-'denʃəl] a di residenza; (area) residenziale.

residue ['rezɪdjuː] n resto; (CHEM, PHYSICS) residuo.

resign [rɪ'zaɪn] vt (one's post) dimettersi da // vi dimettersi; to ~ o.s. to rassegnarsi a; **~ation** [rezɪg'neɪʃən] n dimissioni fpl; rassegnazione f; **~ed** a rassegnato(a).

resilience [rɪ'zɪlɪəns] n (of material) elasticità, resilienza; (of person) capacità di recupero.

resilient [rɪ'zɪlɪənt] a (person) che si riprende facilmente.

resin ['rezɪn] n resina.

resist [rɪ'zɪst] vt resistere a; **~ance** n resistenza.

resolution [rezə'luːʃən] n risoluzione f.

resolve [rɪ'zɒlv] n risoluzione f // vi (decide): to ~ to do decidere di fare // vt (problem) risolvere.

resort [rɪ'zɔːt] n (town) stazione f; (recourse) ricorso // vi: to ~ to aver ricorso a; **as a last ~** come ultimo ricorso.

resounding [rɪ'zaundɪŋ] a risonante; (fig) clamoroso(a).

resource [rɪ'sɔːs] n risorsa; **~s** npl risorse fpl; **~ful** a pieno(a) di risorse, intraprendente.

respect [rɪs'pekt] n rispetto // vt rispettare; **~s** npl ossequi mpl; **with ~ to** rispetto a, riguardo a; **in this ~** per questo riguardo; **~able** a rispettabile; **~ful** a rispettoso(a).

respective [rɪs'pektɪv] a rispettivo(a).

respite ['respaɪt] n respiro, tregua.

resplendent [rɪs'plendənt] a risplendente.

respond [rɪs'pɒnd] vi rispondere.

response [rɪs'pɒns] n risposta.

responsibility [rɪspɒnsɪ'bɪlɪtɪ] n responsabilità f inv.

responsible [rɪs'pɒnsɪbl] a (trustworthy) fidato(a); (job) di (grande) responsabilità; (liable): ~ (for) responsabile (di); **responsibly** ad responsabilmente.

responsive [rɪs'pɒnsɪv] a che reagisce.

rest [rest] n riposo; (stop) sosta, pausa; (MUS) pausa; (support) appoggio, sostegno; (remainder) resto, avanzi mpl // vi riposarsi; (remain) rimanere, restare; (be supported): to ~ on appoggiarsi su // vt (lean): to ~ sth on/against appoggiare qc su/contro; the ~ of them gli altri; it ~s with him to decide sta a lui decidere.

restaurant ['restərɒŋ] n ristorante m; **~ car** n (Brit) vagone m ristorante.

restful ['restful] a riposante.

rest home n casa di riposo.

restitution [restɪ'tjuːʃən] n (act) restituzione f; (reparation) riparazione f.

restive ['restɪv] a agitato(a), impaziente; (horse) restio(a).

restless ['restlɪs] a agitato(a), irrequieto(a).

restoration [restə'reɪʃən] n restauro; restituzione f.

restore [rɪ'stɔː*] vt (building) restaurare; (sth stolen) restituire; (peace, health) ristorare.

restrain [rɪs'treɪn] vt (feeling) contenere, frenare; (person): to ~ (from doing) trattenere (dal fare); **~ed** a (style) contenuto(a), sobrio(a); (manner) riservato(a); **~t** n (restriction) limitazione f; (moderation) ritegno.

restrict [rɪs'trɪkt] vt restringere, limitare; **~ion** [-kʃən] n restrizione f, limitazione f.

rest room n (US) toletta.

restructure [riː'strʌktʃə*] vt ristrutturare.

result [rɪ'zʌlt] n risultato // vi: to ~ in avere per risultato; **as a ~ of** in or di conseguenza a, in seguito a.

resume [rɪ'zjuːm] vt, vi (work, journey) riprendere.

résumé ['reɪzjumeɪ] n riassunto.

resumption [rɪ'zʌmpʃən] n ripresa.

resurgence [rɪ'sɜːdʒəns] n rinascita.

resurrection [rezə'rekʃən] n risurrezione f.

resuscitate [rɪ'sʌsɪteɪt] vt (MED) risuscitare; **resuscitation** [-'teɪʃən] n rianimazione f.

retail ['riːteɪl] n (vendita al) minuto // cpd al minuto // vt vendere al minuto; **~er** n commerciante m/f al minuto, dettagliante m/f; ~ **price** n prezzo al minuto.

retain [rɪ'teɪn] vt (keep) tenere, serbare; **~er** n (servant) servitore m; (fee) onorario.

retaliate [rɪ'tælɪeɪt] vi: to ~ (against) vendicarsi (di); **retaliation** [-'eɪʃən] n rappresaglie fpl.

retarded [rɪ'tɑːdɪd] a ritardato(a); (also: mentally ~) tardo(a) (di mente).

retch [retʃ] vi aver conati di vomito.

retire [rɪ'taɪə*] vi (give up work) andare in pensione; (withdraw) ritirarsi, andarsene; (go to bed) andare a letto, ritirarsi; **~d** a (person) pensionato(a); **~ment** n pensione f; **retiring** a (person) riservato(a).

retort [rɪ'tɔːt] n (reply) rimbecco; (container) storta // vi rimbeccare.

retrace [rɪ'treɪs] vt ricostruire; to ~ one's steps tornare sui passi.

retract [rɪ'trækt] vt (statement) ritrattare; (claws, undercarriage, aerial) ritrarre, ritirare // vi ritrarsi.

retrain [riː'treɪn] vt (worker) riaddestrare.

retread ['riːtred] n (tyre) gomma rigenerata.

retreat [rɪ'triːt] *n* ritirata; *(place)* rifugio // *vi* battere in ritirata; *(flood)* ritirarsi.

retribution [rɛtrɪ'bjuːʃən] *n* castigo.

retrieval [rɪ'triːvəl] *n (see vb)* ricupero; riparazione *f*.

retrieve [rɪ'triːv] *vt (sth lost)* ricuperare, ritrovare; *(situation, honour)* salvare; *(error, loss)* riparare; *(COMPUT)* ricuperare; **~r** *n* cane *m* da riporto.

retrospect ['rɛtrəspɛkt] *n*: in ~ guardando indietro; **~ive** [-'spɛktɪv] *a* retrospettivo(a); *(law)* retroattivo(a).

return [rɪ'təːn] *n (going or coming back)* ritorno; *(of sth stolen etc)* restituzione *f*; *(recompense)* ricompensa; *(FINANCE: from land, shares)* profitto, reddito; *(report)* rapporto // *cpd (journey, match)* di ritorno; *(Brit: ticket)* di andata e ritorno // *vi* tornare, ritornare // *vt* rendere, restituire; *(bring back)* riportare; *(send back)* mandare indietro; *(put back)* rimettere; *(POL: candidate)* eleggere; **~s** *npl (COMM)* incassi *mpl*; profitti *mpl*; in ~ *(for)* in cambio (di); by ~ of post a stretto giro di posta; many happy ~s (of the day)! auguri!, buon compleanno!

reunion [riː'juːnɪən] *n* riunione *f*.

reunite [riːju'naɪt] *vt* riunire.

rev [rɛv] *n abbr* (= *revolution: AUT*) giro. // *vb (also: ~ up) vt* imballare // *vi* imballarsi.

revamp ['riː'væmp] *vt (house)* rinnovare; *(firm)* riorganizzare.

reveal [rɪ'viːl] *vt (make known)* rivelare, svelare; *(display)* rivelare, mostrare; **~ing** *a* rivelatore(trice); *(dress)* scollato(a).

reveille [rɪ'væli] *n (MIL.)* sveglia.

revel ['rɛvl] *vi*: to ~ in sth/in doing dilettarsi di qc/a fare.

revelation [rɛvə'leɪʃən] *n* rivelazione *f*.

revelry ['rɛvlrɪ] *n* baldoria.

revenge [rɪ'vɛndʒ] *n* vendetta; *(in game etc)* rivincita // *vt* vendicare; to take ~ vendicarsi.

revenue ['rɛvənjuː] *n* reddito.

reverberate [rɪ'vəːbəreɪt] *vi (sound)* rimbombare, *(light)* riverberarsi.

reverence ['rɛvərəns] *n* venerazione *f*, riverenza.

Reverend ['rɛvərənd] *a (in titles)* reverendo(a).

reverie ['rɛvərɪ] *n* fantasticheria.

reversal [rɪ'vəːsl] *n* capovolgimento.

reverse [rɪ'vəːs] *n* contrario, opposto; *(back)* rovescio; *(AUT: also:* ~ *gear)* marcia indietro // *a (order, direction)* contrario(a), opposto(a) // *vt (turn)* invertire, rivoltare; *(change)* capovolgere, rovesciare; *(LAW: judgment)* cassare // *vi (Brit AUT)* fare marcia indietro; **~d charge call** *n (Brit TEL)* telefonata con addebito al ricevente; **reversing lights** *npl (Brit AUT)* luci *fpl*

per la retromarcia.

revert [rɪ'vəːt] *vi*: to ~ to tornare a.

review [rɪ'vjuː] *n* rivista; *(of book, film)* recensione *f* // *vt* passare in rivista; fare la recensione di; **~er** *n* recensore/a.

revile [rɪ'vaɪl] *vt* insultare.

revise [rɪ'vaɪz] *vt (manuscript)* rivedere, correggere; *(opinion)* emendare, modificare; *(study: subject, notes)* ripassare; **revision** [rɪ'vɪʒən] *n* revisione *f*; ripasso.

revitalize [riː'vaɪtəlaɪz] *vt* ravvivare.

revival [rɪ'vaɪvəl] *n* ripresa; ristabilimento; *(of faith)* risveglio.

revive [rɪ'vaɪv] *vt (person)* rianimare; *(custom)* far rivivere; *(hope, courage)* ravvivare; *(play, fashion)* riesumare // *vi (person)* rianimarsi; *(hope)* ravvivarsi; *(activity)* riprendersi.

revolt [rɪ'vəult] *n* rivolta, ribellione *f* // *vi* rivoltarsi, ribellarsi // *vt (far)* rivoltare; **~ing** *a* ripugnante.

revolution [rɛvə'luːʃən] *n* rivoluzione *f*; *(of wheel etc)* rivoluzione, giro; **~ary** *a*, *n* rivoluzionario(a).

revolve [rɪ'vɒlv] *vi* girare.

revolver [rɪ'vɒlvə*] *n* rivoltella.

revolving [rɪ'vɒlvɪŋ] *a* girevole.

revue [rɪ'vjuː] *n (THEATRE)* rivista.

revulsion [rɪ'vʌlʃən] *n* ripugnanza.

reward [rɪ'wɔːd] *n* ricompensa, premio // *vt*: to ~ *(for)* ricompensare (per); **~ing** *a (fig)* soddisfacente.

rewind [riː'waɪnd] *vt irg (watch)* ricaricare; *(ribbon etc)* riavvolgere.

rewire [riː'waɪə*] *vt (house)* rifare l'impianto elettrico di.

reword [riː'wəːd] *vt* formulare *or* esprimere con altre parole.

rheumatism ['ruːmətɪzəm] *n* reumatismo.

Rhine [raɪn] *n*: the ~ il Reno.

rhinoceros [raɪ'nɒsərəs] *n* rinoceronte *m*.

rhododendron [rəudə'dɛndrən] *n* rododendro.

Rhone [rəun] *n*: the ~ il Rodano.

rhubarb ['ruːbɑːb] *n* rabarbaro.

rhyme [raɪm] *n* rima; *(verse)* poesia.

rhythm ['rɪðm] *n* ritmo.

rib [rɪb] *n (ANAT)* costola // *vt (tease)* punzecchiare.

ribald ['rɪbəld] *a* licenzioso(a), volgare.

ribbon ['rɪbən] *n* nastro; in ~s *(torn)* a brandelli.

rice [raɪs] *n* riso.

rich [rɪtʃ] *a* ricco(a); *(clothes)* sontuoso(a); the ~ *npl* i ricchi; **~es** *npl* ricchezze *fpl*; **~ly** *ad* riccamente; *(dressed)* sontuosamente; *(deserved)* pienamente; **~ness** *n* ricchezza.

rickets ['rɪkɪts] *n* rachitismo.

rickety ['rɪkɪtɪ] *a* zoppicante.

rickshaw ['rɪkʃɔː] *n* risciò *m inv*.

ricochet ['rɪkəʃeɪ] *n* rimbalzo // *vi* rimbalzare.

rid, *pt*, *pp* **rid** [rɪd] *vt*: to ~ sb of sbarazzare *or* liberare qn di; **to get ~ of** sbarazzarsi di.

ridden ['rɪdn] *pp* of **ride**.

riddle ['rɪdl] *n* (*puzzle*) indovinello // *vt*: **to be ~d with** essere crivellato(a) di.

ride [raɪd] *n* (*on horse*) cavalcata; (*outing*) passeggiata; (*distance covered*) cavalcata; corsa // *vb* (*pt* **rode**, *pp* **ridden**) *vi* (*as sport*) cavalcare; (*go somewhere*: on horse, bicycle) andare (a cavallo *or* in bicicletta *etc*); (*journey*: on bicycle, motorcycle, bus) andare, viaggiare // *vt* (*a horse*) montare, cavalcare; **to ~ a horse/bicycle/camel** montare a cavallo/in bicicletta/in groppa a un cammello; **to ~ at anchor** (*NAUT*) essere alla fonda; **to take sb for a ~** (*fig*) prendere in giro qn; fregare qn; **~r** *n* cavalcatore/trice; (*in race*) fantino; (*on bicycle*) ciclista *m/f*; (*on motorcycle*) motociclista *m/f*; (*in document*) clausola addizionale, aggiunta.

ridge [rɪdʒ] *n* (*of hill*) cresta; (*of roof*) colmo; (*of mountain*) giogo; (*on object*) riga (in rilievo).

ridicule ['rɪdɪkjuːl] *n* ridicolo; scherno // *vt* mettere in ridicolo.

ridiculous [rɪ'dɪkjuləs] *a* ridicolo(a).

riding ['raɪdɪŋ] *n* equitazione *f*; ~ **school** *n* scuola d'equitazione.

rife [raɪf] *a* diffuso(a); **to be ~ with** abbondare di.

riffraff ['rɪfræf] *n* canaglia.

rifle ['raɪfl] *n* carabina // *vt* vuotare; ~ **range** *n* campo di tiro; (*at fair*) tiro a segno.

rift [rɪft] *n* fessura, crepatura; (*fig: disagreement*) incrinatura, disaccordo.

rig [rɪg] *n* (*also: oil ~: on land*) derrick *m inv*; (: *at sea*) piattaforma di trivellazione // *vt* (*election etc*) truccare; **to ~ out** *vt* (*Brit*) attrezzare; (*pej*) abbigliare, agghindare; **to ~ up** *vt* allestire; **~ging** *n* (*NAUT*) attrezzatura.

right [raɪt] *a* giusto(a); (*suitable*) appropriato(a); (*not left*) destro(a) // *n* (*title, claim*) diritto; (*not left*) destra // *ad* (*answer*) correttamente; (*not on the left*) a destra // *vt* raddrizzare; (*fig*) riparare // *excl* bene!; **to be ~** (*person*) aver ragione; (*answer*) essere giusto(a) *or* corretto(a); **by ~s** di diritto; **on the ~** a destra; **to be in the ~** aver ragione, essere nel giusto; ~ **now** proprio adesso; subito; ~ **against the wall** proprio contro il muro; ~ **ahead** sempre diritto; proprio davanti; ~ **in the middle** proprio nel mezzo; ~ **away** subito; ~ **angle** *n* angolo retto; **~eous** ['raɪtʃəs] *a* retto(a), virtuoso(a); (*anger*) giusto(a), giustificato(a); **~ful** *a* (*heir*) legittimo(a); **~-handed** *a* (*person*) che adopera la mano destra; **~-hand man** *n* braccio destro; **~-hand side** *n* lato destro; **~ly**

ad bene, correttamente; (*with reason*) a ragione; ~ **of way** *n* diritto di passaggio; (*AUT*) precedenza; **~-wing** *a* (*POL*) di destra.

rigid ['rɪdʒɪd] *a* rigido(a); (*principle*) rigoroso(a).

rigmarole ['rɪgmərəʊl] *n* tiritera; commedia.

rigorous ['rɪgərəs] *a* rigoroso(a).

rile [raɪl] *vt* irritare, seccare.

rim [rɪm] *n* orlo; (*of spectacles*) montatura; (*of wheel*) cerchione *m*.

rind [raɪnd] *n* (*of bacon*) cotenna; (*of lemon etc*) scorza.

ring [rɪŋ] *n* anello; (*also: wedding ~*) fede *f*; (*of people, objects*) cerchio; (*of spies*) giro; (*of smoke etc*) spirale *m*; (*arena*) pista, arena; (*for boxing*) ring *m inv*; (*sound of bell*) scampanio; (*telephone call*) colpo di telefono // *vb* (*pt* **rang**, *pp* **rung**) *vi* (*person, bell, telephone*) suonare; (*also: ~ out: voice, words*) risuonare; (*TEL*) telefonare // *vt* (*Brit TEL: also: ~ up*) telefonare a; **to ~ the bell** suonare; **to ~ back** *vt, vi* (*TEL*) richiamare; **to ~ off** *vi* (*Brit TEL*) mettere giù, riattaccare; **~ing** *n* (*of bell*) scampanio; (*of telephone*) squillo; (*in ears*) ronzio; **~ing tone** *n* (*Brit TEL*) segnale *m* di libero; **~leader** *n* (*of gang*) capobanda *m*.

ringlets ['rɪŋlɪts] *npl* boccoli *mpl*.

ring road *n* (*Brit*) raccordo anulare.

rink [rɪŋk] *n* (*also: ice ~*) pista di pattinaggio.

rinse [rɪns] *n* risciacquatura; (*hair tint*) cachet *m inv* // *vt* sciacquare.

riot ['raɪət] *n* sommossa, tumulto // *vi* tumultuare; **to run ~** creare disordine; **~ous** *a* tumultuoso(a); che fa crepare dal ridere.

rip [rɪp] *n* strappo // *vt* strappare // *vi* strapparsi; **~cord** *n* cavo di sfilamento.

ripe [raɪp] *a* (*fruit*) maturo(a); (*cheese*) stagionato(a); **~n** *vt* maturare // *vi* maturarsi; stagionarsi.

rip-off ['rɪpɔf] *n* (*col*): **it's a ~!** è un furto!

ripple ['rɪpl] *n* increspamento, ondulazione *f*; mormorio // *vi* incresparsi.

rise [raɪz] *n* (*slope*) salita, pendio; (*hill*) altura; (*increase: in wages: Brit*) aumento; (: *in prices, temperature*) rialzo, aumento; (*fig: to power etc*) ascesa // *vi* (*pt* **rose**, *pp* **risen** [rəʊz, 'rɪzn]) alzarsi, levarsi; (*prices*) aumentare; (*waters, river*) crescere; (*sun, wind, person: from chair, bed*) levarsi; (*also: ~ up: rebel*) insorgere; ribellarsi; **to give ~ to** provocare, dare origine a; **to ~ to the occasion** essere all'altezza; **rising** *a* (*increasing: number*) sempre crescente; (: *prices*) in aumento; (*tide*) montante; (*sun, moon*) nascente, che sorge // *n* (*uprising*) sommossa.

risk [rɪsk] *n* rischio; pericolo // *vt* rischiare; **to take** *or* **run the ~ of doing** correre il rischio di fare; **at ~ in** pericolo; **at one's own ~** a proprio rischio e pericolo; **~y** *a* rischioso(a).

risqué ['riːskeɪ] *a* (*joke*) spinto(a).

rissole ['rɪsəʊl] *n* crocchetta.

rite [raɪt] *n* rito; **last ~s** l'estrema unzione.

ritual ['rɪtjʊəl] *a, n* rituale (*m*).

rival ['raɪvl] *n* rivale *m/f*; (*in business*) concorrente *m/f* // *a* rivale; che fa concorrenza // *vt* essere in concorrenza con; **to ~ sb/sth** in competere con qn/qc in; **~ry** *n* rivalità; concorrenza.

river ['rɪvə*] *n* fiume *m* // *cpd* (*port, traffic*) fluviale; **up/down ~** a monte/valle; **~bank** *n* argine *m*.

rivet ['rɪvɪt] *n* ribattino, rivetto // *vt* ribadire; (*fig*) concentrare, fissare.

Riviera [rɪvɪ'ɛərə] *n*: **the (French) ~** la Costa Azzurra; **the Italian ~** la Riviera.

road [rəʊd] *n* strada; (*small*) cammino; (*in town*) via; **major/minor ~** strada con/senza diritto di precedenza; **~block** *n* blocco stradale; **~hog** *n* guidatore *m* egoista e spericolato; **~ map** *n* carta stradale; **~ safety** *n* sicurezza sulle strade; **~side** *n* margine *m* della strada; **~sign** *n* cartello stradale; **~way** *n* carreggiata; **~works** *npl* lavori *mpl* stradali; **~worthy** *a* in buono stato di marcia.

roam [rəʊm] *vi* errare, vagabondare // *vt* vagare per.

roar [rɔː*] *n* ruggito; (*of crowd*) tumulto; (*of thunder, storm*) muggito // *vi* ruggire; tumultuare; muggire; **to ~ with** laughter scoppiare dalle risa; **to do a ~ing trade** fare affari d'oro.

roast [rəʊst] *n* arrosto // *vt* (*meat*) arrostire; **~ beef** *n* arrosto di manzo.

rob [rɒb] *vt* (*person*) rubare; (*bank*) svaligiare; **to ~ sb of sth** derubare qn di qc; (*fig: deprive*) privare qn di qc; **~ber** *n* ladro; (*armed*) rapinatore *m*; **~bery** *n* furto; rapina.

robe [rəʊb] *n* (*for ceremony etc*) abito; (*also: bath ~*) accappatoio; (*US: cover*) coperta // *vt* vestire.

robin ['rɒbɪn] *n* pettirosso.

robot ['rəʊbɒt] *n* robot *m inv*.

robust [rəʊ'bʌst] *a* robusto(a); (*material*) solido(a).

rock [rɒk] *n* (*substance*) roccia; (*boulder*) masso; roccia; (*in sea*) scoglio; (*Brit: sweet*) zucchero candito // *vt* (*swing gently: cradle*) dondolare; (*child*) cullare; (*shake*) scrollare, far tremare // *vi* dondolarsi; scrollarsi, tremare; **on the ~s** (*drink*) col ghiaccio; (*ship*) sugli scogli; (*marriage etc*) in crisi; **~ and roll** *n* rock and roll *m*; **~-**

bottom *n* (*fig*) stremo // *a* bassissimo(a); **~ery** *n* giardino roccioso.

rocket ['rɒkɪt] *n* razzo; (*MIL*) razzo, missile *m*.

rock fall *n* caduta di massi.

rocking ['rɒkɪŋ]: **~ chair** *n* sedia a dondolo; **~ horse** *n* cavallo a dondolo.

rocky ['rɒkɪ] *a* (*hill*) roccioso(a); (*path*) sassoso(a); (*unsteady: table*) traballante.

rod [rɒd] *n* (*metallic, TECH*) asta; (*wooden*) bacchetta; (*also: fishing ~*) canna da pesca.

rode [rəʊd] *pt of* **ride.**

rodent ['rəʊdnt] *n* roditore *m*.

rodeo ['rəʊdɪəʊ] *n* rodeo.

roe [rəʊ] *n* (*species: also:* **~ deer**) capriolo; (*of fish, also:* **hard ~**) uova *fpl* di pesce; **soft ~** latte *m* di pesce.

rogue [rəʊg] *n* mascalzone *m*.

role [rəʊl] *n* ruolo.

roll [rəʊl] *n* rotolo; (*of banknotes*) mazzo; (*also:* **bread ~**) panino; (*register*) lista; (*sound: of drums etc*) rullo; (*movement: of ship*) rullio // *vt* rotolare; (*also:* **~ up: string**) aggomitolare; (*also:* **~ out: pastry**) stendere // *vi* rotolare; (*wheel*) girare; **to ~ about** *or* **around** *vi* rotolare qua e là; (*person*) rotolarsi; **to ~ by** *vi* (*time*) passare; **to ~ in** *vi* (*mail, cash*) arrivare a bizzeffe; **to ~ over** *vi* rivoltarsi; **to ~ up** *vi* (*col: arrive*) arrivare // *vt* (*carpet*) arrotolare; **~ call** *n* appello; **~er** *n* rullo; (*wheel*) rotella; **~er coaster** *n* montagne *fpl* russe; **~er skates** *npl* pattini *mpl* a rotelle.

rolling ['rəʊlɪŋ] *a* (*landscape*) ondulato(a); **~ pin** *n* matterello; **~ stock** *n* (*RAIL*) materiale *m* rotabile.

ROM [rɒm] *n abbr* (= *read only memory*) memoria di sola lettura.

Roman ['rəʊmən] *a, n* romano(a); **~ Catholic** *a, n* cattolico(a).

romance [rə'mæns] *n* storia (*or* avventura *or* film *m inv*) romantico(a); (*charm*) poesia; (*love affair*) idillio.

Romania [rəʊ'meɪnɪə] *n* = **Rumania.**

Roman numeral *n* numero romano.

romantic [rə'mæntɪk] *a* romantico(a); sentimentale.

romanticism [rə'mæntɪsɪzəm] *n* romanticismo.

Rome [rəʊm] *n* Roma.

romp [rɒmp] *n* gioco rumoroso // *vi* (*also:* **~ about**) far chiasso, giocare in un modo rumoroso.

rompers ['rɒmpəz] *npl* pagliaccetto.

roof, *pl* **~s** [ruːf] *n* tetto; (*of tunnel, cave*) volta // *vt* coprire (con un tetto); **~ of the mouth** palato; **~ing** *n* materiale *m* per copertura; **~ rack** *n* (*AUT*) portabagagli *m inv*.

rook [rʊk] *n* (*bird*) corvo nero; (*CHESS*)

torre f.

room [ru:m] n (in house) stanza; (also: bed~) camera; (in school etc) sala; (space) posto, spazio; ~s npl (lodging) alloggio; "~s to let", (US) "~s for rent" "si affittano camere"; ~**ing house** n (US) casa in cui si affittano camere o appartamentini ammobiliati; ~**mate** n compagno/a di stanza; ~ **service** n servizio da camera; ~**y** a spazioso(a); (garment) ampio(a).

roost [ru:st] n appollaiato // vi appollaiarsi.

rooster ['ru:stə*] n gallo.

root [ru:t] n radice f // vt (plant, belief) far radicare; **to ~ about** vi (fig) frugare; **to ~ for** vt fus fare il tifo per; **to ~ out** vt estirpare.

rope [rəup] n corda, fune f; (NAUT) cavo // vt (box) legare; (climbers) legare in cordata; **to ~ sb in** (fig) coinvolgere qn; **to know the ~s** (fig) conoscere i trucchi del mestiere.

rosary ['rəuzəri] n rosario; roseto.

rose [rəuz] pt of **rise** // n rosa; (also: ~ bush) rosaio; (on watering can) rosetta // a rosa inv.

rosé ['rəuzei] n vino rosato.

rose: ~**bud** n bocciolo di rosa; ~**bush** n rosaio.

rosemary ['rəuzməri] n rosmarino.

rosette [rəu'zet] n coccarda.

roster ['rɔstə*] n: **duty ~** ruolino di servizio.

rostrum ['rɔstrəm] n tribuna.

rosy ['rəuzi] a roseo(a).

rot [rɔt] n (decay) putrefazione f; (col: nonsense) stupidaggini fpl // vt, vi imputridire, marcire.

rota ['rəutə] n tabella dei turni; **on a ~ basis** a turno.

rotary ['rəutəri] a rotante.

rotate [rəu'teit] vt (revolve) far girare; (change round: crops) avvicendare; (: jobs) fare a turno // vi (revolve) girare; **rotating** a (movement) rotante.

rote [rəut] n: **by ~** (by heart) a memoria; (mechanically) meccanicamente.

rotten ['rɔtn] a (decayed) putrido(a), marcio(a); (dishonest) corrotto(a); (col: bad) brutto(a); (: action) vigliacco(a); **to feel ~** (ill) sentirsi proprio male.

rouge [ru:ʒ] n belletto.

rough [rʌf] a aspro(a); (person, manner: coarse) rozzo(a), aspro(a); (: violent) brutale; (district) malfamato(a); (weather) cattivo(a); (plan) abbozzato(a); (guess) approssimativo(a) // n (GOLF) macchia; **to ~ it** far vita dura; **to sleep ~** (Brit) dormire all'addiaccio; **to feel ~** sentirsi male; ~**age** n alimenti mpl ricchi in cellulosa; ~**-and-ready** a rudimentale; ~**cast** n intonaco grezzo; ~ **copy**, ~ **draft** n

brutta copia; ~**ly** ad (handle) rudemente, brutalmente; (make) grossolanamente; (approximately) approssimativamente.

roulette [ru:'let] n roulette f.

Roumania [ru:'meiniə] n = **Rumania**.

round [raund] a rotondo(a) // n tondo, cerchio; (Brit: of toast) fetta; (duty: of policeman, milkman etc) giro; (: of doctor) visite fpl; (game: of cards, in competition) partita; (BOXING) round m inv; (of talks) serie f inv // vt (corner) girare; (bend) prendere; (cape) doppiare // prep intorno a // ad: **all ~** tutt'attorno; **to go the long way ~** fare il giro più lungo; **all the year ~** tutto l'anno; **it's just ~ the corner** (also fig) è dietro; l'angolo; ~ **the clock** ad ininterrottamente; **to go ~** fare il giro; **to go ~ to sb's house** andare da qn; **go ~ the back** passi dietro; **to go ~ a house** visitare una casa; **enough to go ~** abbastanza per tutti; **to go the ~s** (story) circolare; ~ **of ammunition** n cartuccia; ~ **of applause** n applausi mpl; ~ **of drinks** n giro di bibite; ~ **of sandwiches** n sandwich m inv; **to ~ off** vt (speech etc) finire; **to ~ up** vt radunare; (criminals) fare una retata di; (prices) arrotondare; ~**about** n (Brit AUT) rotatoria; (: at fair) giostra // a (route, means) indiretto(a); ~**ers** npl (game) gioco simile al baseball; ~**ly** ad (fig) chiaro e tondo; ~**-shouldered** a dalle spalle tonde; ~ **trip** n (viaggio di) andata e ritorno; ~**up** n raduno; (of criminals) retata.

rouse [rauz] vt (wake up) svegliare; (stir up) destare; provocare; risvegliare; **rousing** a (speech, applause) entusiastico(a).

rout [raut] n (MIL) rotta.

route [ru:t] n itinerario; (of bus) percorso; (of trade, shipping) rotta; ~ **map** n (Brit: for journey) cartina di itinerario.

routine [ru:'ti:n] a (work) corrente, abituale; (procedure) solito(a) // n (pej) routine f, tran tran m; (THEATRE) numero; **daily ~** orario quotidiano.

roving ['rəuvɪŋ] a (life) itinerante.

row [rəu] n (line) riga, fila; (KNITTING) ferro; (behind one another: of cars, people) fila; [rau] (noise) baccano, chiasso; (dispute) lite f // vi (in boat) remare; (as sport) vogare; [rau] litigare // vt (boat) manovrare a remi; **in a ~** (fig) di fila; ~**boat** n (US) barca a remi.

rowdy ['raudi] a chiassoso(a); turbolento(a) // n teppista m/f.

rowing ['rəuɪŋ] n canottaggio; ~ **boat** n (Brit) barca a remi.

royal ['rɔɪəl] a reale; **R~ Air Force (RAF)** n aeronautica militare britannica.

royalty ['rɔɪəltɪ] n (royal persons) (membri *mpl* della) famiglia reale; (*payment: to author*) diritti *mpl* d'autore; (: *to inventor*) diritti di brevetto.

r.p.m. *abbr* (= *revolutions per minute*) giri/min.

R.S.V.P. *abbr* (= *répondez s'il vous plaît*) R.S.V.P.

Rt Hon. *abbr* (*Brit*: = *Right Honourable*) = Onorevole.

rub [rʌb] *n* (*with cloth*) fregata, strofinata; (*on person*) frizione *f*, massaggio // *vt* fregare, strofinare; frizionare; to ~ sb up *or* (*US*) ~ sb the wrong way lisciare qn contro pelo; **to ~ off** *vi* andare via; **to ~ off on** *vt fus* lasciare una traccia su; **to ~ out** *vt* cancellare.

rubber [ˈrʌbə*] *n* gomma; ~ **band** *n* elastico; ~ **plant** *n* ficus *m inv*.

rubbish [ˈrʌbɪʃ] *n* (*from household*) immondizie *fpl*, rifiuti *mpl*; (*fig: pej*) cose *fpl* senza valore; robaccia; sciocchezze *fpl*; ~ **bin** *n* (*Brit*) pattumiera; ~ **dump** *n* (*in town*) immondezzaio.

rubble [ˈrʌbl] *n* macerie *fpl*; (*smaller*) pietrisco.

ruby [ˈruːbɪ] *n* rubino.

rucksack [ˈrʌksæk] *n* zaino.

ructions [ˈrʌkʃənz] *npl* putiferio, finimondo.

rudder [ˈrʌdə*] *n* timone *m*.

ruddy [ˈrʌdɪ] *a* (*face*) fresco(a); (*col: damned*) maledetto(a).

rude [ruːd] *a* (*impolite: person*) scortese, rozzo(a); (: *word, manners*) grossolano(a), rozzo(a); (*shocking*) indecente; ~**ness** *n* scortesia; grossolanità.

rueful [ˈruːful] *a* mesto(a), triste.

ruffian [ˈrʌfɪən] *n* briccone *m*, furfante *m*.

ruffle [ˈrʌfl] *vt* (*hair*) scompigliare; (*clothes, water*) increspare; (*fig: person*) turbare.

rug [rʌg] *n* tappeto; (*Brit: for knees*) coperta.

rugby [ˈrʌgbɪ] *n* (*also*: ~ **football**) rugby *m*.

rugged [ˈrʌgɪd] *a* (*landscape*) aspro(a); (*features, determination*) duro(a); (*character*) brusco(a).

rugger [ˈrʌgə*] *n* (*Brit col*) rugby *m*.

ruin [ˈruːɪn] *n* rovina // *vt* rovinare; (*spoil: clothes*) sciupare; ~s *npl* rovine *fpl*, ruderi *mpl*; ~**ous** *a* rovinoso(a); (*expenditure*) inverosimile.

rule [ruːl] *n* regola; (*regulation*) regolamento, regola; (*government*) governo // *vt* (*country*) governare; (*person*) dominare; (*decide*) decidere // *vi* regnare; decidere; (*LAW*) dichiarare; **as a ~** normalmente; **to ~ out** *vt* escludere; ~**d** *a* (*paper*) vergato(a); ~**r** *n* (*sovereign*) sovrano(a); (*leader*) capo (dello Stato); (*for measuring*)

regolo, riga; **ruling** *a* (*party*) al potere; (*class*) dirigente // *n* (*LAW*) decisione *f*.

rum [rʌm] *n* rum *m* // *a* (*col*) strano(a).

Rumania [ruːˈmeɪnɪə] *n* Romania.

rumble [ˈrʌmbl] *n* rimbombo; brontolio // *vi* rimbombare; (*stomach, pipe*) brontolare.

rummage [ˈrʌmɪdʒ] *vi* frugare.

rumour, (*US*) **rumor** [ˈruːmə*] *n* voce *f* // *vt*: it is ~ed that corre voce che.

rump [rʌmp] *n* (*of animal*) groppa; ~ **steak** *n* bistecca di girello.

rumpus [ˈrʌmpəs] *n* (*col*) baccano; (: *quarrel*) rissa.

run [rʌn] *n* corsa; (*outing*) gita (in macchina); (*distance travelled*) percorso, tragitto; (*series*) serie *f*; (*THEATRE*) periodo di rappresentazione; (*SKI*) pista; (*in tights, stockings*) smagliatura // *vb* (*pt* **ran**, *pp* **run**) *vt* (*operate: business*) gestire, dirigere; (: *competition, course*) organizzare; (: *hotel*) gestire; (: *house*) governare; (*COMPUT*) eseguire; (*water, bath*) far scorrere; (*force through: rope, pipe*): **to ~ sth through** far passare qc attraverso; (*to pass: hand, finger*): **to ~ sth over** passare qc su // *vi* correre; (*pass: road etc*) passare; (*work: machine, factory*) funzionare, andare; (*bus, train: operate*) far servizio; (: *travel*) circolare; (*continue: play, contract*) durare; (*slide: drawer; flow: river, bath*) scorrere; (*colours, washing*) stemperarsi; (*in election*) presentarsi candidato; there was a ~ on ... c'era una corsa a ...; **in the long ~** a lungo andare; **on the ~** in fuga; **I'll ~ you to the station** la porto alla stazione; **to ~ a risk** correre un rischio; **to ~ about** *or* **around** *vi* (*children*) correre qua e là; **to ~ across** *vt fus* (*find*) trovare per caso; **to ~ away** *vi* fuggire; **to ~ down** *vi* (*clock*) scaricarsi // *vt* (*production*) ridurre gradualmente; (*factory*) rallentare l'attività di; (*AUT*) investire; (*criticize*) criticare; **to be ~ down** (*person: tired*) essere esausto(a); **to ~ in** *vt* (*Brit: car*) rodare, fare il rodaggio di; **to ~ into** *vt fus* (*meet: person*) incontrare per caso; (: *trouble*) incontrare, trovare; (*collide with*) andare a sbattere contro; **to ~ off** *vi* fuggire // *vt* (*copies*) fare; **to ~ out** *vi* (*person*) uscire di corsa; (*liquid*) colare; (*lease*) scadere; (*money*) esaurirsi; **to ~ out of** *vt fus* rimanere a corto di; **to ~ over** *vt* (*AUT*) investire, mettere sotto // *vt fus* (*revise*) rivedere; **to ~ through** *vt fus* (*instructions*) dare una scorsa a; **to ~ up** *vt* (*debt*) lasciar accumulare; **to ~ up against** (*difficulties*) incontrare; ~**away** *a* (*person*) fuggiasco(a); (*horse*) in libertà; (*truck*) fuori controllo; (*inflation*) galoppante.

rung [rʌŋ] *pp of* **ring** // *n* (*of ladder*) piolo.

runner ['rʌnə*] *n* (*in race*) corridore *m*; (*on sledge*) pattino; (*for drawer etc, carpet: in hall etc*) guida; **~ bean** *n* (*Brit*) fagiolo rampicante; **~-up** *n* secondo(a) arrivato(a).

running ['rʌnɪŋ] *n* corsa; direzione *f*; organizzazione *f*; funzionamento *m* a (*water*) corrente; (*commentary*) simultaneo(a); **to be in/out of the ~ for sth** essere/non essere più in lizza per qc; **6 days ~** 6 giorni di seguito.

runny ['rʌnɪ] *a* che cola.

run-of-the-mill ['rʌnəvðə'mɪl] *a* solito(a), banale.

runt [rʌnt] *n* (*also pej*) omuncolo; (*zool*) animale *m* più piccolo del normale.

run-through ['rʌnθru:] *n* prova.

run-up ['rʌnʌp] *n*: **~ to** (*election etc*) periodo che precede.

runway ['rʌnweɪ] *n* (*aviat*) pista (di decollo).

rupee [ru:'pi:] *n* rupia.

rupture ['rʌptʃə*] *n* (*med*) ernia.

rural ['ruərl] *a* rurale.

ruse [ru:z] *n* trucco.

rush [rʌʃ] *n* corsa precipitosa; (*of crowd*) afflusso; (*hurry*) furia, fretta; (*current*) flusso // *vt* mandare *or* spedire velocemente; (*attack: town etc*) prendere d'assalto // *vi* precipitarsi; **~es** *npl* (*bot*) giunchi *mpl*; **~ hour** *n* ora di punta.

rusk [rʌsk] *n* biscotto.

Russia ['rʌʃə] *n* Russia; **~n** *a* russo(a) // *n* russo/a; (*ling*) russo.

rust [rʌst] *n* ruggine *f* // *vi* arrugginirsi.

rustic ['rʌstɪk] *a* rustico(a).

rustle ['rʌsl] *vi* frusciare // *vt* (*paper*) far frusciare; (*US: cattle*) rubare.

rustproof ['rʌstpru:f] *a* inossidabile.

rusty ['rʌstɪ] *a* arrugginito(a).

rut [rʌt] *n* solco; (*zool*) fregola; **to get into a ~** (*fig*) adagiarsi troppo.

ruthless ['ru:θlɪs] *a* spietato(a).

rye [raɪ] *n* segale *f*; **~ bread** *n* pane *m* di segale.

S

Sabbath ['sæbəθ] *n* (*Jewish*) sabato; (*Christian*) domenica.

sabotage ['sæbətɑ:ʒ] *n* sabotaggio // *vt* sabotare.

saccharin(e) ['sækərɪn] *n* saccarina.

sachet ['sæʃeɪ] *n* bustina.

sack [sæk] *n* (*bag*) sacco // *vt* (*dismiss*) licenziare, mandare a spasso; (*plunder*) saccheggiare; **to get the ~** essere mandato a spasso; **~ing** *n* tela di sacco; (*dismissal*) licenziamento.

sacrament ['sækrəmənt] *n* sacramento.

sacred ['seɪkrɪd] *a* sacro(a).

sacrifice ['sækrɪfaɪs] *n* sacrificio // *vt* sacrificare.

sad [sæd] *a* triste.

saddle ['sædl] *n* sella // *vt* (*horse*) sellare; **to be ~d with sth** (*col*) avere qc sulle spalle; **~bag** *n* bisaccia; (*on bicycle*) borsa.

sadistic [sə'dɪstɪk] *a* sadico(a).

sadness ['sædnɪs] *n* tristezza.

s.a.e. *n abbr* = *stamped addressed envelope*.

safe [seɪf] *a* sicuro(a); (*out of danger*) salvo(a), al sicuro; (*cautious*) prudente // *n* cassaforte *f*; **~ from** al sicuro da; **~ and sound** sano(a) e salvo(a); (*just*) **to be on the ~ side** per non correre rischi; **~-conduct** *n* salvacondotto; **~-deposit** *n* (*vault*) caveau *m inv*; (*box*) cassetta di sicurezza; **~guard** *n* salvaguardia // *vt* salvaguardare; **~keeping** *n* custodia; **~ly** *ad* sicuramente; sano(a) e salvo(a); prudentemente.

safety ['seɪftɪ] *n* sicurezza; **~ belt** *n* cintura di sicurezza; **~ pin** *n* spilla di sicurezza; **~ valve** *n* valvola di sicurezza.

saffron ['sæfrən] *n* zafferano.

sag [sæg] *vi* incurvarsi; afflosciarsi.

sage [seɪdʒ] *n* (*herb*) salvia; (*man*) saggio.

Sagittarius [sædʒɪ'tɛərɪəs] *n* Sagittario.

Sahara [sə'hɑ:rə] *n*: **the ~** (Desert) il (deserto del) Sahara.

said [sed] *pt, pp of* **say**.

sail [seɪl] *n* (*on boat*) vela; (*trip*): **to go for a ~** fare un giro in barca a vela // *vt* (*boat*) condurre, governare // *vi* (*travel: ship*) navigare; (: *passenger*) viaggiare per mare; (*set off*) salpare; (*sport*) fare della vela; **they ~ed into Genoa** entrarono nel porto di Genova; **to ~ through** (*fig*) *vt fus* superare senza difficoltà // *vi* farcela senza difficoltà; **~boat** *n* (*US*) barca a vela; **~ing** *n* (*sport*) vela; **to go ~ing** fare della vela; **~ing boat** *n* barca a vela; **~ing ship** *n* veliero; **~or** *n* marinaio.

saint [seɪnt] *n* santo/a.

sake [seɪk] *n*: **for the ~ of** per, per amore di.

salad ['sæləd] *n* insalata; **~ bowl** *n* insalatiera; **~ cream** *n* (*Brit*) (tipo di) maionese *f*; **~ dressing** *n* condimento per insalata.

salary ['sælərɪ] *n* stipendio.

sale [seɪl] *n* vendita; (*at reduced prices*) svendita, liquidazione *f*; **"for ~"** "in vendita"; **on ~** in vendita; **on ~ or return** da vendere o rimandare; **~room** *n* sala delle aste; **~s assistant**, (*US*) **~s clerk** *n* commesso/a; **~sman** *n* commesso; (*representative*) rappresentante *m*; **~swoman** *n* commessa.

salient ['seɪlɪənt] *a* saliente.

sallow ['sæləu] *a* giallastro(a).

salmon ['sæmən] *n* (*pl inv*) salmone *m*.

saloon [sə'lu:n] *n* (*US*) saloon *m inv*, bar *m inv*; (*Brit AUT*) berlina; (*ship's lounge*) salone *m*.

salt [sɔlt] *n* sale *m* // *vt* salare // *cpd* di sale; (*CULIN*) salato(a); **to ~ away** *vt* (*col: money*) mettere via; **~ cellar** *n* saliera; **~-water** *a* di mare; **~y** *a* salato(a).

salute [sə'lu:t] *n* saluto // *vt* salutare.

salvage ['sælvidʒ] *n* (*saving*) salvataggio; (*things saved*) beni *mpl* salvati *or* recuperati // *vt* salvare, mettere in salvo.

salvation [sæl'veɪʃən] *n* salvezza; **S~ Army** *n* Esercito della Salvezza.

same [seɪm] *a* stesso(a), medesimo(a) // *pronoun*: **the ~** lo(la) stesso(a), gli(le) stessi(e); **the ~ book** as lo stesso libro di (*o* che); **at the ~ time** allo stesso tempo; **all** *or* **just the ~** tuttavia; **to do the ~** fare la stessa cosa; **to do the ~ as sb** fare come qn; **the ~ to you!** altrettanto a te!

sample ['sɑ:mpl] *n* campione *m* // *vt* (*food*) assaggiare; (*wine*) degustare.

sanctimonious [sæŋktɪ'məunɪəs] *a* bigotto(a), bacchettone(a).

sanction ['sæŋkʃən] *n* sanzione *f* // *vt* sancire, sanzionare.

sanctity ['sæŋktɪtɪ] *n* santità.

sanctuary ['sæŋktjuərɪ] *n* (*holy place*) santuario; (*refuge*) rifugio; (*for wildlife*) riserva.

sand [sænd] *n* sabbia // *vt* cospargere di sabbia.

sandal ['sændl] *n* sandalo.

sandbox ['sændbɔks] *n* (*US*) = **sandpit**.

sandcastle ['sændkɑ:sl] *n* castello di sabbia.

sandpaper ['sændpeɪpə*] *n* carta vetrata.

sandpit ['sændpɪt] *n* (*for children*) buca di sabbia.

sandstone ['sændstəun] *n* arenaria.

sandwich ['sændwɪtʃ] *n* tramezzino, panino, sandwich *m inv* // *vt* (*also: ~ in*) infilare; **~ed between** incastrato fra; **cheese/ham ~** sandwich al formaggio/ prosciutto; **~ course** *n* (*Brit*) corso di formazione professionale; **~ man** *n* uomo *m* sandwich *inv*.

sandy ['sændɪ] *a* sabbioso(a); (*colour*) color sabbia *inv*, biondo(a) rossiccio(a).

sane [seɪn] *a* (*person*) sano(a) di mente; (*outlook*) sensato(a).

sang [sæŋ] *pt of* **sing**.

sanitary ['sænɪtərɪ] *a* (*system, arrangements*) sanitario(a); (*clean*) igienico(a); **~ towel**, (*US*) **~ napkin** *n* assorbente *m* (igienico).

sanitation [sænɪ'teɪʃən] *n* (*in house*) impianti *mpl* sanitari; (*in town*) fognature *fpl*; **~ department** *n* (*US*)

nettezza urbana.

sanity ['sænɪtɪ] *n* sanità mentale; (*common sense*) buon senso.

sank [sæŋk] *pt of* **sink**.

Santa Claus [sæntə'klɔ:z] *n* Babbo Natale.

sap [sæp] *n* (*of plants*) linfa // *vt* (*strength*) fiaccare.

sapling ['sæplɪŋ] *n* alberello.

sapphire ['sæfaɪə*] *n* zaffiro.

sarcasm ['sɑ:kæzm] *n* sarcasmo.

sardine [sɑ:'di:n] *n* sardina.

Sardinia [sɑ:'dɪnɪə] *n* Sardegna.

sash [sæʃ] *n* fascia; **~ window** *n* finestra a ghigliottina.

sat [sæt] *pt, pp of* **sit**.

Satan ['seɪtən] *n* Satana *m*.

satchel ['sætʃl] *n* cartella.

sated ['seɪtɪd] *a* (*appetite*) soddisfatto(a); (*person*): **~ (with)** sazio(a) (di).

satellite ['sætəlaɪt] *a*, *n* satellite (*m*).

satin ['sætɪn] *n* raso // *a* di raso.

satire ['sætaɪə*] *n* satira.

satisfaction [sætɪs'fækʃən] *n* soddisfazione *f*.

satisfactory [sætɪs'fæktərɪ] *a* soddisfacente.

satisfy ['sætɪsfaɪ] *vt* soddisfare; (*convince*) convincere; **~ing** *a* soddisfacente.

Saturday ['sætədɪ] *n* sabato.

sauce [sɔ:s] *n* salsa; (*containing meat, fish*) sugo; **~pan** *n* casseruola.

saucer ['sɔ:sə*] *n* sottocoppa *m*, piattino.

saucy ['sɔ:sɪ] *a* impertinente.

Saudi ['saudɪ]: **~ Arabia** *n* Arabia Saudita; **~ (Arabian)** *a*, *n* arabo(a) saudita.

sauna ['sɔ:nə] *n* sauna.

saunter ['sɔ:ntə*] *vi* andare a zonzo, bighellonare.

sausage ['sɔsɪdʒ] *n* salsiccia; **~ roll** *n* rotolo di pasta sfoglia ripieno di salsiccia.

savage ['sævɪdʒ] *a* (*cruel, fierce*) selvaggio(a), feroce; (*primitive*) primitivo(a) // *n* selvaggio/a // *vt* attaccare selvaggiamente.

save [seɪv] *vt* (*person, belongings, COMPUT*) salvare; (*money*) risparmiare, mettere da parte; (*time*) risparmiare; (*food*) conservare; (*avoid: trouble*) evitare // *vi* (*also: ~ up*) economizzare // *n* (*SPORT*) parata // *prep* salvo, a eccezione di.

saving ['seɪvɪŋ] *n* risparmio // *a*: **the ~ grace of** l'unica cosa buona di; **~s** *npl* risparmi *mpl*; **~s bank** *n* cassa di risparmio.

saviour, (*US*) **savior** ['seɪvjə*] *n* salvatore *m*.

savour, (*US*) **savor** ['seɪvə*] *n* sapore *m*, gusto // *vt* gustare; **~y** *a* saporito(a); (*dish: not sweet*) salato(a).

saw [sɔ:] *pt of* **see** // *n (tool)* sega // *vt (pt* **sawed,** *pp* **sawed** *or* **sawn** [sɔ:n]) segare; **~dust** *n* segatura; **~mill** *n* segheria; **~n-off shotgun** *n* fucile *m* a canne mozze.

saxophone ['sæksəfəun] *n* sassofono.

say [seɪ] *n*: **to have one's ~** fare sentire il proprio parere; **to have a** *or* **some ~** avere voce in capitolo // *vt (pt, pp* **said**) dire; **could you ~ that again?** potrebbe ripeterlo?; **that goes without ~ing** va da sé; **~ing** *n* proverbio, detto.

scab [skæb] *n* crosta; *(pej)* crumiro/a.

scaffold ['skæfəuld] *n* impalcatura; *(gallows)* patibolo; **~ing** *n* impalcatura.

scald [skɔ:ld] *n* scottatura // *vt* scottare.

scale [skeɪl] *n* scala; *(of fish)* squama // *vt (mountain)* scalare; **~s** *npl* bilancia; **on a large ~** su vasta scala; **~ of charges** tariffa; **to ~ down** *vt* ridurre (proporzionalmente); **~ model** *n* modello in scala.

scallop ['skɔləp] *n* pettine *m*.

scalp [skælp] *n* cuoio capelluto // *vt* scotennare.

scalpel ['skælpl] *n* bisturi *m inv*.

scamper ['skæmpə*] *vi*: **to ~ away, ~ off** darsela a gambe.

scampi ['skæmpɪ] *npl* scampi *mpl*.

scan [skæn] *vt* scrutare; *(glance at quickly)* scorrere, dare un'occhiata a; *(poetry)* scandire; *(TV)* analizzare; *(RADAR)* esplorare // *n (MED)* ecografia.

scandal ['skændl] *n* scandalo; *(gossip)* pettegolezzi *mpl*.

Scandinavia [skændɪ'neɪvɪə] *n* Scandinavia; **~n** *a, n* scandinavo(a).

scant [skænt] *a* scarso(a); **~y** *a* insufficiente; *(swimsuit)* ridotto(a).

scapegoat ['skeɪpgəut] *n* capro espiatorio.

scar [skɑ:] *n* cicatrice *f* // *vt* sfregiare.

scarce [skeəs] *a* scarso(a); *(copy, edition)* raro(a); **~ly** *ad* appena; **scarcity** *n* scarsità, mancanza.

scare [skeə*] *n* spavento; panico // *vt* spaventare, atterrire; **there was a bomb ~ at the bank** hanno evacuato la banca per paura di un attentato dinamitardo; **to ~ sb stiff** spaventare a morte qn; **~crow** *n* spaventapasseri *m inv*; **~d** *a*: **to be ~d** aver paura.

scarf, pl scarves [skɑ:f, skɑ:vz] *n (long)* sciarpa; *(square)* fazzoletto da testa, foulard *m inv*.

scarlet ['skɑ:lɪt] *a* scarlatto(a).

scathing ['skeɪðɪŋ] *a* aspro(a).

scatter ['skætə*] *vt* spargere; *(crowd)* disperdere // *vi* disperdersi; **~brained** *a* scervellato(a), sbadato(a).

scavenger ['skævəndʒə*] *n* spazzino.

scenario [sɪ'nɑ:rɪəu] *n (THEATRE, CINEMA)* copione *m*; *(fig)* situazione *f*.

scene [si:n] *n (THEATRE, fig etc)* scena; *(of crime, accident)* scena, luogo; *(sight, view)* vista, veduta; **~ry** *n (THEATRE)* scenario; *(landscape)* panorama *m*; **scenic** *a* scenico(a); panoramico(a).

scent [sɛnt] *n* odore *m*, profumo; *(sense of smell)* olfatto, odorato; *(fig: track)* pista.

sceptical, *(US)* **skeptical** ['skɛptɪkəl] *a* scettico(a).

sceptre, *(US)* **scepter** ['sɛptə*] *n* scettro.

schedule ['ʃɛdju:l, *(US)* 'skɛdju:l] *n* programma *m*, piano; *(of trains)* orario; *(of prices etc)* lista, tabella // *vt* fissare; **on ~** in orario; **to be ahead of/behind ~** essere in anticipo/ritardo sul previsto; **~d flight** *n* volo di linea.

scheme [ski:m] *n* piano, progetto; *(method)* sistema *m*; *(dishonest plan, plot)* intrigo, trama; *(arrangement)* disposizione *f*, sistemazione *f*; *(pension ~ etc)* programma *m* // *vi* fare progetti; *(intrigue)* complottare; **scheming** *a* intrigante // *n* intrighi *mpl*, macchinazioni *fpl*.

schism ['skɪzəm] *n* scisma *m*.

scholar ['skɔlə*] *n* erudito/a; **~ly** *a* dotto(a), erudito(a); **~ship** *n* erudizione *f*; *(grant)* borsa di studio.

school [sku:l] *n* scuola; *(in university)* scuola, facoltà *f inv* // *cpd* scolare, scolastico(a) // *vt (animal)* addestrare; **~book** *n* libro scolastico; **~boy** *n* scolaro; **~children** *npl* scolari *mpl*; **~days** *npl* giorni *mpl* di scuola; **~girl** *n* scolara; **~ing** *n* istruzione *f*; **~master** *n (primary)* maestro; *(secondary)* insegnante *m*; **~mistress** *n* maestra; insegnante *f*; **~teacher** *n* insegnante *m/f*, docente *m/f*; *(primary)* maestro/a.

sciatica [saɪ'ætɪkə] *n* sciatica.

science ['saɪəns] *n* scienza; **~ fiction** *n* fantascienza; **scientific** [-'tɪfɪk] *a* scientifico(a); **scientist** *n* scienziato/a.

scissors ['sɪzəz] *npl* forbici *fpl*.

scoff [skɔf] *vt (Brit col: eat)* trangugiare, ingozzare // *vi*: **to ~ (at)** *(mock)* farsi beffe (di).

scold [skəuld] *vt* rimproverare.

scone [skɔn] *n* focaccina da tè.

scoop [sku:p] *n* mestolo; *(for ice cream)* cucchiaio dosatore; *(PRESS)* colpo giornalistico, notizia (in) esclusiva; **to ~ out** *vt* scavare; **to ~ up** *vt* tirare su, sollevare.

scooter ['sku:tə*] *n (motor cycle)* motoretta, scooter *m inv*; *(toy)* monopattino.

scope [skəup] *n (capacity: of plan, undertaking)* portata; *(: of person)* capacità *fpl*; *(opportunity)* possibilità *fpl*; **within the ~ of** nei limiti di.

scorch [skɔ:tʃ] *vt (clothes)* strinare, bruciacchiare; *(earth, grass)* seccare, bruciare.

score [skɔ:*] *n* punti *mpl*, punteggio;

(MUS) partitura, spartito; (twenty) venti // vt (goal, point) segnare, fare; (success) ottenere // vi segnare; (FOOTBALL) fare un goal; (keep score) segnare i punti; **on that** ~ a questo riguardo; **to** ~ **6 out of 10** prendere 6 su 10; **to** ~ **out** vt cancellare con un segno; ~**board** n tabellone m segnapunti.

scorn [skɔ:n] n disprezzo // vt disprezzare.

Scorpio ['skɔ:prəu] n Scorpione m.

scorpion ['skɔ:prən] n scorpione m.

Scot [skɔt] n scozzese m/f.

scotch [skɔtʃ] vt (rumour etc) soffocare; **S~** n whisky m scozzese, scotch m.

scot-free ['skɔt'fri:] ad: **to get off** ~ farla franca.

Scotland ['skɔtlənd] n Scozia.

Scots [skɔts] a scozzese; ~**man/woman** n scozzese m/f.

Scottish ['skɔtɪʃ] a scozzese.

scoundrel ['skaundrl] n farabutto/a; (child) furfantello/a.

scour ['skauə*] vt (clean) pulire strofinando; raschiare via; ripulire; (search) battere, perlustrare.

scourge [skə:dʒ] n flagello.

scout [skaut] n (MIL) esploratore m; (also: boy ~) giovane esploratore, scout m inv; **to** ~ **around** cercare in giro.

scowl [skaul] vi accigliarsi, aggrottare le sopracciglia; **to** ~ **at** guardare torvo.

scrabble ['skræbl] vi (claw): **to** ~ (**at**) graffiare, grattare; (also: ~ **around**: search) cercare a tentoni // n: **S~** ® Scarabeo ®.

scraggy ['skrægɪ] a scarno(a), molto magro(a).

scram [skræm] vi (col) filare via.

scramble ['skræmbl] n arrampicata // vi inerpicarsi; **to** ~ **out** etc uscire etc in fretta; **to** ~ **for** azzuffarsi per; ~**d eggs** npl uova fpl strapazzate.

scrap [skræp] n pezzo, pezzetto; (fight) zuffa; (also: ~ **iron**) rottami mpl di ferro, ferraglia // vt demolire; (fig) scartare // vi: **to** ~ (**with sb**) fare a botte (con qn); ~**s** npl (waste) scarti mpl; ~**book** n album m inv di ritagli; ~ **dealer** n commerciante m di ferraglia.

scrape [skreip] vt, vi raschiare, grattare // n: **to get into a** ~ cacciarsi in un guaio; **to** ~ **through** vi farcela per un pelo; ~**r** n raschietto.

scrap: ~ **heap** n mucchio di rottami; ~ **merchant** n (Brit) commerciante m di ferraglia; ~ **paper** n cartaccia.

scratch [skrætʃ] n graffio // cpd: ~ **team** squadra raccogliticcia // vt graffiare, rigare // vi grattare, graffiare; **to start from** ~ cominciare or partire da zero; **to be up to** ~ essere all'altezza.

scrawl [skrɔ:l] n scarabocchio // vi scarabocchiare.

scrawny ['skrɔ:nɪ] a scarno(a), pelle e

ossa inv.

scream [skri:m] n grido, urlo // vi urlare, gridare.

scree [skri:] n ghiaione m.

screech [skri:tʃ] n strido; (of tyres, brakes) stridore m // vi stridere.

screen [skri:n] n schermo; (fig) muro, cortina, velo // vt schermare, fare schermo a; (from the wind etc) riparare; (film) proiettare; (book) adattare per lo schermo; (candidates etc) selezionare; ~**ing** n (MED) dépistage m inv; ~**play** n sceneggiatura.

screw [skru:] n vite f; (propeller) elica // vt avvitare; **to** ~ **up** vt (paper etc) spiegazzare; (col: ruin) rovinare; **to** ~ **up one's eyes** strizzare gli occhi; ~**driver** n cacciavite m.

scribble ['skrɪbl] n scarabocchio // vt scribacchiare in fretta // vi scarabocchiare.

script [skrɪpt] n (CINEMA etc) copione m; (in exam) elaborato or compito d'esame.

Scripture ['skrɪptʃə*] n sacre Scritture fpl.

scroll [skrəul] n rotolo di carta.

scrounge [skraundʒ] vt (col): **to** ~ **sth** (off or from sb) scroccare qc (a qn) // vi: **to** ~ **on sb** vivere alle spalle di qn.

scrub [skrʌb] n (clean) strofinata; (land) boscaglia // vt pulire strofinando; (reject) annullare.

scruff [skrʌf] n: **by the** ~ **of the neck** per la collottola.

scruffy ['skrʌfɪ] a sciatto(a).

scrum(mage) ['skrʌm(ɪdʒ)] n mischia.

scruple ['skru:pl] n scrupolo.

scrutiny ['skru:tɪnɪ] n esame m accurato.

scuff [skʌf] vt (shoes) consumare strascicando.

scuffle ['skʌfl] n baruffa, tafferuglio.

scullery ['skʌlərɪ] n retrocucina m or f.

sculptor ['skʌlptə*] n scultore m.

sculpture ['skʌlptʃə*] n scultura.

scum [skʌm] n schiuma; (pej: people) feccia.

scupper ['skʌpə*] vt (NAUT) autoaffondare; (fig) far naufragare.

scurrilous ['skʌrɪləs] a scurrile, volgare.

scurry ['skʌrɪ] vi sgambare, affrettarsi; **to** ~ **off** andarsene a tutta velocità.

scuttle ['skʌtl] n (NAUT) portellino; (also: coal ~) secchio del carbone // vt (ship) autoaffondare // vi (scamper): **to** ~ **away**, ~ **off** darsela a gambe, scappare.

scythe [saɪð] n falce f.

SDP n abbr (Brit) = Social Democratic Party.

sea [si:] n mare m // cpd marino(a), del mare; (ship, sailor, port) marittimo(a), di mare; **by** ~ (travel) per mare; **on the** ~ (boat) in mare; (town) di mare; **to be all at** ~ (fig) non sapere che pesci pigliare; **out to** ~ al largo; (out) **at** ~ in mare; ~**board** n costa; ~**food** n frutti mpl di mare; ~ **front** n lungomare m; ~**gull** n gabbiano.

seal [si:l] n (animal) foca; (stamp) sigillo; (impression) impronta del sigillo // vt sigillare; **to ~ off** vt (close) sigillare; (forbid entry to) bloccare l'accesso a.

sea level n livello del mare.

seam [si:m] n cucitura; (of coal) filone m.

seaman ['si:mən] n marinaio.

seamy ['si:mɪ] a orribile.

seance ['seɪɔns] n seduta spiritica.

seaplane ['si:pleɪn] n idrovolante m.

search [sə:tʃ] n (for person, thing) ricerca; (of drawer, pockets) esame m accurato; (LAW: at sb's home) perquisizione f // vt perlustrare, frugare; (examine) esaminare minuziosamente // vi: **to ~ for** ricercare; **in ~ of** alla ricerca di; **to ~ through** vt fus frugare; ~**ing** a minuzioso(a); penetrante; ~**light** n proiettore m; ~ **party** n squadra di soccorso; ~ **warrant** n mandato di perquisizione.

seashore ['si:ʃɔ:*] n spiaggia.

seasick ['si:sɪk] a che soffre il mal di mare.

seaside ['si:saɪd] n spiaggia, ~ **resort** n stazione f balneare.

season ['si:zn] n stagione f // vt condire, insaporire; ~**al** a stagionale; ~**ed** a (fig) con esperienza; ~**ing** n condimento; ~ **ticket** n abbonamento.

seat [si:t] n sedile m; (in bus, train: place) posto; (PARLIAMENT) seggio; (buttocks) didietro; (of trousers) fondo // vt far sedere; (have room for) avere or essere fornito(a) di posti a sedere per; ~ **belt** n cintura di sicurezza.

sea water n acqua di mare.

seaweed ['si:wi:d] n alghe fpl.

seaworthy ['si:wə:ðɪ] a atto(a) alla navigazione.

sec. abbr = **second(s)**.

secluded [sɪ'klu:dɪd] a isolato(a), appartato(a).

seclusion [sɪ'klu:ʒən] n isolamento.

second ['sɛkənd] num secondo(a) // ad (in race etc) al secondo posto; (RAIL) in seconda // n (unit of time) secondo; (in series, position) secondo/a; (AUT: also: ~ gear) seconda; (COMM: imperfect) scarto; (Brit SCOL: degree) laurea con punteggio discreto // vt (motion) appoggiare; ~**ary** a secondario(a); ~**ary school** n scuola secondaria; ~-**class** a di seconda classe; ~**er** n sostenitore/trice; ~**hand** a di seconda mano, usato(a); ~ **hand** n (on clock) lancetta dei secondi; ~**ly** ad in secondo 'logo; ~**ment** [sɪ'kɔndmənt] n (Brit) distaccamento; ~-**rate** a scadente; ~-**thoughts** npl ripensamenti mpl; on ~

thoughts or (US) thought ripensandoci bene.

secrecy ['si:krəsɪ] n segretezza.

secret ['si:krɪt] a segreto(a) // n segreto; **in ~** in segreto.

secretariat [sɛkrɪ'tɛərɪət] n segretariato.

secretary ['sɛkrətərɪ] n segretario/a; S~ **of State (for)** (Brit POL) ministro (di).

secretive ['si:krətɪv] a riservato(a).

sect [sɛkt] n setta; ~**arian** [-'tɛərɪən] a settario(a).

section ['sɛkʃən] n sezione f.

sector ['sɛktə*] n settore m.

secure [sɪ'kjuə*] a (free from anxiety) sicuro(a); (firmly fixed) assicurato(a), ben fermato(a); (in safe place) al sicuro // vt (fix) fissare, assicurare; (get) ottenere, assicurarsi.

security [sɪ'kjuərɪtɪ] n sicurezza; (for loan) garanzia.

sedan [sɪ'dæn] n (US AUT) berlina.

sedate [sɪ'deɪt] a posato(a); calmo(a) // vt calmare.

sedation [sɪ'deɪʃən] n (MED) l'effetto dei sedativi.

sedative ['sɛdɪtɪv] n sedativo, calmante m.

seduce [sɪ'dju:s] vt sedurre; **seduction** [-'dʌkʃən] n seduzione f; **seductive** [-'dʌktɪv] a seducente.

see [si:] vb (pt saw, pp seen) vt vedere; (accompany): **to ~ sb to the door** accompagnare qn alla porta // vi vedere; (understand) capire // n sede f vescovile; **to ~ that** (ensure) badare che + sub, fare in modo che + sub; ~ **you soon!** a presto!; **to ~ about** vt fus occuparsi di; **to ~ off** vt salutare alla partenza; **to ~ through** vt portare a termine // vt fus non lasciarsi ingannare da; **to ~ to** vt fus occuparsi di.

seed [si:d] n seme m; (fig) germe m; (TENNIS) testa di serie; **to go to ~** fare seme; (fig) scadere; ~**ling** n piantina da semenzaio; ~**y** a (shabby: person) sciatto(a); (: place) cadente.

seeing ['si:ɪŋ] cj: ~ (that) visto che.

seek [si:k], pt, pp **sought** vt cercare.

seem [si:m] vi sembrare, parere; **there** ~**s to be** ... sembra che ci sia ...; ~**ingly** ad apparentemente.

seen [si:n] pp of **see**.

seep [si:p] vi filtrare, trapelare.

seesaw ['si:sɔ:] n altalena a bilico.

seethe [si:ð] vi ribollire; **to ~ with anger** fremere di rabbia.

see-through ['si:θru:] a trasparente.

segregate ['sɛgrɪgeɪt] vt segregare, isolare.

seize [si:z] vt (grasp) afferrare; (take possession of) impadronirsi di; (LAW) sequestrare; **to ~ (up)on** vt fus ricorrere a; **to ~ up** vi (TECH) grippare.

seizure ['si:ʒə*] n (MED) attacco; (LAW)

confisca, sequestro.

seldom ['sɛldəm] *ad* raramente.

select [sɪ'lɛkt] *a* scelto(a) // *vt* scegliere, selezionare; **~ion** [-'lɛkʃən] *n* selezione *f*, scelta.

self [sɛlf] *n* (*pl* **selves** [sɛlvz]): **the ~** l'io *m* // *prefix* auto...; **~-catering** *a* (*Brit*) in cui cf si cucina da sé; **~-centred**, (*US*) **~-centered** *a* egocentrico(a); **~-coloured**, (*US*) **~-colored** *a* monocolore; **~-confidence** *n* sicurezza di sé; **~-conscious** *a* timido(a); **~-contained** *a* (*Brit*: *flat*) indipendente; **~-control** *n* autocontrollo; **~-defence**, (*US*) **~-defense** *n* autodifesa; (*LAW*) legittima difesa; **~-discipline** *n* autodisciplina; **~-employed** *a* che lavora in proprio; **~-evident** *a* evidente; **~-governing** *a* autonomo(a); **~-indulgent** *a* indulgente verso se stesso(a); **~-interest** *n* interesse *m* personale; **~-ish** *a* egoista; **~-ishness** *n* egoismo; **~-less** *a* dimentico(a) di sé, altruista; **~-pity** *n* autocommiserazione *f*; **~-portrait** *n* autoritratto; **~-possessed** *a* controllato(a); **~-preservation** *n* istinto di conservazione; **~-respect** *n* rispetto di sé, amor proprio; **~-righteous** *a* soddisfatto(a) di sé; **~-sacrifice** *n* abnegazione *f*; **~-satisfied** *a* compiaciuto(a) di sé; **~-service** *a* autoservizio, self-service *m*; **~-sufficient** *a* autosufficiente; **~-taught** *a* autodidatta.

sell [sɛl], *pt*, *pp* **sold** *vt* vendere // *vi* vendersi; **to ~ at** *or* **for 1000 lire** essere in vendita a 1000 lire; **to ~ off** *vt* svendere, liquidare; **to ~ out** *vi*: **to ~ out (to sb/sth)** (*COMM*) vendere (tutto) (a qn/qc) // *vt* esaurire; **the tickets are all sold out i** biglietti sono esauriti; **~-by date** *n* data di scadenza; **~er** *n* venditore/trice; **~ing price** *n* prezzo di vendita.

sellotape ['sɛləuteɪp] *n* ® (*Brit*) nastro adesivo, scotch *m* ®.

sellout ['sɛlaut] *n* tradimento; (*of tickets*): **it was a ~** registrò un tutto esaurito.

selves [sɛlvz] *npl of* **self**.

semblance ['sɛmbləns] *n* parvenza, apparenza.

semen ['siːmən] *n* sperma *m*.

semester [sɪ'mɛstə*] *n* (*US*) semestre *m*.

semi... ['sɛmɪ] *prefix* semi...; **~circle** *n* semicerchio; **~colon** *n* punto e virgola; **~detached (house)** *n* (*Brit*) casa gemella; **~final** *n* semifinale *f*.

seminar ['sɛmɪnɑ:*] *n* seminario.

seminary ['sɛmɪnərɪ] *n* (*REL*) seminario.

semiquaver ['sɛmɪkweɪvə*] *n* semicroma.

semiskilled ['sɛmɪ'skɪld] *a* (*worker*) parzialmente qualificato(a); (*work*) che richiede una qualificazione parziale.

senate ['sɛnɪt] *n* senato; **senator** *n* senatore/trice.

send [sɛnd], *pt*, *pp* **sent** *vt* mandare; **to ~ away** *vt* (*letter*, *goods*) spedire; (*person*) mandare via; **to ~ away for** *vt fus* richiedere per posta, farsi spedire; **to ~ back** *vt* rimandare; **to ~ for** *vt fus* mandare a chiamare, far venire; **to ~ off** *vt* (*goods*) spedire; (*Brit SPORT*: *player*) espellere; **to ~ out** *vt* (*invitation*) diramare; **to ~ up** *vt* (*person*, *price*) far salire; (*Brit*: *parody*) mettere in ridicolo; **~er** *n* mittente *m/f*; **~-off** *n*: **to give sb a good ~-off** festeggiare la partenza di qn.

senior ['siːnɪə*] *a* (*older*) più vecchio(a); (*of higher rank*) di grado più elevato // *n* persona più anziana; (*in service*) persona con maggiore anzianità; **~ citizen** *n* persona anziana; **~ity** [-'ɔrɪtɪ] *n* anzianità.

sensation [sɛn'seɪʃən] *n* sensazione *f*; **to create a ~** fare scalpore; **~al** *a* sensazionale; (*marvellous*) eccezionale.

sense [sɛns] *n* senso; (*feeling*) sensazione *f*, senso; (*meaning*) senso, significato; (*wisdom*) buonsenso // *vt* sentire, percepire; **~s** *npl* (*sanity*) ragione *f*; **it makes ~** ha senso; **~less** *a* sciocco(a); (*unconscious*) privo(a) di sensi.

sensibility [sɛnsɪ'bɪlɪtɪ] *n* sensibilità; **sensibilities** *npl* sensibilità *sg*.

sensible ['sɛnsɪbl] *a* sensato(a), ragionevole.

sensitive ['sɛnsɪtɪv] *a*: **~ (to)** sensibile (a).

sensual ['sɛnsjuəl] *a* sensuale.

sensuous ['sɛnsjuəs] *a* sensuale.

sent [sɛnt] *pt*, *pp of* **send**.

sentence ['sɛntns] *n* (*LING*) frase *f*; (*LAW*: *judgment*) sentenza; (: *punishment*) condanna // *vt*: **to ~ sb to death/to 5 years** condannare qn a morte/a 5 anni.

sentiment ['sɛntɪmənt] *n* sentimento; (*opinion*) opinione *f*; **~al** [-'mɛntl] *a* sentimentale.

sentry ['sɛntrɪ] *n* sentinella.

separate *a* ['sɛprɪt] separato(a) // *vb* ['sɛpəreɪt] *vt* separare // *vi* separarsi; **~s** *npl* (*clothes*) coordinati *mpl*; **~ly** *ad* separatamente; **separation** [-'reɪʃən] *n* separazione *f*.

September [sɛp'tɛmbə*] *n* settembre *m*.

septic ['sɛptɪk] *a* settico(a); (*wound*) infettato(a); **~ tank** *n* fossa settica.

sequel ['siːkwl] *n* conseguenza; (*of story*) seguito.

sequence ['siːkwəns] *n* (*series*) serie *f*; (*order*) ordine *m*.

sequin ['siːkwɪn] *n* lustrino, paillette *f* *inv*.

serene [sə'riːn] *a* sereno(a), calmo(a).

sergeant ['sɑːdʒənt] *n* sergente *m*; (*POLICE*) brigadiere *m*.

serial ['sɪərɪəl] n (PRESS) romanzo a puntate; (RADIO, TV) trasmissione f a puntate // a (number) di serie; ~ **number** n numero di serie.
series ['sɪərɪ:z] n (pl inv) serie f inv; (PUBLISHING) collana.
serious ['sɪərɪəs] a serio(a), grave; ~**ly** ad seriamente.
sermon ['sə:mən] n sermone m.
serrated [sɪ'reɪtɪd] a seghettato(a).
serum ['sɪərəm] n siero.
servant ['sə:vənt] n domestico/a.
serve [sə:v] vt (employer etc) servire, essere a servizio di; (purpose) servire a; (customer, food, meal) servire; (apprenticeship) fare; (prison term) scontare // vi (also TENNIS) servire; (be useful): to ~ **as/for/to** do servire da/per/per fare // n (TENNIS) servizio; it ~s him right ben gli sta, se l'è meritata; to ~ **out**, ~ **up** vt (food) servire.
service ['sə:vɪs] n servizio; (AUT: maintenance) assistenza, revisione f // vt (car, washing machine) revisionare; the S~s le forze armate; to be of ~ to sb essere d'aiuto a qn; dinner ~ servizio da tavola; ~**able** a pratico(a), utile; ~ **charge** n (Brit) servizio; ~**man** n militare m; ~ **station** n stazione f di servizio.
serviette [sə:vɪ'et] n (Brit) tovagliolo.
session ['sɛʃən] n (sitting) seduta, sessione f; (SCOL) anno scolastico (or accademico).
set [sɛt] n serie f inv; (RADIO, TV) apparecchio; (TENNIS) set m inv; (group of people) mondo, ambiente m; (CINEMA) scenario; (THEATRE: stage) scene fpl; (: scenery) scenario; (MATH) insieme m; (HAIRDRESSING) messa in piega // a (fixed) stabilito(a), determinato(a); (ready) pronto(a) // vb (pt, pp set) (place) posare, mettere; (fix) fissare; (adjust) regolare; (decide: rules etc) stabilire, fissare; (TYP) comporre // vi (sun) tramontare; (jam, jelly) rapprendersi; (concrete) fare presa; to be ~ **on doing** essere deciso a fare; to ~ **to music** mettere in musica; to ~ **on fire** dare fuoco a; to ~ **free** liberare; to ~ **sth going** mettere in moto qc; to ~ **sail** prendere il mare; to ~ **about** vt fus (task) intraprendere, mettersi a; to ~ **aside** vt mettere da parte; to ~ **back** vt (in time): to ~ **back (by)** mettere indietro (di); to ~ **off** vi partire // vt (bomb) far scoppiare; (cause to start) mettere in moto; (show up well) dare risalto a; to ~ **out** vi partire; (aim): to ~ **out to do** proporsi di fare // vt (arrange) disporre; (state) esporre, presentare; to ~ **up** vt (organization) fondare, costituire; (monument) innalzare; ~**back** n (hitch) contrattempo, inconveniente m; ~

menu n menù m inv fisso.
settee [sɛ'ti:] n divano, sofà m inv.
setting ['sɛtɪŋ] n ambiente m; (of jewel) montatura.
settle ['sɛtl] vt (argument, matter) appianare; (problem) risolvere; (MED: calm) calmare // vi (bird, dust etc) posarsi; (sediment) depositarsi; (also: ~ down) sistemarsi, stabilirsi; calmarsi; to ~ **for sth** accontentarsi di qc; to ~ **on sth** decidersi per qc; to ~ **in** vi sistemarsi; to ~ **up** vi: to ~ **up with sb** regolare i conti con qn; ~**ment** n (payment) pagamento, saldo; (agreement) accordo; (colony) colonia; (village etc) villaggio, comunità f inv; ~**r** n colonizzatore/trice.
setup ['sɛtʌp] n (arrangement) sistemazione f; (situation) situazione f.
seven ['sɛvn] num sette; ~**teen** num diciassette; ~**th** num settimo(a); ~**ty** num settanta.
sever ['sɛvə*] vt recidere, tagliare; (relations) troncare.
several ['sɛvərl] a, pronoun alcuni(e), diversi(e); ~ **of us** alcuni di noi.
severance ['sɛvərəns] n (of relations) rottura; ~ **pay** n indennità di licenziamento.
severe [sɪ'vɪə*] a severo(a); (serious) serio(a), grave; (hard) duro(a); (plain) semplice, sobrio(a); **severity** [sɪ'vɛrɪtɪ] n severità; gravità; (of weather) rigore m.
sew [səu], pt **sewed**, pp **sewn** vt, vi cucire; to ~ **up** vt ricucire.
sewage ['su:ɪdʒ] n acque fpl di scolo.
sewer ['su:ə*] n fogna.
sewing ['səuɪŋ] n cucitura; cucito; ~ **machine** n macchina da cucire.
sewn [səun] pp of **sew**.
sex [sɛks] n sesso; to have ~ **with** avere rapporti sessuali con; ~**ist** a, n sessista (m/f).
sexual ['sɛksjuəl] a sessuale.
sexy ['sɛksɪ] a provocante, sexy inv.
shabby ['ʃæbɪ] a malandato(a); (behaviour) vergognoso(a).
shack [ʃæk] n baracca, capanna.
shackles ['ʃæklz] npl ferri mpl, catene fpl.
shade [ʃeɪd] n ombra; (for lamp) paralume m; (of colour) tonalità f inv; (small quantity): a ~ **of** un po' or un'ombra di // vt ombreggiare, fare ombra a; **in the** ~ all'ombra; a ~ **smaller** un tantino più piccolo.
shadow ['ʃædəu] n ombra // vt (follow) pedinare; ~ **cabinet** n (Brit POL) governo m ombra inv; ~**y** a ombreggiato(a), ombroso(a); (dim) vago(a), indistinto(a).
shady ['ʃeɪdɪ] a ombroso(a); (fig: dishonest) losco(a), equivoco(a).
shaft [ʃɑ:ft] n (of arrow, spear) asta; (AUT, TECH) albero; (of mine) pozzo; (of lift) tromba; (of light) raggio.

shaggy ['ʃægɪ] a ispido(a).

shake [ʃeɪk] vb (pt **shook**, pp **shaken** [ʃuk, 'ʃeɪkn]) vt scuotere; (bottle, cocktail) agitare // vi tremare // n scossa; **to ~ one's head** (in refusal, dismay) scuotere la testa; **to ~ hands with sb** stringere or dare la mano a qn; **to ~ off** vt scrollare (via); (fig) sbarazzarsi di; **to ~ up** vt scuotere; **shaky** a (hand, voice) tremante; (building) traballante.

shale [ʃeɪl] n roccia scistosa.

shall [ʃæl] auxiliary vb: **I ~ go** andrò; **~ I open the door?** apro io la porta?; **I'll get some, ~ I?** ne prendo un po', va bene?

shallow ['ʃæləu] a poco profondo(a); (fig) superficiale.

sham [ʃæm] n finzione f, messinscena; (jewellery, furniture) imitazione f.

shambles ['ʃæmblz] n confusione f, baraonda, scompiglio.

shame [ʃeɪm] n vergogna // vt far vergognare; **it is a ~ (that/to do)** è un peccato (che + sub/fare); **what a ~!** che peccato!; **~faced** a vergognoso(a); **~ful** a vergognoso(a); **~less** a sfrontato(a); (immodest) spudorato(a).

shampoo [ʃæm'pu:] n shampoo m inv // vt fare lo shampoo a; **~ and set** n shampoo e messa in piega.

shamrock ['ʃæmrɔk] n trifoglio (simbolo nazionale dell'Irlanda).

shandy ['ʃændɪ] n birra con gassosa.

shan't [ʃɑ:nt] = **shall not**.

shanty town ['ʃæntɪ-] n bidonville f inv.

shape [ʃeɪp] n forma // vt formare; (statement) formulare; (sb's ideas) condizionare // vi (also: **~ up**) (events) andare, mettersi; (person) cavarsela; **to take ~** prendere forma; **-shaped** suffix: heart-shaped a forma di cuore; **~less** a senza forma, informe; **~ly** a ben proporzionato(a).

share [ʃɛə*] n (thing received, contribution) parte f; (COMM) azione f // vt dividere; (have in common) condividere, avere in comune; **to ~ out** (among or between) dividere (tra); **~holder** n azionista m/f.

shark [ʃɑ:k] n squalo, pescecane m.

sharp [ʃɑ:p] a (razor, knife) affilato(a); (point) acuto(a), acuminato(a); (nose, chin) aguzzo(a); (outline) netto(a); (cold, pain) pungente; (voice) stridulo(a); (person: quick-witted) sveglio(a); (: unscrupulous) disonesto(a); (MUS): **C ~** do diesis // n (MUS) diesis m inv // ad: **at 2 o'clock** alle due in punto; **~en** vt affilare; (pencil) fare la punta a; (fig) aguzzare; **~ener** n (also: **pencil ~ener**) temperamatite m inv; **~-eyed** a dalla vista acuta; **~ly** ad (turn, stop) bruscamente; (stand out, contrast) nettamente; (criticize, retort) duramente, aspramente.

shatter ['ʃætə*] vt mandare in frantumi, frantumare; (fig: upset) distruggere; (: ruin) rovinare // vi frantumarsi, andare in pezzi.

shave [ʃeɪv] vt radere, rasare // vi radersi, farsi la barba // n: **to have a ~** farsi la barba; **~r** n (also: **electric ~r**) rasoio elettrico.

shaving ['ʃeɪvɪŋ] n (action) rasatura; **~s** npl (of wood etc) trucioli mpl; **~ brush** n pennello da barba; **~ cream** n crema da barba.

shawl [ʃɔ:l] n scialle m.

she [ʃi:] pronoun ella, lei; **~-cat** n gatta; **~-elephant** n elefantessa; NB: for ships, countries follow the gender of your translation.

sheaf [ʃi:f], pl **sheaves** n covone m.

shear [ʃɪə*] vt (pt **~ed**, pp **~ed** or **shorn**) (sheep) tosare; **to ~ off** vi spezzarsi; **~s** npl (for hedge) cesoie fpl.

sheath [ʃi:θ] n fodero, guaina; (contraceptive) preservativo.

sheaves [ʃi:vz] npl of **sheaf**.

shed [ʃed] n capannone m // vt (pt, pp **shed**) (leaves, fur etc) perdere; (tears) versare.

she'd [ʃi:d] = **she had, she would**.

sheen [ʃi:n] n lucentezza.

sheep [ʃi:p] n (pl inv) pecora; **~dog** n cane m da pastore; **~ish** a vergognoso(a), timido(a); **~skin** n pelle f di pecora.

sheer [ʃɪə*] a (utter) vero(a) (e proprio(a)); (steep) a picco, perpendicolare; (almost transparent) sottile // ad a picco.

sheet [ʃi:t] n (on bed) lenzuolo; (of paper) foglio; (of glass) lastra; (of metal) foglio, lamina; **~ lightning** n lampo diffuso.

sheik(h) [ʃeɪk] n sceicco.

shelf [ʃelf], pl **shelves** n scaffale m, mensola.

shell [ʃel] n (on beach) conchiglia; (of egg, nut etc) guscio; (explosive) granata; (of building) scheletro // vt (peas) sgranare; (MIL) bombardare, cannoneggiare.

she'll [ʃi:l] = **she will, she shall**.

shellfish ['ʃelfɪʃ] n (pl inv) (crab etc) crostaceo; (scallop etc) mollusco; (pl: as food) crostacei; molluschi.

shelter ['ʃeltə*] n riparo, rifugio // vt riparare, proteggere; (give lodging to) dare rifugio or asilo a // vi ripararsi, mettersi al riparo.

shelve [ʃelv] vt (fig) accantonare, rimandare; **~s** npl of **shelf**.

shepherd ['ʃepəd] n pastore m // vt (guide) guidare; **~'s pie** n timballo di carne macinata e purè di patate.

sheriff ['ʃerɪf] n sceriffo.

sherry ['ʃerɪ] n sherry m inv.

Shetland [ˈʃɛtlənd] n (also: the ~s, the ~ Isles) le isole Shetland, le Shetland.

shield [ʃiːld] n scudo // vt: to ~ (from) riparare (da), proteggere (da or contro).

shift [ʃɪft] n (change) cambiamento; (of workers) turno // vt spostare, muovere; (remove) rimuovere // vi spostarsi, muoversi; **~less** a: a **~less** person un(a) fannullone(a); **~ work** n lavoro a squadre; **~y** a ambiguo(a); (eyes) sfuggente.

shilling [ˈʃɪlɪŋ] n (Brit) scellino (= 12 old pence; 20 in a pound).

shilly-shally [ˈʃɪlɪʃælɪ] vi tentennare, esitare.

shimmer [ˈʃɪmə*] vi brillare, luccicare.

shin [ʃɪn] n tibia.

shine [ʃaɪn] n splendore m, lucentezza // vb (pt, pp **shone**) vi (ri)splendere, brillare // vt far brillare, far risplendere; (torch): to ~ sth on puntare qc verso.

shingle [ˈʃɪŋgl] n (on beach) ciottoli mpl; (on roof) assicella di copertura; **~s** n (MED) herpes zoster m.

shiny [ˈʃaɪnɪ] a lucente, lucido(a).

ship [ʃɪp] n nave f // vt trasportare (via mare); (send) spedire (via mare); (load) imbarcare, caricare; **~building** n costruzione f navale; **~ment** n carico; **~ping** n (ships) naviglio; (traffic) navigazione f; **~shape** a in perfetto ordine; **~wreck** n relitto; (event) naufragio // vt: to be **~wrecked** naufragare, fare naufragio; **~yard** n cantiere m navale.

shire [ˈʃaɪə*] n (Brit) contea.

shirk [ʃəːk] vt sottrarsi a, evitare.

shirt [ʃəːt] n (man's) camicia; in ~ sleeves in maniche di camicia.

shit [ʃɪt] excl (col!) merda (!).

shiver [ˈʃɪvə*] n brivido // vi rabbrividire, tremare.

shoal [ʃəʊl] n (of fish) banco.

shock [ʃɔk] n (impact) urto, colpo; (ELEC) scossa; (emotional) colpo, shock m inv; (MED) shock // vt colpire, scioccare; scandalizzare; **~ absorber** n ammortizzatore m; **~ing** a scioccante, traumatizzante; scandaloso(a).

shod [ʃɔd] pt, pp of **shoe**.

shoddy [ˈʃɔdɪ] a scadente.

shoe [ʃuː] n scarpa; (also: **horse~**) ferro di cavallo // vt (pt, pp **shod**) (horse) ferrare; **~horn** n calzante m; **~lace** n stringa; **~ polish** n lucido per scarpe; **~shop** n calzoleria; **~string** n (fig): on a **~string** con quattro soldi.

shone [ʃɔn] pt, pp of **shine**.

shoo [ʃuː] excl sciò!, via!

shook [ʃuk] pt of **shake**.

shoot [ʃuːt] n (on branch, seedling) germoglio // vb (pt, pp **shot**) vt (game) cacciare, andare a caccia di; (person) sparare a; (execute) fucilare; (film) girare // vi (with gun): to ~ (at) sparare

(a), fare fuoco (su); (with bow): to ~ (at) tirare (su); (FOOTBALL) sparare, tirare (forte); to ~ **down** vt (plane) abbattere; to ~ **in/out** vi entrare/ uscire come una freccia; to ~ **up** vi (fig) salire alle stelle; **~ing** n (shots) sparatoria; (HUNTING) caccia; **~ing star** n stella cadente.

shop [ʃɔp] n negozio; (workshop) officina // vi (also: go **~ping**) fare spese; ~ **assistant** n (Brit) commesso/a; ~ **floor** n officina; (Brit fig) operai mpl, maestranze fpl; **~keeper** n negoziante m/f, bottegaio/a; **~lifting** n taccheggio; **~per** n compratore/trice; **~ping** n (goods) spesa, acquisti mpl; **~ping bag** n borsa per la spesa; **~ping centre**, (US) **~ping center** n centro commerciale; **~-soiled** a sciupato(a) a forza di stare in vetrina; ~ **steward** n (Brit INDUSTRY) rappresentante m sindacale; ~ **window** n vetrina.

shore [ʃɔː*] n (of sea) riva, spiaggia; (of lake) riva // vt: to ~ (up) puntellare.

shorn [ʃɔːn] pp of **shear**.

short [ʃɔːt] a (not long) corto(a); (soon finished) breve; (person) basso(a); (curt) brusco(a), secco(a); (insufficient) insufficiente // n (also: ~ **film**) cortometraggio; (a pair of) ~s (i) calzoncini; to be ~ of sth essere a corto di or mancare di qc; in ~ in breve; ~ of doing a meno che non si faccia; everything ~ of tutto fuorché; it is ~ for è l'abbreviazione or il diminutivo di; to cut ~ (speech, visit) accorciare, abbreviare; (person) interrompere; to fall ~ of venir meno a; non soddisfare; to stop ~ fermarsi di colpo; to stop ~ of non arrivare fino a; **~age** n scarsezza, carenza; **~bread** n biscotto di pasta frolla; **~change** vt: to **~change** sb imbrogliare qn sul resto; **~circuit** n cortocircuito // vt cortocircuitare // vi fare cortocircuito; **~coming** n difetto; **~(crust) pastry** n (Brit) pasta frolla; **~cut** n scorciatoia; **~en** vt accorciare, ridurre; **~fall** n deficit m; **~hand** n (Brit) stenografia; **~hand typist** n (Brit) stenodattilografo/a; ~ **list** n (Brit: for job) rosa dei candidati; **~ly** ad fra poco; **~sighted** a (Brit) miope; **~-staffed** a a corto di personale; ~ **story** n racconto, novella; **~-tempered** a irascibile; **~-term** a (effect) di or a breve durata; ~ **wave** n (RADIO) onde fpl corte.

shot [ʃɔt] pt, pp of **shoot** // n sparo, colpo; (person) tiratore m; (try) prova; (injection) iniezione f; (PHOT) foto f inv; like a ~ come un razzo; (very readily) immediatamente; **~gun** n fucile m da caccia.

should [ʃud] auxiliary vb: I ~ go now dovrei andare ora; he ~ be there now dovrebbe essere arrivato ora; I ~ go if I were you se fossi in te andrei; I ~ like to mi piacerebbe.

shoulder ['ʃəuldə*] n spalla; (Brit: of road): **hard** ~ banchina // vt (fig) addossarsi, prendere sulle proprie spalle; ~ **bag** n borsa a tracolla; ~ **blade** n scapola; ~ **strap** n bretella, spallina.

shouldn't ['ʃudnt] = **should not.**

shout [ʃaut] n urlo, grido // vt gridare // vi urlare, gridare; **to** ~ **down** vt zittire gridando; ~**ing** n urli mpl.

shove [ʃʌv] vt spingere; (col: put): **to** ~ **sth in** ficcare qc in; **to** ~ **off** vi (NAUT) scostarsi.

shovel ['ʃʌvl] n pala // vt spalare.

show [ʃəu] n (of emotion) dimostrazione f, manifestazione f; (semblance) apparenza; (exhibition) mostra, esposizione f; (THEATRE, CINEMA) spettacolo // vb (pt ~**ed**, pp **shown**) vt far vedere, mostrare; (courage etc) dimostrare, dar prova di; (exhibit) esporre // vi vedersi, essere visibile; **on** ~ (exhibits etc) esposto(a); **to** ~ **in** vt (person) far entrare; **to** ~ **off** vi (pej) esibirsi, mettersi in mostra // vt (display) mettere in risalto; (pej) mettere in mostra; **to** ~ **out** vt (person) accompagnare alla porta; **to** ~ **up** vi (stand out) essere ben visibile; (col: turn up) farsi vedere // vt mettere in risalto; (unmask) smascherare; ~ **business** n industria dello spettacolo; ~**down** n prova di forza.

shower ['ʃauə*] n (rain) acquazzone m; (of stones etc) pioggia; (also: ~**bath**) doccia // vi fare la doccia // vt: **to** ~ **sb with** (gifts, abuse etc) coprire qn di; (missiles) lanciare contro qn una pioggia di; ~**proof** a impermeabile.

showing ['ʃəuɪŋ] n (of film) proiezione f.

show jumping n concorso ippico (di salto ad ostacoli).

shown [ʃəun] pp of **show.**

show-off ['ʃəuɔf] n (col: person) esibizionista m/f.

showroom ['ʃəurum] n sala d'esposizione.

shrank [ʃræŋk] pt of **shrink.**

shrapnel ['ʃræpnl] n shrapnel m.

shred [ʃred] n (gen pl) brandello // vt fare a brandelli; (CULIN) sminuzzare, tagliuzzare; ~**der** n (vegetable ~**der**) grattugia; (document ~**der**) distruttore m di documenti.

shrewd [ʃru:d] a astuto(a), scaltro(a).

shriek [ʃri:k] n strillo // vt, vi strillare.

shrill [ʃrɪl] a acuto(a), stridulo(a), stridente.

shrimp [ʃrɪmp] n gamberetto.

shrine [ʃraɪn] n reliquario; (place) santuario.

shrink [ʃrɪŋk] vb (pt **shrank**, pp **shrunk**) vi restringersi; (fig) ridursi // vt (wool) far restringere // n (col: pej) psicanalista m/f; **to** ~ **from doing sth** rifuggire dal fare qc; ~**age** n restringimento; ~**wrap** vt confezionare con pellicola di plastica.

shrivel ['ʃrɪvl] (also: ~ **up**) vt raggrinzare, avvizzire // vi raggrinzirsi, avvizzire.

shroud [ʃraud] n sudario // vt: ~**ed in mystery** avvolto(a) nel mistero.

Shrove Tuesday ['ʃrəuv-] n martedì m grasso.

shrub [ʃrʌb] n arbusto; ~**bery** n arbusti mpl.

shrug [ʃrʌg] n scrollata di spalle // vt, vi: **to** ~ (one's shoulders) alzare le spalle, fare spallucce; **to** ~ **off** vt passare sopra a.

shrunk [ʃrʌŋk] pp of **shrink.**

shudder ['ʃʌdə*] n brivido // vi rabbrividire.

shuffle ['ʃʌfl] vt (cards) mescolare; **to** ~ (one's feet) strascicare i piedi.

shun [ʃʌn] vt sfuggire, evitare.

shunt [ʃʌnt] vt (RAIL: direct) smistare; (: divert) deviare.

shut, pt, pp **shut** [ʃʌt] vt chiudere // vi chiudersi, chiudere; **to** ~ **down** vt, vi chiudere definitivamente; **to** ~ **off** vt fermare, bloccare; **to** ~ **up** vi (col: keep quiet) stare zitto(a), fare silenzio // vt (close) chiudere; (silence) far tacere; ~**ter** n imposta; (PHOT) otturatore m.

shuttle ['ʃʌtl] n spola, navetta; (also: ~ **service**) servizio m navetta inv.

shuttlecock ['ʃʌtlkɔk] n volano.

shy [ʃaɪ] a timido(a).

sibling ['sɪblɪŋ] n fratello/sorella.

Sicily ['sɪsɪlɪ] n Sicilia.

sick [sɪk] a (ill) malato(a); (vomiting): **to be** ~ vomitare; (humour) macabro(a); **to feel** ~ avere la nausea; **to be** ~ **of** (fig) averne abbastanza di; ~ **bay** n infermeria; ~**en** vt nauseare // vi: **to be** ~**ening for sth** (cold etc) cavare qc.

sickle ['sɪkl] n falcetto.

sick: ~ **leave** n congedo per malattia; ~**ly** a malaticcio(a); (causing nausea) nauseante; ~**ness** n malattia; (vomiting) vomito; ~ **pay** n sussidio per malattia.

side [saɪd] n lato; (of lake) riva // cpd (door, entrance) laterale // vi: **to** ~ **with sb** parteggiare per qn, prendere le parti di qn; **by the** ~ **of** a fianco di; (road) sul ciglio di; ~ **by** ~ fianco a fianco; **to take** ~**s (with)** schierarsi (con); ~**board** n credenza; ~**boards** (Brit), ~**burns** npl (whiskers) basette fpl; ~ **effect** n (MED) effetto collaterale; ~**light** n (AUT) luce f di posizione; ~**line** n (SPORT) linea laterale; (fig) attività secondaria; ~**long** a obliquo(a); ~**saddle** ad all'amazzone; ~ **show** n attrazione *f*; **~step** *vt* (*question*) eludere; (*problem*) scavalcare; **~ street** *n* traversa; **~track** *vt* (*fig*) distrarre; **~walk** *n* (*US*) marciapiede *m*; **~ways** *ad* (*move*) di lato, di fianco; (*look*) con la coda dell'occhio.

siding ['saɪdɪŋ] *n* (*RAIL*) binario di raccordo.

sidle ['saɪdl] *vi*: **to ~ up (to)** avvicinarsi furtivamente (a).

siege [si:dʒ] *n* assedio.

sieve [sɪv] *n* setaccio // *vt* setacciare.

sift [sɪft] *vt* passare al crivello; (*fig*) vagliare.

sigh [saɪ] *n* sospiro // *vi* sospirare.

sight [saɪt] *n* (*faculty*) vista; (*spectacle*) spettacolo; (*on gun*) mira // *vt* avvistare; **in ~** in vista; **out of ~** non visibile; **~seeing** *n* giro turistico; **to go ~seeing** visitare una località.

sign [saɪn] *n* segno; (*with hand etc*) segno, gesto; (*notice*) insegna, cartello // *vt* firmare; **to ~ on** *vi* (*MIL*) arruolarsi; (*as unemployed*) iscriversi sulla liste (dell'ufficio di collocamento) // *vt* (*MIL*) arruolare; (*employee*) assumere; **to ~ over** *vt*: **to ~ sth over to sb** cedere qc con scrittura legale a qn; **to ~ up** (*MIL*) *vt* arruolare // *vi* arruolarsi.

signal ['sɪgnl] *n* segnale *m* // *vi* (*AUT*) segnalare, mettere la freccia // *vt* (*person*) fare segno a; (*message*) comunicare per mezzo di segnali; **~man** *n* (*RAIL*) deviatore *m*.

signature ['sɪgnətʃə*] *n* firma; **~ tune** *n* sigla musicale.

signet ring ['sɪgnət-] *n* anello con sigillo.

significance [sɪg'nɪfɪkəns] *n* significato; importanza.

significant [sɪg'nɪfɪkənt] *a* significativo(a).

signpost ['saɪnpəust] *n* cartello indicatore.

silence ['saɪlns] *n* silenzio // *vt* far tacere, ridurre al silenzio; **~r** *n* (*on gun*, *Brit AUT*) silenziatore *m*.

silent ['saɪlnt] *a* silenzioso(a); (*film*) muto(a); **to remain ~** tacere, stare zitto; **~ partner** *n* (*COMM*) socio inattivo.

silhouette [sɪlu:'et] *n* silhouette *f inv*.

silicon chip ['sɪlɪkən-] *n* piastrina di silicio.

silk [sɪlk] *n* seta // *cpd* di seta; **~y** *a* di seta.

silly ['sɪlɪ] *a* stupido(a), sciocco(a).

silt [sɪlt] *n* limo.

silver ['sɪlvə*] *n* argento; (*money*) monete *da 5, 10 or 50 pence*; (*also*: **~ware**) argenteria // *cpd* d'argento; **~ paper** *n* (*Brit*) carta argentata, (carta) stagnola; **~-plated** *a* argentato(a); **~smith** *n* argentiere *m*; **~y** *a* (*colour*) argenteo(a); (*sound*) argentino(a).

similar ['sɪmɪlə*] *a*: **~ (to)** simile (a); **~ly** *ad* allo stesso modo; così pure.

simile ['sɪmɪlɪ] *n* similitudine *f*.

simmer ['sɪmə*] *vi* cuocere a fuoco lento.

simpering ['sɪmpərɪŋ] *a* lezioso(a), smorfioso(a).

simple ['sɪmpl] *a* semplice; **simplicity** [-'plɪsɪtɪ] *n* semplicità.

simultaneous [sɪməl'teɪnɪəs] *a* simultaneo(a).

sin [sɪn] *n* peccato // *vi* peccare.

since [sɪns] *ad* da allora // *prep* da // *cj* (*time*) da quando; (*because*) poiché, dato che; **~ then** da allora.

sincere [sɪn'sɪə*] *a* sincero(a); **~ly** *ad*: **yours ~ly** (*in letters*) distinti saluti; **sincerity** [-'serɪtɪ] *n* sincerità.

sinew ['sɪnju:] *n* tendine *m*; **~s** *npl* (*muscles*) muscoli *mpl*.

sinful ['sɪnful] *a* peccaminoso(a).

sing [sɪŋ], *pt* **sang**, *pp* **sung** *vt*, *vi* cantare.

singe [sɪndʒ] *vt* bruciacchiare.

singer ['sɪŋə*] *n* cantante *m/f*.

singing ['sɪŋɪŋ] *n* canto.

single ['sɪŋgl] *a* solo(a), unico(a); (*unmarried*: *man*) celibe; (: *woman*) nubile; (*not double*) semplice // *n* (*Brit*: *also*: **~ ticket**) biglietto di (sola) andata; (*record*) 45 giri *m*; **~s** *npl* (*TENNIS*) singolo; **to ~ out** *vt* scegliere; (*distinguish*) distinguere; **~ bed** *n* letto a una piazza; **~-breasted** *a* a un petto; **~ file** *n*: **in ~ file** in fila indiana; **~-handed** *ad* senza aiuto, da solo(a); **~-minded** *a* tenace, risoluto(a); **~ room** *n* camera singola.

singlet ['sɪŋglɪt] *n* canottiera.

singly ['sɪŋglɪ] *ad* separatamente.

singular ['sɪŋgjulə*] *a* (*exceptional*, *LING*) singolare; (*unusual*) strano(a) // *n* (*LING*) singolare *m*.

sinister ['sɪnɪstə*] *a* sinistro(a).

sink [sɪŋk] *n* lavandino, acquaio // *vb* (*pt* **sank**, *pp* **sunk**) *vt* (*ship*) (fare) affondare; colare a picco; (*foundations*) scavare; (*piles etc*): **to ~ sth into** conficcare qc in // *vi* affondare, andare a fondo; (*ground etc*) cedere, avvallarsi; **to ~ in** *vi* penetrare.

sinner ['sɪnə*] *n* peccatore/trice.

sinus ['saɪnəs] *n* (*ANAT*) seno.

sip [sɪp] *n* sorso // *vt* sorseggiare.

siphon ['saɪfən] *n* sifone *m*; **to ~ off** *vt* travasare (con un sifone).

sir [sə*] *n* signore *m*; **S~ John Smith** Sir John Smith; **yes ~** sì, signore.

siren ['saɪərn] *n* sirena.

sirloin ['sə:lɔɪn] *n* controfiletto.

sissy ['sɪsɪ] *n* (*col*) femminuccia.

sister ['sɪstə*] *n* sorella; (*nun*) suora; (*Brit*: *nurse*) infermiera *f* caposala *inv*; **~-in-law** *n* cognata.

sit [sɪt], *pt*, *pp* **sat** *vi* sedere, sedersi; (*assembly*) essere in seduta // *vt* (*exam*) sostenere, dare; **to ~ down** *vi* sedersi; **to ~ in on** *vt fus* assistere a; **to ~ up**

vi tirarsi su a sedere; *(not go to bed)* stare alzato(a) fino a tardi.

sitcom ['sɪtkɔm] *n abbr* (= *situation comedy*) commedia di situazione.

site [saɪt] *n* posto; *(also:* building ~*)* cantiere *m* // *vt* situare.

sit-in ['sɪtɪn] *n (demonstration)* sit-in *m inv.*

sitting ['sɪtɪŋ] *n (of assembly etc)* seduta; *(in canteen)* turno; ~ **room** *n* soggiorno.

situated ['sɪtjueɪtɪd] *a* situato(a).

situation [sɪtju'eɪʃən] *n* situazione *f*; "~s vacant" *(Brit)* "offerte *fpl* di impiego".

six [sɪks] *num* sei; ~**teen** *num* sedici; ~**th** *num* sesto(a); ~**ty** *num* sessanta.

size [saɪz] *n* dimensioni *fpl*; *(of clothing)* taglia, misura; *(of shoes)* numero; *(glue)* colla; **to** ~ **up** *vt* giudicare, farsi un'idea di; ~**able** *a* considerevole.

sizzle ['sɪzl] *vi* sfrigolare.

skate [skeɪt] *n* pattino; *(fish: pl inv)* razza // *vi* pattinare; ~**board** *n* skateboard *m inv*; ~**r** *n* pattinatore/ trice; **skating** *n* pattinaggio; **skating rink** *n* pista di pattinaggio.

skeleton ['skɛlɪtn] *n* scheletro; ~ **key** *n* passe-partout *m inv*; ~ **staff** *n* personale *m* ridotto.

skeptical ['skɛptɪkl] *a (US)* = **sceptical.**

sketch [skɛtʃ] *n (drawing)* schizzo, abbozzo; *(THEATRE)* scenetta comica, sketch *m inv* // *vt* abbozzare, schizzare; ~ **book** *n* album *m inv* per schizzi; ~**y** *a* incompleto(a), lacunoso(a).

skewer ['skju:ə*] *n* spiedo.

ski [ski:] *n* sci *m inv* // *vi* sciare; ~ **boot** *n* scarpone *m* da sci.

skid [skɪd] *n* slittamento // *vi* slittare.

skier ['ski:ə*] *n* sciatore/trice.

skiing ['ski:ɪŋ] *n* sci *m*.

ski jump *n (ramp)* trampolino; *(event)* salto con gli sci.

skilful ['skɪlful] *a* abile.

ski lift ['ski:lɪft] *n* sciovia.

skill [skɪl] *n* abilità *f inv*, capacità *f inv*; ~**ed** *a* esperto(a); *(worker)* qualificato(a), specializzato(a).

skim [skɪm] *vt (milk)* scremare; *(soup)* schiumare; *(glide over)* sfiorare // *vi:* **to** ~ **through** *(fig)* scorrere, dare una scorsa a; ~**med milk** *n* latte *m* scremato.

skimp [skɪmp] *vt (work)* fare alla carlona; *(cloth etc)* lesinare; ~**y** *a* misero(a); striminzito(a); frugale.

skin [skɪn] *n* pelle *f* // *vt (fruit etc)* sbucciare; *(animal)* scuoiare, spellare; ~**-deep** *a* superficiale; ~ **diving** *n* nuoto subacqueo; ~**ny** *a* molto magro(a), pelle e ossa *inv*; ~**tight** *a (dress etc)* aderente.

skip [skɪp] *n* saltello, balzo; *(container)* benna // *vi* saltare; *(with rope)* saltare la corda // *vt (pass over)* saltare.

ski: ~ **pants** *npl* pantaloni *mpl* da sci; ~ **pole** *n* racchetta (da sci).

skipper ['skɪpə*] *n (NAUT, SPORT)* capitano.

skipping rope ['skɪpɪŋ-] *n (Brit)* corda per saltare.

skirmish ['skə:mɪʃ] *n* scaramuccia.

skirt [skə:t] *n* gonna, sottana // *vt* fiancheggiare, costeggiare; ~**ing board** *n (Brit)* zoccolo.

ski suit *n* tuta da sci.

skit [skɪt] *n* parodia; scenetta satirica.

skittle ['skɪtl] *n* birillo; ~**s** *n (game)* (gioco dei) birilli *mpl.*

skive [skaɪv] *vi (Brit col)* fare il lavativo.

skulk [skʌlk] *vi* muoversi furtivamente.

skull [skʌl] *n* cranio, teschio.

skunk [skʌŋk] *n* moffetta.

sky [skaɪ] *n* cielo; ~**light** *n* lucernario; ~**scraper** *n* grattacielo.

slab [slæb] *n* lastra.

slack [slæk] *a (loose)* allentato(a); *(slow)* lento(a); *(careless)* negligente // *n (in rope etc)* parte *f* non tesa; ~**s** *npl* pantaloni *mpl*; ~**en** *(also:* ~**en off)** *vi* rallentare, diminuire // *vt* allentare.

slag [slæg] *n* scorie *fpl*; ~ **heap** *n* ammasso di scorie.

slain [sleɪn] *pp of* **slay.**

slam [slæm] *vt (door)* sbattere; *(throw)* scaraventare; *(criticize)* stroncare // *vi* sbattere.

slander ['slɑ:ndə*] *n* calunnia; diffamazione *f* // *vt* calunniare; diffamare.

slang [slæŋ] *n* gergo, slang *m.*

slant [slɑ:nt] *n* pendenza, inclinazione *f*; *(fig)* angolazione *f*, punto di vista; ~**ed** *a* tendenzioso(a); ~**ing** *a* in pendenza, inclinato(a).

slap [slæp] *n* manata, pacca; *(on face)* schiaffo // *vt* dare una manata a; schiaffeggiare // *ad (directly)* in pieno; ~**dash** *a* abborracciato(a); ~**stick** *n (comedy)* farsa grossolana; ~**up** *a:* a ~**up meal** *(Brit)* un pranzo (or una cena) coi fiocchi.

slash [slæʃ] *vt* squarciare; *(face)* sfregiare; *(fig: prices)* ridurre drasticamente, tagliare.

slat [slæt] *n (of wood)* stecca; *(of plastic)* lamina.

slate [sleɪt] *n* ardesia // *vt (fig: criticize)* stroncare, distruggere.

slaughter ['slɔ:tə*] *n* strage *f*, massacro // *vt (animal)* macellare; *(people)* trucidare, massacrare.

slave [sleɪv] *n* schiavo/a // *vi (also:* ~ *away)* lavorare come uno schiavo; ~**ry** *n* schiavitù *f.*

slay [sleɪ], *pt* **slew**, *pp* **slain** *vt (formal)* uccidere.

SLD *n abbr (Brit)* = *Social and Liberal Democrats.*

sleazy ['sli:zɪ] *a* trasandato(a).

sledge [slɛdʒ] *n* slitta; ~**hammer** *n* mazza, martello da fabbro.

sleek [sli:k] *a* (*hair*, *fur*) lucido(a), lucente; (*car*, *boat*) slanciato(a), affusolato(a).

sleep [sli:p] *n* sonno // *vi* (*pt*, *pp* **slept**) dormire; **to go to ~** addormentarsi; **to ~ in** *vi* (*lie late*) alzarsi tardi; (*oversleep*) dormire fino a tardi; ~**er** *n* (*person*) dormiente *m/f*; (*Brit RAIL*: *on track*) traversina; (: *train*) treno di vagoni letto; ~**ing bag** *n* sacco a pelo; ~**ing car** *n* vagone *m* letto *inv*, carrozza *f* letto *inv*; ~**ing pill** *n* sonnifero; ~**less** *a*: **a ~less night** una notte in bianco; ~**walker** *n* sonnambulo/a; ~**y** *a* assonnato(a), sonnolento(a); (*fig*) addormentato(a).

sleet [sli:t] *n* nevischio.

sleeve [sli:v] *n* manica.

sleigh [sleɪ] *n* slitta.

sleight [slaɪt] *n*: ~ **of hand** gioco di destrezza.

slender ['slɛndə*] *a* snello(a), sottile; (*not enough*) scarso(a), esiguo(a).

slept [slɛpt] *pt*, *pp of* **sleep**.

slew [slu:] *vi* girare // *pt of* **slay**.

slice [slaɪs] *n* fetta // *vt* affettare, tagliare a fette.

slick [slɪk] *a* (*clever*) brillante; (*insincere*) untuoso(a), falso(a) // *n* (*also*: oil ~) chiazza di petrolio.

slide [slaɪd] *n* (*in playground*) scivolo; (*PHOT*) diapositiva; (*Brit*: *also*: hair ~) fermaglio (per capelli); (*in prices*) caduta // *vb* (*pt*, *pp* **slid** [slɪd]) *vt* far scivolare // *vi* scivolare; ~ **rule** *n* regolo calcolatore; **sliding** *a* (*door*) scorrevole; **sliding scale** *n* scala mobile.

slight [slaɪt] *a* (*slim*) snello(a), sottile; (*frail*) delicato(a), fragile; (*trivial*) insignificante; (*small*) piccolo(a) // *n* offesa, affronto // *vt* (*offend*) offendere, fare un affronto a; **not in the ~est** affatto, neppure per sogno; ~**ly** *ad* lievemente, un po'.

slim [slɪm] *a* magro(a), snello(a) // *vi* dimagrire; fare (*or* seguire) una dieta dimagrante.

slime [slaɪm] *n* limo, melma; viscidume *m*.

slimming ['slɪmɪŋ] *n* (*diet*) dimagrante; (*food*) ipocalorico(a).

sling [slɪŋ] *n* (*MED*) benda al collo // *vt* (*pt*, *pp* **slung**) lanciare, tirare.

slip [slɪp] *n* scivolata, scivolone *m*; (*mistake*) errore *m*, sbaglio; (*underskirt*) sottoveste *f*; (*of paper*) striscia di carta; tagliando, scontrino // *vt* (*slide*) far scivolare // *vi* (*slide*) scivolare; (*move smoothly*): **to ~** into/out of scivolare in/via da; (*decline*) declinare; **to ~ sth on/off** infilarsi/togliersi qc; **to give sb the ~** sfuggire qn; **a ~ of the tongue** un lapsus linguae; **to ~ away** *vi*

svignarsela; ~**ped disc** *n* spostamento delle vertebre.

slipper ['slɪpə*] *n* pantofola.

slippery ['slɪpərɪ] *a* scivoloso(a).

slip road *n* (*Brit*: *to motorway*) rampa di accesso.

slipshod ['slɪpʃɔd] *a* sciatto(a), trasandato(a).

slip-up ['slɪpʌp] *n* granchio (*fig*).

slipway ['slɪpweɪ] *n* scalo di costruzione.

slit [slɪt] *n* fessura, fenditura; (*cut*) taglio; (*tear*) squarcio; strappo // *vt* (*pt*, *pp* **slit**) tagliare; (*make a slit*) squarciare; strappare.

slither ['slɪðə*] *vi* scivolare, sdrucciolare.

sliver ['slɪvə*] *n* (*of glass*, *wood*) scheggia; (*of cheese etc*) fettina.

slob [slɔb] *n* (*col*) sciattone/a.

slog [slɔg] (*Brit*) *n* faticata // *vi* lavorare con accanimento, sgobbare.

slogan ['sləugən] *n* motto, slogan *m inv*.

slop [slɔp] *vi* (*also*: ~ over) traboccare; versarsi // *vt* spandere; versare.

slope [sləup] *n* pendio; (*side of mountain*) versante *m*; (*of roof*) pendenza; (*of floor*) inclinazione *f* // *vi*: **to ~ down** declinare; **to ~ up** essere in salita.

sloppy ['slɔpɪ] *a* (*work*) tirato(a) via; (*appearance*) sciatto(a); (*film etc*) sdolcinato(a).

slot [slɔt] *n* fessura // *vt*: **to ~ sth into** infilare qc in // *vi*: **to ~ into** inserirsi in.

sloth [sləuθ] *n* (*laziness*) pigrizia, accidia.

slot machine *n* (*Brit*: *vending machine*) distributore *m* automatico; (*for gambling*) slot-machine *f inv*.

slouch [slautʃ] *vi* (*when walking*) camminare dinoccolato(a); **she was ~ing in a chair** era sprofondata in una poltrona; **to ~ about** *vi* (*laze*) oziare.

slovenly ['slʌvənlɪ] *a* sciatto(a), trasandato(a).

slow [sləu] *a* lento(a); (*watch*): **to be ~** essere indietro // *ad* lentamente // *vt*, *vi* (*also*: ~ down, ~ up) rallentare; "~" (*road sign*) "rallentare"; ~**ly** *ad* lentamente; ~ **motion** *n*: in ~ motion al rallentatore.

sludge [slʌdʒ] *n* fanghiglia.

slug [slʌg] *n* lumaca; (*bullet*) pallottola; ~**gish** *a* lento(a).

sluice [slu:s] *n* chiusa.

slum [slʌm] *n* catapecchia.

slumber ['slʌmbə*] *n* sonno.

slump [slʌmp] *n* crollo, caduta; (*economic*) depressione *f*, crisi *f inv* // *vi* crollare.

slung [slʌŋ] *pt*, *pp of* **sling**.

slur [slə:*] *n* pronuncia indistinta; (*stigma*) diffamazione *f*, calunnia; (*smear*): ~ (**on**) macchia (su); (*MUS*) legatura // *vt* pronunciare in modo indistinto.

slush [slʌʃ] *n* neve *f* mista a fango; ~ **fund** *n* fondi *mpl* neri.

slut [slʌt] *n* donna trasandata, sciattona.

sly [slaɪ] *a* furbo(a), scaltro(a).

smack [smæk] *n* (*slap*) pacca; (*on face*) schiaffo // *vt* schiaffeggiare; (*child*) picchiare // *vi*: **to** ~ **of** puzzare di.

small [smɔːl] *a* piccolo(a); ~ **ads** *npl* (*Brit*) piccola pubblicità; ~ **change** *n* moneta, spiccioli *mpl*; ~**holder** *n* piccolo proprietario; ~ **hours** *npl*: **in the** ~ **hours** alle ore piccole; ~**pox** *n* vaiolo; ~ **talk** *n* chiacchiere *fpl*.

smart [smɑːt] *a* elegante; (*clever*) intelligente; (*quick*) sveglio(a) // *vi* bruciare; **to** ~**en up** *vi* farsi bello(a) // *vt* (*people*) fare bello(a); (*things*) abbellire.

smash [smæʃ] *n* (*also*: ~-**up**) scontro, collisione *f* // *vt* frantumare, fracassare; (*opponent*) annientare, schiacciare; (*hopes*) distruggere; (*SPORT*: *record*) battere // *vi* frantumarsi, andare in pezzi; ~**ing** *a* (*col*) favoloso(a), formidabile.

smattering ['smætərɪŋ] *n*: **a** ~ **of** un'infarinatura di.

smear [smɪə*] *n* macchia; (*MED*) striscio // *vt* ungere; (*fig*) denigrare, diffamare.

smell [smɛl] *n* odore *m*; (*sense*) olfatto, odorato // *vb* (*pt, pp* **smelt** *or* **smelled** [smɛlt, smɛld]) *vt* sentire (l')odore di // *vi* (*food etc*): **to** ~ (**of**) avere odore (di); (*pej*) puzzare, avere un cattivo odore; **it** ~**s good** ha un buon odore; ~**y** *a* puzzolente.

smile [smaɪl] *n* sorriso // *vi* sorridere.

smirk [smɜːk] *n* sorriso furbo; sorriso compiaciuto.

smith [smɪθ] *n* fabbro; ~**y** *n* fucina.

smock [smɒk] *n* grembiule *m*, camice *m*.

smog [smɒg] *n* smog *m*.

smoke [sməuk] *n* fumo // *vt*, *vi* fumare; ~**d** *a* (*bacon*, *glass*) affumicato(a); ~ *n* (*person*) fumatore/trice; (*RAIL*) carrozza per fumatori; ~ **screen** *n* (*MIL*) cortina fumogena *or* di fumo; (*fig*) copertura; **smoking** *n* fumo; "no smoking" (*sign*) "vietato fumare"; **smoky** *a* fumoso(a); (*surface*) affumicato(a).

smolder ['sməuldə*] *vi* (*US*) = **smoulder**.

smooth [smuːð] *a* liscio(a); (*sauce*) omogeneo(a); (*flavour*, *whisky*) amabile; (*movement*) regolare; (*person*) mellifluo(a) // *vt* lisciare, spianare; (*also*: ~ **out**: *difficulties*) appianare.

smother ['smʌðə*] *vt* soffocare.

smoulder, (*US*) **smolder** ['sməuldə*] *vi* covare sotto la cenere.

smudge [smʌdʒ] *n* macchia; sbavatura // *vt* imbrattare, sporcare.

smug [smʌg] *a* soddisfatto(a), compiaciuto(a).

smuggle ['smʌgl] *vt* contrabbandare; ~**r** *n* contrabbandiere/a; **smuggling** *n* contrabbando.

smutty ['smʌtɪ] *a* (*fig*) osceno(a), indecente.

snack [snæk] *n* spuntino; ~ **bar** *n* tavola calda, snack bar *m inv*.

snag [snæg] *n* intoppo, ostacolo imprevisto.

snail [sneɪl] *n* chiocciola.

snake [sneɪk] *n* serpente *m*.

snap [snæp] *n* (*sound*) schianto, colpo secco; (*photograph*) istantanea; (*game*) rubamazzo // *a* improvviso(a) // *vt* (far) schioccare; (*break*) spezzare di netto; (*photograph*) scattare un'istantanea di // *vi* spezzarsi con un rumore secco; **to** ~ **open/shut** aprirsi/chiudersi di scatto; **to** ~ **at** *vt fus* (*subj*: *dog*) cercare di mordere; **to** ~ **off** *vt* (*break*) schiantare; **to** ~ **up** *vt* afferrare; ~**py** *a* (*col*: *answer*, *slogan*) d'effetto; **make it** ~**py!** (*hurry up*) sbrigati!, svelto!: ~**shot** *n* istantanea.

snare [snɛə*] *n* trappola.

snarl [snɑːl] *vi* ringhiare.

snatch [snætʃ] *n* (*fig*) furto con strappo, scippo; (*small amount*): ~**es** *of* frammenti *mpl* di // *vt* strappare (con violenza); (*steal*) rubare.

sneak [sniːk] *vi*: **to** ~ **in/out** entrare/uscire di nascosto; ~**ers** *npl* scarpe *fpl* da ginnastica; ~**y** *a* falso(a), disonesto(a).

sneer [snɪə*] *vi* ghignare, sogghignare.

sneeze [sniːz] *vi* starnutire.

sniff [snɪf] *n* fiutata, annusata // *vi* fiutare, annusare; tirare su col naso; (*in contempt*) arricciare il naso // *vt* fiutare, annusare.

snigger ['snɪgə*] *n* riso represso // *vi* ridacchiare, ridere sotto i baffi.

snip [snɪp] *n* pezzetto; (*bargain*) (buon) affare *m*, occasione *f* // *vt* tagliare.

sniper ['snaɪpə*] *n* (*marksman*) franco tiratore *m*, cecchino.

snippet ['snɪpɪt] *n* frammento.

snivelling ['snɪvlɪŋ] *a* (*whimpering*) piagnucoloso(a).

snob [snɒb] *n* snob *m/f inv*; ~**bish** *a* snob *inv*.

snooker ['snuːkə*] *n* tipo di gioco del biliardo.

snoop ['snuːp] *vi*: **to** ~ **on sb** spiare qn; **to** ~ **about** curiosare.

snooty ['snuːtɪ] *a* borioso(a), snob *inv*.

snooze [snuːz] *n* sonnellino, pisolino // *vi* fare un sonnellino.

snore [snɔː*] *vi* russare.

snorkel ['snɔːkl] *n* (*of swimmer*) respiratore *m* a tubo.

snort [snɔːt] *n* sbuffo // *vi* sbuffare.

snotty ['snɒtɪ] *a* moccioso(a).

snout [snaut] *n* muso.

snow [snəu] *n* neve *f* // *vi* nevicare; ~**ball** *n* palla di neve; ~**bound** *a* bloccato(a) dalla neve; ~**drift** n cumulo di neve (ammucchiato dal vento); ~**drop** n bucaneve m inv; ~**fall** n nevicata; ~**flake** n fiocco di neve; ~**man** n pupazzo di neve; ~**plough**, (US) ~**plow** n spazzaneve m inv; ~**shoe** n racchetta da neve; ~**storm** n tormenta.

snub [snʌb] vt snobbare // n offesa, affronto; ~**nosed** a dal naso camuso.

snuff [snʌf] n tabacco da fiuto.

snug [snʌg] a comodo(a); (room, house) accogliente, comodo(a).

snuggle ['snʌgl] vi: to ~ up to sb stringersi a qn.

so [səu] ♦ ad 1 (thus, likewise) così; if ~ se è così, quand'è così; I didn't do it — you did ~! non l'ho fatto io — sì che l'hai fatto!; ~ do I, ~ am I etc anch'io; it's 5 o'clock — ~ it is! sono le 5 — davvero!; I hope ~ lo spero; I think ~ penso di sì; ~ **far** finora, fin qui; (in past) fino ad allora
2 (in comparisons etc: to such a degree) così; ~ **big (that)** così grande (che); she's not ~ **clever as her brother** lei non è (così) intelligente come suo fratello
3: ~ **much** a tanto ◆ ad tanto; I've got ~ **much work/money** ho tanto lavoro/tanti soldi; I love you ~ **much** ti amo tanto; ~ **many** tanti(e)
4 (phrases): 10 or ~ circa 10; ~ **long!** (col: goodbye) ciao!, ci vediamo!
♦ cj 1 (expressing purpose): ~ **as to do** in modo or così da fare; we hurried ~ **as not to be late** ci affrettammo per non fare tardi; ~ **(that)** affinché + sub, perché + sub
2 (expressing result): he didn't arrive ~ I left non è venuto così me ne sono andata; ~ you see, I could have gone vedi, sarei potuto andare.

soak [səuk] vt inzuppare; (clothes) mettere a mollo // vi inzupparsi; (clothes) essere a mollo; to ~ **in** vi penetrare; to ~ **up** vt assorbire.

so-and-so ['səuəndsəu] n (somebody) un tale.

soap [səup] n sapone m; ~**flakes** npl sapone m in scaglie; ~ **opera** n soap opera f inv; ~ **powder** n detersivo; ~**y** a insaponato(a).

soar [sɔ:*] vi volare in alto.

sob [sɔb] n singhiozzo // vi singhiozzare.

sober ['səubə*] a non ubriaco(a); (sedate) serio(a); (moderate) moderato(a); (colour, style) sobrio(a); to ~ **up** vt far passare la sbornia a // vi farsi passare la sbornia.

so-called ['səu'kɔ:ld] a cosiddetto(a).

soccer ['sɔkə*] n calcio.

sociable ['səuʃəbl] a socievole.

social ['səuʃl] a sociale // n festa, serata; ~ **club** n club m inv sociale; ~**ism** n socialismo; ~**ist** a, n socialista (m/f);

~**ize** vi: to ~**ize (with)** socializzare (con); ~ **security** n previdenza sociale; ~ **work** n servizio sociale; ~ **worker** n assistente m/f sociale.

society [sə'saɪətɪ] n società f inv; (club) società, associazione f; (also: high ~) alta società.

sociology [səusɪ'ɔlədʒɪ] n sociologia.

sock [sɔk] n calzino // vt (hit) dare un pugno a.

socket ['sɔkɪt] n cavità f inv; (of eye) orbita; (Brit ELEC: also: wall ~) presa di corrente; (: for light bulb) portalampada m inv.

sod [sɔd] n (of earth) zolla erbosa; (Brit col!) bastardo/a (!).

soda ['səudə] n (CHEM) soda; (also: ~ water) acqua di seltz; (US: also: ~ pop) gassosa.

sodden ['sɔdn] a fradicio(a).

sodium ['səudɪəm] n sodio.

sofa ['səufə] n sofà m inv.

soft [sɔft] a (not rough) morbido(a); (not hard) soffice; (not loud) sommesso(a); (kind) gentile; (weak) debole; (stupid) stupido(a); ~ **drink** n analcolico; ~**en** ['sɔfn] vt ammorbidire; addolcire; attenuare // vi ammorbidirsi; addolcirsi; attenuarsi; ~**ly** ad dolcemente; morbidamente; (weak) dolcezza; morbidezza.

software ['sɔftwɛə*] n (COMPUT) software m.

soggy ['sɔgɪ] a inzuppato(a).

soil [sɔɪl] n (earth) terreno, suolo // vt sporcare; (fig) macchiare.

solace ['sɔlɪs] n consolazione f.

solar ['səulə*] a solare.

sold [səuld] pt, pp of **sell**; ~ **out** a (COMM) esaurito(a).

solder ['səuldə*] vt saldare // n saldatura.

soldier ['səuldʒə*] n soldato, militare m.

sole [səul] n (of foot) pianta (del piede); (of shoe) suola; (fish: pl inv) sogliola // a solo(a), unico(a).

solemn ['sɔləm] a solenne; grave; serio(a).

sole trader n (COMM) commerciante m in proprio.

solicit [sə'lɪsɪt] vt (request) richiedere, sollecitare // vi (prostitute) adescare i passanti.

solicitor [sə'lɪsɪtə*] n (Brit: for wills etc) ≈ notaio; (: in court) ≈ avvocato.

solid ['sɔlɪd] a (not hollow) pieno(a); (strong, sound, reliable, not liquid) solido(a); (meal) sostanzioso(a) // n solido.

solidarity [sɔlɪ'dærɪtɪ] n solidarietà.

solitaire [sɔlɪ'tɛə*] n (games, gem) solitario.

solitary ['sɔlɪtərɪ] a solitario(a); ~ **confinement** n (LAW): in ~ **confinement** in cella d'isolamento.

solo ['səuləu] n assolo; ~**ist** n solista m/ f.

soluble ['sɔljubl] a solubile.

solution [sə'lu:ʃən] n soluzione f.

solve [sɔlv] vt risolvere.

solvent ['sɔlvənt] a (COMM) solvibile // n (CHEM) solvente m.

sombre, (US) **somber** ['sɔmbə*] a scuro(a); (mood, person) triste.

some [sʌm] ♦ a 1 (a certain amount or number of): ~ tea/water/cream del tè/ dell'acqua/della panna; ~ children/apples dei bambini/delle mele
2 (certain: in contrasts) certo(a); ~ people say that ... alcuni dicono che ..., certa gente dice che ...
3 (unspecified) un(a) certo(a), qualche; ~ woman was asking for you una tale chiedeva di lei; ~ day un giorno; ~ day next week un giorno della prossima settimana
♦ pronoun 1 (a certain number) alcuni(e), certi(e); I've got ~ (books etc) ne ho alcuni; ~ (of them) have been sold alcuni sono stati venduti
2 (a certain amount) un po'; I've got ~ (money, milk) ne ho un po'; I've read ~ of the book ho letto parte del libro
♦ ad: ~ 10 people circa 10 persone.

somebody ['sʌmbədɪ] pronoun = **someone.**

somehow ['sʌmhau] ad in un modo o nell'altro, in qualche modo; (for some reason) per qualche ragione.

someone ['sʌmwʌn] pronoun qualcuno.

someplace ['sʌmpleɪs] ad (US) = **somewhere.**

somersault ['sʌməsɔ:lt] n capriola; salto mortale // vi fare una capriola (or un salto mortale); (car) cappottare.

something ['sʌmθɪŋ] pronoun qualcosa, qualche cosa; ~ nice qualcosa di bello; ~ to do qualcosa da fare.

sometime ['sʌmtaɪm] ad (in future) una volta o l'altra; (in past): ~ last month durante il mese scorso.

sometimes ['sʌmtaɪmz] ad qualche volta.

somewhat ['sʌmwɔt] ad piuttosto.

somewhere ['sʌmwɛə*] ad in or da qualche parte.

son [sʌn] n figlio.

song [sɔŋ] n canzone f.

sonic ['sɔnɪk] a (boom) sonico(a).

son-in-law ['sʌnɪnlɔ:] n genero.

sonnet ['sɔnɪt] n sonetto.

sonny ['sʌnɪ] n (col) ragazzo mio.

soon [su:n] ad presto, fra poco; (early) presto; ~ afterwards poco dopo; as ~ as possible prima possibile; I'll do it as ~ as I can lo farò appena posso; ~er ad (time) prima; (preference): I would ~er do preferirei fare; ~er or later prima o poi.

soot [sut] n fuliggine f.

soothe [su:ð] vt calmare.

sophisticated [sə'fɪstɪkeɪtɪd] a sofisticato(a); raffinato(a); complesso(a).

sophomore ['sɔfəmɔ:*] n (US) studente/ essa del secondo anno.

sopping ['sɔpɪŋ] a (also: ~ wet) bagnato(a) fradicio(a).

soppy ['sɔpɪ] a (pej) sentimentale.

soprano [sə'prɑ:nəu] n (voice) soprano m; (singer) soprano m/f.

sorcerer ['sɔ:sərə*] n stregone m, mago.

sore [sɔ:*] a (painful) dolorante; (col: offended) offeso(a) // n piaga; ~**ly** ad (tempted) fortemente.

sorrow ['sɔrəu] n dolore m.

sorry ['sɔrɪ] a spiacente; (condition, excuse) misero(a); ~! scusa! (or scusi! or scusate!); to feel ~ for sb rincrescersi per qn.

sort [sɔ:t] n specie f, genere m // vt (also: ~ out: papers) classificare; ordinare; (: letters etc) smistare; (: problems) risolvere; ~**ing office** n ufficio m smistamento inv.

SOS n abbr (= save our souls) S.O.S. m inv.

so-so ['səusəu] ad così così.

sought [sɔ:t] pt, pp of **seek.**

soul [səul] n anima; ~-**destroying** a demoralizzante; ~**ful** a pieno(a) di sentimento.

sound [saund] a (healthy) sano(a); (safe, not damaged) solido(a), in buono stato; (reliable, not superficial) solido(a); (sensible) giudizioso(a), di buon senso // ad: ~ asleep profondamente addormentato // n (noise) suono; rumore m; (GEO) stretto // vt (alarm) suonare; (also: ~ out: opinions) sondare // vi suonare; (fig: seem) sembrare; to ~ like rassomigliare a; ~ barrier n muro del suono; ~ effects npl effetti sonori; ~**ly** ad (sleep) profondamente; (beat) duramente; ~**proof** vt insonorizzare, isolare acusticamente // a insonorizzato(a), isolato(a) acusticamente; ~**track** n (of film) colonna sonora.

soup [su:p] n minestra; brodo; zuppa; in the ~ (fig) nei guai; ~ **plate** n piatto fondo; ~**spoon** n cucchiaio da minestra.

sour ['sauə*] a aspro(a); (fruit) acerbo(a); (milk) acido(a), fermentato(a); (fig) arcigno(a); acido(a); it's ~ grapes è soltanto invidia.

source [sɔ:s] n fonte f, sorgente f; (fig) fonte.

south [sauθ] n sud m, meridione m, mezzogiorno // a del sud, sud inv, meridionale // ad verso sud; S~ **Africa** n Sudafrica m; S~ **African** a, n sudafricano(a); S~ **America** n Sudamerica m, America del sud; S~ **American** a, n sudamericano(a); ~-**east** n sud-est m; ~**erly** ['sʌðəlɪ] a del sud; ~**ern** ['sʌðən]

a del sud, meridionale; esposto(a) a
sud; **S~ Pole** *n* Polo Sud; **~ward(s)** *ad*
verso sud; **~-west** *n* sud-ovest *m*.

souvenir [su:vəˈnɪə*] *n* ricordo, souvenir
m inv.

sovereign [ˈsɔvrɪn] *a, n* sovrano(a).

soviet [ˈsəʊvɪət] *a* sovietico(a); **the S~
Union** l'Unione *f* Sovietica.

sow *n* [sau] scrofa // *vt* [səu] (*pt* **~ed**, *pp*
sown [səun]) seminare.

soya [ˈsɔɪə], (*US*) **soy** [sɔɪ] *n*: **~ bean** *n*
seme *m* di soia; **~ sauce** *n* salsa di
soia.

spa [spa:] *n* (*resort*) stazione *f* termale;
(*US*: *also*: **health ~**) centro di cure
estetiche.

space [speɪs] *n* spazio; (*room*) posto;
spazio; (*length of time*) intervallo // *cpd*
spaziale // *vt* (*also*: **~ out**) distanziare;
~craft *n* (*pl inv*) veicolo spaziale;
~man/woman *n* astronauta *m/f*, co-
smonauta *m/f*; **~ship** *n* = **~craft**; **spac-
ing** *n* spaziatura.

spacious [ˈspeɪʃəs] *a* spazioso(a),
ampio(a).

spade [speɪd] *n* (*tool*) vanga; pala;
(*child's*) paletta; **~s** *npl* (*CARDS*) picche
fpl.

Spain [speɪn] *n* Spagna.

span [spæn] *pt of* **spin** // *n* (*of bird,
plane*) apertura alare; (*of arch*)
campata; (*in time*) periodo; durata // *vt*
attraversare; (*fig*) abbracciare.

Spaniard [ˈspænjəd] *n* spagnolo/a.

spaniel [ˈspænjəl] *n* spaniel *m inv*.

Spanish [ˈspænɪʃ] *a* spagnolo(a) // *n*
(*LING*) spagnolo; **the ~** *npl* gli Spagnoli.

spank [spæŋk] *vt* sculacciare.

spanner [ˈspænə*] *n* (*Brit*) chiave *f* inglese.

spar [spa:*] *n* asta, palo // *vi* (*BOXING*)
allenarsi.

spare [spɛə*] *a* di riserva, di scorta;
(*surplus*) in più, d'avanzo // *n* (*part*)
pezzo di ricambio // *vt* (*do without*) fare
a meno di; (*afford to give*) concedere;
(*refrain from hurting, using*) risparmiare; **to ~** (*surplus*) d'avanzo; **~
part** *n* pezzo di ricambio; **~ time** *n*
tempo libero; **~ wheel** *n* (*AUT*) ruota di
scorta.

sparing [ˈspɛərɪŋ] *a*: **to be ~ with** sth risparmiare qc; **~ly** *ad* moderatamente.

spark [spa:k] *n* scintilla; **~(ing) plug** *n*
candela.

sparkle [ˈspa:kl] *n* scintillio, sfavillio // *vi*
scintillare, sfavillare; (*bubble*)
spumeggiare, frizzare; **sparkling** *a*
scintillante, sfavillante; (*wine*)
spumante.

sparrow [ˈspærəu] *n* passero.

sparse [spa:s] *a* sparso(a), rado(a).

spartan [ˈspa:tən] *a* (*fig*) spartano(a).

spasm [ˈspæzəm] *n* (*MED*) spasmo; (*fig*)
accesso, attacco; **~odic** [spæzˈmɔdɪk] *a*

spasmodico(a); (*fig*) intermittente.

spastic [ˈspæstɪk] *n* spastico/a.

spat [spæt] *pt, pp of* **spit**.

spate [speɪt] *n* (*fig*): **~ of** diluvio *or*
fiume *m* di; **in ~** (*river*) in piena.

spatter [ˈspætə*] *vt, vi* schizzare.

spawn [spɔ:n] *vt* deporre le uova // *vi* deporre le
uova // *n* uova *fpl*.

speak [spi:k], *pt* **spoke**, *pp* **spoken** *vt*
(*language*) parlare; (*truth*) dire // *vi*
parlare; **to ~ to** sb/of *or* about sth
parlare a qn/di qc; **~ up!** parla più
forte!; **~er** *n* (*in public*) oratore/trice;
(*also*: **loud~er**) altoparlante *m*; (*POL*):
the S~er *il presidente della Camera dei
Comuni* (*Brit*) *or dei Rappresentanti*
(*US*).

spear [spɪə*] *n* lancia; **~head** *vt* (*attack
etc*) condurre.

spec [spɛk] *n* (*col*): **on ~** sperando bene.

special [ˈspɛʃl] *a* speciale; **~ist** *n*
specialista *m/f*; **~ity** [spɛʃɪˈælɪtɪ] *n*
specialità *f inv*; **~ize** *vi*: **to ~ize** (**in**)
specializzarsi (in); **~ly** *ad* specialmente,
particolarmente.

species [ˈspi:ʃi:z] *n* (*pl inv*) specie *f inv*.

specific [spəˈsɪfɪk] *a* specifico(a);
preciso(a); **~ally** *ad* esplicitamente;
(*especially*) appositamente.

specimen [ˈspɛsɪmən] *n* esemplare *m*,
modello; (*MED*) campione *m*.

speck [spɛk] *n* puntino, macchiolina;
(*particle*) granello.

speckled [ˈspɛkld] *a* macchiettato(a).

specs [spɛks] *npl* (*col*) occhiali *mpl*.

spectacle [ˈspɛktəkl] *n* spettacolo; **~s** *npl*
(*glasses*) occhiali *mpl*; **spectacular**
[-ˈtækjulə*] *a* spettacolare // *n* (*CINEMA
etc*) film *m inv etc* spettacolare.

spectator [spɛkˈteɪtə*] *n* spettatore *m*.

spectre, (*US*) **specter** [ˈspɛktə*] *n* spettro.

spectrum, *pl* **spectra** [ˈspɛktrəm, -rə] *n*
spettro; (*fig*) gamma.

speculation [spɛkjuˈleɪʃən] *n*
speculazione *f*; congettura *fpl*.

speech [spi:tʃ] *n* (*faculty*) parola; (*talk*)
discorso; (*manner of speaking*) parlata;
(*enunciation*) elocuzione *f*; **~less** *a*
ammutolito(a), muto(a).

speed [spi:d] *n* velocità *f inv*;
(*promptness*) prontezza; **at full** *or* **top ~**
a tutta velocità; **to ~ up** *vi, vt*
accelerare; **~boat** *n* motoscafo; **~ily**
ad velocemente; prontamente; **~ing** *n*
(*AUT*) eccesso di velocità; **~ limit** *n*
limite *m* di velocità; **~ometer**
[spɪˈdɔmɪtə*] *n* tachimetro; **~way** *n*
(*SPORT*) pista per motociclismo; (*also*:
~way racing) corsa motociclistica (su
pista); **~y** *a* veloce, rapido(a);
pronto(a).

spell [spɛl] *n* (*also*: **magic ~**)
incantesimo; (*period of time*) (breve)
periodo // *vt* (*pt, pp* **spelt** (*Brit*) *or* **~ed**

[spelt, speld]) (*in writing*) scrivere (lettera per lettera); (*aloud*) dire lettera per lettera; (*fig*) significare; **to cast a ~ on sb** fare un incantesimo a qn; **he can't ~ fa** errori di ortografia; **~bound** *a* incantato(a); affascinato(a); **~ing** *n* ortografia.

spend, *pt, pp* **spent** [spend, spent] *vt* (*money*) spendere; (*time, life*) passare; **~thrift** *n* spendaccione/a.

sperm [spə:m] *n* sperma *m*.

spew [spju:] *vt* vomitare.

sphere [sfɪə*] *n* sfera.

spice [spaɪs] *n* spezia // *vt* aromatizzare.

spick-and-span ['spɪkən'spæn] *a* impeccabile.

spicy ['spaɪsɪ] *a* piccante.

spider ['spaɪdə*] *n* ragno.

spike [spaɪk] *n* punta.

spill, *pt, pp* **spilt** or **~ed** [spɪl, -t, -d] *vt* versare, rovesciare // *vi* versarsi, rovesciarsi, **to ~ over** *vi* (*liquid*) versarsi; (*crowd*) riversarsi.

spin [spɪn] *n* (*revolution of wheel*) rotazione *f*; (*AVIAT*) avvitamento; (*trip in car*) giretto // *vb* (*pt* **spun, span,** *pp* **spun**) *vt* (*wool etc*) filare; (*wheel*) far girare // *vi* girare; **to ~ out** *vt* far durare.

spinach ['spɪnɪtʃ] *n* spinacio; (*as food*) spinaci *mpl*.

spinal ['spaɪnl] *a* spinale; **~ cord** *n* midollo spinale.

spindly ['spɪndlɪ] *a* lungo(a) e sottile, filiforme.

spin-dryer [spɪn'draɪə*] *n* (*Brit*) centrifuga.

spine [spaɪn] *n* spina dorsale; (*thorn*) spina.

spinning ['spɪnɪŋ] *n* filatura; **~ top** *n* trottola; **~ wheel** *n* filatoio.

spin-off ['spɪnɔf] *n* applicazione *f* secondaria; (*product*) prodotto secondario.

spinster ['spɪnstə*] *n* nubile *f*; zitella.

spiral ['spaɪərl] *n* spirale *f* // *a* a spirale // *vi* (*fig*) salire a spirale; **~ staircase** *n* scala a chiocciola.

spire ['spaɪə*] *n* guglia.

spirit ['spɪrɪt] *n* (*soul*) spirito, anima; (*ghost*) spirito, fantasma *m*; (*mood*) stato d'animo, umore *m*; (*courage*) coraggio; **~s** *npl* (*drink*) alcolici *mpl*; **in good ~s** di buon umore; **~ed** *a* vivace, vigoroso(a); (*horse*) focoso(a); **~ level** *n* livella a bolla (d'aria).

spiritual ['spɪrɪtjuəl] *a* spirituale.

spit [spɪt] *n* (*for roasting*) spiedo // *vi* (*pt, pp* **spat**) sputare; (*fire, fat*) scoppiettare.

spite [spaɪt] *n* dispetto // *vt* contrariare, far dispetto a; **in ~ of** nonostante, malgrado; **~ful** *a* dispettoso(a).

spittle ['spɪtl] *n* saliva; sputo.

splash [splæʃ] *n* spruzzo; (*sound*) ciac *m*

inv; (*of colour*) schizzo // *vt* spruzzare // *vi* (*also*: **~ about**) sguazzare.

spleen [spli:n] *n* (*ANAT*) milza.

splendid ['splendɪd] *a* splendido(a), magnifico(a).

splint [splɪnt] *n* (*MED*) stecca.

splinter ['splɪntə*] *n* scheggia // *vi* scheggiarsi.

split [splɪt] *n* spaccatura; (*fig: division, quarrel*) scissione *f* // *vb* (*pt, pp* **split**) *vt* spaccare; (*party*) dividere; (*work, profits*) spartire, ripartire // *vi* (*divide*) dividersi; **to ~ up** *vi* (*couple*) separarsi, rompere; (*meeting*) sciogliersi.

splutter ['splʌtə*] *vi* farfugliare; sputacchiare.

spoil, *pt, pp* **spoilt** or **~ed** [spɔɪl, -t, -d] *vt* (*damage*) rovinare, guastare; (*mar*) sciupare; (*child*) viziare; **~s** *npl* bottino; **~sport** *n* guastafeste *m/f inv*.

spoke [spəuk] *pt of* **speak** // *n* raggio.

spoken ['spəukn] *pp of* **speak**.

spokesman ['spəuksmən], **spokeswoman** [-wumən] *n* portavoce *m/f inv*.

sponge [spʌndʒ] *n* spugna // *vt* spugnare, pulire con una spugna // *vi*; **to ~ off** or **on** scroccare a; **~ bag** *n* (*Brit*) nécessaire *m inv*; **~ (cake)** *n* pan *m* di Spagna.

sponsor ['spɔnsə*] *n* (*RADIO, TV, SPORT etc*) finanziatore/trice (a scopo pubblicitario) // *vt* sostenere; patrocinare; **~ship** *n* finanziamento (a scopo pubblicitario); patrocinio.

spontaneous [spɔn'teɪnɪəs] *a* spontaneo(a).

spooky ['spu:kɪ] *a* che fa accapponare la pelle.

spool [spu:l] *n* bobina.

spoon [spu:n] *n* cucchiaio; **~-feed** *vt* nutrire con il cucchiaio; (*fig*) imboccare; **~ful** *n* cucchiaiata.

sport [spɔ:t] *n* sport *m inv*; (*person*) persona di spirito // *vt* sfoggiare; **~ing** *a* sportivo(a); **to give sb a ~ing chance** dare a qn una possibilità (di vincere); **~ jacket** *n* (*US*) = **~s jacket**; **~s car** *n* automobile *f* sportiva; **~s jacket** *n* giacca sportiva; **~sman** *n* sportivo; **~smanship** *n* spirito sportivo; **~swear** *n* abiti *mpl* sportivi; **~swoman** *n* sportiva; **~y** *a* sportivo(a).

spot [spɔt] *n* punto; (*mark*) macchia; (*dot: on pattern*) pallino; (*pimple*) foruncolo; (*place*) posto; (*small amount*): **a ~ of** un po' di // *vt* (*notice*) individuare, distinguere; **on the ~** sul posto; su due piedi; **~ check** *n* controllo senza preavviso; **~less** *a* immacolato(a); **~light** *n* proiettore *m*; (*AUT*) faro ausiliario; **~ted** *a* macchiato(a); a puntini, a pallini; **~ty** *a* (*face*) foruncoloso(a).

spouse [spauz] *n* sposo/a.

spout [spaʊt] *n* (*of jug*) beccuccio; (*of liquid*) zampillo, getto // *vi* zampillare.

sprain [spreɪn] *n* storta, distorsione *f* // *vt*: **to ~ one's ankle** storcersi una caviglia.

sprang [spræŋ] *pt of* **spring**.

sprawl [sprɔ:l] *vi* sdraiarsi (in modo scomposto).

spray [spreɪ] *n* spruzzo; (*container*) nebulizzatore *m*, spray *m inv*; (*of flowers*) mazzetto // *vt* spruzzare; (*crops*) irrorare.

spread [spred] *n* diffusione *f*; (*distribution*) distribuzione *f*; (*CULIN*) pasta (da spalmare) // *vb* (*pt, pp* **spread**) *vt* (*cloth*) stendere, distendere; (*butter etc*) spalmare; (*disease, knowledge*) propagare, diffondere // *vi* stendersi, distendersi; spalmarsi; propagarsi, diffondersi; **~-eagled** ['spred:gld] *a* a gambe e braccia aperte; **~sheet** *n* (*COMPUT*) foglio elettronico ad espansione.

spree [spri:] *n*: **to go on a ~** fare baldoria.

sprightly ['spraɪtlɪ] *a* vivace.

spring [sprɪŋ] *n* (*leap*) salto, balzo; (*coiled metal*) molla; (*season*) primavera; (*of water*) sorgente *f* // *vi* (*pt* **sprang**, *pp* **sprung**) saltare, balzare; **to ~ from** provenire da; **to ~ up** *vi* (*problem*) presentarsi; **~board** *n* trampolino; **~-clean** *n* (*also:* **~-cleaning**) grandi pulizie *fpl* di primavera; **~time** *n* primavera; **~y** *a* elastico(a).

sprinkle ['sprɪŋkl] *vt* spruzzare; spargere; **to ~ water etc on, ~ with water etc** spruzzare dell'acqua *etc* su; **~ sugar etc on, ~ with sugar etc** spolverizzare di zucchero *etc*; **~r** *n* (*for lawn*) irrigatore *m*; (*to put out fire*) sprinkler *m inv*.

sprint [sprɪnt] *n* scatto // *vi* scattare; **~er** *n* (*SPORT*) velocista *m/f*.

sprout [spraʊt] *vi* germogliare; **~s** *npl* (*also:* **Brussels ~s**) cavolini *mpl* di Bruxelles.

spruce [spru:s] *n* abete *m* rosso // *a* lindo(a); azzimato(a).

sprung [sprʌŋ] *pp of* **spring**.

spry [spraɪ] *a* arzillo(a), sveglio(a).

spun [spʌn] *pt, pp cf* **spin**.

spur [spə:*] *n* sperone *m*; (*fig*) sprone *m*, incentivo // *vt* (*also:* **~ on**) spronare; **on the ~ of the moment** lì per lì.

spurious ['spjʊərɪəs] *a* falso(a).

spurn [spə:n] *vt* rifiutare con disprezzo, sdegnare.

spurt [spə:t] *vi* sgorgare; zampillare.

spy [spaɪ] *n* spia // *vi*: **to ~ on** spiare // *vt* (*see*) scorgere; **~ing** *n* spionaggio.

Sq. *abbr* (*in address*) = **square**.

sq. *abbr* (*MATH*) = **square**.

squabble ['skwɒbl] *vi* bisticciarsi.

squad [skwɒd] *n* (*MIL*) plotone *m*; (*POLICE*) squadra.

squadron ['skwɒdrn] *n* (*MIL*) squadrone *m*; (*AVIAT, NAUT*) squadriglia.

squalid ['skwɒlɪd] *a* sordido(a).

squall [skwɔ:l] *n* raffica; burrasca.

squalor ['skwɒlə*] *n* squallore *m*.

squander ['skwɒndə*] *vt* dissipare.

square [skwɛə*] *n* quadrato; (*in town*) piazza; (*instrument*) squadra // *a* quadrato(a); (*honest*) onesto(a); (*col: ideas, person*) di vecchio stampo // *vt* (*arrange*) regolare; (*MATH*) elevare al quadrato // *vi* (*agree*) quadrare; **all ~** pari; **a ~ meal** un pasto abbondante; **2 metres ~** di 2 metri per 2; **1 ~ metre** 1 metro quadrato; **~ly** *ad* diritto; fermamente.

squash [skwɒʃ] *n* (*SPORT*) squash *m*; (*Brit: drink*): **lemon/orange ~** sciroppo di limone/arancia // *vt* schiacciare.

squat [skwɒt] *a* tarchiato(a), tozzo(a) // *vi* accovacciarsi; **~ter** *n* occupante *m/f* abusivo(a).

squawk [skwɔ:k] *vi* emettere strida rauche.

squeak [skwi:k] *vi* squittire.

squeal [skwi:l] *vi* strillare.

squeamish ['skwi:mɪʃ] *a* schizzinoso(a); disgustato(a).

squeeze [skwi:z] *n* pressione *f*; (*also ECON*) stretta // *vt* premere; (*hand, arm*) stringere; **to ~ out** *vt* spremere.

squelch [skwɛltʃ] *vi* fare ciac; sguazzare.

squib [skwɪb] *n* petardo.

squid [skwɪd] *n* calamaro.

squiggle ['skwɪgl] *n* ghirigoro.

squint [skwɪnt] *vi* essere strabico(a) // *n*: **he has a ~** è strabico; **to ~ at sth** guardare qc di traverso; (*quickly*) dare un'occhiata a qc.

squire ['skwaɪə*] *n* (*Brit*) proprietario terriero.

squirm [skwə:m] *vi* contorcersi.

squirrel ['skwɪrəl] *n* scoiattolo.

squirt [skwə:t] *vi* schizzare; zampillare.

Sr *abbr* = **senior**.

St *abbr* = **saint, street**.

stab [stæb] *n* (*with knife etc*) pugnalata; (*col: try*): **to have a ~ at (doing) sth** provare a fare qc // *vt* pugnalare.

stable ['steɪbl] *n* (*for horses*) scuderia; (*for cattle*) stalla // *a* stabile.

stack [stæk] *n* catasta, pila // *vt* accatastare, ammucchiare.

stadium ['steɪdɪəm] *n* stadio.

staff [stɑ:f] *n* (*work force: gen*) personale *m*; (: *Brit SCOL*) personale insegnante; (: *servants*) personale di servizio; (*MIL*) stato maggiore; (*stick*) bastone *m* // *vt* fornire di personale.

stag [stæg] *n* cervo.

stage [steɪdʒ] *n* palcoscenico; (*profession*): **the ~** il teatro, la scena;

(*point*) punto; (*platform*) palco // vt
(*play*) allestire, mettere in scena;
(*demonstration*) organizzare; (*fig*:
perform: *recovery etc*) effettuare; **in ~s**
per gradi; a tappe; **~coach** n diligenza;
~ door n ingresso degli artisti; **~**
manager n direttore m di scena.

stagger ['stægə*] vi barcollare // vt
(*person*) sbalordire; (*hours, holidays*)
scaglionare.

stagnate [stæg'neɪt] vi stagnare.

stag party n festa di addio al celibato.

staid [steɪd] a posato(a), serio(a).

stain [steɪn] n macchia; (*colouring*)
colorante m // vt macchiare; (*wood*)
tingere; **~ed glass window** n vetrata;
~less (*steel*) inossidabile; **~ re-**
mover n smacchiatore m.

stair [steə*] n (*step*) gradino; **~s** npl
(*flight of ~s*) scale fpl, scala; **on the ~s**
sulle scale; **~case, ~way** n scale fpl,
scala.

stake [steɪk] n palo, piolo; (*BETTING*)
puntata, scommessa // vt (*bet*)
scommettere; (*risk*) rischiare; **to be at**
~ essere in gioco.

stale [steɪl] a (*bread*) raffermo(a),
stantio(a); (*beer*) svaporato(a); (*smell*)
di chiuso.

stalemate ['steɪlmeɪt] n stallo; (*fig*)
punto morto.

stalk [stɔːk] n gambo, stelo // vt inseguire
// vi camminare con sussiego.

stall [stɔːl] n bancarella; (*in stable*) box
m inv di stalla // vt (*AUT*) far spegnere //
vi (*AUT*) spegnersi, fermarsi; (*fig*) tem-
poreggiare; **~s** npl (*Brit*: *in cinema,
theatre*) platea.

stallion ['stæljən] n stallone m.

stalwart ['stɔːlwət] n membro fidato.

stamina ['stæmɪnə] n vigore m, resi
stenza.

stammer ['stæmə*] n balbuzie f // vi
balbettare.

stamp [stæmp] n (*postage ~*)
francobollo; (*implement*) timbro;
(*mark, also fig*) marchio, impronta; (*on
document*) bollo, timbro // vt (*also: ~*
one's foot) battere il piede // vt battere;
(*letter*) affrancare; (*mark with a ~*)
timbrare; **~ album** n album m inv per
francobolli; **~ collecting** n filatelia.

stampede [stæm'piːd] n fuggi fuggi m
inv.

stance [stæns] n posizione f.

stand [stænd] n (*position*) posizione f;
(*MIL*) resistenza; (*structure*) supporto,
sostegno; (*at exhibition*) stand m inv;
(*in shop*) banco; (*at market*)
bancarella; (*booth*) chiosco; (*SPORT*)
tribuna // vb (pt, pp **stood**) vi stare in
piedi; (*rise*) alzarsi in piedi; (*be placed*)
trovarsi // vt (*place*) mettere, porre;
(*tolerate, withstand*) resistere,
sopportare; **to make a ~** prendere

posizione; **to ~ for parliament** (*Brit*)
presentarsi come candidato (per il
parlamento); **to ~ by** vi (*be ready*)
tenersi pronto(a) // vt fus (*opinion*) sostenere; **to ~ down** vi (*withdraw*)
ritirarsi; **to ~ for** vt fus (*signify*) rappresentare, significare; (*tolerate*)
sopportare, tollerare; **to ~ in for** vt fus
sostituire; **to ~ out** vi (*be prominent*)
spiccare; **to ~ up** vi (*rise*) alzarsi in
piedi; **to ~ up for** vt fus difendere; **to**
~ up to vt fus tener testa a, resistere
a.

standard ['stændəd] n modello, standard
m inv; (*level*) livello; (*flag*) stendardo //
a (*size etc*) normale, standard inv; **~s**
npl (*morals*) principi mpl, valori mpl; **~**
lamp n (*Brit*) lampada a stelo; **~ of**
living n livello di vita.

stand-by ['stændbaɪ] n riserva, sostituto;
to be on ~ (*gen*) tenersi pronto(a);
(*doctor*) essere di guardia; **~ ticket** n
(*AVIAT*) biglietto senza garanzia.

stand-in ['stændɪn] n sostituto/a;
(*CINEMA*) controfigura.

standing ['stændɪŋ] a diritto(a), in piedi
// n rango, condizione f, posizione f; **of**
many years' ~ che esiste da molti anni;
~ order n (*Brit*: *at bank*) ordine m di
pagamento (permanente); **~ orders** npl
(*MIL*) regolamento; **~ room** n posto
all'impiedi.

standoffish [stænd'ɔfɪʃ] a scostante,
freddo(a).

standpoint ['stændpɔɪnt] n punto di vista.

standstill ['stændstɪl] n: **at a ~**
fermo(a); (*fig*) a un punto morto; **to**
come to a ~ fermarsi; giungere a un
punto morto.

stank [stæŋk] pt of **stink**.

staple ['steɪpl] n (*for papers*) graffetta //
a (*food etc*) di base // vt cucire; **~r** n
cucitrice f.

star [stɑː*] n stella; (*celebrity*) divo/a;
(*principal actor*) vedette f inv // vi: **to ~**
(in) essere il (or la) protagonista (di) //
vt (*CINEMA*) essere interpretato(a) da.

starboard ['stɑːbəd] n dritta.

starch [stɑːtʃ] n amido.

stardom ['stɑːdəm] n celebrità.

stare [steə*] n sguardo fisso // vi: **to ~ at**
fissare.

starfish ['stɑːfɪʃ] n stella di mare.

stark [stɑːk] a (*bleak*) desolato(a) // ad:
~ naked completamente nudo(a).

starling ['stɑːlɪŋ] n storno.

starry ['stɑːrɪ] a stellato(a); **~-eyed** a
(*innocent*) ingenuo(a).

start [stɑːt] n inizio; (*of race*) partenza;
(*sudden movement*) sobbalzo // vt
cominciare, iniziare // vi cominciare; (*on
journey*) partire, mettersi in viaggio;
(*jump*) sobbalzare; **to ~ doing** or **to do**
sth (in)cominciare a fare qc; **to ~ off**

vi cominciare; (*leave*) partire; **to ~ up** *vi* cominciare; (*car*) avviarsi // *vt* iniziare; (*car*) avviare; **~er** *n* (*AUT*) motorino d'avviamento; (*SPORT: official*) starter *m inv*; (: *runner, horse*) partente *m/f*; (*Brit CULIN*) primo piatto; **~ing point** *n* punto di partenza.

startle ['sta:tl] *vt* far trasalire.

starvation [sta:'veɪʃən] *n* fame *f*, inedia.

starve [sta:v] *vi* morire di fame; soffrire la fame // *vt* far morire di fame, affamare.

state [steɪt] *n* stato // *vt* dichiarare, affermare; annunciare; **the S~s** (*USA*) gli Stati Uniti; **to be in a ~** essere agitato(a); **~ly** *a* maestoso(a), imponente; **~ment** *n* dichiarazione *f*; (*LAW*) deposizione *f*; **~sman** *n* statista *m*.

static ['stætɪk] *n* (*RADIO*) scariche *fpl* // *a* statico(a).

station ['steɪʃən] *n* stazione *f*; (*rank*) rango, condizione *f* // *vt* collocare, disporre.

stationary ['steɪʃənərɪ] *a* fermo(a), immobile.

stationer ['steɪʃənə*] *n* cartolaio/a; **~'s (shop)** *n* cartoleria; **~y** *n* articoli *mpl* di cancelleria.

station master *n* (*RAIL*) capostazione *m*.

station wagon *n* (*US*) giardinetta.

statistic [stə'tɪstɪk] *n* statistica; **~s** *n* (*science*) statistica.

statue ['stætju:] *n* statua.

status ['steɪtəs] *n* posizione *f*, condizione *f* sociale; prestigio; stato; **~ symbol** *n* simbolo di prestigio.

statute ['stætju:t] *n* legge *f*; **~s** *npl* (*of club etc*) statuto; **statutory** *a* stabilito(a) dalla legge, statutario(a).

staunch [stɔ:ntʃ] *a* fidato(a), leale.

stave [steɪv] *n* (*MUS*) rigo // *vt*: **to ~ off** (*attack*) respingere; (*threat*) evitare.

stay [steɪ] *n* (*period of time*) soggiorno, permanenza // *vi* rimanere; (*reside*) alloggiare, stare; (*spend some time*) trattenersi, soggiornare; **to ~ put** non muoversi; **to ~ with friends** stare presso amici; **to ~ the night** passare la notte; **to ~ behind** *vi* restare indietro; **to ~ in** *vi* (*at home*) stare in casa; **to ~ on** *vi* restare, rimanere; **to ~ out** *vi* (*of house*) rimanere fuori (di casa); **to ~ up** *vi* (*at night*) rimanere alzato(a); **~ing power** *n* capacità di resistenza.

stead [stɛd] *n*: **in sb's ~** al posto di qn; **to stand sb in good ~** essere utile a qn.

steadfast ['stɛdfɑ:st] *a* fermo(a), risoluto(a).

steadily ['stɛdɪlɪ] *ad* continuamente; (*walk*) con passo sicuro.

steady ['stɛdɪ] *a* stabile, solido(a), fermo(a); (*regular*) costante; (*person*) calmo(a), tranquillo(a) // *vt* stabilizzare;

calmare; **to ~ oneself** ritrovare l'equilibrio.

steak [steɪk] *n* (*meat*) bistecca; (*fish*) trancia.

steal [sti:l], *pt* **stole**, *pp* **stolen** *vt, vi* rubare.

stealth [stɛlθ] *n*: **by ~** furtivamente; **~y** *a* furtivo(a).

steam [sti:m] *n* vapore *m* // *vt* trattare con vapore; (*CULIN*) cuocere a vapore // *vi* fumare; (*ship*): **to ~ along** filare; **~ engine** *n* macchina a vapore; (*RAIL*) locomotiva a vapore; **~er** *n* piroscafo, vapore *m*; **~roller** *n* rullo compressore; **~ship** *n* = **~er**; **~y** *a* (*room*) pieno(a) di vapore; (*window*) appannato(a).

steel [sti:l] *n* acciaio // *cpd* di acciaio; **~works** *n* acciaieria.

steep [sti:p] *a* ripido(a), scosceso(a); (*price*) eccessivo(a) // *vt* inzuppare; (*washing*) mettere a mollo.

steeple ['sti:pl] *n* campanile *m*.

steer [stɪə*] *n* manzo // *vt* (*ship*) governare; (*car*) guidare // *vi* (*NAUT: person*) governare; (: *ship*) rispondere al timone; (*car*) guidarsi; **~ing** *n* (*AUT*) sterzo; **~ing wheel** *n* volante *m*.

stem [stɛm] *n* (*of flower, plant*) stelo; (*of tree*) fusto; (*of glass*) gambo; (*of fruit, leaf*) picciolo // *vt* contenere, arginare; **to ~ from** *vt fus* provenire da, derivare da.

stench [stɛntʃ] *n* puzzo, fetore *m*.

stencil ['stɛnsl] *n* (*of metal, cardboard*) stampino, mascherina; (*in typing*) matrice *f*.

stenographer [stɛ'nɔgrəfə*] *n* (*US*) stenografo/a.

step [stɛp] *n* passo; (*stair*) gradino, scalino; (*action*) mossa, azione *f* // *vi*: **to ~ forward** fare un passo avanti; **~s** *npl* (*Brit*) = **stepladder**; **to be in/out of ~ (with)** stare/non stare al passo (con); **to ~ down** *vi* (*fig*) ritirarsi; **to ~ off** *vt fus* scendere da; **to ~ up** *vt* aumentare; intensificare; **~brother** *n* fratellastro; **~daughter** *n* figliastra; **~father** *n* patrigno; **~ladder** *n* scala a libretto; **~mother** *n* matrigna; **~ping stone** *n* pietra di un guado; (*fig*) trampolino; **~sister** *n* sorellastra; **~son** *n* figliastro.

stereo ['stɛrɪəu] *n* (*system*) sistema *m* stereofonico; (*record player*) stereo *m inv* // *a* (*also*: **~phonic**) stereofonico(a).

sterile ['stɛraɪl] *a* sterile; **sterilize** ['stɛrɪlaɪz] *vt* sterilizzare.

sterling ['stə:lɪŋ] *a* (*gold, silver*) di buona lega; (*fig*) autentico(a), genuino(a) // *n* (*ECON*) (lira) sterlina; **a pound ~** una lira sterlina.

stern [stə:n] *a* severo(a) // *n* (*NAUT*) poppa.

stew [stju:] *n* stufato // *vt, vi* cuocere in

umido.

steward ['stju:əd] n (AVIAT, NAUT, RAIL) steward m inv; (in club etc) dispensiere m; **~ess** n assistente f di volo, hostess f inv.

stick [stɪk] n bastone m; (of rhubarb, celery) gambo // vb (pt, pp **stuck**) vt (glue) attaccare; (thrust): **to ~ sth into** conficcare or piantare or infiggere qc in; (col: put) ficcare; (col: tolerate) sopportare // vi conficcarsi; tenere; (remain) restare, rimanere; **to ~ out, to ~ up** vi sporgere, spuntare; **to ~ up for** vt fus difendere; **~er** n cartellino adesivo; **~ing plaster** n cerotto adesivo.

stickler ['stɪklə*] n: **to be a ~ for** essere pignolo(a) su, tenere molto a.

stick-up ['stɪkʌp] n rapina a mano armata.

sticky ['stɪkɪ] a attaccaticcio(a), vischioso(a); (label) adesivo(a).

stiff [stɪf] a rigido(a), duro(a); (muscle) legato(a), indolenzito(a); (difficult) difficile, arduo(a); (cold) freddo(a), formale; (strong) forte; (high: price) molto alto(a); **~en** vt irrigidire; rinforzare // vi irrigidirsi; indurirsi; **~ neck** n torcicollo.

stifle ['staɪfl] vt soffocare.

stigma ['stɪgmə] n (BOT, fig) stigma m; **~ta** [stɪg'mɑ:tə] npl (REL) stigmate fpl.

stile [staɪl] n cavalcasiepe m; cavalcasteccato.

stiletto [stɪ'letəu] n (Brit: also: **~ heel**) tacco a spillo.

still [stɪl] a fermo(a); silenzioso(a) // ad (up to this time, even) ancora; (nonetheless) tuttavia, ciò nonostante; **~born** a nato(a) morto(a); **~ life** n natura morta.

stilt [stɪlt] n trampolo; (pile) palo.

stilted ['stɪltɪd] a freddo(a), formale; artificiale.

stimulate ['stɪmjuleɪt] vt stimolare.

stimulus, pl **stimuli** ['stɪmjuləs, 'stɪmjulaɪ] n stimolo.

sting [stɪŋ] n puntura; (organ) pungiglione m // vt (pt, pp **stung**) pungere.

stingy ['stɪndʒɪ] a spilorcio(a), tirchio(a).

stink [stɪŋk] n fetore m, puzzo // vi (pt **stank**, pp **stunk**) puzzare; **~ing** a (fig: col): a **~ing ...** uno schifo di ..., un(a) maledetto(a) ... .

stint [stɪnt] n lavoro, compito // vi: **to ~ on** lesinare su.

stir [stə:*] n agitazione f, clamore m // vt rimescolare; (move) smuovere, agitare // vi muoversi; **to ~ up** vt provocare, suscitare.

stirrup ['stɪrəp] n staffa.

stitch [stɪtʃ] n (SEWING) punto; (KNITTING) maglia; (MED) punto (di sutura); (pain) fitta // vt cucire, attaccare; suturare.

stoat [stəut] n ermellino.

stock [stɔk] n riserva, provvista; (COMM) giacenza, stock m inv; (AGR) bestiame m; (CULIN) brodo; (FINANCE) titoli mpl, azioni fpl // a (fig: reply etc) consueto(a); classico(a) // vt (have in stock) avere, vendere; **well-~ed** ben fornito(a); **in ~** in magazzino; **out of ~** esaurito(a); **to take ~ of** (fig) fare il punto di; **~s and shares** valori mpl di borsa; **to ~ up** vi: **to ~ up (with)** fare provvista (di).

stockbroker ['stɔkbrəukə*] n agente m di cambio.

stock cube n (Brit) dado.

stock exchange n Borsa (valori).

stocking ['stɔkɪŋ] n calza.

stockist ['stɔkɪst] n (Brit) fornitore m.

stock: ~ market n Borsa, mercato finanziario; **~ phrase** n cliché m inv; **~pile** n riserva // vt accumulare riserve di; **~taking** n (Brit COMM) inventario.

stocky ['stɔkɪ] a tarchiato(a), tozzo(a).

stodgy ['stɔdʒɪ] a pesante, indigesto(a).

stoke [stəuk] vt alimentare.

stole [stəul] pt of **steal** // n stola.

stolen ['stəuln] pp of **steal**.

stolid ['stɔlɪd] a impassibile.

stomach ['stʌmək] n stomaco; (abdomen) ventre m // vt sopportare, digerire; **~ ache** n mal m di stomaco.

stone [stəun] n pietra; (pebble) sasso, ciottolo; (in fruit) nocciolo; (MED) calcolo; (Brit: weight) = 6.348 kg.; 14 libbre // cpd di pietra // vt lapidare; **~cold** a gelido(a); **~deaf** a sordo(a) come una campana; **~work** n muratura.

stood [stud] pt, pp of **stand**.

stool [stu:l] n sgabello.

stoop [stu:p] vi (also: **have a ~**) avere una curvatura; (bend) chinarsi, curvarsi.

stop [stɔp] n arresto; (stopping place) fermata; (in punctuation) punto // vt arrestare, fermare; (break off) interrompere; (also: **put a ~ to**) porre fine a // vi fermarsi; (rain, noise etc) cessare, finire; **to ~ doing sth** cessare or finire di fare qc; **to ~ dead** fermarsi di colpo; **to ~ off** vi sostare brevemente; **to ~ up** vt (hole) chiudere, turare; **~gap** n (person) tappabuchi m/f inv; (measure) ripiego; **~lights** npl (AUT) stop mpl; **~over** n breve sosta; (AVIAT) scalo.

stoppage ['stɔpɪdʒ] n arresto, fermata; (of pay) trattenuta; (strike) interruzione f del lavoro.

stopper ['stɔpə*] n tappo.

stop press n ultimissime fpl.

stopwatch ['stɔpwɔtʃ] n cronometro.

storage ['stɔ:rɪdʒ] n immagazzinamento; (COMPUT) memoria; **~ heater** n radiatore m elettrico che accumula calore.

store [stɔ:*] n provvista, riserva; (depot)
deposito; (Brit: department ~) grande
magazzino; (US: shop) negozio // vt
immagazzinare; ~s npl (provisions)
rifornimenti mpl, scorte fpl; **to ~ up** vt
mettere in serbo, conservare; **~room** n
dispensa.

storey, (US) **story** ['stɔ:rɪ] n piano.

stork [stɔ:k] n cicogna.

storm [stɔ:m] n tempesta, temporale m,
burrasca; uragano // vi (fig) infuriarsi //
vt prendere d'assalto; **~y** a tempe-
stoso(a), burrascoso(a).

story ['stɔ:rɪ] n storia; favola; racconto;
(US) = **storey**; **~book** n libro di
racconti.

stout [staut] a solido(a), robusto(a);
(brave) coraggioso(a); (fat) corpulen-
to(a), grasso(a) // n birra scura.

stove [stəuv] n (for cooking) fornello; (:
small) fornelletto; (for heating) stufa.

stow [stəu] vt mettere via; **~away** n
passeggero/a clandestino/a.

straddle ['strædl] vt stare a cavalcioni di.

straggle ['strægl] vi crescere (or
estendersi) disordinatamente; trascinarsi; rimanere indietro; **~r** n
sbandato/a.

straight [streɪt] a dritto(a); (frank) one-
sto(a), franco(a) // ad diritto; (drink) liscio // n: **the ~** la linea retta; (RAIL) il
rettilineo; (SPORT) la dirittura d'arrivo;
to put or **get ~** mettere in ordine,
mettere ordine in; **~ away**, **~ off** (at
once) immediatamente; **~en** vt (also:
~en out) raddrizzare; **~-faced** a
impassibile, imperturbabile; **~forward**
a semplice; onesto(a), franco(a).

strain [streɪn] n (TECH) sollecitazione f;
(physical) sforzo; (mental) tensione f;
(MED) strappo; distorsione f; (streak,
trace) tendenza; elemento // vt tendere;
(muscle) sforzare; (ankle) storcere;
(friendship, marriage) mettere a dura
prova; (filter) colare, filtrare // vi
sforzarsi; ~s npl (MUS) note fpl; **~ed** a
(laugh etc) forzato(a); (relations)
teso(a); **~er** n passino, colino.

strait [streɪt] n (GEO) stretto; **~jacket** n
camicia di forza; **~-laced** a bac-
chettone(a).

strand [strænd] n (of thread) filo; **~ed** a
nei guai; senza mezzi di trasporto.

strange [streɪndʒ] a (not known) scono-
sciuto(a); (odd) strano(a), bizzarro(a);
~r n sconosciuto/a; estraneo/a.

strangle ['stræŋgl] vt strangolare; **~hold**
n (fig) stretta (mortale).

strap [stræp] n cinghia; (of slip, dress)
spallina, bretella // vt legare con una cinghia; (child etc) punire (con una cinghia).

strategic [strə'ti:dʒɪk] a strategico(a).

strategy ['strætɪdʒɪ] n strategia.

straw [strɔ:] n paglia; (drinking ~)
cannuccia; that's the last ~! è la goccia
che fa traboccare il vaso!

strawberry ['strɔ:bərɪ] n fragola.

stray [streɪ] a (animal) randagio(a) // vi
perdersi; **~ bullet** n proiettile m
vagante.

streak [stri:k] n striscia; (fig: of madness
etc): **a ~ of** una vena di // vt striare,
screziare // vi: **to ~ past** passare come
un fulmine.

stream [stri:m] n ruscello; corrente f; (of
people) fiume m // vt (SCOL) dividere in
livelli di rendimento // vi scorrere; **to ~
in/out** entrare/uscire a fiotti.

streamer ['stri:mə*] n (of paper) stella
filante.

streamlined ['stri:mlaɪnd] a
aerodinamico(a), affusolato(a); (fig)
razionalizzato(a).

street [stri:t] n strada, via // cpd stradale,
di strada; **~car** n (US) tram m inv; **~
lamp** n lampione m; **~ plan** n pianta
(di una città); **~wise** a (col) esperto(a)
dei bassifondi.

strength [streŋθ] n forza; (of girder,
knot etc) resistenza, solidità; **~en** vt
rinforzare; fortificare; consolidare.

strenuous ['strenjuəs] a vigoroso(a),
energico(a); (tiring) duro(a), pesante.

stress [stres] n (force, pressure)
pressione f; (mental strain) tensione f;
(accent) accento // vt insistere su,
sottolineare.

stretch [stretʃ] n (of sand etc) distesa //
vi stirarsi; (extend): **to ~ to** or **as far as**
estendersi fino a // vt tendere, allungare;
(spread) distendere; (fig) spingere (al
massimo); **to ~ out** vi allungarsi,
estendersi // vt (arm etc) allungare,
tendere; (to spread) distendere.

stretcher ['stretʃə*] n barella, lettiga.

strewn [stru:n] a: **~ with** cosparso(a) di.

stricken ['strɪkən] a (person) provato(a);
(city, industry etc) colpito(a); **~ with**
(disease etc) colpito(a) da.

strict [strɪkt] a (severe) rigido(a),
severo(a); (precise) preciso(a),
stretto(a).

stride [straɪd] n passo lungo // vi (pt
strode, pp **stridden** [strəud, 'strɪdn])
camminare a grandi passi.

strife [straɪf] n conflitto; litigi mpl.

strike [straɪk] n sciopero; (of oil etc)
scoperta; (attack) attacco // vb (pt, pp
struck) vt colpire; (oil etc) scoprire,
trovare // vi far sciopero, scioperare;
(attack) attaccare; (clock) suonare; **on
~** (workers) in sciopero; **to ~ a match**
accendere un fiammifero; **to ~ down**
vt (fig) atterrare; **to ~ out** vt
depennare; **to ~ up** vt (MUS)
attaccare; **to ~ up a friendship** fare
amicizia con; **~r** n scioperante m/f;
(SPORT) attaccante m; **striking** a che

colpisce.

string [strɪŋ] n spago; (row) fila; sequenza; catena; (MUS) corda // vt (pt, pp **strung**): to ~ out disporre di fianco; to ~ **together** (words, ideas) mettere insieme; the ~s npl (MUS) gli archi; to **pull** ~s **for sb** (fig) raccomandare qn; ~ **bean** n fagiolino; ~**(ed) instrument** n (MUS) strumento a corda.

stringent ['strɪndʒənt] a rigoroso(a); (reasons, arguments) stringente, impellente.

strip [strɪp] n striscia // vt spogliare; (also: ~ **down**: machine) smontare // vi spogliarsi; ~ **cartoon** n fumetto.

stripe [straɪp] n striscia, riga; ~**d** a a strisce or righe.

strip lighting n illuminazione f al neon.

stripper ['strɪpə*] n spogliarellista.

striptease ['strɪptiːz] n spogliarello.

strive [straɪv], pt **strove**, pp **striven** [straɪv, strəʊv, 'strɪvn] vi: to ~ to do sforzarsi di fare.

strode [strəʊd] pt of **stride**.

stroke [strəʊk] n colpo; (MED) colpo apoplettico; (caress) carezza // vt accarezzare; at a ~ in un attimo.

stroll [strəʊl] n giretto, passeggiatina // vi andare a spasso; ~**er** n (US) passeggino.

strong [strɒŋ] a (gen) forte; (sturdy: table, fabric etc) solido(a); they are 50 ~ sono in 50; ~**box** n cassaforte f; ~**hold** n fortezza, roccaforte f; ~**ly** ad fortemente, con forza; energicamente; vivamente; ~**room** n camera di sicurezza.

strove [strəʊv] pt of **strive**.

struck [strʌk] pt, pp of **strike**.

structural ['strʌktʃərəl] a strutturale; (CONSTR) di costruzione; di struttura.

structure ['strʌktʃə*] n struttura; (building) costruzione f, fabbricato.

struggle ['strʌgl] n lotta // vi lottare.

strum [strʌm] vt (guitar) strimpellare.

strung [strʌŋ] pt, pp of **string**.

strut [strʌt] n sostegno, supporto // vi pavoneggiarsi.

stub [stʌb] n mozzicone m; (of ticket etc) matrice f, talloncino // vt: to ~ **one's toe** urtare or sbattere il dito del piede; **to ~ out** vt schiacciare.

stubble ['stʌbl] n stoppia; (on chin) barba ispida.

stubborn ['stʌbən] a testardo(a), ostinato(a).

stuck [stʌk] pt, pp of **stick** // a (jammed) bloccato(a); ~-**up** a presuntuoso(a).

stud [stʌd] n bottoncino; borchia; (of horses) scuderia, allevamento di cavalli; (also: ~ **horse**) stallone m // vt (fig): ~**ded with** tempestato(a) di.

student ['stjuːdənt] n studente/essa // cpd studentesco(a); universitario(a); degli studenti; ~ **driver** n (US) conducente

m/f principiante.

studio ['stjuːdɪəʊ] n studio; ~ **flat**, (US) ~ **apartment** n appartamento monolocale.

studious ['stjuːdɪəs] a studioso(a); (studied) studiato(a), voluto(a); ~**ly** ad (carefully) deliberatamente, di proposito.

study ['stʌdɪ] n studio // vt studiare; esaminare // vi studiare.

stuff [stʌf] n cosa, roba; (belongings) cose fpl, roba; (substance) sostanza, materiale m // vt imbottire; (CULIN) farcire; ~**ing** n imbottitura; (CULIN) ripieno; ~**y** a (room) mal ventilato(a), senz'aria; (ideas) antiquato(a).

stumble ['stʌmbl] vi inciampare; to ~ **across** (fig) imbattersi in; **stumbling block** n ostacolo, scoglio.

stump [stʌmp] n ceppo; (of limb) moncone m // vt sconcertare, lasciare perplesso(a).

stun [stʌn] vt stordire; (amaze) sbalordire.

stung [stʌŋ] pt, pp of **sting**.

stunk [stʌŋk] pp of **stink**.

stunt [stʌnt] n bravata; trucco pubblicitario; (AVIAT) acrobazia // vt arrestare; ~**ed** a stentato(a), rachitico(a); ~**man** n cascatore m.

stupefy ['stjuːpɪfaɪ] vt stordire; intontire; (fig) stupire.

stupendous [stjuː'pendəs] a stupendo(a), meraviglioso(a).

stupid ['stjuːpɪd] a stupido(a); ~**ity** [-'pɪdɪtɪ] n stupidità f inv, stupidaggine f.

stupor ['stjuːpə*] n torpore m.

sturdy ['stəːdɪ] a robusto(a), vigoroso(a); solido(a).

sturgeon ['stəːdʒən] n storione m.

stutter ['stʌtə*] n balbuzie f // vi balbettare.

sty [staɪ] n (of pigs) porcile m.

stye [staɪ] n (MED) orzaiolo.

style [staɪl] n stile m; (distinction) eleganza, classe f; **stylish** a elegante; **stylist** n (hair stylist) parrucchiere/a.

stylus ['staɪləs] n (of record player) puntina.

suave [swɑːv] a untuoso(a).

sub... [sʌb] prefix sub..., sotto...; ~**conscious** a, n subcosciente (m); ~**contract** n subappaltare.

subdue [səb'djuː] vt sottomettere, soggiogare; ~**d** a pacato(a); (light) attenuato(a); (person) poco esuberante.

subject n ['sʌbdʒɪkt] soggetto; (citizen etc) cittadino/a; (SCOL) materia // vt [səb'dʒɛkt]: to ~ to sottomettere a; esporre a; to be ~ to (law) essere sottomesso(a) a; (disease) essere soggetto(a) a; ~**ive** [-'dʒɛktɪv] a soggettivo(a); ~ **matter** n argomento; contenuto.

subjunctive [səb'dʒʌŋktɪv] a

congiuntivo(a) // n congiuntivo.

sublet [sʌb'lɛt] vt subaffittare.

submachine gun ['sʌbmə'ʃiːn-] n mitra m inv.

submarine [sʌbmə'riːn] n sommergibile m.

submerge [səb'məːdʒ] vt sommergere; immergere // vi immergersi.

submission [səb'mɪʃən] n sottomissione f.

submissive [səb'mɪsɪv] a remissivo(a).

submit [səb'mɪt] vt sottomettere // vi sottomettersi.

subnormal [sʌb'nɔːməl] a subnormale.

subordinate [sə'bɔːdɪnət] a, n subordinato(a).

subpoena [səb'piːnə] n (LAW) citazione f, mandato di comparizione.

subscribe [səb'skraɪb] vi contribuire; to ~ to (opinion) approvare, condividere; (fund) sottoscrivere; (newspaper) abbonarsi a; essere abbonato(a) a; ~r (to periodical, telephone) abbonato/a.

subscription [səb'skrɪpʃən] n sottoscrizione f; abbonamento.

subsequent ['sʌbsɪkwənt] a successivo(a), seguente; conseguente; ~ly ad in seguito, successivamente.

subside [səb'saɪd] vi cedere, abbassarsi; (flood) decrescere; (wind) calmarsi; ~nce [-'saɪdns] n cedimento, abbassamento.

subsidiary [səb'sɪdɪərɪ] a sussidiario(a); accessorio(a) // n filiale f.

subsidize ['sʌbsɪdaɪz] vt sovvenzionare.

subsidy ['sʌbsɪdɪ] n sovvenzione f.

subsistence [səb'sɪstəns] n esistenza; mezzi mpl di sostentamento.

substance ['sʌbstəns] n sostanza; (fig) essenza.

substantial [səb'stænʃl] a solido(a); (amount, progress etc) notevole; (meal) sostanzioso(a).

substantiate [səb'stænʃɪeɪt] vt comprovare.

substitute ['sʌbstɪtjuːt] n (person) sostituto/a; (thing) succedaneo, surrogato // vt: to ~ sth/sb for sostituire qc/qn a.

subterfuge ['sʌbtəfjuːdʒ] n sotterfugio.

subterranean [sʌbtə'reɪnɪən] a sotterraneo(a).

subtitle ['sʌbtaɪtl] n (CINEMA) sottotitolo.

subtle ['sʌtl] a sottile.

subtotal [sʌb'təʊtl] n somma parziale.

subtract [səb'trækt] vt sottrarre; ~ion [-'trækʃən] n sottrazione f.

suburb ['sʌbəːb] n sobborgo; the ~s la periferia; ~an [sə'bəːbən] a suburbano(a); ~ia n periferia, sobborghi mpl.

subversive [səb'vəːsɪv] a sovversivo(a).

subway ['sʌbweɪ] n (US: underground) metropolitana; (Brit: underpass) sottopassaggio.

succeed [sək'siːd] vi riuscire; avere successo // vt succedere a; to ~ in doing riuscire a fare; ~ing a (following) successivo(a).

success [sək'sɛs] n successo; ~ful a (venture) coronato(a) da successo, riuscito(a); to be ~ful (in doing) riuscire (a fare); ~fully ad con successo.

succession [sək'sɛʃən] n successione f.

successive [sək'sɛsɪv] a successivo(a); consecutivo(a).

succumb [sə'kʌm] vi soccombere.

such [sʌtʃ] a tale; (of that kind): ~ a book un tale libro, un libro del genere; ~ books tali libri, libri del genere; (so much): ~ courage tanto coraggio // ad talmente, così; ~ a long trip un viaggio così lungo; ~ good books libri così buoni; ~ a lot of talmente or così tanto(a); ~ as (like) come; a noise ~ as to un rumore tale da; as ~ ad come or in quanto tale; ~-and-~ a tale (after noun).

suck [sʌk] vt succhiare; (breast, bottle) poppare; ~er n (ZOOL, TECH) ventosa; (BOT) pollone m; (col) gonzo/a, babbeo/a.

suction ['sʌkʃən] n succhiamento; (TECH) aspirazione f.

sudden ['sʌdn] a improvviso(a); all of a ~ improvvisamente, all'improvviso; ~ly ad bruscamente, improvvisamente, di colpo.

suds [sʌdz] npl schiuma (di sapone).

sue [suː] vt citare in giudizio.

suede [sweɪd] n pelle f scamosciata // cpd scamosciato(a).

suet ['suːɪt] n grasso di rognone.

suffer ['sʌfə*] vt soffrire, patire; (bear) sopportare, tollerare // vi soffrire; ~er n malato/a; ~ing n sofferenza.

suffice [sə'faɪs] vi essere sufficiente, bastare.

sufficient [sə'fɪʃənt] a sufficiente; ~ money abbastanza soldi; ~ly ad sufficientemente, abbastanza.

suffocate ['sʌfəkeɪt] vi (have difficulty breathing) soffocare; (die through lack of air) asfissiare.

suffused [sə'fjuːzd] a: ~ with (colour) tinto(a) di; the room was ~ with light nella stanza c'era una luce soffusa.

sugar ['ʃʊgə*] n zucchero // vt zuccherare; ~ beet n barbabietola da zucchero; ~ cane n canna da zucchero; ~y a zuccherino(a), dolce; (fig) sdolcinato(a).

suggest [sə'dʒɛst] vt proporre, suggerire; indicare; ~ion [-'dʒɛstʃən] n suggerimento, proposta.

suicide ['sʊɪsaɪd] n (person) suicida m/f; (act) suicidio.

suit [suːt] n (man's) vestito; (woman's) completo, tailleur m inv; (CARDS) seme m, colore m // vt andar bene a or per;

essere adatto(a) a *or* per; (*adapt*): to ~ sth to adattare qc a; **~able** *a* adatto(a); appropriato(a); **~ably** *ad* (*dress*) in modo adatto; (*thank*) adeguatamente.

suitcase ['su:tkeɪs] *n* valigia.

suite [swi:t] *n* (*of rooms*) appartamento; (*MUS*) suite *f inv*; (*furniture*): bedroom/ dining room ~ arredo *or* mobilia per la camera da letto/sala da pranzo.

suitor ['su:tə*] *n* corteggiatore *m*, spasimante *m*.

sulfur ['sʌlfə*] *n* (*US*) = **sulphur**.

sulk [sʌlk] *vi* fare il broncio; **~y** *a* imbronciato(a).

sullen ['sʌlən] *a* scontroso(a); cupo(a).

sulphur, (*US*) **sulfur** ['sʌlfə*] *n* zolfo.

sultana [sʌl'tɑ:nə] *n* (*fruit*) uva (secca) sultanina.

sultry ['sʌltrɪ] *a* afoso(a).

sum [sʌm] *n* somma; (*SCOL etc*) addizione *f*; **to ~ up** *vt, vi* riassumere.

summarize ['sʌmərauz] *vt* riassumere, riepilogare.

summary ['sʌmərɪ] *n* riassunto // *a* (*justice*) sommario(a.).

summer ['sʌmə*] *n* estate *f* // *cpd* d'estate, estivo(a); **~house** *n* (*in garden*) padiglione *m*; **~time** *n* (*season*) estate *f*; **~ time** *n* (*by clock*) ora legale (estiva).

summit ['sʌmɪt] *n* cima, sommità; (*POL*) vertice *m*.

summon ['sʌmən] *vt* chiamare, convocare; **to ~ up** *vt* raccogliere, fare appello a; **~s** *n* ordine *m* di comparizione // *vt* citare.

sump [sʌmp] *n* (*Brit AUT*) coppa dell'olio.

sumptuous ['sʌmptjuəs] *a* sontuoso(a).

sun [sʌn] *n* sole *m*; in the ~ al sole; **~bathe** *vi* prendere un bagno di sole; **~burn** *n* abbronzatura; (*painful*) scottatura; ~ **cream** *n* crema solare.

Sunday ['sʌndɪ] *n* domenica; ~ **school** *n* = scuola di catechismo.

sundial ['sʌndaɪəl] *n* meridiana.

sundown ['sʌndaun] *n* tramonto.

sundry ['sʌndrɪ] *a* vari(e), diversi(e); all and ~ tutti quanti; **sundries** *npl* articoli diversi, cose diverse.

sunflower ['sʌnflauə*] *n* girasole *m*.

sung [sʌŋ] *pp* of **sing**.

sunglasses ['sʌnglɑ:sɪz] *npl* occhiali *mpl* da sole.

sunk [sʌŋk] *pp* of **sink**.

sun: ~light *n* (luce *f* del) sole *m*; **~ny** *a* assolato(a), soleggiato(a); (*fig*) allegro(a), felice; **~rise** *n* levata del sole, alba; ~ **roof** *n* (*AUT*) tetto apribile; **~set** *n* tramonto; **~shade** *n* parasole *m*; **~shine** *n* (luce *f* del) sole *m*; **~stroke** *n* insolazione *f*, colpo di sole; **~tan** *n* abbronzatura; **~tan oil** *n* olio solare.

super ['su:pə*] *a* (*col*) fantastico(a).

superannuation [su:pərænju'eɪʃən] *n* contributi *mpl* pensionistici; pensione *f*.

superb [su:'pə:b] *a* magnifico(a).

supercilious [su:pə'sɪlɪəs] *a* sprezzante, sdegnoso(a).

superficial [su:pə'fɪʃəl] *a* superficiale.

superhuman [su:pə'hju:mən] *a* sovrumano(a).

superimpose ['su:pərɪm'pəuz] *vt* sovrapporre.

superintendent [su:pərɪn'tɛndənt] *n* direttore/trice; (*POLICE*) ≈ commissario (capo).

superior [su'pɪərɪə*] *a, n* superiore (*m/ f*); **~ity** [-'ɔrɪtɪ] *n* superiorità.

superlative [su'pə:lətɪv] *a* superlativo(a), supremo(a) // *n* (*LING*) superlativo.

superman ['su:pəmæn] *n* superuomo.

supermarket ['su:pəmɑ:kɪt] *n* supermercato.

supernatural [su:pə'nætʃərəl] *a* soprannaturale.

superpower ['su:pəpauə*] *n* (*POL*) superpotenza.

supersede [su:pə'si:d] *vt* sostituire, soppiantare.

superstitious [su:pə'stɪʃəs] *a* superstizioso(a).

supervise ['su:pəvaɪz] *vt* (*person etc*) sorvegliare; (*organization*) soprintendere a; **supervision** [-'vɪʒən] *n* sorveglianza; supervisione *f*; **supervisor** *n* sorvegliante *m/f*; soprintendente *m/f*; (*in shop*) capocommesso/a.

supine ['su:paɪn] *a* supino(a).

supper ['sʌpə*] *n* cena.

supplant [sə'plɑ:nt] *vt* (*person, thing*) soppiantare.

supple ['sʌpl] *a* flessibile; agile.

supplement *n* ['sʌplɪmənt] supplemento // *vt* [sʌplɪ'mɛnt] completare, integrare; **~ary** [-'mɛntərɪ] *a* supplementare.

supplier [sə'plaɪə*] *n* fornitore *m*.

supply [sə'plaɪ] *vt* (*provide*) fornire; (*equip*): to ~ (**with**) approvvigionare (di); attrezzare (con) // *n* riserva, provvista; (*supplying*) approvvigionamento; (*TECH*) alimentazione *f*; **supplies** *npl* (*food*) viveri *mpl*; (*MIL*) sussistenza; ~ **teacher** *n* (*Brit*) supplente *m/f*.

support [sə'pɔ:t] *n* (*moral, financial etc*) sostegno, appoggio; (*TECH*) supporto // *vt* sostenere; (*financially*) mantenere; (*uphold*) sostenere, difendere; **~er** *n* (*POL etc*) sostenitore/trice, fautore/trice; (*SPORT*) tifoso/a.

suppose [sə'pəuz] *vt, vi* supporre; immaginare; to be **~d** to do essere tenuto(a) a fare; **~dly** [sə'pəuzɪdlɪ] *ad* presumibilmente; (*seemingly*) apparentemente; **supposing** *cj* se, ammesso che + *sub*.

suppress [sə'prɛs] *vt* reprimere; sop-

primere; tenere segreto(a).
supreme [su'pri:m] *a* supremo(a).
surcharge ['sə:tʃɑːdʒ] *n* supplemento; (*extra tax*) soprattassa.
sure [ʃuə*] *a* sicuro(a); (*definite, convinced*) sicuro(a), certo(a); ~! (*of course*) senz'altro!, certo!; ~ **enough** infatti; **to make** ~ **of sth/that** assicurarsi di qc/che; ~**ly** *ad* sicuramente; certamente.
surety ['ʃuərəti] *n* garanzia.
surf [sə:f] *n* (*waves*) cavalloni *mpl*; (*foam*) spuma.
surface ['sə:fɪs] *n* superficie *f* // *vt* (*road*) asfaltare // *vi* risalire alla superficie; (*fig: person*) venire a galla, farsi vivo(a); ~ **mail** *n* posta ordinaria.
surfboard ['sə:fbɔːd] *n* tavola per surfing.
surfeit ['sə:fɪt] *n*: **a** ~ **of** un eccesso di; un'indigestione di.
surfing ['sə:fɪŋ] *n* surfing *m*.
surge [sə:dʒ] *n* (*strong movement*) ondata; (*of feeling*) impeto // *vi* (*waves*) gonfiarsi; (*ELEC: power*) aumentare improvvisamente; (*people*) riversarsi.
surgeon ['sə:dʒən] *n* chirurgo.
surgery ['sə:dʒərɪ] *n* chirurgia; (*Brit: room*) studio *or* gabinetto medico, ambulatorio; **to undergo** ~ subire un intervento chirurgico; ~ **hours** *npl* (*Brit*) orario delle visite *or* di consultazione.
surgical ['sə:dʒɪkl] *a* chirurgico(a); ~ **spirit** *n* (*Brit*) alcool *m* denaturato.
surly ['sə:lɪ] *a* scontroso(a), burbero(a).
surname ['sə:neɪm] *n* cognome *m*.
surpass [sə:'pɑːs] *vt* superare.
surplus ['sə:pləs] *n* eccedenza; (*ECON*) surplus *m inv* // *a* eccedente, d'avanzo.
surprise [sə'praɪz] *n* sorpresa; (*astonishment*) stupore *m* // *vt* sorprendere; stupire; **surprising** *a* sorprendente, stupefacente; **surprisingly** *ad* (*easy, helpful*) sorprendentemente.
surrender [sə'rendə*] *n* resa, capitolazione *f* // *vi* arrendersi.
surreptitious [sʌrəp'tɪʃəs] *a* furtivo(a).
surrogate ['sʌrəgɪt] *n* surrogato; ~ **mother** *n* madre *f* sostitutiva.
surround [sə'raund] *vt* circondare; (*MIL etc*) accerchiare; ~**ing** *a* circostante; ~**ings** *npl* dintorni *mpl*; (*fig*) ambiente *m*.
surveillance [sə:'veɪləns] *n* sorveglianza, controllo.
survey *n* ['sə:veɪ] quadro generale; (*study*) esame *m*; (*in housebuying etc*) perizia; (*of land*) rilevamento, rilievo topografico // *vt* [sə:'veɪ] osservare; esaminare; valutare; rilevare; ~**or** *n* perito; geometra *m*; (*of land*) agrimensore *m*.
survival [sə'vaɪvl] *n* sopravvivenza; (*relic*) reliquia, vestigio.

survive [sə'vaɪv] *vi* sopravvivere // *vt* sopravvivere a; **survivor** *n* superstite *m/f*, sopravvissuto/a.
susceptible [sə'septəbl] *a*: ~ (**to**) sensibile (a); (*disease*) predisposto(a) (a).
suspect *a*, *n* ['sʌspekt] *a* sospetto(a) // *n* persona sospetta // *vt* [səs'pekt] sospettare; (*think likely*) supporre; (*doubt*) dubitare.
suspend [səs'pend] *vt* sospendere; ~**ed sentence** *n* condanna con la condizionale; ~**er belt** *n* reggicalze *m inv*; ~**ers** *npl* (*Brit*) giarrettiere *fpl*; (*US*) bretelle *fpl*.
suspense [səs'pens] *n* apprensione *f*; (*in film etc*) suspense *m*.
suspension [səs'penʃən] *n* (*gen AUT*) sospensione *f*; (*of driving licence*) ritiro temporaneo; ~ **bridge** *n* ponte *m* sospeso.
suspicion [səs'pɪʃən] *n* sospetto.
suspicious [səs'pɪʃəs] *a* (*suspecting*) sospettoso(a); (*causing suspicion*) sospetto(a).
sustain [səs'teɪn] *vt* sostenere; sopportare; (*LAW: charge*) confermare; (*suffer*) subire; ~**ed** *a* (*effort*) prolungato(a).
sustenance ['sʌstɪnəns] *n* nutrimento; mezzi *mpl* di sostentamento.
swab [swɔb] *n* (*MED*) tampone *m*.
swagger ['swægə*] *vi* pavoneggiarsi.
swallow ['swɔləu] *n* (*bird*) rondine *f* // *vt* inghiottire; (*fig: story*) bere; **to** ~ **up** *vt* inghiottire.
swam [swæm] *pt of* **swim**.
swamp [swɔmp] *n* palude *f* // *vt* sommergere.
swan [swɔn] *n* cigno.
swap [swɔp] *vt*: **to** ~ (**for**) scambiare (con).
swarm [swɔːm] *n* sciame *m* // *vi* formicolare; (*bees*) sciamare.
swarthy ['swɔːðɪ] *a* di carnagione scura.
swastika ['swɔstɪkə] *n* croce *f* uncinata, svastica.
swat [swɔt] *vt* schiacciare.
sway [sweɪ] *vi* (*building*) oscillare; (*tree*) ondeggiare; (*person*) barcollare // *vt* (*influence*) influenzare, dominare.
swear [swɛə*], *pt* **swore**, *pp* **sworn** *vi* (*witness etc*) giurare; (*curse*) bestemmiare, imprecare; **to** ~ **to sth** giurare qc; ~**word** *n* parolaccia.
sweat [swet] *n* sudore *m*, traspirazione *f* // *vi* sudare.
sweater ['swetə*] *n* maglione *m*.
sweatshirt ['swetʃə:t] *n* felpa.
sweaty ['swetɪ] *a* sudato(a); bagnato(a) di sudore.
Swede [swi:d] *n* svedese *m/f*.
swede [swi:d] *n* (*Brit*) rapa svedese.
Sweden ['swi:dn] *n* Svezia.
Swedish ['swi:dɪʃ] *a* svedese // *n* (*LING*)

svedese m.

sweep [swi:p] n spazzata; (curve) curva; (expanse) distesa; (range) portata; (also: chimney ~) spazzacamino // vb (pt, pp swept) vt spazzare, scopare // vi camminare maestosamente; precipitarsi, lanciarsi; (e)stendersi; **to ~ away** vt spazzare via; trascinare via; **to ~ past** vi sfrecciare accanto; passare accanto maestosamente; **to ~ up** vt, vi spazzare; ~ing a (gesture) largo(a); circolare; a ~ing statement un'affermazione generica.

sweet [swi:t] n (Brit: pudding) dolce m; (candy) caramella // a dolce; (fresh) fresco(a); (fig) piacevole; delicato(a), grazioso(a); gentile; ~corn n granturco dolce; ~en vt addolcire; zuccherare; ~heart n innamorato/a; ~ness n sapore m dolce; dolcezza; ~ pea n pisello odoroso.

swell [swel] n (of sea) mare m lungo // a (col: excellent) favoloso(a) // vb (pt ~ed, pp swollen, ~ed) vt gonfiare, ingrossare; aumentare // vi gonfiarsi, ingrossarsi; (sound) crescere; (MED) gonfiarsi; ~ing n (MED) tumefazione f, gonfiore m.

sweltering ['sweltəriŋ] a soffocante.

swept [swept] pt, pp of sweep.

swerve [swə:v] vi deviare; (driver) sterzare; (boxer) scartare.

swift [swift] n (bird) rondone m // a rapido(a), veloce.

swig [swig] n (col: drink) sorsata.

swill [swil] n broda // vt (also: ~ out, ~ down) risciacquare.

swim [swim] n: to go for a ~ andare a fare una nuotata // vb (pt swam, pp swum) vi nuotare; (SPORT) fare del nuoto; (head, room) girare // vt (river, channel) attraversare or percorrere a nuoto; (length) nuotare; ~mer n nuotatore/trice; ~ming n nuoto; ~ming cap n cuffia; ~ming costume n (Brit) costume m da bagno; ~ming pool n piscina; ~suit n costume m da bagno.

swindle ['swindl] n truffa // vt truffare.

swine [swain] n (pl inv) maiale m, porco; (col!) porco(!).

swing [swiŋ] n altalena; (movement) oscillazione f; (MUS) ritmo; swing m // vb (pt, pp swung) vt dondolare, far oscillare; (also: ~ round) far girare // vi oscillare, dondolare; (also: ~ round: object) roteare; (: person) girarsi, voltarsi; **to be in full ~** (activity) essere in piena attività; (party etc) essere nel pieno; **~ door**, (US) **~ing door** n porta battente.

swingeing ['swindʒiŋ] a (Brit: defeat) violento(a); (: price increase) enorme.

swipe [swaip] vt (hit) colpire con forza; dare uno schiaffo a; (col: steal) sgraffi-gnare.

swirl [swə:l] vi turbinare, far mulinello.

swish [swiʃ] a (col: smart) all'ultimo grido, alla moda // vi sibilare.

Swiss [swis] a, n (pl inv) svizzero(a).

switch [switʃ] n (for light, radio etc) interruttore m; (change) cambiamento // vt (change) cambiare; scambiare; **to ~ off** vt spegnere; **to ~ on** vt accendere; (engine, machine) mettere in moto, avviare; ~board n (TEL) centralino.

Switzerland ['switsələnd] n Svizzera.

swivel ['swivl] vi (also: ~ round) girare.

swollen ['swəulən] pp of swell.

swoon [swu:n] vi svenire.

swoop [swu:p] vi (also: ~ down) scendere in picchiata, piombare.

swop [swɔp] n, vt = swap.

sword [sɔ:d] n spada; ~fish n pesce m spada inv.

swore [swɔ:*] pt of swear.

sworn [swɔ:n] pp of swear.

swot [swɔt] vt sgobbare su // vi sgobbare.

swum [swam] pp of swim.

swung [swʌŋ] pt, pp of swing.

syllable ['siləbl] n sillaba.

syllabus ['siləbəs] n programma m.

symbol ['simbl] n simbolo.

symmetry ['simitri] n simmetria.

sympathetic [simpə'θetik] a (showing pity) compassionevole; (kind) comprensivo(a); ~ towards ben disposto(a) verso.

sympathize ['simpəθaiz] vi: to ~ with sb compatire qn; partecipare al dolore di qn; ~r n (POL) simpatizzante m/f.

sympathy ['simpəθi] n compassione f; in ~ with d'accordo con; (strike) per solidarietà con; **with our deepest ~** con le nostre più sincere condoglianze.

symphony ['simfəni] n sinfonia.

symptom ['simptəm] n sintomo; indizio.

synagogue ['sinəgɔg] n sinagoga.

syndicate ['sindikit] n sindacato.

synonym ['sinənim] n sinonimo.

synopsis, pl **synopses** [si'nɔpsis, -si:z] n sommario, sinossi f inv.

syntax ['sintæks] n sintassi f inv.

synthesis, pl **syntheses** ['sinθəsis, -si:z] n sintesi f inv.

synthetic [sin'θetik] a sintetico(a).

syphilis ['sifilis] n sifilide f.

syphon ['saifən] n, vb = siphon.

Syria ['siriə] n Siria.

syringe [si'rindʒ] n siringa.

syrup ['sirəp] n sciroppo; (also: golden ~) melassa raffinata.

system ['sistəm] n sistema m; (order) metodo; (ANAT) organismo; ~atic [-'mætik] a sistematico(a); metodico(a); ~ disk n (COMPUT) disco del sistema; ~s analyst n analista m programmatore.

T

ta [tɑ:] *excl* (*Brit col*) grazie!

tab [tæb] *n* (*loop on coat etc*) laccetto; (*label*) etichetta; **to keep ~s on** (*fig*) tenere d'occhio.

tabby ['tæbɪ] *n* (*also:* ~ **cat**) (gatto) soriano, gatto tigrato.

table ['teɪbl] *n* tavolo, tavola // *vt* (*Brit: motion etc*) presentare; **to lay** *or* **set the** ~ apparecchiare *or* preparare la tavola; ~**cloth** *n* tovaglia; ~ **of contents** *n* indice *m*; ~ **d'hôte** [tɑ:bl'dəut] *a* (*meal*) a prezzo fisso; ~ **lamp** *n* lampada da tavolo; ~**mat** *n* sottopiatto; ~**spoon** *n* cucchiaio da tavola; (*also:* ~**spoonful:** *as measurement*) cucchiaiata.

tablet ['tæblɪt] *n* (*MED*) compressa; (: *for sucking*) pastiglia; (*for writing*) blocco; (*of stone*) targa.

table: ~ **tennis** *n* tennis *m* da tavolo, ping-pong *m* ®; ~ **wine** *n* vino da tavola.

tabulate ['tæbjuleɪt] *vt* (*data, figures*) tabulare, disporre in tabelle.

tacit ['tæsɪt] *a* tacito(a).

tack [tæk] *n* (*nail*) bulletta; (*stitch*) punto d'imbastitura; (*NAUT*) bordo, bordata // *vt* imbullettare; imbastire // *vi* bordeggiare.

tackle ['tækl] *n* attrezzatura, equipaggiamento; (*for lifting*) paranco; (*RUGBY*) placcaggio // *vt* (*difficulty*) affrontare; (*RUGBY*) placcare.

tacky ['tækɪ] *a* colloso(a), appiccicaticcio(a); ancora bagnato(a).

tact [tækt] *n* tatto; ~**ful** *a* delicato(a), discreto(a).

tactical ['tæktɪkl] *a* tattico(a).

tactics ['tæktɪks] *n, npl* tattica.

tactless ['tæktlɪs] *a* che manca di tatto.

tadpole ['tædpəul] *n* girino.

taffy ['tæfɪ] *n* (*US*) caramella *f* mou *inv*.

tag [tæg] *n* etichetta; **to ~ along** *vi* seguire.

tail [teɪl] *n* coda; (*of shirt*) falda // *vt* (*follow*) seguire, pedinare; **to ~ away**, ~ **off** *vi* (*in size, quality etc*) diminuire gradatamente; ~**back** *n* (*Brit AUT*) ingorgo; ~ **coat** *n* marsina; ~ **end** *n* (*of train, procession etc*) coda; (*of meeting etc*) fine *f*; ~**gate** *n* (*AUT*) portellone *m* posteriore.

tailor ['teɪlə*] *n* sarto; ~**ing** *n* (*cut*) stile *m*; ~**made** *a* (*also fig*) fatto(a) su misura.

tailwind ['teɪlwɪnd] *n* vento di coda.

tainted ['teɪntɪd] *a* (*food*) guasto(a); (*water, air*) infetto(a); (*fig*) corrotto(a).

take, *pt* **took**, *pp* **taken** [teɪk, tuk, 'teɪkn] *vt* prendere; (*gain: prize*) ottenere, vincere; (*require: effort, courage*) occorrere, volerci; (*tolerate*) accettare, sopportare; (*hold: passengers etc*) contenere; (*accompany*) accompagnare; (*bring, carry*) portare; (*exam*) sostenere, presentarsi a; **I ~ it** that suppongo che; **to ~ for a walk** (*child, dog*) portare a fare una passeggiata; **to ~ after** *vt fus* assomigliare a; **to ~ apart** *vt* smontare; **to ~ away** *vt* portare via; togliere; **to ~ back** *vt* (*return*) restituire; riportare; (*one's words*) ritirare; **to ~ down** *vt* (*building*) demolire; (*letter etc*) scrivere; **to ~ in** *vt* (*deceive*) imbrogliare, abbindolare; (*understand*) capire; (*include*) comprendere, includere; (*lodger*) prendere, ospitare; **to ~ off** *vi* (*AVIAT*) decollare // *vt* (*remove*) togliere; (*imitate*) imitare; **to ~ on** *vt* (*work*) accettare, intraprendere; (*employee*) assumere; (*opponent*) sfidare, affrontare; **to ~ out** *vt* portare fuori; (*remove*) togliere; (*licence*) prendere, ottenere; **to ~ sth out of sth** (*drawer, pocket etc*) tirare qc fuori da qc; estrarre qc da qc; **to ~ over** *vt* (*business*) rilevare // *vi*: **to ~ over from** sb prendere le consegne *or* il controllo da qn; **to ~ to** *vt fus* (*person*) prendere in simpatia; (*activity*) prendere gusto a; **to ~ up** *vt* (*one's story*) riprendere; (*dress*) accorciare; (*occupy: time, space*) occupare; (*engage in: hobby etc*) mettersi a; ~**away** *a* (*food*) da portar via; ~**home pay** *n* stipendio netto; ~**off** *n* (*AVIAT*) decollo; ~**out** *a* (*US*) = ~**away**; ~**over** *n* (*COMM*) assorbimento.

takings ['teɪkɪŋz] *npl* (*COMM*) incasso.

talc [tælk] *n* (*also:* ~**um powder**) talco.

tale [teɪl] *n* racconto, storia; (*pej*) fandonia; **to tell ~s** (*fig: to teacher, parent etc*) fare la spia.

talent ['tælnt] *n* talento; ~**ed** *a* di talento.

talk [tɔ:k] *n* discorso; (*gossip*) chiacchiere *fpl*; (*conversation*) conversazione *f*; (*interview*) discussione *f* // *vi* (*chatter*) chiacchierare; ~**s** *npl* (*POL etc*) colloqui *mpl*; **to ~ about** parlare di; (*converse*) discorrere *or* conversare su; **to ~ sb out of/into doing** dissuadere qn da/convincere qn a fare; **to ~ shop** parlare del lavoro *or* degli affari; **to ~ over** *vt* discutere; ~**ative** *a* loquace, ciarliero(a); ~ **show** *n* conversazione *f* televisiva, talk show *m inv*.

tall [tɔ:l] *a* alto(a); **to be 6 feet ~** ≈ essere alto 1 metro e 80; ~**boy** *n* (*Brit*) cassettone *m* alto; ~ **story** *n* panzana, frottola.

tally ['tælɪ] *n* conto, conteggio // *vi*: **to ~ (with)** corrispondere (a).

talon ['tælən] *n* artiglio.

tambourine [tæmbə'ri:n] *n* tamburello.

tame [teɪm] *a* addomesticato(a); (*fig:*

story, style) insipido(a), scialbo(a).

tamper ['tæmpə*] *vi:* to ~ with manomettere.

tampon ['tæmpon] *n* tampone *m*.

tan [tæn] *n (also:* sun~) abbronzatura // *vt* abbronzare // *vi* abbronzarsi // *a (colour)* marrone rossiccio *inv*.

tang [tæŋ] *n* odore *m* penetrante; sapore *m* piccante.

tangent ['tændʒənt] *n (MATH)* tangente *f*; to go off at a ~ *(fig)* partire per la tangente.

tangerine [tændʒə'ri:n] *n* mandarino.

tangle ['tæŋgl] *n* groviglio // *vt* aggrovigliare.

tank [tæŋk] *n* serbatoio; *(for processing)* vasca; *(for fish)* acquario; *(MIL)* carro armato.

tanker ['tæŋkə*] *n (ship)* nave *f* cisterna *inv*; *(truck)* autobotte *f*, autocisterna.

tantalizing ['tæntəlaɪzɪŋ] *a* allettante.

tantamount ['tæntəmaunt] *a:* ~ to equivalente a.

tantrum ['tæntrəm] *n* accesso di collera.

tap [tæp] *n (on sink etc)* rubinetto; *(gentle blow)* colpetto // *vt* dare un colpetto a; *(resources)* sfruttare, utilizzare; *(telephone)* mettere sotto controllo; on ~ *(fig: resources)* a disposizione; ~ **dancing** *n* tip tap *m*.

tape [teɪp] *n* nastro; *(also: magnetic* ~) nastro (magnetico) // *vt (record)* registrare (su nastro); ~ **measure** *n* metro a nastro.

taper ['teɪpə*] *n* candelina // *vi* assottigliarsi.

tape recorder *n* registratore *m* (a nastro).

tapestry ['tæpɪstrɪ] *n* arazzo; tappezzeria.

tar [tɑ:*] *n* catrame *m*.

target ['tɑ:gɪt] *n* bersaglio; *(fig: objective)* obiettivo.

tariff ['tærɪf] *n (COMM)* tariffa; *(taxes)* tariffe *fpl* doganali.

tarmac ['tɑ:mæk] *n (Brit: on road)* macadam *m* al catrame; *(AVIAT)* pista di decollo.

tarnish ['tɑ:nɪʃ] *vt* offuscare, annerire; *(fig)* macchiare.

tarpaulin [tɑ:'pɔ:lɪn] *n* tela incatramata.

tarragon ['tærəgən] *n* dragoncello.

tart [tɑ:t] *n (CULIN)* crostata; *(Brit col: pej: woman)* sgualdrina // *a (flavour)* aspro(a), agro(a); to ~ up *vt (col):* to ~ o.s. up farsi bello(a); *(pej)* agghindarsi.

tartan ['tɑ:tn] *n* tartan *m inv*.

tartar ['tɑ:tə*] *n (on teeth)* tartaro; ~ **sauce** *n* salsa tartara.

task [tɑ:sk] *n* compito; to take to ~ rimproverare; ~ **force** *n (MIL, POLICE)* unità operativa.

tassel ['tæsl] *n* fiocco.

taste [teɪst] *n* gusto; *(flavour)* sapore *m*, gusto; *(fig: glimpse, idea)* idea // *vt* gu-

stare; *(sample)* assaggiare // *vi:* to ~ of *(fish etc)* sapere or avere sapore di; it ~s like fish sa di pesce; can I have a ~ of this wine? posso assaggiare un po' di questo vino?; to have a ~ for sth avere un'inclinazione per qc; in good/bad ~ di buon/cattivo gusto; ~**ful** *a* di buon gusto; ~**less** *a (food)* insipido(a); *(remark)* di cattivo gusto; **tasty** *a* saporito(a), gustoso(a).

tatters ['tætəz] *npl:* in ~ *(also:* tattered) a brandelli, sbrindellato(a).

tattoo [tə'tu:] *n* tatuaggio; *(spectacle)* parata militare // *vt* tatuare.

taught [tɔ:t] *pt, pp of* **teach**.

taunt [tɔ:nt] *n* scherno // *vt* schernire.

Taurus ['tɔ:rəs] *n* Toro.

taut [tɔ:t] *a* teso(a).

tawdry ['tɔ:drɪ] *a* pacchiano(a).

tax [tæks] *n (on goods)* imposta; *(on services)* tassa; *(on income)* imposte *fpl*, tasse *fpl* // *vt* tassare; *(fig: strain: patience etc)* mettere alla prova; ~**able** *a (income)* imponibile; ~**ation** [-'seɪʃən] *n* tassazione *f*; tasse *fpl*, imposte *fpl*; ~ **avoidance** *n* l'evitare legalmente il pagamento di imposte; ~ **collector** *n* esattore *m* delle imposte; ~ **disc** *n (Brit AUT)* ≈ bollo; ~ **evasion** *n* evasione *f* fiscale; ~**-free** *a* esente da imposte.

taxi ['tæksɪ] *n* taxi *m inv* // *vi (AVIAT)* rullare; ~ **driver** *n* tassista *m/f*; ~ **rank** *(Brit)*, ~ **stand** *n* posteggio dei taxi.

tax: ~ **payer** *n* contribuente *m/f*; ~ **relief** *n* agevolazioni *fpl* fiscali; ~ **return** *n* dichiarazione *f* dei redditi.

TB *n abbr* = **tuberculosis**.

tea [ti:] *n* tè *m inv*; *(Brit: snack: for children)* merenda; **high** ~ *(Brit)* cena leggera *(presa nel tardo pomeriggio)*; ~ **bag** *n* bustina di tè; ~ **break** *n (Brit)* intervallo per il tè.

teach [ti:tʃ], *pt, pp* **taught** *vt:* to ~ sb sth, ~ sth to sb insegnare qc a qn // *vi* insegnare; ~**er** *n* insegnante *m/f*; *(in secondary school)* professore/essa, *(in primary school)* maestro/a; ~**ing** *n* insegnamento.

tea cosy *n* copriteiera *m inv*.

teacup ['ti:kʌp] *n* tazza da tè.

teak [ti:k] *n* teak *m*.

team [ti:m] *n* squadra; *(of animals)* tiro; ~**work** *n* lavoro di squadra.

teapot ['ti:pɔt] *n* teiera.

tear *n* [tɛə*] strappo; [tɪə*] lacrima // *vb* [tɛə*] *(pt* tore, *pp* torn) *vt* strappare // *vi* strapparsi; in ~s in lacrime; to ~ **along** *vi (rush)* correre all'impazzata; to ~ up *vt (sheet of paper etc)* strappare; ~**ful** *a* piangente, lacrimoso(a); ~ **gas** *n* gas *m* lacrimogeno.

tearoom ['ti:ru:m] *n* sala da tè.

tease [ti:z] *vt* canzonare; *(unkindly)*

tormentare.
tea set n servizio da tè.
teaspoon ['ti:spu:n] n cucchiaino da tè; (also: ~**ful**: as measurement) cucchiaino.
teat [ti:t] n capezzolo.
teatime ['ti:taim] n ora del tè.
tea towel n (Brit) strofinaccio (per i piatti).
technical ['tɛknɪkl] a tecnico(a); ~**ity** [-'kælɪtɪ] n tecnicità; (detail) dettaglio tecnico.
technician [tɛk'nɪʃən] n tecnico/a.
technique [tɛk'ni:k] n tecnica.
technological [tɛknə'lɔdʒɪkl] a tecnologico(a).
technology [tɛk'nɔlədʒɪ] n tecnologia.
teddy (bear) ['tɛdɪ-] n orsacchiotto.
tedious ['ti:dɪəs] a noioso(a), tedioso(a).
tee [ti:] n (GOLF) tee m inv.
teem [ti:m] vi abbondare, brulicare; to ~ with brulicare di; it is ~ing (with rain) piove a dirotto.
teenage ['ti:neɪdʒ] a (fashions etc) per giovani, per adolescenti; ~**r** n adolescente m/f.
teens [ti:nz] npl: to be in one's ~ essere adolescente.
tee-shirt ['ti:ʃə:t] n = T-shirt.
teeter ['ti:tə*] vi barcollare, vacillare.
teeth [ti:θ] npl of tooth.
teethe [ti:ð] vi mettere i denti.
teething ['ti:ðɪŋ]: ~ **ring** n dentaruolo; ~ **troubles** npl (fig) difficoltà fpl iniziali.
teetotal ['ti:'təutl] a astemio(a).
telegram ['tɛlɪɡræm] n telegramma m.
telegraph ['tɛlɪɡrɑ:f] n telegrafo.
telepathy [tə'lɛpəθɪ] n telepatia.
telephone ['tɛlɪfəun] n telefono // vt (person) telefonare a; (message) telefonare; ~ **booth**, (Brit) ~ **box** n cabina telefonica; ~ **call** n telefonata; ~ **directory** n elenco telefonico; ~ **number** n numero di telefono; **telephonist** [tə'lɛfənɪst] n (Brit) telefonista m/f.
telephoto ['tɛlɪ'fəutəu] a: ~ **lens** teleobiettivo.
telescope ['tɛlɪskəup] n telescopio // vt incastrare a cannocchiale.
televise ['tɛlɪvaɪz] vt teletrasmettere.
television ['tɛlɪvɪʒən] n televisione f; ~ **set** n televisore m.
telex ['tɛlɛks] n telex m inv // vt, vi trasmettere per telex; to ~ sb contattare qn via telex.
tell [tɛl], pt, pp **told** vt dire; (relate: story) raccontare; (distinguish): to ~ sth from distinguere qc da // vi (talk): to ~ (of) parlare (di); (have effect) farsi sentire, avere effetto; to ~ sb to do dire a qn di fare; **to ~ off** vt rimproverare, sgridare; ~**er** n (in bank) cassiere/a; ~**ing** a (remark, detail)

rivelatore(trice); ~**tale** a (sign) rivelatore(trice).
telly ['tɛlɪ] n abbr (Brit col: = television) tivù f inv.
temerity [tə'mɛrɪtɪ] n temerarietà.
temp [tɛmp] n abbr (= temporary) segretaria temporanea.
temper ['tɛmpə*] n (nature) carattere m; (mood) umore m; (fit of anger) collera // vt (moderate) temperare, moderare; **to be in a** ~ essere in collera; **to lose one's** ~ andare in collera.
temperament ['tɛmprəmənt] n (nature) temperamento; ~**al** [-'mɛntl] a capriccioso(a).
temperate ['tɛmprət] a moderato(a); (climate) temperato(a).
temperature ['tɛmprətʃə*] n temperatura; **to have** or **run a** ~ avere la febbre.
tempest ['tɛmpɪst] n tempesta.
template ['tɛmplɪt] n sagoma.
temple ['tɛmpl] n (building) tempio; (ANAT) tempia.
temporary ['tɛmpərərɪ] a temporaneo(a); (job, worker) avventizio(a), temporaneo(a); ~ **secretary** n segretaria temporanea.
tempt [tɛmpt] vt tentare; to ~ sb into doing indurre qn a fare; ~**ation** [-'teɪʃən] n tentazione f.
ten [tɛn] num dieci.
tenable ['tɛnəbl] a sostenibile.
tenacity [tə'næsɪtɪ] n tenacia.
tenancy ['tɛnənsɪ] n affitto; condizione f di inquilino.
tenant ['tɛnənt] n inquilino/a.
tend [tɛnd] vt badare a, occuparsi di // vi: to ~ to do tendere a fare.
tendency ['tɛndənsɪ] n tendenza.
tender ['tɛndə*] a tenero(a); (delicate) fragile; (sore) dolorante; (affectionate) affettuoso(a) // n (COMM: offer) offerta // vt offrire.
tendon ['tɛndən] n tendine m.
tenement ['tɛnəmənt] n casamento.
tenet ['tɛnət] n principio.
tennis ['tɛnɪs] n tennis m; ~ **ball** n palla da tennis; ~ **court** n campo da tennis; ~ **player** n tennista m/f; ~ **racket** n racchetta da tennis; ~ **shoes** npl scarpe fpl da tennis.
tenor ['tɛnə*] n (MUS, of speech etc) tenore m.
tense [tɛns] a teso(a) // n (LING) tempo.
tension ['tɛnʃən] n tensione f.
tent [tɛnt] n tenda.
tentative ['tɛntətɪv] a esitante, incerto(a); (conclusion) provvisorio(a).
tenterhooks ['tɛntəhuks] npl: on ~ sulle spine.
tenth [tɛnθ] num decimo(a).
tent: ~ **peg** n picchetto da tenda; ~ **pole** n palo da tenda, montante m.
tenuous ['tɛnjuəs] a tenue.

tenure ['tɛnjuə*] *n* (*of property*) possesso; (*of job*) permanenza; titolarità.

tepid ['tɛpɪd] *a* tiepido(a).

term [tə:m] *n* (*limit*) termine *m*; (*word*) vocabolo, termine; (*SCOL*) trimestre *m*; (*LAW*) sessione *f* // *vt* chiamare, definire; ~s *npl* (*conditions*) condizioni *fpl*; (*COMM*) prezzi *mpl*, tariffe *fpl*; ~ of imprisonment periodo di prigionia; in the short/long ~ a breve/lunga scadenza; to come to ~s with (*problem*) affrontare.

terminal ['tə:mɪnl] *a* finale, terminale; (*disease*) nella fase terminale // *n* (*ELEC*) morsetto; (*COMPUT*) terminale *m*; (*AVIAT*, *for oil, ore etc*) terminal *m* *inv*; (*Brit*: *also*: **coach ~**) capolinea *m*.

terminate ['tə:mɪneɪt] *vt* mettere fine a // *vi*: **to ~ in** finire in *or* con.

terminus, *pl* **termini** ['tə:mɪnəs, 'tə:mɪnaɪ] *n* (*for buses*) capolinea *m*; (*for trains*) stazione *f* terminale.

terrace ['tɛrəs] *n* terrazza; (*Brit*: *row of houses*) fila di case a schiera; **the ~s** *npl* (*Brit SPORT*) le gradinate; **~d** *a* (*garden*) a terrazze.

terracotta ['tɛrə'kɔtə] *n* terracotta.

terrain [tɛ'reɪn] *n* terreno.

terrible ['tɛrɪbl] *a* terribile; (*weather*) bruttissimo(a); (*work*) orribile, **terribly** *ad* terribilmente; (*very badly*) malissimo.

terrier ['tɛrɪə*] *n* terrier *m* *inv*.

terrific [tə'rɪfɪk] *a* incredibile, fantastico(a); (*wonderful*) formidabile, eccezionale.

terrify ['tɛrɪfaɪ] *vt* terrorizzare.

territory ['tɛrɪtərɪ] *n* territorio.

terror ['tɛrə*] *n* terrore *m*; **~ism** *n* terrorismo; **~ist** *n* terrorista *m/f*.

terse [tə:s] *a* (*style*) conciso(a); (*reply*) laconico(a).

Terylene ['tɛrəliːn] *n* ® terital *m* ®, terilene *m* ®.

test [tɛst] *n* (*trial, check, of courage etc*) prova; (: *of goods in factory*) controllo, collaudo; (*MED*) esame *m*; (*CHEM*) analisi *f* *inv*; (*exam*: *of intelligence etc*) test *m* *inv*; (: *in school*) compito in classe; (*also*: **driving ~**) esame *m* di guida // *vt* provare; controllare, collaudare; esaminare; analizzare; sottoporre ad esame; **to ~ sb in history** esaminare qn in storia.

testament ['tɛstəmənt] *n* testamento; the **Old/New T~** il Vecchio/Nuovo testamento.

testicle ['tɛstɪkl] *n* testicolo.

testify ['tɛstɪfaɪ] *vi* (*LAW*) testimoniare, deporre; **to ~ to sth** (*LAW*) testimoniare qc; (*gen*) comprovare *or* dimostrare qc; (: *be sign of*) essere una prova di qc.

testimony ['tɛstɪmənɪ] *n* (*LAW*) testimonianza, deposizione *f*.

test: **~ match** *n* (*CRICKET, RUGBY*) partita internazionale; **~ pilot** *n* pilota *m* collaudatore; **~ tube** *n* provetta.

tetanus ['tɛtənəs] *n* tetano.

tether ['tɛðə*] *vt* legare // *n*: **at the end of one's ~** al limite (della pazienza).

text [tɛkst] *n* testo; **~book** *n* libro di testo.

textile ['tɛkstaɪl] *n* tessile *m*.

texture ['tɛkstʃə*] *n* tessitura; (*of skin, paper etc*) struttura.

Thames [tɛmz] *n*: **the ~** il Tamigi.

than [ðæn, ðən] *cj* (*in comparisons*) che; (*with numerals, pronouns, proper names*) di; **more ~** 10/once più di 10/una volta; **I have more/less ~ you** ne ho più/meno di te; **I have more pens ~ pencils** ho più penne che matite; **she is older ~ you think** è più vecchia di quanto tu (non) pensi.

thank [θæŋk] *vt* ringraziare; **~ you (very much)** grazie (tante); **~s** *npl* ringraziamenti *mpl*, grazie *fpl* // *excl* grazie!; **~s to** *prep* grazie a; **~ful** *a*: **~ful (for)** riconoscente (per); **~less** *a* ingrato(a); **T~sgiving (Day)** *n* giorno del ringraziamento.

that [ðæt] ♦ *a* (*demonstrative*: *pl* **those**) quel(quell', quello) *m*; quella(quell') *f*; **~ man/woman/book** quell'uomo/quella donna/quel libro; (*not "this"*) quell'uomo/quella donna/quel libro là; **~ one** quello(a) là

♦ *pronoun* **1** (*demonstrative*: *pl* **those**) ciò; (*not "this one"*) quello(a); **who's ~?** chi è?; **what's ~?** cos'è quello?; **is ~ you?** sei tu?; **I prefer this to ~** preferisco questo a quello; **~'s what he said** questo è ciò che ha detto; **what happened after ~?** che è successo dopo?; **~ is (to say)** cioè

2 (*relative*: *direct*) che; (: *indirect*) cui; **the book (~)** I read il libro che ho letto; **the box (~)** I put it in la scatola in cui l'ho messo; **the people (~)** I spoke to le persone con cui *or* con le quali ho parlato

3 (*relative*: *of time*) in cui; **the day (~)** he came il giorno in cui è venuto

♦ *cj* che; **he thought ~** I was ill pensava che io fossi malato

♦ *ad* (*demonstrative*) così; **I can't work ~ much** non posso lavorare (così) tanto; **~ high** così alto; **the wall's about ~ high and ~ thick** il muro è alto circa così e spesso circa così.

thatched [θætʃt] *a* (*roof*) di paglia; **~ cottage** *n* cottage *m* *inv* col tetto di paglia.

thaw [θɔ:] *n* disgelo // *vi* (*ice*) sciogliersi; (*food*) scongelarsi // *vt* (*food*) (fare) scongelare; **it's ~ing** (*weather*) sta sgelando.

the [ðiː, ðə] *definite article* **1** (*gen*) il(lo, l') *m*; la(l') *f*; i(gli) *mpl*; le *fpl*; **~ boy/girl/ink** il ragazzo/la ragazza/l'inchiostro;

~ books/pencils i libri/le matite; ~ history of ~ world la storia del mondo; give it to ~ postman dallo al postino; I haven't ~ time/money non ho tempo/soldi; ~ rich and ~ poor i ricchi e i poveri

2 (in titles): Elizabeth ~ First Elisabetta prima; Peter ~ Great Pietro il grande

3 (in comparisons): ~ more he works, ~ more he earns più lavora più guadagna.

theatre, (US) **theater** ['θɪətə*] n teatro; ~-**goer** n frequentatore/trice di teatri.

theatrical [θɪ'ætrɪkl] a teatrale.

theft [θeft] n furto.

their [ðeə*] a il(la) loro, pl i(le) loro; ~s pronoun il(la) loro, pl i(le) loro; see also **my, mine.**

them [ðem, ðəm] pronoun (direct) li(le); (indirect) gli, loro (after vb); (stressed, after prep: people) loro; (: people, things) essi(e); see also **me.**

theme [θi:m] n tema m; ~ **song** n tema musicale.

themselves [ðəm'sɛlvz] pl pronoun (reflexive) si; (emphatic) loro stessi(e); (after prep) se stessi(e); between ~ tra (di) loro; see also **oneself.**

then [ðen] ad (at that time) allora; (next) poi, dopo; (and also) e poi // cj (therefore) perciò, dunque, quindi // a: the ~ president il presidente di allora; by ~ allora; from ~ on da allora in poi.

theologian [θɪə'ləudʒən] n teologo/a.

theology [θɪ'ɔlədʒɪ] n teologia.

theorem ['θɪərəm] n teorema m.

theoretical [θɪə'rɛtɪkl] a teorico(a).

theory ['θɪərɪ] n teoria.

therapeutic(al) [θɛrə'pju:tɪk(l)] a terapeutico(a).

therapy ['θɛrəpɪ] n terapia.

there [ðeə*] ad **1:** ~ is, ~ are c'è, ci sono; ~ are 3 of them (people) sono in 3; (things) ce ne sono 3; ~ is no-one here non c'è nessuno qui; ~ has been an accident c'è stato un incidente

2 (referring to place) là, lì; up/in/down ~ lassù/là dentro/laggiù; he went ~ on Friday ci è andato venerdì; I want that book ~ voglio quel libro là or lì; ~ he is! eccolo!

3: ~, ~ (esp to child) su, su.

thereabouts [ðeərə'bauts] ad (place) nei pressi, da quelle parti; (amount) giù di lì, all'incirca.

thereafter [ðeər'ɑ:ftə*] ad da allora in poi.

thereby [ðeə'baɪ] ad con ciò.

therefore ['ðeəfɔ:*] ad perciò, quindi.

there's [ðeəz] = **there is, there has.**

thermal ['θə:ml] a termico(a).

thermometer [θə'mɔmɪtə*] n termometro.

thermonuclear ['θə:məu'nju:klɪə*] a termonucleare.

Thermos ['θə:məs] n ® (also: ~ **flask**) thermos m inv ®.

thermostat ['θə:məstæt] n termostato.

thesaurus [θɪ'sɔ:rəs] n dizionario dei sinonimi.

these [ði:z] pl pronoun, a questi(e).

thesis, pl **theses** ['θi:sɪs, 'θi:si:z] n tesi f inv.

they [ðeɪ] pl pronoun essi(esse); (people only) loro; ~ say that ... (it is said that) si dice che ...; ~'d = they had, they would; ~'ll = they shall, they will; ~'re = they are; ~'ve = they have.

thick [θɪk] a spesso(a); (crowd) compatto(a); (stupid) ottuso(a), lento(a) // n: in the ~ of nel folto di; it's 20 cm ~ ha uno spessore di 20 cm; ~**en** vi ispessire // vt (sauce etc) ispessire, rendere più denso(a); ~**ly** ad (spread) a strati spessi; (cut) a fette grosse; (populated) densamente; ~**ness** n spessore m; ~**set** a tarchiato(a), tozzo(a); ~**skinned** a (fig) insensibile.

thief, pl **thieves** [θi:f, θi:vz] n ladro/a.

thigh [θaɪ] n coscia.

thimble ['θɪmbl] n ditale m.

thin [θɪn] a sottile; (person) magro(a); (soup) poco denso(a); (hair, crowd) rado(a); (fog) leggero(a) // vt (hair) sfoltire; to ~ (down) (sauce, paint) diluire.

thing [θɪŋ] n cosa; (object) oggetto; (contraption) aggeggio; ~s npl (belongings) cose fpl; for one ~ tanto per cominciare; the best ~ would be to la cosa migliore sarebbe di; how are ~s? come va?

think [θɪŋk] vb (pt, pp thought) vi pensare, riflettere // vt pensare, credere; (imagine) immaginare; to ~ of pensare a; what did you ~ of them? cosa ne hai pensato?; to ~ about sth/sb pensare a qc/qn; I'll ~ about it ci penserò; to ~ of doing pensare di fare; I ~ so/not penso di sì/no; to ~ well of avere una buona opinione di; to ~ out vt (plan) elaborare; (solution) trovare; to ~ over vt riflettere su; to ~ through vt riflettere a fondo su; to ~ up vt ideare; ~ **tank** n commissione f di esperti.

third [θə:d] num terzo(a) // n terzo/a; (fraction) terzo, terza parte f; (Brit SCOL: degree) laurea col minimo dei voti; ~**ly** ad in terzo luogo; ~ **party insurance** n (Brit) assicurazione f contro terzi; ~-**rate** a di qualità scadente; the T~ **World** n il Terzo Mondo.

thirst [θə:st] n sete f; ~**y** a (person) assetato(a), che ha sete.

thirteen [θə:'ti:n] num tredici.

thirty ['θə:tɪ] num trenta.

this [ðɪs] ◆ a (demonstrative: pl these) questo(a); ~ **man/woman/book** quest'uomo/questa donna/questo libro; (not "that") quest'uomo/questa donna/

questo libro qui; ~ one questo(a) qui
◆ *pronoun* (*demonstrative*: *pl* these) questo(a); (*not ''that one''*) questo(a) qui; who/what is ~? chi è/che cos'è questo?; I prefer ~ to that preferisco questo a quello; ~ is where I live io abito qui; ~ is what he said questo è ciò che ha detto; ~ is Mr Brown (*in introductions, photo*) questo è il signor Brown; (*on telephone*) sono il signor Brown
◆ *ad* (*demonstrative*): ~ high/long *etc* alto/lungo *etc* così; I didn't know things were ~ bad non sapevo andasse così male.

thistle ['θɪsl] *n* cardo.
thong [θɔŋ] *n* cinghia.
thorn [θɔːn] *n* spina.
thorough ['θʌrə] *a* (*search*) minuzioso(a); (*knowledge, research*) approfondito(a), profondo(a); coscienzioso(a); (*cleaning*) a fondo; ~bred *n* (*horse*) purosangue *m/f inv*; ~fare *n* strada transitabile; ''no ~fare'' ''divieto di transito''; ~ly *ad* minuziosamente; in profondità; a fondo; he ~ly agreed fu completamente d'accordo.
those [ðəuz] *pl pronoun* quelli(e) // *pl a* quei(quegli) *mpl*; quelle *fpl*.
though [ðəu] *cj* benché, sebbene // *ad* comunque.
thought [θɔːt] *pt, pp of* think // *n* pensiero; (*opinion*) opinione *f*; (*intention*) intenzione *f*; ~ful *a* pensieroso(a), pensoso(a); (*considerate*) premuroso(a); ~less *a* sconsiderato(a); (*behaviour*) scortese.
thousand ['θauzənd] *num* mille; one ~ mille; ~s of migliaia di; ~th *num* millesimo(a).
thrash [θræʃ] *vt* picchiare; bastonare, (*defeat*) battere; to ~ about *vi* dibattersi; to ~ out *vt* dibattere.
thread [θrɛd] *n* filo; (*of screw*) filetto // *vt* (*needle*) infilare; ~bare *a* consumato(a), logoro(a).
threat [θrɛt] *n* minaccia; ~en *vi* (*storm*) minacciare // *vt*: to ~en sb with sth/to do minacciare qn con qc/di fare.
three [θriː] *num* tre; ~-dimensional *a* tridimensionale; (*film*) stereoscopico(a); ~-piece suit *n* completo (con gilè); ~-piece suite *n* salotto comprendente un divano e due poltrone; ~-ply *a* (*wood*) a tre strati; (*wool*) a tre fili.
thresh [θrɛʃ] *vt* (*AGR*) trebbiare.
threshold ['θrɛʃhəuld] *n* soglia.
threw [θruː] *pt of* throw.
thrifty ['θrɪftɪ] *a* economico(a).
thrill [θrɪl] *n* brivido // *vi* eccitarsi, tremare // *vt* (*audience*) elettrizzare; to be ~ed (*with gift etc*) essere commosso(a); ~er *n* film *m inv* (o dramma *m* or libro) del brivido; ~ing *a* (*book*) pieno(a) di suspense; (*news,*

discovery) entusiasmante.
thrive, *pt* thrived, throve, *pp* thrived, thriven [θraɪv, θrəuv, 'θrɪvn] *vi* crescere or svilupparsi bene; (*business*) prosperare; he ~s on it gli fa bene, ne gode; thriving *a* fiorente.
throat [θrəut] *n* gola; to have a sore ~ avere (un or il) mal di gola.
throb [θrɔb] *vi* (*heart*) palpitare; (*engine*) vibrare; (*with pain*) pulsare.
throes [θrəuz] *npl*: in the ~ of alle prese con; in preda a.
thrombosis [θrɔm'bəusɪs] *n* trombosi *f*.
throne [θrəun] *n* trono.
throng [θrɔŋ] *n* moltitudine *f* // *vt* affollare.
throttle ['θrɔtl] *n* (*AUT*) valvola a farfalla // *vt* strangolare.
through [θruː] *prep* attraverso; (*time*) per, durante; (*by means of*) per mezzo di; (*owing to*) a causa di // *a* (*train, passage*) diretto(a) // *ad* at traverso; to put sb ~ to sb (*TEL*) passare qn a qn; to be ~ (*TEL*) ottenere la comunicazione; (*have finished*) avere finito; ''no ~ way'' (*Brit*) ''strada senza sbocco''; ~out *prep* (*place*) dappertutto in; (*time*) per or durante tutto(a) // *ad* dappertutto; sempre.
throve [θrəuv] *pt of* thrive.
throw [θrəu] *n* tiro, getto; (*SPORT*) lancio // *vt* (*pt* threw, *pp* thrown [θruː, θrəun]) tirare, gettare; (*SPORT*) lanciare; (*rider*) disarcionare; (*fig*) confondere; (*pottery*) formare al tornio; to ~ a party dare una festa; to ~ away *vt* gettare or buttare via; to ~ off *vt* sbarazzarsi di; to ~ out *vt* buttare fuori; (*reject*) respingere; to ~ up *vi* vomitare; ~away *a* da buttare; ~-in *n* (*SPORT*) rimessa in gioco.
thru [θruː] *prep, a, ad* (*US*) = through.
thrush [θrʌʃ] *n* tordo.
thrust [θrʌst] *n* (*TECH*) spinta // *vt* (*pt, pp* thrust) spingere con forza; (*push in*) conficcare.
thud [θʌd] *n* tonfo.
thug [θʌg] *n* delinquente *m*.
thumb [θʌm] *n* (*ANAT*) pollice *m* // *vt* (*book*) sfogliare; to ~ a lift fare l'autostop; ~tack *n* (*US*) puntina da disegno.
thump [θʌmp] *n* colpo forte; (*sound*) tonfo // *vt* battere su // *vi* picchiare, battere.
thunder ['θʌndə*] *n* tuono // *vi* tuonare; (*train etc*): to ~ past passare con un rombo; ~bolt *n* fulmine *m*; ~clap *n* rombo di tuono; ~ous ['θʌndrəs] *a* fragoroso(a); ~storm *n* temporale *m*; ~y *a* temporalesco(a).
Thursday ['θəːzdɪ] *n* giovedì *m inv*.
thus [ðʌs] *ad* così.
thwart [θwɔːt] *vt* contrastare.
thyme [taɪm] *n* timo.
thyroid ['θaɪrɔɪd] *n* tiroide *f*.

tiara [tɪ'ɑːrə] n (woman's) diadema m.
Tiber ['taɪbə*] n: the ~ il Tevere.
tick [tɪk] n (sound: of clock) tic tac m
inv; (mark) segno; spunta; (ZOOL)
zecca; (Brit col): in a ~ in un attimo //
vi fare tic tac // vt spuntare; **to ~ off**
vt spuntare; (person) sgridare; **to ~
over** vi (engine) andare al minimo;
(fig) andare avanti come al solito.
ticket ['tɪkɪt] n biglietto; (in shop: on
goods) etichetta; (: from cash register)
scontrino; (for library) scheda; ~
collector n bigliettaio; ~ **office** n biglietteria.
tickle ['tɪkl] n solletico // vt fare il
solletico a, solleticare; (fig) stuzzicare;
piacere a; far ridere.
tidal ['taɪdl] a di marea; ~ **wave** n onda
anomala.
tidbit ['tɪdbɪt] n (US) = **titbit**.
tiddlywinks ['tɪdlɪwɪŋks] n gioco della
pulce.
tide [taɪd] n marea; (fig: of events)
corso; **to ~ sb over** dare una mano a qn;
high/low ~ alta/bassa marea.
tidy ['taɪdɪ] a (room) ordinato(a),
lindo(a); (dress, work) curato(a), in
ordine; (person) ordinato(a) // vt (also:
~ up) riordinare, mettere in ordine; **to ~
o.s. up** rassettarsi.
tie [taɪ] n (string etc) legaccio; (Brit:
also: **neck~**) cravatta; (fig: link)
legame m; (SPORT: draw) pareggio // vt
(parcel) legare; (ribbon) annodare // vi
(SPORT) pareggiare; **to ~ sth in a bow**
annodare qc; **to ~ a knot in sth** fare un
nodo a qc; **to ~ down** vt fissare con
una corda; (fig): **to ~ sb down to** costringere qn a accettare; **to ~ up** vt
(parcel, dog) legare; (boat) ormeggiare;
(arrangements) concludere; **to be ~d up**
(busy) essere occupato or preso.
tier [tɪə*] n fila; (of cake) piano, strato.
tiff [tɪf] n battibecco.
tiger ['taɪgə*] n tigre f.
tight [taɪt] a (rope) teso(a), tirato(a);
(clothes) stretto(a); (budget, programme, bend) stretto(a); (control)
severo(a), fermo(a); (col: drunk)
sbronzo(a) // ad (squeeze) fortemente;
(shut) ermeticamente; ~**s** npl (Brit)
collant m inv; ~**en** vt (rope) tendere;
(screw) stringere; (control) rinforzare //
vi tendersi; stringersi; ~-**fisted** a
avaro(a); ~**ly** ad (grasp) bene,
saldamente; ~**rope** n corda (da
acrobata).
tile [taɪl] n (on roof) tegola; (on wall or
floor) piastrella, mattonella.
till [tɪl] n registratore m di cassa // vt
(land) coltivare // prep, cj = **until**.
tiller ['tɪlə*] n (NAUT) barra del timone.
tilt [tɪlt] vt inclinare, far pendere // vi inclinarsi, pendere.
timber ['tɪmbə*] n (material) legname

m; (trees) alberi mpl da legname.
time [taɪm] n tempo; (epoch: often pl)
epoca, tempo; (by clock) ora; (moment)
momento; (occasion, also MATH) volta;
(MUS) tempo // vt (race) cronometrare;
(programme) calcolare la durata di; (remark etc) dire (or fare) al momento giusto; **a long ~** molto tempo; **for the ~
being** per il momento; **4 at a ~** 4 per or
alla volta; **from ~ to ~** ogni tanto; **in ~**
(soon enough) in tempo; (after some
time) col tempo; (MUS) a tempo; **in a
week's ~** fra una settimana; **in no ~** in
un attimo; **any ~** in qualsiasi momento;
on ~ puntualmente; **5 ~s 5** 5 volte 5, 5
per 5; **what ~ is it?** che ora è?, che ore
sono?; **to have a good ~** divertirsi; ~'s
up! è (l')ora!; ~ **bomb** n bomba a
orologeria; ~ **lag** n intervallo, ritardo;
(in travel) differenza di fuso orario;
~**less** a eterno(a); ~**ly** a opportuno(a);
~ **off** n tempo libero; ~**r** n (~ switch)
temporizzatore m; (in kitchen)
contaminuti m inv; ~ **scale** n periodo;
~ **switch** n (Brit) temporizzatore m;
~**table** n orario; ~ **zone** n fuso orario.
timid ['tɪmɪd] a timido(a); (easily
scared) pauroso(a).
timing ['taɪmɪŋ] n sincronizzazione f;
(fig) scelta del momento opportuno,
tempismo; (SPORT) cronometraggio.
timpani ['tɪmpənɪ] npl timpani mpl.
tin [tɪn] n stagno; (also: ~ **plate**) latta;
(Brit: can) barattolo (di latta), lattina,
scatola; (for baking) teglia; ~**foil** n stagnola.
tinge [tɪndʒ] n sfumatura // vt: ~**d with**
tinto(a) di.
tingle ['tɪŋgl] vi pizzicare.
tinker ['tɪŋkə*] n stagnino ambulante;
(gipsy) zingaro(a); **to ~ with** vt fus
armeggiare intorno a; cercare di
riparare.
tinkle ['tɪŋkl] vi tintinnare.
tinned [tɪnd] a (Brit: food) in scatola.
tin opener ['-əupnə*] n (Brit) apriscatole m inv.
tinsel ['tɪnsl] n decorazioni fpl natalizie
(argentate).
tint [tɪnt] n tinta; ~**ed** a (hair) tinto(a);
(spectacles, glass) colorato(a).
tiny ['taɪnɪ] a minuscolo(a).
tip [tɪp] n (end) punta; (protective: on
umbrella etc) puntale m; (gratuity)
mancia; (for coal) discarica; (Brit: for
rubbish) immondezzaio; (advice)
suggerimento // vt (waiter) dare la
mancia a; (tilt) inclinare; (overturn:
also: ~ **over**) capovolgere; (empty:
also: ~ **out**) scaricare; ~**off** n (hint)
soffiata; ~**ped** a (Brit: cigarette) col
filtro.
Tipp-Ex ['tɪpɛks] n ® correttore m.
tipsy ['tɪpsɪ] a brillo(a).
tiptoe ['tɪptəu] n: **on ~** in punta di piedi.

tiptop ['tɪp'tɔp] a: in ~ **condition** in ottime condizioni.

tire ['taɪə*] n (US) = **tyre** // vt stancare // vi stancarsi; ~**d** a stanco(a); to be ~**d** of essere stanco or stufo di; ~**some** a noioso(a); **tiring** a faticoso(a).

tissue ['tɪʃuː] n tessuto; (paper handkerchief) fazzoletto di carta; ~ **paper** n carta velina.

tit [tɪt] n (bird) cinciallegra; to give ~ for tat rendere pan per focaccia.

titbit ['tɪtbɪt], (US) **tidbit** ['tɪdbɪt] n (food) leccornia; (news) notizia ghiotta.

titivate ['tɪtɪveɪt] vt agghindare.

title ['taɪtl] n titolo; ~ **deed** n (LAW) titolo di proprietà; ~ **role** n ruolo or parte f principale.

titter ['tɪtə*] vi ridere scioccamente.

TM abbr = **trademark**.

to [tuː, tə] ♦ prep **1** (direction) a; to go ~ France/London/school andare in Francia/a Londra/a scuola; to go ~ Paul's/the doctor's andare da Paul/dal dottore; the road ~ Edinburgh la strada per Edimburgo; ~ the left/right a sinistra/destra

2 (as far as) (fino) a; from here ~ London da qui a Londra; to count ~ 10 contare fino a 10; from 40 ~ 50 people da 40 a 50 persone

3 (with expressions of time): a quarter ~ 5 le 5 meno un quarto; it's twenty ~ 3 sono le 3 meno venti

4 (for, of): the key ~ the front door la chiave della porta d'ingresso; a letter ~ his wife una lettera per la moglie

5 (expressing indirect object) a; to give sth ~ sb dare qc a qn; to talk ~ sb parlare a qn; to be a danger ~ sb/sth rappresentare un pericolo per qn/qc

6 (in relation to) a; 3 goals ~ 2 3 goal a 2; 30 miles ~ the gallon ~ 11 chilometri con un litro

7 (purpose, result): to come ~ sb's aid venire in aiuto a qn; to sentence sb ~ death condannare a morte qn; ~ my surprise con mia sorpresa

♦ with vb **1** (simple infinitive): ~ go/eat etc andare/mangiare etc

2 (following another vb): to want/try/start ~ do volere/cercare di/cominciare a fare

3 (with vb omitted): I don't want ~ non voglio (farlo); you ought ~ devi (farlo)

4 (purpose, result): I did it ~ help you l'ho fatto per aiutarti

5 (equivalent to relative clause): I have things ~ do ho da fare; the main thing is ~ try la cosa più importante è provare

6 (after adjective etc): ready ~ go pronto a partire; too old/young ~ ... troppo vecchio/giovane per ...

♦ ad: to push the door ~ accostare la porta.

toad [təud] n rospo; ~**stool** n fungo (velenoso).

toast [təust] n (CULIN) toast m, pane m abbrustolito; (drink, speech) brindisi m inv // vt (CULIN) abbrustolire; (drink to) brindare a; a piece or slice of ~ una fetta di pane abbrustolito; ~**er** n tostapane m inv.

tobacco [tə'bækəu] n tabacco; ~**nist** n tabaccaio/a; ~**nist's (shop)** n tabaccheria.

toboggan [tə'bɔgən] n toboga m inv; (child's) slitta.

today [tə'deɪ] ad, n (also fig) oggi (m).

toddler ['tɔdlə*] n bambino/a che impara a camminare.

toddy ['tɔdɪ] n grog m inv.

to-do [tə'duː] n (fuss) storie fpl.

toe [təu] n dito del piede; (of shoe) punta; to ~ the line (fig) stare in riga, conformarsi.

toffee ['tɔfɪ] n caramella.

toga ['təugə] n toga.

together [tə'geðə*] ad insieme; (at same time) allo stesso tempo; ~ **with** insieme a.

toil [tɔɪl] n travaglio, fatica // vi affannarsi; sgobbare.

toilet ['tɔɪlət] n (Brit: lavatory) gabinetto // cpd (bag, soap etc) da toletta; ~ **bowl** n vaso or tazza del gabinetto; ~ **paper** n carta igienica; ~**ries** npl articoli mpl da toletta; ~ **roll** n rotolo di carta igienica; ~ **water** n acqua di colonia.

token ['təukən] n (sign) segno; (voucher) buono; **book/record** ~ (Brit) buono-libro/disco.

told [təuld] pt, pp of **tell**.

tolerable ['tɔlərəbl] a (bearable) tollerabile; (fairly good) passabile.

tolerant ['tɔlərnt] a: ~ (of) tollerante (nei confronti di).

tolerate ['tɔləreɪt] vt sopportare; (MED, TECH) tollerare.

toll [təul] n (tax, charge) pedaggio // vi (bell) suonare; the accident ~ on the roads il numero delle vittime della strada.

tomato, ~es [tə'mɑːtəu] n pomodoro.

tomb [tuːm] n tomba.

tomboy ['tɔmbɔɪ] n maschiaccio.

tombstone ['tuːmstəun] n pietra tombale.

tomcat ['tɔmkæt] n gatto.

tomorrow [tə'mɔrəu] ad, n (also fig) domani (m inv); the **day after** ~ dopodomani; a week ~ domani a otto; ~ **morning** domani mattina.

ton [tʌn] n tonnellata (Brit = 1016 kg; US = 907 kg; metric = 1000 kg); (NAUT: also: register ~) tonnellata di stazza (= 2.83 cu.m); ~**s** of (col) un mucchio or sacco di.

tone [təun] n tono // vi intonarsi; to ~ **down** vt (colour, criticism, sound) attenuare; **to ~ up** vt (muscles) tonificare; **~-deaf** a che non ha orecchio (musicale).

tongs [tɒŋz] npl tenaglie fpl; (for coal) molle fpl; (for hair) arricciacapelli m inv.

tongue [tʌŋ] n lingua; **~ in cheek** ad ironicamente; **~-tied** a (fig) muto(a); **~-twister** n scioglilingua m inv.

tonic [tɒnɪk] n (MED) tonico; (MUS) nota tonica; (also: ~ water) acqua tonica.

tonight [tə'naɪt] ad stanotte; (this evening) stasera // n questa notte; questa sera.

tonnage [tʌnɪdʒ] n (NAUT) tonnellaggio, stazza.

tonne [tʌn] n (metric ton) tonnellata.

tonsil [tɒnsl] n tonsilla; **~litis** [-'laɪtɪs] n tonsillite f.

too [tu:] ad (excessively) troppo; (also) anche; **~ much** ad troppo // a troppo(a); **~ many** a troppi(e); **~ bad!** tanto peggio!, peggio così!

took [tuk] pt of **take**.

tool [tu:l] n utensile m, attrezzo // vt lavorare con un attrezzo; **~ box/kit** n cassetta f portautensili/attrezzi inv.

toot [tu:t] vi suonare; (with car horn) suonare il clacson.

tooth [tu:θ], pl **teeth** n (ANAT, TECH) dente m; **~ache** n mal m di denti; **~brush** n spazzolino da denti; **~paste** n dentifricio; **~pick** n stuzzicadenti m inv.

top [tɒp] n (of mountain, page, ladder) cima; (of box, cupboard, table) sopra m inv, parte f superiore; (lid: of box, jar) coperchio; (: of bottle) tappo; (toy) trottola // a più alto(a); (in rank) primo(a); (best) migliore // vt (exceed) superare; (be first in) essere in testa a; **on ~ of** sopra, in cima a; (in addition to) oltre a; **from ~ to bottom** da cima a fondo; **to ~ up**, (US) **~ off** vt riempire; **~ floor** n ultimo piano; **~ hat** n cilindro; **~-heavy** a (object) con la parte superiore troppo pesante.

topic [tɒpɪk] n argomento; **~al** a d'attualità.

top: ~less a (bather etc) col seno scoperto; **~-level** a (talks) ad alto livello; **~most** a il(la) più alto(a).

topple [tɒpl] vt rovesciare, far cadere // vi cadere; traballare.

top-secret [tɒp'si:krɪt] a segretissimo(a).

topsy-turvy [tɒpsɪ'tɜ:vɪ] a, ad sottosopra (inv).

torch [tɔ:tʃ] n torcia; (Brit: electric) lampadina tascabile.

tore [tɔ:*] pt of **tear**.

torment n [tɔ:mɛnt] tormento // vt [tɔ:'mɛnt] tormentare; (fig: annoy) infastidire.

torn [tɔ:n] pp of **tear**.

tornado, **~es** [tɔ:'neɪdəu] n tornado.

torpedo, **~es** [tɔ:'pi:dəu] n siluro.

torrent [tɒrnt] n torrente m.

tortoise [tɔ:təs] n tartaruga; **~shell** [tɔ:təʃɛl] a di tartaruga.

torture [tɔ:tʃə*] n tortura // vt torturare.

Tory [tɔ:rɪ] (Brit POL) a dei tories, conservatore(trice) // n tory m/f inv, conservatore/trice.

toss [tɒs] vt gettare, lanciare; (pancake) far saltare; (head) scuotere; **to ~ a coin** fare a testa o croce; **to ~ up for sth** fare a testa o croce per qc; **to ~ and turn** (in bed) girarsi e rigirarsi.

tot [tɒt] n (Brit: drink) bicchierino; (child) bimbo/a.

total [təutl] a totale // n totale m // vt (add up) sommare; (amount to) ammontare a.

totally [təutəlɪ] ad completamente.

totter [tɒtə*] vi barcollare.

touch [tʌtʃ] n tocco; (sense) tatto; (contact) contatto; (FOOTBALL) fuori gioco m // vt toccare; **a ~ of** (fig) un tocco di; un pizzico di; **in ~ with** in contatto con; **to get in ~ with** mettersi in contatto con; **to lose ~** (friends) perdersi di vista; **to ~ on** vt fus (topic) sfiorare, accennare a; **to ~ up** vt (paint) ritoccare; **~-and-go** a incerto(a); **~down** n atterraggio; (on sea) ammaraggio; (US FOOTBALL) meta; **~ed** a commosso(a); (col) tocco(a), toccato(a); **~ing** a commovente; **~line** n (SPORT) linea laterale; **~y** a (person) suscettibile.

tough [tʌf] a duro(a); (resistant) resistente; (meat) duro(a), tiglioso(a).

toupee [tu:peɪ] n parrucchino.

tour [tuə*] n viaggio; (also: **package ~**) viaggio organizzato or tutto compreso; (of town, museum) visita; (by artist) tournée f inv // vt visitare; **~ing** n turismo.

tourism [tuərɪzəm] n turismo.

tourist [tuərɪst] n turista m/f // ad (travel) in classe turistica // cpd turistico(a); **~ office** n pro loco f inv.

tournament [tuənəmənt] n torneo.

tousled [tauzld] a (hair) arruffato(a).

tout [taut] vi: **to ~ for** procacciare, raccogliere; cercare clienti per // n (also: **ticket ~**) bagarino.

tow [təu] vt rimorchiare; "**on** or (US) **in ~**" (AUT) "veicolo rimorchiato".

toward(s) [tə'wɔ:d(z)] prep verso; (of attitude) nei confronti di; (of purpose) per.

towel [tauəl] n asciugamano; (also: **tea ~**) strofinaccio; **~ling** n (fabric) spugna; **~ rail**, (US) **~ rack** n portasciugamano.

tower [tauə*] n torre f; **~ block** n (Brit) palazzone m; **~ing** a altissimo(a), imponente.

town [taun] *n* città *f inv*; **to go to** ~
andare in città; *(fig)* mettercela tutta; ~
centre *n* centro (città); ~ **clerk** *n* segretario comunale; ~ **council** *n* consiglio comunale; ~ **hall** *n* ≈ municipio; ~
plan *n* pianta della città; ~ **planning** *n*
urbanistica.

towrope ['təurəup] *n* (cavo da) rimorchio.

tow truck *n* *(US)* carro *m* attrezzi *inv*.

toxic ['tɔksɪk] *a* tossico(a).

toy [tɔɪ] *n* giocattolo; **to** ~ **with** *vt fus*
giocare con; *(idea)* accarezzare, trastullarsi con.

trace [treɪs] *n* traccia // *vt (draw)*
tracciare; *(follow)* seguire; *(locate)* rintracciare; **tracing paper** *n* carta da
ricalco.

track [træk] *n (of person, animal)*
traccia; *(on tape, SPORT, path: gen)* pista; *(: of bullet etc)* traiettoria; *(: of
suspect, animal)* pista, tracce *fpl*;
(RAIL) binario, rotaie *fpl* // *vt* seguire le
tracce di; **to keep** ~ **of** seguire; **to** ~
down *vt (prey)* scovare; snidare; *(sth
lost)* rintracciare; ~**suit** *n* tuta sportiva.

tract [trækt] *n (GEO)* tratto, estensione *f*;
(pamphlet) opuscolo, libretto.

tractor ['træktə*] *n* trattore *m*.

trade [treɪd] *n* commercio; *(skill, job)*
mestiere *m* // *vi* commerciare; **to** ~
with/in commerciare con/in; **to** ~ **in** *vt
(old car etc)* dare come pagamento
parziale; ~ **fair** *n* fiera commerciale;
~-**in price** *n* prezzo di permuta; ~**mark**
n marchio di fabbrica; ~ **name** *n*
marca, nome *m* depositato; ~**r** *n*
commerciante *m/f*; ~**sman** *n* fornitore
m; *(shopkeeper)* negoziante *m*; ~
union *n* sindacato; ~ **unionist**
sindacalista *m/f*; **trading** *n* commercio;
trading estate *n (Brit)* zona industriale.

tradition [trə'dɪʃən] *n* tradizione *f*; ~**al** *a*
tradizionale.

traffic ['træfɪk] *n* traffico // *vi*: **to** ~ **in**
(pej: liquor, drugs) trafficare in; ~
circle *n (US)* isola rotatoria; ~ **jam** *n*
ingorgo (del traffico); ~ **lights** *npl*
semaforo; ~ **warden** *n* addetto/a al
controllo del traffico e del parcheggio.

tragedy ['trædʒədɪ] *n* tragedia.

tragic ['trædʒɪk] *a* tragico(a).

trail [treɪl] *n (tracks)* tracce *fpl*, pista;
(path) sentiero; *(of smoke etc)* scia // *vt*
trascinare, strascicare; *(follow)* seguire
// *vi* essere al traino; *(dress etc)* stru-
sciare; *(plant)* arrampicarsi; strisciare;
to ~ **behind** *vi* essere al traino; ~**er** *n*
(AUT) rimorchio; *(US)* roulotte *f inv*;
(CINEMA) prossimamente *m inv*; ~**er
truck** *n (US: articulated lorry)*
autoarticolato.

train [treɪn] *n* treno; *(of dress)* coda,
strascico // *vt (apprentice, doctor etc)*

formare; *(sportsman)* allenare; *(dog)*
addestrare; *(memory)* esercitare;
(point: gun etc): **to** ~ **sth on** puntare qc
contro // *vi* formarsi; allenarsi; **one's** ~
of thought il filo dei propri pensieri; ~**ed**
a qualificato(a); allenato(a); adde-
strato(a); ~**ee** [treɪ'niː] *n* allievo/a; *(in
trade)* apprendista *m/f*; ~**er** *n (SPORT)*
allenatore/trice; *(of dogs etc)*
addestratore/trice; ~**ing** *n* formazione *f*;
allenamento; addestramento; **in** ~**ing**
(SPORT) in allenamento; *(fit)* in forma;
~**ing college** *n* istituto professionale;
(for teachers) ≈ istituto magistrale;
~**ing shoes** *npl* scarpe *fpl* da ginnastica.

traipse [treɪps] *vi* girovagare, andare a
zonzo.

trait [treɪt] *n* tratto.

traitor ['treɪtə*] *n* traditore *m*.

trajectory [trə'dʒɛktərɪ] *n* traiettoria.

tram [træm] *n (Brit: also:* ~**car)** tram *m
inv*.

tramp [træmp] *n (person)* vagabondo/a;
(col: pej: woman) sgualdrina // *vi*
camminare con passo pesante // *vt (walk
through: town, streets)* percorrere a
piedi.

trample ['træmpl] *vt*: **to** ~ **(underfoot)**
calpestare.

trampoline ['træmpəliːn] *n* trampolino.

tranquil ['træŋkwɪl] *a* tranquillo(a);
~**lizer** *n (MED)* tranquillante *m*.

transact [træn'zækt] *vt (business)*
trattare; ~**ion** [-'zækʃən] *n* transazione
f; ~**ions** *npl (minutes)* atti *mpl*.

transatlantic ['trænzət'læntɪk] *a* transat-
lantico(a).

transcript ['trænskrɪpt] *n* trascrizione *f*.

transfer *n* ['trænsfə*] *(gen, also SPORT)*
trasferimento; *(POL: of power)*
passaggio; *(picture, design)* decal-
comania; *(: stick-on)* autoadesivo // *vt*
[træns'fə:*] trasferire; passare; decal-
care.

transform [træns'fɔːm] *vt* trasformare.

transfusion [træns'fjuːʒən] *n* trasfusione
f.

transient ['trænzɪənt] *a* transitorio(a),
fugace.

transistor [træn'zɪstə*] *n (ELEC)* transistor *m inv*; *(also:* ~ **radio)** radio *f inv* a
transistor.

transit ['trænzɪt] *n*: **in** ~ in transito.

transitive ['trænzɪtɪv] *a (LING)*
transitivo(a).

translate [trænz'leɪt] *vt* tradurre;
translation [-'leɪʃən] *n* traduzione *f*;
(SCOL: as opposed to prose) versione *f*;
translator *n* traduttore/trice.

transmission [trænz'mɪʃən] *n* trasmissione *f*.

transmit [trænz'mɪt] *vt* trasmettere;
~**ter** *n* trasmettitore *m*.

transparency [træns'pɛərnsɪ] *n (Brit:*

PHOT) diapositiva.

transparent [træns'pærnt] _a_ trasparente.

transpire [træn'spaɪə*] _vi_ (_happen_) succedere; (_turn out_): it ~d that si venne a sapere che.

transplant _vt_ [træns'plɑːnt] trapiantare // _n_ ['trænsplɑːnt] (_MED_) trapianto.

transport _n_ ['trænspɔːt] trasporto // _vt_ [træns'pɔːt] trasportare; **~ation** [-'teɪʃən] _n_ (mezzo di) trasporto; (_of prisoners_) deportazione _f_; ~ **café** _n_ (_Brit_) trattoria per camionisti.

trap [træp] _n_ (_snare, trick_) trappola; (_carriage_) calesse _m_ // _vt_ prendere in trappola, intrappolare; (_immobilize_) bloccare; (_jam_) chiudere, schiacciare; ~ **door** _n_ botola.

trapeze [trə'piːz] _n_ trapezio.

trapper ['træpə*] _n_ cacciatore _m_ di animali da pelliccia.

trappings ['træpɪŋz] _npl_ ornamenti _mpl_; indoratura, sfarzo.

trash [træʃ] _n_ (_pej: goods_) ciarpame _m_; (: _nonsense_) sciocchezze _fpl_; ~ **can** _n_ (_US_) secchio della spazzatura.

trauma ['trɔːmə] _n_ trauma _m_; **~tic** [-'mætɪk] _a_ traumatico(a).

travel ['trævl] _n_ viaggio; viaggi _mpl_ // _vi_ viaggiare; (_move_) andare, spostarsi // _vt_ (_distance_) percorrere; ~ **agency** _n_ agenzia (di) viaggi; ~ **agent** _n_ agente _m_ di viaggio; **~ler**, (_US_) **~er** _n_ viaggiatore/trice; **~ler's cheque** _n_ assegno turistico; **~ling**, (_US_) **~ing** _n_ viaggi _mpl_ // _cpd_ (_bag, clock_) da viaggio; (_expenses_) di viaggio; ~ **sickness** _n_ mal _m_ d'auto (_or_ di mare _or_ d'aria).

travesty ['trævəstɪ] _n_ parodia.

trawler ['trɔːlə*] _n_ peschereccio (a strascico).

tray [treɪ] _n_ (_for carrying_) vassoio; (_on desk_) vaschetta.

treachery ['tretʃərɪ] _n_ tradimento.

treacle ['triːkl] _n_ melassa.

tread [tred] _n_ passo; (_sound_) rumore _m_ di passi; (_of tyre_) battistrada _m inv_ // _vi_ (_pt_ **trod**, _pp_ **trodden**) camminare; **to** ~ **on** _vt fus_ calpestare.

treason ['triːzn] _n_ tradimento.

treasure ['treʒə*] _n_ tesoro // _vt_ (_value_) tenere in gran conto, apprezzare molto; (_store_) custodire gelosamente.

treasurer ['treʒərə*] _n_ tesoriere/a.

treasury ['treʒərɪ] _n_ tesoreria; **the T~**, (_US_) **the T~ Department** il ministero del Tesoro.

treat [triːt] _n_ regalo // _vt_ trattare; (_MED_) curare; **to** ~ **sb to sth** offrire qc a qn.

treatise ['triːtɪz] _n_ trattato.

treatment ['triːtmənt] _n_ trattamento.

treaty ['triːtɪ] _n_ patto, trattato.

treble ['trebl] _a_ triplo(a), triplice // _vt_ triplicare // _vi_ triplicarsi; ~ **clef** _n_ chiave _f_ di violino.

tree [triː] _n_ albero.

trek [trek] _n_ viaggio; camminata; (_tiring walk_) tirata a piedi // _vi_ (_as holiday_) fare dell'escursionismo.

trellis ['trelɪs] _n_ graticcio.

tremble ['trembl] _vi_ tremare; (_machine_) vibrare.

tremendous [trɪ'mendəs] _a_ (_enormous_) enorme; (_excellent_) meraviglioso(a), formidabile.

tremor ['tremə*] _n_ tremore _m_, tremito; (_also: earth ~_) scossa sismica.

trench [trentʃ] _n_ trincea.

trend [trend] _n_ (_tendency_) tendenza; (_of events_) corso; (_fashion_) moda; **~y** _a_ (_idea_) di moda; (_clothes_) all'ultima moda.

trepidation [trepɪ'deɪʃən] _n_ trepidazione _f_, agitazione _f_.

trespass ['trespəs] _vi:_ **to** ~ **on** entrare abusivamente in; (_fig_) abusare di; "**no ~ing**" "proprietà privata", "vietato l'accesso".

trestle ['tresl] _n_ cavalletto; ~ **table** _n_ tavolo su cavalletti.

trial ['traɪəl] _n_ (_LAW_) processo; (_test: of machine etc_) collaudo; (_hardship_) prova, difficoltà _f inv_; (_worry_) cruccio; **by** ~ **and error** a tentoni.

triangle ['traɪæŋgl] _n_ (_MATH, MUS_) triangolo.

tribe [traɪb] _n_ tribù _f inv_.

tribunal [traɪ'bjuːnl] _n_ tribunale _m_.

tributary ['trɪbjutərɪ] _n_ (_river_) tributario, affluente _m_.

tribute ['trɪbjuːt] _n_ tributo, omaggio; **to pay** ~ **to** rendere omaggio a.

trice [traɪs] _n:_ **in a** ~ in un attimo.

trick [trɪk] _n_ trucco; (_joke_) tiro; (_CARDS_) presa // _vt_ imbrogliare, ingannare; **to play a** ~ **on sb** giocare un tiro a qn; **that should do the** ~ vedrai che funziona; **~ery** _n_ inganno.

trickle ['trɪkl] _n_ (_of water etc_) rivolo; gocciolio // _vi_ gocciolare.

tricky ['trɪkɪ] _a_ difficile, delicato(a).

tricycle ['traɪsɪkl] _n_ triciclo.

trifle ['traɪfl] _n_ sciocchezza; (_Brit CULIN_) ≈ zuppa inglese // _ad:_ **a** ~ **long** un po' lungo; **trifling** _a_ insignificante.

trigger ['trɪgə*] _n_ (_of gun_) grilletto; **to** ~ **off** _vt_ dare l'avvio a.

trim [trɪm] _a_ ordinato(a); (_house, garden_) ben tenuto(a); (_figure_) snello(a) // _n_ (_haircut etc_) spuntata, regolata; (_embellishment_) finiture _fpl_; (_on car_) guarnizioni _fpl_ // _vt_ spuntare; (_decorate_): **to** ~ (**with**) decorare (con); (_NAUT: a sail_) orientare; **~mings** _npl_ decorazioni _fpl_; (_extras: gen CULIN_) guarnizione _f_.

trinket ['trɪŋkɪt] _n_ gingillo; (_piece of jewellery_) ciondolo.

trip [trɪp] _n_ viaggio; (_excursion_) gita, escursione _f_; (_stumble_) passo falso // _vi_ inciampare; (*go lightly*) camminare con passo leggero; **on a ~** in viaggio; **to ~ up** *vi* inciampare // *vt* fare lo sgambetto a.

tripe [traɪp] *n* (*CULIN*) trippa; (*pej*: *rubbish*) sciocchezze *fpl*, fesserie *fpl*.

triple ['trɪpl] *a* triplo(a).

triplets ['trɪplɪts] *npl* bambini(e) trigemini(e).

tripod ['traɪpɔd] *n* treppiede *m*.

trite [traɪt] *a* banale, trito(a).

triumph ['traɪʌmf] *n* trionfo // *vi*: **to ~** (**over**) trionfare (su).

trivia ['trɪvɪə] *npl* banalità *fpl*.

trivial ['trɪvɪəl] *a* insignificante; (*commonplace*) banale.

trod [trɔd] *pt of* **tread**; **~den** *pp of* **tread**.

trolley ['trɔlɪ] *n* carrello; **~ bus** *n* filobus *m inv*.

trombone [trɔm'bəʊn] *n* trombone *m*.

troop [tru:p] *n* gruppo; (*MIL*) squadrone *m*; **~s** *npl* (*MIL*) truppe *fpl*; **to ~ in/out** *vi* entrare/uscire a frotte; **~er** *n* (*MIL*) soldato di cavalleria; **~ing the colour** *n* (*ceremony*) sfilata della bandiera.

trophy ['trəʊfɪ] *n* trofeo.

tropic ['trɔpɪk] *n* tropico; **~al** *a* tropicale.

trot [trɔt] *n* trotto // *vi* trottare; **on the ~** (*Brit: fig*) di fila, uno(a) dopo l'altro(a).

trouble ['trʌbl] *n* difficoltà *f inv*, problema *m*; difficoltà *fpl*, problemi (*worry*) preoccupazione *f*; (*bother, effort*) sforzo; (*POL*) conflitti *mpl*, disordine *m*; (*MED*): **stomach** *etc* **~** disturbi *mpl* gastrici *etc* // *vt* disturbare; (*worry*) preoccupare // *vi*: **to ~ to do** disturbarsi a fare; **~s** *npl* (*POL etc*) disordini *mpl*; **to be in ~** avere dei problemi; **it's no ~!** di niente!; **what's the ~?** cosa c'è che non va?; **~d** *a* (*person*) preoccupato(a), inquieto(a); (*epoch, life*) agitato(a), difficile; **~maker** *n* elemento disturbatore, agitatore/trice; **~shooter** *n* (*in conflict*) conciliatore *m*; **~some** *a* fastidioso(a), seccante.

trough [trɔf] *n* (*also*: **drinking ~**) abbeveratoio; (*also*: **feeding ~**) trogolo, mangiatoia; (*channel*) canale *m*.

trousers ['traʊzəz] *npl* pantaloni *mpl*, calzoni *mpl*; **short ~** calzoncini *mpl*.

trousseau, *pl* **~x** *or* **~s** ['tru:səʊ, -z] *n* corredo da sposa.

trout [traʊt] *n* (*pl inv*) trota.

trowel ['traʊəl] *n* cazzuola.

truant ['truənt] *n*: **to play ~** (*Brit*) marinare la scuola.

truce [tru:s] *n* tregua.

truck [trʌk] *n* autocarro, camion *m inv*; (*RAIL*) carro merci aperto; (*for luggage*) carrello *m* portabagagli *inv*; **~ driver** *n* camionista *m/f*; **~ farm** *n* (*US*) orto industriale.

truculent ['trʌkjʊlənt] *a* aggressivo(a), brutale.

trudge [trʌdʒ] *vi* trascinarsi pesantemente.

true [tru:] *a* vero(a); (*accurate*) accurato(a), esatto(a); (*genuine*) reale; (*faithful*) fedele.

truffle ['trʌfl] *n* tartufo.

truly ['tru:lɪ] *ad* veramente; (*truthfully*) sinceramente; (*faithfully*) fedelmente.

trump [trʌmp] *n* atout *m inv*; **~ed-up** *a* inventato(a).

trumpet ['trʌmpɪt] *n* tromba.

truncheon ['trʌntʃən] *n* sfollagente *m inv*.

trundle ['trʌndl] *vt*, *vi*: **to ~ along** rotolare rumorosamente.

trunk [trʌŋk] *n* (*of tree, person*) tronco; (*of elephant*) proboscide *f*; (*case*) baule *m*; (*US AUT*) bagagliaio; **~s** *npl* (*also*: **swimming ~s**) calzoncini *mpl* da bagno.

truss [trʌs] *n* (*MED*) cinto erniario; **to ~ (up)** *vt* (*CULIN*) legare.

trust [trʌst] *n* fiducia; (*LAW*) amministrazione *f* fiduciaria; (*COMM*) trust *m inv* // *vt* (*rely on*) contare su; (*entrust*): **to ~ sth to sb** affidare qc a qn; **~ed** *a* fidato(a); **~ee** [trʌs'ti:] *n* (*LAW*) amministratore(trice) fiduciario(a); (*of school etc*) amministratore/trice; **~ful, ~ing** *a* fiducioso(a); **~worthy** *a* fidato(a), degno(a) di fiducia.

truth, **~s** [tru:θ, tru:ðz] *n* verità *f inv*; **~ful** *a* (*person*) sincero(a); (*description*) veritiero(a), esatto(a).

try [traɪ] *n* prova, tentativo; (*RUGBY*) meta // *vt* (*LAW*) giudicare; (*test: sth new*) provare; (*strain*) mettere alla prova // *vi* provare; **to ~ to do** provare a fare; (*seek*) cercare di fare; **to ~ on** *vt* (*clothes*) provare; **to ~ out** *vt* provare, mettere alla prova; **~ing** *a* (*day, experience*) logorante, pesante; (*child*) difficile, insopportabile.

tsar [zɑ:*] *n* zar *m inv*.

T-shirt ['ti:ʃə:t] *n* maglietta.

T-square ['ti:skwɛə*] *n* riga a T.

tub [tʌb] *n* tinozza; mastello; (*bath*) bagno.

tuba ['tju:bə] *n* tuba.

tubby ['tʌbɪ] *a* grassoccio(a).

tube [tju:b] *n* tubo; (*Brit: underground*) metropolitana, metrò *m inv*; (*for tyre*) camera d'aria.

tubing ['tju:bɪŋ] *n* tubazione *f*; **a piece of ~** un tubo.

tubular ['tju:bjʊlə*] *a* tubolare.

TUC *n abbr* (*Brit*: = *Trades Union Congress*) confederazione *f* dei sindacati britannici.

tuck [tʌk] *n* (*SEWING*) piega // *vt* (*put*) mettere; **to ~ away** *vt* riporre; **to ~ in** *vt* mettere dentro; (*child*) rimboccare // *vi* (*eat*) mangiare di buon appetito; abbuffarsi; **to ~ up** *vt* (*child*)

rimboccare; ~ **shop** n negozio di pasticceria (in una scuola).

Tuesday ['tju:zdɪ] n martedì m inv.

tuft [tʌft] n ciuffo.

tug [tʌg] n (ship) rimorchiatore m // vt
tirare con forza; **~-of-war** n tiro alla
fune.

tuition [tju:'ɪʃən] n (Brit) lezioni fpl; (:
private ~) lezioni fpl private; (US:
school fees) tasse fpl scolastiche.

tulip ['tju:lɪp] n tulipano.

tumble ['tʌmbl] n (fall) capitombolo // vi
capitombolare, ruzzolare; (somersault)
fare capriole; **to ~ to sth** (col) realizzare
qc; **~down** a cadente, diroccato(a); **~
dryer** n (Brit) asciugatrice f.

tumbler ['tʌmblə*] n bicchiere m (senza
stelo); acrobata m/f.

tummy ['tʌmɪ] n (col) pancia.

tumour, (US) **tumor** ['tju:mə*] n tumore
m.

tuna ['tju:nə] n (pl inv) (also: ~ **fish**)
tonno.

tune [tju:n] n (melody) melodia, aria // vt
(MUS) accordare; (RADIO, TV, AUT)
regolare, mettere a punto; **to be in/out of
~** (instrument) essere accordato(a)/
scordato(a); (singer) essere intonato(a)/
stonato(a); **to ~ in** vi: **to ~ in (to)**
(RADIO, TV) sintonizzarsi (su); **to ~ up**
vi (musician) accordare lo strumento;
~ful a melodioso(a).

tunic ['tju:nɪk] n tunica.

tuning ['tju:nɪŋ] n messa a punto; **~
fork** n diapason m inv.

Tunisia [tju:'nɪzɪə] n Tunisia.

tunnel ['tʌnl] n galleria // vi scavare una
galleria.

turban ['tə:bən] n turbante m.

turbot ['tə:bət] n (pl inv) rombo gigante.

turbulence ['tə:bjuləns] n (AVIAT)
turbolenza.

tureen [tə'ri:n] n zuppiera.

turf [tə:f] n terreno erboso; (clod) zolla //
vt coprire di zolle erbose; **to ~ out** vt
(col) buttar fuori.

turgid ['tə:dʒɪd] a (speech) ampolloso(a),
pomposo(a).

Turin [tjuə'rɪn] n Torino f.

Turk [tə:k] n turco/a.

Turkey ['tə:kɪ] n Turchia.

turkey ['tə:kɪ] n tacchino.

Turkish ['tə:kɪʃ] a turco(a) // n (LING)
turco.

turmoil ['tə:mɔɪl] n confusione f, tumulto.

turn [tə:n] n giro; (in road) curva;
(tendency: of mind, events) tendenza;
(performance) numero; (MED) crisi f
inv, attacco // vt girare, voltare; (milk)
far andare a male; (change): **to ~ sth
into** trasformare qc in // vi girare;
(person: look back) girarsi, voltarsi;
(reverse direction) girarsi indietro;
(change) cambiare; (become)
diventare; **to ~ into** trasformarsi in; a

good ~ un buon servizio; it gave me
quite a ~ mi ha fatto prendere un bello
spavento; "no left ~" (AUT) "divieto di
svolta a sinistra"; it's your ~ tocca a
lei; in ~ a sua volta; a turno; to take ~s
(at sth) fare (qc) a turno; **to ~ away**
vi girarsi (dall'altra parte); **to ~ back**
vi ritornare, tornare indietro; **to ~
down** vt (refuse) rifiutare; (reduce)
abbassare; (fold) ripiegare; **to ~ in**
(col: go to bed) andare a letto // vt (fold)
voltare in dentro; **to ~ off** vi (from
road) girare, voltare // vt (light, radio,
engine etc) spegnere; **to ~ on** vt (light,
radio etc) accendere; (engine) avviare;
to ~ out vt (light, gas) chiudere, spegnere // vi: **to ~ out to be** ... rivelarsi ...,
risultare ...; **to ~ over** vi (person)
girarsi // vt girare; **to ~ round** vi
girare; (person) girarsi; **to ~ up** vi
(person) arrivare, presentarsi; (lost
object) saltar fuori // vt (collar, sound)
alzare; **~ing** n (in road) curva; **~ing
point** n (fig) svolta decisiva.

turnip ['tə:nɪp] n rapa.

turnout ['tə:naut] n presenza, affluenza.

turnover ['tə:nəuvə*] n (COMM) giro di
affari.

turnpike ['tə:npaɪk] n (US) autostrada a
pedaggio.

turnstile ['tə:nstaɪl] n tornella.

turntable ['tə:nteɪbl] n (on record
player) piatto.

turn-up ['tə:nʌp] n (Brit: on trousers) risvolto.

turpentine ['tə:pəntaɪn] n (also: **turps**)
acqua ragia.

turquoise ['tə:kwɔɪz] n (stone) turchese
m // a color turchese; di turchese.

turret ['tʌrɪt] n torretta.

turtle ['tə:tl] n testuggine f; **~neck
(sweater)** n maglione m con il collo
alto.

tusk [tʌsk] n zanna.

tussle ['tʌsl] n baruffa, mischia.

tutor ['tju:tə*] n (in college) docente m/f
(responsabile di un gruppo di studenti);
(private teacher) precettore m; **~ial**
[-'tɔ:rɪəl] n (SCOL) lezione f con discussione (a un gruppo limitato).

tuxedo [tʌk'si:dəu] n (US) smoking m
inv.

TV [ti:'vi:] n abbr (= television) tivù f
inv.

twang [twæŋ] n (of instrument) suono vi-
brante; (of voice) accento nasale.

tweed [twi:d] n tweed m inv.

tweezers ['twi:zəz] npl pinzette fpl.

twelfth [twelfθ] num dodicesimo(a).

twelve [twelv] num dodici; at ~ (o'clock)
alle dodici, a mezzogiorno; (midnight) a
mezzanotte.

twentieth ['twentɪθ] num ventesimo(a).

twenty ['twentɪ] num venti.

twice [twaɪs] ad due volte; ~ as much

due volte tanto.

twiddle ['twɪdl] *vt, vi*: to ~ (with) sth giocherellare con qc; to ~ one's thumbs (*fig*) girarsi i pollici.

twig [twɪg] *n* ramoscello // *vt, vi* (*col*) capire.

twilight ['twaɪlaɪt] *n* crepuscolo.

twin [twɪn] *a, n* gemello(a) // *vt*: to ~ one town with another fare il gemellaggio di una città con un'altra; **~-bedded room** *n* stanza con letti gemelli.

twine [twaɪn] *n* spago, cordicella // *vi* attorcigliarsi.

twinge [twɪndʒ] *n* (*of pain*) fitta; a ~ of conscience/regret un rimorso/rimpianto.

twinkle ['twɪŋkl] *n* scintillio // *vi* scintillare; (*eyes*) brillare.

twirl [twəːl] *n* piroetta // *vt* far roteare // *vi* roteare.

twist [twɪst] *n* torsione *f*; (*in wire, flex*) storta; (*in story*) colpo di scena // *vt* attorcigliare; (*weave*) intrecciare; (*roll around*) arrotolare; (*fig*) deformare // *vi* attorcigliarsi; arrotolarsi; (*road*) serpeggiare.

twit [twɪt] *n* (*col*) minchione/a.

twitch [twɪtʃ] *n* tiratina; (*nervous*) tic *m inv* // *vi* contrarsi; avere un tic.

two [tuː] *num* due; to put ~ and ~ together (*fig*) trarre le conclusioni; **~-door** *a* (*AUT*) a due porte; **~-faced** *a* (*pej: person*) falso(a); **~fold** *ad*: to increase **~fold** aumentare del doppio; **~-piece (suit)** *n* due pezzi *m inv*; **~-piece (swimsuit)** *n* (*costume m* da bagno a) due pezzi *m inv*; **~-seater** *n* (*plane*) biposto; (*car*) macchina a due posti; **~some** *n* (*people*) coppia; **~-way** *a* (*traffic*) a due sensi.

tycoon [taɪˈkuːn] *n*: (*business*) ~ magnate *m*.

type [taɪp] *n* (*category*) genere *m*; (*model*) modello; (*example*) tipo; (*TYP*) tipo, carattere *m* // *vt* (*letter etc*) battere (a macchina), dattilografare; **~-cast** *a* (*actor*) a ruolo fisso; **~face** *n* carattere *m* tipografico; **~script** *n* dattiloscritto; **~writer** *n* macchina da scrivere; **~written** *a* dattiloscritto(a), battuto(a) a macchina.

typhoid ['taɪfɔɪd] *n* tifoidea.

typhoon [taɪˈfuːn] *n* tifone *m*.

typhus ['taɪfəs] *n* tifo.

typical ['tɪpɪkl] *a* tipico(a).

typing ['taɪpɪŋ] *n* dattilografia.

typist ['taɪpɪst] *n* dattilografo/a.

tyrant ['taɪərnt] *n* tiranno.

tyre, (*US*) **tire** ['taɪə*] *n* pneumatico, gomma; ~ **pressure** *n* pressione *f* (delle gomme).

tzar [zɑː*] *n* = **tsar.**

U

U-bend ['juːˈbɛnd] *n* (*in pipe*) sifone *m*.

udder ['ʌdə*] *n* mammella.

UFO ['juːfəu] *n abbr* (= *unidentified flying object*) UFO *m inv.*

ugh [əːh] *excl* puah!

ugly ['ʌglɪ] *a* brutto(a).

UK *n abbr* = **United Kingdom.**

ulcer ['ʌlsə*] *n* ulcera; (*also:* mouth ~) afta.

Ulster ['ʌlstə*] *n* Ulster *m.*

ulterior [ʌlˈtɪərɪə*] *a* ulteriore; ~ **motive** *n* secondo fine *m.*

ultimate ['ʌltɪmət] *a* ultimo(a), finale; (*authority*) massimo(a), supremo(a); **~ly** *ad* alla fine; in definitiva, in fin dei conti.

ultrasound [ʌltrəˈsaund] *n* (*MED*) ultrasuono.

umbilical cord [ʌmbɪˈlaɪkl-] *n* cordone *m* ombelicale.

umbrage ['ʌmbrɪdʒ] *n*: to take ~ offendersi, impermalirsi.

umbrella [ʌmˈbrɛlə] *n* ombrello.

umpire ['ʌmpaɪə*] *n* arbitro.

umpteen [ʌmpˈtiːn] *a* non so quanti(e); for the **~th** time per l'ennesima volta.

UN, UNO *n abbr* = **United Nations (Organization).**

unable [ʌnˈeɪbl] *a*: to be ~ to non potere, essere nell'impossibilità di; essere incapace di.

unaccompanied [ʌnəˈkʌmpənɪd] *a* (*child, lady*) non accompagnato(a).

unaccountably [ʌnəˈkauntəblɪ] *ad* inesplicabilmente.

unaccustomed [ʌnəˈkʌstəmd] *a* insolito(a); to be ~ to sth non essere abituato a qc.

unanimous [juːˈnænɪməs] *a* unanime; **~ly** *ad* all'unanimità.

unarmed [ʌnˈɑːmd] *a* (*without a weapon*) disarmato(a); (*combat*) senz'armi.

unassuming [ʌnəˈsjuːmɪŋ] *a* modesto(a), senza pretese.

unattached [ʌnəˈtætʃt] *a* senza legami, libero(a).

unattended [ʌnəˈtɛndɪd] *a* (*car, child, luggage*) incustodito(a).

unauthorized [ʌnˈɔːθəraɪzd] *a* non autorizzato(a).

unavoidable [ʌnəˈvɔɪdəbl] *a* inevitabile.

unaware [ʌnəˈwɛə*] *a*: to be ~ of non sapere, ignorare; **~s** *ad* di sorpresa, alla sprovvista.

unbalanced [ʌnˈbælənst] *a* squilibrato(a).

unbearable [ʌnˈbɛərəbl] *a* insopportabile.

unbeknown(st) [ʌnbɪˈnəun(st)] *ad*: ~ to all'insaputa di.

unbelievable [ʌnbɪ'liːvəbl] a incredibile.
unbend [ʌn'bend] vb (irg) vi distendersi // vt (wire) raddrizzare.
unbias(s)ed [ʌn'baɪəst] a (person, report) obiettivo(a), imparziale.
unborn [ʌn'bɔːn] a non ancora nato(a).
unbreakable [ʌn'breɪkəbl] a infrangibile.
unbroken [ʌn'brəukən] a intero(a); continuo(a).
unbutton [ʌn'bʌtn] vt sbottonare.
uncalled-for [ʌn'kɔːldfɔː*] a (remark) fuori luogo inv; (action) ingiustificato(a).
uncanny [ʌn'kænɪ] a misterioso(a), strano(a).
unceasing [ʌn'siːsɪŋ] a incessante.
unceremonious ['ʌnserɪ'məʊnɪəs] a (abrupt, rude) senza tante cerimonie.
uncertain [ʌn'sɜːtn] a incerto(a); dubbio(a); **~ty** n incertezza.
unchecked [ʌn'tʃekt] a incontrollato(a).
uncivilized [ʌn'sɪvɪlaɪzd] a (gen) selvaggio(a); (fig) incivile, barbaro(a).
uncle ['ʌŋkl] n zio.
uncomfortable [ʌn'kʌmfətəbl] a scomodo(a); (uneasy) a disagio, agitato(a); fastidioso(a).
uncommon [ʌn'kɔmən] a raro(a), insolito(a), non comune.
uncompromising [ʌn'kɔmprəmaɪzɪŋ] a intransigente, inflessibile.
unconcerned [ʌnkən'sɜːnd] a: to be ~ (about) non preoccuparsi (di or per).
unconditional [ʌnkən'dɪʃənl] a incondizionato(a), senza condizioni.
unconscious [ʌn'kɔnʃəs] a privo(a) di sensi, svenuto(a); (unaware) inconsapevole, inconscio(a) // n: the ~ l'inconscio; **~ly** ad inconsciamente.
uncontrollable [ʌnkən'trəuləbl] a incontrollabile; indisciplinato(a).
unconventional [ʌnkən'venʃənl] a poco convenzionale.
uncouth [ʌn'kuːθ] a maleducato(a), grossolano(a).
uncover [ʌn'kʌvə*] vt scoprire.
undecided [ʌndɪ'saɪdɪd] a indeciso(a).
under ['ʌndə*] prep sotto; (less than) meno di; al disotto di; (according to) secondo, in conformità a // ad (al) disotto; **from ~ sth** da sotto a or dal disotto di qc; **~ there** là sotto; **~ repair** in riparazione.
under... ['ʌndə*] prefix sotto..., sub...; **~ age** a minorenne; **~carriage** n (Brit) carrello (d'atterraggio); **~charge** vt far pagare di meno a; **~coat** n (paint) mano f di fondo; **~cover** a segreto(a), clandestino(a); **~current** n corrente f sottomarina; **~cut** vt irg vendere a prezzo minore di; **~developed** a sottosviluppato(a); **~dog** n oppresso/a; **~done** a (CULIN) al sangue; (pej) poco cotto(a); **~estimate** vt sottovalutare; **~fed** a

denutrito(a); **~foot** ad sotto i piedi; **~go** vt irg subire; (treatment) sottoporsi a; **~graduate** n studente(essa) universitario(a); **~ground** n (Brit: railway) metropolitana; (POL) movimento clandestino // a sotterraneo(a); (fig) clandestino(a); **~growth** n sottobosco; **~hand(ed)** a (fig) furtivo(a), subdolo(a); **~lie** vt irg essere alla base di; **~line** vt sottolineare; **~ling** ['ʌndəlɪŋ] n (pej) subalterno/a, tirapiedi m/f inv; **~mine** vt minare; **~neath** [ʌndə'niːθ] ad sotto, disotto // prep sotto, al di sotto di; **~paid** a mal pagato(a); **~pants** npl mutande fpl, slip m inv; **~pass** n (Brit) sottopassaggio; **~privileged** a non abbiente; meno favorito(a); **~rate** vt sottovalutare; **~shirt** n (US) maglietta; **~shorts** npl (US) mutande fpl, slip m inv; **~side** n disotto; **~skirt** n (Brit) sottoveste f.
understand [ʌndə'stænd] vb (irg: like stand) vt, vi capire, comprendere; I ~ that ... sento che ...; credo di capire che ...; **~able** a comprensibile; **~ing** a comprensivo(a) // n comprensione f; (agreement) accordo.
understatement [ʌndə'steɪtmənt] n: that's an ~! a dire poco!
understood [ʌndə'stud] pt, pp of **understand** // a inteso(a); (implied) sottinteso(a).
understudy ['ʌndəstʌdɪ] n sostituto/a, attore/trice supplente.
undertake [ʌndə'teɪk] vt irg intraprendere; to ~ to do sth impegnarsi a fare qc.
undertaker ['ʌndəteɪkə*] n impresario di pompe funebri.
undertaking [ʌndə'teɪkɪŋ] n impresa; (promise) promessa.
undertone ['ʌndətəun] n: in an ~ a mezza voce, a voce bassa.
underwater [ʌndə'wɔːtə*] ad sott'acqua // a subacqueo(a).
underwear ['ʌndəwɛə*] n biancheria (intima).
underworld ['ʌndəwɜːld] n (of crime) malavita.
underwriter ['ʌndəraɪtə*] n (INSURANCE) sottoscrittore/trice.
undies ['ʌndɪz] npl (col) robina, biancheria intima da donna.
undo [ʌn'duː] vt irg disfare; **~ing** n rovina, perdita.
undoubted [ʌn'dautɪd] a sicuro(a), certo(a); **~ly** ad senza alcun dubbio.
undress [ʌn'dres] vi spogliarsi.
undue [ʌn'djuː] a eccessivo(a).
undulating ['ʌndjuleɪtɪŋ] a ondeggiante; ondulato(a).
unduly [ʌn'djuːlɪ] ad eccessivamente.
unearth [ʌn'ɜːθ] vt dissotterrare; (fig) scoprire.

unearthly [ʌn'ə:θlɪ] *a* soprannaturale; (*hour*) impossibile.

uneasy [ʌn'i:zɪ] *a* a disagio; (*worried*) preoccupato(a).

unemployed [ʌnɪm'plɔɪd] *a* disoccupato(a) // *npl*: the ~ i disoccupati.

unemployment [ʌnɪm'plɔɪmənt] *n* disoccupazione *f*.

unending [ʌn'endɪŋ] *a* senza fine.

unerring [ʌn'ə:rɪŋ] *a* infallibile.

uneven [ʌn'i:vn] *a* ineguale; irregolare.

unexpected [ʌnɪk'spektɪd] *a* inatteso(a), imprevisto(a); ~**ly** *ad* inaspettatamente.

unfailing [ʌn'feɪlɪŋ] *a* (*supply, energy*) inesauribile; (*remedy*) infallibile.

unfair [ʌn'fɛə*] *a*: ~ (**to**) ingiusto(a) (nei confronti di).

unfaithful [ʌn'feɪθful] *a* infedele.

unfamiliar [ʌnfə'mɪlɪə*] *a* sconosciuto(a), strano(a).

unfashionable [ʌn'fæʃnəbl] *a* (*clothes*) fuori moda; (*district*) non alla moda.

unfasten [ʌn'fɑ:sn] *vt* slacciare; sciogliere.

unfavourable, (*US*) **unfavorable** [ʌn'feɪvərəbl] *a* sfavorevole.

unfeeling [ʌn'fi:lɪŋ] *a* insensibile, duro(a).

unfit [ʌn'fɪt] *a* inadatto(a); (*ill*) malato(a), in cattiva salute; (*incompetent*): ~ (**for**) incompetente (in); (: *work, MIL*) inabile (a).

unfold [ʌn'fəuld] *vt* spiegare; (*fig*) rivelare // *vi* (*view, countryside*) distendersi; (*story, plot*) svelarsi.

unforeseen ['ʌnfɔ:'si:n] *a* imprevisto(a).

unforgettable [ʌnfə'getəbl] *a* indimenticabile.

unfortunate [ʌn'fɔ:tʃnət] *a* sfortunato(a); (*event, remark*) infelice; ~**ly** *ad* sfortunatamente, purtroppo.

unfounded [ʌn'faundɪd] *a* infondato(a).

unfriendly [ʌn'frendlɪ] *a* poco amichevole, freddo(a).

ungainly [ʌn'geɪnlɪ] *a* goffo(a), impacciato(a).

ungodly [ʌn'gɔdlɪ] *a* empio(a); at an ~ hour a un'ora impossibile.

ungrateful [ʌn'greɪtful] *a* ingrato(a).

unhappiness [ʌn'hæpɪnɪs] *n* infelicità.

unhappy [ʌn'hæpɪ] *a* infelice; ~ **with** (*arrangements etc*) insoddisfatto(a) di.

unharmed [ʌn'hɑ:md] *a* incolume, sano(a) e salvo(a).

unhealthy [ʌn'hɛlθɪ] *a* (*gen*) malsano(a); (*person*) malaticcio(a).

unheard-of [ʌn'hə:dɔv] *a* inaudito(a), senza precedenti.

uniform ['ju:nɪfɔ:m] *n* uniforme *f*, divisa // *a* uniforme.

uninhabited [ʌnɪn'hæbɪtɪd] *a* disabitato(a).

union ['ju:njən] *n* unione *f*; (*also*: trade ~) sindacato // *cpd* sindacale, dei sindacati; **U~ Jack** *n* bandiera nazionale britannica.

unique [ju:'ni:k] *a* unico(a).

unit ['ju:nɪt] *n* unità *f inv*; (*section: of furniture etc*) elemento; (*team, squad*) reparto, squadra.

unite [ju:'naɪt] *vt* unire // *vi* unirsi; ~**d** *a* unito(a); unificato(a); (*efforts*) congiunto(a); **U~d Kingdom (UK)** *n* Regno Unito; **U~d Nations (Organization) (UN, UNO)** *n* (Organizzazione *f* delle) Nazioni Unite (O.N.U.); **U~d States (of America) (US, USA)** *n* Stati *mpl* Uniti (d'America) (USA).

unit trust *n* (*Brit*) fondo d'investimento.

unity ['ju:nɪtɪ] *n* unità.

universal [ju:nɪ'və:sl] *a* universale.

universe ['ju:nɪvə:s] *n* universo.

university [ju:nɪ'və:sɪtɪ] *n* università *f inv*.

unjust [ʌn'dʒʌst] *a* ingiusto(a).

unkempt [ʌn'kempt] *a* trasandato(a); spettinato(a).

unkind [ʌn'kaɪnd] *a* scortese; crudele.

unknown [ʌn'nəun] *a* sconosciuto(a).

unlawful [ʌn'lɔ:ful] *a* illecito(a), illegale.

unleash [ʌn'li:ʃ] *vt* sguinzagliare; (*fig*) scatenare.

unless [ʌn'lɛs] *cj* a meno che (non) + *sub*; ~ **otherwise stated** salvo indicazione contraria.

unlike [ʌn'laɪk] *a* diverso(a) // *prep* a differenza di, contrariamente a.

unlikely [ʌn'laɪklɪ] *a* improbabile; inverosimile.

unlisted [ʌn'lɪstɪd] *a* (*US TEL*): to be ~ non essere sull'elenco.

unload [ʌn'ləud] *vt* scaricare.

unlock [ʌn'lɔk] *vt* aprire.

unlucky [ʌn'lʌkɪ] *a* sfortunato(a); (*object, number*) che porta sfortuna, di malaugurio; **to be** ~ essere sfortunato, non aver fortuna.

unmarried [ʌn'mærɪd] *a* non sposato(a); (*man only*) scapolo, celibe; (*woman only*) nubile.

unmistakable [ʌnmɪs'teɪkəbl] *a* indubbio(a); facilmente riconoscibile.

unmitigated [ʌn'mɪtɪgeɪtɪd] *a* non mitigato(a), assoluto(a), vero(a) e proprio(a).

unnatural [ʌn'nætʃrəl] *a* innaturale; contro natura.

unnecessary [ʌn'nɛsəsərɪ] *a* inutile, superfluo(a).

unnoticed [ʌn'nəutɪst] *a*: (to go) ~ (passare) inosservato(a).

UNO ['ju:nəu] *n abbr* = **United Nations Organization**.

unobtainable [ʌnəb'teɪnəbl] *a* (*TEL*) non ottenibile.

unobtrusive [ʌnəb'tru:sɪv] *a* discreto(a).

unofficial [ʌnə'fɪʃl] *a* non ufficiale; (*strike*) non dichiarato(a) dal sindacato.

unpack [ʌn'pæk] *vi* disfare la valigia (or

le valigie).

unpalatable [ʌn'pælətəbl] a (truth) sgradevole.

unparalleled [ʌn'pærəleld] a incomparabile, impareggiabile.

unpleasant [ʌn'pleznt] a spiacevole.

unplug [ʌn'plʌg] vt staccare.

unpopular [ʌn'pɒpjulə*] a impopolare.

unprecedented [ʌn'presɪdəntɪd] a senza precedenti.

unpredictable [ʌnprɪ'dɪktəbl] a imprevedibile.

unprofessional [ʌnprə'feʃənl] a: ~ conduct scorrettezza professionale.

unqualified [ʌn'kwɒlɪfaɪd] a (teacher) non abilitato(a); (success) assoluto(a), senza riserve.

unquestionably [ʌn'kwestʃənəblɪ] ad indiscutibilmente.

unravel [ʌn'rævl] vt dipanare, districare.

unreal [ʌn'rɪəl] a irreale.

unrealistic [ʌnrɪə'lɪstɪk] a (idea) illusorio(a); (estimate) non realistico(a).

unreasonable [ʌn'ri:znəbl] a irragionevole.

unrelated [ʌnrɪ'leɪtɪd] a: ~ (to) senza rapporto (con); non imparentato(a) (con).

unreliable [ʌnrɪ'laɪəbl] a (person, machine) che non dà affidamento; (news, source of information) inattendibile.

unremitting [ʌnrɪ'mɪtɪŋ] a incessante.

unreservedly [ʌnrɪ'zə:vɪdlɪ] ad senza riserve.

unrest [ʌn'rest] n agitazione f.

unroll [ʌn'rəʊl] vt srotolare.

unruly [ʌn'ru:lɪ] a indisciplinato(a).

unsafe [ʌn'seɪf] a pericoloso(a), rischioso(a).

unsaid [ʌn'sed] a: to leave sth ~ passare qc sotto silenzio.

unsatisfactory ['ʌnsætɪs'fæktərɪ] a che lascia a desiderare, insufficiente.

unsavoury, (US) **unsavory** [ʌn'seɪvərɪ] a (fig: person) losco(a); (: reputation, subject) disgustoso(a), ripugnante.

unscathed [ʌn'skeɪðd] a incolume.

unscrew [ʌn'skru:] vt svitare.

unscrupulous [ʌn'skru:pjuləs] a senza scrupoli.

unsettled [ʌn'setld] a turbato(a); instabile; indeciso(a).

unshaven [ʌn'ʃeɪvn] a non rasato(a).

unsightly [ʌn'saɪtlɪ] a brutto(a), sgradevole a vedersi.

unskilled [ʌn'skɪld] a: ~ worker manovale m.

unspeakable [ʌn'spi:kəbl] a (awful) abominevole.

unstable [ʌn'steɪbl] a (gen) instabile; (mentally) squilibrato(a).

unsteady [ʌn'stedɪ] a instabile, malsicuro(a).

unstuck [ʌn'stʌk] a: to come ~ scollarsi; (fig) fare fiasco.

unsuccessful [ʌnsək'sesful] a (writer, proposal) che non ha successo; (marriage, attempt) mal riuscito(a), fallito(a); to be ~ (in attempting sth) non riuscire; non avere successo; (application) non essere considerato(a).

unsuitable [ʌn'su:təbl] a inadatto(a); inopportuno(a); sconveniente.

unsure [ʌn'ʃuə*] a incerto(a); to be ~ of o.s. essere insicuro(a).

unsympathetic [ʌnsɪmpə'θetɪk] a (person) antipatico(a); (attitude) poco incoraggiante.

untapped [ʌn'tæpt] a (resources) non sfruttato(a).

unthinkable [ʌn'θɪŋkəbl] a impensabile, inconcepibile.

untidy [ʌn'taɪdɪ] a (room) in disordine; (appearance, work) trascurato(a); (person, writing) disordinato(a).

untie [ʌn'taɪ] vt (knot, parcel) disfare; (prisoner, dog) slegare.

until [ʌn'tɪl] prep fino a; (after negative) prima di // finché, fino a quando; (in past, after negative) prima che + sub, prima di + infinitive; ~ now finora; ~ then fino ad allora.

untimely [ʌn'taɪmlɪ] a intempestivo(a), inopportuno(a); (death) prematuro(a).

untold [ʌn'təʊld] a incalcolabile; indescrivibile.

untoward [ʌntə'wɔ:d] a sfortunato(a), sconveniente.

untranslatable [ʌntrænz'leɪtəbl] a intraducibile.

unused [ʌn'ju:zd] a nuovo(a).

unusual [ʌn'ju:ʒuəl] a insolito(a), eccezionale, raro(a).

unveil [ʌn'veɪl] vt scoprire; svelare.

unwavering [ʌn'weɪvərɪŋ] a fermo(a), incrollabile.

unwelcome [ʌn'welkəm] a non gradito(a).

unwell [ʌn'wel] a indisposto(a); to feel ~ non sentirsi bene.

unwieldy [ʌn'wi:ldɪ] a poco maneggevole.

unwilling [ʌn'wɪlɪŋ] a: to be ~ to do non voler fare; ~ly ad malvolentieri.

unwind [ʌn'waɪnd] vb (irg) vt svolgere, srotolare // vi (relax) rilassarsi.

unwise [ʌn'waɪz] a poco saggio(a); (decision) avventato(a).

unwitting [ʌn'wɪtɪŋ] a involontario(a).

unworkable [ʌn'wə:kəbl] a (plan) inattuabile.

unworthy [ʌn'wə:ðɪ] a indegno(a).

unwrap [ʌn'ræp] vt disfare; aprire.

unwritten [ʌn'rɪtn] a (agreement) tacito(a); (law) non scritto(a).

up [ʌp] ♦ prep: he went ~ the stairs/the hill è salito su per le scale/sulla collina; the cat was ~ a tree il gatto era su un albero; they live further ~ the street vivono un po' più su nella stessa strada

◆ *ad* **1** (*upwards, higher*) su, in alto; ~ **in the sky/the mountains** su nel cielo/in montagna; ~ **there** lassù; ~ **above** su in alto

2: to be ~ (*out of bed*) essere alzato(a); (*prices, level*) essere salito(a)

3: ~ **to** (*as far as*) fino a; ~ **to now** finora

4: to be ~ **to** (*depending on*): **it's** ~ **to you** sta a lei, dipende da lei; (*equal to*): **he's not** ~ **to it** (*job, task etc*) non ne è all'altezza; (*col: be doing*): **what is he** ~ **to?** cosa sta combinando?

◆ *n*: ~**s and downs** alti e bassi *mpl*.

up-and-coming [ʌpənd'kʌmɪŋ] *a* pieno(a) di promesse, promettente.

upbringing ['ʌpbrɪŋɪŋ] *n* educazione *f*.

update [ʌp'deɪt] *vt* aggiornare.

upheaval [ʌp'hiːvl] *n* sconvolgimento, tumulto.

uphill [ʌp'hɪl] *a* in salita; (*fig: task*) difficile // *ad*: **to go** ~ andare in salita, salire.

uphold [ʌp'həuld] *vt irg* approvare; sostenere.

upholstery [ʌp'həulstərɪ] *n* tappezzeria.

upkeep ['ʌpkiːp] *n* manutenzione *f*.

upon [ə'pɔn] *prep* su.

upper ['ʌpə*] *a* superiore // *n* (*of shoe*) tomaia; ~**-class** *a* dell'alta borghesia; ~ **hand** *n*: **to have the** ~ **hand** avere il coltello dalla parte del manico; ~**most** *a* il(la) più alto(a); predominante.

upright ['ʌpraɪt] *a* diritto(a); verticale; (*fig*) diritto(a), onesto(a) // *n* montante *m*.

uprising ['ʌpraɪzɪŋ] *n* insurrezione *f*, rivolta.

uproar ['ʌprɔː*] *n* tumulto, clamore *m*.

uproot [ʌp'ruːt] *vt* sradicare.

upset *n* ['ʌpsɛt] turbamento // *vt* [ʌp'sɛt] (*irg: like set*) (*glass etc*) rovesciare; (*plan, stomach*) scombussolare; (*person: offend*) contrariare; (*: grieve*) addolorare; sconvolgere // *a* [ʌp'sɛt] contrariato(a); addolorato(a); (*stomach*) scombussolato(a), disturbato(a).

upshot ['ʌpʃɔt] *n* risultato.

upside-down ['ʌpsaɪd'daun] *ad* sottosopra.

upstairs [ʌp'stɛəz] *ad*, *a* di sopra, al piano superiore.

upstart ['ʌpstɑːt] *n* parvenu *m inv*.

upstream [ʌp'striːm] *ad* a monte.

uptake ['ʌpteɪk] *n*: **he is quick/slow on the** ~ è pronto/lento di comprendonio.

uptight [ʌp'taɪt] *a* (*col*) teso(a).

up-to-date ['ʌptə'deɪt] *a* moderno(a); aggiornato(a).

upturn ['ʌptəːn] *n* (*in luck*) svolta favorevole; (*COMM: in market*) rialzo.

upward ['ʌpwəd] *a* ascendente; verso l'alto; ~**(s)** *ad* in su, verso l'alto.

urban ['əːbən] *a* urbano(a).

urbane [əː'beɪn] *a* civile, urbano(a),

educato(a).

urchin ['əːtʃɪn] *n* monello.

urge [əːdʒ] *n* impulso; stimolo; forte desiderio // *vt*: **to** ~ **sb to do** esortare qn a fare, spingere qn a fare; raccomandare a qn di fare.

urgency ['əːdʒənsɪ] *n* urgenza; (*of tone*) insistenza.

urgent ['əːdʒənt] *a* urgente.

urinate ['juərɪneɪt] *vi* orinare.

urine ['juərɪn] *n* orina.

urn [əːn] *n* urna; (*also*: **tea** ~) bollitore *m* per il tè.

US, USA *n abbr* = **United States (of America).**

us [ʌs] *pronoun* ci; (*stressed, after prep*) noi; *see also* **me.**

usage ['juːzɪdʒ] *n* uso.

use *n* [juːs] uso; impiego, utilizzazione *f* // *vt* [juːz] usare, utilizzare, servirsi di; **she** ~**d to do it** lo faceva (una volta), era solita farlo; **in** ~ in uso; **out of** ~ fuori uso; **to be of** ~ essere utile, servire; **it's no** ~ non serve, è inutile; **to be** ~**d to** avere l'abitudine di; **to** ~ **up** *vt* consumare; esaurire; ~**d** *a* (*car*) d'occasione; ~**ful** *a* utile; ~**fulness** *n* utilità; ~**less** *a* inutile; ~**r** *n* utente *m/f*; ~**r-friendly** *a* (*computer*) di facile uso.

usher ['ʌʃə*] *n* usciere *m*; (*in cinema*) maschera; ~**ette** [-'rɛt] *n* (*in cinema*) maschera.

USSR *n*: **the** ~ l'URSS *f*.

usual ['juːʒuəl] *a* solito(a); **as** ~ come al solito, come d'abitudine; ~**ly** *ad* di solito.

utensil [juː'tɛnsl] *n* utensile *m*; **kitchen** ~**s** utensili da cucina.

uterus ['juːtərəs] *n* utero.

utility [juː'tɪlɪtɪ] *n* utilità; (*also*: **public** ~) servizio pubblico; ~ **room** *n* locale adibito alla stiratura dei panni etc.

utmost ['ʌtməust] *a* estremo(a) // *n*: **to do one's** ~ fare il possibile *or* di tutto.

utter ['ʌtə*] *a* assoluto(a), totale // *vt* pronunciare, proferire; emettere; ~**ance** *n* espressione *f*; parole *fpl*; ~**ly** *ad* completamente, del tutto.

U-turn ['juː'təːn] *n* inversione *f* a U.

V

v. *abbr* = **verse, versus, volt**; (= *vide*) vedi, vedere.

vacancy ['veɪkənsɪ] *n* (*Brit: job*) posto libero; (*room*) stanza libera.

vacant ['veɪkənt] *a* (*job, seat etc*) libero(a); (*expression*) assente; ~ **lot** *n* (*US*) terreno non occupato; (*: for sale*) terreno in vendita.

vacate [və'keɪt] *vt* lasciare libero(a).

vacation [və'keɪʃən] *n* vacanze *fpl*.

vaccinate ['væksɪneɪt] *vt* vaccinare.

vacuum ['vækjum] n vuoto; ~ **bottle** n (US) = ~ **flask**; ~ **cleaner** n aspirapolvere m inv; ~ **flask** n (Brit) thermos m inv ®; ~-**packed** a confezionato (a) sottovuoto.

vagina [və'dʒaɪnə] n vagina.

vagrant ['veɪgrnt] n vagabondo/a.

vague [veɪg] a vago (a); (blurred: photo, memory) sfocato (a); ~**ly** ad vagamente.

vain [veɪn] a (useless) inutile, vano (a); (conceited) vanitoso (a); **in** ~ inutilmente, invano.

valentine ['væləntaɪn] n (also: ~ **card**) cartolina or biglietto di San Valentino.

valet ['væleɪ] n cameriere m personale.

valiant ['væliənt] a valoroso (a), coraggioso (a).

valid ['vælɪd] a valido (a), valevole; (excuse) valido (a).

valley ['vælɪ] n valle f.

valour, (US) **valor** ['vælə*] n valore m.

valuable ['væljuəbl] a (jewel) di (grande) valore; (time) prezioso (a); ~**s** npl oggetti mpl di valore.

valuation [vælju'eɪʃən] n valutazione f, stima.

value ['vælju:] n valore m // vt (fix price) valutare, dare un prezzo a; (cherish) apprezzare, tenere a; ~ **added tax (VAT)** n (Brit) imposta sul valore aggiunto (I.V.A.); ~**d** a (appreciated) stimato (a), apprezzato (a).

valve [vælv] n valvola f.

van [væn] n (AUT) furgone m; (Brit RAIL) vagone m.

vandal ['vændl] n vandalo/a; ~**ism** n vandalismo.

vanilla [və'nɪlə] n vaniglia // cpd (ice cream) alla vaniglia.

vanish ['vænɪʃ] vi svanire, scomparire.

vanity ['vænɪtɪ] n vanità; ~ **case** n valigetta per cosmetici.

vantage ['vɑːntɪdʒ] n: ~ **point** posizione f or punto di osservazione; (fig) posizione vantaggiosa.

vapour, (US) **vapor** ['veɪpə*] n vapore m.

variable ['vɛərɪəbl] a variabile; (mood) mutevole.

variance ['vɛərɪəns] n: **to be at** ~ (**with**) essere in disaccordo (con); (facts) essere in contraddizione (con).

varicose ['værɪkəus] a: ~ **veins** varici fpl.

varied ['vɛərɪd] a vario (a), diverso (a).

variety [və'raɪətɪ] n varietà f inv; (quantity) quantità, numero; ~ **show** n varietà m inv.

various ['vɛərɪəs] a vario (a), diverso (a); (several) parecchi (e), molti (e).

varnish ['vɑːnɪʃ] n vernice f // vt verniciare.

vary ['vɛərɪ] vt, vi variare, mutare.

vase [vɑːz] n vaso.

vaseline ['væsɪliːn] n ® vaselina.

vast [vɑːst] a vasto (a); (amount, success) enorme; ~**ly** ad enormemente.

VAT [væt] n abbr = **value added tax**.

vat [væt] n tino.

Vatican ['vætɪkən] n: **the** ~ il Vaticano.

vault [vɔːlt] n (of roof) volta; (tomb) tomba; (in bank) camera blindata; (jump) salto // vt (also: ~ **over**) saltare (d'un balzo).

vaunted ['vɔːntɪd] a: **much-**~ tanto celebrato (a).

VCR n abbr = **video cassette recorder**.

VD n abbr = **venereal disease**.

VDU n abbr = **visual display unit**.

veal [viːl] n vitello.

veer [vɪə*] vi girare; virare.

vegetable ['vedʒtəbl] n verdura, ortaggio // a vegetale.

vegetarian [vedʒɪ'tɛərɪən] a, n vegetariano (a).

vehement ['viːmənt] a veemente, violento (a).

vehicle ['viːɪkl] n veicolo.

veil [veɪl] n velo // vt velare.

vein [veɪn] n vena; (on leaf) nervatura; (fig: mood) vena, umore m.

velvet ['vɛlvɪt] n velluto.

vending machine ['vendɪŋ-] n distributore m automatico.

veneer [və'nɪə*] n impiallacciatura; (fig) vernice f.

venereal [vɪ'nɪərɪəl] a: ~ **disease (VD)** malattia venerea.

Venetian [vɪ'niːʃən] a veneziano (a); ~ **blind** n (tenda alla) veneziana.

vengeance ['vendʒəns] n vendetta; **with a** ~ (fig) davvero; furiosamente.

Venice ['venɪs] n Venezia.

venison ['venɪsn] n carne f di cervo.

venom ['venəm] n veleno.

vent [vent] n foro, apertura; (in dress, jacket) spacco // vt (fig: one's feelings) sfogare, dare sfogo a.

ventilate ['ventɪleɪt] vt (room) dare aria a, arieggiare; **ventilator** n ventilatore m.

ventriloquist [ven'trɪləkwɪst] n ventriloquo/a.

venture ['ventʃə*] n impresa (rischiosa) // vt rischiare, azzardare // vi arrischiarsi, azzardarsi.

venue ['venjuː] n luogo di incontro; (SPORT) luogo (designato) per l'incontro.

verb [vəːb] n verbo; ~**al** a verbale; (translation) letterale.

verbatim [vəː'beɪtɪm] a, ad parola per parola.

verdict ['vəːdɪkt] n verdetto.

verge [vəːdʒ] n (Brit) bordo, orlo; **on the** ~ **of doing** sul punto di fare; **to** ~ **on** vt fus rasentare.

verification [verɪfɪ'keɪʃən] n verifica.

veritable ['verɪtəbl] a vero (a).

vermin ['vəːmɪn] npl animali mpl nocivi;

(insects) insetti *mpl* parassiti.
vermouth ['vɜːməθ] *n* vermut *m inv*.
versatile ['vɜːsətaɪl] *a (person)* versatile; *(machine, tool etc)* (che si presta) a molti usi.
verse [vɜːs] *n* versi *mpl*; *(stanza)* stanza, strofa; *(in bible)* versetto.
version ['vɜːʃən] *n* versione *f*.
versus ['vɜːsəs] *prep* contro.
vertical ['vɜːtɪkl] *a, n* verticale *(m)*; ~ly *ad* verticalmente.
vertigo ['vɜːtɪgəʊ] *n* vertigine *f*.
verve [vɜːv] *n* brio; entusiasmo.
very ['verɪ] *ad* molto // *a*: the ~ book which proprio il libro che; at the ~ end proprio alla fine; the ~ last proprio l'ultimo; at the ~ least almeno; ~ much moltissimo.
vessel ['vesl] *n (ANAT)* vaso; *(NAUT)* nave *f*; *(container)* recipiente *m*.
vest [vest] *n (Brit)* maglia; (: *sleeveless*) canottiera; *(US: waistcoat)* gilè *m inv*; ~ed **interests** *npl (COMM)* diritti *mpl* acquisiti.
vestment ['vestmənt] *n (REL)* paramento liturgico.
vestry ['vestrɪ] *n* sagrestia.
vet [vet] *n abbr (= veterinary surgeon)* veterinario // *vt* esaminare minuziosamente; *(text)* rivedere.
veteran ['vetərn] *n* veterano; *(also: war ~)* reduce *m*.
veterinary ['vetrɪnərɪ] *a* veterinario(a); ~ **surgeon**, *(US)* **veterinarian** *n* veterinario.
veto ['viːtəʊ] *n, pl* ~**es** veto // *vt* opporre il veto a.
vex [veks] *vt* irritare, contrariare; ~ed *a (question)* controverso(a), dibattuto(a).
VHF *abbr (= very high frequency)* VHF, altissima frequenza.
via ['vaɪə] *prep (by way of)* via; *(by means of)* tramite.
viable ['vaɪəbl] *a* attuabile; vitale.
viaduct ['vaɪədʌkt] *n* viadotto.
vibrate [vaɪ'breɪt] *vi*: to ~ (**with**) vibrare (di); *(resound)* risonare (di).
vicar ['vɪkə*] *n* pastore *m*; ~**age** *n* presbiterio.
vicarious [vɪ'keərɪəs] *a* indiretto(a).
vice [vaɪs] *n (evil)* vizio; *(TECH)* morsa.
vice- [vaɪs] *prefix* vice....
vice squad *n* (squadra del) buon costume *f*.
vice versa ['vaɪsɪ'vɜːsə] *ad* viceversa.
vicinity [vɪ'sɪnɪtɪ] *n* vicinanze *fpl*.
vicious ['vɪʃəs] *a (remark)* maligno(a), cattivo(a); *(blow)* violento(a); ~ **circle** *n* circolo vizioso.
victim ['vɪktɪm] *n* vittima *f*.
victor ['vɪktə*] *n* vincitore *m*.
Victorian [vɪk'tɔːrɪən] *a* vittoriano(a).
victory ['vɪktərɪ] *n* vittoria.
video ['vɪdɪəʊ] *cpd* video... // *n (~ film)* video *m inv*; *(also: ~ cassette)*

videocassetta; *(also:* ~ **cassette recorder)** videoregistratore *m*; ~ **tape** *n* videotape *m inv*.
vie [vaɪ] *vi*: to ~ **with** competere con, rivaleggiare con.
Vienna [vɪ'enə] *n* Vienna.
Vietnam [vjet'næm] *n* Vietnam *m*; ~**ese** *a, n (pl inv)* vietnamita *(m/f)*.
view [vjuː] *n* vista, veduta; *(opinion)* opinione *f* // *vt (situation)* considerare; *(house)* visitare; **on** ~ *(in museum etc)* esposto(a); **in full** ~ **of** sotto gli occhi di; **in** ~ **of the fact that** considerato che; ~**er** *n (viewfinder)* mirino; *(small projector)* visore *m*; *(TV)* telespettatore/trice; ~**finder** *n* mirino; ~**point** *n* punto di vista.
vigil ['vɪdʒɪl] *n* veglia.
vigorous ['vɪgərəs] *a* vigoroso(a).
vile [vaɪl] *a (action)* vile; *(smell)* disgustoso(a), nauseante; *(temper)* pessimo(a).
villa ['vɪlə] *n* villa.
village ['vɪlɪdʒ] *n* villaggio; ~**r** *n* abitante *m/f* di villaggio.
villain ['vɪlən] *n (scoundrel)* canaglia; *(criminal)* criminale *m*; *(in novel etc)* cattivo.
vindicate ['vɪndɪkeɪt] *vt* comprovare; giustificare.
vindictive [vɪn'dɪktɪv] *a* vendicativo(a).
vine [vaɪn] *n* vite *f*; *(climbing plant)* rampicante *m*.
vinegar ['vɪnɪgə*] *n* aceto.
vineyard ['vɪnjɑːd] *n* vigna, vigneto.
vintage ['vɪntɪdʒ] *n (year)* annata, produzione *f*; ~ **wine** *n* vino d'annata.
vinyl ['vaɪnl] *n* vinile *m*.
violate ['vaɪəleɪt] *vt* violare.
violence ['vaɪələns] *n* violenza; *(POL etc)* incidenti *mpl* violenti.
violent ['vaɪələnt] *a* violento(a).
violet ['vaɪələt] *a (colour)* viola *inv*, violetto(a) // *n (plant)* violetta.
violin [vaɪə'lɪn] *n* violino; ~**ist** *n* violinista *m/f*.
VIP *n abbr (= very important person)* V.I.P. *m/f inv*.
virgin ['vɜːdʒɪn] *n* vergine *f* // *a* vergine *inv*.
Virgo ['vɜːgəʊ] *n (sign)* Vergine *f*.
virile ['vɪraɪl] *a* virile.
virtually ['vɜːtjuəlɪ] *ad (almost)* praticamente.
virtue ['vɜːtjuː] *n* virtù *f inv*; *(advantage)* pregio, vantaggio; **by** ~ **of** grazie a.
virtuous ['vɜːtjuəs] *a* virtuoso(a).
virus ['vaɪərəs] *n* virus *m inv*.
visa ['viːzə] *n* visto.
vis-à-vis [viːzə'viː] *prep* rispetto a, nei riguardi di.
visibility [vɪzɪ'bɪlɪtɪ] *n* visibilità.
visible ['vɪzəbl] *a* visibile.
vision ['vɪʒən] *n (sight)* vista; *(foresight, in dream)* visione *f*.

visit ['vizit] *n* visita; *(stay)* soggiorno // *vt (person)* andare a trovare; *(place)* visitare; ~**ing hours** *npl (in hospital etc)* orario delle visite; ~**or** *κ* visitatore/trice; *(guest)* ospite *m/f*; *(in hotel)* cliente *m/f*; ~**ors' book** *n* libro d'oro; *(in hotel)* registro.

visor ['vaizə*] *n* visiera.

vista ['vistə] *n* vista, prospettiva.

visual ['vizjuəl] *a* visivo(a); visuale; ottico(a); ~ **aid** *n* sussidio visivo; ~ **display unit (VDU)** *n* visualizzatore *m*.

visualize ['vizjuəlaiz] *vt* immaginare, figurarsi; *(foresee)* prevedere.

vital ['vaitl] *a* vitale; ~**ly** *ad* estremamente; ~ **statistics** *npl (fig)* misure *fpl*.

vitamin ['vitəmin] *n* vitamina.

vivacious [vi'veifəs] *a* vivace.

vivid ['vivid] *a* vivido(a); ~**ly** *ad (describe)* vividamente; *(remember)* con precisione.

V-neck ['vi:nɛk] *n* maglione *m* con lo scollo a V.

vocabulary [vəu'kæbjuləri] *n* vocabolario.

vocal ['vəukl] *a (MUS)* vocale; *(communication)* verbale; ~ **chords** *npl* corde *fpl* vocali.

vocation [vəu'keifən] *n* vocazione *f*; ~**al** *a* professionale.

vociferous [və'sifərəs] *a* rumoroso(a).

vodka ['vɔdkə] *n* vodka *f inv*.

vogue [vəug] *n* moda; *(popularity)* popolarità, voga.

voice [vɔis] *n* voce *f* // *vt (opinion)* esprimere.

void [vɔid] *n* vuoto // *a (invalid)* nullo(a); *(empty)* vuoto(a); ~ **of** privo(a) di.

volatile ['vɔlətail] *a* volatile; *(fig)* volubile.

volcano, ~es [vɔl'keinəu] *n* vulcano.

volition [və'lifən] *n*: **of one's own ~** di sua volontà.

volley ['vɔli] *n (of gunfire)* salva; *(of stones etc)* raffica, gragnola; *(TENNIS etc)* volata; ~**ball** *n* pallavolo *f*.

volt [vəult] *n* volt *m inv*; ~**age** *n* tensione *f*, voltaggio.

voluble ['vɔljubl] *a* loquace, ciarliero(a).

volume ['vɔlju:m] *n* volume *m*; ~ **control** *n (RADIO, TV)* regolatore *m or* manopola del volume.

voluntarily ['vɔləntrili] *ad* volontariamente; gratuitamente.

voluntary ['vɔləntəri] *a* volontario(a); *(unpaid)* gratuito(a), non retribuito(a).

volunteer [vɔlən'tiə*] *n* volontario/a // *vi (MIL)* arruolarsi volontario; **to ~ to do** offrire (volontariamente) di fare.

voluptuous [və'lʌptjuəs] *a* voluttuoso(a).

vomit ['vɔmit] *n* vomito // *vt, vi* vomitare.

vote [vəut] *n* voto, suffragio; *(cast)* voto; *(franchise)* diritto di voto // *vi* votare; ~

of thanks discorso di ringraziamento; ~**r** *n* elettore/trice; **voting** *n* scrutinio.

vouch [vautf]: **to ~ for** *vt fus* farsi garante di.

voucher ['vautfə*] *n (for meal, petrol)* buono; *(receipt)* ricevuta.

vow [vau] *n* voto, promessa solenne // *vi* giurare.

vowel ['vauəl] *n* vocale *f*.

voyage ['vɔiidʒ] *n* viaggio per mare, traversata.

vulgar ['vʌlgə*] *a* volgare.

vulnerable ['vʌlnərəbl] *a* vulnerabile.

vulture ['vʌltfə*] *n* avvoltoio.

W

wad [wɔd] *n (of cotton wool, paper)* tampone *m*; *(of banknotes etc)* fascio.

waddle ['wɔdl] *vi* camminare come una papera.

wade [weid] *vi*: **to ~ through** camminare a stento in // *vt* guadare.

wafer ['weifə*] *n (CULIN)* cialda; *(REL)* ostia; *(COMPUT)* wafer *m inv*.

waffle ['wɔfl] *n (CULIN)* cialda; *(col)* ciance *fpl*; riempitivo // *vi* cianciare; parlare a vuoto.

waft [wɔft] *vt* portare // *vi* diffondersi.

wag [wæg] *vt* agitare, muovere // *vi* agitarsi.

wage [weidʒ] *n (also: ~s)* salario, paga // *vt*: **to ~ war** fare la guerra; ~ **packet** *n* busta *f* paga *inv*.

wager ['weidʒə*] *n* scommessa.

waggle ['wægl] *vt* dimenare, agitare // *vi* dimenarsi, agitarsi.

wag(g)on ['wægən] *n (horse-drawn)* carro; *(Brit RAIL)* vagone *m* (merci).

wail [weil] *n* gemito; *(of siren)* urlo // *vi* gemere; urlare.

waist [weist] *n* vita, cintola; ~**coat** *n (Brit)* panciotto, gilè *m inv*; ~**line** *n* (giro di) vita.

wait [weit] *n* attesa // *vi* aspettare, attendere; **to lie in ~ for** stare in agguato a; **to ~ for** aspettare; **I can't ~ to** *(fig)* non vedo l'ora di; **to ~ behind** *vi* rimanere (ad aspettare); **to ~ on** *vt fus* servire; ~**er** *n* cameriere *m*; ~**ing** *n*: "**no ~ing**" *(Brit AUT)* "divieto di sosta"; ~**ing list** *n* lista di attesa; ~**ing room** *n* sala d'aspetto *or* d'attesa; ~**ress** *n* cameriera.

waive [weiv] *vt* rinunciare a, abbandonare.

wake [weik] *vb (pt* **woke,** ~**d,** *pp* **woken,** ~**d)** *vt (also:* ~ **up)** svegliare // *vi (also:* ~ **up)** svegliarsi // *n (for dead person)* veglia funebre; *(NAUT)* scia; ~**n** *vt, vi* = **wake.**

Wales [weilz] *n* Galles *m*.

walk [wɔ:k] *n* passeggiata; *(short)* giretto; *(gait)* passo, andatura; *(path)* sentiero; (*in park etc*) sentiero, vialetto // *vi* camminare; (*for pleasure, exercise*) passeggiare // *vt* (*distance*) fare or percorrere a piedi; (*dog*) accompagnare, portare a passeggiare; **10 minutes' ~ from 10** minuti di cammino or a piedi da; **from all ~s of life** di tutte le condizioni sociali; **to ~ out on** *vt fus* (*col*) piantare in asso; **~er** *n* (*person*) camminatore/trice; **~ie-talkie** ['wɔ:kɪ'tɔ:kɪ] *n* walkie-talkie *m inv*; **~ing** *n* camminare *m*; **~ing stick** *n* bastone *m* da passeggio; **~out** *n* (*of workers*) sciopero senza preavviso or a sorpresa; **~over** *n* (*col*) vittoria facile, gioco da ragazzi; **~way** *n* passaggio pedonale.

wall [wɔ:l] *n* muro; (*internal, of tunnel, cave*) parete *f*; **~ed** *a* (*city*) fortificato(a).

wallet ['wɔlɪt] *n* portafoglio.

wallflower ['wɔ:lflauə*] *n* violacciocca; **to be a ~** (*fig*) fare da tappezzeria.

wallop ['wɔləp] *vt* (*col*) pestare.

wallow ['wɔləu] *vi* sguazzare, voltolarsi.

wallpaper ['wɔ:lpeɪpə*] *n* carta da parati.

wally ['wɔlɪ] *n* (*col*) imbecille *m/f*.

walnut ['wɔ:lnʌt] *n* noce *f*; (*tree*) noce *m*.

walrus, *pl* ~ *or* **~es** ['wɔ:lrəs] *n* tricheco.

waltz [wɔ:lts] *n* valzer *m inv* // *vi* ballare il valzer.

wan [wɔn] *a* pallido(a), smorto(a); triste.

wand [wɔnd] *n* (*also:* **magic ~**) bacchetta (magica).

wander ['wɔndə*] *vi* (*person*) girare senza meta, girovagare; (*thoughts*) vagare; (*river*) serpeggiare // *vt* girovagare per.

wane [weɪn] *vi* (*moon*) calare; (*reputation*) declinare.

wangle ['wæŋgl] *vt* (*Brit col*): **to ~ sth** procurare qc con l'astuzia.

want [wɔnt] *vt* volere; (*need*) aver bisogno di; (*lack*) mancare di // *n*: **for ~ of** per mancanza di; **~s** *npl* (*needs*) bisogni *mpl*; **to ~ to do** volere fare; **to ~ sb to do** volere che qn faccia; **~ing** *a*: **to be found ~ing** non risultare all'altezza.

wanton ['wɔntn] *a* sfrenato(a); senza motivo.

war [wɔ:*] *n* guerra; **to go to ~** entrare in guerra.

ward [wɔ:d] *n* (*in hospital: room*) corsia; (: *section*) reparto; (*POL*) circoscrizione *f*; (*LAW: child*) pupillo/a; **to ~ off** *vt* parare, schivare.

warden ['wɔ:dn] *n* (*Brit: of institution*) direttore/trice; (*of park, game reserve*) guardiano/a; (*Brit: also:* **traffic ~**) addetto/a al controllo del traffico e del parcheggio.

warder ['wɔ:də*] *n* (*Brit*) guardia carceraria.

wardrobe ['wɔ:drəub] *n* (*cupboard*) guardaroba *m inv*, armadio; (*clothes*) guardaroba; (*THEATRE*) costumi *mpl*.

warehouse ['wɛəhaus] *n* magazzino.

wares [wɛəz] *npl* merci *fpl*.

warfare ['wɔ:fɛə*] *n* guerra.

warhead ['wɔ:hɛd] *n* (*MIL*) testata.

warily ['wɛərɪlɪ] *ad* cautamente, con prudenza.

warm [wɔ:m] *a* caldo(a); (*thanks, welcome, applause*) caloroso(a); **it's ~** fa caldo; **I'm ~** ho caldo; **to ~ up** *vi* scaldarsi, riscaldarsi; (*athlete, discussion*) riscaldarsi // *vt* scaldare, riscaldare; (*engine*) far scaldare; **~hearted** *a* affettuoso(a); **~ly** *ad* caldamente; calorosamente; vivamente; **~th** *n* calore *m*.

warn [wɔ:n] *vt* avvertire, avvisare; **~ing** *n* avvertimento; (*notice*) avviso; **~ing light** *n* spia luminosa, **~ing triangle** *n* (*AUT*) triangolo.

warp [wɔ:p] *vi* deformarsi // *vt* deformare; (*fig*) corrompere.

warrant ['wɔrnt] *n* (*LAW: to arrest*) mandato di cattura; (: *to search*) mandato di perquisizione.

warranty ['wɔrəntɪ] *n* garanzia.

warren ['wɔrən] *n* (*of rabbits*) tana.

warrior ['wɔrɪə*] *n* guerriero/a.

Warsaw ['wɔ:sɔ:] *n* Varsavia.

warship ['wɔ:ʃɪp] *n* nave *f* da guerra.

wart [wɔ:t] *n* verruca.

wartime ['wɔ:taɪm] *n*: **in ~** in tempo di guerra.

wary ['wɛərɪ] *a* prudente.

was [wɔz] *pt of* **be**.

wash [wɔʃ] *vt* lavare // *vi* lavarsi // *n*: **to give sth a ~** lavare qc, dare una lavata a qc; **to have a ~** lavarsi; **to ~ away** *vt* (*stain*) togliere lavando; (*subj: river etc*) trascinare via; **to ~ off** *vi* andare via con il lavaggio; **to ~ up** *vi* (*Brit*) lavare i piatti; (*US*) darsi una lavata; **~able** *a* lavabile; **~basin**, (*US*) **~bowl** *n* lavabo; **~cloth** *n* (*US: face cloth*) pezzuola (per lavarsi); **~er** *n* (*TECH*) rondella; **~ing** *n* (*linen etc*) bucato; **~ing machine** *n* lavatrice *f*; **~ing powder** *n* (*Brit*) detersivo (in polvere); **~ing-up** *n* rigovernatura, lavatura dei piatti; **~ing-up liquid** *n* detersivo liquido (per stoviglie); **~-out** *n* (*col*) disastro; **~room** *n* gabinetto.

wasn't ['wɔznt] = **was not**.

wasp [wɔsp] *n* vespa.

wastage ['weɪstɪdʒ] *n* spreco; (*in manufacturing*) scarti *mpl*; **natural ~** diminuzione *f* di manodopera (*per pensionamento, decesso etc*).

waste [weɪst] *n* spreco; (*of time*) perdita; (*rubbish*) rifiuti *mpl* // *a* (*material*) di scarto; (*food*) avanzato(a)

// vt sprecare; (*time, opportunity*) perdere; ~s *npl* distesa desolata; **to lay ~** (*destroy*) devastare; **to ~ away** *vi* deperire; **~ disposal unit** *n* (*Brit*) eliminatore *m* di rifiuti; **~ful** *a* sprecone(a); (*process*) dispendioso(a); **~ ground** *n* (*Brit*) terreno incolto *or* abbandonato; **~paper basket** *n* cestino per la carta straccia; **~pipe** *n* tubo di scarico.

watch [wɔtʃ] *n* orologio; (*act of watching*) sorveglianza; (*guard: MIL, NAUT*) guardia; (*NAUT: spell of duty*) quarto // vt (*look at*) osservare; (: *match, programme*) guardare; (*spy on, guard*) sorvegliare, tenere d'occhio; (*be careful of*) fare attenzione a // vi osservare, guardare; (*keep guard*) fare *or* montare la guardia; **to ~ out** *vi* fare attenzione; **~dog** *n* cane *m* da guardia; **~ful** *a* attento(a), vigile; **~maker** *n* orologiaio/a; **~man** *n* guardiano; (*also:* **night ~man**) guardiano notturno; **~ strap** *n* cinturino da orologio.

water ['wɔːtə*] *n* acqua // vt (*plant*) annaffiare // vi (*eyes*) lacrimare; in British ~s nelle acque territoriali britanniche; **to ~ down** vt (*milk*) diluire; (*fig: story*) edulcorare; **~colour** *n* acquerello; **~colours** *npl* colori *mpl* per acquarello; **~cress** *n* crescione *m*; **~fall** *n* cascata; **~ heater** *n* scaldabagno; **~ lily** *n* ninfea; **~line** *n* (*NAUT*) linea di galleggiamento; **~logged** *a* saturo(a) d'acqua; imbevuto(a) d'acqua; (*football pitch etc*) allagato(a); **~ main** *n* conduttura dell'acqua; **~mark** *n* (*on paper*) filigrana; **~melon** *n* anguria, cocomero; **~proof** *a* impermeabile; **~shed** *n* (*GEO, fig*) spartiacque *m*; **~-skiing** *n* sci *m* acquatico; **~tight** *a* stagno(a); **~way** *n* corso d'acqua navigabile; **~works** *npl* impianto idrico; **~y** *a* (*colour*) slavato(a); (*coffee*) acquoso(a).

watt [wɔt] *n* watt *m inv*.

wave [weɪv] *n* onda; (*of hand*) gesto, segno; (*in hair*) ondulazione *f* // vi fare un cenno con la mano; (*flag*) sventolare // vt (*handkerchief*) sventolare; (*stick*) brandire; **~length** *n* lunghezza d'onda.

waver ['weɪvə*] *vi* vacillare; (*voice*) tremolare.

wavy ['weɪvɪ] *a* ondulato(a); ondeggiante.

wax [wæks] *n* cera // vt dare la cera a; (*car*) lucidare // vi (*moon*) crescere; **~works** *npl* cere *fpl*; museo delle cere.

way [weɪ] *n* via, strada; (*path, access*) passaggio; (*distance*) distanza; (*direction*) parte *f*, direzione *f*; (*manner*) modo, stile *m*; (*habit*) abitudine *f*; (*condition*) condizione *f*; **which ~?** — **this ~** da che parte *or* in quale direzione? — da questa parte *or* per di

qua; **on the ~** (*en route*) per strada; **to be on one's ~** essere in cammino *or* sulla strada; **to be in the ~** bloccare il passaggio; (*fig*) essere tra i piedi *or* d'impiccio; **to go out of one's ~ to do** (*fig*) mettercela tutta *or* fare di tutto per fare; **to lose one's ~** perdere la strada; **in a ~** in un certo senso; **in some ~s** sotto certi aspetti; **by the ~** ... a proposito ...; **"~ in"** (*Brit*) "entrata", "ingresso"; **"~ out"** (*Brit*) "uscita".

waylay [weɪ'leɪ] *vt irg* tendere un agguato a; attendere al passaggio.

wayward ['weɪwəd] *a* capriccioso(a); testardo(a).

W.C. ['dʌblju'siː] *n* (*Brit*) W.C. *m inv*, gabinetto.

we [wiː] *pl pronoun* noi.

weak [wiːk] *a* debole; (*health*) precario(a); (*beam etc*) fragile; **~en** *vi* indebolirsi // vt indebolire; **~ling** ['wiːklɪŋ] *n* smidollato/a; debole *m/f*; **~ness** *n* debolezza; (*fault*) punto debole, difetto.

wealth [wɛlθ] *n* (*money, resources*) ricchezza, ricchezze *fpl*; (*of details*) abbondanza, profusione *f*; **~y** *a* ricco(a).

wean [wiːn] *vt* svezzare.

weapon ['wɛpən] *n* arma.

wear [wɛə*] *n* (*use*) uso; (*deterioration through use*) logorio, usura; (*clothing*): **sports/baby ~** abbigliamento sportivo/per neonati // vb (*pt* **wore**, *pp* **worn**) vt (*clothes*) portare; mettersi; (*damage: through use*) consumare // vi (*last*) durare; (*rub etc through*) consumarsi; **evening ~** abiti *mpl* *or* tenuta da sera; **to ~ away** vt consumare; erodere // vi consumarsi; essere eroso(a); **to ~ down** vt consumare; (*strength*) esaurire; **to ~ off** vi sparire lentamente; **to ~ on** vi passare; **to ~ out** vt consumare; (*person, strength*) esaurire; **~ and tear** *n* usura, consumo.

weary ['wɪərɪ] *a* stanco(a); (*tiring*) faticoso(a).

weasel ['wiːzl] *n* (*ZOOL*) donnola.

weather ['wɛðə*] *n* tempo // vt (*wood*) stagionare; (*storm, crisis*) superare; **under the ~** (*fig: ill*) poco bene; **~beaten** *a* (*person*) segnato(a) dalle intemperie; (*building*) logorato(a) dalle intemperie; **~cock** *n* banderuola; **~ forecast** *n* previsioni *fpl* del tempo, bollettino meteorologico; **~ vane** *n* = **~cock**.

weave [wiːv], *pt* **wove**, *pp* **woven** vt (*cloth*) tessere; (*basket*) intrecciare; **~r** *n* tessitore/trice; **weaving** *n* tessitura.

web [wɛb] *n* (*of spider*) ragnatela; (*on foot*) palma; (*fabric, also fig*) tessuto.

wed [wɛd] vt (*pt, pp* **wedded**) sposare // vi sposarsi.

we'd [wiːd] = **we had**, **we would**.

wedding ['wedıŋ] n matrimonio; **silver/ golden ~ anniversary** n nozze fpl d'argento/d'oro; **~ day** n giorno delle nozze or del matrimonio; **~ dress** n abito nuziale; **~ ring** n fede f.

wedge [wedʒ] n (of wood etc) cuneo; (under door etc) zeppa; (of cake) spicchio, fetta // vt (fix) fissare con zeppe; (push) incuneare.

wedlock ['wedlɔk] n vincolo matrimoniale.

Wednesday ['wednzdı] n mercoledì m inv.

wee [wi:] a (Scottish) piccolo(a).

weed [wi:d] n erbaccia // vt diserbare; **~killer** n diserbante m; **~y** a (person) allampanato(a).

week [wi:k] n settimana; a ~ today/on Friday oggi/venerdì a otto; **~day** n giorno feriale; (COMM) giornata lavorativa; **~end** n fine settimana m or f inv, weekend m inv; **~ly** ad ogni settimana, settimanalmente // a, n settimanale (m).

weep [wi:p], pt, pp **wept** vi (person) plangere; **~ing willow** n salice m piangente.

weigh [weı] vt, vi pesare; **to ~ down** vt (branch) piegare; (fig: with worry) opprimere, caricare; **to ~ up** vt valutare.

weight [weıt] n peso; **to lose/put on ~** dimagrire/ingrassare; **~ing** n (allowance) indennità; **~ lifter** n pesista m; **~y** a pesante; (fig) importante, grave.

weir [wıə*] n diga.

weird [wıəd] a strano(a), bizzarro(a); (eerie) soprannaturale.

welcome ['welkəm] a benvenuto(a) // n accoglienza, benvenuto // vt accogliere cordialmente; (also: bid ~) dare il benvenuto a; (be glad of) rallegrarsi di; **to be ~** essere il(la) benvenuto(a); thank you — you're ~! grazie — prego!

weld [weld] n saldatura // vt saldare.

welfare ['welfɛə*] n benessere m; **~ state** n stato assistenziale.

well [wel] n pozzo // ad bene // a: **to be ~** andare bene; (person) stare bene // excl allora!; ma!; ebbene!; as ~ anche; as ~ as così come; oltre a; X as ~ as Y sia X che Y; he did as ~ as he could ha fatto come meglio poteva; **~ done!** bravo(a)!; get ~ soon! guarisci presto!; **to do ~** in sth riuscire in qc; **to ~ up** vi sgorgare.

we'll [wi:l] = we will, we shall.

well: **~-behaved** a ubbidiente; **~-being** n benessere m; **~-built** a (person) ben fatto(a); **~-dressed** a ben vestito(a), vestito(a) bene; **~-heeled** a (col: wealthy) agiato(a), facoltoso(a).

wellingtons ['welıŋtənz] npl (also: wellington boots) stivali mpl di gomma.

well: **~-known** a noto(a), famoso(a); **~-mannered** a ben educato(a); **~-meaning** a ben intenzionato(a); **~-off** a benestante, danaroso(a); **~-read** a colto(a), **~-to-do** a abbiente, benestante; **~-wisher** n ammiratore/trice.

Welsh [welʃ] a gallese // n (LING) gallese m; the ~ npl i Gallesi; **~man/woman** n gallese m/f; **~ rarebit** n crostino al formaggio.

went [went] pt of go.

wept [wept] pt, pp of weep.

were [wə:*] pt of be.

we're [wıə*] = we are.

weren't [wə:nt] = were not.

west [west] n ovest m, occidente m, ponente m // a (o) ovest inv, occidentale // ad verso ovest; the W~ l'Occidente m; the W~ Country n (Brit) il sudovest dell'Inghilterra; **~erly** a (wind) occidentale, da ovest; **~ern** a occidentale, dell'ovest // n (CINEMA) western m inv; W~ **Germany** n Germania Occidentale; W~ **Indian** a delle Indie Occidentali // n abitante m/f delle Indie Occidentali; W~ **Indies** npl Indie fpl Occidentali; **~ward(s)** ad verso ovest.

wet [wet] a umido(a), bagnato(a); (soaked) fradicio(a), (rainy) piovoso(a); **to get ~** bagnarsi; "~ paint" "vernice fresca"; **~ blanket** n (fig) guastafeste m/f; **~ suit** n tuta da sub.

we've [wi:v] = we have.

whack [wæk] vt picchiare, battere.

whale [weıl] n (ZOOL) balena.

wharf, pl **wharves** [wɔ:f, wɔ:vz] n banchina.

what [wɔt] ◆ ad **1** (in direct/indirect questions) che; quanto; ~ **size** is it? che taglia è?; ~ **colour** is it? di che colore è?; ~ **books do you want?** quali or che libri vuole?

2 (in exclamations) che; ~ **a mess!** che disordine!

◆ pronoun **1** (interrogative) che cosa, cosa, che; ~ **are you doing?** che or (che) cosa fai?; ~ **are you talking about?** di che cosa parli?; ~ **is it called?** come si chiama?; ~ **about me?** e io?; ~ **about doing ...?** e se facessimo ...?

2 (relative) ciò che, quello che; I saw ~ **you did/was on the table** ho visto quello che hai fatto/quello che era sul tavolo

3 (indirect use) (che) cosa; **he asked me** ~ **she had said** mi ha chiesto che cosa avesse detto; **tell me** ~ **you're thinking about** dimmi a cosa stai pensando

◆ excl (disbelieving) cosa!, come!

whatever [wɔt'evə*] a: ~ **book** qualunque or qualsiasi libro + sub // pronoun: **do** ~ **is necessary/you want** faccia qualunque or qualsiasi cosa sia necessaria/lei voglia; ~ **happens** qualunque cosa accada; **no reason ~** *or* whatsoever nessuna ragione affatto *or* al mondo; **nothing ~** proprio niente.

whatsoever [wɔtsəu'evə*] *a see* **whatever**.

wheat [wi:t] *n* grano, frumento.

wheedle ['wi:dl] *vt*: **to ~ sb into doing** sth convincere qn a fare qc (con lusinghe); **to ~ sth out of sb** ottenere qc da qn (con lusinghe).

wheel [wi:l] *n* ruota; (*AUT*: *also*: steering ~) volante *m*; (*NAUT*) (ruota del) timone *m* // *vt* spingere // *vi* (*also*: ~ **round**) girare; **~barrow** *n* carriola; **~chair** *n* sedia a rotelle; **~ clamp** *n* (*AUT*) morsa che blocca la ruota di una vettura in sosta vietata.

wheeze [wi:z] *vi* ansimare.

when [wɛn] ♦ *ad* quando; **~ did it happen?** quando è successo? ♦ *cj* **1** (*at, during, after the time that*) quando; **she was reading ~ I came in** quando sono entrato lei leggeva; **that was ~ I needed you** era allora che avevo bisogno di te

2 (*on, at which*): **on the day ~ I met him** il giorno in cui l'ho incontrato; **one day ~ it was raining** un giorno che pioveva

3 (*whereas*) quando, mentre; **you said I was wrong ~ in fact I was right** mi hai detto che avevo torto, quando in realtà avevo ragione.

whenever [wɛn'evə*] *ad* quando mai // *cj* quando; (*every time that*) ogni volta che.

where [wɛə*] *ad, cj* dove; **this is ~** è qui che; **~abouts** *ad* dove // *n*: **sb's ~abouts** luogo dove qn si trova; **~as** *cj* mentre; **~by** *pronoun* per cui; **~upon** *cj* al che; **wherever** [-'ɛvə*] *ad* dove mai // *cj* dovunque + *sub*; **~withal** *n* mezzi *mpl*.

whet [wɛt] *vt* (*tool*) affilare; (*appetite etc*) stimolare.

whether ['wɛðə*] *cj* se; **I don't know ~ to accept or not** non so se accettare o no; **it's doubtful ~** è poco probabile che; **~ you go or not** che lei vada o no.

which [witʃ] ♦ *a* **1** (*interrogative: direct, indirect*) quale; **~ picture do you want?** quale quadro vuole?; **~ one?** quale?; **~ one of you did it?** chi di voi lo ha fatto?

2: **in ~ case** nel qual caso

♦ *pronoun* **1** (*interrogative*) quale; **~ (of these) are yours?** quali di questi sono suoi?; **~ of you are coming?** chi di voi viene?

2 (*relative*) che; (: *indirect*) cui, il(la) quale; **the apple ~ you ate/~ is on the table** la mela che hai mangiato/che è sul tavolo; **the chair on ~ you are sitting** la sedia sulla quale *or* su cui sei seduto; **he**

said he knew, **~ is true** ha detto che lo sapeva, il che è vero; **after ~** dopo di che.

whichever [witʃ'evə*] *a*: **take ~ book you prefer** prenda qualsiasi libro che preferisce; **~ book you take** qualsiasi libro prenda.

whiff [wif] *n* soffio; sbuffo; odore *m*.

while [wail] *n* momento // *cj* mentre; (*as long as*) finché; (*although*) sebbene + *sub*; per quanto + *sub*; **for a ~** per un po'; **to ~ away** *vt* (*time*) far passare.

whim [wim] *n* capriccio.

whimper ['wimpə*] *n* piagnucolio // *vi* piagnucolare.

whimsical ['wimzikl] *a* (*person*) capriccioso(a); (*look*) strano(a).

whine [wain] *n* gemito // *vi* gemere; uggiolare; piagnucolare.

whip [wip] *n* frusta; (*for riding*) frustino; (*POL*: *person*) capogruppo (*che sovrintende alla disciplina dei colleghi di partito*) // *vt* frustare; (*snatch*) sollevare (*or* estrarre) bruscamente; **~ped cream** *n* panna montata; **~-round** *n* (*Brit*) colletta.

whirl [wə:l] *n* turbine *m* // *vt* (far) girare rapidamente; (far) turbinare // *vi* turbinare; **~pool** *n* mulinello; **~wind** *n* turbine *m*.

whirr [wə:*] *vi* ronzare; rombare; frullare.

whisk [wisk] *n* (*CULIN*) frusta; frullino // *vt* sbattere, frullare; **to ~ sb away** *or* **off** portar via qn a tutta velocità.

whiskers ['wiskəz] *npl* (*of animal*) baffi *mpl*; (*of man*) favoriti *mpl*.

whisky, (*US, Ireland*) **whiskey** ['wiski] *n* whisky *m inv*.

whisper ['wispə*] *n* sussurro; (*rumour*) voce *f* // *vt, vi* sussurrare.

whistle ['wisl] *n* (*sound*) fischio; (*object*) fischietto // *vi* fischiare.

white [wait] *a* bianco(a); (*with fear*) pallido(a) // *n* bianco; (*person*) bianco/a; **~ coffee** *n* (*Brit*) caffellatte *m inv*; **~-collar worker** *n* impiegato; **~ elephant** *n* (*fig*) oggetto (*or* progetto) costoso ma inutile; **~ lie** *n* bugia pietosa; **~ paper** *n* (*POL*) libro bianco; **~wash** *n* (*paint*) bianco di calce // *vt* imbiancare; (*fig*) coprire.

whiting ['waitiŋ] *n* (*pl inv*) (*fish*) merlango.

Whitsun ['witsn] *n* Pentecoste *f*.

whittle ['witl] *vt*: **to ~ away, ~ down** ridurre, tagliare.

whizz [wiz] *vi* sfrecciare; **~ kid** *n* (*col*) prodigio.

who [hu:] *pronoun* **1** (*interrogative*) chi; **~ is it?, ~'s there?** chi è?

2 (*relative*) che; **the man ~ spoke to me** l'uomo che ha parlato con me; **those ~ can swim** quelli che sanno nuotare.

whodunit [hu:'dʌnit] *n* (*col*) giallo.

whoever [hu:'ɛvə*] *pronoun*: ~ **finds it** chiunque lo trovi; **ask** ~ **you like to** chieda a chiunque vuole; ~ **she marries** chiunque sposerà, non importa chi sposerà; ~ **told you that?** chi mai gliel'ha detto?

whole [həul] *a* (*complete*) tutto(a), completo(a); (*not broken*) intero(a), intatto(a) // *n* (*total*) totale *m*; (*sth not broken*) tutto; **the ~ of the** time tutto il tempo; **on the ~, as a ~** nel complesso, nell'insieme; **~hearted** *a* sincero(a); **~meal** *a* (*bread, flour*) integrale; **~sale** *n* commercio *or* vendita all'ingrosso // *a* all'ingrosso; (*destruction*) totale; **~saler** *n* grossista *m/f*; **~some** *a* sano(a); salutare; **~wheat** *a* = **~meal**; **wholly** *ad* completamente, del tutto.

whom [hu:m] *pronoun* 1 (*interrogative*) chi; ~ **did you see?** chi hai visto?; **to ~ did you give it?** a chi lo hai dato? 2 (*relative*) che, *prep* + il (la) quale (*check syntax of Italian verb used*); **the man ~ I saw/to ~ I spoke** l'uomo che ho visto/al quale ho parlato.

whooping cough ['hu:pɪŋ-] *n* pertosse *f*.

whore [hɔ:*] *n* (*pej*) puttana.

whose [hu:z] ♦ *a* 1 (*possessive: interrogative*) di chi; ~ **book is this?**, ~ **is this book?** di chi è questo libro?; ~ **daughter are you?** di chi sei figlia? 2 (*possessive: relative*): **the man ~ son you rescued** l'uomo il cui figlio hai salvato; **the girl ~ sister you were speaking to** la ragazza alla cui sorella stavi parlando
♦ *pronoun* di chi; ~ **is this?** di chi è questo?; **I know ~ it is** so di chi è.

why [waɪ] *ad, cj* perché // *excl* (*surprise*) ma guarda un po'!; (*remonstrating*) ma (via)!; (*explaining*) ebbene!; ~ **not?** perché no?; ~ **not do it now?** perché non farlo adesso?; **that's not ~ I'm here** non è questo il motivo per cui sono qui; **the reason ~** il motivo per cui; **~ever** *ad* perché mai.

wick [wɪk] *n* lucignolo, stoppino.

wicked ['wɪkɪd] *a* cattivo(a), malvagio(a); maligno(a); perfido(a); (*mischievous*) malizioso(a).

wicker ['wɪkə*] *n* vimine *m*; (*also:* **~work**) articoli *mpl* di vimini.

wicket ['wɪkɪt] *n* (*CRICKET*) porta; area tra le due porte.

wide [waɪd] *a* largo(a); (*area, knowledge*) vasto(a); (*choice*) ampio(a) // *ad*: **to open ~** spalancare; **to shoot ~** tirare a vuoto *or* fuori bersaglio; **~angle lens** *n* grandangolare *m*; **~awake** *a* completamente sveglio(a); **~ly** *ad* (*differing*) molto, completamente; (*believed*) generalmente; **~ly spaced** molto distanziati(e); **~n** *vt* allargare, ampliare; ~ **open** *a*

spalancato(a); **~spread** *a* (*belief etc*) molto *or* assai diffuso(a).

widow ['wɪdəu] *n* vedova; **~er** *n* vedovo.

width [wɪdθ] *n* larghezza.

wield [wi:ld] *vt* (*sword*) maneggiare; (*power*) esercitare.

wife [waɪf], *pl* **wives** *n* moglie *f*.

wig [wɪg] *n* parrucca.

wiggle ['wɪgl] *vt* dimenare, agitare.

wild [waɪld] *a* selvatico(a); selvaggio(a); (*sea*) tempestoso(a); (*idea, life*) folle; stravagante; **~s** *npl* regione *f* selvaggia; **~erness** ['wɪldənɪs] *n* deserto; **~goose chase** *n* (*fig*) pista falsa; **~life** *n* natura; **~ly** *ad* (*applaud*) freneticamente; (*hit, guess*) a casaccio; (*happy*) follemente.

wilful ['wɪlful] *a* (*person*) testardo(a), ostinato(a); (*action*) intenzionale; (*crime*) premeditato(a).

will [wɪl] ♦ *auxiliary vb* 1 (*forming future tense*): **I ~ finish it tomorrow** lo finirò domani; **I ~ have finished it by tomorrow** lo finirò entro domani; ~ **you do it?** — **yes I ~/no I won't** lo farai? — sì (lo farò)/no (non lo farò)
2 (*in conjectures, predictions*): **he ~ or he'll be there by now** dovrebbe essere arrivato ora; **that ~ be the postman** sarà il postino
3 (*in commands, requests, offers*): ~ **you be quiet!** vuoi stare zitto?; ~ **you come?** vieni anche tu?; ~ **you help me?** mi aiuti?, mi puoi aiutare?; ~ **you have a cup of tea?** vorrebbe una tazza di tè?; **I won't put up with it!** non lo accetterò!
♦ *vt* (*pt, pp* **~ed**): **to ~ sb to do** volere che qn faccia; **he ~ed himself to go on** continuò grazie a un grande sforzo di volontà ♦ *n* volontà; testamento.

willing ['wɪlɪŋ] *a* volonteroso(a); ~ **to do** disposto(a) a fare; **~ly** *ad* volontieri; **~ness** *n* buona volontà.

willow ['wɪləu] *n* salice *m*.

will power *n* forza di volontà.

willy-nilly ['wɪlɪ'nɪlɪ] *ad* volente o nolente.

wilt [wɪlt] *vi* appassire.

wily ['waɪlɪ] *a* furbo(a).

win [wɪn] *n* (*in sports etc*) vittoria // *vb* (*pt, pp* **won** [wʌn]) *vt* (*battle, prize*) vincere; (*money*) guadagnare; (*popularity*) conquistare // *vi* vincere; **to ~ over**, (*Brit*) ~ **round** *vt* convincere.

wince [wɪns] *n* trasalimento, sussulto // *vi* trasalire.

winch [wɪntʃ] *n* verricello, argano.

wind *n* [wɪnd] vento; (*MED*) flatulenza // *vb* [waɪnd] (*pt, pp* **wound** [waund]) *vt* attorcigliare; (*wrap*) avvolgere; (*clock, toy*) caricare; (*take breath away*: [wɪnd]) far restare senza fiato // *vi* (*road, river*) serpeggiare; **to ~ up** *vt* (*clock*) caricare; (*debate*) concludere; **~fall** *n* colpo di fortuna; **~ing** ['waɪndɪŋ] *a* (*road*) serpeggiante; (*staircase*) a chiocciola; ~ **instrument** n (MUS) strumento a fiato; ~**mill** n mulino a vento.

window ['wɪndəʊ] n finestra; (in car, train) finestrino; (in shop etc) vetrina; (also: ~ **pane**) vetro; ~ **box** n cassetta da fiori; ~ **cleaner** n (person) pulitore m di finestre; ~ **ledge** n davanzale m; ~ **pane** n vetro; ~**sill** n davanzale m.

windpipe ['wɪndpaɪp] n trachea.

windscreen, (US) **windshield** ['wɪndskriːn, 'wɪndʃiːld] n parabrezza m inv; ~ **washer** n lavacristallo; ~ **wiper** n tergicristallo.

windswept ['wɪndswept] a spazzato(a) dal vento.

windy ['wɪndɪ] a ventoso(a); it's ~ c'è vento.

wine [waɪn] n vino; ~ **cellar** n cantina; ~ **glass** n bicchiere m da vino; ~ **list** n lista dei vini; ~ **tasting** n degustazione f dei vini; ~ **waiter** n sommelier m inv.

wing [wɪŋ] n ala; ~**s** fpl (THEATRE) quinte fpl; ~**er** n (SPORT) ala.

wink [wɪŋk] n ammiccamento // vi ammiccare, fare l'occhiolino.

winner ['wɪnə*] n vincitore/trice.

winning ['wɪnɪŋ] a (team) vincente; (goal) decisivo(a); ~**s** npl vincite fpl; ~ **post** n traguardo.

winter ['wɪntə*] n inverno; ~ **sports** npl sport mpl invernali.

wintry ['wɪntrɪ] a invernale.

wipe [waɪp] n pulita, passata // vt pulire (strofinando); (dishes) asciugare; **to** ~ **off** vt cancellare; (stains) togliere strofinando; **to** ~ **out** vt (debt) pagare, liquidare; (memory) cancellare; (destroy) annientare; **to** ~ **up** vt asciugare.

wire ['waɪə*] n filo; (ELEC) filo elettrico; (TEL) telegramma m // vt (house) fare l'impianto elettrico di; (also: ~ **up**) collegare, allacciare.

wireless ['waɪəlɪs] n (Brit) telegrafia senza fili; (set) (apparecchio m) radio f inv.

wiring ['waɪərɪŋ] n impianto elettrico.

wiry ['waɪərɪ] a magro(a) e nerboruto(a).

wisdom ['wɪzdəm] n saggezza; (of action) prudenza; ~ **tooth** n dente m del giudizio.

wise [waɪz] a saggio(a); prudente; giudizioso(a).

...wise [waɪz] suffix: time~ per quanto riguarda il tempo, in termini di tempo.

wish [wɪʃ] n (desire) desiderio; (specific desire) richiesta // vt desiderare, volere; best ~**es** (on birthday etc) i migliori auguri; with best ~**es** (in letter) cordiali saluti, con i migliori saluti; **to** ~ **sb** good-bye dire arrivederci a qn; he ~**ed** me well mi augurò di riuscire; **to** ~ **to do**/**that** sb do desiderare o volere fare/che qn faccia; **to** ~ **for** desiderare; it's ~**ful**

thinking è prendere i desideri per realtà.

wishy-washy ['wɪʃɪ'wɒʃɪ] a (col: colour) slavato(a); (: ideas, argument) insulso(a).

wisp [wɪsp] n ciuffo, ciocca; (of smoke, straw) filo.

wistful ['wɪstful] a malinconico(a).

wit [wɪt] n (gen pl) intelligenza; presenza di spirito; (wittiness) spirito, arguzia; (person) bello spirito; **to be at one's ~s'** **end** (fig) non sapere più cosa fare; **to** ~ ad cioè.

witch [wɪtʃ] n strega.

with [wɪð, wɪθ] prep **1** (in the company of) con; I was ~ **him** ero con lui; we stayed ~ **friends** siamo stati da amici; I'll be ~ **you** in a minute vengo subito

2 (descriptive) con; a room ~ **a view** una stanza con vista sul mare (or sulle montagne etc); the man ~ **the grey hat**/ **blue eyes** l'uomo con il cappello grigio/ gli occhi blu

3 (indicating manner, means, cause): ~ **tears** in her eyes con le lacrime agli occhi; red ~ **anger** rosso dalla rabbia; **to shake** ~ **fear** tremare di paura

4: I'm ~ **you** (I understand) la seguo; **to be** ~ **it** (col: up-to-date) essere alla moda; (: alert) essere sveglio(a).

withdraw [wɪθ'drɔː] vb (irg) vt ritirare; (money from bank) ritirare; prelevare // vi ritirarsi; ~**al** n ritiro; prelievo; (of army) ritirata; (MED) stato di privazione; ~**n** a (person) distaccato(a).

wither ['wɪðə*] vi appassire.

withhold [wɪθ'həʊld] vt irg (money) trattenere; (decision) rimettere, rimandare; (permission): **to** ~ (**from**) rifiutare (a); (information): **to** ~ (**from**) nascondere (a).

within [wɪð'ɪn] prep all'interno; (in time, distances) entro // ad all'interno, dentro; ~ **sight of** in vista di; ~ **a mile of** entro un miglio da; ~ **the week** prima della fine della settimana.

without [wɪð'aʊt] prep senza.

withstand [wɪθ'stænd] vt irg resistere a.

witness ['wɪtnɪs] n (person) testimone m/f // vt (event) essere testimone di; (document) attestare l'autenticità di; ~ **box**, (US) ~ **stand** n banco dei testimoni.

witticism ['wɪtɪsɪzm] n spiritosaggine f.

witty ['wɪtɪ] a spiritoso(a).

wives [waɪvz] npl of **wife**.

wizard ['wɪzəd] n mago.

wk abbr = **week**.

wobble ['wɒbl] vi tremare; (chair) traballare.

woe [wəʊ] n dolore m; disgrazia.

woke [wəʊk] pt of **wake**; ~**n** pp of **wake**.

wolf, pl **wolves** [wʊlf, wʊlvz] n lupo.

woman ['wʊmən], pl **women** n donna; ~ **doctor** n dottoressa; **women's lib** n (col) movimento femminista.

womb [wu:m] n (ANAT) utero.

women ['wɪmɪn] npl di **woman**.

won [wʌn] pt, pp of **win**.

wonder ['wʌndə*] n meraviglia // vi: to ~ whether domandarsi se; to ~ at essere sorpreso(a) di; meravigliarsi di; to ~ about domandarsi di; pensare a; it's no ~ that c'è poco or non c'è da meravigliarsi che + sub; **~ful** a meraviglioso(a).

won't [wəunt] = **will not**.

woo [wu:] vt (woman) fare la corte a.

wood [wud] n legno; (timber) legname m; (forest) bosco; ~ **carving** n scultura in legno, intaglio; **~ed** a boschivo(a); boscoso(a); **~en** a di legno; (fig) rigido(a); inespressivo(a); **~pecker** n picchio; **~ wind** npl (MUS): the **~wind** i legni; **~work** n parti fpl in legno; (craft, subject) falegnameria; **~worm** n tarlo del legno.

wool [wul] n lana; to pull the ~ over sb's eyes (fig) imbrogliare qn; **~len**, (US) **~en** a di lana; **~lens** npl indumenti mpl di lana; **~ly**, (US) **~y** a lanoso(a); (fig: ideas) confuso(a).

word [wə:d] n parola; (news) notizie fpl // vt esprimere, formulare; in other **~s** in altre parole; to break/keep one's ~ non mantenere/mantenere la propria parola; **~ing** n formulazione f; ~ **processing** n elaborazione f di testi, word processing m; ~ **processor** n word processor m inv; **~y** a verboso(a).

wore [wɔ:*] pt of **wear**.

work [wə:k] n lavoro; (ART, LITERATURE) opera // vi lavorare; (mechanism, plan etc) funzionare; (medicine) essere efficace // vt (clay, wood etc) lavorare; (mine etc) sfruttare; (machine) far funzionare; to be out of ~ essere disoccupato(a); **~s** n (Brit: factory) fabbrica // npl (of clock, machine) meccanismo; to ~ **loose** vi allentarsi; to ~ **on** vt fus lavorare a; (principle) basarsi su; to ~ **out** vi (plans etc) riuscire, andare bene // vt (problem) risolvere; (plan) elaborare; it ~s out at £100 fa 100 sterline; to get ~ed up andare su tutte le furie; eccitarsi; **~able** a (solution) realizzabile; **~aholic** n maniaco/a del lavoro; **~er** n lavoratore/trice, operaio/a; **~force** n forza lavoro; **~ing class** n classe f operaia or lavoratrice; **~ing-class** a operaio(a); **~ing man** n lavoratore m; **~ing order** n: in **~ing order** funzionante; **~man** n operaio; **~manship** n abilità; lavoro; fattura; **~sheet** n foglio col programma di lavoro; **~shop** n officina; ~ **station** n stazione f di lavoro; **~-to-rule** n (Brit) sciopero bianco.

world [wə:ld] n mondo // cpd (champion)

del mondo; (power, war) mondiale; to think the ~ of sb (fig) pensare un gran bene di qn; **~ly** a di questo mondo; **~wide** a universale.

worm [wə:m] n verme m.

worn [wɔ:n] pp of **wear** // a usato(a); **~out** a (object) consumato(a), logoro(a); (person) sfinito(a).

worried ['wʌrɪd] a preoccupato(a).

worry ['wʌrɪ] n preoccupazione f // vt preoccupare // vi preoccuparsi.

worse [wə:s] a peggiore // ad, n peggio; a change for the ~ un peggioramento; ~ **off** a in condizioni (economiche) peggiori; **~n** vt, vi peggiorare.

worship ['wə:ʃɪp] n culto // vt (God) adorare, venerare; (person) adorare; Your W~ (Brit: to mayor) signor sindaco; (: to judge) signor giudice.

worst [wə:st] a il(la) peggiore // ad, n peggio; at ~ al peggio, per male che vada.

worsted ['wustɪd] n: (wool) ~ lana pettinata.

worth [wə:θ] n valore m // a: to be ~ valere; it's ~ it ne vale la pena; it is ~ one's while to (do) vale la pena (fare); **~less** a di nessun valore; **~while** a (activity) utile; (cause) lodevole.

worthy ['wə:ði] a (person) degno(a); (motive) lodevole; ~ of degno di.

would [wud] auxiliary vb 1 (conditional tense): if you asked him he ~ do it se glielo chiedesse lo farebbe; if you had asked him he ~ have done it se glielo avesse chiesto lo avrebbe fatto
2 (in offers, invitations, requests): ~ you like a biscuit? vorrebbe or vuole un biscotto?; ~ you ask him to come in? lo faccia entrare, per cortesia; ~ you open the window please? apra la finestra, per favore
3 (in indirect speech): I said I ~ do it ho detto che l'avrei fatto
4 (emphatic): it WOULD have to snow today! doveva proprio nevicare oggi!
5 (insistence): she ~n't do it non ha voluto farlo
6 (conjecture): it ~ have been midnight sarà stato mezzanotte; it ~ seem so sembrerebbe proprio di sì
7 (indicating habit): he ~ go there on Mondays andava lì ogni lunedì.

would-be ['wudbi:] a (pej) sedicente.

wouldn't ['wudnt] = **would not**.

wound vb [waund] pt, pp of **wind** // n, vt [wu:nd] n ferita // vt ferire.

wove [wəuv] pt of **weave**; **~n** pp of **weave**.

wrangle ['ræŋgl] n litigio // vi litigare.

wrap [ræp] n (stole) scialle m; (cape) mantellina // vt (also: ~ up) avvolgere; (parcel) incartare; **~per** n (Brit: of book) copertina; **~ping paper** n carta da pacchi; (for gift) carta da regali.

wrath [rɔθ] n collera, ira.
wreak [ri:k] vt (havoc) portare, causare;
to ~ vengeance on vendicarsi su.
wreath, ~s [ri:θ, ri:ðz] n corona.
wreck [rɛk] n (sea disaster) naufragio;
(ship) relitto; (pej: person) rottame m //
vt demolire; (ship) far naufragare; (fig)
rovinare; **~age** n rottami mpl; (of
building) macerie fpl; (of ship) relitti
mpl.
wren [rɛn] n (ZOOL) scricciolo.
wrench [rɛntʃ] n (TECH) chiave f; (tug)
torsione f brusca; (fig) strazio // vt
strappare; storcere; to ~ sth from
strappare qc a or da.
wrestle ['rɛsl] vi: to ~ (with sb) lottare
(con qn); to ~ with (fig) combattere or
lottare contro; **~r** n lottatore/trice;
wrestling n lotta; (also: all-in wrestling) catch m, lotta libera.
wretched ['rɛtʃɪd] a disgraziato(a);
(col: weather, holiday) orrendo(a),
orribile; (: child, dog) pestifero(a).
wriggle ['rɪgl] vi dimenarsi; (snake,
worm) serpeggiare, muoversi
serpeggiando.
wring [rɪŋ], pt, pp **wrung** vt torcere;
(wet clothes) strizzare; (fig): to ~ sth
out of strappare qc a.
wrinkle ['rɪŋkl] n (on skin) ruga; (on
paper etc) grinza // vt corrugare; rag-
grinzire // vi corrugarsi; raggrinzirsi.
wrist [rɪst] n polso; **~watch** n orologio
da polso.
writ [rɪt] n ordine m; mandato.
write [raɪt], pt **wrote**, pp **written** vt, vi
scrivere; to ~ down vt annotare; (put
in writing) mettere per iscritto; to ~
off (debt) cancellare; (depreciate)
deprezzare; to ~ out vt scrivere;
(copy) ricopiare; to ~ up vt redigere;
~-off n perdita completa; **~r** n autore/
trice, scrittore/trice.
writhe [raɪð] vi contorcersi.
writing ['raɪtɪŋ] n scrittura; (of author)
scritto, opera; in ~ per iscritto; ~
paper n carta da scrivere.
written ['rɪtn] pp of **write**.
wrong [rɔŋ] a sbagliato(a); (not suitable) inadatto(a); (wicked) cattivo(a);
(unfair) ingiusto(a) // ad in modo sbagliato, erroneamente // n (evil) male m;
(injustice) torto // vt fare torto a; you
are ~ to do it ha torto a farlo; you are ~
about that, you've got it ~ si sbaglia; to
be in the ~ avere torto; what's ~? cosa
c'è che non va?; to go ~ (person) sbagliarsi; (plan) fallire, non riuscire; (machine) guastarsi; **~ful** a illegittimo(a);
ingiusto(a); **~ly** ad a torto.
wrote [rəut] pt of **write**.
wrought [rɔ:t] a: ~ iron ferro battuto.
wrung [rʌŋ] pt, pp of **wring**.
wry [raɪ] a storto(a).
wt. abbr = **weight**.

X

Xmas ['ɛksməs] n abbr = **Christmas**.
X-ray ['ɛks'reɪ] n raggio X; (photograph)
radiografia // vt radiografare.
xylophone ['zaɪləfəun] n xilofono.

Y

yacht [jɔt] n panfilo, yacht m inv; **~ing**
n yachting m, sport m della vela.
Yank [jæŋk], **Yankee** ['jæŋkɪ] n (pej)
yankee m/f inv.
yap [jæp] vi (dog) guaire.
yard [jɑ:d] n (of house etc) cortile m;
(measure) iarda (= 914 mm; 3 feet);
~stick n (fig) misura, criterio.
yarn [jɑ:n] n filato; (tale) lunga storia.
yawn [jɔ:n] n sbadiglio // vi sbadigliare;
~ing a (gap) spalancato(a).
yd. abbr = **yard(s)**.
yeah [jɛə] ad (col) sì.
year [jɪə*] n anno; (referring to harvest,
wine etc) annata; he is 8 ~s old ha 8
anni; an eight-~-old child un(a)
bambino/a di otto anni; **~ly** a annuale
// ad annualmente.
yearn [jə:n] vi: to ~ for sth/to do
desiderare ardentemente qc/di fare;
~ing n desiderio intenso.
yeast [ji:st] n lievito.
yell [jɛl] n urlo // vi urlare.
yellow ['jɛləu] a giallo(a).
yelp [jɛlp] vi guaire, uggiolare.
yeoman ['jəumən] n: Y~ of the Guard
guardiano della Torre di Londra.
yes [jɛs] ad, n sì (m inv); to say/answer
~ dire/rispondere di sì.
yesterday ['jɛstədɪ] ad, n ieri (m inv); ~
morning/evening ieri mattina/sera; all
day ~ ieri per tutta la giornata.
yet [jɛt] ad ancora; già // cj ma, tuttavia;
it is not finished ~ non è ancora finito;
the best ~ finora il migliore; as ~ finora.
yew [ju:] n tasso (albero).
yield [ji:ld] n produzione f, resa; reddito
// vt produrre, rendere; (surrender)
cedere // vi cedere; (US AUT) dare la
precedenza.
YMCA n abbr (= Young Men's Christian
Association) Y.M.C.A. m.
yoga ['jəugə] n yoga m.
yog(h)ourt, yog(h)urt ['jəugət] n iogurt
m inv.
yoke [jəuk] n giogo.
yolk [jəuk] n tuorlo, rosso d'uovo.
yonder ['jɔndə*] ad là.
you [ju:] pronoun **1** (subject) tu; (: polite
form) lei; (: pl) voi; (: very formal)
loro; ~ Italians enjoy your food a voi
Italiani piace mangiare bene; ~ and I
will go tu ed io or lei ed io andiamo

2 (object: direct) ti; la; vi; loro (after vb); (: indirect) ti; le; vi; loro (after vb); **I know** ~ ti or la or vi conosco; **I gave it to** ~ te l'ho dato; gliel'ho dato; ve l'ho dato; l'ho dato loro

3 (stressed, after prep, in comparisons) te; lei; voi; loro; **I told** you **to do it** ho detto a TE (or a LEI etc) di farlo; **she's younger than** ~ è più giovane di te (or lei etc)

4 (impersonal: one) si; **fresh air does** ~ **good** l'aria fresca fa bene; ~ **never know** non si sa mai.

you'd [juːd] = **you had, you would**.

you'll [juːl] = **you will, you shall**.

young [jʌŋ] a giovane // npl (of animal) piccoli mpl; (people): **the** ~ i giovani, la gioventù; ~**ster** n giovanotto, ragazzo; (child) bambino/a.

your [jɔː*] a il(la) tuo(a), pl i(le) tuoi(tue); il(la) suo(a), pl i(le) suoi(sue); il(la) vostro(a), pl i(le) vostri(e); il(la) loro, pl i(le) loro; see also **my**.

you're [juə*] = **you are**.

yours [jɔːz] pronoun il(la) tuo(a), pl i(le) tuoi(tue); (polite form) il(la) suo(a), pl i(le) suoi(sue); (pl) il(la) vostro(a), pl i(le) vostri(e); (: very formal) il(la) loro, pl i(le) loro; ~ **sincerely/faithfully** cordiali/distinti saluti; see also **mine**.

yourself [jɔːˈsɛlf] pronoun (reflexive) ti; si; (after prep) te; sé; (emphatic) tu stesso(a); lei stesso(a); **yourselves** pl pronoun (reflexive) vi; si; (after prep) voi; loro; (emphatic) voi stessi(e); loro stessi(e); see also **oneself**.

youth [juːθ] n gioventù f; (young man: pl ~**s** [juːðz]) giovane m, ragazzo; ~**club** n centro giovanile; ~**ful** a giovane; da giovane; giovanile; ~ **hostel** n ostello della gioventù.

you've [juːv] = **you have**.

YTS n abbr (Brit: = Youth Training Scheme) programma di addestramento professionale per giovani.

Yugoslav [ˈjuːgəuˈslaːv] a, n jugoslavo(a).

Yugoslavia [ˈjuːgəuˈslaːvɪə] n Jugoslavia.

yuppie [ˈjʌpɪ] n, a (col) yuppie (m/f inv).

YWCA n abbr (= Young Women's Christian Association) Y.W.C.A. m.

Z

zany [ˈzeɪnɪ] a un po' pazzo(a).

zap [zæp] vt (COMPUT) cancellare.

zeal [ziːl] n zelo; entusiasmo.

zebra [ˈziːbrə] n zebra; ~ **crossing** n (Brit) (passaggio pedonale a) strisce fpl, zebre fpl.

zero [ˈzɪərəu] n zero.

zest [zɛst] n gusto; (CULIN) buccia.

zigzag [ˈzɪgzæg] n zigzag m inv // vi zigzagare.

Zimbabwe [zɪmˈbɑːbwɪ] n Zimbabwe m.

zinc [zɪŋk] n zinco.

zip [zɪp] n (also: ~ **fastener**, (US) ~**per**) chiusura f or cerniera f lampo inv // vt (also: ~ **up**) chiudere con una cerniera lampo; ~ **code** n (US) codice m di avviamento postale.

zodiac [ˈzəudɪæk] n zodiaco.

zombie [ˈzɔmbɪ] n (fig): **like a** ~ come un morto che cammina.

zone [zəun] n zona; (subdivision of town) quartiere m.

zoo [zuː] n zoo m inv.

zoology [zuːˈɔlədʒɪ] n zoologia.

zoom [zuːm] vi: **to** ~ **past** sfrecciare; ~ **lens** n zoom m inv, obiettivo a focale variabile.

zucchini [zuːˈkiːnɪ] npl (US: courgettes) zucchine fpl.

ITALIAN VERBS

1 Gerundio *2* Participio passato *3* Presente *4* Imperfetto *5* Passato remoto *6* Futuro *7* Condizionale *8* Congiuntivo presente *9* Congiuntivo passato *10* Imperativo

andare *3* vado, vai, va, andiamo, andate, vanno *6* andrò *etc* *8* vada *10* va'!, vada!, andate!, vadano!

apparire *2* apparso *3* appaio, appari *o* apparisci, appare *o* apparisce, appaiono *o* appariscono *5* apparvi *o* apparsi, apparisti, apparve *o* apparì *o* apparse, apparvero *o* apparirono *o* apparsero *8* appaia *o* apparisca

aprire *2* aperto *3* apro *5* aprii *o* apersi, apristi *8* apra

AVERE *3* ho, hai, ha, abbiamo, avete, hanno *5* ebbi, avesti, ebbe, avemmo, aveste, ebbero *6* avrò *etc* *8* abbia *etc* *10* abbi!, abbia!, abbiate!, abbiano!

bere *1* bevendo *2* bevuto *3* bevo *etc* *4* bevevo *etc* *8* beva *etc* *9* bevessi *etc*

cadere *5* caddi, cadesti *6* cadrò *etc*

cogliere *2* colto *3* colgo, colgono *5* colsi, cogliesti *8* colga

correre *2* corso *5* corsi, corresti

cuocere *2* cotto *3* cuocio, cociamo, cuociono *5* cossi, cocesti

dare *3* do, dai, dà, diamo, date, danno *5* diedi *o* detti, desti *6* darò *etc* *8* dia *etc* *9* dessi *etc* *10* da'!, dia!, date!, diano!

dire *1* dicendo *2* detto *3* dico, dici, dice, diciamo, dite, dicono *4* dicevo *etc* *5* dissi, dicesti *6* dirò *etc* *8* dica, diciamo, diciate, dicano *9* dicessi *etc* *10* di'!, dica!, dite!, dicano!

dolere *3* dolgo, duoli, duole, dolgono *5* dolsi, dolesti *6* dorrò *etc* *8* dolga

dovere *3* devo *o* debbo, devi, deve, dobbiamo, dovete, devono *o* debbono *6* dovrò *etc* *8* debba, dobbiamo, dobbiate, devano *o* debbano

ESSERE *2* stato *3* sono, sei, è, siamo, siete, sono *4* ero, eri, era, eravamo, eravate, erano *5* fui, fosti, fu, fummo, foste, furono *6* sarò *etc* *8* sia *etc* *9* fossi, fossi, fosse, fossimo, foste, fossero *10* sii!, sia!, siate!, siano!

fare *1* facendo *2* fatto *3* faccio, fai, fa, facciamo, fate, fanno *4* facevo *etc* *5* feci, facesti *6* farò *etc* *8* faccia *etc* *9* facessi *etc* *10* fa'!, faccia!, fate!, facciano!

FINIRE *1* finendo *2* finito *3* finisco, finisci, finisce, finiamo, finite, finiscono *4* finivo, finivi, finiva, finivamo, finivate, finivano *5* finii, finisti, finì, finimmo, finiste, finirono *6* finirò, finirai, finirà, finiremo, finirete, finiranno *7* finirei, finiresti, finirebbe, finiremmo, finireste, finirebbero *8* finisca, finisca, finisca, finiamo, finiate, finiscano *9* finissi, finissi, finisse, finissimo, finiste, finissero *10* finisci!, finisca!, finite!, finiscano!

giungere *2* giunto *5* giunsi, giungesti

leggere *2* letto *5* lessi, leggesti

mettere *2* messo *5* misi, mettesti

morire *2* morto *3* muoio, muori, muore, moriamo, morite, muoiono *6* morirò *o* morrò *etc* *8* muoia

muovere *2* mosso *5* mossi, movesti

nascere *2* nato *5* nacqui, nascesti

nuocere *2* nuociuto *3* nuoccio, nuoci, nuoce, nociamo *o* nuociamo, nuocete, nuocciono *4* nuocevo *etc* *5* nocqui, nuocesti *6* nuocerò *etc* *7* nuoccia

offrire *2* offerto *3* offro *5* offersi *o* offrii, offristi *8* offra

parere *2* parso *3* paio, paiamo, paiono *5* parvi *o* parsi, paresti *6* parrò *etc* *8* paia, paiamo, palate, paiano

PARLARE *1* parlando *2* parlato *3* parlo, parli, parla, parliamo, parlate, parlano *4* parlavo, parlavi, parlava, parlavamo, parlavate, parlavano *5* parlai, parlasti, parlò, parlammo, parlaste, parlarono *6* parlerò, parlerai, parlerà, parleremo, parlerete, parleranno *7* parlerei, parleresti, parlerebbe, parleremmo, parlereste, parlerebbero *8* parli, parli, parli, parliamo, parliate, parlino *9* parlassi, parlassi, parlasse, parlassimo, parlaste, parlassero *10* parla!, parli!, parlate!, parlino!

piacere *2* piaciuto *3* piaccio, piacciamo, piacciono *5* piacqui, piacesti *8* piaccia *etc*

porre *1* ponendo *2* posto *3* pongo, poni, pone, poniamo, ponete, pongono *4* ponevo *etc* *5* posi, ponesti *6* porrò *etc* *8* ponga, poniamo, poniate, pongano *9* ponessi *etc*

potere *3* posso, puoi, può, possiamo, potete, possono *6* potrò *etc* *8* possa, siamo, possiate, possano

prendere *2* preso *5* presi, prendesti

ridurre *1* riducendo *2* ridotto *3* riduco *etc* *4* riducevo *etc* *5* ridussi, riducesti *6* ridurrò *etc* *8* riduca *etc* *9* riducessi *etc*

riempire *1* riempiendo *3* riempio, riempi, riempie, riempiono *4* riempivo *etc* *5* riempii, riempisti *8* riempia

rimanere *2* rimasto *3* rimango, rimangono *5* rimasi, rimanesti *6* rimarrò *etc* *8* rimanga

rispondere *2* risposto *5* risposi, rispondesti

salire *3* salgo, sali, salgono *8* salga

sapere *3* so, sai, sa, sappiamo, sapete, sanno *5* seppi, sapesti *6* saprò *etc* *8* sappia *etc* *10* sappi!, sappia!, sappiate!, sappiano!

scrivere *2* scritto *5* scrissi, scrivesti

sedere *3* siedo, siedi, siede, siedono *8* sieda

spegnere *2* spento *3* spengo, spengono *5*

spensi, spegnesti 8 spenga

stare 2 stato 3 sto, stai, sta, stiamo, state, stanno 5 stetti, stesti 6 starò etc 8 stia etc 9 stessi etc 10 sta'!, stia!, state!, stiano!

tacere 2 taciuto 3 taccio, tacciono 5 tacqui, tacesti 8 taccia

tenere 3 tengo, tieni, tiene, tengono 5 tenni, tenesti 6 terrò etc 8 tenga

trarre 1 traendo 2 tratto 3 traggo, trai, trae, traiamo, traete, traggono 4 traevo etc 5 trassi, traesti 6 trarrò etc 8 tragga 9 traessi etc

udire 3 odo, odi, ode, odono 8 oda

uscire 3 esco, esci, esce, escono 8 esca

valere 2 valso 3 valgo, valgono 5 valsi, valesti 6 varrò etc 8 valga

vedere 2 visto o veduto 5 vidi, vedesti 6 vedrò etc

VENDERE 1 vendendo 2 venduto 3 vendo, vendi, vende, vendiamo, vendete, vendono 4 vendevo, vendevi, vendeva, vendevamo, vendevate, vendevano 5 vendei o vendetti, vendesti, vendé o vendette, vendemmo, vendeste, venderono o vendettero 6 venderò, venderai, venderà, venderemo, venderete, venderanno 7 venderei, venderesti, venderebbe, venderemmo, vendereste, venderebbero 8 venda, venda, venda, vendiamo, vendiate, vendano 9 vendessi, vendessi, vendesse, vendessimo, vendeste, vendessero 10 vendi!, venda!, vendete!, vendano!

venire 2 venuto 3 vengo, vieni, viene, vengono 5 venni, venisti 6 verrò etc 8 venga

vivere 2 vissuto 5 vissi, vivesti

volere 3 voglio, vuoi, vuole, vogliamo, volete, vogliono 5 volli, volesti 6 vorrò etc 8 voglia etc 10 vogli!, voglia!, vogliate!, vogliano!

VERBI INGLESI

present	pt	pp	present	pt	pp
arise	arose	arisen	fly (flies)	flew	flown
awake	awoke	awaked	forbid	forbade	forbidden
be (am, is, are; being)	was, were	been	forecast	forecast	forecast
			forego	forewent	foregone
bear	bore	born(e)	foresee	foresaw	foreseen
beat	beat	beaten	foretell	foretold	foretold
become	became	become	forget	forgot	forgotten
begin	began	begun	forgive	forgave	forgiven
behold	beheld	beheld	forsake	forsook	forsaken
bend	bent	bent	freeze	froze	frozen
beseech	besought	besought	get	got	got, (US) gotten
beset	beset	beset			
bet	bet, betted	bet, betted	give	gave	given
bid	bid, bade	bid, bidden	go (goes)	went	gone
bind	bound	bound	grind	ground	ground
bite	bit	bitten	grow	grew	grown
bleed	bled	bled	hang	hung, hanged	hung, hanged
blow	blew	blown			
break	broke	broken	have (has; having)	had	had
breed	bred	bred			
bring	brought	brought	hear	heard	heard
build	built	built	hide	hid	hidden
burn	burnt, burned	burnt, burned	hit	hit	hit
			hold	held	held
burst	burst	burst	hurt	hurt	hurt
buy	bought	bought	keep	kept	kept
can	could	(been able)	kneel	knelt, kneeled	knelt, kneeled
cast	cast	cast			
catch	caught	caught	know	knew	known
choose	chose	chosen	lay	laid	laid
cling	clung	clung	lead	led	led
come	came	come	lean	leant, leaned	leant, leaned
cost	cost	cost	leap	leapt, leaped	leapt, leaped
creep	crept	crept	learn	learnt, learned	learnt, learned
cut	cut	cut			
deal	dealt	dealt	leave	left	left
dig	dug	dug	lend	lent	lent
do (3rd person; he/she/it does)	did	done	let	let	let
			lie (lying)	lay	lain
			light	lit, lighted	lit, lighted
			lose	lost	lost
draw	drew	drawn	make	made	made
dream	dreamed, dreamt	dreamed, dreamt	may	might	—
			mean	meant	meant
drink	drank	drunk	meet	met	met
drive	drove	driven	mistake	mistook	mistaken
dwell	dwelt	dwelt	mow	mowed	mown, mowed
eat	ate	eaten			
fall	fell	fallen	must	(had to)	(had to)
feed	fed	fed	pay	paid	paid
feel	felt	felt	put	put	put
fight	fought	fought	quit	quit, quitted	quit, quitted
find	found	found	read	read	read
flee	fled	fled	rid	rid	rid
fling	flung	flung	ride	rode	ridden

present	pt	pp	present	pt	pp
ring	rang	rung	spoil	spoiled, spoilt	spoiled, spoilt
rise	rose	risen			
run	ran	run	spread	spread	spread
saw	sawed	sawn	spring	sprang	sprung
say	said	said	stand	stood	stood
see	saw	seen	steal	stole	stolen
seek	sought	sought	stick	stuck	stuck
sell	sold	sold	sting	stung	stung
send	sent	sent	stink	stank	stunk
set	set	set	stride	strode	stridden
shake	shook	shaken	strike	struck	struck, stricken
shall	should	—			
shear	sheared	shorn, sheared	strive	strove	striven
			swear	swore	sworn
shed	shed	shed	sweep	swept	swept
shine	shone	shone	swell	swelled	swollen, swelled
shoot	shot	shot			
show	showed	shown	swim	swam	swum
shrink	shrank	shrunk	swing	swung	swung
shut	shut	shut	take	took	taken
sing	sang	sung	teach	taught	taught
sink	sank	sunk	tear	tore	torn
sit	sat	sat	tell	told	told
slay	slew	slain	think	thought	thought
sleep	slept	slept	throw	threw	thrown
slide	slid	slid	thrust	thrust	thrust
sling	slung	slung	tread	trod	trodden
slit	slit	slit	wake	woke, waked	woken, waked
smell	smelt, smelled	smelt, smelled	waylay	waylaid	waylaid
			wear	wore	worn
sow	sowed	sown, sowed	weave	wove, weaved	woven, weaved
speak	spoke	spoken			
speed	sped, speeded	sped, speeded	wed	wedded, wed	wedded, wed
			weep	wept	wept
spell	spelt, spelled	spelt, spelled	win	won	won
			wind	wound	wound
spend	spent	spent	withdraw	withdrew	withdrawn
spill	spilt, spilled	spilt, spilled	withhold	withheld	withheld
spin	spun	spun	withstand	withstood	withstood
spit	spat	spat	wring	wrung	wrung
split	split	split	write	wrote	written

I NUMERI

NUMBERS

uno(a)	1	one
due	2	two
tre	3	three
quattro	4	four
cinque	5	five
sei	6	six
sette	7	seven
otto	8	eight
nove	9	nine
dieci	10	ten
undici	11	eleven
dodici	12	twelve
tredici	13	thirteen
quattordici	14	fourteen
quindici	15	fifteen
sedici	16	sixteen
diciassette	17	seventeen
diciotto	18	eighteen
diciannove	19	nineteen
venti	20	twenty
ventuno	21	twenty-one
ventidue	22	twenty-two
ventitré	23	twenty-three
ventotto	28	twenty-eight
trenta	30	thirty
quaranta	40	forty
cinquanta	50	fifty
sessanta	60	sixty
settanta	70	seventy
ottanta	80	eighty
novanta	90	ninety
cento	100	a hundred, one hundred
cento uno	101	a hundred and one
duecento	200	two hundred
mille	1 000	a thousand, one thousand
milleduecentodue	1 202	one thousand two hundred and two
cinquemila	5 000	five thousand
un milione	1 000 000	a million, one million

primo(a), 1º	first, 1st
secondo(a), 2º	second, 2nd
terzo(a), 3º	third, 3rd
quarto(a)	fourth, 4th
quinto(a)	fifth, 5th
sesto(a)	sixth, 6th
settimo(a)	seventh
ottavo(a)	eighth
nono(a)	ninth
decimo(a)	tenth
undicesimo(a)	eleventh
dodicesimo(a)	twelfth

I NUMERI

tredicesimo(a)	thirteenth
quattordicesimo(a)	fourteenth
quindicesimo(a)	fifteenth
sedicesimo(a)	sixteenth
diciassettesimo(a)	seventeenth
diciottesimo(a)	eighteenth
diciannovesimo(a)	nineteenth
ventesimo(a)	twentieth
ventunesimo(a)	twenty-first
ventiduesimo(a)	twenty-second
ventitreesimo(a)	twenty-third
ventottesimo(a)	twenty-eighth
trentesimo(a)	thirtieth
centesimo(a)	hundredth
centunesimo(a)	hundred-and-first
millesimo(a)	thousandth
milionesimo(a)	millionth

NUMBERS

Frazioni etc

mezzo	half
terzo	third
due terzi	two thirds
quarto	quarter
quinto	fifth
zero virgola cinque, 0,5	(nought) point five, 0.5
tre virgola quattro, 3,4	three point four, 3.4
dieci per cento	ten per cent
cento per cento	a hundred per cent

Fractions etc

Esempi

abita al numero dieci	he lives at number 10
si trova nel capitolo sette, a pagina sette	it's in chapter 7, on page 7
abita al terzo piano	he lives on the 3rd floor
arrivò quarto	he came in 4th
scala uno a venticinquemila	scale 1:25,000

Examples

L'ORA	THE TIME

che ora è?, che ore sono? • *what time is it?*

è …, sono … • *it is …*

mezzanotte	midnight, twelve pm
l'una (della mattina)	one o'clock (in the morning), one (am)
l'una e cinque	five past one
l'una e dieci	ten past one
l'una e un quarto, l'una e quindici	a quarter past one, one fifteen
l'una e venticinque	twenty-five past one, one twenty-five
l'una e mezzo o mezza, l'una e trenta	half-past one, one thirty
le due meno venticinque, l'una e trentacinque	twenty-five to two, one thirty-five
le due meno venti, l'una e quaranta	twenty to two, one forty
le due meno un quarto, l'una e quarantacinque	a quarter to two, one forty-five
le due meno dieci, l'una e cinquanta	ten to two, one fifty
mezzogiorno	twelve o'clock, midday, noon
l'una, le tredici	one o'clock (in the afternoon), one (pm)
le sette (di sera), le diciannove	seven o'clock (in the evening), seven (pm)

a che ora? • *at what time?*

a mezzanotte	at midnight
all'una, alle tredici	at one o'clock

fra venti minuti	in twenty minutes
venti minuti fa	twenty minutes ago